HISTORIC
DOCUMENTS
OF
1992

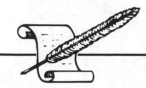

HISTORIC
DOCUMENTS
OF
1992

Cumulative Index, 1988-1992
Congressional Quarterly Inc.

Congressional Quarterly Inc.
1414 22nd St. N.W., Washington, D.C. 20037

The Library of Congress cataloged the first issue of this title as follows:

Historic documents.   1972—
      Washington. Congressional Quarterly Inc.

    1. United States — Politics and government — 1945— — Yearbooks.
2. World politics — 1945— —Yearbooks. I. Congressional Quarterly Inc.

E839.5H57   917.3'03'9205   72-97888
ISBN 0-87187-759-7
ISSN 0892-080X

PREFACE

Domestic concerns—the presidential election, the faltering economy, rioting in Los Angeles, and a devastating hurricane that hit Florida and Louisiana—eclipsed foreign events in the public mind during 1992. One of the oldest political traditions in the United States—the peaceful transition of power from one political party to the other—continued as Bill Clinton, the governor of Arkansas, defeated Republican President George Bush and independent candidate Ross Perot to become the first Democrat elected to the White House since 1976.

Backed by a well-organized campaign organization, Clinton overcame controversies about his draft record and an alleged extramarital affair to lock up the Democratic nomination in a series of hard-fought primaries. With his running mate, Tennessee Sen. Al Gore, Clinton blamed Bush and his predecessor, Ronald Reagan, for the sagging economy, the loss of jobs, and the gaps in health care coverage that left more than 35 million Americans without health insurance. "It's time for a change," Clinton said at virtually every campaign stop.

Although Bush and Vice President Dan Quayle won their party's nominations with ease, the Republican ticket was never able to overcome public dissatisfaction with the slow-growing economy and the soaring federal budget deficit. The president's attempts to focus voter attention on foreign affairs, particularly his leadership of the Persian Gulf war and his role in bringing the Cold War to a close, were to little avail.

Perot, campaigning on a promise to reduce the deficit and get the economy moving again, was the wild card in the race, with political experts unsure whether he would draw more votes from Bush or from Clinton. The Texas billionaire dropped out of the race temporarily but regained much of his support when he re-entered it just five weeks before the November election. His performance in the three presidential debates and his purchase of several half-hour blocks of television time kept his message

How to Use This Book

The documents are arranged in chronological order. If you know the approximate date of the report, speech, statement, court decision, or other document you are looking for, glance through the titles for that month in the table of contents.

If the table of contents does not lead you directly to the document you want, turn to the index at the end of the book. There you may find references not only to the particular document you seek but also to other entries on the same or a related subject. The index in this volume is a five-year cumulative index of *Historic Documents* covering the years 1988-1992. There is a separate volume, *Historic Documents Index, 1972-1989,* which may also be useful.

The introduction to each document is printed in italic type. The document itself, printed in roman type, follows the spelling, capitalization, and punctuation of the original or official copy. Where the full text is not given, omissions of material are indicated by the customary ellipsis points.

before the voters. Although he won no electoral votes, Perot picked up 19 percent of the popular vote, the third highest share ever registered by an independent candidate.

Americans also had to cope with an unusual number of human and natural disasters in 1992. The city of Los Angeles erupted into six days of rioting and looting in late April after a jury acquitted four white police officers of using excessive force in the arrest of Rodney King, a black motorist. In the minds of many who had seen a televised videotape showing the officers hitting King repeatedly with their batons, the acquittal seemed a blatant miscarriage of justice. At year's end the four men were awaiting a second trial on federal charges that they had denied King his civil rights. Meanwhile, a new police chief was trying to respond to criticisms that the Los Angeles Police Department had been unprepared for and had responded slowly to the rioting that followed the acquittal.

The federal government, particularly the Federal Emergency Management Agency, was criticized for its slow response to requests for emergency aid after Hurricane Andrew destroyed great portions of southern Florida and coastal Louisiana in late August. Officials estimated that the full costs of the hurricane would total $20 billion, making it the most damaging in the nation's history. Another hurricane struck the Hawaiian island of Kauai in September, causing about $1 billion in damages.

A storm of an altogether different sort was averted in June, when the conservative-dominated Supreme Court reaffirmed—by a single vote—a woman's basic right to have an abortion. Many Americans had expected that the Court would overturn its 1973 decision in *Roe* v. *Wade*, declaring that a woman's right to choose an abortion was among the personal liberties protected by the Constitution. The Court did allow states to regulate abortion so long as the regulations did not pose an "undue burden" on a woman's right to abortion.

AIDS (acquired immune deficiency syndrome) continued to take its grim toll in 1992. Tennis legend Arthur Ashe announced that he had the disease, a result of AIDS-infected blood he had received during heart bypass surgery some years earlier. Ashe died of AIDS in early 1993. Basketball superstar Earvin "Magic" Johnson resigned from the National Commission on AIDS, charging that President Bush had "dropped the ball" in battling the disease. Bush had asked Johnson to join the commission in November 1991, only days after the basketball player had publicly announced that he had the virus that causes AIDS. Bush appointed Mary D. Fisher to take Johnson's place. Fisher, who was also infected with the virus, had made an emotional speech at the Republican National Convention pleading for more attention to the disease and greater compassion for its victims. Elizabeth Glaser had made a similar plea at the Democratic National Convention.

Although most Americans were focused mainly on domestic issues during the year, events abroad also commanded attention. Russia's uneasy transition toward democracy and a market economy continued. Russian President Boris Yeltsin spoke to a joint session of Congress in June, pressing for enactment of an aid package to Russia. Earlier in the year, former president Richard M. Nixon also strongly urged that the United States provide substantial aid to Russia and the other former Soviet republics to give democratic reforms an opportunity to take root. Yeltsin and Bush also took a major step toward making the world safer when they agreed to cut their countries' nuclear weapons to one-third their current size.

Civil war in the former Yugoslavia worsened in 1992 as reports of "ethnic cleansing," directed primarily at Bosnian Moslems, and other atrocities were confirmed. The United Nations took several actions aimed at punishing Serbian nationalists for their aggression against Bosnia and at getting food and medicine to suffering civilians in Bosnia. But the UN stopped short of voting to use force to stop the fighting. Talks to negotiate a settlement among the warring factions had come to no clear conclusion by year's end. In early December President Bush did send troops to Somalia, where civil war and famine combined to threaten the lives of millions of Somalis. The U.S. troops were joined by units from several other countries in a successful and largely peaceful effort to deliver food and other humanitarian relief to besieged areas of the country. But it was unclear what the future held for the country, which had no functioning government.

These are but some of the topics of national and international interest chosen for *Historic Documents of 1992*. This edition marks the twenty-first year of a Congressional Quarterly project that began with *Historic Documents of 1972*. The purpose of this continuing series is to give students, librarians, journalists, scholars, and others convenient access to important documents on a range of world issues. In our judgment, the official statements, news conferences, speeches, special studies, and court decisions presented here will be of lasting interest.

Each document is preceded by an introduction that provides background information and, when relevant, an account of continuing developments during the year. We believe that these introductions will become increasingly useful as memories of current times fade.

Marty Gottron, coeditor
Washington D.C., April 1993

CONTENTS

January

CONTENTS

February

March

April

CONTENTS

May

June

CONTENTS

July

August

September

October

November

December

HISTORIC DOCUMENTS OF 1992

January

GATES ON REFORM OF THE CENTRAL INTELLIGENCE AGENCY
January 6, February 21, 1992

Director of Central Intelligence Robert M. Gates began an effort in early 1992 to lift at least a corner of the CIA's traditional veil of secrecy. Acting on the recommendations of a high-level internal task force, Gates disclosed most of the panel's report and his reaction to it, dated January 6.

On February 21 in Oklahoma he said the planned reforms signal "a real shift on CIA's part toward greater openness and sense of public responsibility." Speaking to the Tulsa Press Association on the "CIA and Openness," Gates pledged to initiate new lines of communication with persons and groups outside the intelligence community.

From now on, he said, senior CIA officials would be more accessible for interviews, and the Office of Public Affairs would provide more background briefings for reporters. He also said he was expanding the CIA's "historical review unit" to include fifteen full-time positions and transferring to it the CIA's Center for the Study of Intelligence, "where there will be a bias toward declassification of historical documents."

Gates announced he was directing the unit to review for declassification all documents more than thirty years old, including some of the close to 300,000 pages of material concerning the assassination of President John F. Kennedy and intelligence estimates on the Soviet Union more than ten years old. At the same time, Gates acknowledged that there were obstacles to instilling openness in an agency where "for many years, armed guards and physical barriers separated some parts of CIA from others."

3

Background

The reconfiguration of the CIA was the product of fourteen task forces that Gates had established in November 1991 to recommend improvements in the management and organization of the agency and the intelligence community in general. Gates had said he would undertake a sweeping reorganization during his Senate confirmation hearings as director of central intelligence in 1991. Somewhat ironically, when reporters asked for a copy of the task force's report on "openness," they were told by the CIA spokesman that it was "an internal document" and parts of it were classified. The fifteen-page report, entitled "Task Force Report on Greater CIA Openness," had been classified "secret" when it was submitted in December 1991. Subsequently, after members of Congress and reporters had raised questions, Gates made the report public, with the exception of a few names. He also released a January 6, 1992, memorandum in which he commended the task force and gave his views on the recommendations. As with the report itself, names in the memo were blacked out in the copies released to the press.

Congressional Testimony; Further Reforms

Gates followed up on his February speech on April 1, outlining to Congress a series of administrative changes in the gathering, analysis, and coordination of intelligence operations. Testifying before the first hearing ever held jointly by the Senate and House Intelligence committees, the CIA director warned against locking into law any new structure for the intelligence community in an effort to take account of the collapse of the Soviet Union and the end of the cold war. "In a world as fast-changing as what we have seen in the last three or four years," he said, "our ability quickly to adjust structurally, as well as reallocate resources, must be preserved and even enhanced."

Gates accepted the recommendations of all but one task force, ordering changes such as a stronger management staff to help him weed out duplication and revised procedures in the production of intelligence estimates to alert policy makers to a wider range of possible interpretations of often ambiguous intelligence data.

Gates described several of the changes as intended to enhance the director's ability to manage the intelligence community efficiently. The existing Intelligence Community Staff would be replaced by a new staff charged with establishing a division of labor among agencies and reducing unneeded duplication. As the new staff's first director, Gates selected Richard Haver, who was Defense Secretary Dick Cheney's assistant for intelligence policy.

Several of Gates's other moves were intended to insulate from bureaucratic pressures the "national intelligence estimates" that the intelligence community produces for the president and other top decision makers. To underscore its independence from any single agency, the

National Intelligence Council, which oversees drafting the estimates, would be moved out of the CIA headquarters complex and given two newly appointed vice chairmen. "We need to be straightforward about what we know, what we're estimating, and what our confidence level is," Gates said. The director also planned to increase the number of academics and other specialists from outside government on the council.

Recognizing the extent to which intelligence agencies relied on publicly available data in media reports and technical journals, Gates said he would name an official on the community management staff responsible for cataloging the "open source" holdings of each agency. To ensure that the CIA placed a higher priority on supporting the military, particularly during crises, Gates created a new office of military affairs.

Other changes announced by Gates included:

- *Managers' performance evaluations would take account of any complaints that they had politicized subordinates' work. This was intended to reduce the risk that analysts would feel pressured to shade their products to back up policies favored by their superiors.*
- *CIA personnel would be trained about their legal obligation to report possible criminal activity they discovered in the course of their work.*
- *An office to review secret documents for possible declassification would be established, as part of Gates's pledge to be more forthcoming with the public.*

The chairmen of the Senate and House Intelligence committees, Sen. David L. Boren, D-Okla., and Rep. Dave McCurdy, D-Okla., who had introduced similar bills to reform the intelligence system, praised the scope and speed of Gates's reforms. But they also said Gates would need legislative authority to carry out some of the changes, and they criticized his decision not to create a new agency in charge of all satellite and aerial reconnaissance—most of which was controlled by the Defense Department—as one of the task forces had recommended. The Pentagon vigorously opposed such an agency.

Following are excerpts from a January 6, 1992, memo to CIA officials from Robert M. Gates, director of central intelligence, concerning the report of the Task Force on Greater CIA Openness (with heavy lines indicating parts blacked out by the CIA), and from Gates's February 21 speech to the Oklahoma Press Association on "CIA and Openness":

GATES'S MEMORANDUM

1. The task force has done a commendable job of examining the challenge of greater CIA openness and presenting a number of useful recommendations for implementing such a policy. Before addressing

specific recommendations, it is important to establish policy and strategy.

2. I endorse the statement in . . . the report that our objective is to make CIA and the intelligence process more visible and understandable rather than to seek inevitably incomplete or unattainable openness on specific substantive issues. In short, we are trying to help people understand better what this Agency does and how it does it.

3. The idea of a strategy or "vision" statement has merit but it should be short—something to the effect that "CIA's approach to public affairs grows out of our belief that it is important that CIA should be accountable to the American public as a law abiding organization comprised of talented people of integrity whose role supporting national security policymakers is important in an increasingly complex and often dangerous world." The Executive Committee should consider such a strategy statement, revise it as appropriate or desired, and submit it by 1 February for my approval.

4. I believe that CIA, whatever the level of its public affairs effort, will find it difficult to win recognition as an "open" institution. What we should do is strive where we can to be as forthcoming, candid, informative, and helpful as possible to the public, the media, and academia consistent with our mission and the protection of sources and methods. My decisions on specific recommendations have been made in this spirit. . . .

I received a number of useful comments from several of the addressees of this memorandum, as well as a number of others in the Agency. As the Executive Committee considers the actions assigned to it above, as well as additional ideas for greater CIA openness, I commend to you:

a. ▮▮▮▮▮▮▮▮ memorandum, particularly that part suggesting that the senior group reviewing our policy and practices relating to declassification and release of records under the historical review and the FOIA programs consider beyond these programs what kinds of information CIA really needs to protect, the criteria for determining when CIA protects its information, and under what circumstances exceptions should be made. As ▮▮▮▮▮▮▮ says, "Mere expedience and a perceived need to respond to the Hill or press quickly should not be the driving factor in whether we declassify information." Above all, ▮▮▮▮▮▮▮ contends we should be consistent in the way that we release information. . . .

OKLAHOMA SPEECH

. . . The bloodiest, most inhumane century in the history of man is drawing to a close. Revolution and war have cost, conservatively, a hundred million lives since 1914—some 50 million in Russia and the Soviet Union alone.

Yet, in the space of three years, the world created by the Bolshevik Revolution and communism, and two world wars, has been turned upside down. 1991 joins 1776, 1789, 1815, 1914 and 1945 as a date fixed in history's firmament, as a turning point, a division between an old world and a new one. . . .

All historical experience suggests to us that while the revolutionary upheavals we have seen and experienced have succeeded in breaking us loose from the past, the final shape of the future is far from established. We should expect continuing change and upheaval around the world— aftershocks if you will—before the form and patterns of a new era settle into place.

Our national security institutions, especially defense and intelligence, must change—and they are changing dramatically—to meet the new and different challenges of this new and different world. But, our changes must also conform to the reality of an unstable, unpredictable, dangerously over-armed, and still transforming world, not yet the world of our hopes and dreams. . . .

With the collapse of the Soviet empire and the end of the cold war, we have an opportunity . . . to examine intelligence institutions created initially to wage the war against communism, and to alter them to meet the needs of the future.

. . . Even before the dramatic changes of the last three years, we had reached the point where half or less of our resources were focused on the USSR. . . .

Now, change is underway or planned in virtually all the major aspects of our work. . . .

These changes, when taken together, will alter dramatically the way we have done our work for decades. . .

In sum, the American intelligence community today, drawing on its own ideas for constructive change as well as ideas from the private sector, the Congress, other elements of government and outside experts, is being transformed. It is changing better to meet the challenges of a different but still unstable and dangerous world—to be more responsive; to improve accountability; to be better, more effectively managed; to reduce costs; to eliminate unneeded redundancy; to be more flexible; and, above all, to improve performance. . . .

CIA is an intelligence organization, many of whose activities are and must be conducted in secrecy. For most of our history, the less anyone knew about those activities the better. Human sources could be protected, our technical capabilities shielded and, for the most part, our hand hidden. Secrecy toward the outside world was paralleled by secrecy internally.

This legitimate need for secrecy and compartmentation even inside unfortunately created an environment in which communication between organizations and people within CIA was too often stifled. Indeed, for many years, armed guards and physical barriers separated some parts of CIA from others. In this environment, there was little sharing of information *inside* CIA across organizational lines, within the same organization, or with rank and file employees—even when their futures, their careers and their daily lives were involved. . . .

There has been improvement in communication within CIA and the intelligence community over the years, but it has been too slow and too uneven. . . .

If communication inside CIA and the intelligence community has been a problem, our relationship to the outside world has been worse still. Over the years, CIA's approach to dealing with the media and the public has been, at best, uneven. . . . For decades, we have sent our substantive experts to universities to speak to classes about their specialty and about CIA. . . . A reluctance to talk at all—much less on the record—about intelligence issues and processes. This is going to change.

. . . [The] CIA is and will remain an intelligence organization which acquires secretly information critical to our national security and which conducts legitimately secret activities. I have statutory responsibility to protect our sources and methods and I will do so vigorously. . . . In short, we still must be able to keep secrets in order to do our work.

The purpose of greater openness is to make CIA and the intelligence process more visible and understandable. . . .

We are under no illusions that CIA, whatever the level of its efforts, will be able to win recognition as an "open" institution. What we hope to do is all we can to be as forthcoming, candid, informative and helpful as possible to the public, the media, and academia consistent with our mission and the protection of sources and methods.

Bearing in mind these considerations, CIA will take the following initiatives with respect to the public and the media, the academic community, and the declassification of historical documents.

First, the public and media:

- The public affairs office will provide more background briefings to the media as opportunities arise, including on intelligence issues, organization, and process. This office also will continue to respond to telephonic inquiries.
- Senior officials of CIA, to include the executive director, deputy director for intelligence, deputy director for administration, deputy director for science and technology, general counsel, director of congressional affairs and director of public affairs, will be available to provide both background and on the record interviews about CIA and the intelligence process.
- CIA will allow, on a case by case basis, individual profiles of CIA officers not under cover to highlight the quality of our people and the diversity of our workforce, as well as to personalize the work of intelligence.
- For decades, CIA has had a high quality classified internal journal, *Studies in Intelligence*. Over the years, many hundreds of articles have been written by intelligence professionals on every aspect of our work. I have directed the open publication of unclassified articles as well as articles that can be declassified from this journal. As one example, I will soon release to the Smithsonian Institution such an

article dealing with CIA's role in the early development and operation of the SR-71. We are currently discussing with several university presses their publishing compendia of these articles. We also are considering publishing them ourselves and making them available to the public in the same way as other unclassified CIA publications.

- CIA will develop additional unclassified information on the agency, its history, mission, function and role, and also will expand its briefing program for schools, civic groups and other organizations.

Second, with respect to academia:

- The officer-in-residence program, by which CIA overt professionals (like diplomats and military officers) spend a year as guest lecturers at universities, will be expanded as opportunities arise and resources allow.
- CIA's center for the study of intelligence will strengthen its outreach program to universities. We will encourage the development of intelligence studies programs at universities and increase the source and teaching materials we can provide to help such programs.
- CIA will support more academic conferences on issues of mutual interest.
- The center for the study of intelligence will sponsor, both unilaterally and in cooperation with academic institutions, conferences on the history and craft of intelligence.
- CIA will expand its program of providing to universities its experts and officials as guest lecturers on specific issues and the intelligence profession.

Third, with respect to declassification:

- CIA for years has complied with requirements to review documents for declassification under the Freedom of Information Act, the privacy act and executive orders. Congress, in recognition of the special sensitivity of intelligence operations, in 1984 passed the CIA Information Act exempting certain categories of operational, security and technical files from search and review under the Freedom of Information Act. In conformity with all these laws, last year CIA received over 4,500 new requests for document declassification and completed action on some 4,000. Some 5,700 pages of CIA documents were declassified.
- Separately, CIA has had a voluntary historical review program since 1985 to review and declassify historical CIA records. However, apart from a very limited volume of documents declassified from the files of CIA's history staff and turned over to the National Archives, we must acknowledge that the results of our historical review program have been quite meager—the consequences of low priority, few resources, and rigid agency policies and procedures heavily biased toward denial of declassification.

I have directed a new approach that will change this situation while still protecting intelligence sources and methods and conforming to the 1984 CIA Information Act.

- I am transferring the unit responsible for historical review for declassification to the center for the study of intelligence, where there will be a bias toward declassification of historical documents. Line components seeking to appeal a decision by the center staff to declassify a document can appeal only to the head of the center and from there only to the DCI, to me.
- In this time of scarce and diminishing resources, as a measure of the priority I attach to this effort, I am directing the allocation of 15 full-time positions to form the historical review unit.
- Subject to the 1984 CIA Information Act, the unit will review for declassification all documents over 30 years old.
- Beyond this, the unit will review for declassification all national intelligence estimates on the former Soviet Union ten years old or older.
- In addition to systematic review of 30 year old and older documents, I have directed that several of the reviewers be assigned to focus on events of particular interest to historians from the late 1940s to the early 1960s so that these materials need not await their turn in the queue. Such events might include the 1954 Guatemalan coup, the Bay of Pigs and the Cuban missile crisis in 1962.
- This unit will be responsible for CIA participation in preparation of the State Department's *Foreign Relations of the United States* series and compliance with related statutes governing the review of historical material.
- CIA will publish on an annual basis an index of all documents it has declassified under all categories of review, including historical review.
- I am transferring custody of all documents CIA possesses relating to the assassination of President Kennedy to the historical review program. As I have told Senator Boren, Congressman McCurdy and Congressman Louis Stokes, CIA will cooperate fully and willingly in any government-wide effort to declassify these documents. Our ability to act unilaterally is hindered by the privacy act, sequestration of many documents we have by the House Select Committee on Assassinations, and the fact that many other documents we hold on this tragedy belong to other agencies. But CIA will not be found lagging in any broader government effort to review and declassify these documents. . . .

BUSH'S TRADE MISSION TO JAPAN; HOSTS' REMARKS ON U.S. WORKERS

January 8-10, 1992

In the unaccustomed role of salesman for American products, President George Bush visited Japan January 8-10 to press for changes in that country's trading policies. The trade mission sought concessions aimed at opening Japanese markets and at narrowing the huge trade deficit between the two economic superpowers. While the president tried to put the best possible face on the outcome, automobile executives accompanying him and some of his own aides said that the U.S. effort fell far short of its goals.

Bush's trip came at a time of heightened tensions between the United States and Japan. The Tokyo meetings did little to soften the anti-American mood in Japan. Indeed, within just a few weeks of the summit, Japanese political leaders made remarks about the United States that were widely viewed as condescending and antagonistic.

The president had postponed his trip twice: first, because of the Persian Gulf War, and again in November 1991 when he was attending to domestic politics. Planned originally as a diplomatic visit, the thrust of the Tokyo meetings was drastically altered to focus on problems of economics and trade. The change was made, observers believed, to meet criticism that the president was paying insufficient attention to the fitful economic recovery at home.

Eighteen American business leaders accompanied Bush. The entourage was led by the three top American car makers, Lee A. Iacocca, chairman of the Chrysler Corp.; Harold A. Poling, chairman of the Ford Motor Co.; and Robert C. Stempel, chairman of General Motors Corp.

The Bush administration hoped for a Japanese response to trade problems that would clearly translate into jobs at home. But Bush's aides acknowledged that the accords reached in Tokyo would do little to spur the sluggish recovery in the United States.

Bush's Collapse

During much of the summit, Japanese opinion was scathingly critical of the proposals the Americans were advancing. But the Japanese public became intensely sympathetic for a time when Bush, at a dinner with Prime Minister Kiichi Miyazawa, suddenly fainted and vomited. Japanese television showed Miyazawa holding the president's head, and moments later, Bush's wife, Barbara, calmly reassuring the frightened Japanese at the dinner. Blaming his collapse on the twenty-four-hour flu, Bush had recovered sufficiently the next day to attend a state dinner.

Tokyo Summit

Press reports described the intense Tokyo negotiations on trade issues as "grueling" and "bitter." At their conclusion, President Bush called the sessions "highly productive." However, Poling told reporters the agreements left him "unsmiling." The Ford chairman pointed to the failure of the Japanese to agree to a "specific objective" in reducing the "imbalance of trade with our country." Three-quarters of the Japanese trade surplus was accounted for by the sale of cars.

The president, however, did not return home empty-handed. The Japanese offered to buy more American cars, and Japanese automobile manufacturers set goals to procure $19 billion in auto parts from the United States by 1994, up from $10 billion in 1990. Bush also could claim breakthroughs on a cumbersome Japanese system of certifying and inspecting foreign cars. Moreover, the American trade mission obtained concrete agreements on the sale of computers, glass, and paper.

Meeting their Japanese counterparts for the first time, the heads of the Big Three American car manufacturers considered assertions by some of the Japanese car makers downright patronizing. For example, Nobuhiko Kawamoto, president of Honda Motor Co., was quoted in the press as saying that Japan could always buy more American cars and parts "but that does not address the basic problem of how American cars can compete against Japanese cars or American parts against Japanese parts. We cannot lower the quality of our cars."

Poling told reporters that American auto executives "did not ask for any concessions. We are not defeated."

Anti-American Mood

In the wake of the Bush visit, commentary about the United States in Japanese newspapers and on Japanese television was surprisingly antagonistic. Generally, it blamed the United States for its own competitiveness problems. The chorus was soon joined by two top political leaders, the Speaker of the powerful lower house of parliament and, less provocatively, by the prime minister himself.

Particularly harsh criticism reportedly was leveled by the Speaker, Yoshio Sakurauchi. Addressing a group of supporters in Masuda City, Japan, about ten days after President Bush's visit, Sakurauchi was quoted as saying American workers were "too lazy" to compete, that one-third of American workers "cannot even read," and that the United States ran the risk of becoming Japan's "subcontractor." Referring indirectly to Bush's trade mission, Sakarauchi commented that the "real reason" for the U.S. trade deficit with Japan was the "deterioration in quality of U.S. workers." Sakurauchi, formerly Japan's foreign minister, said in a January 21 statement that he had been misquoted.

Prime Minister Miyazawa gave voice to his misgivings about the United States during debate on February 3 in a parliamentary commit-tee. The debate had been on an entirely different subject—the Japanese budget.

Miyazawa said America's concept of "producing things or creating value has become very loose." American college graduates, he said, took jobs on Wall Street "for high salaries." As a result, he said, the number of engineers in America "who actually make things" was shrinking. Among young Americans heading for Wall Street, he suggested, the "work ethic" was lacking.

An apology was quickly issued by the Japanese embassy in Washing-ton, D.C. Miyazawa said that he had "no intention whatsoever of criticizing American workers."

Nevertheless, the Bush administration responded coolly to Miyazawa's remarks. "I would say that the American work force is second to none, that the American work ethic is legendary and has promoted the greatest prosperity ... throughout the world, including other countries like Japan," said presidential press secretary Marlin Fitzwater.

The Japanese leaders' assertions, even after they were softened, contrasted sharply with studies published in early 1992 that indicated Americans were working more hours and had less time for leisure. (Report on Trends in Work and Leisure, p. 163)

U.S. Worker Productivity

The assumption underlying Japanese criticism of U.S. industry was that the productivity of American workers was in serious decline.

Somewhat surprisingly, the Japanese government itself released fig-ures showing that American workers actually rated higher in productivity and in buying power per hour of labor than workers in Japan, Germany, France, or Britain. Writing from Tokyo in the February 8 Washington Post, *T. R. Reid quoted Tetsuo Kondo, Japanese labor minister, as saying that his ministry issued the data "on the theory that, if we're going to be talking about productivity, we ought to have the objective facts."*

The Japanese report showed that, on the key measure of purchasing power per hour of manufacturing work, Americans outproduced the

Japanese by 62 percent and led the European countries by smaller margins.

An earlier survey by the U.S. Department of Labor showed the productivity of American workers to be 19 percent higher than that of the Japanese work force. However, the U.S. study also showed worker productivity in Japan growing at twice the rate of productivity growth in the United States.

> *Following are excerpts from the Reuter transcripts of news conferences held in Tokyo January 9, 1992, by U.S. president George Bush and Japanese prime minister Kiichi Miyazawa (who spoke through an interpreter), and by General Motors chairman Robert C. Stempel and Ford chairman Harold A. Poling; the text of Speaker Yoshio Sakurauchi's January 31 statement on his reported remarks about American workers; the unofficial translation of Miyazawa's February 3 response to a member of the Japanese House of Representatives; the Japanese embassy's February 3 comment on the prime minister's remarks; and Miyazawa's further clarification issued February 4. (The bracketed headings in the Bush-Miyazawa news conference were added by Congressional Quarterly to highlight the organization of the text.):*

BUSH-MIYAZAWA NEWS CONFERENCE

PRESIDENT BUSH: . . . The substantive focus of my visit has been the three very productive sessions I had with Prime Minister Miyazawa, an old and respected friend. As leaders of the two largest economies in the world, with a wide range of security and political as well as economic interests, we had an awful lot to talk about. And on the basis of these discussions, I can make three fundamental observations about U.S.-Japan relations.

First, our security alliance is sound. The U.S.-Japan security treaty remains the core of stability in East Asia, a region still beset with the uncertainties of a world in profound change. Japan's generous host-nation support agreement has helped ensure our continuing ability to retain a forward deployed presence in Japan, a presence that is essential to American, Japanese and regional interests.

Second, as we enter the post-Cold War era, with its many challenges and opportunities, increased cooperation between the United States and Japan on global issues and regional problems is absolutely essential to achieve the foreign policy objectives of both countries.

In this visit, we've dedicated ourselves to building a more prosperous and peaceful world, and for this purpose the prime minister and I have stressed the common purposes of our global partnership, and we've set forth the principles for this partnership in a Tokyo Declaration.

And, third, we've made progress in our all-important economic relationship. Over the past few years we've worked with some success to open markets here so both our countries can benefit from increased trade, lower prices, better goods and more jobs. And, indeed, we've increased our exports to Japan some 70 percent since 1987 and cut our trade deficit with Japan by about 30 percent. My administration has negotiated some 11 arrangements to increase our exports in specific sectors.

This trip adds another significant, but interim, step to that progress, and, of course, we will keep pressing ahead and monitoring progress. I believe the U.S. government and our business leaders have sent a strong message about the importance of fair access to markets.

The detail in the action plan, including the voluntary import proposals involving many billions of dollars and increased U.S. content for Japanese cars made in the United States, make it clear that the message has been received.

Our agreement on government computer procurement will open up additional opportunities in a large leading edge industry for the United States. We've worked out specific commitments in other sectors representing increased opportunities for U.S. exports, including auto parts, paper and glass, and resolved over 50 standards problems—this is the key—50 standards problems that have impeded American businesses. And we've agreed to expand our structural impediments initiative by adding new commitments that will help us follow up on this trip. And I'm pleased that we have worked out together the announcement from a day ago, a strategy for world growth. That one will stimulate—be helpful to both economies. . . .

There is no doubt that we have much more work to do abroad and at home to increase U.S. exports and the jobs they create. Yet we've made headway—there's no question about that—and I'm committed to accomplishing more in the future using all available measures. . . .

In conclusion, this visit has been a success. It has reaffirmed our vital political, security and economic relationship. It has advanced our goal of leveling the playing field in U.S.-Japan competition, further opening Japan's markets to our exports. So this progress translates into jobs and economic growth in America, because I know the American worker can compete with anyone around the world if given a fair chance. And that's exactly what we intend to do, and the accomplishments I've mentioned here aim us directly in that direction.

PRIME MINISTER MIYAZAWA: . . . This is the first time in eight years that we've welcomed a U.S. president here, and we had three meetings with him. We were able to have a very candid exchange of views, and I'm also very glad and satisfied that we've been able to strike a very close personal relationship.

As shown by the dismemberment of the Soviet Union at the end of last year, the world as a post-Cold War era doubtless is developing new moves and trends toward the building of a peace and democracy. And in creating such historic developments, I should like to express once again my deep respect to President Bush for his outstanding foresight and leadership. . . .

Japan and the United States have steadfastly maintained freedom and democracy, basic human rights and market economies, together account for 40 percent of the global GNP, establishing unprecedented prosperity together. And I think it's important that we together were able to further promote the building of a new world order—new world.

And it is important that the United States continue to exercise leadership, and Japan wishes to actively support those efforts by the United States. And I believe that the meetings that I had with the president would mark a concrete first step toward the building of a Japan-U.S. global partnership.

I had a candid exchange of views on various trade and economic issues as well. And in addition to steadily implementing our economic policies, as requested in the joint statement issued yesterday, I believe we were able to engage in substantive discussions on various measures relating to automobiles and automotive parts and components, the central area of the Japan-U.S. trade issue today.

In view of the closeness of the economic ties between our two countries, friction would be inevitable from time to time, and of course our agreement at this time would not necessarily resolve all the problems. But I believe that the discussions I had with the president have been very useful, and I am satisfied with the meeting.

Furthermore, on the basis of the discussions that I have had with the president at this time, we've come up with the Tokyo Declaration and the attached document called the Action Plan. These documents are, indeed, very dramatic and epoch making in that they spell out how our bilateral relations ought to be, bearing in mind the 21st century, and also spells out our responsibilities and roles that our two countries respectively should play, and the issues we together ought to address.

And we are determined to further strengthen global partnership between our two countries on the basis of these documents.

I believe it is quite unprecedented that countries in terms of human history, countries with so starkly different cultures and history, have established deep interdependence and cooperation.

And it is unprecedented that countries which have different cultural and historic backgrounds share the future together, and together would work for the world. And I believe we are attracting a lot of attention from around the world, and I'm intent to do my best to get with the president to respond to these adaptations.

Q: . . . Before coming to Japan, Mr. President, you stated that there are two objectives to your visit. One of these is a job-creating trip. You are going to increase jobs for the Americans. I think that was the first objective that you stated.

The second objective, and I think this was stated during the press conference in Singapore, you referred to the sense of dislike for the United

States in Japan. And one of your objectives is to overcome such sentiment in Japan.

In your statement just now you mentioned that you believe your visit has been successful for the first objective, that is for growth. So I should like to ask. . . if your visit this time really has been helpful in overcoming [that sentiment]?

BUSH: . . . I have been troubled about anti-Japanese feeling in the United States and anti-U.S. feeling in Japan. And I think because of the hospitality of Prime Minister Miyazawa, because of the schedule that has been worked out, because of the personal attention to us by their majesties, the emperor and empress, that—and hopefully by the way our business people have moved out and talked to a lot of different folks, and Barbara's visit to the schools—I hope that that has helped in this second category that you properly ask about.

I think time will tell. But I'll tell you from our standpoint, I think that the signals going back to the United States of this kind of hospitality, this kind of genuine friendship, this kind of caring when I have a little tiny bout of flu, sends a good signal.

And sometimes we forget the big picture. And as I tried in my statement to say, this U.S.-Japan relationship is vital to world security and to many other things.

So I hope the visit has helped in that second account, sir.

[Bush's Bout With the Flu]

Q: Mr. President, people all around the world yesterday saw some very disturbing video of you collapsing in apparently very severe distress, that many of us are not accustomed to when we see people with the flu.

Can you describe what you were experiencing there, and also, can you say that your doctors have conclusively ruled out anything other than the flu, or will there be further tests?

BUSH: No further tests. Totally ruled out anything other than the 24-hour flu. I've had an EKG, perfectly normal. Had blood pressure taken and probing around in all kinds of ways, and it's all going very well indeed. . . .

Really, I'm glad to get the question, because it is—they've done all the checking in the world, the heart is normal, the thyroid or whatever's left of it is going fine, and I really have no hesitancy or worry at all.

Q: Are you at all concerned that now that you've had two quite sort of public health episodes that your—some of the Democratic political opponents who are a lot younger than you might make a subtle issue out of the fact that you're somewhat older and perhaps—

BUSH: Do you think only old people get the flu, Rita? I don't even—I think Democrats get the flu from time to time. [Laughter]

So I wouldn't worry about that. I think it would backfire if somebody tried to make an issue.

I've been blessed by good, strong, physical condition. I played tennis yesterday and then wham, got hit with the flu. But that's perfectly normal.

17

So I don't think there's any political downside. I have always said that if I felt I couldn't do my job for serious, you know, some physical reason, I wouldn't run for president. But all signals are still go. . . .

[Japanese Concessions?]

Q: I'd like to ask a question of Prime Minister Miyazawa. I wonder if you've been able to establish the results. It seems that this has been unilateral concessions made by Japan, depending on how you look at it. And I wonder how the Japanese should read the results?

MIYAZAWA: The issues between Japan and the United States, of course, in resolving these problems, the good will and friendship between our two countries would be very important.

But in the midst of such new and major changes in the world, I think it is very important that the United States, the world leader, remains firm and steady. And it would not be good for us, for the United States, to be encumbered with such difficulties and headaches. Now, the president has come, and in welcoming the president we engaged in a long period of preparations. And we've come up with these results.

There are various issues for which we've been thinking about for a long time and we haven't acted on, problems of our own. And more specifically, there have been some actions we have thought it would be better specifically to better the trade balance between Japan and the United States.

So there were areas of betterment of the Japanese economic structure itself, and also betterment of the Japan-U.S. trade balance as well. And I think as a result of the measures we've agreed on, we'll be able to respond to both issues. . . .

Q: Do you feel that the American auto industry has to do more to—

BUSH: Yes. I think we've got to do more as well, and not just in autos. In both the public and the private sector. One of the things that we haven't focused on here today is this economic growth agenda. And there the United States must do something. Japan is growing more than we are. So they should say, well, hey, how about yourselves.

And we're saying we're going to submit a growth package, we're going to fight for it, we're going to try to get our interest rates down.

And we've got to do a better job in all industries, on building quality, improving competitiveness, knowledge and understanding of the Japanese market, so we can be vigorous competitors, based on more cultural understanding and background.

So it isn't a one-way street, and I'm very unreluctant to say that right here. . . .

[Future Bilateral Relations]

Q: Mr. President, in your summit meeting yesterday, Mr. President, you said now that the Cold War is over, the Japan-U.S. relations are at a turning point, or a crossroads, and I think instead of confrontation, what do you think we must do for cooperation?

BUSH: Well, I would say cooperation, the successful conclusion of the GATT Round, although that's multilateral. I would say that Japan and the United States continue to be in such close touch that when it comes to helping other countries, be it in South America, as democracy starts moving there, or be it in Eastern Europe, or indeed in the Commonwealth, that it's the U.S. and Japan that stay in very close touch on those things.

I had a chance today with Prime Minister Miyazawa to take a tour de reason around the world. It also is in—I would also say that it includes cooperation in trading in Asia itself, outside of Japan.

Neither he nor I want to see the world divided up into trading blocs.

And so as I was assuring him that the NAFTA, the North American Free Trade Agreement, which will affect Canada and Mexico, is not a trading bloc, I had an opportunity to glean from him that Japan would lose if, say, there was an Asian trading bloc.

So neither of us—I think in terms of cooperation, your question asks, we will cooperate to be sure that we don't inadvertently fall into trading blocs that will narrow trade rather than increase it.

But Japan is a respected world power. And we must cooperate. I supported publicly the return of the northern islands to Japan. And there's an area where perhaps cooperation between the two parties can be helpful.

We had long talks about [Russian President Boris N.] Yeltsin's coming out and trying to bring democracy and free markets to Russia. And I think that there's an area where we could have cooperation. So as I look around the world, I believe cooperation is called for in almost every instance. I can't think of one where it's not.

The United Nations, working in the U.N. now with Japan on the Security Council for two years, close cooperation on a lot as we try to use international law to solve some of these problems, as we did in the gulf. . . .

JAPANESE TRADE TALKS

Q: Can you tell us, gentlemen, each of you—do you feel that you're going home essentially empty-handed?

STEMPEL: . . . I think what we did today was start a process. We spent a lot of time in meetings. As you know, the automotive side was very active. I think the president was very clear on that when he indicated that the first steps were in place. We've had lengthy discussions, hard discussions. We did not have an automotive agreement. And the Japanese were very clear on that. . . . We had the beginning of a process.

And the process from their side was a first step. Red [Poling] put forth, on behalf of all of us, a very strong proposal, very clearly supporting the president when he said that we really have to work on this chronic trade imbalance. And our proposal was somewhat different, and we feel that it is a first step and a very important step. Red and I will be taking some actions here to again have a follow-up meeting on this. . . .

POLING: I would characterize it as good news and bad news. The good news is I think that this is one of the first times that we've had business and government in the United States coordinating their efforts on a serious national problem. I think that's very positive.

Second, I would say that I believe the message was conveyed to the Japanese of the seriousness of the problem in the strongest language possible. I think the president indicated that it was a serious problem, that progress had to be made, and that all resources would be used to assure that progress was made. . . .

The bad news is, I think, the proposals that are on the table, as far as the auto industry is concerned, are inadequate, and as Bob indicated the agreement is that a process is in place and additional work has to be done. . . .

Q: Mr. Poling, I believe we heard you say when you were leaving that, you were quoted as saying, "I am not smiling."

POLING: That's right.

Q: You obviously are not very happy with what you heard here, and I was told that you were probably the strongest of all in your wording to the Japanese. Why are you not happy?

POLING: I would have been pleased if I had seen an indication of a commitment on the part of the Japanese to a specific objective in terms of a reduction in the imbalance of trade with our country. The fact that we did not have that leaves me unsmiling. . . .

Q: I just wondered if you all felt it was worthwhile having made this trip?

POLING: From my standpoint, and I'll let Bob and Jack speak for themselves, I think it was positive. I have felt for some time that we have not had the relationship between business and government in the United States in the interests of our country's goals, and I think it's time we get it. I think we have begun. And from that standpoint, I think it was very positive.

STEMPEL: I would agree with that. I think this was an important first step. We generally see the Japanese government and industry together in our country when they come in to do business with the U.S. For Red and myself, this was the first time we had the full support of the U.S. Department of Commerce and the president, and so it's very positive in the sense that we acted as one and really came with some strength. . . .

Q: Would you say that the figures in the proposal of the Japanese side were a surprise to you? [Japanese automakers will seek to buy $19 billion annually in U.S. auto parts by 1994 and boost imports of U.S. autos by 20,000 a year.] Would you describe them as almost embarrassingly low?

POLING: You're pretty close.

SPEAKER SAKURAUCHI'S JANUARY 31 COMMENT

It is very regretful that, with regard to the remarks I made in Shimane, there were some expressions which were short of explanation and were liable to cause misunderstanding and that they were taken as if to disparaging or slighting American workers.

I actually did not make such remarks as 'The United States is Japan's subcontractor' or 'Thirty percent of the U.S. workforce are illiterate' as carried in the press. The true gist of what I meant to say was that, taking account of the concerns raised among the general public over the one-sided argument, made in connection with the automobile and autoparts issue which was taken up in the recent meeting between Prime Minister Miyazawa and President Bush, which attributes to the closed nature of the Japanese market the cause for the fact that the American products are not selling in the Japanese market, it is my wish as a statesman to see the United States economy made, together with the Japanese economy, the most competitive in the world, as stated in the Tokyo Declaration, and through the measures committed by the United States in the Structural Impediments Initiative (SII) to improve the quality of the workforce and raise competitiveness.

In any event, I believe that it is vitally important that Japan and the United States resolve economic problems which stand between the two countries and contribute to the world economy in cooperation with each other, and I believe it is rightful for Japan to give her cooperation to the United States.

MIYAZAWA'S FEBRUARY 3 REMARKS

I have heard your comment, which is easy to understand. (Your point would be) there is something that is lacking in America. Looking at what things have come to over the past 10 years: we might say that the interpretation of producing things or creating value has become very loose; it's that no one doubts that value can be created in the money market. Creating things by the sweat of our brows, a kind of work ethic, is related to various things. There is probably even a connection with computers. People graduating from the universities are going to Wall Street for high salaries. As a result, the number of engineers, who actually make things, is shrinking, something Representative [Kabun] Muto and I both see. While we were debating whether this situation was alright or not, the money market advanced and junk bonds appeared—junk bonds, just as their name implies, are very dangerous. We have these leveraged buyouts (LBOs) where those without their own money can buy up things, and then, unable to pay the interest on their debts, [the companies] fall into bankruptcy. It should be obvious to anyone that such a situation could not continue long. Yet, over the past 10 years, this very situation has continued. I have long felt that this might involve something like a lack of a work ethic. I think what you are worrying about is related to this situation. In one sense, there are many of these same elements present in what has been called Japan's bubble economy. After this bubble [burst], both [countries] now have a lot to clean up in the aftermath, and all of our people learned a lot from this. It is very important to build things of value with the sweat of our brows. This may sound like a sermon, but what I have said is what I feel. When President Bush talks about education, I believe he is trying to reiterate the above kind of message.

EMBASSY COMMENT ON MIYAZAWA'S REMARKS

With regard to the statement made by the Prime Minister before the Budget Committee of the House of Representatives on February 3, the Prime Minister himself has described his true intent in making this statement as follows.

"The thrust of what I said in the Diet interpellation was, in recognition of the excesses of Japan's bubble economy, to stress, as a part of my economic philosophy, the importance of producing things and creating values by the sweat of our brow in our approach to work. The phrase 'work ethic' was used to explain such philosophy of work, and I regret any misunderstanding which may have been caused. I had no intention whatsoever of criticizing American workers."

The overall thrust of what the Prime Minister said in the Diet interpellation was, that reconsideration of the excesses of money games thriving in the American and Japanese economy in the past and the recognition of the importance of producing things, can lead our economies to vitalization. He was reiterating the importance of working by the sweat of our brow in our approach to work. This was a reconsideration of not just the U.S. economy, but also Japan, which has experienced this bubble economy. The vast majority of Japanese people respect the vitality of the U.S. economy and the high productivity of American workers, recognizing that there is much we can learn from them.

MIYAZAWA'S FEBRUARY 4 STATEMENT

(I understand the remark I made yesterday in response to Representative Kabun Muto has been extensively reported in the US media and elsewhere, but) the thrust of my remark was, as a part of my economic philosophy, to stress the importance of producing things and creating values by the sweat of our brow in our approach to work, based on reflection on the excess of the so-called "bubble economy" and so forth. I used the phrase "work ethic" to explain such philosophy of work, and it would be against my wish had this phrase caused any misunderstanding. I would like to clarify my remark, since I had no intention whatsoever of criticizing American workers.

EL SALVADOR PEACE TREATY
January 16, 1992

Meeting January 16 at ornate Chapultepec Castle in Mexico City, El Salvador's President Alfredo Cristiani of the ruling Nationalist Republican Alliance (ARENA) and five commanders of the revolutionary Farabundo Marti National Liberation Front (FMLN) signed a comprehensive peace treaty designed to end the twelve-year civil war in El Salvador. The treaty was the product of several years of arduous negotiations, punctuated by numerous stalemates. It represented a delicate compromise wherein the right-wing renounced its longstanding adamant opposition to change and the left-wing relinquished its ambition to seize the government by force. Army and rebel officers stood at attention together at the treaty-signing ceremony while the national anthem was sung. The FMLN officers and Cristiani then lit an eternal flame to commemorate the tens of thousands of Salvadorans who died in the civil war. The ceremony was attended by nine other heads of state.

Among the major features of the complex ninety-four page treaty were: a major reduction in the size of the army; the disbanding of the repressive security forces to be replaced by a new civilian-controlled police force with FMLN participation; and guarantees that would for the first time allow all citizens to take part in the political process. The formal cease-fire began February 1 and was to continue under international supervision until the FMLN disbanded its military forces. Presidential elections were scheduled to be held in March 1994.

"We understand that what begins to happen now in El Salvador is not the re-establishment of a peace that existed before, but the beginning of a

real peace founded on a social consensus," said President Cristiani at the close of the solemn ceremony.

Origins of the Conflict

Although unrest had been simmering for years, the civil war erupted after right-wing military officers seized control of a progressive military coup in October 1979, attempted to block land reforms, and unleashed a wave of repression. In response, a coalition of five armed Communist revolutionary groups formed the FMLN. A wave of political killings on both sides ensued, including the assassination of Archbishop Oscar Romero, three American nuns and a religious laywoman, and the head of the land-redistribution program and two Americans assisting him. By 1983 the FMLN was able to point to substantial military successes and had won the support of France and Mexico as a "representative political force."

By 1989 more than 75,000 Salvadorans had died and one-quarter of the population had been displaced by the violence. Confronted with a shattered economy, El Salvador's war-weary citizens began to call for a negotiated settlement.

A number of events occurring in 1989 served as the catalyst for negotiations. Early in the year, the Soviet Union halted arms shipments to Nicaragua's left-wing Sandinista government, a close ally of the FMLN. At the same time, FMLN leaders began to back away from Socialist revolution and to call for establishing a pluralistic democracy. The outcome of a major rebel military offensive in November demonstrated to the left that it lacked support for a widespread popular uprising. On the other hand, wealthy conservative entrepreneurs were increasingly apprehensive that the military was unable to protect their property. It was becoming apparent that the FMLN could not be defeated by the El Salvadoran military alone. The election of ARENA's Cristiani, who called for an immediate dialogue with the rebels, and the beginning of communism's collapse worldwide with the fall of the Berlin Wall added impetus to moves for a compromise. The November 1989 murders of six Jesuit priests by a group of military officers, combined with intense army bombing of poor Salvadoran neighborhoods, served to heighten international pressure for a negotiated settlement.

In early December, partly as a means of indicating their good faith, FMLN representatives requested a greater United Nations role in the peace process. Costa Rican president Oscar Arias urged Cristiani to respond positively to FMLN overtures. On April 4, 1990, UN Secretary General Javier Perez de Cuellar announced that he personally would oversee negotiations on a political settlement. Meeting in Geneva in April and in Caracas in May, the two sides agreed to negotiate first on a broad range of political issues and then on a cease-fire. They also agreed to establish a "Group of Friends"—Colombia, Mexico, Spain, and Venezuela—to act as mediators. But talks deadlocked for several months over the issue of army reform and a purge of human rights violators; at one point, the FMLN called for abolishing the army entirely.

Agreement was finally reached on establishing a UN human rights verification mission in El Salvador to investigate violations. In October 1990 both sides agreed to "place greater emphasis on the active role of the [UN] secretary general's representative [mediator Alvaro de Soto] and his role as intermediary." Under pressure from the Group of Friends, the European Community, the Central American presidents, the Bush administration, and Congress, the ARENA-dominated National Assembly voted in April 1991 to amend the controversial 1983 constitution to permit judicial, military, and political reforms.

Meeting in September with UN negotiators in New York, the two groups reached further agreements. They agreed to establish a three-member independent commission to evaluate soldiers' human rights records. Under other provisions, the FMLN was allowed to participate in a new national police force; the government pledged to implement land reform; and the FMLN dropped its insistence on participating in the army. The agreement also established a broadly representative National Commission for the Consolidation of Peace to monitor implementation of the agreements once a cease-fire took effect. The preliminary accord was signed December 31, 1991.

Impact of Congress, Change of U.S. Administrations

The change in U.S. administrations in 1988 helped to make the negotiations possible. In its commitment to defeat communism, the Reagan administration had vigorously supported the far-right factions with military aid and firmly opposed any negotiated settlement. However, in the face of growing congressional opposition to military aid and the waning communist threat in Central America, the administration of George Bush took a more pragmatic view after he took office, supporting the Cristiani forces in their attempts to isolate and weaken the ultra-right.

Throughout the 1980s numerous members of Congress had sought to block U.S. military aid to the Salvadoran armed forces, citing a human rights record that "no truly democratic and just society could tolerate," according to a Pentagon study. After the Jesuit murders, House Democrats established a task force on El Salvador chaired by Rep. Joseph Moakley, D-Mass., who charged that high-ranking officers were directly involved in the atrocity. In October 1990 Congress halved military aid to the country and warned that assistance would be totally halted if the murderers of the priests were not brought to trial. However, Bush restored aid in early 1991 after the FMLN shot down a helicopter, killing three U.S. servicemen. Nonetheless, the administration added its voice to those calling for a compromise and hailed the end to hostilities.

As the treaty was signed, church bells rang throughout El Salvador. January 16 was declared a national holiday, and thousands of Salvadorans flocked to San Salvador's Liberty and Civic plazas to celebrate. "In

*the most important moments of our struggle, the combatants of the
FMLN always dreamed of the day of triumph in the plaza of San
Salvador before thousands of Salvadorans," said Juan Ramon Medrano,
a prominent rebel commander, in addressing the jubilant demonstrators.*

*Following is the text of the synthesis of the peace treaty
between the government of El Salvador and the rebel
FMLN, signed January 16, 1992:*

A Synthesis of the Peace Treaty

1. Armed Forces

Accords concerning the Armed Forces comprise structural, doctrinaire
and educational reforms. These are aimed at redefining the role of the
Armed Forces within the context of a democratic society in times of peace,
optimizing the professionalism of its members, defining with greater
clarity its subordination to civil authority, and highlighting the instrumental rather than decision making nature of the same in the political
field as an institution at the permanent service of the nation.

The following are concrete structural reforms:

- a. Separating the authority of the Armed Forces from the public
  security police functions. Public security shall be under the responsibility of the Civil National Police as a new force separated from the
  Armed Forces organic structure and under civil authority.
- b. Separating the authority of the Armed Forces from the State
  intelligence functions. State intelligence shall be under the responsibility of the State Intelligence Organization as a new entity outside
  the Armed Forces organic structure and under the direct command of
  the President of the Republic.
- c. Dissolution of paramilitary bodies which implies the disarmament
  and dissolution of the Civil Defense Force and the substitution of the
  current Territorial Service regime by a new reserve regime of the Armed
  Forces. The purpose of this regime will be to keep an updated record of
  reservists as well as an updated account of their military skills. For its
  enforcement, this regime will be governed by a law to be passed which
  shall also rule military service, recruiting by lottery mechanisms based
  on universality, obligatoriness, equity and impartiality.
- d. Reduction of the Armed Forces in accordance with the plan
  submitted by the Government to the U.N.'s Secretary General, who
  presented it before the FMLN. The plan shall be implemented by
  stages resulting in the reduction of the different areas of the Armed
  Forces. That is, in its organization, units, personnel, supplies, equipment, facilities, administrative and service structures as well as
  military expense.

The dissolution of those units which were created as a result of the conflict will be especially observed.

- e. Modernization of the educational system of the Armed Forces, so that study plans and programs for instruction and training be aimed at achieving an integral education, encouraging its members to follow professional and specialization courses served in the different universities within the country; organization of an Academic Council at the Military School made up of both civilians and the military which will determine entrance procedures and will appoint the teaching body of said School.
- f. Reorganization of the Armed Forces General Inspectorate so as to guarantee its adequate operation.
- g. Creation of the Court of Honour of the Armed Forces to judge those acts, that not being necessarily punishable, oppose military reputation. This shall be without detriment of the subjection of the military to the Courts of Justice.

On the other hand, the following accords stand out in regards to the Armed Forces:

- a. A process for the purging of the Armed Forces to be carried out by an ad hoc commission composed of three Salvadorean citizens well known for their independent criteria and irreproachable democratic line and with the participation of two Armed Forces officers of irreproachable professional career. The conclusions reached by this Commission may include the transfer, and if the case requires, the discharge of the assessed personnel.
- b. Regulations for private security services through a bill yet to be passed. These regulations will be aimed at insuring the transparency as well as the legality of such activities and the respect for human rights.
- c. Cancelling of licenses to carry guns that are the exclusive right of the Armed Forces as well as the collection of the same.

2. Civil National Police (CNP)

- a. General Information
  The Civil National Police is created as a result of the peace accords as a new force with a new organization, new officer schemes, new mechanisms for education and training as well as a new doctrine. This shall be the only armed police force with national competence both at the urban and rural areas, independent from the Armed Forces, under civil authority, and free of any partisan activity.
- b. Organic Position
  At the beginning, for an approximate period of thirty months, the CNP will be under the direct authority of the President of the Republic

and later on it shall be added to the Ministry of the Interior and Public Security. To this effect, the current Ministry of the Interior is being reorganized, including the creation of a Vice-Ministry of Public Security which will be in charge of the relationship with the CNP.

- c. Organization and Territorial Allocation

The General Director will be assisted by the Operational Assistant Director in charge of executing and coordinating the activities of the Police Central Divisions and Department Stations. There will also be an Assistant Management Director in charge of executing and coordinating the Police's administrative and logistics activities.

The Police General inspectorate will be under the General Director, being in charge of overseeing and controlling the performance of the force's operational services.

The CNP will have specialized legal and international advisory services, rendered by high level experts and technicians on a transitory basis. The CNP will be divided into the following Central Divisions: Public Security, Criminal Investigation, Borders, Finance, Armament and Explosives, Protection to VIP's, Environment and all others to be created at the President of the Republic's initiative. Due to the nature of their functions, some of these Divisions, although organically part of the CNP, will remain under the functional supervision of other authorities. For example, the Criminal Investigation Bureau will be under the functional supervision of the Attorney General of the Republic, and the head of said Division will be appointed by the General Director of the Civil National Police in consultation with the Attorney General and the President of the Supreme Court of Justice. There will be a Police Station in each Department (Province) plus a Metropolitan Station in the City of San Salvador. All other police units of the corresponding district will depend on the latter. The organization of the stations will be adapted to the needs and features of each Department.

- d. CNP's Personnel

1) Hierarchic Levels

The CNP's personnel will be classified into three levels: basic, executive and higher levels. There will be different ranks within each level to be provided by law.

2) Profile

Any person may apply entrance to the CNP and to any of the above mentioned levels by studying at the new National Academy of Public Security. This academy shall be in charge of selecting the CNP's personnel, providing basic education, instruction to intermediate and higher officers, and specialized training for the CNP's personnel. To enter the Academy and remain in the force, individuals shall prove to be in the disposition to serve the community, be able to bear good relationships and show emotional stability. Good conduct and physical conditions are necessary to be a police officer.

a) Educational Level

For the basic level, policemen must have passed the ninth grade of basic education; and police sergeants shall hold a high school diploma.

For the executive level, policemen shall have successfully completed three years of university studies or its equivalent.

For the higher level, a university diploma or its equivalent is necessary.

b) General Requirements to Enter the Academy

(1) Be a Salvadorean citizen by birth.

(2) Have attained eighteen years of age before submitting the application.

(3) Fulfill education requirements for the level being applied for.

(4) Be physically fit for service.

(5) Be enjoying his citizenship rights without restrictions.

(6) Lack criminal records; that is those resulting from nonappealable verdict of guilty.

(7) Pass the entrance examinations aimed at verifying that candidates fit the profile required to enter the Civil National Police, according to each level of responsibility. Entrance examinations will include a general culture test, physical examination, medical checkup, and psychotechnical examination. The above mentioned examinations will be complemented with personal interviews.

3) General Regime

Besides other regulations, the CNP's members shall be career officers and shall be obliged to render their services at any place of the national territory. Normally, they will not be subject to the quartering regime (which will be developed progressively) and shall have the right to a salary adequate to a decent standard of life for themselves and their families and according to their rank and service seniority.

Both the CNP as well as the National Academy of Public Security shall be ruled by special laws whose bills will be passed in a short term.

Transitory Regime

During the transitory period, the CNP's General Director will be appointed by the President of the Republic from a list of three candidates proposed by COPAZ [National Comission for the Consolidation of Peace].

The CNP's organization will be headed by the General Director in accordance with the terms of the subscribed accords. COPAZ will supervise said organization; to this end, it will assign a subcommission that will act as an advisory commission to the General Director for decision making purposes or to take relevant measures in regard to the organization of the CNP.

The CNP will stretch out its functions progressively as the contingents of graduates from the National Academy of Public Security allow it to fully assume its corresponding functions. While this is not achieved, the current National Police will continue performing its public security functions, abiding by the CNP Director's dispositions, and particularly by the special regime that the latter will define for the traditional conflictive areas, while the progressive deployment of the new force is carried out.

In regards to the number of effectives of the CNP, the goal is to have 5,700 effectives at the basic level and 240 at the executive and higher levels in the first two years of formation of the new force. Within the following five years there will be an estimate of 10,000 effectives at the basic level and about 500 at the executive and higher levels.

The incorporation of individuals who have not had direct participation in the armed conflict will be promoted, without detriment of the right that former members of the National Police and FMLN combatants have to not be discriminated at the moment of selecting staff. In the first case, applicants will be accepted prior a behavioral assessment, provided they comply with all entrance requirements and that they have attended the Academy. In the second case, applicants may be admitted provided that they meet all entrance requirements and criteria established by COPAZ, have attended the Academy and also that ONUSAL may prove they have truly and definitively abandoned the armed struggle. COPAZ will see that the participation of each group be equally balanced and that the majority of those selected have not participated directly in the armed conflict.

Basic training courses will have a duration of six months, and one year those at the executive and higher levels.

3. Judicial System

a. National Council of the Judicature

It was agreed that the National Council of the Judicature, governed by Article 187 of the Constitution (ref.), be formed in such a way so as to insure its independence from State Bodies and Political Parties, aiming at a multidisciplinary integration.

The Judicial Training School shall also operate in accordance with the above mentioned article and under said Council, to further a better professional education of judges and other judicial officers.

b. Attorney General's Office for the Defense of Human Rights

It was agreed that the Attorney General for the Defense of Human Rights be appointed on March first of this year at the latest, in accordance with the Constitution.

4. Electoral System

The appointment of a Commission by COPAZ comprising representatives of all legally registered parties was agreed upon. This Commission may also include independent experts to promote a general project to reform the electoral system.

5. Socioeconomic Issues

Agreements were reached concerning the agrarian problem and credit for the agrarian and livestock sector. These measures are necessary to relieve the social cost of structural adjustment programs, find better ways to achieve direct external cooperation to propel assistance and community development projects, and to create a Forum for the economic coordination and the National Reconstruction Program. All this with the idea that to achieve the reunification of the Salvadorean society, a sustained socioeconomic development of the country is necessary, and that this will not be possible without reunification.

The philosophy and general direction of the Government's economic policies are not object of the accords.

6. Political Participation of the FMLN

These accords include the promotion of legislative or other measures necessary to insure former FMLN combatants the full exercise of their civilian political rights according to their reincorporation to the civil, political and institutional life of the country within a framework of complete legality.

7. Cease of Armed Confrontation

The cease of the armed confrontation shall go into effect on the first of February, 1992 (D Day) ending on the 31st of October, 1992. It comprises four elements: 1) Cease-fire; 2) Separation of forces; 3) The end of the FMLN military structure and the reincorporation of its members to the civil, political and institutional life of the country, within a framework of complete legality; and 4) UN's verification of said activities.

From D Day on, no hostile action of any type will take place.

The separation of forces will be accomplished in two stages.

The first stage will take five days (D + 5), in which the Armed Forces will go to 100 established sites, and the FMLN to 50 determined sites. The second stage includes days D + 6 (February 6, 1992) to D + 30 (March 1, 1992). The Armed Forces will retreat to the sites it had in times of peace established in 62; and the FMLN in 15 spotted areas. All weapons, ammunitions, military equipment, etc., shall be concentrated in these areas during said period.

All the FMLN weaponry, ammunition, mines, military equipment, etc. shall remain under the control of ONUSAL from the first day of March, 1992, within the framework of the FMLN's military structure termination.

All this until the period comprised between the 15th to the 31st of October, 1992, on which the FMLN will destroy all the aforementioned objects under ONUSAL's supervision.

The reincorporation of former FMLN combatants into the civil, political and institutional life of the country within a framework of complete legality shall be as follows:

— D + 90:   No less than 20%
— D + 120:   No less than 40%
— D + 180:   No less than 60%
— D + 240:   No less than 80%
— 10/31/92: 100%

The FMLN's military structure termination will be completed in the period between 10-15-92 and 10-31-92.

In order to facilitate the enforcement of this accord, a joint task force (JTF) made up by ONUSAL's Head of Military Observers as Chairman, and a representative of each party, will be set up.

BLACK JUDGE'S OPEN LETTER
TO JUSTICE CLARENCE THOMAS

January 17, 1992

Soon after he was confirmed as the second black person to sit on the Supreme Court, Clarence Thomas was sternly admonished by a fellow black jurist to remember his heritage and his responsibility to uphold the Constitution's Bill of Rights, particularly in decisions regarding civil rights. In an open letter to the new associate justice, Judge A. Leon Higginbotham, Jr., of the Philadelphia federal appeals court told Thomas that "it is ... important to remember how you arrived where you are now, because you did not get there by yourself."

A sharply divided Senate confirmed Thomas in October 1991 to succeed Thurgood Marshall, who retired after long service on the Court as a champion of minority rights. The vote came after heated debate concerning Thomas's qualifications, his apparent opposition to Supreme Court "activism" regarding interpretation of the Constitution, and dramatic accusations from former colleague Anita Hill that Thomas had sexually harassed her. (Hearings on Clarence Thomas's Supreme Court Nomination, Historic Documents of 1991, p. 551)

Higginbotham's letter, dated November 29, 1991, prompted a heavy demand for reprints after it appeared in the January 1992 issue of the scholarly publication, the University of Pennsylvania Law Review. *The article was unusual in that it expressed personal opinions in plain terms without "legalese." It was also extremely uncommon for a federal judge to openly criticize a sitting member of the Supreme Court. But Higginbotham was well respected as a pioneer in black progression to the federal court system, having been appointed as the first black member of the Federal Trade Commission in 1962, then to the federal district court in 1964 (becoming the third black district judge to hold such a position), and, in 1977, as the first black judge on the appeals court. He was also well known for his extensive writing on the history of race relations.*

Higginbotham, like Thomas a Yale law graduate but (at sixty-four) twenty years his senior and a more experienced judge, lectured Thomas not to forget the deprivations they both suffered growing up as poor black youngsters. Had it not been for the civil rights movement, he said, it was "highly probable" that neither he nor Thomas would have been appointed to their positions. He urged Thomas to reconsider his past criticism of Marshall, who was a leader for racial equality before he went on the Court. In one of the more personal passages, Higginbotham noted that, if "Virginia's legalized racism had been allowed to continue," Thomas could have been convicted of the crime of marrying a white woman and "could have been in the penitentiary today rather than serving as an associate justice of the United States Supreme Court."

Perhaps more important than personal reminders was Higginbotham's exceptional challenge to Thomas's qualifications. "Candidly, Justice Thomas, I do not believe that you were indeed the most competent person to be on the Supreme Court," Higginbotham wrote. "I have read almost every article you have published, every speech you have given, and virtually every public comment you have made during the past decade. . . . I could not find one shred of evidence suggesting an insightful understanding on your part on how the evolutionary movement of the Constitution and the work of civil rights organizations have benefitted you."

Mixed Reaction; Thomas's Performance

After the law review published the letter, it was inundated with favorable and unfavorable comments. Numerous conservative lawyers attacked the letter, saying it stepped beyond the bounds of judicial decorum. Clint Bolick, a legal activist who supported Thomas's nomination, called the letter "extremely patronizing," adding that "I'm confident he [Thomas] has the intellectual depth to rethink his position" as Supreme Court cases arise.

"It's a remarkable and powerful letter," said Elliot Mincberg, legal director of People for the American Way. "I can only hope that it will have some impact on Justice Thomas. . . ."

"Granted it is unusual for a judge to do this in connection with a sitting judge and certainly a Supreme Court justice, but there was no one better equipped to do this," said U.S. Circuit Appeals Judge Nathaniel R. Jones.

In an April speech at Duke Law School, Higginbotham said he had wrestled with the issue of whether to make his remarks public, but had decided in favor because of "the extraordinary contribution or harm which people in high public office can cause. . . . I think it is essential that the younger generation be concerned about the values they adopt, even if Justice Thomas might repudiate them."

In his first few months on the Court, Thomas provided a generally consistent vote with the narrow conservative majority on a wide range of issues. As expected, he voted with the antiabortion minority on the session's most important abortion decision, Planned Parenthood of Pennsylvania v. Casey, *in which the Court refused to make abortion illegal but upheld state's rights to impose some restrictions on the practice.* (Supreme Court Decision Upholding Abortion Rights, p. 589)

> *Following are excerpts from the "Open Letter to Justice Clarence Thomas from a Federal Judicial Colleague," by A. Leon Higginbotham, Jr., U.S. Circuit Court of Appeals, dated November 29, 1991, and published in the January 1992* University of Pennsylvania Law Review:

Justice Thomas:

The President has signed your Commission and you have now become the 106th Justice of the United States Supreme Court. I congratulate you on this high honor!

It has been a long time since we talked. I believe it was in 1980 during your first year as a Trustee at Holy Cross College. I was there to receive an honorary degree. You were thirty-one years old and on the staff of Senator John Danforth. You had not yet started your meteoric climb through the government and federal judicial hierarchy. Much has changed since then.

At first I thought that I should write you privately—the way one normally corresponds with a colleague or friend. I still feel ambivalent about making this letter public but I do so because your appointment is profoundly important to this country and the world, and because all Americans need to understand the issues you will face on the Supreme Court. In short, Justice Thomas, I write this letter as a public record so that this generation can understand the challenges you face as an Associate Justice to the Supreme Court, and the next can evaluate the choices you have made or will make.

The Supreme Court can be a lonely and insular environment. Eight of the present Justices' lives would not have been very different if the *Brown* case had never been decided as it was. Four attended Harvard Law School, which did not accept women law students until 1950. Two attended Stanford Law School prior to the time when the first Black matriculated there. None has been called a "nigger" or suffered the acute deprivations of poverty. Justice O'Connor is the only other Justice on the Court who at one time was adversely affected by a white-male dominated system that often excludes both women and minorities from equal access to the rewards of hard work and talent.

By elevating you to the Supreme Court, President Bush has suddenly vested in you the option to preserve or dilute the gains this country has made in the struggle for equality. This is a grave responsibility indeed. In order to discharge it you will need to recognize what James Baldwin called the "force of history" within you. You will need to recognize that both your public life and your private life reflect this country's history in the area of racial discrimination and civil rights. And, while much has been said about your admirable determination to overcome terrible obstacles, it is also important to remember how you arrived where you are now, because you did not get there by yourself.

When I think of your appointment to the Supreme Court, I see not only the result of your own ambition, but also the culmination of years of heartbreaking work by thousands who preceded you. I know you may not want to be burdened by the memory of their sacrifices. But I also know that you have no right to forget that history. Your life is very different from what it would have been had these men and women never lived. That is why today I write to you about this country's history of civil rights lawyers and civil rights organizations; its history of voting rights; and its history of housing and privacy rights. This history has affected your past and present life. And forty years from now, when your grandchildren and other Americans measure your performance on the Supreme Court, that same history will determine whether you fulfilled your responsibility with the vision and grace of the Justice whose seat you have been appointed to fill: Thurgood Marshall. . . .

In 1977 a group of one hundred scholars evaluated the first one hundred Justices on the Supreme Court. Eight of the Justices were categorized as failures, six as below average, fifty-five as average, fifteen as near great and twelve as great. Among those ranked as great were John Marshall, Joseph Story, John M. Harlan, Oliver Wendell Holmes, Jr., Charles E. Hughes, Louis D. Brandeis, Harlan F. Stone, Benjamin N. Cardozo, Hugo L. Black, and Felix Frankfurter. Because you have often criticized the Warren Court, you should be interested to know that the list of great jurists on the Supreme Court also included Earl Warren.

Even long after the deaths of the Justices that I have named, informed Americans are grateful for the extraordinary wisdom and compassion they brought to their judicial opinions. Each in his own way viewed the Constitution as an instrument for justice. They made us a far better people and this country a far better place. I think that Justices Thurgood Marshall, William J. Brennan, Harry Blackmun, Lewis Powell, and John Paul Stevens will come to be revered by future scholars and future generations with the same gratitude. Over the next four decades you will cast many historic votes on issues that will profoundly affect the quality of life for our citizens for generations to come. You can become an exemplar of fairness and the rational interpretation of the Constitution, or you can become an archetype of inequality and the retrogressive evaluation of human rights. The choice as to whether you will build a decisional record of true greatness or of mere mediocrity is yours.

My more than twenty-seven years as a federal judge made me listen with intense interest to the many persons who testified both in favor of and against your nomination. I studied the hearings carefully and afterwards pondered your testimony and the comments others made about you. After reading almost every word of your testimony, I concluded that what you and I have most in common is that we are both graduates of Yale Law School. Though our graduation classes are twenty-two years apart, we have both benefitted from our old Eli connections.

If you had gone to one of the law schools in your home state, Georgia, you probably would not have met Senator John Danforth who, more than twenty years ago, served with me as a member of the Yale Corporation. Dean Guido Calabresi mentioned you to Senator Danforth, who hired you right after graduation from law school and became one of your primary sponsors. If I had not gone to Yale Law School, I would probably not have met Justice Curtis Bok, nor Yale Law School alumni such as Austin Norris, a distinguished black lawyer, and Richardson Dilworth, a distinguished white lawyer, who became my mentors and gave me my first jobs. Nevertheless, now that you sit on the Supreme Court, there are issues far more important to the welfare of our nation than our Ivy League connections. I trust that you will not be overly impressed with the fact that all of the other Justices are graduates of what laymen would call the nation's most prestigious law schools.

Black Ivy League alumni in particular should never be too impressed by the educational pedigree of Supreme Court Justices. The most wretched decision ever rendered against black people in the past century was *Plessy v. Ferguson*. It was written in 1896 by Justice Henry Billings Brown, who had attended both Yale and Harvard Law Schools. The opinion was joined by Justice George Shiras, a graduate of Yale Law School, as well as by Chief Justice Melville Fuller and Justice Horace Gray, both alumni of Harvard Law School.

If those four Ivy League alumni on the Supreme Court in 1896 had been as faithful in their interpretation of the Constitution as Justice John Harlan, a graduate of Transylvania, a small law school in Kentucky, then the venal precedent of *Plessy v. Ferguson*, which established the federal "separate but equal" doctrine and legitimized the worst forms of race discrimination, would not have been the law of our nation for sixty years. The separate but equal doctrine, also known as Jim Crow, created the foundations of separate and unequal allocation of resources, and oppression of the human rights of Blacks.

During your confirmation hearing I heard you refer frequently to your grandparents and your experiences in Georgia. Perhaps now is the time to recognize that if the four Ivy League alumni—all northerners—of the *Plessy* majority had been as sensitive to the plight of black people as was Justice John Harlan, a former slave holder from Kentucky, the American statutes that sanctioned racism might not have been on the books—and many of the racial injustices that your grandfather, Myers Anderson, and my grandfather, Moses Higginbotham, endured would never have occurred.

The tragedy with *Plessy v. Ferguson*, is not that the Justices had the "wrong" education, or that they attended the "wrong" law schools. The tragedy is that the Justices had the wrong *values*, and that these values poisoned this society for decades. Even worse, millions of Blacks today still suffer from the tragic sequelae of *Plessy*—a case which Chief Justice Rehnquist, Justice Kennedy, and most scholars now say was wrongly decided.

As you sit on the Supreme Court confronting the profound issues that come before you, never be impressed with how bright your colleagues are. You must always focus on what *values* they bring to the task of interpreting the Constitution. Our Constitution has an unavoidable—though desirable—level of ambiguity, and there are many interstitial spaces which as a Justice of the Supreme Court you will have to fill in. . . .

I have read almost every article you have published, every speech you have given, and virtually every public comment you have made during the past decade. Until your confirmation hearing I could not find one shred of evidence suggesting an insightful understanding on your part on how the evolutionary movement of the Constitution and the work of civil rights organizations have benefited you. . . .

While you were a presidential appointee for eight years, as Chairman of the Equal Opportunity Commission and as an Assistant Secretary at the Department of Education, you made what I would regard as unwarranted criticisms of civil rights organizations, the Warren Court, and even of Justice Thurgood Marshall. Perhaps these criticisms were motivated by what you perceived to be your political duty to the Reagan and Bush administrations. Now that you have assumed what should be the nonpartisan role of a Supreme Court Justice, I hope you will take time out to carefully evaluate some of these unjustified attacks.

In October 1987, you wrote a letter to the *San Diego Union & Tribune* criticizing a speech given by Justice Marshall on the 200th anniversary celebration of the Constitution. Justice Marshall had cautioned all Americans not to overlook the momentous events that followed the drafting of that document, and to "seek . . . a sensitive understanding of the Constitution's inherent defects, and its promising evolution through 200 years of history."

Your response dismissed Justice Marshall's "sensitive understanding" as an "exasperating and incomprehensible . . . assault on the Bicentennial, the Founding, and the Constitution itself." Yet, however high and noble the Founders' intentions may have been, Justice Marshall was correct in believing that the men who gathered in Philadelphia in 1787 "could not have imagined, nor would they have accepted, that the document they were drafting would one day be construed by a Supreme Court to which had been appointed a woman and the descendant of an African slave." That, however, was neither an assault on the Constitution nor an indictment of the Founders. Instead, it was simply a recognition that in the midst of the Bicentennial celebration, "[s]ome may more quietly commemorate the suffering, the struggle and sacrifice that has triumphed over much of what was wrong with the original document, and observe the anniversary with hopes not realized and promises not fulfilled."

Justice Marshall's comments, much like his judicial philosophy, were grounded in history and were driven by the knowledge that even today, for millions of Americans, there still remain "hopes not realized and promises not fulfilled." His reminder to the nation that patriotic feelings should not get in the way of thoughtful reflection on this country's continued struggle for equality was neither new nor misplaced. . . .

Your response to Justice Marshall's speech, as well as your criticisms of the Warren court and civil rights organizations, may have been nothing more than your expression of allegiance to the conservatives who made you Chairman of the EEOC, and who have now elevated you to the Supreme Court. But your comments troubled me then and trouble me still because they convey a stunted knowledge of history and an unformed judicial philosophy. Now that you sit on the Supreme Court you must sort matters out for yourself and form your own judicial philosophy, and you must reflect more deeply on legal history than you ever have before. You are no longer privileged to offer flashy one-liners to delight the conservative establishment. Now what you write must inform, not entertain. Now your statements and your votes can shape the destiny of the entire nation.

Notwithstanding the role you have played in the past, I believe you have the intellectual depth to reflect upon and rethink the great issues the Court has confronted in the past and to become truly your own man. But to be your own man the first in the series of questions you must ask yourself is this: Beyond your own admirable personal drive, what were the primary forces or acts of good fortune that made your major achievements possible? This is a hard and difficult question. Let me suggest that you focus on at least four areas: (1) the impact of the work of civil rights lawyers and civil rights organizations on your life; (2) other than having picked a few individuals to be their favorite colored person, what it is that the conservatives of each generation have done that has been of significant benefit to African-Americans, women, or other minorities; (3) the impact of the eradication of racial barriers in the voting on your own confirmation; and (4) the impact of civil rights victories in the area of housing and privacy on your personal life. . . .

During the time when civil rights organizations were challenging the Reagan Administration, I was frankly dismayed by some of your responses to and denigrations of these organizations. In 1984, the *Washington Post* reported that you had criticized traditional civil rights leaders because, instead of trying to reshape the Administration's policies, they had gone to the news media to " 'bitch, bitch, bitch, moan and moan, whine and whine.' " If that is still your assessment of these civil rights organizations or their leaders, I suggest, Justice Thomas, that you should ask yourself every day what would have happened to you if there had never been a Charles Hamilton Houston, a William Henry Hastie, a Thurgood Marshall, and that small cadre of other lawyers associated with them, who laid the groundwork for success in the twentieth-century racial civil rights cases? Couldn't they have been similarly charged with, as you phrased it, bitching and moaning and whining when they challenged the racism in the administrations of prior presidents, governors, and public officials? If there had never been an effective NAACP, isn't it highly probable that you might still be in Pin Point, Georgia, working as a laborer as some of your relatives did for decades?

Even though you had the good fortune to move to Savannah, Georgia, in 1955, would you have been able to get out of Savannah and get a responsible job if decades earlier the NAACP had not been challenging racial injustice throughout America? If the NAACP had not been lobbying, picketing, protesting, and politicking for a 1964 Civil Rights Act, would Monsanto Chemical Company have opened their doors to you in 1977? If Title VII had not been enacted might not American companies still continue to discriminate on the basis of race, gender, and national origin?

The philosophy of civil rights protest evolved out of the fact that black people were forced to confront this country's racist institutions without the benefit of equal access to those institutions. For example, in January of 1941, A. Philip Randolph planned a march on Washington, D.C., to protest widespread employment discrimination in the defense industry. In order to avoid the prospect of a demonstration by potentially tens of thousands of Blacks, President Franklin Delano Roosevelt issued Executive Order 8802 barring discrimination in defense industries or government. The order led to the inclusion of anti-discrimination clauses in all government defense contracts and the establishment of the Fair Employment Practices Committee.

In 1940, President Roosevelt appointed William Henry Hastie as civilian aide to Secretary of War Henry L. Stimson. Hastie fought tirelessly against discrimination, but when confronted with an unabated program of segregation in all areas of the armed forces, he resigned on January 31, 1943. His visible and dramatic protest sparked the move towards integrating the armed forces, with immediate and far-reaching results in the army air corps.

A. Philip Randolph and William Hastie understood—though I wonder if you do—what Frederick Douglass meant when he wrote:

> The whole history of the progress of human liberty shows that all concessions yet made to her august claims, have been born of earnest struggle.... If there is no struggle there is no progress....
> This struggle may be a moral one, or it may be a physical one, and it may be both moral and physical, but it must be a struggle. Power concedes nothing without a demand. It never did and it never will.

The struggles of civil rights organizations and civil rights lawyers have been both moral and physical, and their victories have been neither easy nor sudden. Though the *Brown* decision was issued only six years after your birth, the road to *Brown* started more than a century earlier. It started when Prudence Crandall was arrested in Connecticut in 1833 for attempting to provide schooling for colored girls. It was continued in 1849 when Charles Sumner, a white lawyer and abolitionist, and Benjamin Roberts, a black lawyer, challenged segregated schools in Boston. It was continued as the NAACP, starting with Charles Hamilton Houston's suit, *Murray v. Pearson*, in 1936, challenged Maryland's policy of excluding Blacks from the University of Maryland Law School. It was continued in *Missouri ex rel. Gaines v. Canada*, when Houston challenged a 1937 decision of the Missouri Supreme Court. The Missouri courts had held that because law schools in the states of Illinois, Iowa, Kansas, and Nebraska accepted Negroes, a twenty-five-year-old black citizen of Missouri was not being denied his constitutional right to equal protection under the law when he was excluded from the only state supported law school in Missouri. It was continued in *Sweatt v. Painter* in 1946, when Heman Marion Sweatt filed suit for admission to the Law School of the University of Texas after his application was rejected solely because he was black. Rather than admit him, the University postponed the matter for years and put up a separate and unaccredited law school for Blacks. It was continued in a series of cases against the University of Oklahoma, when, in 1950, in *McLaurin v. Oklahoma*, G. W. McLaurin, a sixty-eight-year-old man, applied to the University of Oklahoma to obtain a Doctorate in education. He had earned his Master's degree in 1948, and had been teaching at Langston University, the state's college for Negroes. Yet he was "required to sit apart at . . . designated desk[s] in an anteroom adjoining the classroom . . . [and] on the mezzanine floor of the library, . . . and to sit at a designated table and to eat at a different time from the other students in the school cafeteria.

The significance of the victory in the *Brown* case cannot be overstated. *Brown* changed the moral tone of America; by eliminating the legitimization of state-imposed racism it implicitly questioned racism wherever it was used. It created a milieu in which private colleges were forced to recognize their failures in excluding or not welcoming minority students. I submit that even your distinguished undergraduate college, Holy Cross, and Yale University were influenced by the milieu created by *Brown* and thus became more sensitive to the need to create programs for the recruitment of competent minority students. In short, isn't it possible that you might not have gone to Holy Cross if the NAACP and other civil rights organizations, Martin Luther King and the Supreme Court, had not recast the racial mores of America? And if you had not gone to Holy Cross, and instead had gone to some underfunded state college for Negroes in Georgia, would you have been admitted to Yale Law School, and would you have met the alumni who played such a prominent role in maximizing your professional options?

I have cited this litany of NAACP cases because I don't understand why you appeared so eager to criticize civil rights organizations or their leaders. In the 1980s, Benjamin Hooks and John Jacobs worked just as tirelessly in the cause of civil rights as did their predecessors Walter White, Roy Wilkins, Whitney Young, and Vernon Jordan in the 1950s and '60s. As you now start to adjudicate cases involving civil rights, I hope you will have more judicial integrity than to demean those advocates of the disadvantaged who appear before you. If you and I had not gotten many of the positive reinforcements that these organizations fought for and that the post-*Brown* era made possible, probably neither you nor I would be federal judges today. . . .

During the last ten years, you have often described yourself as a black conservative. I must confess that, other than their own self-advancement, I am at a loss to understand what is it that the so-called black conservatives are so anxious to conserve. Now that you no longer have to be outspoken on their behalf, perhaps you will recognize that in the past it was the white "conservatives" who screamed "segregation now, segregation forever!" It was primarily the conservatives who attacked the Warren Court relentlessly because of *Brown v. Board of Education* and who stood in the way of almost every measure to ensure gender and racial advancement. . . .

At every turn, the conservatives, either by tacit approbation or by active complicity, tried to derail the struggle for equal rights in this country. . . .

Thus, I think now is the time for you to reflect on the evolution of American constitutional and statutory law, as it has affected your personal options and improved the options for so many Americans, particularly non-whites, women, and the poor. If the conservative agenda of the 1950s, '60s, and '70s had been implemented, what would have been the results of the important Supreme Court cases that now protect your rights and the rights of millions of other Americans who can now no longer be discriminated against because of their race, religion, national origin, or physical disabilities? If, in 1954, the United States Supreme Court had accepted the traditional rationale that so many conservatives then espoused, would the 1896 *Plessy v. Ferguson* case, which announced the nefarious doctrine of "separate but equal," and which allowed massive inequalities, still be the law of the land? In short, if the conservatives of the 1950s had had their way, would there ever have been a *Brown v. Board of Education* to prohibit state-imposed racial segregation? . . .

Of the fifty-two senators who voted in favor of your confirmation, some thirteen hailed from nine southern states. Some may have voted for you because they agreed with President Bush's assessment that you were "the best person for the position." But, candidly, Justice Thomas, I do not believe that you were indeed the most competent person to be on the Supreme Court. . . .

While there are many other equally important issues that you must consider and on which I have not commented, none will determine your place in history as much as your defense of the weak, the poor, minorities, women, the disabled and the powerless. I trust that you will ponder often the significance of the statement of Justice Blackmun, in a vigorous dissent of two years ago, when he said: "[S]adly ... one wonders whether the majority [of the Court] still believes that ... race discrimination—or more accurately, race discrimination against nonwhites—is a problem in our society, or even remembers that it ever was."

You, however, must try to remember that the fundamental problems of the disadvantaged, women, minorities, and the powerless have not all been solved simply because you have "moved on up" from Pin Point, Georgia, to the Supreme Court. In your opening remarks to the Judiciary Committee, you described your life in Pin Point, Georgia, as " 'far removed in space and time from this room, this day and this moment.' " I have written to tell you that your life today, however, should not be far removed from the visions and struggles of Frederick Douglass, Sojourner Truth, Harriet Tubman, Charles Hamilton Houston, A. Philip Randolph, Mary McLeod Bethune, W. E. B. Dubois, Roy Wilkins, Whitney Young, Martin Luther King, Judge William Henry Hastie, Justices Thurgood Marshall, Earl Warren, and William Brennan, as well as the thousands of others who dedicated much of their lives to create the America that made your opportunities possible. I hope you have the strength of character to exemplify those values so that the sacrifices of all these men and women will not have been in vain. . . .

No one would be happier than I if the record you will establish on the Supreme Court in years to come demonstrates that my apprehensions were unfounded. You were born into injustice, tempered by the hard reality of what it means to be poor and black in America, and especially to be poor because you are black. You have found a door newly cracked open and you have escaped. I trust you shall not forget that many who preceded you and many who follow you have found, and will find, the door of equal opportunity slammed in their faces through no fault of their own. And I also know that time and the tides of history often call out of men and women qualities that even they did not know lay within them. And so, with hope to balance my apprehensions, I wish you well as a thoughtful and worthy successor to Justice Marshall in the ever ongoing struggle to assure equal justice under law for all persons.

Sincerely,

A. Leon Higginbotham, Jr.

REPORT ON NATIONAL STANDARDS FOR EDUCATIONAL TESTING

January 24, 1992

The controversy over America's educational system took on a new dimension on January 24 when a committee of educators, business and community leaders, and government officials recommended establishing national standards to measure students' academic achievement. The controversial report had potentially significant implications for a nation that had traditionally espoused a decentralized education policy, placing education administration, goals, and curriculum in the hands of state and local agencies and individual schools. However, the panel's proposals were a specific response to the concerns of President George Bush and the nation's governors, among others, to put the instruction of America's youth at the front line of national priorities and to try to correct what they considered was lacking in the educational system.

Background and Council Recommendations

Meeting in Virginia in 1989 at an "education summit," the president and governors had drafted an outline to revamp the U.S. education system. Two years later, drawing in part from that blueprint, Bush presented his plans for an AMERICA 2000 project that would give communities and businesses added incentives to assume an active hands-on role in education, extend school readiness opportunities for preschool youngsters, increase students' knowledge in basic curriculum areas (particularly math and science), and better prepare youths to join an increasingly technology-oriented economy. (Bush on National Education Strategy, Historic Documents of 1991, p. 219)

The result of the summit was the establishment of a thirty-two member panel—the National Council on Education Standards and Testing—cochaired by governors Carroll A. Campbell, R-S.C., and Roy Romer, D-Colo., whose mandate was to investigate the idea of setting national standards for education and testing. The conclusion of the group, composed of politicians, educators, and community/ business representatives, was somewhat cautious: Nationwide tests of ability in English, geography, history, science, and mathematics were highly desirable and feasible, but they should be flexible to accommodate students' diverse demographic, ethnic, and socioeconomic backgrounds.

At the same time, the report, entitled "Raising Standards for American Education," contended that standards would provide "an increasingly diverse and mobile population with shared values and knowledge."

"In the absence of demanding content and performance standards, the United States has gravitated toward having a de facto minimal-skills curriculum," the panel said, noting that the United States was the only major industrialized country that did not mandate minimum standards for grade advancement in core subjects.

The proposal would establish benchmarks for schools and school systems, as well as for students. A two-part system would consist of individual student assessments and an overall national assessment. In its report to the U.S. Department of Education, the National Education Goals panel (established in June 1991), and the American people, the panel recommended that:

- *Students should be graded against national standards, rather than against others taking the same test.*
- *More emphasis should be given to testing problem-solving skills rather than relying on multiple choice answers.*
- *A new twenty-one member National Education Goals Panel, composed of educators, public officials, and representatives of the general public, should be established to oversee the establishment of national standards.*

"This is a turning point in American education," said Romer. "We have started down the path and it is hopeful. . . . There is now new energy and new expectations of American education. It signals we are serious about raising standards and finding ways to do it that respect both local control and national leadership." Education Secretary Lamar Alexander, a member of the goals panel, said, "This is a revolutionary step in American education. Before it is through, it will affect every classroom in the nation's 110,000 schools."

Alexander forecasted that the first voluntary tests would be administered in the next two to three years. But the former Tennessee governor also said that "massive teacher retraining" would be needed, since "this affects every classroom in America."

Concerns Raised

The notion of establishing national testing standards was not universally heralded. Even before the panel issued its report, a group of about fifty well-known educators urged caution. Two members of the standards council signed the educators' statement. While the signers agreed that "dramatically higher educational standards are needed for American schools," they went on to say that "the pursuit of such standards does not require—and could be severely compromised by a [single] national examination." The statement recommended that local educational personnel play a role in developing the standards, taking into account local needs and aiming to improve teaching and learning—not to reward or penalize schools. One signer, Marshall S. Smith, dean of the graduate school of education at Stanford University and a member of the standards council, said he saw "remarkable agreement" between the educators' statement and the council's report. "This is new territory for the United States. It deserves a lot of attention," he said.

Educational professionals pointed out that performance-based assessments had never before been attempted on a large scale in the United States and that, even if they were adopted nationwide, they would not guarantee a dramatic improvement in student learning.

Spokesmen for the textbook industry and those who administer standardized tests, such as the Scholastic Aptitude Test (SAT), queried the proposal. "The expectation that any new tests will revolutionize education is no wiser than the hope that a new kind of thermometer will cure a cold," said Michael H. Kean of the Association of American Publishers. "There would be no problem agreeing on certain basics within every curricular focus. Here's the problem. If you stop at these basic, minimum requirements, you haven't accomplished anything very valuable. But if you go on to set higher standards, you move inevitably toward a national plain vanilla curriculum that may leave no one pleased."

Theodore R. Sizer, professor of education at Brown University and chairman of the Coalition of Essential Schools, said, "I see this as the tip of the iceberg. The iceberg is the arrogation of authority over children by the central government, in the name of high standards and international competition. . . . That's a very questionable proposition."

The report responded to these concerns by saying that, instead of developing a single national test or universal curriculum—ideas strongly opposed by many educators—the standards "should serve as a basic core of important understandings that all students need to acquire, but certainly not everything that a student should learn." Thomas A. Shannon, executive director of the National School Boards Association, pointed out that the plan "supports the autonomy of local school boards."

Governor Campbell predicted that standards in the five core subjects could be in place within twelve to eighteen months. But Frank Newman,

president of the Education Commission of the States, noted that con-
troversies over the value of and need to teach multicultural education
might pose obstacles to developing history and geography standards. "In
math, most people don't feel comfortable arguing an ideological side to
the issue. That's not true in other fields. There are powerful arguments
about what kids should learn," he said.

Congress, which established the goals panel and standards council,
moved quickly to address the proposals. The Senate voted unanimously
to establish a new standards oversight council, while the existing goals
panel voted to reconfigure itself along the lines suggested by the report.
The House planned to hold hearings on the proposals before enacting
legislation.

Following are the text of the transmittal letter and excerpts
from the executive summary of the report, "Raising Stan-
dards for American Education," released January 24, 1992,
by the National Council on Education Standards and
Testing:

A LETTER TO CONGRESS, THE SECRETARY OF EDUCATION, THE NATIONAL EDUCATION GOALS PANEL, AND THE AMERICAN PEOPLE

As co-chairs of the National Council on Education Standards and
Testing, it is our privilege to present *Raising Standards For American
Education.* We believe this report is an important contribution in moving
the Nation toward the adoption of high national education standards for
all students and a voluntary, linked system of assessments.

Through its deliberations, the Council found that the absence of explicit
national standards keyed to world class levels of performance severely
hampers our ability to monitor the Nation's progress toward the National
Education Goals. We presently evaluate student and system performance
largely through measures that tell us how many students are above or
below average, or that compare relative performance among schools,
districts, or states. Most measurements cannot tell us whether students are
actually acquiring the skills and knowledge they will need to prosper in the
future. They cannot tell us how good is "good enough".

In the absence of well-defined and demanding standards, education in
the United States has gravitated toward *de facto* national minimum
expectations, with curricula focusing on low-level reading and arithmetic
skills and on small amounts of factual material in other content areas.
Most current assessment methods reinforce the emphasis on these low-
level skills and processing bits of information rather than on problem
solving and critical thinking. The adoption of world-class standards would

force the Nation to confront today's educational performance expectations that are simply too low.

Explicit and high performance standards could provide an appropriate yardstick against which students, parents, teachers, and others could measure individual and system progress toward the Goals. This information would also help to better direct the use of resources and time. Explicit standards would provide a common anchor for reforms in such areas as assessment, curriculum, instruction, and professional development, thereby promoting systemic rather than piecemeal reform.

The United States enjoys a unique and complex blend of state and local control of education and national purposes for education. We propose to build on this system by setting in motion the appropriate mechanisms that will result in *local* commitment to high *national* expectations for achievement for all students. We do not propose a national curriculum. Standards would provide the basic understandings that all students need to acquire, but not everything a student should learn.

Standards and assessments must be accompanied by appropriate federal, state, and local policies that seek to ensure high quality resources, including instructional materials and well-prepared teachers. The considerable technical and political challenges of going forward are detailed in the Council's report. While fully cognizant of these challenges, we urge the Nation and its leaders to move boldly and decisively toward implementation. We strongly endorse national education standards and a voluntary system of assessments as appropriate focal points in ongoing education reform.

Sincerely,

/s/ Carroll A. Campbell, Jr. /s/ Roy Romer
Governor of Governor of
South Carolina Colorado

EXECUTIVE SUMMARY

The National Council on Education Standards and Testing was created in response to interest in national standards and assessments by the Nation's Governors, the Administration, and Congress. In the authorizing legislation (Public Law 102-62), Congress charged the Council to:

- advise on the desirability and feasibility of national standards and tests, and
- recommend long-term policies, structures, and mechanisms for setting voluntary education standards and planning an appropriate system of tests.

The work of the Council follows and complements the President's Education Summit with the Governors held in 1989. This important collaborative effort led to the adoption of six National Education Goals designed to engage all Americans, from young children to adults. The National Education Goals Panel was created to report annually on progress toward the Goals. In its first year, the Panel concluded that to meaningfully measure progress on Goals 3 and 4, consideration should be given to creating national education standards that define what students should know and be able to do and to identifying and developing methods to assess students' success in meeting them. The President similarly has called for the creation of World Class Standards for students and high-quality tests on which they can demonstrate achievement of these standards.

In carrying out its charge to examine a broad range of issues, the Council met eight times between June and December, 1991. Task forces were created and produced background papers that informed the Council's discussions. In response to the congressional call for broad public partici-pation, the Council solicited and received public comment from experts and organizations representing a wide range of constituents and interests. This report to Congress, the Secretary of Education, the National Educa-tion Goals Panel, and the American people provides recommendations reached after intense deliberation and includes concerns that must be addressed as work progresses on developing standards and assessments.

Desirability of High National Standards and a System of Assessments

In the course of its research and discussions, the Council concluded that high national standards tied to assessments are desirable. In the absence of well-defined and demanding standards, education in the United States has gravitated toward *de facto* national minimum expectations. Except for students who are planning to attend selective four-year colleges, current education standards focus on low-level reading and arithmetic skills and on small amounts of factual material in other content areas. Consumers of education in this country have settled for far less than they should and for far less than do their counterparts in other developed nations.

High national standards tied to assessments can create high expecta-tions for all students and help to better target resources. They are critical to the Nation in three primary ways: to promote educational equity, to preserve democracy and enhance the civic culture, and to improve eco-nomic competitiveness. Further, national education standards would help to provide an increasingly diverse and mobile population with shared values and knowledge.

The Council recommends standards for students and standards for schools and school systems. Student standards include specification of the content—what students should know and be able to do—and the level of performance that students are expected to attain—how good is good enough. The Council envisions that the national standards will include substantive content together with complex problem-solving and higher order thinking skills.

To ensure that students do not bear the sole burden of attaining the standards and to encourage assurances that the tools for success will be available at all schools, the Council also recommends that states establish school delivery standards. System performance standards should also be established. School delivery and system performance standards would attest to the provision of opportunities to learn and of appropriate instructional conditions to enable all children to reach high standards.

In endorsing the concept of national standards for all students, the Council stipulates several characteristics these standards should have:

- Standards must reflect high expectations, not expectations of minimal competency.
- Standards must provide focus and direction, not become a national curriculum.
- Standards must be national, not federal.
- Standards must be voluntary, not mandated by the federal government.
- Standards must be dynamic, not static.

The Council's intent in recommending the establishment of national standards is to raise the ceiling for students who are currently above average and to lift the floor for those who now experience the least success in school, including those with special needs. States should work toward reducing gaps in students' opportunities to learn and in their performance, such as those now associated with race, income, gender, and geographical location.

Having reached consensus that standards are desirable, the Council then determined that it is not sufficient just to set standards. Since tests tend to influence what is taught, assessments should be developed that embody the new high standards. The considerable resources and effort the Nation expends on the current patchwork of tests should be redirected toward the development of a new system of assessments. Assessments should be state-of-the-art, building on the best tests available and incorporating new methods. In order to measure individual student progress and to monitor achievement in attaining the National Education Goals, the new system of assessments should have two components—

- individual student assessments, and
- large-scale sample assessments, such as the National Assessment of Educational Progress.

The key features of both components would be alignment with high national standards and the capacity to produce useful, comparable results. In addition, the system of assessments should have a number of other features.

- The system of assessments must consist of multiple methods of measuring progress, not a single test.
- The system of assessments must be voluntary, not mandatory.
- The system of assessments must be developmental, not static.

As these features are put in place, technical and equity issues need to be resolved, and the overriding importance of ensuring fairness for all children needs to be addressed. Resolving issues of validity, reliability, and fairness is critical to the success of the new system.

The Council concludes that the United States, with appropriate safeguards, should initiate the development of a voluntary system of assessments linked to high national standards. These assessments should be created as expeditiously as possible by a wide array of developers and be made available for adoption by states and localities. The Council finds that the assessments eventually could be used for such high-stakes purposes for students as high school graduation, college admission, continuing education, and certification for employment. Assessments could also be used by states and localities as the basis for system accountability.

In the Council's view, it is desirable that national content and performance standards and assessments of the standards be established. Doing so will constitute an essential next step to help the country achieve the National Education Goals. . . .

Feasibility of Creating National Standards and a System of Assessments

As a first step, the Council recommends that standards be developed in the five core subject areas set out in the National Education Goals—English, mathematics, science, history, and geography—with other subjects to follow. The feasibility of setting national standards and their effectiveness in prompting state and local reform and experimentation is demonstrated by the work of several national professional organizations, a number of states, and other countries. The experiences of the National Council of Teachers of Mathematics (NCTM) and of several states demonstrate that standards-setting is feasible—it is being done. Slowly but surely across the country, states and local districts are responding to the NCTM standards by changing the curriculum and style of teaching to reflect the challenging new standards. The Council recommends national support for such efforts and encourages the work by professional organizations, states, and localities in articulating standards, curriculum frameworks, and instructional guidelines.

To make national standards meaningful, it is important that the Nation be able to measure progress toward them. New forms of assessments—tests worth teaching to—are envisioned. A system of student assessments linked to world-class standards would provide information that could be used to:

- exemplify for students, parents, and teachers the kinds and levels of achievement expected;
- improve classroom instruction and learning outcomes for all students;
- inform students, parents, and teachers about student progress;
- measure and hold students, schools, school districts, states, and the Nation accountable for educational performance; and
- assist education policymakers with programmatic decisions.

It is unlikely that all of these purposes could be accomplished with the same assessment. Requirements for validity, reliability, and fairness necessitate on-going, independent reviews of the assessments and their uses. Further, particularly for children who have historically experienced less success in schools, such as the poor, ethnic minorities, and students with disabilities, schools should ensure the opportunity to learn as a critical condition for valid and fair use of assessment results.

Some existing assessments may be retained, while others will need to be replaced to avoid adding to the current patchwork. . . .

The Council notes that if they are to be useful, comparable results should be available to all key levels, including individual students and their parents, schools, districts, states, and the Nation. Assessment outcomes tied to the standards should be widely distributed and communicated in a form that is readily comprehensible to students, parents, policymakers, and the public. States and localities should report results in the context of relevant information on the conditions of learning and students' opportunities to learn.

Developing and Implementing National Standards and a System of Assessments

To ensure that development of national standards and a voluntary system of assessments is done effectively, a coordinating structure needs to be agreed upon and put into place. This structure should benefit from and not duplicate work already being done by existing entities. The Council recommends that a reconfigured National Education Goals Panel and a newly created National Education Standards and Assessments Council work jointly to certify content and student performance standards and criteria for assessments as world class. The Council further recommends that to ensure strong public accountability in this work the Panel would appoint members of the National Education Standards and Assessments Council, which would have the responsibility to coordinate this national effort.

High national standards and a system of assessments, while critically important, are not panaceas for the Nation's educational problems. Other required elements of reform include state curriculum frameworks tied to the standards, professional development opportunities for teaching to the standards, new roles and responsibilities for educators, technology that

53

enhances instructional opportunities, assistance to families and communities in need, incentives to inspire better efforts by students and educators, early intervention where problems are identified, and the reduction of health and social barriers to learning.

Conclusion

The country is engaged in a national debate on what students should know and be able to do and on how to measure achievement toward those ends. This debate is part of a fundamental shift of perspective among educators, policymakers, and the public from examining inputs and elements of the educational process to examining outcomes and results. The Council initially discussed standards and assessments as a way to help measure progress toward the National Education Goals but came to see the movement toward high standards as a means to help achieve the Goals.

While mindful of the technical and political challenges, the Council concludes that national standards and a system of assessments are desirable and feasible mechanisms for raising expectations, revitalizing instruction, and rejuvenating educational reform efforts for all American schools and students. Thus, the National Council on Education Standards and Testing endorses the adoption of high national standards and the development of a system of assessments to measure progress toward those standards.

STATE OF THE UNION ADDRESS
AND DEMOCRATIC RESPONSE
January 28, 1992

President George Bush's third State of the Union address celebrated two successes abroad—the American role in "winning" the cold war and in driving Iraq out of Kuwait—while setting forth a plan for economic recovery at home. The economic plan was also presented in the Bush administration's fiscal 1993 budget.

His address before a joint session of Congress promised that the determination demonstrated a year earlier in the Persian Gulf War would be applied to lifting the nation out of the longest recession since World War II. Employing stirring rhetoric, the president said that "by the grace of God, America won the Cold War." The world was now a safer place to live, he said, because of "changes of almost biblical proportions." And he spoke movingly of the valor of American men and women under arms.

Turning to the Mideast, Bush said, "We liberated Kuwait. Soon after, the Arab world and Israel sat down to talk seriously and comprehensively about peace—an historic first. And soon after that, at Christmas, the last American hostage came home."

But most of the speech focused on the persistent recession that had caused hardship, disrupted lives, and depressed spirits across the country. When Iraq invaded Kuwait in August 1990, Bush had declared, "This will not stand." He repeated the vow in 1992, adding, "[W]e can bring the same courage and sense of common purpose to the economy that we brought to Desert Storm. And we can defeat hard times together."
(Victory in the Gulf, Historic Documents of 1991, p. 97)

Many in the House chamber and many more watching on television thought that the State of the Union address was the opening salvo in Bush's campaign for reelection. When Bush spoke, his ratings in the public approval polls were at an all-time low. Yet, in an analysis in the Sun *(Baltimore) the next day, Paul West said that the president "looked remarkably cool and in command."*

End of Cold War

Moving into the contentious issue of the size of the "peace dividend," the president said that with "imperial communism" gone spending cuts could be made amounting to $50 billion over the next five years. By 1997 such reductions would bring to 30 percent the total cut in defense spending since he took office.

However, Bush warned that the cuts he described were deep, saying, "[Y]ou must know my resolve: this deep and no deeper." He vowed that in his presidency there would be no retreat from global responsibilities. "As long as I am president," he said, he would "continue to lead in support of freedom everywhere...."

In a jab at his Republican primary opponent, Patrick J. Buchanan, who was running on an "America First" theme, Bush said, "This is a fact, strength in the pursuit of peace is no vice; isolationism in the pursuit of security is no virtue." The statement echoed the well-known assertion of Barry Goldwater in 1964 that "extremism in the defense of liberty is no vice, and ... moderation in the pursuit of justice is no virtue."

Bush said that in the aftermath of the Soviet Union's breakup "dramatic changes" could be made in the U.S. strategic nuclear force. The changes would include ending production of the B-2 Stealth bomber, canceling the intercontinental ballistic missile program, halting production of new warheads for the MX missile, and halting purchases of advanced cruise missiles.

The bulk of the savings Bush proposed—about $32 billion—would come from the elimination of just two programs, the B-2 bomber and the Seawolf nuclear submarine. But Bush neglected to mention the Seawolf, which would have been built at Groton, Connecticut. The ending of the submarine program was a politically hot issue involving jobs in Rhode Island and eastern Connecticut. Other sweeping reductions in the U.S. nuclear arsenal, Bush said, would be possible if the republics of the former Soviet Union reciprocated.

Antirecession Proposals

Early in his address, Bush said, "Now we can look homeward even more and move to set right what needs to be set right." He left little doubt that he was thinking chiefly of the sputtering domestic economy. And at the center of his recovery plan was a proposal he had been advancing for three years: a reduction in the capital gains tax. "This time, at this hour, I cannot take no for an answer...." he told the Congress.

The president's new capital gains tax plan would cut the current top rate of 28.0 percent to a rate as low as 15.4 percent for the most affluent earners. It was the lowest rate Bush had ever requested, and reports in the press said the low rate had been pressed on the president by House Republicans.

The recovery program Bush announced included a series of short-term measures designed to quickly boost the economy. He would order the Internal Revenue Service to reduce the amount of taxes withheld from the paychecks of many Americans. The move would permit taxpayers to spend an extra $25 billion during the course of 1992. Obviously, many of those same taxpayers would receive smaller tax refunds in 1993 because of the president's action.

Also on his own authority, Bush said he would impose a ninety-day moratorium on new government regulations, to halt the "regulatory overkill" that, he contended, was hampering growth. And, in another move to quickly put more money into the economy, he said he would order the acceleration of government spending.

To lift the economy in the short term, Bush asked Congress to permit faster depreciation of some plant and equipment purchases; to grant first-time home buyers a tax credit of up to $5,000; to allow withdrawals from Individual Retirement Accounts (IRAs) for first-time home purchases; and to let commercial real estate developers use losses from rental properties to offset nonrental income.

Finally, among long-term economic proposals, Bush urged a permanent research and development (R&D) tax credit, more spending by the government on R&D, more funds to enroll preschool children in Head Start, regulatory and tax relief for businesses investing in poor neighborhoods, and passage of his New American schools program.

Democratic Response

The official Democratic response to the Republican president's address was presented on television immediately afterward by House Speaker Thomas S. Foley of Washington, who said, "We seek a fundamental change from the unsuccessful economic policies of the past 12 years."

Foley attacked Bush's proposal for a capital gains tax cut, contending that two-thirds of all the money from the tax reduction would go to the richest 1 percent of taxpayers. Foley also said that while Bush had taken credit for extending unemployment benefits in his speech, he had earlier vetoed measures calling for such an extension.

Foley said that the "great challenge" of the 1990s was "to reclaim our industrial edge, revive our economic leadership and make America once more the most prosperous and powerful economy on Earth."

Other Reaction

An editorial in the Washington Post on January 29 said Bush's State of the Union address "sort of seemed to dwindle, to shrink in vision as it *moved along." On the other hand, financial writers said the stock market had been buoyed by the fact that the president had not tried to fix the economy in an election year.*

Gov. Bill Clinton of Arkansas, the Democrat who defeated Bush in the presidential election, largely by promising to get the economy growing again, called Bush's economic recovery proposals "a whole bunch of Band-Aids that are good for scratches but won't fix the open wounds of the American economy."

Following are the White House text of President George Bush's State of the Union address, as delivered to a joint session of Congress on January 28, 1992, and the text of the televised Democratic response by House Speaker Thomas S. Foley of Washington:

STATE OF THE UNION ADDRESS

Mr. Speaker and Mr. President, distinguished members of Congress, honored guests and fellow citizens. Thank you very much for that warm reception.

You know, with the big buildup this address has had, I wanted to make sure it would be a big hit, but I couldn't convince Barbara to deliver it for me.

I see the Speaker and the Vice President are laughing. They saw what I did in Japan, and they're just happy they're sitting behind me.

I mean to speak tonight of big things, of big changes and the promises they hold, and of some big problems—and how, together, we can solve them and move our country forward as the undisputed leader of the age.

We gather tonight at a dramatic and deeply promising time in our history, and in the history of man on Earth.

For in the past 12 months, the world has known changes of almost biblical proportions. And even now, months after the failed coup that doomed a failed system, I am not sure we've absorbed the full impact, the full import of what happened. But communism died this year.

Even as President, with the most fascinating possible vantage point, there were times when I was so busy managing progress and helping to lead change that I didn't always show the joy that was in my heart.

But the biggest thing that has happened in the world in my life—in our lives—is this: By the grace of God, America won the Cold War.

I mean to speak this evening of the changes that can take place in our country now that we can stop making the sacrifices we had to make when we had an avowed enemy that was a superpower. Now we can look homeward even more, and move to set right what needs to be set right.

And I will speak of those things.

But let me tell you something I've been thinking these past few months. It's a kind of roll call of honor. For the Cold War didn't "end"—it was won.

And I think of those who won it, in places like Korea and Vietnam. And some of them didn't come back. Back then they were heroes but this year they were victors.

The long roll call—all the G.I. Joes and Janes, all the ones who fought faithfully for freedom, who hit the ground and sucked the dust and knew their share of horror.

This may seem frivolous—and I don't mean it so—but it's moving to me how the world saw them.

The world saw not only their special valor, but their special style—their rambunctious, optimistic bravery, their do-or-die unity unhampered by class or race or region. What a group we've put forth, for generations now, from the ones who wrote "Kilroy was here" on the walls of the German stalags, to those who left signs in the Iraqi desert that said, "I saw Elvis." What a group of kids we've sent into the world.

And there's another to be singled out—though it may seem inelegant. I mean a mass of people called The American Taxpayer. No one ever thinks to thank the people who pay a country's bills, or an alliance's bills. But for half a century now the American people have shouldered the burden and paid taxes that were higher than they would have been to support a defense that was bigger than it would have been if imperial communism had never existed.

But it did—doesn't anymore.

And here is a fact I wouldn't mind the world acknowledging: The American taxpayer bore the brunt of the burden, and deserves a hunk of the glory.

And so now, for the first time in 35 years, our strategic bombers stand down. No longer are they on 'round-the-clock alert. Tomorrow our children will go to school and study history and how plants grow. And they won't have, as my children did, air raid drills in which they crawl under their desks and cover their heads in case of nuclear war. My grandchildren don't have to do that, and won't have the bad dreams children had once, in decades past. There are still threats. But the long, drawn-out dread is over.

A year ago tonight I spoke to you at a moment of high peril. American forces had just unleashed Operation Desert Storm. And after 40 days in the desert skies and four days on the ground, the men and women of America's Armed Forces, and our allies, accomplished the goals that I declared and that you endorsed: We liberated Kuwait.

Soon after, the Arab world and Israel sat down to talk seriously, and comprehensively, about peace—an historic first. And soon after that, at Christmas, the last American hostages came home. Our policies were vindicated.

Much good can come from the prudent use of power. And much good can come of this: A world once divided into two armed camps now recognizes one sole and preeminent power—the United States of America.

And they regard this with no dread. For the world trusts us with power and the world is right. They trust us to be fair and restrained; they trust us to be on the side of decency; they trust us to do what's right.

I use those words advisedly. A few days after the war began, I received a telegram from Joanne Speicher, the wife of the first pilot killed in the Gulf, Lt. Commander. Scott Speicher. Even in her grief she wanted me to know that some day, when her children were old enough, she would tell them "that their father went away to war because it was the right thing to do."

She said it all: It was the right thing to do.

And we did it together. There were honest differences right here in this Chamber. But when the war began, you put partisanship aside, and supported our troops.

This is still a time for pride but this is no time to boast. For problems face us, and we must stand together once again and solve them and not let our country down.

Two years ago, I began planning cuts in military spending that reflected the changes of the new era. But now, this year, with imperial communism gone, that process can be accelerated.

Tonight I can tell you of dramatic changes in our strategic nuclear force. These are actions we are taking on our own because they are the right thing to do.

After completing 20 planes for which we have begun procurement, we will shut down further production of the B-2 bomber.

We will cancel the small ICBM [intercontinental ballistic missile] program. We will cease production of new warheads for our sea-based ballistic missiles. We will stop all new production of the Peacekeeper missile. And we will not purchase any more advanced cruise missiles.

This weekend I will meet at Camp David with Boris Yeltsin of the Russian Federation. I have informed President Yeltsin that if the Commonwealth, the former Soviet Union, will eliminate all land-based multiple warhead ballistic missiles, I will do the following:

We will eliminate all Peacekeeper missiles. We will reduce the number of warheads on Minuteman missiles to one, and reduce the number of warheads on our sea-based missiles by about one-third. And we will convert a substantial portion of our strategic bombers to primarily conventional use.

President Yeltsin's early response has been very positive, and I expect our talks at Camp David to be fruitful.

I want you to know that for half a century, American presidents have longed to make such decisions and say such words. But even in the midst of celebration, we must keep caution as a friend.

For the world is still a dangerous place. Only the dead have seen the end of conflict. And though yesterday's challenges are behind us, tomorrow's are being born.

The Secretary of Defense recommended these cuts after consultation with the Joint Chiefs of Staff. And I make them with confidence. But do not misunderstand me.

The reductions announced tonight will save us $50 billion over the next five years. By 1997, we will have cut defense by 30 percent since I took office. These cuts are deep, and you must know my resolve: This deep, and no deeper.

To do less would be insensible to progress, but to do more would be ignorant of history.

We must not go back to the days of "the hollow army." We cannot repeat the mistakes made twice in this century, when armistice was followed by recklessness, and defense was purged as if the world were permanently safe.

I remind you this evening that I have asked for your support in funding a program to protect our country from limited nuclear missile attack. We must have this protection because too many people in too many countries have access to nuclear arms.

And I urge you again to pass the Strategic Defense Initiative—SDI.

There are those who say that now we can turn away from the world, that we have no special role, no special place.

But we are the United States of America, the leader of the West that has become the leader of the world.

As long as I am President, we will continue to lead in support of freedom everywhere—not out of arrogance, and not out of altruism, but for the safety and security of our children.

This is a fact: Strength in the pursuit of peace is no vice; isolationism in the pursuit of security is no virtue.

And now to our troubles at home. They are not all economic; the primary problem is our economy. There are some good signs: Inflation, that thief, is down, and interest rates are down. But unemployment is too high, some industries are in trouble, and growth is not what it should be.

Let me tell you right from the start and right from the heart: I know we're in hard times, but I know something else: this will not stand.

My friends in this chamber, we can bring the same courage and sense of common purpose to the economy that we brought to Desert Storm. And we can defeat hard times together.

I believe you will help. One reason is that you're patriots, and you want the best for your country. And I believe that in your hearts you want to put partisanship aside and get the job done—because it's the right thing to do.

The power of America rests in a stirring but simple idea—that people will do great things if only you set them free.

Well, we're going to set the economy free, for if this age of miracles and wonders has taught us anything, it's that if we can change the world, we can change America.

We must encourage investment. We must make it easier for people to invest money and create new products, new industries and new jobs. We must clear away the obstacles to growth—high taxes, high regulation, red tape and, yes, wasteful government spending.

None of this will happen with a snap of the fingers—but it will happen. And the test of a plan isn't whether it's called new or dazzling. The American people aren't impressed by gimmicks; they're smarter on this score than all of us in this room. The only test of a plan is, is it sound and will it work.

We must have a short-term plan to address our immediate needs and heat up the economy. And we need a longer-term plan to keep the combustion going and to guarantee our place in the world economy.

There are certain things that a president can do without Congress—and I am going to do them.

I have this evening asked major Cabinet departments and federal agencies to institute a 90-day moratorium on any new federal regulations that could hinder growth.

In those 90 days, major departments and agencies will carry out a top-to-bottom review of all regulations, old and new, to stop the ones that will hurt growth and speed up those that will help growth.

Further, for the untold number of hard-working, responsible American workers and businessmen and women who've been forced to go without needed bank loans—the banking credit crunch must end.

I won't neglect my responsibility for sound regulations that serve the public good, but regulatory overkill must be stopped.

And I have instructed our government regulators to stop it.

I have directed Cabinet departments and federal agencies to speed up pro-growth expenditures as quickly as possible. This should put an extra $10 billion into the economy in the next six months. And our new transportation bill provides more than $150 billion for construction and maintenance projects that are vital to our growth and well-being. That means jobs building roads, jobs building bridges and jobs building railways.

And I have this evening directed the secretary of the Treasury to change the federal tax withholding tables. With this change, millions of Americans from whom the government withholds more than necessary can now choose to have the government withhold less from their paychecks. Something tells me a number of taxpayers may take us up on this one. This initiative could return about $25 billion back into our economy over the next 12 months—money people can use to help pay for clothing, college or to get a new car.

And, finally, working with the Federal Reserve, we will continue to support monetary policy that keeps both interest rates and inflation down.

These are the things that I can do.

And now, members of Congress, let me tell you what you can do for your country.

You must pass the other elements of my plan to meet our economic needs. Everyone knows that investment spurs recovery. And I am proposing this evening a change in the alternative minimum tax and the creation of a new 15 percent investment tax allowance.

This will encourage businesses to accelerate investment and bring people back to work.

Real estate has led our economy out of almost all the tough times we've ever had. Once building starts, carpenters and plumbers work, people buy homes and take out mortgages.

My plan would modify the passive-loss rule for active real estate developers.

And it would make it easier for pension plans to purchase real estate.

For those Americans who dream of buying a first home and who can't quite afford it, my plan would allow first-time buyers to withdraw savings from IRA without penalty—and provide a $5,000 tax credit for the first purchase of that home.

And, finally, my immediate plan calls on Congress to give crucial help to people who own a home, to everyone who has a business, or a farm, or a single investment.

This time, at this hour, I cannot take no for an answer. You must cut the capital gains tax on the people of our country.

Never has an issue been more demagogued by its opponents.

But the demagogues are wrong—and they know it. Sixty percent of the people who benefit from lower capital gains have incomes under $50,000. A cut in the capital gains tax increases jobs and helps just about everyone in our country.

And so I'm asking you to cut the capital gains tax to a maximum of 15.4 percent.

And I'll tell you, those of you who say, oh, no, someone who's comfortable may benefit from this. You kind of remind me of the old definition of the Puritan, who wouldn't sleep at night worrying that somehow someone somewhere was out having a good time.

The opponents of this measure—and those who've authored various so-called soak-the-rich bills that are floating around this chamber—should be reminded of something: When they aim at the big guy they usually hit the little guy. And maybe it's time that stopped.

This then is my short-term plan. Your part, members of Congress, requires enactment of these common-sense proposals that will have a strong effect on the economy without breaking the budget agreement and without raising tax rates.

While my plan is being passed and kicking in, we've got to care for those in trouble today. I have provided up to $4.4 billion in my budget to extend federal unemployment benefits. I ask for congressional action right away. And I thank the committee—

Well, at last.

And let's be frank—let me level with you. I know, and you know, that my plan is unveiled in a political season. And I know, and you know, that everything I propose will be viewed by some in merely partisan terms. But

I ask you to know what is in my heart: And my aim is to increase our nation's good. And I am doing what I think is right; I am proposing what I know will help.

I pride myself that I am a prudent man, and I believe that patience is a virtue. But I understand that politics is for some a game—and that sometimes the game is to stop all progress and then decry the lack of improvement.

But let me tell you: Far more important than my political future—and far more important than yours—is the well-being of our country.

And members of this chamber are practical people, and I know you won't resent some practical advice: When people put their party's fortunes, whatever the party, whatever side of this aisle, before the public good, they court defeat not only for their country, but for themselves. And they will certainly deserve it.

And I submit my plan tomorrow. And I am asking you to pass it by March 20. And I ask the American people to let you know they want this action by March 20.

From the day after that, if it must be: The battle is joined.

And you know when principle is at stake, I relish a good fair fight.

I said my plan has two parts, and it does. And it is the second part that is the heart of the matter. For it's not enough to get an immediate burst. We need long-term improvement in our economic position.

We all know that the key to our economic future is to ensure that America continues as the economic leader of the world. We have that in our power.

Here, then, is my long-term plan to guarantee our future.

First, trade: We will work to break down the walls that stop world trade. We will work to open markets everywhere. And in our major trade negotiations, I will continue pushing to eliminate tariffs and subsidies that damage America's farmers and workers.

And we'll get more good American jobs within our own hemisphere through the North American Free Trade Agreement and through the Enterprise for the Americas Initiative.

But changes are here, and more are coming. The workplace of the future will demand more highly skilled workers than ever—more people who are computer literate, highly educated.

And we must be the world's leader in education. And we must revolutionize America's schools.

My America 2000 education strategy will help us reach that goal. My plan will give parents more choice, give teachers more flexibility and help communities create New American schools.

Thirty states across the nation have established America 2000 programs. Hundreds of cities and towns have joined in.

And now Congress must join this great movement: Pass my proposals for New American schools.

That was my second long-term proposal.

And here's my third: We must make common-sense investments that will help us compete long term in the marketplace. We must encourage research and development. And my plan is to make the R&D [research and development] tax credit permanent and to provide record levels of support—over $76 billion this year alone—for people who will explore the promise of emerging technologies.

Fourth, we must do something about crime and drugs.

And it is time for a major renewed investment in fighting violent street crime. It saps our strength and hurts our faith in our society and in our future together.

Surely a tired woman on her way to work at 6 in the morning on a subway deserves the right to get there safely.

And surely it's true that everyone who changes his or her life because of crime—from those afraid to go out at night to those afraid to walk in the parks they pay for—surely these people have been denied a basic civil right.

It is time to restore it.

Congress, pass my comprehensive crime bill.

It is tough on criminals and supportive of police—and it has been languishing in these hallowed halls for years now. Pass it. Help your country.

And, fifth, I ask you tonight to fund our HOPE housing proposal and to pass my enterprise zone legislation, which will get businesses into the inner city. We must empower the poor with the pride that comes from owning a home, getting a job, becoming a part of things.

My plan would encourage real estate construction by extending tax incentives for mortgage revenue bonds and low-income housing.

And I ask tonight for record expenditures for the program that helps children born into want move into excellence: Head Start.

Step six: We must reform our health-care system.

For this, too, bears on whether or not we can compete in the world. American health costs have been exploding. This year America will spend over $800 billion on health. And that's expected to grow to $1.6 trillion by the end of the decade. We simply cannot afford this.

The cost of health care shows up not only in your family budget but in the price of everything we buy and everything we sell. When health coverage for a fellow on an assembly line costs thousands of dollars, the cost goes into the products he makes—and you pay the bill.

We must make a choice.

Now, some pretend we can have it both ways. They call it "play or pay." But that expensive approach is unstable. It will mean higher taxes, fewer jobs and eventually a system under complete government control.

Really, there are only two options: We can move toward a nationalized system—which will restrict patient choice—a system which will restrict patient choice in picking a doctor and force the government to ration services arbitrarily—and what we'll get is patients in long lines, indifferent service and a huge new tax burden; or we can reform our own private health-care system, which still gives us, for all its flaws, the best-quality health care in the world.

Well, let's build on our strengths.

My plan provides insurance security for all Americans—while preserving and increasing the idea of choice. We make basic health insurance affordable for all low-income people not now covered. And we do it by providing a health insurance tax credit of up to $3,750 for each low-income family.

And the middle class gets new help too. And, by reforming the health insurance market, my plan assures that Americans will have access to basic health insurance even if they change jobs or develop serious health problems.

We must bring costs under control, preserve quality, preserve choice and reduce the people's nagging daily worry about health insurance. My plan, the details of which I will announce very shortly, does just that.

And, seventh, we must get the federal deficit under control.

We now have in law enforceable spending caps and a requirement that we pay for the programs we create.

There are those in Congress who would ease that discipline now. But I cannot let them do it—and I won't.

My plan would freeze all domestic discretionary budget authority— which means "no more next year than this year."

I will not tamper with Social Security.

But I would put real caps on the growth of uncontrolled spending. And I would also freeze federal domestic government employment.

And with the help of Congress, my plan will get rid of 246 programs that don't deserve federal funding.

Some of them have noble titles, but none of them is indispensable. We can get rid of each and every one of them.

You know, it's time we rediscovered a "home truth" the American people have never forgotten: This government is too big and spends too much.

I call upon Congress to adopt a measure that will help put an end to the annual ritual of filling the budget with pork-barrel appropriations. Every year the press has a field day making fun of outrageous examples— Lawrence Welk museum, research grant for Belgian endive.

We all know how these things get into the budget. And maybe you need someone to help you say no. I know how to say it. And I know what I need to make it stick. Give me the same thing 43 governors have—the line item veto and let me help you control spending.

We must put an end to unfinanced federal government mandates. These are the requirements Congress puts on our cities, counties and states— without supplying the money.

And if Congress passes a mandate, it should be forced to pay for it and balance the cost with savings elsewhere. After all, a mandate just increases someone else's burden—and that means higher taxes at the state and local level.

Step eight: Congress should enact the bold reform proposals that are still awaiting congressional action—bank reform, civil justice reform, tort reform and my national energy strategy.

Finally, we must strengthen the family—because it is the family that has the greatest bearing on our future.

When Barbara holds an AIDS baby in her arms and reads to children, she's saying to every person in this country: Family matters.

And I am announcing tonight a new Commission on America's Urban Families. I've asked Missouri's governor, John Ashcroft, to be chairman, former Dallas Mayor Annette Strauss to be co-chair. You know, I had mayors from the League of Cities in the other day at the White House, and they told me something striking. They said that every one of them, Republicans and Democrats, agreed on one thing: that the major cause of the problems of the cities is the dissolution of the family.

And they asked for this commission, and they were right to ask, because it's time to determine what we can do to keep families together, strong and sound.

There's one thing we can do right away: Ease the burden of rearing a child. I ask you tonight to raise the personal exemption by $500 per child for every family.

For a family with four kids, that's an increase of $2,000. And this is a good start in the right direction, and it's what we can afford.

It's time to allow families to deduct the interest they pay on student loans.

I am asking you to do just that. And I'm asking you to allow people to use money from their IRAs to pay medical and education expenses—all without penalties.

And I'm asking for more. Ask American parents what they dislike about how things are in our country and chances are good that pretty soon they'll get to welfare. Americans are the most generous people on Earth. But we have to go back to the insight of [President] Franklin Roosevelt who, when he spoke of what became the welfare program, warned that it must not become "a narcotic" and a "subtle destroyer" of the spirit.

Welfare was never meant to be a lifestyle; it was never meant to be a habit; it was never supposed to be passed from generation to generation like a legacy.

It's time to replace the assumptions of the welfare state and help reform the welfare system.

States throughout the country are beginning to operate with new assumptions: that when able-bodied people receive government assistance, they have responsibilities to the taxpayer, a responsibility to seek work, education or job training; a responsibility to get their lives in order; a responsibility to hold their families together and refrain from having children out of wedlock—and a responsibility to obey the law.

We are going to help this movement.

Often, state reform requires waiving certain federal regulations. I will act to make that process easier and quicker for every state that asks our help.

And I want to add, as we make these changes, we work together to improve this system, that our intention isn't scapegoating or fingerpointing. If you can read the papers or watch TV, you know there's been a rise these days in a certain kind of bitterness, racist comments, anti-Semitism, an increased sense of division.

Really, this is not us—this is not who we are. And this is not acceptable.

And so you have my plan for America. And I am asking for big things— but I believe in my heart you will do what's right.

And, you know, it's kind of an American tradition to show a certain skepticism toward our democratic institutions. I myself have sometimes thought the aging process could be delayed if it had to make its way through Congress.

You will deliberate, and you will discuss, and that is fine. But, my friends, the people cannot wait. They need help now.

And there is a mood among us. People are worried, there has been talk of decline. Someone even said our workers are lazy and uninspired.

And I thought, really, you go tell Neil Armstrong standing on the moon, tell the men and women who put him there, tell the American farmer who feeds his country and the world. Tell the men and women of Desert Storm.

Moods come and go, but greatness endures. Ours does. And maybe for a moment it's good to remember what, in the dailiness of our lives, we forget:

We are still and ever the freest nation on earth—the kindest nation on earth—the strongest nation on earth—and we have always risen to the occasion.

And we are going to lift this nation out of hard times inch by inch and day by day, and those who would stop us had better step aside—because I look at hard times and I make this vow: This will not stand.

And so we move on together, a rising nation, the once and future miracle that is still, this night, the hope of the world.

Thank you. God bless you. And God bless our beloved country. Thank you very, very much.

FOLEY'S DEMOCRATIC RESPONSE

My fellow Americans, tonight I speak for the Democratic Party. But I also speak for working families and the middle class; for those who worked hard to move ahead but now find themselves falling behind; for so many of strength and spirit and skill who watch with increasing uncertainty as so many of their hopes have been threatened.

This should be America's high noon.

But instead, after winning both a war in the Persian Gulf a year ago and the historic struggle of the last half century against communism, we face an ominous, persistent recession, which reminds us anew of President Kennedy's warning that "This nation cannot be strong abroad if it is weak at home."

At home in America today, thousands wait on a frozen morning outside a hotel in Chicago for just a chance to apply for a job, no matter what the work or wages.

At home in America today, the largest automaker in the world, which once seemed to be the most secure of all corporations, announces that it will have to lay off 75,000 people in order to survive.

At home in America today, the average earnings increase of our workers has declined from first in the world to 10th. This year, millions more of our workers find themselves unemployed and their family's health uninsured. Many state governments are slashing education and other services and raising taxes. The nations whose freedom we protected in the past continue to surpass us in high-paying jobs and the industries of the future.

The standard of living of the American people is a first and fundamental measure of the state of the American union.

So the urgent, overriding task of 1992 is to restore growth and jobs. And the great challenge of the 1990s is to reclaim our industrial edge, revive our economic leadership and make America once more the most prosperous and powerful economy on Earth.

For too long, we were told to wait—that things would get better on their own. There was even an effort to talk us out of the recession—or to tell us that it wasn't really happening at all.

But the truth finally became all too painful—and all too clear. The supply-side, trickle-down decade of the 1980s finally led to an economy in decline and left us month after month with a national administration adrift in domestic policy, seemingly without ideas and without apparent commitment or energy to move America ahead.

In the midst of this recession, the administration even resisted extending unemployment benefits; Congress had to pass it three times last year before the president would sign it.

Today, before the president had sent his message, Congress took action to renew that extension, and we now welcome the president's support.

For many months, Democrats have set forth an agenda for change. We have proposed a tax cut for the middle class to help lift the consumer demand that fuels our economy. We have demanded policies to bring down the trade barriers that lock American products out of markets from Europe to Asia. We have called for national health insurance to make health care a fundamental right of all Americans.

Here, too, we will seek common ground with the president and the Republicans. To achieve all this and more, we will work with him and with them to do what is best for the country.

But we will also stand our ground when basic principles are at stake. We will not agree to do the wrong thing simply for the sake of doing something. In short, we seek a fundamental change from the unsuccessful economic polices of the past 12 years.

When we say a middle-class tax cut, we mean exactly that not more of the tax cuts of the 1980s, which gave most of the benefits to the very few and left most of our people actually paying more in taxes.

We will insist that this time the benefits must go to working families, not to the privileged.

We will insist that a middle-class tax cut be paid for not by taking money that should go to schools and health care but by calling on the richest of our citizens at long last to pay their fair share.

We will oppose any effort to misuse the present crisis as an excuse to repeat the worst errors of the last decade. Then we sowed the seeds of the recession we are now in; we must not go down that path again.

During the past two administrations, there have been consistent efforts to undo government protection of public health and safety. Today the hurt of the unemployed is no excuse to undermine regulatory rules that protect their families and all of us from pollution, deceptive advertising, unsafe food and medicine, workplace injury and death. This is not the way to create jobs or make American business prosperous.

Nor will we accept the kind of capital gains tax cut that will lead largely to accelerated profit-taking, not accelerated investment. One can play a lot of games with statistics, but the bottom line is that two-thirds of all the money from the administration's capital gains tax cut would go to the richest 1 percent of taxpayers. Instead, we need targeted incentives to reward companies that build and buy now—that hire instead of laying off.

The president said tonight that when you aim at the well-off, you usually hit the little guy. The truth is: For 12 years they have been promising to help the little guy — and then giving all the breaks to the well-off. And it is time that that stopped.

As Democrats, our purpose is not just to end this recession but to begin a new time of economic growth and progress.

So we will propose a new commitment to civilian technology and research. For half a century, American weapons were the best in the world. As we enter the new century, America must build the best consumer and industrial products.

We will pursue a trade policy that opens markets on equal terms so that when we buy from Europe and Asia, they will be buying from us as well. We will demand far-reaching changes in education and training so that our students will be first, not last, among the industrial nations in science and math—and so our workers will have the skills and the change to compete successfully with anyone, anywhere.

We will also fight for fundamental change in the area of health care.

Today, millions of Americans have no health insurance at all. And even those who do have no assurance that they are safe. People worry that if they get sick, their coverage will be canceled. Premiums and out-of-pocket costs continue to multiply. Workers who lose their jobs suddenly find their children without health insurance.

This issue will be a test of our national character.

Few Americans realize that the United States and South Africa are the only economically advanced nations that do not guarantee the health care of their people.

We will fight to change that in this Congress—and in the next one,—as long as it takes—because lives and health are at stake, and so is the financial health of America's families.

It is not enough to make minor changes—to tinker at the edges while tolerating basic flaws. We want to replace the status quo, not protect it. We want to help the middle-class family—not tax its health-care benefits.

It is time for national health insurance. It is time to cover every American. It is time to control costs.

Because otherwise we will continue to pay more and more for less and less.

And soon, the burden will break the budgets of middle-class families, of business and of government at every level.

Health care is one of the great unfinished tasks of our society. Almost 60 years ago, America decided that people should age with dignity—and we passed Social Security. Now we must decide that families will live with dignity—and pass national health insurance.

Finally, there are other, urgent issues of basic justice that also go to our character as a nation. So we will oppose any effort from any quarter to widen and exploit racial division—or lessen our commitment to break down the barriers and at long last fulfill the pledge that millions of us make every day, from the schoolhouses of America to the floor of the House of Representatives: that we shall be "one nation, under God, indivisible, with liberty and justice for all." Appeals to race should have no place in our politics or our national life.

We will stand for another civil right of every American—the civil right to be protected from violence and crime.

Election after election, we hear tough talk; this year, we will pass tougher laws if the president will ask the Republicans in the Senate to stop filibustering the crime bill that has already been passed by the House of Representatives.

We will stand—and we will fight—for a woman's right to choose. If the Supreme Court removes the guarantees of choice from the Constitution of the United States, this Congress will write it into the laws of the United States.

We will stand for day care and family leave so that workers who take time off to help a sick parent or child will no longer risk their jobs.

In closing, let me reaffirm our essential resolve, which is to make America work again. For when the economy is wrong, nothing else is right.

We cannot undo all the mistakes of the past 12 years in a single year or in a single Congress.

The administration has waited a long time to act. Over and over, we have said we can fight this recession, and we will. We can change this nation fundamentally—and we have to.

It is true—the Cold War is over, the Old World past; the old ways of thinking and leading will not do.

It is time now to turn our attention to our own land and to our own people—to rebuild its economic strength and standard of life, to master the very different challenges of this new era.

Only a few times have Americans stood at so decisive a turning point. Now, with all of us working together, let's get this nation moving again.

February

NASA AND UN REPORTS
ON OZONE DEPLETION
February 3 and 5, 1992

Issued within days of each other, two major scientific reports confirmed apprehensions held by many—that the earth's protective layer of ozone was being depleted at a disturbing rate, indicating worse environmental damage than previously estimated.

The first report, released February 3 by the National Aeronautics and Space Administration (NASA), was part of the agency's series of atmospheric studies. Citing information obtained from a modified spy plane and an orbiting satellite, the NASA report warned that depletion of ozone—a form of oxygen that protects against the sun's damaging ultraviolet (UV) rays—could be occurring much more rapidly than had been expected. The second study, a United Nations report by a panel of international researchers, highlighted the ozone loss's potentially alarming threat to humans, animals, and crops.

Background: Efforts to Curtail
Damaging Gas Emissions

Public attention had first focused on ozone depletion in 1974. Two California scientists hypothesized that the discharge of man-made chlorofluorocarbons (CFCs)—a type of gas widely used as a propellant in aerosol sprays, as fluids to transmit heat in air conditioners and refrigerators, in foam insulation, to wash micro-electronic chips, and in many other industrial products and processes—could be endangering the ozone layer. Their conclusions were substantiated by further scientific evidence that "discarded" CFCs rise to the ozone layer and are decomposed by sunlight, releasing chlorine molecules (ClOs). The ClOs act as a catalyst to break apart ozone molecules. The reaction is so powerful that one chlorine molecule can destroy about 100,000 ozone molecules before drifting out of the atmosphere. Moreover, CFCs can remain in the atmosphere for a hundred years or more after they are emitted.

Faced with heightened concern about these findings, the U.S. Environmental Protection Agency (EPA) and officials from several other nations in 1978 announced a ban on the use of CFCs in aerosol spray cans. Calls for more stringent international action continued to mount, however, following a number of studies and observations, beginning in 1985, that confirmed the existence of an alarming ozone "hole" over the ecologically delicate region of Antarctica.

Reacting to these concerns, twenty-eight nations signed a Vienna Convention for the Protection of the Ozone Layer in 1985. But at that time the governments agreed only to discuss measures to control emissions of CFCs and other potentially harmful gases. After months of negotiation, fifty-seven nations signed the September 1987 Montreal Protocol on Substances that Deplete the Ozone Layer. The treaty would require a 50 percent cut in the production and consumption of CFCs and other gases by 1999. The day before the United States Senate unanimously approved the treaty in March 1988, NASA released findings of research undertaken by more than 100 scientists from the United States and several UN agencies indicating that ozone depletion was more severe than had been indicated earlier. (Scientists' Report on Ozone Depletion, Historic Documents of 1988, p. 221)

A milestone occurred in June 1990 when, meeting in London, ninety-three nations agreed to halt production of ozone-damaging chemicals, generally by the end of the century. Agreement was reached after the Bush administration, apparently responding to intense domestic and international pressure, reversed the United States' position and agreed to contribute to an international fund to help less-developed nations—which were using increasing amounts of the chemicals to boost manufactures—phase out their production by 2010. The United States was expected to contribute about $25 million to the fund, which would total $150 million to $250 million.

On April 4, 1991, EPA issued still another warning on ozone depletion—one that hit closer to home. Based on NASA data analyzed by atmospheric scientists at the Goddard Space Flight Center, the EPA report said ozone loss was occurring more than twice as rapidly as scientists had foreseen. "It's stunning information," said EPA Administrator William K. Reilly. "It is unexpected, it is disturbing, and it possesses implications we have not yet had time to fully explore."

1992 NASA Report Adds Further Evidence

In releasing preliminary findings from its two missions in February 1992, NASA researchers said data gathered from the satellite and airplane had shown "exceptionally high" levels of ClO at northern latitudes, including the northern part of the United States, Canada, Europe, and Russia. "Sustained levels of ClO could lead to significant ozone destruction over the northern hemisphere and perhaps even lead to an ozone hole over the Arctic," the NASA release warned.

"Everybody should be alarmed about this. It's far worse than we thought," said Michael Kurylo, manager of NASA's upper atmosphere research division, at a briefing for reporters.

NASA issued its end-of-mission statement on one of the studies, the Second Airborne Arctic Stratospheric Expedition, on April 30, reaffirming most of the February 3 reports but indicating that ClO abundance had dropped off, averting large-scale ozone depletion over the Arctic. Chief investigator Joe Waters said that the ClOs were "still very much at an unwanted level and of substantial concern. But they were not at the levels we saw in January which, had they persisted, could have led to a substantial northern ozone depletion this year."

UN Assesses Ozone Depletion's Harmful Effects

The UN researchers found that increased exposure to UV radiation was likely to have a "profound influence" on weakening the human immune system, thereby exposing people more readily to infectious diseases, such as AIDS. Pointing in particular to the adverse impact of UV exposure on a person's eyes and skin, they predicted there would be 1.6 million or more new cases of cataracts and 300,000 new instances of skin cancer each year worldwide by the turn of the century. The UN report also strengthened previous warnings that increased UV exposure could stunt the growth and yields of forests and crops. For ocean life, the threat was that UV-B, the most dangerous variety of the sun's ultraviolet rays, can penetrate deeply and destroy plankton, the microscopic organisms that form the basis of the ocean food chain.

Reaction and Prognosis

Acting almost immediately after the reports were released, the Senate February 6 voted to end all production of CFCs as quickly as possible. The Bush administration, which had opposed a similar proposal when it was debated the previous October, sent word that it had changed its position and would support the legislation, sponsored by Sen. Al Gore of Tennessee, who later became the Democratic nominee for vice president. "Now with the potential ozone hole above Kennebunkport [President George Bush's vacation residence in Maine], the message is beginning to get through," Gore said during debate on the measure.

As they had in the past, many industry spokespersons, while supporting restrictions on CFC production, expressed their unhappiness about the uncertainty caused by repeated changes in national regulation and international law.

Among those urging caution was Thomas Gale Moore, a senior fellow at Stanford's Hoover Institution, a conservative think-tank. "Although it *does seem prudent to phase out CFCs, panic is unjustified," Moore wrote. "The ozone layer will be around to protect us in the future, and we will be able to deal with any thinning by avoiding excess sun and using proper protection." According to the UN Environment Program, there had been a 40 percent drop in CFC consumption since 1986, largely because of accelerated phaseouts in industrialized countries.*

Following are the texts of NASA news releases 92-18 and 92-19, both issued February 3, 1992, and the executive summary of the UN report entitled "Environmental Effects of Ozone Depletion: 1991 Update," released February 5, 1992:

NASA PRESS RELEASE

NASA Release 92-18

Recent observations by NASA's Upper Atmosphere Research Satellite (UARS) have shown exceptionally high levels of chlorine monoxide (ClO) at high northern latitudes, raising the possibility of enhanced ozone depletion over populated areas of the Earth, according to a UARS scientist.

UARS' Microwave Limb Sounder (MLS) detected elevated levels of ClO, a key constituent in the chemical processes that leads to ozone depletion over large, populated areas of Europe and Asia north of about 50 degrees latitude, said the principal investigator for the MLS, Dr. Joe Waters of NASA's Jet Propulsion Laboratory, Pasadena, Calif. On Jan. 11, 1992, for example, high ClO levels were observed over Scandinavia and Northern Eurasia, including the cities of London, Moscow and Amsterdam.

These ClO levels, approximately 1 part per billion by volume, are comparable to levels observed within the Antarctic ozone hole. Stratospheric ClO molecules, which result primarily from industrial chemicals such as chlorofluorocarbons (CFCs) released in the lower atmosphere, are the dominant form of chlorine that destroys ozone in a process that starts when sunlight breaks up the CFCs.

Sustained levels of ClO could lead to significant ozone destruction over the northern hemisphere and perhaps, even lead to an ozone hole over the Arctic, Waters said. Whether an ozone hole actually develops will depend on how long the elevated ClO levels persist.

MLS data also show very low ozone levels in the tropical stratosphere over an area roughly coinciding with the Mount Pinatubo volcanic plume. Observation of reduced ozone in the tropics, linked to volcanic plumes, raises the possibility that volcanic eruptions may trigger ozone depletion processes similar to those that occur within the Antarctic ozone hole.

In the tropics, preliminary results show ozone levels at an altitude of 13 miles were about 50 percent less than typical pre-eruption levels observed by other means since UARS was launched Sept. 12, 1991, three months after Mount Pinatubo erupted. MLS total ozone levels in the tropics appear about 10 percent lower than typical. This area of low ozone extends roughly from 10 degrees South latitude to about 20 degrees North latitude. In addition, the MLS observed transient areas of low ozone across the western United States, findings that were corroborated by independent ground-based measurements in Boulder, Colo.

Computer models have predicted that aerosols from Mount Pinatubo would deplete the ozone layer at a greater rate than previous volcanic eruptions because of the additional chlorine. These models assumed that chemical reactions would occur on the surfaces of the stratospheric sulfur compounds within the volcanic cloud that are similar to reactions that occur on the surfaces of stratospheric ice crystals in Antarctica. The possibility also exists, Waters said, that the low tropical ozone is due to atmospheric dynamics rather than chemistry.

UARS is providing the first opportunity to study these processes from a global perspective. During UARS' primary mission, scientists will have the chance to monitor ozone depletion through two northern winters. UARS scientists will combine data from the 10 instruments to develop a long-term three-dimensional profile of the chemistry, dynamics and energetics of the Earth's upper atmosphere. UARS data also will be combined with data collected from ground-based, aircraft and balloon campaigns.

The MLS team announced their results in five scientific papers given at the recent meeting of the American Meteorological Society in Atlanta.

The Goddard Space Flight Center manages the UARS Project for NASA's Office of Space Science and Applications. JPL developed and operates the MLS on UARS with collaboration from Heriot-Watt University, Edinburgh University and Rutherford Appleton Laboratory, in the United Kingdom.

NASA PRESS RELEASE

NASA Release 92-19

Preliminary results from a NASA-led aircraft study of the upper atmosphere over the Arctic and northern mid-latitudes indicate that development of a late-winter "ozone hole" over the Northern Hemisphere is increasingly likely. Data also show a lessening of the atmosphere's ability to recover from periods of ozone depletion.

Scientists working in the second Airborne Arctic Stratospheric Expedition (AASE II), a 6-month, multi-agency program, found the highest levels of chlorine monoxide (ClO), 1.5 parts per billion by volume, ever measured in either polar region during flights over eastern Canada and northern New England. Calculations indicate that such ClO levels, together with smaller amounts of bromine monoxide (BrO), are high enough to destroy ozone at a rate of 1 to 2 percent a day during the relatively brief period of sunlight present at these latitudes in mid-January, said NASA's Dr. Michael Kurylo, the AASE II Program Manager/Program Scientist.

Stratospheric ClO and BrO result primarily from chlorofluorocarbons (CFCs, used as refrigerants) and halons (bromine compounds used as fire suppressants), industrial products that are released at the Earth's surface.

The total amount of ozone depletion and whether an Arctic ozone hole develops depends on meteorological conditions, specifically the size and duration of the polar vortex, a very cold mass of air isolated by high-level winds. When the air within the polar vortex becomes cold enough, small water ice and nitric acid ice particles form. These polar stratospheric clouds, together with stratospheric liquid droplets called aerosols, provide surfaces on which the reactive forms of chlorine are generated.

Ozone destruction then occurs through a series of chemical reactions initiated by sunlight. The possibility of significant ozone loss over the Arctic will be greatest when the vortex remains intact until the end of February, Dr. Kurylo said.

The AASE II program comprises flights of NASA's DC-8 and ER-2 aircraft carrying scientific instruments to make remote and "in situ" observations of actual chemical levels in the Arctic atmosphere. AASE II began with flights from Fairbanks, Alaska, in October and has continued with flights from Bangor, Maine, in December and January. AASE II will continue through March.

As the vortex oscillated in January, covering different regions of the Arctic, the ER-2 was able to make an unprecedented flight into its center. Scientists thus were able to observe the extent to which non-reactive chlorine had been converted to reactive chlorine, and they concluded that virtually the entire vortex had been converted by mid-January.

The AASE II measurements also showed that nitrogen oxides, which help convert reactive chlorine and bromine into non-reactive forms, are significantly depleted throughout the lower polar stratosphere. These findings are direct observational evidence that this important mechanism for checking ozone-depletion is rendered less robust due to chemical reactions of nitrogen oxides on stratospheric aerosols. Thus, the rate at which the atmosphere is able to recover from ozone depletion is reduced, Dr. Kurylo said.

AASE II measurements conducted at latitudes as far south as 22 degrees North also show pervasive elevated levels of reactive chlorine and reduced levels of nitrogen oxides. These conditions provide the first direct evidence in the Northern Hemisphere linking global ozone reductions seen by satellite to catalytic reactions involving chlorine and bromine in the lower stratosphere. The presence of enhanced volcanic aerosols from Mount Pinatubo appears to amplify the increased concentrations of ClO, the reduced concentrations of nitrogen oxides and hence, the loss of ozone.

AASE II is a multi-agency effort involving NASA, the National Oceanic and Atmospheric Administration and the National Science Foundation, as well as the chemical industry's Alternate Flourocarbon Environmental Acceptability Study. Scientists from several U.S. government laboratories and universities are participating. The NASA aircraft are managed by the Ames Research Center, Moffett Field, Calif., for NASA's Office of Space Science and Applications.

UN REPORT EXECUTIVE SUMMARY
ENVIRONMENTAL EFFECTS OF OZONE DEPLETION

Solar Interactions

- Significant global scale decreases in total ozone have occurred over the past ten years.
- All other factors being constant, there is no scientific doubt that decreases in total ozone will increase UV-B [ultraviolet-B] radiation at ground level.
- Tropospheric ozone and aerosols may have masked the consequences of stratospheric ozone depletion for UV-B in some industrialized regions.
- It is likely that in areas remote from anthropogenic emissions, the UV-B changes due to stratospheric ozone depletion would be only partially compensated by tropospheric ozone and aerosol increases.
- There are no reliable estimates of the direction or magnitude of effects of any cloud cover trends on UV-B.
- Efforts to improve local and regional air quality may bring to light the increases in UV-B associated with the depletion of stratospheric ozone.

Human Health

- The induction of immunosuppression by UV-B has now been demonstrated in humans, not only those of light pigmentation, but also deeply pigmented individuals. This places all of the world's populations at risk of the potential adverse impacts of UV-B on the immune system, including possible increases in the incidence or severity of infectious disease.
- An increased number of adverse ocular effects have been associated with exposure to UV. These include age-related nearsightedness, deformation of the lens capsule, and nuclear cataract (a form of cataract which previous information excluded from consideration). These effects appear to be independent of pigmentation. Estimates of risk would increase slightly if one were to include nuclear cataract

among the forms of cataract increasing with ozone depletion. It is now predicted that, all other things being equal, a sustained 10% decrease in ozone will be associated with between 1.6 and 1.75 million additional cases of cataract per year world-wide.

- Recent information on the relationship of non-melanoma skin cancer to UV exposures confirms previous findings and has allowed refinement of the carcinogenic action spectrum. Incorporation of this new information into the risk estimation process has led to slightly lower predictions. It is now predicted that a sustained 10% decrease in ozone will be associated with a 26% increase in non-melanoma skin cancer. All other things remaining constant, this would mean an increase in excess of 300,000 cases per year world-wide.

Terrestrial Plants

- Continued research on plant responses to UV-B radiation underscores the concern for agriculture, forestry, and natural ecosystems as the ozone layer is depleted.
- Growth and photosynthesis of certain plants (e.g., seedlings of rye, maize, and sunflower) can be inhibited even under ambient levels of UV-B radiation.
- Certain environmental factors, both biotic (e.g., plant diseases and competition with other plants) and abiotic (e.g., carbon dioxide, temperature, heavy metals, and water availability), can interact with the effect of UV-B radiation in plants. This makes it difficult to make quantitative predictions.
- Although most research to date has been with plants from temperate regions, data also show that certain tropical species may be adversely affected by enhanced UV-B radiation.

Aquatic Ecosystems

- Marine phytoplankton produces at least as much biomass as all terrestrial ecosystems combined.
- Recent results show that the aquatic ecosystem is already under UV-B stress and there is concern that an increase in UV-B radiation will cause detrimental effects.
- One consequence of losses in phytoplankton is reduced biomass production which is propagated throughout the whole food web. This may result in losses of biomass for human consumption.
- The marine phytoplankton is a major sink for atmospheric carbon dioxide. Any reduction of the populations would decrease the uptake of carbon dioxide and so augment the greenhouse effect. Also, phytoplankton production of DMS (dimethylsulphate), which acts as a precursor of cloud nucleation, would be reduced, hence potentially affecting global climate.
- A UV-B induced decrease in microorganisms fixing atmospheric

nitrogen would require significant substitution by artificial fertilizers, e.g., in rice production.

Tropospheric Air Quality

- Chemical reactivity in the troposphere is expected to increase in response to increases in UV-B.
- Tropospheric ozone concentrations could rise in moderate to heavily polluted areas, but should decrease in unpolluted regions (with low oxides of nitrogen levels), as recently confirmed by measurements in the Antarctic.
- Other potentially harmful substances (hydrogen peroxide, acids, and aerosols) are expected to increase in all regions of the troposphere due to the enhanced chemical reactivity.
- These changes could exacerbate problems of human health and welfare, increase damage to the biosphere, and might make current air quality goals more difficult and expensive to attain.

Materials Damage

- UV-B radiation is particularly effective in light-induced degradation of wood and plastic products, leading to discoloration and loss of strength. Increased UV-B content in sunlight will cause more rapid degradation, resulting in increased costs of using higher levels of conventional light stabilizers, possible design of new stabilizers, and faster replacement of the affected products.
- Available research data are inadequate to reliably estimate the damage from higher UV-B levels to materials. Very limited relevant data are available for important classes of materials such as wood, plastic coatings, plastics used outdoors, and rubber. Data pertaining to performance of plastics in near-equator regions of the world, with the harshest exposure environments, are particularly needed.
- Some on-going work relating to exposure of plastics under desert conditions is likely to contribute some of the needed data within the next few years. This may lead to improved assessment of damage to plastics resulting from partial ozone depletion, at that time.

Key Areas of Uncertainty

The key areas of uncertainty are the following:

- Quantification of the primary effects on food production and quality, on forestry, and on natural ecosystems.
- Clarification and quantification of influences on human health, especially the immune system, and occurrences of melanomas and cataracts.
- Effects on biota of the enhanced UV radiation during the Antarctic springtime ozone depletion.

INTERNATIONAL MATH-SCIENCE TEST OF YOUNG STUDENTS

February 5, 1992

A twenty-nation comparison of 175,000 students' test scores in 1990 and 1991 confirmed the fears of many educators and business leaders that American students were lagging in math and science skills and thus were being less well prepared to compete in an increasingly complex and technologically oriented world. The test scores showed students in several other nations outperforming their U.S. counterparts in those critical areas. The two-volume study, conducted by the Educational Testing Service (ETS) in Princeton, New Jersey, and funded by the U.S. Department of Education, the National Science Foundation, and the Carnegie Foundation, was released February 5—two weeks after the National Council on Education Standards and Testing recommended establishing nationwide "demanding content and performance standards." (Report on National Standards for Educational Testing, p. 45)

The mathematics and science test, conducted in 6,000 classrooms worldwide, was the second such assessment conducted by ETS. The first, released in 1989, measured the math-science performance of thirteen-year-olds in six nations. Japan and Germany did not take part in the second test. (Report on the State of American Education, Historic Documents of 1989, p. 85)

The National Education Goals Panel, established in 1991 to monitor progress toward the six national education goals drawn up by the Bush administration and the nation's governors, decided to use the ETS test results, as well as four studies conducted by the International Association for the Evaluation of Educational Achievement, as measures of progress. (Education Summit, Historic Documents of 1989, p. 561)

Low U.S. Test Scores, Participation

The $2 million ETS study tested nine-year-olds in fourteen countries and thirteen-year-olds in twenty countries. The United States had among the lowest participation rates of any country; between 70 and 80 percent of schools selected agreed to participate in the test—about 1,400 students from 105 schools. The average U.S. thirteen-year-old scored 55 percent in math and 67 percent in science. However, nine-year-olds performed third in science—behind Korea and Taiwan by only 3 percentage points. Archie E. Lapointe, director of the ETS Center for the Assessment of Educational Progress, suggested that the relatively high U.S. performance at that age could be attributed to science learned out of school, such as through museum visits or educational television programs.

There appeared to be no male-female differences in math ability among thirteen-year-olds in most of the countries studied, and almost all students agreed that math "is for boys and girls about equally." Most students from all countries except Korea expressed positive attitudes toward science. American students have "very, very positive attitudes" about science and math, said Diane S. Ravitch, assistant secretary of education for educational research and improvement. "But they are not correlated with achievement. They are not good at it. They are not getting accurate feedback."

Results of the ETS test showed that the top 10 percent of American students "can compete with the best students in any country," said Education Secretary Lamar Alexander. However, noting that the majority performed below the international average, he said, "It means this is not just an inner-city problem or a rural poverty problem. It's a problem in the suburbs and in the middle-class families all over the country." The secretary said the study results reinforced the view that there should be high national performance standards. "Until we change the attitudes and standards for schools and children, we will not reach our goals," he said. "The good news is, we can reach the goals."

ETS president Gregory R. Anrig told a news conference, "There is no single magic key unlocking educational excellence." But, he added, the tests indicated that "nine- and thirteen-year-olds can learn a great deal when there is rigorous content. High expectations produce high achievement. We do a great disservice to students when we set the bar too low."

Impact of Class Size, TV Watching

The survey appeared to challenge commonly held beliefs that small class size, a longer school year, innovative techniques, and greater funding for books, computers, and teachers could boost student achievement. Korea, which along with Taiwan scored at the top in math and science in both age groups, had a comparatively large average class size of forty-nine. Students in Hungary, who also scored near the top, went to school only 177 days a year—about the same as American students.

The amount of time spent watching television, however, did appear to affect students' performance. Twenty percent of U.S. thirteen-year-olds watched at least five hours each day, compared with only 10 percent of the top-scoring Korean children and 7 percent of Taiwanese and Swiss, who ranked second and third in that age group. "This suggests that within all of those countries, the more time students spend watching television, the less well they do in science," said Lapointe. "It is not among the six national goals to lead the world in the amount of TV we watch," commented Education Secretary Alexander.

The study also found that math achievement was positively related to the number of books in the home and to the amount of time thirteen-year-olds spent reading for pleasure. The average American thirteen-year-old spent, at most, only an hour a week on science homework and another on math, compared with Taiwanese students, who devoted at least four hours a week to math homework, and Russian students, four hours a week on science homework. The Soviet Union's nine- and thirteen-year-olds ranked fourth in math and its thirteen-year-olds ranked fifth in science. Soviet nine-year-olds scored seventh in science.

Pros and Cons of International Tests

Iris C. Rotberg, a senior social scientist at the Rand Corporation, was critical of international comparisons. "The practicality of making comparisons across diverse societies and educational systems makes it difficult to interpret the findings," she said, noting that "only elite schools and regions were sampled" in some countries. "There are different curriculum emphases in different countries and the test results could reflect those" Rotberg said. "We make policy based on these findings and the findings could be misleading because of technical glitches on these tests." Moreover, she said, "It is misleading to measure problems or accomplishments simply by scores on multiple-choice tests."

However, other education experts said the ETS test adhered to rigorous technical standards for data collection and analysis. "I have no hesitancy whatsoever saying this is the most consistent, competent, international study to date," said Emerson J. Elliott, acting commissioner of the National Center for Education Statistics.

Even allowing for flaws in the test, results "still show us in a weak position relative to other countries," said Norman M. Bradburn, chairman of the Board on International Comparative Studies in Education of the National Academy of Sciences, and director of the National Opinion Research Center at the University of Chicago.

Lapointe noted that the study identified countries that tested a nonrepresentative sample of their population and separated out those that were too small to give a fair representation. "The ETS is very confident with the quality of the data," he said.

"There is no question we need to raise standards in the U.S. to compete in the world economy," said Willis D. Hawley, director of the Center for

Education and Human-Development Policy at Vanderbilt University. "That's not the issue. The issue is whether international comparisons tell us what to do."

"The test is a thermometer," said Ravitch. "It doesn't tell you what the cure is; it tells you what the problem is. But some people's reaction is to break the thermometer."

Similar Results from Another Science Test

A related science test administered by the congressionally mandated National Assessment of Educational Progress to 20,000 students in fourth, eighth, and twelfth grades showed that fewer than half of high schools seniors could interpret scientific data, evaluate science experiments, or show in-depth knowledge of scientific information. Only 25 percent of high school seniors taking science courses said they were given two or more hours of homework in the subject each week. Results of the test were released March 26. "It's disappointing but we know why," said Alexander. "We have not made science a priority." Parris C. Battle, a member of the National Assessment Governing Board, said the results indicated that "overall, average science achievement in 1990 was just about where it was in 1970, even though the world certainly changed in twenty years and has become more demanding and complex."

Following are excerpts from the introduction to the reports "Learning Mathematics" and "Learning Science," prepared by the Educational Testing Service for the International Assessment of Educational Progress, and released February 5, 1992, and the texts of the highlights sections:

Introduction to the Reports

Each of the countries that participated in the second International Assessment of Educational Progress (IAEP) did so for its own reasons. Some wanted to compare their results with those of neighbors or competitors. Others wanted to learn about the educational policies and practices of countries whose students seem to regularly achieve success in mathematics and science. Still others wanted to establish a baseline of data within their own countries against which they can measure progress in the future.

All participants, however, shared a common interest in identifying what is *possible* for today's 9- and 13-year old children to know and to be able to do in mathematics and science. While critics warn of the dangers of promoting an educational olympiad, the benefits of periodically gathering comparative data must be considered. Knowledge of what is *possible* produces new enthusiasm, raises sights, establishes new challenges, and ultimately can help improve personal and societal performance.

Some might say that a study that compares the United States with

Slovenia or England with Sao Paulo, Brazil is inappropriate or irrelevant. Education is, in fact, imbedded in each society and culture, and performance should not be studied or described without considering the important differences from country to country. The life of a 13-year-old in a rural Chinese community is very different from that of his or her peer growing up in a middle-class Paris apartment. And yet, these two young citizens may well meet in the global marketplace 20 years from now. And if they do, chances are they will rely on the mathematics and science they learned in this decade to succeed in the complex business and technological environment of 2012.

While recognizing the fundamental differences from country to country, the participants in the second IAEP project assembled tests that focus on the common elements of their curriculums, and in order to form the contexts for interpreting the student achievement data, they added sets of questions about students' home background and classroom experiences and the characteristics of the schools they attend.

This report, then, is organized according to those contexts that surround and affect student performance: the curriculum, classroom practices, home environments, and the characteristics of countries and their education systems. While survey research projects like IAEP cannot establish cause-and-effect relationships, these studies can provide clues that may help explain high and low performance.

Occasionally, the findings are counter-intuitive. For example, in some countries, less well-trained teachers with large classes and poor-quality instructional materials sometimes produce students who achieve truly exceptional results. In other countries, students of better paid, better trained teachers, who work in schools that are more generously supported perform less well on the IAEP tests. The results presented in this report will highlight some of these paradoxes.

One possible reaction to this report would be for a country to examine the results and attempt to find out how to become *Number 1* in the world. A more thoughtful course of action would be for each country to use this information to set reasonable goals that are in harmony with its own values and culture.

The achievement results reported here can help identify what is *possible* for 9- and 13-year-olds to achieve and the descriptive information can suggest practices and curriculums that others are using successfully. It seems reasonable to expect that each country may find elements worth emulating in the practices of its neighbors and competitcrs.

About the Project

In 1990-91, a total of 20 countries surveyed the mathematics and science performance of 13-year-old students and 14 also assessed 9-year-olds in the same subjects. An optional short probe of the geography achievement of 13-year-olds and an experimental performance-based assessment of 13-year-olds' ability to use equipment and materials to solve mathematics and science problems were also conducted by some participants and their results will be presented in forthcoming reports.

Some countries drew samples from virtually all children in the appropriate age group; others confined their assessments to specific geographic areas, language groups, or grade levels. The definition of populations often followed the structure of school systems, political divisions, and cultural distinctions. For example, the sample in Israel focused on students in Hebrew-speaking schools, which share a common curriculum, language, and tradition. The assessment in Slovenia reflected the needs and aspirations of this recently separated republic of Yugoslavia. The restriction to certain grades in the Portuguese assessment was necessitated by a very dispersed student population resulting from a unique education system that allows students to repeat any grade up to three times. All countries limited their assessment to students who were in school, which for some participants meant excluding significant numbers of age-eligible children. In a few cases, a sizable proportion of the selected schools or students did not participate in the assessment, and therefore results are subject to possible nonresponse bias.

A list of the participants is provided below with a description of limitations of the populations assessed. Unless noted, 90 percent or more of the age-eligible children in a population are in school. For countries where more than 10 percent of the age-eligible children are out of school a notation of *in-school population* appears after the country's name. In Brazil, two separate samples were drawn, one each from the cities of Sao Paulo and Fortaleza. In Canada, nine out of the 10 provinces drew separate samples of 13-year-olds and five of these drew separate samples of English-speaking and French-speaking schools, for a total of 14 separate samples. Four Canadian provinces, six separate samples, participated in the assessment of 9-year-olds. These distinct Canadian samples coincide with the separate provincial education systems in Canada and reflect their concern for the two language groups they serve.

Participants

Brazil	Cities of Sao Paulo and Fortaleza, restricted grades, in school population
Canada	Four provinces at age 9 and nine out of 10 provinces at age 13
China	20 out of 29 provinces and independent cities, restricted grades, in-school population
England	All students, low participation at ages 9 and 13
France	All students
Hungary	All students
Ireland	All students
Israel	Hebrew-speaking schools
Italy	Province of Emilia-Romogna, low participation at age 9

Jordan	All students
Korea	All students
Mozambique	Cities of Maputo and Beira, in-school population, low participation
Portugal	Restricted grades, in-school population at age 13
Scotland	All students, low participation at age 9
Slovenia	All students
Soviet Union	14 out of 15 republics, Russian-speaking schools
Spain	All regions except Cataluna, Spanish-speaking schools
Switzerland	15 out of 25 cantons
Taiwan	All students
United States	All students

Typically, a representative sample of 3,300 students from 110 different schools was selected from each population at each age level and half were assessed in mathematics and half in science. A total of about 175,000 9- and 13-year-olds (those born in calendar years 1981 and 1977, respectively) were tested in 13 different languages in March 1991.

Steps to ensure the uniformity and quality of the surveys were taken at all stages of the project. While procedures could not always be followed in exactly the same way in each of the separate assessment centers, overall compliance was very high, as shown in the quality control procedures provided in the figure on the next page. Translations and adaptations of assessment materials were carefully checked for accuracy. All questions were pilot-tested in participating countries before they were used in the final assessment. Comparable sampling designs were used by all participants and the quality of their implementation was carefully checked and documented. Participants were provided with training and computer software to facilitate their tasks and to ensure uniformity and quality. Test administrators were trained to administer the tests to students using the same set of instructions and time limits. The standardization of administration procedures was carefully checked within each country and across countries by an international monitoring team. While the reports of the quality control observers were for the most part completed check lists, some impressionistic observations of international monitoring team members are interspersed throughout this report to give a more personal view of the test administration in several countries. The accuracy of the database was validated though independent checks of a random selection of completed student test booklets and school questionnaires; the accuracy of the data analysis was validated by comparing the results obtained using different statistical programs and computer equipment.

A Word About Comparisons

A major challenge of international studies is to provide fair comparisons of student achievement. Some of the problems faced by these studies are similar to those of any survey research project. For example, samples must be adequately drawn, test administration procedures must be scrupulously adhered to, care must be taken to produce accurate data files. These concerns are not trivial. However, international studies must also address a number of unique issues that stem from the differences in language, culture, and education systems of the participating countries.

Three areas of concern warrant special attention: the representativeness of the target population, the appropriateness of the measures, and educational and cultural differences. As indicated earlier, some participants confined assessments to particular geographic areas, language groups, or grade levels and in some cases, significant numbers of age-eligible children were not attending school and in other cases, participation rates of schools or students were low.... There is simply no way to measure the bias introduced when certain groups of children are excluded from a sample or when response rates are low; their participation could have raised performance scores, lowered them, or not affected them at all....

Countries also differ with respect to the appropriateness of the curricular areas the IAEP assessment sought to measure. All countries participated in the development of the mathematics and science frameworks that guided the design of the instruments; curricular experts in each country reviewed all potential questions for their appropriateness for their own students. While acceptable to all, the resulting tests do not match all countries' curricula equally well....

- The highest-achieving countries with the exception of Taiwan do not practice ability grouping within science classes at age 13. In England (low participation) and Taiwan, more than one-half the schools reported this practice. All other populations were likely to form mixed-ability science classes.
- Thirteen-year-old students in most countries do not spend a great deal of time doing science homework. Between 55 and 90 percent of the students reported spending one hour or less *each week* in all populations except the Soviet Union (Russian-speaking schools) where 59 percent of the students spend four hours or more weekly on science homework.
- Thirteen-year-olds are much more likely to spend their spare time watching television than studying. The most common response is two to four hours of television viewing *each day* in all but two IAEP populations. Twenty percent or more of 13-year-olds from Israel (Hebrew), Scotland, the United States, England (low participation), and Fortaleza (restricted grades) indicated that they watch five hours or more of television each school day.
- Most students in most populations have positive attitudes about science, except students from Korea where only one quarter of these top-performing students exhibited positive attitudes; conversely, stu-

dents in Jordan, who are relatively lower-performing have the greatest percentage of students with positive attitudes (82 percent).

- The range of average performance across the 14 populations participating in the IAEP assessment at age 9 was 13 points. In almost all populations, at least 10 percent of the students performed well (15 points or more above the IAEP average) and at least 10 percent performed poorly (15 points or more below the IAEP average).
- The difference in performance between 9- and 13-year-olds in each of the 14 populations ranged from 15 to 25 points.

Furthermore, the testing format—multiple-choice and short-answer questions—is not equally familiar to students from all countries. To address this issue, participants were given the option of administering a practice test to sampled students prior to the assessment. Finally, since countries differ in the age at which students start school and policies for promotion, students at ages 9 and 13 are further along in their schooling in some countries than in others. While all results presented in this report represent performance of all students in each age group, participants were also provided with results broken down by the two most common grade levels for students in each age group.

International results must ultimately be interpreted in light of the educational and cultural context of each country. The countries participating in IAEP are large and small, rich and poor, and have varied ethnic, religious, language, and cultural traditions. Likewise, educational goals, expectations, and even the meaning of achievement vary from nation to nation. As a reminder of these differences among countries, results are presented along with relevant contextual information that is designed to help the reader interpret their significance.

Highlights of Learning Mathematics

- Factors that impact academic performance interact in complex ways and operate differently in various cultural and educational systems. There is no single formula for success.
- The IAEP results demonstrate what is *possible* for 9- and 13-year-olds to achieve in mathematics. This information can be instructive to policy makers as they attempt to set goals and standards for their own young citizens.
- In almost all 13-year-old populations, at least 10 percent of the students performed very well (20 points or more above the IAEP average) and at least 10 percent performed poorly (20 points or more below the IAEP average). In China (in-school population), however, even students in the 10th percentile performed close to the IAEP average.
- In about one-third of the populations, 13-year-old boys performed significantly better than girls that age. Nevertheless, in almost all populations, three quarters or more of the students felt "mathematics

is for boys and girls about equally."

- Most countries include whole-number operations in their instructional programs for age 13. Students in many countries that emphasize geometry or algebra performed well in those topics as well as in mathematics overall. Taiwan, a high-performing population, is an exception: their schools do not emphasize geometry at this age level. Although Spain (except Cataluna), Portugal (restricted grades), Sao Paulo (restricted grades), and Fortaleza (restricted grades) all emphasize algebra at age 13, students in those places were lower performers.
- Teaching practices, types of instructional materials, teacher background, and classroom organization vary from country to country for children at age 13; moreover, these factors do not distinguish between high-performing and low-performing populations.
- Within individual populations, greater frequency of teacher presentation and independent work are associated with higher performance for the majority of IAEP participants, suggesting either the importance of intensity of instruction in general or of these practices in particular.
- Thirteen-year-old students in most participating countries do not spend a great deal of time doing mathematics homework. The most common response is one hour or less *each week* in all populations except Korea and Israel, where the norm is two to three hours weekly and China, where the most common response is four hours or more weekly.
- Thirteen-year-olds are much more likely to spend their spare time watching television than studying. The norm is two to four hours of television viewing *each day* in all but two IAEP populations. In China (in-school population), 65 percent of the students reported watching little or no television on a daily basis. Slightly more than one-half of the students in France reported watching one hour or less of television each day.
- While socioeconomic factors seem to be associated with mathematics performance at age 13 in many IAEP populations, so are students' out-of-school activities. Amount of leisure reading and time spent on all homework is positively related to mathematics achievement, while amount of time spent watching television is negatively related in about one-half participating countries.
- The range of average performance across the 14 populations participating in the IAEP assessment at age 9 was 20 points, and in almost all populations, at least 10 percent of the students performed very well (20 points or more above the IAEP average) and at least 10 percent performed poorly (20 points or more below the IAEP average).
- The difference in performance between 9- and 13-year-olds in each of the 14 populations ranged from a 22- to 32-point increase.

Highlights of Learning Science

- Factors that impact academic performance, interact in complex ways, and operate differently in various cultures and education systems.

There is no single formula for success.

- The IAEP results demonstrate what is *possible* for 9- and 13-year-olds to achieve in science. This information can be instructive for policy makers as they set goals and standards for their own young citizens.
- In almost all 13-year-old populations at least 10 percent of the students performed well (15 points or more above the IAEP average) and at least 10 percent performed poorly (15 points or more below the IAEP average).
- In nearly all populations, 13-year-old boys performed significantly better than girls that age. Nevertheless, in almost all populations, three-quarters or more of the students felt "science is for boys and girls about equally."
- Science tests and quizzes are most frequently used in Taiwan, the Soviet Union (Russian-speaking schools), the United States, and Jordan. From 67 to almost 90 percent of students take tests or quizzes at least once a week compared with fewer than one-half of the students from most other populations.
- Within individual populations, greater frequency of teacher presentations is associated with higher performance for the majority of IAEP participants, suggesting either the importance of the intensity of instruction in general or of this practice in particular.

The highest-achieving countries with the exception of Taiwan do not practice ability grouping within science classes at age 13. In England (low participation) and Taiwan, more than one-half the schools reported this practice. All other populations were likely to form mixed-ability science classes.

Thirteen-year-old students in most countries do not spend a great deal of time doing science homework. Between 55 and 90 percent of the students reported spending one hour or less *each week* in all populations except the Soviet Union (Russian-speaking schools) where 59 percent of the students spend four hours or more weekly on science homework.

Thirteen-year-olds are much more likely to spend their spare time watching television than studying. The most common response is two to four hours of television viewing *each day* in all but two IAEP populations. Twenty percent or more of 13-year-olds from Israel (Hebrew), Scotland, the United States, England (low participation), and Fortaleza (restricted grades) indicated that they watch five hours or more of television each school day.

Most students in most populations have positive attitudes about science, except students from Korea where only one quarter of these top-performing students exhibited positive attitudes; conversely, students in Jordan, who are relatively lower-performing have the greatest percentage of students with positive attitudes (82 percent).

The range of average performance across the 14 populations participating in the IAEP assessment at age 9 was 13 points. In almost all populations, at least 10 percent of the students performed well (15 points or more above the IAEP average) and at least 10 percent performed poorly (15 points or more below the IAEP average).

The difference in performance between 9- and 13-year-olds in each of the 14 populations ranged from 15 to 25 points.

PRESIDENT'S ECONOMIC REPORT; ECONOMIC ADVISERS' REPORT

February 5, 1992

Predicting an early end to the stubborn recession, President George Bush and his Council of Economic Advisers (CEA) presented their third economic reports to Congress on February 5. Both Bush and his advisers stressed the importance of a vigorous economy and pressed for adoption by Congress of the president's recovery plan. Bush had presented the plan in his State of the Union address on January 28 and in his fiscal 1993 budget, released the next day. (State of the Union Address and Democratic Response, p. 55)

With an end to the cold war, the attention of Americans seemed suddenly focused on domestic affairs. The recession, creating widespread hardship and sapping the nation's confidence, had taken a huge toll. Indeed, the bleak economy was a major issue in the 1992 presidential campaign, and it was clear that Bush's reelection prospects would be greatly enhanced if a turnaround came well before the general election in November. That did not happen, and the continuing economic downturn was a major reason behind Democratic challenger Bill Clinton's victory over Bush in November.

In a brief introduction to the 258-page report of his economic advisers, Bush said that "recent economic problems are a reminder that even a well-functioning economy may face the risk of temporary setbacks...."

While devoting many pages in their report to the recession, the president's economists also turned to two long-term issues considered critical to the nation's economic health. They were the persistent slowdown in productivity growth and the increasingly inequality of incomes since the 1960s.

Alternative Forecasts

The economic advisers offered two sets of forecasts: one if Congress approved Bush's package of tax cuts and other measures designed to stimulate growth and another set if Congress failed to pass it. The double forecasts were presented in a section entitled, "The President's Policies or Business as Usual." Writing in the New York Times on February 6, Steven Greenhouse characterized the economists' report as "more partisan than most."

The report said that real gross domestic product (GDP) would increase by 2.2 percent from the fourth quarter of 1991 to the fourth quarter of 1992—if the president's plan were enacted. Otherwise, the economists said, real GDP would increase by a sluggish 1.6 percent. Gross domestic product was a measure of all the goods and services produced in the United States.

The report also projected that the unemployment rate would drop from about 6.9 percent in 1992 to 6.1 percent in 1994. In the same period, interest rates on ninety-day Treasury bills would rise from 4.1 percent to 5.3 percent.

The economists wrote that they expected the economy to be "sluggish in the early part of 1992" but improving by midyear. In mid-March 1992 many private economists thought they could see faint signs of recovery. March 18 reports on housing and industrial activity were described by CEA chairman Michael J. Boskin as "very good news." Still, Boskin cautioned, "We should wait for broader signs of recovery for a longer period of time before jumping to any conclusions." The recession was the ninth in the post-World War II period. It was also the longest.

In their report published one year earlier, the president's economists had predicted that the recession, which began in the summer of 1990, would end by the middle of 1991. In their new report, they analyzed what had actually happened and why their earlier forecast had been wrong. (President's Economic Report, Economic Advisers' Report, Historic Documents of 1991, p. 73)

By late summer of 1991, the recovery "lost momentum," the new report said. "A self-reinforcing process of growth . . . typically occurs in recoveries. In 1991, however, the spending and production gains and the positive feedback between them were not sufficient to sustain a solid recovery. . . ."

The council blamed the recession on the "oil shock" following Iraq's invasion of Kuwait, on serious problems in the financial sector, and on decisions taken by the Federal Reserve Board. The council assigned no blame to the administrations of either Ronald Reagan or George Bush.

With respect to the Federal Reserve Board, the report said that "it appears that monetary policy should have been geared to lowering interest rates faster and earlier." It said that sluggish demand for credit "in a weaker-than-expected economy" and "fallout" from banking problems "prevented the quantity of credit from expanding as the Fed

[Federal Reserve Board] thought, it would when it lowered interest rates."

In early 1992, the report said, interest rates were generally at their lowest levels in at least two decades. Three-month Treasury bills, it said, fell from 7.2 percent in October 1990 to about 3.8 percent early in 1992.

Slowdown in Productivity Growth

The report called productivity growth "the key to each worker's well-being and the Nation's prosperity." From 1937 to 1973 productivity, or output per worker, grew at a rate of 3.0 percent a year. However, since 1973, when the petroleum exporting countries' embargo against the United States caused the first "oil shock," productivity growth had averaged only 0.9 percent a year.

To raise the rate of productivity growth, the report said the national rate of investment should be increased. It also recommended that the government encourage innovation "in areas where private investors find it difficult to capture the full benefits of new knowledge."

In a discussion of the quality of the U.S. labor force, the economists said productive skills were not "perfectly correlated" with the length of classroom education. Significant factors, they said, were the "quality and relevance" of instruction.

New CEA Members

Two of the three members of the Council of Economic Advisers were new, having taken office on November 13, 1991. They were David F. Bradford, professor of economics and public affairs at Princeton University, and Paul Wonnacott, professor of economics at the University of Maryland. They replaced Richard L. Schmalensee and John B. Taylor, who resigned. Boskin continued as chairman.

Following is the text of the Economic Report of the President and excerpts from the Annual Report of the Council of Economic Advisers, both issued by the White House February 5, 1992:

ECONOMIC REPORT OF THE PRESIDENT

To the Congress of the United States:

1991 was a challenging year for the American economy. Output was stagnant and unemployment rose. The recession, which began in the third quarter of 1990, following the longest peacetime expansion in the Nation's history, continued into 1991. The high oil prices and the uncertainty occasioned by events in the Persian Gulf were quickly resolved with the successful completion of Operation Desert Storm early in the year. Most analysts expected a sustained recovery to follow. Indeed, signs of a moderate expansion began to appear in the spring. Industrial production and consumer spending rose for several months. By the late summer, however, the economy flattened out and was sluggish through the rest of the year.

Our recent economic problems are a reminder that even a well-functioning economy faces the risk of temporary setbacks from external shocks or other disturbances. Market economies, such as the United States, are continually restructuring in response to technological changes and external events. Occasionally, structural imbalances develop that can interrupt economic growth. The American economy experienced an unusual confluence of such imbalances in recent years, for example in the financial and real estate sectors, and in household, corporate, and governmental debt. At the same time, a major reallocation of resources from defense to other sectors has been under way. Not least, the lagged effects of a relatively tight monetary policy coupled with problems in the availability of credit, especially for small and medium-sized businesses, dampened economic growth.

The U.S. economy, however, remains the largest and strongest in the world. The American people enjoy the highest standard of living on earth. American productivity is second to none. With less than 5 percent of the world's population, America produces a quarter of the world's output.

As we move into 1992, the fundamental conditions to generate economic growth are falling into place. Interest rates are at their lowest levels in decades and should help boost investment and consumer spending. Inflation is down and expected to remain relatively low. Generally lean inventories imply that increases in demand will be met mainly from new production, which will generate gains in employment and income. America's international competitive position has improved, as evidenced by record levels of exports.

Nevertheless, the United States faces serious economic challenges: to speed, strengthen, and sustain economic recovery; and, simultaneously, to provide a firmer basis for long-term growth in productivity, income, and employment opportunities. In both my State of the Union address and my fiscal 1993 Budget, I presented a comprehensive program to encourage short-term recovery and long-term growth. I have already taken steps to accelerate job-creating Federal spending, to adjust income tax withholding that will add about $25 billion to the economy over the next year, and to renew the attack on excessive regulation and red tape that hamper business formation and expansion and job creation. I will also continue to support a monetary policy that keeps inflation and interest rates low while providing adequate growth of money and credit to support a healthy economic expansion.

Most of my program will require congressional action. In addition to the executive actions I have already announced, my immediate agenda includes:

- Investment incentives to promote economic growth: a reduction in capital gains tax rates; a 15-percent investment tax allowance; and an improved alternative minimum tax.
- Incentives to help revive real estate: a $5,000 tax credit for first-time homebuyers; penalty-free withdrawals from individual retirement accounts for first-time homebuyers; low-income housing credits; tax preferences for mortgage revenue bonds; a modified passive loss tax rule; and a tax deduction for losses on the sale of a personal residence.

My intermediate and longer term agenda includes:

- Investment in the future: record levels of spending for Head Start and for anti-crime and drug abuse programs; a comprehensive Job Training 2000 initiative, which will enhance the skills and flexibility of our work force; record levels of spending for research and development and infrastructure; record spending on math and science education; and Enterprise Zones.
- Pro-family initiatives: an increase in the personal tax exemption for families with children; new flexible individual retirement accounts for health, education, and first home purchases; and tax deductibility of interest paid on student loans.
- Comprehensive health reform: vital cost containment measures and tax credits for the purchase of health insurance.

Also before the Congress is an urgent unfinished agenda that I proposed earlier, including financial sector reform to make our banking system safer, sounder, and more internationally competitive; the America 2000 education reforms necessary to meet the national education goals, produce a new generation of American schools, and provide the choice and competition that will promote better performance and strengthen accountability; the National Energy Strategy to meet our Nation's energy needs through a combination of enhanced production, diversification of sources, and conservation, thereby enhancing our energy security; and legal reforms to reduce the litigiousness that unnecessarily adds to costs and stifles innovation and productivity.

Successful completion of the Uruguay Round of the General Agreement on Tariffs and Trade and a North American free-trade agreement remain major priorities. I also urge congressional action on the Enterprise for the Americas Initiative. These market-opening initiatives will spur growth and create jobs.

My program can be accommodated within the limits established in the budget agreement of 1990. I am also asking the Congress for budget process reforms: a line-item veto and caps on so-called mandatory programs to control the growth of government spending. Maintaining fiscal discipline is essential to reallocating resources toward investment in the future.

These proposals are described in detail in the fiscal 1993 Budget, and in legislative proposals I am forwarding to the Congress. *The Annual Report of the Council of Economic Advisers*, which accompanies this *Report*, discusses the strengths of the U.S. economy and the challenges it faces in the short run and the long run. It also explains how my comprehensive economic growth proposals are designed to move us toward a more prosperous America.

THE ANNUAL REPORT OF THE COUNCIL OF ECONOMIC ADVISERS

The American Economy: Responding to Challenges

The United States is the most prosperous and productive Nation on earth. With less than 5 percent of the world's population, America produces a quarter of the world's total output. The longest peacetime economic expansion in the Nation's history, 1982 to 1990, produced 30 percent more output, 21 million jobs, and 5 million new corporations.

However, no economic system is immune to disruption. Even well-functioning market economies face the risk of temporary setbacks from external shocks, policy mistakes, or other disturbances. This was starkly demonstrated in the first 2 years of the 1990s. The American economy, which already was experiencing slow growth, fell into recession in the second half of 1990. Between the third quarter of 1990 and the first quarter of 1991, output fell 1.6 percent and 1.7 million jobs were lost. The unemployment rate, which had averaged 5-1/4 percent for the 18 months prior to the recession, rose to 7.1 percent in December 1991. Sluggish growth and recession reflect the serious difficulties that the U.S. economy has faced in correcting structural imbalances while adjusting to previous monetary tightening, the credit crunch, and the August 1990 oil shock.

Over the past few years, structural imbalances had developed in the financial and real estate sectors, in household and corporate debt positions, and in governments' fiscal positions. A major reallocation of resources from defense to other sectors is under way, reversing the trend of the 1980s. The economy also has had to deal with changing national demographics, and a productivity growth showdown that began two decades ago.

The monetary policy initiated in the late 1980s to ease incipient inflationary pressure slowed growth by the early 1990s. The anticipated increase in demand for world capital resulting from the historic changes in the former Soviet bloc increased interest rates substantially in early 1990. Problems in financial markets have limited the availability of credit.

Oil prices surged following Iraq's invasion of Kuwait and consumer and business confidence plummeted as the immediate outlook for growth weakened and uncertainty increased about the worldwide consequences of the crisis. The U.S. economy was not resilient enough to grow in the face of the combination of the oil shock, structural adjustments, monetary restraint, and problems of credit availability. The Nation entered 1991 in the midst of the ninth recession since the end of World War II.

The other industrial countries also were buffeted by many of the same problems that hit the United States—the oil shock, sinking consumer and business confidence, and high interest rates. Several of these countries also were experiencing structural problems relating to government budget positions and serious difficulties in their financial and real estate markets. Recessions began in Canada and the United Kingdom earlier in 1990, and with jobless rates at or exceeding 10 percent in late 1991, the recessions have been deeper than in the United States. Growth in other industrial countries, including France and Italy, slowed in 1991, and the unemployment rate for the European Community as a whole was about 9 percent in 1991. Growth in Japan and Germany slowed considerably in the second half of 1991.

The current economic difficulties in the United States and other industrial countries should not obscure the fundamental strengths of market economies. The United States is the world's best example of the interrelated strengths of democratic pluralism and market-oriented economies. Americans have the highest standard of living in the world. U.S. gross domestic product (GDP) per capita of $22,056 in 1990, the latest year for which comparable data are available, places the United States more than 35 percent above Germany and more than 25 percent above Japan, when calculated using purchasing power equivalents (Chapter 7). The United States has the highest level of productivity of any country in the world, with output per worker about 20 percent above the average of the other major industrial countries. As of 1990, the last year for which comparable data are available, the United States produced a larger share of the industrial output of the Organization for Economic Cooperation and Development—24 of the largest industrial economies—than it did in 1970. U.S. firms are competitive internationally, and America is unsurpassed in basic research.

Nor should we ignore the remarkable sweep of countries around the world seeking to emulate our economic and political system. The collapse of central planning and communism—the most important economic and political event of the postwar era—was, in large part, a consequence of these command systems' inability to provide their populations with adequate standards of living and personal freedoms. Change in the former Soviet bloc is only the most conspicuous; countries in Latin America, Asia, and Africa are discarding their centrally controlled economies and privatizing state-owned enterprises. All are embracing market principles conscious that the transition to the market economy can be difficult. On the political side as well, institutional transformations leading to democratic freedoms are in ascendancy. Market reliance and democracy are mutually reinforcing principles and practices; they lead to the highest standards of living and the greatest personal freedoms. . . .

Adjusting to Structural Factors

The unusual confluence of the cyclical factors, structural imbalances, and long-run trends in the U.S. economy has hindered adjustment and slowed the pace of recovery.

The Financial Sector

The financial sector has been buffeted by disturbances of both an external and policy nature, as well as by problems of its own making. The high inflation and interest rates of the 1970s wiped out a large fraction of the value of the assets held by savings and loans (S&Ls), primarily long-run, fixed-rate mortgages. The debt crisis in the developing countries shocked commercial bank portfolios in the 1980s. The expansion of deposit insurance that did not account for the riskiness of an institution's investments enabled weak banks and S&Ls to stay open and to overinvest in risky assets without losing depositor confidence. Many financial institutions already were in poor financial condition when the downturn in real estate markets hit in the late 1980s. Real estate normally is a cyclical part of the economy; but changing tax laws boosted the upturn in real estate activity in the early and mid-1980s, and a reversal in the laws accentuated the downturn that began in some regions of the country in the late 1980s. The downturn has been most pronounced in commercial real estate and has been particularly deep in certain regions of the country.

While prudent supervision of financial institutions is extremely important, it is widely thought that examiners have been discouraging banks and S&Ls from engaging in some sound lending opportunities. In addition, banks have changed the composition of their lending portfolios and have increased their equity in response to the financial markets' demands for more capital as well as to meet domestic capital requirements and to accommodate the new international agreement on bank capital standards. Once monetary policy shifted actively toward the objective of bolstering economic growth, its effectiveness was dampened by these problems. Indeed, growth of commercial and industrial bank loans slowed during 1990 and fell dramatically in 1991.

Taken together, these unexpectedly tight credit conditions created a credit crunch. . . .

Demographics

Some of the slower growth in recent years is a direct consequence of demographic shifts. As the baby-boom generation matured in the late 1970s and early 1980s, the rate of household formation increased. That contributed to higher demand for big-ticket items such as houses, cars, and appliances, and with it higher levels of mortgage and installment debt. . . .

As the baby-boom generation was forming new households in the 1970s and early 1980s, it also was entering the work force in record numbers. Female participation in the labor force was rising particularly quickly.

However, growth of the working-age population has slowed in the late 1980s and early 1990s. Hence, the contribution to economic growth from an expanding labor force has declined.

Private Debt

Private debt increased substantially during the expansion. From 1982 to 1988, household borrowing almost doubled, growing nearly twice as fast as personal income, and corporate borrowing surged. By the end of the expansion, consumers and businesses faced relatively high levels of debt. Although the value of assets grew as well—a point often ignored when the growth of debt is discussed—the high ratios of household debt to income and corporate debt to profits probably were not sustainable. A period of slower consumption and investment naturally results as households and corporations restructure their balance sheets. . . .

Defense Spending

Increases in defense spending were an important contributor to growth in the 1980s. By the end of the decade, fiscal constraints and shifting spending priorities led to cuts in defense spending; real defense purchases of goods and services surged between 1979 and 1987, but fell somewhat from 1987 to 1990. A much larger defense downsizing has already begun to affect employment in defense industries as firms adjust to expected changes.

The United States has accommodated reductions in defense spending before. But the transition is never easy and, in fact, is costly in the short run, as people retrain and industrial resources are retooled for other purposes. Moreover, local economies where defense industries are a primary source of employment can experience significant disruption. Despite these difficulties the long-run potential dividends to the United States that come from turning military capacity to civilian endeavors is large. Obviously, the benefits to the world of the end of the Cold War transcend these economic factors. . . .

The Administration's Agenda to Meet the Challenges

The president has presented a comprehensive and coordinated growth agenda for the Nation. The agenda includes fiscal and other measures that will stimulate the economy in the short run, address the structural imbalances, and promote the Nation's long-term growth.

The Administration's policies for raising long-run productivity growth and thus the standard of living are based on five principles: a pro-growth fiscal policy that enhances incentives for entrepreneurship, saving, and investment, and that continues to reduce the multiyear structural budget deficit; a trade policy that promotes growth through opening markets worldwide; a regulatory policy that avoids unnecessary burdens on business and consumers; a human capital investment policy that focuses on education, training, and preventive health care; and strong support of a monetary policy that keeps inflation and interest rates low, while providing adequate growth of money and credit to support solid real growth.

The agenda focuses directly on increasing economic growth. The short-term agenda includes executive actions and proposed legislation that will stimulate economic growth immediately. Executive actions with immediate impact include a reduction in excessive personal income tax withholding and acceleration of previously appropriated Federal spending. Reinvigorated action to reduce the burden of unnecessary regulation and prudent measures to reduce the credit crunch will improve the environment for growth now. Proposed legislation focuses on spurring job-creating investment. The proposed 15-percent investment tax allowance and simplified and liberalized treatment of depreciation under the alternative tax, as well as the reduction in the capital gain tax rate, will stimulate business investment. The reduction in the capital gains tax rate will quickly raise asset values, improving confidence and encouraging spending. A $5,000 tax credit and penalty-free withdrawal from individual retirement accounts for first-time homebuyers, along with other incentives, will increase housing construction and sales.

Bolstering the short-term agenda are proposals for the long term that invest in the Nation's future by increasing the productivity of people and business. Record Federal investment in research and development and infrastructure, and the extension of the research and development tax credit will help increase business productivity. Record Federal investment in Head Start, children, and education, as well as proposals that strengthen the war on drugs and improve the implementation of job training through Job Training 2000 will help increase labor productivity. The long-term growth agenda also includes continued efforts to expand international markets through multilateral, regional, and bilateral negotiations.

Fiscal discipline has been a centerpiece of all of this Administration's budgets. Fiscal policy is designed to foster long-term growth by encouraging saving and investment as outlined in the Omnibus Budget Reconciliation Act of 1990. Controlling the growth of government spending and deficits so that resources are freed up for investment is but part of a more comprehensive fiscal program that, within proposed spending categories, shifts spending from current consumption to investment, such as expenditures for research and development and investments in public infrastructure that pass cost-benefit tests.

Some of the President's reform proposals are awaiting congressional action. Education reform through America 2000 will revolutionize education, strengthen accountability, and improve performance. Financial sector reform will strengthen the financial system, improve its ability to contribute to business growth, and sustain its international competitiveness. Civil justice reform will curb wasteful litigation and enhance productive activity. And the National Energy Strategy will increase energy security and conservation.

The President has repeatedly proposed reducing the tax rate on capital gains. This will encourage entrepreneurial activity, create new products, new methods of production, and new businesses. These, in turn, will generate new jobs. A capital gains differential will reduce the tax bias against equity financing and the overall cost of capital, thereby increasing investment and growth. Moreover, the Administration has supported a zero capital gains tax for areas designated as Enterprise Zones to spur investment and encourage entrepreneurial activity in inner cities and rural areas.

Innovation increases productivity growth and the standard of living. The Administration has advocated making the research and experimentation tax credit a permanent part of the tax code and has proposed large increases in both basic and applied research and development spending in the Federal Budget.

There are also proposals to assist families. These policies include an increase in the tax exemption for each child, a new flexible individual retirement account, and deductibility of interest paid on student loans. Comprehensive health reform will increase the affordability and security of health insurance at a cost that is economically sustainable. The incentives for first-time homebuyers, mentioned earlier will encourage homeownership—one of the most important ingredients to family financial and social well-being. The homeownership and opportunities for people everywhere (HOPE) program helps low-income residents of public and assisted housing to manage and eventually own their own homes.

Fundamental banking reform is critical to ensuring efficient operation of credit markets. The recent bill passed by the Congress is at best only a start. Important provisions in the Administration's proposal that would remove many unnecessary and antiquated restrictions on the banking industry are missing from the legislation. These reforms are needed to rebuild the soundness of the banking industry and enable it to be internationally competitive.

The Administration believes a well-functioning legal and regulatory system should increase, not impede, economic activity. Through its Agenda for Civil Justice Reform in America, the Administration has proposed a comprehensive set of reforms to the civil justice system that will improve the efficiency of the legal system and reduce unnecessary and costly litigation. This would free up resources and enhance productivity.

The Administration believes that investments in the Nation's human capital increase its productivity and living standards at home and increase its competitiveness abroad. The National Education Goals, America 2000 Excellence in Education Act, and Job Training 2000 all are directed at improving the quality of our most important resource—our people. The American 2000 Excellence in Education Act focuses on setting world-class educational standards, measuring performance against those standards, and increasing the educational choices available to American families so as to generate the competition that will improve performance and accountability of schools. The Administration's Job Training 2000 system is designed to train millions of workers in the skills needed in the evolving labor market. . . .

Moreover, the President has initiated a variety of measures to expand opportunities and improve the well-being of individuals and families. Although not often thought of as economic policy, expanding tax relief for child care, Head Start, Healthy Start, protecting the civil rights of all Americans, the strategy to eliminate substance abuse, and measures against violent crime all serve to improve U.S. productivity in the long term. Starting our children on the right path, providing our children the finest education, and continuing to provide programs that ensure public safety are sound economic policies.

The President's economic and domestic agenda also includes investing in America's future by improving the Nation's infrastructure, enhancing energy efficiency and security, and improving the quality of the environment and life. . . .

This Administration is committed to free and fair trade. Because trade enhances long-term growth, the Administration is following a multi-pronged effort to open markets, expand trade, and spur growth. . . .

Taken together, the President's proposals constitute a comprehensive agenda to stimulate short-term economic growth and support long-term productivity growth. These policies will expand opportunities for workers and families, increase living standards, and support the global competitiveness of the U.S. economy.

Conclusion

The United States confronts serious economic challenges in the 1990s. The flexibility and resilience of the U.S. economy and the resourcefulness of our people provide America the ability to meet these challenges. But as the Council noted when the United States was in the midst of the longest peacetime expansion in American history and the unemployment rate had hit a 15-year low, the Nation cannot take economic growth for granted. The U.S. economy remains the largest and most productive in the world. Sound policies are essential to guarantee that American living standards will continue to rise substantially from one generation to the next and that the United States will remain the world's leading economy.

The President's agenda, based on sound economic policy principles, seeks to achieve the maximum possible rate of sustainable economic growth. If enacted, the President's policies will not only make near-term recovery faster, stronger, and more certain, but also will solidify the foundation for long-term growth and help ensure that the United States remains the world's leading economy in the 1990s and beyond.

Recent Developments and the Economic Outlook

The U.S. economy entered 1991 in the midst of the ninth recession since the end of World War II. The recession began in the second half of 1990, following the longest peacetime expansion in the Nation's history. A recovery appeared to begin in the spring of 1991 and continue into the summer, as production, employment, and spending all rose. Total output grew in the second and third quarters of 1991, recovering about one-half of the decline that occurred during the recession. In midsummer, however, the economy began to flatten out, and then production, employment, and spending faltered late in the year.

Even during the initial months of recovery, many key economic indicators did not improve much. Only about one-fifth of the jobs lost from July 1990 to April 1991 were regained by October 1991, and employment declined toward the end of the year. The unemployment rate hovered around the 6.9-percent level reached in June, before rising to 7.1 percent in December. By June personal income, adjusted for inflation and taxes, recovered about four-fifths of its 1.5-percent decline but then flattened out for most of the second half of the year. Although many indicators were sluggish or fell back at the end of the year, others continued to improve. For example, growth in exports contributed to a further reduction of the Nation's trade deficit and residential investment showed a strong gain.

The economy is expected to be sluggish in early 1992, but growth is expected to pick up in the middle part of the year. With adoption of the Administration's pro-growth policies, real, or inflation-adjusted, growth, as measured by the change in gross domestic product (GDP) in 1987 dollars, is forecast to be 2.2 percent in 1992, and to average 3 percent in the mid-1990s. The unemployment rate is expected to plateau, or perhaps rise slightly, in early 1992 but should begin to decline by midyear. As the economy picks up, inflation and interest rates are expected to rise slightly over the next year from their recent lows, and then stabilize, before gradually falling.

Although the economy is expected to improve in 1992, the magnitude of the improvement is still uncertain. In addition to uncertainties about the economy's short-term cyclical performance, there also are various structural imbalances in the economy that are being worked through. Beyond the short term, the economy faces the serious challenge of improving productivity; slow productivity growth has plagued the economy for two decades.

One of the major cyclical concerns is whether growth of money and credit—which has been quite sluggish—will be sufficient to promote near-term recovery. Also, consumer confidence, which has fallen significantly, likely will be restored only when prospects for employment and income improve and household balance sheets reflect stable or rising asset values. Higher levels of consumer confidence are essential for growth in consumer spending. Because consumer spending accounts for two-thirds of total spending, its growth is a key ingredient for a durable economic recovery. While exports are expected to continue to promote growth in the domestic economy, the export sector faces risks from the possibility that growth abroad will be slower than expected.

Underlying these cyclical issues are structural imbalances and adjustments that also pose potential difficulties. Although the economy is flexible and continuously restructuring, the number of major structural adjustments currently occurring is abnormally large. Changes in world capital markets in recent years have affected the cost of capital in the United States. In early 1990, for example, long-term interest rates were pushed up significantly by expectations of increased demand for capital—associated with German unification, a reemergent Latin America, and the opening up of Eastern Europe—and an abrupt decline in the supply of capital to the rest of the world from Germany and Japan. The availability of credit also has been restricted as financial institutions have moved to shore up their capital positions and as they have faced more stringent regulation. Sufficient credit is necessary to finance expansion. High levels of public and private debt, high vacancy rates in commercial and residential buildings, and failing financial institutions also could limit prospects for spending. Budget problems of State and local governments have resulted in higher taxes and spending constraints, adding a fiscal drag on the recovery. Impediments to free and fair trade must be removed or avoided to bolster international trade and growth of U.S. exports.

Nonetheless, fundamentals are in place to promote growth in the economy. Nominal interest rates are generally at their lowest levels in two decades, and recent declines should help boost interest-sensitive spending. Lower interest rates also are allowing many homeowners to refinance their mortgages, thereby reducing monthly payments and increasing income available for purchases of goods and services. Inflation is relatively low, and is expected to remain low in the near term. Low and stable inflation reduces the uncertainty confronting businesses and consumers about prices and the purchasing power of money and income, and thus provides a better environment for investment, production, and growth. Imbalances in international accounts have been substantially reduced, and the Nation's trade position should improve further over time as exports continue to grow and the Nation's international competitive position strengthens.

As has been stated in previous *Economic Reports* of this Administration, *the Nation faces serious challenges and cannot take economic growth for granted*. The Administration's policies are designed to support sustained increases in the Nation's standard of living by raising long-run productivity growth. Such policies include a pro-growth fiscal policy that enhances incentives for entrepreneurship, saving, and investment and reduces the multiyear structural budget deficit over time; a trade policy that promotes growth through opening markets worldwide; and a regulatory policy that avoids unnecessary burdens on business and consumers. The Administration also supports a monetary policy that promotes solid real growth while gradually reducing inflation pressures. The adoption of the Administration's pro-growth policies would not only boost the expected rate of growth in the near term and beyond but also would reduce uncertainty and the risk that the economy's performance will be worse than expected.

An Overview of the Economy in 1991

The major economic indicators reflected the effects of the recession in the second half of 1990 and the first half of 1991. Payroll employment, industrial production, real sales, and real personal income fell during this period. The unemployment rate rose to 6.9 percent in June 1991, up from 5.2 percent in June 1990—the approximate level for most of the previous 2 years. The unemployment rate then fell slightly and flattened out for several months before rising at the end of the year. Real GDP—the value of all goods and services produced in the United States—rose 0.2 percent during 1991 (on a fourth-quarter-to-fourth-quarter basis), following a 0.1-percent decline in 1990.

Signs of a Recovery

In the spring of 1991 signs of a recovery began to emerge. The index of leading indicators reached its low in January and then rose sharply through July. Production, sales, and income all bottomed out between February and April and then rose into the summer. By July industrial production had recovered about 3 percentage points of the 5-percent decline that occurred from September 1990 to March 1991. Nonfarm payroll employment did not respond very much, however, and after increasing significantly in May, trended up only slightly through October. Total output and spending also rose; following the 1.6-percent decline registered over the fourth quarter of 1990 and the first quarter of 1991, real GDP increased in the second and third quarters, recovering about 0.8 percent, or about half, of the earlier loss.

Other key data also pointed to recovery. Total retail sales and sales of cars and light trucks hit lows in January 1991 and rose into the early summer. Housing starts, which bottomed out in January, rose 25 percent by August. New orders and shipments for manufacturers' durable goods reached lows in March and rose through July; the 11.7-percent increase in new orders in July was the largest monthly increase on record. Initial claims for unemployment insurance reached a peak in March and then fell for 4 consecutive months through July.

Various conditions had emerged in early 1991 that helped set the stage for the pickup in the economy. Oil prices, which had shot up after Iraq invaded Kuwait in August 1990, fell back to their pre-invasion levels within hours of the successful launch of the air-war phase of Operation Desert Storm in January. Prospects for growth in the international economy—and continued growth in U.S. exports—improved as the threat to oil supplies was eliminated. With the successful end of the ground war, consumer and business confidence rebounded in March. Declining interest rates in late 1990 and early 1991—both short and long term—supported an upturn in residential construction and other interest-sensitive sectors. Furthermore, household net worth recovered somewhat in the first half of 1991; the value of owner-occupied housing and land stopped declining, the runup in the stock market boosted the value of financial assets, and the increase in household liabilities was quite modest.

The Economy Flattens Out

By late summer the recovery lost momentum. A self-reinforcing process of growth—in which increases in spending, production, and employment tend to bolster one another—typically occurs in recoveries. In 1991, however, the spending and production gains and the positive feedback between them were not sufficient to sustain a solid recovery. The leading index flattened out in the late summer and early fall and even declined slightly at the end of the year. After rising through the summer from its trough in April, payroll employment fell significantly in November before rising slightly in December. Industrial production rose slightly from July through September and then fell slightly in each of the final 3 months of the year. Real income was sluggish from August through October and fell in November, before rising in December.

Other indicators pointed to a lackluster economy at the end of the year. Retail sales were relatively flat from late summer into the fall but declined at the end of the year. Motor vehicle sales slipped in July and August and then remained weak in the fall and early winter. Initial claims for unemployment insurance were higher at the end of the year than at midyear. Manufacturers' shipments of durable and nondurable goods showed gains throughout most of the second half of the year, but fell significantly in December.

On the positive side, merchandise exports continued to rise, and housing starts continued on an upward trend through the end of the year. Stock prices rose strongly at year-end, with various market indexes hitting record highs. And, according to a government survey, businesses plan to increase spending for plant and equipment by 5.4 percent in 1992, following a 0.5-percent decrease in 1991. Thus, by the end of 1991, the economy was sluggish at best, but some forward-looking indicators were pointing to improvement in mid-1992.

The fundamental causes underlying the faltering recovery likely will be a source of continuing debate. Most forecasts—including the Administration forecast of a year ago—had foreseen a relatively modest rebound from a relatively shallow downturn. Until the last few months, this scenario seemed to be on track. It now appears that the structural imbalances in the economy were larger—and were taking longer to work off—than expected; it soon became evident that the oil shock and the war were not the economy's only problems. Credit remained tight and money growth was slow. Relatively high levels of household debt incurred earlier constrained consumer spending. The weaker outlook for the economy created greater uncertainty about employment and income prospects as businesses became more cautious in hiring and spending plans; several major corporations announced plans for further downsizing in efforts to reduce costs and become more competitive. These factors contributed to lower consumer confidence and restrained consumer spending. The State and local fiscal drag continued. . . .

Reasons for the Sluggish Economy

The recession of 1990-91 followed the longest peacetime expansion in the Nation's history. During the expansion of 1982-90, real output increased by more than 30 percent, more than 21 million jobs were created, and 5 million businesses were incorporated. The unemployment rate fell from a peak of almost 11 percent in late 1982 to 5 percent in March 1989—a level not experienced since 1973. Employment as a percentage of working-age population reached a peacetime high of more than 63 percent in early 1990. Consumer price inflation remained relatively low and stable throughout the expansion, averaging about 4 percent a year. For a year and a half before the recession, however, real GDP grew at an annual rate of only about 1-1/4 percent.

Economic expansions do not end on their own; they end as a result of external shocks to the economy, economic imbalances that must be worked off, or inappropriate economic policies. Hopes that the expansion would continue were dashed in August 1990, when the economy was hit with an external shock—the rise in oil prices resulting from the Iraqi invasion of Kuwait. Oil prices rose sharply, from less than $19 a barrel in July to more than $30 in late August, and peaked at about $40 in early October. It is natural to point to the oil shock—coupled with the resulting declines in consumer and business confidence—as the event that pushed the economy into recession. However, a number of structural imbalances and the lagged effect of tight monetary policy in 1988 and 1989 also slowed the economy. While the oil shock significantly aggravated weakness in the economy, it is a matter of debate whether these other factors on their own eventually would have pushed the economy into recession, or, alternatively, whether the economy would have experienced a prolonged period of sluggish growth.

Structural Adjustments

By the end of the 1980s, economic growth was constrained by various imbalances that had accumulated over the past two decades. Although some of these imbalances were concentrated in specific sectors and regions of the country, their effects generally were felt nationwide. The economy also has had to deal with a reallocation from defense to other sectors and changing national demographic trends.

Demographic Trends

The baby-boom generation matured in the 1970s and early 1980s, boosting the rate of household formation. As household formation rises, so does the demand for houses and big-ticket durable items such as cars and appliances. The assumption of higher levels of mortgage and installment

113

debt in the process of acquiring better housing and durable goods is a natural result of these demographic trends.

The more recent shift to lower growth in residential housing and in the demand for cars and other durable goods also in part reflects demographic trends. . . .

Buildup in Private Debt

Private debt relative to income rose significantly during the expansion. From 1982 to 1988 household borrowing increased at a 12-percent annual rate, while personal income measured in current dollars increased at the much lower rate of 7 percent. Similarly, corporate borrowing surged, rising at an annual rate of 11 percent.

Borrowing to finance real estate purchases grew substantially. From 1982 to 1989 home mortgage borrowing increased at a 12-percent annual rate and commercial mortgage borrowing at a 10-percent rate. During this period, national income increased about 67 percent, but nonfarm mortgage debt more than doubled. The borrowing financed a surge in construction, which began to outstrip demand. By the late 1980s, both commercial and residential real estate showed signs of overbuilding; the problem was particularly acute in commercial real estate. Vacancy rates in rental housing rose from just above 5 percent in 1982 to about 8 percent at the end of 1987. Commercial office vacancy rates in downtown areas increased from less than 8 percent in 1982 to more than 16 percent in 1988, according to the Coldwell Banker Office Vacancy Index. Favorable provisions in the 1981 tax laws had boosted building and contributed to the upswing in the early to mid-1980s, but the changes in 1986 reversed many of those provisions, hitting commercial real estate and building hard.

By the end of the expansion, many consumers had accumulated relatively high levels of debt. At the same time, the value of their largest asset—their homes—was flat or declining. Householders' expectations of continued increases in the equity in their homes were not being realized. . . .

Financial Sector Imbalances

The real estate situation brought about a further erosion of confidence by exacerbating problems in the already troubled financial sector. Also, a shifting financial regulatory environment—from being too lax during the good times of the expansion to being too tight more recently—further aggravated financial sector difficulties and constrained lending activity and economic growth.

Those troubles had begun in the 1970s, when an increase in inflation and interest rates had produced large and widespread losses on mortgage portfolios—the predominant assets on the balance sheets of savings and loans (S&Ls). These assets consisted primarily of fixed-rate, 20- to 30-year mortgages, but deposit liabilities were primarily short term. When interest rates rose, S&Ls had to increase deposit interest rates to retain deposits— the source of their funds. Hence, the cost of funds to S&Ls increased, even though revenues from outstanding mortgages remained fixed. Moreover, because the market value of a fixed-rate asset falls as interest rates rise, the increase in interest rates in the 1970s slashed the market value of the outstanding mortgages held by S&Ls. By 1980 the thrift industry as a whole was already heavily insolvent.

In the 1980s, an extension of deposit insurance that did not account for the riskiness of the institution's investments and a loosening of lending restrictions—both of which came about mainly in response to the problems in the industry—allowed weak S&Ls to stay open and to pursue risky investment strategies without losing the confidence of their depositors. Government insurance meant that shaky S&Ls could continue to attract deposits because depositors knew they were protected. Many of the risky investments were real estate projects that eventually failed as a result of overbuilding and declining real estate prices. The risk ultimately was borne by the insurer—in the end, the Federal Government and the taxpayers. In fact, in 1984, a task force headed by then Vice President Bush proposed risk-based deposit insurance, which would have sharply curtailed the excessive risk-taking by requiring depository institutions to pay higher deposit insurance premiums if they pursued risky investment strategies.

Besides S&Ls, other financial institutions also experienced balance sheet difficulties as the value of commercial real estate assets declined, and many large banks continued to carry problem loans to Third World countries on their balance sheets. As a result of these factors, bankers grew more cautious about extending loans. Their caution also reflected hesitancy over the profitability of lending projects as a result of the slowing economy.

Tighter lending standards cannot be attributed entirely to caution resulting from a weak economy. Banks' balance sheets had deteriorated with the increase in loan losses taken during the 1980s, and banks moved to rebuild equity and shift their portfolios away from business loans and toward assets with lower default risk. Much of this shift in bank portfolios was a response to financial market demands for increased equity.

But bank regulatory policies played a significant role as well. Although tighter supervision clearly was warranted, it appears that examiners overcompensated and discouraged financial institutions from engaging in some viable lending opportunities. Moreover, the phase-in of capital standards established in the 1988 Basle Accords—an agreement among banking regulators in the major industrialized countries that set capital adequacy standards—also caused some banks to reduce business loans and move into assets deemed safer by the accords, such as Treasury notes and securities issued by U.S. Government agencies. . . .

Monetary Policy and Interest Rate Developments

The Federal Reserve has stated a policy goal of achieving, over time, "price stability." Price stability need not literally mean a zero change in the price level, but a change that is low enough so that inflation no longer is an important factor in the economic decisions of consumers and businesses. Over the past few years, the Federal Reserve generally has maintained a relatively tight monetary policy in an attempt to achieve this goal. These efforts have prevented inflation from being higher than it otherwise would have been, but they also have been one of the important factors contributing to slower growth over the past 3 years.

The Nation's long-term growth prospects were enhanced by the reduction of inflation from the double-digit rates experienced in the 1970s. High inflation causes households and businesses to divert effort from productive activities toward preventing the value of their assets from eroding with inflation. High and variable inflation often is associated with increased uncertainty about the future course of the economy; such uncertainty can add a risk premium to interest rates and reduce investment. Variable inflation makes it difficult to judge the change in the prices of items relative to one another; in market economies, relative prices signal suppliers to devote more resources to products that consumers value more. Thus, low and stable inflation is an important ingredient in achieving maximum sustainable long-term growth. But just as high and variable inflation can be costly, lowering inflation sometimes has costly consequences in the short run for economic growth and employment, which also must be considered when implementing monetary policy....

The Attempt to Engineer a Soft Landing in 1988 and 1989

Solid economic growth in 1987 and 1988 pushed capacity utilization up, and unemployment rates fell to their lowest levels in a decade and a half. These developments spurred concerns that the economy might be outstripping its productive capacity, increasing the possibility of rising inflation. Monetary policy moved toward engineering a "soft landing"—slower growth with low inflation but no recession. Beginning in early 1988, the Federal Reserve gradually increased the Federal funds rate and in 1988 and in 1989 it lowered the midpoint of the target range for the growth of M2 a full percentage point from the previous year.

This tight monetary policy removed some of the incipient inflationary pressure from the economy. However, tighter monetary policy also put substantial downward pressure on output and employment growth.

Monetary Policy and Credit Conditions in Late 1989 and 1990

As growth slowed in 1989 and inflation pressures waned, market interest rates began to fall. The Federal Reserve began to reduce the Federal funds rate in the middle of 1989; over the remainder of the year the rate fell from roughly 9-3/4 percent to about 8-1/4 percent.

Despite declining short-term rates, by early 1990 long-term interest rates were rising. Yields on long-term Treasury bonds rose from below 8 percent at the end of 1989 to more than 9 percent in September 1990, and high-grade corporate bond yields rose to more than 9.5 percent. The rise partly reflected the increase in long-term interest rates throughout the world, discussed earlier. Because interest rates in the United States are influenced by developments in world markets, these events put upward pressure on U.S. long-term rates. Furthermore, tighter credit conditions—the credit crunch described in the previous section—held lending by banks and S&Ls to levels below those normally associated with the prevailing market interest rates and the profitability of investment projects. Higher world interest rates and the credit crunch resulted in tighter credit conditions than otherwise would have been associated with the level of the Federal funds rate.

Monetary Policy and Interest Rates From Late 1990

Market interest rates fell in late 1990 and much of 1991, reflecting lower demand for borrowed funds in the weakened economy, and, after early 1991, declining inflation rates. Furthermore, the prospect of reducing the long-term Federal structural budget deficit led many people to expect that improved coordination between monetary and fiscal policy could result in lower interest rates. . . .

In retrospect, it appears that monetary policy should have been geared to lowering interest rates faster and earlier. It is likely that sluggish demand for credit in a weaker-than-expected economy and continued fallout from the problems in the banking industry prevented the quantity of credit from expanding as the Fed thought it would when it lowered interest rates. Indeed, M2 growth did not react as the Fed expected when it lowered the Federal funds rate in the second half of 1991.

At the end of 1991 and into early 1992, interest rates generally were at their lowest levels in 2 decades or more. Three-month Treasury bill rates fell from 7.2 percent in October 1990 to about 3.8 percent in early 1992, the lowest level of nominal Treasury bill rates since 1972. Near troughs of recessions, however, short-term real interest rates—that is, interest rates adjusted for expected inflation—often are quite low, sometimes negative. Currently, real short-term rates are higher than they have been during many comparable periods in the past.

By mid-January 1992, nominal long-term interest rates also were relatively low. Yields on 10-year Treasury notes were about 6.8 percent, the lowest level of nominal interest rates since 1977. Rates on 30-year fixed mortgages fell from a little more than 10 percent in late 1990 to about 8-1/4 percent in mid-January 1992. The decline in mortgage rates has substantially enhanced the affordability of housing. In addition, interest rates on adjustable rate mortgages have come down, many homeowners have refinanced mortgages at lower rates, and interest rates on consumer installment credit also have fallen. These factors have freed up income for other purposes, allowing households to reduce their debt burdens and to enhance their purchasing power. Of course, these effects are offset somewhat by the lower income earned by holders of interest-bearing assets. . . .

Summary

- While a majority of the private Blue Chip forecasters surveyed in January 1992 placed the end of the recession in the second quarter of 1991, as noted above the trough of the recession has not yet been officially determined. Thus, the statements in this section are consistent with the majority Blue Chip view, but it should be borne in mind that the future course of the economy may affect the values for the recession that began in the third quarter of 1990.

- The decline in output from the third quarter of 1990 through the first quarter of 1991 and the number of jobs lost between June 1990 and April 1991 was somewhat less severe than the average for post-World War II recessions. Much of the decline in output occurred in investment, particularly in inventories. There was a smaller decline in consumption, and an improvement in net exports helped to keep the recession from being more severe.

- Sectoral comparisons show that, relative to previous recessions, manufacturing accounted for a smaller proportion of jobs lost; the construction and service-producing sectors accounted for a much larger proportion.

- The rise in white-collar unemployment represented a larger proportion of total unemployment compared to previous recessions. However, blue-collar unemployment still accounted for a larger share of total unemployment than white-collar unemployment did. . . .

Growth Agenda

The President has presented a comprehensive and coordinated growth agenda for the Nation. The agenda includes fiscal and other measures that will stimulate the economy in the short run, address the structural imbalances, and promote the Nation's long-term growth.

The agenda focuses directly on increasing economic growth. The short-term agenda includes executive actions and proposed legislation that will stimulate economic growth immediately. Executive actions with immediate impact include the reduction in excessive personal income tax withholding and acceleration of previously appropriated Federal spending. Reinvigorated action to reduce the burden of unnecessary regulation and prudent measures to reduce the credit crunch will improve the environment for growth now.

Proposed legislation for a 15-percent tax allowance and simplified and liberalized treatment of depreciation under the alternative minimum tax will spur job-creating investment. Penalty-free withdrawal from individual retirement accounts and a $5,000 tax credit for first-time homebuyers along with other incentives will boost real estate. The President has repeatedly proposed reducing the tax rate on capital gains; the first effect of such a reduction would be to raise asset values, bolstering confidence and spending.

There also are proposals to assist families. These include an increase in the tax exemption for each child, a new flexible individual retirement account, and student loan interest deductions. The incentives for first-time homebuyers mentioned above will encourage homeownership—one of the most important ingredients to family financial and social well-being. Comprehensive health reform will increase the affordability and security of health insurance.

Bolstering the short-term agenda are proposals for the long term that invest in the Nation's future by increasing the productivity of people and business. Record Federal investment in research and development and infrastructure, and the extension of the research and experimentation tax credit will help generate new technologies that enhance productivity and employment growth. The Administration also has advocated making the research and experimentation tax credit a permanent part of the tax code. Record Federal investment in Head Start will prepare all eligible disadvantaged 4-year-olds for effective learning when they start school. Record Federal investment in programs for children and education will improve the opportunities for today's youth when they enter the labor market in the future. Record Federal investment in programs designed to deal directly with the crime and drug problems will, in combination with other programs, move many of those from this subculture into socially productive activity. The comprehensive job-training program will help millions of Americans to acquire the skills necessary to succeed in the changing labor market.

A number of Administration proposals aimed at improving economic performance await congressional action. Education reform through America 2000 will revolutionize education, strengthen accountability, and improve performance. Financial sector reform will strengthen the financial system, improve its ability to contribute to business growth, and sustain international competitiveness. Civil justice reform will curb wasteful litigation and enhance productive activity. The National Energy Strategy will increase energy security and conservation. The long-term growth agenda also includes continued efforts to expand international markets through multilateral, regional, and bilateral negotiations.

The proposed cut in the capital gains tax rate is an important element of the long-term growth agenda. The capital gains tax rate cut would encourage entrepreneurial activity, create new products, new methods of production, and new businesses. These, in turn, would generate new jobs. A capital gains differential would reduce the tax bias against equity financing and the overall cost of capital, thereby increasing investment and growth. The Administration also has supported a zero capital gains tax rate for areas designated as Enterprise Zones to spur investments and encourage entrepreneurial activity in inner cities and rural areas.

Fiscal discipline has been a centerpiece of all of this Administration's budgets. The Administration's proposals are designed to foster long-term growth by encouraging saving, investment, and entrepreneurship. Controlling the growth of government spending and deficits frees resources for private investment. This is but one part of a more comprehensive fiscal program that, within proposed spending categories, also shifts spending from current consumption to investment (such as expenditures for research and development and investments in public infrastructure that pass cost-benefit tests).

Summary

- Federal fiscal policy typically provides a significant stimulus to the economy during recessions and early recovery periods. From 1990 to 1991, automatic stabilizers offset other factors, leaving fiscal policy slightly stimulative. Federal fiscal stimulus is projected to be stronger in fiscal 1992, but still within the constraints of the Omnibus Budget Reconciliation Act.
- The prompt enactment of the Administration's pro-growth policy proposals will boost the economy in the short run and will enhance productivity, investment, and economic growth in the long run. . . .

The Economic Outlook

The Administration projects that the economy is likely to remain sluggish in the early part of 1992 but that a renewed pickup is likely to begin by the middle of the year. With the adoption of the President's policy proposals, the economy is then expected to return to solid real GDP growth of about 3 percent a year through the mid-1990s, and the unemployment rate is expected to decline from around 7 percent to less than 5-1/2 percent.

The sluggish performance of the economy and the declines in consumer and business confidence at the end of 1991 all point to a continued slow economy in the early part of 1992. Various recent developments, however, indicate a resumption of stronger growth in the middle of the year. The cuts in interest rates in the second half of 1991 are expected to support gains in consumer and business spending by the middle of 1992. Relatively low interest rates also should help households and businesses reduce debt-servicing costs and improve their financial positions. The improvement in personal finances would help boost consumer confidence and encourage growth in consumer spending. Declines in long-term interest rates should continue to have positive effects on investment spending; low mortgage rates, in particular, should help to boost residential investment. Business inventories remain relatively lean. As a result, production likely will respond quickly to meet increases in demand, and a sustained increase in demand would encourage businesses to rebuild inventories. The relatively low exchange value of the dollar and growth in the world economy should help to promote continued export growth.

Economic forecasting is an imprecise science, however. Unexpected events and policy changes can cause actual events to be substantially different from the forecast. Forecasts are based largely on predictions about human behavior, usually taking previous patterns of behavior as a guide. But human behavior is complex, difficult to predict, and subject to change. People do not always respond the same way, or with the same speed, in what appear to be similar circumstances. Hence, uncertainty remains about the outlook for the economy.

If the problems the economy has been facing are resolved relatively quickly and confidence is restored, growth could rise faster than is expected. The relatively low rate of inflation combined with the large degree of slack in the economy is particularly noteworthy, for it could allow the Federal Reserve to keep interest rates low—or cut them further, if necessary—to help boost growth with little immediate concern about reintroducing inflation pressures. A quick shift to a significant rebuilding of inventories alone could add as much as a percentage point to the rate of growth over the next year. Alternatively, if the problems are resolved slowly, the economy could perform worse than expected. Tight credit and slow money growth, along with the continuing structural adjustments described earlier could continue to hinder the economy. Under those conditions confidence could remain low, and the rate of growth likely would be lower than expected.

The President's Policies or Business As Usual

With the adoption of the President's pro-growth proposals as outlined in the State of the Union address and presented in detail in the budget, the prospects for renewed solid growth improve markedly.... The President's proposals will inspire confidence and provide a stimulus to the economy in the short run, boosting output, income, and employment. The productivity-enhancing nature of the proposals will also improve the economic outlook in future years. If the President's policy proposals are not adopted relatively promptly, however, and a "business-as-usual" situation persists in determining Federal spending and tax policies, the economy is expected to perform worse than projected, as indicated by the business-as-usual forecast.

With the President's pro-growth policies, the Administration expects real GDP to increase 2.2 percent from the fourth quarter of 1991 to the fourth quarter of 1992. This represents a significant improvement from the 0.2-percent growth during 1991 and the 0.1-percent decline during 1990. Inflation in 1992 should be only slightly higher than in 1991. The relatively low inflation pressures in 1991 partly were a result of the fall in oil prices from their peak in late 1990. But several years of slow money growth and a slow economy, which eased tightness in labor markets and created excess capacity in many industries, also kept inflation pressures down. In 1993 real growth is expected to be even stronger than in 1992—at about a 3-percent rate—as the economy continues to rebound from the recession and the sluggish growth over the 1989-91 period.

The President's policies will also improve the outlook in labor markets, and the unemployment rate is expected to fall from about 6.9 percent in 1992 to 6.1 percent in 1994. Interest rates are expected to fall in 1992 from 1991, reflecting the sluggish economy and the low level of interest rates at the end of 1991. As the expansion becomes more robust, however, short-term interest rates are expected to rise somewhat through 1995 before declining slightly in 1996 and 1997. Long-term interest rates are expected to fall gradually through 1995 and then flatten out, reflecting continued, relatively low inflation and lower uncertainty about fiscal policy and the economic outlook.

Under the business-as-usual projection, real growth in 1992 would likely be around 1.6 percent, well below the rate that would be achieved with the adoption of the President's policy proposals. The period of slow growth that has existed since early 1989 would likely continue in 1992. By 1993 business-as-usual growth picks up some, but remains more than a half percentage point below policy growth. The differences in real growth in the policy and business-as-usual forecasts persist beyond the short-term outlook because of the productivity-enhancing nature of the President's proposals. In the policy forecast, real growth in the 3-percent range continues through the mid-1990s. With business-as-usual, growth averages only in the 2.5-percent range. . . .

Summary

- The economy is expected to remain sluggish in early 1992, but a renewed pickup should occur by midyear. The prompt enactment of the President's proposals would boost the economy in the short run and promote higher growth in the long run.
- However, if the President's proposals are not adopted promptly and a "business-as-usual" environment prevails, growth in the economy will be lower in both the short and long run.
- In the long run, the President's proposals will promote higher private capital accumulation and faster productivity growth. The economy's underlying medium-term growth potential is expected to be about 3 percent a year. Inflation and nominal interest rates are projected to rise slightly in the short run, but then fall gradually thereafter.

Conclusion

Following a year and a half of slow growth, the Nation's economy entered a recession in the second half of 1990. In the late spring of 1991, the economy began to recover. However, the recovery lost momentum in mid-summer, and by the end of the year the economy was sluggish at best.

It is natural to point to the oil shock and the resulting decline in confidence as the reason the economy fell into recession. However, growth in the economy already had been slowed by a number of structural imbalances and the lagged effects of tight monetary policy in earlier years. The flat economy at the end of 1991 was evidence that the structural imbalances in the economy were larger and taking longer to work off than had been expected.

Growth is expected to remain sluggish in the early part of 1992. By midyear, however, the economy is expected to improve. The prompt enactment of the President's pro-growth proposals announced in the State of the Union address will spur economic recovery and promote long-term investment and growth, as well as improve the Nation's competitive position in global markets.

Over the longer term, the Omnibus Budget Reconciliation Act establishes discipline to lower the multiyear structural Federal deficit and therefore, Federal borrowing requirements. Combined with a monetary policy aimed at maintaining solid economic growth while gradually reducing the underlying inflation rate, both nominal and real interest rates are likely to remain relatively low. Credible monetary policy and growth-oriented fiscal policy will facilitate higher levels of capital accumulation, raise labor productivity and thereby real wages, and enhance the economy's growth potential.

The American Labor Market

A sluggish economy generally draws attention to short-run labor market conditions that affect the economic well-being of American workers and their families. Concern is naturally focused on the decline in job prospects and the increase in unemployment brought about by recession. Yet, longer run trends that underlie these shorter run events have profound importance as well. Although a temporary spell of unemployment disrupts a worker's earnings for weeks or months, the creation of job opportunities and the growth in real wages over a person's career determine the standard of living over his or her lifetime. . . . This chapter reviews the longer run developments.

Despite the temporary setbacks of several recessions, employment increased by 38 million, from 71 million in 1974 to 109 million in 1991. This 53-percent growth far surpassed that of most other major industrialized countries. Employment in Japan increased only half as fast; employment in France, Germany, and the United Kingdom grew at less than one-fifth the U.S. rate.

The U.S. economy not only provided employment for an extra 38 million workers, it also delivered improved opportunities in the labor market. The average wage level, adjusted for inflation, rose by 18 percent from 1971 to 1990 (the most recent year for which statistics are available.) . . .

Employment Growth

Over the long-term, despite the temporary setbacks of several recessions, the U.S. economy has demonstrated great capacity to provide jobs to an increasing percentage of the population. Significant shifts in demand and supply accompanied this growth in jobs. Technology and product changes increased demand for more educated workers, while the strong demographic forces of the baby-boom generation and changing preferences of workers regarding work and schooling drove much of the change in supply. . . .

Technological Change

Technological changes that have brought about internal restructuring within industries and firms have also increased the demand for workers with greater educational attainment, particularly in the 1980s. The most extensive restructuring in favor of more educated workers occurred in retail trade, government, and professional and financial services. Manufacturing, which 20 years ago had the least educated work force among industrial sectors, has hired increasing proportions of college-educated workers. In 1988, for example, 45 percent of all workers in high-skill manufacturing industries had a college education, up from 28 percent in 1968. Low-skill manufacturing firms have nearly doubled the percentage of such workers in their work forces, from 9 percent to 17 percent.

Computer technology has extensively changed the nature of the workplace and the operations of firms. In 1984, 8 percent of businesses reported using personal computers. By 1989 that figure had climbed to 36 percent. Proficiency in operating computers has become a requisite for an increasing number of jobs, from secretaries to production-line workers. This proficiency is linked to increased years of schooling; college-educated workers are twice as likely to use computers as are workers with only high school degrees.

Another development has been the shift away from material handling to information handling. Within manufacturing, the input of knowledge, rather than the input of material, accounts for an increasing share of the value added in the production process. The cost of the material content, such as the steel and plastic used in the manufacture of an automobile, for example, has steadily declined relative to the price of the automobile. Instead, the price increasingly incorporates the cost of knowledge embedded in features of the automobile and the production process: the car's advanced design, including the use of computer-aided engineering, the substitution of computer-controlled devices for mechanically controlled devices used in the operation of the vehicle, and the use of robotics in the assembly of the automobile. Consequently, the demand for people with the ability to work with and process knowledge and information, rather than with physical inputs, has increased. . . .

Productivity Trends

The key to each worker's well-being and the Nation's prosperity is productivity growth. An increase in the Nation's standard of living, commonly measured as output per person, depends upon three factors: a greater percentage of the population employed, an increase in average hours worked, and greater labor productivity—output per hour worked. The historical trend in the United States has been toward a rising rate of participation in the labor market and lower hours per worker. Labor productivity has also grown historically, although its low rate of advance in the last two decades is a matter of great concern.

Long-term advances in labor productivity and employment have provided the United States with the highest standard of living in the world. Based on the commonly used measure of gross domestic product (GDP), the U.S. economy produced, on average, $45,918 worth of goods and services per worker in 1990, or $22,056 per capita. GDP per person in the United States was 25 percent above Japan and 35 percent above Germany. Another way to measure the relative prosperity of U.S. workers is to compare their purchasing power—the amount of goods and services that workers can purchase per hour worked. American workers have greater purchasing power than workers in most other major industrialized countries, although the leadership gap has narrowed.

The variation in hours worked per worker and in the fraction of the labor force in paid employment is limited. *Therefore, long-run advances in living standards depend upon continuing improvements in productivity.* Even a modest annual growth rate in productivity, compounded over a long time, can make a very large difference. Growth of 2 percent maintained over 50 years would generate an increase in annual output per worker from the current level of $45,918 to $123,592 in today's dollars. A seemingly small increase in growth rates, similarly maintained over years, can have large consequences. A growth rate of 2.5 percent, instead of 2 percent, would raise output per worker to almost $160,000 after 50 years. . . .

Causes of the Slowdown in Productivity Growth

Although many factors have contributed to the recent slowdown in productivity growth, most researchers look to three broad classes of explanations: a reduced rate of capital accumulation, a change in the rate of technological advance, and a reduced rate of improvement in the skill levels of the labor force. Government policies can have important effects on these determinants and hence on productivity growth.

Capital Accumulation

The notion of capital represents an attempt to capture the productive facilities with which an economy is equipped. These facilities are of a great variety—examples range from the storage tanks and pumps at the local gas station to a highly sophisticated complex for manufacturing microprocessing chips for personal computers. In a private enterprise economy, most capital is put in place by people who bear the risk of success or failure of the investments.

Growth in capital per worker is, over long periods of time, closely associated with productivity growth. From 1959 to 1973, for example, capital per worker grew by 2.4 percent a year in the private business sector, while productivity in that sector grew by 2.8 percent. From 1973 to 1989, capital per worker grew at 0.8 percent annually and annual productivity growth was 0.9 percent.

According to generally accepted economic analysis, a higher level of capital per worker should support a higher level of output per worker. A rough rule of thumb is that a 1-percentage-point higher level of capital per worker should lead to between a quarter and a third of a percentage point higher level of productivity.

Such a static view of capital may well understate the effect of the *process* of increasing the amount of capital per worker. The new investment required for such "capital deepening" is often the method for introducing new technology that contributes to the productivity of existing facilities. New investment may also foster learning by doing; in putting new equipment in place, companies discover new ways of doing things that make their further investments more productive.

These hypotheses are consistent with studies that find a high correlation between investment rates and rates of productivity growth in different countries. Among major industrialized countries, the United States had the lowest investment rate and the lowest rate of productivity growth in recent decades. According to a recent OECD survey, U.S. gross investment as a fraction of gross national product averaged 19 percent in 1971-80, and 18 percent in 1981-89; the corresponding figure for Japan was 29 percent. Between 1950 and 1979, the United States had the lowest rate of growth of capital per worker among the "group of seven" industrial countries (the others being Canada, France, Germany, Italy, Japan, and the United Kingdom). In 1979 the U.S. capital stock was estimated to be 73 percent older than Japan's.

A major suspect in the slowdown of U.S. productivity growth is thus to be found not in the labor markets but in the capital markets. To raise the rate of productivity growth, the national rate of investment should be increased. The Administration has stressed the need to encourage investment through numerous avenues of policy, including measures to reduce the tax bias against saving and investment. Capital formation is also a principal reason the Administration insists on maintaining budgetary discipline. Expanded government borrowing diverts saving from private investment that leads to higher productivity growth.

Innovation

The pace of innovation, or technological change, is also an important determinant of productivity growth. No number of barns or buggies could support today's standard of living. New methods of production, new products, new modes of organization, and new possibilities for communication have been essential to increased growth and have been forthcoming in remarkable degree. The rate of technological advance is difficult to measure quantitatively, other than by reference to productivity change that cannot be explained by measurable changes in inputs such as physical capital and labor.

Innovation requires the commitment of resources to development of new products and processes and to institutional change (for example, the intricately coordinated overnight delivery systems that have become part of everyday business life in the United States). Government can help make the most of opportunities to innovate in a wide variety of ways, from supporting basic scientific research to ensuring that tax laws do not discourage innovation.

Government has a particular role in encouraging innovation in areas where private investors find it difficult to capture the full benefits of new knowledge. The patent protection afforded an invention permits an inventor to require payments from users and hence to capture some of the benefits. But the innovation may convey an idea to another inventor, who is thereby able to create further benefits, an effect not captured by the original patent. For this reason, the Administration has favored tax policies that encourage innovation broadly. It has also proposed increased government support for basic and applied civilian research that has widespread benefits exceeding costs and from which the returns are not fully appropriable by the private firms that might undertake the research.

Labor Force Quality

Improvement in the "quality" of the labor force, that is, in the productive abilities of individual workers, is the third major contributor to advances in productivity. The term "human capital" refers to the stock of knowledge and skills possessed by workers and is sometimes used to express the analogy with the stock of facilities discussed above. Economists generally agree that the stock of human capital is an immensely important source of an economy's productive power.

All else being equal, higher levels of schooling in the population would be expected to lead to higher levels of output per worker. Productive skills are not perfectly correlated with years of classroom education, however. The quality and relevance of instruction are significant factors. Moreover, one of the concerns in recent years is how well the educational system prepares students for the demands of the workplace. The Administration has made improvements in the Nation's educational system a high priority, as described in the last section of this chapter.

Summary

- Advances in labor productivity and employment have provided the United States with the highest standard of living in the world.
- In the United States, as in many other industrialized countries, labor productivity growth during the last 20 years has slowed.
- A slowdown in the rate of capital accumulation is one of several factors contributing to the slower productivity advance. . . .

Government and the Level and Distribution of Income

Income for the typical family has risen substantially over the past several decades. Rapid productivity growth and other factors fueled strong income growth from the late 1940s through the late 1960s. Since then, slower productivity growth and shifting demographic patterns have reduced the rate of income growth. Nevertheless, the typical family in 1990 received about $4,100 more in income after adjusting for inflation than the typical family did in 1970. Average incomes for families in each fifth, or quintile, of the income distribution have increased. Income growth, however, has been uneven for different segments of the population, and the distribution of income has gradually grown more dispersed since the mid-1960s.

Trends in the level and distribution of income are closely related and are affected by a variety of factors. The primary source of income for most families is labor earnings. Thus, the primary causes of the continued long-run increase in family income are the long-term increase in productivity, and hence in wages, the historic growth in employment, and related labor market factors. Changes in the distribution of wages and in employment patterns have also had important effects on the distribution of income.

The level of overall economic activity affects the incomes of families in each part of the income distribution. Sustained long-term economic growth has been the most effective and durable way to raise the income of families.

Demographic patterns also have substantial effects on the level and distribution of income. The average number of people per family has fallen significantly over the past three decades, and single-parent families are much more prevalent now than they were in the 1960s.

The level and structure of government taxes and transfers have important effects on the level, structure, and growth rate of overall economic activity. Many tax and transfer programs contain features that discourage people from working, saving, or investing. Some programs, like the earned income tax credit, can encourage work effort.

Many Federal, State, and local government programs and policies redistribute a substantial amount of income, wealth, and opportunities for economic advancement across the population. In 1990 according to estimates by the Census Bureau, the net effects of Federal and State taxes and transfers raised the income of households in the bottom fifth of the income distribution by an average of more than $8,800, from about $2,100 to about $10,900. Households in the top fifth paid $22,000 more in taxes, on average, than they received in transfers, reducing their average income from about $94,000 to under $72,000.

Most of this redistribution occurs through transfer programs. A network of means-tested programs transfers cash and specific goods, such as food, housing, health care, and job training to the Nation's neediest citizens. Other government programs redistribute in ways that are not means-tested. Social insurance programs protect individuals against a variety of contingencies. Recent decades have seen significant growth in spending on means-tested and social insurance programs and a shift in the composition of means-tested assistance toward the provision of specific goods and services rather than cash.

Despite long-term increases in income and transfer payments, poverty remains a serious problem in the United States. Society can and should provide a minimum level of support for those who are unable to provide for themselves. The most effective antidote to general conditions of poverty in the long run is sustained economic growth. Some poor people are unable to benefit from such growth, however, and require targeted programs. The Administration is firmly committed to the goal of alleviating poverty.

The Federal tax system also redistributes income toward lower income households. Major income tax reforms since the late 1970s reduced marginal tax rates, eliminated many tax shelters, broadened the tax base, and removed many low-income households from the income taxrolls. In addition, Social Security tax rate increases, enacted in the 1970s, were accelerated in 1983 to address short- and long-run financing problems in the Social Security trust fund. Amid these sweeping changes, redistribution of income within the Federal tax system has remained about the same as it was in the 1970s before the reforms took place.

Government tax and spending programs also transfer large amounts of wealth across generations. These transfers are sometimes clearly visible, as in the case of the Social Security program, where current workers make payments and current retirees receive benefits. As explained below, however, other policies embody intergenerational transfers that are much less obvious. In both cases, transfers across generations may be larger than transfers across income classes in a particular year.

The Level and Distribution of Income

The most commonly used measure of income, and the one used in this section, is "money income" as defined by the Bureau of the Census. This measure includes all periodic earned and unearned monetary income except capital gains. Money income includes government cash transfers but does not count noncash government transfers, such as medicaid and food stamps, or fringe benefits, such as employer-provided health insurance, and it does not deduct taxes paid.

While wages are earned by individuals, income is typically shared among members of a family or household. Thus, analyses of income typically focus on these groups rather than on individuals. The Census Bureau defines a family as a group of two or more people related by birth, marriage, or adoption who live together. A household is defined as all related family members and all unrelated people living in a given housing unit. A family, a person living alone, or a group of unrelated people living together in a single housing unit each counts as a single household.

To measure the evolution of income over time, adjustments need to be made for the changing cost of living. Estimates of the cost of living are measured in the consumer price index (CPI) published by the Bureau of

Labor Statistics. As discussed in Chapter 7, the CPI was modified in 1983 to incorporate an improved measure of costs on a consistent basis back to 1967. Most analysts believe this index is the more appropriate measure of changes in the cost of living. . . .

The Role of Demographics

Substantial income growth between 1967 and 1990 is particularly noteworthy in light of several long-term demographic trends. During this period, average family size fell by 14 percent, and average household size fell by 19 percent. Income growth rates for families and households thus understate the growth rate of income per person. *Between 1967 and 1990, average, or mean, real money income rose by 62 percent per person*, as opposed to 35 percent per family.

Large shifts in the composition of households have also influenced income growth. Between 1969 and 1989, the proportion of household heads living alone or with unrelated individuals rose from 18.5 percent to 29.1 percent, and the proportion of families with children that have a female householder rose from 11.3 percent to 21.7 percent. In 1990, more than two-thirds of household heads living alone or with unrelated individuals and one-third of female heads of families were under 35 years old. At this age, many workers are still acquiring skills and training and may also have had short job tenure or little overall labor market experience. Female heads of families also often face child care responsibilities that make full-time participation in the labor force difficult. The means-tested transfer system creates incentives for some women to reduce or eliminate work outside the home. For these and other reasons, female-headed families and people living alone or with unrelated individuals have median incomes well below the overall median. One study found that in the absence of these demographic trends, real median household income between 1969 and 1989 would have grown another $3,200, more than doubling its actual rate of growth.

Two-Earner Families

A related issue is the extent to which sustained income growth is due to the increased proportion of married women that work outside the home. In 1970, 39 percent of married women worked outside the home. That figure rose to 50 percent in 1980 and 58 percent in 1990. The number of working married women rose more in absolute and percentage terms in the 1970s than in the 1980s.

Determining the effect of this trend on *median* income is difficult. Determining the contribution of new second earners to overall income growth is much more straightforward. Average income for married couple families rose by $4,232 (in 1990 dollars) between 1970 and 1980, and $6,035 between 1980 and 1990. The role of the increased number of second earners can be calculated using data on the number and average income of married couple families and second earners. *The increased number of married women in the labor force accounts for only about 18 percent of the real increase in income married couple families between 1980 and 1990.* The corresponding figure for the 1970s is 19 percent. For all families, about 14 percent of the increase in income in the 1980s and 16 percent in the 1970s is due to the increase of two-earner families.

The small role of the rising number of two-earner families in income growth can be attributed to two factors. First, average earnings of second earners are lower than average earnings for all earners, in part because a high proportion of second earners work part-time. Second, the recent *increase* in two-earner families is small relative to the total number of families. From 1980 to 1990, the number of married women in the labor force rose by 5.5 million; the total number of families in 1990 was 66.3 million.

Distribution of Annual Income

The long-term and cyclical factors that affect income levels also affect the distribution of income. Incomes in any year can differ across households for many reasons. Because the primary source of income for most people is labor earnings, the determinants of the wage distribution, including workers' education and changes in labor supply and demand, also help determine the distribution of annual income. Because families and households in the United States experience a significant amount of mobility across income classes, the distribution of *long-term* income differs from the distribution of annual income. . . .

The Distribution of Long-Term Income and Wealth

Families and households display a substantial amount of mobility across income classes in the United States. For this reason, *analyses of income distribution that focus only on annual income tend to overstate the degree of income inequality.*

One reason annual income data are misleading is that earnings of individual workers tend to rise as they acquire training and experience and then to fall when they retire. A 20-year-old worker just starting out and a 45-year-old worker who is in his or her peak earning years could have equal incomes over their careers, but very different wages in the same calendar year.

Data on annual income can also prove misleading because of transitory income, that is, income gains or losses that are thought to be temporary. A person who owns a small business, for example, may face greater year-to-year fluctuations in income than someone who works at a steady wage.

There is substantial mobility across income classes from year to year. One study found that in the mid-1980s, *about one-third of all families were in a different income quintile than they had been in the previous year.* In each of the lowest three quintiles, about 18 percent of the families moved to a higher quintile the following year. In each of the highest three quintiles, more than 20 percent of the families moved to lower quintiles the following year. Another study found that more than half of families in the highest quintile in 1971 had fallen into lower quintiles by 1978. Similarly, almost half of those in the lowest quintile had risen to a higher quintile.

Over long periods, the extent of mobility increases. One study, using data from the 1970s and 1980s, found that *more than 75 percent of households are in a different decile when ranked by lifetime income than when ranked by current income.* A decile includes one-tenth of the households. About 44 percent had current income two or more deciles away from their lifetime income. More than half of households in each of the lowest three deciles for annual income had lifetime income in a higher decile. More than half of households in the top three deciles for annual income had lifetime income in a lower decile.

A recent study, using tax return data from the 1960s, 1970s, and 1980s, estimates that the Gini coefficients for income over 4-year or 7-year periods are between 5.0 percent and 7.7 percent less than the average of the Gini coefficients for the individual years. Another study, using data from 1969 to 1981, found that the Gini for lifetime income in the United States was 19 percent lower than the Gini for annual income, indicating less dispersion in lifetime income.

These findings underscore the importance of income mobility for a large number of families. Nevertheless, even after removing temporary income changes and the effects of the life-cycle on income, part of the population still faces very low long-term income prospects.

Because the distribution of long-term income is less dispersed than are annual incomes, trends in the distribution of annual income may not accurately reflect trends in the distribution of long-term income. For example, an increase in income mobility or in the importance of transitory income can increase inequality of annual income but have no effect on the distribution of long-term income. Nevertheless, one study found that, like annual incomes, incomes averaged over 4- and 7-year periods became more dispersed between 1967-73 and 1979-85.

A related issue is the distribution of wealth. A family's wealth holdings consist of financial assets, such as saving accounts; property, such as a house or family business; pensions and future Social Security benefits; and human capital, the value of future labor earnings. For most households, housing, public and private pensions, and human capital constitute the vast bulk of wealth. One study found that between 1983 and 1989 the median value of households' real financial net worth and property rose 11 percent and that holdings of these assets became more concentrated.

Summary

- Median levels of family and household money income have shown sustained long-term growth since the mid-1960s. Median income is influenced by cyclical and long-term economic activity and demographic patterns.
- Since the mid-1960s and in particular since the early 1980s, income growth has occurred in all quintiles and the distribution of annual

money income has become more dispersed in the United States. Earnings distributions have also become more dispersed in several other countries in recent years.

- Because money income omits in-kind transfers, data on money income understate both the level of and improvement in income for the lowest income groups.
- Families and households display significant mobility across income classes. The distribution of long-term income is more equal than the distribution of annual income. . . .

Effects of Taxes and Transfers on the Distribution of Income

Government tax and transfer policies can have large effects on the distribution of income. The effects of taxes and transfers can occur directly, through receipt of transfers from, or payments of taxes to, the government, or indirectly, when the government program changes a person's behavior. The people who are actually affected by a tax or transfer are not necessarily the same people who send the money directly to, or receive the transfer from, the government. . . .

There are many ways to measure and describe the redistribution that occurs within an economic system. One common measure uses the relationship between average ("effective") tax rates—the ratio of taxes to income—and income level. If the average tax rate increases with income, then the tax system is said to be progressive. If the average tax rate falls as income rises, the system is termed regressive. In a proportional tax system, average tax rates are constant across income classes.

This measure can easily be expanded to consider both taxes and transfers by examining the ratio of taxes minus transfers to income as income rises. Thus, a progressive system, for example, would show higher average rates of taxes net of transfers as income rises. . . .

Redistributive Effects of Other Policies

While taxes and transfers represent a broad range of government activities, other government policies redistribute resources as well. For example, the tax deduction for private contributions to charitable organizations raises these contributions. The private contribution does not appear as a government transfer but is nonetheless influenced by the favorable tax treatment.

Direct government purchases of goods and services and government programs that improve the environment, maintain the infrastructure, and provide education, national defense, or other items can also have important distributional effects. These effects, however, are difficult to measure.

Long-Term Redistribution

The impact of government policies on the distribution of long-term income can differ significantly from the effects on the distribution of annual income. Low-skilled workers in their high-earning years may pay a relatively high amount of taxes compared with other taxpayers, even though income over their entire careers may be relatively low. In contrast, medical students pay relatively low amounts of taxes even though their long-term income is relatively high. A tax increase on the older, low-skilled workers combined with a tax cut for the medical students would *reduce* inequality of annual incomes but *raise* inequality of long-term incomes.

One study, using data from 1969 to 1981, found that Federal taxes and cash transfers reduced the Gini for lifetime incomes by 19 percent and reduced the Gini ratio for annual incomes by 13 percent. Therefore, the combined effects of taxes and transfers may reduce inequality in long-term incomes by more than they reduce inequality in annual incomes.

Some government policies have the effect, intended or unintended, of redistributing wealth *across generations*. A well-known example is Social Security, which makes direct payments to the elderly, financed by payments from current workers. Intergenerational transfers can occur in less obvious forms as well. For example, most wealth in the United States is held by people who are older than 40, and most people over the age of 65 are retired. Therefore, a policy that raised tax rates on capital income and reduced rates on labor income would constitute an implicit transfer of wealth from older to younger generations. These transfers can be large.

Government policies can also transfer resources between currently living generations and generations yet to be born. Financing government through debt rather than through current taxes, for example, can push the burden of paying for current obligations onto future generations....

Conclusion

Over the long term, incomes for families and households in each part of the income distribution have increased substantially. Over the past 25 years, the distribution of money income has become more dispersed in the United States. Similar trends are evident in other countries as well. Trends in the level and distribution of income are determined by a complex interplay of aggregate economic activity, demographic changes, labor market changes, and government policy.

Government taxes and transfers redistribute a substantial amount of resources from higher income households to lower income households and across generations. Most of this redistribution occurs through transfer payments. Government spending on transfer programs has increased significantly, starting in the 1960s and continuing to the present. Redistribution within the Federal tax system has not changed substantially since at least the mid-1970s.

The status of low-income households remains an important concern. A combination of continued economic growth and targeted programs is the best strategy for alleviating poverty....

REPORT ON POSSIBLE DISCOVERY
OF THE FIRST NORTH AMERICANS
February 9, 1992

Striking evidence that humans first came to North America at least 28,000 years ago was reported February 9 in Chicago at the annual meeting of the American Association for the Advancement of Science. Previously, the oldest evidence of humans in North America dated to 14,500 years, about 3,000 years earlier than scientists had believed since the 1920s.

The new evidence was described in a paper titled "The Earliest North Americans?" by Richard S. MacNeish, an archaeologist at the Andover Foundation for Archaeological Research in Massachusetts. MacNeish, one of the nation's leading experts on man's earliest days in the New World, directed the team that made the discovery in Pendejo Cave on the grounds of Fort Bliss in New Mexico.

The most dramatic evidence from the shallow cave was a human palm print and possible fingerprint on pieces of fired clay. The clay came from a fire pit, where it had become hardened. According to both carbon dating and thermoluminescence, a newer method of dating archaeological finds, the clay was approximately 28,000 years old. MacNeish said more possible prints were still being found. The archaeologists also found numerous hearths, some still ringed by stones cracked by fire and holding large charred logs, that could date up to 38,000 years ago.

In addition, the archaeologists found thousands of animal bones in the cave's many layers, some from extinct species. The bones came from rabbits, small camels, extinct mice, coyote, antelope, extinct goats, small and large horses, tapirs, giant turtles, weasels, skunks, magpies, salamanders, llama, four-prong sheep, bear, and lion, among other species.

Hair and Prints Make "A Strong Case"

Only months after announcing the finding of the human palm print, the archaeologists said they had found a black human hair that was approximately 19,000 years old in the same cave. If their estimate of the hair's age was correct, it would be the oldest human remain ever found in the Western Hemisphere. The 14,500-year-old evidence found previously was three human hairs found in Montana in 1986. The half-inch-long hair found in the New Mexico cave was analyzed by forensic scientists at the Ontario Provincial Police in Toronto. They determined it was a human body hair that probably came from a Mongoloid, the group that included most Asians, North American Indians, and Eskimos.

"Put this together with the fingerprints and you've got a pretty strong case that humans were here a lot earlier than the skeptics used to think," MacNeish told the Washington Post. *Rob Bonnichsen, an archaeologist at Oregon State University who found the Montana hairs, told the* Post *that hair is "as good as bone when you're trying to establish human presence. Most of us in this field have probably thrown away lots of it over the years without knowing what we had."*

Other Important Finds of 1992

The New Mexico fingerprints and hair constituted only two of several important archaeological finds made during 1992. In Namibia, Glenn C. Conroy of the Washington University Medical School in St. Louis and colleagues from France and the United States found a fragment of lower jaw with teeth that they said was 13 million years old. Scientists believed the fragment came from a creature closely related to the common ancestor of today's humans and apes. For years, experts had searched for this common ancestor, or "missing link," that would tie together the evolutionary lineages of humans and apes. The discovery, reported in the March 12, 1992, issue of Nature, *was so important that twenty-two of the world's leading authorities on early man met in New York to study the fossil and try to figure out its relationship to similar fossils.*

Another major discovery involved a human skull fragment that was actually found in 1967 in Kenya. Using a new method called argon-40/argon-39, scientists from Yale University and Northeastern Ohio Universities College of Medicine determined the fragment was 2.4 million years old, making it the oldest bone from a true human being ever found. The fragment was half a million years older than any human bone found before. The discovery was reported in the February 20, 1992, issue of Nature.

In China, researchers found two human skulls believed to be between 350,000 and 400,000 years old. The skulls' features cast doubt on the theory that all living humans had a common, hypothetical maternal ancestor dubbed "Eve" who supposedly lived about 200,000 years ago in

Africa. The fossils were discussed in a June 4, 1992, Nature article by Li Tianyuan, their discoverer, and Dennis A. Etler.

In Israel, archaeologists discovered what they believed was the family tomb of Caiaphas, the high priest who turned over Jesus to the Romans to be crucified. The discoverers reported in the September-October 1992 issue of Biblical Archaeology Review that they could not be certain the bones were actually Caiaphas. However, the bones' age, the elaborately carved burial box in which they were found, artifacts found with the bones, and writing in the tomb all indicated the bones were Caiaphas's. The tomb was found by accident by workers widening a road in the Peace Forest in Jerusalem.

In Mexico, controversy surrounded an American-led archaeological project designed to explore and restore important ruins found in south-eastern Mexico. The ruins were discovered by American archaeologist S. Jeffrey K. Wilkerson, whose work was supported by the Smithsonian Institution and the National Geographic Society. After Wilkerson submitted a proposal to the Mexican government to restore the site, Mexican officials enthusiastically backed his plan. However, shortly thereafter the government rejected Wilkerson's plan and said that Mexican archaeologists were exploring the ruins. Previously, no Mexican archaeologists had worked at the site. Both American and Mexican archaeologists accused the government of stealing Wilkerson's plan and pushing him aside. Under heavy pressure, the Mexican government relented a few weeks later and permitted Wilkerson to proceed with his project.

Following are excerpts from "The Earliest North Americans?" by Richard S. MacNeish, a paper presented in Chicago, February 9, 1992, to the American Association for the Advancement of Science:

One of the most hotly debated issues in New World Archaeology is "How early are the Paleoindians in the New World?" This debate is of long standing—starting before the American Revolution and continuing to the present. Although the parameters and available data have changed, the controversy continues, often generating more heat than light on the subject. I am certain the new findings from south central New Mexico that I am about to relate will provide further fuel for the fires.

These findings have been made in Orogrande (or more correctly Pendejo) Cave, located 13 miles east of Orogrande, New Mexico, on the MacGregor Firing Range of Fort Bliss, some 45 miles north of El Paso, Texas. The Andover Foundation for Archaeological Research commenced work there in the winter-spring season of 1990, carried through in the same regimen in 1991, and, even as I speak, excavation continues. The cave—originally called FtB162 and now designated FB9366—was discovered in 1976 during a survey prior to the use of this part of this firing range for experimental military purposes. Although the importance of the cave was recognized in the field notes, it was not revisited until 1989. At this time MacNeish, who had been investigating early agriculture in the general Jornada region for five years (1985-1989) inquired of Dr. Glen DeGarmo of the Environmental Office of Fort Bliss if the military reservation included any caves with good plant preservation that had not been excavated (i.e., looted). In response to this inquiry Paul Lukowsky of that office informed us the survey notes mentioned five caves in Rough Canyon. In April of 1989 we visited these caves, saw their potential—particularly Pendejo, which had preserved corncobs even on the surface, and began making plans for their excavation in 1990. . . .

We have uncovered 25 distinctive strata, one on top of another. Even our sternest critics, Dr. Paul Martin and Dr. Vance Haynes, agree the stratigraphy is magnificent. Further, as of this date, 14 strata have valid radiocarbon determinations (made by three different labs) in sequential order. Thirteen of these strata were laid down before 12,970 [years] BP [before the present]. The 4-5 lowest strata have yet to be adequately dated, but could have been deposited before 38,000 BP. . . .

Thus, the magnificent stratigraphy of Orogrande Cave has the potential to yield significant data about paleoecology and climate change during the last 50,000 or more years, but the $64,000 question is, what does it tell us about Paleoindians or the presence of early early humans in the New World? The answer is, a great deal that is all very new (and very, very controversial).

Let us therefore look more closely at these controversial elements. We will start with a major element of the stratigraphy—the charcoal itself and the evidence of firing in the strata. We found the greatest concentration of these elements were in our features that were considered hearths. . . . Supporting this hypothesis are the thermoluminescence analyses now being undertaken by Dr. Ralph Rowlett of the University of Missouri that show a number of these features not only had repeated fires (rather than the single fire that might occur naturally), but the fires reached temperatures that can occur only in man-made hearths, not in natural burning. . . .

Of key importance in this realm is the necessity of proving that many of our so-called lithic artifacts are "exotic" to the cave and had to be brought in by humans from sources not in and of the cave itself. . . . The most likely explanation for the presence of these "exotic" lithics in the cave is that Paleoindians brought (and used) them there at the time of the formation of the various strata or zones since their composition is definitely *not* the same as the rock of the rooffall. Physically, these materials could not have worked up from the subsoils or spread long distances into Orogrande (Pendejo) Cave by natural means. . . .

The presence of a human agency is equally true of our bone tools and of bones in general. The concentration of bones on the floor or in the zones looks like the result of dumping or butchering by humans rather than a random scattering by carnivores. The kind of bones represented by each of our extinct animals supports this idea. We have uncovered an abnormal number of limb bones and jaws with teeth (which went with the edible tongues) but have found few if any vertebrae, skulls, or scapula and pelvis (which should be there if the animal was dragged into the cave by animals other than humans). Also, many of the bones are burned; more important, a number look as if they have been worked by humans. . . . About a dozen bones with cuts or scratches on them have been examined under the electron microscope and, according to Dr. Pat Shipman, they appear to have been cut by artifacts. Moreover we found four bones with (chipped) stones imbedded in them. On of them, recently CAT scan X-ray photographed by Dr. Chrisman, appears to be a whittled point of burned (rabbit) bone that is imbedded more than 4 cm deep in the back of a horse upper toe bone. This bone projectile point tip had to have been stuck into the bone when it was fresh (i.e., the animal was alive) and would have required at least a 40-pound thrust. The only likely agent for doing this was man. . . .

Even more indisputable is our finding of a human palm print and possible fingerprint on two peanut-sized pieces of fired clay in zone I under the stratum of zone H dated at about 27,000 BP. . . . Even as I speak, we are finding more possible prints in baked clay that is too hard to take modern impressions so our evidence of the presence of humans at Orogrande Cave at least 28,000 years ago rests on very solid foundations. . . .

We are therefore confident that we do have definite evidence of pre-Clovis peoples in Orogrande (or Pendejo) Cave in southern New Mexico. This very significant finding will take some rethinking of our ideas about the peopling of the New World and the beginning of human culture here. . . . The Clovis dam has been breached, a flood of new pre-Clovis evidence will be found, and we in the Paleoindian field are now sailing on uncharted waters.

REPORT ON "HOW SCHOOLS SHORTCHANGE GIRLS"

February 12, 1992

Girls confront serious and widespread obstacles to academic achievement, according to a February 12 report by the American Association of University Women (AAUW). Although boys and girls enter public schools with roughly equal capabilities, girls are "systematically discouraged" from pursuing a curriculum that would enhance their likelihood of entering well-paying professions, particularly those in science and math. Although the report noted that variations between the sexes in achievement and performance in math seemed to be decreasing, it warned that such disparities in science were significant and possibly widening. (International Math-Science Test of Young Students, p. 85)

"Construction of the glass ceiling begins not in the executive suite but in the classroom," said Alice McKee, president of the AAUW Educational Foundation. "It starts in preschool. . . . By the time girls reach high school, they have been systematically tracked toward traditional, sex-segregated jobs and away from areas of study that lead to high-paying jobs in science, technology, and engineering."

AAUW Findings

The study was conducted in 1991 by the Wellesley College Center for Research on Women under a $100,000 grant from the AAUW Educational Foundation. It was based on a compilation of existing research, including a 1990 nationwide survey of 3,000 students.

The study's findings indicated that teachers generally did not pay equal attention to girls and boys, favoring boys with more concern and encouragement. The authors pointed to other research that showed boys in elementary and middle school called out answers eight times more often than did girls. When girls did so, teachers told them to "raise your hand [before you] speak." Moreover, black girls had less interaction with teachers than did white girls, despite the fact that black girls tried to initiate such participation more frequently than did their white counterparts or boys of either race.

The AAUW researchers also pointed to a 1989 study finding that, of the ten books most frequently assigned in public high school English classes, only one was written by a woman and none by a minority group member.

Standardized tests also showed sexual bias, according to the report, with the "most obvious" being the disparate numbers of references to women and men in test items and in stereotyped portrayals of men and women. For example, a study of the 1984-85 Scholastic Aptitude Test (SAT) found references to forty-two men and only three women. Moreover, when SAT scores were used as the principal criterion for awarding scholarships, boys were more likely to obtain them than were girls who received equal or slightly better high school grades.

The researchers said that, generally, topics of particular interest to girls were not adequately discussed in schools. These included sex and health education to help prevent pregnancy and the spread of venereal diseases, as well as incest and rape. The "most evaded of all topics" related to sex and power, the researchers concluded. Schools must be made aware of the fact that girls "confront a culture that both idealizes and exploits the sexuality of young women while assigning them roles that are clearly less valued than male roles."

Recommendations

"The implications of the report's findings are enormous," said McKee. "It presents compelling evidence that girls are not receiving the same quality, or even quantity, of education as their brothers." For example, girls' self-esteem (measured by those reporting they were "happy as I am") dropped nearly 40 percent between elementary and high school, compared with a 20 percent decrease for boys.

The report concluded with forty recommendations, among them:

- *Stricter enforcement of Title IX of the 1972 Education Amendments, which bars discrimination on the basis of sex by schools receiving federal funds.* (Supreme Court on Sexual Harassment of Students, p. 187)
- *Teacher training and staff development in boy-girl issues.*
- *Adoption of "gender fair" multicultural curriculums that avoid sex stereotyping.*
- *Revision of standardized texts to eliminate sex bias.*
- *Improved sex education and health programs.*
- *Expanded efforts to encourage girls to take science and math.*

- *More equity in vocational education programs, which tended to be geared to males, although women made up 45 percent of the nation's work force.*
- *A more central role for women in education reform efforts. (Although the overwhelming majority of public school teachers were women, more than 95 percent of the nation's school superintendents and 72 percent of its principals were men.)*
- *Increased emphasis on grades, portfolios of student work, and extra-curricular activities—rather than standardized tests—to measure student ability.*

Reaction: Education Summit on Girls

The report was praised by the National Coalition of Girls Schools, which said that "girls have been shown again and again to be treated as second-class citizens academically in coed learning environments."

However, spokespersons for the U.S. Department of Education contended that sex-equity programs were no longer needed. "You have to look at the larger context, at all the great strides women have made," said Diane S. Ravitch, assistant secretary for educational research and improvement. Ravitch pointed to the fact that the percentage of female high school graduates enrolling in college was greater than men. Women comprised 55 percent of the enrollment in higher education in 1989, compared with 41 percent in 1971. "I think the problem in this country is not gender bias, but bias against academic achievement," she said. Ravitch said the Bush administration sought to remedy that through initiatives such as AMERICA 2000. (Education Summit, Historic Documents of 1989, p. 561)

Ravitch took even stronger exception to the AAUW report in a February 20 appearance on the Diane Rehm radio talk show in Washington, D.C. "I really think the report is a lot of special interest whining" written by "some overheated feminists," she said. What often passes for bias in class, she added, is merely the teacher's effort to compensate for boys' reluctance to answer questions while the girls "are eager to participate and have their hands up." She said the case could just as easily be made that the system is biased against boys.

Other criticism came from the College Board and the Educational Testing Service. The presidents of the two organizations said it was inappropriate to "equate score differences [between boys and girls on standardized tests] with bias in the tests." Rather, they contended, test score differences may indeed be "meaningful indicators that girls may be educationally shortchanged . . . that these scores reflect real differences of concern, not biased tests."

The report was released as leaders from nearly three dozen national education and youth-serving groups met in Washington, D.C., at a "National Education Summit on Girls" to discuss adopting the AAUW's recommendations. Most of them said they would disseminate the report

143

widely and would work to train educators to eliminate sex bias. David G. Imag, executive director of the American Association of Colleges for Teacher Education, said his organization was committed to a "multilayered program of gender-sensitive teacher education." Representing the Council of Chief State School Officers (CCSSO), Florida Commissioner of Education Betty Castor said the CCSSO was calling on states to compile student data in ways that would facilitate better analysis of girls' school experience and academic achievement. She also said the CCSSO was asking the governors to consider sex bias in their education "report cards" and other activities. (Education Summit, Historic Documents of 1989, p. 561)

> *Following is the executive summary of the report, "How Schools Shortchange Girls," prepared for the American Association of University Women, released February 12, 1992:*

Why a Report on Girls?

The invisibility of girls in the current education debate suggests that girls and boys have identical educational experiences in school. Nothing could be further from the truth. Whether one looks at achievement scores, curriculum design, or teacher-student interaction, it is clear that sex and gender make a difference in the nation's public elementary and secondary schools.

The educational system is not meeting girls' needs. Girls and boys enter school roughly equal in measured ability. Twelve years later, girls have fallen behind their male classmates in key areas such as higher-level mathematics and measures of self-esteem. Yet gender equity is still not a part of the national debate on educational reform.

Neither the *National Education Goals* issued by the National Governors Association in 1990 nor *America 2000*, the 1991 plan of the President and the U.S. Department of Education to "move every community in America toward these goals," makes any mention of providing girls equitable opportunities in the nation's public schools. Girls continue to be left out of the debate—despite the fact that for more than two decades researchers have identified gender bias as a major problem at all levels of schooling.

Schools must prepare both girls and boys for full and active roles in the family, the community, and the work force. Whether we look at the issues from an economic, political, or social perspective, girls are one-half of our future. We must move them from the sidelines to the center of the education-reform debate.

A critical step in correcting educational inequities is identifying them publicly. The *AAUW Report: How Schools Shortchange Girls* provides a comprehensive assessment of the status of girls in public education today. It exposes myths about girls and learning, and it supports the work of the many teachers who have struggled to define and combat gender bias in their schools. The report challenges us all—policymakers, educators, administrators, parents, and citizens—to rethink old assumptions and act now to stop schools from shortchanging girls.

Our public education system is plagued by numerous failings that affect boys as negatively as girls. But in many respects girls are put at a disadvantage simply because they are girls. *The AAUW Report* documents this in hundreds of cited studies.

When our schools become more gender-fair, education will improve for all our students—boys as well as girls—because excellence in education cannot be achieved without equity in education. By studying what happens to girls in school, we can gain valuable insights about what has to change in order for each student, every girl and every boy, to do as well as she or he can.

What the Research Reveals

What Happens in the Classroom?

- Girls receive significantly less attention from classroom teachers than do boys.
- African American girls have fewer interactions with teachers than do white girls, despite evidence that they attempt to initiate interactions more frequently.
- Sexual harassment of girls by boys—from innuendo to actual assault—in our nation's schools is increasing.

A large body of research indicates that teachers give more classroom attention and more esteem-building encouragement to boys. In a study conducted by Myra and David Sadker, boys in elementary and middle school called out answers eight times more often than girls. When boys called out, teachers listened. But when girls called out, they were told to "raise your hand if you want to speak." Even when boys do not volunteer, teachers are more likely to encourage them to give an answer or an opinion than they are to encourage girls.

Research reveals a tendency, beginning at the preschool level, for educators to choose classroom activities that appeal to boys' interests and to select presentation formats in which boys excel. The teacher-student interaction patterns in science classes are often particularly biased. Even in math classes, where less-biased patterns are found, psychologist Jacquelynne Eccles reports that select boys in each math class she studied received particular attention to the exclusion of all other students, female and male.

Teaching methods that foster competition are still standard, although a considerable body of research has demonstrated that girls—and many boys

as well—learn better when they undertake projects and activities coopera-
tively rather than competitively.

Researchers, including Sandra Damico, Elois Scott, and Linda Grant,
report that African American girls have fewer interactions with
teachers than do white girls, even though they attempt to initiate
interactions more often. Furthermore, when African American girls do as
well as white boys in school, teachers often attribute their success to
hard work while assuming that the white boys are not working up to their
potential.

Girls do not emerge from our schools with the same degree of confidence
and self-esteem as boys. The 1990 AAUW poll, *Shortchanging Girls,
Shortchanging America*, documents a loss of self-confidence in girls that is
twice that for boys as they move from childhood to adolescence. Schools
play a crucial role in challenging and changing gender-role expectations
that undermine the self-confidence and achievement of girls.

Reports of boys sexually harassing girls in schools are increasing at an
alarming rate. When sexual harassment is treated casually, as in "boys will
be boys," both girls and boys get a dangerous, damaging message: "girls are
not worthy of respect; appropriate behavior for boys includes exerting
power over girls."

What Do We Teach Our Students?

- The contributions and experiences of girls and women are still
  marginalized or ignored in many of the textbooks used in our nation's
  schools.
- Schools, for the most part, provide inadequate education on sexuality
  and healthy development despite national concern about teen pregnancy, the AIDS crisis, and the increase of sexually transmitted
  diseases among adolescents.
- Incest, rape, and other physical violence severely compromise the lives
  of girls and women all across the country. These realities are rarely, if
  ever, discussed in schools.

Curriculum delivers the central messages of education. It can strengthen
or decrease student motivation for engagement, effort, growth, and development through the images it gives to students about themselves and the
world. When the curriculum does not reflect the diversity of students' lives
and cultures, it delivers an incomplete message.

Studies have shown that multicultural readings produced markedly
more favorable attitudes toward nondominant groups than did the traditional reading lists, that academic achievement for all students was linked
to use of nonsexist and multicultural materials, and that sex-role stereotyping was reduced in students whose curriculum portrayed males and
females in nonstereotypical roles. Yet during the 1980s, federal support for
reform regarding sex and race equity dropped, and a 1989 study showed
that of the ten books most frequently assigned in public high school

English courses only one was written by a woman and none by members of minority groups.

The "evaded" curriculum is a term coined in this report to refer to matters central to the lives of students that are touched on only briefly, if at all, in most schools. The United States has the highest rate of teenage childbearing in the Western industrialized world. Syphilis rates are now equal for girls and boys, and more teenage girls than boys contract gonorrhea. Although in the adult population AIDS is nine times more prevalent in men than in women, the same is not true for young people. In a District of Columbia study, the rate of HIV infection for girls was almost three times that for boys. Despite all of this, adequate sex and health education is the exception rather than the rule.

Adolescence is a difficult period for all young people, but it is particularly difficult for girls, who are far more likely to develop eating disorders and experience depression. Adolescent girls attempt suicide four to five times as often as boys (although boys, who choose more lethal methods, are more likely to be successful in their attempts).

Perhaps the most evaded of all topics in schools is the issue of gender and power. As girls mature they confront a culture that both idealizes and exploits the sexuality of young women while assigning them roles that are clearly less valued than male roles. If we do not begin to discuss more openly the ways in which ascribed power—whether on the basis of race, sex, class, sexual orientation, or religion—affects individual lives, we cannot truly prepare our students for responsible citizenship.

How Do Race/Ethnicity and Socioeconomic Status Affect Achievement in School?

- Girls from low-income families face particularly severe obstacles. Socioeconomic status, more than any other variable, affects access to school resources and educational outcomes.
- Test scores of low-socioeconomic-status girls are somewhat better than for boys from the same background in the lower grades, but by high school these differences disappear. Among high-socioeconomic-status students, boys generally outperform girls regardless of race/ethnicity.
- Too little information is available on differences among various groups of girls. While African Americans are compared to whites, or boys to girls, relatively few studies or published data examine differences by sex *and* race/ethnicity.

All girls confront barriers to equal participation in school and society. But minority girls, who must confront racism as well as sexism, and girls from low-income families face particularly severe obstacles. These obstacles can include poor schools in dangerous neighborhoods, low teacher expectations, and inadequate nutrition and health care.

Few studies focus on issues affecting low-income girls and girls from minority groups—unless they are pregnant or drop out of school. In order to develop effective policies and programs, a wide range of issues—from course-taking patterns to academic self-esteem—require further examination by sex, race/ethnicity, and socioeconomic status.

How Are Girls Doing in Math and Science?

- Differences between girls and boys in math achievement are small and declining. Yet in high school, girls are still less likely than boys to take the most advanced courses and be in the top-scoring math groups.
- The gender gap in science, however, is *not* decreasing and may, in fact, be increasing.
- Even girls who are highly competent in math and science are much less likely to pursue scientific or technological careers than are their male classmates.

Girls who see math as "something men do" do less well in math than girls who do not hold this view. In their classic study, Elizabeth Fennema and Julia Sherman reported a drop in both girls' math confidence and their achievement in the middle school years. The drop in confidence *preceded* the decline in achievement.

Researcher Jane Kahle found that boys come to science classes with more out-of-school familiarity and experience with the subject matter. This advantage is furthered in the classroom. One study of science classrooms found that 79 percent of all student-assisted science demonstrations were carried out by boys.

We can no longer afford to disregard half our potential scientists and science-literate citizens of the next generation. Even when girls take math and science courses and do well in them, they do not receive the encouragement they need to pursue scientific careers. A study of high school seniors found that 64 percent of the boys who had taken physics and calculus were planning to major in science and engineering in college, compared to only 18.6 percent of the girls who had taken the same subjects. Support from teachers can make a big difference. Studies report that girls rate teacher support as an important factor in decisions to pursue scientific and technological careers.

Tests: Stepping Stones or Stop Signs?

- Test scores can provide an inaccurate picture of girls' and boys' abilities. Other factors such as grades, portfolios of student work, and out-of-school achievements must be considered in addition to test scores when making judgments about girls' and boys' skills and abilities.
- When scholarships are given based on the Scholastic Aptitude Test (SAT) scores, boys are more apt to receive scholarships than are girls who get equal or slightly better high school grades.

- Girls and boys with the same Math SAT scores do not do equally well in college—girls do better.

In most cases tests reflect rather than cause inequities in American education. The fact that groups score differently on a test does not necessarily mean that the test is biased. If, however, the score differences are related to the validity of the test—for example, if girls and boys know about the same amount of math but boys' test scores are consistently and significantly higher—then the test is biased.

A number of aspects of a test—beyond that which is being tested—can affect the score. For example, girls tend to score better than boys on essay tests, boys better than girls on multiple-choice items. Even today many girls and boys come to a testing situation with different interests and experiences. Thus a reading-comprehension passage that focuses on baseball scores will tend to favor boys, while a question testing the same skills that focuses on child care will tend to favor girls.

Why Do Girls Drop Out and What Are the Consequences?

- Pregnancy is not the only reason girls drop out of school. In fact, less than half the girls who leave school give pregnancy as the reason.
- Dropout rates for Hispanic girls vary considerably by national origin: Puerto Rican and Cuban American girls are more likely to drop out than are boys from the same cultures or other Hispanic girls.
- Childhood poverty is almost inescapable in single-parent families headed by women without a high school diploma: 77 percent for whites and 87 percent for African Americans.

In a recent study, 37 percent of the female drop-outs compared to only 5 percent of the male drop-outs cited "family-related problems" as the reason they left high school. Traditional gender roles place greater family responsibilities on adolescent girls than on their brothers. Girls are often expected to "help out" with caretaking responsibilities; boys rarely encounter this expectation.

However, girls as well as boys also drop out of school simply because they do not consider school pleasant or worthwhile. Asked what a worthwhile school experience would be, a group of teenage girls responded, "School would be fun. Our teachers would be excited and lively, not bored. They would act caring and take time to understand how students feel. . . . Boys would treat us with respect. If they run by and grab your tits, they would get into trouble." *

Women and children are the most impoverished members of our society. Inadequate education not only limits opportunities for women but jeopardizes their children's—and the nation's—future.

*As quoted in *In Their Own Voices: Young Women Talk About Dropping Out*, Project on Equal Education Rights (New York, National Organization for Women Legal Defense and Education Fund, 1988), p. 12.

Recommendations: Action for Change

The research reviewed in *The AAUW Report: How Schools Short-change Girls* challenges traditional assumptions about the egalitarian nature of American schools. Girls do not receive equitable amounts of teacher attention, are less apt than boys to see themselves reflected in the materials they study, and often are not expected or encouraged to pursue higher level math and science.

The current education-reform movement cannot succeed if it continues to ignore half of its constituents. We must move girls from the sidelines to the center of education planning. The issues are urgent; our actions must be swift and effective.

The Recommendations

Strengthened reinforcement of Title IX is essential.

1. Require school districts to assess and report on a regular basis to the Office for Civil Rights in the U.S. Department of Education on their own Title IX compliance measures.
2. Fund the Office for Civil Rights at a level that permits increased compliance reviews and full and prompt investigation of Title IX complaints.
3. In assessing the status of Title IX compliance, school districts must include a review of the treatment of pregnant teens and teen parents. Evidence indicates that these students are still the victims of discriminatory treatment in many schools.

Teachers, administrators, and counselors must be prepared and encouraged to bring gender equity and awareness to every aspect of schooling.

4. State certification standards for teachers and administrators should require course work on gender issues, including new research on women, bias in classroom-interaction patterns, and the ways in which schools can develop and implement gender-fair multicultural curricula.
5. If a national teacher examination is developed, it should include items on methods for achieving gender equity in the classroom and in curricula.
6. Teachers, administrators, and counselors should be evaluated on the degree to which they promote and encourage gender-equitable and multicultural education.
7. Support and released time must be provided by school districts for teacher-initiated research on curricula and classroom variables that affect student learning. Gender equity should be a focus of this research and a criterion for awarding funds.
8. School-improvement efforts must include a focus on the ongoing

professional development of teachers and administrators, including those working in specialized areas such as bilingual, compensatory, special, and vocational education.

9. Teacher-training courses must not perpetuate assumptions about the superiority of traits and activities traditionally ascribed to males in our society. Assertive and affiliative skills as well as verbal and mathematical skills must be fostered in both girls and boys.

10. Teachers must help girls develop positive views of themselves and their futures, as well as an understanding of the obstacles women must overcome in a society where their options and opportunities are still limited by gender stereotypes and assumptions.

The formal school curriculum must include the experiences of women and men from all walks of life. Girls and boys must see women and girls reflected and valued in the materials they study.

11. Federal and state funding must be used to support research, development, and follow-up study of gender-fair multicultural curricular models.

12. The Women's Educational Equity Act Program (WEEAP) in the U.S. Department of Education must receive increased funding in order to continue the development of curricular materials and models, and to assist school districts in Title IX compliance.

13. School curricula should deal directly with issues of power, gender politics, and violence against women. Better-informed girls are better equipped to make decisions about their futures. Girls and young women who have a strong sense of themselves are better able to confront violence and abuse in their lives.

14. Educational organizations must support, via conferences, meetings, budget deliberations, and policy decisions, the development of gender-fair multicultural curricula in all areas of instruction.

15. Curricula for young children must not perpetuate gender stereotypes and should reflect sensitivity to different learning styles.

Girls must be educated and encouraged to understand that mathematics and the sciences are important and relevant to their lives. Girls must be actively supported in pursuing education and employment in these areas.

16. Existing equity guidelines should be effectively implemented in all programs supported by the local, state, and federal governments. Specific attention must be directed toward including women on planning committees and focusing on girls and women in the goals, instructional strategies, teacher training, and research components of these programs.

17. The federal government must fund and encourage research on the effect on girls and boys of new curricula in the sciences and

mathematics. Research is needed particularly in science areas where boys appear to be improving their performance while girls are not.

18. Educational institutions, professional organizations, and the business community must work together to dispel myths about math and science as "inappropriate" fields for women.

19. Local schools and communities must encourage and support girls studying science and mathematics by showcasing women role models in scientific and technological fields, disseminating career information, and offering "hands-on" experiences and work groups in science and math classes.

20. Local schools should seek strong links with youth-serving organizations that have developed successful out-of-school programs for girls in mathematics and science and with those girls' schools that have developed effective programs in these areas.

Continued attention to gender equity in vocational education programs must be a high priority at every level of educational governance and administration.

21. Linkages must be developed with the private sector to help ensure that girls with training in nontraditional areas find appropriate employment.

22. The use of a discretionary process for awarding vocational-education funds should be encouraged to prompt innovative efforts.

23. All states should be required to make support services (such as child care and transportation) available to both vocational and prevocational students.

24. There must be continuing research on the effectiveness of vocational education for girls and the extent to which the 1990 Vocational Education Amendments benefit girls.

Testing and assessment must serve as stepping stones not stop signs. New tests and testing techniques must accurately reflect the abilities of both girls and boys.

25. Test scores should not be the only factor considered in admissions or the awarding of scholarships.

26. General aptitude and achievement tests should balance sex differences in item types and contexts. Tests should favor neither females nor males.

27. Tests that relate to "real life situations" should reflect the experiences of both girls and boys.

Girls and women must play a central role in educational reform. The experiences, strengths, and needs of girls from every race and social class must be considered in order to provide excellence and equity for all our nation's students.

28. National, state, and local governing bodies should ensure that women of diverse backgrounds are equitably represented on committees and commissions on educational reform.

29. Receipt of government funding for in-service and professional development programs should be conditioned upon evidence of efforts to increase the number of women in positions in which they are underrepresented. All levels of government have a role to play in increasing the numbers of women, especially women of color, in education-management and policy positions.

30. The U.S. Department of Education's Office of Educational Research and Improvement (OERI) should establish an advisory panel of gender-equity experts to work with OERI to develop a research and dissemination agenda to foster gender-equitable education in the nation's classrooms.

31. Federal and state agencies must collect, analyze, and report data broken down by race/ethnicity, sex, and some measure of socioeconomic status, such as parental income or education. National standards for use by all school districts should be developed so that data is comparable across district and state lines.

32. National standards for computing dropout rates should be developed for use by all school districts.

33. Professional organizations should ensure that women serve on education-focused committees. Organizations should utilize the expertise of their female membership when developing educational initiatives.

34. Local schools must call on the expertise of teachers, a majority of whom are women, in their restructuring efforts.

35. Women teachers must be encouraged and supported to seek administrative positions and elected office, where they can bring the insights gained in the classroom to the formulation of education policies.

A critical goal of education reform must be to enable students to deal effectively with the realities of their lives, particularly in areas such as sexuality and health.

36. Strong policies against sexual harassment must be developed. All school personnel must take responsibility for enforcing these policies.

37. Federal and state funding should be used to promote partnerships between schools and community groups, including social service agencies, youth-serving organizations, medical facilities, and local businesses. The needs of students, particularly as highlighted by pregnant teens and teen mothers, require a multi-institutional response.

38. Comprehensive school-based health- and sex-education programs must begin in the early grades and continue sequentially through

twelfth grade. These courses must address the topics of reproduction and reproductive health, sexual abuse, drug and alcohol use, and general mental and physical health issues. There must be a special focus on the prevention of AIDS.

39. State and local school board policies should enable and encourage young mothers to complete school, without compromising the quality of education these students receive.

40. Child care for the children of teen mothers must be an integral part of all programs designed to encourage young women to pursue or complete educational programs.

CLINTON LETTER ON DRAFT
February 12, 1992

Like vice presidential nominee Dan Quayle four years earlier, Democratic presidential candidate Bill Clinton was dogged throughout his 1992 campaign by criticism that he had taken extraordinary steps to avoid serving in the Vietnam War. The Arkansas governor was forced to confront the allegations during the primary campaign and again after he won his party's nomination to oppose President George Bush.

The controversy arose with publication of a 1969 letter in which Clinton sought to explain why he decided, after it was clear he was safe from the draft, to revoke an earlier pledge to join an ROTC (Reserve Officers Training Corps) program. The pledge had won him a temporary deferment. The December 3 letter, in which Clinton expressed his strong opposition to the war, was written to Col. Eugene Holmes, then-director of the ROTC program at the University of Arkansas. In it, Clinton, then a student at Oxford University on a Rhodes scholarship, thanked Holmes "for saving me from the draft." After much soul searching, he wrote, "I came to believe that the draft system itself is illegitimate" in a democracy, especially for "a war I opposed and despised with a depth of feeling I had reserved solely for racism in America before Vietnam."

Threat to Presidential Campaign

The draft issue posed the second major setback to Clinton's presidential campaign while it was just getting off the ground. On January 28 a supermarket tabloid, Star, published the claims of Gennifer Flowers, an Arkansas state employee and former nightclub singer, that she had been Clinton's lover for twelve years. She later played tapes of intimate phone conversations purported to be between her and the governor. With Hillary, his wife of fourteen years at his side, Clinton appeared on CBS's "60 Minutes" and denied Flowers's allegations while conceding that there had been problems in their marriage.

As the Flowers story began to fade, new controversy erupted over the draft issue. Again Clinton chose to meet the problem head-on. After ABC News informed him that it had received a copy of the letter and intended to air it that night, February 12, Clinton moved swiftly, calling a news conference to release the letter and explain the circumstances of its being written.

Nonetheless, the episode confronted Clinton with an American public that had still-simmering and mixed sentiments about the Vietnam War. In addition, at the time, he was facing two Democratic primary challengers who had served in Vietnam: Sen. Tom Harkin of Iowa, who fought in Asia but came to oppose the war; and Sen. Bob Kerrey of Nebraska, who served in the navy, lost part of a leg, and earned a Congressional Medal of Honor.

But some observers noted that Clinton's letter—which seemed to have been written by a young person deeply troubled about the course he should have taken or should take—and the empathy of many Americans, who also wanted to "forget" about the war muted what might have been more devastating to political campaigns in previous years. Nationwide opinion polls indicated that Americans were divided on whether Clinton should have acted as he did.

Events Leading to the Letter

The content of Clinton's 1969 letter did not reveal the rather complex events leading up to it, which were on public record or recalled by Clinton after the document was made public.

Having enrolled in November 1964 as an undergraduate at Georgetown University in Washington, D.C., Clinton had been classified 2-A (student deferment) by his Hot Springs, Arkansas, draft board. In March 1968 he was reclassified 1-A (available) but was told by the draft board that he would be given leniency so he could attend Oxford on a Rhodes scholarship. According to subsequent news reports, many residents were proud that a student from their city had won the prestigious award.

Clinton graduated from Georgetown in June and began a term at Oxford that fall, participating in demonstrations against the war in London with thousands of other American students there. After completing his first year of the two-year Oxford program in 1969, Clinton said he was informed that he was likely to lose his draft reprieve because deferments from graduate school had been ended; therefore, he later said, he thought he would be vulnerable to the draft. Meeting with the Arkansas ROTC in August, Clinton was reclassified 1-D after signing a letter of intent that he would enroll in the University of Arkansas's army ROTC program, although, according to many accounts (including that of his mother), he apparently had no intention of entering the university's law school. ("ROTC was the one way in which I could possibly, but not positively, avoid both Vietnam and resistance," Clinton later wrote in his letter to Holmes).

Clinton said he wrote to his draft board September 12 asking to be made 1-A, but he never mailed the letter. On October 1 President Richard Nixon announced that graduate students could complete the school year without being inducted, although they still might be drafted. The measure further reduced Clinton's chances of immediate draft. That month, Clinton's stepfather apparently met with local draft officials and told the University of Arkansas ROTC that his son wanted to rescind his agreement. Clinton was reclassified 1-A after the Arkansas ROTC informed the draft board he would not be attending the University of Arkansas.

Shortly thereafter, on November 26, Congress enacted legislation that reconfigured the draft into a birthdate lottery. On December 1 Clinton was assigned number 311, too high to be called. One day later he applied to Yale Law School and the next day wrote to Colonel Holmes, trying to explain his reasoning for the sequence of events that resulted in his decision to enter and withdraw from ROTC.

According to a Rhodes scholarship questionnaire he filled out in June 1970, Clinton said he had not decided whether he would return to Oxford in the fall because he might be "entering Yale Law School or getting drafted." By then, according to many observers, Clinton could have known that getting drafted was a remote possibility. News accounts at the time said that men with numbers above 250 would almost certainly not be called; in fact, 195 was the highest number drafted. Indeed, some commentators noted that Clinton likely knew that he was unlikely to be drafted.

Reaction to Clinton's Actions

Clinton "signed a contract [with the Arkansas ROTC] and did not honor it," said Clinton Jones, a Democrat who had been second in command of the Arkansas ROTC in 1969 and who furnished ABC News with a copy of the letter. After it was made public, Holmes echoed those sentiments, saying, "Ethically, I think he should have stayed in ROTC. He'd given his word and was backing out."

Beyond service for the ROTC, the Clinton controversy reopened painful new questions about the Vietnam era. News surveys of men around the same age as Clinton brought back mixed memories and opinions about the draft. It "raises the question of whether anyone in my generation will ever be elected president," said Rep. Thomas J. Downey, D-N.Y., who was a student at Cornell University in 1969 but was deferred because of a punctured eardrum. "The problem is that the scar has weakened the tissue of American life, and every time it is rubbed it hurts again."

"I am amazed at how the media are concentrating their coverage on an incident that occurred twenty-two years ago," said Gov. Zell Miller of Georgia. "Millions of Americans are out of work, others don't have an adequate health-care plan to pay for their medical bills. And instead of reporting how Bill Clinton plans to address those problems, we're harping on a letter that was written by a twenty-three-year-old student who had a deep and sincere conviction that the Vietnam War was wrong."

The similar controversy that surfaced during the 1988 presidential campaign about then-senator Dan Quayle concerned charges that he had avoided Vietnam service by using influence to get into the Indiana National Guard, which was closed to most draft-age men. (Republican National Convention, Historic Documents of 1988, p. 591)

An editorial in the February 14 New York Times *noted, "Clinton worked to avoid the draft, at times cleverly, but in ways that accorded with accepted common practice among others of his generation. . . . [He] may or may not have exposed himself to actual risk of induction. But to single him out as some sort of devious draft-dodger does him, and the anguish of Vietnam, an injustice."*

In interviews following release of the letter, several of Clinton's friends and colleagues at Oxford said the contents captured feelings shared by most Americans at Oxford. "The predominant view of all the people I knew at college was . . . you should not only oppose the war, but you should also be an activist against the war," said Thomas Williamson, Jr., a Washington, D.C., lawyer and adviser to the Clinton campaign.

"I have very specific recollections of conversations in which [Clinton] said, 'I must make myself eligible to be drafted because it's just not right to use deferments in this way and, because if I want a political career, this would not be helpful,'" said Robert Reich, a Harvard University economics professor and informal adviser to the Clinton campaign.

The "Character Issue"

Bush supporters stepped up their attacks on Clinton's character after the New York convention at which he won the Democratic nomination. At the Republican convention in Houston in August, Bush's former primary challenger, columnist Pat Buchanan, asked the delegates which of the two men "has the moral authority to send young Americans into war": Clinton, who "sat up in a dormitory in Oxford, England, and figured out how to dodge the draft," or Bush, "the American patriot and war hero?" (Democratic National Convention, p. 667; Republican National Convention, p. 781)

Clinton deflected some of the criticism about his draft decisions by choosing as his running mate a Vietnam veteran, Sen. Al Gore of Tennessee. He also faced the draft issue again on August 25 when he and President Bush separately spoke at the American Legion annual convention. Clinton, speaking first, told the veterans that "if you choose to vote against me because of what happened twenty-three years ago, that's your right and I respect that. But I hope you will cast your vote while looking toward the future with hope, rather than remaining fixed to the problems of the past." Bush made no mention of Clinton in his speech, but his campaign gave reporters a two-page memo citing alleged inconsistencies in Clinton's draft statements.

A week later, on September 2, the Los Angeles Times *published new allegations against Clinton, reporting that his late uncle Raymond Clinton had lobbied the local draft board for the deferment that enabled his nephew to study at Oxford. This time Clinton refused to reply. "Everyone involved in the story is now dead," he told reporters. "I said everything I had to say at the American Legion. I have nothing else to say about that. I have no comment."*

Nevertheless, Clinton was forced to comment on the allegations many more times as the Bush campaign pressed the issue to divert attention from the president's weakest area—the dismal economy. On the defensive, Clinton sometimes contradicted himself with each new disclosure about his actions concerning the draft. More and more the issue became not what he had done to avoid serving in an unpopular and undeclared war, but what his statements revealed about his veracity, his consistency, and his decisiveness—in short, his character.

> *Following is the text of the December 3, 1969, letter, released February 12, 1992, that Bill Clinton, then a Rhodes scholar at Oxford, wrote to Col. Eugene Holmes, director of the ROTC program at the University of Arkansas, setting forth Clinton's decisions on classification for service in the Vietnam War:*

Dear Col. Holmes,

I am sorry to be so long in writing. I know I promised to let you hear from me at least once a month, and from now on you will, but I have had to have some time to think about this first letter. Almost daily since my return to England I have thought about writing, about what I want to and ought to say.

First, I want to thank you, not just for saving me from the draft, but for being so kind and decent to me last summer, when I was as low as I have ever been. One thing which made the bond we struck in good faith somewhat palatable to me was my high regard for you personally. In retrospect, it seems that the admiration might not have been mutual had you known a little more about me, about my political beliefs and activities. At least you might have thought me more fit for the draft than for ROTC.

Let me try to explain. As you know, I worked for two years in a very minor position on the Senate Foreign Relations Committee. I did it for the experience and the salary but also for the opportunity, however small, of working every day against a war I opposed and despised with a depth of feeling I had reserved solely for racism in America before Vietnam. I did not take the matter lightly but studied it carefully, and there was a time when not many people had more information about Vietnam at hand than I did.

I have written and spoken and marched against the war. One of the national organizers of the Vietnam Moratorium is a close friend of mine. After I left Arkansas last summer, I went to Washington to work in the national headquarters of the Moratorium, then to England to organize the Americans here for demonstrations Oct. 15 and Nov. 16.

Interlocked with the war is the draft issue, which I did not begin to consider separately until early 1968. For a law seminar at Georgetown I wrote a paper on the legal arguments for and against allowing, within the Selective Service System, the classification of selective conscientious objection, for those opposed to participation in a particular war, not simply to "participation in war in any form."

From my work I came to believe that the draft system itself is illegitimate. No government really rooted in limited, parliamentary democracy should have the power to make its citizens fight and kill and die in a war they may oppose, a war which even possibly may be wrong, a war which, in any case, does not involve immediately the peace and freedom of the nation. The draft was justified in World War II because the life of the people collectively was at stake. Individuals had to fight, if the nation was to survive, for the lives of their countrymen and their way of life. Vietnam is no such case. Nor was Korea an example where, in my opinion, certain military action was justified but the draft was not, for the reasons stated above.

Because of my opposition to the draft and the war, I am in great sympathy with those who are not willing to fight, kill, and maybe die for their country (i.e. the particular policy of a particular government) right or wrong. Two of my friends at Oxford are conscientious objectors. I wrote a letter of recommendation for one of them to his Mississippi draft board, a letter which I am more proud of than anything else I wrote at Oxford last year. One of my roommates is a draft resister who is possibly under indictment and may never be able to go home again. He is one of the bravest, best men I know. His country needs men like him more than they know. That he is considered a criminal is an obscenity.

The decision not to be a resister and the related subsequent decisions were the most difficult of my life. I decided to accept the draft in spite of my beliefs for one reason: to maintain my political viability within the system. For years I have worked to prepare myself for a political life characterized by both practical political ability and concern for rapid social progress. It is a life I still feel compelled to try to lead. I do not think our system of government is by definition corrupt, however dangerous and inadequate it has been in recent years. (The society may be corrupt, but that is not the same thing, and if that is true we are all finished anyway.)

When the draft came, despite political convictions, I was having a hard time facing the prospect of fighting a war I had been fighting against, and that is why I contacted you. ROTC was the one way left in which I could possibly, but not positively, avoid both Vietnam and resistance. Going on with my education, even coming back to England, played no part in my decision to join ROTC. I am back here, and would have been at Arkansas Law School because there is nothing else I can do. In fact, I would like to have been able to take a year out perhaps to teach in a small college or work on some community action project and in the process to decide whether to attend law school or graduate school and how to begin putting what I have learned to use.

But the particulars of my personal life are not nearly as important to me as the principles involved. After I signed the ROTC letter of intent I began to wonder whether the compromise I had made with myself was not more objectionable than the draft would have been, because I had no interest in the ROTC program in itself and all I seemed to have done was to protect myself from physical harm. Also, I began to think I had deceived you, not by lies—there were none—but by failing to tell you all the things I'm writing now. I doubt that I had the mental coherence to articulate them then.

At that time, after we had made our agreement and you had sent my 1-D deferment to my draft board, the anguish and loss of my self regard and self confidence really set in. I hardly slept for weeks and kept going by eating compulsively and reading until exhaustion brought sleep. Finally, on September 12 I stayed up all night writing a letter to the chairman of my draft board, saying basically what is in the preceding paragraph, thanking him for trying to help in a case where he really couldn't, and stating that I couldn't do the ROTC after all and would he please draft me as soon as possible. I never mailed the letter, but I did carry it on me every day until I got on the plane to return to England. I didn't mail the letter because I didn't see, in the end, how my going in the army and maybe going to Vietnam would achieve anything except a feeling that I had punished myself and gotten what I deserved. So I came back to England to try to make something of this second year of my Rhodes scholarship.

And that is where I am now, writing to you because you have been good to me and have a right to know what I think and feel. I am writing too in the hope that my telling this one story will help you to understand more clearly how so many fine people have come to find themselves still loving their country but loathing the military, to which you and other good men have devoted years, lifetimes, of the best service you could give. To many of us, it is no longer clear what is service and what is disservice, or if it is clear, the conclusion is likely to be illegal.

Forgive the length of this letter. There was much to say. There is still a lot to be said, but it can wait. Please say hello to Col. Jones for me.

Merry Christmas.

Sincerely,
Bill Clinton

REPORT ON TRENDS
IN WORK AND LEISURE
February 17, 1992

Fully employed Americans have been spending progressively more time at their jobs and less time at leisure, according to a report released February 17 by the Economic Policy Institute, a nonprofit, nonpartisan economic research group located in Washington, D.C. The study, entitled The Great American Time Squeeze: Trends in Work and Leisure, 1969-1989, *found that by 1989 Americans were working an average of 158 hours more annually than they did twenty years ago. At the same time, employer-compensated time off for vacations, holidays, sick leave, and personal leave days, as well as time spent relaxing and resting at home, decreased by 15 percent during the 1980s.*

The authors, Laura Leete-Guy, an assistant professor at the Weatherhead School of Management at Case Western Reserve University, and Juliet B. Schor, an associate professor of economics and head tutor of women's studies at Harvard University, found that the increase—which included both hours on the job and time spent on home-related tasks—was steady and cumulative. The trend affected all income classes, occupations, industries, demographic groups, and gender. Indeed, the authors concluded, "America is starved for time; increasing numbers of people are finding themselves overworked, stressed out, and heavily taxed by the joint demands of work and family life." The steady decline in real wages since 1973, combined with rising health care and housing costs, were cited as among the principal reasons that Americans had to work extra hours—simply to maintain their existing standard of living.

Leete-Guy and Schor's findings were reinforced by a number of other studies, including Schor's 1991 book, The Overworked American: The Unexpected Decline of Leisure, *and similar reports indicating that Americans were falling behind financially despite working longer hours. These included "Families on a Treadmill: Work and Income in the 1980s," a January 17 staff study for Congress's Joint Economic Committee; "Vanishing Dreams: The Economic Plight of America's Young Families," an April 14 report by the Children's Defense Fund; and a series of Census Bureau reports on findings of the 1990 census.* (Report on the Economic Plight of American Families, p. 353)

Questions of work and leisure also became an issue in the 1992 presidential campaign, with Democratic challenger Bill Clinton contending that Americans were working harder for less money and President George Bush defending his economic policies. (Democratic National Convention, p. 667; Republican National Convention, p. 781)

Some commentators, however, disputed the less-leisure theory. Newsweek *columnist Robert J. Samuelson, in a discussion of Schor's book, argued that "nearly all of the increase in work time ... occurs among women. This has little to do with the pressure from employers (if it did, similar increases would occur among men).... Women have gone into more occupations, are moving up career ladders and spend more time on the job."*

Wider Impact of Need to Work Longer Hours

Basing their findings primarily on data provided by the March Current Population Survey for market hours and the University of Michigan Time-Use Studies for nonmarket hours, Leete-Guy and Schor concluded that, while fully employed men worked 72 more hours in 1989 than they did in 1969, fully employed women—who had been entering the work force in proportionately greater numbers—were working 287 more hours annually (the equivalent of seven added weeks). (This was partially offset by a 126-hour decline in annual hours spent performing household-related work). Young parents between the ages of eighteen and thirty-nine were particularly affected, with mothers working 241 more hours a year and fathers, 189 more hours. The heavier work burden fell most sharply on single, fully employed parents, whose total work hours rose by 222 hours annually between 1969 and 1989. These increases, the authors pointed out, occurred at a time when the number of single-parent families was steadily growing and while child care arrangements for working parents had not kept pace with need.

In addition to the constant rise in annual hours on the job, Leete-Guy and Schor highlighted several other related findings:

- *Time spent commuting rose by 204 hours between 1975 and 1985.*
- *Between 1969 and 1981 paid time off increased by 3.4 days, but during the 1980s it declined by 3.7 days.*
- *In response to public opinion polls, most Americans said they would*

be willing to forfeit some income in exchange for more vacation time (70 percent of those earning $30,000 a year or more said they would give up a day's pay each week for an extra day off, as did 48 percent of those with annual incomes of $20,000).

- *Household hours (for example, time spent in child care, shopping, cooking, laundry, and household maintenance and repairs) declined somewhat but not enough to compensate for the rise in market hours.*

The authors pointed out that the reduction in U.S. workers' leisure time contradicted previous forecasts by many economic experts that automation, growth in productivity, and other factors would produce a general increase in Americans' free time. They also noted that "the pattern of working hours in the United States presents a sharp contrast with the pattern of working hours in Western Europe. "Although the United States emerged from the Second World War with considerably lower hours then Western Europe, Americans' working hours are now substantially above those of Europe," the report said. Ironically, at the same time that most fully employed Americans were working longer hours, the number of Americans able to work who were unemployed or involuntarily underemployed doubled during the two decades studied, rising from 7.2 percent of the labor force in 1969 to 14.5 percent in 1989.

Japanese Criticism of U.S. Workers

The Economic Policy Institute report was released against a backdrop of harsh criticism of Americans' industrial productivity and management style leveled by top Japanese officials following President Bush's January 8-10 trade mission to Japan. On January 19 Yoshio Sakarauchi, Speaker of Japan's lower house of parliament, who later said he was misquoted, was reported to have called American workers "lazy" and largely illiterate.

Prime Minister Kiichi Miyazawa, who had recently returned from a trip to the United States, said February 3 that America may lack a "work ethic," but he, too, later apologized, saying his remarks had been misinterpreted.

"To think that America would have to send its president over here to beg! To think that all those wonderful department stores ... have gone bankrupt! What is it—a lack of effort?" commented a Japanese business-man to a Washington Post *reporter in Kichijoji.* (Bush's Trade Mission to Japan; Hosts' Remarks on U.S. Workers, p. 11)

> *Following are excerpts from "The Great American Time Squeeze: Trends in Work and Leisure, 1969-1989," a study undertaken for the Economic Policy Institute by Laura Leete-Guy and Juliet B. Schor, released February 17, 1992:*

Introduction

Americans are starved for time. Since 1969, the annual hours of work of employed Americans have risen markedly—by approximately 140 hours, or more than an additional three weeks. *This increase includes both hours on the job and time spent working at home.* As a result, leisure, or free time, has declined as well. Increasing numbers of people are finding themselves overworked, stressed out, and heavily taxed by the joint demands of work and family life.

This lack of leisure has begun to manifest itself in a dramatic shift in public attitudes toward time. For the first time since surveys on time-income tradeoffs have been taken, people are indicating strong desires to trade off income for time away from the job. A 1989 poll found nearly two-thirds expressing the desire to give up an average of 13 percent of their current paycheck for more free time. Eight of ten respondents indicated they would forego a faster career track for a slower one which would allow them more time to spend with their families. A second survey found that 70 percent of those earning $30,000 a year or more would give up a day's pay each week for an extra day of free time. Surprisingly, even among those earning only $20,000 a year, 48 percent said they would do the same. Yet even a decade ago, only a very small percentage of Americans preferred to give up income for time.

The causes of this dramatic shift in public opinion are not hard to find. The rise in working hours has been steady and cumulative. As we shall demonstrate in this paper, the growth of work hours and the decline of leisure have affected a wide spectrum of Americans—across income classes, occupations and industries, demographic groups, and genders. This decline of leisure contains a certain irony. Thirty years ago, it was widely believed that automation, productivity growth, and consumer satiation would bring liberation from work. Predictions were that by the 1980s, the workweek would have fallen to twenty hours. Experts worried about an upcoming "crisis of excess leisure time," and its attendant boredom and ennui. Instead, we have too little time, with its attendant social problems.

Our research reveals a number of striking findings. For example:

- Fully-employed Americans (those not unemployed—i.e., seeking work but unable to find it—or involuntarily underemployed—i.e., working part-time because full-time work is unavailable), worked on average an additional 138 hours annually between 1969 and 1989. If we add in the rise in commuting time and the decline in paid time off, *the increase is 158 hours, or one additional month of work per year.* Since the decline in unpaid household-related work hours (for child care, shopping, repairs, etc.) did not match the increase in paid work, the rise in hours on the job has meant a significant loss of leisure.
- The rise in work has been greatest for women. Fully-employed women

have had a rise in market hours totalling 287 hours over the twenty-year period. This has been partially offset by a 126-hour decline in annual household hours, for a net gain of 161 hours. Among men, the rise in total hours has been 139.

- In striking reversal of thirty years of progress, paid time off (vacations, holidays, sick leave, and personal days) fell roughly 15 percent in the 1980s. U.S. practices provide a sharp contrast to Western Europe, where workers enjoy four to six weeks of paid vacation each year. Even the meager two weeks enjoyed on average by American workers is now in jeopardy. As West Europeans gain free time, Americans are losing it.

- The percentage of the labor force which cannot get enough work has doubled. In 1969, 7.2 percent of the labor force was either unemployed or involuntarily underemployed. In 1989, that figure stood at 14.5 percent. At the same time that most Americans have seen their work schedules rise, a growing minority have been prevented from getting the working hours they want and need.

- The work explosion has been very hard on parents, as they find themselves with less and less time to spend with their children. Among workers with children, total hours have risen by 139 per year. Compared to 1969, today's young parents (ages 18-39) are putting in far more hours of work, 241 more per year by young mothers and 189 more per year by young fathers.

In the pages which follow, we document these claims. Unlike most studies, ours analyzes both paid market hours and hours of unpaid household work (e.g., home repair, child care, shopping, cleaning, and so on). The inclusion of household hours is necessary in order to avoid finding a spurious increase in market hours generated by shifts away from goods and services produced at home. We have also calculated annual hours, rather than the more common weekly hours. The annual hours measure allows us to account for intra-year variations in labor force participation. We have corrected for business cycle effects, a correction which has not been made in any previous studies. The data sets we have used are the March Current Population Survey (CPS) for market hours and the University of Michigan Time-Use Studies for non-market hours.... To our knowledge, ours are the only recent estimates from the CPS of total annual hours worked.

The Growth of Market Hours

... [M]arket hours of work have risen over the period we are considering. In 1989, the average adult American was working 86 more hours annually than in 1969, with an increase of 65 hours since 1979. As we will show, this overall increase in market hours reflects both a rise in the proportion of the population employed and an increase in annual hours worked per employed person.

One reason for the rise in average hours worked is simply that a greater proportion of the adult population is in the labor force.... [T]he percentage of the adult population in the labor force has risen in the last twenty years, from 68.5 to 71.6 percent. Women's labor force participation rose from 53.1 to 63.5 percent, while men's fell from 86.6 to 80.5 percent. However, because women participants work fewer hours in the market than men, equal changes in participation rates do not yield equal changes in market hours. The decline of men's market hours is largely the result of lower participation, given that among employed men weekly hours fell only slightly and weeks per year rose slightly. As a result, increasing numbers of men are working fewer hours. Among women, the opposite tendency is occurring, as participation rates rise and specialization in household work becomes less common.

There has not only been an increase in labor force participation among all adults, there has also been a significant rise in the working time of those in the labor market.... The major reason that working hours of employed workers has risen is that there was a rise in weeks worked, rather than changes in weekly hours. On average, weekly hours have risen only slightly, from 27.0 to 27.9....

... The discussion so far has falsely assumed that there has not been growing underemployment in the labor market. However, the unemployment rate at business cycle peaks has risen, from 3.4 percent in 1969 to 5.3 percent in 1989. It is important to recognize growing unemployment and underemployment in order to distinguish between voluntary and involuntary changes in hours, which previous studies have not done. We find that persons subject to *involuntary* leisure have been a steadily growing percentage of the labor force. Moreover, when our analysis takes the rise of involuntary leisure into account, we find an even larger rise of market hours worked.

We have defined as "labor market constrained" those who fall into the following categories *and* report that additional work was desired but not available: did not work at all during the year, worked part-year/part-time, worked full-year/part-time, and worked part-year/full-time. (Part-year is defined as less than 50 weeks per year and part-time is less than 35 hours per week.) These are all situations where people have involuntary leisure.

At each business cycle peak in our sample, the percentage of the labor force which is constrained has risen dramatically from 7.2 percent in 1969 to 14.5 percent in 1989.... Roughly two-thirds of those experiencing labor market constraints are part-year/full-time workers. The share of the labor force in this category rose substantially over this period. The shares in every other constraint category are smaller, but show large increases....

If we exclude the constrained portion of the labor force from our measures, the data reveal a much greater rise in work, and provide strong support for the time-squeeze hypothesis. *Among those persons who are fully employed, market hours have increased by 138....* Hours for constrained workers have fallen by 246 per year, revealing a growing gap between those who are able to secure market work and those who are not. We define as "unprovided hours," those which labor market participants indicate they would like to work, but during which they are unable to find employment. We find that the average "unprovided hours" per constrained labor force participant rose from 718 per year in 1969 to 803 in 1989. Projected onto the entire labor force, this implies an aggregate level in the economy of unprovided hours in 1989 of 14.6 billion, up from 4.2 billion in 1969.

Among the unconstrained, the breakdown for men and women shows lengthening market hours for both. Employed men are working seventy-two more hours per year. Employed women have added 287 hours. This is the equivalent of seven weeks of additional market work each year. The irrationality of this result is striking. At a time when majorities are articulating a desire for less demanding jobs (in terms of hours), a growing minority finds itself unable to secure enough hours. . . .

As noted above, the upward trend has been most pronounced for women, whose additional work burden has mainly taken the form of working a greater fraction of the year. Women are now less likely to leave paid work during the summer recess in order to care for children; they take less time off around the birth of a child. . . . The proportion of women who work full-time, year round, has risen steadily and substantially for twenty years. Women's pattern of labor force participation is getting to look more and more like men's.

Adjustments to Market Hours: Vacations, Holidays, Sick Leave, and Commuting

The CPS data on which our analysis is based include paid time off in its definition of work time. . . .

Surprisingly, these data show no net increase in paid time off between 1969 and 1989. Moreover, a 3.4 day *increase* in paid time off between 1969 and 1981 was followed by a 3.7 *decline* between 1981 and 1989, leaving a net decline in paid time off of 0.3 days (or roughly 2.5 hours per year). . . . This suggests that our prior analysis overstated the rise in working hours in the 1970s but *understated* the rise in working hours in the 1980s.

Commuting time has also risen, further increasing total "work" time. The length of the average daily trip to and from work remained steady between 1969 and 1975, but rose thereafter. The average commuting time for employed workers rose from 181 hours per year in 1975 to 204 hours in 1985, an increase of 23 hours. Combining trends in paid time off and commuting, it appears that we have understated the upward trend in market hours over the last two decades by about 25.5 hours per employed person.

The Decline of Household Hours

We now turn our attention to trends in household hours, the time spent doing child care, shopping, cooking, laundry, making repairs, and doing other household maintenance activities. . . . Even though hours of market work have risen, there may not be a loss of leisure time if unpaid household hours have fallen commensurately.

In fact, as market hours have risen, average annual household hours have fallen. The decline in household hours, however, has not been as large as the rise of market hours. . . . This means there has been a loss of leisure time, especially among people in the unconstrained workforce. . . .

. . . [A]s women have left the home, men are entering it, doing on average an additional 161 hours of work a year. As a consequence, the ratio of all men's household labor to women's rose from 41 to 59 percent. This increase has been driven by the exit of men from the labor force, because men who are out of the labor force do far more household work than their counterparts who are in it. This trend has also reduced domestic hours for the subset of Americans who are at home full-time (i.e., out of the labor force). This is because men without paying jobs do much less work than women without paying jobs. (The average difference is about 800 hours.)

While shifts in the gender composition of the labor force have been the largest factor in the decline of household labor, falling rates of marriage and childbearing have also played a major role. The percentage of the population which has not married (i.e., has no spouse present) has risen from 31.4 to 40.6 percent. At the same time, people are having far fewer children. The percentage of the population with no children has risen from 57.7 to 67.3 percent. The percentage with two or more children has fallen from 28.7 to 19.0 percent. For women, these shifts account for 25 percent of the reduction in household work. For men, these factors have reduced the rise in household hours by 20 percent.

Working . . . With Children

Since the mid 1970s, stagnant real wages have sent a larger share of women with children into the labor force than ever before. This addition to family income has come at the cost, however, of leisure time for parents. While parents have typically had longer work hours than non-parents, between 1969 and 1989 the gap widened considerably between the number of hours worked by parents with one or two children, and those of non-parents. . . . [T]he total hours worked by parents with one or two children at home rose by 123 and 107, respectively, per year. This compares to a ninety-one hour increase in total hours worked by non-parents. The increase in total hours worked is somewhat lower for those with three or more children at home. This is because the extent to which women work outside the home diminishes as the size of a family grows. And when women enter the labor force under today's market conditions, the family work burden rapidly rises.

While concerns about "time-squeeze" have often been associated with working mothers only, our calculations show that total hours worked have risen for working men and women alike who have children under age eighteen living at home. Between 1969 and 1989, the work burden of employed parents rose considerably (in this section we will only consider those not constrained in the labor market). Employed, unconstrained mothers are working a total of 165 more hours per year, while employed, unconstrained fathers are putting in an additional 142 hours. . . .

During the late 1970s and the 1980s, wages of young people faltered more than those of older workers. Thus, one might expect the effect of market conditions on hours worked to be more pronounced among these recent labor market entrants. This is, in fact, the case. Young working parents have experienced a considerable increase in total hours worked. . . . Employed parents aged 18-39 were working 169 more hours per year in 1989 than in 1969; for mothers in this group, the additional work comes to 241 hours per year, while these fathers are working an additional 189 hours per year.

These changes in work patterns have taken place coincident with the rapid alteration of marriage and family patterns. Marriage rates have fallen dramatically in the last twenty years and, as is well known, the single working parent is more prevalent than ever. The work burden is increasing most rapidly among members of this growing group. Total hours worked by single employed parents, aged 18-39, rose by 222 between 1969 and 1989. This increase is nearly half again as large as that shouldered by their married counterparts. In the face of stagnating wages, parents needing to support one or more children on the wages of one adult are being more "time-squeezed" than those who can rely on two incomes.

The changes in the total hours of working parents are rooted in the patterns of change in market and non-market hours discussed earlier in this paper. As women's hours of paid employment rise, the hours they work at home decline less than proportionately. Among employed mothers (who are unconstrained in the labor market), hours of paid work per year have risen over 25 percent from 1,281 to 1,627 (an increase of 346 hours), while their hours of unpaid household work have dropped by only 181 per year. . . . At the same time, the amount of household work done by men has risen. Among employed fathers, this increase in unpaid work amounts to an additional 128 hours per year, while the hours spent in paid employment have remained virtually unchanged.

Comparison With Western Europe

In recent years the pattern of working hours in the United States presents a sharp contrast with the pattern of working hours in Western Europe. Although the United States emerged from the Second World War with considerably lower hours than Western Europe, Americans' working hours are now substantially above those of Europeans. The major difference is that vacation time has increased in Europe, while in the United States, a modest rise in vacation time between the 1950s and 1980 is in the process of being eroded. Unfortunately, there are no comprehensive, internationally consistent and up-to-date data which would allow us to compare all-economy annual hours between the two regions. . . .

The major difference between the United States and Europe is vacation time. Our estimate for paid time off in the United States in 1989 is 16.1 days per year. Paid time off in Europe is considerably longer. . . . Most European countries now give paid vacations of at least five weeks. In France, Denmark, Finland, and Sweden the legal minimum is five weeks, with average vacation time ranging between five and eight weeks. Paid holidays are also slightly higher in most European countries than in the United States. . . .

The pieces of evidence we have available do not permit us to calculate total annual hours for European countries. However, they do point to the conclusion that European countries are providing more leisure for their citizens than does the United States. The United States ranks higher on all measures of working hours, with the exception of having more part-time work. But it is unlikely that the higher incidence of part-time work (some of which is involuntary) is sufficient to offset less paid time off and higher participation. This conclusion is strengthened if we consider that hours of housework are greater for women working part-time. Finally, we might note that Japan is the only major industrialized country with longer hours than the United States, primarily on account of days worked per year. There is now considerable pressure in Japan to reduce work time, as it has become a source of social and economic problems.

Conclusion

Our research finds that Americans are indeed "squeezed" for time. Despite skepticism from some academics (Burtless 1990; Juster and Stafford 1991; Robinson 1989), the opinion polls and media attention have focused on a serious problem: Americans *are* finding themselves with progressively less leisure. Compared with twenty years ago, those Americans who have jobs (and are not experiencing "involuntary leisure") work an additional 149 hours a year, calculated as the sum of changes in market and household hours. . . . This is nearly an extra month of work each year. The increase is smaller for the general population, averaging twenty-seven hours a year.

Despite the common belief that time squeeze is a problem only for working mothers, both men and women have experienced declining leisure. Our research also shows that although parents are the most pressed for time—their work burden exceeds that of non-parents by 6 to 700 hours a year—both parents and those without children are working longer hours. . . . Nevertheless, the time-squeeze would have been far more severe had Americans not reduced their rates of marriage and childbearing so significantly during the last twenty years. While the causes of the former may be obscure, there is little question that women's labor market advances have discouraged childbearing. . . .

Time-squeeze has been caused by a number of factors. For women, the rise in market hours has not been fully offset by a decline in household work—in part because men have not compensated them by working sufficiently more at home. Among men, the surprising result is that those with jobs have actually experienced a rise in hours. We have argued elsewhere that employers exhibit a bias against declines in market hours, because firms find long hours to be profit-maximizing. We suspect this is an important part of why men's hours have not fallen more. . . .

SUPREME COURT ON BEATING OF INMATES BY PRISON GUARDS

February 25, 1992

In a 7-2 ruling February 25 the Supreme Court held that the use of excessive physical force against a prisoner could constitute cruel and unusual punishment under the Eighth Amendment to the Constitution, even though the inmate did not suffer serious injury. Justices Clarence Thomas and Antonin Scalia dissented from the decision, which many viewed as a departure from the Court's increasingly conservative opinions on prisoners' rights. The Bush administration supported the majority position.

The case involved Keith Hudson, an inmate at the state penitentiary in Angola, Louisiana. Hudson testified that he received bruises, facial swelling, loosened teeth, and a cracked dental plate in a beating by prison guards early on the morning of October 30, 1983. Following an argument with security officer Jack McMillian, Hudson was handcuffed, shackled, and beaten by McMillian and a colleague, Marvin Woods. Arthur Mezo, the supervisor on duty, allegedly looked on and merely told the officers "not to have too much fun."

A federal district court magistrate found that the officers used undue brutality and awarded Hudson $800 in damages. The Fifth Circuit Court of Appeals subsequently reversed, holding that inmates alleging use of excessive force in violation of the Eighth Amendment must prove "significant injury" and that Hudson could not prevail because his injuries were "minor" and required no medical attention.

Majority Decision and Dissent

Writing for the majority, Justice Sandra Day O'Connor disputed contentions that the Eighth Amendment did not protect prisoners who were the subject of "malicious" force that did not cause serious injury. If the constitutional protection did not offer such a shield, O'Connor wrote, the amendment would "permit any physical punishment, no matter now diabolic or inhuman, inflicting less than some arbitrary quantity of injury. Such a result would have been as unacceptable to the drafters of the Eighth Amendment as it is today." O'Connor referred much of the majority's reasoning to a 1986 decision, Whitley v. Albers, *which concerned the claim of an inmate who was shot by a guard during a prison riot. In that case the Court made a distinction between "force . . . applied in a good faith effort to maintain or restore discipline" and that used "maliciously and sadistically for the very purpose of causing harm."*

In his dissent, Thomas, joined by Scalia, said the majority had given the Eighth Amendment protection clause a scope that exceeded history and precedent. "Surely prison was not a more congenial place in the early years of the Republic than it is today; nor were our judges . . . so naive as to be unaware of the often harsh conditions of prison life. Rather, they simply did not conceive of the Eighth Amendment as protecting inmates from harsh treatment," he concluded. "I see no reason why our society's standards of decency should be more readily offended when officials, with a culpable state of mind, subject a prisoner to a deprivation on one discrete occasion than when they subject him to continuous deprivation [such as uncivilized confinement] inflicted over time. . . ."

O'Connor was firm in challenging that interpretation. "To deny . . . the difference between punching a prisoner in the face and serving him unappetizing food is to ignore the concepts of dignity, civilized standards, humanity, and decency that animate the Eighth Amendment," she wrote.

In addition to O'Connor, the majority consisted of Chief Justice William H. Rehnquist and Justices Byron R. White, Anthony M. Kennedy, and David H. Souter. John Paul Stevens and Harry A. Blackmun, while concurring in the judgment, offered separate views that the majority's "malicious or sadistic" standard was too stringent.

Reaction and Impact

Besides arousing speculation that the decision could signal a moderation of the Court's increasing tendency to construe prisoners' rights narrowly, the split indicated that the still-controversial, newly seated Justice Thomas appeared to be fulfilling predictions that he would be a firm conservative in the manner of his mentor, Scalia.

The practical impact on the court system also was mixed: some observers said it could mean that federal courts would have more influence and activism with respect to the treatment of prisons' inmates as compared with state courts, which usually handled such cases. A number of state officials said that the shift might overburden the judicial system at all levels, resulting in an increase in unjustifiable claims— which might harm those with legitimate grievances.

Alvin J. Bronstein, director of the National Prison Project of the

American Civil Liberties Union, praised the ruling, saying, "A court that we don't expect a lot of prisoners' rights victories from today showed concern for human decency and sent a message to prison officials that you cannot beat up prisoners, cannot treat them brutally, without federal court intervention." Thomas's dissent was "very disappointing," he added, "because it really says where Justice Thomas is on human rights kinds of concerns."

"[T]he dissenters' argument is mind-boggling," said an editorial in the February 26 Washington Post. When excessive force "amounts to the purposeful, unnecessary and wanton infliction of pain, it is clearly unconstitutional. The dissenters respond that the Eighth Amendment should not be turned into 'a National Code of Prison Regulation,' but their argument that prison beatings are no business of the federal courts is a tortured exercise in avoidance." The majority's "new, broader interpretation of the Eighth Amendment, based on 'evolving standards of decency that mark the progress of a maturing society,' is welcome and absolutely needed," the Post said.

> *Following are excerpts from the February 25, 1992, Supreme Court decision in* Hudson v. McMillian et al., *holding that the "cruel and unusual punishment" clause of the Eighth Amendment may protect inmates from beatings by prison guards, from a concurring opinion by Justice Harry A. Blackmun, and from the dissenting opinion by Justice Clarence Thomas.*

No. 90-6531

Keith J. Hudson, Petitioner *v.* Jack McMillian et al.	On writ of certiorari to the United States Court of Appeals for the Fifth Circuit

[February 25, 1992]

JUSTICE O'CONNOR delivered the opinion of the Court.

This case requires us to decide whether the use of excessive physical force against a prisoner may constitute cruel and unusual punishment when the inmate does not suffer serious injury. We answer that question in the affirmative.

[I Omitted]

II

In *Whitley* v. *Albers* (1986), the principal question before us was what legal standard should govern the Eighth Amendment claim of an inmate shot by a guard during a prison riot. We based our answer on the settled rule that " 'the unnecessary and wanton infliction of pain ... constitutes cruel and unusual punishment forbidden by the Eighth Amendment.' " (quoting *Ingraham* v. *Wright* (1977)).

[Establishing] an "unnecessary and wanton infliction of pain" varies according to the nature of the alleged constitutional violation. For example, the appropriate inquiry when an inmate alleges that prison officials failed to attend to serious medical needs is whether the officials exhibited "deliberate indifference." See *Estelle* v. *Gamble* (1976). This standard is appropriate because the State's responsibility to provide inmates with medical care ordinarily does not conflict with competing administrative concerns.

By contrast, officials confronted with a prison disturbance must balance the threat unrest poses to inmates, prison workers, administrators, and visitors against the harm inmates may suffer if guards use force. Despite the weight of these competing concerns, corrections officials must make their decisions "in haste, under pressure, and frequently without the luxury of a second chance." We accordingly concluded in *Whitley* that application of the deliberate indifference standard is inappropriate when authorities use force to put down a prison disturbance. Instead, "the question whether the measure taken inflicted unnecessary and wanton pain and suffering ultimately turns on 'whether force was applied in a good faith effort to maintain or restore discipline or maliciously and sadistically for the very purpose of causing harm.' " (quoting *Johnson* v. *Glick*, cert. denied *sub nom. John* v. *Johnson* (1973)).

Many of the concerns underlying our holding in *Whitley* arise whenever guards use force to keep order. Whether the prison disturbance is a riot or a lesser disruption, corrections officers must balance the need "to maintain or restore discipline" through force against the risk of injury to inmates. Both situations may require prison officials to act quickly and decisively. Likewise, both implicate the principle that "'[p]rison administrators ... should be accorded wide-ranging deference in the adoption and execution of policies and practices that in their judgment are needed to preserve internal order and discipline and to maintain institutional security.'" (quoting *Bell* v. *Wolfish* (1979)). In recognition of these similarities, we hold that whenever prison officials stand accused of using excessive physical force in violation of the Cruel and Unusual Punishments Clause, the core judicial inquiry is that set out in *Whitley*: whether force was applied in a good-faith effort to maintain or restore discipline, or maliciously and sadistically to cause harm.

Extending *Whitley*'s application of the "unnecessary and wanton infliction of pain" standard to all allegations of excessive force works no innovation. This Court derived the *Whitley* test from one articulated by Judge Friendly in *Johnson* v. *Glick, supra*, a case arising out of a prisoner's claim to have been beaten and harassed by a guard. Moreover, many Courts of Appeals already apply the *Whitley* standard to allegations of excessive force outside of the riot situation....

A

Under the *Whitley* approach, the extent of injury suffered by an inmate is one factor that may suggest "whether the use of force could plausibly have been thought necessary" in a particular situation, "or instead evinced such wantonness with respect to the unjustified infliction of harm as is tantamount to a knowing willingness that it occur." *Whitley*. In determining whether the use of force was wanton and unnecessary, it may also be proper to evaluate the need for application of force, the relationship between that need and the amount of force used, the threat "reasonably perceived by the responsible officials," and "any efforts made to temper the severity of a forceful response." *Ibid.* The absence of serious injury is therefore relevant to the Eighth Amendment inquiry, but does not end it.

Respondents nonetheless assert that a significant injury requirement of the sort imposed by the Fifth Circuit is mandated by what we have termed the "objective component" of Eighth Amendment analysis. See *Wilson* v. *Seiter* (1991). *Wilson* extended the deliberate indifference standard applied to Eighth Amendment claims involving medical care to claims about conditions of confinement. In taking this step, we suggested that the subjective aspect of an Eighth Amendment claim (with which the Court was concerned) can be distinguished from the objective facet of the same claim. Thus, courts considering a prisoner's claim must ask both if "the officials act[ed] with a sufficiently culpable state of mind" and if the alleged wrongdoing was objectively "harmful enough" to establish a constitutional violation.

With respect to the objective component of an Eighth Amendment violation, *Wilson* announced no new rule. Instead, that decision suggested a relationship between the requirements applicable to different types of Eighth Amendment claims. What is necessary to show sufficient harm for purposes of the Cruel and Unusual Punishments Clause depends upon the claim at issue, for two reasons. First, "[t]he general requirement that an Eighth Amendment claimant allege and prove the unnecessary and wanton infliction of pain should . . . be applied with due regard for differences in the kind of conduct against which an Eighth Amendment objection is lodged." *Whitley, supra*. Second, the Eighth Amendment's prohibition of cruel and unusual punishments " 'draw[s] its meaning from the evolving standards of decency that mark the progress of a maturing society,' " and so admits of few absolute limitations. *Rhodes* v. *Chapman* (1981) (quoting *Trop* v. *Dulles* (1958)).

The objective component of an Eighth Amendment claim is therefore contextual and responsive to "contemporary standards of decency." *Estelle*. For instance, extreme deprivations are required to make out a conditions-of-confinement claim. Because routine discomfort is "part of the penalty that criminal offenders pay for their offenses against society," *Rhodes, supra*, at 347, "only those deprivations denying 'the minimal civilized measure of life's necessities' are sufficiently grave to form the basis of an Eighth Amendment violation." *Wilson* (quoting *Rhodes*) (internal citation omitted). A similar analysis applies to medical needs. Because society does not expect that prisoners will have unqualified access to health care, deliberate indifference to medical needs amounts to an Eighth Amendment violation only if those needs are "serious." See *Estelle* v. *Gamble*.

In the excessive force context, society's expectations are different. When prison officials maliciously and sadistically use force to cause harm, contemporary standards of decency always are violated. See *Whitley*. This is true whether or not significant injury is evident. Otherwise, the Eighth Amendment would permit any physical punishment, no matter how diabolic or inhuman, inflicting less than some arbitrary quantity of injury. Such a result would have been as unacceptable to the drafters of the Eighth Amendment as it is today. See *Estelle* (proscribing torture and barbarous punishment was "the primary concern of the drafters" of the Eighth Amendment); *Wilkerson* v. *Utah* (1879) ("[I]t is safe to affirm that punishments of torture . . . and all others in the same line of unnecessary cruelty, are forbidden by [the Eighth Amendment]").

That is not to say that every malevolent touch by a prison guard gives rise to a federal cause of action. See *Johnson* v. *Glick* ("Not every push or shove, even if it may later seem unnecessary in the peace of a judge's chambers, violates a prisoner's constitutional rights"). The Eighth Amendment's prohibition of "cruel and unusual" punishment necessarily excludes from constitutional recognition *de minimis* uses of physical force, provided that the use of force is not of a sort " 'repugnant to the conscience of mankind.' " *Whitley* (quoting *Estelle*).

In this case, the Fifth Circuit found Hudson's claim untenable because his injuries were "minor." Yet the blows directed at Hudson, which caused bruises, swelling, loosened teeth, and a cracked dental plate, are not *de minimis* for Eighth Amendment purposes. The extent of Hudson's injuries thus provides no basis for dismissal of his claim.

B

The dissent's theory that *Wilson* requires an inmate who alleges excessive use of force to show serious injury *in addition to* the unnecessary and wanton infliction of pain misapplies *Wilson* and ignores the body of our Eighth Amendment jurisprudence. As we have already suggested, the question before the Court in *Wilson* was "[w]hether a prisoner claiming that conditions of confinement constitute cruel and unusual punishment must show a culpable state of mind on the part of prison officials and, if so, what state of mind is required." *Wilson*. *Wilson* presented neither an allegation of excessive force nor any issue relating to what was dubbed the "objective component" of an Eighth Amendment claim.

Wilson did touch on these matters in the course of summarizing our prior holdings, beginning with *Estelle* v. *Gamble*. *Estelle*, we noted, first applied the Cruel and Unusual Punishments Clause to deprivations that were not specifically part of the prisoner's sentence. *Wilson*. As might be expected from this primacy, *Estelle* stated the principle underlying the cases discussed in *Wilson*: punishments "incompatible with the evolving standards of decency that mark the progress of a maturing society" or "involv[ing] the unnecessary and wanton infliction of pain" are "repugnant to the Eighth Amendment." *Estelle*. This is the same rule the dissent would reject. With respect to the objective component of an Eighth Amendment claim, however, *Wilson* suggested no departure from *Estelle* and its progeny.

The dissent's argument that claims based on excessive force and claims based on conditions of confinement are no different in kind is likewise unfounded. Far from rejecting *Whitley*'s insight that the unnecessary and wanton infliction of pain standard must be applied with regard for the nature of the alleged Eighth Amendment violation, the *Wilson* Court adopted it. See *Wilson*. How could it be otherwise when the constitutional touchstone is whether punishment is cruel and unusual? To deny, as the dissent does, the difference between punching a prisoner in the face and serving him unappetizing food is to ignore the " 'concepts of dignity, civilized standards, humanity, and decency' " that animate the Eighth Amendment. *Estelle* (quoting *Jackson* v. *Bishop* (1968)).

C

Respondents argue that, aside from the significant injury test applied by the Fifth Circuit, their conduct cannot constitute an Eighth Amendment violation because it was "isolated and unauthorized." The beating of Hudson, they contend, arose from "a personal dispute between correctional security officers and a prisoner," and was against prison policy. Respondents invoke the reasoning of courts that have held the use of force by prison officers under such circumstances beyond the scope of "punishment" prohibited by the Eighth Amendment. See *Johnson* v. *Glick*, ("[A]lthough a spontaneous attack by a guard is 'cruel' and, we hope, 'unusual,' it does not fit any ordinary concept of 'punishment' "); *George* v. *Evans* (1980) ("[A] single, unauthorized assault by a guard does not constitute cruel and unusual punishment ... "). But see *Duckworth* v. *Franzen* (1985) ("If a guard decided to supplement a prisoner's official punishment by beating him, this would be punishment ... "), cert. denied (1986).

We take no position on respondents' legal argument because we find it inapposite on this record. The Court of Appeals left intact the Magistrate's determination that the violence at issue in this case was "not an isolated assault." Indeed, there was testimony that McMillian and Woods beat another prisoner shortly after they finished with Hudson. To the extent that respondents rely on the unauthorized nature of their acts, they make a claim not addressed by the Fifth Circuit, not presented by the question on which we granted certiorari, and, accordingly, not before this Court.

Moreover, respondents ignore the Magistrate's finding that Lieutenant Mezo, acting as a supervisor, "expressly condoned the use of force in this instance."

The judgment of the Court of Appeals is   *Reversed.*

JUSTICE BLACKMUN, concurring in the judgment.

The Court today appropriately puts to rest a seriously misguided view that pain inflicted by an excessive use of force is actionable under the Eighth Amendment only when coupled with "significant injury," *e.g.*, injury that requires medical attention or leaves permanent marks. Indeed, were we to hold to the contrary, we might place various kinds of state-sponsored torture and abuse—of the kind ingeniously designed to cause pain but without a telltale "significant injury—entirely beyond the pale of the Constitution. In other words, the constitutional prohibition of "cruel and unusual punishments" then might not constrain prison officials from lashing prisoners with leather straps, whipping them with rubber hoses, beating them with naked fists, shocking them with electric currents, asphyxiating them short of death, intentionally exposing them to undue heat or cold, or forcibly injecting them with psychosis-inducing drugs. These techniques, commonly thought to be practiced only outside this Nation's borders, are hardly unknown within this Nation's prisons. . . .

JUSTICE THOMAS, with whom JUSTICE SCALIA joins, dissenting.

We granted certiorari in this case "limited to the following question," which we formulated for the parties:

> " 'Did the Fifth Circuit apply the correct legal test when determining that petitioner's claim that his Eighth Amendment rights under the Cruel and Unusual Punishment Clause were not violated as a result of a single incident of force by respondents which did not cause a significant injury?' " (1991).

Guided by what it considers "the evolving standards of decency that mark the progress of a maturing society," the Court today answers that question in the negative. I would answer it in the affirmative, and would therefore affirm the judgment of the Fifth Circuit. I respectfully dissent.

I

The magistrate who found the facts in this case emphasized that petitioner's injuries were "minor." The three judges of the Fifth Circuit who heard the case on appeal did not disturb that assessment, and it has not been challenged here. The sole issue in this case, as it comes to us, is a legal one: must a prisoner who claims to have been subjected to "cruel and unusual punishment" establish at a minimum that he has suffered a significant injury? The Court today not only responds in the negative, but broadly asserts that *any* "unnecessary and wanton" use of physical force against a prisoner *automatically* amounts to "cruel and unusual punishment," whenever more than *de minimis* force is involved. Even a *de minimis* use of force, the Court goes on to declare, inflicts cruel and unusual punishment where it is "repugnant to the conscience of mankind." *Ante*, at 7 (internal quotations omitted). The extent to which a prisoner is *injured* by the force—indeed, whether he is injured at all—is in the Court's view irrelevant.

In my view, a use of force that causes only insignificant harm to a prisoner may be immoral, it may be tortious, it may be criminal, and it may even be remediable under other provisions of the Federal Constitution, but it is not "cruel and unusual punishment." In concluding to the contrary, the Court today goes far beyond our precedents.

A

Until recent years, the Cruel and Unusual Punishment Clause was not deemed to apply at all to deprivations that were not inflicted as part of the sentence for a crime. For generations, judges and commentators regarded the Eighth Amendment as applying only to torturous punishments meted out by statutes or sentencing judges, and not generally to any hardship that might befall a prisoner during incarceration. . . .

Surely prison was not a more congenial place in the early years of the Republic than it is today; nor were our judges and commentators so naive as to be unaware of the often harsh conditions of prison life. Rather, they simply did not conceive of the Eighth Amendment as protecting inmates from harsh treatment. Thus, historically, the lower courts routinely rejected prisoner grievances by explaining that the courts had no role in regulating prison life. "[I]t is well settled that it is not the function of the courts to superintend the treatment and discipline of prisoners in penitentiaries, but only to deliver from imprisonment those who are illegally confined." *Stroud* v. *Swope*. . . .

B

We made clear in *Estelle* [1976] that the Eighth Amendment plays a very limited role in regulating prison administration. The case involved a claim that prison doctors had inadequately attended an inmate's medical needs. We rejected the claim because the inmate failed to allege "acts or omissions sufficiently harmful to evidence *deliberate indifference* to *serious* medical needs." From the outset, thus, we specified that the Eighth Amendment does not apply to every deprivation, or even every unnecessary deprivation, suffered by a prisoner, but *only* that narrow class of deprivations involving "serious" injury inflicted by prison officials acting with a culpable state of mind. We have since described these twin elements as the "objective" and "subjective" components of an Eighth Amendment prison claim. See *Wilson* v. *Seiter* (1991). . . .

We synthesized our Eighth Amendment prison jurisprudence last Term in *Wilson, supra*. There the inmate alleged that the poor conditions of his confinement *per se* amounted to cruel and unusual punishment, and argued that he should not be required in addition to establish that officials acted culpably. We rejected that argument, emphasizing that an inmate seeking to establish that a prison deprivation amounts to cruel and unusual punishment always must satisfy *both* the "objective component . . . (was the deprivation sufficiently serious?)" *and* the "subjective component (did the officials act with a sufficiently culpable state of mind?)" of the Eighth Amendment. Both are necessary components; neither suffices by itself. . . .

[C omitted]

D

The Court's attempts to distinguish the cases expressly resting upon the objective component are equally unconvincing. As noted above, we have required an extreme deprivation in cases challenging conditions of confinement, *Rhodes* v. *Chapman* (1981). Why should such an objectively serious deprivation be required there and not here? The Court's explanation is that "routine discomfort is 'part of the penalty that criminal offenders pay for their offenses against society.'" But there is quite a gap between "routine discomfort" and the denial of "the minimal civilized measure of life's necessities" required to establish an Eighth Amendment violation. In the Court's view, then, our society's standards of decency are not violated by anything short of uncivilized conditions of confinement (no matter how malicious the mental state of the officials involved), but are automatically violated by any malicious use of force, regardless of whether it even causes an injury. This is puzzling. I see no reason why our society's standards of decency should be more readily offended when officials, with a culpable state of mind, subject a prisoner to a deprivation on one discrete occasion than when they subject him to continuous deprivations over time. If anything, I would think that a deprivation inflicted continuously over a long period would be of greater concern to society than a deprivation inflicted on one particular occasion. . . .

II

Today's expansion of the Cruel and Unusual Punishment Clause beyond all bounds of history and precedent is, I suspect, yet another manifestation of the pervasive view that the Federal Constitution must address all ills in our society. Abusive behavior by prison guards is deplorable conduct that properly evokes outrage and contempt. But that does not mean that it is invariably unconstitutional. The Eighth Amendment is not, and should not be turned into, a National Code of Prison Regulation. To reject the notion that the infliction of concededly "minor" injuries can be considered either "cruel" or "unusual" punishment" (much less cruel *and* unusual punishment) is not to say that it amounts to acceptable conduct. Rather, it is to recognize that primary responsibility for preventing and punishing such conduct rests not with the Federal Constitution but with the laws and regulations of the various States. . . .

Because I conclude that, under our precedents, a prisoner seeking to establish that he has been subjected to "cruel and unusual punishment" must always show that he has suffered a serious injury, I would affirm the judgment of the Fifth Circuit.

SUPREME COURT ON SEXUAL HARASSMENT OF STUDENTS

February 26, 1992

In a surprisingly broad 9-to-0 decision, the Supreme Court held February 26 that students who are victims of sexual harassment and other forms of sex discrimination may sue for money damages from schools and colleges that receive federal funds under Title IX of the Education Amendments of 1972. The Bush administration, in opposing the suit before the Court, had argued that Title IX did not provide for such monetary relief. But Justice Byron R. White, writing for the majority, impatiently rejected the administration's arguments, stating that such relief was available since Congress had never intended to limit damage awards under Title IX.

Having expected defeat from the conservative-leaning Court, advocates for women's groups praised the decision in the case, Franklin v. Gwinnett County Public Schools, *and expressed relief at the Court's action. Women's rights advocates predicted that the little-used law would be converted into a powerful tool to fight sex discrimination at schools and universities. "It's an enormous victory for women and girls across the country because it puts teeth in the federal law that prohibits sex discrimination in schools," said Marcia D. Greenberger, co-president of the National Women's Law Center in Washington, D.C.*

The decision in the case, which involved charges by a Georgia high school student that a teacher had persistently sexually harassed her, came in the wake of sexual harassment allegations made against nominee Clarence Thomas during Senate Judiciary Committee hearings in October 1991 on Thomas's confirmation to the Supreme Court. The sensational charges were brought by University of Oklahoma law professor

Anita F. Hill, who described instances in which she said Thomas had sexually harassed her when she worked for him at the Department of Education and the Equal Employment Opportunity Commission. Thomas categorically denied the charges. Women's rights advocates had expressed concern, in light of the charges against him and the bruising battle surrounding the allegations, that Thomas, once confirmed to the Court, would oppose decisions that expand women's rights. But while expressing reservations in a concurring opinion written by Justice Antonin Scalia, Thomas agreed in the Franklin case that Title IX permits students to sue for sex bias damages. (Thomas Confirmation Hearings, Historic Documents of 1991, p. 551)

Harassment Charges Detailed

The Franklin case began in 1988 with a lawsuit filed in the U.S. District Court for the Northern District of Georgia by student Christine Franklin against the Gwinnett County, Georgia, school system for failing to stop a teacher from sexually harassing her for more than a year. Franklin, then a high school student at North Gwinnett High School, claimed that she was subjected to continual verbal and physical sexual harassment from Andrew Hill, a coach and teacher.

According to Franklin, Hill engaged her in explicitly sexual discussions, in which he asked her probing questions about her sexual experiences with her boyfriend, forcibly kissed her on the mouth in the school parking lot, and in other ways forced unwanted sexual attention on her. At three different occasions during her junior year, Hill asked that Franklin be excused from a class and took the high school student to a private office where she was forced to engage in sexual intercourse. Franklin contended that school officials were aware of the situation but did nothing to stop it and discouraged her from pressing charges. Hill eventually resigned, and the school closed its investigation.

Before bringing suit, Franklin filed a complaint with the U.S. Department of Education, which enforces Title IX. The Department agreed that Franklin's rights had been violated but dropped the investigation because Hill had resigned and the school district had instituted a grievance procedure.

Basis for Monetary Damages

In its ruling, the District Court dismissed Franklin's complaint, saying that Title IX does not authorize monetary damages. Franklin appealed the ruling to the U.S. Court of Appeals for the Eleventh Circuit in Atlanta, Georgia, and the appellate court upheld the order. On further appeal, the Supreme Court agreed to review the matter. In his majority decision, Justice White drew the backing of Justices Harry A. Blackmun, John Paul Stevens, Sandra Day O'Connor, Anthony M. Kennedy, and David H. Souter. A concurring opinion by Justice Scalia was joined by Chief Justice William H. Rehnquist and Justice Thomas. The three justices agreed with the majority that damages ought to be available under Title IX, but they questioned White's reasoning.

White sharply rejected the Bush administration's argument that no monetary relief should be available under Title IX. The administration cited a 1979 court decision, Davis v. Passman, *to bolster its argument that monetary damages should be denied to Franklin. But White, in a verbal slap on the wrist to the administration, contended that Davis "did nothing to interrupt the long line of cases in which the Court has held that if a right of action exists to enforce a federal right and Congress is silent on the question of remedies, a federal court may order any appropriate relief." Citing additional precedents to support his view, White made the Court's position crystal clear: "The general rule, therefore," he wrote, "is that absent clear direction to the contrary by Congress, the federal courts have the power to award any appropriate relief in a cognizable cause of action brought pursuant to a federal statute."*

Hovering over the case was the question of whether any private suit could be brought under Title IX at all. Congress had never spelled out explicitly that the statute could be used for private lawsuits, only making clear that the law could be used to cut off federal funds to schools and colleges that unlawfully discriminated. But, according to White, there was no room for debate on the issue.

First, White called upon a 1979 Court holding, Cannon v. *University of Chicago, to bolster his contention that private individuals could in fact file suit under Title IX. Then, White cited 1986 amendments to Title IX to illustrate his assertion that Congress intended to provide the right not only to file private suits but to collect for damages. In summing up his argument, White declared, "Congress made no effort to restrict the right of action recognized in Cannon and ratified in the 1986 Act or to alter the traditional presumption in favor of any appropriate relief for violation of a federal right. We cannot say, therefore, that Congress has limited the remedies available to a complainant in a suit brought under Title IX."*

White's opinion was marked by an almost scolding tone, nowhere more evident than in his appraisal of the administration and school district's proposed remedies in the case. Back pay, said White, was "clearly inadequate" because Franklin was a student when the discrimination occurred, and an injunction or similar form of relief would not compensate Franklin since she no longer attended the Gwinnett high school and Hill no longer taught there. The administration's two suggested solutions would therefore "leave petitioner remediless," White concluded.

Court observers predicted that the decision might open the door for the awarding of money damages under two other civil rights laws that the Court has treated as closely related to Title IX: Title VI of the Civil Rights Act of 1964 and Section 504 of the Rehabilitation Act of 1973. The former bans racial discrimination in programs receiving federal funds; the latter prohibits discrimination against handicapped individuals in federally funded programs. The new Civil Rights Act of 1991, cleared by Congress November 7, 1991, and signed by President Bush on November 21, allowed for the first time limited money damages for victims of harassment and other discrimination based on sex, religion or disability. But the provision applied to employment bias, not discrimination against students.

The ruling also had possible implications for investigations of much-publicized incidents at the military service academies, where a poll showed many students experienced some form of harassment, and at the 1991 convention of the Tailhook Association, where a number of female officers reported being molested by fellow naval aviators. Navy Secretary H. Lawrence Garrett III resigned in 1992 after the Tailhook incident came to light. (GAO on Student Treatment at Military Academies; p. 481; Pentagon Report on Tailhook Convention; p. 879)

Following is the text of the Supreme Court's February 26, 1992, decision in Franklin v. Gwinnett County Public Schools *et al.:*

No. 90-918

Christine Franklin, Petitioner *v.* Gwinnett County Public Schools and William Prescott	On writ of certiorari to the United States Court of Appeals for the Eleventh Circuit

[February 26, 1992]

Justice White delivered the opinion of the Court.

This case presents the question whether the implied right of action under Title IX of the Education Amendments of 1972, 20 U.S.C. § 1681-1688 (Title IX), which this Court recognized in *Cannon* v. *University of Chicago* (1979), supports a claim for monetary damages.

I

Petitioner Christine Franklin was a student at North Gwinnett High School in Gwinnett County, Georgia, between September 1985 and August 1989. Respondent Gwinnett County School District operates the high school and receives federal funds. According to the complaint filed on December 29, 1988 in the United States District Court for the Northern District of Georgia, Franklin was subjected to continual sexual harassment beginning in the autumn of her tenth grade year (1986) from Andrew Hill, a sports coach and teacher employed by the district. Among other allegations, Franklin avers that Hill engaged her in sexually-oriented conversations in which he asked about her sexual experiences with her boyfriend and whether she would consider having sexual intercourse with an older man; that Hill forcibly kissed her on the mouth in the school parking lot; that he telephoned her at her home and asked if she would meet him socially; and that, on three occasions in her junior year, Hill interrupted a class, requested that the teacher excuse Franklin, and took her to a private office where he subjected her to coercive intercourse. The complaint further alleges that though they became aware of and investigated Hill's sexual harassment of Franklin and other female students, teachers and administrators took no action to halt it and discouraged Franklin from pressing charges against Hill. On April 14, 1988, Hill resigned on the condition that all matters pending against him be dropped. The school thereupon closed its investigation.

In this action, the District Court dismissed the complaint on the ground that Title IX does not authorize an award of damages. The Court of Appeals affirmed. *Franklin* v. *Gwinnett Cty. Public Schools* (CA 11 1990). The court noted that analysis of Title IX and Title VI of the Civil Rights Act of 1964, 42 U.S.C. § 2000d *et seq.* (Title VI), has developed along similar lines. Citing as binding precedent *Drayden* v. *Needville Independent School Dist.* (CA5 1981), a decision rendered prior to the division of the Fifth Circuit, the court concluded that Title VI did not support a claim for monetary damages. The court then analyzed this Court's decision in *Guardians Assn.* v. *Civil Service Comm'n of New York City* (1983), to determine whether it implicitly overruled *Drayden.* The court stated that the absence of a majority opinion left unresolved the question whether a court could award such relief upon a showing of intentional discrimination. As a second basis for its holding that monetary damages were unavailable, the court reasoned that Title IX was enacted under Congress' Spending Clause powers and that "[u]nder such statutes, relief may frequently be limited to that which is equitable in nature, with the recipient of federal funds thus retaining the option of terminating such receipt in order to rid itself of an injunction." *Franklin*, 911 F. 2d, at 621. The court closed by observing it would "proceed with extreme care" to afford compensatory relief absent express provision by Congress or clear direction from this Court. Accordingly, it held that an action for monetary damages could not be sustained for an alleged intentional violation of Title IX, and affirmed the District Court's ruling to that effect.

Because this opinion conflicts with a decision of the Court of Appeals for the Third Circuit, see *Pfeiffer* v. *Marion Center Area School Dist.* (1990), we granted certiorari (1991). We reverse.

II

In *Cannon* v. *University of Chicago* (1979), the Court held that Title IX is enforceable through an implied right of action. We have no occasion here to reconsider that decision. Rather, in this case we must decide what remedies are available in a suit brought pursuant to this implied right. As we have often stated, the question of what remedies are available under a statute that provides a private right of action is "analytically distinct" from the issue of whether such a right exists in the first place. *Davis* v. *Passman* (1979). Thus, although we examine the text and history of a statute to determine whether Congress intended to create a right of action, *Touche Ross & Co.* v. *Redington* (1979), we presume the availability of all appropriate remedies unless Congress has expressly indicated otherwise. This principle has deep roots in our jurisprudence.

A

"[W]here legal rights have been invaded, and a federal statute provides for a general right to sue for such invasion, federal courts may use any available remedy to make good the wrong done." *Bell* v. *Hood* (1946). The Court explained this longstanding rule as jurisdictional, and upheld the exercise of the federal courts' power to award appropriate relief so long as a cause of action existed under the Constitution or laws of the United States.

The *Bell* Court's reliance on this rule was hardly revolutionary. From the earliest years of the Republic, the Court has recognized the power of the judiciary to award appropriate remedies to redress injuries actionable in federal court, although it did not always distinguish clearly between a right to bring suit and a remedy available under such a right. In *Marbury* v. *Madison*, 1 Cranch 137, 163 (1803), for example, Chief Justice Marshall observed that our government "has been emphatically termed a government of laws, and not of men. It will certainly cease to deserve this high appellation, if the laws furnish no remedy for the violation of a vested legal right." This principle originated in the English common law, and Blackstone described "it is a general and indisputable rule, that where there is a legal right, there is also a legal remedy, by suit or action at law, whenever that right is invaded." 3 W. Blackstone, Commentaries 23 (1783). ...

In *Kendall* v. *United States* (1838), the Court applied these principles to an act of Congress that accorded a right of action in mail carriers to sue for adjustment and settlement of certain claims for extra services but which did not specify the precise remedy available to the carriers. After surveying possible remedies, which included an action against the postmaster general for monetary damages, the Court held that the carriers were entitled to a writ of mandamus compelling payment under the terms of the statute. "It cannot be denied but that congress had the power to command that act to be done," the Court stated; "and the power to enforce the performance of the act must rest somewhere, or it will present a case which has often been said to involve a monstrous absurdity in a well organized government, that there should be no remedy, although a clear and undeniable right should be shown to exist. And if the remedy cannot be applied by the circuit court of this district, it exists nowhere." *Dooley* v. *United States* (1901), also restated "the principle that a liability created by statute without a remedy may be enforced by a common-law action."

The Court relied upon this traditional presumption again after passage of the Federal Safety Appliance Act of 1893, ch. 196, 27 Stat. 531. In *Texas & Pacific R. Co.* v. *Rigsby* (1916), the Court first had to determine whether the Act supported an implied right of action. After answering that question in the affirmative, the Court then upheld a claim for monetary damages: "A disregard of the command of the statute is a wrongful act, and where it results in damage to one of the class for whose especial benefit the statute was enacted, the right to recover the damages from the party in default is implied, according to a doctrine of the common law...." The foundation upon which the *Bell* v. *Hood* Court articulated this traditional presumption, therefore, was well settled. See also *Texas & New Orleans R. Co.* v. *Railway & Steamship Clerks* (1930).

B

Respondents and the United States as *amicus curiae*, however, maintain that whatever the traditional presumption may have been when the Court decided *Bell* v. *Hood*, it has disappeared in succeeding decades. We do not agree. In *J.I. Case Co.* v. *Borak* (1964), the Court adhered to the general rule that all appropriate relief is available in an action brought to vindicate a federal right when Congress has given no indication of its purpose with respect to remedies. Relying on *Bell* v. *Hood*, the *Borak* Court specifically rejected an argument that a court's remedial power to redress violations of the Securities Exchange Act of 1934 was limited to a declaratory judgment. 377 U.S., at 433-434. The Court concluded that the federal courts "have the power to grant all necessary remedial relief" for violations of the Act. As Justice Clark's opinion for the Court observed, this holding closely followed the reasoning of a similar case brought under the Securities Act of 1933, in which the Court had stated:

> " 'The power *to enforce* implies the power to make effective the right of recovery afforded by the Act. And the power to make the right of recovery effective implies the power to utilize any of the procedures or actions normally available to the litigant according to the exigencies of the particular case.' " (quoting *Deckert* v. *Independence Shares Corp.* (1940 0)).

That a statute does not authorize the remedy at issue "in so many words is no more significant than the fact that it does not in terms authorize execution to issue on a judgment." Subsequent cases have been true to this position. See, *e.g.*, *Sullivan* v. *Little Hunting Park, Inc.* (1969), stating that the "existence of a statutory right implies the existence of all necessary and appropriate remedies"; *Carey* v. *Piphus* (1978), upholding damages remedy under 42 U.S.C. § 1983 even though the enacting Congress had not specifically provided such relief.

The United States contends that the traditional presumption in favor of all appropriate relief was abandoned by the Court in *Davis* v. *Passman* (1979), and that the *Bell* v. *Hood* rule was limited to actions claiming constitutional violations.... The Government's position, however, mirrors the very misunderstanding over the difference between a cause of action and the relief afforded under it that sparked the confusion we attempted to clarify in *Davis*. Whether Congress may limit the class of persons who have a right of action under Title IX is irrelevant to the issue in this lawsuit. To reiterate, "the question whether a litigant has a 'cause of action' is analytically distinct and prior to the question of what relief, if any, a litigant may be entitled to receive." *Davis*, therefore, did nothing to interrupt the long line of cases in which the Court has held that if a right of action exists to enforce a federal right and Congress is silent on the question of remedies, a federal court may order any appropriate relief.

Contrary to arguments by respondents and the United States that *Guardians Assn.* v. *Civil Service Comm'n of New York City* (1983), and *Consolidated Rail Corp.* v. *Darrone* (1984), eroded this traditional presumption, those cases in fact support it. Though the multiple opinions in *Guardians* suggest the difficulty of inferring the common ground among the Justices in that case, a clear majority expressed the view that damages were available under Title VI in an action seeking remedies for an intentional violation, and no Justice challenged the traditional presumption in favor of a federal court's power to award appropriate relief in a cognizable cause of action. The correctness of this inference was made clear the following Term when the Court unanimously held that the 1978 amendment to § 504 of the Rehabilitation Act of 1973—which had expressly incorporated the "remedies, procedures, and rights set forth in title VI" (29 U.S.C. § 794a(a)(2))—authorizes an award of backpay. In *Darrone*, the Court observed that a majority in *Guardians* had "agreed that retroactive relief is available to private plaintiffs for all discrimination ... that is actionable under Title VI." The general rule, therefore, is that absent clear direction to the contrary by Congress, the federal courts have the power to award any appropriate relief in a cognizable cause of action brought pursuant to a federal statute.

III

We now address whether Congress intended to limit application of this general principle in the enforcement of Title IX. See *Bush* v. *Lucas* (1983); *Wyandotte Transp. Co.* v. *United States* (1967). Because the cause of action was inferred by the Court in *Cannon*, the usual recourse to statutory text and legislative history in the period prior to that decision necessarily will not enlighten our analysis. Respondents and the United States fundamentally misunderstand the nature of the inquiry, therefore, by needlessly dedicating large portions of their briefs to discussions of how the text and legislative intent behind Title IX are "silent" on the issue of available remedies. Since the Court in *Cannon* concluded that this statute supported no express right of action, it is hardly surprising that Congress also said nothing about the applicable remedies for an implied right of action.

During the period prior to the decision in *Cannon*, the inquiry in any event is *not* " 'basically a matter of statutory construction,' " as the

United States asserts. Brief for United States as *Amicus Curiae* 8 (quoting *Transamerica Mortgage Advisors, Inc.* v. *Lewis* (1979)). Rather, in determining Congress's intent to limit application of the traditional presumption in favor of all appropriate relief, we evaluate the state of the law when the legislature passed Title IX. *Merrill Lynch, Pierce, Fenner & Smith, Inc.* v. *Curran,* (1982). In the years before and after Congress enacted this statute, the Court "follow[ed] a common-law tradition [and] regarded the denial of a remedy as the exception rather than the rule." *Id.,* at 375 (footnote omitted). As we outlined in Part II, this has been the prevailing presumption in our federal courts since at least the early nineteenth century. In *Cannon,* the majority upheld an implied right of action in part because in the decade immediately preceding enactment of Title IX in 1972, this Court had found implied rights of action in six cases. In three of those cases, the Court had approved a damages remedy. See, *e.g., J. I. Case Co., Wyandotte Transp. Co., supra,* at 207; *Sullivan* v. *Little Hunting Park, Inc.* (1969). Wholly apart from the wisdom of the *Cannon* holding, therefore, the same contextual approach used to justify an implied right of action more than amply demonstrates the lack of any legislative intent to abandon the traditional presumption in favor of all available remedies.

In the years *after* the announcement of *Cannon,* on the other hand, a more traditional method of statutory analysis is possible, because Congress was legislating with full cognizance of that decision. Our reading of the two amendments to Title IX enacted after *Cannon* leads us to conclude that Congress did not intend to limit the remedies available in a suit brought under Title IX. In the Civil Rights Remedies Equalization Amendment of 1986, 42 U.S.C. § 2000d-7, Congress abrogated the States' Eleventh Amendment immunity under Title IX, Title VI, § 504 of the Rehabilitation Act of 1973, and the Age Discrimination Act of 1975. This statute cannot be read except as a validation of *Cannon*'s holding. A subsection of the 1986 law provides that in a suit against a State, "remedies (including remedies both at law and in equity) are available for such a violation to the same extent as such remedies are available for such a violation in the suit against any public or private entity other than a State." 42 U.S.C. § 2000d-7(a)(2). While it is true that this savings clause says nothing about the nature of those other available remedies, *Milwaukee* v. *Illinois,* (1981), absent any contrary indication in the text or history of the statute, we presume Congress enacted this statute with the prevailing traditional rule in mind.

In addition to the Civil Rights Remedies Equalization Amendment of 1986, Congress also enacted the Civil Rights Restoration Act of 1987, Pub. L. 100-259, 102 Stat. 28 (1988). Without in any way altering the existing rights of action and the corresponding remedies permissible under Title IX, Title VI, § 504 of the Rehabilitation Act, and the Age Discrimination Act, Congress broadened the coverage of these antidiscrimination provisions in this legislation. In seeking to correct what it considered to be an unacceptable decision on our part in *Grove City College* v. *Bell* (1984), Congress made no effort to restrict the right of action recognized in *Cannon* and ratified in the 1986 Act or to alter the traditional presumption in favor of any appropriate relief for violation of a federal right. We cannot say, therefore, that Congress has limited the remedies available to a complainant in a suit brought under Title IX.

IV

Respondents and the United States nevertheless suggest three reasons why we should not apply the traditional presumption in favor of appropriate relief in this case.

A

First, respondents argue that an award of damages violates separation of powers principles because it unduly expands the federal courts' power into a sphere properly reserved to the Executive and Legislative Branches. Brief for Respondents 22-25. In making this argument, respondents misconceive the difference between a cause of action and a remedy. Unlike the finding of a cause of action, which authorizes a court to hear a case or controversy, the discretion to award appropriate relief involves no such increase in judicial power. Federal courts cannot reach out to award remedies when the Constitution or laws of the United States do not support a cause of action. Indeed, properly understood respondents' position invites us to *abdicate* our historic judicial authority to award appropriate relief in cases brought in our court system. It is well to recall that such authority historically has been thought necessary to provide an important safeguard against abuses of legislative and executive power, see *Kendall* v. *United States* (1838), as well as to insure an independent judiciary. See generally Katz, The Jurisprudence of Remedies: Constitutional Legality and the Law of Torts in *Bell* v. *Hood* (1968). Moreover, selective abdication of the sort advocated here would harm separation of powers principles in another way, by giving judges the power to render inutile causes of action authorized by Congress through a decision that *no* remedy is available.

B

Next, consistent with the Court of Appeals's reasoning, respondents and the United States contend that the normal presumption in favor of all appropriate remedies should not apply because Title IX was enacted pursuant to Congress's Spending Clause power. In *Pennhurst State School and Hospital* v. *Halderman* (1981), the Court observed that remedies were limited under such Spending Clause statutes when the alleged violation was *unintentional*. Respondents and the United States maintain that this presumption should apply equally to *intentional* violations. We disagree. The point of not permitting monetary damages for an unintentional violation is that the receiving entity of federal funds lacks notice that it will be liable for a monetary award. This notice problem does not arise in a case such as this, in which intentional discrimination is alleged. Unquestionably, Title IX placed on the Gwinnett County Schools the duty not to discriminate on the basis of sex, and "when a supervisor sexually harasses a subordinate because of the subordinate's sex, that supervisor 'discriminate[s]' on the basis of sex." *Meritor Savings Bank, FSB* v. *Vinson* (1986). We believe the same rule should apply when a teacher sexually harasses and abuses a student. Congress surely did not intend for federal monies to be expended to support the intentional actions it sought by statute to proscribe. Moreover, the notion that Spending Clause statutes do not authorize monetary awards for intentional violations is belied by our unanimous holding in *Darrone*. Respondents and the United States characterize the backpay remedy in *Darrone* as equitable relief, but this description is irrelevant to their underlying objection: that application of the traditional rule in this case will require state entities to pay monetary awards out of their treasuries for intentional violations of federal statutes.

C

Finally, the United States asserts that the remedies permissible under Title IX should nevertheless be limited to backpay and prospective relief. In addition to diverging from our traditional approach to deciding what remedies are available for violation of a federal right, this position conflicts with sound logic. First, both remedies are equitable in nature, and it is axiomatic that a court should determine the adequacy of a remedy in law before resorting to equitable relief. Under the ordinary convention, the proper inquiry would be whether monetary damages provided an adequate remedy, and if not, whether equitable relief would be appropriate. *Whitehead* v. *Shattuck* (1891). Moreover, in this case the equitable remedies suggested by respondent and the Federal Government are clearly inadequate. Backpay does nothing for petitioner, because she was a student when the alleged discrimination occurred. Similarly, because Hill—the person she claims subjected her to sexual harassment—no longer teaches at the school and she herself no longer attends a school in the Gwinnett system, prospective relief accords her no remedy at all. The government's answer that administrative action helps other similarly-situated students in effect acknowledges that its approach would leave petitioner remediless.

V

In sum, we conclude that a damages remedy is available for an action brought to enforce Title IX. The judgment of the Court of Appeals, therefore, is reversed and the case is remanded for further proceedings consistent with this opinion.

So ordered.

JUSTICE SCALIA, with whom the CHIEF JUSTICE and JUSTICE THOMAS join, concurring in the judgment.

The substantive right at issue here is one that Congress did not expressly create, but that this Court found to be "implied." See *Cannon* v. *University of Chicago* (1979). Quite obviously, the search for what was Congress's *remedial* intent as to a right whose very existence Congress did not expressly acknowledge is unlikely to succeed; it is "hardly surprising,", as the Court says, that the usual sources yield no explicit answer.

The Court finds an implicit answer, however, in the legislators' presumptive awareness of our practice of using "any available remedy" to redress violations of legal rights. *Bell* v. *Hood* (1946). This strikes me as question-begging. We can plausibly assume acquiescence in our *Bell* v. *Hood* presumption when the legislature says nothing about remedy in expressly creating a private right of action; perhaps even when it says nothing about remedy in creating a private right of action by clear textual implication; but not, I think, when it says nothing about remedy in a statute in which the courts divine a private right of action on the basis of "contextual" evidence such as that in *Cannon*, which charged Congress with knowledge of a court of appeals' creation of a cause of action under a similarly worded statute. Whatever one thinks of the validity of the last approach, it surely rests on attributed rather than actual congressional knowledge. It does not demonstrate an explicit legislative decision to create a cause of action, and so could not be expected to be accompanied by a legislative decision to alter the application of *Bell* v. *Hood*. Given the nature of *Cannon* and some of our earlier "implied right of action" cases, what the Court's analytical construct comes down to is this: Unless Congress expressly legislates a more limited remedial policy with respect to rights of action it does not know it is creating, it intends the full gamut of remedies to be applied.

In my view, when rights of action are judicially "implied," categorical limitations upon their remedial scope may be judicially implied as well. Although we have abandoned the expansive rights-creating approach exemplified by *Cannon*, see *Touche Ross & Co.* v. *Redington* (1979); *Transamerica Mortgage Advisors, Inc.* v. *Lewis* (1979)—and perhaps ought to abandon the notion of implied causes of action entirely, see *Thompson* v. *Thompson* (1988) (SCALIA, J., concurring in judgment)— causes of action that came into existence under the *ancien regime* should be limited by the same logic that gave them birth. To require, with respect to a right that is not consciously and intentionally created, that any limitation of remedies must be express, is to provide, in effect, that the most questionable of private rights will also be the most expansively remediable. As the United States puts it, "[w]hatever the merits of 'implying' rights of action may be, there is no justification for treating [congressional] silence as the equivalent of the broadest imaginable grant of remedial authority." . . .

I nonetheless agree with the Court's disposition of this case. Because of legislation enacted subsequent to *Cannon*, it is too late in the day to address whether a judicially implied exclusion of damages under Title IX would be appropriate. The Civil Rights Remedies Equalization Amendment of 1986, 42 U.S.C. § 2000d-7(a)(2), must be read, in my view, not only "as a validation of *Cannon*'s holding," but also as an implicit acknowledgment that damages are available. . . . I therefore concur in the judgment.

U.S.-LATIN AMERICAN DRUG SUMMIT AT SAN ANTONIO
February 27, 1992

Convening in San Antonio February 26 and 27, President George Bush and leaders from six Latin American nations pledged greater cooperation in the effort to halt drug smuggling and production in a region increasingly plagued by the crisis. The leaders met for five hours, in between Bush's campaign appearances in California and Texas.

Attending the conference were Presidents Bush, Jaime Paz Zamora of Bolivia, Cesar Gaviria Trujillo of Colombia, Rodrigo Borja Cevallos of Ecuador, Carlos Salinas de Gortari of Mexico, and Alberto Fujimori of Peru. Venezuelan President Carlos Andres Perez, who was embroiled in a domestic crisis following a coup attempt earlier in the month, was represented by a delegation. The Texas meeting followed up on a previous regional summit held in Cartagena, Colombia, in February 1990. At that meeting, Bush and the presidents of Peru, Colombia, and Bolivia had agreed on general pledges of cooperation in the drug war. Mexico, Venezuela, and Ecuador had not attended the 1990 summit but were invited to the San Antonio meeting because of growing drug problems in those countries. (Drug Summit Agreements at Cartagena, Colombia, Historic Documents of 1990, p. 115)

Major Points of Agreement; No Added U.S. Aid

At a news conference following the meeting, Bush said the participating nations had "established an aggressive agenda for the rest of the century" for combatting drug traffic. Although the Bush administration did not commit the United States to additional funding for the international effort, it did agree to exert greater control over exports of chemicals used to process cocaine from raw coca leaves. The president explained that the U.S. economic recession prevented further financial assistance to the regional effort. "We are operating under enormous deficits that concern the American people enormously," he said. "So we don't have all the money to spend on all the programs that we think are worthwhile."

At Peru's insistence, the seven agreed to drop a proposal to set specific goals for reducing drug production, cultivation, and consumption. Among the major features of the accord, the participants agreed to:

- *Establish training centers for antidrug law enforcement agents*
- *Create a common database to exchange information "concerning the activities of organizations, groups and persons engaged in illicit drug trafficking*
- *Sign legal-assistance pacts to facilitate sharing evidence in drug trafficking cases*
- *Meet annually at the cabinet level to review progress in the war against drugs*
- *Form a civil-aviation registration exchange designed to prevent drug traffickers from registering private planes in different countries under the same numbers—a practice that made it difficult for police to prove that a specific plane was involved in drug trafficking*

The participants also agreed to send a cabinet-level delegation to Europe and Japan to request additional international funding for their efforts.

Immediately after the accord was reached, the Bush administration signed a bilateral mutual legal assistance agreement with Colombia. The President also directed the Defense Department to provide Mexico with twelve UH-1H helicopters, along with spare parts, to use in trailing drug traffickers.

Major Issues: Economic vs. Military Aid

A major issue that surfaced during the negotiations concerned Fujimori's rejection of Colombian proposals, supported by the United States, designed to reduce the harvesting of coca. Noting that about 250,000 peasants in his country produced 60 percent of the world's cocaine, the Peruvian president argued that a crackdown on production might spark violence led by Sendero Luminoso (Shining Path) rebel forces. The group controlled much of the territory in the Upper Huallaga Valley, where most of Peru's cocaine was produced. In September, however, Shining Path received a major setback with the capture of its leader, Abimael Guzman Reynoso. (Fujimori on Capture of Peruvian Shining Path Leader, p. 859)

Fujimori also said that U.S. antidrug aid was too heavily geared to military measures and should focus instead on fostering alternative economic incentives to coca growers. (Since 1991 the United States had provided Peru with more than $100 million in military aid for the *antidrug effort; Congress had, for a time, held up delivery of much of the aid on the grounds of human rights violations.)*

Agreeing with Fujimori, the presidents of Ecuador and Bolivia also pressed for U.S. grants to establish new industries and agricultural markets in their countries, as well as incentives for increased investment by U.S. businesses. "Up to now, all our struggles against the drug traffic basically have been financed with Ecuadoran capital," said President Cevallos.

(The United States in 1992 spent less than 5 percent of its $12.7 billion annual drug-control budget in Latin America.)

The leaders of the more developed nations of Mexico, Colombia, and Venezuela expressed particular interest in launching new measures that would further open U.S. markets to their exports, helping stimulate job creation and economic growth.

Another issue concerned the sharp three-year increase in the amount of U.S. military aid given to the Colombian and Bolivian armies to fight drugs. Government officials in those countries, as well as civil rights groups, objected that armies strengthened by antidrug funds might challenge civilian governments, engage in human rights abuses, and use the money to fight guerrillas rather than drug traffickers. In a statement issued February 26, the U.S. Embassy in Bogota agreed to stop financing the army and, instead, direct more of the military aid to the police.

Mixed Success of Past Efforts

Although Bush administration officials had pointed to modest success in the war against drugs since 1990, a number of drug experts and members of Congress said drug trafficking in the region had increased, with cocaine continuing to flow into the United States and new markets being opened in Europe, Japan, and other Asian countries. "By every objective standard, the president's Andean strategy has failed," said Rep. Charles E. Schumer, D-N.Y., chairman of the House Subcommittee on Crime and Criminal Justice, which oversees the Drug Enforcement Administration. Drug experts also pointed out that Colombia had refused to extradite traffickers; moreover, both Colombia and Bolivia had accepted plea bargains from prominent drug traffickers, who then received lenient sentences.

"[T]he overriding reality is that more drugs are coming in" to the United States, said Bruce M. Bagley, a specialist on drug trafficking and Latin America at the University of Miami. "To improve the situation, we're going to have to move away from the supply side and military tactics to a stronger focus on demand in this country."

Following are the texts of President Bush's remarks at the opening session of the U.S.-Latin American drug summit in San Antonio and the seven-nation declaration on cooperative measures to combat drug trafficking, February 27, 1992:

REMARKS AT THE OPENING SESSION
OF THE DRUG SUMMIT

It is a great honor and pleasure to call to order an historic meeting, in a historic city, in a historic State, my home State of Texas. We are all here to make this San Antonio drug summit as successful as the first summit called by President Barco 2 years ago in beautiful, heroic Cartagena. It is fitting to begin this meeting with a warm tribute to the great, visionary man who first brought us together on this issue, Virgilio Barco.

In Cartagena, as President Paz Zamora, who is also here today, will recall, we faced a daunting, unprecedented, some thought hopeless, challenge: How to unite against the scourge of drugs, violence, and corruption that was undermining our democratic societies, our institutions, our economies, and our environment.

That meeting gave birth to a new alliance to strengthen our democracies by attacking the drug trafficking and consumption with greater resolve than ever before. Cartagena was when we stopped the finger-pointing and committed ourselves to cooperation, when we recognized that drugs are an international plague caused by both consumer and supplier.

Two years later the situation has markedly improved. We are facing the challenge. We are united. We are resolute. We are prevailing. We are now seven, not four. We welcome to this group Mexico, Venezuela, and Ecuador, all of whom have shown firm leadership and courage in this struggle. Others in the Americas and Europe are with us, seeing the threat more clearly. Progress is being made. We have courageously faced those who would subvert our societies, break our laws, and kill thousands of innocents. Top traffickers are dead or jailed. Record levels of cocaine and other drugs have been seized. Cultivation has leveled off. Interdiction is up worldwide. We have cracked down on drug users. Consumption is declining as our people increasingly reject drugs, especially our youth. Our judicial institutions are stronger, better able to meet the challenge. Our efforts against money laundering, chemical diversion, and illegal arms exports are improving.

But, we are here today because the job is not yet done. We have not yet won this fight. It is time to assess our accomplishments and our plans, to learn from the past and look to the future. Let me mention what seems to me to be some priority areas.

First and foremost, we must reduce demand. All else will fail if we do not do that. I know that task falls heaviest on the United States, and we have made a good beginning. Since I came to office, there has been a 35 percent decrease in current cocaine users, and 27 percent fewer young people are using drugs.

Second, we must continue the economic reform, economic assistance, debt, trade, and investment measures which are so important to our antinarcotics programs. The United States wants alternative development to succeed. I am sure Peruvian and Bolivian peasants will stop growing illegal coca if there is an alternative besides starvation. The stick of law enforcement must have a carrot, an offer of viable economic alternatives for poor peasants.

Third, we must continue and enhance our effectiveness in eradication, interdiction, and law enforcement that have been so critical to our success thus far. Just as demand reduction will lower supply, so also supply reduction will lessen demand. We have laid this out in the "Strategy for Action" that is part of our declaration. We must make it happen.

Fourth, we must look carefully and imaginatively at what might be called nonviolent law enforcement measures. We must strengthen and harmonize our laws on money laundering, arms, exports, chemical controls, asset seizure, and in other areas. It is here that the long arm of the law can fracture the power of the traffickers. The antiracketeering laws in the United States have proven to be one of the strongest measures we have developed in recent years.

Fifth, our judicial systems need our attention. Many of us have underway legal reforms so that we can handle criminal cases faster, more securely, and more effectively. These are important and should proceed. We must also cooperate by sharing information about traffickers and their crimes so they can be brought to justice.

Sixth, our cooperation has developed in the past 2 years, and I welcome that. We need to keep in close touch so that we can coordinate strategy and understand each others' perspectives and needs. That makes the high-level follow-on meeting very important. It will be the first review of how our "Strategies for Action" are progressing. We also must enlist the cooperation of the Europeans and Asians. To do that we should send a delegation to those countries to talk to their leaders.

Seventh, heroin production is a worrisome problem which Mexico and Colombia are moving against with some success. This is a sign the traffickers believe the cocaine trade is declining. We cannot ignore this new threat, or we risk a surprise in the future.

Eighth, we must do a better job educating our press and our publics about our progress. In the United States, for example, we are seeing a downturn in demand that was purchased at great cost in money and effort. Another example is the story of the drop in cultivation in the Chapare in Bolivia.

Ninth, as we take up the struggle within our own countries with renewed vigor, we must bear in mind that our efforts transcend borders. We must respect sovereignty, or our cooperation will not be sustained. But as sovereign states, we can agree to cooperate against the traffickers who trample on the sovereignty. If we do not work together, the traffickers will destroy us separately.

Finally, one more note of great importance. Everything we do must conform to our democratic principles. None of us wants a drug-free dictatorship. We must protect the human and civil rights of our citizens.

We are all committed to defending democracy and its principles as we defeat the scourge of drugs.

DECLARATION OF SAN ANTONIO

San Antonio Drug Summit 1992

We, the Presidents of Bolivia, Colombia, Ecuador, Mexico, Peru, and the United States of America, and the Minister of Foreign Relations of Venezuela, met in San Antonio, Texas, on the 26th and 27th of February, one thousand nine hundred and ninety-two and issued the following

Declaration of San Antonio

We recognize that the Cartagena Declaration, issued on February 15, 1990, by the Presidents of Bolivia, Colombia, Peru, and the United States of America, laid the foundation for the development of a comprehensive and multilateral strategy to address the problem of illegal drugs. Those of us who represent the countries that met in Cartagena strongly reaffirm the commitments assumed at that time. Meeting now as representatives of seven governments, we express our determination to move beyond the achievements of Cartagena, build upon the progress attained, and adapt international cooperation to the new challenges arising from worldwide changes in the drug problem.

We recognize that the overall problem of illegal drugs and related crimes represents a direct threat to the health and well-being of our peoples, to their economies, the national security of our countries, and to harmony in international relations. Drugs lead to violence and addiction, threaten democratic institutions, and waste economic and human resources that could be used for the benefit of our societies.

We applaud the progress achieved over the past two years in reducing cocaine production, in lowering demand, in reducing cultivation for illicit purposes, in carrying out alternative development programs, and in dismantling and disrupting transnational drug trafficking organizations and their financial support networks. The close cooperation among our governments and their political will have led to an encouraging increasing in drug seizures and in the effectiveness of law enforcement actions. Also as a result of this cooperation and political will, a number of the principal drug lords who were actively engaged in the drug trade two years ago are in prison in several countries. Alternative development programs have proven to be an effective strategy for replacing coca cultivation in producer countries.

Although we are encouraged by these achievements, we recognize that mutual cooperative efforts must be expanded and strengthened in all areas. We call on all sectors of society, notably the media, to increase their efforts in the anti-drug struggle. The role of the media is very important, and we urge them to intensify their valuable efforts. We undertake to promote, through the media, the values essential to a healthy society.

In addition to the cocaine problem, we recognize the need to remain alert to the expansion of the production, trafficking, and consumption of heroin, marijuana, and other drugs. We emphasize the need to exert greater control over substances used in the production of these drugs, and to broaden consultations on the eradication of these illegal crops.

We are convinced that our anti-drug efforts must be conducted on the basis of the principle of shared responsibility and in a balanced manner. It is essential to confront the drug problem through an integrated approach, addressing demand, cultivation for illicit purposes, production, trafficking, and illegal distribution networks, as well as related crimes, such as traffic in firearms and in essential and precursor chemicals, and money laundering. In addition, our governments will continue to perfect strategies that include alternative development, eradication, control and interdiction, the strengthening of judicial systems, and the prevention of illicit drug use.

We recognize the fundamental importance of strengthening judicial systems to ensure that effective institutions exist to bring criminals to justice. We assume responsibility for strengthening judicial cooperation among our countries to attain these objectives. We reaffirm our intention to carry out these efforts in full compliance with the international legal framework for the protection of human rights.

We reaffirm that cooperation among us must be carried out in accordance with our national laws, with full respect for the sovereignty and territorial integrity of our nations, and in strict observance of international law.

We recognize that the problem of illicit drugs is international. All countries directly or indirectly affected by the drug problem should take upon themselves clear responsibilities and actions in the anti-drug effort. We call on the countries of the region to strengthen national and international cooperative efforts and to participate actively in regional programs. We recognize that in the case of Peru, complicity between narco-trafficking and terrorism greatly complicates the anti-drug effort, threatens democratic institutions, and undermines the viability of the Peruvian economy.

We express our support for the anti-drug struggle being carried out by our sister nations of the Western Hemisphere, we call on them to increase their efforts, and we offer to strengthen our governments' cooperation with them through specific agreements they may wish to sign. We value and encourage regional unity in this effort.

We note with concern the opening and expansion of markets for illicit drugs, particularly cocaine, in Europe and Asia. We call upon the nations of those continents and on other member countries of the international community to strengthen, through bilateral or multilateral agreements, cooperation in the anti-drug effort in which the nations of the Western Hemisphere are engaged. To this end, we have agreed to form a high-level group with representatives designated by the signatory countries of this Declaration, to visit other countries of this Hemisphere, Europe, and Japan, with the purpose of inviting them to participate actively in the efforts and cooperative strategies described in this Declaration.

We reaffirm our solid commitment to the anti-drug efforts of international organizations, notably the United Nations and the Organization of American States. Inspired by the mandate of the Inter-American Commission on the Control of Drug Abuse, we express our full support for its programs.

We recognize the fundamental importance of strong economies and innovative economic initiatives to the successful conduct of the anti-drug effort. Further progress in the areas of trade and investment will be essential. We support the Enterprise for the Americas Initiative as a means of improving economic conditions in the Hemisphere, and we are encouraged by the progress the countries of the region have made in restructuring their economies.

We reaffirm the importance of alternative development in the anti-drug effort. We note that the victims of narco-trafficking in the region include those sectors of society that live in extreme poverty and that are attracted to illicit drug production and trafficking as a means of livelihood. We consider that if our efforts to reduce illegal drug trafficking are to be successful, it will be essential to offer legitimate options that generate employment and income.

We propose to achieve the objectives and goals defined above in this Declaration and in its attached Strategies for Action.

Recognizing the need to ensure cohesion and progress in our anti-drug efforts, our governments intend to hold a high-level meeting on an annual basis.

In order to broaden international anti-drug efforts still further, we invite additional countries or representatives of groups of countries to associate themselves with this Declaration.

Done at San Antonio, Texas, on this, the 27th day of February, 1992, in the English and Spanish languages.

Strategies for Drug Control and the Strengthening of the Administration of Justice

The Countries intend to strengthen unilateral, bilateral, and multilateral enforcement efforts and strengthen judicial systems to attack illicit trafficking in narcotic drugs, psychotropic substances, and precursor and essential chemicals. The Countries are determined to combat drug trafficking organizations through the arrest, prosecution, sentencing, and imprisonment of their leaders, lieutenants, members, accomplices, and accessories through the seizure and forfeiture of their assets, pursuant to the Countries' respective domestic legal systems and laws in force. To attain these objectives, the Countries intend to carry out coordinated cooperative actions through their national institutions.

Enforcement efforts cannot be carried out without economic programs such as alternative development.

The Countries request financial support from the international community in order to obtain funds for alternative development programs in nations that require assistance.

Training Centers

The Countries intend to provide training for the personnel who are responsible for or support the counter-drug battle in the signatory Countries at national training centers already in existence in the region. Emphasis will be given to the specialties of each of these centers in which personnel from governments of the other Countries may be enrolled as appropriate, in accordance with their respective legal systems. The signatory Countries, other governments, and international organizations are encouraged to provide financial and technical support for this training.

Regional Information Sharing

The Countries intend to expand reciprocal information sharing concerning the activities of organizations, groups, and persons engaged in illicit drug trafficking. The Countries will establish channels of communication to ensure the rapid dissemination of information for purposes of effective enforcement. This information sharing will be consistent with the security procedures, laws, and regulations of each country.

Control of Sovereign Air Space

The Countries recognize that drug traffickers move illicit drugs via identified air corridors and without regard to international borders or national airspace. The Countries also recognize that monitoring of airspace is an important factor in the apprehension of aircraft and crews involved in illicit drug traffic.

The Countries recognize that there is a need to exchange timely information on potential drug traffickers in and around each country's sovereign air space.

The Countries also agree to exchange information on their experiences and to provide one another with technical assistance in detecting, monitoring, and controlling aerial drug trafficking, when such assistance is requested in accordance with the domestic laws of each country and international laws in force.

Aircraft, Airfield, and Landing Strip Control

The Countries, recognizing that private and commercial aircraft are being utilized with increasing frequency in illicit trafficking of narcotic drugs and psychotropic substances, intend to establish and increase the necessary enforcement actions to prevent the utilization of such aircraft, pursuant to the domestic laws of each country and international regulations in force.

The Countries also intend, if necessary, to examine their domestic regulations pertaining to civil aviation in order to prevent the illicit use of aircraft and airports. They will also take the enforcement measures necessary to prevent the establishment of clandestine landing strips and eliminate those already in existence.

The Countries will cooperate closely with each other in providing mutual assistance when requested in order to investigate aircraft suspected of illicit drug trafficking. The Countries, pursuant to their domestic legal systems, also intend to seize and confiscate private aircraft when it has been proven that they have been used in the illicit traffic of narcotic drugs and psychotropic substances.

Maritime Control Actions

As called for in Article 17 of the 1988 United Nations Convention against Illicit Traffic in Narcotic Drugs and Psychotropic Substances, the Countries intend to strengthen cooperation to eliminate to the extent possible illicit trafficking by sea. To this end, they will endeavor to establish mechanisms to determine the most expeditious means to verify the registry and ownership of vessels suspected of illicit trafficking that are operating seaward of the territorial sea of any nation. The Countries further intend to punish illicit traffic in narcotic drugs and psychotropic substances by sea under their national laws.

Chemical Control Regimes

The Countries recognize that progress has been made in international efforts to eliminate the diversion of chemicals used in the illicit production of narcotic drugs and psychotropic substances. They specifically support the "Model Regulations to Control Chemical Precursors and Chemical Substances, Machines and Materials" of the Organization of American States, the chemical control measures adopted at the April 1991 International Drug Enforcement Conference (IDEC) meeting, and the recommendations in the Final Report of the Group of Seven Chemical Action Task Force, published in June 1991. The Countries call on all nations, and in particular, chemical exporting countries, to adopt the recommendations of the Group of Seven Chemical Action Task Force. They welcome the work of the above-mentioned Task Force and await with interest its report to the 1992 Economic Summit, in which it will make recommendations for the proper organization of worldwide control of those chemical products.

The Countries express their support for including ten additional chemicals in the United Nations Convention Against Illicit Traffic in Narcotic Drugs and Psychotropic Substances, as proposed by the United States on behalf of the Chemical Action Task Force in the U.S. notification to the Secretary General.

The Countries call on the International Narcotics Control Board to strengthen its actions aimed at controlling essential and precursor chemicals.

The Countries intend to investigate, in their respective countries, the legitimacy of significant commercial transactions in controlled chemical products. The Countries call on the chemical producing nations to establish an effective system for certification of end uses and end users.

The Countries will take appropriate legal action against companies violating chemical control regulations.

Studies will be conducted in the countries where narcotic drugs and psychotropic substances are produced in order to quantify the demand for chemicals for legitimate purposes in order to assist in the control of these products. The United States intends to provide financial and technical assistance for conducting the aforementioned studies and for setting up national data banks.

The Countries urge all nations and international organizations to cooperate effectively with programs aimed at strengthening border control in order to prevent the illegal entry of chemicals.

Port and Free Trade Zone Control

The Countries intend to implement measures to suppress illicit drug trafficking in free trade zones and ports, as called for in Article 18 of the 1988 United Nations Convention Against Illicit Traffic in Narcotic Drugs and Psychotropic Substances and in accordance with the recommendations of the Ninth International Drug Enforcement Conference. A group of experts may be required to conduct a specialized study in order to identify the ports and free trade zones and identify the vulnerable points in the ports and free trade zones in the region that could be utilized for illicit traffic in drugs and chemicals. This study and subsequent reviews will serve as the basis for adopting measures to prevent illicit traffic in drugs and controlled substances in ports and free trade zones.

Carrier Cooperation Agreement

The Countries are concerned about the difficulties inherent in the identification of suspicious shipments included in the great volume of legitimate commerce. In order to improve the effectiveness of border controls and also facilitate the transit of legitimate merchandise, the Countries intend to enlist the cooperation of air, land, and maritime transport companies. The Countries agree, in principle, to implement common standards and practices in order to include carriers in measure to improve anti-drug security.

Money Laundering

The 1988 United Nations Convention Against Illicit Traffic in Narcotic Drugs and Psychotropic Substances establishes a series of measures related to the control of financial assets to which the Countries intend to conform their domestic laws. The Countries support full implementation of this Convention, which requires, inter alia, the criminalization of all money laundering operations related to illicit drug traffic.

The Countries recognize and support the efforts of the Group of Seven Financial Action Task Force. The Countries call upon the Eleventh Meeting of senior-level OAS/CICAD officials to approve the Model Regulations on Money Laundering related to illicit drug traffic.

The Countries intend to make recommendations regarding the following:

- The elements of a comprehensive financial enforcement and money laundering control program;
- Exchange of financial information among governments in accordance with bilateral understandings.

Strengthening the Administration of Justice

The Countries recognize and support efforts designed to improve their judicial systems, in those cases in which this may be necessary, in order to ensure the effectiveness of those systems in establishing the culpability and penalties applicable to traffickers in illicit drugs. They recognize the need for adequate protection for the persons responsible for administering justice in this area inasmuch as effective legal systems are essential for democracy and economic programs.

The Countries call on all nations to strengthen the United Nations Drug Control Program.

Strengthening Judicial Cooperation

The Countries support the provisions of the 1988 United Nations Convention Against Illicit Traffic in Narcotic Drugs and Psychotropic Substances related to increased cooperation and mutual legal assistance in the battle against illicit drug trafficking, money laundering, and investigations and proceedings involving seizure and forfeiture. The Countries must consider approval of the projects of the OAS Inter-American Judicial Committee on mutual legal assistance in criminal matters and on precautionary measures.

The Countries will encourage the expeditious exchange of information and evidence needed for legal proceedings involving illicit drug trafficking, pursuant to their domestic laws and bilateral and multilateral agreements.

Sharing of Assets and Property

The Countries shall seek to conclude bilateral or multilateral agreements on the sharing of property seized and forfeited in the struggle against drug trafficking in accordance with the laws in force and the practices in each country. The Countries also consider that asset sharing would encourage international cooperation among law enforcement officials, and that confiscated property would be a valuable source of funds and equipment for combatting drug production and trafficking and for preventing drug consumption and treating addicts.

Firearms Control

The Countries recommend that measures to control firearms, ammunition, and explosives be strengthened in order to avoid their diversion to drug traffickers. The Countries also call for an enhanced exchange of detailed and complete information regarding seized weapons in order to facilitate the identification and determination of origin of such weapons, as well as the prosecution of those responsible for their illegal export.

To this end, the United States intends to tighten its export controls and to cooperate with the Governments of the other Countries to verify the legitimacy of end users.

The Countries consider that close cooperation with the OAS/CICAD is essential in such firearms, ammunition, and explosives control efforts.

Other Cooperative Arrangements

The Countries recognize that cooperative operations have been a useful tool in the war against drug traffickers in the past. The Countries intend to continue and expand such cooperative measures through their national organizations responsible for the struggle against illegal drug trafficking.

Strategies in the Economic and Financial Areas

The Countries propose to strengthen unilateral, bilateral and multilateral efforts aimed at improving economic conditions in the countries involved in the cycle of illegal drug production and trafficking. Extreme poverty and the growth of the drug problem are the main reasons that peasants become involved in illegal coca leaf production. The Countries reaffirm the principles in the Declaration of Cartagena, which accept that alternative economic development is an essential part of the comprehensive plan to reduce illegal trade in narcotic drugs and psychotropic substances. Alternative development cannot succeed in the absence of enforcement and interdiction efforts that effectively reduce this illegal drug trafficking.

The Countries recognize and approve of the structural changes that have taken place in the economies of the Andean countries and Mexico. These changes strengthen stability and increase prospects for economic growth. The Countries recognize that these reforms merit full support. Efforts to attract an increased flow of private investment will provide opportunities for sustained economic growth.

Economic Issues

The Countries recognize that the Enterprise for the Americas Initiative (EAI) with its three pillars—investment, trade, and debt—offers important means of improving economic conditions in the Hemisphere.

All of the Countries have signed bilateral trade and investment framework agreements with the United States. The Countries recognize that these agreements are important to encourage investment and trade liberalization, and they intend to move ahead with the three pillars of the EAI as follows:

Investment

The Countries recognize the critical importance of enacting laws and taking steps that encourage private investment and economic development. In this regard, the Countries have expressed their willingness to negotiate parallel bilateral agreements to protect intellectual property rights, as well as bilateral investment agreements, and others that promote trade liberalization. For this purpose, the Enterprise for the Americas Initiative includes trade and investment framework agreements.

The Countries express their satisfaction with the establishment of the Multilateral Investment Fund under the aegis of the Inter-American Development Bank. The Countries consider this Fund important to provide technical assistance and to encourage private investment.

The Countries note that the move towards a market economy in Latin America is a good vehicle for generating sustained economic growth, with benefits throughout society. They therefore view with interest experiences in privatizing services and industries that can serve to attract a significant flow of direct foreign investment. The initiation of operations by the Multilateral Investment Fund and technical assistance in support of privatization efforts will aid in the development of market economies. Some Andean countries plan to proceed with privatization programs and reforms of financial systems to the degree and depth possible in each country.

The Andean countries state that facilitating access to the 936 funds would have a catalytic effect in attracting private investment to that subregion.

The profound structural changes in the region make the active participation of financial entities in funding private projects more important than ever before. The Countries urge entities such as the International Finance Corporation (IFC) and the Inter-American Investment Corporation (IIC) to continue working with the Andean region. The countries of the Andean region are pleased by Mexico's participation as a stockholder in the Andean Development Corporation (ADC), which is a suitable channel for development activity in the subregion, particularly for the private sector, within a framework of productive integration. These countries express their interest in also being able to count on active participation by the United States Government in the ADC. The United States takes note of that interest.

Trade

The Countries express their satisfaction regarding enactment of the Andean Trade Preference Act which allows the countries of the Andean region to export a wide variety of products to the United States for a ten-year period without paying duties. Those eligible countries that wish to benefit from this law will take the required steps. The United States, furthermore, plans to implement the provisions of this law as rapidly as possible in order to extend its benefits to the countries determined to fulfill the criteria in the Law. The Andean countries also express their interest in having these preferences extended to Venezuela.

The Countries recognize that the proposed North American Free Trade Agreement will be an important step in the process of creating a hemispheric free trade agreement in accordance with the Enterprise for the Americas Initiative. The Countries stress the importance of continued economic integration and trade liberalization efforts.

Debt

The Countries express their satisfaction with the progress achieved by some Andean countries and Mexico in renegotiating their debt with the private international banking system and intend, when appropriate, to continue to support reduction of this debt. The Countries point out that the economic reforms implemented by Bolivia have already made it possible for that country to benefit from the reduction of a large part of its bilateral debt with the United States under the auspices and in the spirit of the Enterprise for the Americas Initiative, which will make it possible to implement environmental projects in Bolivia. The Government of the United States will continue to take the necessary steps to obtain the legislative approval required for the debt categories that still do not have this authorization.

Alternative Development

The Countries acknowledge that the goals of the Cartagena Declaration regarding the substitution of other agricultural products for coca and other plants that feed the drug cycle, and the creation of new sources of licit income, have not yet been fully achieved. The Countries note that in a major new initiative, the United States—in consultation with Bolivia, Colombia, Ecuador and Peru—is engaged in a program to provide training and technical assistance in agricultural marketing that will stress participation by the private sector as well as assistance for animal and plant health. The Countries applaud this program and intend to facilitate its implementation to the maximum extent possible.

Notwithstanding assistance already pledged by the United States and the United Nations, the Countries recognize the need to establish a broad basis of funding for alternative development. For this reason, and given the worldwide range of illicit narcotics, the Countries intend to strive for increased participation of countries such as Japan and others as well as international financial agencies and institutions such as the World Bank, the Inter-American Development Bank, the European Community, the OAS, the OECD and others. The Andean nations believe, and the United States takes note, that such actions should also include the establishment of a facility for alternative development in an international financial institution. The Countries are determined to enlist the support of the international community in their fight against drugs.

The Countries support the work of the OAS/CICAD Group of Experts charged with reviewing the alternative development approach and recommending ways to enhance it.

Under the alternative development program, the Countries recognize the importance of implementing short-term projects such as emergency food programs, food for work, and income and employment generation. The Countries recognize that these efforts must simultaneously accompany eradication efforts in order to reduce the economic impact on coca leaf producers. These short-term actions must be aimed at producing jobs and temporary income until such time as the alternative development projects are fully developed.

The Countries underscore the need for alternative development programs to be strengthened in coca leaf producing countries, or in those countries with areas that have potential for producing plants from which elements utilizable in the production of narcotics and psychotropic drugs can be extracted, so as to reduce the supply of raw material that feeds the narco-trafficking cycle. These programs will help farmers have different economic alternatives, which will allow them to move away from illegal coca production.

The Countries acknowledge the progress achieved in alternative development in Bolivia and the beginning of alternative development activities in Peru. In this context, the Countries note the bilateral agreements with the United States signed by Peru and by Bolivia to implement alternative economic development and drug control programs, as useful experiences applicable to other countries. These two most salient examples are summarized as follows:

Bolivia

In Bolivia, with the firm support of the United States, efforts undertaken to develop other crops in coca producing zones, as well as in those areas from which people have been expelled, are having some success, starting with the production of genetic material with a proven biological viability, acceptable rate of return and a potential for export. Technical assistance and credit, as well as continuing training of farmers, permits the achievement of a good level of technology transfer.

Actions taken in the infrastructure area have made it possible to improve the means of transporting agricultural products to consumer markets and processing them.

Aggressive marketing is slowly allowing the opening of internal markets to the first items of this production, in accordance with phytosanitary and quality control requirements. The support being given to the social dimension by providing infrastructure in the health and education sectors is making it possible to improve the quality of life of the rural population.

A new five-year project, which will start in early June of 1992, will provide continuity and strengthen key activities, such as marketing and private investment.

Multilateral cooperation through the United Nations Drug Control Program (UNDCP) has also assisted in the alternative development process, especially in basic sanitation, roads, energy and agroindustry.

Nevertheless, based on the above-mentioned Bolivian experiences it is recommended that:

1. Recognition be given to the fact that implementation of coca reduction policy has to be adapted to the pace of alternative development in order to reduce the gap between the loss of income and its replacement. It is evident that the success in alternative development will discourage farmers from growing coca.

2. Recognition be given to the importance of full and active participation by the farmers in alternative development processes.

3. Bilateral and multilateral cooperation in alternative development be considered with regard to its specificity. It should include comprehensive, multisectoral and long-term program guidance and should also be sufficiently flexible, broad and timely to be able to promote qualitative changes beyond the short term.

Peru

In the case of Peru, progress can be summarized by the following points:

- The participation of the United States Government and Japan in the support group for the reentry of Peru into the international financial community. This allows the IDB and other bilateral donors to provide funds.
- The carrying out of massive food aid programs, promotion of a favorable economic policy framework for the development of the private sector and the liberalization of two-way trade.
- The existence of projects, especially in the Upper Huallaga Valley where 14,000 farmers have received technical assistance in seed research, production, and marketing. The project provided credit and land titles and made it possible to resurface 1,200 kilometers of roads and to set up potable water systems, health posts and latrines.
- The massive support received by President Fujimori from the rural population in coca producing areas.
- Plans for 1992 that call for the resurfacing of the road linking the Upper Huallaga Valley to the coast, a program for recognizing and awarding property rights, and the participation of multinational firms interested in investing in alternative development projects.
- All this has been achieved in spite of insidious narco-trafficking, terrorism and the alliance between the two. Under the Agreement on Narcotics Control and Alternative Development signed on May 14, 1991, which includes aspects relating to interdiction and security, an

autonomous Peruvian institution will be responsible for distributing the necessary resources. This institution and its U.S. counterpart will hold meetings to implement the shared strategy, immediately after the Presidential Summit in San Antonio.

- With respect to respect to human rights, the importance of conducting the anti-drug struggle within the framework of international standards is stressed.
- With respect to the citizens' commitment to the anti-drug effort, emphasis is placed on the need for them to have access to information and for efficient legal and administrative systems to exist.
- In order to have adequate farmer participation, consideration should be given, among other requirements, to:
  a. Creating the democratic tools that make it possible to involve the people directly in the decision-making process;
  b. Recognizing, awarding, and registering property rights;
  c. Concluding crop substitution agreements with farmers;
  d. Ensuring that eradication programs take into account the safeguarding of human health and preservation of the ecosystem;
  e. Fostering new economic opportunities, such as alternative development and crop substitution programs, that will help to dissuade growers from initiating or expanding illegal cultivation;
  f. Implementing reforestation programs in those areas where coca has been eradicated but where the land is not suitable for farming;
  g. Substantially facilitating access to business activity and to credit;
  h. Abolishing bureaucratic obstacles and mechanisms, particularly those that limit the production, marketing, and exploration of alternative goods;
  i. Promoting the participation of all countries interested in providing technical solutions and conducting specific alternative development projects with the peasants and/or their organizations.

The Environment

The Countries express their concern regarding the severe damage that coca cultivation and illegal processing of coca derivatives are causing to the environment of the Andean region. The slash-and-burn method employed by coca and opium poppy growers causes severe erosion of the soil, and indiscriminate disposal of the toxic chemicals used to produce coca derivatives is poisoning the rivers and the water table. These activities enrich a small group of traffickers and cause harm to thousands of people.

The United States Government notes that it is helping the Andean governments address the serious environmental problems caused by illegal coca and opium production. The United States is providing technical assistance and training under comprehensive environmental management programs that are important components of alternative development projects. The United States is providing assistance for watershed management, farm-level and community forestry, reforestation and environmental restoration, education on environmental problems, and environmental monitoring programs. These efforts are designed to prevent damage to—and to restore—the soil, water, and forest resources, thereby improving the quality of life and expanding opportunities for those who abandon, or never initiate, coca production in favor of alternative crops. The Countries agree that such technical assistance and training services must be designed to strengthen the capacity of Andean governments to protect their countries' natural environment.

The Countries agree to design and implement suitable programs to reduce the negative ecological impact of coca production and ensure that security, interdiction, and substitution activities take the protection of the ecosystem into account.

Strategies for Prevention and Demand Reduction

The Countries recognize that consumption of, and illicit traffic in, drugs and psychotropic substances are a comprehensive problem, and that it can therefore be resolved only if control, interdiction, and supply reduction measures are accompanied by vigorous and effective action in demand reduction.

It is also necessary for society, including its members who consume illegal drugs and those who are involved in illicit drug traffic or the cultivation of plants intended for conversion into illicit drugs, to be made aware of the harmful consequences of the production, traffic, and consumption of illicit drugs. It is imperative to provide warnings about the dangers of violence, crime, corruption, environmental damage, addiction, and the dissolution of society and the family resulting from the drug problem.

The Countries are convinced that raising awareness regarding the harmful impact of drug-related offenses will motivate society to develop a culture that rejects drug use and to support vigorously efforts to combat supply and demand. In order to support this awareness campaign, the Countries agree to assume the responsibility, either individually or jointly, to conduct long-term programs to inform the public through the appropriate mass media and other information resources.

The Countries also call on their respective private sectors to combine efforts to create a culture that rejects drugs.

In this regard, the Countries are aware that demand can be controlled and reduced and that the basis can be laid for increasing awareness by means of continuous, systematic actions that include:

Prevention

The Countries consider that prevention must be a priority aspect of national strategies to reduce the demand for drugs.

In order to prevent consumption of drugs and dissuade occasional users, the Countries must include in their national and drug control strategies comprehensive prevention programs that include, among other things:

Education

The Countries recognize that education is fundamental in the upbringing of the individual and the creation of positive values and attitudes toward life, and that the educational system at all levels and in all its forms is a suitable tool to reach most of the people. Consequently, the Countries undertake to engage in additional educational efforts for comprehensive prevention of drug use from pre-school through higher education, by means of scientific research, in order to create an attitude and a culture that rejects drugs and in which the family and the community play a fundamental role.

Community Mobilization

The Countries wish to emphasize the importance mobilizing all sectors of society against drugs as a fundamental part of national prevention efforts. This mobilization includes carrying out actions at the individual, family, and social levels by means of activities that include recreation, sports, and cultural events that make it possible to achieve a total rejection of drug consumption.

Treatment and Rehabilitation

In order for drug addicts to receive suitable assistance, the Countries consider that it is necessary to increase their capacity with regard to treatment and rehabilitation, in addition to improving the quality of services. The Countries consider that these programs must be designed not only to rehabilitate drug addicts but also to help them reenter society.

The Countries believe that treatment and rehabilitation are basic in reducing the consequences arising from drug use, including AIDS transmission, societal violence, and the destruction of the family and social structure.

Scientific Research

The Countries recognize that it is necessary to establish programs for basic and social research, including epidemiology, in their national strategies. Epidemiological programs must be conducted using a methodology that makes it possible to compare findings at the regional and international levels. These findings will also be useful in evaluating prevention programs. The Countries undertake to exchange information on drug abuse through a regional information network and to support initiatives to establish a data bank on this subject, especially within the framework of CICAD.

Training

The Countries undertake to cooperate by providing appropriate technical assistance for the education and training of human resources in these areas.

The Countries will also endeavor to consult with one another and exchange information on the prevention of illicit drug use, treatment, rehabilitation, and scientific research. In this regard, they agree to cooperate in order to determine the most effective ways to utilize the research findings in implementing the various programs.

National Councils

The Countries are convinced that the creation of national councils to coordinate efforts to develop strategies against illicit drugs has made an important contribution to the development of prevention, treatment, and rehabilitation programs in all countries.

Follow-Up

The Countries undertake to engage in on-going follow-up of the actions described above. To that end, they will assign responsibility to their national councils in line with OAS/CICAD programs.

March

SAUDI ARABIA'S
FIRST CONSTITUTION
March 1, 1992

Without relinquishing any of his own power, King Fahd ibn Abdul-Aziz on March 1 decreed the rudiments of a new "main law" for Saudi Arabia that would expand citizens' participation in government and guarantee certain protections in writing for the first time. Fahd emphasized that Moslem "general principles" would continue to guide the nation and that "The kingdom of Saudi Arabia is an Arab and Islamic sovereign state, its religion is Islam, and its constitution the Holy Quran [Koran]" and the teachings of the prophet Muhammad. As the document made clear, the three authorities of government were "the judicial, executive, and organizational," and the "king is the reference to all of these...."

The order was issued by a king whose family members held many, if not most, of the prominent government posts, as had long been the royal family's prerogative. The lengthy and detailed statement marked the first time in the monarchy's sixty-year history—which dated from the founding of the nation—that it had tried to fashion a constitution.

Background: U.S. Interest

The United States followed the Saudi developments with particular interest, for several reasons. Saudi Arabia had provided the launching point for much of the U.S. and allied actions in Kuwait and Iraq during the "Desert Storm" operation of early 1991. (Related Stories, Historic Documents of 1991, pp. 3, 15, 97, 121) The Saudi government, although autocratic by most assessments, had been considered somewhat moderate regarding Middle East politics. The United States, members of the European Community, Japan, and others had a sizable stake in guaran-

teeing imports of Saudi oil, although global reliance on Middle East oil supplies had diminished considerably during the 1980s.

As with many nations in the region, Saudi Arabia was somewhat of an enigma for the United States; it provided crucial launching stations for joint U.S./Saudi surveillance aircraft over the neighboring Middle East and other countries during numerous crises, but Saudi Arabia remained adamantly opposed to the existence of the Jewish nation of Israel.

Particularly after the "Desert Storm" operation, some observers questioned the condoning of autocratic regimes such as those in Saudi Arabia and Kuwait, while openly opposing that of Saddam Hussein, the tenacious dictator who still held power in Iraq despite efforts of the United States and its allies to unseat him. Some speculated that it was partly in response to these concerns that Saudi King Fahd announced the changes in his government. Indeed, Fahd acknowledged this pressure, saying that "momentous events in the recent past ... have made it necessary to develop the country's administrative structure."

Monarchy Remains, with Modifications

Although the monarchy remained, strongly embedded in Islam, King Fahd acknowledged that Saudi Arabia had been in a "constitutional vacuum." The king announced plans to expand political participation by establishing a sixty-one-member advisory council, whose members he would name, to oversee the royal court. The council would have the authority to question cabinet ministers and propose laws.

For the first time in Saudi history, Fahd's document spelled out rules for succession, stating that the crown would be given to "the most suitable" son and grandson of the kingdom's founder, King Abdul Aziz ibn Saud, rather than the eldest, as had been the case. The seventy-year-old Fahd declared that "the king will choose his crown prince and relieve him from his duty by a royal order," suggesting that the crown prince would not necessarily be made the permanent ruler. That was a major break in a tradition, where the crown prince—whose appointment was the result of negotiations within the ruling house—had been routinely considered to be the successor. However, Fahd also declared that succession would "be confined" to the sons and grandsons of the kingdom's founder.

The document contained elements of the U.S. Constitution's Bill of Rights in that it prohibited arbitrary arrest and entry into private homes, but the rights to free speech and free press were not mentioned. The plan provided for the king's appointment of provincial councils, which would have limited authority over local matters. The king decreed that judges should be independent.

Mixed Assessment

Outside attention focused mostly on the constitution's provisions for succession, which reportedly had been controversial within the royal family (which included more than thirty of Fahd's surviving sons) and the establishment of a consultative assembly. "They are conceding the principle of political participation and political institutionalization," said one Saudi professional.

Regarding the provision that allowed the king to fire the crown prince, Brookings Institution analyst William Quandt said, "That's new. Normally the king wouldn't have the unilateral power" to designate another successor. Article Five states that "When the king dies, the crown prince succeeds him until enthronement." The current crown prince is Abdullah, Fahd's half-brother.

An unidentified Saudi official close to the royal court was quoted in the March 2 Washington Post as saying, "The ultra-left will not see enough reform and the ultra-right will be very, very disappointed that the emphasis on sharia [Islamic law] will only be in general terms." Other observers noted that the king still retained principal power over the government, armed forces, and billions of dollars of treasury funds.

Following is the text of the "basic system of government" decreed March 1, 1992, by King Fahd ibn Abdul-Aziz, as provided by the official Saudi Press Agency in Washington, D.C.:

The basic system of government, the consultative council, and the provincial system were announced by the custodian of the two holy mosques, King Fahd ibn Abdul-Aziz, during an extraordinary session of the council of ministers.

'While taking into account the public interests and developments in all spheres, I, King Fahd ibn Adul-Aziz al-saud, the king of the Kingdom of Saudi Arabia, order the following:

Firstly:

issuance of the basic system as in the attached formula.

Secondly:

work will continue by all ongoing regulations, instructions and resolutions when this system is implemented until amendments take place.

Thirdly:

this system should be published in the official gazette. In the name of Allah, the most merciful and beneficient.

I.

Chapter One: The General Principles:

The First Article:

The kingdom of Saudi Arabia is an Arab and Islamic sovereign state, its religion is Islam, and its constitution the Holy Quran [Koran] and the prophet's Sunnah. Its language is Arabic and capital Riyadh.

The Second Article:

The festivals of the state are eid al-fitr and eid al-adha and its calender is the hijri calender.

The Third Article:

The flag of the state is as follows:

- A-its colour is green.
- B-its width is equal to the third of its length.
- C-it will carry 'La Ilah Illah Allah and Mohammed Rasoul Ullah and it will never be unfurled.

The Fourth Article:

The emblem of the state is two intersected swords and a palm tree. The system determines the national anthem and the medals.

The Second Chapter:

The Fifth Article:

- A-the system of the Kingdom of Saudi Arabia is a monarchy.
- B-its rule will be confined to the sons of the kingdom's founder Abdul-Aziz Ibn Abdel-Rahman Al-Faisal Al-Saud and grandsons. The most suitable of them will be enthroned to rule under the guidance of the Holy Quran and the prophet's Sunnah.
- C-the king will choose his crown prince and relieve him from his duty by a royal order.
- D-the crown prince will be assigned to carry out the work of the crown prince and the duties delegated to him by the king.
- E-when the king dies, the crown prince succeeds him until enthronement.

The Sixth Article:

The citizens will take allegiance before the monarch in line with the Holy Quran and the prophet's Sunnah.

The Seventh Article:

The rule in the kingdom depends on the Holy Quran and the prophet's Sunnah.

The Eighth Article:

The rule in the kingdom is based on justice, consultations and equality in accordance with the Islamic Shariah.

[The Third Chapter]: The Constituents of the Saudi Society:

The Ninth Article:

The family is the nucleus of the Saudi society and its members are grown up on the basis of the Islamic Creed and obedience to the almighty God, prophet and rulers and respect of the system, love of the homeland and pride of its history.

The Tenth Article:

The state is keen on enhancing relations among members of the family, preserving the Arab and Islamic values and taking care of all members and enable them to develop their skills.

The 11th Article:

The Saudi society is based on dependence on the almighty God and cooperation.

The 12th Article:

The state is keen on enhancing national unity and prevention of all kinds of seditions.

The 13th Article:

The education aims at implantation of the Islamic Creed in the new generations, development of their skills so as to enable them to contribute to the building of their society.

The Fourth Chapter: The Economic Principles:

The 14th Article:

All the wealth inside the ground or on its surface or in the territorial waters or in the land and sea-range as well as all resources of these wealth is owned by the state as will be shown by the system. The system shows means for the exploitation of the wealth, its protection and development in a manner that serves the interests of the state, its security and economy.

The 15th Article:

There will be no concessions or investment for one of the resources of the country, except those allowed only according to the system.

The 16th Article:

The state should protect the public properties and the citizens and residents should preserve them.

The 17th Article:

Ownership, capital and work are basic constituents of the kingdom's economic and social system.

The 18th Article:

The state allows the freedom of personal property and could not be expropriated except for the public sake after compensation.

The 19th Article:

Confiscation of public properties is prohibited. Confiscation is only according to the judicial verdict.

The 20th Article:

Taxes and fees are not levied except when there is a need for that on just bases. They are not levied, amended or canceled except in accordance to the system.

The 21st Article:

Zakat (Alms) is to be collected and spent according to the Sharia teachings.

The 22nd Article:

The economic and social development is carried out in the light of a scientific and just plan.

The Fifth Chapter: Duties and Rights:

The 23rd Article:

The state protects the Islamic Creed and carries out its shari'a and undertakes its duty towards the Islamic call.

The 24th Article:

The state services the two Holy Mosques and ensures the security and safety of their visitors so as to enable them to perform their rituals in comfort and ease.

The 25th Article:

The state is keen on realization of the hopes of the Arab and Muslim nation in solidarity and unity and at the same time enhances its relations with the friendly states.

The 26th Article:

The state protects the rights of the people in line with the Islamic Sharia.

The 27th Article:

The state ensures the rights of the citizens and their families in case of emergency, disease, disability and eldership and supports the social insurance system and encourages the establishments and individuals to contribute to charitable works.

The 28th Article:

The state helps all abled-people to obtain jobs and enacts laws to protect the worker and the owner of the work.

The 29th Article:

The state takes care of sciences, arts, culture and encourages scientific research, preserves the Arab and Islamic heritage and contributes to the Arab, Islamic and human civilization.

The 30th Article:

The state makes education available and adheres to the principle of illiteracy eradication.

The 31st Article:

The state takes care of public health and makes health care available.

The 32nd Article:

The state undertakes preservation, protection and development of the environment and prevents pollution.

The 33rd Article:

The state establishes the armed forces and enables them to take their responsibility towards the defence of the Islamic Creed, the two Holy Mosques, the society and the homeland.

The 34th Article:

Defence of the Islamic Creed, society, and the homeland are the responsibility of all. The system clarifies the rules of military services.

The 35th Article:

The system clarifies the rules of Saudi Arabian nationality.

The 36th Article:

The state ensures the security of all citizens and residents and nobody has the right to harass, arrest or imprison anyone except under the rules of the system.

The 37th Article:

Nobody is allowed to enter the houses without the permission of their owners and nobody has the right to probe them except in accordance with the system.

The 38th Article:

The penalty is personal, and no crime or penalty except in the line of a Shariah text or the regulations and no penalty except in accordance to the regulations.

The 39th Article:

The information and publication media should express in a good manner and abide by the regulations of the state and contribute to the culturing of the nation and supporting its unity. All that lead to sedition and disunity or undermines the state's security and public relations or insults the dignity and rights of the people. The regulations will clarify this.

The 40th Article:

Nobody has the right to confiscate, delay or get informed with the cables, postal items, or telephone call and other means of telecommunications except according to the regulations set by the system.

The 41st Article:

The residents in the kingdom of Saudi Arabia will adhere to its regulations and they should respect the values of the Saudi society, traditions and feelings.

The 42nd Article:

The state gives political asylum if the public interest necessitates that and the regulations and international agreements will clarify the procedures pertaining to extradition of the criminals.

The 43rd Article:

The council of the king and the council of the crown prince are open for all citizens and everyone has the right to clarify his problem.

The Sixth Chapter: The State's Authorities:

The 44th Article:

The authorities of the state comprise the judicial authority, the executive authority and the organizational authority.

All these authorities cooperate in performing their responsibilities and the king is the reference of all these authorities.

The 45th Article:

The source of ifta in the kingdom of Saudi Arabia is the Holy Quran and the prophet's Sunna and the system clarifies the hierarchy of the senior Ulama and the administration of the scientific researches and ifta and their responsibilities.

The 46th Article:

The judicial authority is an independent organ and nobody has an authority on the judges except the authority of the Islamic Shariah.

The 47th Article:

All people either citizens or residents in the kingdom are entitled to suit files on equal basis, the system will clarify the required procedures.

The 48th Article:

The system of judges is applied on all cases presented before the Shari'a rules according to the teachings of the Holy Quran and Sunnah and the regulations set by the ruler provided that they do not contradict with the Holy Quran and Sunnah.

The 49th Article:

In the light of what has been stipulated in the Article 53 of this system, the courts will be specialized for the settlement of the disputes.

The 50th Article:

The king or whomsoever he may deputize will be concerned about the implementation of the judicial rules.

The 51st Article:

The system will determine the formation of the supreme judicial council and its specialization as well as the organization and specializations of various courts.

The 52nd Article:

Judges will be appointed and relieved of their duties by a royal decree according to a proposal by the supreme judicial council and according to the system's regulations.

The 53rd Article:

The system will determine the organization and specializations of the board of grievances.

The 54th Article:

The system will determine the organization and specializations of the department of investigations and public prosecution.

The 55th Article:

The king will rule the nation according to the rulings of Islam and supervise the application of Sharia (Islamic laws), the state's general policy and the protection and defence of the country.

The 56th Article:

The king acts as prime minister and is assisted in the performance of his duties by members of the council of ministers, according to the rulings of this and other systems. The system of the council of ministers will determine the authorities of the council, in connection with internal and external affairs. The organization of government authorities and coordinating their work. It will also determine the qualities that must be found in ministers, the authorities invested in them, the method of questioning them and all their affairs. The system and specializations of the council of ministers will be modified according to this system.

The 57th Article:

A-the king will appoint deputy prime ministers and cabinet ministers and relieve them of their duties by a royal decree.

B-the deputy prime ministers and cabinet ministers are responsible before the king for the application of Islamic Sharia, systems and the state's general policy.

C-the king has the right to dissolve the council of ministers and re-structure it.

The 58th Article:

The king will appoint ministers, deputy ministers and officials of the excellent grade or relieve them of their duties by a royal decree and according to the rulings of the system.

Ministers and heads of independent authorities are responsible for their ministries or authorities before the prime minister.

The 59th Article:

The system will determine the rulings of civil service, including salaries, rewards, compensations, privileges and retirement pensions.

The 60th Article:

The king is the supreme commander of all armed forces and he appoints officers or ends their service according to the system.

The 61st Article:

The king has the right to declare a state of emergency, general recruitment and war. The system will determine relevant rulings.

The 62nd Article:

If a danger threatens the safety of the kingdom, the unity of its lands or impede the state institutions' performance of their duties, the king has the right to take the necessary speedy measures to face this danger. If the king decides that these measures should be continuous, he would make the necessary decision to make them so.

The 63rd Article:

The king will receive heads of states, appoint his representatives in other countries and accept accredition of the representatives of other countries in the kingdom.

The 64th Article:

The king will award medals according to the relevant clauses of the system.

The 65th Article:

The king has the right to delegate some authorities to the crown prince by a royal decree.

The 66th Article:

In case of his travel abroad, the king will issue a royal decree to deputize the crown prince in running the affairs of the state and look after the interests of the people as stated in the royal decree.

The 67th Article:

The organizational authority will draw up systems and regulations to realize interests or eliminate corruption in the affairs of the state, according to the rulings of the Islamic Shari'a, and practice its specializations according to this system and the systems of the councils of ministers and Shura.

The 68th Article:

The system of the Shura council will determine the method of its formation, the method of practicing its specializations and selecting its members.

The king has the right to dissolve the Shura council and re-structure it.

The 69th Article:

The king has the right to call the council of ministers and Shura for a joint meeting and invite whoever he wishes to attend this meeting and discuss whatever issues he raises.

The 70th Article:

Systems, treaties, international agreements and privileges will be issued and modified by royal decrees.

The 71st Article:

Systems will be published in the official Gazette and deemed effective as of the date of their publication, unless another date is mentioned.

Section 7: Financial Affairs:

The 72nd Article:

The system will determine the rulings of the state revenues and their delivery to the state treasury.

The 73rd Article:

No obligation should be made to pay funds from the state treasury except in accordance with the provisions of the budget. Should the provisions of the budget not suffice for paying such funds, a royal decree must be issued for their payment.

The 74th Article:

The assets of the state should not be sold, rented or dealt with except in accordance with the systems.

The 75th Article:

The system will determine the rulings of monetary agencies, banks, standards, measures, and weights.

The 76th Article:

The system will determine the state's fiscal year. The budget will be issued by a royal decree and will include an estimate of this year's revenues and expenditures. It will be issued at least one month before the beginning of the fiscal year. Should emergency reasons arise and prevent its issuance before the beginning of the new fiscal year, the budget of the previous fiscal year should be followed until a new one has been issued.

The 77th Article:

The concerned authority will prepare the state's final accounts for the ending fiscal year and submit it to the prime minister.

The 78th Article:

The budgets and final accounts of authorities of generally moral nature will be subject to the rulings of the state budget and its final account.

Section 8: Control Authorities:

The 79th Article:

All revenues, expenditures, and fixed aid mobile assets of the state will be controlled and made sure they are well-utilized and kept. An annual report on this control will be submitted to the prime minister. The system will determine the relevant control authority and its specializations.

The 80th Article:

Government authorities will be controlled to ensure their good performance and the application of systems. Financial and administrative violations will be investigated and annual report on them will be submitted to the prime minister.

The systems will determine the relevant authority and its specializations.

Section 9: General Rulings:

The 81st Article:

The implementation of this system does not violate the treaties and agreements the kingdom is committed to with other countries, or international organizations and institutions.

The 82nd Article:

Noting that the seventh article of this system should not be violated, no one of the rulings of this system should, in any way, be obstructed, unless it is a temporary measure during a time of war and as shown in the system.

The 83rd Article:

No amendment of this system should be made except in the same manner of its issuance.

II.

In line with the requirements of the public interest and the desire to achieve the state's goals pertaining to the upgrading of the performance of the government organs at different parts and to develop them in a manner fit with the development achieved by the state, custodian of the two Holy Mosques King Fahd announced the provincial system according to the attached draft.

The system will be put into effect within one year from its publication.

The system shall be published in the official gazette.

Article 1:

This system aims at upgrading the level of the administrative work and development in all parts of the kingdom. It also aims at the preservation of security and order, the rights of citizens and their freedom in the framework of the Islamic Sharia.

Article 2:

The kingdom's regions and the headquarters of each governorate shall be approved by a royal decree upon the recommendation of the minister of interior.

Article 3:

Each province shall be made of a number of governorates, districts and centers. This division shall take into consideration the population, the geography, security, environment and transportation means in each region. The organisation of the province shall be according to a royal decree upon the recommendation of the minister of interior. The districts and centers shall be organized according to a resolution to be issued by the minister of interior and upon the proposal to be made by the governor of the province.

Article 4:

Each province shall have a governor with the rank of a minister and shall have a deputy at the excellent grade who shall assist the governor in the discharge of his works and acting for him during his absence. Governors and their deputies shall be appointed and relieved by a royal decree upon the recommendation of the minister of interior.

Article 5:

The governor of the province shall answer to the minister of interior.

Article 6:

The governor and his deputy shall be sworn in before the king before they assume their works.

Article 7:

Each governor shall administer his province according to the state's general policy, the provisions of this system and other rules and regulations.

He shall be responsible for the following:

- A-preservation of security, order and stability and to take the necessary measures in this connection according to rules and regulations.
- B-implementation of the judicial rules after their final endorsement.
- C-insure the rights of individuals and their freedom and refrain from any act that will affect these rights and freedom except within the limits stipulated in the laws and regulations.
- D-work to develop the province in social, economic and urban terms.

- E-work to develop the public services in the province and promote their efficiency.
- F-management of the provinces, districts and centers and supervision of the works of the governors of provinces, directors of districts and heads of centers to make sure of their compatibility to carry out their duties.
- G-preservation of the state's wealth and properties and prevention of any trespassing.
- H-supervision of the government departments and their personnel in the region to make sure of their good performance of their duties with full honesty and diligence. Consideration shall be given to the fact that the employees of the ministries and departments in the region are answerable to their ministries and departments.
- I-direct contact with ministers and heads of departments for discussing affairs of the region with them with the aim of promoting the performance of the departments.
- J-present annual reports to the minister of interior on the efficiency of the public utilities in the region and other affairs of the region according to the implementing rules of the system.

Article 8:

An annual meeting will be held for province governors, under the chairmanship of the minister of interior, to discuss issues pertaining to the provinces and the minister of the interior will submit a report on it to the prime minister.

Article 9:

The governor of each province will hold a meeting for rulers of governorates and directors of districts at least twice a year to discuss the affairs of the province. The governor will submit a report on the outcome to the minister of the interior.

Article 10:

- A-One or more deputy governors will be appointed for each province, at an administrative grade not less than the 14th grade, with cabinet resolutions, according to the recommendation of the minister of the interior.
- B-Each governorate will have a governor, whose administrative grade will not be less than the 14th grade. He will be appointed by the prime minister's order and according to the recommendation of the minister of the interior. Each governorate will have a deputy governor, whose administrative grade will not be less than the 12th. He will be appointed by an interior minister's decision and according to the recommendation of the province's governor.
- C-Each district will have a director, whose administrative grade should

not be less than the 8th. He will be appointed by the minister of the interior according to the recommendation of the province governor.
- D-Each centre will have a chairman, whose administrative grade should not be less than the 5th. He will be appointed by the province governor according to the recommendation of a governorate ruler.

Article 11:

Province governors, governorate governors, district directors and centre chairmen will preside at their place of work and should not leave it without a permission from their superiors.

Article 12:

Governorate governors, district directors and centre chairmen will perform their duties within the administrative framework of their assignments and the limits of the authorities invested in them.

Article 13:

Governorate governors should run their governorates within the framework of the specializations outlined in the seventh article with the exception of provisions F, I and J of this article. They will control the work of district directors and centre chairmen affiliated to them and make sure of their efficiency. They will submit regular reports to the province governor on the performance of public services and other government affairs, according to the executive regulations of this system.

Article 14:

Every ministry or government authority serving the province must appoint a chairman of its branches in the province with an administrative grade not less than the 12th. He will be directly linked with the central authority and should coordinate his work with the province governor.

Article 15:

Each province will have a provincial council at the province headquarters.

Article 16:

The province council will comprise:

- A-The province governor as a chairman of the council.
- B-The vice-governor of the province as deputy chairman of the council.
- C-The deputy governor of the province and governors of the governorates.
- D-The heads of government authorities named by the prime minister in the province, according to the recommendation of the minister of the interior.

- E-At least 10 well-qualified and experienced citizens will be appointed by the prime minister, according to the recommendation of the province governor and pursuant to the approval of the minister of the interior. Their membership will last for four years and will be renewable.

Article 17:

Members of the council must be a Saudi, born and raised in the kingdom, known for his efficiency and righteousness, not younger than thirty and living in the province.

Article 18:

A member can submit written proposals to the province council's chairman, if it is related to the council's affairs. The chairman will include every proposal in the council's agenda to be studied.

Article 19:

A province council member should not attend the discussions of the council or its committees, if the issue is related to a personal interest of his, the interest of some one the member can not testify for or if he is a guardian or a deputy of somebody who has a personal interest.

Article 20:

If an appointed member wishes to resign, he should submit a request to this effect to the minister of the interior through the province governor. The resignation will not be considered effective unless the prime minister approves, according to the recommendation of the minister of the interior.

Article 21:

In circumstances not mentioned in this system, an appointed member can not be sacked before the end of his term except with an order from the prime minister according to the recommendation of the minister of the interior.

Article 22:

In case a member's seat becomes vacant for any reason, another member would be appointed within three months. The term of office of the new member would be the remaining period of his predecessor's term as stated in item E of article 16 of this system.

Article 23:

The province council will study all elements aiming at upgrading services in the province and perform the following duties:

- A-Determining the needs of the province and suggesting including them in the state development plan.

- B-Determining the useful projects according to their priorities and proposing their approval in the annual state budget.
- C-Studying the organizational plans of the province's cities and villages and following up their implementation after approving them.
- D-Following up the implementation of clauses of the development plan and budget related to the province.

Article 24:

The province council will propose any useful work for the citizens of the province and encourage citizens to participate in it. It will also submit a report on it to the minister of the interior.

Article 25:

The province council will be prevented from probing any issue different from its specializations named in this system. Its resolutions on such issues would be null and void and the minister of the interior would issue a decision to this effect.

Article 26:

The province council will hold an ordinary session every 3 months at the invitation of its chairman. The chairman can call an extraordinary meeting if the need for it arises.

The council session will include the sitting or sittings held according to one call and it can not be terminated before probing all issues on the agenda.

Article 27:

Attending the meetings of the province council will be considered a duty for the members mentioned in terms C and D of Article 16 of this system. They should attend in person or send their deputies in case of their absence.

As for members mentioned in item E, the absence of a member during two successive sessions without an accepted excuse will obligate relieving him of his duties. In that case this member should not be re-appointed before at least two years of relieving him of his duties.

Article 28:

The meetings of the province council will not be considered effective unless at least two-thirds of members attend. Resolutions will be issued by absolute majority of votes. Should both sides get the same number of votes, the side for which the chairman votes wins.

Article 29:

The province council can have special committees, when needed, to study any issue related to its specialization. It can also use experienced specialized personnel for this purpose and call anybody to attend the meetings and participate in discussions without voting.

Article 30:

The minister of the interior can call the province council to meet under his chairmanship in any place he sees fit and he can chair any meeting that he attends.

Article 31:

The province council can not meet except by the call of its chairman, his deputy or by an order of the minister of the interior.

Article 32:

The council chairman has to submit a copy of the resolutions to the minister of the interior.

Article 33:

The province council chairman should inform ministries and government authorities of resolutions related to them.

Article 34:

Ministries and government authorities should take into account the resolutions of the province council mentioned in items A and B of Article 23 of this system. If the ministry or authority decides not to implement the resolution of the council, and if the council is not convinced by the reasons given by the ministry or authority, the issue should be raised to the attention of the minister of the interior to submit it to the prime minister.

Article 35:

Every ministry or authority that has services in the province should inform the province council of the projects approved for the province in the budget or development plan, as soon as they are issued.

Article 36:

Each minister or head of authority can sound the opinion of the province council on any issue pertaining to its specialization in the province. The council should give its opinion on it.

Article 37:

The council of ministers will determine, according to a proposal by the minister of the interior, the rewards of the council chairman and members. The expenses of transport and accomodation should be taken into account.

Article 38:

The Council can not be dissolved except by a prime minister's order, according to the recommendations of the minister of the interior. In that case new members should be appointed within 3 months. During that period, members mentioned in items C and D of article 16 of this system, will perform duties of the council under the chairmanship of the province governor.

Article 39:

The province council will have a secretariat in the province headquarters to prepare the council's agenda, call meetings, record the minutes of the meetings, issue resolutions, taking the necessary measure to organize the sittings and take down the council's resolutions.

Article 40:

The minister of the interior will issue the necessary regulations to implement the system.

III.

Referring to the system of the consultative council (Majlis Al-Shura) issued under the royal decree in 1347 AH, custodian of the two Holy Mosques King Fahd Ibn Abdu-Aziz ordered the following:

- Firstly: Issuing of the consultative council's system with the enclosed formula.
- Secondly: This system will replace the system of the Shura council of 1347 AH and situations of this council would be regulated by a royal decree.
- Thirdly: All regulations, instructions and resolutions valid until the implementation of this system would continue until they are accordingly amended.
- Fourthly: This system will be implemented with a period of six months from the publication date.
- Fifthly: This system should be published in the official gazette.

In the name of God, most gracious, most merciful:
The system of Majlis Al-Shura (consultative council):

Article 1:

In line with the almighty God's saying "It is part of the mercy of God that thou dost deal gently with them, wert thou severe or harsh-hearted, they would have broken away. From about thee, so pass over (their faults), and ask for (God's) forgiveness for them, and consult them in affairs of the moment, then when thou hast, taken a decision thy trust in God" and the God's saying: "Those who hearken to their Lord and establish regular prayer, who conduct their affairs in mutual consultation, who spend out of what we bestow on them for sustenance."

And in line with the tradition of the messenger of Allah (peace be upon him), in consulting his companions and pursuation of the nation to do the same.

The consultative council has been set-up to undertake proper tasks in compliance with this system and the basic system of ruling in adherence to the book of God and the tradition of his messenger, preserving the bonds of brotherhood and cooperation for righteousness.

Article 2:

The consultative council, is based on holding fast all together by the rope which the God stretches out, strict adherence to the sources of the islamic legislation. The members of the council would devote themselves to serve the common interest, preservation of the unity of the people, the entity of the state and the interests of the nation.

Article 3:

The consultative council consists of a speaker, sixty well-educated and qualified members to be selected by the king. The rights and duties of the members and their affairs would be identified by a royal decree.

Article 4:

A member of the consultative member should be:

- A-Saudi National in terms of origin and by birth.
- B-He should be famous for being well-qualified and of a good reputation.
- C-He should not be less than 30 years old.

Article 5:

A member of the Shura council has the right to apply for exemption to the speaker and in turn the speaker should submit the matter to the king.

Article 6:

If a member of the Shura council neglects his duties, investigation should be conducted against him and should be tried in accordance to rules and procedures to be issued by a royal decree.

Article 7:

If, for any reason, a seat of a member of the Shura council, falls vacant, the king will name an alternative by a royal decree.

Article 8:

A member of the Shura council should not exploit the membership to serve his own interest.

Article 9:

Membership of the Shura council should not be joined with any other private or public job unless the king sees a need for this.

Article 10:

Speaker of the Shura council could appoint his deputy and the secretary general of the council, their resignation will be determined by royal decrees, their salaries, rights and duties and various affairs would be determined by a royal decree.

Article 11:

Speaker, members and secretary general of the Shura council should take the following oath before undertaking their work in the council:

> "I swear with great Allah, that I shall be faithful to my religion, then to my king and country, and never uncover a secret of the state, and to preserve the interests of state, its regulations and to perform my duties with truth, honesty, justice, and faithfulness."

Article 12:

The city of Riyadh will be the headquarters of the consultative council but the council could hold a meeting at any other place inside the kingdom if approved by the king.

Article 13:

The term of the Shura council will be four years (Hijri calendar) as of the date set on the royal decree on the formation of the council. The new council should be formed at least two months ahead of the expiration date of the preceding one. If the term finishes before the formation of a new council, the old one should perform its duties until a new one is formed. When a new council is formed, it should be noticed that the number of the new members of the council should at least be half the members of the council.

Article 14:

The king, or whomsoever he delegates at the council of Shura, should deliver an annual royal speech before the council on the domestic and foreign policies of the state.

Article 15:

The council shall give its opinion in the general policies of the state which are referred to it by the prime minister. The council's specific duties are:

- A-To review the general plans for economic and social development rendering its opinion about those plans;

- B-To study laws, agreements, alliances, international accords and concessions and to give its opinions concerning them;
- C-To debate annual reports submitted by ministries and other government organizations and to issue its opinion concerning them.

Article 16:

A quorum of two-thirds of the membership, including the president or the deputy, is required to hold a meeting. Resolutions are only valid if passed by a majority.

Article 17:

Resolutions of the Shura council would be submitted to the prime minister, who would refer them to the council of ministers for discussion and if viewpoints of the two councils are identical, a royal approval will be issued, but if the viewpoints differ, then, the king would undertake a proper decision.

Article 18:

Regulations, conventions, international agreements, privileges, would be only issued and amended by royal decrees after being reviewed by the Shura council.

Article 19:

It is up to the Shura council to assign specialized committees of its members to practice its specializations and it has the right to form specialized committees of its members to discuss items on its agenda.

Article 20:

The council's affiliated committees could seek the help of whoever it sees suitable from non-members after the approval of the speaker of the council.

Article 21:

A general commission should be set up for the council of Shura comprising the speaker, his deputy and heads of specialized committees of the council.

Article 22:

Speaker of the Shura council should submit to the prime minister an application if any official has to attend the council's sessions provided that the council is discussing concerned matters and the official would have the right of discussion but not the right of voting.

Article 23:

Every group of ten members of the Shura council, has the right to propose a new system, or amendment of an implemented one and to submit the matter to the speaker of the council who, in turn, should raise the proposal to the king.

Article 24:

The speaker of the Shura council must submit an application to the prime minister for providing the council with governmental documents and statements which the council sees necessary to accelerate its functions.

Article 25:

Civil services regulations are applied to the personnel of the council's bodies unless the internal regulations stipulates otherwise.

Article 27:

The Shura council would have a special budget ratified by the king and should be spent within regulations and rules issued by a royal decree.

Article 28:

Organization of financial affairs of the council, financial control and final account would be done in line with special rules to be identified by a royal decree.

Article 29:

The internal regulation of the Shura council should organize the duties of its speaker and his deputy, the council's secretary general, the bodies of the council, management of the sessions, work process, functions of committees, method of voting, discussion regulation, answering rules besides all matters that would provide control and perfectness inside the council so that it could be able to exercise its duties in a manner that would serve the best interests of the kingdom and its people, and such regulation would be issued by a royal decree.

Article 30:

The amendment of this system would not be made except in the method it had been issued.

IRISH ABORTION CASE
March 5, 1992

In a case that deeply divided Ireland and threatened to have international repercussions, the Irish Supreme Court ruled February 26 that a pregnant fourteen-year-old girl could travel to England to get an abortion. The court issued its written decision in the case March 5.

According to court documents and press reports, the unidentified girl alleged that a friend's father raped her. When the girl learned she was pregnant, she and her parents decided to go to England so she could get an abortion. Abortion in Ireland was illegal unless a woman's life was at risk. The ban on abortion became part of the Irish constitution in 1983, when 69 percent of those voting in a referendum backed the measure. Some 95 percent of the Irish population was Roman-Catholic.

Ireland's attorney general, Harry Whelehan, learned of the case when the girl's parents contacted local police before leaving for England to see if they needed any genetic evidence from the operation to help them prosecute the alleged rapist. Whelehan then obtained an injunction barring the girl from traveling to England to get the abortion. Already in England when the injunction was issued, the girl and her parents voluntarily returned to Ireland to fight the court order.

The Irish government officially estimated that more than 4,000 Irish women a year went to England to get abortions, but it was believed that several thousand additional Irish woman obtained abortions in England each year, giving British addresses to keep their abortions secret. Before this case, the Irish government had never sought to block a woman from getting an abortion in England and had not prosecuted those who got abortions there.

The injunction ignited a hot debate both inside and outside Ireland. "The state appears more concerned with protecting the procreative rights of rapists than with protecting the rights of their victims," said Jon O'Brien of the Irish Family Planning Association. Pro-life activists, on the other hand, charged that abortion rights supporters were using the girl as a test case to get abortion legalized in Ireland.

Pressure on the Court

Officials in other European Community nations expressed dismay at the injunction because citizens in EC nations were supposed to have a right to travel freely among the countries. Some feared that the EC might retaliate by reducing the hundreds of millions of dollars in subsidies that it gave Ireland annually.

Ireland's powerful Catholic Bishops' Conference initially stayed out of the dispute. Only days before the court's ruling, though, the Conference announced that it opposed restrictions on travel. The government, too, at first tried to remain above the debate. However, after several government ministers criticized the injunction, newly installed Prime Minister Albert Reynolds on February 22 said that Ireland should be "a society which respects the rights of the living, as well as the unborn." The Irish press reported that the government had told the Supreme Court it wanted the travel ban struck down.

In its ruling, the court sidestepped the issue of the travel ban. It said the girl could travel to England to get an abortion because a psychologist who examined her said she was intent on committing suicide if she couldn't end the pregnancy. The court said there was "a real and substantial risk" to the mother's life that could only be avoided by allowing her to get an abortion. Because the court avoided the major legal issues, its ruling pleased few other than the girl and her parents, who quickly returned to England so she could get an abortion.

In a referendum held November 25, Irish voters, by a three-to-two margin, approved a proposed constitutional amendment lifting the ban on traveling abroad to get an abortion. The voters also approved an amendment guaranteeing women access to information on abortions. But the voters rejected, by a two-to-one margin, a proposed amendment that would have allowed abortions in Ireland to save the life of the mother. The language of the amendment apparently angered many women, and several newly elected female members of the Irish Parliament promised to press for new consideration of an amendment to liberalize the abortion law.

Following are excerpts from the Irish Supreme Court's decision in the case of X and Others v. The Attorney General, issued March 5, 1992:

No. 47/92

X and Others, Appellants   }   The Supreme Court of Ireland
v.
The Attorney General   }

[March 5, 1992]

JUDGMENT delivered on the 5th day of March 1992 by FINLAY C. J.
... The first issue submitted before the High Court on behalf of the
Appellants was that because the Oireachtas had not enacted any law
regulating the manner in which the right to life of the unborn and the right
to life of the mother, referred to in the Eighth Amendment, could be
reconciled the Court could make no order in a case in which an issue of
reconciliation arose. The learned trial Judge in rejecting this submission
stated as follows:

> It seems to me that if the Court is apprised of a situation in which the life of
> the unborn is threatened, then it would be failing in its constitutional duty to
> protect it merely because the Oireachtas had failed to legislate on how it was to
> have regard to the equal right of the mother as provided for in the Eighth
> Amendment. Complicated and difficult issues of fact may, of course, arise in
> individual cases, but that does not inhibit the Court from applying the clear
> rule of law laid down in the Amendment.

The second issue which was submitted on behalf of the Appellants in the
High Court was that although the Eighth Amendment required the courts
to defend and vindicate the life of the unborn; that they were in doing so to
have regard to the equal right to life of the mother; that in doing so in this
case the Court should not make the order sought because this would
prejudice the mother's right to life, because of the very real danger which,
it was said, the evidence established that she would take her own life if the
order was made and she was unable to procure an abortion. Dealing with
this issue the learned trial Judge stated as follows:

> I am quite satisfied that there is a real and imminent danger to the life of the
> unborn and that if the Court does not step in to protect it by means of the
> injunction sought, its life will be terminated. The evidence also establishes that
> if the Court grants the injunction sought there is a risk that the Defendant may
> take her own life. But the risk that the Defendant may take her own life, if an
> order is made, is much less and of a different order of magnitude than the
> certainty that the life of the unborn will be terminated if the order is not made. I
> am strengthened in this view by the knowledge that the young girl has the
> benefit of the love and care and support of devoted parents who will help her
> through the difficult months ahead. It seems to me, therefore, that having had
> regard to the rights of the mother in this case, the Court's duty to protect the
> life of the unborn requires it to make the order sought."

Article 40.3.3 of the Constitution
as inserted by the Eighth Amendment

The State acknowledges the right to life of the unborn and, with due regard to the equal right to life of the mother, guarantees in its laws to respect, and as far as practicable, by its laws to defend and vindicate that right.

Interpretation of Article 40.3.3

In the course of his judgment in *McGee* v. *The Attorney General* 1974 IR, Walsh J. at p. 318, stated as follows:

> In this country, it falls finally upon the judges to interpret the Constitution and in doing so to determine, where necessary, the rights which are superior or antecedent to positive law or which are imprescriptible or inalienable. In the performance of this difficult duty there are certain guidelines laid down in the Constitution for the judge. The very structure and content of the Articles dealing with fundamental rights clearly indicate that justice is not subordinate to the law. In particular, the terms of Section 3 of Article 40 expressly subordinate the law to justice. Both Aristotle and the Christian philosophers have regarded justice as the highest human virtue. The virtue of prudence was also esteemed by Aristotle, as by the philosophers of the Christian world. But the great additional virtue introduced by Christianity was that of charity—not the charity which consists of giving the deserving for that is justice, but the charity which is also called mercy. According to the Preamble, the People gave themselves the Constitution to promote the common good, with due observance of prudence, justice and charity so that the dignity and freedom of the individual might be assured. The judges must, therefore, as best they can from their training and their experience interpret these rights in accordance with their ideas of prudence, justice and charity. It is but natural that from time to time the prevailing ideas of these virtues may be conditioned by the passage of time; no interpretation of the Constitution is intended to be final for all time. It is given in the light of prevailing ideas and concepts.

In the course of his judgment in *The State (Healy)* v. *O'Donoghue* 1976 IR, O'Higgins C. J., at p. 347, stated as follows:

> The Preamble to the Constitution records that the People "seeking to promote the common good, with due observance of prudence, justice and charity, so that the dignity and freedom of the individual may be assured, true social order attained, the unity of our country restored and concord established with other nations, do hereby adopt, enact, and give to ourselves this Constitution."
>
> In my view, this Preamble makes it clear that rights given by the Constitution must be considered in accordance with concepts of prudence, justice and charity, which may gradually change or develop as society changes and develops and which fail to be interpreted from time to time in accordance with prevailing ideas. The Preamble envisages a Constitution which can absorb or be adapted to such changes. In other words, the Constitution did not seek to impose for all time the ideas prevalent or accepted with regard to these virtues at the time of its enactment. . . .

I accept . . . that the doctrine of the harmonious interpretation of the Constitution involves in this case a consideration of the constitutional rights and obligations of the mother of the unborn child and the interrelation of those rights and obligations with the rights and obligations of other people and, of course, with the right to life of the unborn child as well.

Such a harmonious interpretation of the Constitution carried out in accordance with concepts of prudence, justice and charity, as they have been explained in the judgment of Walsh J. in *McGee* v. *The Attorney General* leads me to the conclusion that in vindicating and defending as far as practicable the right of the unborn to life but at the same time giving due regard to the right of the mother to life, that the Court must, amongst the matters to be so regarded, concern itself with the position of the mother within a family group, with persons on whom she is dependent, with, in other instances, persons who are dependent upon her and her interaction with other citizens and members of society in the areas in which her activities occur. Having regard to that conclusion, I am satisfied that the test proposed on behalf of the Attorney General that the life of the unborn could only be terminated if it were established that an inevitable or immediate risk to the life of the mother existed, for the avoidance of which a termination of the pregnancy was necessary, insufficiently vindicates the mother's right to life.

I, therefore, conclude that the proper test to be applied is that if it is established as a matter of probability that there is a real and substantial risk to the life as distinct from the health of the mother, which can only be avoided by the termination of her pregnancy, that such termination is permissible, having regard to the true interpretation of Article 40.3.3 of the Constitution.

Has the appellant by evidence satisfied this test?

With regard to this issue, the findings of fact made by the learned trial judge in the High Court are as follows:

> When the Defendant learned that she was pregnant she naturally was greatly distraught and upset. Later she confided in her mother that when she learned she was pregnant she had wanted to kill herself by throwing herself downstairs. On the journey back from London she told her mother that she had wanted to throw herself under a train when she was in London, that as she had put her parents through so much trouble she would rather be dead than continue as she was. On the 31st January, in the course of a long discussion with a member of the Garda Siochana, she said: "I wish it were all over; sometimes I feel like throwing myself downstairs." And in the presence of another member of the Garda Siochana, when her father commented that the "situation was worse than a death in the family" she commented: "Not if it was me".
>
> On the day of her return from London the Defendant's parents brought her to a very experienced clinical psychologist. He explained in his report that he had been asked to assess her emotional state, that whilst she was co-operative she was emotionally withdrawn, that he had concluded that she was in a state of shock and that she had lost touch with her feelings. She told him that she had been crying on her own, but had hid her feelings from her parents to protect them. His opinion was that her vacant, expressionless manner indicated that she was coping with the appalling crisis she faced by a denial of her emotions. She did not seem depressed, but he said that she "coldly expressed a desire to solve

matters by ending her life." In his opinion, in her withdrawn state "she was capable of such an act, not so much because she is depressed but because she could calculatingly reach the conclusion that death is the best solution." He considered that the psychological damage to her of carrying a child would be considerable, and that the damage to her mental health would be devastating. His report was supplemented by oral testimony. He explained in the course of his consultation with the Defendant she had said to him: "It is hard at fourteen to go through the nine months" and that she said: "It is better to end it now than in nine months' time." The psychologist understood this to mean that by ending her life she would end the problems through which she was putting her parents with whom she has a very strong and loving relationship.

The psychologist . . . stated that when he had interviewed this young girl and was anxious to have a continuing discussion with her parents who accompanied her and not having anybody available to remain with the young girl in the waiting room, his view of the risk of her committing suicide was so real, on his past experience in this field of medicine, that notwithstanding its obvious inappropriateness he requested her to remain in the room while he discussed the problem with her parents.

I am satisfied that the only risk put forward in this case to the life of the mother is the risk of self-destruction. I agree with the conclusion reached by the learned trial judge in the High Court that that was a risk which, as would be appropriate in any other form of risk to the life of the mother, must be taken into account in reconciling the right of the unborn to life and the rights of the mother to life. Such a risk to the life of a young mother, in particular, has it seems to me, a particular characteristic which is relevant to the question of whether the evidence in this case justifies a conclusion that it constitutes a real and substantial risk to life.

If a physical condition emanating from a pregnancy occurs in a mother, it may be that a decision to terminate the pregnancy in order to save her life can be postponed for a significant period in order to monitor the progress of the physical condition, and that there are diagnostic warning signs which can readily be relied upon during such postponement.

In my view, it is common sense that a threat of self-destruction . . . which the psychologist clearly believes to be a very real threat, cannot be monitored in that sense and that it is almost impossible to prevent self-destruction in a young girl in the situation in which this Defendant is if she were to decide to carry out her threat of suicide.

I am, therefore, satisfied that on the evidence before the learned trial judge, which was in no way contested, and on the findings which he has made, that the Defendant Appellants have satisfied the test which I have laid down as being appropriate and have established as a matter of probability that there is a real and substantial risk to the life of the mother by self-destruction which can only be avoided by termination of her pregnancy.

It is for this reason that, in my view, the Defendants were entitled to succeed in this appeal, and the orders made in the High Court have been set aside.

NIXON'S SPEECH ON RUSSIAN AID
March 11, 1992

Projecting himself into an opening in the national political discourse, former president Richard Nixon early in 1992 pressed his view that the United States should provide substantial aid to Russia, the Ukraine, and the other former republics of the Soviet Union. Only such assistance, he argued, would give democratic reforms a chance to take root in the formerly communist lands. The earlier response of the Bush administration to Russia's urgent requests for aid, the former president said, had been "pathetically inadequate."

Many of Nixon's arguments, advanced at first in articles and in memorandums to friends, were cogently marshaled in a speech in Washington, D.C., on March 11 before an audience of 200 foreign policy experts, officials in Nixon's own administration, and foreign ambassadors. Nixon's strongly expressed views pierced a profound silence surrounding the issue of extensive aid to the former Soviet republics. Neither the Bush administration nor most members of Congress, observers said, had wanted to bring up the touchy subject. An inward-turning electorate, presidential politics, and a domestic economy barely inching its way out of recession had rendered foreign aid an unwelcome issue.

Bush Action Follows

On April 1, about three weeks after Nixon's speech, President George Bush announced that the United States would participate in a $24 billion international aid initiative designed to stabilize Russia's economy. Under the plan, additional U.S. assistance would include food credits to Russia *and the other former Soviet republics. Analysts estimated that the program would require between $3 billion and $4 billion in U.S. outlays.*

Writing in the New York Times *on March 11, journalist Thomas L. Friedman said Nixon's harsh criticism had "stung" the Bush administration. But William Hyland, editor of the prestigious* Foreign Affairs *magazine, who was in the audience when Nixon spoke, suggested that "one thing Nixon [was] doing" was giving President Bush "political cover" with the conservatives in his party to go ahead with the assistance program. Indeed, observers said, Nixon's efforts probably would help the Bush administration to obtain crucial congressional support for the aid package.*

Emerging Elder Statesman

The forum Nixon chose for his speech was a conference on "America's Role in the Emerging World," sponsored by the Richard M. Nixon Library and Birthplace in Yorba Linda, California. The Washington Post *said the conference and speech marked the "most explicit and highest-profile foreign policy role" Nixon had taken since resigning the presidency in August 1974, disgraced by his part in the scandals known collectively as Watergate.* (Nixon Resignation, Historic Documents of 1974, p. 683.) *The only speaker at the forum to touch publicly on that aspect of Nixon's past was James R. Schlesinger, who had been CIA director and secretary of defense under Nixon. Schlesinger said the former president had weathered a storm that would have destroyed most other public figures.*

The seventy-nine-year-old Nixon spoke in a hotel ballroom without notes, teleprompter, or lectern. He omitted the criticism of Bush contained in his earlier memorandums.

Decrying what he called "a new isolationism," Nixon told his audience that without major outside aid Russia might turn to "a new despotism" that could be "a far more dangerous threat to peace and freedom, and particularly to peace, than was the old totalitarianism." Referring to Boris N. Yeltsin, Russia's first postcommunist president, Nixon said that if freedom failed under Yeltsin the likely new despotism could wipe out any peace dividend gained from the end of the cold war.

Noting estimates that it would cost about $20 billion a year over five years "to cover some of these items I have mentioned," Nixon said the Financial Times *had pointed out that the West spent twenty times that much just in the previous year to defend against Soviet communism.*

"Who Lost China?"

In the memos he circulated in the weeks before his speech, Nixon wrote that "the hot-button issue in the 1950s was 'who lost China?' If Yeltsin goes down, the question 'who lost Russia?' will be an infinitely more devastating issue in the 1990s."

Press accounts reminded readers that Nixon himself was one of a number of Republican politicians who had advanced their careers by raising the question "who lost China?" after the takeover of that country by a communist regime in 1949. Still, Nixon's stark warning resonated with Bush administration policy makers, who were said to realize they would be blamed if disaster were to overtake the new regime in Russia.

Russian Aid Package

There were signs that the aid program Bush announced April 1 had been hastily assembled. But administration officials denied that it was put together in response to Nixon's criticisms or to counter a long-scheduled foreign policy speech that Arkansas governor Bill Clinton, then the Democratic presidential front-runner, gave in New York the same day the Bush program was announced.

Actually, the officials said, various approaches to Russian aid had been under consideration for more than six months. But the process had been sped up to show support for Yeltsin before a crucial meeting he was to have with the Congress of People's deputies—the Russian parliament. Conservative "old thinkers" were expected to attack Yeltsin's reforms.

The Bush package contained three parts: a multinational initiative spearheaded by the Group of Seven industrialized nations, the extension of additional food credits, and a legislative package authorizing several additional aid proposals. The initiative called for $24 billion in aid in 1992, much of it as loans and guarantees rather than as direct assistance.

In the second part, Bush proposed to increase by $1.1 billion the export credits available for purchase of U.S. agricultural goods by the former Soviet republics. Of that amount, $600 million would be earmarked for Russia. The remaining $500 million would be available for the other former republics.

The third component would provide congressional endorsement of all the proposals, together with waivers of laws of the cold war era limiting U.S. assistance for, and business activities in, the former Soviet republics. Much of the aid package would be channeled through the International Monetary Fund, the World Bank, and the European Bank for Reconstruction and Development. (Munich Economic Summit, p. 637)

Lobbying for passage of the aid legislation, Secretary of State James A. Baker III told congressional committees that it was as much a policy statement as it was an authorization bill. Baker urged Congress to approve the legislation before Yeltsin visited Washington in mid-June 1992. (Yeltsin's Summit with Bush, Address to Congress, p. 519) *That deadline was not met, but the assistance legislation was enacted on October 3, just before final adjournment of the 102d Congress.*

> *Following is the text of former president Richard Nixon's speech on aid to Russia and the other former Soviet republics, delivered in Washington, D.C., on March 11, 1992.* (The bracketed headings have been added by Congressional Quarterly to highlight the organization of the text.):

Thank you very much. Thank you very much. May I express my appreciation to Secretary [James R.] Schlesinger for his much-too-generous introduction, and particularly for his reference to Mrs. Nixon. She would like to have been here, but I can assure you she is watching on CNN right now. (Laughter.) I also want to say that we don't plan to have a big party for her 80th birthday, so I consider this to be the celebration of that 80th birthday. And I know we all want to send, as you have already by your applause when she was mentioned, our best wishes to her. I also want to express appreciation particularly—not only to Jim Schlesinger and Dimitri Simes, but all of those who have participated in and who have made this conference possible.

We meet at a very challenging time, a challenging time in America's history. We meet at a time when we have been through three years of events that have changed the world. I refer, of course, to the collapse of communism in Eastern Europe and in the Soviet Union, to our victory over aggression in the Gulf War. As a result of those events, we live in a new world, and the question now is, what should the leadership position of the United States be in that new world.

Other participants in this conference and the various fora, some of which I will attend and I hope all of you can attend, will address what the policy of the United States should be in this new world ideally.

I'm going to direct my remarks in this political year not just to what our policy should be, but what is possible politically. In that respect, incidentally, I should point out that if you follow political campaigns, it's rather standard practice for the candidate to get up and say, "This is the most important election in history." I know, I said it a lot of times. (Laughter.) And of course every campaign is very important to the candidate. In this case it's very important to the nation.

Now over the past 44 years I have had the opportunity to observe 12 presidential elections, I have been a candidate in five of them, and in that period of time there has never been a campaign in those 44 years in which foreign policy was less discussed, and there has never been a time in which foreign policy was more important, because whoever is President in the next four years will provide the leadership that will make the difference as to whether peace and freedom survive in the world. Since that is the case then, it is vitally important that foreign policy be front and center, front and center in our considerations.

We have been on a rollercoaster ride as far as foreign policy is concerned. After the Communist victory in Vietnam the attitude of most Americans was that there was nothing we could do in foreign policy, then after our victory in the Gulf War the conventional wisdom [was] that we could do anything, and then after the collapse of Communism, particularly in the Soviet Union, the conventional wisdom was that there was nothing left to do.

As a result of these events we see developing a new isolationism in both of the political parties. The general theme which runs through the new isolationist is somewhat like this, that the United States no longer should play or can play a leadership role in the world. There are some who say we can't afford to, there are others who say it is not necessary for us to play that role, and there are still others who say that others should play that role.

When we consider what they are saying I would say that it sort of reminds me of a pickup band, a ragtime band. Some are marching to different drummers, some are singing off key, but all of them have the same tune, the same theme, come home America.

As a matter of fact, what we find is that even some of those who have been the strongest supporters of a strong foreign policy role for the United States now say it's time to turn our efforts inward, we can't afford it, as far as foreign policy is concerned, and our domestic concerns are so great we should look inward.

[Inseparable: Foreign and Domestic Policy]

What they fail to realize, those who take that line, is that foreign and domestic policy are like Siamese twins: neither can survive without the other. What they fail to realize is that the American people will not support a strong foreign policy unless we have a strong policy dealing with problems at home. And what they fail to realize is that as far as foreign policy is concerned, it has an impact on what we do at home. We can't be at peace in a world of wars, and we can't have a healthy American economy in a sick world economy. For example, we all can recall—I can, at least, you've read about it, I lived through it—the Great Depression. It began as a recession in 1931, became a depression in 1932 in great part because the United States adopted a protectionist policy as far as the Smoot-Hawley Tariff Act was concerned.

So we leave that particular position. We come now to the fundamental question: Is it necessary for the United States to play a role in this new world since all of these events have occurred? And those who answer no begin with what I think is a false premise. It goes something like this: The Cold War is over, and we have won it. It's time to come home. That's only half true. It is true that as far as the Cold War is concerned, the communists have lost it. It is not true, however, that the free world has won it.

What we have to realize is that the Cold War was not the traditional war over territory by great powers. It was a war of ideas, the ideas of communism versus the ideas of freedom. We can see that war most clearly in Russia, in Russia, the place where the seeds of the idea of communism were first planted. The Russian people reaped the very bitter harvest from those seeds that had been planted, and as a result, the Russian people rejected communism. They rejected it because it didn't work.

["A New Despotism"]

But now, freedom is on trial, and if freedom does not work, the Russian people are not going to return to communism, because it failed, but they will return, in my view, to what I would call a new despotism, in which they trade their freedom for security and as to which they in effect provide for leadership and put their future in the hands of those who are going to make sure that they can have the necessities of life, and who make the promises, and then of course will have the opportunity to carry them out. This new despotism, which would be shorn of the baggage of the dying faith of communism, this new despotism, which would have the overtones of imperialist Russian activities which have been traditional in Russian history, that new despotism could be a far more dangerous threat to peace and freedom in the world, and particularly to peace, than was the old Soviet totalitarianism. And it is that, therefore, that we have to address today.

So let us turn to Russia. And in turning to Russia, as I was saying to Dr. [Zbigniew] Brzezinski during lunch, that does not mean that I believe we should ignore what is happening in Ukraine and the other republics that have become independent in Eastern Europe and the rest, but I use Russia only as the prime example of the problem. What I say about Russia would apply to the others as well.

As we look at Russia today, the question somebody asked me at the table was briefly this: Is it going to work? Are they going to survive? Is freedom going to survive? And the answer is it is going to be a very close-run thing.

It's going to be close-run because there are many minus factors at this time. Among them, as Dmitri Simes has pointed out in a recent article, corruption is rampant. Among them we have the problem of ethnic quarrels. Among them we have the problem of enormous suffering because of the changes that have been made economically by the attempt to build a free market society in Russia.

And one of the major reasons that there is a serious question as to whether freedom can succeed in Russia is the lack of a management class. When I say the lack of a management class, that indicates why the Marshall Plan analogy will not work, because when we look at Russia and when we compare the situation in Europe, and for that matter, in Japan at the end of World War II, five years of war did not destroy the management class in Western Europe or in Japan. Seventy years of totalitarian communism did destroy the management class in Russia. And therefore, you have to have a different approach than simply the Marshall Plan approach. Those are the negatives.

There are some positive factors which we sometimes overlook, and one is that Russia is a very rich country, rich in resources and rich in its people. It's a highly industrialized society. The Russian people are a great people, they are a strong people. We have to realize that 95 percent of the Russian people are literate. We have to realize that in their workforce, 90 percent have the equivalent of a high school education. We have to recognize, too, that Russia produces some of the great scientists, the great engineers, particularly in military activities. Some people forget that the first man in space was not an American, it was a Russian.

[Gorbachev and Yeltsin: "Political Heavyweights"]

There's another factor on the plus side, which is often overlooked. Pushkin in the 19th century wrote that rebellions in Russia tend to be senseless and violent. What is particularly significant about the revolution that has occurred is that is was neither violent nor, of course, was it senseless. And this is to the great credit, we would have to say, to both [former Soviet president Mikhail] Gorbachev and [Russian president Boris] Yeltsin.

The major factor on the plus side, however, is that Russia, the new Russia, has a strong leader. Now, there's a tendency to underestimate Yeltsin, Boris Yeltsin. Some say that democratically that he simply isn't— that politically, he isn't democratic enough; and others say that intellectually, he's not smart enough; socially that he's not smooth enough.

I have seen many great leaders over the past 44 years. I would rate Gorbachev and Yeltsin as political heavyweights. Both were born as peasants. Gorbachev became a man of the world; Yeltsin remained a man of the people. And Yeltsin right now must never forget that.

As he moves onto the world scene, he must always remember that if he's going to change the world, he first has to change Russia. He has to change it from dictatorship to democracy. He has to change it from a command economy to a free market economy. And if he's going to be able to do that, he is going to need help. The question is, should we provide that help.

Let's look at the positive factors as far is Yeltsin is concerned. Yeltsin has demonstrated his physical courage by standing on top of a tank and facing down a gang of card-carrying killers who were trying, or course, to run a counter—a Stalinist coup.

We also find that Yeltsin, in addition to that—and this is even more important in my view—he has political courage. He risked his immense popularity by adopting policies which let the ruble float. They have enormous inflation that caused enormous hardship, and as a result has brought its popularity down. But it was a necessary first step in moving from a command to a freemarket economy.

He is one who, unlike Gorbachev, if you read Gorbachev's first column in the New York Times a few days ago, Yeltsin is one who has repudiated not just communism but socialism, as well. He is one, too, who has completely vetoed all of the foreign aid programs that he inherited from Gorbachev, which in the year 1990 took $15 billion from the Russian budget, which provided aid to a number of countries including Cuba which were antagonistic to the West and to the United States. And we all know that in the field of arms control, for example, he not only has matched what President Bush has courageously taken the initiative on, he has exceeded it.

So what do we find? We find that Yeltsin is the most pro-Western leader in Russian history. Under those circumstances, then, he deserves our help.

What does he need? He needs a number of things. Just to tick off a few of them, he needs, for example, help from the IMF and other sources, and that will take billions of dollars to stabilize the ruble. He needs more open markets for the exports which Russia would want to make, the new Russia, to the West and to other parts of the world. He needs, in addition, the help of the West insofar as humanitarian aid is concerned. And there needs to be, without question, one facility, a Western group which would analyze and assess all of the needs and then would develop a program for working out with private enterprise and with governments how they meet those needs.

I won't go into further detail because the experts can fill you in on it. But to summarize very briefly, it is important for us to recognize that Yeltsin is going to need very substantial economic aid from the West. Not just the United States, I emphasize, but from the West. The New York Times in its editorial today estimated that that cost of the aid to cover some of these items that I have mentioned and others would be approximately $20 billion a year over a period of five years. That's a great deal of money. However, the London Financial Times, in its report yesterday pointed out that $20 billion a year has to be compared with 20 times that much that the West spent even last year, before the collapse of Communism, to defend against the Soviet Communism. So under the circumstances this puts it all in perspective.

Now we come to the hard political questions. What does the United States do? How do we meet this problem, particularly when we are in the midst of a presidential campaign and in the middle of a recession? And the first argument that is made, and it's one that is well taken, is that the United States has carried this burden long enough, it is time for others to take it, that after World War II we provided aid to our allies of course, but also to our defeated enemies and enabled them to recover from World War II. Now it's time, therefore, for those that we helped then to assume the burden for helping the Soviet Union, the other countries in the former Soviet Union—I mean helping Russia, the other independent countries in the former Soviet Union and those in Eastern Europe, that it's time for the ones we helped recover from World War II, help them recover from the Cold War. They are right.

The major burden for meeting the needs that Russia has and the other countries that need the help, that must be carried by the countries in Europe and in Japan that we helped after World War II. But the United States is the richest and strongest nation in the world and we must provide the leadership. We cannot provide the leadership unless we have a seat at the table. To paraphrase Ben Stein in another context, you can't have a seat at the table unless you have chips to put in the pot. And we have to have enough chips to be a serious contender for that leadership role.

["What's in It for Us?"]

Now we come to basically a fundamentally basic question in a campaign year. What's in it for us? What's in it for us to help the Russians, Ukraine, the other independent countries in the Soviet Union and the countries of Eastern Europe? And the answer is that a great deal is in it for us.

Charity, it is said, begins at home and I agree. But aid to Russia, just speaking of Russia specifically, is not charity. We have to realize that if Yeltsin fails the alternative is not going to be somebody better, it's going to be somebody infinitely worse. We have to realize that if Yeltsin fails, if freedom fails, the new despotism which will take its place will mean that the peace dividend is finished, we will have to rearm, and that's going to cost infinitely more than would the aid that we provide at the present time. It would also mean, if Yeltsin failed, if freedom fails in Russia, it means that a great wave of freedom that has been going all over the world in these recent two or three years, that it will begin to ebb, and that dictatorship, rather than democracy, will be the wave of the future.

On the other hand, if freedom succeeds in Russia, let's see what it means. It means that Russia will be an example to others, particularly in China, particularly in the other communist countries—the remaining ones—and in the non-communist dictatorships around the world, an example for the others to follow, a powerful magnet drawing them to that.

It would mean, too, that we have, with Russia succeeding, a totally new world—a new world in the sense of what it can mean to everybody, particularly to us in the United States as well. Just think. For seventy years, communist Russia has been trying to export communism around the world. If Yeltsin and the reforms succeed, democratic, free Russia will be exporting the goods and ideas of freedom around the world. And that means that, in the years ahead, that will have an impact going far beyond Russia, far beyond Europe, all over the world. And economically speaking, it means that the new Russia, with all of the production that we'll be able to have with a free economy, will provide great markets for the products of the United States. That means billions of dollars in trade and potentially millions of jobs.

It also means, if Yeltsin succeeds, if democracy survives, that our children and grandchildren will have removed a fear of a possible world nuclear war that now haunts them, because democracies do not begin wars.

We come now, however, to another political question, and I understand that people are interested in politics these days. And the political question is this: All of the pollsters are telling their candidates, don't tackle foreign policy, and particularly not foreign aid, because foreign aid is poison as a political issue. They're wrong and history proves it.

[Truman's "Indispensable Act"]

In 1947, I recall vividly as if it were yesterday what Harry Truman did. Let me lay the foundation of what he did and why. In that year, Harry Truman's popularity in January of that year, 1947, was 35 percent. The Congress was overwhelmingly Republican. He had suffered an enormous defeat, electing the 80th Congress in the previous November. And yet, I remember as if it were yesterday Harry Truman—jaunty, some said a little cocky—coming down before a joint session of the Congress and asking for millions of dollars in aid to Greece and Turkey to prevent communist subversion and possibly communist aggression. It was a very tough vote for two very young and both, as history later indicated, rather ambitious young congressmen.

The liberal Democrats in Jack Kennedy's Massachusetts district were against military foreign aid. And the conservative Republicans in my California district were against all foreign aid. Under the circumstances, however, after considering it, we both voted for it, and a majority in that Republican House and the Senate, voted for that program and that was the program which later was developed into the Marshall Plan and later into NATO, which not only contained communism but bought the time that was essential for communism to fail as it inevitably did fail last year in the Soviet Union as well as, of course, in Eastern Europe two years before.

That was an indispensable act. The following year, Harry Truman who had been 35 percent in January of 1947, won the election for president. What is more important, however, is that that action by a Democratic president supported by a Republican Congress, providing aid to Greece and Turkey laid the foundation. It was the indispensable step toward containing communism and eventually providing the basis for the victory of freedom in Russia and in the Soviet Union. And then you have a situation at the present time where we have a Republican president with a Democratic Congress with the opportunity to take action which would provide aid to Russia and the other countries that we have mentioned here which would assure the victory of freedom. That is the political issue and that is the foreign policy issue, as well.

We have, then, a situation which can be summarized in this way. During the Cold War, the United States and the other nations were doing everything that we could to prevent the success of what were basically evil ideas. Now we have to do what we can to assure the success of those ideas that are good. If, for example, the United States, the people of the United States could so splendidly react as they did and support that program that I have referred to, which Harry Truman asked for 47 years ago, if they could do that, a program which had for its purpose preventing and defending against war, isn't it also now even a greater inspiration that the United States would join other nations in a program that will bring the blessings of peace?

In other words, putting it simply, war brings out the worst and the best in men; real peace can bring out and will bring out only the best. That is the question, then, that Americans must face today, political Americans, all Americans, and I think we know what the answer should be.

As we look, then, to the future, I think it is important for us to recognize that we have this great responsibility but it's also a very great opportunity. Consider this, the 20th century will be remembered as a century of war. By our leadership at this time we can help make the 21st century a century of peace and freedom. That is our challenge.

In his Iron Curtain speech, Winston Churchill said, "America at this time stands at the pinnacle of world power. This is a solemn moment for the American democracy, because with primacy in power is joined an awesome accountability for the future."

Despite what the pessimists say, despite what the negatives say, those words are as true today as they were when he spoke them exactly 45 years ago today.

America today has that responsibility and we say why not someone else? And if America does not lead, who? The Japanese? The Chinese? The Russians? The Germans? They are the only nations in the world that have the potential economic and military power to lead in the next century. This is our moment of greatness. It's our moment of truth. We must seize this moment because we hold the future in our hands. (Applause.)

SURGEON GENERAL'S REPORT ON SMOKING IN THE AMERICAS

March 12, 1992

The countries of Latin America and the Caribbean face a smoking epidemic just as serious as the one afflicting their North American neighbors, warned U.S. Surgeon General Antonia Novello in a report issued March 12.

Novello said the report, "Smoking and Health in the Americas," represented "an important step toward a recognition of the international threat posed by tobacco use." It examined the historical, social, economic, and regulatory aspects of smoking in the Western Hemisphere. The study was a joint two-and-a-half-year effort by the U.S. Public Health Service and the Pan American Health Organization. Simultaneously with its release, the PAHO issued a companion document listing country by country the status of tobacco prevention and control in the Americas.

By the mid-1980s at least 526,000 people in the Americas died annually of diseases directly attributable to smoking, the surgeon general's report said. These diseases included cancer, heart disease, and chronic obstructive lung disease. Most of the deaths occurred in the United States and Canada. However, about 100,000 of the deaths occurred in Latin America and the Caribbean, and the toll was likely to climb much higher in coming years without strong anti-smoking efforts.

"The confluence of social, economic, and political forces in Latin America and the Caribbean today is conducive to marked increases in the prevalence of smoking," Novello said in releasing the report. "Young people in the Americas are susceptible to the allure of smoking, and if

current trends continue, ten years from now we will be witnessing the presence of yet another addicted generation."

The increased smoking would inevitably lead to high levels of disease, two senior U.S. health officials said in the report's foreword. "We are in the unfortunate position of watching an epidemic—like the one we are currently living with in the United States—begin to gather momentum among our neighbors," they wrote.

Temporary Dropoff

Per capita tobacco consumption grew sharply in Latin America and the Caribbean during the 1960s and 1970s, but it fell in the 1980s because of a severe economic downturn. The report warned that an economic recovery would likely boost tobacco use once again. In addition, changing demographics, growing urbanization, rising education levels, and the increasing entry of women into the work force also made it likely that smoking rates would climb.

A lack of sound numbers made it hard to estimate how many people smoked in Latin America and the Caribbean, the report said. However, available data indicated that 37 percent of men and 20 percent of women smoked. A significant number of women had started smoking in recent years.

The prevalence of smoking varied widely among countries and was linked largely to economic conditions. The poorest nations still had low smoking rates. In nations with greater economic development, the prevalence of smoking was high among young people in urban areas—reaching 50 percent or more in some cases. Moreover, diseases associated with smoking were already major causes of death in these countries. And in the most industrialized nations previously high levels of smoking were tapering off.

Countries also varied widely in their efforts to halt the spread of smoking. Most countries had taken some type of action, such as levying taxes, restricting advertising, requiring health warnings, developing national health coalitions, promoting antismoking education efforts, and improving data collection about smoking. Yet few had adopted a comprehensive, unified approach. In some nations, other urgent health problems resulted in smoking control receiving a low priority. In others, economic problems caused governments to do little.

Government efforts to control smoking were also hampered by the domination of the tobacco industry by transnational corporations. These corporations "have directed their efforts toward penetrating developing economies" and present "a formidable obstacle to smoking-control efforts," the report said.

Benefits Outweigh Effect on Economies

Claims that curtailing smoking would harm the economies of Latin America and the Caribbean were unfounded, the report said. Tobacco production was a major contributor to the economies of only a few countries. Overall, the long-term costs of smoking-related diseases offset the economic benefits of tobacco production.

Each country must deal with the smoking problem "in its own political, economic, and cultural context," the report said, yet the nations of the Americas "face a common threat." It urged them to take a common approach "characterized by agreement on goals, objectives, and means" that would benefit the whole region. Without such coordinated action, Novello warned that "the epidemic of tobacco use is likely to proceed according to a well-defined script: gradual adoption of the smoking habit, long-term entrenchment of tobacco use, and a major loss of human life."

Countries covered by the report included the Latin American nations of Bolivia, Colombia, Ecuador, Peru, Venezuela, Argentina, Chile, Paraguay, Uruguay, Brazil, Belize, Costa Rica, El Salvador, Guatemala, Honduras, Nicaragua, Panama, Mexico, Cuba, Dominican Republic, Haiti, and Puerto Rico; the Caribbean nations of Anguilla, Antigua and Barbuda, Bahamas, Barbados, Bermuda, British Virgin Islands, Cayman Islands, Dominica, French Guiana, Grenada, Guadeloupe, Guyana, Jamaica, Martinique, Montserrat, Netherlands Antilles and Aruba, Saint Kitts and Nevis, Saint Lucia, Saint Vincent and the Grenadines, Suriname, Trinidad and Tobago, Turks and Caicos Islands, and the Virgin Islands; and the North American nations of Canada and the United States.

The 1992 report, the twenty-second in a series about smoking issued by various surgeon generals, also examined the status of smoking in the United States and Canada. It said "considerable gains" have been made in reducing smoking, and that the prevalence of smoking continues to fall by about one-half percent annually in the United States. However, that rate of decline was insufficient to meet the goal of reducing smoking prevalence to 15 percent by the year 2000. "It is clear that the efforts under way in the United States and Canada are important in maintaining the momentum of smoking abatement," the report said, "but it is equally clear that they are insufficient."

Following are excerpts from the executive summary to the report "Smoking and Health in the Americas," released March 12, 1992, including the prefaces by Antonia C. Novello, U.S. surgeon general, and Carlyle Guerra de Macedo, director of the Pan American Health Organization, and the major conclusions and summary:

NOVELLO'S PREFACE

This 1992 report of the Surgeon General, *Smoking and Health in the Americas*, is the second on smoking and health during my tenure as Surgeon General. Over the years, the reports have systematically examined the effect of smoking on human health: the biologic effects of substances in tobacco, the risks of disease, the susceptibility of target organs, the addictive nature of nicotine, and the evolving epidemiology of the problem. The reports summarize a massive amount of information that has accumulated on the untoward effects of tobacco use, now easily designated the single most important risk to human health in the United States. The 1990 report, *The Health Benefits of Smoking Cessation*, documented the positive impact of quitting and thus furthered the logical argument leading to a smoke-free society.

This report is a departure from its predecessors in that it treats the evidence against smoking as an underlying assumption. The issue for the future is how we will go about achieving a smoke-free society, and a consideration of smoking in the Americas is an early step in that direction. The report explores the historical, epidemiologic, economic, and social issues that surround tobacco use in the Americas. It focuses on cultural antecedents and trends, on social and economic structure, and on the local, national, and regional efforts that are currently under way to control tobacco use.

One of the striking inferences to be drawn from the report is that the countries of the Americas occupy a continuum of consequences related to smoking. This continuum appears to be related to overall economic development. Countries that are furthest along the path of industrialization have gone through a period of high smoking prevalence and are now experiencing the incongruous combination of declining prevalence and increasing morbidity and mortality from smoking. Other countries, substantially along the path, are entering a period of high prevalence and may also be experiencing some of the disease and disability associated with smoking. Still others, less developed industrially, have low prevalences of smoking and relatively lower estimates for smoking-attributable mortality, but must contend with numerous other public health issues.

Not all countries fit easily into such a simple classification. Within countries, there is considerable diversity in the pace of industrialization, urbanization, and general development as well as in the manifestation of the effects of tobacco use. But the classification is useful in defining the pathway that all countries are likely to take. In the absence of coordinated action, the epidemic of tobacco use is likely to proceed according to a well-defined script: gradual adoption of the smoking habit, long-term entrenchment of tobacco use, and a major loss of human life.

The forces that create this script are complex and often difficult to untangle. One of the major findings of the report is the crucial role of surveillance in understanding the intricate interrelationship of the factors that influence smoking. The educational level of the population, for example, illustrates the complexity. Data from selected sources indicate that smoking is more prevalent among highly educated women than among less-educated women. One would think that increased education would be linked to a greater awareness of and concern about the health consequences of smoking, but this assumption appears incorrect. It may be that a higher educational level, especially in developing countries, imparts greater susceptibility to messages that promote positive associations with smoking. Only through systematic monitoring of smoking prevalence as well as of the knowledge, attitudes, and behaviors of the population can we appreciate the underlying reasons for the current epidemiologic configuration. Such appreciation, in turn, is the basis for a rational prevention and control program.

Another area in which surveillance is critical is in the monitoring of the tobacco sector of the economy. Such monitoring should include production, consumption, price structure, and taxation policy as well as advertising and promotion of tobacco products. The structure of the industry in any country will have important ramifications for the growth and "success" of the commodity. One of the fundamental paradoxes of market-oriented societies is that some entrepreneurs—even acting completely within the prescribed rules of business practice—will come into conflict with public health goals. The market structure of the tobacco industry constitutes a major threat to public health simply because the product is tobacco. In the tobacco industry, attempts to control a large market share, marketing to target groups, widespread use of innovative promotional techniques, and corporate growth, development, and consolidation—in short, the traditional elements of successful entrepreneurial activity—are ultimately inimical to the public health. Each country faces its own resolution of this paradox, but recognizing and monitoring it is fundamental to the prevention and control of tobacco use.

Most countries of the Americas have begun to face these complex issues. Several have taken major steps, others tentative ones, but all should recognize the crucial role of international coordination and cooperation. It is clear that although most countries can have significant impact on their own smoking-related problems, the international community can become smoke-free only by acting in concert. The process is an arduous one that begins with multifaceted efforts to change social norms regarding smoking and that moves ultimately to a disappearance of demand for tobacco products. I hope that the current report will serve as an impetus for continuing activity in the control of smoking and for mobilization of international resources toward the goal of a smoke-free society.

MACEDO'S PREFACE

Diseases related to smoking are an important cause of premature deaths in the world, both in developed and developing countries. Eliminating smoking can do more to improve health and prolong life than any other measure in the field of preventive medicine.

Developing countries, including those of Latin America and the Caribbean, are not behind their neighbors in the north with regard to the tremendous growing problem of noncommunicable diseases related to tobacco consumption.

Over the last three decades, the countries of Latin America and the Caribbean have experienced important changes in their demographic, socioeconomic, and epidemiologic profiles. Increasing numbers of the older, more urban, and especially the poorer populations of the region, are dying of diseases related to lifestyle determinants. Consumption of tobacco is one of these harmful threats to the health and well-being of our populations.

Despite that, in most of the developing countries of our region, not enough attention has been given to generate actions and the kind of information needed for policy and program formulation with regard to tobacco control. It is also unfortunate that while the transnational conglomerates in control of almost all tobacco production and marketing have directed their efforts toward penetrating developing economies, many governments, given the urgent needs created by other health problems, and in some cases due to financial or economic reasons, consider tobacco control a low priority.

The United States Government and the Pan American Health Organization (PAHO) have been working in a joint effort to generate the information included in the Surgeon General's report, and the PAHO country report, which hopefully will bring more awareness and promote action against smoking in the region of the Americas.

Our collaboration with the Office of the Surgeon General has been highly satisfactory, and it will encourage the development of a regional network for implementing research and exchange of successful experiences in the control of tobacco addiction.

Major Conclusions

Five major conclusions have emerged from review of the complex factors affecting smoking in the Americas. The first two relate to the current size of the problem; the latter three, to current conditions that have an important influence on the prevention and control of tobacco use.

1. The prevalence of smoking in Latin America and the Caribbean is variable but reaches 50 percent or more among young people in some urban areas. Significant numbers of women have taken up smoking in recent years.
2. By 1985, an estimated minimum of 526,000 smoking-attributable deaths were occurring yearly in the Americas; 100,000 of these deaths occurred in Latin America and the Caribbean.
3. In Latin America and the Caribbean, the current structure of the tobacco industry, which is dominated by transnational corporations, presents a formidable obstacle to smoking-control efforts.
4. The economic arguments for support of tobacco production are offset by the long-term economic effects of smoking-related disease.

5. Commitment to surveillance of tobacco-related factors—such as prevalence of smoking; morbidity and mortality; knowledge, attitudes, and practices; tobacco consumption and production; and taxation and legislation—is crucial to the development of a systemic program for prevention and control of tobacco use.

Summary

The use of tobacco in the Americas long predates the European voyages of discovery. Among indigenous populations, tobacco was used primarily for the pharmacologic effects of high doses of nicotine, and it played an important role in shamanistic and other spiritual practices. Its growth as a cash crop began only after the European market was opened to tobacco in the early and mid-seventeenth century. During early colonial times, the focus for tobacco cultivation shifted from Latin America and the Caribbean to North America, where a light, mellow brand of tobacco was grown. Despite antitobacco movements, the popularity of tobacco increased dramatically after the U.S. Civil War, and by the early part of the twentieth century, the cigarette had emerged as the tobacco product of choice in the United States.

The first half of the twentieth century witnessed a spectacular increase in the popularity of cigarettes and in the growth of several major cigarette manufacturing companies in the United States. Interest in international expansion was minimal until after World War II. In the early 1950s, preliminary reports of the health effects of tobacco first appeared; these were followed in 1964 by the first report of the Surgeon General on the health effects of smoking (Public Health Service 1964). These events, which were accompanied by a downturn in U.S. tobacco consumption, ushered in a period of rapid international expansion by the tobacco companies. Their expansion into Latin America and the Caribbean was typified by a process of denationalization—that is, the abandonment of local government tobacco monopolies and the creation of subsidiaries by U.S. and British transnational tobacco corporations. The transnational companies were particularly successful in altering local demand by influencing consumer preferences. Local taste for dark tobacco in a variety of forms was largely replaced by demand for the long, filtered, light-tobacco cigarettes produced by the transnational companies.

During the 1980s, several divergent forces influenced the consumption of tobacco in Latin America and the Caribbean. Changing demographics (primarily declining birth and death rates and an overall growth in the population), increasing urbanization, improving education, and the growing entry of women into the labor force—all expanded the potential market for tobacco. Although systematic surveillance evidence is lacking, an increased prevalence of smoking among young people, particularly women in urban areas, appears to have occurred during this period. A countervailing force, however, was the major economic downturn experienced by most countries of Latin America and the Caribbean during the

1980s. The result was that despite the increasing prevalence of smoking in some sectors of the population, overall consumption of tobacco declined. Unlike the decline in North America, however, the decline in Latin America and the Caribbean seems to have been based on income elasticity rather than on health concerns.

The health burden imposed by smoking in Latin America and the Caribbean is currently smaller than that in North America. A conservative estimate is that, by the mid-1980s, at least 526,000 deaths from smoking-related diseases were occurring annually in the Americas and that approximately 100,000 of these deaths occurred in Latin America and the Caribbean. Since the smoking epidemic is more recent, less widespread, and less entrenched in Latin America and the Caribbean than in North America, it may be thought of as less "mature"—that is, sufficient time has not yet elapsed for the cumulative effects of tobacco use to become manifest. Because health data from Latin American and Caribbean countries vary in consistency and comprehensiveness, establishing overall trends for morbidity and mortality is difficult. Nonetheless, the available evidence suggests an important contrast between North America on the one hand, and Latin America and the Caribbean on the other. In the United States and Canada, smoking-associated mortality is high and increasing because of high consumption levels in the past, but prevalence of smoking is declining. In Latin America and the Caribbean, prevalence of smoking is high in some sectors, but smoking-attributable mortality is still low compared with that for North America. This contrast augurs poorly for public health in Latin America and the Caribbean, unless action is taken.

The health costs of smoking are considerable. The U.S. population of civilian, noninstitutionalized persons aged 25 years or older who ever smoked cigarettes will incur lifetime excess medical care costs of $501 billion. The estimated average lifetime medical costs for a smoker exceed those for a nonsmoker by over $6,000. This excess is a weighted average of the costs incurred by all smokers, whether or not they develop smoking-related illness. For smokers who do develop such illnesses, the personal financial impact is much higher.

Available data do not permit a firm estimate for Latin America and the Caribbean. The estimate will probably vary with the health care structure of the country, but the burden is likely to increase with increasing development and industrialization. Nonetheless, early evidence suggests that smoking-prevention programs can be cost-effective under current economic circumstances.

The economics of the tobacco industry in the Americas are complex. Although tobacco had long been thought to be an inelastic commodity, it has been demonstrated to be both price and income elastic. Such elasticity renders tobacco use susceptible to control through taxation and other disincentives. Revenues from tobacco have been an important, though variable, source of funds for governments, but the case for promoting tobacco production on economic grounds is weak. Currently, only a few countries of Latin America and the Caribbean have economies that are largely dependent on tobacco production. The current economic picture, coupled with consumer responsiveness to income and price and the potential health hazards, has created a significant opportunity for tobacco control in Latin America and the Caribbean.

This opportunity is reflected, to some extent, in the fact that most countries of the Americas have legislation that controls tobacco use. Restrictions on advertising, the requirement of health warnings on tobacco products, limits on access to tobacco, and restrictions on public smoking have all been invoked. The legislative approach is not systematic, however, and in many countries, the programs have gaps. Furthermore, the extent to which such legislation is enforced is not fully known. Nonetheless, the pace of enactment suggests a growing awareness of the potential efficacy of the legislative approach.

Overall, the public health approach to tobacco control in Latin America and the Caribbean is variable. Many countries have adopted some elements of comprehensive control, including (in addition to legislation and taxation) the development of national coalitions, the promotion of education and media-based activities, and the development and refinement of surveillance systems. Few countries, however, have adopted the unified approach that characterizes, for example, the program in Canada.

The potential exists in the Americas for a strong, coordinated effort in smoking control at the local, national, and regional levels. The high prevalence of smoking that is emerging in many areas is a clear indicator of an approaching epidemic of smoking-related disease. The potential for decreasing consumption in Latin America and the Caribbean has been well demonstrated, albeit by the unfortunate mechanism of an economic downturn. The potential for a decline in smoking prevalence motivated by health concerns has been well demonstrated in North America. Furthermore, the importance of tobacco manufacturing and production to local economies is undergoing considerable scrutiny. Regional and international plans for tobacco control have been developed and are being implemented. For persons in the Americas in the coming years, the individual decision to smoke may well be made in an environment that is increasingly cognizant of the costs and hazards of smoking.

STUDY ON CANCER-PREVENTION PROPERTIES OF BROCCOLI

March 15, 1992

A team of scientists announced March 15 that they had isolated a potent, cancer-fighting chemical in the popular vegetable broccoli. Paul Talalay, a molecular pharmacologist at Johns Hopkins University School of Medicine, supervised a five-year series of controlled experiments that indicated a compound present in broccoli, sulforaphane, may help to prevent cancer. This conclusion was published in the Proceedings of the National Academy of Sciences.

The Hopkins study was widely reported both in the United States and abroad. Scientific studies, even ones with potentially important implications for medical science, such as the Hopkins findings, rarely receive so much attention. President George Bush was at least partially responsible for the added publicity. His now-famous 1991 declaration—"I do not like broccoli and I haven't liked it since I was a little kid and my mother made me eat it and I'm president of the United States and I'm not going to eat any more broccoli"—gave the story a news angle it otherwise would not have had. In a Science News *interview, Talalay took a bipartisan stance on the president's dislike for the vegetable. "Broccoli should protect both Republicans and Democrats equally well," he said. "The president may not want to change his mind, but we are hoping to encourage others to eat better."*

American opinion of broccoli is considerably higher than President Bush's. Per capita consumption of the vegetable shot up 800 percent from 1970 to 1989, from half a pound to four and a half pounds. A third of Americans ate broccoli at least once every two weeks, an increase of 33 percent over the previous decade. As consumption of broccoli rose, so did prices, and the publicity surrounding the Hopkins study made prices go up even further. Soon after the study was released, the wholesale price of broccoli doubled.

Beneficial Results Foreseen

Since the mid-1970s epidemiologists have reported that high intake of green and yellow vegetables was helpful in protecting the body against carcinogens. Increased comsumption of cruciferous vegetables (those belonging to the mustard family and including broccoli, brussels sprouts, cabbage, cauliflower) correlated with lowered risk of colon, breast, and prostate cancer. A few animal experiments with such vegetables also supported this conclusion.

Eating more vegetables results in a variety of complex dietary alterations, including higher fiber and vitamin consumption and lower fat intake. The Johns Hopkins study identified in vegetables known to reduce cancer risk in man a specific compound that raises the activities of enzymes that can neutralize cancer-causing chemicals. "This is the first time that a compound of such high potency in accelerating the detoxication processes has been isolated from vegetables," said Talalay.

The experiments did not prove that sulforaphane protects human cells against cancer. But, based on knowledge that other agents that raise the levels of these enzymes in animals block cancer, and that compounds chemically related to sulforaphane are anticarcinogens, Talalay was optimistic that additional research would demonstrate the natural compound's benefits in humans. If Talalay's prediction proves correct, consumption of vegetables containing sulforaphane or related compounds would be expected to reduce the risk of developing various types of cancer. An attractive aspect of this strategy of "chemoprotection" is that it is not specific for a single type of cancer, but that it usually protects against a variety of malignancies.

The Hopkins scientists chose to study broccoli because their cell culture test had shown that, among many vegetables examined, it is especially rich in its ability to raise the activities of the protective enzymes. In the experiments, solvent extracts of SAGA broccoli (grown in Maine, and a rich source of enzyme-boosting activity) were separated into many component fractions. Each fraction was then introduced separately into a culture of mouse liver cells. A single component, ultimately identified as sulforaphane, caused the mouse cells to produce cancer-fighting—so-called Phase II—enzymes, which detoxify cancer-causing molecules and prevent them from damaging a cell's deoxyribonucleic acid (DNA), or genetic material.

Phase II enzymes are opposed in their protective role by phase I enzymes, which can transform innocuous molecules into toxic ones. It is the balance between the phase I and phase II enzymes that determines whether a cell will become cancerous. Although most foods contain substances that stimulate cell production of both phase I and phase II enzymes, sulforaphane induces production only of phase II enzymes. Although some scientists speculated that even phase II enzymes could cause toxicity, there was general agreement that phase II enzymes have mostly beneficial effects. In fact, Talalay said he believed phase II enzymes may hold the key to cancer prevention. "There is mounting evidence that if you are able to raise the phase II enzymes, this will divert the carcinogenic compounds from damaging the [genes]."

Talalay said many years of research would be needed to prove conclusively how broccoli prevents cancer. In future experiments, many of which were to be performed on human cells, the Hopkins scientists hoped to determine how much sulforaphane is an effective cancer-fighting dose, how the human body responds to sulforaphane, and which foods are best at preventing cancer.

Following are excerpts from the two papers on the cancer-prevention properties of broccoli that appeared in the March 15, 1992, Proceedings of the National Academy of Sciences:

ABSTRACT

Dietary composition is a major determinant of cancer risk in humans and experimental animals. Major and minor components of the diet may enhance or suppress the development of malignancy. Many dietary constituents also modify the metabolism of carcinogens by induction of enzymes involved in xenobiotic metabolism, and this is one well-established mechanism for modulating the risk of cancer. . . .

Survey of extracts of a variety of commonly consumed, organically grown vegetables for quinone reductase inducer activity identified crucifers (and particularly those of the genus *Brassica*) as singularly rich sources. It is therefore of interest that high consumption of these types of vegetables has been correlated with decreased cancer risk in humans. . . .

Extrinsic factors, including personal life-styles, play a major role in the development of most human malignancies. Cigarette smoking and consumption of alcohol, exposure to synthetic and naturally occurring carcinogens, radiation, drugs, infectious agents, and reproductive and behavioral practices are now widely recognized as important contributors to the etiology of cancer. But perhaps most surprising is the inference that normal human diets play causative roles in more than one-third (and possibly even two-thirds) of human neoplasia. Our food contains not only numerous mutagens and carcinogens but also a variety of chemicals that block carcinogenesis in animal models. Furthermore, carcinogens can even protect against their own toxic and neoplastic effects or those of other carcinogens—i.e., carcinogens may act as anticarcinogens. Clearly, dietary modifications modulate cancer risk in various ways: for instance, through changes in caloric intake, by altering the consumption of nutritive and nonnutritive major components, and by providing exposure to numerous minor chemicals that may be genotoxic or protective. Rational recommendations for modifying human diets to reduce the risk of cancer require identification of dietary carcinogens and chemoprotectors, even though interactions among such factors in the etiology of cancer are complex. Whereas extensive efforts have been made to identify dietary carcinogens and mutagens, chemoprotective components have received far less attention. This paper describes a method for detecting and identifying anticarcinogenic components in human diets.

Since a major mechanism regulating neoplasia is the balance between phase I enzymes, which activate carcinogens, and phase II enzymes, which detoxify them, we have developed a cell culture system for simple and rapid detection of dietary components that enhance phase II detoxication enzymes. With this procedure we surveyed extracts of a variety of vegetables for their ability to induce such protective enzymes. In the accompanying paper we describe use of this method to isolate and identify a major inducer of protective enzymes from broccoli.

We chose vegetables as sources of inducers of detoxication enzymes for the following reasons. First, numerous epidemiological studies suggest that high consumption of yellow and green vegetables, especially those of the family Cruciferae (mustards) and the genus *Brassica* (cauliflower, cress, brussels sprouts, cabbage, broccoli), reduces the risk of developing cancer of various organs. Moreover, administration of vegetables or of some of their chemical components to rodents also protects against chemical carcinogenesis. Second, well-documented evidence established that feeding of certain vegetables (e.g., brussels sprouts and cabbage) induces both phase I and phase II enzymes in animal tissues and stimulates the metabolism of drugs in humans. The elevations of enzymes that metabolize xenobiotics may be highly relevant to the protective effects of vegetables, since relatively modest dietary changes not only affected the metabolism of drugs but also modified the ability of carcinogens to cause tumors in rodents. . . .

Since some crucifers (broccoli, brussels sprouts, cauliflower, cabbage) are consumed in substantial quantities in Western diets and are believed to protect against cancer, we examined the relation of inducer potency to variety, strain, location of growth, time of sowing, and time of harvest. Although systematic examination of these factors under field conditions would require extensive studies over several years of cultivation, it was important to determine whether such variables significantly affected the inducer activity. Except for a sample of kohlrabi, Cruciferae belonging to the species *Brassica oleracea* consistently and potently induced QR with broccoli and brussels sprouts generally the most potent inducers. The inductive capacity of most crucifers appears to be independent of geographic location of growth and time of harvest, although late sowing may have enhanced modestly the potency of the induction. On the basis of these results a particular variety of broccoli (SAGA) was selected for isolation and identification of monofunctional inducer activity as described in the accompanying paper.

In summary, epidemiological studies point to the inverse relationship between vegetable consumption and the risk of epithelial cancer, and they suggest a practical approach to achieving protection by emphasizing that the typical Western diet is low in fruits and vegetables....

ABSTRACT

Consumption of vegetables, especially crucifers, reduces the risk of developing cancer. Although the mechanisms of this protection are unclear, feeding of vegetables induces enzymes of xenobiotic metabolism and thereby accelerates the metabolic disposal of xenobiotics. Induction of phase II detoxication enzymes, such as quinone reductase ... and glutathione S-transferases ... in rodent tissues affords protection against carcinogens and other toxic electrophiles.... Sulforaphane is a monofunctional inducer, like other anticarcinogenic isothiocyanates, and induces phase II enzymes selectively.... Sulforaphane is the most potent inducer.... The induction of detoxication enzymes by sulforaphane may be a significant component of the anticarcinogenic action of broccoli.

Individuals who consume large amounts of green and yellow vegetables have a lower risk of developing cancer. Feeding of such vegetables to rodents also protects against chemical carcinogenesis.... Although much evidence suggests that induction of these enzymes is a major mechanism responsible for this protection, the precise role of enzyme induction in protection of humans requires clarification. ... [W]e found that cruciferous vegetables (broccoli, cauliflower, mustard, cress, brussels sprouts) were a rich source of inducer activity. We chose to investigate broccoli (*Brassica oleracea italica*) specifically because it is consumed in substantial quantities by Western societies and has been shown to contain abundant phase II enzyme inducer activity. In this paper we describe the isolation and identification of a potent major phase II enzyme inducer from broccoli.... We selected SAGA broccoli for study because acetonitrile extracts of lyophilized homogenates of this variety were especially rich in inducer activity in comparison with other vegetables....

... [S]ulforaphane is a major and probably the principal inducer of phase II enzymes present in extracts of SAGA broccoli....

It will be important to establish whether the alterations of drug metabolism observed in humans and rodents after the ingestion of cruciferous vegetables can be ascribed to their content of sulforaphane.

DE KLERK'S REMARKS ON NEW CONSTITUTION

March 18, 1992

The effort to move away from apartheid in South Africa was given a major boost on March 17, when a solid majority of the nation's whites voted in favor of negotiating a new constitution that would provide power-sharing between South Africa's minority white and overwhelmingly majority black populations (4.5 million and 33 million, respectively). The referendum was the progeny of South African President Frederik W. de Klerk, who launched a vigorous American-style campaign to persuade whites to accept the change. "It doesn't often happen that in one generation a nation gets the opportunity to rise above itself," said de Klerk on March 18, the day after the vote, which occurred on his 56th birthday. "The white electorate has risen above itself in this referendum. . . . Today we have closed the books on apartheid."

More than two-thirds of the white voters—68.7 percent—voted "yes" on the go-ahead for a new constitution. In only one of fifteen voting districts, Pietersburg, a conservative stronghold, did a majority vote in opposition. The margin of victory—much greater than had been foreseen—was the result of a well-orchestrated campaign by government officials, business and civic leaders, and the media.

Most newspapers ran prominent front-page editorials strongly endorsing the constitutional initiative. Both moderate black and white leaders had predicted "unprecedented political turmoil" and renewed international sanctions if the Conservative party and other right-wing groups succeeded in their concerted campaign to defeat the initiative.

Moving Toward Ending Apartheid

The referendum vote was one of many significant steps toward elimi-nating South Africa's fifty-year-old segregationist political, economic, and social system. After he became president, de Klerk began to move pragmatically but steadily to institute political reforms. One of his first moves, in February 1990, was to release African National Congress (ANC) leader Nelson Mandela and other political prisoners. At the same time, the president legalized the ANC and other anti-apartheid groups, allowing them to hold marches and rallies. Early in 1991 he called for an end to the remaining basic laws separating the races, including scrapping the Lands Acts that effectively made 87 percent of the country a white preserve, and he canceled the Group Areas Act, a vehicle for strictly segregating the races. The president also hinted that he needed a mandate to negotiate a new constitution and called for establishing an interim government based on a power-sharing formula among the races. Responding to these and other measures, a number of governments—including the Bush administration—which had imposed economic and diplomatic sanctions against South Africa, eased or lifted the restric-tions. Despite these actions, however, violence in South Africa continued. (De Klerk and Mandela on South African Changes, Historic Documents of 1990, p. 65; De Klerk on Racial Laws; Bush on Economic Sanctions, Historic Documents of 1991, p. 53)

With the release of Mandela—a highly respected leader among blacks whose fate was seen as a bellwether by many persons—de Klerk had a negotiating partner. Unlike more militant and uncompromising black groups, which called for absolute black majority rule, the ANC urged nonviolence and a South Africa that respected all citizens equally. Under de Klerk's and the ANC's initiative, more moderate political groups formed the CODESA (Convention for a Democratic South Africa) negoti-ating body. First meeting in February 1992, about 300 delegates from nineteen groups approved a declaration of intent committing them to adhere to the basic tenets of multiparty democracy. (The existing constitu-tion excludes blacks from voting and from representation in the tricameral parliament composed of whites, Indians, and mixed-race coloreds.)

CODESA Process and Referendum

In campaigning for the referendum to proceed with the CODESA process, de Klerk threatened to resign and call a general election if a majority of whites voted "no." Although many white South Africans feared that a "yes" vote would lead to black majority rule and economic catastrophe, de Klerk emphasized that a retreat to apartheid was "too ghastly to contemplate." Turning back the clock, he said, would plunge the nation into further violence and economic depression.

De Klerk seemed to have plucked underlying sentiment in favor of a "yes" vote. A majority of the nation's white community had become increasingly uneasy with South Africa's status as an international outcast. They feared that a "no" vote would lead to renewed international economic sanctions, discourage foreign investment in the country, and reimpose a ban on South African participation in the Olympics and the upcoming World Cup cricket competition.

Reaction to the Referendum

After the referendum, Mandela said the vote meant the peace process was "definitely on course" and that there was "great relief" among black leaders about the outcome. But he also said, "apartheid is still very much alive. I still cannot vote in my own country" and warned that this should be the "absolute last" all-white vote.

White House press spokesman Marlin Fitzwater praised the vote "for a just and democratic future" and said "the United States firmly and fully supports" the constitutional negotiations. Members of the Organization of African Unity also generally praised the vote, as did other world leaders, including those in the European Community. The referendum "will bring South Africa back into the international community," said British prime minister John Major.

The reaction from radical South African right- and left-wing groups was strident. The radical black Pan-Africanist Congress, which had refused to participate in the constitutional negotiations, called the referendum "an obscenity and an insult to the dispossessed masses of our country." Conservative party leader Andries Treurnicht said that, despite defeat, "the struggle for freedom and survival is now continuing in even greater earnestness than before. . . . This vote signals the end of parliamentary politics as we have known it."

Violence Escalates

Despite de Klerk's victory on the referendum, reform still had a long way to go; at the end of the year, the apartheid system and existing constitution remained largely intact, with no new laws on the books that protected or extended blacks' rights.

Relations between de Klerk and Mandela, at first cordial, became laced with acrimony. Mandela broke off constitutional negotiations June 23, accusing the government of permitting Zulu supporters of ANC's rival Inkatha Freedom Party to kill forty-three residents of the pro-ANC township of Boipatong. In the aftermath, the ANC launched a "mass action" campaign of general strikes and stay-aways.

Violence continued, with twenty-eight killed in September in a confrontation between ANC demonstrators and soldiers from the Ciskei "homeland" town of Bisho, who fired on the marchers indiscriminately. Nonetheless, Mandela indicated that he was ready to resume negotiations. Meeting September 26, the two leaders pledged "with all urgency" to create an interim government of national unity. But their harmony was marred by the opposition of Mangosuthu Buthelezi, leader of the nation's 7 million Zulus, who broke off his participation in protest of the "illegitimate" ANC-government arrangements.

> *Following are excerpts from the March 18, 1992, news conference held by South African President F. W. de Klerk following a referendum in which a large majority of whites voted in favor of negotiations to work out a new constitution:*

Good Afternoon, ladies and gentlemen. I would like to start out by first saying thank you to all of you, because all of you have participated in this referendum as much as I and all the other political leaders have participated, and without your involvement, the electorate would not have been properly informed. So thank you to the media for making available so much space and so much time, and to play an informative role.

I would also like to address a special word of appreciation towards the Department of Internal Affairs. I think they excelled themselves. They rendered a marvelous service to the public, those who lost their documents; to immigrants who wanted to naturalize. They managed to cut red tape in an admirable manner, and they did a sterling job, also yesterday, and also today.

Ladies and gentlemen, the result was an extraordinary one. It is one which creates confidence. It should create confidence internationally, and hopefully it will also create confidence internally. The massive positive result sends out a powerful message to all South Africans, that those who have the power in terms of the present, imperfect Constitution really mean it when they say: We want to share power, we want a new dispensation, we want it to be fair, we want it to be equitable, we believe in one undivided South Africa, within which power must be shared on the basis of no suppression, no domination, effective protection of minorities, and all the other important checks and balances which we have emphasized and for which we now have a very clear mandate.

I also wish to say that we are entering a new phase, and I wish to express the hope that those who voted no will accept this clear, democratic answer from the electorate as a clear statement, and that they will also exhibit a new approach within this new reality. It is important that the negotiation process become even more representative.

I believe it is important that they accept that the process is indeed irreversible, and that a final no has been said by the yes victory against attempts to return to the old days and the policy which could not succeed over a period of 40 years; that they should enjoy the opportunity which exists to become part of the negotiation process and to come and compete creatively. There is room for differences, and I am not asking them to agree with every point of view supported by the yes voters, but to support the reform process. The basis, namely that we should offer a just solution within the reality that we are living in the same country; to find a way of living together; and the method, namely that we should talk and place our different views on the table—all this, I hope, will now also become part of the planning and activity of those who voted no, and their leaders.

We must guard against radicalism. We must guard against frustration due to lack of success for support of your views leading to negative results. Today I also extend a hand of friendship to all who voted yes, and I call on them and their leaders to come and work with us, to come and build with us. We have reached a turning point in our history, and everyone now has the opportunity to make this turning point its departure point to long term stability and security and peace. There is enough room and a place for everyone in South Africa, and there are ways other than those advocated up to now by the no voters, to give the Afrikaner people security, a secure society, to secure everything which is so important to all the minorities in South Africa effectively. I did not ask for a blank check. I am committed to the mandate given to me, and you may come and assist to ensure that the new constitution we are working on will be a constitution which will offer real security and peace and prosperity and stability for all in South Africa, and on which the future must be built.

Any questions ladies and gentlemen?

[Moderator] Mr. Hilton-Barber. The mike.

[Hilton-Barber] Brett Hilton-Barber, Radio 702. Sir, do you feel that the right-wing will now try to take an unconstitutional approach to halting your reforms, including widespread violence?

[De Klerk] No, I don't fear that. I am convinced that the majority of those who voted no and the majority of the leadership on the right are responsible people. They are against violence, as we are, and I hope that the no-voters won't allow themselves to be misled or to be wrongly influenced by a very small handful of radicals who might entertain such thoughts. We will continue to stand firm against radicalism, whether it's on the right or the left, and I think one of the important interpretations of today's outcome is that the overwhelming majority of voters within the House of Assembly reject violence and are reaching out to peaceful negotiated solutions.

[Moderator] That gentleman please.

[Mopane] Israel Mopane, Bop [Bophuthatswana] TV News. Mr. President, you have been given a landslide victory. How fast will you be moving to bring about democracy in South Africa?

[De Klerk] The test for success is to be found in the tempo of success of negotiation. I think that this landslide victory will have a positive influence also on the tempo. I think it will give impetus to the whole process of negotiation, but the final acid test lies in us reaching agreement around the negotiation table and nobody can really put an exact timetable on when that will be attained, but I think the foundation has been laid by the landslide victory to get there sooner.

[Moderator] Mr. (Bell) please.

[(Bell)] (Gavin Bell), London TIMES. Mr. President, on a specific point on the negotiations, the relevant Codesa [Convention for a Democratic South Africa] working group recently agreed on the need to establish an interim government council. Have you any idea whether this might be installed this year?

[De Klerk] Well there was an agreement in principal with regard to certain basic principles. Further discussions will continue. This only laid a foundation and gave structure to the discussions. There was no final agreement on specific installation of an interim or transitional government, we prefer the term transitional, and once again I think nobody can put an exact timetable because there are important aspects in that regard also still to be negotiated.

[Moderator] Gentleman next to Mr. (Bell). Thank you.

[(O'Hare)] (Julian O'Hare), from BBC television Newsnight program, London. You have won this referendum, sir, and the yes-campaign has won it, partly on the pledge to white voters of a power-sharing government in the future, yet Mr. Mandela, even as he congratulates you today, is still talking about majority government in which the party with the greatest number of votes or a majority is asked to form a government. How will you bridge that gap?

[De Klerk] The only way to bridge gaps, and that is what we have been mandated to do, is to do that through negotiation. It is an important gap and, therefore, it is difficult to put timetables because when you get to those fundamentals then there is no quick fix. It's easy to bridge gaps when the gaps relate to mere practicalities, but this will be obviously one of the fundamental aspects where we need to find accommodation. I have a clear mandate to do so now within a particular framework.

We believe that we are in step with the rest of the world when we say it must be power sharing. Some of the most successful democracies avoid the possibility of domination just on a winner takes all basis. There are so many successful democracies which have succeeded in avoiding that and the rest of the world, wherever you find the type of complexity, and nowhere is it as complex as our complexities, have found it necessary to build in checks and balances which can prevent the misuse of power, which does offer effective security to minorities against domination.

It's common sense for us to do so too, and therefore, I believe that I have a very good case and a very good cause and I am in step with the rest of the world on this issue and hopefully, wisdom will prevail at the negotiation table and we will be able to find a formula which will clearly, on the one hand, attain this, and on the other hand, will in no way detract from the essential democratic nature because we don't have a hidden agenda when we say these things. We don't want a majority, however it is made up, to be relegated into an inferior position or into a weak position. It is a question of, if you have 51 percent of the vote you shouldn't have a hundred percent of the power.

Mr. Mandela, if that is a correct reflection of his point of view, stands on the Westminster system. The Westminster system isn't a good system for our type of society. It's a marvelous one for Great Britain and, therefore, some tough negotiations lie ahead.

[Moderator] Mr. Ottaway.

[Ottaway] Dave Ottaway, WASHINGTON POST. Mr. President, I'm wondering, now that you have a clear mandate, I'm wondering whether we can expect that there will be any changes in the top levels of your security forces, and whether you will finally take any steps against the AWB [Afrikaner Resistance Movement], as it seems to be a private army on its own in the country.

[De Klerk] Yes, I've heard about the speculation that I felt I needed a mandate to do something with regard to the security forces. I want to reject it as I've done already during the campaign. There's a very, very good relationship between me and the top echelon of the security forces, the defense force, as well as the South African Police, and this story that I might be contemplating a purge of the security forces has no factual basis whatsoever. With regard to the question of acting against the AWB, we are not acting, since the 2nd of February 1990, against organizations per se. We act against illegal activities. We act against people who break the law. If intimidation is part of the policy of any movement, yes, we will act against intimidation. If unlawful interference with the ordinary run of democracy is contemplated by anybody, we will act against them. But against organizations per se, since we revoked the state of emergency, and since 2 February 1990, we are not dealing with it in that specific way.

[Moderator] [name indistinct].

[Unidentified reporter] Mr. President, why are you insisting that the MK [Umkhonto we Sizwe, Spear of the Nation—ANC Military wing] be dissolved, if you're not insisting the AWB be dissolved.

[De Klerk] The MK finds itself in a position of being offered as a private army, as a military wing of a political party, participating in the negotiation process. We've signed an accord, in the peace accord, which says that no political party should have private armies. Inasmuch as AWB could be coupled in that very same sense, our attitude with regard to the AWB would be exactly the same. We are not discriminating in any direction whatsoever, but the AWB, thus far, has not looked upon itself as a military wing of the CP [Conservative Party], and the CP has not accepted them formally, with fôrmal links, as its military wing. So really there are some differences, but I have no sympathy for the AWB. I think that fascism and a form of neo-Nazism is absolutely unacceptable. We totally reject it. I regard that organization as a dangerous organization. They are our political opponents, and we fought them tooth and nail during the referendum, and will continue to do so after the referendum. But any organization breaking the law will be dealt with in terms of the law.

[Moderator] Mr. (Martin).

[Martin] Martin, CBC Television. Just a follow-up on that question regarding checks and balances. How far are you prepared to go to ensure that checks and balances are put in place, given the stance of the ANC [African National Congress]? How far would you be able to go?

[De Klerk] Well, it's absolutely fundamental, and therefore we will put very strong emphasis on that. We will continue negotiating until we are also satisfied that a new constitution to which we agree will be able to accommodate the needs arising from the complexity of our society, and from the many minorities of cultural diversity, etcetera. So for us it's fundamental, and we're not just playing with words. I believe it must be part of a new constitution. It is part of our bottom line.

[Moderator] Mr. Tony Johnson.

[Johnson] Anthony Johnson, CAPE TIMES. Mr. de Klerk, given the resounding victory the yes vote has just received, what do you think the prospects are that elements of the right-wing will join the negotiations, and what's the implications of this for the Conservative Party?

[De Klerk] I definitely believe that there's a strong element within the CP and those who voted no who felt, even before the referendum was called, that they should change their stance on negotiations, and should find ways and means of becoming participants in negotiations. If I can facilitate in the sense of meeting them, they are welcome to come and see me. It's an open invitation, which I issued a long time ago, and my door remains open. Many of the objections which have been offered are not valid objections. The declaration of intent does not exclude, in any way whatsoever, the type of reasonable proposals which I think some—I don't agree that they can work—but which some people within the CP would like to bring into the negotiation process. Therefore I do expect some form of realignment within the allies to the right which fought for the no vote. Alternatively, I expect a repositioning and hopefully a more realistic policy approach after some internal agonizing within the ranks of the right. But I do think that the political scene to the right of us will be very active and extremely interesting in the weeks to follow.

[Moderator] Mr. Contreras.

[Contreras] Joe Contreras, from NEWSWEEK magazine. Mr. President, you said in the past that creating a single united education department required a change to the constitution of this country. You said earlier today that this country has closed the book on apartheid. I want to ask you whether the landslide victory in the referendum will in anyway change your feelings about the possibility of creating a single unified educational department before a new dispensation is negotiated?

[De Klerk] Inasmuch as it requires fundamental changes to the Constitution, the position remains the same. Yes, it must be changed, but only after negotiation. On that there is consensus. There is already consensus in Codesa that we must not change the constitution unilaterally. That fundamental changes to the constitution must flow from negotiation and from agreements reached there. In that sense of the word I won't, because of the landslide win now, suddenly start doing important things unilaterally which we have already agreed upon should flow from negotiation.

But administratively, we have already started to do fundamental reforms with regard to education, and we cannot wait necessarily to prepare the ground for a more acceptable educational system which will also stop to be controversial in the political sense of the word because we really need in this country—looking upon education as one of our highest priorities—we really need to start working together to upgrade education and training wherever it is possible and not to keep it in the political arena where it wrongly is at the moment. So, as I've said during the opening of Parliament almost a year ago, little bit more than a year ago, what we can do administratively to remove discrimination, to improve education, we will continue to do, but the Constitution itself is a matter to be negotiated.

[Moderator] Mr. Johnson.

[Johnson] Shawn Johnson, from THE STAR. Mr. de Klerk, did we today experience the last white referendum in South African history, and if the answer is no could you perhaps sketch for us the precise circumstances under which it's conceivable that we would go through another exercise of this sort?

[De Klerk] I made this very clear when I announced the referendum that we will be asking for a specific mandate. If we deliver on that mandate which I now have, then there won't be need again. If we don't deliver, and if on fundamentals we cannot give effect to the promises which we made and on the basis of which we gained the landslide win, than obviously I'm bound by previous assurances that, once again, I will have to somehow or another come back to the electorate, but I foresee that we will be able to deliver. And therefore I think it is improbable that we will have such a specific referendum again. . . .

[Moderator] The last question. Mr. Christopher Wren at the back please.

[Wren] Mr. President, how calculated was the risk that you took in calling the referendum? Did it ever. . . . [Wren changes thought] Were you ever worried that you might lose or did you feel that you had support all along, to carry it off?

[De Klerk] I'm not a gambling man as NEWSWEEK called me on their front cover. No, I was confident when I called it that I could at that stage command nowhere near the type of support which the yes vote brought, but definitely that I had majority support. That was based not on a guess, but obviously in modern times we all have the benefit of opinion polls from time to time and all the opinion polls also indicated that countrywide, where every vote has the same weight, I started off with basic assurance that I could win. But then a campaign of course holds its risks. Sometimes things can go wrong during a campaign and we are very grateful that in our case, instead of going wrong it really came together.

We had a marvelous campaign. We succeeded in one of, what I would describe, one of our main goals, and that was to get each and every voter who had the opportunity to vote, an opportunity to decide for himself or herself and to really divorce grievances, and there are many. People feel uncertain. The economy is bad. Many people are going through a bad time at the moment and we have the greatest sympathy with that, but we really gave them the opportunity and they helped us by putting that aside and by focusing on the content of the question and by committing themselves to a peaceful solution through negotiation, and this was wonderful for South Africa and all its people.

I thank, therefore, in closing, the electorate for the way in which they applied their minds, they accepted our bona fides and gave us the benefit of what they believe, gave us the benefit of making a personal choice and a personal commitment. This referendum, more than the 2 February 1990, has changed and will change the face of South Africa. Thank you very much ladies and gentlemen. Everything of the best, and I hope that some of you will get in some rest now as well.

ETHICS OFFICE REPORTS ON SUNUNU'S TRAVELS

March 23, April 7, 1992

A report released April 7 by the Office of Government Ethics (OGE) criticized both the travel practices of former White House chief of staff John H. Sununu and a previous memorandum on the matter prepared by presidential counsel C. Boyden Gray. The thirty-eight-page OGE analysis challenged the White House's justification of Sununu's use of military aircraft for extensive travel, including political and personal trips.

Before releasing its report, OGE sent the review and questions to Gray's office for comment on March 23. After the counsel's office responded to OGE's satisfaction, Sununu, who had already reimbursed the government $1,423, paid an additional $4,243.

During his two years as President, George Bush's chief of staff, the former New Hampshire governor, had taken seventy-six trips on military aircraft at a total cost of more than $500,000. Of that amount, Sununu had reimbursed the government $17,578, and political sponsors had paid $53,000. Sununu claimed that forty-nine trips—including two ski trips to Colorado—were entirely on "official business," which meant that he traveled free and reimbursed the government coach fare plus one dollar for any family members who traveled with him. On several occasions, however, he classified as "official" trips that combined government business with Republican political events. For example, in 1990 he took two trips that included political functions in Akron, Ohio, and Milwaukee, Wisconsin, billing the government for the entire cost of $19,582 for use of the Air Force Gulfstream jet. Only four trips, including two to a dentist in Boston, were listed as personal.

Publicity Prompts Policy Review, Revision

In April 1991 news reports began circulating about Sununu's extensive travel, using military aircraft and billing the government for expenses that were sometimes nonofficial. Apparently, Bush—who had said he would institute rigorous ethical standards in the White House—had been unaware of a Reagan administration policy that allowed the chief of staff and national security adviser almost total freedom to use military aircraft. In response to the news reports, the White House released the records of Sununu's travels, which provoked additional publicity. At the same time, Bush asked Gray to review the White House travel policy "in light of practice and see if it should be altered in any way." On May 9 the counsel sent a memorandum to the chief of staff. Sununu promptly released the memorandum to the press with a statement that "the White House Counsel's Office . . . has concluded that 'these trips were properly classified . . . and appropriate reimbursements have been made.'" Sununu also contended that his use of military aircraft was not only permitted but also required under the policy established October 1, 1987, by President Ronald Reagan for his chief of staff and national security adviser.

In a press release May 9, the White House announced a policy revision "designed to avoid any questions about their [chief of staff and national security adviser] use of military aircraft." Henceforth, the White House counsel's office would review requests for travel on military aircraft on a case-by-case basis and would authorize use "where security, communications or scheduling needs require the use of military aircraft." The existing reimbursement policy for personal or political travel on military planes would remain in effect. The new policy would not affect cabinet officers, such as the secretary of state, whose responsibilities required "instantaneous secure communications" with the White House and other agencies.

Shortly thereafter, responding to numerous requests that an independent executive branch agency investigate Sununu's travel, the OGE undertook its review. In December the White House adopted further regulations designed to clarify travel authorization, voucher, and billing procedures.

The travel issue added to the controversy already swirling around Sununu. Finally, on December 10, 1991, after several advisers warned Bush that his autocratic, high-profile chief of staff could be a liability to the president's reelection, Bush forced Sununu to resign. In his resignation letter, Sununu—who had been instrumental in Bush's 1988 victory in the New Hampshire primary—said he would continue to support Bush "in pit bull mode or pussy cat mode (your choice, as always)." Sununu remained in the White House as a counselor to the president. (Sununu's Resignation as Bush's Chief of Staff, Historic Documents of 1991, p. 769)

Bush replaced Sununu with the lower-key, congenial, and less imperious transportation secretary, Samuel K. Skinner. But by the spring of 1992 questions about Skinner's travel practices were also being raised in the press. Skinner reimbursed the government $3,275.50.

Ethics Agency Questions Practices

In its report the OGE suggested that initial White House investigations were inadequate and that policy changes had been made only in response to widespread public revelations of Sununu's extensive travel. The OGE also disputed Sununu's contention that the government mandated all his travel on military aircraft for security reasons. The ethics office report said that "putting aside the question of whether the Governor [Sununu] should have relied upon the policy of a previous President without confirming it with the President he served, that policy clearly required that the Chief of Staff and National Security Advisor exercise some discretion when using Government aircraft for vacation or similar travel. In short, the policy allowed him to use the aircraft when appropriate and make whatever reimbursements were necessary, but it did not require him to use it for all purposes. Assuming the Governor attempted to adhere to this policy, we must conclude he substantially erred in his analysis of an appearance of impropriety. . . ."

The report also questioned the government's policy of requiring reimbursement at commercial rates, rather than the full cost of using much more expensive military aircraft, as well as the White House's determination that for the eleven times he used a government car and driver, Sununu would reimburse the government less than $600—a rate based on the cost of a rental car and a driver for only the hours the car was in use. Rep. Robert E. Wise, Jr., D-W. Va., said April 7 that the minimal amount of reimbursements meant that taxpayers were paying large sums for the former chief of staff's personal travel.

The OGE challenged a number of Sununu's trips, including ski vacations, that he had labeled as official. For example, he classified a three-day vacation in Aspen, Colorado, in December 1990 as official business, based on remarks he said he made about his job at breakfast the first day at a Ski magazine event. Industry sponsors paid for all of the Sununu's ground expenses; taxpayers paid for $31,954 in military air fare. Sununu reimbursed the government $802 for his wife's air travel on the Gulfstream.

Gray did not comment on the OGE's suggestion that he had undertaken an inadequate inquiry; his office said that Gray had not questioned whether Sununu had categorized his travel appropriately, saying that there was a "presumption" that a high-ranking official would correctly determine whether his travel was official.

Following are the texts of the March 23, 1992, letter from Office of Government Ethics director Stephen D. Potts to Counsel to the President C. Boyden Gray summarizing the OGE's findings concerning travel by former White House chief of staff John H. Sununu, and the April 7, 1992, White House statement announcing release of the OGE report:

POTTS'S LETTER TO GRAY

Dear Mr. Gray:

Last May, after you issued your memorandum to Governor Sununu on his use of Government aircraft, I wrote to you asking to see the background documents that you and your staff relied upon in coming to your conclusions in that memorandum. Your office provided a member of my staff with access to copies of these travel documents and miscellaneous letters. The Governor's staff was also very cooperative with regard to access to the Governor's daily schedules. I thank you, your staff and the Governor's staff for that assistance.

On February 5, 1992, consistent with OGE's policy of providing a draft analysis of any review done by it of any agency review of an individual's conduct, I provided you with this Office's draft analysis of the May 9 memorandum. On February 11, my staff met with yours to discuss the draft. At that time, your staff provided additional memoranda supplementing your May 9 memorandum and detailing changes in White House procedures that had occurred since the issuance of your memorandum. Your staff also provided copies of all available letters of invitation to the Governor for the trips. These letters had not been made available to your staff at the time of your review but were subsequently made available to the General Accounting Office (GAO). Your staff asked that this Office take the information in these documents, as well as information provided orally, into consideration before issuing a final analysis. After discussions with my staff, I asked that your office provide your comments in writing. I received a memorandum incorporating your comments on February 26, 1992. I have considered carefully the written and oral input from your office. My conclusions are set forth in the enclosed analysis.

The enclosed analysis contains a section entitled "Other Issues." We recognize that the primary focus of your May 9 memorandum was the use of Government aircraft. In the days preceding issuance of your memorandum, these other issues, understandably, did not appear as pressing as the issue involving use of Government aircraft. We raise these issues now, however, because they need to be addressed by your office. We assume that the GAO, with its team of auditors and its expanded scope of review, may have questions other than those of our offices. In those instances where we noticed issues that may be the source of criticism of the Executive Office of the President (EOP) by the GAO, but which are not traditionally within the ambit of an "ethics" review, we have taken the liberty of mentioning them so that the appropriate offices within the EOP can take any necessary steps to address those issues as well.

One very important issue that must be raised in the context of this review concerns the procedures followed by Governor Sununu's

Office and by the Military Office for the Governor's travel. These procedures—or lack thereof—resulted in so little proper travel documentation as to make adequate review difficult. I was dismayed to learn from my staff that of 76 listed trips, travel authorizations had been issued for only 29 and 15 of those were issued after the trips had been taken. There were travel vouchers for only 5 trips and, apparently, the only reason these vouchers were completed is because a part of each of these trips was with the President and some office other than the Chief of Staff's was, therefore, responsible for assisting with the preparation of the documents. Travel vouchers are normally a primary source of information about the characterization of trips by individuals. Vouchers also can provide answers to questions about the source of travel expenses.

In addition we, as did your office, found there was no established written procedure for requesting an aircraft or for documenting an oral request. There was no procedure for formally notifying the Military Office whether a trip was to be considered official, political or personal and thus there were no standard billing procedures. Had the Governor or his office followed the proper procedures, or had the Military Office employed a more formalized billing procedure, appropriate questions would have arisen early, and the Governor's use of government aircraft probably would not have become the issue it did.

From the additional memoranda you provided my Office on February 11, I now know that on December 12, 1991, you submitted a memorandum to Andy Card, then Assistant to the President and Deputy Chief of Staff, in which you outlined several areas in which changes would significantly improve the review and approval process of travel by White House staff. The subjects covered were travel authorizations, travel vouchers, procedures for determining the status of travelers, billing and reimbursement procedures, and the use of military aircraft approval forms. I understand that Mr. Card approved these procedures on December 19, 1991, and that they may be incorporated into the White House Staff Manual and a future White House Travel Guide. I believe that these changes, like the President's change of policy issued on May 9, should ensure that the Government does not inadvertently provide personal or political travel to individuals without seeking appropriate reimbursements.

The enclosed analysis begins with an introductory section which is intended to set forth the basis for the analysis so that it can be read and understood without this letter. It also sets forth the standard of review used by our Office. We appreciate that your Office, acting under time constraints to which our Office was not subject, of necessity employed a different standard of review. The introduction is followed by an analysis of the general statements made at the beginning of your May 9 memorandum. The analysis proceeds to specific issues addressed in that memorandum and ends with specific issues not addressed by the memorandum. You will find throughout that I occasionally suggest that your office seek additional information and, based upon that information, revisit your analysis of certain trips to determine if the proper source paid for the travel expenses. In addition, for three trips not previously considered personal, I have determined, based upon the information now available to both of our offices, that the Governor should reimburse the Government for these trips.

The Governor in a May 9, 1991 press release stated that your memorandum "made it clear that all travel expense payments and reimbursements received were consistent with applicable ethics laws and regulations. . . ." Your memorandum did not specifically state that conclusion, but it may have created that impression. The Governor's statement is discussed in some detail in the enclosed analysis. In brief, however, it is the conclusion of this Office that Governor Sununu's actions clearly implicated specific regulations dealing with the standards of conduct required of executive branch officials. Additionally, documents reviewed by my Office suggest that Governor Sununu, while the Chief of Staff, was not sensitive to the Principles of Ethical Conduct for Government Officers and Employees set forth by President Bush in his Executive Order in April of 1989. As I know you agree, high ranking Government officials should not be given favored treatment. The rules apply to all alike and the higher the position in Government the greater the responsibility to adhere to the highest principles of public service.

Individuals who serve the Government in the Cabinet or as Chief of Staff or National Security Advisor must, of course, have the ability to use available Government resources whenever necessary to carry out their duties in a responsible manner. However, because a higher level review of travel-related decisions by such individuals is typically not conducted, such individuals bear a significant duty of care in exercising personal judgment with respect to such decisions. Unfortunately, I can only conclude that Governor Sununu failed to meet this responsibility.

I can appreciate the difficulties you faced in issuing your memorandum to the Governor, and I applaud your acting quickly to recommend to the President a change in the policy concerning the use of military aircraft. Given the time in which your review had to be conducted and the disarray of the documents your staff had to review, I believe that your office did an admirable preliminary job. I concur in your judgment that it was more important to stop the questionable conduct than to conduct a more thorough review, which would have prolonged the issue. Your prompt action also made it possible for my Office to begin its review early.

The enclosed analysis asks that your Office obtain additional information and that the Governor reimburse the Government for at least three more trips. I now ask that you proceed with these matters. When this Office reviews an agency ethics program, we provide that agency with 60 days in which to respond to the issues contained in that memorandum. I would appreciate your concluding this matter and providing me with a

final report on your actions within 60 days. If you have any questions, please do not hesitate to contact me.
Sincerely,

Stephen D. Potts
Director

WHITE HOUSE PRESS RELEASE

Today the White House released a report prepared by the Office of Government Ethics (OGE) regarding former Chief of Staff John H. Sununu's travel on military aircraft. At the same time, the White House released a response to the report prepared by the Office of the Counsel to the President, and a letter from the Director of the Office of Government Ethics stating that OGE's review is concluded.

In his letter to the Counsel to the President, the Director of the Office of Government Ethics stated, "I am very pleased with your response and the actions the Governor has chosen to take. I believe that this now ends any open question about the issues raised by his use of military aircraft."

The OGE report identified several matters that it believed warranted further inquiry. In each case, the Office of Counsel to the President resolved the matter to the satisfaction of OGE. The report also recommended in several instances that Governor Sununu should provide additional reimbursement to the Government. To avoid any further question regarding his travel, Governor Sununu has reimbursed $4242.80 to the Government.

The OGE report noted that the White House has instituted numerous changes in policy and procedure since May 9, 1991. On May 9, 1991, the White House issued a revised travel policy that requires trip-by-trip review and approval by the Counsel's office to ensure that military aircraft are used only when necessary. That policy also tightened the standards for use of military aircraft in cases of personal or political travel.

In December 1991, the White House adopted a series of improvements in the review and approval process for travel of White House staff. These improvements include:

- a strict requirement that travel authorizations be completed in advance of travel for all travel of White House staff;
- a strict requirement that travel vouchers be completed for all travel of White House staff within two weeks following travel;
- a process to ensure that the status of all travellers on military aircraft is determined before travel begins and confirmed after travel is completed; and
- procedures to ensure prompt billing for political and personal travel and prompt payment of reimbursements.

The OGE report stated that these changes should prevent any recurrence of the events in question.

 **HISTORIC DOCUMENTS OF 1992**

April

REPORT ON SPENDING HABITS
OF UNITED WAY'S EX-PRESIDENT
April 2, 1992

Five weeks after William Aramony was forced from office as president of United Way of America (UWA), a report commissioned by the board of governors concluded that he had developed a "lavish lifestyle" that "constituted a lack of judgment" and "tragically jeopardized" the network of charitable organizations he had developed during twenty-two years in office.

Personal spending by the sixty-four-year-old Aramony ranged from purchases of flowers and golf equipment to flights to Europe on the supersonic Concorde—all at UWA's expense. The report showed some reimbursements by Aramony, who claimed he repaid "everything" and denied any misuse of funds.

In December 1991, after UWA officials learned that allegations concerning Aramony's use of the charity's funds were about to be made public, they hired the Investigative Group Inc. (IGI), with Aramony's consent, to look into the charges. In February news reports disclosed Aramony's salary ($390,000, plus $73,000 in other compensation during his last year as president) and reported on his unusual management style. The UWA board then expanded the investigation, retaining the Washington law firm of Verner, Liipfert, Bernhard, McPherson, and Hand. On February 28 the board removed Aramony and Thomas J. Merlo, chief financial officer, from UWA payrolls.

History of United Way System

As a national organization, UWA came into being in 1918 to provide services to local "Community Chests," which were established to coordi-

nate community fund raising for various charities. The national organization, "Community Chests and Councils Inc.," was incorporated in 1932. By 1944 there were approximately 800 local United Ways or Community Chests; in 1967 United Way campaigns raised more than $700 million to fund 31,300 agencies; in 1990 the system raised $3.11 billion to fund an estimated 44,000 agencies nationwide.

In 1992 approximately 1,400 local United Ways belonged to the national UWA; the local members are independent, separately incorporated organizations governed by local boards of volunteers. The UWA is a tax-exempt organization ruled by a thirty-seven-member board of governors elected by the member organizations and reflecting business, industry, labor, and not-for-profit sectors. UWA provides technical support and services to more than 2,100 local community-based organizations. Local United Ways pay annual dues to the national office in an amount equal to approximately 1 percent of the community-wide campaign contributions raised by each local. The dues represent the primary financial support for UWA's operating budget. Of its total revenues of almost $30 million in 1991, $24.2 million was derived from dues. UWA services to members include consulting on volunteer and professional training and marketing, advertising, conferencing, and fund distribution.

Report Findings

"These allegations suggest that Aramony manipulated the design and operation of UWA so that it served not only its charitable purpose . . . but also provided benefits to Mr. Aramony personally and to certain of his friends and family members," the fifty-nine-page report said. Although they lauded Aramony's accomplishments at UWA, the investigators concluded that he used his position as president to write his own rules. "Obedience to authority was the rule, and financial controls failed to take into account the power of the president and his assistants," the report said.

Among the expenditures documented were $92,000 in limousine service over four years; almost $38,000 on at least twenty-nine trips to Las Vegas for Aramony and others; more than $72,000 on international air fare for Aramony, his wife, and others; and more than $33,000 on numerous trips to Gainesville, Florida, the home of a female companion.

In addition to spending excesses, the report criticized Aramony's lax management. "The looseness and independence of Mr. Aramony's management style over the course of more than two decades resulted in a breach of . . . trust. . . . As a result, what developed was a haphazard practice of expenditures without adequate documentation, the proliferation of spin-offs [corporations created by the UWA board but independently run] not accountable to UWA, the payment of unjustified consulting fees, and the hiring or supporting of a number of persons who were either related to or personally associated with Mr. Aramony."

Interim president Kenneth W. Dam said after the report was released that "these conclusions are disturbing, and they will certainly outrage people. They will and should feel betrayed."

Impact on UWA and Affiliates: Government Probe

Following revelations of Aramony's spending habits, hundreds of the 1,400 local United Way organization members stopped paying dues to the national organization. As of June, only 532 local affiliates were paying some or all of their dues. Representatives from thirteen of the largest locals urged Dam to drastically reduce the 260-employee staff of the national organization. Responding to the boycott, which had halved UWA income, Dam announced June 2 that employees would be encouraged to take time off or resign and that all salary increases would be frozen.

In the months following Aramony's resignation, nearly $9 million had been cut from UWA's $29 million operating budget. By July the staff was down to 185, and new rules had been instituted to safeguard against a repetition of the scandal. "People realize that we are closing the book on the past," Dam said. "We are going to have a new United Way around here."

The federal government also launched a probe of Aramony's administration, issuing subpoenas for records—including minutes of board meetings, financial ledgers, credit card bills, spending on gifts, and travel—covering the final ten years of his tenure. The investigation, operating from the U.S. attorney's office in Alexandria, Virginia, was being conducted by FBI and Internal Revenue Service agents. The subpoenas listed thirteen companies that were spin-offs of UWA during Aramony's tenure, among them companies involved in buying condominiums in New York City and Coral Gables, Florida. (After he left UWA, Aramony continued to serve as chairman of the board of one of them, Partnership Umbrella Inc., a discount buying service.)

The government probe placed further financial and public relations strains on the already beleaguered organization and its smaller local affiliates, which would have to gather and copy thousands of pages of documents. The possibility of criminal indictments added further fuel to the existing eagerness of many local organizations to distance themselves from the national office.

Appearing on television April 2, Aramony charged that "the report's wrong" and "to my knowledge" he had paid for everything. In an angry letter to the UWA board, Aramony complained that he had not been given a chance to review the report or defend himself. "I repeatedly requested a due process opportunity to hear and answer the charges made against me," Aramony's April 3 letter said. "Your response was to convene a modern-day Salem witch trial-by-press-release." Moreover, Aramony wrote, "I reject categorically any suggestion of misappropriation or breach of trust during my tenure at United Way of America."

Aramony reiterated his position in a May 5 letter to UWA board members. "I can demonstrate that I had put into place policies and procedures to ensure that any items of personal expense were either charged to me or reimbursed by me. . . . Of course I will repay to the UWA the cost of any of my personal expense items that have not heretofore been reimbursed."

Aramony had been scheduled to receive $4.4 million in pension benefits, but UWA officials said they would not pay him that amount.

New President

In August the United Way announced the appointment of a new president, thirty-nine-year-old Elaine L. Chao, who had been director of the federal Peace Corps. Her salary was set at $195,000 a year, about half of what Aramony had been paid.

UWA officials said that "integrity, honesty, and a commitment to volunteerism" were among the primary qualifications in the selection of Chao from among 600 candidates. Chao, a former deputy secretary of transportation, was one of the highest ranking women and Asian-Americans in the Bush administration.

Dam, a vice president of International Business Machines and a former deputy secretary of state, stepped down as interim president following Chao's appointment.

Following is the executive summary of the "Report to the Board of Governors of United Way of America," by Verner, Liipfert, Bernhard, McPherson, and Hand and the Investigative Group Inc., released April 2, 1992:

This Report describes what will surely be disturbing findings to the tens of millions of Americans who give of themselves to help others. It reveals a story of excess and of values lost. Mr. William Aramony served the United Way of America as its President for twenty-two years; he served various segments of the United Way system for a total of thirty-seven years. He devoted the greater part of his life to unifying and empowering local United Way organizations around the country. He led a not-for-profit institution to record contributions and worldwide renown, and because of this background of success and commitment, UWA's Board of Governors placed a high degree of trust in him.

Tragically, the informality and independence of Mr. Aramony's management style over the course of more than two decades resulted in a breach of that trust. Under Mr. Aramony's stewardship, UWA did not have a strong institutional culture open to examination by its local members and contributors. UWA sponsored the creation of an intricate network of "spin-off" organizations, managed significant amounts of charitable contributions, and adopted costly retirement plans often without the benefit of expert and informed analysis.

The results were a haphazard practice of expenditures without adequate documentation, a proliferation of loosely related spin-off organizations with ill-defined financial structures and markets to serve, and a series of employment offers and consulting contracts that too often brought little demonstrable benefit—and some outright harm—to UWA.

As we noted above, this Report undoubtedly provides disturbing findings. It is our profound hope that this Report will also provide this reassurance: that although individual abuses can occur in almost any environment, the UWA has already moved quickly to rectify those that were discovered within its senior management. The services provided by UWA and the United Way local organizations around the country deserve to continue; they are indispensable to philanthropy in America.

* * *

In December 1991, UWA learned that allegations of certain improprieties would soon be publicly lodged against then-UWA President William Aramony. Generally, it was alleged that Mr. Aramony maintained a lifestyle exceeding the level of comfort and convenience which most people would accept from the leader of a charitable organization. Specifically, it was alleged that Mr. Aramony used UWA funds, both directly and through the use of organizations which had been spun off from UWA operations, to rent limousines, to take transatlantic flights on the Concorde, and to reward friends and family members with jobs, board memberships, and consulting contracts.

These allegations suggest that Mr. Aramony manipulated the design and operation of UWA so that it served not only its charitable purpose of providing targeted and effective assistance to the needy but also provided benefits to Mr. Aramony personally and to certain of his friends and family members. The alleged improper expenditures constituted a fraction of UWA's budget, and UWA's entire budget has been only about one percent of the amount donated annually to local United Way organizations around the country. Nevertheless, public reaction to these allegations was understandably furious.

The UWA Board of Governors was quick to respond. UWA, with the concurrence of Mr. Aramony, hired the Investigative Group Inc. (IGI) to ascertain the truth behind the allegations. IGI is an international investigative group which specializes in gathering intelligence in complex corporate, financial, and legal matters. The Chairman of IGI's Washington, D.C., office, Terry Lenzner, served as assistant chief counsel to the Senate Watergate Committee in 1974 and was formerly a Justice Department attorney and a federal prosecutor.

During this part of its investigation, IGI interviewed Mr. Aramony and reviewed various corporate and personal documents related to him, including expense reports, travel records, corporate credit card records, telephone logs and bills, check vouchers, appointment calendars, and certain personal records provided by Mr. Aramony. UWA then retained Verner, Liipfert, Bernhard, McPherson and Hand to work with the investigative firm in identifying and pursuing additional areas of concern. At the direction of UWA's Board of Governors, Verner, Liipfert expanded the scope of the investigation. Additional information was sought regarding Mr. Aramony's travel and other expenditures, the purchase of apartments in New York and Florida, expenditures authorized by Mr. Thomas Merlo, then-Chief Financial Officer of UWA and a close friend to Mr. Aramony, and other transactions. At the same time, Verner, Liipfert examined both the relationship of UWA to the various spin-off organizations—from their design and start-up through their current operations—and the personnel practices within UWA governing hiring decisions, consultant arrangements and the establishment of executive compensation.

Kenneth W. Dam, who was elected interim UWA President on March 6, 1992, following Mr. Aramony's departure, worked closely with the investigators to identify those areas in which immediate financial and procedural controls could be put into effect. Within the two-week period following his election, Mr. Dam had:

- subjected all transactions between UWA and spin-off organizations to his personal preapproval;
- secured agreement from the spin-offs that each will cooperate with UWA's investigators;
- ordered the sale of all automobiles owned by UWA;
- terminated all club memberships paid for by UWA;
- prohibited the use of limousines by UWA officers;
- enforced at the top executive level the same policies requiring coach travel by air, economical travel by ground, and modest lodging that applied to other UWA employees;
- suspended potentially costly modifications to executives' pension plans;
- and discontinued payment under consulting contracts pending review and specific approval.

*   *   *

This Report provides detailed information, produced through our nine-week investigation, which strongly suggests the need for additional reforms. For example, this Report shows that:

The rationale cited by Mr. Aramony as justifying the creation of certain separate spin-off organizations to undertake activities previously performed within UWA—namely, that performance within UWA would jeopardize its tax-exempt status—was not accurate. UWA could have maintained certain activities in-house without inviting jeopardy. The spin off of certain activities—not all—has needlessly cost UWA the income stream which those activities would otherwise have generated and placed the spin-off organizations outside the ready oversight of the UWA Board.

Mr. Aramony persuaded the Executive Committee of UWA's Board to approve the transfer of almost $1 million to another spin-off organization. This amount represented half of the rebate provided by a vendor from whom UWA and local United Ways purchased a volume of services and equipment. Mr. Aramony justified this transfer on the basis that the spin-off organization had been primarily responsible for achievement of the purchase target. However, the spin-off organization was not yet in existence when efforts by UWA and local United Ways to reach the purchase target began.

As a not-for-profit organization, circumstances in which it would be appropriate for UWA to purchase property—for example, condominiums—are very limited. However, one of the spin-off organizations utilized money received from UWA to purchase condominiums in New York and Miami for purposes not essential to fulfill a charitable mandate.

UWA loaned more than $2 million to one of the spin-off organizations during the time that UWA's Chief Financial Officer was also a director of the spin-off. This loan violates applicable not-for-profit corporation law. Although UWA published a report which mentioned this loan, there is no record demonstrating that the Board was expressly informed of the loan or the fact that UWA and the spin-off shared an officer or director in common. In a similar instance, UWA agreed to guarantee a bank loan taken out by one of the spin-off organizations. This arrangement, too, is an apparent violation of applicable not-for-profit corporation law. No UWA records demonstrate that the Board was given an opportunity to disapprove this transaction.

Expense claims which Mr. Aramony submitted to UWA for such items as first class travel, limousine service and gifts to friends are dwarfed by the expenditures Mr. Aramony approved for questionable consulting fees, ill-founded transfers of funds to spin-offs, high salaries and benefits for senior executives. However, it is the former expenditures which are most offensive when subjected to public scrutiny. That is understandable. They evidence, at best, insensitivity to the loss of confidence they engender in a public that gives, often at personal sacrifice, to meet the needs and relieve the suffering of others. At worst, they convey to the public a disregard for UWA's very mission.

We are satisfied that some of the expenditures described below are business-related while others are personal. UWA's files are so inadequate with respect to justification of expenditures that attempting to distinguish precisely business and personal expenditures without a full outside audit is impossible.

- From 1988 through 1991, UWA spent more than $92,265 for limousine services for Mr. Aramony.
- From 1987 through 1990, UWA spent at least $40,762 for airfare on the Concorde for Mr. Aramony or others flying with him.
- From 1988 through 1990, UWA spent more than $33,650 for Mr. Aramony for airfare to or through Gainesville, Florida, although there is no record of UWA business in Gainesville during this time period.
- From 1988 through 1991, UWA spent more than $19,700 for meals, entertainment expenses, gifts, clothes, flowers, purchases from mail-order catalogs and golf equipment purchased by Mr. Aramony.
- From 1988 through 1990, UWA spent more than $37,894 on at least twenty-nine trips to Las Vegas, Nevada for Mr. Aramony and others.
- From 1987 through 1991, UWA spent more than $72,509 on international airfare—sometimes first class—for Mr. Aramony, his wife, and others. Hotel bills and other expenses related to these trips totalled more than $58,943. Destinations included England, France, Norway, Turkey, Germany, Russia and Italy.
- In December 1989, UWA spent $6,100 for first class air fare for Mr. Aramony and a companion to travel to Egypt. Corporate documents state that the trip was not business-related. This fare was reportedly repaid by Mr. Aramony on March 20, 1992, more than two years later.

Mr. Aramony has presented to UWA a demand for pension benefits he believes are worth in excess of $4.4 million. However, UWA's and Mutual of America's documentation of such important items as the texts of UWA's pension plans was incomplete. It is unclear the extent to which the anticipated costs and benefits, the contemplated means of calculating those benefits and funding them, as well as the general administration of the plans, were adequately disclosed to the Board. Such capricious pension plan management and administration is inconsistent with a demand for millions in benefits from a not-for-profit institution. We have recommended that no pension distributions be made until all legal rights have been clearly determined.

Mr. Aramony's failure to observe the kind of spending constraints which must control not-for-profit institutions constituted a lack of judgment which has tragically jeopardized the philanthropic goals to which he had otherwise successfully devoted so much of his life.

However, with the financial controls now in place at UWA—the limitations on spending by UWA executives; the requirements for specific documentation of the purpose for travel, and for the anticipated cost of certain expenditures such as benefit plans; the necessity to get preapproval for major expenditures—these abuses will not and cannot be repeated.

Only two categories of issues remain open at this point:

First: There are accounting issues which will require extensive requests for additional documentation from certain former officers and employees. We recommend in several places within this Report, that independent auditors be directed to establish the exact amounts which certain individuals should reimburse to UWA.

Second: There are policy issues on which the Board will want to consult with local United Way organizations before taking final action. For example, although this Report notes problematic transactions between UWA and certain spin-offs, those can be addressed by the specific recommendations included within this Report. What this Report cannot decide, but the Board must, is whether or which of the spin-offs should remain independent, which should be brought back within UWA, which should be terminated, and which can provide desirable and affordable services in a mechanism involving appropriate levels of accountability to UWA and the local United Ways. The first constituency to be consulted regarding these issues is the local United Ways, but clearly the ultimate concern is whether the organization of UWA and the spin-offs best serves the purpose of efficient and effective philanthropy.

Trust and confidence are fragile commodities. Once tarnished, they are difficult to restore. The actions taken by Chairman Akers, President Dam, along with the steps recommended for Board action should, we believe, generate a renewal of public confidence. They do not make it impossible for individuals to abuse the system; no procedure can ensure that. They do, however, provide a framework for renewed vigor and oversight by UWA's Board of Directors. The public must be satisfied that when it gives to charity, its money goes to charity. That goal of UWA is again achievable.

SUPREME COURT ON ENTRAPMENT IN CHILD PORNOGRAPHY CASE

April 6, 1992

In a ruling that could affect similar sting operations, the Supreme Court on April 6 overturned the conviction of a man who finally took the bait after being enticed by the government for more than two years to buy child pornography. The Court said that prosecutors had not proved their case that the purchaser, Keith Jacobson, might have bought such material without government provocation. Postal authorities had personally delivered the sexually explicit matter to Jacobson, a sixty-year-old Nebraskan farmer, then arrested him for receiving it through the mail.

Justice Byron R. White wrote the 5-4 opinion, which was joined by Harry A. Blackmun and John Paul Stevens—considered by most observers to be the most liberal on the Court—as well as by the newest appointees, moderate/conservative David H. Souter and conservative Clarence Thomas. Justice Sandra Day O'Connor dissented, joined by Chief Justice William H. Rehnquist and Justices Antonin Scalia and Anthony M. Kennedy.

The decision was somewhat of a departure from recent federal court decisions upholding law enforcement agents' increasing use of controversial sting techniques to obtain evidence against common criminals, drug dealers, crime bosses, and politicians—including members of Congress and former District of Columbia mayor Marion Barry. Barry went to prison for cocaine possession, and several members of Congress were convicted of accepting bribes from bogus Arab sheiks. (Abscam investigation, Historic Documents of 1980, p. 899)

Government Persistence against Defendant

The case against Jacobson began in 1984 when he ordered two magazines, Bare Boys I and Bare Boys II, containing pictures of nude preteen and teenage boys, from a California adult bookstore. (Jacobson later testified that he did not know the magazines would contain pictures of minors.) At the time of his purchase, there was no federal law prohibiting mail-order receipt of such material. Shortly thereafter, however, Congress enacted the Child Protection Act of 1984, making it illegal to receive sexually explicit depictions of children through the mail.

After they discovered Jacobson's name on the bookstore mailing list, two government agencies, conducting an undercover operation called Project Looking Glass, sent mail to him through five fictitious organizations and a "pen pal," to test his willingness to break the law. Many of the bogus organizations alleged that their aim was to promote sexual freedom and lobby against censorship. Jacobson responded to some of the correspondence and finally ordered from one of the fake catalogs, Boys Who Love Boys, a magazine that depicted young boys engaged in sexual activities. He was arrested by officials who delivered the photocopied magazine, but a search of his home revealed no pornographic materials other than those the government had sent him, as well as the Bare Boys magazines.

Jacobson pleaded entrapment at his trial but was found guilty and sentenced to two years on probation and 250 hours of community service, which he had performed before the Supreme Court overturned his conviction.

"Predisposition": A Principal Issue

Writing for the majority, Justice White held that the prosecution failed to show that Jacobson had been predisposed, independent of the government's acts and beyond a reasonable doubt, to violate the law by soliciting child pornography through the mail. Moreover, in acting to enforce the law, government agents could not carry out criminal schemes designed to persuade an otherwise innocent and law-abiding person to commit a crime and thereby face prosecution.

Postal inspectors "overstepped the line between setting a trap for the 'unwary innocent' and the 'unwary criminal'," White concluded. "When the government's quest for convictions leads to the apprehension of an otherwise law-abiding citizen who, if left to his own devices, likely would have never run afoul of the law, the courts should intervene." When a defendant claimed entrapment, "the prosecution must prove beyond reasonable doubt that the defendant was disposed to commit the criminal act prior to first being approached by government agents."

White wrote that the ruling "in no way encroaches on government investigatory activities," but O'Connor disagreed, arguing that it "introduces a new requirement that Government sting operations have a *reasonable suspicion of illegal activity before contacting a suspect" and might thereby hamper law enforcement operations. The decision could lead to a situation in which "every defendant will claim that something the government agent did before soliciting the crime 'created' a predisposition that was not there before. For example a drug buyer will claim that the description of the drug's purity and effects was so tempting that it created the urge to try it for the first time."*

Effect on Future Investigations

The decision "essentially tells the government to be more careful about how they target people and implant things in their minds," said Jacobson after the Court exonerated him from criminal wrongdoing. "I think it's important because as American citizens living in a democratic country we have a right to be left alone if we're not breaking the law."

Commenting after the Court acted, Daniel Mihalko, the postal inspector in charge of Project Looking Glass (which resulted in 147 convictions), said the agents had acted conservatively and cautiously "to make sure that no innocent person was targeted." If Jacobson had not responded to the government's solicitations, "we would not have gone forward with any type of investigation," Mihalko contended.

Calling the decision a "disappointment," U.S. Solicitor General Kenneth W. Starr noted that the effort to ensnare Jacobson involved "rather unusual circumstances" and was also "unusual in its length and intensity." "This is a Court that says there are limits to what the government can do but it has not embarked on a new approach to a case that should in any way jeopardize law enforcement efforts including sting operations," he said. A number of legal experts agreed with Starr that, in general, the decision would not constrain the government's ability to set legal traps, but that it might result in more lawsuits from the persons caught in them.

Following are excerpts from the April 6, 1992, 5-4 Supreme Court decision and dissent in Jacobson v. United States, *overturning Keith Jacobson's conviction for illegally requesting child pornography offered by government agents:*

No. 90-1124

Keith Jacobson, Petitioner *v.* United States	On writ of certiorari to the United States Court of Appeals for the Eighth Circuit

[April 6, 1992]

JUSTICE WHITE delivered the opinion of the Court.

On September 24, 1987, petitioner Keith Jacobson was indicted for violating a provision of the Child Protection Act of 1987 which criminalizes the knowing receipt through the mails of a "visual depiction [that] involves the use of a minor engaging in sexually explicit conduct. . . . " Petitioner defended on the ground that the Government entrapped him into committing the crime through a series of communications from undercover agents that spanned the 26 months preceding his arrest. Petitioner was found guilty after a jury trial. The Court of Appeals affirmed his conviction . . . holding that the Government had carried its burden of proving beyond reasonable doubt that petitioner was predisposed to break the law and hence was not entrapped.

Because the Government overstepped the line between setting a trap for the "unwary innocent" and the "unwary criminal," *Sherman* v. *United States* (1958), and as a matter of law failed to establish that petitioner was independently predisposed to commit the crime for which he was arrested, we reverse the Court of Appeals' judgment affirming his conviction.

I

In February 1984, petitioner [Keith Jacobson], a 56-year-old veteran-turned-farmer who supported his elderly father in Nebraska, ordered two magazines and a brochure from a California adult bookstore. The magazines, entitled Bare Boys I and Bare Boys II, contained photographs of nude preteen and teenage boys. The contents of the magazines startled petitioner, who testified that he had expected to receive photographs of "young men 18 years or older." Tr. 425. On cross-examination, he explained his response to the magazines:

> "[PROSECUTOR]: [Y]ou were shocked and surprised that there were pictures of very young boys without clothes on, is that correct?
>
> "[JACOBSON]: Yes, I was.
>
> "[PROSECUTOR]: Were you offended?
>
> "[JACOBSON]: I was not offended because I thought these were a nudist type publication. Many of the pictures were out in a rural or outdoor setting. There was—I didn't draw any sexual connotation or connection with that." *Id.*, at 463.

The young men depicted in the magazines were not engaged in sexual activity, and petitioner's receipt of the magazines was legal under both federal and Nebraska law. Within three months, the law with respect to child pornography changed; Congress passed the Act illegalizing the receipt through the mails of sexually explicit depictions of children. In the very month that the new provision became law, postal inspectors found petitioner's name on the mailing list of the California bookstore that had mailed him Bare Boys I and II. There followed over the next 2½ years, repeated efforts by two Government agencies, through five fictitious organizations and a bogus pen pal, to explore petitioner's willingness to break the new law by ordering sexually explicit photographs of children through the mail.

The Government began its efforts in January 1985 when a postal inspector sent petitioner a letter supposedly from the American Hedonist Society, which in fact was a fictitious organization. The letter included a membership application and stated the Society's doctrine: that members had the "right to read what we desire, the right to discuss similar interests with those who share our philosophy, and finally that we have the right to seek pleasure without restrictions being placed on us by outdated puritan morality." Record, Government Exhibit 7. Petitioner enrolled in the organization and returned a sexual attitude questionnaire that asked him to rank on a scale of one to four his enjoyment of various sexual materials, with one being "really enjoy," two being "enjoy," three being "somewhat enjoy," and four being "do not enjoy." Petitioner ranked the entry "[p]reteen sex" as a two, but indicated that he was opposed to pedophilia. *Ibid.*

For a time, the Government left petitioner alone. But then a new "prohibited mail specialist" in the Postal Service found petitioner's name in a file, Tr. 328-331, and in May 1986, petitioner received a solicitation from a second fictitious consumer research company, "Midlands Data Research," seeking a response from those who "believe in the joys of sex and the complete awareness of those lusty and youthful lads and lasses of the neophite *[sic]* age." Record Government Exhibit 8. The letter never explained whether "neophite" referred to minors or young adults. Petitioner responded: "Please feel free to send me more information, I am interested in teenage sexuality. Please keep my name confidential." *Ibid.*

Petitioner then heard from yet another Government creation, "Heartland Institute for a New Tomorrow" (HINT), which proclaimed that it was "an organization founded to protect and promote sexual freedom and freedom of choice. We believe that arbitrarily imposed legislative sanctions restricting *your* sexual freedom should be rescinded through the legislative process." *Id.*, Defendant's Exhibit 102. The letter also enclosed a second survey. Petitioner indicated that his interest in "[p]reteen sex-homosexual" material was above average, but not high. In response to another question, petitioner wrote: "Not only sexual expression but freedom of the press is under attack. We must be ever vigilant to counter attack right wing fundamentalists who are determined to curtail our freedoms." *Id.*, Government Exhibit 9.

"HINT" replied, portraying itself as a lobbying organization seeking to repeal "all statutes which regulate sexual activities, except those laws which deal with violent behavior, such as rape. HINT is also lobbying to eliminate any legal definition of 'the age of consent'." *Id.*, at Defendant's Exhibit 113. These lobbying efforts were to be funded by sales from a catalog to be published in the future "offering the sale of various items which we believe you will find to be both interesting and stimulating." *Ibid.* HINT also provided computer matching of group members with similar survey responses; and, although petitioner was supplied with a list of potential "pen pals," he did not initiate any correspondence.

Nevertheless, the Government's "prohibited mail specialist" began writing to petitioner, using the pseudonym "Carl Long." The letters employed a tactic known as "mirroring," which the inspector described as "reflect[ing] whatever the interests are of the person we are writing to." Tr. 342. Petitioner responded at first, indicating that his interest was primarily in "male-male items." Record, Government Exhibit 9A. Inspector "Long" wrote back:

> "My interests too are primarily male-male items. Are you satisfied with the type of VCR tapes available? Personally, I like the amateur stuff better if its [sic] well produced as it can get more kinky and also seems more real. I think the actors enjoy it more." *Id.,* Government Exhibit 13.

Petitioner responded:

> "As far as my likes are concerned, I like good looking young guys (in their late teens and early 20's) doing their thing together." *Id.,* Government Exhibit 14.

Petitioner's letters to "Long" made no reference to child pornography. After writing two letters, petitioner discontinued the correspondence.

By March 1987, 34 months had passed since the Government obtained petitioner's name from the mailing list of the California bookstore, and 26 months had passed since the Postal Service had commenced its mailings to petitioner. Although petitioner had responded to surveys and letters, the Government had no evidence that petitioner had ever intentionally possessed or been exposed to child pornography. The Postal Service had not checked petitioner's mail to determine whether he was receiving questionable mailings from persons—other than the Government—involved in the child pornography industry.

At this point, a second Government agency, the Customs Service, included petitioner in its own child pornography sting, "Operation Borderline," after receiving his name on lists submitted by the Postal Service. *Id.,* at 71-72. Using the name of a fictitious Canadian company called "Produit Outaouais," the Customs Service mailed petitioner a brochure advertising photographs of young boys engaging in sex. Record, Government Exhibit 22. Petitioner placed an order that was never filled. *Id.,* Government Exhibit 24.

The Postal Service also continued its efforts in the Jacobson case, writing to petitioner as the "Far Eastern Trading Company Ltd." The letter began:

> "As many of you know, much hysterical nonsense has appeared in the American media concerning 'pornography' and what must be done to stop it from coming across your borders. This brief letter does not allow us to give much comments; however, why is your government spending millions of

dollars to exercise international censorship while tons of drugs, which makes yours the world's most crime ridden country are passed through easily." *Id.,* Government Exhibit 1.

The letter went on to say:

> "[W]e have devised a method of getting these to you without prying eyes of U.S. Customs seizing your mail. . . . After consultations with American solicitors, we have been advised that once we have posted our material through your system, it cannot be opened for any inspection without authorization of a judge." *Ibid.*

The letter invited petitioner to send for more information. It also asked petitioner to sign an affirmation that he was "not a law enforcement officer or agent of the U.S. Government acting in an undercover capacity for the purpose of entrapping Far Eastern Trading Company, its agents or customers." Petitioner responded. *Ibid.* A catalogue was sent, *id.,* Government Exhibit 2, and petitioner ordered Boys Who Love Boys, *id.,* Government Exhibit 3, a pornographic magazine depicting young boys engaged in various sexual activities. Petitioner was arrested after a controlled delivery of a photocopy of the magazine.

When petitioner was asked at trial why he placed such an order, he explained that the Government had succeeded in piquing his curiosity:

> "Well, the statement was made of all the trouble and the hysteria over pornography and I wanted to see what the material was. It didn't describe the—I didn't know for sure what kind of sexual action they were referring to in the Canadian letter. . . ." Tr. 427-428.

In petitioner's home, the Government found the Bare Boys magazines and materials that the Government had sent to him in the course of its protracted investigation, but no other materials that would indicate that petitioner collected or was actively interested in child pornography.

Petitioner was indicted for violating 18 U.S.C. §2552(a)(2)(A). The trial court instructed the jury on the petitioner's entrapment defense, petitioner was convicted, and a divided Court of Appeals for the Eighth Circuit, sitting *en banc,* affirmed, concluding that "Jacobson was not entrapped as a matter of law." (1990). We granted certiorari. (1991).

II

There can be no dispute about the evils of child pornography or the difficulties that laws and law enforcement have encountered in eliminating it. See generally *Osborne* v. *Ohio* (1990); *New York* v. *Ferber* (1982). Likewise, there can be no dispute that the Government may use undercover agents to enforce the law. "It is well settled that the fact that officers or employees of the Government merely afford opportunities or facilities for the commission of the offense does not defeat the prosecution. Artifice and stratagem may be employed to catch those engaged in criminal enterprises." *Sorrells* v. *United States* (1932); *Sherman* v. *United States; United States* v. *Russell* (1973).

In their zeal to enforce the law, however, Government agents may not originate a criminal design, implant in an innocent person's mind the disposition to commit a criminal act, and then induce commission of the crime so that the Government may prosecute. *Sorrells, supra,* at 442; *Sherman, supra,* at 372. Where the Government has induced an individual to break the law and the defense of entrapment is at issue, as it was in this case, the prosecution must prove beyond reasonable doubt that the defendant was disposed to commit the criminal act prior to first being approached by Government agents. *United States* v. *Whoie* (1991).

Thus, an agent deployed to stop the traffic in illegal drugs may offer the opportunity to buy or sell drugs, and, if the offer is accepted, make an arrest on the spot or later. In such a typical case, or in a more elaborate "sting" operation involving government-sponsored fencing where the defendant is simply provided with the opportunity to commit a crime, the entrapment defense is of little use because the ready commission of the criminal act amply demonstrates the defendant's predisposition. See *United States* v. *Sherman* (CA2 1952). Had the agents in this case simply offered petitioner the opportunity to order child pornography through the mails, and petitioner—who must be presumed to know the law—had promptly availed himself of this criminal opportunity, it is unlikely that his entrapment defense would have warranted a jury instruction. *Mathews* v. *United States* (1988).

But that is not what happened here. By the time petitioner finally placed his order, he had already been the target of 26 months of repeated mailings and communications from Government agents and fictitious organizations. Therefore, although he had become predisposed to break the law by May 1987, it is our view that the Government did not prove that this predisposition was independent and not the product of the attention that the Government had directed at petitioner since January 1985. *Sorrells, supra,* at 442; *Sherman.*

The prosecution's evidence of predisposition falls into two categories: evidence developed prior to the Postal Service's mail campaign, and that developed during the course of the investigation. The sole piece of preinvestigation evidence is petitioner's 1984 order and receipt of the Bare Boys magazines. But this is scant if any proof of petitioner's predisposition to commit an illegal act, the criminal character of which a defendant is presumed to know. It may indicate a predisposition to view sexually-oriented photographs that are responsive to his sexual tastes; but evidence that merely indicates a generic inclination to act within a broad range, not all of which is criminal, is of little probative value in establishing predisposition.

Furthermore, petitioner was acting within the law at the time he received these magazines. Receipt through the mails of sexually explicit depictions of children for noncommercial use did not become illegal under federal law until May 1984, and Nebraska had no law that forbade petitioner's possession of such material until 1988. Neb Rev. Stat.

§28-813.01 (1989). Evidence of predisposition to do what once was lawful is not, by itself, sufficient to show predisposition to do what is now illegal, for there is a common understanding that most people obey the law even when they disapprove of it. This obedience may reflect a generalized respect for legality or the fear of prosecution, but for whatever reason, the law's prohibitions are matters of consequence. Hence, the fact that petitioner legally ordered and received the Bare Boys magazines does little to further the Government's burden of proving that petitioner was predisposed to commit a criminal act. This is particularly true given petitioner's unchallenged testimony was that he did not know until they arrived that the magazines would depict minors.

The prosecution's evidence gathered during the investigation also fails to carry the Government's burden. Petitioner's responses to the many communications prior to the ultimate criminal act were at most indicative of certain personal inclinations, including a predisposition to view photographs of preteen sex and a willingness to promote a given agenda by supporting lobbying organizations. Even so, petitioner's responses hardly support an inference that he would commit the crime of receiving child pornography through the mails. Furthermore, a person's inclinations and "fantasies ... are his own and beyond the reach of government.... *Paris Adult Theatre I* v. *Slaton* (1973); *Stanley* v. *Georgia* (1969).

On the other hand, the strong arguable inference is that, by waving the banner of individual rights and disparaging the legitimacy and constitutionality of efforts to restrict the availability of sexually explicit materials, the Government not only excited petitioner's interest in sexually explicit materials banned by law but also exerted substantial pressure on petitioner to obtain and read such material as part of a fight against censorship and the infringement of individual rights. For instance, HINT described itself as "an organization founded to protect and promote sexual freedom and freedom of choice" and stated that "the most appropriate means to accomplish [its] objectives is to promote honest dialogue among concerned individuals and to continue its lobbying efforts with State Legislators." Record, Defendant's Exhibit 113. These lobbying efforts were to be financed through catalogue sales. *Ibid.* Mailings from the equally fictitious American Hedonist Society, *id.,* Government Exhibit 7, and the correspondence from the non-existent Carl Long, *id.,* Defendant's Exhibit 5, endorsed these themes.

Similarly, the two solicitations in the spring of 1987 raised the spectre of censorship while suggesting that petitioner ought to be allowed to do what he had been solicited to do. The mailing from the Customs Service referred to "the worldwide ban and intense enforcement on this type of material," observed that "what was legal and commonplace is now an 'underground' and secretive service," and emphasized that "[t]his environment forces us to take extreme measures" to insure delivery. *Id.,* Government Exhibit 22. The Postal Service solicitation described the concern about child pornography as "hysterical nonsense," decried "international censorship," and assured petitioner, based on consultation with "American solicitors" that an order that had been posted could not be opened for inspection without authorization of a judge. *Id.,* Government Exhibit 1. It further asked petitioner to affirm that he was not a government agent attempting to entrap the mail order company or its customers. *Ibid.* In these particulars, both government solicitations suggested that receiving this material was something that petitioner ought to be allowed to do.

Petitioner's ready response to these solicitations cannot be enough to establish beyond reasonable doubt that he was predisposed, prior to the Government acts intended to create predisposition, to commit the crime of receiving child pornography through the mails. See *Sherman,* 356 U.S., at 374. The evidence that petitioner was ready and willing to commit the offense came only after the Government had devoted 2½ years to convincing him that he had or should have the right to engage in the very behavior proscribed by law. Rational jurors could not say beyond a reasonable doubt that petitioner possessed the requisite predisposition prior to the Government's investigation and that it existed independent of the Government's many and varied approaches to petitioner. As was explained in *Sherman,* where entrapment was found as a matter of law, "the Government [may not] pla[y] on the weaknesses of an innocent party and beguil[e] him into committing crimes which he otherwise would not have attempted." *Id.,* at 376.

Law enforcement officials go too far when they "implant in the mind of an innocent person the *disposition* to commit the alleged offense and induce its commission in order that they may prosecute." *Sorrells,* 287 U.S., at 442 (emphasis added). Like the *Sorrells* court, we are "unable to conclude that it was the intention of the Congress in enacting this statute that its processes of detection and enforcement should be abused by the instigation by government officials of an act on the part of persons otherwise innocent in order to lure them to its commission and to punish them." *Id.,* at 448. When the Government's quest for convictions leads to the apprehension of an otherwise law-abiding citizen who, if left to his own devices, likely would have never run afoul of the law, the courts should intervene.

Because we conclude that this is such a case and that the prosecution failed, as a matter of law, to adduce evidence to support the jury verdict that petitioner was predisposed, independent of the Government's acts and beyond a reasonable doubt, to violate the law by receiving child pornography through the mails, we reverse the Court of Appeals' judgment affirming the conviction of Keith Jacobson.

It is so ordered.

JUSTICE O'CONNOR, with whom the CHIEF JUSTICE and JUSTICE KENNEDY join, and with whom JUSTICE SCALIA joins except as to Part II, dissenting.

Keith Jacobson was offered only two opportunities to buy child pornography through the mail. Both times, he ordered. Both times, he asked for opportunities to buy more. He needed no Government agent to coax, threaten, or persuade him; no one played on his sympathies, friendship, or suggested that his committing the crime would further a greater good. In fact, no Government agent even contacted him face-to-face. The Government contends that from the enthusiasm with which Mr. Jacobson responded to the chance to commit a crime, a reasonable jury could permissibly infer beyond a reasonable doubt that he was predisposed to commit the crime. I agree....

The first time the Government sent Mr. Jacobson a catalog of illegal materials, he ordered a set of photographs advertised as picturing "young boys in sex action fun." He enclosed the following note with his order: "I received your brochure and decided to place an order. If I like your product, I will order more later." Record, Government Exhibit 24. For reasons undisclosed in the record, Mr. Jacobson's order was never delivered.

The second time the Government sent a catalog of illegal materials, Mr. Jacobson ordered a magazine called "Boys Who Love Boys," described as: "11 year old and 14 year old boys get it on in every way possible. Oral, anal sex and heavy masturbation. If you love boys, you will be delighted with this." *Id.,* Government Exhibit 2. Along with his order, Mr. Jacobson sent the following note: "Will order other items later. I want to be discreet in order to protect you and me." *Id.,* Government Exhibit 3.

Government agents admittedly did not offer Mr. Jacobson the chance to buy child pornography right away. Instead, they first sent questionnaires in order to make sure that he was generally interested in the subject matter. Indeed, a "cold call" in such a business would not only risk rebuff and suspicion, but might also shock and offend the uninitiated, or expose minors to suggestive materials. *Pacifica Foundation* (1978) (right to be free from offensive material in one's home); 39 U.S.C. §3010 (regulating the mailing of sexually explicit advertising materials). Mr. Jacobson's responses to the questionnaires gave the investigators reason to think he would be interested in photographs depicting preteen sex.

The Court, however, concludes that a reasonable jury could not have found Mr. Jacobson to be predisposed beyond a reasonable doubt on the basis of his responses to the Government's catalogs, even though it admits that, by that time, he was predisposed to commit the crime. The Government, the Court holds, failed to provide evidence that Mr. Jacobson's obvious predisposition at the time of the crime "was independent and not the product of the attention that the Government had directed at petitioner." *Ante,* at 9. In so holding, I believe the Court fails to acknowledge the reasonableness of the jury's inference from the evidence, redefines "predisposition," and introduces a new requirement that Government sting operations have a reasonable suspicion of illegal activity before contacting a suspect.

I

This Court has held previously that a defendant's predisposition is to be assessed as of the time the Government agent first suggested the crime, not when the Government agent first became involved. *Sherman* v. *United States* (1958). See also, *United States* v. *Williams* (1983). Until the Government actually makes a suggestion of criminal conduct, it could not be said to have "implant[ed] in the mind of an innocent person the disposition to commit the alleged offense and induce its commission. . . ." *Sorrells* v. *United States* (1932). Even in *Sherman* v. *United States, supra,* in which the Court held that the defendant had been entrapped as a matter of law, the Government agent had repeatedly and unsuccessfully coaxed the defendant to buy drugs, ultimately succeeding only by playing on the defendant's sympathy. The Court found lack of predisposition based on the Government's numerous unsuccessful attempts to induce the crime, not on the basis of preliminary contacts with the defendant.

Today, the Court holds that Government conduct may be considered to create a predisposition to commit a crime, even before any Government action to induce the commission of the crime. In my view, this holding changes entrapment doctrine. Generally, the inquiry is whether a suspect is predisposed before the Government induces the commission of the crime, not before the Government makes initial contact with him. There is no dispute here that the Government's questionnaires and letters were not sufficient to establish inducement; they did not even suggest that Mr. Jacobson should engage in any illegal activity. If all the Government had done was to send these materials, Mr. Jacobson's entrapment defense would fail. Yet the Court holds that the Government must prove not only that a suspect was predisposed to commit the crime before the opportunity to commit it arose, but also before the Government came on the scene. *Ante,* at 8.

The rule that preliminary Government contact can create a predisposition has the potential to be misread by lower courts as well as criminal investigators as requiring that the Government must have sufficient evidence of a defendant's predisposition *before it ever seeks to contact him.* Surely the Court cannot intend to impose such a requirement, for it would mean that the Government must have a reasonable suspicion of criminal activity before it begins an investigation, a condition that we have never before imposed. The Court denies that its new rule will affect run-of-the-mill sting operations, *ante,* at 8, and one hopes that it means what it says. Nonetheless, after this case, every defendant will claim that something the Government agent did before soliciting the crime "created" a predisposition that was not there before. For example, a bribe taker will claim that the description of the amount of money available was so enticing that it implanted a disposition to accept the bribe later offered. A drug buyer will claim that the description of the drug's purity and effects was so tempting that it created the urge to try it for the first time. In short, the Court's opinion could be read to prohibit the Government from advertising the seductions of criminal activity as part of its sting operation, for fear of creating a predisposition in its suspects. That limitation would be especially likely to hamper sting operations such as this one, which mimic the advertising done by genuine purveyors of pornography. No doubt the Court would protest that its opinion does not stand for so broad a proposition, but the apparent lack of a principled basis for distinguishing these scenarios exposes a flaw in the more limited rule the Court today adopts.

The Court's rule is all the more troubling because it does not distinguish between Government conduct that merely highlights the temptation of the crime itself, and Government conduct that threatens, coerces, or leads a suspect to commit a crime in order to fulfill some other obligation. For example, in *Sorrells,* the Government agent repeatedly asked for illegal liquor, coaxing the defendant to accede on the ground that "one former war buddy would get liquor for another." *Sorrells* v. *United States, supra,* at 440. In *Sherman,* the Government agent played on the defendant's sympathies, pretending to be going through drug withdrawal and begging the defendant to relieve his distress by helping him buy drugs. *Sherman, supra,* at 371.

The Government conduct in this case is not comparable. While the Court states that the Government "exerted substantial pressure on petitioner to obtain and read such material as part of a fight against censorship and the infringement of individual rights," *ante,* at 10, one looks at the record in vain for evidence of such "substantial pressure." The most one finds is letters advocating legislative action to liberalize obscenity laws, letters which could easily be ignored or thrown away. Much later, the Government sent separate mailings of catalogs of illegal materials. Nowhere did the Government suggest that the proceeds of the sale of the illegal materials would be used to support legislative reforms. While one of the HINT letters suggested that lobbying efforts would be funded by sales from a catalog, Record, Defendant's Exhibit 113, the catalogs actually sent, nearly a year later, were from different fictitious entities (Produit Outaouais and Far Eastern Trading Company), and gave no suggestion that money would be used for any political purposes. *Id.,* Government Exhibit 22, Government Exhibit 2. Nor did the Government claim to be organizing a civil disobedience movement, which would protest the pornography laws by breaking them. Contrary to the gloss given the evidence by the Court, the Government's suggestions of illegality may also have made buyers beware, and increased the mystique of the materials offered: "[f]or those of you who have enjoyed youthful material . . . we have devised a method of getting these to you without prying eyes of U.S. Customs seizing your mail." *Id.,* Government Exhibit 1. Mr. Jacobson's curiosity to see what " 'all the trouble and the hysteria' " was about, *ante,* at 6, is certainly susceptible of more than one interpretation. And it is the jury that is charged with the obligation of interpreting it. In sum, the Court fails to construe the evidence in the light most favorable to the Government, and fails to draw all reasonable inferences in the Government's favor. It was surely reasonable for the jury to infer that Mr. Jacobson was predisposed beyond a reasonable doubt, even if other inferences from the evidence were also possible.

II

The second puzzling thing about the Court's opinion is its redefinition of predisposition. The Court acknowledges that "[p]etitioner's responses to the many communications prior to the ultimate criminal act were ... indicative of certain personal inclinations, including a predisposition to view photographs of preteen sex. . . ." *Ante,* at 10. If true, this should have settled the matter; Mr. Jacobson was predisposed to engage in the illegal conduct. Yet, the Court concludes, "petitioner's responses hardly support an inference that he would commit the crime of receiving child pornography through the mails." *Ibid.*

The Court seems to add something new to the burden of proving predisposition. Not only must the Government show that a defendant was predisposed to engage in the illegal conduct, here, receiving photographs of minors engaged in sex, but also that the defendant was predisposed to break the law knowingly in order to do so. The statute violated here, however, does not require proof of specific intent to break the law; it requires only knowing receipt of visual depictions produced by using minors engaged in sexually explicit conduct. See 18 U.S.C. §2252(a)(2); *United States* v. *Moncini,* 882 F.2d 401, 404-406 (CA9 1989). Under the Court's analysis, however, the Government must prove *more* to show predisposition than it need prove in order to convict.

The Court ignores the judgment of Congress that specific intent is not an element of the crime of receiving sexually explicit photographs of minors. The elements of predisposition should track the elements of the crime. The predisposition requirement is meant to eliminate the entrapment defense for those defendants who would have committed the crime anyway, even absent Government inducement. Because a defendant might very well be convicted of the crime here absent Government inducement even though he did not know his conduct was illegal, a specific intent requirement does little to distinguish between those who would commit the crime without the inducement and those who would not. In sum, although the fact that Mr. Jacobson's purchases of *Bare Boys I* and *Bare Boys II* were legal at the time may have some relevance to the question of predisposition, it is not, as the Court suggests, dispositive.

The crux of the Court's concern in this case is that the Government went too far and "abused" the "processes of detection and enforcement" by luring an innocent person to violate the law. *Ante,* at 12, quoting *Sorrells.* Consequently, the Court holds that the Government failed to prove beyond a reasonable doubt that Mr. Jacobson was predisposed to commit the crime. It was, however, the jury's task, as the conscience of the

community, to decide whether or not Mr. Jacobson was a willing participant in the criminal activity here or an innocent dupe. The jury is the
traditional "defense against arbitrary law enforcement." *Duncan* v. *Louisiana* (1968). Indeed, in *Sorrells,* in which the Court was also concerned
about overzealous law enforcement, the Court did not decide itself that the
Government conduct constituted entrapment, but left the issue to the jury.
Sorrells, supra, at 452. There is no dispute that the jury in this case was
fully and accurately instructed on the law of entrapment, and nonetheless
found Mr. Jacobson guilty. Because I believe there was sufficient evidence
to uphold the jury's verdict, I respectfully dissent.

THE VAIL AGENDA
FOR NATIONAL PARKS
April 8, 1992

The National Park Service faced "severe challenges" that threatened its continuing ability to manage and protect "the nation's most spectacular natural areas, the 'crown jewels,'" according to a report that examined the agency on its seventy-fifth anniversary.

The "Vail Agenda" report, released April 8, was prepared by a fourteen-member committee of Park Service officials, conservationists, and university professors. The report grew out of an anniversary symposium held in the fall of 1991 in Vail, Colorado. Hundreds of Park Service employees, park users, academics, state and local officials, and others examined the agency's performance. Throughout the process, the committee said, it "heard variations on a repetitive theme: The National Park Service has lost the ability to exercise leadership in determining the fate of the resources and programs it manages. At the level of the overall system, the Park Service is variously seen as run and overrun by Congress, the White House, the Secretary of the Interior, private interest groups, or public interest groups."

Created by an act of Congress on August 25, 1916, during the administration of Woodrow Wilson, the National Park Service administered 359 units in more than twenty categories, ranging from sprawling national parks such as Yellowstone to tiny historic sites. Its budget was $1.4 billion at the time of the report.

Treatment of Employees

Much of the panel's criticism was directed at how the Park Service treated its 20,000 employees, who it called the agency's "greatest strength." The employees made less money than comparable federal workers, found their initiative "thwarted by inadequately trained managers and politicized decision making," and suffered from inadequate training and employment standards that resulted in "eroding professionalism," the panel said.

The report emphasized the need to improve working conditions. "To some extent, they are a paradox," the panel said of Park Service employees. "At all levels, they are striking in their commitment; yet, they confront an organization that repeatedly frustrates their development, professionalism, and initiative." The panel warned that if this paradox persisted, the Park Service would "decline into mediocrity." To prevent it, the Park Service should improve employment standards, training, pay grades, management of job assignments, and career opportunities.

The committee did not limit its criticisms to actions by the National Park Service. It also said the Park Service was being forced to take on "inappropriate new units." That was an indirect criticism of Congress for creating new, questionable parks, such as the expensive "Steamtown" railroad history project in Pennsylvania.

The blunt report drew praise from Park Service employees. "The excitement this is generating inside is extraordinary because it tells it like it is," a Park Service official who requested anonymity told the Washington Post. *"The question is, what next? The issue here is the absence of leadership." James Ridenour, the Park Service's director, also praised the report. "It doesn't hold back any punches," Ridenour told the* Post. *"It really gives us an outline for where they think we should be going."*

Usage and Encroachments

The Park Service's top goal must be to protect park resources "from internal and external impairment," the panel said. Internally, parks were most threatened by the sheer number of people using them, with more than 258 million recreation visits a year. Only 58 million visits were to national parks. The others were to other units of the system, such as recreation areas, monuments, seashores, and historic sites.

The heavy usage creates an "inherent tension" between making parks accessible to the public while also protecting the facilities. The committee said that without proper management, "public access can degrade park resources such that the very values that public access is intended to provide cannot be perpetuated." When public access and park protection conflicted, the committee came down firmly on the side of protection. "Limitations on access and use are appropriate where they threaten impairment of a unit's special qualities, and where they significantly threaten the quality of overall visitor experience ...," the committee said. It especially urged the Park Service to protect wilderness areas.

Externally, parks were threatened by activities and developments immediately outside their boundaries. These included construction of suburban homes, clear-cutting of adjacent forests, and mining. The panel said the Park Service should provide technical and planning assistance to public agencies or private individuals planning developments near park boundaries. The Park Service also should aggressively use its legal authority to block external threats and seek additional legislative authority where needed, according to the panel.

The committee also urged the Park Service to beef up its educational activities, saying that its commitment to education had "waxed and waned." The agency should provide visitor centers, interpretation by either service employees or concessionaires, written and visual materials, educational outreach to area schools, and research opportunities for professionals, the panel said.

The committee admitted that implementing its recommendations would cost money. It said that funding for park protection "has been neglected and deferred in the past. Simultaneously, a number of new, costly, and sometimes ill-conceived responsibilities have been added to the Park Service's charge." It said Congress must provide adequate basic funding, but that the Park Service also needed to look at additional revenue options. These included a gasoline tax increase earmarked for the Park Service, user fees, income tax check-offs, sale of commerative tokens, and creation of passes for visitors and donors.

> *Following is an excerpt entitled "A Statement of Condition" from "National Parks for the 21st Century: The Vail Agenda," a report prepared for the director of the National Park Service by the Steering Committee of the 75th Anniversary Symposium and released April 8, 1992:*

The National Park Service has great strengths—and it has major problems. Without question, its greatest strength is its employees. For the vast majority of its employees, to work for the Park Service is to engage in an ever-renewing project of preserving and protecting some of the nation's and the world's most meaningful and enriching—and, often, most fragile and threatened—natural and cultural resources. Throughout the organization, the individuals who work for the Park Service are precisely those who are drawn to this challenge and who hold forcefully to personal stakes in the units and programs for which they are responsible. They are drawn despite a pay scale that is commonly one or two steps below that of comparably responsible and experienced employees in other sister federal agencies, and despite the common frustrations associated with bureaucracies and politics.

When individuals with this much dedication encounter roadblocks to performance, the result is a weakening of morale and effectiveness. Perceptions exist among many employees and observers—and not without bases in reality—that good job performance is impeded by lowered educational requirements and eroding professionalism; that initiative is thwarted by inadequately trained managers and politicized decision making; that the Park Service lacks the information and resource management/research capability it needs to be able to pursue and defend its mission and resources in Washington, D.C. and in the communities that surround the park units; that the mission and the budget of the Service is being diluted by increasing and tangential responsibilities; that there is a mismatch between the demand that the park units be protected and the tools available when the threats to park resources and values are increasingly coming from outside unit boundaries; and that communication within the Service repeatedly breaks down between field personnel and regional and headquarters management. The result of these perceptions is that the National Park Service faces significant morale and performance problems. These threaten the agency's capacity to manage and protect park resources in the short run, and can impede the agency's future ability to attract and retain employees with the education, skills and dedication of the current workforce. Many of the recommendations of the Working Groups aim accurately at overturning the realities that underlie these perceptions.

Beyond the energy and dedication of its employees, the second great strength of the Park Service is the quality of the heritage and recreational resources under its management. These resources are the foundation of the broad base of public support for the Service, and they are the source of the natural inclination to look to the Park Service to manage new resources that might warrant protection. Notwithstanding their quality, the resources of the Park System now encompass a markedly diffuse range of public values. Citizen support for and interest in individual units varies greatly, as do the contributions each unit makes to the national heritage. Requisite personnel skills, organizational structures, and management demands also vary greatly.

The 359 units of the park system arrayed in more than 20 separate classifications which aptly describe the system's dispersion, including: national battlefield, national battlefield site, national battlefield park, national historical park, national historic site, national lakeshore, national monument, national memorial, national military park, national park, national preserve, national river, wild and scenic riverway, national recreation area, national seashore, national scenic trail, international historic site, national heritage corridor and national parkway. In addition, the National Park Service is responsible for numerous and valuable external programs of support and assistance which have impact beyond the boundaries of the National Park System and even beyond the United States.

Some specific park units or programmatic responsibilities might, arguably, be better placed with other private, state, local, tribal, or federal agencies. Nevertheless, the broad range of resources and functions now managed by the National Park Service represents a permanent reality.

Effective management of such a diffuse system requires the abandonment of any hope for a single, simple management philosophy. This is particularly difficult for an agency with its origins—and its identification in the public's mind—in the management and protection of the nation's most spectacular natural areas, the "crown jewels".

The Symposium process elicited numerous proposals that do not and should not apply to all units of the system: "The parks should be managed as environmental classrooms"; "The parks should be managed for recreation"; "The parks should be managed to teach American history." The challenge for the Park Service is to enunciate objectives which match the breadth of its responsibilities and alleviate intra-agency conflicts which result from the desire for a single, narrowly-focused management strategy. The National Park Service manages a portfolio of assets; it must learn and implement the strategies of a portfolio manager. This means recognizing that all of the units and programs of the agency contribute to public value, but that the ways that these contributions are made and the forms that they take are varied.

The units and programs of the National Park System, taken together, have an important story to tell—a story that is, at once, interesting, instructive, and inspiring. The National Park System has the potential to bring together the landscapes, places, people and events that contribute in unique ways to the shared national experience and values of an otherwise highly diverse people. Unfortunately, there is widespread concern that the story is going untold; that, without resources, training, research, appropriate facilities and leadership, the Park Service is in danger of becoming merely a provider of "drive through" tourism or, perhaps, merely a traffic cop stationed at scenic, interesting or old places.

There are multiple sources for this concern. Managing and protecting the System's natural, cultural and recreational sites and programs are tasks for professionals—rangers, interpreters, scientists, planners, managers. The same can be said of the tasks of understanding and communicating history, or biology, or cultural significance, or archeology, or geology. Meeting these responsibilities requires education, research and experience in specialized and technical fields. But professionals are expensive, and low grade structures have impaired the ability of the Park Service to attract and retain qualified personnel. They have also gradually forced the weakening of many educational standards for employment. Training budgets, meanwhile, have tended to be focused on mandated law enforcement and administrative compliance responsibilities. The problems of maintaining a professional workforce are only exacerbated by perceptions that management itself faces the need to enhance its professional competency, or is subject to political interference that dilutes any bolstering sense of mission.

Additionally, as the National Park System has expanded, units and programs have been added that arguably have lacked sufficient national significance to warrant National Park Service designation. Yet, such additions to the system have had sufficient constituent appeal and/or economic development benefits in selected regions to secure their inclusion in the Park Service portfolio.

At the same time as new responsibilities have been added (and have attracted at least initial funding), the core operational budget of the Park Service has remained flat in real terms since 1983. Meanwhile, recreational visits to park units have risen sharply (25%) over the same period, reaching almost 260 million in 1990. Clearly, the capability of the Park Service to pursue its most central purposes of resource protection and public enjoyment is being stretched thinner and thinner. These disturbing problems are not the sole responsibility of Congress. The Park Service, partly through its own inaction and partly due to constraints emanating from the Executive Branch during the 1970s and 1980s, has lost the credibility and capability it must possess in order to play a proactive role in charting its own course, in defining and defending its core mission.

The National Park System should be a source of national pride, community, and consensus. It should represent the land, the cultures and the experiences that have defined and sustained the people of the nation in the past, and upon which we must continue to depend in the future. But, today, the ability of the National Park Service to achieve the most fundamental aspects of its mission has been compromised. There is a wide and discouraging gap between the Service's potential and its current state, and the Service has arrived at a crossroads in its history.

The basic facts and dimensions of the issues, problems, opportunities and solutions have been articulated and defined throughout the 75th Anniversary Symposium process. An opportunity for change has been created-nothing more and nothing less. Choices must now be made and action must now be taken by those who are responsible for the future of the National Park System—the Director and employees of the National Park Service, the Administration, Congress, and the concerned and committed public. If we fail to seize this opportunity for change, our common heritage will surely suffer.

ARTHUR ASHE, JR.,
ON AIDS STATUS
April 8, 1992

Tennis legend Arthur R. Ashe, Jr., so choked up with emotion that his wife had to read part of his statement, announced on April 8 that he had AIDS (acquired immune deficiency syndrome). His statement came only five months after basketball superstar Earvin "Magic" Johnson became the first major sports figure to announce that he had tested positive for HIV (human immunodeficiency syndrome), which can lead to AIDS. Ashe died of AIDS-related pneumonia on February 6, 1993. (Magic Johnson on His Retirement from Basketball, Historic Documents of 1991, p. 747).

Ashe, twice ranked the top tennis player in the world and winner of the U.S. Open in 1968 and Wimbledon in 1975, learned in September 1988 that he had AIDS. However, he shared the news only with a relatively few family members and close friends. Ashe said he kept his condition secret to protect his family's privacy. He decided to make his condition public after a sports reporter from USA Today *called and asked him about rumors that he had the disease. During the conversation Ashe refused to confirm or deny the rumors and asked the paper to delay running a story so he could prepare a public statement. The paper did not agree to that request but said it would not publish a story until it had solid confirmation its information was correct.*

At his press conference Ashe said he was "sorry that I have been forced to make this revelation . . . . After all, I am not running for some office of public trust, nor do I have stockholders to account to. It is only that I fall under the dubious umbrella of 'public figure.' "

His attack on the media for forcing him to go public touched off a fierce debate about where the line should be drawn between the public's right to know and a person's right to privacy. Courts had ruled that public figures such as Ashe enjoyed fewer privacy rights than private citizens but had never clearly delineated who had what rights. That left the media free to make its own rules.

Most editors of major newspapers said USA Today *did nothing wrong in pursuing the Ashe story. "I would've done the same thing," Bob Ingle, executive editor of the* San Jose Mercury News, *told the* Washington Journalism Review. *"This was not a minor figure in American sports. Probably the interest was heightened because the disease was AIDS. But even if Arthur Ashe had bone cancer, I think we would have covered it."*

Gene Policinski, USA Today's *managing editor for sports, agreed. "Any time a public figure is ill, it's news," he told the* Washington Post. *"If he has a heart attack, as Arthur Ashe did in 1979, it's news. We have no special zone of treatment for AIDS. It's a disease." Policinski said the story was particularly newsworthy because Ashe's "fame exists far beyond tennis."*

However, Floyd Abrams, a renowned attorney who had represented the media in some of the biggest First Amendment cases in recent decades, said the story was so unimportant and the potential for harm so high that USA Today *should have left Ashe alone. "It also is a case of press survival," he said. "The press should realize the harm this story does to them. It makes the public angry and it makes the courts angry. . . . To pursue [Ashe] under these circumstances is unseemly and self-destructive." It was later learned that a number of reporters had known for years that Ashe had AIDS but had not reported the news.*

Ashe was certainly not the first person to believe that the media had infringed upon his right to privacy. In 1988 presidential candidate Gary Hart lashed out at the media for staking out his townhouse to learn whether he was having affairs. Later, NBC News and the New York Times *were criticized when they named the woman who alleged that William Kennedy Smith had raped her.*

Ashe said his doctors were "one hundred percent sure" he contracted HIV, the virus that causes AIDS, during transfusions he received as part of heart bypass surgery. Ashe underwent bypass surgery twice, in December 1979 and June 1983, and doctors were certain that Ashe received the contaminated blood in 1983. The second operation came two years before the Food and Drug Administration approved a blood screening test to detect HIV. By the time Ashe announced he had AIDS, some 4,400 Americans had contracted AIDS through blood transfusions. They represented about 2 percent of all AIDS patients. However, only 20 of the patients contracted AIDS from blood that had been screened for HIV, according to the U.S. Centers for Disease Control. In March 1992, the month before Ashe's press conference, blood centers started using a new test that could screen blood for both HIV 1, the initial virus, and HIV 2, a new strain that was common in West Africa but had not yet appeared in the U.S. blood supply.

Ashe learned he had AIDS in 1988 after doctors started conducting tests to see why his right hand had lost all motor function. Brain surgery revealed the presence of toxoplasmosis, a marker for the AIDS virus, and subsequent blood tests confirmed that Ashe had AIDS. At his press conference Ashe said his wife, Jeanne, and his 5-year-old daughter, Camera, had both tested negative for HIV.

Ironically, months after the press conference Ashe admitted that being forced to go public about his illness had resulted in many benefits. Most importantly, Ashe said, the strain of keeping his illness secret had ended for his wife and other members of his family. Ashe also could and did start working publicly on AIDS education projects.

Following are comments made by Arthur R. Ashe, Jr., at a press conference on April 8, 1992:

I thank all of you for coming on such short notice. Rumors and half-truths have been floating about concerning my medical condition since my heart attack on July 31, 1979. Most of you know I had my first heart bypass operation six months later on December 13, 1979. But beginning with my admittance to New York Hospital for brain surgery in September 1988, many of you heard that I had tested positive for HIV, the virus that causes AIDS. That was indeed the case. It was transmitted through a blood transfusion after my first or my second open-heart bypass operation in June 1983. I have known since, September 1988, that I had AIDS.

My right hand had lost all motor function and a biopsy of brain tissue removed detected the presence of toxoplasmosis, a marker for the AIDS virus which is relatively harmless in people with normally-functioning immune systems. Subsequent blood tests proved positive for HIV.

So, some may ask, why not admit it earlier? Why hide it? The answer is simple: any admission of HIV infection at that time would have seriously, permanently, and, my wife Jeanne and I believed, unnecessarily infringed upon our family's right to privacy. Just as I am sure everyone in this room has some personal matter he or she would like to keep private, so did we. There was certainly no compelling medical or physical necessity to "go public" with my condition. I had it on good authority that my status was common knowledge in the medical community. However, I am truly grateful to all of you—medical and otherwise—who know but either didn't even ask me or never made it public. What I came to feel about a year ago was that there was a silent and unspoken conspiracy and complicity to assist me in maintaining my privacy.

This has meant a great deal to me, Jeanne and my daughter Camera (although she doesn't know it yet). She already knows that perfect strangers come up to daddy on the street and say "hi." Beginning tonight, Jeanne and I must teach her how to react to new, different, and sometimes cruel comments, that have little to do with reality.

Particularly for the sake of our family, Jeanne and I and some close friends have often talked about how long we could conceal this secret. Then, sometime last week, someone telephoned *USA Today* and told them. After several days of checking it out they decided to confront me with the rumors. It put me in the unenviable position of having to lie if I wanted to protect our privacy. *No one should have to make that choice.* I am sorry that I have been forced to make this revelation. I am not sick, and I can function very well in all that I have been involved in for the past 3 years. After all, I am not running for some office of public trust, nor do I have stockholders to account to. It is only that I fall under the dubious umbrella of "public figure."

As for my family, my wife and daughter are in excellent health and both are HIV-negative.

I have been an activist on many issues in the past—against apartheid, for education and the athlete, the need for better, faster change in tennis. I will continue with projects, and will certainly get involved with the AIDS crisis. I will be talking with several people and experts about how I might best help the cause. I have gained much insight in watching Magic Johnson weave his magic among school children, and I suspect we may join hands to work together.

The quality of one's life changes irrevocably when something like this becomes public. Reason and rational thought are too often waived out of fear, caution, or just plain ignorance. My family and I must now learn a new set of behavioral standards to function in the everyday world, and sadly, there really was no good reason for this to have to happen now. But, it has happened, and we will adjust and go forward.

REPORT ON UNSAFE SEX RISKS
AMONG HIGH SCHOOL STUDENTS
April 10, 1992

Despite years of highly publicized warnings, large numbers of high school students continued to engage in sexual and drug-use behavior that placed them at risk of infection by HIV, the virus that causes AIDS, according to a report released April 10 by the Centers for Disease Control. The report, "Selected Behaviors that Increase Risk for HIV Infection Among High School Students—United States, 1990," was based on a survey of 11,600 students in grades nine through twelve in the fifty states, the District of Columbia, Puerto Rico, and the Virgin Islands.

The survey found that students began engaging in sex at early ages, with many having had intercourse with multiple partners before they reached adulthood. Sexual intercourse is one of the chief methods for transmitting HIV, and the risk increases with the number of sexual partners. One-third of males and one-fifth of females first had intercourse before age fifteen, according to the survey. By the time they turned seventeen, nearly two-thirds of males and half the females had engaged in sex. Among all students, 19 percent reported having had sex with four or more people. The rate was significantly higher for males (27 percent) than for females (12 percent).

Although condom use reduces the risk of HIV infection, more than half of the sexually active students were unprotected the last time they had intercourse. Only 45 percent said they or their partner had used a condom. Students with the most sexual partners used condoms significantly less than those with fewer partners, the study found.

Only 1.5 percent of the students said they had injected drugs, another primary method for transmitting HIV. However, the rate of drug use was much higher for those who had had four or more sexual partners. Among these students, 5.1 percent said they had injected drugs.

"Like Playing Russian Roulette"

Health officials noted that a single act of unprotected sex or of injecting drugs could lead to HIV infection. "The best way to explain it to kids is that it's like playing Russian roulette and not knowing how many live bullets are in the chambers," Lloyd Kolbe, director of the CDC's Division of Adolescent and School Health, told the Associated Press. "If you pull the trigger once, it can cause you to become infected."

The cumulative number of AIDS cases among persons ages thirteen through nineteen rose from 127 in January 1987 to 789 in December 1991, the CDC reported. By 1989 AIDS had become the sixth leading cause of death for people ages fifteen through twenty-four. The full impact of current risky behaviors by teenagers would not be known for at least a decade, however, because the average incubation period between HIV infection and the onset of AIDS was nearly ten years.

Public health officials hoped that the experience of celebrity AIDS victims, such as basketball star Earvin "Magic" Johnson, would influence teenagers to change their sexual practices for the better. Any widespread improvement would be detected by future studies. (Magic Johnson's Retirement from Basketball, Historic Documents of 1991, p. 747; Magic Johnson's Resignation from AIDS Commission, p. 891)

The survey released in 1992 was part of the Youth Risk Behavior Surveillance System that CDC implemented two years earlier. The system was developed to measure periodically changes in health-risk practices such as HIV-related behavior; drug, alcohol, and tobacco use; improper dietary patterns; and inadequate physical activity, among others. To increase the comparability of data among sites, the CDC provided technical assistance to state and local departments of education that helped with CDC-sponsored surveys.

Follow-up to Earlier Study

An earlier CDC report found that many high school students were poorly informed about AIDS prevention. The report, "HIV-Related Knowledge and Behaviors Among High School Students—Selected U.S. Sites, 1989," was based on surveys of thirteen-to-eighteen-year-old high school students by departments of education in thirty states, ten cities, and two territories during February-May 1989.

An average of 38 percent of the students said they had not been taught about AIDS or HIV infection in school, and 44 percent said they had not discussed AIDS or HIV infection with their parents or other adults in their families. The surveys found that high school students were still confused about how HIV was transmitted. On average, 98 percent knew it could be transmitted by sharing drug needles and 88 percent knew they could get the virus by having sexual intercourse without a condom.

However, large numbers of students were unaware they could not get the HIV virus through blood donations (42 percent), bites by mosquitos or other insects (52 percent), public toilets (27 percent), or blood tests (27 percent).

Like the later survey, the 1989 report found that large numbers of students engaged in unsafe behavior. For example, 56 percent of the students said they had engaged in sexual intercourse at least once, and 21 percent said they had had sex with four or more people. At every site surveyed, more boys than girls had engaged in intercourse and had had sex with four or more partners. An average of 3 percent of students said they had injected drugs, with just under 1 percent saying they had shared needles while doing so.

"HIV-related knowledge and behaviors among high school students are cause for concern throughout the United States," the CDC concluded in the 1989 report.

> *Following is the text (footnotes and tables omitted) of the report by the U.S. Department of Health and Human Services' Centers for Disease Control, "Selected Behaviors that Increase Risk for HIV Infection Among High School Students—United States, 1990," released April 10, 1992:*

From January 1987 through December 1991, the cumulative number of acquired immunodeficiency syndrome (AIDS) cases among adolescents aged 13-19 years in the United States increased from 127 to 789, and in 1989, AIDS became the sixth leading cause of death for persons aged 15-24 years. Because the median incubation period between infection with human immunodeficiency virus (HIV) and onset of AIDS is nearly 10 years, many 20-29-year-olds with AIDS may have been infected during adolescence. Surveillance of selected sexual and injecting-drug-use (IDU) behaviors among adolescents can provide critical information about the risk for HIV infection among this group. This article presents self-reported data from 1990 about HIV-risk behaviors among U.S. high school students and describes strategies to reduce HIV infection among adolescents.

The national school-based Youth Risk Behavior Survey is a component of CDC's Youth Risk Behavior Surveillance System that periodically measures the prevalence of priority health-risk behaviors among youth through representative national, state, and local surveys. A three-stage sample design was used to obtain a representative sample of 11,631 students in grades 9-12 in the 50 states, the District of Columbia, Puerto Rico, and the Virgin Islands. Students were asked: "How old were you the first time you had sexual intercourse?"; "With how many persons have you had sexual intercourse in your life?"; "The last time you had sexual intercourse, did you or your partner use a condom to prevent sexually transmitted diseases such as genital herpes, genital warts, gonorrhea, syphilis, clap, drip, or AIDS/HIV infection?"; and "During your life, have you ever injected (shot up) any drug not prescribed by a doctor, such as steriods, cocaine, amphetamines, or heroin?"

Of all students in grades 9-12, the median age of reported first intercourse was 16.1 years (95% confidence interval [CI] = ± 0.1) for male students and 16.9 years (95% CI = ± 0.1) for female students. About one third (33.5%) of male students and 20.0% of female students initiated sexual intercourse before age 15 years. Nearly two thirds (64.8%) of male students and 52.4% of female students initiated sexual intercourse before age 17 years.

Of all students, 19.0% reported having had four or more sex partners during their lifetime. Male students (26.7%) were significantly more likely than female students (11.8%) to report having had four or more sex partners. Black male students (60.4%) were most likely to report having had four or more sex partners. The percentage of students who had four or more sex partners increased significantly by grade from 9th (12.4%) and 10th (14.8%) to 12th (28.6%) grade.

Among students who reported sexual intercourse during the 3 months preceding the survey (i.e., currently sexually active), 44.9% reported that they or their partners had used a condom at last sexual intercourse. Male students (49.4%) were significantly more likely than female students (40.0%) to report condom use at last sexual intercourse. Students who had four or more sex partners were significantly less likely to have used a condom at last sexual intercourse (40.6%) than were students with fewer lifetime sex partners (48.3%).

Of all students in grades 9-12, 1.5% reported IDU. Male students (2.3%) were significantly more likely than female students (0.7%) to report IDU. Students with four or more sex partners were significantly more likely to report IDU (5.1%) than were students with fewer lifetime sex partners.

Editorial Note: Although the risk for HIV infection is decreased by correct use of condoms and reduction of the number of sex partners, these approaches do not completely eliminate risk. The most effective means of preventing HIV infection are refraining from sexual intercourse, maintaining monogamous sexual relationships with an uninfected sex partner, and avoiding IDU. The findings in this report and previous reports from the United States and Italy indicate that a substantial proportion of students engage in behaviors that place them at risk for HIV infection.

CDC is working with national, state, and local health and education agencies to help decrease the proportion of 9th-12th-grade students who have initiated sexual intercourse; decrease the proportion of sexually active 9th-12-grade students who are currently sexually active; increase the proportion of currently sexually active 9th-12th-grade students who used a condom at last sexual intercourse; and decrease the proportion of 9th-12th-grade students who use injecting drugs.

Strategies to address these risk behaviors should include 1) using public health surveillance data to assist agencies in reducing HIV-risk behaviors among adolescents; 2) enhancing the capacity of state and local health and education agencies and national organizations to implement effective HIV-prevention education within comprehensive school health education programs; 3) using research to identify effective HIV-risk behavior interventions and applying these interventions through training centers; and 4) combining the efforts of numerous groups and organizations (e.g. families, public health agencies, schools, community and religious organizations, and media) to prevent HIV-risk behaviors among adolescents.

EXECUTIVE ORDER ON UNION POLITICAL ACTIVITY
April 13, 1992

In a move that was widely viewed to have election-year implications, President George Bush April 13 issued an executive order designed to ensure that union dues paid by nonunion employees of federal contractors would not be used for political activities the employees opposed. Issued the same day that the AFL-CIO executive committee endorsed Governor Bill Clinton of Arkansas for the presidency, the order reaffirmed a 1988 Supreme Court ruling in Communications Workers of America v. Beck *that a union may not use fees collected from a nonunion employee, if that employee objects, on activities not related to collective bargaining, contract administration, or grievance adjustment. Clinton later won both the Democratic nomination and the general election.* (Postelection Statements of Perot, Bush, and Clinton, p. 1019)

Bush's order required all federal contractors to post notices informing employees of their rights under Beck. *These included the right to refrain from joining a union, the right of nonmembers to object to the use of their mandatory union payments for purposes unrelated to collective bargaining, and the right to seek appropriate refunds and reductions in future payments.*

The case had been brought to the Supreme Court by Harry F. Beck, an electronics technician, who was guest of honor at a White House Rose Garden ceremony Bush used as the occasion to sign the executive order. Beck, a Republican, said his complaint had been prompted by union support for Democratic presidential nominee Hubert H. Humphrey in 1968. In comments after the signing ceremony, he said that the National Labor Relations Board (NLRB), which had authority over mediating worker complaints arising after the 1988 Court ruling, had been lax in acting on grievances brought before it.

In his remarks, Bush quoted Thomas Jefferson as saying in 1779, " 'To compel a man to furnish contributions of money for the propagation of opinions which he disbelieves and abhors is sinful and tyrannical.' It is this Jeffersonian insight that we reaffirm today with reforms to strengthen the political rights of American workers." The president also noted the presence of conservative actor Charlton Heston, whom he called "one of America's most intrepid fighters for individual rights ... [who has] been a member of four different labor organizations, and ... a member of the Screen Actors Guild."

Asked why the president was just now signing an executive order related to a four-year-old Court decision, Press Secretary Marlin Fitzwater said, "The timing now is dictated because with the national campaign coming upon us, this is a point where this law has its most usefulness, and the campaign activities are the ones it was designed to protect." A senior administration official said that politically "it makes our base [Republican conservatives] happy," and that "if it is seen as an effort to change the corrupt systems that run America, that works, too."

While conservatives in Congress and in Bush's reelection campaign, who had considered enforcement of Beck to be a priority, hailed the action as enhancing individual freedom for workers, labor leaders called it a "political gesture" that would not have much impact on their activities. They said it would affect only around 1 million workers, in contrast to the White House estimate of 3 million. AFL-CIO President Lane Kirkland said Bush's order represented "obsequious pandering to the ultra-right wing of his party," stating that its impact would be inconsequential because most union political contributions came from voluntary dues checkoffs. However, questions remained concerning how the NLRB would proceed on enforcing the order—whether it would require unions to provide information on their spending on a national or unit-by-unit basis, with the latter requiring considerably more paperwork.

> *Following are excerpts from President Bush's remarks at an April 13, 1992, signing ceremony for the Beck executive order and the text of the executive order requiring federal contractors to notify nonunion employees that any union dues they are required to pay could not be used for political activities they opposed:*

EXCERPTS OF PRESIDENT BUSH'S REMARKS

... Today happens to be a very special anniversary. Two hundred and forty nine years ago today, Thomas Jefferson was born. And there is a renewed spirit of Jeffersonian reform sweeping through this nation today. It is therefore a fitting occasion for putting into effect new reforms that will protect Americans' fundamental rights against political abuse by special interest groups.

For brilliance, for courage, for passion in the cause of freedom and democracy, no one has ever surpassed Thomas Jefferson. He eloquently stated a principle of fundamental fairness in 1779 when he declared, "To compel a man to furnish contributions of money for the propagation of opinions which he disbelieves and abhors is sinful and tyrannical."

Now not long ago in Philadelphia, I spoke of the wisdom of the founders on the subject of government reform. It is this Jeffersonian insight that we reaffirm today with reforms to strengthen the political rights of American workers.

In the Executive Order I will sign in just a few minutes, I am directing that companies performing federal contract work must inform their employees in the clearest possible terms of their legal rights as affirmed in the Supreme Court's landmark Beck decision....

The Beck decision is one of a series of cases protecting American workers from being compelled against their will to pay union or agency dues in excess of what is actually used for collective bargaining purposes and contract administration. Full implementation of this principle will guarantee that no American will have his job or livelihood threatened for refusing to contribute to political activities against his will.

The Executive Order that I sign today will make it easier for employees of federal contractors to understand and then exercise their political rights.

The Secretary of Labor is separately proposing a rule clarifying and then bringing up to date requirements for labor organizations to account for how workers' dues are spent. This rule aims to foster union democracy and it also will have the effect of helping employees protect their Beck rights.

The trial court in the Beck case found, for instance, that in plaintiff Beck's workplace—Harry Beck's workplace—79 percent of the compulsory dues collected went to purposes unrelated to collective bargaining and contract administration. Our new rule will assist union members in discovering how their dues are being spent. And perhaps most important of all, I expect the NLRB, the National Labor Relations Board, to carry out its responsibilities to enforce the principles of the Beck decision....

EXECUTIVE ORDER

By the authority vested in me as President by the Constitution and the laws of the United States, in order to provide employees, labor organizations, and contracting employers with information concerning the rights of employees, and thereby to promote harmonious relations in the workplace

347

for purposes of ensuring the economical and efficient administration and completion of Government contracts, it is hereby ordered as follows:

Section 1. The Secretary of Labor ("Secretary") shall be responsible for the administration and enforcement of this order. The Secretary shall adopt such rules and regulations and issue such orders as are deemed necessary and appropriate to achieve the purposes of this order.

Sec. 2. (a) Except in contracts exempted in accordance with section 3 of this order, all Government contracting departments and agencies shall, to the extent consistent with law, include the following provisions in every Government contract, other than collective bargaining agreements as defined in 5 U.S.C. 7103(a)(8) and small purchase contracts governed by Part 13 of the Federal Acquisition Regulation (48 C.F.R. 13.000-13.507), entered into, amended, renegotiated, or renewed, after the effective date of this order:

1. During the term of this contract, the contractor agrees to post a notice, of such size and in such form as the Secretary of Labor may prescribe, in conspicuous places in and about its plants and offices, including all places where notices to employees are customarily posted. The notice shall include the following information (except that the last sentence shall not be included in notices posted in the plants or offices of carriers subject to the Railway Labor Act, as amended (45 U.S.C. 151-188)):

   Notice to Employees
   Under Federal law, employees cannot be required to join a union or maintain membership in a union in order to retain their jobs. Under certain conditions, the law permits a union and an employer to enter into a union-security agreement requiring employees to pay uniform periodic dues and initiation fees. However, employees who are not union members can object to the use of their payments for certain purposes and can only be required to pay their share of union costs relating to collective bargaining, contract administration, and grievance adjustment.

   If you believe that you have been required to pay dues or fees used in part to support activities not related to collective bargaining, contract administration, or grievance adjustment, you may be entitled to a refund and to an appropriate reduction in future payments. . . .

2. The contractor will comply with all provisions of Executive Order No. 12800 of April 13, 1992, and related rules, regulations, and orders of the Secretary of Labor.

3. In the event that the contractor does not comply with any of the requirements set forth in paragraphs (1) or (2) above, this contract may be canceled, terminated, or suspended in whole or in part, and the contractor may be declared ineligible for further Government contracts in accordance with procedures authorized in or adopted pursuant to Executive Order No. 12800 of April 13, 1992. Such other sanctions or remedies may be imposed as are provided in Executive Order No. 12800 of April 13, 1992, or by rule, regulation, or order of

the Secretary of Labor, or as are otherwise provided by law.

4. The contractor will include the provisions of paragraphs (1) through (3) in every subcontract or purchase order entered into in connection with this contract unless exempted by rules, regulations, or orders of the Secretary of Labor issued pursuant to section 3 of Executive Order No. 12800 of April 13, 1992, so that such provisions will be binding upon each subcontractor or vendor. The contractor will take such action with respect to any such subcontract or purchase order as may be directed by the Secretary of Labor as a means of enforcing such provisions, including the imposition of sanctions for noncompliance: *Provided, however,* that if the contractor becomes involved in litigation with a subcontractor or vendor, or is threatened with such involvement, as a result of such direction, the contractor may request the United States to enter into such litigation to protect the interests of the United States.

(b) Whenever, through Acts of Congress or through clarification of existing law by the courts or otherwise, it appears that contractual provisions other than, or in addition to, those set out in subsection (a) of this section are needed to inform employees fully and accurately of their rights with respect to union dues, union-security agreements, or the like, the Secretary shall promptly issue such rules, regulations, or orders as are needed to cause the substitution or addition of appropriate contractual provisions in Government contracts thereafter entered into.

Sec. 3. (a) The Secretary may, if the Secretary finds that special circumstances require such an exemption in order to serve the national interest, exempt a contracting department or agency from the requirements of any or all of the provisions of section 2 of this order with respect to a particular contract, subcontract, or purchase order.

(b) The Secretary may, by rule, regulation, or order, exempt from the provisions of section 2 of this order certain classes of contracts (i) to the extent that they involve work outside the United States and do not involve the recruitment or employment of workers within the United States; (ii) to the extent that they involve work in jurisdictions where State law forbids enforcement of union-security agreements; (iii) to the extent that they involve work at sites where the notice to employees described in section 2(a) of this order would be unnecessary because the employees are not represented by a union; (iv) to the extent that they involve numbers of workers below appropriate thresholds set by the Secretary; or (v) to the extent that they involve subcontracts below an appropriate tier set by the Secretary.

(c) The Secretary may provide, by rule, regulation, or order, for the exemption of facilities of a contractor, subcontractor, or vendor that are in all respects separate and distinct from activities related to the performance of the contract: *Provided,* that such exemption will not interfere with or impede the effectuation of the purposes of this order: *And provided further,* that in the absence of such an exemption all facilities shall be covered by the provisions of this order.

Sec. 4. (a) The Secretary may investigate any Government contractor, subcontractor, or vendor to determine whether the contractual provisions required by section 2 of this order have been violated. Such investigation shall be conducted in accordance with procedures established by the Secretary.

(b) The Secretary shall receive and investigate complaints by employees of a Government contractor, subcontractor, or vendor where such complaints allege a failure to perform or a violation of the contractual provisions required by section 2 of this order.

Sec. 5. (a) The Secretary, or any agency or officer in the executive branch of the Government designated by rule, regulation, or order of the Secretary, may hold such hearings, public or private, regarding compliance with this order as the Secretary may deem advisable.

(b) The Secretary may hold hearings, or cause hearings to be held, in accordance with subsection (a) of this section prior to imposing, ordering, or recommending the imposition of sanctions under this order. Neither an order for debarment of any contractor from further Government contracts under section 6(b) of this order nor the inclusion of a contractor on a published list of noncomplying contractors under section 6(c) of this order shall be carried out without affording the contractor an opportunity for a hearing.

Sec. 6. In accordance with such rules, regulations, or orders as the Secretary may issue or adopt, the Secretary may:

(a) after consulting with the contracting department or agency, direct that department or agency to cancel , terminate, suspend, or cause to be cancelled, terminated, or suspended, any contract, or any portion or portions thereof, for failure of the contractor to comply with the contractual provisions required by section 2 of this order; contracts may be cancelled, terminated, or suspended absolutely, or continuance of contracts may be conditioned upon future compliance: *Provided,* that before issuing a directive under this subsection, the Secretary shall provide the head of the contracting department or agency an opportunity to offer written objections, which shall include a complete statement of reasons for the objections, among which reasons shall be a finding that completion of the contract is essential to the agency's mission, to the issuance of such a directive: *And provided further,* that no directive shall be issued by the Secretary under this subsection so long as the head of the contracting department or agency continues personally to object to the issuance of such directive;

(b) after consulting with each affected contracting department or agency, provide that one or more contracting departments or agencies shall refrain from entering into further contracts, or extensions or other modifications of existing contracts, with any noncomplying contractor, until such contractor has satisfied the Secretary that such contractor has complied with and will carry out the provisions of this order: *Provided,* that before issuing a directive under this subsection, the Secretary shall provide the head of each contracting department or agency an opportunity to offer written objections, which shall include a complete statement of reasons for the objections, among which reasons shall be a finding that further contracts or extensions or other modifications of existing contracts with the noncomplying contractor are essential to the agency's mission, to the issuance of such a directive: *And provided further,* that no directive shall be issued by the Secretary under this subsection so long as the head of a contracting department or agency continues personally to object to the issuance of such directive; and

(c) publish, or cause to be published, the names of contractors that have, in the judgment of the Secretary, failed to comply with the provisions of this order or of related rules, regulations, and orders of the Secretary.

Sec. 7. Whenever the Secretary invokes section 6(a) or 6(b) of this order, the contracting department or agency shall report the results of the action it has taken to the Secretary within such time as the Secretary shall specify.

Sec. 8. Each contracting department and agency shall cooperate with the Secretary and provide such information and assistance as the Secretary may require in the performance of the Secretary's functions under this order.

Sec. 9. The Secretary may delegate any function or duty of the Secretary under this order to any officer in the Department of Labor or to any other officer in the executive branch of the Government, with the consent of the head of the department or agency in which that officer serves.

Sec. 10. The Federal Acquisition Regulatory Council shall take whatever action is required to implement in the Federal Acquisition Regulation the provisions of this order and of any related rules, regulations, or orders of the Secretary.

Sec. 11. Nothing contained in this order or promulgated pursuant to this order is intended to confer any substantive or procedural right, benefit, or privilege enforceable at law by a party against the United States, its agencies or instrumentalities, its officers, or its employees, nor to authorize the assessment of any dues or fees by any labor organization.

Sec. 12. This order shall become effective 30 days after the date of this order.

GEORGE BUSH
THE WHITE HOUSE,
April 13, 1992.

REPORT ON ECONOMIC PLIGHT
OF AMERICA'S YOUNG FAMILIES
April 14, 1992

The American Dream was becoming increasingly unattainable for young families with children as the decade of the 1990s began, according to a report issued April 14. The Children's Defense Fund prepared the report, "Vanishing Dreams: The Economic Plight of America's Young Families," in cooperation with Northeastern University's Center for Labor Market Studies. The report examined economic trends affecting families with children where the head of the household was under age thirty.

The study found that, after adjusting for inflation, the median income of these young families fell 32 percent between 1973 and 1990. For families headed by someone age thirty or over, the median income dropped by 6 percent. And in families without children, the median income rose 11 percent.

"The implicit message to young Americans is frighteningly clear: bearing and raising and nurturing children may no longer be compatible with active pursuit of the American Dream," said Marian Wright Edelman, president of the Children's Defense Fund, in releasing the report. "No society can convey this message for long if it hopes to survive and prosper." Edelman charged that "the nation has marginalized and pauperized much of two generations of Americans—young parents and young children."

The economic losses struck virtually all families with young children, crossing racial, educational, and economic lines, the report said. However, the losses hit people with low levels of education particularly hard. Between 1973 and 1990, the median income of a young family with children headed by a high school dropout fell 46 percent in 1990 dollars. Median incomes fell 30 percent for families headed by a high school graduate, and 15 percent for those headed by a person who attended some college classes. Only young families headed by a college graduate experienced a slight increase—3 percent—in their median income.

The falling incomes caused poverty rates to soar, according to the report. Between 1973 and 1990, the poverty rate for young white families with children rose from 10.2 percent to 23.8 percent; for blacks, from 37.9 percent to 57.9 percent; and for Latinos, from 27.8 percent to 43.5 percent. By 1990, two out of every five children in young families were poor. This included one out of four white children, two of three black children, and one of two Latino children.

Poor families lacked money for adequate food, shelter, and health care. The study said that a low-income family of three needed $309 monthly for food, and an average of $482 for rent and utilities on a modest two-bedroom apartment. That left $33 for all other expenses, including car costs, clothing, insurance, school costs, health care, and child care.

The report attributed a wide range of "devastating consequences" to the decline in income. These included increases in hunger, homelessness, low-birthweight babies, infant deaths, child disability, substance abuse, crime, violence, school failure, teen pregnancy, and racial tension.

Government programs aimed at helping these poor families were inadequate, the report said. In 1989 the average poor family with children received only $141 worth of monthly food and housing benefits. That left many poor families "just one illness, job loss, or family crisis away from homelessness or family dissolution," the report said.

Several factors caused the economic troubles of young families, the report said, including changes in the American economy, a lack of government assistance for families in trouble, and changes in the composition of the families themselves. It placed part of the blame on falling real wages, caused partially by a drop in the value of the minimum wage, and the growth of part-time and temporary jobs.

The federal government cut programs aimed at helping young families at the same time upheavals in the economy were causing them hardships. Public programs for young families with children were already inadequate in the 1970s, the report said, but they were "further weakened by spasms of deep retrenchment" that hit especially hard in 1981 and 1982. The federal government reduced food stamp benefits for all families, and it eliminated pregnant women, eighteen-to-twenty-year-old students, and teen parents from eligibility for Aid to Families with Dependent Children and Medicaid. In addition, the government eliminated a major job creation program and slashed job training funds in half.

The report admitted that actions by the families themselves sometimes added to their difficulties. For example, 33 percent of all children born to women under age thirty in 1989 were born out of wedlock, up from just 12 percent in 1970. In 1989 alone, 941,000 children were born to unmarried women under age thirty. These children faced a tremendous risk of living in poverty. In 1990 more than three-fourths of all children living in families headed by females under thirty were poor. "Changing values" were partially to blame for the growth in single-parent households, according to the report. But it contended that economic hardships and persistent joblessness also "contributed significantly" to falling marriage rates and the increase in babies born out of wedlock.

Many families responded to their falling earnings by sending a second worker to the market. This strategy only partly succeeded in boosting incomes, according to the report. In addition, several other problems resulted: higher costs for child care, less time with children, and more stress for families.

The government needed to take several actions to stop the earnings decline and to help young families get back on their feet, the report concluded. The highlights included enactment of a refundable children's tax credit, improved governmental efforts to collect child support and governmental payments to make up for support that could not be collected, universal health insurance, and full funding of Head Start.

Following are excerpts from the Children's Defense Fund report "Vanishing Dreams: The Economic Plight of America's Young Families," released April 14, 1992:

Throughout American history most young families have struggled, to some degree, to get a foothold in the job and housing markets and embark on the path toward the American dream. Most older adults remember leaner times—years when they worked hard to establish a career, to start a family, and to purchase a home. They also often remember it fondly as a time of hope and opportunity. Typically, young adults were confident that within a short period the future would bring enough financial security to build strong families. And as a nation, we generally assumed that each future generation of young families would be better off than its predecessors.

That time may now have passed us by. During the past two decades, the economic struggle for many young Americans has become desperate. Today's young families are bearing the brunt of massive economic and social change and an increasingly unequal apportioning of the nation's loss in jobs and incomes.

The current generation of young adults is no less educated, motivated, or responsible in most areas of life than its predecessors. As a group, they are more likely to complete high school, enroll in college, delay childbearing, and prepare for their futures than the generations before them. But in fundamental ways, the rules of the game have changed. Young Americans now are less able to build an early foundation for their own economic security, form stable families, provide adequate support for their children, or have hope and confidence in the future. In the process, they as a group increasingly are falling further behind older Americans.

In 1988 the Children's Defense Fund and Northeastern University's Center for Labor Market Studies published *Vanishing Dreams: The Growing Economic Plight of America's Young Families*. The report documented that young families with children in 1986 were far worse off economically than the previous generation. This report provides a new look at America's young workers and families, using more recent data from the U.S. Census Bureau and the U.S. Bureau of Labor Statistics. The data show that young families with children were barely helped at all by the economic growth of the mid- to late-1980s, and that the tiny gains they achieved during this period were more than wiped out in 1990 by the effects of the current recession. Families without children actually achieved modest gains between 1973 and 1990.

The huge economic losses sustained by young families with children since 1973 do not reflect short-term or cyclical trends that will be reversed quickly or easily. They are the product of sweeping changes in the U.S. economy and the American family, with far-reaching consequences for children and for the nation.

Young families—those headed by someone younger than 30—numbered 9.0 million in March 1991. Young families are the crucible for America's next generation of children and youths: Most children spend at least part of their lives—their earliest and most developmentally vulnerable months or years—in a young family. Two in three young families in 1991 had at least one child. In total, young families contained 10.6 million children— one in six of all American children—and more than one-third of all children younger than six.

Children in young families will be the workers, leaders, parents, taxpayers, soldiers, and hope of America's twenty-first century. The nation neglects them at its peril.

Yet young adults increasingly are forced to make a difficult choice between perilous economic insecurity for themselves and their children and postponing or perhaps forsaking plans for childbearing altogether. American families with children receive so few public and private supports that changes in the labor market and in family structure have left millions of young parents and their children virtually defenseless against the ravages of poverty.

The implicit message to many young Americans is frighteningly clear: bearing and raising children may no longer be compatible with active pursuit of the American dream. No society can convey this message for long if it hopes to survive and prosper....

Summary and Key Findings

Young families always have faced an uphill struggle starting out in life, with a considerable gap between them and older, more established families. But today's young families have been so battered by economic and social changes that the hill is becoming impossible to climb and the gap has widened into a chasm.

Between 1973 and 1989—two years when the business cycle reached its peak—young families with children (those headed by persons younger than 30) suffered terribly. Poverty among children in young families skyrocketed as the median income (after adjusting for inflation) of such families plunged. The much-heralded period of economic growth from 1982 to 1989 bypassed young families, and they now are suffering dramatic additional losses from the current recession.

These trends pose grave threats to the more than one-half of all American children who start their lives in young families and who are becoming poorer and poorer—both absolutely and in relation to the rest of the nation. Older families with children hardly prospered between 1973 and 1990, but they avoided major economic losses. Families without children actually achieved modest gains during this period.

Income

- After adjusting for inflation, the median income of young families with children plunged by nearly one-third—32 percent—between 1973 and 1990. For older families with children it dropped by 6 percent, and for families without children it increased by 11 percent.
- These income losses have affected virtually every group of young families with children: white, black, and Latino; married-couple and single-parent; and those headed by high school graduates as well as dropouts. Only young families with children headed by a college graduate experienced a slight increase in their median income between 1973 and 1990.
- The greatest part of these income losses for young families with children occurred during the 1980s. Their median income fell by 19 percent as a result of back-to-back recessions in 1980 and 1981-1982, and rose by an insignificant 1.4 percent during the remainder of the decade. Then the current recession sent young families with children into an economic freefall, with their median income plunging by 9 percent in a single year from 1989 to 1990.
- The median income for young families with children was more than two-thirds that of older families with children in 1973; by 1990 it had fallen to less than one-half.

Poverty

- As a result of these income losses, the poverty rate for children in young families doubled—from 20 percent in 1973 to a shocking 40 percent in 1990.
- In virtually every critical area of development and healthy maturation, child poverty creates major roadblocks to individual accomplishment,

future economic self-sufficiency, and national progress. Studies show, unsurprisingly, that a poor child is more likely than a nonpoor child to go without necessary food, shelter, and health care and to die in infancy. Poor children also are less likely than nonpoor children to be in good preschool programs or child care settings, and more likely to fall behind in school, drop out, get pregnant too soon, and be unemployed or sporadically employed.

- Dramatically increased child poverty in young families does not reflect only the problems of America's most vulnerable groups, although the child poverty rates for young black families (68 percent), young Latino families (51 percent), young female-headed families (77 percent), and young families headed by high school dropouts (64 percent) are astronomical. Between 1973 and 1990 child poverty rates more than doubled in young white families (to 27 percent in 1990), young married-couple families (to 20 percent), and young families headed by high school graduates (to 33 percent).

- More than half of the increase in the number of poor children in America since 1973 has been the result of falling incomes and rising poverty among young families.

- The economic plight of young families is a national, not an urban or a regional, problem. Nearly three-fourths of the increase in the number of young families with children living in poverty has occurred outside the nation's central cities. Young families with children in every region of the country suffered sharp declines in median income and steep increases in poverty between 1973 and 1989, even before the current recession further battered regional economies.

Causes

Young families are in trouble because of a devastating combination of profound changes in the American economy, government's inadequate response to families in trouble, and changes in the composition of young families themselves.

- Slightly less than one-half of the increase in poverty among young families and children between 1973 and 1989 (before the start of the current recession) can be attributed to economic shifts and government policies that have made it more difficult for young families to obtain adequate incomes. These changes have hurt all young families with children, regardless of their family structure, race or ethnicity, or educational attainment.

- Staggering declines in the annual earnings of heads of young families with children between 1973 and 1990 played a major role in pushing poverty rates higher: For all heads of young families with children, annual earnings (after adjusting for inflation) plummeted by 44 percent. These earnings losses were dramatic for heads of young white families with children (40 percent), for high school graduates heading young families with children (41 percent), and for heads of young married-couple families with children (33 percent).

- The rest of the increase in poverty among young families and children reflects changing family composition. Today's young family heads are somewhat better educated than those in the generation preceding them, but they also are more likely to be minorities or single women struggling to raise children on their own. Because these groups have considerably higher poverty rates to begin with, poverty among young families and children rises as their share of the total pool of young families rises.
- The growth in young female-headed families with children is in part a reflection of changing values. But the economic hardships associated with falling earnings and persistent joblessness among young adults also have contributed significantly to falling marriage rates and the increasing rates of out-of-wedlock childbearing.
- Increases in poverty among young families with children are not the result of young Americans having more children. Indeed, young families as a group have responded to a tightening economic vise by postponing childbearing and choosing to have fewer children. But these attempts to adapt their behavior have been overwhelmed by the sweeping economic and social changes that now jeopardize young families with children.

Recommendations

America's young families cannot wait another year for a response to the economic disaster that has struck them. While the deterioration of their economic status will not be reversed quickly or easily, immediate steps must be taken by Congress in 1992 to ensure that every child has a Fair Start, a Healthy Start, and a Head Start:

- *Enactment of a refundable children's tax credit.* As proposed in recent months in various forms and amounts by the National Commission on Children and key members of Congress from both parties, the federal government should bolster the incomes of families with children through the establishment of a refundable tax credit for children. Such a credit would reduce federal income taxes for middle- and low-income families and help the lowest income families that have no tax liability through a tax refund. While creating no new bureaucracies, a refundable children's credit would target tax relief and economic support precisely to the group—families with children—that has been hardest hit by declining incomes and rising poverty rates since 1973.
- *Creation of a child support assurance system.* To combat extremely high poverty rates among young female-headed families and to give all single parents the chance to lift their families out of poverty through work, federal and state governments should join in assuring that all children who are not living with both parents receive a minimally

adequate child support payment from the absent parent. If adequate payments cannot be collected on the child's behalf, despite the best feasible federal and state child support enforcement efforts, the federal government should make up the difference and guarantee that children do not suffer as a result of the shortcomings of the child support system.

- *Health insurance coverage and access.* The nation must enact a national health plan to ensure insurance coverage for all Americans. Children and pregnant women need basic health care now—including prenatal and maternity care, checkups, immunizations, and care for children who are sick or disabled. As an immediate step, the president and Congress must extend Medicaid coverage to every low-income child and pregnant woman. Steps also must be taken to ensure that this insurance provides real access to essential health services, not merely theoretical coverage. Necessary steps include universal access to childhood vaccines and increased funding for community and migrant health centers, the National Health Service Corps, and other public health activities.
- *Full funding of Head Start.* A first step in bolstering the productivity of our next generation of workers lies in early investments in education for America's children. Head Start and other quality preschool and child care programs help keep children at grade level, help children get ready for school, and help prevent the need for costly special education programs in later years. Yet Head Start still reaches only one in three eligible preschool children. As recommended by prominent business groups, educators, and a broad range of study commissions that have examined the educational problems of disadvantaged children and youths, the president and Congress should act to ensure every child a Head Start by 1995 by enacting immediately S. 911, the School Readiness Act, and accelerating the funding increases it provides to boost the program's appropriation by $2.1 billion this year.

Numerous other steps, detailed further in the Recommendations section . . . , are necessary to help today's young families with children and provide a strong foundation for future generations. Increases in the federal minimum wage, expanded health insurance coverage and access to health care, and other initiatives to supplement low earnings all would help young parents support their children through work. Greater investments in the skills and productivity of America's future work force through education and job training programs also are essential. Finally, the nation must maintain an adequate safety net to protect children when their young parents are unable to support them by aggressively pursuing full employment conditions, broadening eligibility for unemployment compensation, and ensuring that AFDC benefits are minimally adequate. . . .

USE OF DNA "FINGERPRINTS" AS EVIDENCE IN CRIMINAL CASES
April 14, 1992

The controversial and relatively new use of DNA typing to identify criminal suspects received a boost April 14 from the National Research Council, an arm of the National Academy of Sciences. The council endorsed the DNA procedure as "fundamentally sound" while calling for a laboratory accreditation program and other improvements to ensure accurate tests.

However, the report, "DNA Technology in Forensic Science," did not immediately resolve the dispute over whether DNA tests should be admitted as evidence in court. Experts came up with different interpretations of the report's key findings, indicating that the controversy would likely continue.

DNA, or deoxyribonucleic acid, is the genetic material that carries the coded messages of heredity. Scientists could extract DNA, which is unique for everyone except identical twins, from blood, semen, saliva, skin, or hair found at crime scenes. They then compared that DNA with DNA from a criminal suspect. If the DNA "fingerprint" did not match, the suspect could be ruled out. But if it did match, the fingerprint could be extremely powerful evidence in court.

Accuracy and Statistical Odds

In trials where attorneys sought to introduce DNA evidence, two major arguments usually arose: Was the test itself accurate? And what were the statistical odds that other people could have the same DNA pattern as the suspect?

Both sides of the DNA dispute agreed there was "a lack of standardiza-

tion of practices and a lack of uniformly accepted methods for quality assurance," said the NRC report, which was prepared by a panel of molecular biologists, forensic scientists, and legal scholars. "The deficiencies are due largely to the rapid emergence of DNA typing and its introduction in the United States through the private sector," the report said. Although DNA laboratories were unregulated, it concluded, the tests could be highly accurate if DNA samples were collected and analyzed properly.

The statistical question arose in courtrooms because it was scientifically impossible to examine the entire DNA sequence, which contained between 50,000 and 100,000 genes. In DNA tests, technicians compared only certain parts of the sequence. With only the partial test, it was possible for many people to show the same DNA pattern. After performing the analysis, technicians used various statistical models to determine what the odds were that someone other than the suspect could have the same DNA pattern. The NRC panel said laboratories used two different methods to calculate the odds. It recommended several measures to improve the statistical reliability of those calculations.

In general, the NRC panel said, courts should admit DNA evidence in trials. However, it also recommended that judges continue considering the reliability of specific laboratory techniques on a case-by-case basis. The panel listed a number of standards a laboratory should meet before a judge admitted a DNA test it performed.

Several law professors and defense attorneys interviewed by the New York Times *said no existing forensic laboratory met the NRC standards. They thus interpreted the report as saying that DNA tests should not be admitted until the standards could be implemented. However, at a press conference the NRC panel's chairman, Victor A. McKusick of Johns Hopkins University in Baltimore, said, "We think that DNA can be used in court without interruption." He said standards "of sorts" were already in place in that laboratories already adhered to good laboratory practices. "The present methods are good," he said, "but this doesn't mean they can't be better."*

DNA testing was developed in 1985. Since then, DNA tests had been admitted in several hundred legal cases. They were used most commonly in criminal cases such as murder or rape where there might not be regular fingerprints in civil proceedings such as paternity cases.

Reliance on DNA Data Banks

The need to establish standards for DNA testing was becoming critical because police agencies and courts were increasingly relying upon the tests. Twenty states had developed data banks of DNA records from convicted criminals, three-quarters of them within just the prior two years. Some experts estimated that thirty states would have such data banks by 1995. The use of data banks was expected to grow after 1993, when the FBI was scheduled to link the state files in a computerized network. The network was designed to help law enforcement officials search for suspects who crossed state lines.

The proliferation of data banks also was expected to help in solving crimes. Before creation of the banks, DNA tests were primarily used to match samples from a crime scene with those of a suspect. But with creation of the data banks, law enforcement officers could take DNA information from a crime scene and see if there were any matches with records on a computer. Automated fingerprint analysis, a similar process that was already available, had been credited with solving tens of thousands of crimes, the NRC said.

Four months after the DNA report was released, scientists at the National Institute of Standards and Technology announced they had developed a new procedure to help improve the accuracy of DNA tests. The NIST scientists created a set of DNA samples from human cells grown in their laboratory and found the samples' DNA fingerprint. The scientists offered laboratories kits containing the samples and the fingerprint. They said lab technicians should analyze an NIST sample at the same time they analyzed a "live" sample. If the NIST sample lined up correctly with its fingerprint, the test of the live sample should be accurate as well, NIST officials said.

Following is the text of a news release, "Study Supports Use of DNA Typing in Forensic Science," issued by the National Research Council on April 14, 1992, to accompany the report, "DNA Technology in Forensic Science:"

A report released today by the National Research Council confirms the general reliability of using DNA typing evidence in criminal cases, a practice that has been challenged in some legal and scientific circles.

However, reliability depends upon a high level of quality control in the process of collecting, analyzing, and interpreting the data, the report states.

When collected and analyzed properly, DNA samples are capable of providing "strong evidence" for pointing to the perpetrator of a crime or clearing an innocent suspect. Genetic differences within ethnic groups must be accounted for in calculating the probability of a chance match between an innocent person and a sample left at the crime scene. But these differences do not undermine the essential reliability of DNA evidence, according to the report.

The study committee's endorsement of DNA typing came with a number of recommendations to resolve deficiencies in the system. These include:

- Using a method, termed the "ceiling principle," to calculate statistical probabilities. This method would allow forensic scientists to take into account the greater likelihood of a match within ethnic groups, without requiring knowledge of the race of the perpetrator.

- Studying DNA patterns in a random sample of 15 to 20 ethnic groups, and preserving the blood cells collected in these studies for future research.
- Forming a National Committee on Forensic DNA Typing to provide the forensic community with advice about rapid changes in DNA typing technology and statistical interpretation of results.
- Establishing detailed quality assurance and quality control programs to monitor laboratory work and ensure consistent reliability of the techniques employed. A mandatory accreditation program should be initiated under the responsibility of the U.S. Department of Health and Human Services (DHHS) in consultation with the Department of Justice.
- Establishing federal and state policies concerning the access to and use of DNA samples and information.
- Creating, if pilot studies confirm its value, a national DNA profile databank that contains information on felons convicted of crimes.

"DNA typing for personal identification is a powerful tool for criminal investigation and justice," said Victor A. McKusick, committee chair and University Professor of Medical Genetics at The Johns Hopkins University. "But there are certain standards that need to be met consistently from a technical point of view, and aspects of the statistical interpretation of the findings that need to be taken into account in reporting the results of tests."

Calculating the Odds

DNA is shorthand for deoxyribonucleic acid, the genetic material that carries the coded messages of heredity that determine appearance and physiological function. Forensic scientists extract DNA from samples of blood, semen, saliva, skin, and hair follicles found at the scene of the crime, then develop a "DNA profile" by analyzing three to five locations in the DNA where individual variations are common. This profile is compared with DNA taken directly from the suspect. If the profiles do not match, the suspect is excluded. DNA typing often is helpful in ruling out suspects during criminal investigations. If the profiles match, the next step is calculating the odds that another person could share the same DNA pattern at the sites studies.

Scientists currently use one of two methods to calculate the odds, McKusick said. Laboratories employ the multiplication rule, which uses probabilities to predict how many matches would occur in a population.

Another is the counting method, which uses the actual matches found within a certain databank.

Differences in estimates using the two methods can be extraordinary. In one Manhattan murder case noted in the report, odds ranged from 1 in 500, based on counting matches of DNA patterns to those in a databank, to

1 in 739 billion, based on multiplying the lowest frequencies possible at each DNA site.

The report questions applications of the multiplication rule when they do not reflect the increased chance of a match within subpopulations. However, while some population geneticists believe multiplication-rule calculations are invalid until comprehensive population studies are completed, the study committee offers an alternative approach. The committee recommends that DNA profiles be performed on 100 people from each of 15 to 20 major populations to determine frequencies of sites currently used in forensic applications. In applying the multiplication rule to these and existing data, forensic practitioners should use the highest observed frequency for each DNA site. This method, termed the "ceiling principle," accounts for the greater likelihood of a match within subpopulations, but would not require scientists to know the race of the perpetrator to calculate the odds.

The report recommends that these population studies and other developments be overseen by the proposed National Committee on Forensic DNA Typing, which primarily would provide scientific and technical advice on rapidly evolving DNA technology.

Until further population data are available, forensic scientists can still use DNA typing data. But they should opt for calculations based on application of the multiplication rule with the ceiling principle.

Laboratory Standards

The FBI's DNA typing technique is the most prevalent one in use in the United States. However, a number of private and public forensic science laboratories employ other methods.

DNA typing is "so powerful, so complex, and so important that some degree of standardization of the laboratory procedures is necessary to assure the courts of high-quality results," the study committee concluded. DNA typing is capable, in principle, of an extremely low rate of "false-positive results"—or results that would incriminate an innocent person—so the risk of error will come from poor laboratory practice or poor sample handling and labeling.

To remedy the situation, the report recommends that a mandatory accreditation program be established and administered by DHHS, in consultation with the Justice Department.

Courtroom Concerns

While most courts have ruled that DNA typing evidence is admissible, some have barred it on grounds that the techniques must first be proven to be generally accepted within the scientific community.

The study committee recommended that courts accept the reliability of DNA typing and recognize that current laboratory techniques are fundamentally sound. However, in determining admissibility of evidence, courts must continue to consider on a case-by-case basis the reliability of specific techniques used to analyze samples. For example, courts should require that laboratories providing DNA typing evidence show proper accreditation for each DNA typing technique used or demonstrate their ability to operate at the same level of standards as those accredited, the report said.

Social Impact

The report also points to a number of ethical and social concerns raised with this powerful new technology. DNA is capable of revealing information about inherited diseases and other traits. Because of this, DNA databanks set up for law enforcement purposes could also be of interest to potential employers and insurance companies. Given the usefulness of DNA typing in forensic science, databanks and storage of samples will continue to proliferate. Laws must be enacted soon, the committee said, to control both the access to and the use of this vital information.

The report was sponsored by the Federal Bureau of Investigation, National Institutes of Health National Center for Human Genome Research, National Institute of Justice, National Science Foundation, Alfred P. Sloan Foundation, and the State Justice Institute.

FDA'S LIMITED APPROVAL
OF SILICONE BREAST IMPLANTS
April 16, 1992

*Addressing a highly emotional issue, Food and Drug Administration
(FDA) Commissioner David A. Kessler announced April 16 that the
agency was ending its three-month moratorium on the use of silicone gel
breast implants and would permit their restricted use while gathering
additional information about their safety. The announcement was made
after a twenty-four-member advisory panel of scientists and physicians
was unable to reach a firm conclusion regarding the safety of the
implants.*

*Following reports that rupture or leakage of the devices—used by an
estimated half-million to one million women—could cause serious health
problems, the FDA January 6 had called for a voluntary ban on their use.
In February the FDA advisory panel recommended restricting access to
the devices and called for expensive new safety tests. Data suggested that
between 3 and 10 percent of implants had ruptured, considerably higher
than the 1 percent claimed by manufacturers. Preliminary data indicated
that silicone could migrate through the body, irritating tissues, and that
leaks could possibly cause scleroderma (an immune system disorder
characterized by thickened and tightened skin) as well as lupus
erythematosus (a connective-tissue disorder that causes rashes, flulike
symptoms, and joint pain).*

*"I am highly conscious that some women need these implants for
reconstruction after cancer surgery or traumatic injury, or for certain
congenital disorders," Kessler said in answer to questions about his
statement. "While this policy is meant to be compassionate toward these
patients, it is not to be interpreted as 'business as usual.' Our primary*

goal is to put in place a process to obtain adequate information about the safety of these devices." Under the FDA ruling, women who sought implants solely for cosmetic reasons would have to enroll in clinical studies and agree to close medical monitoring and frequent testing over a number of years. However, all women would still be able to obtain saline-filled implants.

The FDA advised women who already had silicone gel implants to see their physician and be alert to signs of possible problems, such as breast pain; a burning sensation, hardness, or change in the shape of the breast; skin rashes; and prolonged joint and muscle pain. The only clear case for immediate removal was outright rupture. Experts advised that women diagnosed with a disease possibly related to implants should also consider having them removed—a procedure that cost between $1,000 and $5,000, with a risk of surgical complications of less than 1 percent.

Lack of Safety Information

Silicone breast implants were first introduced on the market in 1962. At that time, no federal law existed to require manufacturers to prove that their products were safe. The FDA obtained that authority in 1976 but did not ask companies to provide safety data until 1988. During highly publicized hearings in late 1991 and February 1992, the FDA advisory panel concluded that although there were insufficient data on the long-term effects of implants, consideration should be given to special psychological needs for them, particularly among women who had had surgery for breast cancer.

Because of its stability, resistance to bodily fluids, and ability to be implanted without tissue rejection, silicone was used in a wide variety of devices—including wrist implants and pacemakers—before being used in breast reconstruction. However, no statistically reliable information existed on how often leaks occur in breast implants, what happens when they do, and whether and how the amount and effects of leakage change over time. "The window of opportunity for assessing these devices properly was lost ten, fifteen, or even twenty-five years ago," said Mark Lappe, a professor at the University of Illinois medical school. "We are facing the consequences of twenty-five years of suppression of data."

On February 10 Dow Corning—a joint venture of Dow Chemical and Corning, Inc., and a pioneer in the manufacture of the implants—had made public an 800-page document that contained twenty-seven scientific studies undertaken over a twenty-five-year period as well as internal memos that revealed concern on the part of some company officials that the implants could rupture under certain circumstances. In March the company's new chief executive, Keith McKennon, said Dow would cease manufacturing implants (which accounted for only 1 percent of the firm's business), saying, "It seems fairly clear that the future use of these products will be curtailed to a considerable extent." However, he said Dow would honor its commitment to carry out safety studies and fund

$10 million in research. The company also pledged to pay up to $1,000 toward a removal operation for women who could not afford the surgery and whose doctors determined it was medically necessary.

After the Dow Corning decision, Sidney Wolfe, director of Public Citizen's Health Research Group, said, "this is a strong signal that there is something very wrong with these products. The good news is that this has finally happened. The bad news is that it didn't happen much sooner."

Reaction to FDA Decision

"I think it's a very fair decision for everyone," said Dennis Condon, president of Mentor Corp., one of the two remaining breast-implant manufacturers (the other was McGhan Medical Corp.). "The patients who really need this device will continue to have access to it. The agency will be able to answer its questions and the manufacturers will be able to continue with their testing." Condon predicted that the clinical tests required by the FDA ruling—focusing on the frequency with which implants rupture and leak—would probably take three or four years.

Speaking for Mentor, Noel Rose, chairman of immunology at Johns Hopkins University, said that many symptoms thought to be caused by leaky implants might in fact be due to much less serious and more common reactions.

A more skeptical opinion on the FDA ruling was expressed by Mary McGrath, a plastic surgeon from George Washington University and a member of the expert panel. "If there are dangers to implants, then those dangers apply to all users." Permitting only some women to have them was "judgmental and paternalistic," she said. "It is a ruling on the validity of plastic surgery, and that is not [the panel's] business."

"This is the first sign that science, logic, and compassion are being returned to the review process for these devices," said Norman Cole, president of the American Society of Plastic and Reconstructive Surgeons. "Throughout this debate, our great concern has been for the women who are most affected by the restrictions on the use of this device. We are relieved that their most pressing needs will now be addressed."

The Washington Post *said in a March 22 editorial that "this radical shrinkage of the market is sure to spark criticism of . . . Kessler for unnecessarily taking a 'choice' away from women by scaring off first the consumers, then the maker. But the criticism is misguided. The 'choice' being offered was no informed choice at all."*

The silicone gel implant controversy prompted the FDA to announce a new agency program to reassess the safety and effectiveness of older medical devices, including those that contained silicone such as testicular protheses. Among products facing scrutiny were orthopedic devices (artificial knee and shoulder joints); cardiovascular devices; and ear, nose and throat devices.

Following is the text of the April 16, 1992, statement by U.S. Food and Drug Administration Commissioner David A. Kessler announcing that a moratorium on silicone gel breast implants would be lifted, permitting women to have them under restricted and closely regulated conditions:

Good Morning.

Today, I am announcing our decision that silicone breast implants will be available only under controlled clinical studies.

Patients who need these implants for breast reconstruction will be assured access to these studies.

This decision reflects the recommendations of the General and Plastic Surgery Devices Panel issued on February 20.

We are going to acquire, once and for all, the information necessary to establish the safety of these devices.

And most importantly, we want to give women who already have these implants the scientific data they need to make sound decisions related to their health.

The FDA decision is based on a key regulatory principle that applies to breast implants and other medical devices that require premarket approval.

The principle is these types of products have to be shown by their manufacturer to be safe and effective before they may be distributed and used.

Some people argue that the devices have to be proven unsafe before the FDA can act to protect patients against their use. This is NOT so.

The burden of proof is an affirmative one, and it rests with the manufacturer.

In this instance, the manufacturers have *not shown* these devices to be safe.

After three full decades on the market, what do we know about these devices?

The list of unanswered questions is long.

- We do not know how long these devices will last.

    In the apt observation of one member of FDA's advisory board on breast implants, we know more about the lifespan of automobile tires than we do about the longevity of breast implants.

- We know that some of these implants will rupture, but we don't know how many of them will rupture.

    The data on failed implants that we've seen so far raises concerns. The manufacturers' reports suggest a range of ruptures between 0.2 percent and 1.1 percent. Yet the medical literature contains figures that are significantly higher.

    Recent preliminary findings presented at the advisory panel suggested that between 4 and 6 percent of asymptomatic women have ruptured devices.

Considering that more than a million women are using these implants, even low rupture rates are unacceptable.

- Furthermore, we're not sure of the chemical composition of the gel that leaks into the body once the shell ruptures.
- And we do not know whether there is any link between the implants and immune-related disorders and other systemic diseases.

Until these basic questions are satisfactorily answered, we cannot approve these devices.

The central aim of FDA's decision is to significantly limit the use of silicone gel breast implants while vigorously pursuing the necessary research about their safety.

Let me underscore: while these devices are being studied, their availability will be limited.

Yet, as I have said, women who require them as part of reconstructive surgery will be provided ready access to these studies.

Further, important and needed research will be carried out on the safety of breast implants when they are used for augmentation and reconstructive purposes.

As is the case with any investigational product, the use of these breast implants involves certain risks, as well as potential benefits.

Participation in these studies will therefore be predicated on the informed consent of all enrolled patients.

In addition, each medical facility participating in the breast implant studies will have to have the protocol and informed consent document reviewed by an Institutional Review Board that oversees medical research projects.

Similarly as with any research studies, close follow-up of all patients will be required and all patients will become part of a prospective registry so they will have access not only to the information generated as part of the study in which they participate, but all studies of these devices.

The FDA will implement the breast implant decision in three stages.

- Stage One, which goes into effect next week, makes silicone gel implants available to women whose need for them is most urgent, and whose emotional and physical distress has been very much on our mind.

  This group includes patients who have in place, for reconstruction purposes, a temporary breast tissue expander, who need a permanent silicone implant.

  It also includes all women who have a ruptured implant that needs to be replaced for medical reasons.

  These women, upon signing the informed consent form and after obtaining a doctor's certification that they need a silicone gel implant, can have the necessary operation as early as next Tuesday.

I have to add one caveat—namely, that manufacturers will be able to distribute these devices only if they are in compliance with Good Manufacturing Practices.

The FDA field staff is now completing the necessary inspections to verify such compliance.

- Stage Two, which will start in a number of months, will include a protocol for women who elect breast reconstruction because of cancer, or who have had serious trauma to a breast, or a disease or congenital disorder causing a severe breast abnormality.

  Implementation of this stage will begin as soon as the participating device manufacturers develop the protocol for the studies and meet other FDA prerequisites, including the preparation of a distribution and accountability system for the implants.

- Stage Three will be the availability of more intensive research protocol for a limited number of women for reconstruction or augmentation purposes. These women will need to meet the eligibility requirements as stipulated by the clinical protocol sponsored by the device manufacturers.

Again, these studies will evaluate the risks of the implants as well as their potential benefits, including psychological benefits.

Each study will include fundamental questions such as the frequency of implant rupture; the frequency of implant leakage or "bleed"; the frequency and severity of capsular contracture which can cause pain and change in the shape of the breast; the frequency of change in the sensation of breast or nipple; and the extent to which the implants interfere with mammography.

I stress that this is a limited access program.

The devices will not be available for any other users outside these protocols until all pertinent safety concerns are resolved.

Let me now turn to the future legal status of this product.

As a matter of law, today we are denying premarket approval applications for distribution and use of these devices for cosmetic purposes or for augmentation of the healthy breasts.

The use of the device for reconstructive purposes in approved research protocols will be permitted under the public health need extension of the application review period which allows the availability of the device for reasons of public health.

Any use of the product for augmentation purposes will be permitted only under investigational device status.

While reimbursement for breast implants is not under the FDA jurisdiction, the extension of the review period under the public health need clause provides insurers with the option to continue reimbursement for these devices in reconstruction patients if they so choose.

Let me now address women who already have implants.

You should be aware that we have entered into discussions with both the current and past manufacturers of breast implants about establishing a registry.

We expect that the results of these discussions will be the development of an independent, retrospective registry that will enable us to tell you about further information involving the devices you have in place.

If you are not experiencing any difficulties, there is no need to have the implants removed. However, you should have periodic checkups for such potential problems as rupture.

If you are having symptoms you think may be related to your implants, you should see your doctor.

And if you have any questions, feel free to call our hot line on breast implants, which will continue operating as usual.

The toll free number is 1-800-532-4440. For the hearing impaired the TTY number is 1-800-688-6167. (The hours of operation are 9 AM-7 PM Eastern Standard Time—Monday through Friday.)

We understand your concerns and anxieties, and we're doing our utmost to relieve them.

The studies that will be undertaken are designed to provide the information you need and have every right to expect.

JUSTICE DEPARTMENT REPORTS ON RISE OF VIOLENT CRIME

April 19 and 26, 1992

Violent crime rose dramatically in the United States in 1991, according to two different reports issued a week apart by agencies of the Department of Justice. Both reports were based on preliminary figures.

The Bureau of Justice Statistics issued the first report, the National Crime Victimization Survey, on April 19. For the survey, about 95,000 people were asked if they had been a victim of crime in the previous six months. The report counted both crimes reported to police and those not reported. Just under half of all violent crimes were not reported to police in 1991.

Violent crimes rose by 8 percent, according to the report, from 2.4 million in 1990 to 2.6 million in 1991. Another 3.8 million violent crimes were attempted in 1991, up 6 percent from 1990. The figures include rapes, robberies, and assaults, but not murders. Big increases in rapes and assaults spurred the surge in violent crime. The number of attempted and completed rapes rose by 59 percent, from 130,000 to 208,000, and assaults climbed 7.5 percent, from 4.7 million to 5 million.

Justice Department officials said the increase in rapes was statistically significant, but cautioned that the number was an estimate based on a survey rather than a count of actual cases. Patsy Klaus, a Justice Department statistician, told the Associated Press the 59 percent increase "looks dramatic" because "you are dealing with a small number to begin with. We don't know if it's a trend. If we continue to get these numbers over the years, it would be of concern."

There were 31.3 violent crimes per 1,000 people in 1991, the report said. That was an increase from 29.6 per 1,000 in 1990. However, it was well below the record rate of 35.3 per 1,000 set in 1981.

In contrast to rates for violent crimes, those for property crimes generally fell or remained virtually unchanged. For example, the rates for theft and burglary remained constant, while motor vehicle thefts fell 6 percent and personal larceny with contact declined 13 percent.

FBI Statistics

The FBI issued the second document, the Uniform Crime Report, on April 26. Unlike the earlier report, it only covered crimes that had been reported to police. The FBI said violent crime rose 5 percent in 1991. That jump followed increases of 6 percent in 1988, 5 percent in 1989, and 11 percent in 1990. In contrast to the earlier report, the FBI said that rapes and assaults rose by relatively small amounts. Both climbed 3 percent in 1991, the FBI said. Among other violent crimes, murder rose 7 percent and robbery rose 8 percent.

Mid-sized and smaller cities experienced bigger increases in violent crime than the largest metropolitan areas, according to the FBI. Violent crime rose 4 percent in cities with populations over 1 million, and 2 percent in those with populations of 500,000 to 1 million. By contrast, violent crime jumped 8 percent in cities with populations of 100,000 to 500,000, 6 percent in those with 50,000 to 100,000 people, 5 percent in cities with 10,000 to 50,000 people, and 4 percent in cities with under 10,000 people. The Uniform Crime Report, like the earlier document, found smaller increases in property crimes than in violent crimes. The number of property crimes rose 2 percent, compared to 5 percent for violent crimes.

Although fighting violent crime is largely a state and local responsibility, the crime increases were not expected to help President George Bush's reelection effort. Arkansas Governor Bill Clinton, the eventual Democratic candidate, immediately used the violent crime figures to attack Bush. "President Bush has used an expansion of the death penalty as a cover for actually weakening the partnership of the federal government in the fight against crime," Clinton said in a speech.

Attorney General on Reducing Violent Crime

In a report titled Combatting Violent Crime: 24 Recommendations to Strengthen Criminal Justice, *Attorney General William P. Barr July 28 urged a continuation of tough law enforcement policies. "While we can debate the rehabilitative and deterrent effect of imprisonment," Barr said, "there can be no doubt that chronic criminals are not committing crimes while they are in prison."*

Noting that violent crime was "primarily a state and local problem"— 95 percent of all violent crimes were prosecuted in state and local courts—Barr urged the states to adopt several measures to strengthen the criminal justice system. These included mandatory minimum penalties for gun offenders and habitual violent offenders, "an effective death penalty for the most heinous crimes," and treating chronic violent juvenile defenders as adults. Earlier in the year Barr had ordered 300 FBI agents transferred from the foreign counterintelligence division to violent crime investigations and created task forces in several cities to fight violent crime.

> *Following is the text of a press release, "Personal and Household Crimes Rose Less Than 2 Percent Last Year," issued April 19, 1992, by the Bureau of Justice Statistics to accompany the National Crime Victimization Survey, and an untitled press release issued April 26, by the FBI to accompany the Uniform Crime Report:*

BUREAU OF JUSTICE STATISTICS RELEASE

Washington, D.C.—The Bureau of Justice Statistics (BJS) said today that the estimated number of personal and household crimes in the U.S. rose 1.9 percent last year, increasing from 34.4 million in 1990 to 35.1 million in 1991.

BJS, a Department of Justice component in the Office of Justice Programs, said the preliminary crime rate estimates are from its National Crime Victimization Survey (NCVS), which is an on-going data collection program that uses U.S. Bureau of the Census interviewers.

During 1991 approximately 95,000 people in about 48,000 nationally representative U.S. households were asked about crimes they might have experienced during the preceding six months.

The data include both crimes reported to police and those that go unreported. Because the BJS survey includes unreported crime, there may be differences in these data from what the Federal Bureau of Investigation publishes in its Uniform Crime Reports, which are based on police reports. About 37 percent of all crimes and 49 percent of all violent crimes were reported to law enforcement agencies last year. An estimated 22 million personal and household crimes were not reported to the police during 1991. The percentage of unreported crime last year was almost identical to the percentage in 1990.

"Last year's estimated increase brings the total number of victimizations during 1991 to a level that is still well below the peak number of almost 41.5 million recorded in 1981," noted BJS Director Steven D. Dillingham. "In 1981 the survey estimated there were about 6.6 million violent crimes—that is, about 35.3 violent crimes for every 1,000 people 12 years old or older, compared to an estimated 6.4 million such crimes, or 31.3 per 1,000 people last year."

BJS commented that statistically significant increases in the preliminary estimates of rape and simple assault occurred last year, but the rates per capita were only marginally higher than in 1990.

The preliminary estimates of the rape rate rose to 1.0 per 1,000 in 1991. This estimate, which was higher than the rate for the preceding year, is similar to rates BJS reported in previous years. For example, in 1978, 1979 and 1981 the per capita rape rates were at or near the 1991 estimate.

Last year's ratio of simple assaults per 1,000 U.S. inhabitants 12 years old and older was only marginally higher than the 1990 rate. The estimated 52.6 burglaries per 1,000 U.S. households last year was at or near the lowest rate since the survey began in 1973. Between 1981 and 1991 burglary rates declined 40 percent. During the same period robbery rates declined 24 percent—from 7.4 robberies per 1,000 people to 5.6 per 1,000 in 1991. . . .

FBI RELEASE ON UNIFORM CRIME REPORTS

FBI Director William S. Sessions announced today that the number of serious crimes in the Nation rose 3 percent from 1990 to 1991, according to preliminary Uniform Crime Reporting statistics. Based on an Index of selected offenses, Uniform Crime Reporting figures measure changes in the level of crimes reported to law enforcement agencies across the country. The Index has shown increases since 1985—5 percent in 1985, 6 percent in 1986, 2 percent in 1987, 3 percent in 1988, and 2 percent in both 1989 and 1990.

Violent crime overall rose 5 percent in 1991 as compared to 1990. Among the reported violent crimes, robbery showed the greatest increase, 8 percent. Murder was up 7 percent, and forcible rape and aggravated assault each increased 3 percent.

The property crime total increased 2 percent in 1991. Of the property crimes reported, burglary was up 3 percent; both larceny-theft and motor vehicle theft rose 2 percent. Arson showed no change.

Geographically, three of the four regions recorded increases in the Crime Index total, 1991 versus 1990. The Midwest reported a 4-percent rise, and the South and the West registered 3-percent upswings. The Northeast showed no change.

Both suburban county and rural county law enforcement agencies experienced increases in Crime Index offenses reported, 4 and 5 percent, respectively. Cities outside of metropolitan areas recorded an upswing of 4 percent. By population size, the Nation's cities showed Crime Index increases of 4-percent in all groups except cities from 25,000 to 49,999, which recorded a 3-percent rise, and cities with 500,000 or more inhabitants, which showed no change. . . .

NEW EVIDENCE OF UNIVERSE'S "BIG BANG" ORIGINS

April 23, 1992

New evidence supporting the theory that the universe began with a cataclysmic explosion 15 billion years ago was released April 23 at the American Physical Society's meeting in Washington, D.C.

Scientists around the world said the latest reinforcement for the so-called Big Bang theory was one of the most important discoveries ever made in cosmology—the study of the universe's earliest beginnings and largest structures. "If they are right, this is a Nobel-class discovery," said Stephen Maran, editor of the Astronomy and Astrophysics Encyclopedia. *He told the* Washington Post: *"They've found the first evidence of shape arising in the universe. It's like Genesis."*

Physicist Stephen Hawking of Cambridge University agreed. "It is the discovery of the century, if not of all time," he told Reuters. Hawking, who wrote the best-selling book A Brief History of Time, *is often considered Albert Einstein's successor.*

In announcing the findings, scientist George Smoot said that "English doesn't have enough superlatives to convey" the importance of the discovery. "It's going to mean a revolution in the understanding of the early universe." Smoot, a Lawrence Berkeley Laboratory astrophysicist, directed the project.

The new evidence came from millions of measurements made by NASA's Cosmic Background Explorer (COBE) satellite, which detected minute temperature differences in background radiation that scientists believed came from the Big Bang explosion.

The Big Bang theory was first proposed in 1927 by an obscure Belgian priest named Georges Lemaitre, who believed that the universe was created when a dense clump of material exploded. But much of the scientific community dismissed Lemaitre's theory. Two years later American astronomer Edwin Hubble discovered that distant galaxies were racing away from Earth at enormous speeds, which increased the farther away they got. This finding suggested that the universe was expanding. It also suggested that some event had triggered the expansion.

Cosmic Noise from the Explosion

In the 1940s other researchers theorized that in its early days the universe was both extremely hot and dense. They believed that nuclear reactions occurring in this environment accounted for the large quantity of hydrogen and helium found in the universe. They also noted that if this hot matter exploded, as the Big Bang theory proposed, the universe should still contain great amounts of radiation from the explosion. This raised the possibility that if scientists could peer far enough into space, they might see the glow of the initial fireball.

The first glimpse of that fireball came in 1964, when Arno Penzias and Robert Wilson received unexplained noise using a new, extremely sensitive microwave receiver and antenna. The noise came equally from all parts of the universe. Eventually, scientists realized this noise was cosmic background radiation and postulated that it emanated from the Big Bang explosion some 15 billion years ago. The uniform radiation was the strongest piece of evidence supporting the Big Bang theory because it could not be explained except as the remnant of a primeval explosion. Penzias and Wilson eventually received the Nobel Prize for their discovery.

Scientists embarked on hundreds of experiments that examined the radiation, looking for clues to the first moments of the universe. However, their research was hampered by the radiation's faintness and distortions caused by the Earth's atmosphere.

That led to COBE, which was launched aboard a Delta rocket on November 17, 1989. COBE's mission was to measure the diffuse-infrared radiation that bombarded Earth. Its instruments were far more sensitive than anything ever used before.

What COBE found was tiny but startling: "ripples" in the radiation that showed up as temperature fluctuations. The fluctuations were extraordinarily faint, just about thirty millionths of a degree warmer or cooler than the rest of the sky. The temperature variations were "the imprints of tiny ripples in the fabric of space-time put there by the primeval explosion process," Smoot told the Post. *"Over billions of years, the smaller of these ripples have grown into galaxies, clusters of galaxies, and the great voids in space." The ripples help to explain one of the universe's great mysteries: its lumpiness. Without ripples, radiation from the Big Bang should have created a uniformly smooth universe.*

The ripples may date from when the universe was less than one-trillionth of a second old, Smoot said. "It's as close to the start as we're ever likely to get," said COBE scientist Alan Kogut.

From its orbit 559 miles above Earth, COBE made hundreds of millions of measurements that were later analyzed by computer. These measurements allowed scientists to "map" the entire sky, with accuracy equal to measuring the height of Mount Everest to within one inch, Smoot said.

Implications for Religious Theory

Some theologians saw no conflict between COBE's findings and the religious belief that divine intervention created order out of chaos. "Christian cosmology and the Big Bang are very compatible understandings of the arrow of time," the Rev. Frederic B. Burnham, a science historian and director of the Trinity Institute in New York City, told the Associated Press. "There was a beginning and there will be an end."

Even COBE scientists agreed that their findings did not contradict religious beliefs about the creation of the universe. "The story we found is very parallel to the story in Genesis," said John Mather, one of the key COBE scientists. "The Bible has things in the same sequence as we have. It's just a question of what you mean by a 'day.'"

Following is the text of a press release, "COBE Detects Structure of Early Universe," released by the National Aeronautics and Space Administration on April 23, 1992:

Scientists announced today, at the American Physical Society's meeting held in Washington, D.C., that they have detected the long-sought variations within the glow from the Big Bang—the primeval explosion that began the Universe 15 billion years ago—using NASA's Cosmic Background Explorer (COBE). This detection is a major milestone in a 25-year search and supports theories explaining how the initial expansion happened.

These variations show up as temperature fluctuations in the sky, revealed by statistical analysis of maps made by the Differential Microwave Radiometers (DMR) on the COBE satellite. The fluctuations are extremely faint, only about thirty millionths of a degree warmer or cooler than the rest of the sky, which is itself very cold—only 2.73 degrees above absolute zero. The DMR is still gathering data and the measurements are expected to become ever more precise.

The Big Bang theory was initially suggested because it explains why distant galaxies are receding from us at enormous speeds, as though all galaxies started moving away from the same location a long time ago. The theory also predicts the existence of cosmic background radiation—the glow left over from the explosion itself. The Big Bang theory received its strongest confirmation when this radiation was discovered in 1964 by Arno Penzias and Robert Wilson, who later won the Nobel Prize for this discovery.

Although the Big Bang theory is widely accepted, there have been several unresolved mysteries. How could all of the matter and energy in the Universe become so evenly mixed in the instant following the Big Bang? How could this evenly distributed matter then break up spontaneously into objects of all sizes, such as galaxies and clusters of galaxies? The temperature variations seen by COBE help to resolve these mysteries.

"The COBE receivers mapped the sky as it would appear if our eyes could see microwaves at the wavelengths 3.3, 5.7 and 9.6 mm, which is about 10,000 times longer than the wavelength of ordinary light," explained Dr. George Smoot, University of California, Berkeley, the leader of the team that made this discovery. "Most of the energy received from the sky at these wavelengths is from the cosmic background radiation of the Big Bang, but it is extremely faint by human standards.

"Hundreds of millions of measurements were made by the DMR over the course of a year, and then combined to make pictures of the sky. Making sure all the measurements were combined correctly required exquisitely careful computer analysis," Smoot explained.

Another COBE scientist, Dr. Charles Bennett of the Goddard Space Flight Center, Greenbelt, Md., explained that a major challenge for the team was to distinguish the Big Bang signals from those coming from our own Milky Way Galaxy. "The Milky Way emits microwaves that appear mostly concentrated in a narrow zone around the sky. We compared the signals at different positions and at different wavelengths to separate the radiation of the Big Bang from that of the Milky Way Galaxy," said Dr. Bennett.

The temperatures and sizes of the fluctuations in the background radiation COBE detected agree with the predictions of "inflationary cosmology," a theory that says the structure and behavior of the Universe were determined by minute fluctuations occurring when the Universe was much younger than one-trillionth of a second. The COBE results provide new evidence in support of the "inflationary" scenario.

The amount of gravity provided by these visible fluctuations was inadequate to draw together the galaxies and clusters of galaxies. Instead, astronomers conclude that the galaxies formed only because most of the material in the Universe is invisible and totally unlike ordinary matter.

This "dark matter" provides the necessary gravitational attraction for forming galaxies. The fluctuations seen by COBE are too small to explain how the visible matter in the young Universe could condense into the galaxies that now exist. According to COBE scientist Dr. Edward Wright from the University of California, Los Angeles, the COBE measurements support theories postulating large amounts of dark matter.

"These theories say that most of the matter in the Universe is invisible to us and must be a new kind of matter, not yet detected in our laboratories," he explained. "Nevertheless, we need such invisible matter to explain how galaxies formed in the early Universe and gathered themselves together into huge clusters. Ordinary matter would be attracted into regions of concentrated dark matter, and the Universe as we know it today could develop, eventually leading to the formation of galaxies, stars and planets," Wright said.

COBE was launched in November, 1989, from Vandenberg Air Force Base, Calif., aboard a Goddard-managed Delta launch vehicle. The Goddard Space Flight Center, Greenbelt, Md., manages COBE for NASA's Office of Space Science and Applications, Astrophysics Division, Washington, D.C.

REPORT ON RAPE IN AMERICA
April 23, 1992

Women suffer rape in much higher numbers than previously estimated, with only 16 percent of the crimes being reported to police, according to an in-depth National Women's Study. Based on 1990 data, 683,000 women are forcibly raped annually—an average of 1.3 per minute, 78 per hour, and 1,871 each day—with as many as 12.1 million American women (one out of every eight) having been rape victims at least once in their lifetimes.

The researchers arrived at their figures by interviewing a large cross-section of women and projecting their experiences against the total of 96.8 million adult American women. The three-year study—funded by the National Institute on Drug Abuse and conducted by the National Victim Center, the Crime Victims Research and Treatment Center, and the University of South Carolina Medical School—surveyed 4,008 women age eighteen or older. The study was described as longitudinal because it included follow-up interviews with most of the women initially polled.

The April 23 interim report, entitled Rape in America: A Report to the Nation, *was based on interviews with 2,785 respondents who had completed all three years of interviews. Of those, 507 women reported they had been raped—more than once in some cases (among the 507 there were 714 cases of rape). The report also included data on "the State of Services for Victims of Rape," based on information collected in 1992 by the National Victim Center from 370 agencies that provided crisis assistance to rape victims. The survey obtained information on up to three rapes from each victim—the first ever experienced, the most recent, and the "worst" if other than the first or most recent. According to the researchers' definition, rape occurred when there was sexual penetration without consent, involving the use or threat of violence.*

Rape: An Underreported Crime

The study's estimated number of rape victims was more than five times larger than the Justice Department's National Crime Survey figure of 130,000 attempted and completed rapes in 1990. (Justice Department Reports on Rise of Violent Crime, p. 375)

Justice Department officials, while questioning some of the study's methodology, acknowledged that rape was dramatically underreported. "We have significant differences in sample size, estimation, procedures," noted Steven Dillingham, director of the Bureau of Justice Statistics, who did not dispute the National Women's Study figures. "Our point of view is that exact levels of rape are always going to be problematic. . . ."

Cassandra Thomas, president of the National Coalition Against Sexual Assault, a coordinating center for rape crisis programs, said, "I don't think this is a high number. It falls in line with what we see in crisis centers across the country."

The figures support what some experts have believed all along, said Mary P. Koss, a University of Arizona professor of family and community medicine who conducted a study of rape involving college women in 1987. "There is a lot more rape than has been reflected by federal statistics, and that observation is more important than whether these are the exact right numbers."

"A Tragedy of Youth"

" . . . [R]ape in America is a tragedy of youth, with the majority of rape cases occurring during childhood and adolescence," the report said. Although the study did not cover rapes of girls under eighteen or of boys and men, many of the surveyed women had been raped when they were younger. Responses indicated that 61 percent of all rapes occurred before the victim reached the age of eighteen; 29 percent were ten or younger.

"I was really shocked that such a large percentage of rapes happen so early in life," said study coauthor Dean Kilpatrick, a nationally known expert on rape. "We may have severely underestimated the degree of violence involved in the sexual assault of our youth."

"We may be making progress in encouraging women to report rapes, but we still have a long way to go in getting children to report rapes," said Lucy Berliner of Seattle's Sexual Assault Project.

Study Findings: Cause for Concern

"The startling number of rape victims, and the early age at which many of these rapes occur, are examples of a terrible truth that defies simple explanation, easy understanding, or quick remedies," the researchers stated. "These facts tear at the very fabric of our individual and collective values."

Among the study's major findings:

- *Only 22 percent of rape victims were assaulted by someone they had never seen before or did not know well; the rest were assaulted by husbands, ex-husbands, fathers, stepfathers, boyfriends, ex-boyfriends, other relatives, and nonrelatives such as friends and neighbors.*

- *Rape victims expressed concern about the following in particular: the family knowing they had been sexually assaulted (71 percent), people thinking it was their fault or that they were responsible (69 percent), people outside the family knowing they had been sexually assaulted (68 percent), and their names being made public by the news media (50 percent). Only 29 ranked as "most important" fear of contracting AIDS or another sexually transmitted disease.*

- *Only 17 percent of all victims reported having a medical exam after such an assault; 60 percent were not advised about pregnancy testing or how to prevent pregnancy; and more than 73 percent were not given information about testing for exposure to HIV/AIDS.*

- *Only 16 percent of rapes were ever reported to police; however, 61 percent of victims said they would report a similar future incident.*

- *Sixty-six percent of rape victims surveyed stated they would be "a lot" or "somewhat" more likely to report assaults to police if there was a law prohibiting media disclosure of their identities. Ninety-one percent favored a "privacy law."*

- *Rape victims were three times more likely than nonvictims to suffer major bouts of depression; those suffering from rape-related post-traumatic stress disorder were thirteen times more likely to have two or more major alcohol problems and twenty-six times more likely to have two or more major drug abuse problems.*

- *Contrary to some perceptions, extreme violence is rare, with only 4 percent of victims reporting they were seriously hurt, compared with 70 percent unharmed and 24 percent suffering minor injuries.*

Recommendations: Legislation, Education

"[I]t is imperative that rape be classified as a major public health issue in the United States," the report concluded. "The traumatic consequences of rape—ranging from severe mental health problems, to substance abuse problems, to victims' fears about privacy, to the tragic youth of its victims—affect the long-term physical, mental and emotional health of millions of American women. The 'domino effect' rape has on victims' families and friends also contributes to detrimental public health consequences."

Among the report's recommendations were:

- *Enactment of legislation to prevent media disclosure of victims' names and addresses*

- *Education about rape in primary and secondary grades*
- *More comprehensive training for the medical, including mental health, community about the appropriate treatment of rape victims*
- *Initiation of public education programs to dispel widely held stereotypes about rape, the characteristics of rape victims, and how they responded after the assault*

Effect of Smith and Tyson "Date Rape" Cases

Some observers questioned the need for legislation preventing media disclosure of victims' names, noting that most newspapers and television already concealed the names of victims, which did not appear to encourage women to come forward. Interviews with rape service agency personnel concerning two highly publicized "date rape" incidents revealed their thoughts about the likelihood that victims would come forward to press charges against their attacker. Of the agencies responding, 71 percent said that the outcome of the 1991 case acquitting William Kennedy Smith (nephew of Sen. Edward M. Kennedy, D-Mass.) of raping his date would make other victims less likely to report assaults to the police. (Kennedy Apology for Faults in Private Life, Historic Documents of 1991, p. 713)

Conversely, 82 percent of agency personnel thought that the 1992 conviction of heavyweight boxing champion Mike Tyson for "date rape" would have a positive effect on women's willingness to report such crimes.

During both the Smith and Tyson trials, most of the news media withheld the names of the alleged victims, but in both cases the accusers later "went public" and told their stories on television.

> *Following are excerpts from "Rape in America: A Report to the Nation," prepared by the National Victim Center and the Crime Victims Research and Treatment Center and released April 23, 1992:*

The past year has witnessed unprecedented interest in crimes against women, from Congressional hearings to several high profile rape trials to media scrutiny of rape issues. This intense public concern has produced more questions than answers about crimes against women:

- What is forcible rape?
- How much rape is there in the United States?
- What are rape victims' key concerns?
- How many rapes are actually reported to police, and does media disclosure of rape victims' names affect such reporting?
- What has been the impact of recent high profile rape cases on reporting of rapes?

Rape in America: A Report to the Nation addresses these and other pertinent questions, providing the first national empirical data about forcible rape of women in America. The results of two nationwide studies conducted by the National Victim Center and the Crime Victims Research and Treatment Center at the Medical University of South Carolina are summarized in this *Report*.

The National Women's Study, funded by the National Institute of Drug Abuse, is a three-year longitudinal study of a national probability sample of 4,008 adult women. In *The State of Services for Victims of Rape*, sponsored by the National Victim Center, 370 agencies which provide crisis assistance to rape victims were survey respondents.

The National Women's Study is a longitudinal survey of a large national probability sample of 4,008 adult American women (age 18 or older), 2,008 of whom represent a cross section of all adult women and 2,000 of whom are an oversample of younger women between the ages of 18 and 34. Eighty-five percent of women contacted agreed to participate and completed the initial (Wave One) telephone interview. At the one year follow-up (Wave Two), 81% of *The National Women's Study* participants (n=3220) were located and re-interviewed. The two year follow-up (Wave Three) is currently in progress, but preliminary data from the first 2,785 women who completed the 45-minute Wave Three interview are included in this Report. In addition to gathering information about forcible rapes that occurred throughout women's lifetimes, *The National Women's Study* also assessed such major mental health problems as depression, Post-traumatic Stress Disorder, suicide attempts, as well as alcohol and drug-related problems and consumption. . . .

The National Women's Study

During Wave One of the study, information was gathered about forcible rape experiences occurring *any time* during a woman's lifetime. Thirteen percent of women surveyed reported having been victims of *at least one completed rape* in their lifetimes. Based on U.S. Census estimates of the number of adult women in America, one out of every eight adult women, or at least *12.1 million American women,* has been the victim of forcible rate sometime in her lifetime.

Many American women were raped more than once. While 56%, or an estimated 6.8 million women experienced only one rape, 39%, or an estimated 4.7 million women were raped more than once, and five percent were unsure as to the number of times they were raped.

Prior to this study, national information about rape was limited to data on reported rapes from the *FBI Uniform Crime Reports* or data from the *Bureau of Justice Statistics, National Crime Survey (NCS)* on reported and non-reported rapes occurring in the past year. However, the *NCS* provides no information about rapes occurring over the lifetime of a victim, and has been recently redesigned due to criticisms that it failed to detect a substantial proportion of rape cases. Therefore, the results of these two new surveys fill a large gap in current knowledge about rape at the national level.

Information from *The National Women's Study* indicates that 0.7% of all women surveyed had experienced a completed forcible rape in the past year. This equates to an estimated *683,000 adult American women who were raped during a twelve-month period.*

The National Women's Study estimate that 683,000 adult American women were raped in a one year period *does not include all rapes that occurred in America that year.* Rapes that occurred to female children and adolescents under the age of 18—which comprised more than six out of ten of all rapes occurring over women's lifetimes—were not included, nor were any rapes of boys or men.

Thus the 683,000 rapes of adult women probably constitute well less than half of all the rapes that were experienced by all Americans of all ages and genders during that one year period.

How do these estimates from *The National Women's Study* compare with those from the *FBI Uniform Crime Reports* and from the *National Crime Survey?* The FBI estimate of the number of attempted or completed forcible rapes that were reported to police in 1990 was 102,560. The *National Crime Survey* estimates include both reported and non-reported rapes that are either attempted or completed. The *NCS* estimate for 1990 is 130,000 attempted or completed rapes of female Americans age 12 or older. *The National Women's Study* estimate was based on completed rapes of adult women (age 18 or older) that occurred between Wave One (conducted in the fall of 1989), and Wave Two (conducted in the fall of 1990). Thus, the time periods were not identical, but were roughly comparable.... Although it did not include attempted rapes or rapes of adolescents between the ages of 12 and 18 as did the *NCS, The National Women's Study* estimate was still 5.3 times larger than the *NCS* estimate.

In *The National Women's Study,* information was gathered regarding up to three rapes per person: the first rape she ever experienced, the most recent rape, and the "worst" rape if other than the first or most recent. Information was available from Wave One about 714 such *cases* of rape that 507 *victims* of rape had experienced. The survey found that rape in America is a tragedy of youth, with the majority of rape cases occurring during childhood and adolescence. Twenty-nine percent of all forcible rapes occurred when the victim was *less than 11 years old,* while another 32% occurred *between the ages of 11 and 17.* Slightly more than one in five rapes (22%) occurred between the ages of 18 and 24; seven percent occurred between the ages of 25 and 29, with *only six percent* occurring when the victim was older than 29 years old. Three percent of the respondents were not sure or refused to answer.

Characteristics of Rape

The National Women's Survey clearly dispels the common myth that most women are raped by strangers. To the contrary, only 22% of rape victims were assaulted by someone they had never seen before or did not know well. Nine percent of victims were raped by husbands or ex-husbands; eleven percent by their fathers or step-fathers; ten percent by boyfriends or ex-boyfriends; sixteen percent by other relatives; and twenty-nine percent by other non-relatives, such as friends and neighbors.

Another common misconception about rape is that most victims sustain serious physical injuries. Over two-thirds (70%) of rape victims reported no physical injuries; only 4% sustained serious physical injuries, with 24% receiving minor physical injuries. Of considerable importance is the fact that many victims who did *not* sustain physical injuries nonetheless *feared being seriously injured or killed* during the rape. Almost half of all rape victims (49%) described being fearful of serious injury or death during the rape. ....

Without accurate information about victims' concerns after rape, it is difficult to create and implement policies and programs to meet their most critical needs. Therefore, rape victims were asked about the extent to which they were concerned about issues specific to their personal rape experiences.

Rape victims were at least somewhat or extremely concerned about the following:

- Her family knowing she had been sexually assaulted (71%);
- People thinking it was her fault or that she was responsible (69%);
- People outside her family knowing she had been sexually assaulted (68%);
- Her name being made public by the news media (50%);
- Becoming pregnant (34%);
- Contracting a sexually transmitted disease not including HIV/AIDS (19%); and
- Contracting HIV/AIDS (10%).

The combination of concerns about being blamed (which reflect the stigma still associated with rape) and people finding out they had been victims (which reflects confidentiality concerns) may explain why more than half of rape victims in America express concern about the news media disclosing their names.

It is clear that rape victims are extremely concerned about people *finding out* and *finding reasons* to blame them for the rape. If the *stigma* of rape was not *still* a very real concern in victims' eyes, perhaps fewer rape victims in America would be concerned about invasion of their privacy and other disclosure issues.

Somewhat surprisingly, concerns about exposure to sexually transmittable diseases and HIV/AIDS were lower than might be expected. However, many victims were raped years ago as children, prior to America's AIDS epidemic.

Victims were asked if they had a medical examination following the assault. In *only 17%* of all rape cases did such an exam occur. Of these, 60% of rape victims who did receive a medical examination had it within 24 hours of the assault. However, in 40% of the cases, the exam occurred more than 24 hours *after* the assault. Victims told their doctors in only two-thirds of rape cases that they had been sexually assaulted; the doctor was never told about the rape in one-third of such cases. . . .

Rape remains the most underreported violent crime in America. *The National Women's Study* found that only 16%, or approximately one out of every six rapes, are ever reported to police. Of reported rapes, one-quarter (25%) were reported to police more than 24 hours *after* the rape occurred.

Rape victims were asked about the likelihood of reporting to police if a similar incident happened in the future. The surprising (and encouraging) responses indicated that 61% definitely would report and 25% probably would report a future rape to the police.

The National Women's Study findings show that 84% of rape victims do not report to the police. What implications does this have for public safety and public policy?

If the assumption is made that each rapist in America rapes only once in his life, then each unreported rape results in an injustice to that victim, but has no further impact on public safety. However, there is clear evidence that most rapists are recidivists. A respected study of unincarcerated sex offenders provides dramatic evidence of the extent of recidivism and why it is so important for rape victims to report. Dr. Gene Abel and his colleagues studied 561 unincarcerated sex offenders, of whom 126 admitted to having committed rape. *These 126 rapists had committed a total of 907 rapes involving 882 different victims. The average number of different victims per rapist was seven.*

Unreported rapes are a threat to public safety in America. After all, rapists cannot be apprehended, indicted, prosecuted, and incarcerated if the criminal justice system does not know that a rape has occurred. Such undetected rapists remain invisible to the criminal justice system. If rape victims are reluctant to report, then rapists will remain free to continue raping America's women, men and children.

Therefore, the dire need for public safety dictates what America's public policy should be: to do everything possible to encourage reporting of *all* alleged rapes to police.

During the past year, several high profile rape cases received vast publicity, with several respected news agencies straying from their standard wise policies of *not* disclosing rape victims' names. The argument has been made that disclosing rape victims' names would "destigmatize" the crime of rape and encourage victims to report rapes to police. It is extremely significant that rape victims appear to strongly disagree with this argument.

Half of rape victims surveyed (50%) stated they would be *a lot more likely* to report rapes to police if there was a law prohibiting the news media from getting and disclosing their names and addresses, with an additional 16% *somewhat more likely* to report.

Opposition to media disclosure of rape victims' names is *not* limited to victims themselves. All participants in *The National Women's Survey* were asked if they personally favored or opposed laws which prevent the disclosure of the names and addresses of sexual assault victims. More than three-quarters (76%) of American women strongly favor or somewhat favor such laws.

When asked how they think the risk of being identified in the news media affects rape reporting to the police, almost nine out of ten American women (86%) felt victims would be *less likely* to report rapes if they felt their names would be disclosed by the news media.

A disturbing pattern emerges when one looks at shifts of concerns of rape victims over these years. It appears that women are *just as likely* in recent years to fear negative evaluation by others if a rape is disclosed, and are *more concerned* about the possibility of their names being made public. In addition, they are more likely to be concerned about their risk of developing sexually transmitted diseases and HIV/AIDS. Finally, even in the minority of cases where victims *do* seek information and health care, their legitimate concerns are frequently not addressed. At the very least, these women should be encouraged to feel comfortable and should be supported in seeking adequate health care and information to quell fears about exposure to disease, regardless of the criminal justice or civil justice consequences of cases. . . .

The Mental Health Impact of Rape

. . . Almost one-third (31%) of all rape victims developed PTSD [post-traumatic stress disorder] sometime during their lifetimes, and more than one in ten rape victims (11%) still has PTSD at the present time. Rape victims were 6.2 times more likely to develop PTSD than women who had never been victims of crime (31% vs. 5%). Rape victims were also 5.5 times more likely to have current PTSD than their counterparts who had never been victims of crime (11% vs. 2%). . . .

[R]ape victims were *three times more likely than non-victims of crime* to have ever had a major depressive episode (30% vs. 10%), and were 3.5 times more likely to be currently experiencing a major depressive episode (21% vs. 6%).

Some mental health problems are life-threatening in nature. When asked if they ever thought seriously about committing suicide, 33% of the rape victims and 8% of the non-victims of crime stated that they had seriously considered suicide. Thus, rape victims were *4.1 times more likely* than non-crime victims *to have contemplated suicide*. Rape victims were also *13 times more likely* than non-crime victims to have *actually made a suicide* attempt (13% vs. 1%). The fact that 13% of all rape victims had actually attempted suicide confirms the devastating and potentially life-threatening mental health impact of rape.

Finally, there was substantial evidence that rape victims had higher rates of drug and alcohol consumption and a greater likelihood of having drug and alcohol-related problems than non-victims of crime....

Thus, rape is a problem for America's mental health and public health systems as well as for the criminal justice system.

The dramatically higher risk of substance abuse problems among American women who have been raped and develop PTSD suggests that America may need to commit greater resources to the war on rape, as it has to win its war on drugs.

State of Services for Victims of Rape

The tragedy of rape is confronted daily by a remarkable group of advocates nationwide who devote their collective energies to crisis intervention, victim assistance and support, and rape prevention. Over two thousand organizations have emerged in the past twenty years to support rape victims....

Because of their contact with rape victims, including those who choose not to report to police, such agencies are in a unique position to help determine the scope and nature of both rape in America and, more specifically, rape victims' most prevalent concerns. *The State of Services for Victims of Rape* included responses from staff at 370 agencies that provide crisis counseling to rape victims, including those who may not report to police....

The results of this *Report* clearly refute the assertion that media disclosure of rape victims' names would *increase* victims' willingness to report to police. To the contrary, almost all respondents to both studies highlighted in this *Report* felt that rape victims' privacy rights should not only be respected, but protected by law.

The privacy rights of persons accused of rape were also addressed in this survey. A majority of rape crisis centers (63%) favored laws that would prohibit the disclosure of the names of persons accused of rape until *after* an arrest is made. However, support for protecting the privacy of persons *indicted* for rape decreased significantly, with 40% of respondents strongly or somewhat favoring laws prohibiting media disclosure of *indicted defendants'* names. Support for protecting the privacy for persons *convicted* of rape was even less, with less than one-fourth (24%) believing that convicted rapists' privacy rights in the news media should be protected by law.

Agencies were asked what percentage of rape victims they served were unwilling to report the crime to police. Forty-two percent of the agencies said that *more than half* of all their sexually assaulted clients were unwilling to report to the police....

High Profile Rape Cases: What Is the Impact?

Based upon their personal experiences and the victims to whom they talked, agencies were asked if they thought the highly publicized West

Palm Beach sexual battery trial [of William Kennedy Smith] had an effect on women's willingness to report rapes to police. Almost two-thirds (66%) of all rape service agencies thought this trial and its outcome, indeed, affected rape reporting. Of those agencies that thought the trial had an effect:

- Seven out of ten agencies (71%) thought victims would be *somewhat less likely* to report rapes to police;
- One out of five (20%) thought victims would be *much less likely to report;*
- Less than one in ten agencies (9%) thought victims would be *somewhat more likely* to report; and
- *Not one agency* thought victims would be *much more likely* to report.

In summary, almost two-thirds of agencies thought the West Palm Beach trial made rape victims *somewhat or much less likely* to report to police.

Agencies were also asked whether they thought the highly publicized Indianapolis trial [of boxer Mike Tyson] had any effect on women's willingness to report rapes to police. Almost half the agencies (48%) thought the trial had an effect on rape reporting. Of those agencies that thought the trial had an effect:

- Eighty-two percent of the agencies thought that women would be *somewhat or much more likely* to report rapes to police; and
- Eighteen percent of the agencies surveyed said that victims would be *much or somewhat less* likely to report rapes to the police.

Clearly, agencies that work directly with rape victims believe that the conviction in the Indianapolis trial had a salutary effect on a victim's likelihood to report. This is in stark contrast to their perception of the impact of the West Palm Beach trial....

NUTRITION REVISIONISM: FOODS, CHOLESTEROL, MILK, MARGARINE

April 28, September 29, and October 7, 1992

Just when it seemed safe to eat again, a spate of new reports issued in 1992 revised nutrition knowledge and raised questions about the safety of everything from low cholesterol levels to milk. In an August editorial, the New York Times *summed up the reactions of many people to the new studies. "To read the ever-changing reports about diet and health is to fear that you're damned if you do, damned if you don't," the newspaper said.*

The U.S. Department of Agriculture kicked off the changes April 28 when it released the long-delayed "Food Guide Pyramid." The pyramid represented a refinement of the Basic Four Food Groups, a nutrition education mainstay dating back to the 1950s. Instead of just urging Americans to eat a variety of foods, as the Basic Four did, the pyramid said Americans should eat more of certain types of foods and less of others. The pyramid advised people to eat daily nine to eleven servings of grains such as bread, cereal, rice and pasta; three to five servings of vegetables; two to three servings of fruit; two to three servings of dairy products; two to three servings of meat, poultry, fish, dry beans, eggs, and nuts; and to consume fats, oils, and sweets "sparingly." The pyramid did not specify the size of a "serving."

The Agriculture Department was originally scheduled to release the pyramid in 1991. However, Agriculture Secretary Edward Madigan halted publication after the meat and dairy industries strongly objected to the new graphic, which made it clear their products should be eaten only in relatively small amounts. The Agriculture Department then spent $855,000 to study the pyramid again before finally issuing a graphic that was nearly identical to the first one.

Dangers of Too-Low Cholesterol

Later in the year, several studies were released which indicated that having a blood cholesterol count below certain levels could increase the risk of death from a variety of causes. One of the biggest studies appeared in the July issue of The Archives of Internal Medicine. The study tracked 350,000 healthy middle-aged men for twelve years. Those men with very low blood cholesterol levels had hardly any heart disease by the end of the study, and their death rate from heart attacks was about half that of men with higher cholesterol levels.

However, they had higher rates of other diseases than men with higher cholesterol levels. They were twice as likely to have an intracranial hemorrhage, to die from lung disease, or to kill themselves; three times as likely to have liver cancer; and five times as likely to die of alcoholism.

Results from the various studies confounded scientists, who for several years had urged all Americans to lower their blood cholesterol levels. "What it comes down to is that there is an extraordinary set of observations that have emerged this year because for the first time we have large enough studies to really see them," Dr. Stephen Hulley, a heart disease researcher at the University of California in San Francisco, told the New York Times. He called the observations "very serious and disconcerting."

Scientists offered a variety of theories to explain the results, but said too many specifics remained unknown and that numerous explanations made sense. Several researchers said the studies indicated that cholesterol levels should not drop below 160 milligrams per deciliter of blood. The average cholesterol level in the nation was just over 200. In 1987, the National Cholesterol Education Program, a project of the National Heart, Lung, and Blood Institute, said it was "desirable" for Americans to have cholesterol levels below 200.

The year 1992 also gave some official recognition to what became known as the "French Paradox," a finding that the French generally have a lower rate of heart disease than Americans, despite their fondness for cheeses and other dairy products that are thought to raise cholesterol levels. One theory, broadcast in 1991 on CBS's "Sixty Minutes," is that the wine consumed by the French with their meals somehow counteracts the artery-clogging effect of cholesterol. So persuasive was the argument that the U.S. Bureau of Alcohol, Tobacco, and Firearms for the first time permitted bottles of red wine to carry tags, beginning in 1992, citing the benefits of moderate drinking. The tags were to carry a six-paragraph excerpt from the TV segment.

Milk and Margarine Harmful?

On September 29 Dr. Benjamin Spock, the nation's best-known pediatrician, joined with members of the Physicians Committee for

Responsible Medicine, which supports animal rights and vegetarian diets, in urging parents to reconsider whether their children should drink milk. The committee contended that many infants could not properly digest milk, the fat in milk could start children on the road toward heart disease, proteins in milk could predispose susceptible children to diabetes, and milk was often contaminated with traces of antibiotics.

The committee added that other foods, such as kale, broccoli, collard greens, or fish, provided more calcium than milk without milk's risks. The panel did not, however, explain how parents could persuade their children to eat collard greens and kale.

The benefits of eating broccoli received another boost in a much-publicized study that indicated the vegetable may help to prevent certain types of cancer. (Story on Cancer-Prevention Properties of Broccoli, p. 277)

Earlier in the year, the American Academy of Pediatrics had recommended that infants not receive whole milk during their first year because it could lead to iron deficiency. Also, a study published in July in the New England Journal of Medicine *indicated there might be a link between drinking cow's milk during infancy and the onset of juvenile diabetes in people who were genetically prone to the disease. Nonetheless, most major medical authorities continued to recommend that children over age one drink milk, although they urged parents not to force milk on their children.*

Finally, on October 7 the Department of Agriculture released a preliminary study indicating that the oils in margarine, vegetable shortening, and processed foods such as cookies were linked to heart disease. The culprits, according to the study, were trans fatty acids created when manufacturers processed soybean and corn oils into solid or semisolid form. Manufacturers had been switching to those oils because of concerns that palm and coconut oils and lard had high amounts of saturated fat, which caused heart disease. However, the USDA study suggested that trans fatty acids worked similarly to saturated fat in raising blood cholesterol levels.

Following are the "Food Guide Pyramid," issued April 28, 1992, by the U.S. Department of Agriculture; "Milk: No Longer Recommended or Required," issued September 29 by the Physicians Committee for Responsible Medicine (footnotes omitted); and "Summary of Trans Fatty Acid Study Results," issued October 7 by the U.S. Department of Agriculture:

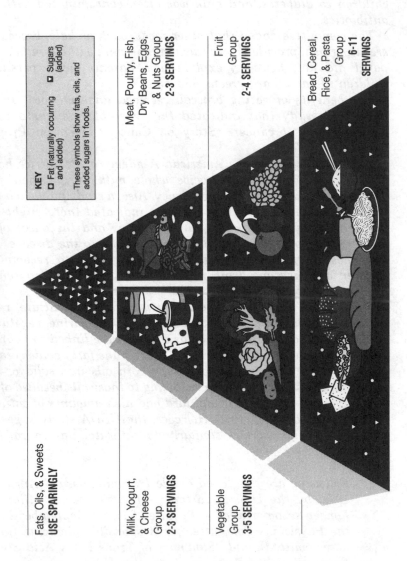

Food Guide Pyramid
A Guide to Daily Food Choices

KEY
◻ Fat (naturally occurring and added)
◪ Sugars (added)

These symbols show fats, oils, and added sugars in foods.

Fats, Oils, & Sweets
USE SPARINGLY

Milk, Yogurt, & Cheese Group
2-3 SERVINGS

Meat, Poultry, Fish, Dry Beans, Eggs, & Nuts Group
2-3 SERVINGS

Vegetable Group
3-5 SERVINGS

Fruit Group
2-4 SERVINGS

Bread, Cereal, Rice, & Pasta Group
6-11 SERVINGS

PHYSICIANS' REPORT ON MILK

A substantial body of scientific evidence raises concerns about health risks from cow's milk products. These problems relate to the proteins, sugar, fat, and contaminants in dairy products, and the inadequacy of whole cow's milk for infant nutrition.

Health risks from milk consumption are greatest for infants less than one year of age, in whom whole cow's milk can contribute to deficiencies in several nutrients, including iron, essential fatty acids, and vitamin E. The American Academy of Pediatrics recommends that infants under a year of age not receive whole cow's milk.

Cow's milk products are very low in iron, containing only about one-tenth of a milligram per eight-ounce serving. To get the U.S. Recommended Daily Allowance of 15 mg of iron, an infant would have to drink more than 31 quarts of milk per day. Milk can also cause blood loss from the intestinal tract, which, over time, reduces the body's iron stores. Researchers speculate that the blood loss may be a reaction to proteins present in milk. Pasteurization does not eliminate the problem. Researchers from the University of Iowa recently wrote in the Journal of Pediatrics: "...In a large proportion of infants, the feeding of cow milk causes a substantial increase of hemoglobin loss. Some infants are exquisitely sensitive to cow milk and can lose large quantities of blood."

Although concerns are greatest for children in the first year of life, there are also health concerns related to milk use among older children and some problems associated with cow's milk formulas:

Milk Proteins and Diabetes: Several reports link insulin-dependent diabetes to a specific protein in dairy products. This form of diabetes usually begins in childhood. It is a leading cause of blindness and contributes to heart disease, kidney damage, and amputations due to poor circulation.

Studies of various countries show a strong correlation between the use of dairy products and the incidence of diabetes. A recent report in the New England Journal of Medicine adds substantial support to the long-standing theory that cow's milk proteins stimulate the production of the antibodies which, in turn, destroy the insulin-producing pancreatic cells. In the new report, researchers from Canada and Finland found high levels of antibodies to a specific portion of a cow's milk protein, called bovine serum albumin, in 100% of the 142 diabetic children they studied at the time the disease was diagnosed. Non-diabetic children may have such antibodies, but only at much lower levels. Evidence suggests that the combination of a genetic predisposition and cow's milk exposure is the major cause of the childhood form of diabetes, although there is no way of determining which children are genetically predisposed. Antibodies can apparently form in response to even small quantities of milk products, including infant formulas.

401

Pancreatic cell destruction occurs gradually, especially after infections, which cause the cellular proteins to be exposed to the damage of antibodies. Diabetes becomes evident when 80 to 90 percent of the insulin-producing beta cells are destroyed.

Milk proteins are also among the most common causes of food allergies. Often, the cause of the symptoms is not recognized for substantial periods of time.

Milk Sugar and Health Problems: Many people, particularly those of Asian and African ancestry, are unable to digest the milk sugar, lactose. The result is diarrhea and gas. For those who can digest lactose, its breakdown products are two simple sugars: glucose and galactose. Galactose has been implicated in ovarian cancer and cataracts. Nursing children have active enzymes that break down galactose. As we age, many of us lose much of this capacity.

Fat Content: Whole milk, cheese, cream, butter, ice cream, sour cream, and all other dairy products aside from skim and non-fat products contain significant amounts of saturated fat, as well as cholesterol, contributing to cardiovascular diseases and certain forms of cancer. The early changes of heart disease have been documented in American teenagers. While children do need a certain amount of fat in their diets, there is no nutritional requirement for cow's milk fat. On the contrary, cow's milk is high in saturated fats, but low in the essential fatty acid linoleic acid.

Contaminants: Milk contains frequent contaminants, from pesticides to drugs. About a third of milk products have been shown to be contaminated with antibiotic traces. The vitamin D content of milk has been poorly regulated. Recent testing of 42 milk samples found only 12% within the expected range of vitamin D content. Testing of 10 samples of infant formula revealed seven with more than twice the vitamin D content reported on the label, one of which had more than four times the label amount. Vitamin D is toxic in overdose.

Osteoporosis: Dairy products offer a false sense of security to those concerned about osteoporosis. In countries where dairy products are not generally consumed, there is actually less osteoporosis than in the United States. Studies have shown little effect of dairy products on osteoporosis. In postmenopausal women, most studies show little effect of calcium intake on the bone density of the spine. There is also little or no effect on bone at the hip, where very serious breaks can occur. Some studies have found an effect of calcium intake on bone density in the forearm. Studies of premenopausal women have likewise shown that calcium intake has relatively little effect on bone density. Boosting calcium intake may be useful only for those who consume very little calcium, e.g., less than 400 mg of calcium per day. For those who are not grossly deficient in calcium, supplements and dairy products have little or no effect. Science magazine of August 1, 1986, noted "the large body of evidence indicating no relationship between calcium intake and bone density."

There are many other good sources of calcium. Kale, broccoli, and other green leafy vegetables contain calcium that is readily absorbed by the body. A recent report in the American Journal of Clinical Nutrition found that calcium absorbability was actually higher for kale than from milk, and concluded, "greens such as kale can be considered to be at least as good as milk in terms of their calcium absorbability." Broccoli actually contains more calcium per calorie than does milk. Beans are also rich in calcium. Fortified orange juice supplies large amounts of calcium in a palatable form. Calcium is only one of many factors that affect the bone. Other factors include hormones, phosphorus, boron, exercise, smoking, alcohol, and drugs. Protein is also important in calcium balance. Diets that are rich in protein, particularly animal proteins, encourage calcium loss.

Recommendations

In summary, there is no nutritional requirement for dairy products, and there are serious problems that can result from the proteins, sugar, fat, and contaminants in milk products. Therefore, the following recommendations are offered:

- Breast-feeding is the preferred method of infant feeding. As recommended by the American Academy of Pediatrics, whole cow's milk should not be given to infants under one year of age.
- Parents should be alerted to the potential risks to their children from cow's milk use.
- Cow's milk should not be required or recommended in government guidelines.
- Government programs, such as school lunch programs and the WIC program, should be consistent with these recommendations.

SUMMARY OF TRANS FATTY ACID STUDY

Experimental

The dietary study was a carefully controlled, blinded trial whose objective was to clarify realistic effects of dietary *trans* fatty acids on blood lipid levels compared to saturated and *cis* fatty acids. Fifty-eight healthy adult subjects (29 men and 29 women) consumed each of four experimental diets in a random manner. Each experimental period was six weeks. One diet was high in the saturated fatty acids, lauric, myristic, and palmitic, but low in *trans*. A second diet was high in oleic acid (high *cis*) but low in *trans*. The third diet was moderate in *trans* (about 10 g/day at 3000 kcal/day), similar to the level the ISEO has calculated to be available for consumption in the U.S. diet, namely, about 8 g/person/day. The fourth diet was high in *trans* (about 20 g/day at 3000 kcal). During week-six on each diet, blood samples were taken and plasmas were analyzed for blood lipid and lipoprotein levels.

Key Results

Preliminary results indicate that some *trans* fatty acids may be cholesterol raising in a similar direction as certain saturated fatty acids. Cholesterol levels on the oleic (OLEIC), moderate *trans* (MOD TRANS), high *trans* (HIGH TRANS), and saturated (SAT) diets were 203, 211, 214, and 217 mg/dl, respectively. Statistically, plasma cholesterol after MOD TRANS and HIGH TRANS were higher than after OLEIC and lower than after SAT. The difference in plasma cholesterol level between MOD TRANS and HIGH TRANS was not statistically significant. Changes in LDL cholesterol corresponded to changes in total cholesterol. HDL cholesterol levels were not significantly different after OLEIC and MOD TRANS. After HIGH TRANS, HDL cholesterol was slightly, though significantly, lower than after either OLEIC or SAT.

Overall Perspective

Results of this research need to be interpreted in the broad context of existing knowledge on fatty acid metabolism including *trans* fatty acids. Whereas indications are that *trans* fatty acids are similar to saturates in raising plasma cholesterol, available information does not show if such elevation results from the same physiological effects or mechanisms of action. Caution should be exercised in recommending dietary changes based on plasma cholesterol effects alone. Risk factors for heart disease include not only blood lipid levels, but also blood clotting, blood pressure, and other factors known to be affected by the amount and type of fat in the diet. Saturated fatty acids have been implicated in increased risk from several of these factors, *trans* fatty acids in only one. Replacement of *trans* fatty acids in the American food supply with saturates, and especially with lauric, myristic, and palmitic acids which are the most hypercholesterolemic, should not be encouraged until their role is fully defined. Further, we do not know what effect *trans* fatty acids might have if consumed in diets having lower total fat together with lower saturated fat (such as the NCEP Step 1 diet, where lowering total fat to 30% of energy and saturates to 10% of energy is recommended). Results of the present research strongly support the need for additional investigation.

May

BUSH AND KING ON L.A. RIOTS; REPORT ON POLICE RESPONSE
May 1, October 21, 1992

A few hours after four white Los Angeles police officers were acquitted April 29 of virtually all charges in the beating of black motorist Rodney King, the city erupted into riots. The massive civil disturbance, which lasted for nearly six days, left at least forty-four people dead and about 2,000 injured. Thousands of businesses were destroyed by arson and looting, with losses estimated at $1 billion.

Most of the rioting took place in South Central Los Angeles, an economically depressed area of the city populated largely by blacks and Hispanics, but even the more affluent neighborhoods of Los Angeles reported some incidents. Protests and scattered violence broke out in other cities, but none turned into wholesale rioting.

The convulsive events quickly became the subject of charges in the presidential politics of the 1992 election year. White House press secretary Marlin Fitzwater suggested May 4 that the riots were the result of the social welfare legislation passed by a Congress controlled by the Democrats in the 1960s and 1970s.

Two days later, Arkansas Governor Bill Clinton, who later won the Democratic presidential nomination and then the presidential election, retorted that in part the Los Angeles crisis was the consequence of "twelve years of denial and neglect" of burgeoning social problems in the inner cities by the Republican administrations of Ronald Reagan and George Bush. However, the riots and the deteriorating conditions in the nation's inner cities soon faded as an issue in the 1992 political debate.

Unexpected Acquittal

The seeds of the riot had been sown more than a year earlier on March 3, 1991, when the four policemen caught King after a high-speed auto chase and beat him repeatedly with long batons while eleven other white officers stood by and watched. A nearby resident recorded the incident on videotape, and in the following days the tape was played repeatedly on newscasts throughout the world.

Reaction was swift and nearly unanimous in condemning the brutal beating. President Bush called the incident "sickening." The four officers were indicted in Los Angeles court for assault and related charges. Later in the summer a judge granted a change of venue, citing his belief that the officers could not receive a fair trial in Los Angeles. The trial eventually took place in Ventura County, northeast of Los Angeles, where only 2 percent of the residents were black.

After seven days of deliberations, the jury, which included one Asian and one Hispanic but no blacks, acquitted the four officers of all counts except one, and that one resulted in a hung jury. Many observers attributed the acquittals to the change in venue. "We are convinced that the change of venue that produced an all-white jury and Mr. King's race were major factors in the acquittals," Benjamin L. Hooks, the executive director of the NAACP, said April 30.

Days of Violence

Blacks as well as many whites saw the acquittals as a miscarriage of justice. Speaking at a rally in the first hours after the verdict but before the violence started, Los Angeles Mayor Tom Bradley said that "we have come tonight to say that we have had enough!" Bradley later appealed to city residents to refrain from rioting.

But it was too late. Angry mobs were already forming. With the rioting barely slowing after two days, President Bush appealed for calm in a nationally televised address on May 1, but said he understood the anger. People waited fourteen months for the justice system to work, he said. "And when the verdict came in, they felt betrayed. Viewed from outside the trial, it was hard to understand how the verdict could possibly square with the video," he said.

Rodney King himself appeared before the public for the first time since his beating to plea for an end to the rioting. "People, I just want to say, can we all get along?" the visibly distraught King said. "We're all stuck here for a while. Let's try to work it out." King had not testified at the trial.

By May 2, 5,000 state and local police and 6,000 National Guardsmen were on duty in the city, and Bush had put 4,500 soldiers and marines on standby. The Los Angeles Police Department was later heavily criticized both for its slowness in responding to early violence and for its strategy in containing the burning and looting.

The resentment and rage of the black community in South Central Los Angeles had been mounting for many years. Black leaders and others had frequently identified and decried examples of the use of excessive force by the police.

After the King beating, a commission appointed by Mayor Bradley and headed by Warren M. Christopher, a prominent Los Angeles attorney who became secretary of state in the Clinton administration, reported that a "significant number of officers in the Los Angeles Police Department ... repetitively use excessive force against the public...." The commission recommended that police chief Daryl F. Gates, a principal target of black anger, be replaced. Gates resigned June 26, 1992, several weeks after the riots, steadfastly defending the police force and his leadership of it. Gates was replaced by Willie L. Williams, the former Philadelphia police commissioner.

Political observers had warned for years that deteriorating inner cities throughout the country were explosive because of poverty, unemployment, street crime, drug use, and poor schools and housing. All of those problems afflicted South-Central Los Angeles, which was overrun by gangs and drug-dealing criminals and had recently lost 70,000 previously stable jobs when companies such as General Motors and Bethlehem Steel closed plants in the area or relocated them.

Aftermath of the Riot

In the days immediately following the riots, the White House said the administration would provide $100 million in disaster aid to victims and another $200 million to rebuild damaged areas. Officials also said that the Small Business Administration would provide up to $400 million in loans to rebuild businesses that had been gutted and looted.

On August 5 a federal grand jury in Los Angeles brought federal civil rights charges against the four policemen involved in the King beating: Stacey C. Koon, Laurence M. Powell, Theodore J. Briseno, and Timothy E. Wind. Wind, a rookie, had been dismissed from the force after the beating; the other three men had been suspended without pay. The federal indictment charged that the officers "willfully and intentionally used unreasonable force" under color of the law during King's arrest.

Videotapes also figured in another case related to the riots—the near-fatal beating of a white truck driver, Reginald Denny. Identified from tapes of the beating, three men were charged with attempted murder and robbery, and a fourth was accused of picking Denny's pocket. The four men were black. Both trails were scheduled to be heard at approximately the same time in early 1993, making many apprehensive about what might happen if one of the groups was acquitted, while the other was convicted.

In October 1992 a special commission headed by former CIA and FBI director William H. Webster issued its report on the riots, criticizing the

*city government and police department for being unprepared to handle
such emergencies.*

> *Following are texts of President George Bush's May 1
> nationally televised address and Rodney King's May 1 plea
> for calm to the residents of Los Angeles, together with
> excerpts from the Webster report on "The City in Crisis,"
> issued October 21, 1992:*

BUSH ADDRESS ON THE CIVIL DISTURBANCES IN LOS ANGELES, CALIFORNIA

Tonight I want to talk to you about violence in our cities and justice for our citizens, two big issues that have collided on the streets of Los Angeles. First, an update on where matters stand in Los Angeles.

Fifteen minutes ago I talked to California's Governor Pete Wilson and Los Angeles Mayor Tom Bradley. They told me that last night was better than the night before; today, calmer than yesterday. But there were still incidents of random terror and lawlessness this afternoon.

In the wake of the first night's violence, I spoke directly to both Governor Wilson and Mayor Bradley to assess the situation and to offer assistance. There are two very different issues at hand. One is the urgent need to restore order. What followed Wednesday's jury verdict in the Rodney King case was a tragic series of events for the city of Los Angeles: Nearly 4,000 fires, staggering property damage, hundreds of injuries, and the senseless deaths of over 30 people.

To restore order right now, there are 3,000 National Guardsmen on duty in the city of Los Angeles. Another 2,200 stand ready to provide immediate support. To supplement this effort I've taken several additional actions. First, this morning I've ordered the Justice Department to dispatch 1,000 Federal riot-trained law enforcement officials to help restore order in Los Angeles beginning tonight. These officials include FBI SWAT teams, special riot control units of the U.S. Marshals Service, the border patrol, and other Federal law enforcement agencies. Second, another 1,000 Federal law enforcement officials are on standby alert, should they be needed. Third, early today I directed 3,000 members of the 7th Infantry and 1,500 marines to stand by at El Toro Air Station, California. Tonight, at the request of the Governor and the mayor, I have committed these troops to help restore order. I'm also federalizing the National Guard, and I'm instructing General Colin Powell to place all those troops under a central command.

What we saw last night and the night before in Los Angeles is not about civil rights. It's not about the great cause of equality that all Americans must uphold. It's not a message of protest. It's been the brutality of a mob, pure and simple. And let me assure you: I will use whatever force is necessary to restore order. What is going on in L.A. must and will stop. As your President I guarantee you this violence will end.

Now let's talk about the beating of Rodney King, because beyond the urgent need to restore order is the second issue, the question of justice: Whether Rodney King's Federal civil rights were violated. What you saw and what I saw on the TV video was revolting. I felt anger. I felt pain. I thought: How can I explain this to my grandchildren?

Civil rights leaders and just plain citizens fearful of, and sometimes victimized by, police brutality were deeply hurt. And I know good and decent policemen who were equally appalled.

I spoke this morning to many leaders of the civil rights community. And they saw the video, as we all did. For 14 months they waited patiently, hopefully. They waited for the system to work. And when the verdict came in, they felt betrayed. Viewed from outside the trial, it was hard to understand how the verdict could possibly square with the video. Those civil rights leaders with whom I met were stunned, and so was I and so was Barbara and so were my kids.

But the verdict Wednesday was not the end of the process. The Department of Justice had started its own investigation immediately after the Rodney King incident and was monitoring the State investigation and trial. And so let me tell you what actions we are taking on the Federal level to ensure that justice is served.

Within one hour of the verdict, I directed the Justice Department to move into high gear on its own independent criminal investigation into the case. And next, on Thursday, five Federal prosecutors were on their way to Los Angeles. Our Justice Department has consistently demonstrated its ability to investigate fully a matter like this.

Since 1988, the Justice Department has successfully prosecuted over 100 law enforcement officials for excessive violence. I am confident that in this case, the Department of Justice will act as it should. Federal grand jury action is underway today in Los Angeles. Subpoenas are being issued. Evidence is being reviewed. The Federal effort in this case will be expeditious, and it will be fair. It will not be driven by mob violence but by respect for due process and the rule of law.

We owe it to all Americans who put their faith in the law to see that justice is served. But as we move forward on this or any other case, we must remember the fundamental tenet of our legal system. Every American, whether accused or accuser, is entitled to protection of his or her rights.

In this highly controversial court case, a verdict was handed down by a California jury. To Americans of all races who were shocked by the verdict, let me say this: You must understand that our system of justice provides for the peaceful, orderly means of addressing this frustration. We must respect the process of law whether or not we agree with the outcome. There's a difference between frustration with the law and direct assaults upon our legal system.

In a civilized society, there can be no excuse, no excuse for the murder, arson, theft and vandalism that have terrorized the law-abiding citizens of Los Angeles. Mayor Bradley, just a few minutes ago, mentioned to me his particular concern, among others, regarding the safety of the Korean community. My heart goes out to them and all others who have suffered losses.

The wanton destruction of life and property is not a legitimate expression of outrage with injustice. It is itself injustice. And no rationalization, no matter how heartfelt, no matter how eloquent, can make it otherwise.

Television has become a medium that often brings us together. But its vivid display of Rodney King's beating shocked us. The America it has shown us on our screens these last 48 hours has appalled us. None of this is what we wish to think of as American. It's as if we were looking in a mirror that distorted our better selves and turned us ugly. We cannot let that happen. We cannot do that to ourselves.

We've seen images in the last 48 hours that we will never forget. Some were horrifying almost beyond belief. But there were other acts, small but significant acts in all this ugliness that give us hope. I'm one who respects our police. They keep the peace. They face danger every day. They help kids. They don't make a lot of money, but they care about their communities and their country. Thousands of police officers and firefighters are risking their lives right now on the streets of L.A., and they deserve our support. Then there are the people who have spent each night not in the streets but in the churches of Los Angeles, praying that man's gentler instincts be revealed in the hearts of people driven by hate. And finally, there were the citizens who showed great personal responsibility, who ignored the mob, who at great personal danger helped the victims of violence, regardless of race.

Among the many stories I've seen and heard about these past few days, one sticks in my mind, the story of one savagely beaten white truck driver, alive tonight because four strangers, four black strangers, came to his aid. Two were men who had been watching television and saw the beating as it was happening, and came out into the street to help; another was a woman on her way home from work; and the fourth, a young man whose name we may never know. The injured driver was able to get behind the wheel of his truck and tried to drive away. But his eyes were swollen shut. The woman asked him if he could see. He answered, "No." She said, "Well, then I will be your eyes." Together those four people braved the mob and drove that truck driver to the hospital. He's alive today only because they stepped in to help.

It is for every one of them that we must rebuild the community of Los Angeles, for these four people and the others like them who in the midst of this nightmare acted with simple human decency.

We must understand that no one in Los Angeles or any other city has rendered a verdict on America. If we are to remain the most vibrant and hopeful Nation on Earth we must allow our diversity to bring us together, not drive us apart. This must be the rallying cry of good and decent people.

For their sake, for all our sakes, we must build a future where, in every city across this country, empty rage gives way to hope, where poverty and despair give way to opportunity. After peace is restored to Los Angeles, we must then turn again to the underlying causes of such tragic events. We must keep on working to create a climate of understanding and tolerance, a climate that refuses to accept racism, bigotry, anti-Semitism, and hate of any kind, anytime, anywhere.

Tonight, I ask all Americans to lend their hearts, their voices, and their prayers to the healing of hatred. As President, I took an oath to preserve, protect, and defend the Constitution, an oath that requires every President to establish justice and ensure domestic tranquility. That duty is foremost in my mind tonight.

Let me say to the people saddened by the spectacle of the past few days, to the good people of Los Angeles, caught at the center of this senseless suffering: The violence will end. Justice will be served. Hope will return.

Thank you, and may God bless the United States of America.

RODNEY G. KING'S STATEMENT

People, I just want to say, can we all get along? Can we get along? Can we stop making it horrible for older people and the kids?

I mean, we've got enough smog here in Los Angeles, let alone to deal with setting these fires and things. It's just not right; it's not right. And it's not going to change anything. We'll get our justice. They've won the battle, but they haven't won the war. We'll have our day in court, and that's all we want.

I'm neutral. I love everybody. I love people of color. You know, I'm not like they're making me out to be. We've got to quit. We've got to quit. After all, I mean, I can understand the first upset, for the first two hours after the verdict. But to go on—to keep going on like this and to see this security guard shot on the ground, it's just not right. It's just not right because those people will never go home to their families again.

I mean, please, we can get along here. We can all get along. We've just got to. I mean, we're all stuck here for a while. Let's try to work it out. Let's try to beat it. Let's try to work it out.

THE CITY IN CRISIS

The City Caught Unprepared

The "not guilty" verdicts from the jury trial of four police officers who arrested Rodney King sparked an unprecedented firestorm of violence in Los Angeles. Our inquiry will focus upon the preparation for, and response to, this disorder. We begin with an overview of what happened before and after the announcement of the verdicts.

At approximately 1:00 p.m. on April 29, 1992, the District Attorney's office was informed by Court personnel that the jury deliberating in the trial of the four police officers accused of beating Rodney King had reached verdicts. Although they did not know the content of the verdicts, prosecutors did learn that the jury had not reached a verdict on all counts. At the request of prosecutors, Judge Weisberg ordered a two-hour delay prior to announcing the verdicts to enable the media, who had been providing unprecedented live coverage of the trial, to ready themselves to broadcast the event.

When the jury's verdicts were read to a packed courtroom in the Simi Valley courthouse at 3:00 p.m., they were simultaneously broadcast by the media to the entire City—indeed, to the entire country and many parts of the world. The reaction to the verdicts in many quarters of the City was one of shock and anger. Although there were limited expressions of support for the verdicts and the operation of the criminal justice system, many who had seen the taped beating replayed over and over again during the preceding weeks and months found it hard to accept the outcome.

Almost immediately, crowds began to congregate in South Central Los Angeles to protest the verdicts. As these street corner protests began to grow in number and size, they first became angry and then turned violent, a situation dramatized most vividly by the beating of Reginald Denny just about four hours after the verdicts were announced. Over the course of the next six days, the reaction escalated into a terrifying reign of violence, widespread looting, and mass destruction of property in many communities across the City. The swiftness and ferocity of these events stunned the entire City and its people.

Common sense, as well as substantial available information, indicated in advance of these events that some manner of public outcry to a verdict other than conviction was predictable. It is thus reasonable to want to know why it was that the City was so apparently unprepared and unable to respond when the reaction in fact occurred. Despite the many months that passed between the beating and the trial, the more than 12 weeks of trial, the week of jury deliberations and the two hours advance warning that a verdict other than guilty on all counts would be handed down, City leaders and LAPD commanders alike seem to have been caught by surprise as the lawlessness escalated following the verdict. Although a handful of public officials appeared to have realized that a total failure to convict was a possibility, particularly after the case was transferred to Simi Valley, most public officials, including members of the City Council, the Mayor's Office, the Police Commission, and the District Attorney's Office, apparently did not seriously anticipate the possibility of a *complete* acquittal. Indeed, the most commonly expressed response on the part of the City's leaders to the absence of even one conviction was one of shock and disbelief. Even those who had contemplated the possibility of disorder following the verdicts were unprepared to deal with the violence.

The initial response of City officials was marked by uncertainty, some confusion, and an almost total lack of coordination. Within the police department, there was initially no meaningful integration with any of the other arms of City government, and uncharacteristic hesitancy in responding to initial incidents of disorder. Indeed, the tentativeness of the response to initial incidents now appears to have been a factor that enabled the violence, looting and destruction to take hold and grow. It now appears that the Command Staff had no specific plan in place for dealing with potential unrest following the verdicts. It was therefore unable to implement any preconceived and carefully thought out response. The absence of such a plan, coupled with holes in the Department's command structure and a generally poor state of mental readiness, severely hampered the performance of many commanders and the overall response.

The Approach of "Zero Hour"

During the two hours that elapsed between the time prosecutors were notified that the jury had reached verdicts and the actual reading of the verdicts, little was done to prepare for the possibility of a widespread and disorderly reaction. The failure of City and police leaders to position the City's resources properly to respond to the coming firestorm, however, started long before this two-hour window. The videotaped beating of Rodney King and the indictment and trial that followed were the subject of intense public scrutiny and unprecedented media attention for months before the jury reached its verdicts on April 29th.

The Rodney King beating was a racially charged event from the moment of its occurrence, and, as discussed below, took place against a backdrop of racial and ethnic tension in the City. Existing passions were fueled by the fact that, unlike most controverted events, the King beating was captured on video that was shown over and over again on television. Moreover, even before the trial commenced, the decision to transfer the case from Los Angeles County to Simi Valley caused concern among many people, in particular many within the African-American community, that a fair and just outcome might not be achieved. By the time the trial finally began on February 3, 1992, the event had been subjected to such an exhaustive blitz of media coverage and public debate—much of which discussed the racial overtones of the incident—that it is hard to imagine any resident of the City who was not aware of the beating incident, the pending trail, and the significant social and political issues they raised.

The trial itself lasted 12½ weeks—from February 3 through April 22, 1992. The entire trial was carried live on cable television and was the subject of extensive daily publicity and commentary in all forms of local and national media. During this extended period, the trial was one of the most extensively covered and publicized events in the City, if not the country, and was at the forefront of public discussion and debate. As the trial neared its end in late April, that fact was known not just to those who were involved in the trial or followed it closely, but to residents throughout

415

the City who were anticipating the trial's conclusion. Indeed, the closing arguments of the prosecution and of attorneys for the four police officers were publicly broadcast, replayed, and dissected as the City openly debated the jury's possible decision.

The jury spent seven days deliberating before rendering its verdicts. Given the length of the deliberations and certain questions that were asked by the jury during the process, people began to speculate openly that acquittals were possible. While the jury was deliberating, the press reported a statement by Chief Gates that an overtime allocation of $1 million had been set aside in the event extra police manpower was required. Some City leaders publicly urged restraint by the community and the police no matter what the jury's verdicts might turn out to be. Thus, when the jury's verdicts were read on April 29, the announcement marked the much-anticipated culmination of an event that was at the forefront of the City's collective conscience. At the same time, the reading of the verdicts fell like a matchstick upon the dry tinder of the City's already tense climate.

The Pre-Trial Temperature of the City

The Rodney King incident did not occur in a vacuum but within the context of the entire social, economic, and political climate of the City. The tensions that existed in these areas undoubtedly had a profound impact on the public's perception of and reaction to the videotaped beating and on the nature of the LAPD Command Staff's response to the lawlessness that followed the jury verdicts.

Tensions in the Community

In the past decade, Los Angeles has experienced rapid demographic and economic changes. The population of the City as a whole has grown by 17 percent during that period and now exceeds 3.5 million people. At the same time, the make-up of the population has shifted to 40 percent Hispanic, 37 percent Anglo, 13 percent African-American, nine percent Asian-American, and one percent Native American. As the ethnic makeup of the City has changed fundamentally, so too has the economic stratification of its population. By 1990, more than 18.5 percent of Los Angeles residents were living below the poverty line. These changes in the City's makeup have caused significant stratification of Los Angeles by neighborhood. Thus, those areas of South and Central Los Angeles that are overwhelmingly populated by African-American and Hispanic citizens are the same areas that have experienced despairingly high unemployment and in which 20-40 percent of the residents are living below the poverty line. By contrast, several of the elite communities on the Westside of Los Angeles remain fairly homogenous Anglo neighborhoods and have minimal levels of poverty.

These profound shifts have contributed to greatly increased tensions between the City's affluent and less well off citizens, and among members of different racial and ethnic groups. Notable among these tensions is the conflict in South Central Los Angeles, between African-Americans and Korean-Americans who live alongside one another but who have in the main experienced dramatically different economic success during the past decade. Existing tensions in this community were heightened by the Harlins-Du incident just several months before the King verdict. The sentence of five-years' probation imposed in that case on a middle-aged Korean-American grocery store owner, who was found by a jury to be guilty of fatally shooting a fifteen-year-old African-American girl, deeply angered and caused many in the African-American community to lose confidence in the law enforcement and judicial systems. Without question the apparent leniency shown to Ms. Du inflamed racial and political tensions and contributed to the brittle atmosphere preceding the unrest.

Los Angeles on the eve of the verdicts was also in the midst of a worsening economic downturn. Although the strain of the deepening recession had been hard on the entire City, it was hitting the African-American community especially severely. The disproportionately high levels of unemployment, poverty, and homelessness in Los Angeles' African-American neighborhoods was by most accounts giving rise to a growing level of tension, frustration, and anger that contributed to the tense atmosphere preceding the unrest.

Tensions Between the Community and LAPD

The atmosphere preceding the verdicts was also characterized by widespread tension between minority communities and the LAPD. African-Americans, especially young African-American males, widely perceive that they are frequently the victims of police mistreatment, racism, and abuse. The result of this belief is an apparently large reservoir of anger and frustration directed at the LAPD, which has been exacerbated by a commonly-held belief in Los Angeles' minority communities that the legal system does not work to discipline officers who mistreat people of color or to vindicate the rights of the victims of this unfair treatment. For many, the videotaped King beating merely confirmed their perception of widespread abuse of force by the LAPD against people of color.

Perceptions of improper and biased treatment by the LAPD are not confined to the African-American community. Leaders of Los Angeles' Hispanic communities believe that their communities receive inadequate police protection, and that Hispanics are victims of prejudice and racism by the LAPD and are frequent victims of police excessive force. Leaders of the Korean-American communities express a similar view that Korean-Americans do not receive adequate protection from the LAPD. . . .

Tensions Between the Chief of Police and Other City Leaders

When the unrest began on April 29, the City's Mayor and Chief of Police had not spoken to one another directly for more than one year.

417

Some observers felt that latent dislike between Mayor Tom Bradley and Chief Daryl Gates escalated to a complete rupture of their relationship in April, 1991, when the Mayor openly called upon the Chief to resign. That rupture significantly changed the way the Office of the Mayor related to the LAPD. At the same time, relations between the Chief and the Police Commission had become severely strained. The City Council's decision to reverse the attempt by the Police Commission to suspend the Chief in the wake of the King incident and the subsequent adoption on June 4, 1991 of Charter Amendment 5—granting the Council power to override actions of the City's citizen commissions—led to virtually a complete turnover of the membership of the Police Commission, including the election of a new President. Whereas previous Commissions had been relatively passive in their dealings with the Chief, the new Commission tried to adopt a more proactive stance that did not necessarily increase the effectiveness of their oversight of the Department. The Chief had been given clear signals by the Council that he could safely ignore the Commission.

Tensions Within the Police Department

Finally, by April 29, 1992 there had been a recognizable deterioration in the motivational level and state of mental readiness within the LAPD. To start, there appears to have been a significant level of polarization and dysfunction within the senior ranks. Observers noted the evidently displeased reaction of the Chief to the cooperation by some of his subordinates with the police department investigation conducted by the Christopher Commission. This appears to have resulted in a measure of estrangement of the Chief from some of his key subordinates. Still another factor contributing to a widely-perceived breakdown in cooperation amongst top commanders was the intense competition to replace Gates and become the new Chief. These problems at the top levels all contributed to a lessening of confidence within the Department.

At the same time, the report of the Christopher Commission itself, while properly identifying significant problems within the Department, had the unfortunate side-effect of doing further damage to the professional self-confidence of many rank and file police officers who had not themselves done anything wrong. Not the least among these changes was the community-based policing plan that required seven police Areas—including 77th Street, Harbor and Southeast Areas—to report directly to Chief Gates for some purposes.

Taken together these factors combined to seriously undermine the morale of the Department and its police officers, and leave it in a poor state of psychological preparedness for the events of April 29. The situation was made all the worse by critical retirements, transfers and command changes that left significant vacancies in parts of the command structure and created critical vulnerabilities of inexperience in other parts.

Preparation for the Verdict

In addition to whatever planning and training is carried out generally to prepare for emergency situations, Los Angeles City officials had months to prepare specifically for the possibility of a public reaction to a verdict in the King beating case. Yet, apart from relatively limited efforts in particular LAPD Areas and isolated consideration by the Mayor's office and in other City agencies of the possibility of a public outcry, there seems to have been very little meaningful preparation for the King verdicts. There was no City-wide planning effort, no specific coordination with county, state, and federal authorities and, indeed, no event-specific planning within the LAPD itself. The City's standing emergency "plan" was so general and unspecific, untested, unfamiliar to those who were later called upon to carry it out, and in large part non-responsive to the nature of the civil disturbance that occurred, that it proved to be essentially useless. The police department's "plan" consisted of its Tactical Manual and its "standing plans" which together proved to be equally unspecific and non-responsive. As a result, when the violence and destruction did come, City officials and police commanders had given little specific thought to the problem of what strategies were appropriate to implement.

Under the City's Local Emergencies Ordinance, which is discussed in detail in Chapter Three, the Emergency Operations Organization is charged with responsibility for "direction and control of local emergency preparation, response and recovery." Upon activation of the Emergency Operations Organization, the Mayor becomes its "Director" and is given direct supervisory control over all of its operations and personnel, including the Emergency Operations Board established to manage preparations for and response to emergencies. As Director, the Mayor is also given extraordinarily broad discretionary power during the period of the emergency to promulgate, issue and enforce rules, regulations and orders for the purpose of protecting life and property. The Emergency Operations Board is made responsible for supervising, regulating, controlling and managing the affairs of the Emergency Operations Organization. However, the Board is not brought into existence only in times of emergency. The Board was created to oversee and direct City-wide emergency planning and training activities as well. Hence, it has been given the power to make and enforce all necessary and desirable rules and regulations for the purpose of governing the Emergency Operations Organization during periods of preparation, local emergency, response and recovery, including the right to issue instructions to the heads of the City's departments and the power to appoint any committees it needs to do its work.

The Board reports directly to the Mayor in his capacity as Director of The Emergency Operations Organization. In its day-to-day operations, however, there is a split of responsibility under the ordinance. The Board is chaired permanently by the Chief of Police, who is also designated as the Deputy Director of the Emergency Operations Organization. At the same time, the City Administrative Officer ("CAO") is designated as the Emergency Operations Organization Coordinator. From the ordinance, it is evident that the City Council intended that the Chief of Police be in charge of the Board, subject to the direction of the Mayor, during actual periods of local emergency, when its activities must be directed toward emergency response. On the other hand, the City Administrative Officer is charged with responsibility for management of the Board in nonemergency times, when its activities must be directed toward emergency preparedness.

This split of responsibilities explains why Chief Administrative Officer Keith Comrie is responsible for directing the activities of the Emergency Management Committee ("committee"), which forms the working arm or staff of the Emergency Operations Organization and consists of representatives from all of the involved City departments and agencies. The primary responsibility of the Committee is to manage the City's planning and training activities. Unfortunately, the Committee's preparatory activities have been confined almost exclusively to earthquake "recovery," with virtually no attention being devoted to civil disorder preparation.

It is now evident that the Emergency Operations Organization was not used in any way to plan for the possibility of a reaction to a verdict in the King beating trial. Mayor Bradley, as the Director of the Emergency Operations Organization, did not direct the Emergency Operations Organization to develop any planned response to that threat. Similarly, neither Chief Gates, the Deputy Director of the Emergency Operations Organization and Chairman of the Emergency Operations Board, nor City Administrative Officer Comrie, the Emergency Operations Organization Coordinator, nor any of their staffs, sought to develop a coordinated plan for response through the Emergency Operations Organization.

Although Chief Gates claimed that the LAPD had a plan to deal with the possibility of violent public reaction following a verdict, he apparently was talking only about the LAPD Tactical Manual and the so-called "standing plans" of the Department's geographical Areas. The Tactical Manual is a basic procedures and training manual that provides general concepts to deal with a City-wide disorder. The "standing plans" consist of a collection of lists and procedure manuals for a wide range of situations from civil defense to flood control, and again offer no specific plans for responding to a massive disturbance. Indeed, Chief Gates rejected a suggestion beforehand by one Deputy Chief that the Department needed to be more concerned about the possibility of civil disorder. In so doing, he implicitly decided not to develop a single event plan, although in the past such plans had been developed by the Department in special circumstances, such as the 1984 Olympic Games. As a result, the Department was caught flat-footed on April 29. It should have been part of an LAPD plan to place the entire department on alert as soon as it was learned that verdicts were imminent. However, more than an hour after the LAPD learned that the jury had reached verdicts, there still was no Department-wide declaration of a Tactical Alert, no contemplation of mobilization, nor even a decision as to whether officers should be held over at the end of their watches, although individual Watch Commanders made decisions on their own to do so.

Neither the Mayor, the Council nor the Police Commission made any adequate efforts to determine if there really was a plan. All appear to have simply accepted the Chief's representation that his Department was ready without further verification. In retrospect, all plainly had a duty to do more than this.

In the absence of any specific plan, preparation within the LAPD beforehand had been limited to a review of Area "standing plans," checks of disturbance equipment in some bureaus, and sporadic roll call discussions and drills. Under the guise of "earthquake preparedness," some individual units held disturbance-control drills on station rooftops or in their parking lots. However, no practical training was given to members of the Department Command Staff, and no Department-wide drills were carried out. Nor was there any effort to establish liaisons or coordinate preparation and planning with law enforcement agencies outside the LAPD.

Although he did not use the Emergency Operations Organization framework, the Mayor evidently anticipated the possibility of an adverse reaction to the trial verdicts and directed his staff to map out a response plan with community leaders. His staff claims to have focused their energies in this direction after receiving assurances from Chief Gates, as well as Deputy Chiefs Matthew Hunt and Bernard Parks, that the police department was ready to respond to any possible disturbance.

The Mayor's plan seems to have been a relatively good one, as far as it went. Working with community leaders, the Mayor planned to provide a centralized forum at the First A.M.E. Church from which the congregated community could voice its reaction to a verdict. In addition, "talking points" were developed for use by officials and community leaders to help calm public reaction. Patrols from local churches were arranged to fan out through the community to calm tensions following the verdicts. While various community leaders assisted with this process, however, it is unclear whether any City Council members or Chief Gates were involved or received copies of the "talking points." In any event, before the verdicts were announced the Mayor had four different speeches prepared and he delivered one of them on television at about 5:00 p.m. on the evening of April 29.

The Post-Verdict Firestorm

The public reaction to the verdicts began almost immediately after they were broadcast live at 3:00 p.m. on April 29. Initial demonstrations of protest quickly sprung up outside the Simi Valley courthouse and on street corners in South Central Los Angeles. These protests grew angrier as the afternoon progressed.

The initial incidents in the City, which occurred within an hour or so after the verdicts were announced, took place in the Hyde Park neighbor-hood of the 77th Street police Area. The intersection of Florence and Normandie, which was the subject of live television coverage and was widely regarded as one of the "flash points" for the disorder, experienced repeated violent activity beginning before 4:00 p.m. Events there reached their peak at approximately 6:45 p.m., when cameras captured live several young African-American males dragging Reginald Denny, a passing motor-ist, from his truck and beating him close to death. It was shortly after the Denny beating that the violence began to spread and accelerate.

By 6:30 p.m., a crowd of about 150 protesters had also assembled outside of Parker Center, which was stormed and vandalized within the hour. This incident appears to have riveted the attention of police commanders, although their focus should have been on South Bureau where the first incidents of arson were beginning to occur. Firefighters responding to initial incidents were attacked by protesters, and one firefighter was hospitalized early in the evening after being shot while responding to a call. The first fatality, the death by shooting of an 18-year-old youth, occurred at approximately 8:15 p.m. The youth was shot by an unknown assailant at the corner of Vernon and Vermont.

Our analysis of events shows, however, that as late as 7:00 p.m., outbreaks of violence were largely confined to part of the 77th Street and Southwest Areas. As we document in Chapter Eight, it was within the next hour after 7:00 p.m. that the fires started and the violence began to spread. Thus, any chance the Command Staff had to contain the disturbance at the onset ended around 7:00 p.m. the first night. After that, the violence steadily worked its way north and west.

The lawlessness that occurred involved physical violence, looting and massive destruction of property, primarily through arson. The lawlessness was cyclical in nature but, unlike past disorders, occurred with equal intensity in daylight hours and during the nighttime. Thus, after the destruction on the first night, in each of the next five days the activity tended to start in the morning, build during the day, reach a high point in the evening and then tail off in the early morning hours. . . . [T]he second day of violence was the most severe in terms of the overall number of incidents. However, even on the third day the level of lawlessness was more severe than the first day. Only on the fourth and fifth days did the levels begin to fall off.

By the time the mayhem subsided some six days later, violence, looting and arson engulfed seven police Areas that make up the core of the central City: Southeast, 77th Street, Southwest, Newton Street, Rampart, Wilshire and Hollywood Areas. . . . Lesser incidents also occurred in Westwood, Venice, San Pedro, and Culver City. . . .

Given the widespread looting that occurred during the disorder, it is not surprising to find that most of the reported incidents involved property crimes. . . . [F]ully 58 percent of the incidents fell into this category, followed by 19 percent reported crimes against persons, and 17 percent reported in the category for unruly crowds and other disturbances. In the seven most active Areas, property crimes overwhelmingly predominated as well, with the largest numbers of incidents occurring in the Rampart, Wilshire and Newton Areas.

In the end, during the six days of the disturbance, at least 42 people lost their lives, more than 700 businesses were burned, and some $1 billion in property was damaged or destroyed. Although the violence stretched to many areas in the City, the hardest hit remained the communities of South and South Central Los Angeles and Koreatown. On many of the major commercial streets in these communities, 50 percent or more of the buildings were damaged or destroyed. In South and South Central, more than 560 businesses were destroyed by fire, hundreds more were victimized by looters, more than 21,000 people were left without electricity, and the entire area was left without mail service or public transportation. During the six days of rioting and for days beyond, it became impossible in these communities to purchase the bare necessities of life.

In Koreatown, located partly in Central but mostly in West Bureau, more than 100 fires were reported on the first night alone, and over 300 businesses were burned and looted before the terror ended. Damage in Koreatown alone is estimated to exceed $200 million. It thus is understandable—although seriously troubling—that many in the Korean-American community saw the need to arm and defend themselves and their property from the attacks of lawbreakers. Gunfights between these citizens and their attackers tragically were an all too frequent occurrence during the disorder. . . .

The perpetrators of this violence were not confined to any single racial or ethnic classification. Although the initial violent incidents immediately following the verdicts appear for the most part to have involved African-American males, members of all racial groups were involved in the spreading physical assaults and looting. People of all ages and gender participated in the looting, although the preponderance of participants were young males. In one widely publicized incident on the second day of the violence, for example, men, women and children of all ages and races could be seen lining up in order to loot an enormous Fedco store in Culver City.

The widespread violence does not appear to have been directed by any single individual or group. Although gang members seem to have been involved in many cases, the scope of the violence was massive and appears to have gone far beyond gang activity. Moreover, although persistent rumors suggest that there might have been pre-conceived plans among gangs or others to carry out the pattern of violence and destruction that occurred, our study has uncovered no hard evidence to confirm such a supposition. A notable exception, discussed in Chapter Eight, was the evidently organized assault by gang members on gun and sporting goods stores and pawnshops that resulted in the taking of more than 4,300 firearms from just 19 locations. On the whole, however, the disturbance seems to have largely begun with explosive outbursts of physical assaults and property destruction that took place as a result of pent-up anger and frustration. However, once the violence began and it became evident that the police were not able to check the lawbreaking, others apparently joined in, fueling the expansion of the disturbance.

The City's Response

With few exceptions, the failure of City officials and police department commanders adequately to prepare specifically for the possibility of the public reaction to the verdicts seems to have left many of these leaders— and the rank and file of the police department—mentally unready to confront the disorder when it came. It is therefore not surprising that when the verdicts arrived, the response suffered from a lack of leadership. The failure of individual commanders to react quickly, as contemplated by Department policy, to the initial incidents of violence led to situations that spread, intensified and careened out of control.

The Emergency Operations Organization

The Emergency Operations Organization ("EOO") should have been the nerve center of the City's emergency response. In this case, however, the EOO was largely dysfunctional. The Emergency Operations Center ("EOC"), located four stories underground in City Hall East, was supposed to swing into action as the City's central command and coordination location. It was designed to be staffed during an emergency by representatives of each City department or agency involved in the response. Less than an hour after the verdicts were announced, but more than three hours after he learned that the verdicts had come down, Chief Gates activated the EOC. However, activation appears to have accomplished little more than turning on lights in an almost empty room.

At the time the City's emergency apparatus was theoretically activated, the Mayor and Chief of Police still had not spoken with one another and seem to have taken no steps to coordinate their activities. Shortly after "activating" the EOC, Chief Gates left City Hall for a political fundraiser in Brentwood. Members of the LAPD division specifically-trained to staff the EOC were allowed to go home at 4:00 p.m., at the end of their regular shift. It was hours before these individuals could be located and ordered back into action. The other City agencies whose presence is necessary to staff the EOC did not even begin to learn that it had been activated until after 4:45 p.m., when someone asked a City Hall operator to start making telephone calls to them. Mayor Bradley left for the preplanned meeting at the First A.M.E. Church intended to provide an outlet for the community's anger. No one thus appears to have been left at the EOC to direct the City's response.

Beyond staffing problems, the EOC mechanism did not work well. At the beginning, the EOC was unable to obtain timely and reliable information from the police field commands. Late in the night of April 29, the EOC still had not been able to establish a direct telephone link with the

LAPD's South Bureau Field Command Post. Moreover, within the EOC, procedures for communication and routing of information were apparently overwhelmed by the volume of information and did not work. Virtually every element of the EOC's command, control, communications and information network seems to have broken down, with the result that the EOC never seems to have been in a "catch up" position for most of the disorder period. While there seems to have been modest improvement in conditions by the third day, it does not appear that the EOC ever provided effective command and control. Hence, it is questionable whether the EOC ever served as an effective mechanism to coordinate the activities of either the police or the many other agencies called upon to assist in the response.

The LAPD

Although the LAPD appeared to stay on top of events in much of the City—responding effectively to troublesome situations, for example, in Westwood Village and at the Foothill station—they could not keep up with the violence that erupted in the seven most active police Areas. Handicapped by the failure at the highest levels of the Command Staff to engage in specific planning and preparation for the possibility of unrest, rank and file police officers in the seven most active Areas seemed to have been put on the defensive and forced to react to the race of events. During the entire crisis, the Chief of Police appears never actively to have taken command of the Department and its response, preferring to leave that critical responsibility in the hands of less experienced subordinates.

In the 77th Street Area, where the initial violence occurred, officers responding to the first incidents were outnumbered by demonstrators and ordered to retreat by their Watch Commander, Lieutenant Michael Moulin. This decision appears to have made sense under the circumstances, but the failure after that to regroup and return rapidly to the scene appears to have been a critical error. At approximately 6:15 p.m., an order went out for all South Bureau units, which included the 77th, to report to a command post that was being established at an RTD facility at 54th and Arlington. While all units were being drawn from the streets into this staging area, none were being sent back out to deal with the growing violence, with the consequence that the 77th—and ultimately much of South Bureau—was left with a much-reduced police presence during the critical first hours of the disorder.

At the Field Command Post, the commanding officers on the scene appear to have been given very little information about the situation in the rest of South Bureau or the City at large, and communications difficulties made it almost impossible for them to receive guidance from the Department Commander. The rest of the City watched on live television as the incidents became more violent, more numerous and quickly grew out of control in the absence of any LAPD response. All of the Los Angeles television networks had helicopters continuously in the air from the outbreak of violence through the end of the disturbance—thereby enabling the public to watch the violence spread throughout the City. Many LAPD commanders, however, were unable to watch the television reports from these helicopters and did not get the benefit of reports from the Department's own helicopter units which generally were not used for reconnaissance. Television commentators openly remarked on the absence of police.

At around 6:45 p.m., the explosion of 9-1-1 emergency calls caused the LAPD Communications Division Commander to broadcast a City-wide Tactical Alert. Just after 8:00 p.m., the LAPD was put into emergency mobilization, a process that took several hours more to complete. At 8:45 p.m., the Mayor declared a local state of emergency and, shortly thereafter requested that the Governor mobilize 2,000 National Guard troops. This occurred almost immediately after Chief Gates returned to City Hall from the fundraiser. When the Mayor requested National Guard troops from the Governor, he evidently did so without calling upon local police agency mutual aid resources intended to provide the first line of additional support in such a situation.

During the first evening of the disorder, the LAPD seems to have lost all control over the mobs of demonstrators in South Bureau, who looted and burned at will. Circumstances did not improve on Day Two, as the violence spread north and west. The best strategy would seem to have been to get people off the streets and to arrest lawbreakers. However, confusion over the City's curfew order may have hampered this effort and the failure specifically to plan in advance for this contingency seems to have inhibited implementation of a City-wide arrest strategy. Few arrests were made the first night. Although the level of arrests began to pick up the next day, it did not keep pace with the explosion of looting and violence. Over the entire six days of mayhem, a total of only 5,002 arrests were made in the entire City of Los Angeles. Of this number 4,880 were made by the LAPD and 122 by other law enforcement agencies. Once the LAPD began making arrests, the system for processing lawbreakers rapidly appears to have bogged down in many instances, with the result that fewer arrests were made than seemingly were required by the circumstances.

The Response from Outside

The sheer size of the deployment of mutual aid resources to assist the City and the LAPD in responding to the disturbance points to the importance of mutual aid to both preparation and response. The California National Guard was called out during the first evening of rioting. However, a significant number of troops do not appear to have reached the streets until May 1. The initial deployment of 2,000 was augmented by two subsequent call ups, reaching a maximum Guard deployment of over 7,000 troops. Federal forces were deployed to bases around Los Angeles beginning on May 1st, although they did not reach their street assignments until Sunday, May 3rd. All told, federal troops numbered 3,500, and were supplemented by a deployment of more than 1,200 riot-trained law officers. At the regional level, the California Highway Patrol ("CHP") deployed 1,500 officers to assist the local efforts, and the Los Angeles Sheriff's Department ("LASD") mobilized all of its forces, although only a small number were deployed inside City boundaries.

Although large in scale and clearly essential to the ability of the City and the LAPD to control the disturbance, response was hindered by a lack of planning and coordination with, and effective use of, these outside resources, including the region's mutual aid resources, the National Guard, and federal troops. It is apparent that prior to April 29th neither the City nor the LAPD participated in any meaningful preparations with outside resources for the possibility of a civil disturbance that would exhaust City and Department resources.

The result of this lack of planning was a parallel lack of understanding of the function of the mutual aid system as soon as the unrest broke out. On the evening of April 29, when it was determined that outside assistance would be needed by the City, Police commanders did not call upon the local police resources most readily available under the California Law Enforcement Mutual Aid Plan. Instead they bypassed local mutual aid entirely and urged the Mayor directly to request of the Governor that the California National Guard be deployed, even though the first elements of such a deployment could have been anticipated to—and did in fact—take 17 hours or more to effectuate. As the National Guard began to deploy on April 30, the City's "out-of-channel request" caused some temporary confusion as to whether the National Guard was to function under the direction of the LAPD or the Sheriff, who actually appears to have assigned initial Guard units to duty in parts of the County outside of City boundaries.

Additional problems arose when the President ordered federal troops to be deployed to assist in the response. At the forefront was confusion as to the proper role of the military. Despite an express written declaration by the President to the contrary, the federal troop commander, Major General Covault, took the position that the defense Department's internal plan for handling domestic civil disturbances coupled with the *posse comitatus* statute prohibited the military from engaging in any law enforcement functions. This position required each request for assistance to be subjected to a nebulous test to determine whether the requested assignment constituted a law enforcement or a military function. As a result, after the federalization on May 1, not only were the federal troops rendered largely unavailable for most assignments requested by the LAPD, but the National Guard, under federal command, was made subject to the same restrictions, and therefore had to refuse many post-federalization requests for help. . . .

. . . To remedy the situation for the future, we make the following recommendations:

- The Mayor should direct the Emergency Operations Board as soon as possible to put in place a true master plan for City emergency preparedness, including preparedness for civil disorders. This plan should be developed through an integrated inter-departmental planning process that identifies all reasonably probable contingencies, establishes relevant priorities for emergency response, and puts in place the resource assignments and action steps necessary for the City to achieve these priorities. Specific attention should be given in this process to comprehensive plans that identify probable needs for the use of mutual aid resources and the means of securing such aid in emergencies. As part of this process, all City departments should be required to develop detailed emergency plans for performing their specific assignments.

- The City Administrative Officer should be placed in charge of completing this process and of producing an adequate master plan, together with adequate departmental plans, under the overall direction of the Mayor. There is some urgency to this task, so it should be completed as soon as possible and, in all events, no later than February 15, 1993. . . .

- The Mayor should also direct the Emergency Operations Board to develop and put in place a comprehensive program for emergency preparedness training. . . . Specific attention should be given to putting in place a training program for elected officials, senior managers, and uniformed service commanders to ensure the development of crisis management leadership skills and experience.

- The Chief of Police should actively participate in this process of developing City-wide priorities, plans, and training programs for emergency preparedness, and should oversee the development of a true Department emergency preparedness plan and training program that reasonably anticipates contingencies and permits the LAPD to operate effectively in support of the City's priorities in cases of civil disorder and other emergencies. Specific attention should be given to the following:

1. The Department's mechanisms for tactical alert and mobilization during emergencies should be streamlined and made more specific.
2. Concepts of command and control for emergency response should be simplified. Consideration should be given to reducing or even eliminating requirements for the use of a duplicate command structure and Field Command Posts.
3. Some method must be found to establish and maintain communications during emergencies from the field to headquarters, between LAPD field units, and between LAPD and non-LAPD field units.
4. Attention must be given to logistical support during emergencies, such as transportation, equipment, food, and the like.
5. Specific plans must be developed for use of mutual aid resources, including especially what assignments to make to mutual aid resources, what command and control to use and how to operate with them.

6. Strategies and tactics for civil disorder response should be reviewed in light of recent experience in Los Angeles and elsewhere. Particular attention should be given to development of coordinated Department-wide approaches for use in a City-wide emergency, such as improved initial response capability, rapid containment, and an arrest strategy that is fully coordinated with all other agencies that must be involved.

7. A triage scheme should be developed for the 9-1-1 response system that permits the Department to reduce and restore service according to pre-selected priorities as needed in the event of an emergency.

8. Plans should be developed to make use of all the Department's personnel during emergencies. In this connection, consideration should be given to requiring Department personnel who are not involved in undercover work to report periodically and train in uniform to improve readiness.

9. In addition, the Department should implement a comprehensive program of integrated emergency response training, that includes training for all levels within the Department as well as combined training with inter-departmental and mutual aid resources. Field exercises should be routinely carried out as part of the Department's normal training cycle. Significant attention should be given in this program to training officers at the Command Staff level in classroom, tabletop and field exercise settings to improve their leadership and decision-making skills.

- A comprehensive review should be conducted of the quality and quantity of emergency equipment available for use by the Department. Special attention should be given in this review to the need for higher-quality personal gear (helmets, face-guards and bullet-proof vests); the availability of tear gas and masks; and mobile communications equipment, including hand-held ROVER radios for all police use and cellular telephones for commanders.

- We recognize that some of our recommendations may result in additional costs. However, even in this time of severe budgetary constraints, the Mayor and Council should ensure that the City budget, and all relevant departmental budgets, includes sufficient funding for adequate emergency preparedness activities and equipment. . . .

- The Chief of Police as general manager and chief administrative officer of the Department must be responsible for the day-to-day management of the police department. However, it is in the best interests of the City and the Department that the citizen Police Commission perform real oversight functions in connection with the Department's operations. To this end, we urge implementation of recommendations by the Christopher Commission that call for establishment of an independent staff to support the Police Commission.

GORBACHEV ON THE END OF THE COLD WAR
May 6, 1992

Forty-six years after former British prime minister Winston Churchill proclaimed in a speech at Fulton, Missouri, that an iron curtain was descending across Europe, former Soviet president Mikhail Gorbachev traveled to Fulton May 6 to hail the end of the Cold War and warn that the world faces "the most difficult transition in the history of mankind."

Gorbachev stood at the same lectern at Westminster College that Churchill had used when he pronounced on March 5, 1946, that "a shadow has fallen upon the scenes so lately lighted by the Allied victory. From Stettin in the Baltic to Trieste in the Adriatic an iron curtain has descended across the Continent." Churchill's speech has often been cited as the opening of the Cold War.

Gorbachev said the Cold War never should have happened. At the end of World War II the world community—particularly the Soviet Union and the United States—had a unique opportunity to end the reliance on force to resolve conflicts, he said. "If the United States and the Soviet Union had been capable of understanding their responsibility and sensibly correlating their national interests and strivings with the rights and interests of other states and peoples, the planet today would be a much more suitable and favorable place for human life," he said.

Shared Blame

Both superpowers made mistakes that led to the Cold War, Gorbachev said, but he particularly blamed the United States. Western countries misread Joseph Stalin's intentions at the end of World War II, Gorbachev maintained. The West believed that Stalin was a dangerous aggres-

sor, Gorbachev said, when he actually never would have initiated a major war. In addition, the Soviet Union was in no position to fight another war because it had been "exhausted and destroyed" by World War II. Nonetheless, the United States touched off the arms race by developing nuclear weapons, Gorbachev said, an action that was "a fateful error."

The end of the Cold War should not be interpreted as a victory of one way of life over another, Gorbachev said. Instead, it "was altogether a victory for common sense, reason, democracy, and common human values." His view contrasted with that of President George Bush, who said repeatedly during the election year that the United States had won the Cold War.

The relaxation of tensions between the two superpowers brought changes in relationships among various countries, Gorbachev said. It also unleashed an "exaggerated nationalism" that led to an increasing number of regional conflicts. To help countries make the transition and resolve future disputes, Gorbachev advocated restructuring the United Nations to make it stronger. Ironically, forty-six years earlier Churchill also had called for strengthening the United Nations.

Strengthening the United Nations

The United Nations had changed little since its creation at the end of World War II, Gorbachev said. To improve the authority and potential of the UN Security Council, he said, its permanent membership needed to be expanded to include Germany, Japan, India, Italy, Indonesia, Canada, Poland, Brazil, Mexico, and Egypt. In addition, the Security Council needed better support from nations and additional peacekeeping forces.

Gorbachev said the UN secretary-general needed authority to act before a conflict became violent. He also proposed that a special body be created under the Security Council that would have the power to use political, diplomatic, economic, and military means to prevent or settle regional conflicts. And finally, he said closer coordination between UN organizations and regional bodies would help settle disputes throughout the world.

In a veiled warning directed at the United States, Gorbachev said new international relationships would not allow one nation or group of nations to "monopolize the international arena." Instead, world integration brought about by common economic, environmental, and political problems should result in a multipolar system, he said.

The estimated 10,000 to 15,000 spectators repeatedly interrupted Gorbachev with strong applause. During the speech, students raised a series of blue and white placards that said: "Cold war, nyet. Gorby, da."

Gorbachev's speech at the tiny liberal arts college, which has 750 undergraduates, was the highlight of a thirteen-day tour of the United States. The trip was partially a goodwill mission and partially an effort to raise funds for the Gorbachev Foundation. Trip organizers said that Gorbachev hoped to raise $3 million for the foundation, although Gorba-

chev did not charge for his Fulton speech. Two days before the speech, Gorbachev was the guest of honor at a $5,000-a-plate luncheon in Simi Valley, California, hosted by former president Ronald Reagan. Gorbachev also met in Los Angeles with Hollywood stars and business executives.

Following is the text of Mikhail Gorbachev's speech, "The River of Time and the Imperative of Action," presented May 6, 1992, at Westminster College in Fulton, Missouri (The bracketed headings have been added by Congressional Quarterly to highlight the organization of the text.):

Here we stand, before a sculpture in which the sculptor's imagination and fantasy, with remarkable expressiveness and laconism, convey the drama of the "Cold War", the irrepressible human striving to penetrate the barriers of alienation and confrontation. It is symbolic that this artist was the granddaughter of Winston Churchill and that this sculpture should be in Fulton.

More than 46 years ago Winston Churchill spoke in Fulton and in my country this speech was interpreted as the formal declaration of the "Cold War." This was indeed the first time the words, "Iron Curtain," were pronounced, and the whole Western world was challenged to close ranks against the threat of tyranny in the form of the Soviet Union and Communist expansion. Everything else in this speech, including Churchill's analysis of the postwar situation in the world, his thoughts about the possibility of preventing a third world war, the prospects for progress, and methods of reconstructing the postwar world, remained unknown to the Soviet people.

Today, in paying tribute to this eminent statesman, we can evaluate more quietly and objectively both the merits of his speech and the limitations of the analysis which it included, his ideas and predictions, and his strategic principles.

Since that time the world in which we live has undergone tremendous changes. Even so, however paradoxical it may sound, there is a certain similarity between the situation then and today. Then, the prewar structure of international relations had virtually collapsed, a new pattern of forces had emerged along with a new set of interests and claims.

Different trends in world development could be discerned, but their prospects were not clearly outlined. New possibilities for progress had appeared. Answers had to be found to the challenges posed by new subjects of international law. The atmosphere was heavy—not only with hope, but also with suspicion, lack of understanding, unpredictability.

In other words, a situation had emerged in which a decision with universal implications had to be taken. Churchill's greatness is seen in the fact that he was the first among prominent political figures to understand that.

Indeed, the world community which had at that time already established the United Nations, was faced with a unique opportunity to change the course of world development, fundamentally altering the role in it of force and of war. And, of course, this depended to a decisive degree on the Soviet Union and the United States—here I hardly need to explain why.

[Both Countries Missed the Chance]

So I would like to commence my remarks by noting that the U.S.S.R. and the U.S. missed that chance—the chance to establish their relationship on a new basis of principle and thereby to initiate a world order different from that which existed before the war. I think it is clear that I am not suggesting that they should have established a sort of condominium over the rest of the world. The opportunity was on a different plane altogether.

If the United States and the Soviet Union had been capable of understanding their responsibility and sensibly correlating their national interests and strivings with the rights and interests of other states and peoples, the planet today would be a much more suitable and favorable place for human life. I have more than once criticized the foreign policy of the Stalinist leadership in those years. Not only was it incapable of reevaluating the historical logic of the interwar period, taking into account the experience and results of the war, and following a course which corresponded to the changed reality, it committed a major error in equating the victory of democracy over fascism with the victory of socialism and aiming to spread socialism throughout the world.

But the West, and the United States in particular, also committed an error. Its conclusion about the probability of open Soviet military aggression was unrealistic and dangerous. This could never have happened, not only because Stalin, as in 1939-1941, was afraid of war, did not want war, and never would have engaged in a major war. But primarily because the country was exhausted and destroyed; it had lost tens of millions of people, and the public hated war. Having won a victory, the army and the soldiers were dying to get home and get back to a normal life.

By including the "nuclear component" in world politics, and on this basis unleashing a monstrous arms race—and here the initiator was the United States, the West—"sufficient defense was exceeded," as the lawyers would say. This was a fateful error. . . .

So I would be so bold as to affirm that the governing circles of the victorious powers lacked an adequate strategic vision of the possibilities for world development as they emerged after the war—and, consequently, a true understanding of their own countries' national interests. Hiding behind slogans of "striving for peace" and defense of their people's interests on both sides, decisions were taken which split asunder the world which had just succeeded in overcoming fascism because it was united.

And on both sides this was justified ideologically. The conflict was presented as the inevitable opposition between good and evil—all the evil, of course, being attributed to the opponent. This continued for decades until it became evident that we were approaching the abyss. I am stating this because the world community has paid dearly for the errors committed at this turning-point in world history.

In the major centers of world politics the choice, it would seem, has today been made in favor of peace, cooperation, interaction, and common security. And in pushing forward to a new civilization we should under no circumstances again make the intellectual, and consequently political, error of interpreting victory in the "Cold War" narrowly as a victory for oneself, one's own way of life, for one's own values and merits. This was a victory over a scheme for the development of humanity which was becoming slowly congealed and leading us to destruction. It was a shattering of the vicious circle into which we had driven ourselves. This was altogether a victory for common sense, reason, democracy, and common human values.

... In thinking over the processes which we ourselves have witnessed, we are forced to conclude that humanity is at a major turning-point. Not only the peoples of the former U.S.S.R., but the whole world is living through this watershed situation. This is not just some ordinary stage of development, like many others in world history. This is a turning-point on a historic and worldwide scale and signifies the incipient substitution of one paradigm of civilization by another....

This existing and intensifying integration of the world reveals a broad spectrum of favorable opportunities for the future of mankind.

First and foremost, it signifies the possibility of creating a global international security system, thus preventing large-scale military conflicts like the world wars of the 20th century and facilitating a radical reduction in levels of armaments and reducing the burden of military expenditures. This signifies that the attention, and the resources, of the world community can be focussed on solving problems in non-military areas: population, environment, food production, energy sources, and the like. This means new opportunities for economic progress, ensuring normal conditions of life for the Earth's growing population and improved living conditions.

We have, in fact, already starting moving in that direction. But the significance of these changes, while a great source of hope, should not blind us to the dangers—some of which we have already encountered. It would be a supreme tragedy if the world, having overcome the "1946 model," were to find itself once again in a "1914 model" world. A major international effort will be needed to render irreversible the shift in favor of a democratic world—and democratic for the whole of humanity, not just for half of it.

[New Dangers]

I am in full agreement with Secretary of State James Baker's formulation. The existing dangers are largely a function of the watershed character of the times we live in. It is quite clear that the enhanced integration and interdependence of the world at the same time creates new strains—both domestically and internationally—unleashing processes which earlier were hidden from view. The very fact that the two world alliances are no longer in confrontation and that the collapse of totalitarian regimes has released centrifugal forces which had been temporarily frozen—territorial and intergovernmental contradictions and claims—has encouraged an exaggerated nationalism. And this has already led to much bloodshed.

The ending of the global confrontation of nuclear superpowers, and of the ideological opposition between the two world systems, has rendered even more visible today's major contradiction—between the rich and poor countries, between "North" and "South", even though these terms today are merely conventional. . . .

One of the worst of the new dangers is ecological. When Winston Churchill gave his speech here, most people on this planet did not even suspect a mortal threat from that direction.

But today, global climatic shifts, the greenhouse effect, the "ozone hole," acid rain, contamination of the atmosphere, soil, and water by industrial and household waste, the destruction of the forests, etc. all threaten the stability of the planet. Despite all the efforts being made to prevent ecological catastrophe, the destruction of nature is intensifying. And the effects of our poisoning of the spiritual sphere—drug addiction, alcoholism, terrorism, crime—become further ecological threats. All of this together heightens the probability of social, national, and international conflicts.

If they do not understand the transitional character of the present international system, with all its inherent contradictions and conflicts, politicians again risk committing errors which would have the most baneful consequences for all. The prospect of catastrophic climatic changes, more frequent droughts, floods, hunger, epidemics, national-ethnic conflicts, and other similar catastrophes compels governments to adopt a world perspective and seek generally applicable solutions. The only alternative would be an intensification of conflicts throughout the world, instability of political systems, civil wars, i.e., ultimately, a threat to world peace. . . .

What has to be done is to create the necessary mechanisms. In my position it is not very appropriate to name them. It is important that they should be authorized by the world community to deal with problems. Without that there is no point in talking about a new era or a new civilization. I will limit myself to designating the lines of activity and the competence of such mechanisms.

Nuclear and Chemical Weapons. Rigid controls must be instituted to prevent their proliferation, including enforcement measures in cases of violation. An agreement must be concluded among all present nuclear states on procedures for cutting back on such weapons and liquidating them. Finally a world convention prohibiting chemical weapons should be signed.

The Peaceful Uses of Nuclear Energy. The powers of the IAEA [International Atomic Energy Agency] must be strengthened, and it is imperative that all countries working in this area be included in the IAEA system. The procedures of the IAEA should be tightened up and the work performed in a more open and aboveboard manner. Under United Nations auspices a powerful consortium should be created to finance the modernization or liquidation of high-risk nuclear power stations, and also to store spent fuel. A set of world standards for nuclear power plants should be established. Work on nuclear fusion must be expanded and intensified.

The Export of Conventional Weapons. Governmental exports of such weapons should be ended by the year 2000, and, in regions of armed conflict, it should be stopped at once. The illegal trade in such arms must be equated with international terrorism and the drug trade. With respect to these questions the intelligence services of the states which are permanent members of the Security Council should be coordinated. And the Security Council itself must be expanded, which I will mention in a moment.

Regional Conflicts. Considering the impartially examined experience obtained in the Middle East, in Africa, in Southeast Asia, Korea, Yugoslavia, the Caucasus, and Afghanistan, a special body should be set up under the United Nations Security Council with the right to employ political, diplomatic, economic, and military means to settle and prevent such conflicts.

Human Rights. The European process has officially recognized the universality of this common human value, i.e., the acceptability of the international interference wherever human rights are being violated. This task is not easy even for states which signed the Paris Charter of 1990 and even less so for all states members of the United Nations. However, I believe that the new world order will not be fully realized unless the United Nations and its Security Council create structures (taking into consideration existing United Nations and regional structures) authorized to impose sanctions and to make use of other enforcement measures.

Food, Population, Economic Assistance. It is no accident that these problems should be dealt with in this connection. Upon their solution depends the biological viability of the Earth's population and the minimal social stability needed for a civilized existence of states and peoples. Major scientific, financial, political, and public organizations—among them, the authoritative Club of Rome—have long been occupied with these problems. However, the newly emerging type of international interaction will make possible a breakthrough in our practical approach to them. I would propose that next year a world conference be held on this subject, one similar to the forthcoming conference on the environment.

Ladies and Gentlemen! All of these problems demand an enhanced level of organization of the international community. . . .

Here the decisive role may and must be played by the United Nations. Of course, it must be restructured, together with its component bodies, in order to be capable of confronting the new tasks. . . .

The United Nations, which emerged from the results and the lessons of the Second World War, is still marked by the period of its creation. This is true both with respect to the makeup of its subsidiary bodies and auxiliary institutions and with respect to its functioning. Nothing, for instance, other than the division into victors and vanquished, explains why such countries as Germany and Japan do not figure among the permanent members of the Security Council.

In general, I feel Article 53 on "enemy states" should be immediately deleted from the UN Charter. Also, the criterion of possession of nuclear weapons would be archaic in the new era before us. The great country of India should be represented in the Security Council. The authority and potential of the Council would also be enhanced by incorporation on a permanent basis of Italy, Indonesia, Canada, Poland, Brazil, Mexico, and Egypt, even if initially they do not possess the veto. . . .

It is clear that the 20th century nurtured immense opportunities. And from it we are inheriting frightful, apocalyptic threats. But we have at our disposal a great science, one which will help us avoid crude miscalculations. Moral values have survived in this frightful century, and these will assist and support us in this, the most difficult, transition in the history of humanity—from one qualitative state to another.

In concluding I would like to return to my starting-point. From this tribune Churchill appealed to the United Nations to rescue peace and progress, but he appealed primarily to Anglo-Saxon unity as the nucleus to which others could adhere. In the achievement of this goal the decisive role, in his view, was to be played by force, above all, by armed force. He even entitled his speech "The Sinews of Peace."

The goal today has not changed: peace and progress for all. But now we have the capacity to approach it without paying the heavy price we have been paying these past 50 years or so, without having to resort to means which put the very goal itself in doubt, which even constitute a threat to civilization. And while continuing to recognize the outstanding role of the United States of America, and today of other rich and highly developed countries, we must not limit our appeal to the elect, but call upon the whole world community.

In a qualitatively new and different world situation the overwhelming majority of the United Nations will, I hope, be capable of organizing themselves and acting in concert on the principles of democracy, equality of rights, balance of interests, common sense, freedom of choice, and willingness to cooperate. Made wise by bitter experience, they will, I think, be capable of dispensing, when necessary, with egoistic considerations in order to arrive at the exalted goal which is man's destiny on earth.

TWENTY-SEVENTH AMENDMENT
TO THE CONSTITUTION
May 18, 1993

Nearly 203 years after it was first proposed and accepted by Congress, an amendment that bars congressional pay raises from taking effect in midterm was officially certified May 18 by the United States Archivist as the Twenty-seventh Amendment to the Constitution. The amendment states: "No law varying the compensation for the services of the Senators and Representatives shall take effect, until an election of Representatives shall have intervened."

The amendment was proposed by James Madison. "[T]here is a seeming impropriety in leaving any set of men without control to put their hand into the public coffers, to take out money to put in their pockets," he told his fellow members of the first House of Representatives. The Madison amendment was sent to the states in September 1789 as part of a package of twelve proposed amendments. Ten became the Bill of Rights, but the pay raise amendment was ratified by only six states and then languished until 1873, when Ohio ratified it. More than a century elapsed before Wyoming ratified the amendment, in 1978. The amendment gained momentum, and by May 12, 1992, a total of forty states had ratified it, two more than necessary to make the amendment part of the Constitution. (Three-fourths of the states—thirty-eight of fifty—must ratify an amendment to make it legal.)

Some members of the House and Senate questioned whether the amendment was valid because so much time had passed since the first states had acted on the amendment. In 1921 the Supreme Court ruled that ratification must reflect a "contemporaneous consensus," and recent constitutional amendments have contained deadlines (seven years has become standard). In 1982, the Equal Rights Amendment, which barred discrimination on the basis of sex, was declared dead when only thirty-five of the required thirty-eight states had ratified the amendment within the ten-year time period. (Equal Rights Amendment, Historic Documents of 1982, p. 611).

When word came that the thirty-eighth state, Michigan, had ratified the pay raise amendment on May 7, House Speaker Thomas S. Foley, D-Wash., and Senator Robert C. Byrd, D-W. Va., a former majority leader who has written a history of the Senate, suggested hearings to explore whether too much time had elapsed. "As the actions of the states become more and more separated in time from each other and from the Congress that promulgated the amendment, the question can be raised about whether their actions truly represent the will of the people," Byrd said in a floor speech.

On May 13, however, the archivist of the United States, Don W. Wilson, notified Congress that he would recognize the amendment. "Upon receipt of formal notification of ratification of the Congressional Pay Amendment by three-fourths of the states, I will ... certify the adoption of the amendment," he said. Wilson's decision, a formality for most amendments, proved pivotal. Already on the defensive for recent sizable pay raises and wracked by a series of other scandals and abuses of personal privilege, Congress had little desire to challenge Wilson's declaration.

Instead, the House and Senate each passed resolutions May 20 accepting the amendment. The Senate adopted two resolutions recognizing the validity of the Twenty-seventh Amendment by votes of 99-0. Byrd, who sponsored the resolutions, said that "in most circumstances, I believe that a lapse of this length would be too great to sustain ratification of an amendment. The congressional pay amendment deserves a different fate." Byrd, however, scolded Wilson for not following "historic tradition." When questions about the validity of ratification arose in the past, Byrd said, certification by the archivist or secretary of State was postponed pending congressional discussion and resolution.

The House passed a resolution similar to Byrd's by a vote of 414-3. Most members who spoke on the House floor said that the passage of time had not robbed the amendment of its relevance. Rep. Jack Brooks, D-Tx., said the amendment "has the same meaning, the same goal, the same aim, and the same intended effect when it was ratified in 1992 as it did when it was first ratified in 1789." Indeed, said Hamilton Fish, Jr., R-N.Y., the "rash of recent ratifications" was enough to validate the timeliness of the amendment. Only one member spoke against the amendment. "The principle of contemporary consensus ... is just too important to waive just because it appears popular at the moment," Neal Smith, D-Iowa, argued.

Between 1789 and 1924 four other amendments were sent to the states without a deadline for ratification and remain unratified. They include a proposal to change the apportionment of the House of Representatives (sent to the states in 1789), a stricture forbidding American officials from accepting titles of nobility (1810), language prohibiting federal laws against slavery (1861), and a proposal allowing Congress to regulate child labor (1924). It is highly unlikely that interest in any of these proposed amendments would ever revive. The last amendment to the Constitution took effect in 1971; it gave eighteen-year-olds the right to vote.

Following is the declaration of the archivist of the United States certifying the Twenty-seventh Amendment to the U.S. Constitution, as released by the National Archives on May 18, 1992:

To All To Whom These Presents Shall Come, Greeting:

Know ye, that the first Congress of the United States, at its first session, held in New York, New York, on the twenty-fifth day of September, in the year one thousand seven hundred and eighty-nine, passed the following resolution to amend the Constitution of the United States of America, in the following words and figures in part, to wit:

The Conventions of a number of the States having at the time of their adopting the Constitution, expressed a desire, in order to prevent misconstruction or abuse of its powers, that further declaratory and restrictive clauses should be added: And as extending the ground of public confidence in the Government will best ensure the beneficent ends of its institution;

Resolved by the Senate and House of Representatives of the United States of America in Congress assembled, two thirds of both Houses concurring, that the following Articles be proposed to the Legislatures of the several States, as Amendments to the Constitution of the United States, all or any of which Articles, when ratified by three fourths of the said Legislatures, to be valid to all intents and purposes, as part of the said Constitution, viz.:

Articles in addition to, and amendment of, the Constitution of the United States of America, proposed by Congress and ratified by the Legislatures of the several States, pursuant to the fifth Article of the original Constitution.

* * *

Article the Second . . . No law, varying the compensation for the services of the Senators and Representatives, shall take effect, until an election of Representatives shall have intervened.

* * *

And, further, that Section 106b, Title 1 of the United States Code provides that whenever official notice is received at the National Archives and Records Administration that any amendment proposed to the Constitution of the United States has been adopted, according to the provisions of the Constitution, the Archivist of the United States shall forthwith cause the amendment to be published, with his certificate, specifying the States by which the same may have been adopted, and that the same has become valid, to all intents and purposes, as a part of the Constitution of the United States.

And, further, that it appears from official documents on file in the National Archives of the United States that the Amendment to the Constitution of the United States proposed as aforesaid has been ratified by the Legislatures of the States of Alabama, Alaska, Arizona, Arkansas, Colorado, Connecticut, Delaware, Florida, Georgia, Idaho, Illinois, Indiana, Iowa, Kansas, Louisiana, Maine, Maryland, Michigan, Minnesota, Missouri, Montana, Nevada, New Hampshire, New Jersey, New Mexico, North Carolina, North Dakota, Ohio, Oklahoma, Oregon, South Carolina, South Dakota, Tennessee, Texas, Utah, Vermont, Virginia, West Virginia, Wisconsin, and Wyoming.

And, further, that the States whose Legislatures have so ratified the said proposed Amendment constitute the requisite three fourths of the whole number of States in the United States.

NOW, Therefore, be it known that I, Don W. Wilson, Archivist of the United States, by virtue and in pursuance of Section 106b, Title 1 of the United States Code, do hereby certify that the aforesaid Amendment has become valid, to all intents and purposes, as a part of the Constitution of the United States.

IN TESTIMONY WHEREOF,
I have hereunto set my hand and
caused the seal of the National
Archives and Records
Administration to be affixed.

DONE at the City of Washington
this 18th day of May
in the year of our Lord one
thousand nine hundred and ninety-two.

DON W. WILSON

VICE PRESIDENT QUAYLE'S "MURPHY BROWN" SPEECH

May 19, 1992

With a single reference to Murphy Brown, a television character who gave birth out of wedlock, Vice President Dan Quayle set off a national uproar in a speech May 19 to the Commonwealth Club of California.

In the speech, Quayle placed much of the blame for the nation's problems, including the recent Los Angeles riots, on the decline of moral values and the family. Near the end of his thirty-minute talk Quayle said: "It doesn't help matters when prime time TV has Murphy Brown— a character who supposedly epitomizes today's intelligent, highly paid, professional woman—mocking the importance of fathers by bearing a child alone, and calling it just another 'lifestyle choice.'" Much of the substance of Quayle's speech got lost in the ensuing hubbub over his criticism of the situation comedy.

The program's story line had Murphy getting pregnant accidentally by her ex-husband. She rejected marriage to him and abortion, and decided to have the baby on her own. More than 38 million Americans watched the season-ending episode where Murphy gave birth, but Quayle and President George Bush were not among them.

Newspaper headline writers had a field day with Quayle's speech. "MURPHY HAS A BABY ... QUAYLE HAS A COW," said the Philadelphia Daily News. *"Quayle to Murphy Brown: YOU TRAMP!" said the* New York Daily News. *Editorial writers tended to attack the speech's substance. The* Washington Post *said: "For Dan Quayle, of all people, to be giving instruction on how poor people must buckle down and get their values together and pull themselves up by their bootstraps and the rest from the cushy perch of the vice presidency of this particular administration is, at the very least, ironic and morally klunkish."*

Quayle's reference to Murphy Brown clearly caught the White House by surprise. Bush at first refused to comment, but he was unable to avoid the question May 20 at a news conference with a baffled Canadian prime minister Brian Mulroney, who asked, "Who is Murphy Brown?"

Bush said that "children should have the benefit of being born into families where the mother and a father will give them love and attention all their lives." But he conceded, "it's not always possible."

"Family Values" and Abortion Politics

White House spokesman Marlin Fitzwater, while agreeing that Quayle made a good point, also praised the program's "prolife values" for showing a leading character deciding against having an abortion. The next day, Quayle said Fitzwater was wrong and that the program "does not represent the prolife policies."

Some political pundits and the show's executive producer, Diane English, assailed the vice president for attacking a woman who rejected abortion when the Bush administration was doing everything it could to ban abortion nationwide. "If the vice president thinks it's disgraceful for an unmarried woman to bear a child, and if he believes that a woman cannot adequately raise a child without a father, then he'd better make sure abortion remains safe and legal," English said.

Others accused Quayle of echoing the cultural populism first expressed by Vice President Spiro T. Agnew in his 1970 assault on the news media as "nattering nabobs of negativism." Quayle's remark also revived the debate over whether television really influenced American society. Conservatives had long contended that television was a powerful force in establishing social norms. Others, though, argued that it was ridiculous to believe that a television sitcom could influence attitudes and actions.

Other critics viewed Quayle's remark as an attack on single mothers and working women. They noted the irony that Bush's daughter Dorothy was divorced and raising two young children by herself. (She married again a month later.) The day after the speech, Quayle denied that he meant to attack single mothers, who made up a large and growing segment of the population. The nation had 10.1 million single mothers, although few met Murphy Brown's profile as an upper-income, professional woman. There were only 15,000 single mothers ages thirty-five to forty-four who had never married and had family incomes of $50,000 or more, according to the Census Bureau.

A few days after Quayle's speech, Democratic presidential candidate Bill Clinton criticized the broad theme underlying it. "The president's notion that we can do nothing for a community but rebuild the American family is as wrongheaded and simplistic as the Democrats' old notion that there is a social program answer for every social problem," Clinton said in a Cleveland speech. "Family values alone won't feed a hungry child, and material security will not provide a moral compass. We need both."

Attack on the "Cultural Elite"

Quayle was unfazed by all the criticism. He told reporters: "It's a speech that had to be given, an important speech .... The discussion will get beyond Murphy Brown and it will give me an opportunity to talk about values .... Values are going to be very important to this campaign." Several weeks later he went on the offensive once again with an assault on the "cultural elite," including its members in Hollywood. In a speech June 9, 1992, at the Southern Baptist convention, Quayle said: "As I discovered recently, to appeal to our country's enduring, basic moral values is to invite the scorn and laughter of the elite culture. Talk about right and wrong, and they'll try to mock us in newsrooms, sitcom studios, and faculty lounges across America. But in the heart of America, in the homes and workplaces and churches, the message is heard."

Both speeches by the vice president were seen as attempts to embrace icons such as family, law-and-order, and the flag that helped Ronald Reagan to win the presidency in 1980 and 1984 and Bush to win in 1988. The speeches were reportedly part of a strategy by the vice president and his advisers to take a more aggressive approach as the presidential campaign heated up.

Ironically, three months after Quayle's Murphy Brown speech the show won an Emmy as best comedy series and star Candice Bergen won an Emmy as best actress. "I would like to thank the vice president," Bergen said in her acceptance speech to loud applause. "And I would like to thank the television academy and the members of the cultural elite."

Lingering Repercussions

The heated discussion touched off by the vice president continued throughout the summer and fall, especially after the Republicans at their Houston convention in August renominated Bush and Quayle on a "family values" platform that called for an absolute ban on abortions. (Republican National Convention, p. 781; Republican Party Platform, p. 799)

Candice Bergen as Murphy Brown made the cover of Time magazine, and there was nonpartisan consensus on talk shows that Quayle had opened a significant dialogue. Commentators agreed that Hollywood "doesn't get it" and was continuing to pump out sex and violence despite declining profits and box office statistics that indicated the public wanted more wholesome fare. Clinton supporters, however, resented the Republicans' efforts to turn shared values and concerns into a partisan issue.

In a bizarre turnabout to the episode, the "Murphy Brown" show opened its new season on September 21 with the fictional unmarried newswoman replying to the real-life vice president. News clips of the Quayle speech and the headlines it generated were interspersed with *scenes of the harried "new mother" reacting to the criticism. "Glamorize single motherhood?" Brown asks in disbelief. "Look at me, ... Am I glamorous?"*

This time, Quayle was among the millions of viewers. He watched the show with a group that included an unwed mother and other single parents. Afterward he said again that he meant no offense to single mothers and was merely trying to get Hollywood "to begin reflecting our values."

> *Following are excerpts from the speech delivered by Vice President Dan Quayle on May 19, 1992, before the Commonwealth Club of California in San Francisco, and from President George Bush's news conference May 20, 1992, with Prime Minister Brian Mulroney of Canada. (The bracketed headings have been added by Congressional Quarterly to highlight the organization of the text.):*

QUAYLE SPEECH

... When I have been asked during these last weeks who caused the riots and the killing in L.A., my answer has been direct and simple: Who is to blame for the riots? The rioters are to blame. Who is to blame for the killings? The killers are to blame. Yes, I can understand how people were shocked and outraged by the verdict in the Rodney King trial. But there is simply no excuse for the mayhem that followed. To apologize or in any way to excuse what happened is wrong. It is a betrayal of all those people equally outraged and equally disadvantaged who did not loot and did not riot—and who were in many cases victims of the rioters. No matter how much you may disagree with the verdict, the riots were wrong. And if we as a society don't condemn what is wrong, how can we teach our children what is right?

But after condemning the riots, we do need to try to understand the underlying situation.

In a nutshell: I believe the lawless social anarchy which we saw is directly related to the breakdown of family structure, personal responsibility and social order in too many areas of our society. For the poor the situation is compounded by a welfare ethos that impedes individual efforts to move ahead in society, and hampers their ability to take advantage of the opportunities America offers.

If we don't succeed in addressing these fundamental problems, and in restoring basic values, any attempt to fix what's broken will fail. But one reason I believe we won't fail is that we have come so far in the last 25 years.

There is no question that this country has had a terrible problem with race and racism. The evil of slavery has left a long legacy. But we have faced racism squarely, and we have made progress in the past quarter century. The landmark civil rights bills of the 1960's removed legal barriers to allow full participation by blacks in the economic, social and political life of the nation. By any measure the America of 1992 is more egalitarian, more integrated, and offers more opportunities to black Americans—and all other minority group members—than the America of 1964. There is more to be done. But I think that all of us can be proud of our progress.

And let's be specific about one aspect of this progress: This country now has a black middle class that barely existed a quarter century ago. Since 1967 the median income of black two parent families has risen by 60 percent in real terms. The number of black college graduates has skyrocketed. Black men and women have achieved real political power—black mayors head 48 of our largest cities, including Los Angeles. These are achievements.

[New Black Underclass]

But as we all know, there is another side to that bright landscape. During this period of progress, we have also developed a culture of poverty—some call it an underclass—that is far more violent and harder to escape than it was a generation ago.

The poor you always have with you, Scripture tells us. And in America we have always had poor people. But in this dynamic, prosperous nation, poverty has traditionally been a stage through which people pass on their way to joining the great middle class. And if one generation didn't get very far up the ladder—their ambitious, better-educated children would.

But the underclass seems to be a new phenomenon. It is a group whose members are dependent on welfare for very long stretches, and whose men are often drawn into lives of crime. There is far too little upward mobility, because the underclass is disconnected from the rules of American society. And these problems have, unfortunately, been particularly acute for Black Americans.

Let me share with you a few statistics on the difference between black poverty in particular in the 1960's and now.

- In 1967 68% of black families were headed by married couples. In 1991, only 48% of black families were headed by both a husband and wife.
- In 1965 the illegitimacy rate among black families was 28%. In 1989, 65%—two thirds—of all black children were born to never-married mothers.
- In 1951 9.2% of black youth between 16 -19 were unemployed. In 1965, it was 23%. In 1980 it was 35%. By 1989, the number had declined slightly, but was still 32%.
- The leading cause of death of young black males today is homicide.

It would be overly simplistic to blame this social breakdown on the programs of the Great Society alone. It would be absolutely wrong to blame it on the growth and success most Americans enjoyed during the

1980's. Rather, we are in large measure reaping the whirlwind of decades of changes in social mores.

I was born in 1947, so I'm considered one of those "Baby Boomers" we keep reading about. But let's look at one unfortunate legacy of the "Boomer" generation. When we were young, it was fashionable to declare war against traditional values. Indulgence and self-gratification seemed to have no consequences. Many of our generation glamorized casual sex and drug use, evaded responsibility and trashed authority. Today the "Boomers" are middle-aged and middle class. The responsibility of having families has helped many recover traditional values. And, of course, the great majority of those in the middle class survived the turbulent legacy of the 60's and 70's. But many of the poor, with less to fall back on, did not.

The intergenerational poverty that troubles us so much today is predominantly a poverty of values. Our inner cities are filled with children having children; with people who have not been able to take advantage of educational opportunities; with people who are dependent on drugs or the narcotic of welfare. To be sure, many people in the ghettos struggle very hard against these tides—and sometimes win. But too many feel they have no hope and nothing to lose. This poverty is, again, fundamentally a poverty of values.

Unless we change the basic rules of society in our inner cities, we cannot expect anything else to change. We will simply get more of what we saw three weeks ago. New thinking, new ideas, new strategies are needed.

[Role of Government]

For the government, transforming underclass culture means that our policies and programs must create a different incentive system. Our policies must be premised on, and must reinforce, values such as: family, hard work, integrity and personal responsibility.

I think we can all agree that government's first obligation is to maintain order. We are a nation of laws, not looting. It has become clear that the riots were fueled by the vicious gangs that terrorize the inner cities. We are committed to breaking those gangs and restoring law and order. As James Q. Wilson has written, "Programs of economic restructuring will not work so long as gangs control the streets."

Some people say "law and order," are code words. Well, they are code words. Code words for safety, getting control of the streets, and freedom from fear. And let's not forget that, in 1990, 84 percent of the crimes committed by blacks were committed against blacks.

We are for law and order. If a single mother raising her children in the ghetto has to worry about drive-by shootings, drug deals, or whether her children will join gangs and die violently, her difficult task becomes impossible. We're for law and order because we can't expect children to learn in dangerous schools. We're for law and order because if property isn't protected, who will build businesses?

As one step on behalf of law and order—and on behalf of opportunity as well—the President has initiated the "Weed and Seed" program— to "weed out" criminals and "seed" neighborhoods with programs that address root causes of crime. And we have encouraged community-based policing, which gets the police on the street so they interact with citizens.

Safety is absolutely necessary. But it's not sufficient. Our urban strategy is to empower the poor by giving them control over their lives. To do that, our urban agenda includes:

- Fully funding the Home-ownership and Opportunity for People Everywhere program. HOPE—as we call it—will help public housing residents become home-owners. Subsidized housing all too often merely made rich investors richer. Home ownership will give the poor a stake in the neighborhoods, and a chance to build equity.
- Creating enterprise zones by slashing taxes in targeted areas, including a zero capital gains tax, to spur entrepreneurship, economic development, and job creation in inner cities.
- Instituting our education strategy, AMERICA 2000, to raise academic standards and to give the poor the same choices about how and where to educate their children that rich people.
- Promoting welfare reform to remove the penalities for marriage, create incentives for saving, and give communities greater control over how the programs are administered.

These programs are empowerment programs. They are based on the same principles as the Job Training Partnership Act, which aimed to help disadvantaged young people and dislocated workers to develop their skills to give them an opportunity to get ahead. Empowering the poor will strengthen families. And right now, the failure of our families is hurting America deeply. When families fail, society fails. The anarchy and lack of structure in our inner cities are testament to how quickly civilization falls apart when the family foundation cracks. Children need love and discipline. They need mothers and fathers. A welfare check is not a husband. The state is not a father. It is from parents that children learn how to behave in society; it is from parents above all that children come to understand values and themselves as men and women, mothers and fathers.

[Gangs as Surrogate Families]

And for those concerned about children growing up in poverty, we should know this: marriage is probably the best anti-poverty program of all. Among families headed by married couples today, there is a poverty rate of 5.7 percent. But 33.4 percent of families headed by a single mother are in poverty today.

Nature abhors a vacuum. Where there are no mature, responsible men around to teach boys how to be good men, gangs serve in their place. In fact, gangs have become a surrogate family for much of a generation of inner-city boys. I recently visited with some former gang members in Albuquerque, New Mexico. In a private meeting, they told me why they had joined gangs. These teenage boys said that gangs gave them a sense of security. They made them feel wanted, and useful. They got support from their friends. And, they said, "It was like having a family." "Like family"— unfortunately, that says it all.

The system perpetuates itself as these young men father children whom they have no intention of caring for, by women whose welfare checks support them. Teenage girls, mired in the same hopelessness, lack sufficient motive to say no to this trap.

Answers to our problems won't be easy.

We can start by dismantling a welfare system that encourages dependency and subsidizes broken families. We can attach conditions—such as school attendance, or work—to welfare. We can limit the time a recipient gets benefits. We can stop penalizing marriage for welfare mothers. We can enforce child support payments.

Ultimately, however, marriage is a moral issue that requires cultural consensus, and the use of social sanctions. Bearing babies irresponsibly is, simply, wrong. Failing to support children one has fathered is wrong. We must be unequivocal about this.

[Influence of TV]

It doesn't help matters when prime time TV has Murphy Brown—a character who supposedly epitomizes today's intelligent, highly paid, professional woman—mocking the importance of fathers, by bearing a child alone, and calling it just another "lifestyle choice."

I know it is not fashionable to talk about moral values, but we need to do it. Even though our cultural leaders in Hollywood, network TV, the national newspapers routinely jeer at them, I think that most of us in this room know that some things are good, and other things are wrong. Now it's time to make the discussion public.

It's time to talk again about family, hard work, integrity and personal responsibility. We cannot be embarrassed out of our belief that two parents, married to each other, are better in most cases for children than one. That honest work is better than hand-outs—or crime. That we are our brothers' keepers. That it's worth making an effort, even when the rewards aren't immediate.

So I think the time has come to renew our public commitment to our Judeo-Christian values—in our churches and synagogues, our civic organizations and our schools. We are, as our children recite each morning, "one nation under God." That's a useful framework for acknowledging a duty and an authority higher than our own pleasures and personal ambitions.

If we lived more thoroughly by these values, we would live in a better society. For the poor, renewing these values will give people the strength to help themselves by acquiring the tools to achieve self-sufficiency, a good education, job training, and property. Then they will move from permanent dependence to dignified independence.

Shelby Steele, in his great book, *The Content of Our Character*, writes,

"Personal responsibility is the brick and mortar of power. The responsible person knows that the quality of his life is something that he will have to make inside the limits of his fate.... The quality of his life will pretty much reflect his efforts."

I believe that the Bush Administration's empowerment agenda will help the poor gain that power, by creating opportunity, and letting people make the choices that free citizens must make.

Though our hearts have been pained by the events in Los Angeles, we should take this tragedy as an opportunity for self-examination and progress. So let the national debate roar on. I, for one, will join it. The president will lead it. The American people will participate in it. And as a result, we will become an even stronger nation.

BUSH NEWS CONFERENCE

... **Q.** Lets get it over with, sir—Murphy Brown. [*Laughter*]

Q. —Vice President Quayle's criticism of Murphy Brown, and also his statement that a lack of family values led to the L.A. riots?

The President. Everybody give me a Murphy Brown question. I've got one answer right here for you. [*Laughter*] What's your Murphy Brown question?

Q. What's your answer?

The President. What's the question? You're getting four different questions.

Q. Do you agree that she's not a good role model?

Q. Can a TV sitcom really influence a legitimate—

The President. All right, are you ready for the answer?

Q. Yes.

The President. All right, this is the last Murphy Brown question.

Q. Maybe.

The President. This is the last Murphy Brown answer, put it that way. [*Laughter*]

No, I believe that children should have the benefit of being born into families where the mother and a father will give them love and care and attention all their lives. I spoke on this family point in Notre Dame the other day. I talked to Barbara about it a lot, and we both feel strongly that that is the best environment in which to raise kids. It's not always possible, but that's the best environment. I think it results in giving a kid the best shot at the American dream, incidentally. It's a certain discipline, a certain affection. One of the things that concerns me deeply is the fact that there are an awful lot of broken families. So that's really the kind of guidance I would place on that. I'm not going to get into the details of a very popular television show....

The Prime Minister. I'll be happy to take these domestic questions at—

Q. Murphy Brown was more important, sir?

The Prime Minister. I didn't take Murphy Brown. Let me ask a question: Who is Murphy Brown? [Laughter]. . . .

Q. Was it a mistake for Murphy Brown to portray an unwed mother in that show?

The President. I told you. . . . I said I've just taken the last Murphy Brown question and tried to put it in a serious context that I hope the American people can understand. That's it. . . .

BUSH AND COURT ON RETURN
OF HAITIAN REFUGEES
May 24, July 29, 1992

In a highly controversial action on May 24, President George Bush halted the entrance into the United States of Haitians seeking political asylum. By executive order he authorized the U.S. Coast Guard to begin repatriating boatloads of people attempting to escape Haiti's oppressive economic and political conditions.

Two months later, on July 29, a federal appeals court declared that Bush had acted illegally. Federal courts rarely overturn a president's action, but in this case, the court said, a 1980 law clearly states that the United States "may not return aliens to their persecutors."

The court granted an injunction preventing the Coast Guard from returning any Haitian "whose life or freedom would be threatened." The Justice Department promptly sought a reversal from the Supreme Court, which on August 1 allowed the Bush administration policy to remain in effect until it decides whether to rule on the policy's legality. Justices Harry Blackmun and John Paul Stevens dissented from the decision to allow the temporary continuation.

In the first few weeks after it took effect, the administration's turn-back policy caused a sharp drop in the number of Haitians attempting the risky boat trip. Their immediate destination was Guantanamo Bay, the only remaining U.S. military installation on the island of Cuba, but most of them hoped to be allowed to enter the United States.

A press release accompanying the May 24 executive order cited the necessity of protecting "the lives of the Haitians, whose boats are not equipped for the 600-mile sea journey." The order empowered the secretary of state to make "appropriate arrangements" with all involved foreign governments to prevent further illegal migrations and instructed that the Coast Guard be provided with guidelines for further interdiction and return of "undocumented aliens."

Coup and Embargo

The exodus resulted from a September 30, 1991, violent coup that ousted Haiti's democratically elected president, Jean Bertrand Aristide, who was replaced by a harsh and repressive military dictatorship headed by Gen. Raoul Cedras. Responding to reports of widespread harassment, intimidation, and terrorism throughout the country, the thirty-four-member Organization of American States (OAS) voted in October to impose a trade embargo on Haiti. The OAS action was designed to extract from the ruling junta a pledge to restore constitutional government to a country that had suffered a long history of despotic rule and extreme poverty. But the effort was only partially successful; the junta remained uncompromising, and other nations, among them those in the European Community, continued to deliver supplies—particularly oil (which directly supported the military)—to the beleaguered country. Meanwhile, confronted with increasingly severe economic and political conditions, thousands of desperate Haitians began to flee their homeland.

Meeting on May 17, 1992, members of the OAS unanimously adopted a resolution on measures intended to tighten the embargo. Henceforth, all ships that continued to deliver oil and other products to Haiti would be barred from all other harbors in the hemisphere. The organization stopped short of instituting other sanctions, however, such as calling for a ban on commercial passenger flights to and from Haiti or severing diplomatic relations.

Noting that there had been "a lot of leakage" in the October embargo, U.S. Deputy Secretary of State Lawrence Eagleburger expressed support for the OAS resolution but also noted that more stringent enforcement could damage Haiti's economic climate to a degree that would promote serious increases in the number of Haitian refugees. "You're on the horns of a dilemma, but you can't sit there and do nothing," he said.

Refugee Deluge

Soon after the coup, the U.S. base at Guantanamo Bay was inundated with Haitian refugees. Most had escaped on boats so rickety and crowded that Coast Guard spokesmen referred to them as "unseaworthy," placing many of the passengers in "imminent danger."

Despite the risks, the number of Haitians arriving at Guantanamo rose from almost 6,000 in March 1992 to more than 8,000 in mid-May. As of May 22, 34,560 refugees had been lodged at Guantanamo for temporary periods; 13,524 were returned to Haiti; 1,176 were being held on Coast Guard cutters; and 6,691 were allowed to immigrate under U.S. regulations governing political refugee status, which allowed immigration for refugees who would face severe persecution if repatriated.

Executive Order and Aftermath

The mass flight of refugees created an embroglio for the U.S. government. On a single day in May, for example, the Coast Guard rescued a thousand Haitians on boats and transported them to Guantanamo Bay. Government officials expressed concern that the situation was becoming intolerable in the refugee tent camps on the base; facilities were inadequate, and disease and weather-related dangers loomed large. Officers from the Immigration and Naturalization Service said about 30 percent of the refugees had a credible case for entering the United States on grounds of political asylum. State and Defense Department officials contended that the estimate was inflated.

Noting that eighteen Haitians had perished off the Cuban coast in one week alone, the White House press release stated that "both the temporary processing facility at the U.S. Naval base Guantanamo and the Coast Guard cutters on patrol are filled to capacity." The administration's action seemed to have had an effect, albeit controversial. The State Department reported that the number of Haitians intercepted daily peaked at 1,074 on May 29 and declined thereafter until June 3, when no refugees were intercepted.

The embargo, and the repatriation of Haitians fleeing its effects, drew fire from several human rights organizations, which contended that the rejection and return of refugees violated existing United Nations conventions protecting refugees from forced repatriation. Joseph Eldridge of the Lawyers Committee for Human Rights said the strategy of forced repatriation was "unconscionable" and violated the UN Convention of Civil and Political Rights. Perhaps anticipating such objections, Bush's executive order noted: "The international legal obligations of the United States under the United Nations Protocol Relating to the Status of Refugees . . . do not extend to persons located outside the territory of the United States."

In early June the State Department asked members of the OAS to consider supporting a mission to oversee the return of a constitutional government in Haiti and measures to provide security for the country's citizens. If the OAS was unable to provide such a force, the UN might be regarded as an alternative, the department suggested. Sanctions against Haiti would be lifted if this proposal was accepted, OAS officials said. But, under pressure from his soldiers, Cedras continued to reject an agreement that might lead to the reinstatement of Aristide, who had pledged to reform and discipline the military.

Appeals Court Decision

The U.S. Court of Appeals for the 2d Circuit in New York split 2-1 in its highly unusual ruling against the president. The lone dissenter was Judge John M. Walker, Jr., a cousin of Bush's.

Overturning a lower court, the appeals court agreed with the Haitians' lawyers that the 1980 U.S. law applied to boat interceptions in international waters. One attorney, Michael Ratner of the Center for Constitutional Rights, said that it was a "historic, incredible opinion. The court declared a president's order illegal. How many times has that ever happened? Only a handful."

The Justice Department said the administration stood by its policy, fearing that the court's action might lure more Haitians into "embarking on dangerous journeys on the high seas in the false hope of reaching the United States."

Following are the executive order issued May 24, 1992, by President George Bush on the interdiction of illegal aliens from Haiti, the White House press release issued the same day, and excerpts from the July 29, 1992, decision of the U.S. Court of Appeals for the 2d Circuit holding that the executive order violated the Immigration and Nationality Act:

EXECUTIVE ORDER

Interdiction of Illegal Aliens

By the authority vested in me as President by the Constitution and the laws of the United States of America, including sections 212(f) and 215(a)(1) of the Immigration and Nationality Act, as amended (8 U.S.C. 1182(f) and 1185(a)(1)), and whereas:

(1) The President has authority to suspend the entry of aliens coming by sea to the United States without necessary documentation, to establish reasonable rules and regulations regarding, and other limitations on, the entry or attempted entry of aliens into the United States, and to repatriate aliens interdicted beyond the territorial sea of the United States;

(2) The international legal obligations of the United States under the United Nations Protocol Relating to the Status of Refugees (U.S. T.I.A.S. 6577; 19 U.S.T. 6223) to apply Article 33 of the United National Convention Relating to the Status of Refugees do not extend to persons located outside the territory of the United States;

(3) Proclamation No. 4865 suspends the entry of all undocumented aliens into the United States by the high seas; and

(4) There continues to be a serious problem of persons attempting to come to the United States by sea without necessary documentation and otherwise illegally;

I, GEORGE BUSH, President of the United States of America, hereby order as follows:

Section 1. The Secretary of State shall undertake to enter into, on behalf of the United States, cooperative arrangements with appropriate foreign governments for the purpose of preventing illegal migration to the United States by sea.

Sec. 2. (a) The Secretary of the Department in which the Coast Guard is operating, in consultation, where appropriate, with the Secretary of Defense, the Attorney General, and the Secretary of State, shall issue appropriate instructions to the Coast Guard in order to enforce the suspension of the entry of undocumented aliens by sea and the interdiction of any defined vessel carrying such aliens.

(b) Those instructions shall apply to any of the following defined vessels:

(1) Vessels of the United States, meaning any vessel documented or numbered pursuant to the laws of the United States, or owned in whole or in part by the United States, a citizen of the United States, or a corporation incorporated under the laws of the United States or any State, Territory, District, Commonwealth, or possession thereof, unless the vessel has been granted nationality by a foreign nation in accord with Article 5 of the Convention on the High Seas of 1958 (U.S. T.I.A.S. 5200; 13 U.S.T. 2312).

(2) Vessels without nationality or vessels assimilated to vessels without nationality in accordance with paragraph (2) of Article 6 of the Convention on the High Seas of 1958 (U.S. T.I.A.S. 5200; 13 U.S.T. 2312).

(3) Vessels of foreign nations with whom we have arrangements authorizing the United States to stop and board such vessels.

(c) Those instructions to the Coast Guard shall include appropriate directives providing for the Coast Guard:

(1) To stop and board defined vessels, when there is reason to believe that such vessels are engaged in the irregular transportation of persons or violations of United States law or the law of a country with which the United States has an arrangement authorizing such action.

(2) To make inquiries of those on board, examine documents and take such actions as are necessary to carry out this order.

(3) To return the vessel and its passengers to the country from which it came, or to another country, when there is reason to believe that an offense is being committed against the United States immigration laws, or appropriate laws of a foreign country with which we have an arrangement to assist; provided, however, that the Attorney General, in his unreviewable discretion, may decide that a person who is a refugee will not be returned without his consent.

(d) These actions, pursuant to this section, are authorized to be undertaken only beyond the territorial sea of the United States.

Sec. 3. This order is intended only to improve the internal management of the Executive Branch. Neither this order nor any agency guidelines, procedures, instructions, directives, rules or regulations implementing this order shall create, or shall be construed to create, any right or benefit, substantive or procedural (including without limitation any right or benefit under the Administrative Procedure Act), legally enforceable by any party against the United States, its agencies or instrumentalities, officers, employees, or any other person. Nor shall this order be construed to require any procedures to determine whether a person is a refugee.

Sec. 4. Executive Order No. 12324 is hereby revoked and replaced by this order.

Sec. 5. This order shall be effective immediately.

GEORGE BUSH

THE WHITE HOUSE

PRESS RELEASE

President Bush has issued an executive order which will permit the U.S. Coast Guard to begin returning Haitians picked up at sea directly to Haiti. This action follows a large surge in Haitian boat people seeking to enter the United States and is necessary to protect the lives of the Haitians, whose boats are not equipped for the 600-mile sea journal.

The large number of Haitian migrants has led to a dangerous and unmanageable situation. Both the temporary processing facility at the U.S. Naval base Guantanamo and the Coast Guard cutters on patrol are filled to capacity. The President's action will also allow continued orderly processing of more than 12,000 Haitians presently at Guantanamo.

Through broadcasts on the Voice of America and public statements in the Haitian media we continue to urge Haitians not to attempt the dangerous sea journey to the United States. Last week alone eighteen Haitians perished when their vessel capsized off the Cuban coast.

Under current circumstances, the safety of Haitians is best assured by remaining in their country. We urge any Haitians who fear persecution to avail themselves of our refugee processing service at our Embassy in Port-au-Prince. The Embassy has been processing refugee claims since February. We utilize this special procedure in only four countries in the world. We are prepared to increase the American embassy staff in Haiti for refugee processing if necessary.

The United States Coast Guard has picked up over 34,000 since the coup in Haiti last September 30. Senior U.S. officials are seeking the assistance of other countries and the United Nations to help deal with the plight of Haitian boat people, and we will continue our intensive efforts to find alternative solutions to avoid further tragedies on the high seas.

The President has also directed an intensification of our ongoing humanitarian assistance efforts in Haiti. Our current programs total 47 million dollars and provide food for over 600,000 Haitians and health care services which reach nearly two million. We hope other nations will also increase their humanitarian assistance as called for in the resolution on Haiti passed by the OAS Foreign Ministers on May 17.

No. 2023

Gene McNary, Commissioner, Immigration and Naturalization Service; et al.	August Term 1991
v.	Decided:
Haitian Centers Council, Inc.; et al.	Docket No. 92-6144

[Argued: June 26, 1992]

BEFORE: NEWMAN, PRATT, and WALKER, *Circuit Judges.*

Appeal from an order of the United States District Court for the Eastern District of New York, Sterling Johnson, Jr., *Judge,* denying plaintiffs' motion to preliminarily enjoin defendants from returning to Haiti any interdicted Haitian "whose life or freedom would be threatened on account of his race, religion, nationality, membership of a particular social group or political opinion."

We reverse the order of the district court and remand with a direction to grant the injunction requested by plaintiffs.

Judge Newman, with whom Judge Pratt joins, concurs in a separate opinion.

Judge Walker dissents in a separate opinion. . . .

PRATT, *Circuit Judge:*

On May 23, 1992, President George Bush issued an executive order which allowed the Coast Guard to intercept boatloads of Haitian refugees at sea and to return them to their persecutors in Haiti. The narrow issue we decide on this appeal is whether the government's actions, taken to implement this order, comport with § 243(h)(1) of the Immigration and Nationality Act, 8 U.S.C. § 1253(h)(1). We hold that they do not. . . .

On May 28, 1992, plaintiffs sought a temporary restraining order before Judge Johnson, challenging the actions under the new policy as *ultra vires,* as well as violative of (1) § 243(h)(1) of the INA, (2) Article 33 of the 1954 Convention relating to the Status of Refugees, (3) the 1981 U.S.-Haiti Executive Agreement, (4) the Administrative Procedure Act, and (5) the equal protection component of the fifth amendment's due process clause. The district court held a hearing, at which the plaintiffs presented not only evidence demonstrating the heightened political repression currently occurring in Haiti, but also evidence that specific plaintiffs who had been returned have since been abused, were tortured, and were hiding in fear of their lives.

Judge Johnson construed the plaintiffs' motion as one for a preliminary injunction. Although he called the United States' actions "unconscionable", "particularly hypocritical", and "a cruel hoax", he nonetheless denied the injunction. Relying on his prior decision that the right to counsel under 8 U.S.C. § 1362 and 8 C.F.R. § 208.9 is limited to aliens found in the United states, Judge Johnson concluded that "Section 243(h) is similarly unavailable as a source of relief for Haitian aliens in international waters." He also concluded that although "[o]n its face, Article 33 imposes a mandatory duty upon contracting states such as the United States not to return refugees to countries in which they face political persecution", our prior decision in *Bertrand* v. *Sava* (1982) held that the Convention's provisions are not self-executing; thus, Judge Johnson felt he could not grant plaintiffs the requested relief. He did not address the other issues raised by the plaintiffs....

Discussion

Although this is an appeal from the denial of a preliminary injunction, only questions of law are presented, and our usual *de novo* review applies. There is no challenge to Judge Johnson's finding that "the Plaintiffs undeniably make a substantial showing of irreparable harm"; thus, if the district court's view of the law was incorrect, then an injunction should issue.

On appeal, the plaintiffs wield the full arsenal of arguments that they wielded in the district court—§ 243(h) of the INA, Article 33 of the Refugee Convention, the 1981 U.S.-Haiti agreement, the APA, and the fifth amendment's equal protection component. The government addresses each of these contentions, and adds two of their own: (1) that since the subject plaintiffs are now back in Haiti, they stand in the same position as the "screened-out" plaintiffs in a similar federal action commenced in Florida, and are thus bound under principles of collateral estoppel by the eleventh circuit's holding in *Haitian Refugee Center, Inc.* v. *Baker* (1992); and that the executive order falls within the President's constitutional powers as commander-in-chief and his inherent authority over foreign relations, and was issued "pursuant to an express or implied authorization of Congress." *Youngstown Sheet & Tube Co.* v. *Sawyer* (1952) (Jackson, J., concurring).

We address the dispositive contentions in turn.

[A omitted]

B. *Section 243*(h)*(1) of the INA*
  Before 1980, § 243(h) of the INA read as follows:

> The Attorney General is authorized to withhold deportation of any alien within the United States to any country in which in his opinion the alien would be subject to persecution on account of race, religion, or political opinion and for such period of time he deems to be necessary for such reason.

In 1980 this section was replaced by a new § 243(h)....

> The Attorney General shall not deport or return any alien ... to a country if the Attorney general determines that such aliens's life or freedom would be threatened in such country on account of race, religion, nationality, membership in a particular social group, or political opinion.

8 U.S.C. § 1253(h)(1). This new statute makes the following textual changes: it strips the attorney general of the discretion formerly granted him under the old § 243(h) and makes his obligations under this new section mandatory; it applies now to "any alien", rather than "any alien within the United States"; and instead of authorizing the attorney general to "withhold deportation", it states that he shall not deport or return" an alien found to have been threatened by persecution.

These amendments to this statute present us with two problems of construction and interpretation. First, we must determine whether Haitians intercepted in international waters fall within the scope of "any alien" in § 243(h)(1). If so, we must turn to the second problem: whether intercepting Haitians in international waters and returning them to Haiti constitutes the "return" of an alien, conduct that would be impermissible under § 243(h)(1).

1. Congress has already resolved the first problem for us, for in § 101a(a)(3) of the INA, 8 U.S.C. § 1101(a)(3), it has provided that, as used in the INA, "[t]he term 'alien' means any person not a citizen or national of the United States." The plain language of this provision makes clear that aliens are aliens, regardless of where they are located. Since the words of the statute are unambiguous, " 'judicial inquiry is complete.' " *Connecticut Nat'l Bank* v. *Germain* (1992) (quoting *Rubin* v. *United States* (1981)). In light of this congressional definition, the plaintiffs in this case, who are citizens of Haiti, not of the United states, are plainly designated by the term "any alien", used by congress in § 243(h)(1).

Since the plain language of § 243(h)(1) and § 101(a)(3) appears to resolve the first statutory problem before us, we may turn to other canons of construction only to determine whether there is a "clearly expressed legislative intention" contrary to that language, which would require us to question the virtually-conclusive presumption that congress meant what it said.... The government nevertheless tenders numerous reasons—the presumption against extraterritorial application, an assertedly inconsistent provision in § 243(h)(2)(C), § 243's placement in part V of the INA, and other provisions of the INA which expressly limit their application to aliens "within the United States"—to support its argument that § 243(h)(1) does not apply to these plaintiffs. We reject all of these arguments, none of which is sufficient to overcome the plain language of § 243(h)(1).

First, the presumption that laws of the United States have no extraterritorial application has no relevance in the present context. That presumption is a canon of construction "whereby *unexpressed* congressional intent may be ascertained", *Foley Bros., Inc.* v. *Filardo* (1949) (emphasis added), which "serves to protect against unintended clashes between our laws and those of other nations which could result in international discord." *EEOC* v. *Arabian American Oil Co.* (1991). But congress knew "how to place the high seas within the jurisdictional reach of a statute", *Argentine Republic* v. *Amerada Hess Shipping Corp.* (1989), and it did so here by making § 243(h)(1) apply to "any alien" without regard to location. Additionally, comity is of reduced concern here, as the Haitians are being intercepted in international (i.e., non-sovereign) waters. We are thus not faced with the spectre of forum-shopping refugees coming into United States courts in order to enforce some right that courts in Haiti would not recognize; on the contrary, § 243(h)(1) may be invoked only in United States courts, and only against the United States government. Only when the United States itself acts extraterritorially does § 243(h)(1) have extraterritorial application. Absent proactive government intervention of the sort presented here, § 243(h)(1)'s ban on "return" of aliens to their persecutors could not be invoked by persons located outside the borders of the United States.

Second, the government points us to § 243(h)(2)(C) of the INA, which directs that the provisions of § 243(h)(1) shall not apply if "there are serious reasons for considering that the alien has committed a serious nonpolitical crime outside the United States prior to the arrival of the alien in the United States." 8 U.S.C. § 1253(h)(2)(C). The government argues that the language "prior to the arrival of the alien in the United States" means that § 243(h)(1) cannot apply to these plaintiffs, who have not arrived in the United States. We disagree.

To accept the government's reading of the statute, we would, in effect, be reading the words "within the United States" back into § 243(h)(1), which would counter congress's plainly expressed intent to eliminate those limiting words in 1980. The Supreme Court only recently reminded us of "the canon of statutory construction requiring a change in language to be read, if possible, to have some effect, see *e.g.*, *Brewster* v. *Gage* (1930); 2A N. Singer, Sutherland Statutory Construction § 46.06 (5th ed. 1992)." *American Nat'l Red Cross* v. *S.G.* (1992). Our reading, on the other hand, gives full vitality to all portions of § 243(h), as actually written by congress. True, the "serious nonpolitical crime" exception in § 243(h)(2)(C) does not apply to an alien who has not arrived in the United States, but that seems to be precisely what congress meant to accomplish. Not only is that the way they worded the exception, but it also comports with common sense. The United States would have a strong domestic interest in keeping alien criminals out of its territory (and out of its prisons), and a strong foreign policy interest in refraining from granting safe haven to nonpolitical criminals fleeing from other countries.

Before 1980, § 243(h) distinguished between two groups of aliens: those "within the United States", and all others. After 1980, § 243(h)(1) no longer recognized that distinction, although § 243(h)(2)(C) preserves it for the limited purposes of the "serious nonpolitical crime" exception. The government's reading would require us to rewrite § 243(h)(1) into its pre-

1980 status, but we may not add terms or provisions where congress has omitted them, *see, Gregory* v. *Ashcroft; West Virginia Univ. Hosps., Inc.* v. *Casey* (1991), and this restraint is even more compelling when congress has specifically removed a term from a statute: "Few principles of statutory construction are more compelling than the proposition that Congress does not intend *sub silentio* to enact statutory language that it has earlier discarded". *Nachman Corp.* v. *Pension Benefit Guaranty Corp.* (1980) (Stewart, J., dissenting) (quoted with approval in *INS* v. *Cardoza-Fonseca.* "To supply omissions transcends the judicial function." *Iselin* v. *United States* (1926) (Brandeis, J.).

The third reason urged by the government for not reading the statute literally, is that § 243(h)(1) is located in Part V of the INA. This argument similarly fails. Part V of the INA deals primarily with deportation and adjustment of status. The eleventh circuit relied on this fact—almost exclusively—to conclude that "[t]he provisions of Part V of the INA dealing with deportation only apply to aliens 'in the United States.'" *HRC* v. *Baker,* 953 F.2d at 1510 (citing, *inter alia,* 8 U.S.C. §§ 1251, 1253(a)). Putting aside the fact that it ignores the plain language of § 243(h), this argument ascribes entirely unwarranted weight to the location of the provision: of course, the provisions of Part V "dealing with deportation" must apply only to aliens "in the United States", since an alien must be "in" the "port" of a country in order to be "de-ported" from it. . . .

The statute's location in Part V reflects its original placement there before 1980—when § 243(h) applied by its terms only to "deportation". Since 1980, however, § 243(h)(1) has applied to more than just "deportation"—it applies to "return" as well (the former is necessarily limited to aliens "in the United States", the latter applies to all aliens). Thus, § 243, which applies to all aliens, regardless of whereabouts, has broader application than most other portions of Part V, each of which is limited by its terms to aliens "in" or "within" the United States; but the fact that § 243 is surrounded by sections more limited in application has no bearing on the proper reading of § 243 itself. If anything, it has an effect opposite to what the government suggests: it tends to prove that if congress had meant to limit § 243(h)(1)'s scope to aliens "in the United States", it surely knew how to do that. " ' "[W]here Congress includes particular language in one section of a statute but omits it in another section of the same Act, it is generally presumed that Congress acts intentionally and purposely in the disparate inclusion or exclusion." ' " *INS* v. *Cardoza-Fonseca* (citations omitted).

Lastly, we reject the government's suggestion that since § 243(h) restricts actions of only the attorney general, the President might in any event assign the same "return" function to some other government official. Congress understood that the President's agent for dealing with immigration matters is the attorney general, *see* 8 U.S.C. § 1103(a); *cf. Kleindienst* v. *Mandel* (1972), and we would find it difficult to believe that the proscription of § 243(h)(1)—returning an alien to his persecutors—was forbidden if done by the attorney general but permitted if done by some other arm of the executive branch.

In sum on this point, the district court erred in concluding that § 243(h)(1) does not apply to aliens outside the United States. By drawing its conclusion from its earlier right-to-counsel ruling, the district court failed to appreciate the differences in the plain language of the two statutes. The INA's right-to-counsel provision, 8 U.S.C. § 1362, applies to "the person concerned" in "any exclusion or deportation proceeding[]", whereas, as we have already noted, § 243(h)(1) applies by its terms to a much broader class of persons—all "aliens", no matter where located.

2. Having concluded that § 243(h)(1) applies to all "aliens", we must face the other textual problem posed by the statute: whether the government's interception and forcible repatriation of Haitian refugees constitutes a "return" of those refugees to their persecutors in violation of § 243(h)(1). We conclude that it does.

Section 243(h)(1) prohibits the government from both *deporting* and *returning* an alien. Virtually all prior litigation under this subsection has focused on the term "deport"; not until the executive's recent actions in "reaching out" to repatriate Haitians has litigation attention shifted to the term "return", which is nowhere defined in the INA. Since congress provided no special definition, we must interpret § 243(h)(1) by "giving the 'words used' their 'ordinary meaning'". *Moskal* v. *United States,* (1962). The rule is no different for the INA: we " 'assume "that the legislative purpose is expressed by the ordinary meaning of the words used." ' " *INS* v. *Phinpathya* (1984) (citations omitted).

Congress directed that the "Attorney General shall not . . . return any alien to a country" that would persecute the alien. When used, as here, in its transitive mode, the word "return" means "to bring, send, or put (a person or thing) back to or in a former position". *Webster's Third New International Dictionary* 1941 (1971). Here, congress has amplified the meaning of "return" by adding after the word "return", the prepositional phrase "to a country [where he would be persecuted]"; significantly, congress made no mention of where the alien (who may be anywhere, within or without the United States) must be returned "from". Of parallel significance, the Kennebunkport Order itself directs the Coast Guard to "return the vessel and its passengers *to* the country from which it came". (emphasis added). As we do with congress, we presume that the President of the United States uses words with their "ordinary meaning"; thus, when the "return" directed by the President is *to* a persecuting country, it is exactly the kind of "return" that is prohibited by § 243(h)(1) of the INA.

Since the plain language of § 243(h) demonstrates that what is important is the place "to" which, not "from" which, the refugee is returned, and since § 243(h)(1) by its terms (a) applies to all "aliens" regardless of their location, and (b) prohibits their "return . . . to a country" where they would likely be persecuted, we conclude that the executive's action of reaching out into international waters, intercepting Haitian refugees, and returning them without determining whether the return is to their persecutors, violates § 243(h)(1) of the Immigration and Nationality Act.

The government does not offer a contrary view of the term "return" in § 243(h)(1), rather, it argues that the 1980 amendment to § 243(h) merely "makes the language read like article 33; which, the government assures us, prohibits the "return" only of refugees who have entered the territory of the contracting state. Thus, we must turn our attention to the government's reading of Article 33.

3. Article 33 of the Refugee Convention, which is entitled "Prohibition of expulsion or return ('refoulement')", reads:

> 1. No Contracting State shall expel or return (*"refouler"*) a refugee in any manner whatsoever to the frontiers of territories where his life or freedom would be threatened on account of his race, religion, nationality, membership of a particular social group or political opinion.

> 2. The benefits of the present provision may not, however, be claimed by a refugee whom there are reasonable grounds for regarding as a danger to the security of the country in which he is, or who, having been convicted by a final judgment of a particularly serious crime, constitutes a danger to the community of that country.

United Nations Convention relating to the Status of Refugees, 189 U.N.T.S. 150, 176 (1954). Although the United States was not a party to the original Refugee Convention, the provisions of that Convention were nonetheless ratified by the United States when it acceded to the 1967 Protocol relating to the Status of Refugees ("Protocol").

The Supreme Court has recognized "that one of Congress' primary purposes [in passing the Refugee Act of 1980] was to bring United States refugee law into conformance with the 1967 United Nations Protocol Relating to the Status of Refugees, ... to which the United States acceded in 1968." *INS.* v. *Cardoza-Fonseca....*

As with statutes, treaties are to be construed first with reference to their terms' "ordinary meaning ... in their context", and "in light of their object and purpose." Vienna Convention, art. 31(1). The plain meaning of treaty terms controls " 'unless "application of the words of the treaty according to their obvious meaning effects a result inconsistent with the intent or expectations of its signatories." ' " *United States* v. *Stuart* (citations omitted). To stray from clear treaty language, there must be "extraordinarily strong contrary evidence." *Sumitomo Shoji America, Inc.* v. *Avagliano* (1982). According to article 32 of the Vienna Convention, "supplementary means of interpretation", which consist primarily of the preparatory and conclusory circumstances of a treaty (the interpertation enumerated in Article 31 of the Vienna Convention "leave [] the meaning ambiguous or obscure" or lead to an "manifestly absurd or unreasonable result."

The plain language of Article 33.1 of the Refugee Convention leads us to conclude that, just as with § 243(h)(1), the word "return" means "return", without regard to where the refugee is to be returned *from,* and, just as with 243(h)(1), what *is* important under Article 33.1 is where the refugee is to be returned *to.* The Protocol's definition of "refugee" is extremely persuasive on this point. Under the Protocol, a "refugee" is "any person who . . . owing to a well-founded fear of being persecuted . . . is outside the country of his nationality". Thus, a "refugee" under the Protocol, just as with "any alien" under § 243(h)(1) of the INA, is defined not with regard to his current location but with regard to his past location.

Article 33.1's prohibition against "return" plainly applies to *all* refugees, regardless of location. This reading is borne out by the language used in other articles of the Refugee Convention that have a more limiting effect on the term "refugee". . . . The government's position, that Article 33.1 applies only to refugees who have entered the territory of the contracting state, is therefore untenable in view of the plain language of that section. Had the parties to the Refugee Convention meant to limit its application in that way, we would expect a wording of that section in line with, for instance, Article ("refugees within their territories"). But the contracting states did not so limit Article 33.1; instead, the term "a refugee" in Article 33.1 encompasses all "refugees". *Accord* Office of the United Nations High Commissioner for Refugees, *Handbook on Procedures and Criteria for Determining Refugee Status* 9 (1979) ("A person is a refugee within the meaning of the 1951 Convention as soon as he fulfills the criteria contained in the definition. This would necessarily occur prior to the time at which his refugee status is formally determined.").

This reading of Article 33.1 is further supported by the "object and purpose" not only of that article, but also of the Refugee Convention as a whole. It is clear that the purpose of Article 33.1 is to prevent all "refugees", "in any manner whatsoever", from being put into the hands of those who would persecute them. One of the considerations stated in the Preamble to the Convention is that the United Nations has "endeavoured to assure refugees the widest possible exercise of . . . fundamental rights and freedoms." The government's offered reading of Article 33.1, however, would narrow the exercise of those freedoms, since refugees in transit, but not present in a sovereign area, could freely be returned to their persecutors. This would hardly provide refugees with "the widest possible exercise" of fundamental human rights, and would indeed render Article 33.1 "a cruel hoax". . . .

C. Article II Powers and Other Justifications for the Kennebunkport Order

Finally, the government offers numerous reasons why the summary return of Haitians is authorized by law. We find none of these arguments sufficient to overcome the will of congress as expressed in § 243(h)(1) of the INA, for "[w]hen the President takes measures incompatible with the expressed or implied will of Congress, his power is at its lowest ebb, for then he can rely only upon his own constitutional powers minus any constitutional powers of Congress over the matter". *Youngstown Sheet & Tube Co. v. Sawyer.*

The government suggests that both the President's constitutional position as "Commander in Chief of the Army and Navy of the United States", U.S. Const. art. II, § 2, cl. 1, and his "inherent authority as ' "the sole organ of the nation in its external relations" ' ", Brief for the United States at 27 (quoting *United States* v. *Curtiss-Wright Export Corp.* (Mar. 7, 1899)), justify the Kennebunkport Order. We disagree.

The Supreme Court said, in *United States ex. rel. Knauff* v. *Shaughnessy* (1950), that "[t]he exclusion of aliens is a fundamental act of sovereignty. The right to do so stems not alone from legislative power but is inherent in the executive power to control the foreign affairs of the nation." But the reason for that rule is absent here, for this case does not deal with the sovereign right "to turn back from our gates any alien or class of aliens." *Id.* at 550 (Jackson, J., dissenting). To the contrary, when seized, these aliens were far from, and by no means necessarily heading for, our gates.

Similarly, we reject the government's arguments that §§ 212(f) and 215(a)(1) of the INA, which allow the President to "suspend the entry of all aliens or any class of aliens" and to place such "reasonable rules, regulations . . . limitations and exceptions" on the entry of aliens as he deems appropriate, also allow him to order the summary return to their persecutors of aliens intercepted on the high seas. The President's power to regulate "entry" into the United States is not questioned on this appeal. Even through the executive's actions have the practical effect of prohibiting some Haitians' entry into the United States, they also have the effect of prohibiting the Haitians from gaining entry into the Bahamas, Jamaica, Cuba, Mexico, the Cayman Islands, or any other country in which they might seek safe haven. By enforcing the INA's prohibition against forcible return of refugees, we leave unimpaired the President's authority to regulate entry into this country.

The government says that this is "an absurd result", since, under this reading, "the President could authorize the Coast Guard to block the path of Haitian vessels sailing toward Miami and force them back to sea without regard for their safety, but could not return them to land." Brief for United States at 30. We do not see the absurdity. This argument fails because it embraces two unwarranted assumptions—one express, the other not. While some intercepted Haitians may in fact be heading for Miami, some may also be heading toward other nations. The government's actions prevent the Haitians from seeking asylum in *any* country. Also, the unstated premise—that returning these Haitians to their persecutors is somehow "in regard for their safety"—is itself absurd.

Likewise, while the President is entitled to lead the country's external relations, he apparently did not view the Kennebunkport Order as addressing a foreign policy concern; on the contrary, the executive order specifically states that it was "intended only to improve the internal management of the Executive Branch." Exec. Order 12,807, 57 Fed. Reg. at 23,134. In any event, congress, wielding its "complete", "plenary" legislative power over immigration matters, *see Oceanic Navigation Co.* v. *Stranahan* (1909); *Boutelier* v. *INS* (1967), has spoken directly at the question at issue so that "[t]his is a job for the Nation's lawmakers, not for its military authorities." *Youngstown Sheet & Tube Co.* v. *Sawyer*. Similarly, we reject any suggestion that the Kennebunkport Order was issued "pursuant to an express or implied authorization of Congress", *id.* at 635 (Jackson, J., concurring), for we can hardly infer congress's permission for the executive to do what it *expressly* forbade him from doing by § 243(h)(1) of the INA.

The government also argues that the Kennebunkport Order draws on the authority that congress gave to the Coast Guard to compel compliance with the laws of the United States on the high seas, including the power to use "all necessary force to compel compliance." 14. U.S.C. § 89(a). According to the government, the Haitians are somehow violating the INA's prohibition on illegal entry while afloat on the international waters of the Windward Passage. This argument is perplexing at best, and in any event provides no ground for sustaining the current interdiction program.

Lastly, although not raised in so many words, there is an undercurrent in the government's brief to the effect that this case presents a "political question" which is beyond the scope of judicial decisionmaking. We strongly disagree, for this case involves a determination of whether the current interdiction program itself (a creation of an executive order and thus of law, *see Acevedo* v. *Nassau Country, NY* (1974) is consistent with a federal statute. As our discussion above amply illustrates, there exists no "lack of judicially discoverable and manageable standards" to apply. *See Baker* v. *Carr* (1962). "The federal courts may review a case such as this one to insure that 'the executive departments abide by the legislatively mandated procedures.'" *Haitian Refugee Center* v. *Gracey* (Edwards, J., concurring) (quoting *International Union of Bricklayers* v. *Meese* (D.C. Cir. 1985)).

Conclusion

The plain language of § 243(h)(1) of the Immigration and Nationality Act clearly states that the United States may not return aliens to their persecutors, no matter where in the world those actions are taken. In view of this, plaintiffs' arguments regarding the self-executing nature of Article 33.1 of the Refugee Convention are largely academic, since § 243(h)(1) provides coextensive protection.

In light of our conclusion that § 243(h)(1) prohibits the actions at issue, we need not address the plaintiffs' remaining arguments in favor of reversal. The order of the district court is reversed, and the case is remanded to the district court with instructions to enter an injunction prohibiting the defendants from returning to Haiti any interdicted Haitian whose life or freedom would be threatened on account of his or her race, religion, nationality, membership in a particular social group, or political opinion.

Reversed and remanded with instructions. The mandate shall issue forthwith.

REGULATION OF GENETICALLY ENGINEERED FOODS

May 26, 1992

In a policy statement issued May 26, the White House announced that biologically engineered foods would be regulated no differently than other foods, clearing the way for the rise of the American biotechnology industry. The $4 billion industry was expected to be worth $50 billion by the end of the decade.

A cloud of uncertainty had hovered over the biotechnology industry since the early 1980s. Until the May announcement companies had not known how their products would be regulated by the Food and Drug Administration (FDA). Companies had feared they would be required to submit each new product to the FDA for premarket testing, a complicated process that delayed product development and marketing. Potential investors had hesitated to commit capital to an industry whose future was in doubt.

The new policy, a component of President Bush's regulatory reform initiative, removed much of that uncertainty. Developed by the FDA and Vice President Dan Quayle's Council on Competitiveness, the policy required that genetically engineered foods be held to a regulatory standard no more rigorous than that governing other foods. For purposes of regulation, genetic manipulation would be considered a food additive, no different from a sweetener or a preservative. Biotechnology firms seeking to introduce a new product would not need to consult with the FDA beforehand unless the product was decidedly novel, a determination to be made by the firms themselves using FDA guidelines. Labeling of genetically engineered foods would not be required unless they posed a unique safety risk, such as causing an allergic reaction in some people.

Both the Agriculture Department and the Environmental Protection Agency planned to use the new policy as a model in developing regulations of their own. The Agriculture Department oversees food products not regulated by the FDA, including livestock, fish, and poultry. The EPA has jurisdiction over genetically engineered pesticides and disease resistant plants.

As expected, the biotechnology industry welcomed the new policy, which reflected the growing consensus in the scientific community that genetic engineering was not as dangerous as once thought. For years representatives of the industry had lobbied the government to accept a risk-based approach to regulation, as opposed to a process-based one. New products, the industry argued, should be evaluated on the basis of risk posed to consumers, with special emphasis placed on food product itself, not on the process used to make it. That an organism was produced genetically was no reason to condemn it outright, the industry said. Furthermore, there was nothing inherently risky about taking a gene from one source and implanting it in another. Genetic engineering was no different, in principle, from more conventional methods of plant breeding. Whether one manipulated genes or plant tissue, the goal was still the same: selecting for favorable characteristics to improve product quality.

Criticisms of the New Policy

Charging that the scientific community had not properly assessed the risks of biotechnology, critics of the new policy upbraided the FDA for moving too quickly and for placing excessive trust in industry. Calling for extensive premarket testing and labeling of all genetically produced foods, they questioned the wisdom of what seemed to them a policy of self-regulation. Jeremy Rifkin, president of the Washington-based Foundation on Economic Trends, filed a petition with the FDA demanding that all new genetic substances be regulated as food additives and that all genetically engineered products be labeled as such. Another critic, Margaret Mellon, the National Wildlife Federation's biotechnology expert, said the new policy put the public at risk and could be responsible for releasing dangerous organisms into the air and endangering the food supply.

The FDA downplayed the concerns of critics, reaffirming its commitment to the national health. Mechanisms were in place, it said, to prevent dangerous products from being unleashed on the public. Its safety criteria were one such mechanism. Biotechnology firms were prohibited from marketing foods that differed significantly from those already known to be safe. A significant difference was thought to exist if the product, as a result of gene splicing, contained 1) an unfamiliar toxic substance or one that heightened the levels of a naturally occurring toxicant, 2) a compound uncommon to the food supply, 3) an allergen, or an ingredient that would cause an allergic reaction in humans, or 4) a high enough concentration of important nutrients to raise safety con-

cerns. Products meeting any one of these four criteria would be subjected to rigorous premarket testing. Those that posed a significant health risk to a segment of the population, such as allergy sufferers, would likely be labeled.

As additional evidence of the policy's safety, the FDA cited the self-interest of biotechnology companies, who needed the agency's approval to gain public trust and as protection against liability. Even in the unlikely event of a dangerous product's being introduced, the FDA could immediately take it off the market.

Consumer Benefits Promised

Both the FDA and biotechnology companies argued that the benefits of genetic engineering to consumers far outweighed the costs. In exchange for regulatory relief, the industry promised better vegetables, fruits, and grains needing less fertilizer and pesticides. It also promised lower retail prices. Operating in a climate free of excessive, costly regulation (applying to the FDA for premarket approval can be a long, expensive process), companies would pass on cost savings to consumers.

More than a dozen biotechnology companies were poised to deliver nearly seventy new food products to the American market. They held out the prospect of sweeter potatoes, longer-lasting peppers, leaner pork, healthier cooking oils, drought-resistant grains, and insect-resistant cotton. One company developed a strain of corn that could be used to make fully biodegradable plastic.

In addition to plant genes, biotechnology companies experimented with genes from animals. A gene from the winter flounder that enables it to endure low temperatures was added to vegetables to prevent them from becoming mushy in cold weather. Firms did not rule out the possibility of using human genes to enhance product quality.

> *Following is the text of a fact sheet outlining the Food and Drug Administration's regulatory policy for foods developed through biotechnology, issued by the White House on May 26, 1992:*

As part of the President's regulatory reform initiative, the Administration today announced its policy for foods developed through biotechnology. This policy builds upon the Administration's "Scope Document" for biotechnology, which was released last February. The Scope Document sets forth a scientifically sound, risk-based approach for streamlining the regulation of biotechnology products.

Biotechnology is one of the most rapidly growing industries in America. Among other benefits, it has the potential to provide consumers with innovative new food products that are more nutritious, better tasting, and more resistant to cold, drought, and pests.

Until now, however, uncertainty about how the government might regulate these products has inhibited the commercialization of foods developed through biotechnology. To eliminate such uncertainty, the Food and Drug Administration (FDA) is today issuing for public comment a policy statement that clarifies its interpretation of the Federal Food, Drug, and Cosmetic Act with respect to these products.

The policy provides a "road map" that will allow the biotechnology industry to plan for the commercialization of improved food products. By providing regulatory certainty, the policy will help maintain U.S. competitiveness in both the biotechnology and the food industries.

1. The Policy. The policy statement clarifies that the standards for federal regulation of new food varieties developed through biotechnology will be the same as they are for all other foods. The policy is based upon a determination by the FDA that new biotechnology techniques do not raise new or unique safety issues that warrant additional regulatory oversight. The level of oversight should depend on the food's characteristics, not on the method by which it was derived.

- Under the new policy, FDA will not ordinarily require premarket review if the food constituents of new plant varieties are the same or substantially similar to substances currently found in other foods, such as proteins, fats, oils, and carbohydrates.

  For example, if a high quality protein already found in bananas were added to a variety of tomato, then premarket review would not be required.

- Premarket approval would be required, however, when the characteristics of these food substances raise significant safety questions so that they are not considered substantially similar to existing foods.

  For example, if a novel sweetening agent that has never been an ingredient in any other food were added to a variety of grapefruit, then premarket review would be required.

2. Benefits for Consumers and Industry. This policy will provide substantial benefits to both consumers and industry.

- It will give consumers sooner access to innovative new food products, such as vegetable oils with lower levels of saturated fat, and tomatoes that ripen more quickly, last longer, and taste better.
- It will keep the U.S. food supply among the safest in the world.
- It will enable FDA to focus its resources on products presenting legitimate safety questions without unnecessarily inhibiting innovation.
- It will enable the industry to begin to consider early in the research and development process the steps necessary to ensure food safety. The policy will do this by pointing companies toward the relevant

food safety issues that need to be considered. As with all food products, companies will continue to have the primary responsibility for ensuring food safety.

- It will demonstrate to other countries a scientifically sound, risk-based approach for the oversight of foods derived from new plant varieties. Adoption of this type of oversight by other countries will encourage international commerce in food products and discourage non-tariff trade barriers.
- It will benefit farmers by providing products that require less fertilizer and pesticides, and spoil less quickly.

CENSUS PORTRAIT OF THE NATION'S SOCIAL, ECONOMIC STATUS
May 29, 1992

The fullest economic and social portrait of the nation to emerge from the 1990 census was presented May 29 by the U.S. Bureau of the Census. It released a sheaf of statistics drawn from the responses of 17.7 million American households, one of every six, to the 1990 "long form" questionnaires. Other Americans had been asked fewer questions.

In all, the answers provided a close look at various trends in American life, from levels of income to immigration flow to commuting patterns. They showed the largest foreign-born population in history, some 19.7 million, of whom 8.6 million entered the United States in the 1980s. Moreover, 31.8 million persons above age five spoke a language other than English at home, and nearly half of them said they did not speak English "very well." Spanish was the predominant foreign tongue, spoken by 17.3 million people.

Economically as well as culturally, the United States appeared to have grown more diverse—and possibly stratified. The numbers of rich and poor increased as the middle class shrank in size. The Census Bureau reported earlier in the year that the middle-income categories accounted for 63 percent of the people in 1989, in contrast to 63 percent twenty years earlier. During that time, the high-income share of the population grew to 14.7 percent, up from 10.9. During the past decade poverty rates took a steep upward climb, especially among children and female-headed households. In 1989 some 31.7 million Americans were living in poverty, as officially defined, about 4.3 million more than in 1979. Nearly one-fifth of all American children (17.9 percent) lived in poverty, as did about one-eighth of the people sixty-five and older.

Incomes Rise But Spread Unevenly

Median household income rose to $30,056 in 1989, an increase of 6.5 percent in ten years after adjusting for higher consumer prices. Half of the American households earned more and half less. And on a per-person basis, income also rose. It went to $14,420, a ten-year increase of 17.9 percent after inflation. But much of the increased income was siphoned away by the soaring cost of housing during the 1980s. The portion of households that paid more than 30 percent of their income for housing—the "affordability" standard defined by the federal government—grew to nearly 20 percent for home owners and to more than 40 percent for renters. During the decade, the median costs of mortgages rose 27 percent above inflation, to $737 a month, and median rent prices went up 16 percent, to $447.

Moreover, the increases in income were spread unevenly across the country. Household income in Mississippi, the poorest state by that measure, was less than half what it was in Connecticut, the wealthiest. A quarter of all Mississippians lived in poverty, more than in any other state. However, the rates in several other states, mostly in the South, approached that figure. As in previous censuses, poverty was especially prevalent among blacks, Hispanics, and American Indians.

Nationally, total employment continued to grow; men and women above age fifteen held a total of 115.6 million jobs. But many of the new jobs were in low-paying service industries, while higher-paying manufacturing jobs declined. The farm population continued to shrink, accounting for 3.8 million Americans in 1990, less than 2 percent of the total.

Urban Migration Unchecked

A longstanding migration to urban areas continued. Three-fourths of the 248.7 million people recorded in the 1990 census lived in cities or their suburban surroundings. According to data cited by bureau officials in congressional testimony May 26, the proportion of the total population living in the suburbs reached a record high 46.2 percent. Suburbanites outnumbered central-city inhabitants, 115 million to 78 million.

As Americans continued to fill in the outer reaches of expanding metropolitan areas, their commuting habits remained firmly fixed on the automobile. The census showed that 73 percent of all workers drove to work alone, while 13.4 percent were in car pools. Only 5.3 percent used public transportation to get to work.

> Following are excerpts from a Bureau of the Census news release, May 29, 1992, titled "The Nation's Economic, Social, and Housing Portrait Drawn from 1990 Census Long Form":

The Commerce Department's Census Bureau today completed the release of Summary Tape File 3A that provides economic, social, and housing data from the 1990 census. Illinois, Oklahoma, Minnesota, and Wisconsin were the last states to receive their data in a distribution that started on March 19. . . .

Information provided on STF 3A is from the long-form questionnaire that was mailed to about one in six or 17.7 million housing units. These sample data are subject to sampling error and other limitations. Also, STF 3A contains only limited information for racial and Hispanic origin groups. Population and housing counts and basic characteristics for these groups from the census short-form questionnaire were released previously in STFs 1 and 2. Detailed economic, social, and housing characteristics for about 40 separate racial and Hispanic origin groups may be obtained from STF 4, scheduled for release later in 1992. Because of differences in questionnaire wording and procedures, these figures do not necessarily agree with official statistics which are based on current surveys. . . .

Social Characteristics

- Among the nation's population aged 25 and over in 1990, about 75.2 percent were at least high school graduates and 20.3 percent had at least a bachelor's degree.
- 31,844,979 persons aged 5 years and over (13.8 percent) spoke a language other than English at home, and 43.9 percent of those persons said they do not speak English "very well."
- About 7.9 percent of all persons living in the nation were foreign born.
- Among persons aged 5 years and over, 21,585,297 or 9.4 percent moved to a different state between 1985 and 1990.
- 73.2 percent of workers drove to work alone, 13.4 percent were in carpools, and 5.3 percent used public transportation to get to work.
- Median household income for the nation rose from $28,226 in 1979 to $30,056 in 1989, an increase of 6.5 percent, after adjusting for the increase in consumer prices. The 1979-1989 inflation factor is 1.676.
- Real per capita income rose from $12,226 in 1979 to $14,420 in 1989, an increase of 17.9 percent. The 1979-1989 inflation factor is 1.676.
- 65.3 percent of persons aged 16 and over were in the labor force in 1990: 74.4 percent of males compared with 56.8 percent of females. Also, 59.7 percent of mothers with children under age 6 were in the labor force.
- 6.3 percent of persons in the civilian labor force in 1990 were unemployed: 6.4 percent of males compared with 6.2 percent of females.
- The poverty rate for persons went up from 12.4 percent in 1979 to 13.1 percent in 1989, while the number of persons in poverty rose from 27,392,580 in 1979 to 31,742,864 in 1989.
- The poverty rate for related children under 18 years was 17.9 percent in 1989, while the poverty rate for persons 65 and over was 12.8 percent.
- The poverty rate for families went up to 10.0 percent in 1989 from 9.6 percent in 1979, while the number of families in poverty rose from 5,670,215 in 1979 to 6,487,515 in 1989.

- The poverty rate for families with a female householder and no spouse present was 31.1 percent in 1989.
- 11.2 percent of teenagers aged 16 to 19 were high school dropouts—not enrolled in school and not a high school graduate. Of these, about 59.6 percent were unemployed or not in the labor force.

Housing Characteristics

- A median monthly owner cost for homeowners with a mortgage was $737 in 1990, compared with $581 in 1980, an increase of 26.9 percent after adjusting for the increase in consumer prices. The comparable figures for owners without mortgages was $209 in 1990 and $206 in 1980. The 1980-1990 inflation factor is 1.588.
- 19.5 percent of homeowners had owner costs that were 30 percent or more of their household income in 1990, compared with 17.6 percent in 1980.
- The median monthly gross rent was $447 in 1990 and $385 in 1980, an increase of 16.1 percent in real terms. The 1980-1990 inflation factor is 1.588.
- 41.2 percent of renters had monthly costs that were 30 percent or more of their household income in 1990, compared with 38.9 percent in 1980.
- 20.7 percent of all housing units in the nation were built between 1980 and March 1990, while 18.4 percent were built before 1940.
- 20.9 percent of all householders moved into their homes between 1989 and March 1990, while 9.1 percent moved in before 1960.
- 51.0 percent of the nation's occupied homes were heated by utility gas, 25.8 percent by electricity, 12.2 percent by fuel oil or kerosene, and 10.5 percent by some other fuel.
- 1.1 percent of the nation's homes in 1990 lacked complete plumbing facilities.
- 1.1 percent of the nation's homes in 1990 lacked complete kitchen facilities.

All the estimates in this release are from the 1990 Decennial Census of Population and Housing. These sample data are not entirely comparable with those collected in the bureau's various surveys (such as the monthly Current Population Survey) which also yield information on labor force status, income and poverty levels, education, and so on. Differences in the data may be because of enumeration procedures, processing techniques, etc.

The user should note that these data are based on a sample, they may differ from comparable figures shown in 100-percent tabulations, and that they are subject to sampling variability and nonsampling error such as coverage error or processing error. . . .

June

GAO ON STUDENT TREATMENT
AT MILITARY ACADEMIES
June 2, 1992

In a year marked by several highly publicized incidents of sexual harassment involving Navy personnel, Congress was told June 2 that women midshipmen at Annapolis reported fewer such problems than their counterparts at the other military service academies. Appearing before the Senate Armed Services Subcommittee on Manpower and Personnel, Paul L. Jones, director of defense force management issues for the General Accounting Office (GAO), provided preliminary results of the GAO's review of hazing and other student treatment issues at the U.S. Military Academy, the U.S. Naval Academy, and the U.S. Air Force Academy. Summarizing the work to date, Jones noted that:

- *"hazing has not completely disappeared from the academies, despite prohibitions against it;*
- *"women and minorities have not reached the same level of achievement as white males in a number of areas, although we found no evidence of deliberate or systematic efforts to treat these groups differently;*
- *"sexual harassment occurs more frequently than is reported. Most students, both men and women, believe that reported harassment will be investigated and offenders appropriately punished. However, there are significant negative consequences to reporting it;*
- *"military performance systems could be improved through elimination of subjective elements; and*
- *"academy adjudicatory systems provide the minimum due process rights stipulated by the courts and some additional rights, with limitations."*

Jones testified that "the incidents of harassment are still occurring as we complete our focus groups at the academies."

Congressional interest in student treatment at the academies was provoked by several incidents that occurred at the Naval Academy in 1989 and 1990. In one, a woman complained that she had been hand-cuffed to a urinal. Subsequently, several members of Congress asked the GAO to investigate, focusing on hazing, treatment and performance of women and minorities, harassment, the effectiveness of the military performance systems, and the fairness of academies' adjudicatory sys-tems, such as the honor system.

The GAO reviewed case files and administered questionnaires to academy students, faculty, and the commandant's staff at each of the academies. The GAO also conducted focus group meetings and walk-in student meetings. The data covered the classes of 1988-91, with partial data on later classes. The review began with the Naval Academy in Annapolis in 1990 and was extended to the Air Force Academy in Colorado Springs and the Military Academy at West Point in 1991.

The preliminary findings showed that the Naval Academy had fewer incidents of sexual harassment than the two other academies. About a third of the female midshipmen surveyed in 1990 said that they had experienced some form of sexual harassment a few times a month or more, compared with 64 percent at West Point and 39 percent at the Air Force Academy. The most frequent complaints concerned derogatory comments (28 percent at the Naval Academy, 63 percent at West Point, and 40 percent at the Air Force Academy), and comments by male students that standards had been lowered to admit women (33, 64, and 38 percent, respectively). Fourteen percent of female students at West Point reported receiving unwanted sexual advances, compared with 4 percent at Annapolis and 5 percent at the Air Force.

Assistant Secretary of the Navy Barbara Spyridon Pope testified that officials at Annapolis had made considerable progress in changing attitudes and policies after the 1989 and 1990 incidents were reported. "I think it's a serious problem and we have a lot of work to do. A lot has gone on since then. I would wager if the GAO went out this fall, they would see even lower numbers [of sexual harassment]."

Subcommittee Chairman John Glenn, D-Ohio, a former astronaut and Marine Corps pilot, told Navy officials at the hearing, "You took your lumps a while ago, and I have to congratulate you on having the lowest incidence of sexual harassment in this survey."

Two weeks after the hearing, however, the Navy began receiving even more bad publicity. Newspapers reported that Naval aviators molested at least twenty-six women, half of them officers, at a September 1991 convention in Las Vegas of the Tailhook Association, a nonofficial organization of Naval and Marine Corps pilots. The disclosure reverber-ated throughout the Navy, resulting in the resignation of Navy Secretary H. Lawrence Garrett III, reprimands for more than seventy officers, a *congressional delay on promotions of Navy officers, and a global "stand down" order for every officer and enlisted person to take a full day of training on sexual harassment rules.* (Pentagon Report on Tailhook Incident, p. 879)

> *Following are excerpts from congressional testimony on June 2, 1992, by Paul L. Jones of the U.S. General Accounting Office, regarding GAO's preliminary review of student treatment in the military service academies:*

Despite its being outlawed, hazing has never completely disappeared from the academies. At all three academies, hazing-type treatment occurs more frequently than officially filed charges would imply. The distinction between hazing and legitimate fourth class (freshmen) indoctrination is somewhat unclear. Many of the traditional elements of the fourth class systems are subject to potential abuse by upper-class students. The academies have rarely charged anyone with hazing and have usually chosen to pursue hazing-type offenses using lesser charges.

Hazing-type treatment is not harmless. A strong correlation exists between exposure to such treatment and a number of undesirable outcomes, including higher levels of physical and psychological stress among cadets and midshipmen, lower grade point averages, attrition from the academies, and reduced career motivation.

Recent systemic changes to the fourth class systems at the Military and Naval Academies appear to have had some success at reducing the extent of hazing-type treatment. For example, the class entering after the changes reported a lower frequency of hazing-type treatment than the previous three classes. However, some kinds of hazing-type activities continue. The Air Force Academy has not conducted an in-depth review of its fourth class system similar to those conducted at the other academies. Air Force Academy officials commented that the Academy reviews its fourth class system annually and has made several changes in the last 2 years, such as reducing fourth class training by 50 percent in academic year 1990-91 and converting the third class (sophomore) indoctrination training responsibility from an unsupervised role to a supervised one.

We found that the distinction between hazing and legitimate fourth class indoctrination was somewhat unclear to questionnaire respondents at the Naval Academy. DOD commented that the term "hazing-type" treatment can mean different things to different people and that being able to make this distinction is recognized as part of the process of effective leadership training at the academies.

Treatment and Performance of Women and Minorities

In the area of how women and minorities are faring at the academies, we found no evidence of deliberate or systematic efforts to treat these groups differently. We found that while the majority of students responding to our questionnaires perceived that women and minorities received the same treatment as their counterparts, significant numbers of men and whites, respectively, perceived that women and minorities received preferential treatment.

In reviewing a wide variety of indicators, we found that generally women and minorities did not fare as well as other groups with respect to academic, physical education, and military performance grades. For example, while women generally have had Academy success predictor scores higher than men, their academic, physical education, and military performance grades were about the same or lower than men. In addition, women and minorities were generally charged with disciplinary and honor code offenses at higher rates than other groups. At the Naval Academy, in academic year 1989-90, 7 out of 115 (6.1 percent) freshman women were convicted of the most serious level of conduct offenses (such as being under the influence of alcohol or drinking while on duty), compared to 9 out of 1,155 (0.8 percent) freshman men. We found that academically deficient women were generally disenrolled by the academies at lower rates than academically deficient men at the Naval and Air Force Academies.

We found that not all the subgroups within the minorities category fared the same. The category of minorities is made up of blacks, hispanics, asians, and native americans. We found that generally blacks fared the worst of the various subgroups in terms of academic, physical education, and military performance grades.

The academies have taken some steps to address the negative perceptions regarding women and minorities, as well as the performance differences. Students at all three academies receive equal opportunity/human relations training where these issues are covered. In addition, the Naval Academy established an academic center for academically at-risk students. Further, each academy monitors perceptual and performance data by gender and race to varying degrees.

We identified a number of possible factors that may be contributing to the gender and racial disparities we found at the academies. These include the traditional white male cultures of the services and the academies, the stressful environment at the academies being magnified for some subgroups, the small numbers of women and minorities in the student populations, and the influence of gender and racial stereotypes. When the size of a subgroup within a population is 15 percent or less, such as the case for women and the various minority subgroups at the academies, behavioral scientists have found it can have negative effects in terms of intergroup dynamics. One of the negative effects of being such a small minority is accentuated personal stress. While the academies are stressful for all students, they tend to be even more stressful for women and minorities. This extra stress can take a toll. For example, we found a correlation between female and minority questionnaire respondents who had experienced high levels of stress and low grades. Other negative effects of minority subgroup status are being stereotyped and seen as "not fitting in". We found evidence of negative sentiments toward women at the academies, in terms of questionnaire write-in comments expressing views that women did not belong at the Academy because they could not go into combat.

Harassment

In the area of harassment, we found that sexual harassment occurs more frequently than is reported to officials. In response to our survey questions about the types and extent of harassment experienced, significant numbers of female respondents at all academies reported personally experiencing various types of verbal and visual (graphic) harassment fairly often (once or twice a month or more)....

The most frequently experienced types of harassment were derogatory comments, comments that standards have been lowered, comments that women don't belong, offensive posters, and mocking gestures. For example, the percentage of women indicating they had experienced comments that standards had been lowered a couple of times a month or more was about 33 percent at the Naval Academy, about 38 percent at the Air Force Academy, and about 64 percent at the Military Academy. More extreme forms of sexual harassment, such as pressure for dates and unwanted sexual advances, appear to be less frequent among academy students.

Although there was general agreement among the respondents that if the harassment were reported, the incident would be thoroughly investigated and the offender would be appropriately disciplined, there was also general consensus that there were significant negative consequences to reporting the harassment. The perceived negative consequences could include loss of support by fellow students, being viewed as a crybaby and less favorably by the student and officer chains of command, being shunned, and receiving lower military performance grades. Consistent with these perceptions of the negative consequences of reporting harassment, we found relatively small numbers of conduct cases involving harassment charges at all three academies. We also found a correlation between the female and minority questionnaire respondents who had experienced high levels of harassment and stress.

The academies have taken some steps to address harassment. For example, the Naval Academy established an ombudsman program, staffed by commissioned officers and senior non-commissioned officers, as a channel to air grievances and seek advice on human relations matters. The Military Academy established a human resources council, staffed by faculty members and Commandant's staff, to address issues related to race, ethnicity, culture, religion, and gender. This group has researched the issue of date rape, as well as having held sensing sessions with small groups of cadets on the issue of racial insensitivity. The Air Force Academy has an organization called the Cadet Counseling and Leadership Development Center that both offers reactive services of counseling cadets one-on-one and develops military training sessions dealing with human relations. The Center also administers the Social Action Program that investigates allegations of sexual and racial harassment.

Effectiveness of Military Performance Systems

In terms of the effectiveness of military performance systems at the academies, we found the systems contained some design flaws that would limit their effectiveness because of their subjective nature. The military performance systems are intended to measure each student's officer potential. The design flaws limiting the effectiveness of these systems are the trait-oriented rather than performance-oriented aspects of the evaluations, the comparisons of students to each other through rankings or forced grade distributions rather than against standards, and the limited feedback value of such evaluations. In addition, we found that these systems had disparate effects in terms of minorities' grades and to a lesser extent in women's grades.

Due Process in Adjudicatory Systems

Although we have not completed our analysis of the due process aspects of the adjudicatory systems at the academies, we have found that the academies generally provide the minimal due process rights that the courts have stipulated apply to them. These rights are the right to have a hearing, the right to be apprised of the charges, and the right to have an adequate opportunity to present a defense.

While the courts have stated that the academies must provide due process, they have largely deferred to the academies the question of what due process rights are appropriate. The academies maintain that the administrative nature of their systems do not require the full range of due process rights that are necessary for criminal systems. In addition to the basic rights, the academies have provided other due process rights, with some limitations, to their students. For example, a student charged with a serious disciplinary or honor offense would be entitled to legal counsel. The right to legal counsel is limited to legal advice from an academy- or service-provided attorney or a privately retained attorney outside of a hearing. However, the attorney would not be allowed to participate in the hearing and the student would be expected to conduct his/her own defense.

In reviewing case files, we have also found some apparent inconsistencies in decisions and punishments across subgroups of students, across cases of similar offenses, and across the systems. Academy officials stated the decisions and punishments in the cases involving their adjudicatory systems are made on a case by case basis, taking into account the specifics of each case and prior individual conduct. Nevertheless, bearing this explanation in mind, we found decisions that appeared inconsistent, perhaps in part because the case file documents generally contain little or no explanation of the rationales for the decisions.

Honor Systems

With respect to the honor systems of the academies, we found a lack of consensus as to what constitutes an honor offense. To an even greater extent, we found a reluctance to report others for suspected honor offenses. Our examination of honor case files revealed instances of individuals charged and sometimes disenrolled based solely on oral evidence for offenses that seem trivial or "catch-22" in nature. For example, an upperclassman ordered a freshman to buy some food at a snack bar that is off-limits to freshmen as a condition for losing a bet. The freshman, feeling that the order must be obeyed, did as the upperclassman requested. In the snack bar food line, another upperclass student asked the freshman if he was a freshman. If the freshman answered yes, he could get into trouble, and if he answered no, he could be charged with the honor offense of lying. The freshman answered "no". Then the upperclass student asked, "So, you're not a freshman?" Again the freshman answered "no". The freshman was charged with and found guilty of the honor offense of lying. The freshman resigned from the Academy. . . .

FOREST SERVICE ORDER ON CLEAR-CUTTING AND SPOTTED OWL

June 4, 1992

A new policy aimed at sharply reducing clear-cutting in national forests and managing the forests based on "ecosystem management" principles was announced June 4 by F. Dale Robertson, chief of the U.S. Forest Service.

Robertson said the policy shift could reduce the controversial practice of clear-cutting by 70 percent. However, it was not expected to significantly reduce the amount of timber harvested from the 191 million acres of federally owned forests. Over the short term timber harvests could be reduced by 5 percent, Robertson said, but there would be no long-term reduction. In 1991 logging companies harvested 8.5 million board feet of timber from the 156 national forests.

The new policy was designed to place greater emphasis on protecting wildlife habitat and keeping air and water clean. Some environmentalists said the policy represented a major change for the Forest Service, which in the past managed forests to maximize timber production. "They will try to keep the system intact and harvest the product, rather than just harvest the product," Neil Sampson, executive vice president of American Forest, told the Washington Post. *However, other environmentalists said the policy actually changed very little.*

The policy came amidst growing criticism of the Forest Service and the National Park Service over their management of federal lands. Earlier in the year, a report known as "The Vail Agenda" sharply criticized the National Park Service's stewardship. (The Vail Agenda for National Parks, p. 329)

In addition, the policy was announced as the fight over protection of the northern spotted owl continued. Just a week earlier, a federal judge had ruled that the Forest Service's plan for protecting the owl was inadequate. The judge's ruling—the latest in a long line of court orders aimed at protecting the owls—meant that a court-imposed ban on logging millions of acres of Forest Service land in the Pacific Northwest would continue. (Ruling on Protecting the Spotted Owl, Historic Documents of 1991, p. 275)

In May, Interior Secretary Manuel Lujan, Jr., made public an official and an alternative version of a recovery plan for the owl, which was declared a threatened species in 1990. The official version called for restoring owl populations to levels that would lead to removal of the bird from the threatened species list, thus complying with the Endangered Species Act. The alternative version, prepared at Lujan's direction, would preserve some owls but not enough to get the bird off the list.

The official recovery plan would set aside 5.4 million acres of forest in the Pacific Northwest and cost about 32,000 jobs in the timber industry, according to the Interior Department. The alternative plan would set aside about half the number of acres, 2.8 million, and cost half the number of jobs, about 15,000. Environmentalists labeled the alternative version the "extinction plan." They pointed out that the document itself said it was "highly likely" that the plan would "eventually result in extinction or near complete extirpation of northern spotted owls" after more than a century. The alternative plan would require approval by Congress, and such approval appeared unlikely.

Also in May, a panel composed primarily of Bush administration officials voted to override the Endangered Species Act and allow logging of about 1,700 acres of federal land in Oregon that were home to spotted owls. The decision was made by the seven-member Endangered Species Committee, a panel chaired by Lujan and commonly known as the "God Squad." The decision, which allowed logging on thirteen parcels of land managed by the federal Bureau of Land Management (BLM), angered logging interest groups and environmentalists. Loggers were unhappy because the committee denied exemptions for another thirty-one tracts requested by the BLM. They also were displeased because the panel told the BLM not to sell any more timber until it had developed a plan for "recovering" owl populations on land it managed. Environmentalists, on the other hand, said it was improper to allow logging on any of the parcels. The environmentalists said they would immediately file suit in an effort to block logging on the land. Despite all the rhetoric, the panel's decision had little immediate impact because earlier in the year courts had enjoined the BLM from selling timber on the lands in question.

The controversy over the spotted owl also came up during the presidential campaign. In a September campaign swing through the Pacific Northwest, President George Bush proposed a major amendment to the Endangered Species Act of 1973. The amendment would require the Interior Department to balance the environmental benefits of protecting

threatened animals and plants against the economic benefits of employ-
ment. "It's time," the president said, "to put people ahead of owls."

Although the spotted owl was the symbol of the fight in the Northwest,
the real battle was over preservation of old-growth forests that the owls
lived in. The timber industry claimed that preserving the owl's habitat
would cost tens of thousands of jobs. Environmentalists said there would
be neither timber industry jobs nor spotted owls if clear-cutting of the
old-growth forests continued.

> *Following is the U.S. Department of Agriculture news*
> *release of June 4, 1992, on the policy entitled "Ecosystem*
> *Management of the National Forests and Grasslands,"*
> *announced the same day by F. Dale Robertson, chief of the*
> *U.S. Forest Service:*

Clearcutting will no longer be a standard way of harvesting national
forest timber under a proposal announced today by the U.S. Department
of Agriculture.

"The new policy will limit clearcutting to areas where it is essential to
meet forest plan objectives, such as establishing habitat for endangered
species of wildlife," said USDA's Forest Service Chief F. Dale Robertson.

Robertson said the proposed clearcutting policy is part of a more
ecological approach to management of the Forest Service's 191-million-
acre national forest system.

Clearcutting is a harvest method in which all trees are removed at the
same time from a site. It is used primarily to reforest tree species which
require full sunlight to grow and to create habitat for certain kinds of
wildlife, such as deer and elk.

"Although it is a proven forest management tool, clearcutting has
become increasingly controversial on national forests because of its appearance and impacts on other resources," Robertson said. "The new
policy addresses public concerns and expands current efforts to decrease
the use of this harvesting method on national forest lands."

Current regulations, established under the National Forest Management
Act of 1976, limit national forest clearcuts to 40 acres or less except for
Douglas-fir, southern yellow pine, and Alaskan hemlock-sitka spruce
forests where they may be larger. In the past few years, the Forest Service
has decreased the number of clearcuts and substituted more visually
acceptable harvest methods, Robertson said.

In 1988, clearcutting was used on 310,000 of the 728,424 acres of national
forest that was harvested.

"The new policy, in conjunction with the Forest Service's new ecological
approach to land management, can reduce clearcutting by as much as 70
percent from 1988 levels," Robertson said.

In 1990, the Forest Service initiated a program, called New Perspectives, to practice more environmentally sensitive forestry. This approach calls for greater use of harvesting methods that leave green trees and downed woody material on site.

The proposed reduction in clearcutting may reduce timber yields on national forests by about 10 percent in the short run, Robertson said, and there will be some increases in timber sale costs.

"However," he said, "we believe the long term environmental and esthetic benefits of reduced clearcutting and its accompanying controversy will outweigh any possible short term losses. Judicious use of alternative harvest methods such as selective cutting can be substituted for clearcutting on most national forest areas. And, in the long run, timber yields will be about the same."

Under the proposed policy, clearcutting would no longer be allowed as a standard commercial harvesting practice. Instead it would be allowed only under one or more of the following circumstances:

1. To establish, enhance, or maintain habitat for threatened, endangered, or sensitive species.
2. To enhance wildlife habitat or walter yield values, or to provide for recreation, scenic vistas, utility lines, road corridors, facility sites, reservoirs, or similar developments.
3. To rehabilitate lands adversely impacted by events such as fires, windstorms, or insect or disease infestations.
4. To preclude or minimize the occurrence of potentially adverse impacts of insects or disease infestations, windthrow, logging damage or other factors affecting forest health.
5. To provide for the establishment and growth of desired trees or other vegetative species that are shade intolerant.
6. To rehabilitate poorly stocked stands due to past management practices or natural events.
7. To meet research needs.

REPORT ON GUN VIOLENCE
June 10, 1992

Declaring violence in the United States to be a "public health emergency," an editorial in the Journal of the American Medical Association *called for a national system of gun registration and licensing. The editorial, signed by former surgeon general C. Everett Koop and JAMA editor George Lundberg, was one of more than seventy articles and editorials about violence published June 10 by the AMA's ten scientific journals. JAMA devoted its entire issue to the topic.*

The editorial said a system like that used to license automobile drivers was needed for gun owners. To get a license, gun owners would have to be above a certain age, not suffer from unspecified physical or mental conditions, be able to demonstrate knowledge about proper gun use, and be monitored in using guns. Owners who violated the rules would lose their right to own or use guns. The editorial did not specify details of the proposed rules.

While he was surgeon general from 1981 to 1989, Koop avoided the debate on gun control by contending that gun violence was not a health issue. However, he reversed his position at a press conference. "If the violence report being published this month in the Journal of the American Medical Association *were due to a virus, the American people and their leaders would be shouting for a cure," he said.*

In an article accompanying the editorial, researchers from the National Center for Health Statistics reported that murders with guns were the leading cause of death among black males ages fifteen to nineteen in the United States. In addition, the article reported that from 1987 to 1989 the firearm homicide rate for black teenage males increased 71 percent. During the same period, the death rate from motor vehicle accidents (the second leading cause of death among black teenage males) fell 3 percent.

Other articles in JAMA and the other AMA publications reported that:

- *Gun wounds killed more youths ages fifteen to nineteen, both black and white, than anything else other than automobile accidents. Between 1979 and 1989, the number of teenagers killed by guns in either homicides or suicides rose from twelve per 100,000 to eighteen per 100,000. During the same period, the number killed in automobile accidents fell from forty-four per 100,000 to thirty-four per 100,000.*
- *Murders of fifteen-to-nineteen-year-olds with guns declined from 1979 to 1984. However, they started climbing in mid-decade and jumped sharply at the decade's end. Meanwhile, murders with other weapons fell.*
- *One-third of Seattle high school students said they could easily get a handgun, and 6 percent said they had brought a handgun to school.*
- *Most handgun owners said they bought the weapon for protection from crime. Handgun owners, however, were forty-two times more likely to kill either themselves or a family member than to shoot a criminal at home.*
- *Domestic fights involving guns were twelve times more likely to result in death than domestic fights involving other weapons.*
- *More than one-third of gun owners kept their weapons loaded, and more than half kept them in places that were not locked.*

James Baker, chief Washington lobbyist for the National Rifle Association, told the New York Times *that doctors had no place commenting about deaths from guns. "Statistics show that 93,000 accidental deaths are caused by the medical profession annually," he said. "It would make more sense for these doctors to look at their own house first."*

> *Following is the text of an editorial titled "Violence in America: A Public Health Emergency," published June 10, 1992, in the* Journal of the American Medical Association:

Violence, according to one dictionary, is defined as "(1) exertion of any physical force so as to injure or abuse, (2) injury by or as if by distortion, infringement, or profanation, (3) intense, turbulent and often destructive action, or force." In his book *Powershift* Alvin Toffler identifies violence or the threat of violence as one of the three fundamental sources of all human power, the other two being money and knowledge. Toffler convincingly argues that these power sources influence every person and all groups including government. Of the three, violence is the lowest form of power because it can only be used to punish. Knowledge and money are far more versatile and can be used in an infinite variety of positive as well as negative or manipulative ways. The violence referred to in this issue of *JAMA* is the interpersonal kind rather than such types as war or that produced by forces of nature.

Response to *JAMA's* Call for Papers

The response to a call for papers on any aspects of interpersonal violence, made last August on behalf of the editors of JAMA and all nine AMA specialty journals, was extraordinary. *JAMA* alone received 131 topical papers for peer review and consideration. Of these, 12 appear in this issue; one relevant paper has been published in each *JAMA* since May 5, and another cluster of papers emphasizing domestic violence will appear in the June 17 issue. The specialty journals also received a great many manuscripts and published from one to 12 articles each in their June issues, in total 59. This outpouring of manuscripts not only confirms what we all know—that violence in the United States is a major issue—it underscores that violence is also a medical/public health issue, which is keenly felt by innumerable physicians and subject to medical/epidemiologic research.

The 1985 Surgeon General's Conference

One of us (C.E.K.) convened the Surgeon General's Workshop on Violence and Public Health at Leesburg, Va, in October 1985. The recommendations of the 150 assembled experts were reported by the Surgeon General to the Senate Committee on Children, Families, Drugs and Alcoholism. Regional, state, and local workshops followed to create a new awareness of the possibilities for understanding and dealing with violence provided by multidisciplinary approaches. Pediatricians, psychiatrists, and other physicians, along with administrators and the public, were challenged to consider violence as a public health issue and to seek out its root causes and best treatments.

Seven years later, violence in our country has not diminished; instead, violence makes constant headlines. In fact, the incidence of violence has increased, especially among some groups.

- One million US inhabitants die prematurely each year as the result of intentional homicide or suicide.
- From 1960 to 1980 the population of the United States increased by 26%; the homicide rate due to guns increased 160%.
- The leading cause of death in both black and white teenage boys in America is gunshot wounds.
- The number of deaths due to firearms is seven times greater in the United States than in the United Kingdom.
- The death rate from trauma in France is 66% that of the US rate, and the rate in the Netherlands is only 39%.
- Armed assaults in California schools are on a sharp increase
- One third of students in 31 Illinois high schools have brought some weapons to school for self-defense.

- Suicide is the third leading cause of death among children and adolescents in the United States, a rate that has doubled in the last 30 years, the increase almost solely due to firearms.
- Of the fatalities in the 1992 Los Angeles, Calif, riots, the vast majority occurred as a result of gunshot wounds.

New Research in Firearm Fatalities/Deaths by Gunshot Wounds

- In this issue of *JAMA*, Fingerhut and colleagues document extraordinarily high firearm fatality rates in many core metropolitan counties, with rates for black male and female teenagers increasing sharply in recent years to reach alarming levels.
- Saltzman et al demonstrate that firearm-associated family and intimate assaults in Atlanta, Ga, are 12 times more likely to result in death than nonfirearm assaults.
- Weil and Hemenway document in a national sample that large numbers of handgun owners keep their guns loaded in their homes and that many loaded weapons are not locked up, even if children are in the household. This dangerous behavior seemed not to be altered with training.
- Callahan and Rivara show that one third of Seattle, Wash, high school students report easy access to handguns, 6% own a handgun and 6% of males have carried a handgun to school.

These research findings, together with other articles in these issues, and an array of related data paint a grotesque picture of a society steeped in violence, especially by firearms, and so numbed by the ubiquity and prevalence of violence as to seemingly accept it as inevitable. We do not agree. No society, including ours, need be permeated by firearm homicide. This is unacceptable. Prior solutions have not succeeded. New approaches are required. Two such are included in adjacent commentaries.

What Now?

Regarding violence in our society as purely a sociologic matter, or one of law enforcement, has led to unmitigated failure. It is time to test further whether violence can be amenable to medical/public health interventions.

We believe violence in America to be a public health emergency, largely unresponsive to methods thus far used in its control. The solutions are very complex, but possible. We urge all persons in authority to take the following actions:

1. Support additional major research on the causes, prevention, and cures of violence.
2. Stimulate the education of all Americans about what is now known and what can now be done to address this emergency.
3. Demand legislation intended to reverse the upward trend of firearm injuries and deaths, the end result that is most out of control.

Proposed New Legislation

Automobiles, intended to be a means of transportation, when used inappropriately frequently become lethal weapons and kill human beings. Firearms are intended to be lethal weapons. When used inappropriately in peace time, they, too, frequently kill human beings.

In the state of Texas in 1990, deaths from firearms, for the first time in many decades, surpassed deaths from motor vehicles, 3443 to 3309, respectively, as the leading cause of injury mortality. In the 1970s and 1980s, defining motor vehicle casualties as a public health issue and initiating intervention activity succeeded in reversing the upward trend of such fatalities, without banning or confiscating automobiles. We believe that comparable results can be anticipated by similarly treating gunshot wound casualties. But the decline in fatalities will not occur overnight and will require a major coordinated effort.

The right to own or operate a motor vehicle carries with it certain responsibilities. Among them are that the operator meet certain criteria:

- be a certain age and physical/mental condition;
- be identifiable as owner or operator;
- be able to demonstrate knowledge and skill in operating the motor vehicle safely;
- be subject to performance monitoring; and
- be willing to forfeit the right to operate or own a vehicle if these responsibilities are abrogated.

We propose that the right to own or operate a firearm carries with it the same prior conditions, namely, that the owner and operator of a firearm also meet specific criteria:

- be of a certain age and physical/mental condition;
- be required to demonstrate knowledge and skill in proper use of that firearm;
- be monitored in the firearm's use; and
- forfeit the right to own or operate the firearm if these conditions are abrogated.

These restrictions should apply uniformly to all firearms and to all US inhabitants across all states through a system of gun registration and licensing for gun owners and users. No grandfather clauses should be allowed.

Anticipated Resistance and Support

We recognize the enormous amount of change and expense necessary to effect any major proposal such as this having to do with guns. But we believe that anything short of this proposed registration and licensing for gun ownership and use would be too little action to recommend at this time. We also believe that there is great public sentiment in support of this proposal.

A vast lobby of special interests supports the utterly unfettered ownership and use of firearms. It is certain vigorously to oppose this proposal at any cost. One of us (G.D.L.) has met with representatives of the National Rifle Association in Washington, DC, to discuss ways to counter the acknowledged epidemic of firearm homicides. We invite that organization and any other dissenting persons and groups to make their own rational proposals for countering this acute public health emergency of injuries and homicides, especially those occurring in young black men and women. We can wait no longer to act.

C. Everett Koop, MD
George D. Lundberg, MD

EARTH SUMMIT IN RIO
June 12, 1992

A dispute within the Bush administration helped create harsh feelings toward the United States at the Earth Summit held June 3-13 in Rio de Janeiro, Brazil. The summit, a gathering of delegates from 178 nations sponsored by the United Nations, was aimed at finding cures for the world's environmental ills.

The dispute centered on one of the summit's showpieces, a biodiversity treaty designed to protect rare plant and wildlife species. Experts predicted that if current development continued, between 10 percent and 20 percent of the earth's estimated 10 million species of plants and animals would become extinct by the year 2020.

Biodiversity and Greenhouse Gases

Before the summit William K. Reilly, administrator of the Environmental Protection Agency and chief of the U.S. delegation at Rio, wrote a confidential memo proposing that the United States sign the biodiversity treaty. Some White House officials opposed the treaty, however, arguing that it would hurt U.S. biotechnology companies. They won the debate, and the United States was the only nation at the summit that did not sign the accord.

In a memo written after the summit, Reilly said the U.S. decision was so unpopular that other nations virtually ignored any other ideas proposed by American delegates. "We assigned a low priority to the negotiations of the biodiversity treaty," Reilly wrote, "were slow to engage the climate issue, were last to commit our President to attend Rio. We put our delegation together late, and we committed few resources. No doubt, this contributed to negative feelings toward the United States."

In a June 12 speech at the summit, President George Bush defended the decision and said that U.S. efforts to protect biodiversity would exceed the treaty's requirements. He also defended the nation's environmental record in general. "America's record on environmental protection is second to none, so I did not come here to apologize," he said.

Some 116 heads of state attended the summit, but Bush agreed to attend only at the last minute. His reticence was apparently part of a U.S. negotiating strategy aimed at weakening a treaty that would have strictly limited emissions of "greenhouse" gases, such as carbon dioxide, methane, and nitrogen oxide, which are thought to cause global warming. In negotiations before the summit, the United States persuaded other nations to drop provisions requiring reductions by specific levels and dates. The Wall Street Journal *reported that U.S. delegates won the debate by threatening that Bush would boycott the summit. U.S. officials reportedly believed that the specific emissions cuts and timetables in the original treaty would harm economic growth. Under the final treaty, developed countries agreed to try to reduce emissions of greenhouse gases to 1990 levels by the year 2000. Although the treaty was significantly weakened, it still represented the first international attempt to limit greenhouse gases.*

North-South Split

Many disputes at the summit pitted the industrialized nations of the North against the developing countries of the South. Countries from the South criticized those from the North for using too many resources and causing a disproportionate share of global pollution, while the North criticized the South for failing to protect critical resources such as tropical rain forests and for allowing population growth to continue unchecked. The United Nations Population Fund estimated that the world population of 5.4 billion would more than double to 11.6 billion by the year 2150, with much of the growth occurring in developing nations.

Poor countries in the South also demanded that richer nations of the North give them money to help protect natural resources and clean up pollution. Maurice Strong, secretary-general of the summit, said before the meeting that the industrialized nations needed to give developing nations $125 billion annually for environmental projects. At the summit, though, industrialized nations pledged far less. Japan agreed to contribute $1.4 billion annually, a 50 percent increase from previous levels. The United States also pledged a 50 percent increase, to $750 million annually.

Besides the biodiversity and global warming treaties, delegates also signed accords aimed at setting environmental priorities; conserving forests; and fighting toxic waste, ocean pollution, and energy inefficiency. Critics said the agreements were far too weak to solve the earth's myriad environmental problems. Some treaties, critics noted, simply called for conducting studies or creating plans for later use in developing specific agreements. Other accords used vague generalities instead of specific details to describe what nations would do. For example, the biodiversity treaty required nations to inventory their plant and animal species to establish a base line for protection. Yet there was no deadline for completing the survey, no framework for sharing the findings, and no requirement that nations determine how many of the species were actually endangered.

At the summit's conclusion Strong, the organizer of a similar meeting twenty years earlier in Stockholm, criticized the Rio effort as an "agreement without sufficient commitment." Choking back tears, he noted that the Stockholm meeting failed to solve the world's environmental problems. "We don't have another 20 years now," he said. "I believe we are on the road to tragedy."

Following is the text of President George Bush's statement at the UN Conference on Environment and Development, on June 12, 1992, and excerpts from a news conference on June 13, both at Rio de Janeiro, Brazil:

BUSH'S STATEMENT

.... This is truly an historic gathering.

And the Chinese have a proverb, if a man cheats the Earth, the Earth will cheat man. And the idea of sustaining the planet so that it may sustain us is as old as life itself. We must leave this Earth in better condition than we found it.

And today this old truth must be applied to new threats facing the resources which sustain us all—the atmosphere and the ocean, the stratosphere and the biosphere. Our village is truly global. Some find the challenges ahead overwhelming. I believe that their pessimism is unfounded.

Twenty years ago, at the Stockholm Conference, the chief concern of our predecessors was the horrible threat of nuclear war, the ultimate pollutant. No more. Upon my return from Rio, I will meet with Russian President [Boris N.] Yeltsin in Washington, and the subject we will discuss is cooperation, not confrontation.

Twenty years ago, some spoke of the limits to growth, and today we realize that growth is the engine of change, and the friend of the environment. Today an unprecedented era of peace, freedom and stability makes concerted action on the environment possible as never before.

This summit is but one key step in the process of international cooperation on environment and development. The United States will work to carry forward the promise of Rio. And because as important as the road to Rio has been, what matters more is the road from Rio.

There are those who say that cooperation between developed and developing countries is impossible. Well, let them come to Latin America, where debt-for-nature swaps are protecting forests in Costa Rica and funding pollution control in Chile. There are those who say that it takes state control to protect the environment. Well, let them go to Eastern Europe, where the poisoned bodies of children now pay for the sins of fallen dictators, and only the new breeze of freedom is allowing for cleanup.

There are those who say that change can never come because the interests of the status quo are too powerful. Well, let them come right here to Brazil, where President [Fernando] Collor [de Mello] is forging a new approach that recognizes the economic value of sustaining the rain forest.

There are those who say that economic growth and environmental protection cannot be compatible. Well, let them come to the United States, where in the 20 years since Stockholm, our economy has grown by 57 percent and yet we've cut the lead going into the air by 97 percent, the carbon monoxide by 41 percent, the particulates by 59 percent. We've cleaned up our water and preserved our parks, wilderness and wildlife.

There are those who say that the leaders of the world do not care about the Earth and the environment. Well, let them all come here to Rio.

Mr. President, we have come to Rio. We've not only seen the concern; we share it. We not only care; we're taking action.

We come to Rio with an action plan on climate change. It stresses energy efficiency, cleaner air, reforestation, new technology. And I'm happy to report that I've just signed that framework convention on climate change.

And today I invite my colleagues from the industrialized world to join in a prompt start on the convention's implementation. I propose that our countries meet by Jan. 1 to lay out our national plans for meeting the specific commitments in the framework convention. Let us join in translating the words spoken here into concrete action to protect the planet.

We come to Rio with a proposal to double global forest assistance, and we stand ready to work together, respecting national sovereignty, on new strategies for forests for the future.

As a down payment, we will double U.S. forest bilateral assistance next year and we will reform at home, phasing out clear-cutting as a standard practice on U.S. national forests and working to plant 1 billion trees a year.

We come to Rio with an extensive program of technology cooperation. We stand ready, government and private sector, to help spread green technology and launch a new generation of clean growth. We come to Rio recognizing that the developing countries must play a role in protecting the global environment but will need assistance in pursuing this cleaner growth.

So we stand ready to increase U.S. international environmental aid by 66 percent above the 1990 levels, on top of the more than $2.5 billion that we provide through the world's development banks for Agenda 21 projects.

We come to Rio with more scientific knowledge about the environment than ever before and with the wisdom that there is much, much we [can] do that's not yet known. And we stand ready to share our science and to lead the world in a program of continued research.

We come to Rio prepared to continue America's unparalleled efforts to preserve species and habitat. And let me be clear: Our efforts to protect biodiversity itself will exceed, will exceed the requirements of the treaty. But that proposed agreement threatens to retard biotechnology and undermine the protection of ideas, and unlike the climate agreement, its financing scheme will not work. And it is never easy, it is never easy to stand alone on principle, but sometimes leadership requires that you do. And now is such a time.

Let's face it, there has been some criticism of the United States, but I must tell you, we come to Rio proud of what we have accomplished, and committed to extending the record on American leadership on the environment. In the United States we have the world's tightest air quality standards on cars and factories, the most advanced laws for protecting lands and waters, and the most open processes for public participation.

And now for a simple truth. America's record on environmental protection is second to none, so I did not come here to apologize. We come to press on with deliberate purpose and forceful action, and such action will demonstrate our continuing commitment to leadership and to international cooperation on the environment.

We believe that the road to Rio must point toward both environmental protection and economic growth, environment and development, and by now it's clear [that] to sustain development we must protect the environment and to protect the environment we must sustain development.

It's been said that we don't inherit the Earth from our ancestors, we borrow it from our children, and when our children look back on this time and this place they will be grateful that we met at Rio and they will certainly be pleased with the intentions stated and the commitments made. But they will judge us by the actions we take from this day forward.

Let us not disappoint them.

Mr. President, once again my congratulations to you, sir; Mr. [U.N.] Secretary General [Boutros Boutros-Ghali], our sincere thanks, and thank you all very, very much.

NEWS CONFERENCE

PRESIDENT BUSH: ... We've had a very successful visit. We've signed a climate convention. We've asked others to join us in presenting action plans for the implementation of the climate convention. We've won agreement on forest principles.

We found a warm reception among the G-7 [the group of seven leading industrialized nations] and many developing countries to our forests-for-the-future initiative. And many U.S. proposals on oceans and public participation, on the importance of economic instruments and free markets were included in this mammoth Agenda 21 document and the Rio Declaration.

Let me be clear on one fundamental point. The United States fully intends to be the world's pre-eminent leader in protecting the global environment. And we have been that for many years. We will remain so. And we believe that environment and development, the two subjects of this conference, can and should go hand in hand.

A growing economy creates the resources necessary for environmental protection, and environmental protection makes growth sustainable over the long term. I think that recognition of that fact by leaders from around the world is the central accomplishment of this important Rio conference.

Q: Mr. President, to what extent do the images that Americans have seen back home of your being hustled off the stage in Panama, not being allowed to finish your — to give your speech, and the isolation that the United States has had in Rio: To what extent does this erode into what Americans seem to still feel is your strong suit, your ability to conduct foreign policy?

P: Well, I think in both instances, the reality will prevail. In Panama, Panama has made dramatic strides. They're a free country. They're a democratic country. I think everybody was there, saw the warmth of the reception from the people of Panama along the streets. And it was tremendous. And what got the news, of course, was a handful of demonstrators in demonstration. The smoke blew the wrong way as the police tried to contain that small group, and that permitted the disruption of an outdoor rally. But that should not obscure the fact that Panama is democratic, Panama is free, Panama is growing at 9.6 percent, and the warmth from the Panamanian people was overwhelming. Can you let 300 people, or 200—whichever it is—carry the day in terms of—in terms of the reality? And the answer is no. The hundreds of thousands of people were much more representative of the change.

And then I heard an interview from a prison today by Mr. [Gen. Manuel Antonio] Noriega, the discredited drug lord who's had a fair trial, as though his criticism means anything. I mean, come on. Panama's doing well, and I was very proud to be there, and so I'd like to go back.

And what we did in helping, in the first place, protect American lives, secondly, restore democracy, is—it's good, it's very, very positive.

In terms of Rio, as I said yesterday, we are the leaders. We are not the followers. And the fact that we don't go along with every single covenant— I don't think that means a relinquishment of leadership. I think we are, and I think the record shows we are the leading environmental nation in the world.

And so I, you know, I would just reject the premise for saying no, this doesn't concern me.

Q: If I could do a follow-up, Mr. President, along those lines. You set a Jan. 1st target for another meeting of the conference to discuss global warming. You've set a lot of deadlines for Congress that haven't been heeded. Your proposal yesterday wasn't particularly well received by the other nations. Why do you think that that Jan. 1st deadline will be heeded any more than your congressional deadlines?

P: Well, we—I don't think there's any comparison. Because I think the G-7 nations and the developed nations want to meet the commitments that they've signed up for. And so I've not found that it wasn't received well at all. In fact, [Environmental Protection Agency Administrator] Bill Reilly told me it was well received, and we will be there with specific plans.

Now, you want to talk about leadership? We will be there with specific plans prepared to share, but, more important, that others who have signed these documents ought to have specific plans. So, I think this is a leadership role. We are challenging them to come forward. We will be there. And I think the Third World and others are entitled to know that the commitments made are going to be commitments kept.

* * *

Q: . . . In one remark you made and members of your administration have indicated that there were other nations here, some of whose officials were critical of your positions, who are in no position themselves, or their countries are in no position, to meet the terms of the climate change treaty, for example, and yet they were privately critical of you. And you suggested that that was so. Would you care to elaborate on who they were and what—

P: No, I don't think I suggested that at all. What I'm saying is let's go forward.

Q: You're glad that you've taken the position that you've taken?

P: Well, I think most are. I think most people are glad that we've taken this position to go forward. And I was very pleased, incidentally, with the remarks by [West German Chancellor Helmut] Kohl, by [Canadian Prime Minister] Brian Mulroney. I had a good talk with the prime minister of Japan before getting here. I'm most appreciative of [British Prime Minister] John Major for what he said. And so I think there's not only understanding, but support for American positions.

And I—Bill Reilly told me and I'll let — I don't want to get into private conversations, but yesterday evening he talked to some of the developing nations' representatives, and they were rather supportive of what we said.

So it's—the fact that we didn't sign that one treaty does not diminish in my view the U.S. leadership role. Sometimes leadership is not going along with everybody else.

* * *

Q: Some respected environmentalists here at the Earth Summit say that poverty leads to many of the environmental problems and that poverty in developing nations is perpetuated by unending foreign debt and an unfair trade balance that funnels money from the South to the North. They criticize the Earth Summit and wealthy nations like the United States for not focusing on these issues here.

How would you respond to that criticism, please?

P: Well, I would take great credit for the fact that the United States has taken the leadership role, a unique one that's been well received, in debt-for-equity swaps or forgiveness of debt or debt-for-environmental swaps, and I think that shows that we are sensitive to the problems of the Third World in terms of the economy.

I happen to believe that a successful conclusion to the GATT [General Agreement on Tariffs and Trade] Round, the Uruguay Round of GATT, will do more than any foreign aid program of any country to help the Third World because I believe their products will be able to flow more freely and they will be able to prosper by the market that they've been denied access to through various forms of protection.

So both those areas, I think, would refute the allegation.

Q: Follow-up. There are those who say that if the GATT is successful and these barriers are dropped, these developing nations will not be able to protect their own developing industries from the multilaterals coming in. How do you respond to that?

P: Well, I say that the things they do best they'll be able to get into the world markets. And I just am convinced that free and fair trade is best for everybody. If you don't believe me, take a country that is now moving well along on the development path: talk to President Carlos Salinas of Mexico. He is convinced that the free trade agreement with Mexico will be good for him, Mexico, good for the United States and good for the environment. And he's right.

He believes that Mexico—and he's made this point over and over again—can do much more in environmental cleanup, environmental progress, if this free trade agreement is met. Now, there's a very good refutation to the criticism you say some are making.

* * *

Q: Sir, you talk about not wanting to jeopardize jobs by being overly conscious of the environmental concerns, but you've never really been very specific about which jobs you would save with your policies....

P: I would give you—I will give you an example and that was on the owl decision [to allow some timber cutting in areas inhabited by the northern spotted owl]. There, what was clearly at stake was some 30,000 jobs in the Northwest. That decision was met with some opposition by certain environmentalists. But it was a good decision and it found some people, regrettably, will still be put out of work, but not near as many as if that arrangement had not been achieved.

JOSEPH CARDINAL BERNARDIN ON SEXUAL ABUSE BY PRIESTS
June 15, September 21, 1992

The Archdiocese of Chicago, the nation's second-largest Roman Catho-lic diocese, must take strong measures to protect children from sexual abuse by priests, according to a commission appointed by the Archbishop of Chicago. The commission's report, released by Joseph Cardinal Ber-nardin June 15, said the Catholic Church frequently failed to investigate properly sexual abuse charges against priests. "Very often, allegations of child sexual abuse have not been handled well in the Church because the overriding concern has been to do everything possible to protect the rights of priests, at times leading to an infringement of the rights of the victims," the commission said. Some critics of the Catholic Church were even harsher. They alleged that priests who molested children were simply moved from parish to parish without any warning to the new parishioners or reports to police.

Such a case had prompted Bernardin to appoint the commission in October 1991. Several years earlier a priest had been accused of sexual misconduct, been removed from two parishes, and entered therapy. After a sexual disorder clinic said he no longer posed a threat to children, he was appointed pastor of a suburban Chicago parish in the spring of 1990. Shortly after arriving, however, he allegedly propositioned a young man and sexually molested a young girl. The archdiocese immediately re-moved him from his post, but his parishioners became angry when they learned that the church had keep his past from them.

A similar case received national attention in September when prosecu-tors charged James R. Porter, a former Roman Catholic priest, with sexually molesting thirty-two male and female children three decades earlier in southeastern Massachusetts. After assaulting the children, Porter allegedly told them that God would get them and their families if they ever told anyone what had happened. Shortly before his arrest Porter admitted sexually abusing children while he was a priest in the 1960s. At his arraignment, however, he pleaded not guilty to forty-six counts of indecent assault, sodomy, and committing unnatural acts.

More than 200 people in three states alleged that Porter had assaulted them. Some of the alleged victims charged in civil suits against Porter and the Catholic Church that the church knew of his attacks but simply kept moving him from parish to parish. In December sixty-eight men and women who alleged that Porter sexually abused them settled a suit with the Diocese of Fall River, Massachusetts. Although details of the settlement were not made public, it reportedly involved substantial payments to each victim and changes in church policy.

Porter worked at three different parishes in Massachusetts in the 1960s before leaving in 1967 to enroll in a pedophilia treatment program for priests in New Mexico. The church decided he was cured in 1970 and sent him to a parish in Minnesota. He left the priesthood in 1974, later married, and had four children.

In an unrelated case, the same day Porter was arrested a Roman Catholic priest in Worcester, Massachusetts, was charged with soliciting a child to pose nude. Prosecutors alleged that Father Ronald D. Provost, 53, took a photograph of a nude ten-year-old boy. They said police found photos of other nude boys at the rectory where Provost lived.

In its report, the Chicago Archdiocese committee said that priests who sexually abused children should never return to any kind of ministry involving children, even after treatment. "We have identified no conditions in which an exception can be made to this," the committee said.

At a September 21 news conference, Bernardin said he agreed with the committee's recommendation. "I accept the clinical data which suggest that once it has been demonstrated that a priest is an abuser, he should never again return to parish ministry or any ministry which might place a child at risk," Bernardin said. He also announced a series of measures growing out of the committee's report to protect children against abuse by priests. The major provisions included appointment of a nine-member board to investigate future charges of sexual abuse by priests, hiring of a full-time administrator and support staff to investigate reports of sexual abuse by priests, and creation of a toll-free, twenty-four-hour telephone hotline to report sexual abuse by priests.

> *Following is an excerpt of the report, "The Cardinal's Commission on Clerical Sexual Misconduct with Minors," and a statement by Joseph Cardinal Bernardin, Archbishop of Chicago, implementing the commission's recommendations, as issued at a press conference on September 21, 1992:*

THE CARDINAL'S COMMISSION ON CLERICAL SEXUAL MISCONDUCT WITH MINORS

[A omitted]

B. Scope of the Problem

In 1980, the National Center on Child Abuse and Neglect (NCCAN) published a study, in which it estimated that professionals knew about nearly 45,000 cases of child sexual abuse in 1979. *In a follow-up study in 1988, NCCAN estimated that the number of known cases had more than tripled. The study attributed this dramatic increase to better awareness of the symptoms, and hence better diagnosis, rather than to an increase in the number of actual cases.* However, it also estimated that the number of new cases of child sexual abuse may be as high as 200,000.

There is another way of ascertaining the number of cases. Several often-quoted studies have estimated that, by the time they reach the age of 18, 1 out of 4 girls in the U.S., and 1 out of 6 to 10 boys, have been sexually abused. Clearly the matter has already reached epidemic proportions. Imagine yourself as a teacher looking out over a class of 24 students—or a priest looking out over a congregation of 1000 parishioners. Estimate the number of victims who may be sitting right before your eyes!

Dr. Gene Abel, Dr. Judith Becker, and their colleagues reported in the 1987 *Journal of Interpersonal Violence* that, in a study they conducted of paraphilic acts committed by 561 subjects, only .3% involved rape of an adult, while 21.9% involved molestation of a child. As the authors commented on this surprising finding:

> This is certainly in contrast to the media depictions of these two offenses, which suggest that rape is more frequent or as frequent as child molestation. Since adults have greater access to the media than children, it is not surprising that our current media presentations focus more on crimes affecting adult victims and less on the more frequent crime of child molestation.

We tend to defend ourselves from such statistics about child abuse by claiming that our class or our parish is different from others. Such things do not happen here, we may argue. However, all the literature we surveyed indicated that child sexual abuse has no boundaries. It cuts across all racial, ethnic, cultural, and socioeconomic borders. It pervades our entire society.

Even if no priest in the Archdiocese had ever been accused of sexual misconduct with minors, the Church—bishops, priests, deacons, religious laypersons—need to address the issue of child sexual abuse because it is undermining the stability of our society and ruining the lives of its victims. However, the focus of this Report is primarily on sexual misconduct by the clergy, and we need to look at the pastoral dimensions of that behavior.

C. Pastoral Dimensions

Each day, parents and governmental agencies entrust tens of thousands of children and adolescents to the care of the Archdiocese of Chicago—in its schools and religious education programs, in residential care institutions (for example, the Maryville Academy, Misericordia North and South, and Mercy Home for Boys and Girls), in sports and youth activities, in social and cultural programs. That is a very sacred trust, indeed.

Most Catholics experience the Church most directly in their parish community. It is there that they celebrate the important events of their lives—from baptisms to funerals. They gather there often with other believers to celebrate the Eucharist and to ask God's forgiveness and help. While there has been an expansion of lay ministries in the last thirty years, the priest remains an indispensable part of parish life. Not only is he empowered to celebrate the sacraments with us; his leadership abilities and capacity to work with others are also important assets in building a true community of faith.

His understanding of Scripture and the Church's teaching help to guide and form Catholics of all ages. People entrust him with some of the most private concerns of their lives. Moreover, because of his ordination, he does not act on his own. He represents the Church and helps carry out the Church's mission and ministry, which is Jesus' own mission and ministry. A priest mediates between God and the people he serves.

Because of the nature of the priest's role in the Church, there is a sacred trust between him and those he serves. This is necessary for him to be accepted in the local community and effective in his ministry. People simply must be able to trust him.

In accord with long-standing tradition in the Latin Rite, the revised Code of Canon Law makes it quite clear that

> Clerics are obliged to observe perfect and perpetual continence for the sake of the kingdom of heaven and therefore are obliged to observe celibacy, which is a special gift of God ... (Cannon 277,§ 1).

Any sexual misconduct by a priest ... is a clear violation of celibacy and chastity. It also has the potential for causing considerable harm to the Church and the persons involved, especially if the matter becomes publicly known. Catholics have a right to expect their priests to live in accord with the Church's teaching and discipline. Sexual misconduct undermines people's trust in a priest. As noted above, the focus of this Report is on sexual misconduct with minors.

Impact on the Victim(s)

Sexual misconduct by a priest with a minor, in addition to being a violation of celibacy and chastity, almost always has serious harmful effects on the victims, whether the matter becomes publicly known or not. They suffer a loss of self-esteem. They often find it difficult to trust an adult again. They may feel guilty, or be made to feel guilty by the abuser.

They often experience sexual confusion. They may not feel they will be believed, or they encounter actual disbelief on the part of significant persons in their lives, for example, a parent, a pastor. They may keep the matter hidden or repress it, displacing their anger at the Church, the priesthood, even God.

Victims' capacity to develop a trusting relationship with other clergy is impeded. They may begin to lose faith in the sacraments of the Eucharist and Penance because they are administered by priests. If diocesan leaders do not respond effectively to victims' reports of sexual abuse by clergy, the victims often become further alienated from the Church. They may also ask themselves why God is allowing all this to happen to them. Often, they cease being an active member of the Church, a tragic loss for the community of faith. The psychological impact upon victims will be discussed in more detail below; here the issue is the spiritual harm caused and the need for a compassionate, effective pastoral response.

Impact on the Victim's Families

When the victim's family learns of the sexual abuse or misconduct, they too experience a serious trauma. How parents respond to the information plays an important role on how much of an emotional impact the experience has. If they do not believe what their child tells them, or if they react in a highly emotional way, the impact may be much greater on an individual who has already been victimized. So, families, too, need help in responding to these incidents. In the past, the Church, like many other communities and institutions, has not shown sufficient awareness of the harmful effects of sexual abuse on the victims and, therefore, has not adequately reached out to them and their families in an appropriate way. More recently, the Archdiocese has moved more in that direction by offering victims counseling and helping their families cope with the traumatic experience they have undergone. But much more needs to be done, as the Commission itself recognizes, and as all of the victims it interviewed pointed out.

Impact on the Priest

Sexual misconduct or abuse with any minor is a tragedy. But when the offender is a priest, or when a priest is falsely accused of such a transgression, the tragedy is greatly heightened. Both sexual misconduct and false accusations breach the sacred trust that must exist between a priest and the people he serves.

Because sexual misconduct involves a serious breach of trust by the priest, one may rightly ask whether the necessary trust between that person and a community can ever be sufficiently restored to allow him to minister again effectively in a parish setting or—in certain serious, notorious cases—anywhere again. With his future priestly ministry in jeopardy, the priest himself may find it difficult to pray and may also feel alienated from the Church he has served—often well.

Impact on his Family, Friends, Classmates

It does not take much imagination to assume the trauma which his family, friends, and classmates go through when their priest, son or brother is accused of sexual misconduct with minors. They, too, need understanding, compassion, and healing.

Impact on the Parishes

Incidents of sexual misconduct with minors, when they become known, also have a severely negative impact on the parish communities where the priests have served. As we have seen this past year, some of the communities have become divided between a priest's supporters and opponents. The Commission received letters from both groups. On the one hand, some excoriated us and the Archdiocese for the "shameful," "unchristian" way we treated a particular priest who had engaged in sexual misconduct with minors. Others were very angry that they had not been told in advance of earlier allegations against him, indicating that they might well not have accepted him into their parish had they known about his background.

It will take time for these communities to be healed. If an individual priest's supporters understood the nature of his illness or knew the details of his misconduct, they might still be willing to forgive the priest's actions, but they would also understand why certain decisions had to be made in order to remove the risk he posed to further potential victims. In these situations, that must be the Church's *primary concern:* to ensure the safety of the people the Church serves and to do all that it reasonably can do to ensure that no harm comes to our children and teenagers.

Some may ask, Why not make all the cases and details public? This will be discussed in more detail below, in the section of this chapter on the legal dimensions of the problem. Suffice it to say here that, often, victims who have come forward with allegations of sexual misconduct have requested that the matter be kept confidential in order to protect their right to privacy. When some have come forward and this has become public knowledge, they have suffered the reproach of their fellow parishioners and/or the additional trauma of media coverage of very painful experiences. Moreover, many victims and their families wanted the priest to get the psychological help he needed, but did not want to make the matter public.

This may appear to be a "dodge" or a "cover-up," but the Church also must respect the request for confidentiality or privacy under these circumstances. At the same time, archdiocesan officials also have a responsibility to the larger community of faith in terms of damage control. Often when the sexual misconduct was eventually made public, it was because the victims and their families were dissatisfied with the Church's response to the matter and felt they had no resort but to go to civil authorities with the allegation.

Impact on the Priests in the Archdiocese

The priests who serve in the Archdiocese have also suffered from the revelation of multiple cases of fellow priest's sexual misconduct with minors. Priests have been put on the defensive, and their morale has been seriously affected. While some appear to be relieved that these matters have finally come out into the open, many resent the fact that some of the cases have become public. At the same time, there are rumors that many priests knew of the sexual misconduct of some of the priests who have been charged or investigated recently but did not come forward with that information—because of a cynicism that nothing would be done to remedy the situation or simply because of an unwillingness to confront a fellow priest with his misconduct.

Priests' ministry to children and teenagers may be hampered by the present situation. They may be fearful of touching or even blessing children. This would be a great tragedy—for the young people as well as for the priests themselves.

Very often, allegations of child sexual abuse have not been handled well in the Church because the overriding concern has been to do everything possible to protect the rights of priests, at times leading to an infringement of the rights of the victims. This dimension of the problem will be taken up in more detail below under legal dimensions of the problem of sexual misconduct with minors.

Impact on the Whole Church

The members of the Commission are personally well aware of the negative effect which the issue of sexual misconduct by the clergy has had on the entire Archdiocese and the wider Church. Our friends and relatives have broached the topic with us often since we were appointed to the Commission. In many cases, it has eroded Catholics' confidence in their priests and bishops. They are embarrassed by the revelations of sexual misconduct by clergy. Those who are struggling with their faith find it eroded by these reports. It has attracted considerable media attention, much of the reporting quite careful, some of it quite exploitative and sensational, all of it painful to see and hear. The letters we received from concerned laity and clergy were often as eloquent as they were poignant. Many simply wish that the whole matter would go away and never be raised again.

However, we must put this problem into its appropriate context. Several people whom we interviewed told us that the Catholic Church, and specifically the Archdiocese of Chicago, is one of the first large communities or organizations in this nation which is now facing this complex issue directly, despite the pain associated with it. We have an opportunity to educate ourselves and others about the nature of this problem and the necessary steps we must take in order to prevent child abuse to the extent that we can and to respond to its victims, their families, and their communities with compassion and assistance—and to help those who have committed the abuse in ways that are consonant with the Church's mission and ministry.

Child abuse is clearly one of the "signs of the times" in the 1990's. It has already reached epidemic proportions. The Church can be a leader in raising people's consciousness about the problem and its impact on young people and in helping to bring healing to their lives. In other words, this is a time of opportunity to be prophetic like the Lord Jesus and to learn from the Good Shepherd to take better care of our younger brothers and sisters. . . .

STATEMENT BY JOSEPH CARDINAL BERNARDIN

Overview

Today the Archdiocese of Chicago takes the next step in its mission to ensure that no minors will suffer sexual misconduct by priests. We are instituting new policies entitled, "Clerical Sexual Misconduct with Minors: Policies for Education, Prevention, Assistance to Victims and Procedures for Determination of Fitness for Ministry." The new policies place primary concern on the safety of all children and the well being of the community. This is a comprehensive, pastoral response of education, prevention and prompt action to address a problem of great concern to all of us.

Here's an overview:

- The new policies are built around an independent lay/clergy Review Board and Administrator charged with a stringent process to determine fitness for ministry.
- The policies will be triggered immediately upon receipt of an allegation of sexual misconduct by a priest with a minor.
- An 800-telephone number will be opened to receive information of an allegation.
- A Victim Assistance Minister backed up by a team of trained specialists will be available to move quickly to provide assistance to a victim and any other affected person or community.
- Psychological screening of seminarians will be improved and courses in sexual development will be evaluated and enhanced.
- Unified personnel records will follow a priest from early studies throughout his entire career.
- For the priests against whom allegations have been made, the Vicars for priests will continue to offer counsel, support and referral to professional resources.

The new policies are directed to the safety of children and to helping the Church make more informed decisions about returning priests to ministry. They formalize our efforts to cooperate with civil authorities.

The new policies require:

- All clergy, religious order members, employees and volunteers working for the Archdiocese to comply fully with the letter and spirit of the new program.
- All priests who have or request authorization to serve in the Archdiocese must certify in writing that they are familiar with the new policies, that is, they must know and understand what is expected of them.
- Compliance with all civil reporting requirements related to sexual misconduct with a minor and cooperation with official investigations.

I share the anguish of all those affected by this tragedy: the victims, their families, their communities and priests. These new policies are designed to accommodate the needs of all these people whose lives have been changed forever by these tragic encounters. I accept the clinical data which suggest that once it has been demonstrated that a priest is an abuser, he should never again return to parish ministry or any ministry which might place a child at risk.

New Policies

The blueprint for this program was outlined in the report of the Commission on Clerical Sexual Misconduct with Minors, released on June 15, 1992. You will recall that I accepted the Commission's recommendations in principle and authorized an extensive consultation with Archdiocesan advisory groups.

During the intervening weeks, a solid foundation for the new policies has been built through extensive consultation and discussion with: the special Commission itself, the Cabinet, the College of Consultors, the Presbyteral Council and the Archdiocesan Pastoral Council. These advisory groups overwhelmingly support both the Commission's recommendations and these new policies. The problem of clerical sexual misconduct with minors affects the entire Church, so the whole Church must be involved in its solution. These policies make this possible.

Independent Review Board

Today, representatives of the whole Church, a nine-member, independent Review Board is being established. This Board, consisting of six lay persons and three priests, will now be responsible for the processing and management of all cases of priests against whom allegations are made. This Board will now determine the fitness for ministry of any priests against whom allegations of sexual misconduct are made and will report their findings directly to me. . . .

This Review Board will be supported by a full-time Fitness Review Administrator, a lay professional with qualifications and experience in addressing the sexual abuse of children. The Review Board, together with the Administrator, will serve as my principal advisors in these matters.

The details of their respective duties are outlined in the policy document.

The Review Board's charge is to move promptly and credibly to determine the fitness for ministry of any priest accused of sexual misconduct with a minor and the conditions under which it may be possible for the priest to return to ministry. You will recall that in June 1992 the Commission Report disclosed that eight priests, who had been accused of sexual misconduct with minors, were in the process of being reassigned to non-parish ministries. The Commission felt that such reassignments should be made, even though the allegations against these priests were, for the most part made years ago and, currently, there was no risk to children or adolescents. Since then all eight cases have been resolved, either through reassignment to non-parish ministry or resignation. One of the first tasks of the new Board will be to review and monitor the disposition of these cases.

Victim Assistance

Should allegations of sexual misconduct with minors by priests be made in the future, we now have in place a new Victim Assistance Minister. This person's task will be to identify the professional resources available for the care of victims and their families or others who may have been affected by the sexual misconduct. . . .

Community Outreach

In addition, a series of programs designed to promote healing and understanding by the communities affected by this issue has been established. This program involves a team of psychologists, social workers, educators and pastoral ministers, who have responded in recent months on short notice to parish communities affected by this issue.

Assistance to Priests

The Vicars for Priests will continue to provide assistance, advice, and support to priests in many areas of ministerial and human needs. The Vicars facilitate referrals to professional resources as needed.

In the case of any disclosure of sexual misconduct with a minor by a priest to a Vicar, the Vicar will immediately report the fact to the Administrator, who will, in turn, begin the initial inquiry involving the priest, victim and Review Board. The Administrator will make prompt reports to the Illinois Department of Children and Family Services and help the victim to do the same with all public authorities. This is a significant departure from the past, when the Vicars for Priests had the sole responsibility to maintain contact with the priest, manage the inquiry and follow up and notify the proper authorities. To help prevent incidents from occurring in the future, the Archdiocese will organize substantive continuing education programs for all Archdiocesan personnel about the nature and effect of sexual misconduct with a minor.

Screening and Education

Full psychological profiles of seminarians will be created, updated and maintained as part of their permanent personnel file. Age appropriate courses on sexual development, which are part of the Archdiocesan seminary curriculum, will be reviewed and enhanced.

Priest Personnel Board

The new policies establish a unified priest personnel record-keeping system, from seminary training throughout a priest's entire career, to enable those responsible for ministerial assignments to consider the full record of a priest.

Review Process

An equitable review process, modeled after other professions, has been structured so the fitness of a priest accused of sexual misconduct with a minor can be determined promptly and credibly. The process is centered around the nine-member Review Board and its Administrator. Once the administrator is on board, we shall establish a 24-hour 800 number to receive initial information of any allegation of sexual misconduct by priests with minors. The process demands strict confidentiality. It also requires immediate disclosure of information to appropriate civil authorities and cooperation with those authorities. The process begins with a First-Stage Review by the Board within 48 hours of an allegation; a Second-Stage Review is held within 30 to 120 days; and Supplementary Reviews are scheduled as needed.

If the safety of children is ever an issue, the priest will immediately be withdrawn from his ministerial assignment. The Review Board's standard will be to determine whether there is "reasonable cause to suspect" that the accused priest engaged in sexual misconduct with a minor.

Return to Ministry

Priests who are withdrawn from ministry must undergo a psychiatric examination by an independent professional organization designated by the Archdiocese. If a Second Stage or Supplementary Review of the Board does not recommend return to ministry, the priest may never return to parish ministry or a ministry that includes access to minors. Such a priest may return to a restricted ministry with no access to minors only if the Archdiocese permits him to do so and if he undergoes a stringent treatment program of no less than two years, followed by a supervised aftercare program.

Conclusion

In the past three months, much has been accomplished. We have embarked upon a course that will serve well all the people of the Archdiocese. These new policies will enable the people of the Church to protect children, assist those affected, promote healing and address the fitness of those who have failed. These actions, in the long term, will also ensure the integrity of the priesthood.

While I cannot change the past, I can do something about the future. My pledge to the children, the people and the priests of the Archdiocese is that I will do everything in my power to accelerate the implementation of these new policies, which will give assurance and hope to all.

YELTSIN'S SUMMIT WITH BUSH, ADDRESS TO CONGRESS
June 16-17, 1992

In a historic breakthrough, President George Bush of the United States and President Boris Yeltsin of Russia, meeting at the White House in Washington, June 16, 1992, signed an agreement that would slash their countries' nuclear arsenals to one-third their current size. The accord was reached only after Yeltsin consented to abandon the concept of "strategic parity," a governing principle in all arms negotiations between the United States and the former Soviet Union during the Cold War. In an editorial June 17, 1992, the Baltimore Sun *called the arms agreement an "extraordinary step forward."*

But the emotional climax of Yeltsin's stunning visit to Washington came June 17 when he addressed a joint meeting of Congress in the House chamber. Referring to what he called the "idol of communism," Yeltsin told members of Congress, "It has collapsed never to rise again. I am here to assure you we will not let it rise again in our land." Yeltsin's deftly composed and delivered address was repeatedly interrupted by standing ovations and by chants of "Boris! Boris!" "It was an electrifying speech," Rep. Lee H. Hamilton, D-Ind., told reporters.

In his speech, in an interview, and with President Bush, Yeltsin spoke of American servicemen who might have been imprisoned in the Soviet Union during conflicts beginning with World War II. However, his suggestion that Americans in the Vietnam War had been sent to the Soviet Union puzzled U.S. and some Russian officials. Yet in his address he spoke with passion of his intention to have Russian archives combed for information about Americans from any war. He told members of Congress that "even if one American has been detained in my country, and still can be found, I will get him back to his family."

The Russian president pressed Congress to pass the Freedom Support Act, a part of a massive aid effort for Russia and the other former republics of the Soviet Union that President Bush had announced April 1. The Economist *of London said that Yeltsin's "forceful" speech "did more to make the case for an aid package ... than Mr. Bush has ever done."* (Nixon's Speech on Russian Aid, p. 255)

Yeltsin's Success

Yeltsin's performance during his Washington visit, and especially during his appearance before Congress, drew raves from the American press. Newsweek *magazine, in its June 29, 1992, issue, said that the Russian leader "took Congress by storm with a triumphant speech that sharply redefined the Russian-American relationship."*

Writing in the June 18, 1992, New York Times, *Michael Wines noted that when Yeltsin arrived in Washington he had a "lingering reputation as a rough-hewn politician,... his past strewn with rumors of heavy drinking and disappearances at odd times." Wines added, "But Yeltsin now seems to have dispatched all that."*

Referring to action in Congress on the Russian aid legislation, Pamela Fessler in the June 20 CQ Weekly Report quoted a Democratic congressional aide as saying, "It's not so much that Yeltsin won them all over ... as [it is that] his appearance improved the climate in which a vote will be taken."

Massive Nuclear Cuts

Negotiated over only five months, the arms cuts that Bush and Yeltsin agreed to went far beyond those achieved in nine years of negotiations over the Strategic Arms Reduction Treaty (START), which was signed July 31, 1991, by President Bush and Mikhail S. Gorbachev, then president of the Soviet Union. (London Economic Summit, Historic Documents of 1991, p. 451; Decisions to Reduce U.S.-Soviet Nuclear Weaponry, p. 475.)

The Bush-Yeltsin agreement would cut the total U.S. and Russian strategic arsenals by the year 2003 to no more than 6,500 weapons—about one fourth of the 25,000 long-range nuclear weapons in the countries' arsenals in 1990.

Appearing together at a news conference in the White House Rose Garden June 16, Bush and Yeltsin attributed the relative ease with which the accord was negotiated to the profoundly changed relationship between the two Cold War adversaries. Summing up the epochal agreement, President Bush said that "the nuclear nightmare recedes."

Under the agreement, in the year 2003, the United States would have 3,500 warheads and Russia would have 3,000. Thus, Yeltsin gave up nuclear parity, making the boldest concession. Both sides would eliminate all of their land-based missiles with multiple warheads by 2003.

Most of Russia's weapons were in those missiles, while the United States was more dependent on submarine-based missiles.

A 50-percent cut in submarine-launched ballistic missile warheads was considered the Americans' chief concession. The United States would carry out the reduction either by cutting the number of warheads per missile or by reducing the number of its submarines.

Russian Aid Legislation

Six months after Bush proposed it, and more than three months after Yeltsin's address to Congress, the House cleared the Freedom Support Act on October 3, 1992, providing aid for the former republics of the Soviet Union. President Bush signed the measure into law on October 24, 1992. The measure represented the part of Bush's total aid program that required congressional authorization. The $24-billion multilateral aid initiative that Bush and other Western leaders promised was dependent on the legislation.

The legislation authorized $460 million in bilateral assistance to the republics and a $12.3-billion increase in the U.S. contribution to the International Monetary Fund. The package also expanded U.S. efforts to help dismantle the former Soviet nuclear arsenal and to assist in converting the military establishment to civilian activities. The law also endorsed U.S. participation in currency stabilization funds for the republics.

American MIAs

In an interview with NBC News as he was flying to Washington from Moscow, Yeltsin said that Russian archives showed that some American prisoners from the Vietnam War "were transferred" to the Soviet Union "and were kept in labor camps." Some of the Americans, he said, might still be alive.

Bush on June 16 said that Yeltsin had told him the Russian government was investigating new information regarding U.S. servicemen from the Vietnam War. Praising Yeltsin for his frankness, Bush said he was persuaded the Russian president was prepared "to go the last mile" to find any missing Americans. Bush immediately dispatched Malcolm Toon, the co-chairman of a joint Russian-U.S. commission on POWs and MIAs, to Russia to review any new evidence.

Many Defense Department and other U.S. officials were skeptical of Yeltsin's information. Sen. John Kerry, D-Mass., chairman of the Senate Select Committee on POW/MIA Affairs, reacting cautiously to Yeltsin's assertions, noted that the Russian leader had only mentioned the possibility Americans could be alive.

Following is the transcript of the announcement June 16 by
Russian President Boris Yeltsin and President George Bush
on the new strategic arms agreement and of Yeltsin's

address to Congress, delivered on June 17 through an interpreter. (The bracketed headings have been added by Congressional Quarterly to highlight the organization of the text.)

BUSH AND YELTSIN ON ARMS REDUCTIONS ACCORD

PRESIDENT BUSH: ... Let me just say that I'm pleased to announce that President Yeltsin and I have just reached an extraordinary agreement on two areas of vital importance to our countries and to the world. First, we have agreed on far-reaching new strategic arms reductions, building on the agreement reached with Russia, Ukraine, Kazakhstan and Belarus. Our two countries are now agreeing to even further dramatic strategic arms reductions substantially below the levels determined by START [Strategic Arms Reduction Treaty].

We have agreed to eliminate the world's most dangerous weapons, heavy ICBMs [intercontinental ballistic missiles], and all other multiple-warhead ICBMs, and dramatically reduce our total strategic nuclear weapons.

Those dramatic reductions will take place in two phases. They will be completed no later than the year 2003 and may be completed as early as the year 2000 if the United States can assist Russia in the required destruction of ballistic missile systems.

With this agreement, the nuclear nightmare recedes more and more for ourselves, for our children and for our grandchildren.

Just a few years ago, the United States was planning a strategic nuclear stockpile of about 13,000 warheads. Now President Yeltsin and I have agreed that both sides will go down to 3,000 to 3,500 warheads, with each nation determining its own force structure within that range.

And I'd like to point out that this fundamental agreement, which in earlier years could not have been completed even in a decade, has been completed in only five months.

Our ability to reach this agreement so quickly is a tribute to the new relationship between the United States and Russia and to the personal leadership of our guest, Boris Yeltsin.

In the near future, the United States and Russia will record our agreement in a brief treaty document that President Yeltsin and I will sign and submit for ratification in our countries.

President Yeltsin and I have also agreed to work together, along with the allies and other interested states, to develop a concept for a global protection system against limited ballistic missile attack.

And we will explore a senior group—or we will establish a senior group—to explore practical steps toward that end, including the sharing of early warning and cooperation in developing ballistic missile defense capabilities and technologies.

This group will also explore the development of a legal basis for cooperation, including new treaties and agreements, and possible changes to existing treaties and agreements necessary to implement the global protection system.

That group is headed by [Policy Planning State Director] Dennis Ross for the United States [and] will first meet in Moscow within the next 30 days.

In conclusion, these are remarkable steps for our two countries, a departure from the tensions and the suspicions of the past, and a tangible, important expression of our new relationship. They also hold major promise for a future world protected against the danger of limited ballistic missile attack.

[Yeltsin Responds]

PRESIDENT YELTSIN: Mr. President, ladies and gentlemen, I'd like to add a few words to what President Bush has just announced here.

What we have achieved is an unparalleled and probably an unexpected thing for you and for the whole world. You are the first to hear about this historic decision, which has been reached today after just five months of negotiations. We are in fact meeting a sharp, dramatic reduction in the total number for the two sides of the number of nuclear warheads, from 21,000 to 6,000 or 7,000 for the United States of America and Russia.

Indeed, we have been able to cut over those five months of negotiations the total number of nuclear warheads to one-third, while it took 15 years under the START treaty to make some reductions.

This is an expression of the fundamental change in the political and economic relations between the United States of America and Russia.

It is also an expression and a proof of the personal trust and confidence that has been established between the presidents of these countries, President Bush of the United States of America and [the] president of Russia, and these things have been achieved without deception, without anybody wishing to gain unilateral advantages.

This is a result of the trust entertained by the president of democratic Russia toward America and by the president of the United States toward the new Russia.

This is the result of a carefully measured balance of security. We were not going in for numbers, for just 1,000, 2,000 or 3,000 pieces. Rather we have established a record for each country to elect the number, the figure that it will consider appropriate for its own defense and security.

As I have told you, the total number will go down from 21,000 to 6,000 for the two sides. Under the first phase, the reductions for the two sides will be down to the 3,800-to-4,250 bracket: including ICBMs, 1,250; and heavy missiles, 650; SLBMs, 2,250. Under the second phase we shall go down to, respectively, 3,000 and 3,500, including total reduction and destruction of heavy missiles.

Land-based MIRVs [multiple warhead missiles] will be reduced as well.

SLBMs [submarine-launched ballistic missiles] will go down to 1,750.

Each country will elect the figure that it will consider appropriate to ensure its defense and security.

Thus we are departing from the ominous parity where each country was exerting every effort to stay in line, which has led Russia, for instance, to have half of its population living below the poverty line. We cannot afford it, and therefore we must have a minimum-security level to deal with any possible eventuality which might arise anywhere in the world and threaten our security.

But we know one thing: We shall not fight against each other. This is a solemn undertaking that we are taking today, and it will be reflected as a matter of partnership and friendship in the charter that we are going to sign.

Our proposal is to cut the process of destruction from the proposed 13 years down to nine years. So the things that I have been mentioning before will materialize by the year 2000.

I am happy to be involved here in this historic occasion, and I will also hope that I will be as happy when this thing materializes and President Bush and I will be celebrating together the implementation of that agreement in the year 2000.

I thank you.

I want to add that these figures have been agreed with and ratified by the secretary for Defense, Mr. [Dick] Cheney, and the defense minister, Pavel Grachev, of the Russian Federation.

I thank you.

P: And I would only add to that my gratitude to the secretary of State, to Mr. [Andrei V.] Kozyrev, his counterpart, and also to Gen. [Brent] Scowcroft and others that have worked on this and accomplished all this in record time. . . .

Q: Would you explain for people who might not understand why friends who trust each other and who do not plan to attack would still need 7,000 nuclear warheads—

P: What I'm saying is, we've moved dramatically down from 13,000. It's going to be a—this will be seen as an enormous move forward toward the relaxation of tension and toward the friendship that we feel for each other.

The elimination of these—the most destabilizing of weapons—is extraordinarily positive. And the fact that each country at this juncture in history retains some nuclear weapons speaks for itself.

Who knows what lies out there ahead? But certainly I agree with what President Yeltsin said, that there is no animosity. The Cold War days are over, and he came here in a spirit of forward movement on these arms control agreements, and that speaks for itself.

YELTSIN: I would like to amplify on that.

I would say that in response to your question that the technical and financial resources that are required in order to destroy, dismantle and reduce the total number of warheads and missiles from 21,000 to 6,000 or

7,000 is enormous, and this is the only thing that conditions this figure.

[American POWs]

Q: [Question on the status of possible American POWs in Russia].

P: ... President Yeltsin and I discussed this morning the issue that is of the highest priority for our administration and, I know, for every American—the fate of American POWs and MIAs from World War II, Korea, the Cold War period and Vietnam.

President Yeltsin informed me for the first time that Russia may have information about the fate of some of our servicemen from Vietnam. And he said the Russian government is pursuing this information vigorously, just as we speak.

And with us today are President Yeltsin's adviser, Dmitri Volkogonov over here, and our able former ambassador to the U.S.S.R., Ambassador Malcolm Toon. Now they are the co-chairs of the Joint U.S.-Russian Commission on POW-MIAs, and they've met during the last few months along with the members of the United States Congress who are also part of this bipartisan U.S. delegation to unearth information on American POWs and MIAs from 1945 on, and Russian POWs and MIAs from the Afghan war.

President Yeltsin and I have instructed both of these gentlemen to begin immediately a joint U.S.-Russian pursuit of the latest information—it was given to me today.

I have asked Ambassador Toon to return immediately to Moscow to work on this issue, and I want to assure all Americans, and particularly those families of the American POWs and MIAs, that we will spare no effort in working with our Russian colleagues to investigate all information in the Russian archives concerning our servicemen.

And while we do not have any specific information to make public today, I pledge to keep the American people informed of developments on this issue as we find out more about these latest leads.

And let me just point out that the forthcoming comments by President Yeltsin are just one more sign of this improved new relationship between Russia and the United States of America. For him to go back and dig into these records, without fear of embarrassment, is of enormous consequence to the people of the United States of America.

And I salute him for this. He has told me he will go the last mile to find whatever ... [information exists about] American POWs and MIAs, and to clear this record once and for all, and in so many other fields this demonstrates his leadership and the period of change that we are saluting and I saluted here today on the South Lawn of the White House. So we're very grateful to you, Mr. President.

YELTSIN: I will only add a couple of points, Mr. President.

Our commission, headed and chaired by Dmitri Volkogonov, has been meeting for several months now, and it has already met with some success, and I can promise that the joint commission which will be established following this press conference will be working hard and will report to the American public all the information that will be found in the archives that we are going to open for it, in . . . [opening] the archives in the KGB, in the Central Committee of the Communist Party, regarding the fate of American POWs and MIAs.

Q: Do you agree it's possible some of those Americans may still be alive?

P: I would simply say that this—I have no evidence of that, but the cooperation that is, has been extended, and again is being extended by the president of Russia will guarantee to the American people that if anyone's alive, that person, those people would be found. And equally as important to the loved ones is the accounting for any possible MIA.

And so we have no evidence of anyone being alive, but I would simply say again that this, this is the best way to get to the bottom of it, and this new approach by the president of Russia to go into these archives and to try to find missing records will be the best assurance that I can give the American people that the truth will, will be revealed, finally.

Q: Is there a danger of raising false hopes?

P: You got to be careful of that, yeah.

YELTSIN ADDRESS TO CONGRESS

Mr. Speaker, Mr. President, members of Congress, ladies and gentlemen:

It is indeed a great honor for me to address the Congress of the great land of freedom as the first-ever, over 1,000 years of history of Russia, popularly elected president, as a citizen of the great country which has made its choice in favor of liberty and democracy.

For many years, our two nations were the two poles, the two opposites. They wanted to make us implacable enemies. That affected the destinies of the world in a most tragic way.

The world was shaken by the storms of confrontation. It was close to exploding; close to perishing beyond salvation.

That evil scenario is becoming a thing of the past. Reason begins to triumph over madness. We have left behind the period when America and Russia looked at each other through gun sights, ready to pull the trigger at any time.

Despite what we saw in the well-known American film, "The Day After," it can be said today, tomorrow will be a day of peace, less of fear and more of hope for the happiness of our children.

The world can sigh in relief. The idol of communism, which spread everywhere social strife, animosity and unparalleled brutality, which instilled fear in humanity, has collapsed.

It has collapsed never to rise again. I am here to assure you, we will not let it rise again in our land.

I am glad that the people of Russia have found strength to shake off the crushing burden of the totalitarian system. I am proud that I am addressing you on behalf of the great people whose dignity is restored.

I admire ordinary Russian men and women who, in spite of severe trials, have preserved their intellectual integrity and are enduring tremendous hardships for the sake of the revival of their country.

Russia has made its final choice in favor of a civilized way of life, common sense and universal human heritage. I am convinced that our people will reach that goal. There is no people on this earth who could be harmed by the air of freedom. There are no exceptions to that rule.

Liberty sets the mind free, fosters independence and unorthodox thinking and ideas. But it does not offer instant prosperity or happiness and wealth to everyone. This is something that politicians in particular must keep in mind. Even the most benevolent intentions will inevitably be abandoned and committed to oblivion if they are not translated into everyday efforts.

Our experience of the recent years has conclusively pointed that out. Liberty will not be fooled. There can be no coexistence between democracy and a totalitarian state system. There can be no coexistence between market economy and powers who control everything and everyone.

There can be no coexistence between a civic society, which is pluralist by definition, and communist intolerance to dissent. The experience of the past decade has taught us: Communism has no human face. Freedom and communism are incompatible.

You will recall August 1991, when for three days Russia was under the dark cloud of dictatorship.

I addressed the Muscovites who were defending the White House of Russia. I addressed all the people of Russia. I addressed them standing on top of the tank whose crew had disobeyed criminal orders.

I will be candid with you: At that moment, I feared. But I had no fear for myself. I feared for the future of democracy in Russia and throughout the world. Because I was aware what could happen if we failed to win.

Citizens of Russia upheld their freedom and did not allow the continuation of the 75 years of nightmare. From this high rostrum I want to express our sincere thanks and gratitude to President Bush and to the American people for their invaluable moral support for the just cause of the people of Russia.

Last year citizens of Russia passed another difficult test of maturity. We chose to forgo vengeance and the intoxicating craving for summary justice over the fallen collosus known under the name of the CPSU [Communist Party of the Soviet Union].

There was no replay of history. The Communist Party citadel, next to the Kremlin, the Communist Bastille, was not destroyed. There was not a hint of violence against Communists in Russia. People simply brushed off the venomous dust of the past and went about their business.

There were no lynch law trials in Russia. The doings of the Communist Party over many years have been referred to the constitutional court of the Russian Federation. I am confident that its verdict will be fair.

Russia has seen for itself that any delay in strengthening the foundations of freedom and democracy can throw the society far back. For us the ominous lesson of the past is relevant today as never before. It was precisely in a devastated country, with an economy in near paralysis, that Bolshevism succeeded in building a totalitarian regime, creating a gigantic war machine and an insatiable military-industrial complex.

[Economic and Political Reforms]

This must not be allowed to happen again. That is why economic and political reforms are the primary tasks for Russia today. We are facing the challenges that no one has ever faced before at any one time.

We must carry through unprecedented reforms in the economy, which over the seven decades has been stripped of all market infrastructure; lay the foundations for democracy; and restore the rule of law in the country that for scores of years was poisoned with political strife and political oppression.

We have no right to fail in this most difficult endeavor, for there will be no second try, as in sports. Our predecessors have used them all up. The reforms must succeed.

I am given strength by the support of the majority of the citizens of Russia. The people of Russia are aware that there is no alternative to reform, and that this is very important.

My job, as everybody else's in Russia, is not an easy one. But in everything I do, I have the reliable and invaluable support of my wife, and of my entire large family.

Today I am telling you what I tell my fellow countrymen: I will not go back on the reforms. And it is practically impossible to topple Yeltsin in Russia. I am in good health, and I will not say "uncle" before I make the reforms irreversible.

We realize our great responsibility for the success of our changes, not only toward the people of Russia but also toward the citizens of America and of the entire world.

Today the freedom of America is being upheld in Russia. Should the reforms fail, it will cost hundreds of billions to upset that failure.

[New Arms Treaty]

Yesterday we concluded an unprecedented agreement on cutting down strategic offensive arsenals. They will be reduced radically in two phases, not by 30 or 40 percent, as negotiated previously over 15 years. They will be slashed to less than one-third of today's strength—from 21,000 nuclear warheads on both sides down to 6,000 to 7,000 by the year 2000. And it has taken us only five months to negotiate. And I fervently hope that George Bush and myself will be there in the year 2000 to preside over that.

We have simply no right to miss this unique opportunity, the more so that arms and the future of Russian reforms designed to make impossible any restoration of the totalitarian dictatorship in Russia are so dramatically interrelated.

I am here to say that we have the firm determination and the political will to move forward. We have proved that by what we have done.

It is Russia that has put an end to the imperial policies and was the first to recognize the independence of the Baltic republics.

Russia is a founding member of the Commonwealth of Independent States, which has averted uncontrolled disintegration of the former empire and the threat of a general interethnic blood bath.

Russia has granted tangible powers to its autonomous republics. The treaty of federation has been signed, and our nation has escaped the fate of the Soviet Union.

Russia has preserved its unity. It was Russia that substantially slowed down the flywheel of militarization and is doing all it can to stop it altogether.

I am formally announcing that, without waiting for the treaty to be signed, we have begun taking off alert the heavy SS-18 missiles targeted on the United States of America.

And the defense minister of Russia is here in this room to confirm that.

Russia has brought its policies toward a number of countries in line with its solemn declarations of the recent years. We have stopped arms deliveries to Afghanistan, where the senseless military adventure has taken thousands of Russian and hundreds of thousands of Afghan lives.

With external props removed, the puppet regime collapsed.

We have corrected the well-known imbalances in relations with Cuba. At present that country is one of our Latin American partners. Our commerce with Cuba is based on universally accepted principles and world prices.

[An End to Double Standards]

It is Russia that once and for all has done away with double standards in foreign policy. We are firmly resolved not to lie any more, either to our negotiating partners, or to the Russian or American or any other people.

There will be no more lies—ever.

The same applies to biological weapons experiments and the facts that have been revealed about American prisoners of war, the KAL 007 flight and many other things. That list could be continued.

The archives of the KGB and the Communist Party Central Committee are being opened.

Moreover, we are inviting the cooperation of the United States and other nations to investigate these dark pages.

I promise you that each and every document in each and every archive will be examined in order to investigate the fate of every American unaccounted for. As president of Russia, I assure you that even if one American has been detained in my country, and can still be found, I will find him; I will get him back to his family.

(sustained applause)

I thank you for the applause. I could see everybody rise.

Some of you who have just risen here to applaud me have also written in the press that until Yeltsin gets things done and gets all the jobs done, there should be no Freedom Support Act passing through the Congress.

Well, I don't really quite understand you, ladies and gentlemen. This matter has been investigated, and is being investigated. Yeltsin has already opened the archives, and is inviting you to join us in investigating the fate of each and every unaccounted American.

So now you are telling me, first, do the job, and then we shall support you in passing that act? I don't quite understand you.

We have made tangible moves to make contact between Russia and foreign business communities much easier. Under the recent legislation, foreign nationals who privatize a facility or a building in Russia are given property rights to the plot of land on which they are located.

Legislation on bankruptcy has been recently enacted.

Mandatory sale of foreign currency to the state, at an artificially low rate of exchange, has been ended.

We are ready to bring our legal practice, as much as possible, in line with world standards, of course on the basis of symmetry with each country.

We are inviting the private sector of the United States to invest in the unique and untapped Russian market. And I am saying: Do not be late.

[U. S. Policy]

Now that the period of global confrontation is behind us, I call upon you to take a fresh look at the current policy of the United States toward Russia, and also to take a fresh look at the longer-term prospects of our relations.

Russia is a different country today. Sometimes the obsolete standards brought into being by a different era are artificially imposed on new realities.

True, that equally applies to us. Let us together, therefore, master the art of reconciling differences on the basis of partnership, which is the most efficient and democratic way.

This would come naturally both for the Russians and the Americans. If this is done, many of the problems which are now impeding mutual advantageous cooperation between Russia and the United States will become irrelevant, and I mean legislative frameworks too.

It will not be a wasteful endeavor. On the contrary, it will promote a more efficient solution of your problems, as well as of ours. And of course it will create new jobs, in Russia as well as in the United States.

History is giving us a chance to fulfill President [Woodrow] Wilson's dream, namely, to make the world safe for democracy.

More than 30 years ago, President [John F.] Kennedy addressed these words to humanity: "My fellow citizens of the world, ask not what America can do for you, but what together we can do for the freedom of man."

I believe that his inspired call for working together toward a democratic world is addressed above all to our two peoples, to the people of America and to the people of Russia.

Partnership and friendship of our two largest democracies, in strengthening democracy, is indeed a great goal.

Joining the world community, we wish to preserve our identity, our own image and history, promote culture, strengthen moral standards of our people.

We find relevant the warning of the great Russian philosopher, Berdyaev, who said to negate Russia in the name of humankind is to rob humankind.

At the same time, Russia does not aspire to change the world in its own image. It is the fundamental principle of the new Russia to be generous and to share experience, moral values and emotional warmth, rather than to impose and curse.

It is the tradition of the Russian people to repay kindness with kindness. This is the bedrock of the Russian lifestyle, the underlying truth revealed by the great Russian culture.

Free and democratic Russia will remain committed to this tenet. Today, free and democratic Russia is extending its hand of friendship to the people of America. Acting on the will of the people of Russia, I am inviting you, and through you, the people of the United States, to join us in partnership in the quest for freedom and justice in the 21st century.

The Russo-American dialogue has gone through many a dramatic moment. But the peoples of Russia and America have never gone to war against each other. Even in the darkest periods, our affinity prevailed over our hatred.

In this context, I would like to recall something that took place 50 years ago. The unprecedented war, world war, was waging. Russia, which was bleeding white, and all our people were looking forward to the opening of the second front. And it was opened, first and foremost, thanks to the active stance taken by President [Franklin D.] Roosevelt and by the entire American people.

Sometimes I think that if today, like during that war, a second but peaceful front could be opened to promote democratic market reforms, their success would be guaranteed early.

The passing by Congress of the Freedom Support Act could become the first step in that direction.

Today legislation promoting reforms is much more important than appropriation of funds.

May I express the hope that the United States Congress, as the staunch advocate of freedom, will remain faithful to its strategic course on this occasion as well.

Members of Congress, every man is a man of his own time. No exception is ever made for anyone, whether an ordinary citizen or the president. Much experience has been gained; many things have been reassessed.

I would like now to conclude my statement with the words from a song by Irving Berlin, an American of Russian descent: God bless America, to which I add, and Russia.

REPORT ON THE FEDERAL EMERGENCY MANAGEMENT AGENCY

June 22, 1992

A congressional investigation of the Federal Emergency Management Agency (FEMA), the agency responsible for coordinating the nation's disaster relief programs, charged in June that the agency was grossly mismanaged and wracked by internal feuding, power struggles, and overt hostility by FEMA executives toward career employees.

The probe, conducted by staff of the House Appropriations Committee and labeled an interim point paper, concluded that the agency had become a "political dumping ground" for inexperienced Bush administration loyalists.

Established by President Jimmy Carter in 1979, FEMA was an amalgam of several agencies and departments that dealt with all types of domestic natural, manmade, and nuclear emergencies. The agency had been under attack long before the House panel's investigation. In 1989 the agency was the target of stinging criticism for its handling of disaster relief in the wake of Hurricane Hugo in South Carolina and a major earthquake in San Francisco. But FEMA was to face its severest challenges in 1992. First came the House committee's scrutiny of its operations and then the major disaster in Florida and Louisiana caused by Hurricane Andrew, the costliest hurricane in U.S. history. (Damage of Hurricanes Andrew and Iniki, p. 843; Relief Effort in Hurricane, Earthquake Disasters, Historic Documents of 1989, p. 667)

FEMA's Role in Hurricane Andrew

FEMA's handling of the disaster in Florida was criticized almost as soon as the hurricane hit August 24, destroying some 85,000 houses and leaving a quarter of a million Floridians homeless. Two days later President George Bush ordered Transportation Secretary Andrew H. Card, Jr., to coordinate all relief efforts, replacing FEMA as Washington's chief coordinator of emergency relief. Bush also directed the Defense Department to provide comprehensive assistance, including the use of regular Army troops. Frustrated local officials had denounced the apparent political infighting between the White House and Florida Governor Lawton Chiles. In the midst of the turmoil, an exasperated Kate Hale, director of emergency operations in Dade County (Miami), said, "For God's sake, where are they? ... Get those services down here.... Sort out your political feuds afterwards."

Some members of Congress later urged that the Pentagon be made responsible for coordinating major disaster relief activities. Senator John B. Breaux of Louisiana, said, "If there's one thing we learned from Hurricane Andrew [it] is that the military ought to be put ... in the predominant role for responding to natural disasters along with the National Guard from the respective states."

The point paper, prepared by the committee's surveys and investigations staff, contained a host of criticisms covering virtually every aspect of FEMA's management and activities. The three top executives were singled out for various personal indiscretions, inappropriate behavior, self-aggrandizement, and possibly illegal management actions.

FEMA director Wallace E. Stickney, a protege of former White House chief of staff John Sununu, was called ineffective and uninterested in FEMA's programs and mission. Instead, Stickney was said to have busied himself with public relations, reorganization schemes aimed at placing his friends in agency jobs, and ways to expand top officials' perquisites and upgrade their office accommodations.

Stickney handed over day-to-day operations to his deputy, Jerry D. Jennings, a former White House aide. Both officials initiated job realignments, personnel transfers, and forced retirements that, according to the report, "created a situation where a once well-regarded, efficient management structure" was now in disarray. Jennings's hand-picked executive director, Thomas R. McQuillan, had allegedly pressured a homosexual employee to provide, as a precondition for a job assignment, a list of all other homosexuals who worked at FEMA. Both McQuillan and Jennings were subsequently forced from their executive posts.

Investigation's Findings

The investigation found that FEMA had a disproportionate number of political appointees for an agency of its size. As a result, the federal government's principal agency for coordinating relief measures was led by officials with little or no experience in disaster and emergency management. And the inordinate number of noncareer appointees had caused serious morale problems among the career staff.

FEMA management had "abrogated its fiduciary responsibilities,"
according to the report. There was a perception that some consultants
were hired solely because of their friendship with the executive director,
who hired them. For example, the report noted one outside consultant
who had been hired to explore leases at alternative buildings even though
FEMA had its own personnel to work on such matters. Unnecessary and
costly renovations had been made at the agency's headquarters, and
other projects were approved under the guise of benefiting all employees,
while in actuality they were initiated for the benefit of FEMA executives
alone or to give FEMA headquarters a corporate appearance, with little
regard to cost.

FEMA responded to these charges in August, calling the report's
conclusions unfounded and full of innuendo and hallway speculation. It
nevertheless said the agency was confident the final report would
"provide a logically reasoned objective" evaluation. It contended that the
squabbling that had "occupied the time and attention of a few FEMA
employees and the interest of some in Congress" had not affected the
agency's effectiveness, which included support to state and local agencies
battered by thirty-two major disasters in 1992 alone.

Following are excerpts of the preliminary findings of the
point paper, prepared by the surveys and investigations
staff of the House Appropriations Committee, regarding the
management and administration of the Federal Emergency
Management Agency, issued June 22, 1992:

Federal Emergency Management Agency Management and Administration Activities

Issue 1: The Organization and Administration of the Federal Emergency Management Agency

The Federal Emergency Management Agency (FEMA) was established
in 1979 to provide a focal point of accountability at the Federal level for
emergency preparedness, mitigation, and response activities. FEMA's
mission is to coordinate the resources of Federal, state, and local governments in preparing for and in responding to a full range of emergencies,
including natural, manmade, and nuclear emergencies. . . .

The current Director, according to interviews of career FEMA employees, is considered to be weak, reluctant to interact with agency personnel,
and uninterested in the substantive programs of FEMA, preferring instead
to participate in external public relations activities. In fact, shortly after
his arrival in August 1990, the Director executed a memorandum delegat-
ing his authority as Director to his Deputy, presumably in order to
distance himself from the day-to-day management of the agency.

The Director has reportedly made statements at staff meetings indicating an apparent resentment of career Federal employees which, in turn, have alienated him from them. In response to a question on the importance of FEMA's career employees to the agency, the Director is quoted as stating that "the only thing that is important is what the White House thinks of this agency."

Accordingly, a number of FEMA employees advised that morale at the agency is at an all-time low, in part because of the perceived lack of leadership displayed by both the Director and his Deputy and also because of "the way the agency is being managed or mismanaged." One result of this perceived mismanagement was the unionization of FEMA's headquarters in February 1992. Although a few regional offices have been unionized for several years, the unionization of FEMA's headquarters is cited as an example of the antagonistic "we" versus "they" attitude between FEMA's politically appointed top managers and the career civil service employees at the agency.

The current Director and Deputy Director of FEMA were appointed in mid-1990 and fill two of the nine Presidential appointees with Senate confirmation (PAS) positions at the agency. FEMA has 56 Senior Executive Service (SES) positions, fourteen of which are non-career political appointees, including the 10 Regional Directors, the General Counsel, the Superintendent of the Fire Administration, a Senior Policy Advisor, and the Deputy Associate Director for External Affairs. In the past year alone, four new SES positions, which were formerly non-SES jobs, have been created and filled by individuals new to FEMA.

FEMA also has 14 Schedule C employees, non-career political appointees hired at the GM/GS-15 level and below. . . .

Statistically, FEMA does have a disproportionate number of PAS, SES, and Schedule C positions. According to the Office of Personnel Management, as of December 1991, the average Government-wide ratio of PAS employees to total FTE's is 1 to 2,993, whereas FEMA's corresponding ratio is 1 to 314. The average ratio of SES employees to FTE's is 1 to 262, whereas FEMA's ratio is 1 to 50. For Schedule C employees, the Government-wide ratio is 1 to 1,225 versus the ratio at FEMA of 1 to 202.

Issue 2: Reorganization of the Management and Administration Component

The third highest ranking official at FEMA headquarters is currently the Executive Director, who serves immediately under and reports to the agency's Deputy Director. Shortly after his appointment in May 1990, the Deputy Director began a reorganization of FEMA's Headquarters. According to former senior officials, the Deputy Director made it clear he was going to "go after" every subordinate office Director at FEMA Headquarters because he felt "old was bad" and that he was more interested in the benefits associated with his position and cosmetic changes to FEMA's offices than with the missions and programs of FEMA.

Subsequently, in November 1990, the Chief of Staff position, formerly the number 3 position at headquarters, was abolished following the lateral transfer of the incumbent to a less influential position several months earlier. Thereafter, a new SES position, entitled Executive Director, Office of Management Services, was created to replace the Chief of Staff position. The responsibilities of this new position were identical to those of the old Chief of Staff position and included oversight and supervision of the Offices of Administrative Support, Acquisition Management, Security, and Program Analysis and Evaluation. In March 1991, an Executive Director was hired to fill the new position. By removing the previous Chief of Staff and hiring a new Executive Director, the Deputy Director was thus in position to undertake further reorganization through his subordinate. Although the Executive Director is a self-described "can do" executive, many FEMA employees contend he is in reality only a "hatchet man" for the Deputy Director. The Executive Director has subsequently effected many of the aesthetic and personnel changes originally contemplated and discussed by the Deputy Director when he took office in May of 1990.

According to FEMA employees, the Executive Director made it clear early in his tenure that he had a number of administrative and renovational plans on his agenda and would brook no resistance, legitimate or otherwise, to these plans. Objections by subordinates, citing either non-compliance with Government regulations, an appearance of impropriety, or budgetary constraints, were interpreted by the Executive Director as "disloyalty," to be dealt with accordingly at a later date. According to employees under his supervision, the Executive Director indicated many of the organizational changes were made based on his assessment of a subordinate's loyalty to the Deputy, to him and to management.

Substantive administrative changes began in the summer of 1991 when the Executive Director announced to his subordinate Office Directors that "all your money is mine and I will give you what I think you need." As a result, although each Division has its own budgetary allocation, most of the Office Directors interviewed were unaware of their respective Division's obligations and remaining balances. For example, one was surprised to learn that $118,000 had been allocated for travel for his Division for FY 1992 and that $75,000 of this amount had already been committed in the first quarter. He stated his Division has had minimal travel this fiscal year and these funds might have been used by other FEMA offices. By comparison, this Division was allocated $5,000 for FY 1991 travel and had committed only $236 by the first quarter of FY 1991. The FY 1993 budget request reflects a proposal to consolidate the five subordinate offices into a single line item called the Office of the Executive Director.

In November 1991, the Office of Administrative Support was restructured. Although the Office Director of this organizationally-powerful office retained his position, three of his six directorates were removed and placed under the supervision of his deputy, who became the head of a new entity, the Office of Operations Support. The removal of the three most important directorates (Space and Property Management, Headquarters Services, and Management Analysis) left this Office Director with the three less substantive directorates (Records and Information Systems Management, Graphic Arts and Design, and Printing and Publications), which in effect reduced the stature of the Office of Administrative Support. This Office Director believes the dismantling of his division was malpurposeful because he had previously challenged the propriety and/or legality of a number of the Executive Director's actions. . . .

In December 1991, a new Office Director was installed in the Office of Acquisition Management. By way of background, in early March 1991, prior to the new Executive Director's arrival, the position of Director, Office of Acquisition Management, had been upgraded and advertised as an SES position. The Director of Acquisition Management, who had more than 7 years experience in the position, was asked to write the justification for the upgrade of his position. He did so, but in November 1991, he was notified that he had not been selected for the job because the Executive Director felt "there was no chemistry between us." The Executive Director then offered the deposed Office Director an opportunity to serve as the deputy in the same office. . . .

Illustrative of the organizational chaos at FEMA is an action which also occurred in December 1991, when the Executive Director changed the name of his office (Office of Management Services) to the Office of the Executive Director, which he felt was more descriptive of his responsibilities. In late April 1992, the name was changed back to the Office of Management Services by order of FEMA's Director, but not before delivery had been accepted earlier that month of 500 lapel buttons which read "FEMA's Office of the Executive Director-At Your Service!" It should be noted that all references to this Management and Administration line item activity in FEMA's FY 1993 budget request reflect the previous name, "Office of the Executive Director," rather than the current name, "Office of Management Services."

Consequently, in May 1992, FEMA's Director relieved the Executive Director of his responsibilities, in response to several administrative issues, including the Executive Director's alleged threat to a homosexual FEMA employee to deny his request for participation in a scientific expedition if he did not provide a list of other homosexual employees at FEMA. The Executive Director was then ordered to report to an off-site facility in Virginia and although he has relinquished his position, he has refused to vacate the headquarters building. He has also retained counsel in an attempt to regain the position of Executive Director. . . .

Issue 3: Use of Consultants for the Headquarters Building Lease and Other Matters

The 10-year lease on FEMA's headquarters facility was scheduled to expire in August 1991. Although the General Services Administration (GSA) had advocated a move by FEMA to a proposed new Federal building and had issued a Solicitation for Offers in August 1990, relatively little internal work had been done by FEMA by March 1991 to either renew the lease or to relocate the agency. FEMA's Director delegated this task to the Executive Director.

Before the Congressional hearings on March 25, 1992, (Subcommittee on VA, HUD, and Independent Agencies, House Appropriations Committee) in response to a direct question concerning the use of space consultants by FEMA, the Executive Director testified that only one consultant and two members of his staff had worked on a relocation survey project. He further testified that the total costs associated with this survey were $2,477.

Contrary to his testimony, the Executive Director had in fact hired two consultants and had eschewed the use of personnel from FEMA's Space and Property Management Division. One consultant was hired in July 1991 for 1 year at $69,000 and was tasked initially to work on space and lease matters. The Executive Director provided him with the parameters FEMA considered essential for a new facility, including a minimum of 250,000 square feet of stand-alone space and close proximity to public transportation. . . .

The second consultant was hired by a non-competitive acquisition process in August 1991 to identify potential headquarters sites in the metropolitan area at a daily rate of $260 plus expenses, the total not to exceed $2,500. He was paid $2,477 for 8 days work but had no dealings with GSA nor did he review any GSA regulations. Furthermore, the consultant was told to keep his search confidential and not to mention the agency to prospective landlords. It remains to be resolved as to whether these or other FEMA lease activities were in violation of the Federal Property Management Regulations.

This consultant ultimately recommended four sites, three in Virginia and one in the District. Although a significant number of FEMA employees reside in Maryland, no sites were identified in that jurisdiction because "nothing was available in Maryland which met the specifications." In August 1991, an extension to the existing lease was executed by GSA to allow FEMA to remain in its current location until August 2001, with a commensurate increase in the rent.

Both of these consultants had a pre-existing relationship with the Executive Director and were recruited by him to work at FEMA. The first consultant had worked with the Executive Director at another agency in 1990. . . .

The second consultant has been a close friend of the Executive Director for approximately 20 years. In December 1991, he was appointed on a temporary basis not to exceed 1 year to the position of Program Specialist in the Space and Property Management Division. He recently applied for a permanent position in this same Division.

In addition to these consultants hired by FEMA to assist with lease matters, FEMA has regularly hired consultants since 1979 to work in a variety of programmatic areas. However, the use of outside consultants under the present administration increased substantially during FY 1991. Whereas 42 consultants were hired in FY 1990 at a cost of approximately $8.7 million, the number increased to 63 in FY 1991 at a cost of $11.5 million.

One such consultant hired in FY 1991 through the efforts of the Executive Director was a "facilitator." His company was awarded a sole-source contract to conduct a teambuilding meeting in Washington and three retreat-style teambuilding sessions at resorts in Virginia and West Virginia. According to employees who attended the first retreat in West Virginia, it did not produce positive results, but produced instead a greater chasm between the Executive Director and his subordinates.

The facilitator was paid a total of $12,675 for the first retreat, at a rate of $1,650 per day plus expenses for 6.5 days. The additional days were attributed to travel, preparatory work, and post-retreat feedback. The same fees were charged for subsequent sessions. . . .

Issue 4: Renovations at Headquarters and Related Expenditures

A top priority of the new Executive Director in April 1991 was to expeditiously renovate and re-carpet the executive floor of FEMA's headquarters, despite the fact that FEMA's lease on the building was due to expire in August 1991. As previously noted, there was an effort underway, supported by contractors hired by the Executive Director, to relocate the headquarters to new space.

In May and August 1991, a total of approximately $4,400 from Salaries and Expenses funding was expended to procure carpeting for the executive eighth floor. Another $2,442 was spent on installation. In August and September 1991, over $10,000 was spent to replace the solid doors with glass doors in the Offices of the Director, the Deputy Director, the Inspector General and the General Counsel, again in spite of the possibility that FEMA might vacate the building in the near future. By the time a new lease for FEMA's old headquarters building was executed in December 1991, FEMA had already expended almost $10,000 on renovations that the landlord would have implemented as part of a new lease arrangement.

Another top priority of both the Executive Director and the Deputy Director was to obtain parking for the employees at headquarters. However, one official stated "the real reason that FEMA has parking is because the Executive Director and Deputy Director wanted it for themselves; the parking for everyone else was just a cover for these two."

In 1985, the then-Director of FEMA issued a memorandum which reiterated the opinion of FEMA's Office of General Counsel that it was not permissible for FEMA to provide parking for any employee except on those days when that employee actually used his vehicle for official business. A subsequent memorandum from the Office of General Counsel dated April 1991, stated that, in general, a Government agency can only provide parking for its employees either when the Government owns a building and parking spaces or when an agency leases a building and the lease includes parking spaces. Neither situation was applicable to FEMA.

Disregarding these prior opinions, the Executive Director subsequently established a FEMA headquarters parking program and entered into discussions with a newly-appointed General Counsel. In June 1991, the Executive Director submitted a letter to GSA requesting a delegation of authority for FEMA to operate a parking program. With the letter, the Executive Director included a certification that funds were available to pay for 209 parking spaces. Although several FEMA officials indicated to him that funds were not available and such a costly program had not been budgeted for, the Executive Director assured them the money would be available. . . .

In conjunction with his office enhancement project, the Executive Director spent approximately $7,000 for new furnishings for his own office. The Executive Director also proposed that FEMA maintain an elevator to be used exclusively for eighth floor executives and staff because he felt that they were spending too much time waiting in the lobby for the elevators and that a dedicated elevator would provide the executive look he desired. Because this project would have cost approximately $50,000, it has been temporarily tabled.

Other lobby improvement projects included the purchase of "more professional" uniforms costing more than $16,000 for the contract security guards, who are not FEMA employees, and a review of optical style passageway systems to replace the security turnstiles currently in place. . . .

Preliminary Investigative Staff Findings

An Inordinate Number of Political Appointee Positions has Adversely Impacted FEMA

FEMA has a disproportionate number of authorized PAS, SES, and Schedule C positions, when compared to other executive agencies, and far exceeds the Government-wide average. These inordinate numbers, and the temporality of the PAS officials and non-career political appointees, have resulted in a lack of continuity in management and administration policy and style and a deep skepticism of management's commitment to the mission of the agency. FEMA is widely viewed as a political "dumping ground," a turkey farm if you will, where large numbers of positions exist that can be conveniently and quietly filled by political appointment. This has led to a situation where top officials, having little or no experience in disaster and emergency management, are creating substantial morale problems among careerists and professionals.

FEMA Headquarters Reorganization Has Been Counter Productive

While it is not uncommon for incoming senior officials to effect agency reorganizations, the restructuring at FEMA by its present administration is noteworthy in that its efforts have been both capricious and detrimental to the mission and programs of the agency.

Substantive actions, ranging from office realignments to transfers and forced retirement of acknowledged professionals by the Deputy Director, and his principal assistant, the Executive Director, have created a situation where a once well regarded, efficient management structure is now viewed as being in disarray. Severe morale problems exist because of the seemingly haphazard nature of the reorganizational changes and employees constantly wonder who or what will be next.

In acknowledgment of this situation, some reorganization actions have recently been countermanded by the FEMA Director, albeit under pressure, and the Executive Director has been relieved of his duties following revelations that he was allegedly involved in the forced production of a list of homosexuals at the agency....

FEMA's Use of Outside Consultants Is Neither Warranted Nor Cost Effective

The present FEMA administration spent $11.5 million during FY 1991 for outside consultants, an increase of 35 percent over the agency's FY 1990 total of $8.5 million. In one case, consultants were hired to conduct relocation surveys even though the agency had an indigenous entity responsible for such leasing matters. Another consultant was hired to conduct seminars, of dubious value and results, at Virginia and West Virginia resorts, with little apparent regard to cost.

At a minimum, there is a perception that some consultants were hired solely due to their pre-existing relationships with the Executive Director, who was responsible for their hiring. More importantly, however, there is a perception that senior management has abrogated its fiduciary responsibilities and in at least one case, testimony before a Congressional hearing substantially understated the cost of consultants conducting FEMA's relocation project.

FEMA Headquarters Renovations Have Been Costly and Unnecessary

FEMA's senior officials have undertaken headquarters renovations that were premature, ill-advised, and seemingly driven by a desire for aggrandizement. FEMA wasted almost $10,000 on renovations that the landlord would have implemented had agency officials had the fortitude to simply wait a few months for the lease to be renewed.

Some projects were undertaken under the guise of benefiting all employees, but in reality, were initiated to either accommodate FEMA executives or to create a corporate headquarters appearance, with little regard to cost. Parking, previously not permissible under Government regulations, was obtained for employees at a cost of almost $25,000 per month....

SUPREME COURT ON
HATE-CRIME LAW
June 22, 1992

The Supreme Court declared June 22 that a hate-crime law used to prosecute an alleged cross-burner in St. Paul, Minnesota, violated the constitutional right of free speech. In nullifying that city's ordinance, the Court jeopardized perhaps hundreds of local and state antibias laws, and campus codes that punish offensive remarks motivated by prejudice.

The St. Paul law prohibited the use of symbols, including burning crosses and swastikas, likely to create "anger, alarm, or resentment" on the basis of race, color, creed, religion, or gender. The Court held that the law was fatally flawed by specifying certain kinds of offensive expressions for punishment. "The First Amendment does not permit St. Paul to impose special prohibitions on those speakers who express views on disfavored subjects," said Justice Antonin Scalia, writing for five of the justices. Although four other justices disagreed with Scalia's reasoning, the Court was unanimous in its judgment that the ordinance was unconstitutional.

A key question was whether the ruling would undercut not just laws that banned specific acts as so-called hate crimes but also less direct measures—such as laws that required stiffer penalties for crimes if there was evidence that they were motivated by racial bias or prejudice. The Court did not directly address such measures, but some analysts suggested that Scalia's broad argument could cast doubt on their constitutionality as well. The ruling did not affect a 1990 federal law in which Congress directed the Justice Department to gather and publish statistics on hate crimes.

Cross-Burning on Black Family's Lawn

The case, R. A. V. *v.* City of St. Paul, *was the most important one involving political expression the Supreme Court had decided since it ruled in 1989 and 1990 that statutes barring flag-burning were unconstitutional. The St. Paul ordinance was challenged on behalf of a white teenager, Robert Viktora, who was arrested and charged under the law with burning a cross on the lawn of a black family that had moved into an all-white block. The incident occurred June 21, 1990. The trial judge, ruling that the law was too broad and content-laden to be constitutional, dismissed the count against Viktora. But the Minnesota Supreme Court reversed the lower court's ruling, saying that the law outlawed only "fighting words"—words that simply by being spoken inflict injury or incite violence. "Fighting words," along with libel and obscenity, are not protected by the First Amendment.*

But Scalia argued that the ordinance was unconstitutional because it barred only specified categories of "fighting words," based on the content of speech. "Those who wish to use 'fighting words' in connection with other ideas—to express hostility, for example, on the basis of political affiliation, union membership or homosexuality—are not covered," Scalia wrote in an opinion joined by Chief Justice William H. Rehnquist and Justices Anthony M. Kennedy, David H. Souter, and Clarence Thomas. "Selectivity of this sort creates the possibility that the city is seeking to handicap the expression of particular ideas," he added.

Scalia said that cross-burning and other bias-inspired acts are "reprehensible" but could be prosecuted as other kinds of crime, such as arson. "St. Paul has sufficient means at its disposal to prevent such behavior without adding the First Amendment to the fire," he wrote.

Court Debates "Fighting Words" Doctrine

Four other justices—Byron R. White, Harry A. Blackmun, John Paul Stevens, and Sandra Day O'Connor—agreed that the law was unconstitutional but for other reasons. Writing for the four, White argued that it outlawed not just fighting words but also "expressive conduct that causes only hurt feelings, offense or resentment and is protected by the First Amendment." White contended, however, that the majority's reasoning was faulty. It abandoned "long established First Amendment doctrine" and wrongly maintained that the government could not legitimately distinguish between categories of "fighting words," White wrote.

"The selective regulation reflects the city's judgment that harms based on race, color, creed, religion or gender are more pressing public concerns than harms caused by other fighting words," he added. "In light of our nation's long and painful experience with discrimination, this determination is plainly reasonable." In a separate opinion, Blackmun said the majority "manipulated doctrine to strike down an ordinance whose premise it opposed, namely that racial threats and verbal assaults are of

greater harm than other fighting words." He added: "I fear that the court has been distracted from its proper mission by the temptation to decide the issue over 'politically correct speech' and 'cultural diversity,' neither of which is presented here."

Case Splits Various Rights Groups

Among several normally allied organizations, the case created a conflict between their concerns for free speech and punishing racist intimidation. For instance, the Anti-Defamation League, the NAACP, and the People for the American Way supported the law's constitutionality. The American Civil Liberties Union and the American Jewish Congress argued against it.

One of the first results of the Supreme Court's decision followed in September. The University of Wisconsin voted to repeal its speech code that punished students who uttered racist or sexist slurs. "There was concern that it violated the First Amendment," said Patricia Hodulik, the university's senior counsel. Other universities were reported to be ready to rescind or modify their similar codes. "Speech codes were unwise and for the most part unnecessary, even though they were adopted for the best of reasons," Robert M. O'Neill, a University of Virginia law professor who directs the Thomas Jefferson Center for the Protection of Free Expression, said after the University of Wisconsin acted.

Following are excerpts from the majority opinion of Justice Antonin Scalia in the Supreme Court case of R. A. V. *v.* City of St. Paul, *decided June 22, 1992, holding that the St. Paul, Minnesota, antibias ordinance violated free-speech rights:*

No. 90-7675

R.A.V., Petitioner *v.* City of St. Paul, Minnesota	On writ of certiorari to the Supreme Court of Minnesota

[June 22, 1992]

JUSTICE SCALIA delivered the opinion of the Court.

In the predawn hours of June 21, 1990, petitioner and several other teenagers allegedly assembled a crudely-made cross by taping together broken chair legs. They then allegedly burned the cross inside the fenced yard of a black family that lived across the street from the house where the petitioner was staying. Although this conduct could have been punished under any number of laws, one of the two provisions under which respondent city of St. Paul chose to charge petitioner (then a juvenile) was the St. Paul Bias-Motivated Crime Ordinance....

545

I

In construing the St. Paul ordinance, we are bound by the construction given to it by the Minnesota court. Accordingly, we accept the Minnesota Supreme Court's authoritative statement that the ordinance reaches only those expressions that constitute "fighting words" within the meaning of *Chaplinsky* [v. *New Hampshire,* 1942]. Petitioner . . . urge[s] us to modify the scope of the *Chaplinsky* formulation, thereby invalidating the ordinance as "substantially overbroad." We find it unnecessary to consider this issue. Assuming, *arguendo,* that all of the expression reached by the ordinance is proscribable under the "fighting words" doctrine, we nonetheless conclude that the ordinance is facially unconstitutional in that it prohibits otherwise permitted speech solely on the basis of the subjects the speech addresses.

The First Amendment generally prevents government from proscribing speech, *Cantwell* v. *Connecticut* (1940) or even expressive conduct, see *Texas* v. *Johnson* (1989), because of disapproval of the ideas expressed. Content-based regulations are presumptively invalid. *Simon & Shuster, Inc.* v. *Members of N.Y. State Crime Victims Bd.* (1991). From 1791 to the present, however, our society, like other free but civilized societies, has permitted restrictions upon the content of speech in a few limited areas, which are "of such slight social value as a step to truth that any benefit that may be derived from them is clearly outweighed by the social interest in order and morality." *Chaplinsky.* We have recognized that "the freedom of speech" referred to by the First Amendment does not include a freedom to disregard these traditional limitations. See, *e.g.,* *Roth* v. *United States* (1957) (obscenity); *Beauharnais* v. *Illinois* (1952) (defamation); *Chaplinsky* v. *New Hampshire* ("fighting words"). Our decisions since the 1960's have narrowed the scope of the traditional categorical exceptions for defamation and for obscenity, but a limited categorical approach has remained an important part of our First Amendment jurisprudence.

We have sometimes said that these categories of expression are "not within the area of constitutionally protected speech" or that the "protection of the First Amendment does not extend" to them. Such statements must be taken in context, however, and are no more literally true than is the occasionally repeated shorthand characterizing obscenity "as not being speech at all." What they mean is that these areas of speech can, consistently with the First Amendment, be regulated *because of their constitutionally proscribable content* (obscenity, defamation, etc.)—not that they are categories of speech entirely invisible to the Constitution, so that they may be made the vehicles for content discrimination unrelated to their distinctively proscribable content. Thus, the government may proscribe libel; but it may not make the further content discrimination of proscribing *only* libel critical of the government. We recently acknowledged this distinction in [*New York* v.] *Ferber* [1982], where, in upholding

New York's child pornography law, we expressly recognized that there was no "question here of censoring a particular literary theme. . . ."

Our cases surely do not establish the proposition that the First Amendment imposes no obstacle whatsoever to regulation of particular instances of such proscribable expression, so that the government "may regulate [them] freely. That would mean that a city council could enact an ordinance prohibiting only those legally obscene works that contain criticism of the city government or, indeed, that do not include endorsement of the city government. Such a simplistic, all-or-nothing-at-all approach to First Amendment protection is at odds with common sense and with our jurisprudence as well. It is not true that "fighting words" have at most a *"de minimis"* expressive content, or that their content is *in all respects* "worthless and undeserving of constitutional protection"; sometimes they are quite expressive indeed. We have not said that they constitute *"no* part of the expression of ideas," but only that they constitute "no *essential* part of any exposition of ideas."

The proposition that a particular instance of speech can be proscribable on the basis of one feature (*e.g.*, obscenity) but not on the basis of another (*e.g.*, opposition to the city government) is commonplace, and has found application in many contexts. We have long held, for example, that nonverbal expressive activity can be banned because of the action it entails, but not because of the ideas it expresses—so that burning a flag in violation of an ordinance against outdoor fires could be punishable, whereas burning a flag in violation of an ordinance against dishonoring the flag is not. . . .

In other words, the exclusion of "fighting words" from the scope of the First Amendment simply means that, for purposes of that Amendment, the unprotected features of the words are, despite their verbal character, essentially a "nonspeech" element of communication. Fighting words are thus analogous to a noisy sound truck: Each is, as Justice Frankfurter recognized, a "mode of speech"; both can be used to convey an idea; but neither has, in and of itself, a claim upon the First Amendment. As with the sound truck, however, so also with fighting words: The government may not regulate use based on hostility—or favoritism—towards the underlying message expressed.

The concurrences describe us as setting forth a new First Amendment principle that prohibition of constitutionally proscribable speech cannot be "underinclusiv[e]"—a First Amendment "absolutism" whereby "within a particular 'proscribable' category of expression, . . . a government must either proscribe *all* speech or no speech at all." That easy target is of the concurrences' own invention. In our view, the First Amendment imposes not an "underinclusiveness" limitation but a "content discrimination" limitation upon a State's prohibition of proscribable speech. There is no problem whatever, for example, with a State's prohibiting obscenity (and other forms of proscribable expression) only in certain media or markets, for although that prohibition would be "underinclusive," it would not discriminate on the basis of content.

Even the prohibition against content discrimination that we assert the First Amendment requires is not absolute. It applies differently in the context of proscribable speech than in the area of fully protected speech. The rationale of the general prohibition, after all, is that content discrimination "rais[es] the specter that the Government may effectively drive certain ideas or viewpoints from the marketplace." *Simon & Schuster*. But content discrimination among various instances of a class of proscribable speech often does not pose this threat.

When the basis for the content discrimination consists entirely of the very reason the entire class of speech at issue is proscribable, no significant danger of idea or viewpoint discrimination exists. Such a reason, having been adjudged neutral enough to support exclusion of the entire class of speech from First Amendment protection, is also neutral enough to form the basis of distinction within the class. To illustrate: A State might choose to prohibit only that obscenity which is the most patently offensive *in its prurience—i.e.,* that which involves the most lascivious displays of sexual activity. But it may not prohibit, for example, only that obscenity which includes offensive *political* messages. . . .

Another valid basis for according differential treatment to even a content-defined subclass of proscribable speech is that the subclass happens to be associated with particular "secondary effects" of the speech, so that the regulation is "*justified* without reference to the content of the . . . speech." A State could, for example, permit all obscene live performances except those involving minors. Moreover, since words can in some circumstances violate laws directed not against speech but against conduct (a law against treason, for example, is violated by telling the enemy the nation's defense secrets), a particular content-based subcategory of a proscribable class of speech can be swept up incidentally within the reach of a statute directed at conduct rather than speech. Thus, for example, sexually derogatory "fighting words," among other words, may produce a violation of Title VII's general prohibition against sexual discrimination in employment practices. Where the government does not target conduct on the basis of its expressive content, acts are not shielded from regulation merely because they express a discriminatory idea or philosophy.

These bases for distinction refute the proposition that the selectivity of the restriction is "even arguably 'conditioned upon the sovereign's agreement with what a speaker may intend to say.' " There may be other such bases as well. Indeed, to validate such selectivity (where totally proscribable speech is at issue) it may not even be necessary to identify any particular "neutral" basis, so long as the nature of the content discrimination is such that there is no realistic possibility that official suppression of ideas is afoot. (We cannot think of any First Amendment interest that would stand in the way of a State's prohibiting only those obscene motion pictures with blue-eyed actresses.) Save for that limitation, the regulation of "fighting words," like the regulation of noisy speech, may address some offensive instances and leave other, equally offensive, instances alone.

II

Applying these principles to the St. Paul ordinance, we conclude that, even as narrowly construed by the Minnesota Supreme Court, the ordinance is facially unconstitutional. Although the phrase in the ordinance, "arouses anger, alarm or resentment in others," has been limited by the Minnesota Supreme Court's construction to reach only those symbols or displays that amount to "fighting words," the remaining, unmodified terms make clear that the ordinance applies only to "fighting words" that insult, or provoke violence, "on the basis of race, color, creed, religion or gender." Displays containing abusive invective, no matter how vicious or severe, are permissible unless they are addressed to one of the specified disfavored topics. Those who wish to use "fighting words" in connection with other ideas—to express hostility, for example, on the basis of political affiliation, union membership, or homosexuality—are not covered. The First Amendment does not permit St. Paul to impose special prohibitions on those speakers who express views on disfavored subjects.

In its practical operation, moreover, the ordinance goes even beyond mere content discrimination, to actual viewpoint discrimination. Displays containing some words—odious racial epithets, for example—would be prohibited to proponents of all views. But "fighting words" that do not themselves invoke race, color, creed, religion, or gender—aspersions upon a person's mother, for example—would seemingly be usable *ad libitum* in the placards of those arguing *in favor* of racial, color, etc. tolerance and equality, but could not be used by that speaker's opponents. One could hold up a sign saying, for example, that all "anti-Catholic bigots" are misbegotten; but not that all "papists" are, for that would insult and provoke violence "on the basis of religion." St. Paul has no such authority to license one side of a debate to fight freestyle, while requiring the other to follow Marquis of Queensbury Rules.

What we have here, it must be emphasized, is not a prohibition of fighting words that are directed at certain persons or groups (which would be *facially* valid if it met the requirements of the Equal Protection Clause); but rather, a prohibition of fighting words that contain (as the Minnesota Supreme Court repeatedly emphasized) messages of "bias-motivated" hatred and in particular, as applied to this case, messages "based on virulent notions of racial supremacy." One must wholeheartedly agree with the Minnesota Supreme Court that "[i]t is the responsibility, even the obligation, of diverse communities to confront such notions in whatever form they appear," but the manner of that confrontation cannot consist of selective limitations upon speech. St. Paul's brief asserts that a general "fighting words" law would not meet the city's needs because only a content-specific measure can communicate to minority groups that the "group hatred" aspect of such speech "is not condoned by the majority."

The point of the First Amendment is that majority preferences must be expressed in some fashion other than silencing speech on the basis of its content. . . .

The content-based discrimination reflected in the St. Paul ordinance comes within neither any of the specific exceptions to the First Amendment prohibition we discussed earlier, nor within a more general exception for content discrimination that does not threaten censorship of ideas. It assuredly does not fall within the exception for content discrimination based on the very reasons why the particular class of speech at issue (here, fighting words) is proscribable. . . . [T]he reason why fighting words are categorically excluded from the protection of the First Amendment is not that their content communicates any particular idea, but that their content embodies a particularly intolerable (and socially unnecessary) *mode* of expressing *whatever* idea the speaker wishes to convey. St. Paul has not singled out an especially offensive mode of expression—it has not, for example, selected for prohibition only those fighting words that communicate ideas in a threatening (as opposed to a merely obnoxious) manner. Rather, it has proscribed fighting words of whatever manner that communicate messages of racial, gender, or religious intolerance. Selectivity of this sort creates the possibility that the city is seeking to handicap the expression of particular ideas. That possibility would alone be enough to render the ordinance presumptively invalid, but St. Paul's comments and concessions in this case elevate the possibility to a certainty.

St. Paul argues that the ordinance comes within another of the specific exceptions we mentioned, the one that allows content discrimination aimed only at the "secondary effects" of the speech. According to St. Paul, the ordinance is intended, "not to impact on [*sic*] the right of free expression of the accused," but rather to "protect against the victimization of a person or persons who are particularly vulnerable because of their membership in a group that historically has been discriminated against." Even assuming that an ordinance that completely proscribes, rather than merely regulates, a specified category of speech can ever be considered to be directed only to the secondary effects of such speech, it is clear that the St. Paul ordinance is not directed to secondary effects within the meaning of *Renton*. . . .

It hardly needs discussion that the ordinance does not fall within some more general exception permitting *all* selectivity that for any reason is beyond the suspicion of official suppression of ideas. The statements of St. Paul in this very case afford ample basis for, if not full confirmation of, that suspicion.

Finally, St. Paul . . . defend[s] the conclusion of the Minnesota Supreme Court that, even if the ordinance regulates expression based on hostility towards its protected ideological content, this discrimination is nonetheless justified because it is narrowly tailored to serve compelling state interests. Specifically, they assert that the ordinance helps to ensure the basic human rights of members of groups that have historically been subjected to discrimination, including the right of such group members to live in peace where they wish. We do not doubt that these interests are compelling, and that the ordinance can be said to promote them. But the "danger of censorship" presented by a facially content-based statute requires that that weapon be employed only where it is "*necessary* to serve the asserted [compelling] interest.". . . The dispositive question in this case, therefore, is whether content discrimination is reasonably necessary to achieve St. Paul's compelling interests; it plainly is not. An ordinance not limited to the favored topics, for example, would have precisely the same beneficial effect. In fact the only interest distinctively served by the content limitation is that of displaying the city council's special hostility towards the particular biases thus singled out. That is precisely what the First Amendment forbids. The politicians of St. Paul are entitled to express that hostility—but not through the means of imposing unique limitations upon speakers who (however benightedly) disagree.

Let there be no mistake about our belief that burning a cross is someone's front yard is reprehensible. But St. Paul has sufficient means at its disposal to prevent such behavior without adding the First Amendment to the fire.

The judgment of the Minnesota Supreme Court is reversed, and the case is remanded for proceedings not inconsistent with this opinion.

It is so ordered.

SUPREME COURT ON PRAYER AT PUBLIC SCHOOL GRADUATION
June 24, 1992

Prayer at a public school graduation ceremony violates the constitutional doctrine of separation of church and state, the Supreme Court ruled in a 5-4 decision June 24. Even a nonsectarian prayer, as in this case, Lee v. Weisman, *has the effect of coercing youngsters to participate in a religious exercise, the court said.*

The decision was a defeat for President George Bush, whose Justice Department had urged the Court to use the case to discard restrictive past rulings on school prayer. Instead the Court drew on precedents in a thirty-year series of decisions holding that prayers sanctioned by public schools violated the First Amendment. Its provisions guarantee religious freedom and forbid the establishment of a state religion. This case resulted in the Court's first major school prayer ruling since 1985, when it struck down an Alabama law permitting a moment of silent prayer in the classroom.

Bush was "very disappointed" in the latest decision, according to a White House statement. "The Court has unnecessarily cast away a venerable and proper American tradition of non-sectarian prayer at public celebrations," the president said. Undoubtedly contributing to Bush's disappointment was the fact that the majority opinion was written by Justice Anthony M. Kennedy and supported by Justice Sandra Day O'Connor—both appointees of Ronald Reagan—and by David H. Souter, Bush's first Supreme Court nominee.

Bush, following the pattern of his predecessor, sought to fill the Court with conservative-minded justices with views attuned to his own. Justices Harry A. Blackmun and John Paul Stevens, who represent the Court's once-dominant liberal-moderate wing, cast their votes with centrists

Kennedy, O'Connor, and Souter to uphold lower-court rulings that had barred a public school in Providence, Rhode Island, from inviting clergy to deliver benedictions and invocations at future ceremonies.

Objection to Prayer at Girl's Graduation

The case arose when Daniel Weisman objected to prayers at graduation ceremonies at which his daughter, Deborah, participated at Nathan Bishop Middle School in Providence. Two brief nonsectarian prayers, an invocation and benediction, were delivered by a rabbi. The school's principal, Robert E. Lee, provided the rabbi a pamphlet entitled "Guidelines for Civic Occasions," prepared by the National Conference of Christians and Jews. The guidelines recommended that public prayers at nonsectarian civil ceremonies be composed with "inclusiveness and sensitivity," though acknowledging that "prayer of any kind might be inappropriate on some civic occasions."

Shortly before the graduation ceremony, on June 29, 1989, the girl's father sought an injunction in federal district court to bar the prayer. That court denied the motion for lack of adequate time to consider it. The next month he filed an amended complaint seeking a permanent injunction to bar various public school officials from inviting clergy to deliver prayers at future graduations. He argued that his daughter, moving into high school, was likely to hear prayers recited at her high school graduation.

1971 Case Precedent Upheld

In deciding for Weisman, the district court relied on a three-part test set forth by the Supreme Court in a 1971 case, Lemon v. Kurtzman. *That test required the state to show that the disputed activity had a secular purpose, that its primary effect neither advanced nor inhibited religion, and that it did not foster excessive church-state entanglement.*

The lower court decided that the effects test is violated whenever government action "creates an identification of the state with a religion, or with religion in general." By sponsoring the graduation prayers, even though nonsectarian, the school had created such an identification, the district court said.

After the U.S. Court of Appeals for the First Circuit upheld the lower court ruling, the Justice Department asked the Supreme Court to adopt a more lenient standard to allow prayer and other religious elements in public life so long as they did not "coerce participation" or establish an official religion. Some analysts had expected an increasingly conservative court to be sympathetic with that view.

But Kennedy wrote on behalf of the Court that it did not need to reconsider the Lemon *decision because the Rhode Island incident clearly violated the Constitution's ban on the establishment of religion. "The state, in a school setting, in effect required participation in a religious exercise," Kennedy wrote. He noted that the Supreme Court, in other rulings, had allowed prayer at beginning sessions of Congress and state legislatures. But he said those uses of prayer, "cannot compare with the constraining potential of the one school event most important for the student to attend."*

Emphatic Dissent and Surprise

Justice Antonin Scalia wrote a strongly worded dissenting opinion, which he took the unusual step of reading aloud from the bench to emphasize his disagreement with the majority's view. His opinion was endorsed by Chief Justice William H. Rehnquist and Justices Byron R. White and Clarence Thomas. Scalia called the ruling "as senseless in policy as it is unsupported by law." He went on to say that the ruling "lays waste a tradition that is as old as public-school graduation ceremonies themselves, and that is a component of an even more longstanding American tradition of nonsectarian prayer to God at public celebrations generally."

Steven Shapiro of the American Civil Liberties Union, which aided the Rhode Island family who challenged the graduation prayer, praised the decision and said it "should put an end to any lingering debate about prayer in school" Solicitor General Kenneth W. Starr, who argued before the Supreme Court on behalf of the Bush administration, said he was "disappointed" and "surprised" by the Court's "willingness to strike down a well-settled tradition and historical practice." Starr said he did not interpret the ruling as an absolute barrier to prayer at school graduation ceremonies. He suggested that student-initiated prayers, unsupervised by school officials, might be permissible.

> *Following are excerpts from the Supreme Court's majority opinion in* Lee v. Weisman, *issued June 24, 1992, declaring that a nonsectarian prayer at a public school graduation violates the Constitution's separation of church and state doctrine:*

No. 90-1014

Robert E. Lee, Individually and as Principal of Nathan Bishop Middle School, et al., Petitioners

v.

Daniel Weisman etc.

On writ of certiorari to the United States Court of Appeals for the First Circuit

[June 24, 1992]

JUSTICE KENNEDY delivered the opinion of the Court.

School principals in the public school system of the city of Providence,

Rhode Island, are permitted to invite members of the clergy to offer invocation and benediction prayers as part of the formal graduation ceremonies for middle schools and for high schools. The question before us is whether including clerical members who offer prayers as part of the official school graduation ceremony is consistent with the Religion Clauses of the First Amendment, provisions the Fourteenth Amendment makes applicable with full force to the States and their school districts. . . .

[I omitted]

II

These dominant facts mark and control the confines of our decision: State officials direct the performance of a formal religious exercise at promotional and graduation ceremonies for secondary schools. Even for those students who object to the religious exercise, their attendance and participation in the state-sponsored religious activity are in a fair and real sense obligatory, though the school district does not require attendance as a condition for receipt of the diploma.

This case does not require us to revisit the difficult questions dividing us in recent cases, questions of the definition and full scope of the principles governing the extent of permitted accommodation by the State for the religious beliefs and practices of many of its citizens. See *Allegheny County* v. *Greater Pittsburgh ACLU* (1989); *Wallace* v. *Jaffree* (1985); *Lynch* v. *Donnelly* (1984). For without reference to those principles in other contexts, the controlling precedents as they relate to prayer and religious exercise in primary and secondary public schools compel the holding here that the policy of the city of Providence is an unconstitutional one. We can decide the case without reconsidering the general constitutional framework by which public schools' efforts to accommodate religion are measured. Thus we do not accept the invitation of petitioners and *amicus* the United States to reconsider our decision in *Lemon* v. *Kurtzman, supra*. The government involvement with religious activity in this case is pervasive, to the point of creating a state-sponsored and state-directed religious exercise in a public school. Conducting this formal religious observance conflicts with settled rules pertaining to prayer exercises for students, and that suffices to determine the question before us.

The principle that government may accommodate the free exercise of religion does not supersede the fundamental limitations imposed by the Establishment Clause. It is beyond dispute that, at a minimum, the Constitution guarantees that government may not coerce anyone to support or participate in religion or its exercise, or otherwise act in a way which "establishes a [state] religion or religious faith, or tends to do so." *Lynch*, quoting *Everson* v. *Board of Education of Ewing* (1947). The State's involvement in the school prayers challenged today violates these central principles.

That involvement is as troubling as it is undenied. A school official, the principal, decided that an invocation and a benediction should be given; this is a choice attributable to the State, and from a constitutional perspective it is as if a state statute decreed that the prayers must occur. The principal chose the religious participant, here a rabbi, and that choice is also attributable to the State. . . .

The State's role did not end with the decision to include a prayer and with the choice of clergyman. Principal Lee provided Rabbi Gutterman with a copy of the "Guidelines for Civic Occasions," and advised him that his prayers should be nonsectarian. Through these means the principal directed and controlled the content of the prayer. Even if the only sanction for ignoring the instructions were that the rabbi would not be invited back, we think no religious representative who valued his or her continued reputation and effectiveness in the community would incur the State's displeasure in this regard. It is a cornerstone principle of our Establishment Clause jurisprudence that "it is no part of the business of government to compose official prayers for any group of the American people to recite as a part of a religious program carried on by government," *Engel* v. *Vitale* (1962), and that is what the school officials attempted to do.

Petitioners argue, and we find nothing in the case to refute it, that the directions for the content of the prayers were a good-faith attempt by the school to ensure that the sectarianism which is so often the flashpoint for religious animosity be removed from the graduation ceremony. The concern is understandable, as a prayer which uses ideas or images identified with a particular religion may foster a different sort of sectarian rivalry than an invocation or benediction in terms more neutral. The school's explanation, however, does not resolve the dilemma caused by its participation. The question is not the good faith of the school in attempting to make the prayer acceptable to most persons, but the legitimacy of its undertaking that enterprise at all when the object is to produce a prayer to be used in a formal religious exercise which students, for all practical purposes, are obliged to attend.

We are asked to recognize the existence of a practice of nonsectarian prayer, prayer within the embrace of what is known as the Judeo-Christian tradition, prayer which is more acceptable than one which, for example, makes explicit references to the God of Israel, or to Jesus Christ, or to a patron saint. There may be some support, as an empirical observation, to the statement of the Court of Appeals for the Sixth Circuit, picked up by Judge Campbell's dissent in the Court of Appeals in this case, that there has emerged in the country a civic religion, one which is tolerated when sectarian exercises are not. . . . If common ground can be defined which permits once conflicting faiths to express the shared conviction that there is an ethic and a morality which transcend human invention, the sense of community and purpose sought by all decent societies might be advanced. But though the First Amendment does not allow the government to stifle prayers which aspire to these ends, neither does it permit the government to undertake that task for itself. . . .

The degree of school involvement here made it clear that the graduation prayers bore the imprint of the State and thus put school-age children who objected in an untenable position. We turn our attention now to consider the position of the students, both those who desired the prayer and she who did not.

To endure the speech of false ideas or offensive content and then to counter it is part of learning how to live in a pluralistic society, a society which insists upon open discourse towards the end of a tolerant citizenry. And tolerance presupposes some mutuality of obligation. It is argued that our constitutional vision of a free society requires confidence in our own ability to accept or reject ideas of which we do not approve, and that prayer at a high school graduation does nothing more than offer a choice. By the time they are seniors, high school students no doubt have been required to attend classes and assemblies and to complete assignments exposing them to ideas they find distasteful or immoral or absurd or all of these. Against this background, students may consider it an odd measure of justice to be subjected during the course of their educations to ideas deemed offensive and irreligious, but to be denied a brief, formal prayer ceremony that the school offers in return. This argument cannot prevail, however. It overlooks a fundamental dynamic of the Constitution.

The First Amendment protects speech and religion by quite different mechanisms. Speech is protected by insuring its full expression even when the government participates, for the very object of some of our most important speech is to persuade the government to adopt an idea as its own.... The method for protecting freedom of worship and freedom of conscience in religious matters is quite the reverse. In religious debate or expression the government is not a prime participant, for the Framers deemed religious establishment antithetical to the freedom of all. The Free Exercise Clause embraces a freedom of conscience and worship that has close parallels in the speech provisions of the First Amendment, but the Establishment Clause is a specific prohibition on forms of state intervention in religious affairs with no precise counterpart in the speech provisions.... The explanation lies in the lesson of history that was and is the inspiration for the Establishment Clause, the lesson that in the hands of government what might begin as a tolerant expression of religious views may end in a policy to indoctrinate and coerce. A state-created orthodoxy puts at grave risk that freedom of belief and conscience which are the sole assurance that religious faith is real, not imposed.

The lessons of the First Amendment are as urgent in the modern world as in the 18th Century when it was written. One timeless lesson is that if citizens are subjected to state-sponsored religious exercises, the State disavows its own duty to guard and respect that sphere of inviolable conscience and belief which is the mark of a free people. To compromise that principle today would be to deny our own tradition and forfeit our standing to urge others to secure the protections of that tradition for themselves.

As we have observed before, there are heightened concerns with protecting freedom of conscience from subtle coercive pressure in the elementary and secondary public schools. . . . Our decisions in *Engle* v. *Vitale* (1962), and *Abington School District* [v. *Schempp,* 1963] recognize, among other things, that prayer exercises in public schools carry a particular risk of indirect coercion. The concern may not be limited to the context of schools, but it is most pronounced there. See *Allegheny County* v. *Greater Pittsburgh ACLU* (Kennedy J., concurring in judgment in part and dissenting in part). What to most believers may seem nothing more than a reasonable request that the nonbeliever respect their religious practices, in a school context may appear to the nonbeliever or dissenter to be an attempt to employ the machinery of the State to enforce a religious orthodoxy.

We need not look beyond the circumstances of this case to see the phenomenon at work. The undeniable fact is that the school district's supervision and control of a high school graduation ceremony places public pressure, as well as peer pressure, on attending students to stand as a group or, at least, maintain respectful silence during the Invocation and Benediction. This pressure, though subtle and indirect, can be as real as any overt compulsion. Of course, in our culture standing or remaining silent can signify adherence to a view or simple respect for the views of others. And no doubt some persons who have no desire to join a prayer have little objection to standing as a sign of respect for those who do. But for the dissenter of high school age, who has a reasonable perception that she is being forced by the state to pray in a manner her conscience will not allow, the injury is no less real. There can be no doubt that for many, if not most, of the students at the graduation, the act of standing or remaining silent was an expression of participation in the Rabbi's prayer. That was the very point of the religious exercise. It is of little comfort to a dissenter, then, to be told that for her the act of standing or remaining in silence signifies mere respect, rather than participation. What matters is that, given our social conventions, a reasonable dissenter in this milieu could believe that the group exercise signified her own participation or approval of it.

Finding no violation under these circumstances would place objectors in the dilemma of participating, with all that implies, or protesting. We do not address whether that choice is acceptable if the affected citizens are mature adults, but we think the State may not, consistent with the Establishment Clause, place primary and secondary school children in this position. Research in psychology supports the common assumption that adolescents are often susceptible to pressure from their peers towards conformity, and that the influence is strongest in matters of social convention. . . . To recognize that the choice imposed by the State constitutes an unacceptable constraint only acknowledges that the government may no more use social pressure to enforce orthodoxy than it may use more direct means.

The injury caused by the government's action, and the reason why Daniel and Deborah Weisman object to it, is that the State, in a school setting, in effect required participation in a religious exercise. It is, we concede, a brief exercise during which the individual can concentrate on joining its message, meditate on her own religion, or let her mind wander. But the embarrassment and the intrusion of the religious exercise cannot be refuted by arguing that these prayers, and similar ones to be said in the future, are of a *de minimis* character. To do so would be an affront to the Rabbi who offered them and to all those for whom the prayers were an essential and profound recognition of divine authority. And for the same reason, we think that the intrusion is greater than the two minutes or so of time consumed for prayers like these. Assuming, as we must, that the prayers were offensive to the student and the parent who now object, the intrusion was both real and, in the context of a secondary school, a violation of the objectors' rights. That the intrusion was in the course of promulgating religion that sought to be civic or nonsectarian rather than pertaining to one sect does not lessen the offense or isolation to the objectors. At best it narrows their number, at worse increases their sense of isolation and affront.

There was a stipulation in the District Court that attendance at graduation and promotional ceremonies is voluntary.... Petitioners and the United States, as *amicus,* made this a center point of the case, arguing that the option of not attending the graduation excuses any inducement or coercion in the ceremony itself. The argument lacks all persuasion. Law reaches past formalism. And to say a teenage student has a real choice not to attend her high school graduation is formalistic in the extreme. True, Deborah could elect not to attend commencement without renouncing her diploma; but we shall not allow the case to turn on this point. Everyone knows that in our society and in our culture high school graduation is one of life's most significant occasions. A school rule which excuses attendance is beside the point. Attendence may not be required by official decree, yet it is apparent that a student is not free to absent herself from the graduation exercise in any real sense of the term "voluntary," for absence would require forfeiture of those intangible benefits which have motivated the student through youth and all her high school years. Graduation is a time for family and those closest to the student to celebrate success and express mutual wishes of gratitude and respect, all to the end of impressing upon the young person the role that it is his or her right and duty to assume in the community and all of its diverse parts.

The importance of the event is the point the school district and the United States rely upon to argue that a formal prayer ought to be permitted, but it becomes one of the principal reasons why their argument must fail. Their contention, one of considerable force were it not for the constitutional constraints applied to state action, is that the prayers are an essential part of these ceremonies because for many persons an occasion of this significance lacks meaning if there is no recognition, however brief, that human achievements cannot be understood apart from their spiritual essence. We think the Government's position that this interest suffices to force students to choose between compliance or forfeiture demonstrates fundamental inconsistency in its argumentation. It fails to acknowledge that what for many of Deborah's classmates and their parents was a spiritual imperative was for Daniel and Deborah Weisman religious conformance compelled by the State. While in some societies the wishes of the majority might prevail, the Establishment Clause of the First Amendment is addressed to this contingency and rejects the balance urged upon us. The Constitution forbids the State to exact religious conformity from a student as the price of attending her own high school graduation. This is the calculus the Constitution commands.

The Government's argument gives insufficient recognition to the real conflict of conscience faced by the young student. The essence of the Government's position is that with regard to a civic occasion of this importance it is the objector, not the majority, who must take unilateral and private action to avoid compromising religious scruples, here by electing to miss the graduation exercise. This turns conventional First Amendment analysis on its head. It is a tenet of the First Amendment that the State cannot require one of its citizens to forfeit his or her rights and benefits as the price of resisting conformance to state-sponsored religious practice. To say that a student must remain apart from the ceremony at the opening invocation and closing benediction is to risk compelling conformity in an environment analogous to the classroom setting, where we have said the risk of compulsion is especially high.... Just as in *Engel v. Vitale* and *Abington School District* v. *Schempp,* we found that provisions within the challenged legislation permitting a student to be voluntarily excused from attendance or participation in the daily prayers did not shield those practices from invalidation; the fact that attendance at the graduation ceremonies is voluntary in a legal sense does not save the religious exercise.

Inherent differences between the public school system and a session of a State Legislature distinguish this case from *Marsh* v. *Chambers* (1983). The considerations we have raised in objection to the invocation and benediction are in many respects similar to the arguments we considered in *Marsh*. But there are also obvious differences. The atmosphere at the opening of a session of a state legislature where adults are free to enter and leave with little comment and for any number of reasons cannot compare with the constraining potential of the one school event most important for the student to attend. The influence and force of a formal exercise in a school graduation are far greater than the prayer exercise we condoned in *Marsh*. The *Marsh* majority in fact gave specific recognition to this distinction and placed particular reliance on it in upholding the prayers at issue there.... Today's case is different. At a high school graduation, teachers and principals must and do retain a high degree of control over the precise contents of the program, the speeches, the timing, the movements, the dress, and the decorum of the students.... In this atmosphere the state-imposed character of an invocation and benediction by clergy selected by the school combine to make the prayer a state-sanctioned religious exercise in which the student was left with no alternative but to submit. This is different from *Marsh* and suffices to make the religious exercise a First Amendment violation. Our Establishment Clause jurisprudence remains a delicate and fact-sensitive one, and we cannot accept the parallel relied upon by petitioners and the United States between the facts of *Marsh* and the case now before us. Our decisions in *Engel* v. *Vitale, supra,* and *Abington School District* v. *Schempp, supra,* require us to distinguish the public school context.

We do not hold that every state action implicating religion is invalid if one or a few citizens find it offensive. People may take offense at all manner of religious as well as nonreligious messages, but offense alone does not in every case show a violation. We know too that sometimes to endure social isolation or even anger may be the price of conscience or nonconformity. But, by any reading of our cases, the conformity required of the student in this case was too high an exaction to withstand the test of the Establishment Clause. The prayer exercises in this case are especially improper because the State has in every practical sense compelled attendance and participation in an explicit religious exercise at an event of singular importance to every student, one the objecting student had no real alternative to avoid....

Our society would be less than true to its heritage if it lacked abiding concern for the values of its young people, and we acknowledge the profound belief of adherents to many faiths that there must be a place in the student's life for precepts of a morality higher even than the law we today enforce. We express no hostility to those aspirations, nor would our oath permit us to do so. A relentless and all-pervasive attempt to exclude religion from every aspect of public life could itself become inconsistent with the Constitution.... We recognize that, at graduation time and throughout the course of the educational process, there will be instances when religious values, religious practices, and religious persons will have some interaction with the public schools and their students.... But these matters, often questions of accommodation of religion, are not before us. The sole question presented is whether a religious exercise may be conducted at a graduation ceremony in circumstances where, as we have found, young graduates who object are induced to conform. No holding by this Court suggests that a school can persuade or compel a student to participate in a religious exercise. That is being done here, and it is forbidden by the Establishment Clause of the First Amendment.

For the reasons we have stated, the judgment of the Court of Appeals is
Affirmed.

SUPREME COURT ON DAMAGE SUITS FOR TOBACCO-RELATED ILLS

June 24, 1992

The Supreme Court held June 24 that health-warning labels on cigarette packs do not protect tobacco companies from personal-injury claims if the companies misled the public about the risks of smoking. The court thus cleared the way for such lawsuits to proceed if they allege that important health information was concealed or falsified. If fraud were proven, the labels would not shield the companies from liability for illnesses or deaths attributed to smoking.

Deciding that question was the most important in a series of complicated rulings the Court issued in the case of Cipollone v. Liggett Group, Inc. *It involved the family of a woman, Rose Cipollone, who died of lung cancer in 1984 after forty-two years of smoking. The suit invoked New Jersey law to seek compensation for her death from Liggett and other tobacco companies whose brands she smoked. A federal district court rejected Liggett's argument that federal law pre-empted the New Jersey statute, but an appellate court agreed that it did.*

At issue was a federal law enacted in 1965 and revised in 1969 that required the health-warning labels. The law specifically barred states from requiring tobacco companies to provide additional warnings. The 1969 version also said that the states could not prohibit or restrict tobacco advertising or promotion as long as the packages were labeled in accordance with federal law.

Tobacco companies argued that Congress had intended to pre-empt all health-related damage claims filed under state law, saying that the purpose of the statute was to impose uniform standards on cigarette manufacturers.

The Court took a narrower view, saying that Congress would have to be more explicit if federal law is to supersede state law so broadly. Justice John Paul Stevens, writing for the Court, said that by naming some areas of state law to be pre-empted Congress had defined its reach. State law would prevail in other areas, Stevens added in a passage that some legal analysts viewed as an important departure from past decisions that took a broader view of pre-emption.

Although the Court ruled 7-2 in rejecting the industry's position that it should be shielded from all health claims, the majority split on the question of whether any claims were barred. Stevens and three other justices—Byron R. White, Sandra Day O'Connor, and Chief Justice William H. Rehnquist—argued that the federal law did pre-empt some claims—principally those asserting that smokers had not been adequately warned about health hazards after 1969. But these justices, who formed a plurality, said that tobacco companies could be sued for damages on other grounds, including allegations that they withheld information and intentionally misrepresented the health hazards of smoking. "Congress offered no sign that it wished to insulate cigarette manufacturers from fraud," Stevens wrote.

In a concurring opinion for himself and two others—Justices Anthony M. Kennedy and David H. Souter—Justice Harry A. Blackmun said the Court should not have disallowed any claims. The federal law, he said, did not provide enough "unambiguous evidence of congressional intent" to justify any pre-emption of state damage suits. By allowing some claims and disallowing others, Blackmun added, the Court created a "crazy quilt of pre-emption." Justice Antonin Scalia, in a written dissent, agreed with Blackmun's concerns that the Court's complex opinion would confuse lower courts. But Scalia—joined by Justice Clarence Thomas—argued that the tobacco companies should have been shielded from all damage suits.

Phillip Morris, Inc., one of the cigarette companies involved in the case, contended that the decision would have "little practical effect" on litigation. The company called the decision a "significant victory" for the defendants because it barred lawsuits based on claims that smokers were not warned of health hazards after 1969.

Anti-smoking activists disagreed that the decision favored the industry. "It's a compromise—but a compromise that vastly favors the plaintiffs and disadvantages the tobacco industry," said Alan B. Morrison, a lawyer with the Public Citizen Litigation Group, which filed a legal brief on behalf of several health groups supporting the Cipollone family. Morrison said the conspiracy and fraud suits allowed by the Court were the ones juries were most likely to receive sympathetically.

The Bush administration did not take part in the case, but Health and Human Services Secretary Louis W. Sullivan said, "I applaud the Supreme Court's decision to hold the tobacco industry at least partly accountable for the millions of deaths and billions of dollars in medical costs associated with smoking-related illnesses." According to government estimates, some 434,000 deaths a year in the United States are attributable to smoking.

Following are excerpts from Justice John Paul Stevens's opinion on behalf of the Supreme Court in the case of Cipollone v. Liggett Group, Inc., *issued June 24, 1992:*

<u>No. 90-1038</u>

Thomas Cipollone, Individually and as Executor of the Estate of Rose D. Cipollone, Petitioner

v.

Liggett Group, Inc., et al.

On writ of certiorari to the United States Court of Appeals for the Third Circuit

[June 24, 1992]

JUSTICE JOHN PAUL STEVENS delivered the opinion of the Court except as to Parts V and VI.

"WARNING: THE SURGEON GENERAL HAS DETERMINED THAT CIGARETTE SMOKING IS DANGEROUS TO YOUR HEALTH." A federal statute enacted in 1969 requires that warning (or a variation thereof) to appear in a conspicuous place on every package of cigarettes sold in the United States. The questions presented to us by this case are whether that statute, or its 1965 predecessor which required a less alarming label, pre-empted petitioner's common law claims against respondent cigarette manufacturers. . . .

[I omitted]

II

Although physicians had suspected a link between smoking and illness for centuries, the first medical studies of that connection did not appear until the 1920s. The ensuing decades saw a wide range of epidemiologic and laboratory studies on the health hazards of smoking. Thus, by the time the Surgeon General convened an advisory committee to examine the issue in 1962, there were more than 7,000 publications examining the relationship between smoking and health.

In 1964, the advisory committee issued its report, which stated as its central conclusion: "Cigarette smoking is a health hazard of sufficient importance in the United States to warrant appropriate remedial action." Relying in part on that report, the Federal Trade Commission (FTC), which had long regulated unfair and deceptive advertising practices in the cigarette industry, promulgated a new trade regulation rule. That rule, which was to take effect January 1, 1965, established that it would be a violation of the Federal Trade Commission Act "to fail to disclose, clearly and prominently, in all advertising and on every pack, box, carton, or container [of cigarettes] that cigarette smoking is dangerous to health and may cause death from cancer and other diseases." Several States also moved to regulate the advertising and labeling of cigarettes. Upon a congressional request, the FTC postponed enforcement of its new regulation for six months. In July 1965, Congress enacted the Federal Cigarette Labeling and Advertising Act. The 1965 Act effectively adopted half of the FTC's regulation: the Act mandated warnings on cigarette packages (§ 5(a)), but barred the requirement of such warnings in cigarette advertising (§ 5(b)).

Section 2 of the Act declares the statute's two purposes: (1) adequately informing the public that cigarette smoking may be hazardous to health, and (2) protecting the national economy from the burden imposed by diverse, nonuniform and confusing cigarette labeling and advertising regulations. In furtherance of the first purpose, § 4 of the Act made it unlawful to sell or distribute any cigarettes in the United States unless the package bore a conspicuous label stating: "CAUTION: CIGARETTE SMOKING MAY BE HAZARDOUS TO YOUR HEALTH." In furtherance of the second purpose, § 5, captioned "Preemption," provided in part:

> "(a) No statement relating to smoking and health, other than the statement required by section 4 of this Act, shall be required on any cigarette package.
> "(b) No statement relating to smoking and health shall be required in the advertising of any cigarettes the packages of which are labeled in conformity with the provisions of this Act."

Although the Act took effect January 1, 1966, § 10 of the of the Act provided that its provisions affecting the regulation of advertising would terminate on July 1, 1969.

As that termination date approached, federal authorities prepared to issue further regulations on cigarette advertising. The FTC announced the reinstitution of its 1964 proceedings concerning a warning requirement for cigarette advertisements. The Federal Communications Commission (FCC) announced that it would consider "a proposed rule which would ban the broadcast of cigarette commercials by radio and television stations." State authorities also prepared to take actions regulating cigarette advertisements.

It was in this context that Congress enacted the Public Health Cigarette Smoking Act of 1969, which amended the 1965 Act in several ways. First, the 1969 Act strengthened the warning label, in part by requiring a statement that cigarette smoking "is dangerous" rather than that it "may be hazardous." Second, the 1969 Act banned cigarette advertising in "any medium of electronic communication subject to [FCC] jurisdiction."

Third, and related, the 1969 Act modified the pre-emption provision by replacing the original § 5(b) with a provision that reads:

"(b) No requirement or prohibition based on smoking and health shall be imposed under State law with respect to the advertising or promotion of any cigarettes the packages of which are labeled in conformity with the provisions of this Act."...

III

... Article VI of the Constitution provides that the laws of the United States "shall be the supreme Law of the Land; ... any Thing in the Constitution or Laws of any state to the Contrary notwithstanding." Art. VI, cl. 2. Thus, since our decision in *McCulloch* v. *Maryland* (1819), it has been settled that state law that conflicts with federal law is "without effect." Consideration of issues arising under the Supremacy Clause "start[s] with the assumption that the historic police powers of the States [are] not to be superseded by ... Federal Act unless that [is] the clear and manifest purpose of Congress." *Rice* v. *Santa Fe Elevator Corp.* (1947). Accordingly, " '[t]he purpose of Congress is the ultimate touchstone' " of preemption analysis.

Congress' intent may be "explicitly stated in the statute's language or implicitly contained in its structure and purpose." In the absence of an express congressional command, state law is pre-empted if that law actually conflicts with federal law, or if federal law so thoroughly occupies a legislative field " 'as to make reasonable the inference that Congress left no room for the States to supplement it.' "...

In our opinion, the pre-emptive scope of the 1965 Act and the 1969 Act is governed entirely by the express language in § 5 of each Act. When Congress has considered the issue of pre-emption and has included in the enacted legislation a provision explicitly addressing that issue, and when that provision provides a "reliable indicium of congressional intent with respect to state authority, there is no need to infer congressional intent to pre-empt state laws from the substantive provisions" of the legislation. Such reasoning is a variant of the familiar principle of *expressio unius est exclusio alterius:* Congress' enactment of a provision defining the pre-emptive reach of a statute implies that matters beyond that reach are not pre-empted. In this case, the other provisions of the 1965 and 1969 Acts offer no cause to look beyond § 5 of each Act. Therefore, we need only identify the domain expressly pre-empted by each of those sections. As the 1965 and 1969 provisions differ substantially, we consider each in turn.

IV

In the 1965 pre-emption provision regarding advertising (§ 5(b)), Congress spoke precisely and narrowly: "No *statement* relating to smoking and health shall be required *in the advertising* of [properly labeled] cigarettes." Section 5(a) used the same phrase ("No *statement* relating to smoking and health") with regard to cigarette labeling. As § 5(a) made clear, that phrase referred to the sort of warning provided for in § 4, which set forth verbatim the warning Congress determined to be appropriate. Thus, on their face, these provisions merely prohibited state and federal rule-making bodies from mandating particular cautionary statements on cigarette labels (§ 5(a)) or in cigarette advertisements (§ 5(b)).

Beyond the precise words of these provisions, this reading is appropriate for several reasons. First, as discussed above, we must construe these provisions in light of the presumption against the pre-emption of state police power regulations. This presumption reinforces the appropriateness of a narrow reading of § 5. Second, the warning required in § 4 does not by its own effect foreclose additional obligations imposed under state law. That Congress requires a particular warning label does not automatically pre-empt a regulatory field. Third, there is no general, inherent conflict between federal pre-emption of state warning requirements and the continued vitality of state common law damages actions. For example, in the Comprehensive Smokeless Tobacco Health Education Act of 1986, Congress expressly pre-empted State or local imposition of a "statement relating to the use of smokeless tobacco products and health" but, at the same time, preserved state law damages actions based on those products. All of these considerations indicate that § 5 is best read as having superseded only positive enactments by legislatures or administrative agencies that mandate particular warning labels.

This reading comports with the 1965 Act's statement of purpose, which expressed an intent to avoid "diverse, nonuniform, and confusing labeling and advertising *regulations* with respect to any relationship between smoking and health." Read against the backdrop of regulatory activity undertaken by state legislatures and federal agencies in response to the Surgeon General's report, the term "regulation" most naturally refers to positive enactments by those bodies, not to common law damages actions. . . .

For these reasons, we conclude that § 5 of the 1965 Act only pre-empted state and federal rulemaking bodies from mandating particular cautionary statements and did not pre-empt state law damages actions.

V

Compared to its predecessor in the 1965 Act, the plain language of the pre-emption provision in the 1969 Act is much broader. First, the later Act bars not simply "statements" but rather "requirement[s] or prohibition[s] . . . imposed under State law." Second, the later Act reaches beyond statements "in the advertising" to obligations "with respect to the advertising or promotion" of cigarettes.

. . . The 1969 Act worked substantial changes in the law: rewriting the label warning, banning broadcast advertising, and allowing the FTC to regulate print advertising. . . .

Petitioner . . . contends that § 5(b), however broadened by the 1969 Act, does not pre-empt *common law* actions. He offers two theories for limiting the reach of the amended § 5(b). First, he argues that common law damages actions do not impose "requirement[s] or prohibition[s]" and that Congress intended only to trump "state statute[s], injunction[s], or executive pronouncement[s]." We disagree; such an analysis is at odds both with the plain words of the 1969 Act and with the general understanding of common law damages actions. The phrase "[n]o requirement or prohibition" sweeps broadly and suggests no distinction between positive enactments and common law; to the contrary, those words easily encompass obligations that take the form of common law rules. As we noted in another context, "[state] regulation can be as effectively exerted through an award of damages as through some form of preventive relief. The obligation to pay compensation can be, indeed is designed to be, a potent method of governing conduct and controlling policy."

Although portions of the legislative history of the 1969 Act suggest that Congress was primarily concerned with positive enactments by States and localities, the language of the Act plainly reaches beyond such enactments. "We must give effect to this plain language unless there is a good reason to believe Congress intended the language to have some more restrictive meaning." In this case there is no "good reason to believe" that Congress meant less than what it said: indeed, in light of the narrowness of the 1965 Act, there is "good reason to believe" that Congress meant precisely what it said in amending the Act.

Moreover, common law damages actions of the sort raised by petitioner are premised on the existence of a legal duty and it is difficult to say that such actions do not impose "requirements or prohibitions."... It is in this way that the 1969 version of § 5(b) differs from its predecessor. Whereas the common law would not normally require a vendor to use any specific *statement* on its packages or in its advertisements, it is the essence of the common law to enforce duties that are either affirmative *requirements* or negative *prohibitions*. We therefore reject petitioner's argument that the phrase "requirement or prohibition" limits the 1969 Act's pre-emptive scope to positive enactments by legislatures and agencies.

Petitioner's second argument for excluding common law rules from the reach of § 5(b) hinges on the phrase "imposed under State law." This argument fails as well. At least since *Erie R.* v. *Tompkins* (1938), we have recognized the phrase "state law" to include common law as well as statutes and regulations.... Although the presumption against pre-emption might give good reason to construe the phrase "state law" in a pre-emption provision more narrowly than an identical phrase in another context, in this case such a construction is not appropriate. As explained above, the 1965 version of § 5 was precise and narrow on its face; the obviously broader language of the 1969 version extended that section's pre-emptive reach. Moreover, while the version of the 1969 Act passed by the Senate pre-empted "any State *statute or regulation* with respect to ... advertising or promotion," the Conference Committee replaced this language with "State *law* with respect to advertising or promotion." In such a situation, § 5(b)'s pre-emption of "state law" cannot fairly be limited to positive enactments.

That the pre-emptive scope of § 5(b) cannot be limited to positive enactments does not mean that that section pre-empts all common law claims. . . .

Nor does the statute indicate that any familiar subdivision of common law claims is or is not pre-empted. We therefore cannot follow petitioner's passing suggestion that § 5(b) pre-empts liability for omissions but not for acts, or that § 5(b) pre-empts liability for unintentional torts but not for intentional torts. Instead we must fairly but—in light of the strong presumption against pre-emption—narrowly construe the precise language of § 5(b) and we must look to each of petitioner's common law claims to determine whether it is in fact pre-empted. The central inquiry in each case is straightforward: we ask whether the legal duty that is the predicate of the common law damages action constitutes a "requirement or prohibition based on smoking and health . . . imposed under State law with respect to . . . advertising or promotion," giving that clause a fair but narrow reading. As discussed below, each phrase within that clause limits the universe of common law claims pre-empted by the statute.

We consider each category of damages actions in turn. . . .

Failure to Warn

To establish liability for a failure to warn, petitioner must show that "a warning is necessary to make a product . . . reasonably safe, suitable and fit for its intended use," that respondents failed to provide such a warning, and that that failure was a proximate cause of petitioner's injury. In this case, petitioner offered two closely related theories concerning the failure to warn: first, that respondents "were negligent in the manner [that] they tested, researched, sold, promoted, and advertised" their cigarettes; and second, that respondents failed to provide "adequate warnings of the health consequences of cigarette smoking."

Petitioner's claims are pre-empted to the extent that they rely on a state law "requirement or prohibition . . . with respect to . . . advertising or promotion." Thus, insofar as claims under either failure to warn theory require a showing that respondents' post-1969 advertising or promotions should have included additional, or more clearly stated, warnings, those claims are pre-empted. The Act does not, however, pre-empt petitioner's claims that rely solely on respondents' testing or research practices or other actions unrelated to advertising or promotion.

Breach of Express Warranty

Petitioner's claim for breach of an express warranty arises under N.J. Stat. Ann. § 12A:2-313(1)(a) [(West 1991)], which provides:

> Any affirmation of fact or promise made by the seller to the buyer which relates to the goods and becomes part of the basis of the bargain creates an express warranty that the goods shall conform to the affirmation or promise.

Petitioner's evidence of an express warranty consists largely of statements made in respondents' advertising. . . .

A manufacturer's liability for breach of an express warranty derives from, and is measured by, the terms of that warranty. Accordingly, the "requirements" imposed by an express warranty claim are not "imposed under State law," but rather imposed *by the warrantor*. If, for example, a manufacturer expressly promised to pay a smoker's medical bills if she contracted emphysema, the duty to honor that promise could not fairly be said to be "imposed under state law," but rather is best understood as undertaken by the manufacturer itself. While the general duty not to breach warranties arises under state law, the particular "requirement . . . based on smoking and health . . . with respect to the advertising or promotion [of] cigarettes" in an express warranty claim arises from the manufacturer's statements in its advertisements. In short, a common law remedy for a contractual commitment voluntarily undertaken should not be regarded as a "requirement . . . *imposed under State law*" within the meaning of § 5(b).

That the terms of the warranty may have been set forth in advertisements rather than in separate documents is irrelevant to the pre-emption issue . . . because although the breach of warranty claim is made "with respect to advertising" it does not rest on a duty imposed under state law. Accordingly, to the extent that petitioner has a viable claim for breach of express warranties made by respondents, that claim is not pre-empted by the 1969 Act.

Fraudulent Misrepresentation

Petitioner alleges two theories of fraudulent misrepresentation. First, petitioner alleges that respondents, through their advertising, neutralized the effect of federally mandated warning labels. Such a claim is predicated on a state-law prohibition against statements in advertising and promotional materials that tend to minimize the health hazards associated with smoking. Such a *prohibition*, however, is merely the converse of a state law *requirement* that warnings be included in advertising and promotional materials. Section 5(b) of the 1969 Act pre-empts both requirements and prohibitions; it therefore supersedes petitioner's first fraudulent misrepresentation theory. . . .

Petitioner's second theory . . . alleges intentional fraud and misrepresentation both by "false representation of a material fact [and by] conceal-[ment of] a material fact." The predicate of this claim is a state law duty not to make false statements of material fact or to conceal such facts. . . .

Section 5(b) pre-empts only the imposition of state law obligations "with respect to the advertising or promotion" of cigarettes. Petitioner's claims that respondents concealed material facts are therefore not pre-empted insofar as those claims rely on a state law duty to disclose such facts through channels of communication other than advertising or promotion. Thus, for example, if state law obliged respondents to disclose material facts about smoking and health to an administrative agency, § 5(b) would not pre-empt a state law claim based on a failure to fulfill that obligation.

Moreover, petitioner's fraudulent misrepresentation claims that do arise with respect to advertising and promotions (most notably claims based on allegedly false statements of material fact made in advertisements) are not pre-empted by § 5(b). Such claims are not predicated on a duty "based on smoking and health" but rather on a more general obligation—the duty not to deceive. This understanding of fraud by intentional misstatement is appropriate for several reasons. First, in the 1969 Act, Congress offered no sign that it wished to insulate cigarette manufacturers from longstanding rules governing fraud. To the contrary, both the 1965 and the 1969 Acts explicitly reserved the FTC's authority to identify and punish deceptive advertising practices—an authority that the FTC had long exercised and continues to exercise. This indicates that Congress intended the phrase "relating to smoking and health" (which was essentially unchanged by the 1969 Act) to be construed narrowly, so as not to proscribe the regulation of deceptive advertising.

Moreover, this reading of "based on smoking and health" is wholly consistent with the purposes of the 1969 Act. State law prohibitions on false statements of material fact do not create "diverse, nonuniform, and confusing" standards. Unlike state law obligations concerning the warning necessary to render a product "reasonably safe," state law proscriptions on intentional fraud rely only on a single, uniform standard: falsity. Thus we conclude that the phrase "based on smoking and health" fairly but narrowly construed does not encompass the more general duty not to make fraudulent statements. Accordingly, petitioner's claim based on allegedly fraudulent statements made in respondents' advertisements are not pre-empted by § 5(b) of the 1969 Act.

Conspiracy to Misrepresent or Conceal Material Facts

Petitioner's final claim alleges a conspiracy among respondents to misrepresent or conceal material facts concerning the health hazards of smoking. The predicate duty underlying this claim is a duty not to conspire to commit fraud. For the reasons stated in our analysis of petitioner's intentional fraud claim, this duty is not pre-empted by § 5(b) for it is not a prohibition "based on smoking and health" as that phrase is properly construed. Accordingly, we conclude that the 1969 Act does not pre-empt petitioner's conspiracy claim.

VI

To summarize our holding: The 1965 Act did not pre-empt state law damages actions; the 1969 Act pre-empts petitioner's claims based on a failure to warn and the neutralization of federally mandated warnings to the extent that those claims rely on omissions or inclusions in respondents' advertising or promotions; the 1969 Act does not pre-empt petitioner's claims based on express warranty, intentional fraud and misrepresentation, or conspiracy.

The judgment of the Court of Appeals is accordingly reversed in part and affirmed in part, and the case is remanded for further proceedings consistent with this opinion.

It is so ordered.

SUPREME COURT ON DESEGREGATION AT MISSISSIPPI COLLEGES

June 26, 1992

Moving into a new field of inquiry, the Supreme Court on June 26 held that Mississippi had not gone far enough toward eliminating racial barriers in its state-supported universities. The Court had outlawed segregation in primary and secondary schools in 1954 and upheld mandatory integration in dozens of rulings since then. But never before had it decided whether a state had met its constitutional obligation to dismantle a formerly segregated system of higher education.

The case, U.S. v. Fordice, resulted from a 1975 lawsuit brought against Mississippi by several black plaintiffs and joined by the Justice Department. Kirk Fordice, then the state's governor, was named defendant. The plaintiffs argued that Mississippi carried out policies that perpetuated segregation at its eight state-supported universities despite the adoption of a "race neutral" admission standard. Saying that some of the challenged policies were rooted in a segregationist past and thus "constitutionally suspect," the Supreme Court sent the case back to federal district court for reconsideration under new guidelines.

The lower court had found no violations of federal law and concluded that "the defendants are fulfilling their affirmative duty to disestablish the former de jure [in law] segregated system of higher education." A federal appeals court reheard the case and affirmed that decision. Justice Byron R. White, writing for the Supreme Court, said that the lower and appellate courts failed "to consider the State's duties in their proper light." White wrote that the courts had erred in holding that race-neutral policies alone demonstrated that Mississippi had completely abandoned its prior dual system of separate education for black and white college students.

For twelve years after the lawsuit was filed, the plaintiffs and the state were unable to resolve their differences. Then in 1987 each side presented in federal district court voluminous evidence to support the contention that Mississippi had, or had not, continued or adopted policies that had the effect of restricting the number of black students at formerly white institutions.

The court record showed that in 1986, about 99 percent of the white students in the state university system attended one or another of the five formerly all-white schools (the University of Mississippi, Mississippi State University, Mississippi University for Women, University of Southern Mississippi, and Delta State University), where 80 to 91 percent of the student bodies were white. At the other three universities (Alcorn State, Jackson State, and Mississippi Valley State), which had been exclusively for black students, their student bodies remained 92 to 99 percent black.

"That an institution is predominately white or black does not in itself make a constitutional violation," White wrote. But he added that a "freedom of choice" policy adopted by the Mississippi university system "did not compensate for other practices that fostered segregation." He went on to say that "several surviving aspects" of the old system were constitutionally suspect" and had not been examined with proper care by the other courts.

One practice, originally enacted in 1963 by three of the white universities, set a minimum American College Testing (ACT) score for admission that disqualified most of the black high school graduates. The state refused to consider other admission criteria such as high school grades. The Supreme Court also cited a duplication of "unnecessary programs" at the two sets of universities, disregarded by the lower court, as a vestige of the old "separate but equal" system. In another practice that may perpetuate segregation, White wrote, the university system in 1981 issued "mission statements" for each of the universities that could restrict the range of choices as to where an entering student might attend.

All the other justices except Antonin Scalia endorsed the high court's opinion. Scalia, in a dissenting opinion, warned that the decision could result in the "elimination of predominantly black institutions" of learning. "Not only Mississippi but Congress itself seems to be out of step with the drum that the Court beats today," Scalia wrote, "judging by its passage of an Act entitled 'Strengthening Historically Black Colleges and Universities' authorizing federal grants for those institutions."

Clarence Thomas, the Supreme Court's only black member, wrote a separate opinion concurring in the Court's decision but arguing that it did not "foreclose the possibility that there exists 'sound educational justification' for maintaining historically black colleges as such." He said that "a state could operate a diverse assortment of institutions— including historically black institutions—open to all on a race-neutral basis, but with established traditions and programs that might dispropor-

tionately appeal to one race or another."

According to press reports of responses from administrators among the sixty-five predominantly black public universities, opinion was divided as to whether the Supreme Court decision might threaten the existence of those institutions. Robert Albright, the president of Johnson C. Smith University in Charlotte, North Carolina, was quoted as saying: "This may leave a loophole for states interested in the demise of black colleges." Some civil-rights advocates expressed hope that the decision would result in better financing for the black universities. Many of them had been hurt in recent years by cutbacks of state funding for public education.

Following are excerpts from the opinion of Justice Byron R. White, writing for the Supreme Court, in the case U.S. v. Fordice, issued June 26, 1992, holding that Mississippi must answer further questions in lower court before its state-supported university system could be declared free of its racially segregated past and in compliance with the U.S. Constitution:

Nos. 90-1205 and 90-6588

United States, Petitioner *v.* Kirk Fordice, Governor of Mississippi, et al. Jake Ayers, et al., Petitioners *v.* Kirk Fordice, Governor of Mississippi, et al.	On writs of certiorari to the United States Court of Appeals for the Fifth Circuit

[June 26, 1992]

JUSTICE WHITE delivered the opinion of the Court.

In 1954, this Court held that the concept of " 'separate but equal' " has no place in the field of public education. *Brown* v. *Board of Education (Brown I)* (1954). The following year, the Court ordered an end to segregated public education "with all deliberate speed." *Brown* v. *Board of Education (Brown II)* (1955). Since these decisions, the Court has had many occasions to evaluate whether a public school district has met its affirmative obligation to dismantle its prior *de jure* segregated system in elementary and secondary schools. In this case we decide what standards to apply in determining whether the State of Mississippi has met this obligation in the university context.

I

Mississippi launched its public university system in 1848 by establishing the University of Mississippi, an institution dedicated to the higher education exclusively of white persons. In succeeding decades, the State erected additional post-secondary, single-race educational facilities. Alcorn State University opened its doors in 1871 as "an agricultural college for the education of Mississippi's black youth." ... Creation of four more exclusively white institutions followed: Mississippi State University (1880), Mississippi University for Women (1885), University of Southern Mississippi (1912), and Delta State University (1925). The State added two more solely black institutions in 1940 and 1950: in the former year, Jackson State University, which was charged with training "black teachers for the black public schools," and in the latter year, Mississippi Valley State University, whose functions were to educate teachers primarily for rural and elementary schools and to provide vocational instruction to black students.

Despite this Court's decisions in *Brown I* and *Brown II,* Mississippi's policy of *de jure* segregation continued. The first black student was not admitted to the University of Mississippi until 1962, and then only by court order.... For the next 12 years the segregated public university system in the State remained largely intact. Mississippi State University, Mississippi University for Women, University of Southern Mississippi, and Delta State University each admitted at least one black student during these years, but the student composition of these institutions was still almost completely white. During this period, Jackson State and Mississippi Valley State were exclusively black; Alcorn State had admitted five white students by 1968.

In 1969, the United States Department of Health, Education and Welfare (HEW) initiated efforts to enforce Title VI of the Civil Rights Act of 1964.... HEW requested that the State devise a plan to disestablish the formerly *de jure* segregated university system. In June 1973, the Board of Trustees of State Institutions of Higher Learning submitted a Plan of Compliance, which expressed the aims of improving educational opportunities for all Mississippi citizens by setting numerical goals on the enrollment of other-race students at State universities, hiring other-race faculty members, and instituting remedial programs and special recruitment efforts to achieve those goals.... HEW rejected this Plan as failing to comply with Title VI because it did not go far enough in the areas of student recruitment and enrollment, faculty hiring, elimination of unnecessary program duplication, and institutional funding practices to ensure that "a student's choice of institution or campus, henceforth, will be based on other than racial criteria." The Board reluctantly offered amendments, prefacing its reform pledge to HEW with this statement: "With deference, it is the position of the Board of Trustees ... that the Mississippi system of higher education is in compliance with Title VI of the Civil Rights Act of 1964." ... At this time, the racial composition of the State's universities had changed only marginally from the levels of 1968, which were almost exclusively single-race. Though HEW refused to accept the modified Plan, the Board adopted it anyway.... But even the limited effects of this Plan in disestablishing the prior *de jure* segregated system were substantially constricted by the state legislature, which refused to fund it until Fiscal Year 1978, and even then at well under half the amount sought by the Board....

Private petitioners initiated this lawsuit in 1975. They complained that Mississippi had maintained the racially segregative effects of its prior dual system of post-secondary education in violation of the Fifth, Ninth, Thirteenth, and Fourteenth Amendments, and Title VI of the Civil Rights Act of 1964.... Shortly thereafter, the United States filed its complaint in intervention, charging that State officials had failed to satisfy their obligation under the Equal Protection Clause of the Fourteenth Amendment and Title VI to dismantle Mississippi's dual system of higher education.

After this lawsuit was filed, the parties attempted for 12 years to achieve a consensual resolution of their differences through voluntary dismantlement by the State of its prior separated system. The Board of Trustees implemented reviews of existing curricula and program "mission" at each institution. In 1981, the Board issued "Mission Statements" that identified the extant purpose of each public university. These "missions" were clustered into three categories: comprehensive, urban, and regional. "Comprehensive" universities were classified as those with the greatest existing resources and program offerings. All three such institutions (University of Mississippi, Mississippi State, and Southern Mississippi) were exclusively white under the prior *de jure* segregated system. The Board authorized each to continue offering doctoral degrees and to assert leadership in certain disciplines. Jackson State, the sole urban university, was assigned a more limited research and degree mission, with both functions geared toward its urban setting. It was exclusively black at its inception. The "regional" designation was something of a misnomer, as the Board envisioned those institutions primarily in an undergraduate role, rather than a "regional" one in the geographical sense of serving just the localities in which they were based. Only the universities classified as "regional" included institutions that, prior to desegregation, had been either exclusively white—Delta State and Mississippi University for Women—or exclusively black—Alcorn State and Mississippi Valley.

By the mid-1980's, 30 years after *Brown,* more than 99 percent of Mississippi's white students were enrolled at University of Mississippi, Mississippi State, Southern Mississippi, Delta State, and Mississippi University for Women. The student bodies at these universities remained predominantly white, averaging between 80 and 91 percent white students. Seventy-one percent of the State's black students attended Jackson State, Alcorn State, and Mississippi Valley, where the racial composition ranged from 92 to 99 percent black....

II

By 1987, the parties concluded that they could not agree on whether the State had taken the requisite affirmative steps to dismantle its prior *de jure* segregated system. They proceeded to trial. Both sides presented voluminous evidence on a full range of educational issues spanning admissions standards, faculty and administrative staff recruitment, program duplication, on-campus discrimination, institutional funding disparities, and satellite campuses. Petitioners argued that in various ways the State continued to reinforce historic, race-based distinctions among the universities. Respondents argued generally that the State had fulfilled its duty to disestablish its state-imposed segregative system by implementing and maintaining good-faith, nondiscriminatory race-neutral policies and practices in student admission, faculty hiring, and operations. Moreover, they suggested, the State had attracted significant numbers of qualified black students to those universities composed mostly of white persons. Respondents averred that the mere continued existence of racially identifiable universities was not unlawful given the freedom of students to choose which institution to attend and the varying objectives and features of the State's universities.

At trial's end, based on the testimony of 71 witnesses and 56,700 pages of exhibits, the District Court entered extensive findings of fact. The court first offered a historical overview of the higher education institutions in Mississippi and the developments in the system between 1954 and the filing of this suit in 1975. . . . It then made specific findings recounting post-1975 developments, including a description at the time of trial, in those areas of the higher education system under attack by plaintiffs: admission requirements and recruitment; institutional classification and assignment of missions; duplication of programs; facilities and finance; the land grant institutions; faculty and staff; and governance. . . .

The court's conclusions of law followed. As an overview, the court outlined the common ground in the case: "Where a state has previously maintained a racially dual system of public education established by law, it assumes an 'affirmative duty' to reform those policies and practices which required or contributed to the separation of the races.". . . [T]he court stated: "While student enrollment and faculty and staff hiring patterns are to be examined, greater emphasis should instead be placed on current state higher education policies and practices in order to insure that such policies and practices are racially neutral, developed and implemented in good faith, and do not substantially contribute to the continued racial identifiability of individual institutions." . . .

When it addressed the same aspects of the university system covered by the fact-findings in light of the foregoing standard, the court found no violation of federal law in any of them. "In summary, the court finds that current actions on the part of the defendants demonstrate conclusively that the defendants are fulfilling their affirmative duty to disestablish the former *de jure* segregated system of higher education." . . .

The Court of Appeals reheard the case en banc and affirmed the decision of the District Court.... With a single exception ... it did not disturb the District Court's findings of fact or conclusions of law....

III

The District Court, the Court of Appeals, and respondents recognize and acknowledge that the State of Mississippi had the constitutional duty to dismantle the dual school system that its laws once mandated. Nor is there any dispute that this obligation applies to its higher education system. If the State has not discharged this duty, it remains in violation of the Fourteenth Amendment. *Brown* v. *Board of Education* and its progeny clearly mandate this observation. Thus, the primary issue in this case is whether the State has met its affirmative duty to dismantle its prior dual university system

Our decisions establish that a State does not discharge its constitutional obligations until it eradicates policies and practices traceable to its prior *de jure* dual system that continue to foster segregation. Thus we have consistently asked whether existing racial identifiability is attributable to the State; and examined a wide range of factors to determine whether the State has perpetuated its formerly *de jure* segregation in any facet of its institutional system....

Like the United States, we do not disagree with the Court of Appeals' observation that a state university system is quite different in very relevant respects from primary and secondary schools. Unlike attendance at the lower level schools, a student's decision to seek higher education has been a matter of choice. The State historically has not assigned university students to a particular institution. Moreover, like public universities throughout the country Mississippi's institutions of higher learning are not fungible—they have been designated to perform certain missions. Students who qualify for admission enjoy a range of choices of which institution to attend. Thus, as the Court of Appeals stated, "[i]t hardly needs mention that remedies common to public school desegregation, such as pupil assignments, busing, attendance quotas, and zoning, are unavailable when persons may freely choose whether to pursue an advanced education and, when the choice is made, which of several universities to attend."

We do not agree with the Court of Appeals or the District Court, however, that the adoption and implementation of race-neutral policies alone suffice to demonstrate that the State has completely abandoned its prior dual system. That college attendance is by choice and not by assignment does not mean that a race-neutral admissions policy cures the constitutional violation of a dual system. In a system based on choice, student attendance is determined not simply by admissions policies, but also by many other factors. Although some of these factors clearly cannot be attributed to State policies, many can be. Thus, even after a State dismantles its segregative *admissions* policy, there may still be state action that is traceable to the State's prior *de jure* segregation and that continues to foster segregation. . . . If policies traceable to the *de jure* system are still in force and have discriminatory effects, those policies too must be reformed to the extent practicable and consistent with sound educational practices. . . . We also disagree with respondents that the Court of Appeals and District Court properly relied on our decision in *Bazemore* v. *Friday* (1986). *Bazemore* neither requires nor justifies the conclusions reached by the two courts below.

Bazemore raised the issue whether the financing and operational assistance provided by a state university's extension service to voluntary 4-H and Homemaker Clubs was inconsistent with the Equal Protection Clause because of the existence of numerous all-white and all-black clubs. Though prior to 1965 the clubs were supported on a segregated basis, the District Court had found that the policy of segregation had been completely abandoned and that no evidence existed of any lingering discrimination in either services or membership; any racial imbalance resulted from the wholly voluntary and unfettered choice of private individuals. . . . In this context, we held inapplicable the *Green* [v. *New Kent County School Bd.*, 1968] Court's judgment that a voluntary choice program was insufficient to dismantle a *de jure* dual system in public primary and secondary schools, but only after satisfying ourselves that the State had not fostered segregation by playing a part in the decision of which club an individual chose to join.

Bazemore plainly does not excuse inquiry into whether Mississippi has left in place certain aspects of its prior dual system that perpetuate the racially segregated higher education system. If the State perpetuates policies and practices traceable to its prior system that continue to have segregative effects—whether by influencing student enrollment decisions or by fostering segregation in other facets of the university system—and such policies are without sound educational justification and can be practicably eliminated, the State has not satisfied its burden of proving that it has dismantled its prior system. Such policies run afoul of the Equal Protection Clause, even though the State has abolished the legal requirement that whites and blacks be educated separately and has established racially neutral policies not animated by a discriminatory purpose. Because the standard applied by the District Court did not make these inquiries, we hold that the Court of Appeals erred in affirming the District Court's ruling that the State had brought itself into compliance with the Equal Protection Clause in the operation of its higher education system.

IV

Had the Court of Appeals applied the correct legal standard, it would have been apparent from the undisturbed factual findings of the District Court that there are several surviving aspects of Mississippi's prior dual system which are constitutionally suspect; for even though such policies may be race-neutral on their face, they substantially restrict a person's choice of which institution to enter and they contribute to the racial identifiability of the eight public universities. Mississippi must justify these policies or eliminate them.

It is important to state at the outset that we make no effort to identify an exclusive list of unconstitutional remnants of Mississippi's prior *de jure* system.... With this caveat in mind, we address four policies of the present system: admission standards, program duplication, institutional mission assignments, and continued operation of all eight public universities.

We deal first with the current admissions policies of Mississippi's public universities. As the District Court found, the three flagship historically white universities in the system—University of Mississippi, Mississippi State University, and University of Southern Mississippi—enacted policies in 1963 requiring all entrants to achieve a minimum composite score of 15 on the American College Testing Program (ACT).... The court described the "discriminatory taint" of this policy, an obvious reference to the fact that, at the time, the average ACT score for white students was 18 and the average score for blacks was 7.... The District Court concluded, and the en banc Court of Appeals agreed, that present admissions standards derived from policies enacted in the 1970's to redress the problem of student unpreparedness.... Obviously, this mid-passage justification for perpetuating a policy enacted originally to discriminate against black students does not make the present admissions standards any less constitutionally suspect.

The present admission standards are not only traceable to the *de jure* system and were originally adopted for a discriminatory purpose, but they also have present discriminatory effects. Every Mississippi resident under 21 seeking admission to the university system must take the ACT. Any applicant who scores at least 15 qualifies for automatic admission to any of the five historically white institutions except Mississippi University for Women, which requires a score of 18 for automatic admission unless the student has a 3.0 high school grade average. Those scoring less than 15 but at least 13 automatically qualify to enter Jackson State University, Alcorn State University, and Mississippi Valley State University. Without doubt, these requirements restrict the range of choices of entering students as to which institution they may attend in a way that perpetuates segregation....

The segregative effect of this automatic entrance standard is especially striking in light of the differences in minimum automatic entrance scores among the regional universities in Mississippi's system. The minimum score for automatic admission to Mississippi University for Women (MUW) is 18; it is 13 for the historically black universities. Yet MUW is assigned the same institutional mission as two other regional universities, Alcorn State and Mississippi Valley—that of providing quality undergraduate education. The effects of the policy fall disproportionately on black students who might wish to attend MUW; and though the disparate impact is not as great, the same is true of the minimum standard ACT score of 15 at Delta State University—the other "regional" university—as compared to the historically black "regional" universities where a score of 13 suffices for automatic admission. The courts below made little if any effort to justify in educational terms those particular disparities in entrance requirements or to inquire whether it was practicable to eliminate them.

We also find inadequately justified by the courts below or by the record before us the differential admissions requirements between universities with dissimilar programmatic missions. We do not suggest that absent a discriminatory purpose different programmatic missions accompanied by different admissions standards would be constitutionally suspect simply because one or more schools are racially identifiable. But here the differential admission standards are remnants of the dual system with a continuing discriminatory effect, and the mission assignments "to some degree follow the historical racial assignments." Moreover, the District Court did not justify the differing admission standards based on the different mission assignments. It observed only that in the 1970's, the Board of Trustees justified a minimum ACT score of 15 because too many students with lower scores were not prepared for the historically white institutions and that imposing the 15 score requirement on admissions to the historically black institutions would decimate attendance at those universities. The District Court also stated that the mission of the regional universities had the more modest function of providing quality undergraduate education. Certainly the comprehensive universities are also, among other things, educating undergraduates. But we think the 15 ACT test score for automatic admission to the comprehensive universities, as compared with a score of 13 for the regionals, requires further justification in terms of sound educational policy.

Another constitutionally problematic aspect of the State's use of the ACT test scores is its policy of denying automatic admission if an applicant fails to earn the minimum ACT score specified for the particular institution, without also resorting to the applicant's high school grades as an additional factor in predicting college performance. The United States produced evidence that the American College Testing Program (ACTP), the administering organization of the ACT, discourages use of ACT scores as the sole admissions criterion on the ground that it gives an incomplete "picture" of the student applicant's ability to perform adequately in college. . . . The record also indicated that the disparity between black and white students' high school grade averages was much narrower than the gap between their average ACT scores, thereby suggesting that an admissions formula which included grades would increase the number of black students eligible for automatic admission to all of Mississippi's public universities. . . .

A second aspect of the present system that necessitates further inquiry is the widespread duplication of programs. "Unnecessary" duplication refers, under the District Court's definition, "to those instances where two or more institutions offer the same nonessential or noncore program. Under this definition, all duplication at the bachelor's level of nonbasic liberal arts and sciences course work and all duplication at the master's level and above are considered to be unnecessary." The District Court found that 34.6 percent of the 29 undergraduate programs at historically black institutions are "unnecessarily duplicated" by the historically white universities, and that 90 percent of the graduate programs at the historically black institutions are unnecessarily duplicated at the historically white institutions.... In its conclusions of law on this point, the District Court nevertheless determined that "there is no proof" that such duplication "is directly associated with the racial identifiability of institutions," and that "there is no proof that the elimination of unnecessary program duplication would be justifiable from an educational standpoint or that its elimination would have a substantial effect on student choice." ...

The District Court's treatment of this issue is problematic from several different perspectives. First, the court appeared to impose the burden of proof on the plaintiffs to meet a legal standard the court itself acknowledged was not yet formulated. It can hardly be denied that such duplication was part and parcel of the prior dual system of higher education—the whole notion of "separate but equal" required duplicative programs in two sets of schools—and that the present unnecessary duplication is a continuation of that practice. *Brown* and its progeny, however, established that the burden of proof falls on the *State,* and not the aggrieved plaintiffs, to establish that it has dismantled its prior *de jure* segregated system.... The court's holding that petitioners could not establish the constitutional defect of unnecessary duplication, therefore, improperly shifted the burden away from the State. Second, implicit in the District Court's finding of "unnecessary" duplication is the absence of any educational justification and the fact that some if not all duplication may be practicably eliminated. Indeed, the District Court observed that such duplication "cannot be justified economically or in terms of providing quality education." ... Yet by stating that "there is no proof" that elimination of unnecessary duplication would decrease institutional racial identifiability, affect student choice, and promote educationally sound policies, the court did not make clear whether it had directed the parties to develop evidence on these points, and if so, what that evidence revealed.... Finally, by treating this issue in isolation, the court failed to consider the combined effects of unnecessary program duplication with other policies, such as differential admissions standards, in evaluating whether the State had met its duty to dismantle its prior *de jure* segregated system.

We next address Mississippi's scheme of institutional mission classification, and whether it perpetuates the State's formerly *de jure* dual system. The District Court found that, throughout the period of *de jure* segregation, University of Mississippi, Mississippi State University, and University of Southern Mississippi were the flagship institutions in the state system. They received the most funds, initiated the most advanced and specialized programs, and developed the widest range of curricular functions. At their inception, each was restricted for the education solely of white persons.... The missions of Mississippi University for Women and Delta State University (DSU), by contrast, were more limited than their other all-white counterparts during the period of legalized segregation. MUW and DSU were each established to provide undergraduate education solely for white students in the liberal arts and such other fields as music, art, education, and home economics.... When they were founded, the three exclusively black universities were more limited in their assigned academic missions than the five all-white institutions. Alcorn State, for example, was designated to serve as "an agricultural college for the education of Mississippi's black youth.'....

In 1981, the State assigned certain missions to Mississippi's public universities as they then existed. It classified University of Mississippi, Mississippi State, and Southern Mississippi as "comprehensive" universities having the most varied programs and offering graduate degrees. Two of the historically white institutions, Delta State University and Mississippi University for Women, along with two of the historically black institutions, Alcorn State University and Mississippi Valley State University, were designated as "regional" universities with more limited programs and devoted primarily to undergraduate education. Jackson State University was classified as an "urban" university whose mission was defined by its urban location.

The institutional mission designations adopted in 1981 have as their antecedents the policies enacted to perpetuate racial separation during the *de jure* segregated regime.... That different missions are assigned to the universities surely limits to some extent an entering student's choice as to which university to seek admittance.... We do not suggest that absent discriminatory purpose the assignment of different missions to various institutions in a State's higher education system would raise an equal protection issue where one or more of the institutions become or remain predominantly black or white. But here the issue is whether the State has sufficiently dismantled its prior dual system; and when combined with the differential admission practices and unnecessary program duplication, it is likely that the mission designations interfere with student choice and tend to perpetuate the segregated system. On remand, the court should inquire whether it would be practicable and consistent with sound educational practices to eliminate any such discriminatory effects of the State's present policy of mission assignments.

Fourth, the State attempted to bring itself into compliance with the Constitution by continuing to maintain and operate all eight higher educational institutions. The existence of eight instead of some lesser number was undoubtedly occasioned by State laws forbidding the mingling of the races. And as the District Court recognized, continuing to maintain all eight universities in Mississippi is wasteful and irrational. The District

Court pointed especially to the facts that Delta State and Mississippi Valley are only 35 miles apart and that only 20 miles separate Mississippi State and Mississippi University for Women.... It was evident to the District Court that "the defendants undertake to fund more institutions of higher learning than are justified by the amount of financial resources available to the state," but the court concluded that such fiscal irresponsibility was a policy choice of the legislature rather than a feature of a system subject to constitutional scrutiny.

Unquestionably, a larger rather than a smaller number of institutions from which to choose in itself makes for different choices, particularly when examined in the light of other factors present in the operation of the system, such as admissions, program duplication, and institutional mission designations. Though certainly closure of one or more institutions would decrease the discriminatory effects of the present system, based on the present record we are unable to say whether such action is constitutionally required. Elimination of program duplication and revision of admissions criteria may make institutional closure unnecessary. However, on remand this issue should be carefully explored by inquiring and determining whether retention of all eight institutions itself affects student choice and perpetuates the segregated higher education system, whether maintenance of each of the universities is educationally justifiable, and whether one or more of them can be practicably closed or merged with other existing institutions.

Because the former *de jure* segregated system of public universities in Mississippi impeded the free choice of prospective students, the State in dismantling that system must take the necessary steps to ensure that this choice now is truly free. The full range of policies and practices must be examined with this duty in mind. That an institution is predominantly white or black does not in itself make out a constitutional violation. But surely the State may not leave in place policies rooted in its prior officially-segregated system that serve to maintain the racial identifiability of its universities if those policies can practicably be eliminated without eroding sound educational policies....

Because the District Court and the Court of Appeals failed to reconsider the State's duties in their proper light, the cases must be remanded. To the extent that the State has not met its affirmative obligation to dismantle its prior dual system, it shall be adjudged in violation of the Constitution and Title VI and remedial proceedings shall be conducted. The decision of the Court of Appeals is vacated, and the cases are remanded for further proceedings consistent with this opinion.

It is so ordered.

SUPREME COURT ON
ABORTION RIGHTS
June 29, 1992

The Supreme Court confounded both sides in the national abortion-rights debate by taking a middle position in a decision June 29, upholding most provisions of a restrictive Pennsylvania abortion law but, by a 5-4 majority, reaffirming a woman's basic right to have an abortion. The conservative-dominated Court surprised many Americans by falling one vote short of overturning the 1973 Roe v. *Wade decision, which declared that a woman's right to choose abortion was among the personal liberties protected by the Constitution.*

Three Court appointees of President Ronald Reagan and George Bush—both outspoken foes of abortion—staked out the prevailing centrist position in the case, Planned Parenthood of Southeastern Pennsylvania v. Casey, *The three justices—Sandra Day O'Connor, Anthony M. Kennedy, and David H. Souter—upheld the central ruling of* Roe *but effectively offered the states wider latitude in regulating abortion. That position drew the backing of the Court's two longstanding supporters of abortion rights, Harry A. Blackmun, author of the* Roe *decision, and John Paul Stevens, despite their dislike of the Pennsylvania law's restrictions.*

Four justices, including Chief Justice William H. Rehnquist, voted to override Roe *entirely and thus free the states to regulate or outlaw abortion as they saw fit. Joined by Justices Byron R. White, Antonin Scalia, and Clarence Thomas, Rehnquist contended that the Court had left the 1973 decision but a shell—a "judicial Potemkin Village"—that should be further dismantled. Scalia, in a separate dissenting opinion, accused the Court of "foreclosing all democratic outlet for the deep passion this issues arises, by banishing the issue from the political forum. . . . [with a rigid national rule]. . . ."*

The Court's middle-course ruling appeared to neutralize debate on the issue, at least during the presidential election campaign. Many abortion-rights advocates had expected the Court to ban abortion, a decision that would have been certain to ignite the issue on the political hustings. As it happened, the decision appeared to catch both the leading advocates and foes of abortion by surprise. Each side quickly portrayed the ruling as a defeat for themselves, in the apparent hope of galvanizing further support for their separate causes. But as indicated by opinion polls, the thinking of a majority of Americans coincided with the ruling. Polls consistently had shown strong support for a woman's right to choose to terminate a pregnancy but also strong support for the kinds of restrictions upheld in the Pennsylvania law.

Court's New 'Undue Burden' Test

Pennsylvania's Abortion Control Act of 1989, one of the nation's strictest, was challenged in court by five abortion clinics and a physician before it went into effect. They named Governor Robert P. Casey of Pennsylvania the defendant. A federal district court declared all the challenged provisions unconstitutional and blocked their enforcement. The U.S. Circuit Court of Appeals for the Third Circuit, drawing on a subsequent Supreme Court decision (Webster v. Reproductive Health Services) that gave states new leeway to regulate abortion, upheld four provisions and struck down one. It required women to notify husbands of their intent to undergo an abortion.

The Supreme Court let stand the appeals court's findings. The four provisions required doctors and clinics to present abortion-seekers with information about risks of and alternatives to abortion and mandated a twenty-four-hour waiting period, required women under age eighteen to obtain the consent of one parent or a judge, permitted no abortions after twenty-four weeks of pregnancy unless needed to protect the woman's life or prevent permanent physical harm, and compelled physicians to keep detailed records of abortions and the reason for performing later-term abortions.

The Supreme Court judged the provisions by a new "undue burden" test—whether the restrictions placed an undue state-imposed burden on the woman's right to abortion. This standard replaced Roe's trimester framework—which held that abortion was a woman's absolute right during her first three months of pregnancy, subject to reasonable restrictions during the second three months to protect maternal health, and could be performed during the final three months only to save her life or health. The spousal requirement did not pass the undue burden test because it permitted husbands to exercise a veto over their wives' decisions. "Women do not lose their constitutionally protected liberty when they marry," said the prevailing opinion, jointly written by

O'Connor, Kennedy, and Souter. It was the first time since the Court reinstated the death penalty in 1976 that it had handed down a jointly written opinion—which emphasized the importance the authors attached to the case. In addition, four separate opinions were issued—by Rehnquist, Scalia, Blackmun, and Stevens. All five opinions amounted to 157 printed pages.

Three-Way Split Among Justices

The main opinion acknowledged that "men and women of good conscience can disagree ... about the profound moral and spiritual implications of terminating a pregnancy, even at its earlier stage...." Indeed, said the three authors, "some of us as individuals find abortion morally offensive ... but that cannot control our decision. Our obligation is to define the liberty of all, not to mandate our own moral code." The Constitution, they declared, affords protection "to personal decisions relating to marriage, procreation, contraception, family relationships, child rearing and education."

Blackmun wrote in an impassioned separate opinion that beginning with the 1989 Webster *decision the Court appeared poised to "cast into darkness the hopes and visions of every woman in this country." But now, he added, "just when so many expected the darkness to fall, the flame has grown brighter." Blackmun praised the joint opinion "as an act of personal courage and constitutional principle."*

He cautioned, however, that the distance between the two sides on the issue was but a single vote. "I am 83 years old. I cannot remain on this court forever, and when I do step down, the confirmation process for my successor well may focus on the issue before us today."

Although O'Connor, Kennedy, and Souter were all Reagan-Bush appointees, Kennedy's vote was the biggest surprise to Court-watchers. Souter addressed the question for the first time, O'Connor had indicated in previous cases that she might go either way, but Kennedy had previously endorsed the view that abortion was not a fundamental right.

More State Regulation Expected

The Court's affirmation of the public's sentiment—at least to some degree—did not diminish a flurry of rhetoric in the days that followed. Bush drew the ire of anti-abortionists by initially praising the decision for upholding most of the Pennsylvania restrictions. Wanda Franz, president of the National Right to Life Committee, called the ruling a "loss for unborn children and a victory of pro-abortion forces." But Kate Michelman, president of the National Abortion Rights Action League, saw the Court's action as moving women "one step closer to the back alleys [to illegal abortion]."

There was general agreement on one matter, that the Casey *decision would increase the amount of activity in state legislatures on regulation.* Casey *put the focus on the critical components of state waiting periods, and parental consent or notification for minors. Mississippi, North Dakota, and Ohio had passed laws with informed consent and waiting period provisions. Kansas, Maryland, Michigan, Nebraska, and South Carolina required parental consent or notification. However, the decision left in doubt stringent laws enacted in Louisiana and Utah that prohibited abortion in almost all circumstances.*

Following are excerpts from the Supreme Court's opinions of June 29, 1992, in Planned Parenthood of Southeastern Pennsylvania *v.* Casey, *upholding but modifying the right to abortion:*

Nos. 91-744 and 91-902

Planned Parenthood of Southeastern Pennsylvania, et al., Petitioners

v.

Robert P. Casey, et al., etc.

On writs of certiorari to the United States Court of Appeals for the Third Circuit

[June 29, 1992]

JUSTICE O'CONNOR, JUSTICE KENNEDY, and JUSTICE SOUTER announced the judgment of the Court [JUSTICE STEVENS joins, concurring in part and dissenting in part]....

I

Liberty finds no refuge in a jurisprudence of doubt. Yet 19 years after our holding that the Constitution protects a woman's right to terminate her pregnancy in its early stages, *Roe* v. *Wade* (1973), that definition of liberty is still questioned. Joining the respondents as *amicus curiae*, the United States, as it has done in five other cases in the last decade, again asks us to overrule *Roe*....

... And at oral argument in this Court, the attorney for the parties challenging the statute took the position that none of the enactments can be upheld without overruling *Roe* v. *Wade*. We disagree with that analysis; but we acknowledge that our decisions after *Roe* cast doubt upon the meaning and reach of its holding. Further, the Chief Justice admits that he would overrule the central holding of *Roe* and adopt the rational relationship test as the sole criterion of constitutionality. ... State and federal courts as well as legislatures throughout the Union must have guidance as they seek to address this subject in conformance with the Constitution. Given these premises, we find it imperative to review once more the principles that define the rights of the woman and the legitimate authority of the State respecting the termination of pregnancies by abortion procedures.

After considering the fundamental constitutional questions resolved by *Roe,* principles of institutional integrity, and the rule of *stare decisis,* we are led to conclude this: the essential holding of *Roe* v. *Wade* should be retained and once again reaffirmed.

It must be stated at the outset and with clarity that *Roe*'s essential holding, the holding we reaffirm, has three parts. First is a recognition of the right of the woman to choose to have an abortion before viability and to obtain it without undue interference from the State. Before viability, the State's interests are not strong enough to support a prohibition of abortion or the imposition of a substantial obstacle to the woman's effective right to elect the procedure. Second is a confirmation of the State's power to restrict abortions after fetal viability, if the law contains exceptions for pregnancies which endanger a woman's life or health. And third is the principle that the State has legitimate interests from the outset of the pregnancy in protecting the health of the woman and the life of the fetus that may become a child. These principles do not contradict one another; and we adhere to each.

II

... Men and women of good conscience can disagree, and we suppose some always shall disagree, about the profound moral and spiritual implications of terminating a pregnancy, even in its earliest stage. Some of us as individuals find abortion offensive to our most basic principles of morality, but that cannot control our decision. Our obligation is to define the liberty of all, not to mandate our own moral code. The underlying constitutional issue is whether the State can resolve these philosophic questions in such a definitive way that a woman lacks all choice in the matter, except perhaps in those rare circumstances in which the pregnancy is itself a danger to her own life or health, or is the result of rape or incest.

It is conventional constitutional doctrine that where reasonable people disagree the government can adopt one position or the other.... That theorem, however, assumes a state of affairs in which the choice does not intrude upon a protected liberty. Thus, while some people might disagree about whether or not the flag should be saluted, or disagree about the proposition that it may not be defiled, we have ruled that a State may not compel or enforce one view or the other....

Our law affords constitutional protection to personal decisions relating to marriage, procreation, contraception, family relationships, child rearing, and education.... Our cases recognize "the right of the *individual,* married or single, to be free from unwarranted governmental intrusion into matters so fundamentally affecting a person as the decision whether to bear or beget a child." (emphasis in original). Our precedents "have respected the private realm of family life which the state cannot enter." These matters, involving the most intimate and personal choices a person may make in a lifetime, choices central to personal dignity and autonomy, are central to the liberty protected by the Fourteenth Amendment. At the heart of liberty is the right to define one's own concept of existence, of meaning, of the universe, and of the mystery of human life. Beliefs about these matters could not define the attributes of personhood were they formed under compulsion of the State.

These considerations begin our analysis of the woman's interest in terminating her pregnancy but cannot end it, for this reason: though the abortion decision may originate within the zone of conscience and belief, it is more than a philosophic exercise. Abortion is a unique act. It is an act fraught with consequences for others: for the woman who must live with the implications of her decision, for the persons who perform and assist in the procedure; for the spouse, family, and society which must confront the knowledge that these procedures exist, procedures some deem nothing short of an act of violence against innocent human life; and, depending on one's beliefs, for the life or potential life that is aborted. Though abortion is conduct, it does not follow that the State is entitled to proscribe it in all instances. That is because the liberty of the woman is at stake in a sense unique to the human condition and so unique to the law. The mother who carries a child to full term is subject to anxieties, to physical constraints, to pain that only she must bear. That these sacrifices have from the beginning of the human race been endured by woman with a pride that ennobles her in the eyes of others and gives to the infant a bond of love cannot alone be grounds for the State to insist she make the sacrifice. Her suffering is too intimate and personal for the State to insist, without more, upon its own vision of the woman's role, however dominant that vision has been in the course of our history and our culture. The destiny of the woman must be shaped to a large extent on her conception of her spiritual imperatives and her place in society.

It should be recognized, moreover, that in some critical respects the abortion decision is of the same character as the decision to use contraception, to which *Griswold* v. *Connecticut, Eisenstadt* v. *Baird,* and *Carey* v. *Population Services International,* afford constitutional protection. We have no doubt as to the correctness of those decisions. They support the reasoning in *Roe* relating to the woman's liberty because they involve personal decisions concerning not only the meaning of procreation but also human responsibility and respect for it. . . .

It was this dimension of personal liberty that *Roe* sought to protect, and its holding invoked the reasoning and the tradition of the precedents we have discussed, granting protection to substantive liberties of the person. *Roe* was, of course, an extension of those cases and, as the decision itself indicated, the separate States could act in some degree to further their own legitimate interests in protecting pre-natal life. The extent to which the legislatures of the States might act to outweigh the interests of the woman in choosing to terminate her pregnancy was a subject of debate both in *Roe* itself and in decisions following it.

While we appreciate the weight of the arguments made on behalf of the State in the case before us, arguments which in their ultimate formulation conclude that *Roe* should be overruled, the reservations any of us may have in reaffirming the central holding of *Roe* are outweighed by the explication of individual liberty we have given combined with the force of *stare decisis*. We turn now to that doctrine.

III

A

The obligation to follow precedent begins with necessity, and a contrary necessity marks its outer limit. With Cardozo, we recognize that no judicial system could do society's work if it eyed each issue afresh in every case that raised it. See B. Cardozo, The Nature of the Judicial Process (1921). Indeed, the very concept of the rule of law underlying our own Constitution requires such continuity over time that a respect for precedent is, by definition, indispensable.... At the other extreme, a different necessity would make itself felt if a prior judicial ruling should come to be seen so clearly as error that its enforcement was for that very reason doomed....

So in this case we may inquire whether *Roe*'s central rule has been found unworkable; whether the rule's limitation on state power could be removed without serious inequity to those who have relied upon it or significant damage to the stability of the society governed by the rule in question; whether the law's growth in the intervening years has left *Roe*'s central rule a doctrinal anachronism discounted by society; and whether *Roe*'s premises of fact have so far changed in the ensuing two decades as to render its central holding somehow irrelevant or unjustifiable in dealing with the issue it addressed.

1

Although *Roe* has engendered opposition, it has in no sense proven "unworkable," representing as it does a simple limitation beyond which a state law is unenforceable. While *Roe* has, of course, required judicial assessment of state laws affecting the exercise of the choice guaranteed against government infringement, and although the need for such review will remain as a consequence of today's decision, the required determinations fall within judicial competence.

2

The inquiry into reliance counts the cost of a rule's repudiation as it would fall on those who have relied reasonably on the rule's continued application. Since the classic case for weighing reliance heavily in favor of following the earlier rule occurs in the commercial context ... where advance planning of great precision is most obviously a necessity, it is no cause for surprise that some would find no reliance worthy of consideration in support of *Roe*.

While neither respondents nor their *amici* in so many words deny that the abortion right invites some reliance prior to its actual exercise, one can readily imagine an argument stressing the dissimilarity of this case to one involving property or contract. Abortion is customarily chosen as an unplanned response to the consequence of unplanned activity or to the failure of conventional birth control, and except on the assumption that no intercourse would have occurred but for *Roe*'s holding, such behavior may appear to justify no reliance claim. Even if reliance could be claimed on that unrealistic assumption, the argument might run, any reliance interest would be *de minimis*. This argument would be premised on the hypothesis that reproductive planning could take virtually immediate account of any sudden restoration of state authority to ban abortions.

To eliminate the issue of reliance that easily, however, one would need to limit cognizable reliance to specific instances of sexual activity. But to do this would be simply to refuse to face the fact that for two decades of economic and social developments, people have organized intimate relationships and made choices that define their views of themselves and their places in society, in reliance on the availability of abortion in the event that contraception should fail. The ability of women to participate equally in the economic and social life of the Nation has been facilitated by their ability to control their reproductive lives.... The Constitution serves human values, and while the effect of reliance on *Roe* cannot be exactly measured, neither can the certain cost of overruling *Roe* for people who have ordered their thinking and living around that case be dismissed.

3

No evolution of legal principle has left *Roe*'s doctrinal footings weaker than they were in 1973. No development of constitutional law since the case was decided has implicitly or explicitly left *Roe* behind as a mere survivor of obsolete constitutional thinking.

It will be recognized, of course, that *Roe* stands at an intersection of two lines of decisions, but in whichever doctrinal category one reads the case, the result for present purposes will be the same. The *Roe* Court itself placed its holding in the succession of cases most prominently exemplified by *Griswold* v. *Connecticut* (1965). When it is so seen, *Roe* is clearly in no jeopardy, since subsequent constitutional developments have neither disturbed, nor do they threaten to diminish, the scope of recognized protection accorded to the liberty relating to intimate relationships, the family, and decisions about whether or not to beget or bear a child....

Roe, however, may be seen not only as an exemplar of *Griswold* liberty but as a rule (whether or not mistaken) of personal autonomy and bodily integrity, with doctrinal affinity to cases recognizing limits on governmental power to mandate medical treatment or to bar its rejection. If so, our cases since *Roe* accord with *Roe*'s view that a State's interest in the protection of life falls short of justifying any plenary override of individual liberty claims....

Finally, one could classify *Roe* as *sui generis*. If the case is so viewed, then there clearly has been no erosion of its central determination. The original holding resting on the concurrence of seven Members of the Court in 1973 was expressly affirmed by a majority of six in 1983, see *Akron* v. *Akron Center for Reproductive Health, Inc.* (1983) *(Akron I)*, and by a majority of five in 1986, see *Thornburgh* v. *American College of Obstetricians and Gynecologists* (1986), expressing adherence to the constitutional ruling despite legislative efforts in some States to test its limits. More recently, in *Webster* v. *Reproductive Health Services* (1989), although two of the present authors questioned the trimester framework in a way consistent with our judgment today, a majority of the Court either decided to reaffirm or declined to address the constitutional validity of the central holding of *Roe*. . . .

4

We have seen how time has overtaken some of *Roe*'s factual assumptions: advances in maternal health care allow for abortions safe to the mother later in pregnancy than was true in 1973, and advances in neonatal care have advanced viability to a point somewhat earlier. . . . But these facts go only to the scheme of time limits on the realization of competing interests, and the divergences from the factual premises of 1973 have no bearing on the validity of *Roe*'s central holding, that viability marks the earliest point at which the State's interest in fetal life is constitutionally adequate to justify a legislative ban on nontherapeutic abortions. The soundness or unsoundness of that constitutional judgment in no sense turns on whether viability occurs at approximately 28 weeks, as was usual at the time of *Roe,* at 23 to 24 weeks, as it sometimes does today, or at some moment even slightly earlier in pregnancy, as it may if fetal respiratory capacity can somehow be enhanced in the future. Whenever it may occur, the attainment of viability may continue to serve as the critical fact, just as it has done since *Roe* was decided; which is to say that no change in *Roe*'s factual underpinning has left its central holding obsolete, and none supports an argument for overruling it.

5

The sum of the precedential inquiry to this point shows *Roe*'s underpinnings unweakened in any way affecting its central holding. While it has engendered disapproval, it has not been unworkable. An entire generation has come of age free to assume *Roe*'s concept of liberty in defining the capacity of women to act in society, and to make reproductive decisions; no erosion of principle going to liberty or personal autonomy has left *Roe*'s central holding a doctrinal remnant; *Roe* portends no developments at odds with other precedent for the analysis of personal liberty; and no changes of fact have rendered viability more or less appropriate as the point at which the balance of interests tips. Within the bounds of normal *stare decisis* analysis, then, and subject to the considerations on which it customarily turns, the stronger argument is for affirming *Roe*'s central holding, with whatever degree of personal reluctance any of us may have, for not overruling it.

B

In a less significant case, *stare decisis* analysis could, and would, stop at the point we have reached. . . .

C

. . . Our analysis would not be complete, however, without explaining why overruling *Roe*'s central holding would not only reach an unjustifiable result under principles of *stare decisis,* but would seriously weaken the Court's-capacity to exercise the judicial power and to function as the Supreme Court of a Nation dedicated to the rule of law. To understand why this would be so it is necessary to understand the source of this Court's authority, the conditions necessary for its preservation, and its relationship to the country's understanding of itself as a constitutional Republic.

The root of American governmental power is revealed most clearly in the instance of the power conferred by the Constitution upon the Judiciary of the United States and specifically upon this Court. As Americans of each succeeding generation are rightly told, the Court cannot buy support for its decisions by spending money and, except to a minor degree, it cannot independently coerce obedience to its decrees. The Court's power lies, rather, in its legitimacy, a product of substance and perception that shows itself in the people's acceptance of the Judiciary as fit to determine what the Nation's law means and to declare what it demands.

The underlying substance of this legitimacy is of course the warrant for the Court's decisions in the Constitution and the lesser sources of legal principle on which the Court draws. That substance is expressed in the Court's opinions, and our contemporary understanding is such that a decision without principled justification would be no judicial act at all. But even when justification is furnished by apposite legal principle, something more is required. Because not every conscientious claim of principled justification will be accepted as such, the justification claimed must be beyond dispute. The Court must take care to speak and act in ways that allow people to accept its decisions on the terms the Court claims for them, as grounded truly in principle, not as compromises with social and political pressures having, as such, no bearing on the principled choices that the Court is obliged to make. Thus, the Court's legitimacy depends on making legally principled decisions under circumstances in which their principled character is sufficiently plausible to be accepted by the Nation.

The need for principled action to be perceived as such is implicated to some degree whenever this, or any other appellate court, overrules a prior case. This is not to say, of course, that this Court cannot give a perfectly satisfactory explanation in most cases. People understand that some of the

Constitution's language is hard to fathom and that the Court's Justices are sometimes able to perceive significant facts or to understand principles of law that eluded their predecessors and that justify departures from existing decisions. However upsetting it may be to those most directly affected when one judicially derived rule replaces another, the country can accept some correction of error without necessarily questioning the legitimacy of the Court.

In two circumstances, however, the Court would almost certainly fail to receive the benefit of the doubt in overruling prior cases. There is, first, a point beyond which frequent overruling would overtax the country's belief in the Court's good faith. Despite the variety of reasons that may inform and justify a decision to overrule, we cannot forget that such a decision is usually perceived (and perceived correctly) as, at the least, a statement that a prior decision was wrong. There is a limit to the amount of error that can plausibly be imputed to prior courts. If that limit should be exceeded, disturbance of prior rulings would be taken as evidence that justifiable reexamination of principle had given way to drives for particular results in the short term. The legitimacy of the Court would fade with the frequency of its vacillation.

That first circumstance can be described as hypothetical; the second is to the point here and now. Where, in the performance of its judicial duties, the Court decides a case in such a way as to resolve the sort of intensely divisive controversy reflected in *Roe* and those rare, comparable cases, its decision has a dimension that the resolution of the normal case does not carry. It is the dimension present whenever the Court's interpretation of the Constitution calls the contending sides of a national controversy to end their national division by accepting a common mandate rooted in the Constitution.

The Court is not asked to do this very often, having thus addressed the Nation only twice in our lifetime, in the decisions of *Brown* and *Roe*. But when the Court does act in this way, its decision requires an equally rare precedential force to counter the inevitable efforts to overturn it and to thwart its implementation. Some of those efforts may be mere unprincipled emotional reactions; others may proceed from principles worthy of profound respect. But whatever the premises of opposition may be, only the most convincing justification under accepted standards of precedent could suffice to demonstrate that a later decision overruling the first was anything but a surrender to political pressure, and an unjustified repudiation of the principle on which the Court staked its authority in the first instance. So to overrule under fire in the absence of the most compelling reason to reexamine a watershed decision would subvert the Court's legitimacy beyond any serious question. . . .

The country's loss of confidence in the judiciary would be underscored by an equally certain and equally reasonable condemnation for another failing in overruling unnecessarily and under pressure. Some cost will be paid by anyone who approves or implements a constitutional decision where it is unpopular, or who refuses to work to undermine the decision or to force its reversal. The price may be criticism or ostracism, or it may be violence. An extra price will be paid by those who themselves disapprove of the decision's results when viewed outside of constitutional terms, but who nevertheless struggle to accept it, because they respect the rule of law. To all those who will be so tested by following, the Court implicitly undertakes to remain steadfast, lest in the end a price be paid for nothing. The promise of constancy, once given, binds its maker for as long as the power to stand by the decision survives and the understanding of the issue has not changed so fundamentally as to render the commitment obsolete. From the obligation of this promise this Court cannot and should not assume any exemption when duty requires it to decide a case in conformance with the Constitution. A willing breach of it would be nothing less than a breach of faith, and no Court that broke its faith with the people could sensibly expect credit for principle in the decision by which it did that.

It is true that diminished legitimacy may be restored, but only slowly. Unlike the political branches, a Court thus weakened could not seek to regain its position with a new mandate from the voters, and even if the Court could somehow go to the polls, the loss of its principled character could not be retrieved by the casting of so many votes. Like the character of an individual, the legitimacy of the Court must be earned over time. So, indeed, must be the character of the Nation of people who aspire to live according to the rule of law. Their belief in themselves as such a people is not readily separable from their understanding of the Court invested with the authority to decide their constitutional cases and speak before all others for their constitutional ideals. If the Court's legitimacy should be undermined, then, so would the country be in its very ability to see itself through its constitutional ideals. The Court's concern with legitimacy is not for the sake of the Court but for the sake of the Nation to which it is responsible.

The Court's duty in the present case is clear. In 1973, it confronted the already-divisive issue of governmental power to limit personal choice to undergo abortion, for which it provided a new resolution based on the due process guaranteed by the Fourteenth Amendment. Whether or not a new social consensus is developing on that issue, its divisiveness is no less today than in 1973, and pressure to overrule the decision, like pressure to retain it, has grown only more intense. A decision to overrule *Roe*'s essential holding under the existing circumstances would address error, if error there was, at the cost of both profound and unnecessary damage to the Court's legitimacy, and to the Nation's commitment to the rule of law. It is therefore imperative to adhere to the essence of *Roe*'s original decision, and we do so today.

IV

From what we have said so far it follows that it is a constitutional liberty of the woman to have some freedom to terminate her pregnancy. We conclude that the basic decision in *Roe* was based on a constitutional analysis which we cannot now repudiate. The woman's liberty is not so unlimited, however, that from the outset the State cannot show its concern for the life of the unborn, and at a later point in fetal development the State's interest in life has sufficient force so that the right of the woman to terminate the pregnancy can be restricted.

That brings us, of course, to the point where much criticism has been directed at *Roe,* a criticism that always inheres when the Court draws a specific rule from what in the Constitution is but a general standard. We conclude, however, that the urgent claims of the woman to retain the ultimate control over her destiny and her body, claims implicit in the meaning of liberty, require us to perform that function. Liberty must not be extinguished for want of a line that is clear. And it falls to us to give some real substance to the woman's liberty to determine whether to carry her pregnancy to full term.

We conclude the line should be drawn at viability, so that before that time the woman has a right to choose to terminate her pregnancy. We adhere to this principle for two reasons. First, as we have said, is the doctrine of *stare decisis.* Any judicial act of line-drawing may seem somewhat arbitrary, but *Roe* was a reasoned statement, elaborated with great care. We have twice reaffirmed it in the face of great opposition. . . . Although we must overrule those parts of *Thornburgh* and *Akron I* which, in our view, are inconsistent with *Roe*'s statement that the State has a legitimate interest in promoting the life or potential life of the unborn, the central premise of those cases represents an unbroken commitment by this Court to the essential holding of *Roe.* It is that premise which we reaffirm today.

The second reason is that the concept of viability, as we noted in *Roe,* is the time at which there is a realistic possibility of maintaining and nourishing a life outside the womb, so that the independent existence of the second life can in reason and all fairness be the object of state protection that now overrides the rights of the woman. . . . Consistent with other constitutional norms, legislatures may draw lines which appear arbitrary without the necessity of offering a justification. But courts may not. We must justify the lines we draw. And there is no line other than viability which is more workable. To be sure, as we have said, there may be some medical developments that affect the precise point of viability, but this is an imprecision within tolerable limits given that the medical community and all those who must apply its discoveries will continue to explore the matter. The viability line also has, as a practical matter, an element of fairness. In some broad sense it might be said that a woman who fails to act before viability has consented to the State's intervention on behalf of the developing child.

The woman's right to terminate her pregnancy before viability is the most central principle of *Roe* v. *Wade.* It is a rule of law and a component of liberty we cannot renounce. . . .

Yet it must be remembered that *Roe* v. *Wade* speaks with clarity in establishing not only the woman's liberty but also the State's "important and legitimate interest in potential life." That portion of the decision in *Roe* has been given too little acknowledgement and implementation by the Court in its subsequent cases. Those cases decided that any regulation touching upon the abortion decision must survive strict scrutiny, to be sustained only if drawn in narrow terms to further a compelling state interest.... Not all of the cases decided under that formulation can be reconciled with the holding in *Roe* itself that the State has legitimate interests in the health of the woman and in protecting the potential life within her. In resolving this tension, we choose to rely upon *Roe*, as against the later cases.

Roe established a trimester framework to govern abortion regulations. Under this elaborate but rigid construct, almost no regulation at all is permitted during the first trimester of pregnancy; regulations designed to protect the woman's health, but not to further the State's interest in potential life, are permitted during the second trimester; and during the third trimester, when the fetus is viable, prohibitions are permitted provided the life or health of the mother is not at stake. Most of our cases since *Roe* have involved the application of rules derived from the trimester framework.

The trimester framework no doubt was erected to ensure that the woman's right to choose not become so subordinate to the State's interest in promoting fetal life that her choice exists in theory but not in fact. We do not agree, however, that the trimester approach is necessary to accomplish this objective. A framework of this rigidity was unnecessary and in its later interpretation sometimes contradicted the State's permissible exercise of its powers.

Though the woman has a right to choose to terminate or continue her pregnancy before viability, it does not at all follow that the State is prohibited from taking steps to ensure that this choice is thoughtful and informed. Even in the earliest stages of pregnancy, the State may enact rules and regulations designed to encourage her to know that there are philosophic and social arguments of great weight that can be brought to bear in favor of continuing the pregnancy to full term and that there are procedures and institutions to allow adoption of unwanted children as well as a certain degree of state assistance if the mother chooses to raise the child herself. It follows that States are free to enact laws to provide a reasonable framework for a woman to make a decision that has such profound and lasting meaning. This, too, we find consistent with *Roe's* central premises, and indeed the inevitable consequence of our holding that the State has an interest in protecting the life of the unborn.

We reject the trimester framework, which we do not consider to be part of the essential holding of *Roe*. Measures aimed at ensuring that a woman's choice contemplates the consequences for the fetus do not necessarily interfere with the right recognized in *Roe*, although those measures have been found to be inconsistent with the rigid trimester framework announced in that case. A logical reading of the central holding in *Roe* itself, and a necessary reconciliation of the liberty of the woman and the interest of the State in promoting prenatal life, require, in our view, that we abandon the trimester framework as a rigid prohibition on all previability regulation aimed at the protection of fetal life. The trimester framework suffers from these basic flaws: in its formulation it misconceives the nature of the pregnant woman's interest; and in practice it undervalues the State's interest in potential life, as recognized in *Roe*.

As our jurisprudence relating to all liberties save perhaps abortion has recognized, not every law which makes a right more difficult to exercise is *ipso facto,* an infringement of that right. An example clarifies the point. We have held that not every ballot access limitation amounts to an infringement of the right to vote. Rather, the States are granted substantial flexibility in establishing the framework within which voters choose the candidates for whom they wish to vote. . . .

The abortion right is similar. Numerous forms of state regulation might have the incidental effect of increasing the cost or decreasing the availability of medical care, whether for abortion or any other medical procedure. The fact that a law which serves a valid purpose, one not designed to strike at the right itself, has the incidental effect of making it more difficult or more expensive to procure an abortion cannot be enough to invalidate it. Only where state regulation imposes an undue burden on a woman's ability to make this decision does the power of the State reach into the heart of the liberty protected by the Due Process Clause. . . .

Not all government intrusion is of necessity unwarranted; and that brings us to the other basic flaw in the trimester framework: even in *Roe's* terms, in practice it undervalues the State's interest in the potential life within the woman.

Roe v. Wade was express in its recognition of the State's "important and legitimate interest[s] in preserving and protecting the health of the pregnant woman [and] in protecting the potentiality of human life." 410 U.S., at 162. The trimester framework, however, does not fulfill *Roe's* own promise that the State has an interest in protecting fetal life or potential life. *Roe* began the contradiction by using the trimester framework to forbid any regulation of abortion designed to advance that interest before viability. Before viability, *Roe* and subsequent cases treat all governmental attempts to influence a woman's decision on behalf of the potential life within her as unwarranted. This treatment is, in our judgment, incompatible with the recognition that there is a substantial state interest in potential life throughout pregnancy.

The very notion that the State has a substantial interest in potential life leads to the conclusion that not all regulations must be deemed unwarranted. Not all burdens on the right to decide whether to terminate a pregnancy will be undue. In our view, the undue burden standard is the appropriate means of reconciling the State's interest with the woman's constitutionally protected liberty.

The concept of an undue burden has been utilized by the Court as well as individual members of the Court, including two of us, in ways that could be considered inconsistent. Because we set forth a standard of general application to which we intend to adhere, it is important to clarify what is meant by an undue burden.

A finding of an undue burden is a shorthand for the conclusion that a state regulation has the purpose or effect of placing a substantial obstacle in the path of a woman seeking an abortion of a nonviable fetus. A statute with this purpose is invalid because the means chosen by the State to further the interest in potential life must be calculated to inform the woman's free choice, not hinder it. And a statute which, while furthering the interest in potential life or some other valid state interest, has the effect of placing a substantial obstacle in the path of a woman's choice cannot be considered a permissible means of serving its legitimate ends. To the extent that the opinions of the Court or of individual Justices use the undue burden standard in a manner that is inconsistent with this analysis, we set out what in our view should be the controlling standard. . . . Understood another way, we answer the question, left open in previous opinions discussing the undue burden formulation, whether a law designed to further the State's interest in fetal life which imposes an undue burden on the woman's decision before fetal viability could be constitutional. . . . The answer is no.

Some guiding principles should emerge. What is at stake is the woman's right to make the ultimate decision, not a right to be insulated from all others in doing so. Regulations which do no more than create a structural mechanism by which the State, or the parent or guardian of a minor, may express profound respect for the life of the unborn are permitted, if they are not a substantial obstacle to the woman's exercise of the right to choose. . . . Unless it has that effect on her right of choice, a state measure designed to persuade her to choose childbirth over abortion will be upheld if reasonably related to that goal. Regulations designed to foster the health of a woman seeking an abortion are valid if they do not constitute an undue burden.

Even when jurists reason from shared premises, some disagreement is inevitable. . . . That is to be expected in the application of any legal standard which must accommodate life's complexity. We do not expect it to be otherwise with respect to the undue burden standard. We give this summary:

(a) To protect the central right recognized by *Roe* v. *Wade* while at the same time accommodating the State's profound interest in potential life, we will employ the undue burden analysis as explained in this opinion. An undue burden exists, and therefore a provision of law is invalid, if its purpose or effect is to place a substantial obstacle in the path of a woman seeking an abortion before the fetus attains viability.

(b) We reject the rigid trimester framework of *Roe* v. *Wade*. To promote the State's profound interest in potential life, throughout pregnancy the State may take measures to ensure that the woman's choice is informed, and measures designed to advance this interest will not be invalidated as long as their purpose is to persuade the woman to choose childbirth over abortion. These measures must not be an undue burden on the right.

(c) As with any medical procedure, the State may enact regulations to further the health or safety of a woman seeking an abortion. Unnecessary health regulations that have the purpose or effect of presenting a substantial obstacle to a woman seeking an abortion impose an undue burden on the right.

(d) Our adoption of the undue burden analysis does not disturb the central holding of *Roe* v. *Wade,* and we reaffirm that holding. Regardless of whether exceptions are made for particular circumstances, a State may not prohibit any woman from making the ultimate decision to terminate her pregnancy before viability.

(e) We also affirm *Roe*'s holding that "subsequent to viability, the State in promoting its interest in the potentiality of human life may, if it chooses, regulate, and even proscribe, abortion except where it is necessary, in appropriate medical judgment, for the preservation of the life or health of the mother." ...

These principles control our assessment of the Pennsylvania statute, and we now turn to the issue of the validity of the challenged provisions.

V

The Court of Appeals applied what it believed to be the undue burden standard and upheld each of the provisions except for the husband notification requirement. We agree generally with this conclusion, but refine the undue burden analysis in accordance with the principles articulated above. We now consider the separate statutory sections at issue. ...

[A omitted]

B

... Except in a medical emergency, the statute requires that at least 24 hours before performing an abortion a physician inform the woman of the nature of the procedure, the health risks of the abortion and of childbirth, and the "probable gestational age of the unborn child." ...

In *Akron I* (1983), we invalidated an ordinance which required that a woman seeking an abortion be provided by her physician with specific information "designed to influence the woman's informed choice between abortion or childbirth." ... As we later described the *Akron I* holding in *Thornburgh* v. *American College of Obstetricians and Gynecologists,* there were two purported flaws in the Akron ordinance: the information was designed to dissuade the woman from having an abortion and the ordinance imposed "a rigid requirement that a specific body of information be given in all cases, irrespective of the particular needs of the patient. ..." *Ibid.*

To the extent *Akron I* and *Thornburgh* find a constitutional violation when the government requires, as it does here, the giving of truthful, nonmisleading information about the nature of the procedure, the attendant health risks and those of childbirth, and the "probable gestational age" of the fetus, those cases go too far, are inconsistent with *Roe*'s acknowledgment of an important interest in potential life, and are overruled. . . .

We also see no reason why the State may not require doctors to inform a woman seeking an abortion of the availability of materials relating to the consequences to the fetus, even when those consequences have no direct relation to her health. An example illustrates the point. We would think it constitutional for the State to require that in order for there to be informed consent to a kidney transplant operation the recipient must be supplied with information about risks to the donor as well as risks to himself or herself. . . . In short, requiring that the woman be informed of the availability of information relating to fetal development and the assistance available should she decide to carry the pregnancy to full term is a reasonable measure to insure an informed choice, one which might cause the woman to choose childbirth over abortion. This requirement cannot be considered a substantial obstacle to obtaining an abortion, and, it follows, there is no undue burden. . . .

Our analysis of Pennsylvania's 24-hour waiting period between the provision of the information deemed necessary to informed consent and the performance of an abortion under the undue burden standard requires us to reconsider the premise behind the decision in *Akron I* invalidating a parallel requirement. In *Akron I* we said: "Nor are we convinced that the State's legitimate concern that the woman's decision be informed is reasonably served by requiring a 24-hour delay as a matter of course." . . . We consider that conclusion to be wrong. The idea that important decisions will be more informed and deliberate if they follow some period of reflection does not strike us as unreasonable, particularly where the statute directs that important information become part of the background of the decision. The statute, as construed by the Court of Appeals, permits avoidance of the waiting period in the event of a medical emergency and the record evidence shows that in the vast majority of cases, a 24-hour delay does not create any appreciable health risk. In theory, at least, the waiting period is a reasonable measure to implement the State's interest in protecting the life of the unborn, a measure that does not amount to an undue burden.

Whether the mandatory 24-hour waiting period is nonetheless invalid because in practice it is a substantial obstacle to a woman's choice to terminate her pregnancy is a closer question. The findings of fact by the District Court indicate that because of the distances many women must travel to reach an abortion provider, the practical effect will often be a delay of much more than a day because the waiting period requires that a woman seeking an abortion make at least two visits to the doctor. The

District Court also found that in many instances this will increase the exposure of women seeking abortions to "the harassment and hostility of anti-abortion protesters demonstrating outside a clinic." As a result, the District Court found that for those women who have the fewest financial resources, those who must travel long distances, and those who have difficulty explaining their whereabouts to husbands, employers, or others, the 24-hour waiting period will be "particularly burdensome." ...

These findings are troubling in some respects, but they do not demonstrate that the waiting period constitutes an undue burden. ...

We are left with the argument that the various aspects of the informed consent requirement are unconstitutional because they place barriers in the way of abortion on demand. Even the broadest reading of *Roe,* however, has not suggested that there is a constitutional right to abortion on demand. ... Rather, the right protected by *Roe* is a right to decide to terminate a pregnancy free of undue interference by the State. Because the informed consent requirement facilitates the wise exercise of that right it cannot be classified as an interference with the right *Roe* protects. The informed consent requirement is not an undue burden on that right.

C

Section 3209 of Pennsylvania's abortion law provides, except in cases of medical emergency, that no physician shall perform an abortion on a married woman without receiving a signed statement from the woman that she has notified her spouse that she is about to undergo an abortion. ...

... The American Medical Association (AMA) has published a summary of the recent research ... which indicates that in an average 12-month period in this country, approximately two million women are the victims of severe assaults by their male partners. In a 1985 survey, women reported that nearly one of every eight husbands had assaulted their wives during the past year. The AMA views these figures as "marked underestimates," because the nature of these incidents discourages women from reporting them, and because surveys typically exclude the very poor, those who do not speak English well, and women who are homeless or in institutions or hospitals when the survey is conducted. ...

Other studies fill in the rest of this troubling picture. Physical violence is only the most visible form of abuse. Psychological abuse, particularly forced social and economic isolation of women, is also common. ... Many victims of domestic violence remain with their abusers, perhaps because they perceive no superior alternative. ...

The limited research that has been conducted with respect to notifying one's husband about an abortion, although involving samples too small to be representative, also supports the District Court's findings of fact. The vast majority of women notify their male partners of their decision to obtain an abortion. In many cases in which married women do not notify their husbands, the pregnancy is the result of an extramarital affair. Where the husband is the father, the primary reason women do not notify their husbands is that the husband and wife are experiencing marital difficulties, often accompanied by incidents of violence. . . .

This information . . . reinforce[s] what common sense would suggest. In well-functioning marriages, spouses discuss important intimate decisions such as whether to bear a child. But there are millions of women in this country who are the victims of regular physical and psychological abuse at the hands of their husbands. Should these women become pregnant, they may have very good reasons for not wishing to inform their husbands of their decision to obtain an abortion. . . .

The spousal notification requirement is thus likely to prevent a significant number of women from obtaining an abortion. It does not merely make abortions a little more difficult or expensive to obtain; for many women, it will impose a substantial obstacle. We must not blind ourselves to the fact that the significant number of women who fear for their safety and the safety of their children are likely to be deterred from procuring an abortion as surely as if the Commonwealth had outlawed abortion in all cases. . . .

Section 3209 embodies a view of marriage consonant with the common-law status of married women but repugnant to our present understanding of marriage and of the nature of the rights secured by the Constitution. Women do not lose their constitutionally protected liberty when they marry. The Constitution protects all individuals, male or female, married or unmarried, from the abuse of governmental power, even where that power is employed for the supposed benefit of a member of the individual's family. These considerations confirm our conclusion that § 3209 is invalid.

D

We next consider the parental consent provision. . . .

We have been over most of this ground before. Our cases establish, and we reaffirm today, that a State may require a minor seeking an abortion to obtain the consent of a parent or guardian, provided that there is an adequate judicial bypass procedure. . . . [I]n our view, the one-parent consent requirement and judicial bypass procedure are constitutional. . . .

E

Under the recordkeeping and reporting requirements of the statute, every facility which performs abortions is required to file a report stating its name and address as well as the name and address of any related entity, such as a controlling or subsidiary organization. In the case of state-funded institutions, the information becomes public. . . .

In *Danforth* . . . we held that recordkeeping and reporting provisions "that are reasonably directed to the preservation of maternal health and that properly respect a patient's confidentiality and privacy are permissible." We think that under this standard, all the provisions at issue here except that relating to spousal notice are constitutional. Although they do not relate to the State's interest in informing the woman's choice, they do relate to health. The collection of information with respect to actual patients is a vital element of medical research, and so it cannot be said that the requirements serve no purpose other than to make abortions more difficult. Nor do we find that the requirements impose a substantial obstacle to a woman's choice. At most they might increase the cost of some abortions by a slight amount. While at some point increased cost could become a substantial obstacle, there is no such showing on the record before us.

Subsection (12) of the reporting provision requires the reporting of, among other things, a married woman's "reason for failure to provide notice" to her husband. . . . This provision in effect requires women, as a condition of obtaining an abortion, to provide the Commonwealth with the precise information we have already recognized that many women have pressing reasons not to reveal. Like the spousal notice requirement itself, this provision places an undue burden on a woman's choice, and must be invalidated for that reason.

VI

Our Constitution is a covenant running from the first generation of Americans to us and then to future generations. It is a coherent succession. Each generation must learn anew that the Constitution's written terms embody ideas and aspirations that must survive more ages than one. We accept our responsibility not to retreat from interpreting the full meaning of the covenant in light of all of our precedents. We invoke it once again to define the freedom guaranteed by the Constitution's own promise, the promise of liberty. . . .

It is so ordered.

I

JUSTICE STEVENS, concurring in part and dissenting in part. . . .

The Court is unquestionably correct in concluding that the doctrine of *stare decisis* has controlling significance in a case of this kind, notwithstanding an individual justice's concerns about the merits. . . . The societal costs of overruling *Roe* at this late date would be enormous. *Roe* is an integral part of a correct understanding of both the concept of liberty and the basic equality of men and women. . . .

I also accept what is implicit in the Court's analysis, namely, a reaffirmation of *Roe's* explanation of *why* the State's obligation to protect the life or health of the mother must take precedence over any duty to the unborn. . . . From this holding, there was no dissent . . . indeed, no member of the Court has ever questioned this fundamental proposition. Thus, as a matter of federal constitutional law, a developing organism that is not yet a "person" does not have what is sometimes described as a "right to life." This has been and, by the Court's holding today, remains a fundamental premise of our constitutional law governing reproductive autonomy.

II

My disagreement with the joint opinion begins with its understanding of the trimester framework established in *Roe*. Contrary to the suggestion of the joint opinion, it is not a "contradiction" to recognize that the State may have a legitimate interest in potential human life and, at the same time, to conclude that that interest does not justify the regulation of abortion before viability (although other interests, such as maternal health, may). The fact that the State's interest is legitimate does not tell us when, if ever, that interest outweighs the pregnant woman's interest in personal liberty. . . .

Weighing the State's interest in potential life and the woman's liberty interest, I agree with the joint opinion that the State may " 'expres[s] a preference for normal childbirth,' " that the State may take steps to ensure that a woman's choice "is thoughtful and informed," and that "States are free to enact laws to provide a reasonable framework for a woman to make a decision that has such profound and lasting meaning." Serious questions arise, however, when a State attempts to "persuade the woman to choose childbirth over abortion." Decisional autonomy must limit the State's power to inject into a woman's most personal deliberations its own views of what is best. The State may promote its preferences by funding childbirth, by creating and maintaining alternatives to abortion, and by espousing the virtues of family; but it must respect the individual's freedom to make such judgments. . . .

III

The 24-hour waiting period required by . . . the Pennsylvania statute raises even more serious concerns. Such a requirement arguably furthers the State's interests in two ways, neither of which is constitutionally permissible.

First, it may be argued that the 24-hour delay is justified by the mere fact that it is likely to reduce the number of abortions, thus furthering the State's interest in potential life. But such an argument would justify any form of coercion that placed an obstacle in the woman's path. The State cannot further its interests by simply wearing down the ability of the pregnant woman to exercise her constitutional right.

Second, it can more reasonably be argued that the 24-hour delay furthers the State's interest in ensuring that the woman's decision is informed and thoughtful. But there is no evidence that the mandated delay benefits women or that it is necessary to enable the physician to convey any relevant information to the patient. The mandatory delay thus appears to rest on outmoded and unacceptable assumptions about the decisionmaking capacity of women. . . .

In the alternative, the delay requirement may be premised on the belief that the decision to terminate a pregnancy is presumptively wrong. This premise is illegitimate. Those who disagree vehemently about the legality and morality of abortion agree about one thing: The decision to terminate a pregnancy is profound and difficult. No person undertakes such a decision lightly—and States may not presume that a woman has failed to reflect adequately merely because her conclusion differs from the State's preference. A woman who has, in the privacy of her thoughts and conscience, weighed the options and made her decision cannot be forced to reconsider all, simply because the State believes she has come to the wrong conclusion.[5]

Part of the constitutional liberty to choose is the equal dignity to which each of us is entitled. A woman who decides to terminate her pregnancy is entitled to the same respect as a woman who decides to carry the fetus to term. The mandatory waiting period denies women that equal respect. . . .

JUSTICE BLACKMUN, concurring in part, concurring in the judgment in part, and dissenting in part. . . .

Three years ago, in *Webster* v. *Reproductive Health Serv.* (1989), four Members of this Court appeared poised to "cas[t] into darkness the hopes and visions of every woman in this country" who had come to believe that the Constitution guaranteed her the right to reproductive choice. . . . All that remained between the promise of *Roe* and the darkness of the plurality was a single, flickering flame. Decisions since *Webster* gave little reason to hope that this flame would cast much light. But now, just when so many expected the darkness to fall, the flame has grown bright.

I do not underestimate the significance of today's joint opinion. Yet I remain steadfast in my belief that the right to reproductive choice is entitled to the full protection afforded by this Court before *Webster*. And I fear for the darkness as four Justices anxiously await the single vote necessary to extinguish the light.

Make no mistake, the joint opinion of JUSTICES O'CONNOR, KENNEDY, and SOUTER is an act of personal courage and constitutional principle. In contrast to previous decisions in which JUSTICES O'CONNOR and KENNEDY postponed reconsideration of *Roe* v. *Wade* (1973), the authors of the joint opinion today join JUSTICE STEVENS and me in concluding that "the essential holding of *Roe* should be retained and once again reaffirmed." . . . In brief, five Members of this Court today recognize that "the Constitution protects a woman's right to terminate her pregnancy in its early stages." . . .

In one sense, the Court's approach is worlds apart from that of THE CHIEF JUSTICE and JUSTICE SCALIA. And yet, in another sense, the distance between the two approaches is short—the distance is but a single vote.

I am 83 years old. I cannot remain on this Court forever, and when I do step down, the confirmation process for my successor well may focus on the issue before us today. That, I regret, may be exactly where the choice between the two worlds will be made.

CHIEF JUSTICE REHNQUIST, with whom JUSTICE WHITE, JUSTICE SCALIA, and JUSTICE THOMAS join, concurring in the judgment in part and dissenting in part.

The joint opinion, following its newly-minted variation on *stare decisis,* retains the outer shell of *Roe* v. *Wade,* but beats a wholesale retreat from the substance of that case. We believe that *Roe* was wrongly decided, and that it can and should be overruled consistently with our traditional approach to *stare decisis* in constitutional cases. We would adopt the approach of the plurality in *Webster* v. *Reproductive Health Services* and uphold the challenged provisions of the Pennsylvania statute in their entirety. . . .

JUSTICE SCALIA, with whom THE CHIEF JUSTICE, JUSTICE WHITE, and JUSTICE THOMAS join, concurring in the judgment in part and dissenting in part.

My views on this matter are unchanged from those I set forth in my separate opinions in *Webster* v. *Reproductive Health Services.* . . . The States may, if they wish, permit abortion-on-demand, but the Constitution does not *require* them to do so. The permissibility of abortion, and the limitations upon it, are to be resolved like most important questions in our democracy: by citizens trying to persuade one another and then voting. As the Court acknowledges, "where reasonable people disagree the government can adopt one position or the other." The Court is correct in adding the qualification that this "assumes a state of affairs in which the choice does not intrude upon a protected liberty," but the crucial part of that qualification is the penultimate word. A State's choice between two positions on which reasonable people can disagree is constitutional even when (as is often the case) it intrudes upon a "liberty" in the absolute sense. Laws against bigamy, for example—which entire societies of reasonable people disagree with—intrude upon men and women's liberty to marry and live with one another. But bigamy happens not to be a liberty specially "protected" by the Constitution.

That is, quite simply, the issue in this case: not whether the power of a woman to abort her unborn child is a "liberty" in the absolute sense; or even whether it is a liberty of great importance to many women. Of course it is both. The issue is whether it is a liberty protected by the Constitution of the United States. I am sure it is not. I reach that conclusion not because of anything so exalted as my views concerning the "concept of existence, of meaning, of the universe, and of the mystery of human life." Rather, I reach it for the same reason I reach the conclusion that bigamy is not constitutionally protected—because of two simple facts: (1) the Constitution says absolutely nothing about it, and (2) the longstanding traditions of American society have permitted it to be legally proscribed. . . .

There is a poignant aspect to today's opinion. Its length, and what might be called its epic tone, suggest that its authors believe they are bringing to an end a troublesome era in the history of our Nation and of our Court. "It is the dimension" of authority, they say, to "cal[l] the contending sides of national controversy to end their national division by accepting a common mandate rooted in the Constitution."

There comes vividly to mind a portrait by Emanuel Leutze that hangs in the Harvard Law School: Roger Brooke Taney, painted in 1859, the 82d year of his life, the 24th of his Chief Justiceship, the second after his opinion in *Dred Scott*. He is all in black, sitting in a shadowed red armchair, left hand resting upon a pad of paper in his lap, right hand hanging limply, almost lifelessly, beside the inner arm of the chair. He sits facing the viewer, and staring straight out. There seems to be on his face, and in his deep-set eyes, an expression of profound sadness and disillusionment. Perhaps he always looked that way, even when dwelling upon the happiest of thoughts. But those of us who know how the lustre of his great Chief Justiceship came to be eclipsed by *Dred Scott* cannot help believing that he had that case—its already apparent consequences for the Court, and its soon-to-be-played-out consequences for the Nation—burning on his mind. I expect that two years earlier he, too, had thought himself "call[ing] the contending sides of national controversy to end their national division by accepting a common mandate rooted in the Constitution." ...

It is no more realistic for us in this case, than it was for him in that, to think that an issue of the sort they both involved—an issue involving life and death, freedom and subjugation—can be "speedily and finally settled" by the Supreme Court, as President James Buchanan in his inaugural address said the issue of slavery in the territories would be.... Quite to the contrary, by foreclosing all democratic outlet for the deep passions this issue arouses, by banishing the issue from the political forum that gives all participants, even the losers, the satisfaction of a fair hearing and an honest fight, by continuing the imposition of a rigid national rule instead of allowing for regional differences, the Court merely prolongs and intensifies the anguish.

We should get out of this area, where we have no right to be, and where we do neither ourselves nor the country any good by remaining.

SUPREME COURT ON LAND-TAKING COMPENSATION

June 29, 1992

In a case widely expected to be the vehicle for a broad expansion of property rights, the Supreme Court June 29 required South Carolina to reconsider its refusal to pay a property owner for economic losses when a new state land-use regulation prevented him from building on environmentally fragile coastal land. But the ruling was narrowly based, leaving the state with power to continue to regulate land use.

The case, Lucas v. South Carolina Coastal Council, *was the last legal test of land-use rights in the Court's 1991-92 term. Two previous cases similarly were pressed by property owners and allied organizations in the hope that the conservative majority of justices would expand the Fifth Amendment's prohibition against taking private property without just compensation. In one case,* EFZ Properties v. Rodriguez, *the Court said it had mistakenly accepted the case and declined to rule. In the other case,* Yee v. Escondido, *the Court decided on more limited grounds than the plaintiff sought and ruled that a mobile home rent-control ordinance was valid.*

Lucas came to the high court on appeal from the South Carolina Supreme Court. It had overruled a lower court's award of $1,232,387 to David H. Lucas, who in 1986 paid $975,000 for two lots on the Isle of Palms, a barrier island near Charleston then being developed for residential use. Before Lucas put up any housing, the state legislature in 1988 passed the Beachfront Management Act establishing a Coastal Council and directing it to determine where development should be prohibited along the seashore. The council placed Lucas's property within the prohibited area. He thereupon sued for damages, saying that the state's action had made his property worthless.

The South Carolina Supreme Court held that the state had acted "to prevent serious public harm" to the coastline and was not compelled to pay compensation. Justice Antonin Scalia, writing for the high court, said that the decision not to compensate the landowner had to be justified on the basis of laws in force when Lucas acquired the property. It sent the case back to the state court to make that determination. At issue was whether Lucas's plan for housebuilding could be considered a "noxious" use of the property. A line of prior U.S. Supreme Court decisions had affirmed the right to take private property without compensation if it fit that legal description.

Chief Justice William H. Rehnquist and Justices Byron R. White, Sandra Day O'Connor, and Clarence Thomas endorsed Scalia's views. Justice Anthony M. Kennedy wrote a concurring opinion defending the court's decision to review the case—a decision that was strongly attacked in separate dissents by Justices Harry A. Blackmun and John Paul Stevens, and in a "statement" by Justice David H. Souter. All three noted that the law was amended in 1990 to permit relief for property owners who might be harmed by the law. Since Lucas had not sought that relief, they said, the court acted prematurely in agreeing to rule on the case.

Souter said such issues as what constitutes total deprivation of private property should be confronted directly but could not be in this case. He said the court should dismiss it "and await an opportunity to face the total deprivation question entirely."

The majority ruling held to precedents that a property owner must be deprived of the entire economic use of the land that is taken by the government to claim compensation for it. Chip Mellor, president of the Institute for Justice, a nonprofit law center that filed a brief on behalf of Lucas, said that the decision was "another evolutionary step toward greater protection for property owners." But environmental groups appeared relieved that the decision had placed heavy restrictions on the government's ability to regulate the use of land for public purposes. "From our point of view, the case is a partial victory," said John Echeverria, counsel for the National Audubon Society.

Following are excerpts from the majority opinion in the case of Lucas v. South Carolina Coastal Council, *issued June 29, 1992, as written by Justice Antonin Scalia:*

No. 91/453

David H. Lucas, Petitioner   }   On writ of certiorari to the Su-
v.   preme Court of South Carolina
South Carolina Coastal Council }

[March 5, 1992]

JUSTICE SCALIA delivered the opinion of the Court.

A

Prior to Justice Holmes' exposition in *Pennsylvania Coal Co.* v. *Mahon* (1922), it was generally thought that the Takings Clause reached only a "direct appropriation" of property or the functional equivalent of a "practical ouster of [the owner's] possession." Justice Holmes recognized in *Mahon,* however, that if the protection against physical appropriations of private property was to be meaningfully enforced, the government's power to redefine the range of interests included in the ownership of property was necessarily constrained by constitutional limits. If, instead, the uses of private property were subject to unbridled, uncompensated qualification under the police power, "the natural tendency of human nature [would be] to extend the qualification more and more until at last private property disappear[ed]." These considerations gave birth in that case to the oft-cited maxim that, "while property may be regulated to a certain extent, if regulation goes too far it will be recognized as a taking."

Nevertheless, our decision in *Mahon* offered little insight into when, and under what circumstances, a given regulation would be seen as going "too far" for purposes of the Fifth Amendment.... We have, however, described at least two discrete categories of regulatory action as compensable without case-specific inquiry into the public interest advanced in support of the restraint. The first encompasses regulations that compel the property owner to suffer a physical "invasion" of his property. In general (at least with regard to permanent invasions), no matter how minute the intrusion, and no matter how weighty the public purpose behind it, we have required compensation....

The second situation in which we have found categorical treatment appropriate is where regulation denies all economically beneficial or productive use of land. As we have said on numerous occasions, the Fifth Amendment is violated when land-use regulation "does not substantially advance legitimate state interests *or denies an owner economically viable use of his land.*"...

We think ... that there are good reasons for our frequently expressed belief that when the owner of real property has been called upon to sacrifice *all* economically beneficial uses in the name of the common good, that is, to leave his property economically idle, he has suffered a taking.

B

The trial court found Lucas's two beachfront lots to have been rendered valueless by respondent's enforcement of the coastal-zone construction ban. Under Lucas's theory of the case, which rested upon our "no economically viable use" statements, that finding entitled him to compensation.... The South Carolina Supreme Court, however, thought otherwise. In its view, the Beachfront Management Act was no ordinary enactment, but involved an exercise of South Carolina's "police powers" to mitigate the harm to the public interest that petitioner's use of his land might occasion....

It is correct that many of our prior opinions have suggested that "harmful or noxious uses" of property may be proscribed by government regulation without the requirement of compensation. For a number of reasons, however, we think the South Carolina Supreme Court was too quick to conclude that that principle decides the present case. The "harmful or noxious uses" principle was the Court's early attempt to describe in theoretical terms why government may, consistent with the Takings Clause, affect property values by regulation without incurring an obligation to compensate—a reality we nowadays acknowledge explicitly with respect to the full scope of the State's police power.... "Harmful or noxious use" analysis was, in other words, simply the progenitor of our more contemporary statements that "land-use regulation does not effect a taking if it 'substantially advance[s] legitimate state interests'...."

The transition from our early focus on control of "noxious" uses to our contemporary understanding of the broad realm within which government may regulate without compensation was an easy one, since the distinction between "harm-preventing" and "benefit-conferring" regulation is often in the eye of the beholder. It is quite possible, for example, to describe in *either* fashion the ecological, economic, and aesthetic concerns that inspired the South Carolina legislature in the present case. One could say that imposing a servitude on Lucas's land is necessary in order to prevent his use of it from "harming" South Carolina's ecological resources; or, instead, in order to achieve the "benefits" of an ecological preserve.... Whether Lucas's construction of single-family residences on his parcels should be described as bringing "harm" to South Carolina's adjacent ecological resources thus depends principally upon whether the describer believes that the State's use interest in nurturing those resources is so important that *any* competing adjacent use must yield.

When it is understood that "prevention of harmful use" was merely our early formulation of the police power justification necessary to sustain (without compensation) *any* regulatory diminution in value; and that the distinction between regulation that "prevents harmful use" and that which "confers benefits" is difficult, if not impossible, to discern on an objective, value-free basis; it becomes self-evident that noxious-use logic cannot serve as a touchstone to distinguish regulatory "takings"—which require compensation—from regulatory deprivations that do not require compensation. *A fortiori* the legislature's recitation of a noxious-use justification cannot be the basis for departing from our categorical rule that total regulatory takings must be compensated. If it were, departure would virtually always be allowed....

Where the State seeks to sustain regulation that deprives land of all economically beneficial use, we think it may resist compensation only if the logically antecedent inquiry into the nature of the owner's estate shows that the proscribed use interests were not part of his title to begin with.

This accords, we think, with our "takings" jurisprudence, which has traditionally been guided by the understandings of our citizens regarding the content of, and the State's power over, the "bundle of rights" that they acquire when they obtain title to property. It seems to us that the property owner necessarily expects the uses of his property to be restricted, from time to time, by various measures newly enacted by the State in legitimate exercise of its police powers; "[a]s long recognized, some values are enjoyed under an implied limitation and must yield to the police power." And in the case of personal property, by reason of the State's traditionally high degree of control over commercial dealings, he ought to be aware of the possibility that new regulation might even render his property economically worthless (at least if the property's only economically productive use is sale or manufacture for sale). In the case of land, however, we think the notion pressed by the Council that title is somehow held subject to the "implied limitation" that the State may subsequently eliminate all economically valuable use is inconsistent with the historical compact recorded in the Takings Clause that has become part of our constitutional culture.

Where "permanent physical occupation" of land is concerned, we have refused to allow the government to decree it anew (without compensation), no matter how weighty the asserted "public interests" involved.... We believe similar treatment must be accorded confiscatory regulations, i.e., regulations that prohibit all economically beneficial use of land: Any limitation so severe cannot be newly legislated or decreed (without compensation), but must inhere in the title itself, in the restrictions that background principles of the State's law of property and nuisance already place upon land ownership. A law or decree with such an effect must, in other words, do no more than duplicate the result that could have been achieved in the courts—by adjacent landowners (or other uniquely affected persons) under the State's law of private nuisance, or by the State under its complementary power to abate nuisances that affect the public generally, or otherwise.

On this analysis, the owner of a lake bed, for example, would not be entitled to compensation when he is denied the requisite permit to engage in a landfilling operation that would have the effect of flooding others' land. Nor the corporate owner of a nuclear generating plant, when it is directed to remove all improvements from its land upon discovery that the plant sits astride an earthquake fault. Such regulatory action may well have the effect of eliminating the land's only economically productive use, but it does not proscribe a productive use that was previously permissible under relevant property and nuisance principles. The use of these properties for what are now expressly prohibited purposes was *always* unlawful, and (subject to other constitutional limitations) it was open to the State at any point to make the implication of those background principles of nuisance and property law explicit.... When, however, a regulation that declares "off-limits" all economically productive or beneficial uses of land goes beyond what the relevant background principles would dictate, compensation must be paid to sustain it.

The "total taking" inquiry we require today will ordinarily entail (as the application of state nuisance law ordinarily entails) analysis of, among other things, the degree of harm to public lands and resources, or adjacent private property, posed by the claimant's proposed activities, the social value of the claimant's activities and their suitability to the locality in question, and the relative ease with which the alleged harm can be avoided through measures taken by the claimant and the government (or adjacent private landowners) alike. The fact that a particular use has long been engaged in by similarly situated owners ordinarily imports a lack of any common-law prohibition (though changed circumstances or new knowledge may make what was previously permissible no longer so). So also does the fact that other landowners, similarly situated, are permitted to continue the use denied to the claimant.

It seems unlikely that common-law principles would have prevented the erection of any habitable or productive improvements on petitioner's land; they rarely support prohibition of the "essential use" of land. The question, however, is one of state law to be dealt with on remand. We emphasize that to win its case South Carolina must do more than proffer the legislature's declaration that the uses Lucas desires are inconsistent with the public interest, or the conclusory assertion that they violate a common-law maxim. . . . As we have said, a "State, by *ipse dixit,* may not transform private property into public property without compensation. . . ." Instead, as it would be required to do if it sought to restrain Lucas in a common-law action for public nuisance, South Carolina must identify background principles of nuisance and property law that prohibit the uses he now intends in the circumstances in which the property is presently found. Only on this showing can the State fairly claim that, in proscribing all such beneficial uses, the Beachfront Management Act is taking nothing.

The judgment is reversed and the cause remanded for proceedings not inconsistent with this opinion.

So ordered.

July

NCES REPORT ON EDUCATION
July 7, 1992

In an annual report released July 7, the U.S. Department of Education's National Center for Education Statistics (NCES) offered its annual comprehensive review of education in the United States. The 421-page report, The Condition of Education 1992, *was based on sixty indicators, divided into six groups: (1) access, participation, and progress; (2) achievement, attainment, and curriculum; (3) economic and other outcomes of education; (4) size, growth, and output of educational institutions; (5) climate, classrooms, and diversity in educational institutions; and (6) human and financial resources of educational institutions. The study compared indicators in twenty nations between 1969 and 1991.*

The researchers found that 96 percent of U.S. students enrolled in grades ten-twelve in the fall of 1989 either were enrolled again in the fall of 1990 or had graduated during the year. The percentage broke down to 97 percent for whites, 95 percent for blacks, and 92 percent for Hispanics. The other 4 percent of the total dropped out of school during the year or failed to return in the fall. As of March 1991, 85 percent of adults ages twenty-five to twenty-nine had completed high school, up from 78 percent two decades earlier and higher than the percentages in Japan, Germany, France, the United Kingdom, Italy, and Canada.

Focusing on the transition from school to work, the report found that labor market opportunities for U.S. high school graduates, at any age, have consistently been better than for those who have not completed high school. For males between the ages of twenty-five and thirty-four, 85 percent of high school graduates were employed in 1991 versus 70 percent of those who had not finished high school. For females, the disparity was

*even greater—67 versus 42 percent. Fewer than half of recent high school
dropouts had a job in October 1990, whereas 68 percent of high school
graduates were employed. However, there was a significant racial disparity, with only 45 percent of black recent high school graduates holding
jobs, compared with 75 percent of white graduates.*

*The study also contained information on drug and alcohol use. The
percentage of high school students reporting having used alcohol has
been high since 1975; in 1991, 54 percent of high school seniors reported
having used alcohol in the previous thirty days. The percentage reporting
having used illegal drugs within thirty days was substantial (16 percent
in 1991), but the figure had declined sharply since 1979, when 39 percent
reported doing so. The percentage reporting having ever used cocaine was
8 percent in 1991, down from 17 percent in 1981. Whites were about twice
as likely as blacks to report having used cocaine.*

International Comparisons

*In comparisons with other nations, the report found that the United
States spent more on elementary and secondary education ($3,846 per
pupil) than any other nation, with Japan leading in expenditures for
higher education ($7,221 per student, compared with $4,643 in the United
States). American women had more education than their counterparts in
other nations; 82.1 percent of U.S. females ages twenty-five to sixty-four
had high school diplomas, and 20.5 percent held postsecondary degrees.
This compared with 72.2 percent and 13 percent in Canada and 68.5
percent and 5.2 percent in Japan, respectively.*

*In the area of comparative academic performance and achievement,
the report referred to studies conducted over a twenty-year period by two
groups—the National and the International Assessment of Educational
Progress (NAEP and IAEP)—on what students know and can do in
reading, writing, science, mathematics, and other subjects. The NAEP
found that average reading proficiency among nine- and thirteen-year-
olds was about the same in 1990 as in 1971; among seventeen-year-olds, it
was slightly higher in 1991. Average mathematics proficiency among
nine- and thirteen-year-olds showed slight gains, while that of seventeen-
year-olds remained about the same. The IAEP found that both the math
and science assessment for nine- and thirteen-year-olds was lower in the
United States than in Korea, Taiwan, and the former Soviet Union.*
(International Math-Science Test of Young Students, p. 85)

Shift Toward Vocational Courses

*In 1987, 68.5 percent of the courses taken by high school students were
academic rather than vocational, a drop from 73 percent in 1969. Between
1969 and 1987, however, black and Hispanic students increased the
percentage of academic courses they took, from 65.6 to 67.5 percent and
61.9 to 66.7 percent, respectively, while the percentage of academic
courses taken by whites decreased to 68.5 percent from 75.1 percent.*

Diane S. Ravitch, assistant secretary for educational research and improvement, said the report presented a "complicated picture." "We are the most schooled people in the world," she noted, but cautioned that "the question remains as to whether we are the most educated people in the world." Ravitch noted in particular what she called "a decline in white male achievement" as measured by the percentage of academic courses taken (down from 74.2 in 1969 to 67.3 percent in 1987).

However, some education experts questioned the validity of tying overall educational achievement to the number of academic courses students took. "It's not so much taking the course but what you get out of it," said Jacqueline Ancess of Columbia University's National Center for Restructuring Education, Schools and Teaching. "You may force more academic standards, but it does not mean that anyone is going to learn any more." Others noted that the range of courses offered in high schools had broadened since the 1970s, enabling non-college-bound students to take vocational courses that better prepared them to enter the workplace.

Following are excerpts from the "Overview" of the report on The Condition of Education 1992 *by the U.S. Department of Education's National Center for Education Statistics, released July 7, 1992:*

Introduction

During the 1980s, the country became increasingly aware of the range of critical issues facing education. These issues were nationwide in scope, and included inequality of opportunity for a good education for all segments of the population, general low academic performance, drug use and violence in the schools, unacceptably high dropout rates, high cost of a college education, and slowing productivity growth of workers. These concerns continue to have serious implications, not only for schools and colleges, but for the future of individual citizens, U.S. economic competitiveness, and ultimately the structure and cohesiveness of American society and culture.

The Condition of Education provides a means to report where progress is being made and where it is not, to draw attention to emerging issues, and to inform the ongoing policy debate.

The Structure of the Condition of Education

A quick tour of the volume may help the reader make the best use of it. The core of the volume consists of 60 indicators. Each indicator is presented on two pages. However, included in the back of the volume are supplemental tables providing additional details, and sometimes an explanatory note on a technical or data-related issue.

The 60 indicators are organized into 6 sections. The 6 sections are: 1) Access, Participation, and Progress; 2) Achievement, Attainment, and

Curriculum; 3) Economic and Other Outcomes of Education; 4) Size, Growth, and Output of Educational Institutions; 5) Climate, Classrooms, and Diversity in Educational Institutions; and 6) Human and Financial Resources of Educational Institutions. Instead of separating elementary and secondary education from postsecondary education indicators, this edition integrates elementary, secondary, and postsecondary education into each of the six sections. One can find information on an issue either by using the table of contents which lists the 60 indicators or by using the index which references not only the indicators but also the supplemental tables. When an updated indicator is not available in this volume, the index references the indicator number and edition of the *Condition of Education* which last published the indicator.

Each of the 6 sections of indicators is introduced with a short essay which interprets and summarizes some of the results that are found in the indicators as they relate to an important issue. In addition, the results from throughout the volume as they relate to particular issues that cut across the sections of the report are pulled together below.

At the bottom of each of the two indicator pages is the source of the data for the indicator. A description of the sources is provided starting on page 375. Sometimes more knowledge about the type of survey used to calculate the indicator can give the reader insights into interpreting the indicator. Some of the terms used in this report may not be familiar to all readers. Thus, a glossary is provided starting on page 401.

An indicator is not the same as a statistic because it is carefully designed to allow comparison, either over time, across countries, between groups, between sectors of education, and so forth. For this reason, the same data may be used to construct several indicators. For example, *Indicator 8* uses data on enrollment in college to calculate the percentage of high school graduates enrolled in college. This percentage is the rate at which a specific population group participates in higher education. This indicator is informative about opportunities available or pursued, and it can be compared over time and between age groups. *Indicator 47* also uses data on enrollment to calculate the percentage of students who are of certain ages. This indicator is informative about the changing age composition of students, and it can be compared over time and between sectors of higher education.

In the remainder of the overview, we gather some of the disparate pieces of evidence on selected issues: math and science education with an emphasis on differences between males and females, the education of minority groups including blacks and Hispanics, and the education of women. References to indicators and tables are given in parentheses. The table references are to the supplemental tables starting on page 157. Occasionally, references to indicators in a previous edition of *The Condition of Education* are given and can be recognized by the year added to the reference.

Math and Science

The President and the governors set a goal that U.S. students be first in the world in math and science achievement by the year 2000. By both highlighting the importance of math and science and setting a high standard for U.S. students to achieve, the hope is to stimulate efforts of schools and teachers to improve math and science education and to encourage more students to study math and science and take pride in doing well. In particular, policymakers hope to increase participation in math and science among women, blacks, Hispanics, and students from low income families. To excel in math and science, possibly more than in other subjects, requires early interest, participation, and achievement, so the indicators range from math and science achievement of 9-year-olds to the fields of conferred doctor's degrees. The results outlined below highlight differences between males and females.

Achievement of girls compared to boys

The National Assessment of Educational Progress (NAEP) has been reporting the performance of students in reading, writing, science, mathematics, and other subjects for the past 20 years. At age 9, there was no difference between boys and girls in average math proficiency from 1973 to 1990. In science, the same general conclusion holds but is weaker. By age 17, girls seem to have fallen a little behind. In 1990, the average mathematics proficiency of 17-year-old men and women were similar, but in earlier years 17-year-old men were a little more proficient than women *(Indicator 14)*. However, among college-bound men and women who take the SAT women on average score 45 points lower on the math component (Table 18-9). In science, the differences were larger, but there is some evidence it has been shrinking *(Indicator 15)*. In 1990, a greater percentage of eighth-grade girls than boys reported that they never used computers or wrote reports or projects in their math classes *(Indicator 42)*.

International comparisons show that patterns of differences between boys and girls in math and science achievement are similar in the United States and other countries. In most of the countries participating in the 1991 International Assessment of Educational Progress (IAEP), 9-year-old boys and girls performed equally well on the mathematics assessment, but, in several countries, girls did slightly less well than boys at age 13 *(Indicator 16)*. Korea was an exception: there, girls' scores were slightly lower than boys' at age 9 but appeared to catch up to them by age 13. In science, 9-year-old girls already were performing poorer than boys in most countries, except for the United States, and by age 13 were behind in even more countries, including the United States *(Indicator 17)*. Taiwan was an exception: there, girls scored lower than boys at age 9 but scored equally well at age 13.

However, girls in the United States seem to fall behind their counterparts in other countries between the ages of 9 and 13. In math, at age 9, girls were already behind their counterparts in Korea, the former Soviet Union, and Taiwan; by age 13 they had also fallen behind their counterparts in Canada. In science, at age 9, girls scored comparably to their counterparts in Korea, Taiwan, and Canada and higher than their counterparts in the Soviet Union; by 13 they had fallen behind their counterparts in Korea, the Soviet Union, and Taiwan *(Indicator 17)*.

Course-taking

In the high school class of 1987, women took slightly more of their credits in academic subjects than men, but slightly fewer credits in math (2.92 v. 3.03) and science (2.53 v. 2.66). Although women were more likely than men to take algebra I and algebra II and as likely to take geometry, they were less likely to take trigonometry, analysis, or calculus. Although women were more likely than men to take biology, they were less likely to take chemistry, and much less likely to take physics.

The differences between men and women in math and science course-taking that have begun to appear in high school become larger in college. In addition, a background in math and science in high school can be important for studying other subjects in college, such as computer science and engineering. In 1990, women were less likely than white men to major in the natural sciences as undergraduates. Asian women were an exception—they were substantially *more* likely than white men to major in the natural sciences *(Indicator 26)*. However, differences between men and women have been narrowing since the early 1970s. Women were much less likely than men to major in computer science or engineering as undergraduates. The situation has changed, however, because women in the 1980s were more likely to choose these fields than they had been in the 1970s (Table 2:10-2, 1991).

At the graduate level, men still are even more likely than women to major in the natural sciences than at the undergraduate level. In 1990, at the master's degree level men were 75 percent more likely than women and at the doctorate level were 53 percent more likely than women to major in the natural sciences. Men were five times more likely than women to major in computer science and engineering at the graduate level, about the same as they were at the bachelor's level *(Indicator 27)*.

Postsecondary degrees

Change in the number of higher education degrees conferred in math, science, and engineering fields is an indication of the supply of new talent. However, the growth or decline in the number of degrees conferred may not be indicative of an oversupply or shortage of scientists and engineers. A shortage would be indicated if graduates in these fields were finding an increasing number of job offers and if the salaries being offered were rising.

The number of bachelor's degrees conferred in the natural sciences has fallen since 1975. While the number of bachelor's degrees in all fields increased between 1975 and 1990, the number in the natural sciences fell.

Fewer college graduates are choosing to study physical and life sciences (Table 28-1). The number of degrees conferred in engineering rose then fell during this period—from 46,900 in 1975, to 96,100 in 1985, and down to 82,100 in 1990. On the other hand, the number of college students earning bachelor's degrees in computer and information sciences increased from 5,000 bachelor's degrees in 1975 to 27,400 in 1990 (Table 28-3). Although there have been shifts in the number of degrees in specific science and engineering fields, the total number of bachelor's degrees in these fields fell significantly between 1986 and 1990—from 214,400 to 177,400 degrees.

At the graduate level, the patterns were generally of stable or falling numbers during the last half of the 1970s and of stable or rising numbers during the 1980s. The total number of science and engineering master's degrees was stable during the last half of the 1970s and grew during the 1980s. The growth was almost entirely in computer science and engineering fields. At the doctorate level the pattern was similar for the total number of science and engineering, but the number of natural science degrees grew 17 percent in the 1980s. It should be noted that a substantial number of graduate level degrees in science and engineering fields are awarded to non-U.S. citizens most of whom do not have definite postgraduate plans in the United States *(Indicator 2:21 and Table 2:21-5, 1991)*.

Minorities

Getting a high quality education is one of the means available to blacks and Hispanics to fight their economic disadvantages. Black and Hispanic children are much more likely to live below the poverty line. In 1990, 44 percent of black children and 38 percent of Hispanic children compared to 15 percent of white children lived in families with income below the poverty line *(Indicator 39)*. The size of the differences and the change over time in differences in educational achievement between blacks and Hispanics on the one hand and whites on the other are outlined below.

Blacks

Starting disadvantaged children in education early is the philosophy behind Head Start, a popular program for disadvantaged preschool children. However, differences in access to education between black and white children start before kindergarten. In 1989, 30 percent of black 3- and 4-year olds were in a nursery school program compared to 40 percent of whites. While there has been an increase in the proportion of both white and black 3- and 4-year-olds attending nursery school, the proportion for whites has increased at a faster rate. On the other hand, in 1989, 78 percent of black 5-year-olds were in kindergarten, similar to the rate (81 percent) for whites *(Indicator 2)*.

Elementary School

Since the mid-1970s the percentage of 8- and 13-year-old children who were "behind," that is, one or more years below the modal (most common) grade for their age, has risen for all children *(Indicator 3)*. However, more black than white children fall behind between ages 8 and 13. In 1989, 29 percent of black 8-year-old boys were in 2nd grade or below, about the same as their white counterparts. However, 49 percent of black 13-year-olds were in 7th grade or below, compared to 32 percent of their white counterparts. Though girls in general are less likely than boys to be below the modal grade for their age, 8-year-old black girls were already behind their white counterparts.

As early as age 9, academic proficiency in reading, math, and science as measured by the National Assessment of Educational Progress (NAEP) is lower for black children than for their white counterparts. However, in recent years the gap was narrower than it was two decades ago. In 1990, black 9-year-olds were 35 scale points behind whites in reading, compared to 44 scale points behind in 1970 *(Indicator 12);* 27 points behind whites in math, compared to 35 points behind in 1973 *(Indicator 14);* and 42 points behind in science, compared to 57 points behind in 1970 *(Indicator 15)*. The patterns for 13-year-olds were similar. As a basis for comparison, consider that, in 1990, the increase per year of age in average proficiency between age 9 and 13 in reading, math, and science was 10, 12, and 7 scale points, respectively.

Secondary School

Black teenagers have substantially increased their efforts in high school. Despite more black 13-year-olds being one or more years below modal grade, fewer black teenagers are dropping out of high school before graduating. Between 1989 and 1990, 5 percent of black high school students 15 or older in grades 10-12 dropped out of school compared to 3.3 percent of whites. Although still considered too high by many educators, the rate among blacks (5 percent) was substantially lower than it was 2 decades earlier (9.9 percent, *Indicator 5*). In 1990, 78 percent of black 19-to 20-year-olds had graduated from high school compared to 68 percent in 1973 *(Indicator 20)*. The completion rate for whites was higher (87 percent) but largely unchanged over the same period, so the black-white differential narrowed considerably.

Near the end of high school, NAEP again gives evidence that there is a large but narrowing gap in achievement between blacks and whites. Blacks have improved relative to whites in reading, mathematics, and science. For example, in 1971 average reading proficiency among 17-year-old blacks was well below (52 scale points) 17-year-old whites and also below (22 points) 13-year-old whites; in 1990, the proficiency of 17-year-old blacks was closer (22 points) to that of 17-year-old whites, and slightly higher than 13-year-old whites. In 1970, average mathematics proficiency among 17-year-old blacks was 40 scale points behind their white counterparts and about the same as 13-year-old whites; in 1990, it was 21 points behind 17-year-old whites, and 13 points above 13-year-old whites.

The Scholastic Aptitude Test (SAT) provides corroborating evidence of the gains made by blacks. In 1991, average black scores were 90 points lower than whites' on the verbal component of the SAT and 104 points lower on the math component; in 1976 they had been 119 and 139 points lower, respectively (Tables 18-8 and 18-9). The conclusion is the same—blacks are behind their white counterparts but catching up.

Higher Education

Gains made by blacks in higher education are not as dramatic as those in elementary and secondary education. The percentage of blacks enrolling in college in the fall following high school graduation was near 50 percent in the late 1980s, about the same as it was in 1978 (an earlier high point for this indicator). The percentage of blacks going immediately on to college has increased since 1983, as has the rate for whites, so the gap remains at about 14 percentage points (Indicator 7). Some of the difference may be made up by delayed entry, as blacks are more likely than whites to enroll in college after a delay (Indicator 2:2, 1991). Overall, about 30 percent of black high school graduates 16-24 years old were enrolled in college as undergraduates during the late 1980s, about the same as were during the last half of the 1970s. In contrast, in 1990, about 38 percent of their white counterparts were enrolled in college, up from 30 percent a decade earlier (Indicator 9).

College attainment among blacks is far lower than it is for whites. In 1991, 41 percent of black high school graduates 25 to 29 years old had completed 1 or more years of college, compared to 55 percent of their white counterparts. In addition, only 14 percent of black high school graduates had completed 4 or more years of college compared to 30 percent of their white counterparts. During the 1970s, the percentage of both white and black high school graduates completing 1 or more or 4 or more years of college grew; during the 1980s, however, there was little change in these college attainment rates (Indicator 22).

Using information on the number of bachelor's degrees awarded, the pattern of change in degrees earned between 1977 and 1990 was different for black men and women. The number earned by men declined each year except for the most recent one, whereas the number earned by women fluctuated up and down. In contrast, the number of bachelor's degrees earned by white women increased each year and, after 1979, the number earned by white men remained stable despite a decline in the number of whites graduating from high school early in the decade (Indicator 24).

The fields of study of black degree recipients often differ from those of whites at both the undergraduate and graduate levels, but these differences have narrowed over time. In 1990, at the bachelor's degree level, black men were less likely than white men to major in the natural sciences but more likely to major in technical/professional fields (other than education and business). At the doctorate level, black men were much less likely than white men to major in the natural sciences or in the computer sciences and engineering, but much more likely to major in education.

Among women, blacks were less likely than whites to major in education at the bachelor's level, but more likely to do so at the doctor's level *(Indicator 26).*

Although blacks generally earn less than whites, among both blacks and whites those with more education have better employment and earnings outcomes. In 1990, only 31 percent of blacks who dropped out of high school between 1989 and 1990 were employed. Among blacks who completed high school but did not enroll in college, 45 percent were employed—higher but still very low *(Indicator 29).* Earnings among 25- to 34-year-old blacks, particularly black women, show that the incentive to pursue additional education is sizeable. In 1990, black males with 9-11 years of schooling earned 28 percent less than those with 12 years of schooling; those with 4 or more years of college earned 66 percent more. Black females with 9-11 years of schooling earned 56 percent less than those with 12 years of schooling; those with 4 or more years of college earned 109 percent more. Between 1974 and 1990, for blacks the earnings advantage of completing college increased *(Indicator 31).*

Hispanics

Hispanics, as a minority group in the United States, have had a very different history than blacks. There is a great deal of diversity among Hispanics. The three largest Hispanic subgroups are Mexican-Americans, Puerto Ricans, and Cubans. Recent immigrants from Central and South America are a fourth group. They live in different parts of the United States, their economic circumstances vary, and their periods of immigration are different. Still, all share the Spanish language in their cultural heritage. Of course, a much higher proportion of Hispanics than non-Hispanics are foreign born. As a result, Hispanic children are more likely not to hear or speak English at home and are more likely to have limited English proficiency. As mentioned earlier, in 1990, 38 percent of Hispanic children lived in families with income below the poverty line, compared to 15 percent of white children *(Indicator 39).* Although the source of their disadvantages are different, the effects on their performance in the education system are not unlike blacks. Highlighted below are noteworthy differences in the education of Hispanics on the one hand, from blacks and whites on the other.

Hispanics, like Asians, are a growing minority group in the United States; the percentage of students who are Hispanic has increased substantially. In 1989, 20 percent of students in public schools in the central cities of metropolitan areas were Hispanic, up from 11 percent in 1972. In public schools in other parts of metropolitan areas 10 percent of the student body were Hispanic; in private schools, 7 percent were Hispanic *(Indicator 37).*

Most racial/ethnic groups reported a similar percentage of occurrence of *most* types of criminal activity in their school in 1989. One exception was that Hispanics were much more likely to report the presence of street gangs in their schools—32 percent, compared to 12 percent of whites and 20 percent of blacks *(Indicator 43)*.

Preprimary

Hispanic 3- and 4-year-olds were less likely than both black and white children to attend nursery school—in 1989, that rate was 20 percent compared to 30 percent of black children and 40 percent of white children. The gap between Hispanics and whites has grown over time—the proportion of white children attending nursery school increased from 22 percent in 1974 to 40 percent in 1990, while for Hispanics it increased from 16 percent in 1974 to only 20 percent in 1990. On the other hand, in 1990, 78 percent of Hispanic 5-year-olds attended kindergarten, comparable to the rate (81 percent) for white 5-year-olds *(Indicator 2)*.

Elementary School

Like black children, Hispanic 13-year-old students generally were more likely to be below the modal grade for their age than their white counterparts. Also, the gap between Hispanics and whites in the proportion of 13-year-old boys below grade level was greater in recent years than it had been in the mid-1970s. The disparity between Hispanic and white 13-year-old girls is large but has not increased over the 1974-1989 period *(Indicator 3)*.

Secondary School

The gains blacks have made in their high school education have not been shared by Hispanics. The number of credits in academic subjects has increased for Hispanics. Hispanics in the high school class of 1987 took 15 credits in academic subjects, up from 13 in 1969 (Table 25-1). On the other hand, improvements in average proficiency in reading, math, and science were not as prevalent among Hispanics as they were among blacks *(Indicators 12, 14, and 15)*. The school persistence rate for Hispanics has been near 90 percent for most of the past two decades, whereas for blacks it has gradually increased *(Indicator 5)*. Fewer Hispanics have completed high school. In 1991, 56 percent of Hispanic 25- to 29-years-old had completed high school, compared to 81 percent of blacks and 90 percent of whites. The high school completion rate of Hispanics has remained fairly stable (fluctuating between 55 and 63 percent) since the mid-1970s while the rate for blacks has increased (from 69 percent in 1975 to 81 percent in 1991, *Indicator 22*).

Higher Education

Hispanics who go on to college are more likely to enroll in a 2-year college than blacks. In the fall of 1990, 55 percent of Hispanic college students were enrolled in 2-year colleges compared to 37 percent of white students and 42 percent of black students (supplemental table 38-1).

While the percentage of Hispanic high school graduates 25 to 29 years old who have completed 4 or more years of college has not increased over the past 2 decades, the percentage with some college has increased, from 25 percent in 1971 to 43 percent in 1978; since then, it's been fairly stable *(Indicator 22)*.

Data of another type are more encouraging. The number of bachelor's degrees conferred to Hispanics increased substantially during the 1980s, particularly for women. In 1990, 62 percent more bachelor's degrees were awarded to Hispanic women than in 1981; 38 percent more were awarded to Hispanic men. These increases appear to be larger than the increase in the number of Hispanics graduating from high school. The number of advanced degrees awarded to Hispanics has also increased, but not as much. In 1990, 21 and 43 percent more advanced degrees were awarded to Hispanic men and women, respectively, than in 1981 *(Indicator 24)*.

Fields of Study

The fields Hispanics chose to study for their bachelor's degrees are largely similar to those whites selected. Hispanics are somewhat more likely than whites to major in the humanities and social/behavioral sciences and somewhat less likely to major in education *(Indicator 26)*.

Labor Market Outcomes

While the employment rate is low both for Hispanics who have graduated from high school but not enrolled in college and for Hispanics who have left high school without graduating (dropouts), there is some evidence that Hispanic dropouts find it somewhat easier than black dropouts to get work *(Indicator 29)*.

Females

Over the last two decades women have made important advances in their education that puts them on a par with men in many areas. Below are summarized some of the differences between boys and girls, as well as men and women on education indicators and where there has been change over time.

Generally girls start school ahead of boys and are less likely to be behind. For example, 22 percent of 8-year-old girls versus 28 percent of boys were in grade 2 or below in October 1989. By age 13 the disparity was larger—26 percent of girls versus 36 percent of boys were in grade 7 or below *(Indicator 3)*. In the high school class of 1987, girls took more credits in academic subjects than boys (16.0 v. 15.3), whereas in the class of 1969 boys and girls took about the same number (14.9, *Indicator 25*). Girls exhibit higher average proficiency in reading and writing than boys at ages 9, 13, and 17 *(Indicators 12 and 13)*. However, among college-bound men and women who take the SAT exam, women have scores about 10 points lower than men on the verbal component (Table 18-8). Girls were more likely than boys to finish high school on time, and among dropouts, girls were as likely as boys to return and finish later *(Indicator 6)*.

From 1976 to 1987, women and men were equally likely to enroll in college in October following graduation, but in the late 1980s women were slightly *more* likely than men to do so *(Indicator 7)*. Women under the age of 25 who have completed high school are somewhat less likely than men to be enrolled in a 4-year college *(Indicator 8)*. However, the number of bachelor's degrees conferred on women has increased more rapidly than it has for men *(Indicator 24)*.

The college attainment of women has caught up to that of men. In the early 1970s, among high school graduates, about 40 percent of women compared to 50 percent of men 25 to 29 years old had completed 1 or more years of college; in the late 1980s, about 52 percent of both women and men had done so (Table 22-2). In the early 1970s, among high school graduates about 20 percent of women compared to 27 percent of men 25 to 29 years old had completed 4 or more years of college; in the late 1980s, about 27 percent of both women and men had done so (Table 22-3).

Data on the number of degrees conferred demonstrate more clearly the educational progress of women. In 1990, more associate's, bachelor's, and master's degrees were awarded to white women than to their male counterparts, whereas in 1977 the reverse was true. Though fewer doctor's degrees were awarded to white women than to white men, the gap has closed considerably. In 1977, almost 3 times as many doctorate degrees were awarded to white men as to white women; in 1990 men were awarded only 41 percent more. Among Hispanics the patterns were similar. Among blacks, women were awarded more of each degree than men in both 1977 and 1990 with the exception of doctor's degrees in 1977. Among Asians the pattern is reversed—women earned fewer of each degree than men in both 1977 and 1990 with the exception of associate's degrees (Table 24-1).

The fields that women and men study in college remain very different despite narrowing of differences at the undergraduate level and in some fields at the graduate level. At the bachelor's level, women were more than 3 times as likely as men to major in education in 1989, but that was down from what it had been in 1971 *(Indicator 2:10, 1991)*. A notable exception is Asian women who were *less* likely than white men but more likely than Asian men to major in education *(Indicator 26)*. At the master's degree level, however, women were 2.8 times as likely as men to major in education, which was up substantially from 1971 *(Indicator 27)*. On the other hand, women are increasingly likely to major in business at the master's level—whereas, women were less than one-tenth as likely as men to major in business in 1971, they were half as likely by 1990.

Despite the lagging achievement of girls in the United States in math and science compared to their counterparts in other countries cited above, women in the United States generally have higher educational attainment than their counterparts in other countries. For example, in 1987 among U.S. women 25-64 years old, 82 percent had completed high school—far more than their counterparts in countries such as Japan, West Germany, the United Kingdom, France, and Canada. Also, 21 percent had completed

4 or more years of college, again far more than their counterparts in other countries (Table 23-1).

In a few countries the educational attainment of younger generations of women has improved rapidly. This is evident in the fact that the attainment of women 25-34 years old was substantially higher than for all women. The result is that the gap is closing between the educational attainment of women in these countries and in the United States. For example, in Japan 92 percent of women 25-34 years old had finished *secondary* education, and in West Germany 88 percent had done so, compared to 87 percent in the United States. Nevertheless, women 25-34 years old in the United States were still much more likely to complete *higher* education than their counterparts in Japan and West Germany *(Indicator 23)*. In addition, the percentage of women graduating in the science fields (including health sciences) was much higher in the U.S. than in Japan or West Germany *(Indicator 2:8, 1991)*.

The labor force participation rates of women rose steadily throughout the 1970s and 1980s for those with a high school education or better. By 1991, for women 25-34 years old who had completed college, the percentage employed was about 9 percentage points lower than for men—83 versus 92 percent, in contrast to a 36 point gap in 1971 *(Indicator 30)*. Women college graduates shared in the growth in earnings for all college graduates in the 1980s. Although women college graduates earn less on average than men college graduates, the earnings advantage women who are college graduates enjoy over their counterparts with only a high school education is greater than that enjoyed by men *(Indicator 31)*. . . .

MUNICH ECONOMIC SUMMIT
July 6-8, 1992

Playing a subdued role compared with his participation in other international conferences, President George Bush joined six other leaders of the world's largest industrialized countries July 6-8 for the annual Group of Seven summit meeting. The summit, held in Munich, Germany, made scant progress toward solving problems related to the world economy, international trade, and war in the former Yugoslavia. Indeed, its most vital work may have come after its official end, when President Boris Yeltsin of Russia met with the Group of Seven, seeking aid and support.

The meeting of the Group of Seven (or G-7) was the first since the end of the Cold War and the break-up of the former Soviet Union. It came at a time of global economic distress and of an inward-turning tendency in large parts of the world. Moreover, the seven leaders seemed themselves to be particularly vulnerable to political changes taking place in their own countries.

The leaders decried the warfare in the former Yugoslavia but stopped well short of threatening military action, which might bring peace. They did warn warring factions against interfering with the humanitarian efforts of the United Nations.

Although the Group of Seven failed to achieve a breakthrough on a revision of world trade rules, the leaders agreed that a new accord would boost the global economy. Lamenting the failure, Britain's prime minister, John Major, said a breakthrough "would have been a huge bonus" for the summit.

Yeltsin's appearance in Munich recalled for many observers the previous year, when then Soviet President Mikhail S. Gorbachev joined *the Group of Seven in London at the end of its meeting. Gorbachev went home empty-handed, but Yeltsin received a promise of $1 billion in immediate assistance. Describing himself as "very satisfied," Yeltsin said, "I didn't expect more, and I didn't want less." (Yeltsin's Summit with Bush, Address to Congress, p. 519; London Economic Summit, Historic Documents of 1991, p. 451)*

Changing U.S. Role

The first of the annual summit meetings of the Group of Seven was held in 1975 at Rambouillet, France. Nearly twenty years later, and in light of the profound changes that had taken place in the world, a number of observers questioned whether the G-7 structure continued to fulfill its original purpose. Indeed, before leaving Washington for the meeting, Treasury Secretary Nicholas Brady told reporters, "Some of the early usefulness of these conferences has begun to wane."

Besides Bush and Major, participants in the Munich meeting included Chancellor Helmut Kohl of Germany, President Francois Mitterrand of France, Prime Minister Giulio Andreotti of Italy; Prime Minister Brian Mulroney of Canada; and Prime Minister Kiichi Miyazawa of Japan. The leaders were joined by officials of the European Community.

A reporter at a news conference July 8, 1992, asked Bush whether he thought that "being a superpower isn't necessarily what it used to be cracked up to be." Bush replied that he thought the United States was the "sole remaining superpower." He added, "And that's when you consider the economic and military and everything else. And I think others see it that way. But that doesn't mean that the way you lead is to dictate."

On the other hand, writing from Munich in the July 9, 1992, Washington Post, Don Oberdofer said the U.S. role had been "questioned unofficially by a spectrum of foreign diplomats." Oberdorfer quoted an unnamed European official who said, "This is the first major summit in which the Americans are just another player."

World Economy and World Trade

Poorly performing economies and political unease in their own countries provided an unwanted backdrop at the Munich summit meeting. Unemployment stood at 7.8 percent in the United States, yet France and Britain had jobless rates of nearly 10 percent, and Italy's rate was more than 11 percent. In the European Community generally, 20 percent of adults under twenty-five-years of age were unemployed.

Huge, unanticipated costs of reunification had driven up Germany's deficit. And in both Germany and the United States budget deficits were preventing political leaders from applying the fiscal measures that might reinvigorate their economies.

A few days before the Munich economic summit, Brady told reporters that if he could "wave a magic wand over one problem" it would be the world trade talks." Brady referred to the effort by 108 nations to revitalize the standing rules of world trade known as the General Agreement on Tariffs and Trade (GATT). Many experts believed a successful outcome to the negotiations would add at least a half of a percentage point to the annual rate of world growth, which currently was less than 1.8 percent. The main sticking point in the talks, which had resisted any solution for several years, was a dispute between the United States and the European Community over subsidies paid to EC farmers growing soybean and other oil seeds. The United States demanded cuts in the EC subsidies so that its farmers could compete in European markets. Despite a few early signs of hope at the Munich meeting, it soon became clear that the Europeans would not move on the issue.

At his July 8, 1992, news conference, President Bush said he was "disappointed" there had been no breakthrough in the trade issue. Bush added that "we're going to keep pushing for it without regard to the U.S. election."

Besides the promise of $1 billion in immediate aid, the Group of Seven also agreed to reschedule repayment of Russia's share of the former Soviet Union's former debt of about $70 billion.

Speaking of the $1 billion in assistance, Chancellor Kohl told reporters at Munich, "This is a harbinger of things to come." He alluded to a $24-billion assistance package for Russia, assembled in the spring of 1992 in a multinational initiative. (Nixon's Speech on Russian Aid, p. 255; Yeltsin's Summit with Bush, Address to Congress, p. 519)

Yeltsin set out a plan in Munich under which Russia would exchange debt relief for Russian land, buildings, raw materials, and oil and gas exploration rights. Observers believed that Western investors would respond favorably to the opportunities.

Following is the declaration issued jointly by the Group of Seven at the Munich Economic Summit on July 7, 1992:

1. We, the Heads of State and Government of seven major industrial nations and the President of the Commission of the European Community, have met in Munich for our eighteenth annual Summit.
2. The international community is at the threshold of a new era, freed from the burden of the East-West conflict. Rarely have conditions been so favorable for shaping a permanent peace, guaranteeing respect for human rights, carrying through the principles of democracy, ensuring free markets, overcoming poverty and safeguarding the environment.
3. We are resolved, by taking action in a spirit of partnership, to seize the unique opportunities now available. While fundamental change entails risk, we place our trust in the creativity, effort and dedication

of people as the true sources of economic and social progress. The global dimension of the challenges and the mutual dependencies call for world-wide cooperation. The close coordination of our policies as part of this cooperation is now more important than ever.

World Economy

4. Strong world economic growth is the prerequisite for solving a variety of challenges we face in the post-Cold War world. Increasingly, there are signs of global economic recovery. But we will not take it for granted and will act together to assure the recovery gathers strength and growth picks up.

5. Too many people are out of work. The potential strength of people, factories and resources is not being fully employed. We are particularly concerned about the hardship unemployment creates.

6. Each of us faces somewhat different economic situations. But we all would gain greatly from stronger, sustainable non-inflationary growth.

7. Higher growth will help other countries, too. Growth generates trade. More trade will give a boost to developing nations and to the new democracies seeking to transform command economies into productive participants within the global marketplace. Their economic success is in our common interest.

8. A successful Uruguay Round will be a significant contribution to the future of the world economy. An early conclusion of the negotiations will reinforce our economies, promote the process of reform in Eastern Europe and give new opportunities for the well-being of other nations, including in particular the developing countries.

We regret the slow pace of the negotiations since we met in London last year. But there has been progress in recent months. Therefore we are convinced that a balanced agreement is within reach.

We welcome the reform of the European Community's Common Agricultural Policy which has just been adopted and which should facilitate the settlement of outstanding issues.

Progress has been made on the issue of internal support in a way which is consistent with the reform of the Common Agricultural Policy, on dealing with the volume of subsidized exports and on avoiding future disputes. These topics require further work. In addition, parties still have concerns in the areas of market access and trade in cereal substitutes that the seek to address.

We reaffirm that the negotiations should lead to a globally balanced result. An accord must create more open markets for goods and services and will require comparable efforts from all negotiating partners.

On this basis we expect that an agreement can be reached before the end of 1992.

9. We are committed, through coordinated and individual actions, to build confidence for investors, savers, and consumers: confidence

that hard work will lead to a better quality of life; confidence that investments will be profitable; confidence that savings will be rewarded and that price stability will not be put at risk.

10. We pledge to adopt policies aimed at creating jobs and growth. We will seek to take the appropriate steps, recognizing our individual circumstances, to establish sound macro economic policies to spur stronger sustainable growth. With this in mind we have agreed on the following guidelines:

- to continue to pursue sound monetary and financial policies to support he upturn without rekindling inflation;
- to create the scope for lower interest rates through the reduction of excessive public deficits and the promotion of savings;
- to curb excessive public deficits above all by limiting public spending. Taxpayers' money should be used more economically and more effectively.
- to integrate more closely our environmental and growth objectives, by encouraging market incentives and technological innovation to promote environmentally sound consumption and production.

As the risk of inflation recedes as a result of our policies, it will be increasingly possible for interest rates to come down. This will help promote new investment and therefore stronger growth and more jobs.

11. But good macro economic policies are not enough. All our economies are burdened by structural rigidities that constrain our potential growth rates. We need to encourage competition. We need to create a more hospitable environment for private initiative. We need to cut back excess regulation, which suppresses innovation, enterprise and creativity. We will strengthen employment opportunities through better training, education, and enhanced mobility. We will strengthen the basis for long-term growth through improvements in infrastructure and greater attention to research and development. We are urging these kinds of reforms for new democracies in the transition to market economies. We cannot demand less of ourselves.

12. The coordination of economic and financial policies is a central element in our common strategy for sustained, non- inflationary growth. We request our Finance Ministers to strengthen their cooperation on the basis of our agreed guidelines and to intensify their work to reduce obstacles to growth and therefore foster employment. We ask them to report to our meeting in Japan in 1993.

United Nations Conference on Environment and Development (UNCED)

13. The Earth Summit has been a landmark in heightening the consciousness of the global environmental challenges, and in giving new impetus to the process of creating a world-wide partnership on

development and the environment. Rapid and concrete action is required to follow through on our commitments on climate change, to protect forests and oceans, to preserve marine resources, and to maintain biodiversity. We there fore urge all countries, developed and developing, to direct their policies and resources towards sustainable development which safeguards the interests of both present and future generations.

14. To carry forward the momentum of the Rio Conference, We urge other countries to join us:

- in seeking to ratify the Climate Change Convention by the end of 1993,
- in drawing up and publishing national action plans, as foreseen at UNCED, by the end of 1993,
- in working to protect species and the habitats on which they depend,
- in giving additional financial and technical support to developing countries for substantial development through official development assistance (ODA), in particular by replenishment of IDA, and for actions of global benefit through the Global Environment Facility (GEF) with a view to its being established as a permanent funding mechanism,
- in establishing at the 1992 UN General Assembly the Sustainable Development Commission which will have a vital role to play in monitoring the implementation of Agenda 21,
- in establishing an international review process for the forest principles, in an early dialogue, on the basis of the implementation of these principles, on possible appropriate internationally agreed arrangements, and in increased international assistance,
- in further improving monitoring of the global environment, including through better utilization of data from satellite and other earth observation programs,
- in the promotion of the development and diffusion of energy and environment technologies, including proposals for innovative technology programs,
- by ensuring the international conference on straddling fish stocks and highly migratory fish stocks in the oceans is convened as soon as possible.

Developing Countries

15. We welcome the economic and political progress which many developing countries have made, particularly in East and South-East Asia, but also in Latin America and in some parts of Africa. However, many countries throughout the world are still struggling against poverty. Sub-Sahara Africa, above all, gives cause for concern.

16. We are committed to a dialogue and partnership founded on shared responsibility and a growing consensus on fundamental political and economic principles. Global challenges such as population growth and the environment can only be met through cooperative efforts by all countries. Reforming the economic and social sector of the UN system will be an important step to this end.

17. We welcome the growing acceptance of the principles of good governance. Economic and social progress can only be assured if countries mobilize their own potential, all segments of the population are involved and human rights are respected. Regional cooperation among developing countries enhances development and can contribute to stability, peaceful relations and reduced arms spending.

18. The industrial countries bear a special responsibility for a sound global economy. We shall pay regard to the effects of our policies on the developing countries. We will continue our best efforts to increase the quantity and quality of official development assistance in accordance with our commitments. We shall direct official development assistance more towards the poorest countries. Poverty, population policy, education, health, the role of women and the well-being of children merit special attention. We shall support in particular those countries that undertake credible efforts to help themselves. The more prosperous developing countries are invited to contribute to international assistance.

19. We underline the importance for developing countries of trade, foreign direct investment, and an active private sector. Poor developing countries should be offered technical assistance to establish a more diversified export base especially in manufactured goods.

20. Negotiations on a substantial replenishment of IDA funds should be concluded before the end of 1992. The IMF should continue to provide concessional financing to support the reform programs for the poorest countries. We call for an early decision by the IMF on the extension for one year of the Enhanced Structural Adjustment Facility and for the full examination of options for the subsequent period, including a renewal of the facility.

21. We are deeply concerned about the unprecedented drought in southern Africa. Two thirds of the Drought Appeal target has been met. But much remains to be done. We call on all countries to assist.

22. We welcome the progress achieved by many developing countries in overcoming the debt problems and regaining their creditworthiness. Initiatives of previous Summits have contributed to this. Nevertheless, many developing countries are still in a difficult situation.

23. We confirm the validity of the international debt strategy. We welcome the enhanced debt relief extended to the poorest countries by the Paris Club. We note that the Paris Club has agreed to consider the stock of debt approach, under certain conditions, after

a period of three or four years, for the poorest countries that are prepared to adjust, and we encourage it to recognize the special situation of some highly indebted lower-middle-income countries on a case by case basis. We attach great importance to the enhanced use of voluntary debt conversions, including debt conversions for environmental protection.

Central and Eastern Europe

24. We welcome the progress of the democracies in central and eastern Europe including the Baltic states (CEECs) toward political and economic reform and integration into the world economy. The reform must be pursued vigorously. Great efforts and even sacrifices are still required from their people. They have our continuing support.

25. We welcome the substantial multilateral and bilateral assistance in support of reform in the CEECs. Financing provided by the EBRD is playing a useful role. Since 1989, total assistance and commitments, in the form of grants, loans and credit guarantees by the Group of 24 and the international financial institutions, amounts up to $52 billion. We call upon the Group of 24 to continue its coordination activity and to adapt it to the requirements of each reforming country. We reaffirm our readiness to make fair contributions.

26. We support the idea of working with Poland to reallocate, on the basis of existing arrangements, funds from the currency stabilization fund, upon agreement on an IMF program, towards new uses in support of Poland's market reform effort, in particular by strengthening the competitiveness of Poland's business enterprises.

27. The industrial countries have granted substantial trade concessions to the CEECs in order to ensure that their reform efforts will succeed. But all countries should open their markets further. The agreements of the EC and EFTA countries aiming at the establishment of free trade ares with these countries are a significant contribution. We shall continue to offer the CEECs technical assistance in enhancing their export capacity.

28. We urge all CEECs to develop their economic relations with each other, with the new independent states of the former Soviet Union as well as more widely on a market-oriented basis and consistent with GATT principles. As a step in this direction we welcome the special cooperation among the CSFR, Poland and Hungary, and hope that free trade among them will soon be possible.

29. Investment from abroad should be welcomed. It is important for the development of the full economic potential of the CEECs. We urge the CEECs to focus their policies on the creation of attractive and reliable investment conditions for private capital. We are providing our bilateral credit insurance and guarantee instruments to promote

foreign investment when these conditions, including servicing of debt, are met. We call upon enterprises in the industrial countries to avail themselves of investment opportunities in the CEECs.

New Independent States of the Former Soviet Union

30. The far-reaching changes in the former Soviet Union offer an historic opportunity to make the world a better place: more secure, more democratic and more prosperous. Under President Yeltsin's leadership the Russian government has embarked on a difficult reform process. We look forward to our meeting with him to discuss our cooperation in support of these reforms. We are prepared to work with the leaders of all new states pursuing reforms. The success is in the interest of the international community.

31. We are aware that the transition will involve painful adjustments. We offer the new states our help for their self-help. Our cooperation will be comprehensive and will be tailored to their reform progress and internationally responsible behavior, including further reductions in military spending and fulfillment of obligations already undertaken.

32. We encourage the new states to adopt sound economic policies, above all by brining down budget deficits and inflation. Working with the IMF can bring experience to this task and lend credibility to the efforts being made. Macroeconomic stabilization should not be delayed. It will only succeed if at the same time the building blocks of a market economy are also put into place, through privatization, land reform, measures to promote investment and competition and appropriate social safeguards for the population.

33. Creditworthiness and the establishment of a dependable legal framework are essential if private investors are to be attracted. The creditworthiness of the new states will in particular be assessed by the way in which they discharge their financial obligations.

34. Private capital and entrepreneurial commitment must play a decisive and increasing part in economic reconstructions. We urge the new states to develop an efficient private business sector, in particular the body of small and medium-sized private companies which is indispensable for a market economy.

35. Rapid progress is particularly urgent and attainable in two sectors: agriculture and energy. These sectors are of decisive importance in improving the supply situation and increasing foreign exchange revenue. Trade and industry in our countries are prepared to cooperate. Valuable time has already been lost because barriers to investment remain in place. For energy, we note the importance of the European Energy Charter for encouraging production and ensuring the security of supply. We urge rapid conclusion of the preparatory work.

36. All summit participants have shown solidarity in a critical situation by providing extensive food aid, credits and medical assistance. they also have committed technical assistance. A broad inflow of know-how and experience to the new states is needed to help them realize their own potential. Both private and public sectors can contribute to this. What is needed most of all is concrete advice on the spot and practical assistance. The emphasis should be on projects selected for their value as a model or their strategic importance for the reform process. Partnerships and management assistance at corporate level can be particularly effective.

37. We stress the need for the further opening of international markets to products from the new states. Most-favored-nation treatment should be applied to trade with the new states and consideration given to further preferential access. The new states should not impede reconstruction by setting up barriers to trade between themselves. It is in their own interest to cooperate on economic and monetary policy.

38. We want to help the new states to preserve their highly-developed scientific and technological skills and to make use of them in building up their economies. We call upon industry and science in the industrial countries to promote cooperation and exchange with the new states. By establishing International Science and Technology Centers we are helping to redirect the expertise of scientists and engineers who have sensitive knowledge in the manufacture of weapons of mass destruction towards peaceful purposes. We will continue our efforts to enable highly-qualified civil scientists to remain in the new states and to promote research cooperation with western industrial countries.

39. We welcome the membership of the new states in the international financial institutions. This will allow them to work out economic reform programs in collaboration with these institutions and on this basis to make use of their substantial financial resources. Disbursements of these funds should be linked to progress in implementing reforms.

40. We support the phased strategy of cooperation between the Russian government and the IMF. This will allow the IMF to disburse a first credit tranche in support of the most urgent stabilization measures within the next few weeks while continuing to negotiate a comprehensive reform program with Russia. This will pave the way for the full utilization of the $24 billion support package announced in April. Out of this, $6 billion earmarked for a ruble stabilization fund will be released when the necessary macroeconomic conditions are in place.

41. We suggest that country consultative groups should be set up for the new states, when appropriate, in order to foster close cooperation among the states concerned, international institutions and partners.

The task of these groups would be to encourage structural reforms and to coordinate technical assistance.

Safety of nuclear power plants in the new independent states of the former Soviet Union and in central and eastern Europe.

42. While we recognize the important role nuclear power plays in global energy supplies, the safety of Soviet-design nuclear power plants gives cause for great concern. Each state, through its safety authorities and plant operators, is itself responsible for the safety of its nuclear power plants. The new states concerned of the former Soviet Union and the countries of central and eastern Europe must give high priority to eliminating this danger. These efforts should be part of a market-oriented reform of energy policies encouraging commercial financing for the development of the energy sector.

43. A special effort should be made to improve the safety of these plants. We offer the states concerned our support within the framework of a multilateral program of action. We look to them to cooperate fully. We call upon other interested states to contribute as well.

44. The program of action should comprise immediate measures in the following areas:

- operational safety improvements;
- near-term technical improvements to plants based on safety assessments;
- enhancing regulatory regimes.

Such measures can achieve early and significant safety gains.

45. In addition, the program of action is to create the basis for longer-term safety improvements by the examination of:

- the scope for replacing less safe plants by the development of alternative energy sources and the more efficient use of energy,
- the potential for upgrading plants of more recent design.

Complementary to this, we will pursue the early completion of a convention on nuclear safety.

46. The program of action should develop clear priorities, provide coherence to the measures and ensure their earliest implementation. To implement the immediate measures, the existing G-24 coordination mandate on nuclear safety should be extended to the new states concerned of the former Soviet Union and at the same time made more effective. We all are prepared to strengthen our bilateral assistance.

In addition, we support the setting up of a supplementary multilateral mechanism, as appropriate, to address immediate operational safety and technical safety improvement measures not covered by bilateral programs. We invite the international community to contribute to the funding. The fund would take account of bilateral funding, be administered by a steering body of donors on the basis of consensus, and be coordinated with and assisted by the G-24 and the EBRD.

47. Decisions on upgrading nuclear power plants of more recent design will require prior clarification of issues concerning plant safety, energy policy, alternative energy sources and financing. To establish a suitable basis on which such decisions can be made, we consider the following measures necessary:

• The necessary safety studies should be presented without delay.
• Together with the competent international organizations, in particular the IEA, the World Bank should prepare the required energy studies including replacement sources of energy and the cost implications. Based on these studies, the World Bank and the EBRD should report as expeditiously as possible on potential financing requirements.

48. We shall review the progress made in this action program at our meeting in 1993.

49. We take note of the representations that we received from various heads of state or government and organizations, and we will study them with interest.

Next Meeting

50. We welcome and have accepted Prime Minister Miyazawa's invitation to Tokyo in July 1993.

SENTENCING OF FORMER
PANAMANIAN DICTATOR NORIEGA
July 10, 1992

Former Panamanian strongman General Manuel Antonio Noriega was sentenced in a Miami federal court July 10 to forty years in prison for drug trafficking, money laundering, and racketeering. The sentencing, by U.S. District Judge William M. Hoeveler, climaxed a complicated four-year legal and political battle in which Noriega became the first foreign head of state to be convicted of criminal charges in a U.S. court.

Federal grand juries in Miami and Tampa, Florida, had indicted Noriega on the drug trafficking charges in 1988. In December 1989 the United States invaded Panama, captured Noriega, and returned him to the United States to stand trial. After a seven-month trial, Noriega was convicted April 9, 1992, on eight counts involving drug trafficking and acquitted on two others. (Grand Jury Indictments of General Noriega, Historic Documents of 1988, p. 81; Bush Announces Invasion of Panama, Historic Documents of 1989, p. 701)

Noriega was almost certain to appeal his conviction, and he still was under indictment in Tampa on charges of marijuana trafficking. Meanwhile, questions were raised about where Noriega would serve his prison sentence after Hoeveler December 8 ruled that Noriega was a prisoner of war under the Geneva Conventions.

Despite Noriega's ouster and the installation of a civilian government, Panama still seemed to be a center for money laundering for the Colombia drug cartel. The situation "is not much better" than it was under Noriega, Secretary of State Warren M. Christopher said in January 1993 shortly before sworn into office. Much speculation surrounded allegations that President Guillermo Endara's law firm had links to money-laundering operations. Prominent Panamanians both in government and the private sector were suspected of profiting from drug-related activities.

The Sentencing

Throughout his trial, Noriega's defense attorneys argued that the ousted dictator was a prisoner of war outside the jurisdiction of the U.S. court system and that the charges against him were politically motivated. In a rambling, vitriolic three-hour speech before his sentencing, Noriega said that he had been captured and brought to trial so that the Bush administration could install a puppet government in Panama that would allow the United States to continue to control the Panama Canal after the year 2000. In 1978 President Jimmy Carter had signed a treaty turning over control of the canal to Panama in that year.

As he had throughout the trial, Hoeveler said that the politics of the case were irrelevant. A jury found Noriega guilty "beyond a reasonable doubt" of the drug trafficking charges, the judge said, "and that is the basis on which he shall be sentenced, not on the basis of speculation or what's been in the newspapers about Panama or what the General feels the real reason for his indictment was."

Judge Hoeveler imposed sentences of twenty years each, to be served concurrently, on two racketeering charges, to be followed by concurrent penalties of fifteen years each on five counts of drug trafficking, and then by five years on one count of money laundering. In addition the judge imposed a $100 fine and ordered Noriega to serve three years of special probation if and when he is ever released from prison. Noriega had faced a maximum sentence of 120 years in prison.

In a statement issued after the sentencing, President George Bush said the U.S. invasion of Panama had "freed the people of Panama from a brutal tyranny; the sentence handed down today demonstrates that it also led to the conviction and just punishment of an unrepentant drug criminal. For that, Americans and our allies have reason to be proud."

The P.O.W. Issue

Hoeveler's December 9 opinion that Noriega was a prisoner of war under the terms of the Geneva Conventions could ultimately affect where the general served his sentence. That decision was to be made by the Federal Bureau of Prisons. Noriega's attorneys had argued that his prisoner-of-war status required that he be kept in a military prison. Hoeveler disagreed with that argument on the ground that Noriega had been convicted as a felon in a U.S. civilian court. But he suggested that conditions at the maximum security prison where prosecutors had suggested that Noriega be incarcerated might not meet the standards laid out by the international treaty governing treatment of war prisoners.

The government should "err to the benefit of the P.O.W.," Hoeveler said. It "must keep in mind the importance to our own troops of faithful and, indeed, liberal adherence to the mandates" of the Geneva Conventions. "Regardless of how the Government views the defendant as a person, the implications of a failure to adhere to the Convention are too great to justify departure."

Hoeveler conceded that government prosecutors could challenge his jurisdiction over the issue of whether Noriega was a P.O.W. That was just one of many questions, the judge said, that made this entire case unique.

Noriega's Descent from Power

Before his capture in early 1990, Noriega had been an asset of the U.S. intelligence community for three decades or more, according to numerous reports. He rose through the ranks of the Panamanian military, and after the death of General Omar Torrijos in a plane crash in 1981, he gained control of both the military and the government. Throughout this period he lent valuable assistance to the Central Intelligence Agency and to the Pentagon. During Ronald Reagan's presidency, for example, Noriega supported U.S. efforts to supply the contra forces fighting the Sandinista government in Nicaragua. Somewhere along the line, it is charged, he became involved in drug dealing and money laundering.

In February 1988 two U.S. federal grand juries returned indictments against Noriega, among other things charging him with accepting a $4.6 million bribe from Colombia's Medillin drug cartel to permit the use of Panama as a transshipment point for cocaine and other drugs headed for the United States.

The next month President Ronald Reagan imposed the first of a series of economic sanctions against Panama. In May 1989 Noriega nullified the results of a presidential election that impartial observers said was won overwhelmingly by Endara, who eventually took the oath of office at a U.S. military base.

A failed coup against Noriega, mounted in October 1989 with limited assistance from the United States, spurred planning for the U.S. invasion. The die was cast on December 15, when the Panamanian legislature, appointed by Noriega, declared a "state of war" with the United States. On December 20 Bush announced that the invasion had begun.

Following are excerpts from the transcript of remarks by U.S. District Judge William M. Hoeveler at the sentencing of Panamanian General Manuel Antonio Noriega in Miami on July 10, 1992:

THE COURT: I'm not by a sentence here interested in giving a message to anybody. That indeed is not my function.

Somewhat in response to what the General has said in his comments, and perhaps reflective of a basic lack of understanding of our system, that the health of this system is indeed that it isn't governed by politics. I don't know because I'm not privy to all of the factors that gave rise to the invasion of Panama or the politics behind it. If some of the things happened that General Noriega says happened, that burden is on someone else.

I was presented with an indictment, with legal charges against a defendant and other defendants, and it was my function—and hopefully it was accomplished, but that remains for the Court of Appeals to decide—to see that the General got all of the rights that he was entitled to under the law.

And I might say, I think over the course of two and a half years of this litigation, the General has gotten every right, not necessarily from me but from the entire system, that a defendant could be afforded, including having his very competent counsel paid by the United States Government.

The beauty of this system is that a case that comes into court is and should be uninfluenced by anything except the charges that are made and the defenses that are presented.

The politics of this case were not a part of the case, should not have been a part of the case, and I think everybody did all they could to keep them from being a part of this case, and as I say, what happened outside the four corners of this case and this courtroom is somebody else's burden, not mine.

But now I'm called upon to make a decision on sentencing, and again, I must look not to what the General mentioned but to what happened in this courtroom, the evidence that was presented to a very fine jury of U.S. citizens, who have determined that in eight counts the General had done beyond a reasonable doubt what was charged in those counts, and that is the basis on which he shall be sentenced, not on the basis of speculation or what's been in the newspapers about Panama or what the General feels the real reason for his indictment was.

The real reason why we're here today is because a jury of twelve men and women decided that the Government had proved beyond a reasonable doubt that the charges limited to the indictment were indeed proved to that extent and beyond a reasonable doubt.

And so with that introduction and that conclusion, I will ask you and the General to please rise.

As to Count I of the indictment, the defendant will be committed to the custody of the Attorney General of the United States, or his authorized representative, for confinement for a period of twenty years.

As to Count II, the defendant will be committed to the custody of the Attorney General, or his authorized representative, for a term of twenty years, that term to run concurrent with the sentence in Count I.

As to Counts III, IV, V, VI and VII, the defendant will be committed to the custody of the Attorney General for a period of fifteen years.

Each of those counts will be concurrent with each other but consecutive to the counts set forth in Counts I and II.

As to Count V of the indictment, the defendant will be committed to the custody of the Attorney General for a period of five years—that's Count

XI of the indictment, the defendant will be committed to the custody of the Attorney General for a period of five years, to be consecutive to the sentences imposed in Counts I and II and III through VII.

As to the Counts III, IV, V, VI and VII, the defendant will also serve upon release a three-year special parole term. Those special parole terms will also be concurrent with each other.

Thus, the total sentence is the defendant be committed to the custody of the Attorney General for a period of forty years and he will be assessed fifty dollars for two counts, for a one hundred dollar assessment.

Now, on the question of the remand, I'm going to order that the defendant be held at the Miami Correctional Center for a period of at least sixty days and give an opportunity to the defense to submit a memorandum on the question of whether or not the defendant should be remanded to someone other than the Attorney General.

I don't think that he can be, frankly, but I wanted to give you the opportunity to try to convince me otherwise.

I would say this in connection with the institution: The Government has to this point recognized, although not officially, as I understand it, the defendant and has treated the defendant as a prisoner of war and has stated not only in its memorandum but through Mr. Sullivan here today that he will be treated as a—

Marshals, would you close the door, please?

THE MARSHAL: Yes sir.

Order back in the court, please.

THE COURT: I would presume from the Government's statements that they will continue to regard the General as a prisoner of war and he will be accorded those privileges that are set forth and that are proper in the Geneva Convention.

However, I do believe that he should be remanded to the Attorney General for the fulfillment of those obligations. But, as I've said, in the event you can convince me otherwise, I'll be glad to hear from you when you're ready to submit a memorandum. Of course, the Government will have an opportunity to respond.

In the meantime, the defendant will be housed at Miami Correctional center for at least sixty days.

Now, Mr. Rubino [the defense attorney], does the defendant or do you find any fault with the manner in which the Court has imposed sentence?

MR. RUBINO: Other than the things with the POW.

THE COURT: Other than the comments you've already made.

MR. RUBINO: Yes. Preserving those, no, sir.

THE COURT: All right. And for the defendants, anything to take up with the Court?

MR. SULLIVAN: Nothing from the Government, your Honor.

THE COURT: We'll be in recess. Thank you.

RABIN ON LABOR VICTORY IN ISRAELI ELECTIONS

July 13, 1992

For the first time in fifteen years, Israeli voters returned the Labor Party to power in parliamentary elections that heralded potentially significant changes in the nation's foreign and domestic policies and represented a resounding defeat for the ruling conservative Likud Party headed by Yitzhak Shamir.

Speaking to reporters after the June 23 vote, newly elected Prime Minister Yitzhak Rabin said he would slow the highly controversial process—vigorously pursued by the Likud—of establishing "political" settlements in the territories occupied by Israel after the 1967 Middle East War. And he pledged to take steps to reinvigorate the stalled Middle East peace talks and negotiations over granting Palestinians a greater degree of self-rule in the West Bank and Gaza Strip.

One of Rabin's first actions was to renew Israel's request for $10 billion in U.S.-backed loan guarantees to assist the government in providing housing and jobs for about 400,000 Jewish emigrants from the former Soviet Union. The Bush administration had held up action on the loan guarantees as a gesture of disapproval of the Shamir government's policy of expanding Jewish settlements near large Palestinian population centers. Because the United States would be guaranteeing repayment, the loan would allow Israel to borrow money at lower interest rates.

Cautious Pragmatism

Although the Labor party did not win a majority of seats in the 120-member Knesset (parliament), its victory was large enough to allow it to form a coalition government that excluded the Likud. In the elections, the Likud lost votes to small right-wing parties as well as to Labor and won fewer seats in the Knesset than it had in any election since 1969. Analysts said that the nation's soaring unemployment rate and Israeli concern over deteriorating relations with the United States were major reasons for Likud's defeat. A substantial majority of the immigrant voters from the former Soviet Union voted against the party, largely because they perceived that Likud intransigence on settlements was holding up loan guarantees.

In an address to the Knesset introducing his cabinet July 13, Rabin pledged to give priority to the "war on unemployment and to strengthening the economic and social systems." He also pledged to "take vigorous steps that will lead to the conclusion of the Israeli-Arab conflict" and said he would "spare no effort" to improve U.S.-Israeli relations. The prime minister said he was ready to travel "today, tomorrow" to Amman, Jordan, Damascus, Syria, or Beirut, Lebanon, to expedite the peace process.

Rabin's background might have offset any Israeli fears about the nation's security under the Labor party's more accommodating policy toward the nation's Arab neighbors. Rabin, the nation's first native-born prime minister, had directed the victory in the 1967 war. After a tour as ambassador to the United States, he served for three years as prime minister in the mid-1970s. As defense minister under Shamir from 1984 to 1990, Rabin contended with the Palestinian intifada, exhibiting what many observers saw as a tough policy against the uprising.

Despite his apparent willingness to be more flexible on sensitive issues, Rabin's overall 1992 campaign was cautious, based on the middle-of-the road policies espoused by the Likud-Labor coalition of the 1980s. These included rejection of a sovereign Palestinian state and insistence on maintaining Israeli rule over a unified Jerusalem.

"Rabin managed to convince the Likud voter that by voting for him and against the Likud, you were still voting for something in the very center of the Israeli establishment," commented Yossi Olmert, director of the government press office. "People wanted a change for various reasons, and Rabin offered a change that was not too radical."

Loan Guarantees Approved

Spokespersons for the Bush administration predicted that the Labor victory was likely to ease strained relations between the United States and Israel and improve prospects for progress in Middle East peace negotiations, particularly since Rabin's cabinet had decided to halt new settlements in the West Bank and Gaza pending review of all construction approved by the previous government.

Bush telephoned Rabin July 13 to congratulate him on his victory. The same day the White House announced that Secretary of State James A. Baker III would travel to the Middle East to confer with Rabin and Arab leaders. Baker arrived in Israel July 19, amid reports that the two governments were nearing agreement on the loan issue.

Baker's conferences with Rabin and Arab leaders were viewed as an attempt to spur the stalled Mideast peace process. Baker had been the principal impetus behind the peace initiative, which began with an international conference in Madrid in October 1991 and had then moved to direct talks among Israel, Syria, Lebanon, and a joint Jordanian-Palestinian delegation, held periodically in Washington, D.C. (Secretary Baker's Policy Address on the Middle East, Historic Documents of 1989, p. 289; Bush on War Victory and Mideast Peace Plans, Historic Documents of 1991, p. 121; Madrid Conference on Mideast Peace, Historic Documents of 1991, p. 719).

Three weeks after he met with Baker, Rabin traveled to the United States where he met with Bush August 10-11 at the president's summer home in Kennebunkport, Maine. At the end of the two-day meeting, Bush announced he would send a new loan guarantee proposal to Congress. Under its terms, Israel agreed to deduct the cost of continuing settlement construction from the amount of the guarantee.

Renewed Relations with Egypt

On July 21—only eight days after he assumed office—Rabin flew to Egypt to meet with President Hosni Mubarak for a session of low-key discussions. It was the first meeting between an Israeli head of state and Mubarak in six years. Although no substantive agreements were reached, the fact that Mubarak was willing to meet with Rabin marked a symbolic step forward in relations between the two nations (Egypt was the only nation to have signed a peace treaty with Israel). To indicate his disapproval of Likud policies, Mubarak had repeatedly refused to meet with Shamir.

At the end of Rabin's visit, Mubarak said he had accepted an invitation to visit Israel, which he had never before done in his eleven years as president. "[B]earing in mind that Mr. Rabin is only one week in office . . . we didn't ask for miracles," said Mubarak of the discussions. "We didn't try to reach any agreement or understanding," commented Rabin. "The purpose was to exchange views." But the Israeli prime minister pledged to speed up talks on self-rule for the 1.7 million Palestinians who lived in the Israeli-occupied West Bank and Gaza Strip.

Fitful Peace Talks

Rabin took a number of steps to make the atmosphere more conducive to improving Arab-Israeli relations, but they fell short of supporting Palestinian sovereignty or totally abandoning the settlements policy. The Labor government distinguished between "political" settlements in densely populated Arab areas, which it planned to halt, and "security" settlements in the Golan Heights, around Jerusalem, and along the Jordan Valley, which it said remained necessary. However, Palestinian and Arab leaders rejected the distinction, calling for a total settlement freeze.

Despite lingering Arab-Israeli differences, peace talks, which had broken down in April, resumed in Washington August 24, with officials on both sides saying they were hopeful that major progress could be achieved. The new round of negotiations was expected to be more intense and last longer than the previous five. However, the four-week round of talks ended in an impasse between Israel and Syria concerning the link between Israeli withdrawal from the Golan Heights (demanded by Syria) and Israel's demands that it would not withdraw until Syria agreed to sign a formal peace treaty and normalize relations.

Peace negotiations were left in limbo at year's end, when Israel deported 415 Palestinians it considered to be Islamic militants bent on disrupting the peace process. However, Lebanon refused to take in the deportees, and Israel refused to let them return. The men were caught in the buffer zone between Lebanon and Israel, and for a time both Lebanon and Israel refused to allow relief agencies to bring them water or food.

Following are excerpts of Prime Minister Yitzhak Rabin's address to the Israeli Knesset, July 13, 1992, in English translation, as provided by the Embassy of Israel:

Your Excellency Mr. President, Speaker of the Knesset, Members of the Knesset:

... Members of the Knesset, on the first day of Tamouz 5752, July 2nd, 1992, the President of the State charged me with forming a Government for Israel, and on Friday, the 9th of Tamouz, July 10th, I informed him that I had succeeded in that task. Participating in the Government that is asking for the Knesset's confidence today are the Labor, Democratic Israel (Meretz), and Sephardi Torah Guardians (Shas) parties. Following clarifications regarding its policy regarding the Arab population in Israel, the Government will also be supported by the Democratic Front for Peace and Equality and the Democratic Arab Party. The Government will keep its doors open to parties that are prepared to endorse its basic policies.

Despite possible differences of opinion among the members of the coalition, which have come from various parts of the political spectrum, the new Government is united by the sense permeating the people of Israel that this is a propitious hour, a time of great possibilities and opportunities that we shall do our utmost not to lose or squander.

Mr. Speaker, Members of the Knesset, in the last decade of the twentieth century, the atlases, history and geography books no longer present an up-to-date picture of the world. Walls of enmity have fallen, borders have disappeared, powers have crumbled and ideologies collapsed, states have been born, states have died and also, the gates of emigration have been flung open. And it is our duty, to ourselves and to our children, to see the new world as it is now—to discern its dangers, explore its prospects, and do everything possible so that the State of Israel will fit into this world whose face is changing. No longer are we necessarily "A people that dwells alone," and no longer is it true that 'The whole world is against us.' We must overcome the sense of isolation that has held us in its thrall for almost half a century. We must join the international movement toward peace, reconciliation, and cooperation that is spreading over the entire globe these days—lest we be the last to remain, all alone, in the station.

The new Government has accordingly made it a prime goal to promote the making of peace and take vigorous steps that will lead to the conclusion of the Arab-Israeli conflict. We shall do so based on the recognition by the Arab countries, and the Palestinians, that Israel is a sovereign state with a right to live in peace and security. We believe wholeheartedly that peace is possible, that it is imperative, and that it will ensue. "I shall believe in the future," wrote the poet Shaul Tcherniknovsky. "Even if it is far off, the day will come when peace and blessings are borne from nation to nation"—and I want to believe that that day is not far off.

The Government will propose to the Arab states and the Palestinians the continuation of the peace talks based upon the framework forged at the Madrid Conference. As a first step toward a permanent solution we shall discuss the institution of autonomy in Judea, Samaria, and the Gaza District. We do not intend to lose precious time. The Government's first directive to the negotiating teams will be to step up the talks and hold ongoing discussions between the sides. Within a short time we shall renew the talks in order to diminish the flame of enmity between the Palestinians and the State of Israel.

As a first step, to illustrate our sincerity and good will, I wish to invite the Jordanian-Palestinian delegation to an informal talk, here in Jerusalem, so that we can hear their views, make ours heard, and create an appropriate atmosphere for neighborly relations.

To you, the Palestinians in the territories, I wish to say from this rostrum—We have been fated to live together on the same patch of land, in the same country. We lead our lives with you, beside you and against you. You have failed in the war against us. One hundred years of your bloodshed and terror against us have brought you only suffering, humiliation, bereavement, and pain. You have lost thousands of your sons and daughters, and you are losing ground all the time. For 44 years now, you have been living under a delusion. Your leaders have led you through lies and deceit. They have missed every opportunity, rejected all the proposals for a settlement, and have taken you from one tragedy to another.

And you, Palestinians in the territories, who live in the wretched poverty of Gaza and Khan Yunis, in the refugee camps of Hebron and Shechem; you who have never known a single day of freedom and joy in your lives— listen to us, if only this once. We offer you the fairest and most viable proposal from our standpoint today—autonomy—self-government—with all its advantages and limitations. You will not get everything you want.

Perhaps neither will we. So once and for all, take your destiny in your hands. Don't lose this opportunity that may never return. Take our proposal seriously—to avoid further suffering, and grief; to end the shedding of tears and of blood.

The new Government urges the Palestinians in the territories to give peace a chance—and to cease all violent and terrorist activity for the duration of the negotiations on the subject of autonomy. We are well aware that the Palestinians are not all of a single mold, that there are exceptions and differences among them. But we urge the population, which has been suffering for years, and the perpetrators of the riots in the territories, to forswear stones and knives and await the results of the talks that may well bring peace to the Middle East. If you reject this proposal, we shall go on talking but treat the territories as though there were no dialogue going on between us. Instead of extending a friendly hand, we will employ every possible means to prevent terror and violence. The choice, in this case, is yours.

We have lost our finest sons and daughters in the struggle over this land and in the war against the Arab armies. My comrades in the Israel Defense Forces, and I myself as a former military man who took part in Israel's war, lovingly preserve the memory of the fallen and regard ourselves as sharing in the pain of the families whose sleepless nights, year in and year out, are one long Day of Remembrance to them. Only people who have lost those dearest to them can understand us. Our hearts also go out to the disabled, whose bodies bear the scars of war and terrorism.

Neither have we forgotten, on this distinguished occasion. The IDF soldiers who are prisoners of war or missing in action. We shall continue to make every effort to bring them home, and our thoughts are with their families today, as well.

Members of the Knesset, we shall continue to fight for our right to live here in peace and tranquility. No knife or stone, no fire-bomb or land-mine will stop us. The Government presented here today sees itself as responsible for the security of every one of Israel's citizens, Jews and Arabs, within the State of Israel, in Judea, in Samaria, and in the Gaza District.

We shall strike hard, without flinching, at terrorists and those who abet them. There will be no compromises in the war against terror. The IDF and the other security force will prove to the agents of bloodshed that our lives are not for the taking. We shall act to contain the hostile activities as much as possible and maintain the personal security of the inhabitants of Israel and the territories while both upholding the law and guarding the rights of the individual. . . .

Members of the Knesset, the plan to apply self-government to the Palestinians in Judea, Samaria, and Gaza—the autonomy of the Camp David Accords—is an interim settlement for a period of five years. No later than three years after its institution, discussions will begin on the permanent solution. It is only natural that the holding of talks on the subject creates concern among those among us who have chosen to settle in

Judea, Samaria, and the Gaza District. I hereby inform you that the Government, by means of the IDF and the other security services, will be responsible for the security and welfare of the residents of Judea, Samaria and the Gaza District. However, at the same time, the Government will refrain from any steps and activities that would disrupt the proper conduct of the peace negotiations.

We see the need to stress that the Government will continue to enhance and strengthen Jewish settlement along the lines of confrontation, due to their importance for security, and in Greater Jerusalem.

This Government, like all of its predecessors, believes there is no disagreement in this House concerning Jerusalem as the eternal capital of Israel. United Jerusalem has been and will forever be the capital of the Jewish People, under Israeli sovereignty, a focus of the dreams and longings of every Jew. The Government is firm in its resolve that Jerusalem will not be open to negotiation. The coming years will also be marked by the extension of construction in Greater Jerusalem. All Jews, religious and secular, have vowed "If I forget, thee, O Jerusalem, may my right hand wither." This vow unites us all and certainly includes me as a native of Jerusalem.

The Government will safeguard freedom of worship for the followers of all religions and all communities in Jerusalem. It will rigorously maintain free access to the Holy Places for all sects and ensure the conduct of a normal and pleasant life for those who visit and reside in the city.

Members of the Knesset, the winds of peace have lately been blowing from Moscow to Washington, from Berlin to Beijing. The voluntary liquidation of weapons of mass destruction and the abrogation of military pacts have lessened the risk of war in the Middle East, as well. And yet this region, with Syria and Jordan, Iraq and Lebanon, is still fraught with danger. Thus when it comes to security, we will concede not a thing. From our standpoint, security takes preference even over peace. A number of countries in our region have recently stepped up their efforts to develop and produce nuclear weapons. According to published information, Iraq was very close to attaining nuclear arms. Fortunately, its nuclear capability was discovered in time and, according to various testimonies, was damaged during and following the Gulf War. The possibility that nuclear weapons will be introduced into the Middle East in the coming years is a very grave and negative development from Israel's standpoint. The Government, from its very outset—and possibly in collaboration with other countries— will address itself to thwarting any possibility that one of Israel's enemies will possess nuclear weapons. Israel has long been prepared to face the threat of nuclear arms. At the same time, this situation requires us to give further thought to the urgent need to end the Arab—Israeli conflict and live in peace with our Arab partners.

Members of the Knesset, from this moment forward the concept of "Peace process" is no longer relevant. From now on we shall not speak of a "process" but of making peace. In that peace-making we wish to call upon the aid of Egypt, whose late leader, President Anwar Sadat, exhibited such courage and was able to bequeath to his people—and to us—the first peace agreement. The Government will seek further ways of improving neighborly relations and strengthening ties with Egypt and its president, Hosni Mobarak.

I call upon the leaders of the Arab countries to follow the lead of Egypt and its president and take the step that will bring us—and them—peace. I invite the King of Jordan and the Presidents of Syria and Lebanon to this rostrum in Israel's Knesset, here in Jerusalem, for the purpose of talking peace. In the service of peace, I am prepared to travel to Amman, Damascus, and Beirut today, tomorrow. For there is no greater victory than the victory of peace. Wars have their victors and their vanquished, but everyone is a victor in peace.

Sharing with us in the making of peace will also be the United States, whose friendship and special closeness we prize. We shall spare no effort to strengthen and improve the special relationship we have with the one Power in the world. Of course we shall avail ourselves of its advice, but the decisions will be ours alone, of Israel as a sovereign and independent state. We shall also take care to cultivate and strengthen our ties with the European Community. Even if we've not always seen eye to eye and have had our differences with the Europeans, we have no doubt that the road to peace will pass through Europe as well.

We shall strengthen every possible tie with Russia and the other states of the Commonwealth, with China, and with every country that responds to our outstretched hand.

Mr. Speaker, Members of the Knesset, security is not only the tank, the plane, and the missile boat. Security is also, and perhaps above all, the man; the Israeli citizen. Security is a man's education; it is his home, his school, his street and neighborhood, the society that has fostered him. Security is also a man's hope. It is the peace of mind and livelihood of the immigrant from Leningrad, the roof over the head of the immigrant from Gondar in Ethiopia, the factory that employs a demobilized soldier, a young native son. It means merging into our way of life and culture; that, too, is security.

You ask how we're going to ensure it?

We're going to change the national order of priorities and the allocation of financial resources from the state budget and from funds mobilized abroad.

Preference will be given to the war on unemployment and to strengthening the economic and social systems.

Unemployment is an insidious evil. It deprives a man of his dignity. It destroys the soul of the man who cannot feed his family, for there is no greater ignominy than the shame of hunger.

We intend to increase the rate of economic growth.

To create places of work for the hundreds of thousands of new immigrants and natives of this country who will enter the job market in the coming years. We shall do this by retooling the economy for open management free of administrative restrictions and superfluous government involvement. There's too much paper work—and not enough production.

- We shall promote the sale of Government-owned firms and privatization, and we shall do so in collaboration with the workers, so that they will suffer no harm. A free world demands a free economy.
- We shall invest in basic necessary projects so as to attract entrepreneurs to build enterprises. We shall allocate funds for the infrastructure—transportation, electricity, water and sewage, high-tech industries, research and development. That is the Government's job.
- We shall decrease the Government's involvement in the capital market and open a market for venture capital.
- We shall encourage the creation of small businesses.

We shall establish a basket of social services to be provided, by law, to all citizens covering education, health, welfare, and housing.

We want the new immigrants and our sons and daughters to find work, a livelihood, and a future in this country. We don't want Israel's main export to be our children.

Members of the Knesset, we have resolved to make the citizen our prime concern, and I want that all [of] us, Members of this House, should remember that the people do not serve us, we serve the people.

Chief among the services to the citizenry will be the education of our children. At the start of the coming school year, in another two months, we will already make every effort to institute a long school day in the development towns and poorer neighborhoods. We may face organizational difficulties, but we shall do our best to overcome them.

- We shall ensure equality among all the streams of education, including the Arab and Druze communities.
- We shall make every effort that every student in Israel is able to study, even if there isn't a penny in his pocket—or in that of his parents.

One of our prime objectives will be to strengthen the development towns. We shall give preference to helping them get back on their feet by means of offering incentives. We shall also try to cultivate the poorer neighborhoods in the cities by providing a neighborhood basket of services that will answer educational, health, and welfare needs.

Our concern will be not for the young alone. We intend to introduce a national pension law that will cover all the participants in the economy, salaried and self-employed alike. Pension funds will be subject to government supervision. We owe the elderly among us a life of dignity and shall be faithful to the value expressed in the supplication: "Do not abandon us in our old age."

We shall do everything possible to ensure housing for the new immigrants and to answer the needs of young couples by giving preference and aid to demobilized soldiers. We send our young people on the most difficult and dangerous of national missions and then ignore them after they return from it safely. "More power to the IDF" also means tending to our soldiers once they have completed their army service.

The homeless, families living in overcrowded conditions, and others overburdened by their mortgages will come first in our order of priorities. Israel will be not just a state; it will also be a home.

The Government that embarks on its journey today sees the health of its citizens as one of its highest priorities. "May you enjoy a full recovery" is not just a wish for good health; it will be the right of the ailing according to a national health law. That law will establish the public funding necessary to maintain a high-level public-health system that ensures equality for all. Every citizen in Israel will benefit from health insurance through public health funds. And most important, we should all be healthy.

Members of the Knesset, it is proper to admit that for years we have erred in our treatment of Israel's Arab and Druze citizens. Today, almost 45 years after the establishment of the state, there are substantial gaps between the Jewish and Arab communities in a number of spheres. On behalf of the new Government, I see it as fitting to promise the Arab, Druze, and Bedouin population that we shall do everything possible to close those gaps. We shall try to make the great leap that will enhance the welfare of the minorities that have tied their fate to our own.

Members of the Knesset, Theodor Herzl once said: "All of men's achievements are rooted in dreams." We have dreamed and fought and created—despite all the difficulties, despite all the criticism—a safe haven for the Jewish People. This is the essence of Zionism, the dream of generations come true.

In the last years, the gates have opened up for Jews wishing to emigrate to our country, and hundreds of thousands of Jews who have come from the ends of the earth—and particularly from Russia and the other republics of the Commonwealth—are rebuilding their lives among us. No one is closer to us than they are. We are obliged to show them the way, to absorb them in the spirit of Jewish solidarity.

In the past months the flow of immigrants has dwindled, and that is to our regret. The Government will act to resume and increase immigration, especially from Russia and the other members of the Commonwealth, and will continue the efforts to save Jews who suffer persecution just because they are Jews. Without all this, we will not have a return to Zion. And all of us are returnees to Zion.

In this small country we have gathered dozens of Jewish communities and cultures. It is not easy to meld them all into a single nation, and in the meanwhile we must foster patience and tolerance to help bring people together.

The Jewish heritage has kept the Jewish People alive through all its wanderings and dispersions, and we see it as our duty to preserve the tie between the State of Israel and the Jewish heritage. Safeguarding the unity of the people requires tolerance and the creation of conditions for religious and secular to live together in mutual respect. We shall see to it that all Jewish children are educated in the light of Jewish values.

The Government will refrain from any religious or anti-religious coercion and will provide for the public religious needs of the country's citizens regardless of political affiliation.

The "special funding" will be abolished.

The Minister of Defence will appoint a team, under his auspices, to investigate and determine the criteria for exempting yeshivah students from army service, so as to prevent the abuse of the existing arrangements in this area.

I believe that these steps, taken in full collaboration with the religious and ultra-orthodox parties, will help mitigate the polarization of our society and bring the People of Israel closer together. Members of the Knesset, the road ahead is a long one, and there is much to be accomplished:

- We shall complete the legislation of Basic Laws in order to forge a Constitution for the State.
- We shall take the reports of the State Comptroller very seriously and wipe out every trace of corruption.
- We shall finally implement the law—already passed—for direct election of the Prime Minister and change the system of elections to the Knesset.
- We shall pay special attention to the quality of the environment and to improving roads and transportation.

Members of the Knesset, a few words to our friends in the Opposition. We are not living under any delusions. We know that we face a great task, that there is much work to be done, and that our efforts may encounter difficulties. We shall be engaged in getting things accomplished, and there can be no accomplishment without errors. We expect criticism from you, and it may be as penetrating as you like, as long as it is constructive criticism that is concerned with the future and fate of this people.

This is also an opportunity to request, Members of the Knesset, that we do everything in our power to enhance the prestige of the Knesset by comporting ourselves in a courteous and responsible manner. The people of Israel see us nightly on their television screens, and we cannot blame them if our own image is reflected in the national mirror—and we are treated accordingly. The Government is turning over a new leaf today. I suggest that we too, Members of the Knesset, turn over a new leaf with the people that have sent us here.

Members of the Knesset, we have today presented to the Knesset the basic guidelines of the new Government's policy and all the understandings relating to the formation of that Government, including the coalition agreements. There are no secrets or covert agreements and none will [be] made in the future. Everything is on the table, out in the open, in accordance with the law. . . .

DEMOCRATIC NATIONAL CONVENTION
July 13-16, 1992

Emphasizing youth, traditional family values, and mainstream policy views, a jubilant Democratic party nominated a southern "baby boomer" ticket at its national convention in New York City's Madison Square Garden July 13-16. Named as standard bearers were Arkansas Governor Bill Clinton for president and U.S. Senator Al Gore of Tennessee for vice president.

Clinton, who had locked in his party's presidential nomination during a series of hard-fought primaries, went into the convention with higher poll ratings than the incumbent, President George Bush. Bush and Vice President Dan Quayle won easy renomination a month later at the Republican national convention in Houston. (Republican National Convention, p. 781)

In New York the Democrats' spirits were buoyed by reports that Clinton was a likely election winner because of widespread public dissatisfaction with Bush's handling of the persistently poor economy. But even before the convention ended, it was upstaged by Dallas billionaire Ross Perot's short-lived decision not to make an independent bid for the White House. Perot later rejoined the race and debated Bush and Clinton about the economy and other election issues. It was the first time that an independent or third-party candidate was included in a presidential debate with both major party candidates. (Perot's Statements on Ending and Reviving His Campaign, p. 717; Presidential and Vice Presidential Debates, p. 907)

Perot's temporary withdrawal was the ultimate distraction in the week when Clinton, his campaign, and his party sought to reintroduce the

Democratic presidential nominee to the nation. Holding high his humble origins, Clinton cast himself as the self-made hero of small-town America and the paradigm of old-fashioned virtues. "I am a product of that middle class. And when I am president, you will be forgotten no more," Clinton said in his acceptance speech July 16.

Family values and uprightness rang from every pillar and post in Madison Square Garden. Clinton's acceptance speech was rife with references to God and faith, home and family. He twice quoted from Scripture. And a "New Covenant" was the Arkansan's successor phrase to the New Frontier and the New Deal. "I'm fed up with politicians in Washington lecturing the rest of us about 'family values,'" Clinton said. "Our families have values. But our government doesn't."

Close behind in priority was the theme of Clinton as engineer of change. In the plainspeak that was the hallmark of his appearances all week, Clinton intoned: "Jobs. Education. Health care. These are not just commitments from my lips. They are the work of my life."

The convention also performed its traditional tasks, unifying the party and building steam for the daunting task of toppling an incumbent president. The convention succeeded in this partly because the party's mainstreamers got back behind the wheel. They nominated a ticket consisting of two party moderates and adopted a platform heavily influenced by the centrist ideas of the Democratic Leadership Council (DLC) and its think tank, the Progressive Policy Institute. Clinton had been a founder and leader of the DLC. "These candidates, combined with this platform, mean this party has really changed," said Al From, DLC executive director. (Democratic Party Platform, p. 685)

The convention also laid claim to the legendary youth-and-vigor image of President John F. Kennedy. Clinton imitated his idol in coming to the hall a night early to thank the delegates who voted for him. A film about Robert F. Kennedy was a highlight of one night's program, as was a 1963 film clip of a sixteen-year-old Clinton shaking hands with Kennedy.

In appealing to youth, as in much else, Clinton was ably assisted by his running mate. At forty-four, Gore was a year younger than Clinton, making their ticket the youngest in the twentieth century. After Clinton's speech the Garden rang with a recording of Fleetwood Mac's "Don't Stop (Thinking About Tomorrow)" (a hit in 1977, the last time a Democrat was inaugurated president).

Gore, who brought little of the traditional balance in terms of region or ideology, complemented Clinton in image and in expertise, especially in environmental protection. Throughout the week, Gore and his family were offered up as human symbols of the perfect nuclear family. He gave a confident and even masterful acceptance speech, bringing many in his audience to tears by recounting how his son's near-fatal traffic accident had changed his life. He also rounded out the personal and ideological triumph of the DLC. Clinton ran as the DLC favorite in 1992; Gore had run for president with the group's blessing in 1988.

Gore's speech was the second that moved the convention delegates to tears. The first spellbinder, on July 14, was by Elizabeth Glaser, a victim of HIV, the virus that causes AIDS. (Convention Speeches by Women Infected with HIV, p. 709)

Party Shines

The Democratic National Committee, under Chairman Ronald H. Brown, ran a colorful and energetic show in tune with its youthful ticket. Critical in all these developments was the role of Brown, a glib and dapper Washington lawyer who assumed the chair in 1989 after a brief but sharp campaign. Brown was an unusually visible chairman, dominating much of the convention news even as he acted as Clinton's point man.

Controversy was almost entirely confined to the early going and involved primarily the supporters of former California governor Edmund G. "Jerry" Brown, Jr. Brown arrived with more than 600 delegates, enough to make a fuss on the floor the first night when informed their man would not be addressing the convention from the podium. In the end Brown was given the chance to make his own seconding speech on July 15.

The far more polite challenge posed by another rival from the primaries, former senator Paul E. Tsongas of Massachusetts, was disposed of quietly. Tsongas was allowed to present several amendments to the platform, all of which were defeated.

Along the way the party's powerhouse personalities, such as Jesse L. Jackson and New York governor Mario M. Cuomo, assumed their roles in the process of unifying the party and supporting the ticket. Both gave stirring speeches, then retreated, leaving the limelight at last to the nominee.

The Moment Arrives

Clinton's staff openly compared the challenge facing their candidate in his acceptance speech to the task Bush had tackled in his acceptance four years earlier. Bush wanted to reshape the public perception of him left over from eight years in the No. 2 job and from a brief but nasty primary season. Clinton wanted to erase the notions of privilege, arrogance, and irresponsibility created in the 1992 primaries, less by his rival candidates than by reports in tabloid newspapers and other media.

Commencing the makeover was a short film made by Linda Bloodworth-Thomason and Harry Thomason, producers of the TV comedy "Designing Women." The film was highly effective at evoking the mood and personalities of Clinton's early years. It also presented a more romantic side of Clinton's wife, Hillary, than had been glimpsed during the primaries.

Following the film, Clinton walked unannounced onto the empty stage and spent about one minute waving and acknowledging the crowd. When he began speaking, he was low key and earnest. The words were rarely soaring in their rhetoric and often almost childlike in their simplicity. Like the film before it, the speech ended in Hope, Arkansas, where Clinton was born. It closed with the words, "I still believe in a place called Hope." The speech began about 10:25 p.m. and lasted fifty-five minutes.

Clinton often referred to himself at the convention as "the comeback kid," including when he came to the floor on the roll-call night. He claimed the title after rebounding from damaging stories about his alleged relationship with a singer and about the means by which he avoided the Vietnam War draft. (Clinton Letter on Draft, p. 155)

Following are speeches at the Democratic National Convention in New York City as delivered by Al Gore and Bill Clinton accepting the party's nomination for vice president and president, respectively, on July 16, 1992. (The bracketed headings have been added by Congressional Quarterly to highlight the organization of the texts.):

GORE ACCEPTANCE SPEECH

Thank you. Thank you. Thank you very much.

I have to tell you, I've been dreaming of this moment since I was a kid growing up in Tennessee: that one day I'd have the chance to come here to Madison Square Garden and be the warm-up act for Elvis.

My friends, I thank you for your confidence expressed in the vote this evening. I pledge to pour my heart and soul into this crusade on behalf of the American people. And I accept your nomination for the vice presidency of the United States of America.

I did not seek—I did not seek this nomination nor did I expect it. But I am here to join this team because I love my country and because I believe in my heart that together, Bill Clinton and I offer the American people the best chance we have to move this nation forward in the right direction again.

I am here because the country I love has a government that is failing our people—failing the forgotten majority in your hometown and mine, those who scrimped and saved, who work hard all their lives to build a better life for their children.

I am here to renew a journey our founders began more than 200 years ago. In my lifetime, I have seen America's ideals and dreams change the world, and I believe that now is the time to bring those ideals and dreams home here to change America.

Our country is in trouble. And while George Bush and Dan Quayle have been making excuses for deadlock and delay, people in other nations inspired by the eternal promise of America have torn down the Berlin Wall, brought communism to its knees and forced a racist government in South Africa to turn away from apartheid.

Throughout the world, obstacles to liberty that many thought might stand forever turned out to simply be no match for men and women who decided in their hearts that their future could be much greater than their past would let them dream.

Their faith in the power of conscience and their confidence in the force of truth required a leap of the human spirit. Can we say truthfully that their chance for change was better than ours? And yet we face our own crisis of the spirit here and now in America. We're told we can no longer change; we've seen our better days. They even say we're history.

The cynics are having a field day because across this country millions of American families have been betrayed by a government out of touch with our values and beholden to the privileged few. Millions of people—millions of people are losing faith in the very idea of democracy and are even in danger of losing heart, because they fear their lives may no longer have any deeper meaning or purpose.

But you can't kill hope that easily, not in America, not here, where a cynic is just a disappointed idealist in disguise, a dreamer yearning to dream again.

In every American, no matter how badly betrayed or poorly led, there is always hope. Even now, if you listen, you can hear the pulse of America's true spirit.

No, the American spirit isn't gone. But we vow here tonight that in November George Bush and Dan Quayle will be history.

["Time for Them to Go"]

I'm not saying they're bad people, but their approach to governing this country has badly failed. They have taxed the many to enrich the few, and it is time for them to go.

They have given us false choices, bad choices and no choice. And it is time for them to go.

They have ignored the suffering of those who are victims—of AIDS, of crime, of poverty, of ignorance, of hatred and harassment. It is time for them to go.

They have nourished and appeased tyranny, and endangered America's deepest interest while betraying our cherished ideals. It is time for them to go.

They have mortgaged our children's future to avoid the decisions they lack the courage to make. It is time for them to go.

They embarrassed our nation when the whole world was asking for American leadership in confronting the environmental crisis. It is time for them to go.

They have demeaned our democracy with the politics of distraction, denial and despair. What time is it?

[Audience:] It is time for them to go.

What time is it?

[Audience:] It is time for them to go.

What time is it?

[Audience:] It is time for them to go.

The American people are disgusted with excuses and tired of blame. They know that throughout American history, each generation has passed on leadership to the next. That time has come again. The time for a new generation of leadership for the United States of America to take over from George Bush and Dan Quayle. And you know what that means for them. It is time for them to go.

[President for the Twenty-first Century]

Ladies and gentlemen, in 1992 our challenge is not to elect the last president of the 20th century but to elect the first president of the 21st century, President Bill Clinton.

Bill Clinton has a plan that offers real answers for the real problems of real people, a bold new economic strategy to rebuild this country and put our people back to work.

And if you want to know what Bill Clinton can do, take a look at what he has already done. For more than a decade he has been fighting against incredible odds to bring good jobs, better skills and genuine hope to one of the poorest states in our country.

A decade ago, when his state needed dramatic reform to shake up one of the poorest school systems in America, Bill Clinton took on the established interests and made Arkansas the first state to require teacher testing. He has cut classroom size, raised test scores above the national average and earned the support of both teachers and parents, who now know Bill Clinton will be the real education president for this country.

For most of the last decade, while the Republicans have been trying to use welfare to divide us, Bill Clinton has led the fight to reform the welfare system, to move people off welfare and into the work force.

And he did all this while balancing 11 budgets in a row. Let me say that again: while balancing 11 budgets in a row and giving the people of Arkansas one of the lowest tax burdens in this country. No wonder Arkansas under Bill Clinton has been creating manufacturing jobs at 10 times the national rate. And no wonder when all of the nation's governors, Republicans and Democrats alike, were asked to vote on who was the most effective governor in all the land, by an overwhelming margin they chose Bill Clinton.

What we need in America in 1992 is a president who will unleash the best in us by putting faith in the decency and good judgment of our people. A president who will challenge us to be true to our values and examine the ways in which our own attitudes are sometimes barriers to the progress we seek.

["Relationship to the Earth"]

I'm convinced that America is ready to be inspired and lifted again, by leaders committed to seeking out the best in our society, developing it and strengthening it. I've spent much of my career working to protect the environment, not only because it is vital to the future of my state of Tennessee, our country and our earth but because I believe there is a fundamental link between our current relationship to the earth and the attitudes that stand in the way of human progress.

For generations we have believed that we could abuse the earth because we were somehow not really connected to it. But now we must face the truth. The task of saving the earth's environment must and will become the central organizing principle of the post-Cold War world.

And just as the false assumption that we are not connected to the earth has led to the ecological crisis, so the equally false assumption that we are not connected to each other has led to our social crisis.

Even worse, the evil and mistaken assumption that we have no connection to those generations preceding us or those who will follow us has led to the crisis of values we face today.

Those are the connections that are missing from our politics today. Those are the bridges we must rebuild if we are to rebuild our country. And those are the values we must honor if we are to recapture that faith in the future which has always been the heart of the American Dream.

We have another challenge as well. In the wake of the Cold War, with the re-emergence of ancient ethnic and racial hatreds throughout the world, the United States must once again prove that there is a better way. Just as we accepted as a people on behalf of humankind the historic mission of proving that political freedom is the best form of government and that economic freedom is the best engine of prosperity, and must now accept the obligation of proving that freedom from prejudice is the heart and soul of community, that yes, we can get along.

Yes, people of all backgrounds cannot only live together peacefully but enrich one another, celebrate diversity and come together as one. Yes, we will be one people and live the dream that will make this world free.

In the end, this election isn't about politics. It isn't even about winning, though that's what we are going to do.

This election is about the responsibilities that we owe one another, the responsibilities that we owe our children, the calling we hear to serve our country and to be part of a community larger than ourselves.

You've heard a lot in the past week about how much Bill Clinton and I have in common. Indeed, we both share the values we learned in our hometowns: individual responsibility, faith, family and the belief that hard work should be rewarded. We're both fathers with young children, children who are part of a generation whose very future is very much at stake in this election. And we're both proud of our wives, Hillary Clinton and Tipper Gore—two women who have done more for the children of this country in the last 12 years than the last two men who have sat in the Oval Office have done in their entire lifetimes.

I'm proud my father and mother could be here tonight to see me join a ticket that will make good on the best advice they ever gave me: to tell the truth and always love my country. My sister and I were born to two wonderful people who worked hard to give us a better life. 1992 is the Year of the Woman. It is also the 46th anniversary of the year my mother, born in a time when women weren't even allowed to vote, became one of the first women to graduate from Vanderbilt Law School.

My father was a teacher in a one-room school who worked his way to the United States Senate. I was 8 years old when my father's name was placed in nomination for the vice presidency before the Democratic convention in 1956. And growing up, I watched him stand courageously for civil rights and economic opportunity and a government that worked for ordinary people.

[Almost Lost a Son]

I don't know what it's like to lose a father, but I know what it's like to lose a sister and almost lose a son. I wish my late sister Nancy could be here this evening, but I am grateful beyond words for the blessings that my family has shared. Three years ago, my son Albert was struck by a car crossing the street after watching a baseball game in Baltimore. Tipper and I watched as he was thrown 30 feet in the air and scraped another 20 feet on the pavement after he hit the ground. I ran to his side and called his name, but he was limp and still, without breath or pulse. His eyes were open with the empty stare of death, and we prayed, the two of us, there in the gutter, with only my voice.

His injuries, inside and out, were massive, and for terrible days he lingered between life and death. Tipper and I spent the next 30 days and nights there at his bedside. Our family was lifted and healed, in no small measure by an incredible outpouring of love and compassion and prayers of thousands of people, most of whom we never even knew.

Albert is plenty brave and strong, and with the support of three wonderful sisters—Karenna, Kristin and Sarah—and two loving parents who helped him with his exercises every morning and prayed for him every night, he pulled through. And now, thank God, he has fully recovered, and runs and plays and torments his older sisters like any little boy.

But, ladies and gentlemen, I want to tell you this straight from my heart—that experience changed me forever. When you've seen your 6-year-old son fighting for his life, you realize that some things matter a lot more than winning. You lose patience with the lazy assumption of so many in politics that we can always just muddle through. When you've seen your reflection in the empty stare of a boy waiting for a second breath of life, you realize that we weren't put here on earth to look out for our needs alone; we are part of something much larger than ourselves. All of us are part of something much greater than we are capable of imagining.

And my friends, if you look up for a moment from the rush of your daily lives, you will hear the quiet voices of your country crying out for help. You will see your reflection in the weary eyes of those who are losing hope in

America. And you will see that our democracy is lying there in the gutter, waiting for us to give it a second breath of life.

I don't care what party you're in, whether you are an independent, whether you have been tempted to give up completely on the whole political process or not, or give up on our party or not, we want you to join this common effort to unite our country behind a higher calling. If you have been supporting Ross Perot, I want to make a special plea to you this evening: Stay involved. You have already changed politics in this country for the better. Keep on fighting for change.

The time has come for all Americans to be part of the healing. In the words of the Bible, "Do not lose heart. This nation will be renewed."

In order to renew our nation, we must renew ourselves. Just as America has always transcended the hopes and dreams of every other nation on earth, so must we transcend ourselves, and in Gandhi's words, become the change we wish to see in the world.

Let those of us alive today resolve with one another that we will so conduct ourselves—in this campaign and in our lives—that 200 years from now, Americans will say of our labors that this nation and this earth were healed by people they never even knew.

I'm told that Hope, Ark., is indeed a lot like my hometown of Carthage, Tenn.: a place where people know about it when you're born and care about it when you die. That's the America Bill Clinton and I grew up in. That's the kind of nation we want our children to grow up in. Just as Hope is a community, so is America. When we bring the community of America together, we will rekindle the American spirit and renew this nation for generations to come. And the way to begin is to elect Bill Clinton president of the United States of America.

Thank you very much.

CLINTON ACCEPTANCE SPEECH

Governor [Ann W.] Richards, Chairman [Ronald H.] Brown, Mayor [David N.] Dinkins, our great host—my fellow delegates, and my fellow Americans, I am so proud of Al Gore.

He said he came here tonight because he always wanted to do the warm-up for Elvis. Well, I ran for president this year for one reason and one reason only: I wanted to come back to this convention and finish that speech I started four years ago.

Last night [New York governor] Mario Cuomo taught us how a real nominating speech should be given.

He also made it clear why we have to steer our ship of state on a new course. Tonight I want to talk with you about my hope for the future, my faith in the American people and my vision of the kind of country we can build together.

I salute the good men who were my campaign—companions on the campaign trail: [Iowa senator] Tom Harkin. [Nebraska senator] Bob Kerrey. [Virginia governor] Doug Wilder. [Former California governor] Jerry Brown. And [former Massachusetts senator] Paul Tsongas.

One sentence in the platform we built says it all: "The most important family policy, urban policy, labor policy, minority policy and foreign policy America can have is an expanding entrepreneurial economy of high-wage, high-skill jobs."

And so, in the name of all those who do the work, pay the taxes, raise the kids and play by the rules, in the name of the hard-working Americans who make up our forgotten middle class, I proudly accept your nomination for president of the United States.

["Forgotten No More"]

I am a product of that middle class. And when I am president, you will be forgotten no more.

We meet at a special moment in history, you and I. The Cold War is over. Soviet communism has collapsed. And our values—freedom, democracy, individual rights and free enterprise—they have triumphed all around the world. And yet just as we have won the Cold War abroad, we are losing the battles for economic opportunity and social justice here at home.

Now that we have changed the world, it's time to change America.

I have news for the forces of greed and the defenders of the status quo: Your time has come and gone. It's time for a change in America.

Tonight 10 million of our fellow Americans are out of work. Tens of millions more work harder for lower pay. The incumbent president says unemployment always goes up a little before a recovery begins. But unemployment only has to go up by one more person before a real recovery can begin.

And Mr. President, you are that man.

This election is about putting power back in your hands and putting the government back on your side. It's about putting people first.

You know, I've said that all across the country. And whenever I do, someone always comes back at me, as a young man did this week at a town meeting at the Henry Street Settlement on the Lower East Side of Manhattan. He said, "That sounds good, Bill. But you're a politician. Why should I trust you?"

Tonight, as plainly as I can, I want to tell you who I am, what I believe and where I want to lead America.

I never met my father.

He was killed in a car wreck on a rainy road three months before I was born, driving from Chicago to Arkansas to see my mother.

After that, my mother had to support us. So we lived with my grandparents while she went back to Louisiana to study nursing.

I can still see her clearly tonight through the eyes of a 3-year-old: kneeling at the train station and weeping as she put me back on the train to Arkansas with my grandmother. She endured her pain because she knew her sacrifice was the only way she could support me and give me a better life.

My mother taught me. She taught me about family, and hard work, and sacrifice. She held steady through tragedy after tragedy. And she held our family, my brother and me, together through tough times. As a child, I watched her go off to work each day at a time when it wasn't always easy to be a working mother.

As an adult, I watched her fight off breast cancer. And again she has taught me a lesson in courage. And always, always she taught me to fight.

That's why I'll fight to create high-paying jobs so that parents can afford to raise their children today. That's why I'm so committed to making sure every American gets the health care that saved my mother's life.

And that women's health care gets the same attention as men's.

That's why I'll fight to make sure women in this country receive respect and dignity—whether they work in the home, out of the home or both.

You want to know where I get my fighting spirit? It all started with my mother. Thank you, mother. I love you.

When I think about opportunity for all Americans, I think about my grandfather.

He ran a country store in our little town of Hope. There were no food stamps back then, so when his customers—whether they were white or black—who worked hard and did the best they could came in with no money, well, he gave them food anyway. Just made a note of it. So did I. Before I was big enough to see over the counter, I learned from him to look up to people other folks looked down on.

My grandfather just had a high school education—a grade school education. But in that country store he taught me more about equality in the eyes of the Lord than all my professors at Georgetown; more about the intrinsic worth of every individual than all the philosophers at Oxford; more about the need for equal justice under the law than all the jurists at Yale Law School.

If you want to know where I come by the passionate commitment I have to bringing people together without regard to race, it all started with my grandfather.

["Hillary Taught Me"]

I learned a lot from another person, too. A person who for more than 20 years has worked hard to help our children. Paying the price of time to make sure our schools don't fail them. Someone who traveled our state for a year, studying, learning, listening. Going to PTA meetings, school board meetings, town hall meetings. Putting together a package of school reforms recognized around the nation. Doing it all while building a distinguished legal career and being a wonderful loving mother.

That person is my wife.

Hillary taught me. She taught me that all children can learn, and that each of us has a duty to help them do it. So if you want to know why I care so much about our children and our future, it all started with Hillary. I love you.

Frankly, I'm fed up with politicians in Washington lecturing the rest of us about "family values."

Our families have values. But our government doesn't.

I want an America where "family values" live in our actions, not just in our speeches. An America that includes every family: every traditional family and every extended family, every two-parent family, every single-parent family and every foster family. Every family.

I do want to say something to the fathers in this country who have chosen to abandon their children by neglecting their child support: Take responsibility for your children, or we will force you to do so.

Because governments don't raise children; parents do. And you should.

And I want to say something to every child in America tonight who is out there trying to grow up without a father or a mother: I know how you feel. You're special, too. You matter to America. And don't you ever let anybody tell you you can't become whatever you want to be.

And if other politicians make you feel like you're not a part of their families, come on and be part of ours.

The thing that makes me angriest about what's gone wrong these last 12 years is that our government has lost touch with our values, while politicians continue to shout about them. I'm tired of it.

I was raised to believe the American Dream was built on rewarding hard work. But we have seen the folks in Washington turn the American ethic on its head. For too long those who play by the rules and keep the faith have gotten the shaft. And those who cut corners and cut deals have been rewarded.

People are working harder than ever, spending less time with their children, working nights and weekends on the job instead of going to PTA and Little League or Scouts. And their incomes are still going down, their taxes are going up, and the costs of housing, health care and education are going through the roof. Meanwhile, more and more of our best people are falling into poverty, even though they work 40 hours a week.

Our people are pleading for change, but government is in the way. It's been hijacked by privileged, private interests. It has forgotten who really pays the bills around here. It's taking more of your money and giving you less in return.

We have got to go beyond the brain-dead politics in Washington and give our people the kind of government they deserve: a government that works for them.

The president ought to be a powerful force for progress. But right now I know how President Lincoln felt when General [George B.] McClellan wouldn't attack in the Civil War. He asked him, "If you're not going to use your army, may I borrow it?" And so I say: George Bush, if you won't use your power to help America, step aside. I will.

["Failed Economic Theory"]

Our country is falling behind. The president is caught in the grip of a failed economic theory. We have gone from first to 13th in the world in wages since Reagan and Bush have been in office. Four years ago, candidate Bush said America is a special place, not just "another pleasant country somewhere on the U.N. roll call, between Albania and Zimbabwe."

Now, under President Bush, America has an unpleasant economy stuck somewhere between Germany and Sri Lanka. And for most Americans, Mr. President, life's a lot less kind and a lot less gentle than it was before your administration took office.

Our country has fallen so far, so fast, that just a few months ago the Japanese prime minister actually said he felt sympathy for America. Sympathy. When I am your president, the rest of the world will not look down on us with pity but up to us with respect again.

What is George Bush doing about our economic problems?

Now four years ago he promised us 15 million new jobs by now. And he's over 14 million short. Al Gore and I can do better.

He has raised taxes on the people driving pickup trucks and lowered taxes on people riding in limousines. We can do better.

He promised to balance the budget, but he hasn't even tried. In fact, the budgets he has submitted to Congress nearly doubled the debt. Even worse, he wasted billions and reduced our investments in education and jobs. We can do better.

So if you are sick and tired of a government that doesn't work to create jobs, if you're sick and tired of a tax system that's stacked against you, if you're sick and tired of exploding debt and reduced investments in our future, or if, like the great civil rights pioneer Fannie Lou Hamer, you're just plain old sick and tired of being sick and tired, then join with us, work with us, win with us, and we can make our country the country it was meant to be.

The choice you face is clear.

George Bush talks a good game. But he has no game plan to compete and win in the world economy. I do. He won't take on the big insurance companies to lower costs and provide health care to all Americans. I will.

He won't even implement the recommendations of his own commission on AIDS, but I will.

He won't streamline the federal government and change the way it works; cut 100,000 bureaucrats and put 100,000 new police officers on your streets of American cities, but I will.

He's never balanced a government budget, but I have. Eleven times.

He won't break the stranglehold the special interests have on our elections and lobbyists have on our government, but I will.

He won't give mothers and fathers a chance to take some time off from work when a baby's born or a parent is sick, but I will.

We're losing our farms at a rapid rate and he has no commitment to keep family farms in the family, but I do.

He's talked a lot about drugs but he hasn't helped people on the front line to wage that war on drugs and crime, but I will.

He won't take the lead in protecting the environment and creating new jobs in environmental technologies for the 21st century, but I will.

You know what else? He doesn't have Al Gore, and I do.

Just in case, just in case you didn't notice, that's Gore with an "e" on the end.

And George Bush won't guarantee a woman's right to choose. I will.

Hear me now: I am not pro-abortion. I am pro-choice, firmly. I believe this difficult and painful decision should be left to the women of America.

I hope the right to privacy can be protected and we will never again have to discuss this issue on political platforms.

But I am old enough to remember what it was like before *Roe v. Wade*, and I do not want to return to the time when we make criminals of women and their doctors.

Jobs. Education. Health care. These are not just commitments from my lips. They are the work of my life.

Our priorities are clear: We will put our people first again.

[Need Fundamental Change]

But priorities without a clear plan of action are just empty words. To turn our rhetoric into reality we've got to change the way government does business, fundamentally. Until we do, we'll continue to be pouring billions of dollars down the drain.

The Republicans have campaigned against big government for a generation. But have you noticed? They've run big government for a generation, and they haven't changed a thing. They don't want to fix government; they still want to campaign against it. And that's all.

But, my fellow Democrats, it's time for us to realize that we've got some changing to do too. There is not a program in government for every problem. And if we really want to use government to help people, we've got to make it work again.

Because we are committed in this convention and in this platform to making these changes, we are, as Democrats, in the words that Ross Perot himself spoke today, a revitalized Democratic Party.

I am well aware that all those millions of people who rallied to Ross Perot's cause wanted to be in an army of patriots for change. Tonight I say to them: Join us and together we will revitalize America.

Now, I don't have all the answers. But I do know the old ways don't work. Trickle-down economics has sure failed. And big bureaucracies, both private and public, they fail too.

That's why we need a new approach to government. A government that offers more empowerment and less entitlement, more choices for young people in the schools they attend, in the public schools they attend. And more choices for the elderly and for people with disabilities in the long-term care they receive.

["A New Covenant"]

A government that is leaner, not meaner, a government that expands opportunity, not bureaucracy, a government that understands that jobs must come from growth in a vibrant and vital system of free enterprise. I call this approach a New Covenant, a solemn agreement between the people and their government, based not simply on what each of us can take, but on what all of us must give to our nation.

We offer our people a new choice based on old values. We offer opportunity. We demand responsibility. We will build an American community again. The choice we offer is not conservative or liberal; in many ways it's not even Republican or Democratic. It is different. It is new. And it will work.

It will work because it is rooted in the vision and the values of the American people. Of all the things George Bush has ever said that I disagree with, perhaps the thing that bothers me most is how he derides and degrades the American tradition of seeing and seeking a better future. He mocks it as "the vision thing."

But just remember what the Scripture says: "Where there is no vision, the people perish."

I hope—I hope nobody in this great hall tonight or in our beloved country has to go through tomorrow without a vision. I hope no one ever tries to raise a child without a vision. I hope nobody ever starts a business or plants a crop in the ground without a vision. For where there is no vision the people perish.

One of the reasons we have so many children in so much trouble in so many places in this nation is because they have seen so little opportunity, so little responsibility, so little loving, caring community that they literally cannot imagine the life we are calling them to lead.

And so I say again, where there is no vision, America will perish.

What is the vision of our New Covenant?

An America with millions of new jobs in dozens of new industries moving confidently toward the 21st century. An America that says to entrepreneurs and business people: We will give you more incentives and more opportunity than ever before to develop the skills of your workers and create American jobs and American wealth in the new global economy.

But you must do your part; you must be responsible. American companies must act like American companies again—exporting products, not jobs.

That's what this New Covenant is all about.

An America in which the doors of college are thrown open once again to the sons and daughters of stenographers and steelworkers. We'll say: Everybody can borrow the money to go to college. But you must do your part. You must pay it back—from your paychecks, or better yet, by going back home and serving your communities.

Just think of it, think of it, millions of energetic young men and women serving their country by policing the streets or teaching the children, or caring for the sick, or working with the elderly and people with disabilities, or helping young people stay off drugs and out of gangs, giving us all a sense of new hope and limitless possibilities. That's what this New Covenant is all about.

An America in which health care is a right, not a privilege.

In which we say to all of our people: Your government has the courage—finally—to take on the health-care profiteers and make health care affordable for every family.

But you must do your part: preventive care, prenatal care, child immunization; saving lives, saving money, saving families from heartbreak. That's what the New Covenant is all about.

An America in which middle-class incomes—not middle-class taxes—are going up. An America, yes, in which the wealthiest few—those making over $200,000 a year—are asked to pay their fair share.

An America in which the rich are not soaked—but the middle class is not drowned, either.

Responsibility starts at the top; that's what the New Covenant is all about. An America where we end welfare as we know it. We will say to those on welfare, you will have and you deserve the opportunity through training and education, through child care and medical coverage, to liberate yourself.

But then, when you can, you must work, because welfare should be a second chance, not a way of life. That's what the New Covenant is all about.

An America with the world's strongest defense, ready and willing to use force, when necessary. An America at the forefront of the global effort to preserve and protect our common environment—and promoting global growth. An America that will not coddle tyrants, from Baghdad to Beijing.

An America that champions the cause of freedom and democracy, from Eastern Europe to Southern Africa, and in our own hemisphere, in Haiti and Cuba.

The end of the Cold War permits us to reduce defense spending while still maintaining the strongest defense in the world. But we must plow back every dollar of defense cuts into building American jobs right here at home.

I know well that the world needs a strong America, but we have learned that strength begins at home.

The New Covenant is about more than opportunities and responsibilities for you and your families. It's also about our common community. Tonight every one of you knows deep in your heart that we are too divided. It is time to heal America.

["There Is No Them"]

And so, we must say to every American: Look beyond the stereotypes that blind us. We need each other. All of us, we need each other. We don't have a person to waste. And yet, for too long politicians told the most of us that are doing all right that what's really wrong with America is the rest of us. Them. Them, the minorities. Them, the liberals. Them, the poor. Them, the homeless. Them, the people with disabilities. Them, the gays. We got to where we really "them'ed" ourselves to death. Them and them and them.

But this is America. There is no them. There is only us.

One nation, under God, indivisible, with liberty and justice for all.

That is our Pledge of Allegiance, and that's what the New Covenant is all about.

How do I know we can come together and make change happen? Because I have seen it in my own state. In Arkansas we're working together and we're making progress. No, there is no Arkansas miracle. But there are a lot of miraculous people.

And because of them, our schools are better, our wages are higher, our factories are busier, our water is cleaner, and our budget is balanced. We're moving ahead.

I wish—I wish I could say the same thing about America under the incumbent president. He took the richest country in the world and brought it down.

We took one of the poorest states in America and lifted it up.

I say all, to all those in this campaign season who would criticize Arkansas, come on down.

Especially—especially if you're from Washington—come on down. Sure, you'll see us struggling against some of the problems we haven't solved yet. But you'll also see a lot of great people doing amazing things. And you might even learn a thing or two.

In the end, my fellow Americans, this New Covenant simply asks us all to be Americans again. Old-fashioned Americans for a new time. Opportunity. Responsibility. Community. When we pull together, America will pull ahead. Throughout the whole history of this country, we have seen time and time and time again when we are united, we are unstoppable.

We can seize this moment, make it exciting and energizing and heroic to be an American again.

We can renew our faith in each other and in ourselves. We can restore our sense of unity and community. As the Scripture says, our eyes have not yet seen, nor our ears heard nor our minds imagined what we can build.

["We Can Do It"]

But I can't do this alone. No president can. We must do it together. It won't be easy and it won't be quick. We didn't get into this mess overnight, and we won't get out of it overnight. But we can do it with our commitment, creativity, diversity and drive.

We can do it. We can do it. We can do it.

I want every person in this hall and every person in this land to reach out and join us in a great new adventure to chart a bold new future.

As a teenager I heard John Kennedy's summons to citizenship. And then, as a student at Georgetown, I heard that call clarified by a professor named Carroll Quigley, who said to us that America was the greatest country in the history because our people have always believed in two things, that tomorrow can be better than today, and that every one of us has a personal, moral responsibility to make it so.

That kind of future entered my life the night our daughter Chelsea was born. As I stood in that delivery room, I was overcome with the thought that God had given me a blessing my own father never knew: the chance to hold my child in my arms.

Somewhere at this very moment, another child is born in America. Let it be our cause to give that child a happy home, a healthy family, a hopeful future. Let it be our cause to see that that child has the chance to live to the fullest of her God-given capacities. Let it be our cause to see that child grow up strong and secure, braced by her challenges but never struggling alone; with family and friends and a faith that in America, no one is left out; no one is left behind.

Let it be our cause that when this child is able, she gives something back to her children, her community and her country. Let it be our cause to give her a country that's coming together, not coming apart. A country of boundless hopes and endless dreams; a country that once again lifts its people and inspires the world.

Let that be our cause, our commitment and our New Covenant.

My fellow Americans, I end tonight where it all began for me: I still believe in a place called Hope. God bless you, and God bless America.

DEMOCRATIC PARTY PLATFORM
July 14, 1992

Democrats tried throughout their 1992 convention to send the nation an unmistakable message that they had redefined the party to seize the center. The platform adopted July 14 at the convention in New York City was an integral part of that effort because it straddled traditional Democratic and Republican philosophies. (Democratic National Convention, p. 667)

"We reject both the do-nothing government of the last 12 years and the big government theory that says we can hamstring business and tax and spend our way to prosperity," the platform said. "Instead we offer a third way." The approach emphasized economic growth, the virtues of personal responsibility, the vitality of families, and the need to limit welfare benefits. It called for maintaining law and order in this country and being prepared to use military force when necessary abroad.

Delegates hoped the message would help break a track record that had seen Democrats lose all but one of the previous six presidential races. Tennessee Governor Ned McWherter said the platform would be "a plus in the fall. I believe this country's ready for change, and those of us from all extremes have to come into the middle."

The platform bore the stamp of the Democratic nominee, Arkansas Governor Bill Clinton. He controlled the platform-writing process because he controlled the vast majority of delegates. Many of the platform ideas grew out of the Democratic Leadership Council, which Clinton once chaired. The council was created to separate the party from its reputation as a bedrock of support for old-style New Deal liberalism. And yet the platform still contained much that would be familiar to New Deal

Democrats. It called for more spending on a variety of social programs, higher taxes on the wealthy, civil rights protection for homosexuals (including "an end to Defense Department discrimination"), increases in public works spending, a more liberal unpaid family leave policy, and opposition to private school vouchers.

The document was particularly vague on some issues: It called for "universal access to quality, affordable health care" without specifying how. The only clue was that the reform should be "uniquely American." And it said, "We will relieve the tax burden on middle-class Americans by forcing the rich to pay their fair share," without defining that "fair share."

Setting New Priorities

The platform was written to create new priorities, said John D. Holum, a Washington lawyer and veteran political activist who wrote the original draft. Asked whether the document implicitly criticized some longstanding party views, he replied, "I think it's explicit."

Instead of relying solely on private markets or government programs, he said, the platform focused on "a greater engagement on the whole of a society." Ironically, some of the leading advocates of this more moderate approach were, like Holum, veterans of George McGovern's 1972 presidential campaign. "We fought so many ideological battles that I'm weary of that, and it cost us an opportunity to win a majority of votes," said James Wall, a Clinton delegate who led Illinois's McGovern contingent twenty years ago. "The platform is no place to put in hard-line ideological positions."

In length the platform ran about 10,000 words, twice as long as the 1988 platform, and much shorter than the 1992 Republican platform. (1988 Democratic Party Platform, Historic Documents of 1988, p. 557; 1992 Republican Party Platform, p. 799)

Brown's Delegates Dissatisfied

The platform seemed more palatable to delegates for former Massachusetts Senator Paul E. Tsongas than to supporters of former California Governor Edmund G. "Jerry" Brown, Jr. Brown supporters lacked the delegate strength to bring their objections to the floor. Brown had pressed Clinton to adopt a "humility agenda" of campaign and electoral reforms such as congressional term limits and pay cuts. His delegates expressed their distaste for the product by waving signs that said, "Not!" as adoption neared.

"It's missing solutions for working people in this country," said Sal Roselli, a Brown delegate from San Francisco. Roselli, president of Hospital and Health Care Workers' Union Local 250, was particularly embittered that the platform did not endorse a national health-care plan. "It's like the Republican party and corporate America have taken over the Democratic party."

The Clinton campaign agreed to let Tsongas forces bring four minority planks to a vote. These planks called for an investment tax credit for all businesses, limits on entitlement benefits, a delay on middle-class tax cuts until the federal deficit is under control, and an increase in the gasoline tax to pay for public works projects.

Delegates defeated all four proposals, though Tsongas's supporters generally seemed satisfied. "It's not exactly what we wanted," said Patricia Mitchell of Bastrop, Texas. "But if you look at the economic platform—without saying it, they've adopted a lot of ideas from Tsongas." Patricia Ambinder of Orlando, Florida, agreed: "It's Senator Tsongas's influence."

Calls for Change

The platform sought to distance the party from its image as a defender of bureaucracy. "We vow to make government more decentralized, more flexible and more accountable—to reform public institutions and replace public officials who aren't leading with ones who will."

The platform called for shifting to "a more efficient, flexible and results-oriented government." It borrowed a phrase Clinton had used from the outset, saying there ought to be "a new covenant to repair the damaged bond between the American people and their government."

A striking element was the document's embrace of business and entrepreneurship, and the paucity of references to labor unions. "An expanding, entrepreneurial economy of high-skill, high-wage jobs is the most important family policy, urban policy, labor policy, minority policy and foreign policy America can have," it said. The platform backed an investment tax credit and capital gains reductions for "patient investors in emerging technologies and new business."

Although the platform only generally discussed how to reduce the budget deficit, it specifically named federal programs that ought to be expanded. Among them: education spending, a summer jobs initiative and training programs for inner-city youth, community development programs, public works, enterprise zones, child health and nutrition programs, Head Start, and environmental protection programs. It also proposed a "Domestic GI Bill" to allow all Americans to borrow money for college, as had Clinton. The loan would be paid back as a percentage of the borrower's income or through community service work.

Four years earlier the Democratic party platform on family policy discussed the need for a variety of government programs. In 1992 it highlighted government limits, saying, "governments don't raise children, people do. People who bring children into this world have a responsibility to care for them and give them values, motivation and discipline. Children should not have children."

To preserve the country's national security, the platform backed a survivable nuclear force, shifting some conventional forces from Europe to other potential conflict spots, maintaining the superiority of U.S.

military personnel and technology, and improving intelligence capabilities.

> *Following is the text of the platform adopted July 14, 1992, by delegates to the Democratic National Convention in New York City:*

Two hundred summers ago, this Democratic Party was founded by the man whose burning pen fired the spirit of the American Revolution—who once argued we should overthrow our own government every 20 years to renew our freedom and keep pace with a changing world. In 1992, the party Thomas Jefferson founded invokes his spirit of revolution anew.

Our land reverberates with a battle cry of frustration that emanates from America's very soul—from the families in our bedrock neighborhoods, from the unsung, workaday heroes of the world's greatest democracy and economy. America is on the wrong track. The American people are hurting. The American dream of expanding opportunity has faded. Middle-class families are working hard, playing by the rules, but still falling behind. Poverty has exploded. Our people are torn by divisions.

The last 12 years have been a nightmare of Republican irresponsibility and neglect. America's leadership is indifferent at home and uncertain in the world. Republican mismanagement has disarmed government as an instrument to make our economy work and support the people's most basic values, needs and hopes. The Republicans brought America a false and fragile prosperity based on borrowing, not income, and so will leave behind a mountain of public debt and a backbreaking annual burden in interest. It is wrong to borrow to spend on ourselves, leaving our children to pay our debts.

We hear the anguish and the anger of the American people. We know it is directed not just at the Republican administrations that have had power but at government itself.

Their anger is justified. We can no longer afford business as usual—neither the policies of the last 12 years of tax breaks for the rich, mismanagement, lack of leadership and cuts in services for the middle class and the poor, nor the adoption of new programs and new spending without new thinking.

It is time to listen to the grass roots of America, time to renew the spirit of citizen activism that has always been the touchstone of a free and democratic society.

Therefore we call for *a revolution in government*—to take power away from entrenched bureaucracies and narrow interests in Washington and put it back in the hands of ordinary people. We vow to make government more decentralized, more flexible and more accountable—to reform public institutions and replace public officials who aren't leading with ones who will.

The Revolution of 1992 is about restoring America's economic greatness. We need to rebuild America by abandoning the something-for-nothing ethic of the last decade and putting people first for a change. Only a thriving economy, a strong manufacturing base and growth in creative new enterprise can generate the resources to meet the nation's pressing human and social needs. An expanding, entrepreneurial economy of high-skill, high-wage jobs is the most important family policy, urban policy, labor policy, minority policy and foreign policy America can have.

The Revolution of 1992 is about putting government back on the side of working men and women—to help those who work hard, pay their bills, play by the rules, don't lobby for tax breaks, do their best to give their kids a good education and to keep them away from drugs, who want a safe neighborhood for their families, the security of decent, productive jobs for themselves and a dignified life for their parents.

The Revolution of 1992 is about a radical change in the way government operates—not the Republican proposition that government has no role nor the old notion that there's a program for every problem, but a shift to a more efficient, flexible and results-oriented government that improves services, expands choices, and empowers citizens and communities to change our country from the bottom up. We believe in an activist government, but it must work in a different, more responsive way.

The Revolution of 1992 is about facing up to tough choices. There is no relief for America's frustration in the politics of diversion and evasion, of false choices or of no choices at all. Instead of everyone in Washington blaming one another for inaction, we will act decisively—and ask to be held accountable if we don't.

Above all the Revolution of 1992 is about restoring the basic American values that built this country and will always make it great: personal responsibility, individual liberty, tolerance, faith, family and hard work. We offer the American people not only new ideas, a new course and a new president, but a return to the enduring principles that set our nation apart: the promise of opportunity, the strength of community, the dignity of work and a decent life for senior citizens.

To make this revolution, we seek a *New Covenant* to repair the damaged bond between the American people and their government, that will expand *opportunity,* insist upon greater individual *responsibility* in return, restore *community* and ensure *national security* in a profoundly new era.

We welcome the close scrutiny of the American people, including Americans who may have thought the Democratic Party had forgotten its way, as well as all who know us as the champion for those who have been denied a chance. With this platform we take our case for change to the American people.

Opportunity

Our party's first priority is opportunity—broad-based, non-inflationary economic growth and the opportunity that flows from it. Democrats in

1992 hold nothing more important for America than an economy that offers growth and jobs for all.

President Bush, with no interest in domestic policy, has given America the slowest economic growth, the slowest income growth and the slowest jobs growth since the Great Depression. And the American people know the long Bush recession reflects not just a business cycle, but a long-term slide, so that even in a fragile recovery we're sinking. The ballooning Bush deficits hijacked capital from productive investments. Savings and loan sharks enriched themselves at their country's expense. The stock market tripled, but average incomes stalled, and poverty claimed more of our children.

We reject both the do-nothing government of the last 12 years and the big government theory that says we can hamstring business and tax and spend our way to prosperity. Instead we offer a third way. Just as we have always viewed working men and women as the bedrock of our economy, we honor business as a noble endeavor and vow to create a far better climate for firms and independent contractors of all sizes that empower their workers, revolutionize their workplaces, respect the environment, and serve their communities well.

We believe in free enterprise and the power of market forces. But economic growth will not come without a national economic strategy to invest in people. For 12 years our country has had no economic vision, leadership or strategy. It is time to put our people and our country first.

Investing in America

The only way to lay the foundation for renewed American prosperity is to spur both public and private investment. We must strive to close both the budget deficit and the investment gap. Our major competitors invest far more than we do in roads, bridges and the information networks and technologies of the future. We will rebuild America by investing more in transportation, environmental technologies, defense conversion and a national information network.

To begin making our economy grow, the president and Congress should agree that savings from defense must be reinvested productively at home, including research, education and training, and other productive investments. This will sharply increase the meager 9 percent of the national budget now devoted to the future. We will create a "future budget" for investments that make us richer, to be kept separate from those parts of the budget that pay for the past and present. For the private sector, instead of a sweeping capital gains windfall to the wealthy and those who speculate, we will create an investment tax credit and a capital gains reduction for patient investors in emerging technologies and new business.

Support for Innovation

We will take back the advantage now ceded to Japan and Germany, which invest in new technologies at higher rates than the U.S. and have the growth to show for it. We will make the R&D [research and development] tax credit permanent, double basic research in the key technologies for our future and create a civilian research agency to fast-forward their development.

The Deficit

Addressing the deficit requires fair and shared sacrifice of all Americans for the common good. In 12 Republican years a national debt that took 200 years to accumulate has been *quadrupled.* Rising interest on that debt now swallows one tax dollar in seven. In place of the Republican supply side disaster, the Democratic investment, economic conversion and growth strategy will generate more revenues from a growing economy. We must also tackle spending by putting everything on the table; eliminate non-productive programs; achieve defense savings; reform entitlement programs to control soaring health-care costs; cut federal administrative costs by 3 percent annually for four years; limit increases in the "present budget" to the rate of growth in the average American's paycheck; apply a strict "pay as you go" rule to new non-investment spending; and make the rich pay their fair share in taxes. These choices will be made while protecting senior citizens and without further victimizing the poor. This deficit-reduction effort will encourage private savings, eliminate the budget deficit over time and permit fiscal policies that can restore America's economic health.

Defense Conversion

Our economy needs both the people and the funds released from defense at the Cold War's end. We will help the stalwarts of that struggle—the men and women who served in our armed forces and who work in our defense industries—make the most of a new era. We will provide early notice of program changes to give communities, business and workers enough time to plan. We will honor and support our veterans. Departing military personnel, defense workers and defense support personnel will have access to job retraining, continuing education, placement and relocation assistance, early retirement benefits for military personnel, and incentives to enter teaching, law enforcement and other vital civilian fields. Redirected national laboratories and a new civilian research agency will put defense scientists, engineers and technicians to work at critical civilian technologies. Small business defense firms will have technical assistance and transition grants and loans to help convert to civilian markets, and defense-dependent communities will have similar aid in planning and implementing conversion. We will strongly support our civilian space program, particularly environmental missions.

The Cities

Only a robust economy will revitalize our cities. It is in all Americans' interest that the cities once again be places where hard-working families can put down roots and find good jobs, quality health care, affordable housing and decent schools. Democrats will create a new partnership to rebuild America's cities after 12 years of Republican neglect. This partnership will include consideration of the seven economic growth initiatives set forth by our nation's mayors. We will create jobs by investing significant resources to put people back to work, beginning with a summer jobs initiative and training programs for inner-city youth. We support a stronger community development program and targeted fiscal assistance to cities that need it most. A national public works investment and infrastructure program will provide jobs and strengthen our cities, suburbs, rural communities and country. We will encourage the flow of investment to inner city development and housing through targeted enterprise zones and incentives for private and public pension funds to invest in urban and rural projects. While cracking down on redlining and housing discrimination, we also support and will enforce a revitalized Community Reinvestment Act that challenges banks to lend to entrepreneurs and development projects; a national network of Community Development Banks to invest in urban and rural small businesses; and microenterprise lending for poor people seeking self-employment as an alternative to welfare.

Agriculture and the Rural Community

All Americans, producers and consumers alike, benefit when our food and fiber are produced by hundreds of thousands of family farmers receiving a fair price for their products. The abundance of our nation's food and fiber system should not be taken for granted. The revolution that lifted America to the forefront of world agriculture was achieved through a unique partnership between public and private interests. The inattention and hostility that has characterized Republican food, agriculture and rural development policies of the past 12 years has caused a crisis in rural America. The cost of Republican farm policy has been staggering, and its total failure is demonstrated by the record number of rural bankruptcies.

A sufficient and sustainable agricultural economy can be achieved through fiscally responsible programs. It is time to re-establish the private/public partnership to ensure that family farmers get a fair return for their labor and investment, that consumers receive safe and nutritious foods, and that needed investments are made in basic research, education, rural business development, market development and infrastructure to sustain rural communities.

Workers' Rights

Our workplaces must be revolutionized to make them more flexible and productive. We will reform the job safety laws to empower workers with greater rights and to hold employers accountable for dangers on the job. We will act against sexual harassment in the workplace. We will honor the work ethic—by expanding the earned-income tax credit so no one with children at home who works full time is still in poverty, by fighting on the side of family farmers to ensure they get a fair price for their hard work and working to sustain rural communities; by making work more valuable than welfare; and by supporting the right of workers to organize and bargain collectively without fear of intimidation or permanent replacement during labor disputes.

Lifelong Learning

A competitive American economy requires the global market's best-educated, best-trained, most flexible work force. It's not enough to spend more on our schools; we must insist on results. We oppose the Bush administration's efforts to bankrupt the public school system—the bedrock of democracy—through private school vouchers. To help children reach school ready to learn, we will expand child health and nutrition programs and extend Head Start to all eligible children, and guarantee all children access to quality, affordable child care. We deplore the savage inequalities among public schools across the land and believe every child deserves an equal chance to a world-class education. Reallocating resources toward this goal must be a priority. We support education reforms such as site-based decision-making and public school choice, with strong protections against discrimination. We support the goal of a 90 percent graduation rate and programs to end dropouts. We will invest in educational technology and establish world-class standards in math, science and other core subjects, and support effective tests of progress to meet them. In areas where there are no registered apprenticeship programs, we will adopt a national apprentice-ship-style program to ease the transition from school to work for non-college-bound students, so they can acquire skills that lead to high-wage jobs. In the new economy, opportunity will depend on lifelong learning. We will support the goal of literacy for all Americans. We will ask firms to invest in the training of all workers, not just corporate management.

A Domestic GI Bill

Over the past 12 years, skyrocketing costs and declining middle-class incomes have placed higher education out of reach for millions of Americans. It is time to revolutionize the way student loan programs are run. We will make college affordable to *all* students who are qualified to attend, *regardless of family income*. A Domestic GI Bill will enable all Americans to borrow money for college, so long as they are willing to pay it back as a percentage of their income over time or through national service address-ing unmet community needs.

Affordable Health Care

All Americans should have universal access to quality, affordable health care—not as a privilege but as a right. That requires tough controls on health costs, which are rising at two to three times the rate of inflation, terrorizing American families and businesses and depriving millions of the care they need. We will enact a uniquely American reform of the health-care system to control costs and make health care affordable; ensure quality and choice of health-care providers; cover all Americans regardless of pre-existing conditions; squeeze out waste, bureaucracy and abuse; improve primary and preventive care including child immunization and prevention of diseases like tuberculosis now becoming rampant in our cities; provide expanded education on the relationship between diet and health; expand access to mental health treatment services; provide a safety net through support of public hospitals; provide for the full range of reproductive choice—education, counseling, access to contraceptives and the right to a safe, legal abortion; expand medical research; and provide more long-term care, including home health care. We will make ending the epidemic in breast cancer a major priority, and expand reproductive health services and other special health needs of women. We must be united in declaring war on AIDS and HIV disease, implement the recommendations of the National Commission on AIDS and fully fund the Ryan White Care Act; provide targeted and honest prevention campaigns; combat HIV-related discrimination; make drug treatment available for all addicts who seek it; guarantee access to quality care; expand clinical trials for treatments and vaccines; and speed up the FDA [Food and Drug Administration] drug approval process.

Fairness

Growth and equity work in tandem. People should share in society's common costs according to their ability to pay. In the last decade, mounting payroll and other taxes have fallen disproportionately on the middle class. We will relieve the tax burden on middle-class Americans by forcing the rich to pay their fair share. We will provide long-overdue tax relief to families with children. To broaden opportunity, we will support fair lending practices.

Energy Efficiency and Sustainable Development

We reject the Republican myth that energy efficiency and environmental protection are enemies of economic growth. We will make our economy more efficient, using less energy, reducing our dependence on foreign oil, and producing less solid and toxic waste. We will adopt a coordinated transportation policy, with a strong commitment to mass transit; encourage efficient alternative-fueled vehicles; increase our reliance on clean natural gas; promote clean coal technology; invest in R&D [research and development] on renewable energy sources; strengthen efforts to prevent air and water pollution; support incentives for domestic oil and gas operations; and push for revenue-neutral incentives that reward conservation, prevent pollution and encourage recycling.

Civil and Equal Rights

We don't have an American to waste. Democrats will continue to lead the fight to ensure that no Americans suffer discrimination or deprivation of rights on the basis of race, gender, language, national origin, religion, age, disability, sexual orientation or other characteristics irrelevant to ability. We support ratification of the Equal Rights Amendment, affirmative action, stronger protection of voting rights for racial and ethnic minorities, including language access to voting, and continued resistance to discriminatory English-only pressure groups. We will reverse the Bush administration's assault on civil rights enforcement, and instead work to rebuild and vigorously use machinery for civil rights enforcement; support comparable remedies for women; aggressively prosecute hate crimes; strengthen legal services for the poor; deal with other nations in a way that Americans of any origin do not become scapegoats or victims of foreign policy disputes; provide civil rights protection for gay men and lesbians and an end to Defense Department discrimination; respect Native American culture and our treaty commitments; require the United States government to recognize its trustee obligations to the inhabitants of Hawaii generally and to Native Hawaiians in particular; and fully enforce the Americans with Disability Act to enable people with disabilities to achieve independence and function at their highest possible level.

Commonwealth and Territories

We recognize the existing status of the Commonwealth of Puerto Rico and the strong economic relationship between the people of Puerto Rico and the United States. We pledge to support the right of the people of the Commonwealth of Puerto Rico to choose freely, and in concert with the U.S. Congress their relationship with the United States, either as an enhanced commonwealth, a state or an independent nation.

We pledge to the people of American Samoa, Guam, the Northern Mariana Islands and the Virgin Islands just and fair treatment under federal policies, assisting their economic and social development. We respect their right and that of the people of Palau to decide freely their future relationship with the United States and to be consulted on issues and policies that directly affect them.

Responsibility

Sixty years ago, Franklin Roosevelt gave hope to a nation mired in the Great Depression. While government should promise every American the opportunity to get ahead, it was the people's responsibility, he said, to make the most of that opportunity: "Faith in America demands that we recognize the new terms of the old social contract. In the strength of great hope we must all shoulder our common load."

For 12 years, the Republicans have expected too little of our public institutions and placed too little faith in our people. We offer a new social contract based neither on callous, do-nothing Republican neglect nor on an outdated faith in programs as the solution to every problem. We favor a third way beyond the old approaches—to put government back on the side of citizens who play by the rules. We believe that by what it says and how it conducts its business, government must once again make responsibility an instrument of national purpose. Our future as a nation depends upon the daily assumption of personal responsibility by millions of Americans from all walks of life—for the religious faith they follow, the ethics they practice, the values they instill, the pride they take in their work.

Strengthening the Family

Governments don't raise children, people do. People who bring children into this world have a responsibility to care for them and give them values, motivation and discipline. Children should not have children. We need a national crackdown on deadbeat parents, an effective system of child-support enforcement nationwide and a systematic effort to establish paternity for every child. We must also make it easier for parents to build strong families through pay equity. Family and medical leave will ensure that workers don't have to choose between family and work. We support a family preservation program to reduce child and spousal abuse by providing preventive services and foster care to families in crisis. We favor ensuring quality and affordable child-care opportunities for working parents, and a fair and healthy start for every child, including essential prenatal and well-baby care. We support the needs of our senior citizens for productive and healthy lives, including hunger prevention, income adequacy, transportation access and abuse prevention.

Welfare Reform

Welfare should be a second chance, not a way of life. We want to break the cycle of welfare by adhering to two simple principles: No one who is able to work can stay on welfare forever, and no one who works should live in poverty. We will continue to help those who cannot help themselves. We will offer people on welfare a new social contract. We'll invest in education and job training, and provide the child care and health care they need to go to work and achieve long-term self-sufficiency. We will give them the help they need to make the transition from welfare to work, and require people who can work to go to work within two years in available jobs either in the private sector or in community service to meet unmet needs. That will restore the covenant that welfare was meant to be: a promise of temporary help for people who have fallen on hard times.

Choice

Democrats stand behind the right of every woman to choose, consistent with *Roe v. Wade*, regardless of ability to pay, and support a national law to protect that right. It is a fundamental constitutional liberty that individual Americans—not government—can best take responsibility for making the most difficult and intensely personal decisions regarding reproduction. The goal of our nation must be to make abortion less necessary, not more difficult or more dangerous. We pledge to support contraceptive research, family planning, comprehensive family life education, and policies that support healthy childbearing and enable parents to care most effectively for their children.

Making Schools Work

Education is a cooperative enterprise that can only succeed if everyone accepts and exercises personal responsibility. Students must stay in school and do their best; parents must get involved in their children's education; teachers must attain, maintain and demonstrate classroom competency; school administrators must enforce discipline and high standards of educational attainment; governments must end the inequalities that create educational ghettos among school districts and provide equal educational opportunity for all, and ensure that teachers' pay measures up to their decisive role in children's lives; and the American people should recognize education as the core of our economy, democracy and society.

Labor-Management Responsibilities

The private sector is the engine of our economy and the main source of national wealth. But it is not enough for those in the private sector just to make as much money as they can. The most irresponsible people in all of the 1980s were those at the top of the ladder, the inside traders, quick-buck artists and S&L [savings and loans] kingpins who looked out for themselves and not for the country. America's corporate leaders have a responsibility to invest in their country. CEOs [chief executive officers], who pay themselves 100 times what they pay the average worker, shouldn't get big raises unrelated to performance. If a company wants to overpay its executives and underinvest in the future or transfer jobs overseas, it shouldn't get special treatment and tax breaks from the Treasury. Managers must work with employees to make the workplace safer, more satisfying and more efficient.

Workers must also accept added responsibilities in the new economy. In return for an increased voice and a greater stake in the success of their enterprises, workers should be prepared to join in cooperative efforts to increase productivity, flexibility and quality. Government's neutrality between labor and management cannot mean neutrality about the collective bargaining process, which has been purposely crippled by Republican administrations. Our economic growth depends on processes, including collective bargaining, that permit labor and management to work together on their common interests, even as they work out their conflicts.

Responsibility for the Environment

For ourselves and future generations, we must protect our environment. We will protect our old-growth forests, preserve critical habitats, provide a genuine "no net loss" policy on wetlands, conserve the critical resources of soil, water and air, oppose new offshore oil drilling and mineral exploration and production in our nation's many environmentally critical areas, and address ocean pollution by reducing oil and toxic waste spills at sea. We believe America's youth can serve their country well through a civilian conservation corps. To protect the public health, we will clean up the environmental horrors at federal facilities, insist that private polluters clean up their toxic and hazardous wastes, and vigorously prosecute environmental criminals. We will oppose Republican efforts to gut the Clean Air Act in the guise of competitiveness. We will reduce the volume of solid waste and encourage the use of recycled materials while discouraging excess packaging. To avoid the mistakes of the past, we will actively support energy efficiency, recycling and pollution-prevention strategies.

Responsible Government

Democrats in 1992 intend to lead a revolution in government, challenging it to act responsibly and be accountable, starting with the hardest and most urgent problems of the deficit and economic growth. Rather than throwing money at obsolete programs, we will eliminate unnecessary layers of management, cut administrative costs, give people more choices in the service they get and empower them to make those choices. To foster greater responsibility in government at every level, we support giving greater flexibility to our cities, counties and states in achieving federal mandates and carrying out existing programs.

Responsible Officials

All branches of government must live by the laws the rest of us obey, determine their pay in an open manner that builds public trust and eliminate special privileges. People in public office need to be accessible to the people they represent. It's time to reform the campaign finance system, to get big money out of our politics and let the people back in. We must limit overall campaign spending and limit the disproportionate and excessive role of PACs [political action committees]. We need new voter registration laws that expand the electorate, such as universal same-day registration, along with full political rights and protections for public employees and new regulations to ensure that the airwaves truly help citizens make informed choices among candidates and policies. And we need fair political representation for all sectors of our country—including the District of Columbia, which deserves and must get statehood status.

Restoring Community

The success of democracy in America depends substantially on the strength of our community institutions: families and neighborhoods, public schools, religious institutions, charitable organizations, civic groups and other voluntary associations. In these social networks, the values and character of our citizens are formed as we learn the habits and skills of self-government and acquire an understanding of our common rights and responsibilities as citizens.

Twelve years of Republican rule have undermined the spirit of mutual dependence and obligation that binds us together. Republican leaders have urged Americans to turn inward, to pursue private interests without regard to public responsibilities. By playing racial, ethnic and gender-based politics, they have divided us against each other, created an atmosphere of blame, denial and fear, and undone the hard-fought battles for equality and fairness.

Our communities form a vital "third sector" that lies between government and the marketplace. The wisdom, energy and resources required to solve our problems are not concentrated in Washington but can be found throughout our communities, including America's nonprofit sector, which has grown rapidly over the last decade. Government's best role is to enable people and communities to solve their own problems.

America's special genius has been to forge a community of shared values from people of remarkable and diverse backgrounds. As the party of inclusion, we take special pride in our country's emergence as the world's largest and most successful multiethnic, multiracial republic. We condemn anti-Semitism, racism, homophobia, bigotry and negative stereotyping of all kinds. We must help all Americans understand the diversity of our cultural heritage. But it is also essential that we preserve and pass on to our children the common elements that hold this mosaic together as we work to make our country a land of freedom and opportunity for all.

Both Republican neglect and traditional spending programs have proven unequal to these challenges. Democrats will pursue a new course that stresses work, family and individual responsibility, and that empowers Americans to liberate themselves from poverty and dependence. We pledge to bolster the institutions of civil society and place a new emphasis on civic enterprises that seek solutions to our nation's problems. Through common, cooperative efforts we can rebuild our communities and transform our nation.

Combating Crime and Drugs

Crime is a relentless danger to our communities. Over the last decade, crime has swept through our country at an alarming rate. During the 1980s, more than 200,000 Americans were murdered, four times the number who died in Vietnam. Violent crimes rose by more than 16 percent since 1988 and nearly doubled since 1975. In our country today, a murder is committed every 25 minutes, a rape every six minutes, a burglary every 10 seconds. The pervasive fear of crime disfigures our public life and diminishes our freedom.

None suffer more than the poor: An explosive mixture of blighted prospects, drugs and exotic weaponry has turned many of our inner-city communities into combat zones. As a result, crime is not only a symptom but also a major cause of the worsening poverty and demoralization that afflicts inner city communities.

To empower America's communities, Democrats pledge to restore government as upholder of basic law and order for crime-ravaged communities. The simplest and most direct way to restore order in our cities is to put more police on the streets. America's police are locked in an unequal struggle with crime: Since 1951 the ratio of police officers to reported crimes has reversed, from 3-to-1 to 1-to-3. We will create a Police Corps, in which participants will receive college aid in return for several years of service after graduation in a state or local police department. As we shift people and resources from defense to the civilian economy, we will create new jobs in law enforcement for those leaving the military.

We will expand drug counseling and treatment for those who need it, intensify efforts to educate our children at the earliest ages to the dangers of drug and alcohol abuse, and curb demand from the street corner to the penthouse suite, so that the United States, with 5 percent of the world's population, no longer consumes 50 percent of the world's illegal drugs.

Community Policing

Neighborhoods and police should be partners in the war on crime. Democrats support more community policing, which uses foot patrols and storefront offices to make police officers visible fixtures in urban neighborhoods. We will combat street violence and emphasize building trust and solving the problems that breed crime.

Firearms

It is time to shut down the weapons bazaars in our cities. We support a reasonable waiting period to permit background checks for purchases of handguns, as well as assault weapons controls to ban the possession, sale, importation and manufacture of the most deadly assault weapons. We do not support efforts to restrict weapons used for legitimate hunting and sporting purposes. We will work for swift and certain punishment of all people who violate the country's gun laws and for stronger sentences for criminals who use guns. We will also seek to shut down the black market for guns and impose severe penalties on people who sell guns to children.

Pursuing All Crime Aggressively

In contrast to the Republican policy of leniency toward white-collar crime—which breeds cynicism in poor communities about the impartiality of our justice system—Democrats will redouble efforts to ferret out and punish those who betray the public trust, rig financial markets, misuse their depositors' money or swindle their customers.

Further Initiatives

Democrats also favor innovative sentencing and punishment options, including community service and boot camps for first-time offenders; tougher penalties for rapists; victim-impact statements and restitution to ensure that crime victims will not be lost in the complexities of the criminal justice system; and initiatives to make our schools safe, including alternative schools for disruptive children.

Empowering the Poor and Expanding the Middle Class

We must further the new direction set in the Family Support Act of 1988, away from subsistence and dependence and toward work, family and personal initiative and responsibility. We advocate slower phasing out of Medicaid and other benefits to encourage work; special savings accounts to help low-income families build assets; fair lending; an indexed minimum wage; an expanded Job Corps; and an end to welfare rules that encourage family breakup and penalize individual initiative, such as the $1,000 limit on personal savings.

Immigration

Our nation of immigrants has been invigorated repeatedly as new people, ideas and ways of life have become part of the American tapestry. Democrats support immigration policies that promote fairness, non-discrimination and family reunification and that reflect our constitutional freedoms of speech, association and travel.

Housing

Safe, secure housing is essential to the institutions of community and family. We support homeownership for working families and will honor that commitment through policies to encourage affordable mortgage credit. We must also confront homelessness by renovating, preserving and expanding the stock of affordable low-income housing. We support tenant management and ownership, so public housing residents can manage their own affairs and acquire property worth protecting.

National Service

We will create new opportunities for citizens to serve each other, their communities and their country. By mobilizing hundreds of thousands of volunteers, national service will enhance the role of ordinary citizens in solving unresolved community problems.

The Arts

We believe in public support for the arts, including a National Endowment for the Arts that is free from political manipulation and firmly rooted in the First Amendment's freedom of expression guarantee.

Preserving Our National Security

During the past four years, we have seen the corrosive effect of foreign policies that are rooted in the past, divorced from our values, fearful of change and unable to meet its challenges. Under President Bush, crises have been managed rather than prevented; dictators like Saddam Hussein have been wooed rather than deterred; aggression by the Serbian regime against its neighbors in what was Yugoslavia has been met by American timidity rather than toughness; human rights abusers have been rewarded, not challenged; the environment has been neglected, not protected; and America's competitive edge in the global economy has been dulled, not honed. It is time for new American leadership that can meet the challenges of a changing world.

At the end of World War II, American strength had defeated tyranny and American ingenuity had overcome the Depression. Under President [Harry S] Truman, the United States led the world into a new era, redefining global security with bold approaches to tough challenges: containing communism with the NATO alliance and in Korea; building the peace through organizations such as the United Nations; and advancing global economic security through new multilateral institutions.

Nearly a half century later, we stand at another pivotal point in history. The collapse of communism does not mean the end of danger of threats to our interests. But it does pose an unprecedented opportunity to make our future more secure and prosperous. Once again, we must define a compelling vision for global leadership at the dawn of a new era.

Restructuring Our Military Forces

We have not seen the end of violence, aggression and the conflicts that can threaten American interests and our hopes for a more peaceful world. What the United States needs is not the Bush administration's Cold War thinking on a smaller scale but a comprehensive restructuring of the American military enterprise to meet the threats that remain.

Military Strength

America is the world's strongest military power, and we must remain so. A post-Cold War restructuring of American forces will produce substantial savings beyond those promised by the Bush administration, but that restructuring must be achieved without undermining our ability to meet future threats to our security. A military structure for the 1990s and beyond must be built on four pillars: *First,* a survivable nuclear force to deter any conceivable threat as we reduce our nuclear arsenals through arms control negotiations and other reciprocal action. *Second,* conventional forces shifted toward projecting power wherever our vital national interests are threatened. This means reducing the size of our forces in Europe while meeting our obligations to NATO and strengthening our rapid deployment capabilities to deal with new threats to our security posed by renegade dictators, terrorists, international drug traffickers and the local armed conflicts that can threaten the peace of entire regions. *Third,* maintenance of the two qualities that make America's military the best in the world—the superiority of our military personnel and of our technology. These qualities are vital to shortening any conflict and saving American lives. *Fourth,* intelligence capabilities redirected to develop far more sophisticated, timely and accurate analyses of the economic and political conditions that can fuel new conflicts.

Use of Force

The United States must be prepared to use military force decisively when necessary to defend our vital interests. The burdens of collective security in a new era must be shared fairly, and we should encourage multilateral peacekeeping through the United Nations and other international efforts.

Preventing and Containing Conflict

American policy must be focused on averting military threats as well as meeting them. To halt the spread of nuclear and other weapons of mass destruction, we must lead a renewed international effort to get tough with companies that peddle nuclear and chemical warfare technologies, strengthen the International Atomic Energy Agency and enforce strong sanctions against governments that violate international restraints. A Comprehensive Test Ban would strengthen our ability to stop the spread of nuclear weapons to other countries, which may be our greatest future security threat. We must press for strong international limits on the dangerous and wasteful flow of conventional arms to troubled regions. A U.S. troop presence should be maintained in Korea as long as North Korea presents a threat to South Korea.

Restoring America's Economic Leadership

The United States cannot be strong abroad if it is weak at home. Restoring America's global economic leadership must become a central element of our national security policies. The strength of nations, once defined in military terms, now is measured also by the skills of their workers, the imagination of their managers and the power of their technologies.

Either we develop and pursue a national plan for restoring our economy through a partnership of government, labor and business, or we slip behind the nations that are competing with us and growing. At stake are American jobs, our standard of living and the quality of life for ourselves and our children.

Economic strength—indeed our national security—is grounded on a healthy domestic economy. But we cannot be strong at home unless we are part of a vibrant and expanding global economy that recognizes human rights and seeks to improve the living standards of all the world's people. This is vital to achieving good quality, high-paying jobs for Americans.

Trade

Our government must work to expand trade while insisting that the conduct of world trade is fair. It must fight to uphold American interests—promoting exports, expanding trade in agricultural and other products, opening markets in major product and service sectors with our principal competitors, achieving reciprocal access. This should include renewed authority to use America's trading leverage against the most serious problems. The U.S. government also must firmly enforce U.S. laws against unfair trade.

Trade Agreements

Multilateral trade agreements can advance our economic interests by expanding the global economy. Whether negotiating the North American Free Trade Area (NAFTA) [agreement] or completing the GATT [General Agreement on Tariffs and Trade] negotiations, our government must assure that our legitimate concerns about environmental, health and safety, and labor standards are included. Those American workers whose jobs are affected must have the benefit of effective adjustment assistance.

Promoting Democracy

Brave men and women—like the hero who stood in front of a tank in Beijing and the leader who stood on a tank in Moscow—are putting their lives on the line for democracy around the world. But as the tide of democracy rose in the former Soviet Union and in China, in the Baltics and South Africa, only reluctantly did this administration abandon the status quo and embrace the fight for freedom.

Support for democracy serves our ideals *and* our interests. A more democratic world is a world that is more peaceful and more stable. An American foreign policy of engagement for democracy must effectively address:

Emerging Democracies

Helping to lead an international effort to assist the emerging—and still fragile—democracies in Eastern Europe and the former Soviet Union build democratic institutions in free market settings, demilitarize their societies and integrate their economies into the world trading system. Unlike the Bush administration, which waited too long to recognize the new democratic governments in the Baltic countries and the nations of the former Soviet Union, we must act decisively with our European allies to support freedom, diminish ethnic tensions, and oppose aggression in the former communist countries, such as Bosnia-Herzegovina, which are struggling to make the transition from communism to democracy. As change sweeps through the Balkans, the United States must be sensitive to the concerns of Greece regarding the use of the name Macedonia. And in the post-Cold War era, our foreign assistance programs in Africa, the Caribbean, Latin America and elsewhere should be targeted at helping democracies rather than tyrants.

Democracy Corps

Promoting democratic institutions by creating a Democracy Corps to send American volunteers to countries that seek legal, financial and political expertise to build democratic institutions, and support groups like the National Endowment for Democracy and Asia Foundation and others.

China Trade Terms

Conditioning of favorable trade terms for China on respect for human rights in China and Tibet, greater market access for U.S. goods, and responsible conduct on weapons proliferation.

South Africa

Maintenance of state and local sanctions against South Africa in support of an investment code of conduct, existing limits on deductibility of taxes paid to South Africa and diplomatic pressure until there is an irreversible, full and fair accommodation with the black majority to create a democratic government with full rights for all its citizens. We deplore the continuing violence, especially by Boipatong Township, and are concerned about the collapse of the negotiations. The U.S. government should consider re-imposing federal sanctions. The Democratic Party supports the creation of a South African/American Enterprise Fund that will provide a new interim government with the use of public and private funds to help in the development of democracy in South Africa.

Middle East Peace

Support for the peace process now under way in the Middle East, rooted in the tradition of the Camp David accords. Direct negotiations between Israel, her Arab neighbors and Palestinians, with no imposed solutions, are the only way to achieve enduring security for Israel and full peace for all parties in the region. The end of the Cold War does not alter America's deep interest in our longstanding special relationship with Israel, based on shared values, a mutual commitment to democracy and a strategic alliance that benefits both nations. The United States must act effectively as an honest broker in the peace process. It must not, as has been the case with this administration, encourage one side to believe that it will deliver unilateral concessions from the other. Jerusalem is the capital of the state of Israel and should remain an undivided city accessible to people of all faiths.

Human Rights

Standing everywhere for the rights of individuals and respect for ethnic minorities against the repressive acts of governments—against torture, political imprisonment and all attacks on civilized standards of human freedom. This is a proud tradition of the Democratic Party, which has stood for freedom in South Africa and continues to resist oppression in Cuba. Our nation should once again promote the principle of sanctuary for politically oppressed people everywhere, be they Haitian refugees, Soviet Jews seeking U.S. help in their successful absorption into Israeli society or Vietnamese fleeing communism. Forcible return of anyone fleeing political repression is a betrayal of American values.

Human Needs

Support for the struggle against poverty and disease in the developing world, including the heartbreaking famine in Africa. We must not replace the East-West conflict with one between North and South, a growing divide between the industrialized and developing world. Our development programs must be re-examined and restructured to assure that their benefits truly help those most in need to help themselves. At stake are the lives of millions of human beings who live in hunger, uprooted from their homes, too often without hope. The United States should work to establish a specific plan and timetable for the elimination of world hunger.

Cyprus

A renewed commitment to achieve a Cyprus settlement pursuant to the United Nations resolutions. This goal must now be restored to the diplomatic agenda of the United States.

Northern Ireland

In light of America's historic ties to the people of Great Britain and Ireland, and consistent with our country's commitment to peace, democracy and human rights around the world, a more active United States role in promoting peace and political dialogue, to bring an end to the violence and achieve a negotiated solution in Northern Ireland.

Preserving the Global Environment

As the threat of nuclear holocaust recedes, the future of the Earth is challenged by gathering environmental crises. As governments around the world have sought the path to concerted action, the Bush administration—despite its alleged foreign policy expertise—has been more of an obstacle to progress than a leader for change, practicing isolationism on an issue that affects us all. Democrats know we must act now to save the health of the Earth and the health of our children for generations to come.

Addressing Global Warming

The United States must become a leader, not an impediment, in the fight against global warming. We should join our European allies in agreeing to limit carbon dioxide emissions to 1990 levels by the year 2000.

Ozone Depletion

The United States must be a world leader in finding replacements for CFCs [chlorofluorocarbons] and other ozone-depleting substances.

Biodiversity

We must work actively to protect the planet's biodiversity and preserve its forests. At the Rio Earth Summit, the Bush administration's failure to negotiate a biodiversity treaty it could sign was an abdication of international leadership.

Developing Nations

We must fashion imaginative ways of engaging governments and business in the effort to encourage developing nations to preserve their environmental heritage.

Population Growth

Explosive population growth must be controlled by working closely with other industrialized and developing nations and private organizations to fund greater family-planning efforts.

* * *

As a nation and as a people, we have entered into a new era. The Republican president and his advisers are rooted in Cold War precepts and cannot think or act anew. Through almost a half century of sacrifice, constancy and strength, the American people advanced democracy's triumph in the Cold War. Only new leadership that restores our nation's greatness at home can successfully draw upon these same strengths of the American people to lead the world into a new era of peace and freedom.

In recent years we have seen brave people abroad face down tanks, defy coups and risk exodus by boat on the high seas for a chance at freedom and the kind of opportunities we call the American dream. It is time for Americans to fight against the decline of those same opportunities here at home.

Americans know that, in the end, we will all rise or fall together. To make our society one again, Democrats will restore America's founding values of family, community and common purpose.

We believe in the American people. We will challenge all Americans to give something back to their country. And they will be enriched in return, for when individuals assume responsibility, they acquire dignity. When people go to work, they rediscover a pride that was lost. When absent parents pay child support, they restore a connection they and their children need. When students work harder, they discover they can learn as well as any on Earth. When corporate managers put their workers and long-term success ahead of short-term gain, their companies do well and so do they. When the leaders we elect assume responsibility for America's problems, we will do what is right to move America forward together.

CONVENTION SPEECHES BY WOMEN INFECTED WITH HIV

July 14 and August 19, 1992

Amidst the hoopla of the Democratic and Republican national conventions, two women infected with the virus that causes AIDS brought tears to the eyes of delegates with emotional speeches in which they pleaded for attention to the disease and compassion for its victims.

Elizabeth Glaser, 44, wife of actor Paul Michael Glaser, spoke July 14 at the Democratic National Convention in New York City. She contracted the HIV virus through a blood transfusion. Her seven-year-old daughter died from AIDS in 1988, and her son was infected in utero. Mary D. Fisher, 44, the daughter of a major GOP contributor and the mother of two young sons, spoke August 19 at the Republican National Convention in Houston. She contracted the HIV virus from her former husband.

Ironically, Glaser and Fisher were both white, upper class, heterosexual women, and did not fit the stereotype of those suffering from AIDS. Among many Americans, AIDS was still thought to be a disease affecting gay men, minorities, and drug users. As atypical AIDS patients, Glaser and Fisher joined Ryan White, the Indiana teenager who died of AIDS in 1990, and Kimberly Bergalis, the Florida woman who contracted AIDS from her dentist, in breaking through some of the stereotypes surrounding the disease.

"The messenger is as important as the message," Jim Graham, executive director of the Whitman-Walker Clinic in Washington, D.C., told the Washington Post. *"When a person comes forward whom everybody can identify with, it suddenly humanizes the whole process. The face we have of AIDS is the face of stereotypes. When we see Mary Fisher or Elizabeth*

709

Glaser, we have an understanding of what a leveler AIDS is."

Others agreed that the appearances by Glaser and Fisher helped break through the bigotry that often surrounded the disease. "People will not listen to a gay man," said June E. Osborn, chairperson of the National Commission on AIDS. "It's up to others to be the messengers."

In their speeches, both women focused primarily on building AIDS awareness and seeking compassion for AIDS victims. However, in the context of the political conventions it was inevitable that they would also make partisan comments. At the Democratic convention, Glaser criticized the administration of President George Bush for doing too little to fight AIDS. "When anyone tells President Bush that the battle against AIDS is seriously underfunded, he juggles the numbers to mislead the public into thinking we're spending twice as much as we really are," Glaser said. "While they play games with numbers, people are dying."

At the Republican convention, Fisher praised Bush's leadership on AIDS and said that many of his actions had "gone unheralded." However, she also asked the delegates and those watching the convention on television "to recognize that AIDS virus is not a political creature. It does not care whether you are Democrat or Republican. It does not ask whether you are black or a white, male or female, gay or straight, young or old."

Fisher also emphasized that all people with AIDS were alike, no matter what their skin color or lifestyle. "Though I am white, and a mother, I am one with a black infant struggling with tubes in a Philadelphia hospital," she said. "Though I am female, and contracted this disease in marriage, I am one with the lonely gay man sheltering a flickering candle from the cold wind of his family's rejection."

Fisher's comments came at the convention of a party that many observers charged was hostile to gays and minorities, two groups hard hit by AIDS. The religious right, which targeted homosexuals for attack, had become increasingly influential within the Republican party. The convention itself, President Bush, and Vice President Dan Quayle all stressed the need for family values, a conservative viewpoint that many gays considered hostile. The Republican platform, adopted only days before Fisher spoke, defended Bush's record on AIDS. It also said the disease should be prevented through education that stressed "marital fidelity, abstinence and a drug-free lifestyle."

In the eleven years between the discovery of AIDS in America and the two speeches, nearly 150,000 Americans had died from the disease. By late 1991, it was estimated that between 1 million and 1.5 million Americans were infected with the HIV virus. Many of those infected were gay men, although the number of women and children who were infected was rapidly rising.

Only one month after the Republican convention ended, Bush's commitment to fighting AIDS again became an issue when basketball superstar Earvin "Magic" Johnson resigned from the National Commis-

sion on AIDS. In resigning, Johnson charged that Bush had "dropped the ball" in battling AIDS (Magic Johnson's Resignation from AIDS Commission, p. 891). Bush appointed Fisher to replace Johnson on the panel.

Following are the texts of speeches made by Elizabeth Glaser on July 14, 1992, at the Democratic National Convention and by Mary Fisher on August 19, 1992, at the Republican National Convention:

DEMOCRATIC CONVENTION: ELIZABETH GLASER

I'm Elizabeth Glaser.

Eleven years ago, while giving birth to my first child, I hemorrhaged and was transfused with 7 pints of blood. Four years later, I found out that I had been infected with the AIDS virus and had unknowingly passed it on to my daughter, Ariel, through my breast milk, and my son Jake, in utero.

Twenty years ago I wanted to be at the Democratic Convention because it was a way to participate in our country.

Today I am here because it's a matter of life and death.

Exactly four years ago my daughter died of AIDS—she did not survive the Reagan administration. I am here because my son and I may not survive four more years of leaders who say they care, but do nothing. I am in a race with the clock. This is *not* about being a Republican or an Independent or a Democrat—it's about the future—for each and every one of us.

I started out just a mom—fighting for the life of her child. But along the way I learned how unfair America can be. Not just for people who have HIV, but for many many people—gay people, people of color, children. A strange spokesperson for such a group—a well-to-do white woman—but I have learned my lessons the *hard way*—and I *know* that America has lost her path—and is at *risk* of losing her soul. America wake up—we are all in a struggle between life and death.

I understand the sense of frustration and despair in our country, because I know first hand about screaming for help and getting no answer. I went to Washington to tell Presidents Reagan and Bush we needed to do much, much more for AIDS research and care, and that children couldn't be forgotten. The first time, when nothing happened, I thought—oh, they just didn't hear, the second time, when nothing happened I thought, maybe I didn't shout loud enough. But, now I realize that they don't hear because they don't *want* to listen. When you cry for help and no one listens you start to lose hope.

I began to lose *faith* in America. I felt my country was letting me down—and it was.

This is not the America I was raised to be proud of. I was raised to believe that others problems were my problems as well. But when I tell most people about HIV, hoping they will care and try to help, I see the look in their eyes—it's *not my* problem they're thinking—well, it's *everyone's problem* and we need a leader who will tell us that.

We need a visionary to guide us—to say it *wasn't* all right for Ryan White to be banned from school because he had HIV or a man or woman denied a job because they were infected with this virus. We need a leader who is truly committed to educating us.

I *believe* in America—but *not* with a leadership of selfishness and greed where the wealthy get health care and insurance and the poor don't. Do you know how much my AIDS care costs? Over $40,000 a year. Someone without insurance can't afford this. Even the drugs that I hope will keep me alive are out of reach for others. Is their life any less valuable—of course not. *This* is not the America I was raised to be proud of—where the rich people get care and drugs that poor people can't. We need health care for all. We need a leader to say this, and do something about it.

I believe in America-But not with a leadership that talks about problems but is incapable of solving them. Two HIV commission reports with recommendations about what to do to solve this crisis sitting on shelves, gathering dust. We need a leader who will not only listen to these recommendations, but implement them.

I *believe* in America, but *not* with a leadership that doesn't hold government accountable. I go to Washington to the National Institutes of Health and say "Show me what you're doing on HIV." They hate it when I come because I try to tell them how to do it better. But that's why I *love* being a tax payer because it's *my* money and they *must* become accountable.

I *believe* in an America where our leaders talk straight. When anyone tells President Bush that the battle against AIDS is seriously under-funded, he juggles the numbers to mislead the public into thinking we're spending twice as much as we really are. While they play games with numbers, people are dying.

I believe in America, but an America where there is a light *in every* home—1,000 points of light just wasn't enough—my house has been dark for too long.

Once every generation, history brings us to an important crossroads. Sometimes in life there is that moment when it's possible to make a change for the better. *This* is one of those moments.

For me, this is not politics. It's a crisis of caring.

In this hall is the future: women, men of all colors saying take America back. We are just real people wanting a more hopeful life. But, words and ideas are not enough. Good thoughts won't save my family. What's the point of caring if we don't do something about it. We *must* have ACTION. A President *and* a Congress that can work together so we can get out of this gridlock and move ahead. Because I don't win my war if the Congress cares and the President doesn't—or if the President cares and the Congress doesn't support the ideas.

The people in this hall—this week, the Democratic party—all of us can begin to deliver that partnership, and in November *we can all* bring it home.

My daughter lived seven years, and in her last year, when she couldn't walk or talk, her wisdom shone through. Who taught me to love when all I wanted to do was hate. She taught me to help others, when all I wanted to do was help myself. She taught me to be brave, when all I felt was fear.

My daughter and I loved each other with simplicity. America, we can do the same.

This was the country that offered hope. This was the place where dreams could come true. Not just economic dreams, but dreams of freedom, justice and equality. We *all* need to hope that our dreams can come true. I challenge you to make it happen, because *all our lives,* not just mine, depend on it.

REPUBLICAN CONVENTION: MARY FISHER

Less than three months ago, at Platform Hearings in Salt Lake City, I asked the Republican party to lift the shroud of silence which had been draped over the issue of HIV and AIDS. I have come tonight to bring our silence to an end.

I bear a message of challenge, not self-congratulations. I want your attention, not your applause. I would never have asked to be HIV-positive. But I believe that in all things there is a purpose, and I stand before you, and before the nation, gladly.

The reality of AIDS is brutally clear. Two hundred thousand Americans are dead or dying; a million more are infected. Worldwide, forty million, sixty million, or a hundred million infections will be counted in the coming few years. But despite science and research, White House meetings and congressional hearings; despite good intentions and bold initiatives, campaign slogans and hopeful promises—it is, despite it all, it's the epidemic which is winning tonight.

In the context of an election year, I ask you, here, in this great hall, or listening in the quiet of your home, to recognize that AIDS virus is not a political creature. It does not care whether you are Democrat or Republican. It does not ask whether you are Black or a White, male or female, gay or straight, young or old.

Tonight, I represent an AIDS community whose members have been reluctantly drafted from every segment of American society. Though I am White, and a mother, I am one with a Black infant struggling with tubes in a Philadelphia hospital. Though I am female, and contracted this disease in marriage, and enjoy the warm support of my family, I am one with the lonely gay man sheltering a flickering candle from the cold wind of his family's rejection.

This is not a distant threat; it is a present danger. The rate of infection is increasing fastest among women and children. Largely unknown a decade ago, AIDS is the third leading killer of young-adult Americans today. But it won't be third for long, because, unlike other diseases, this one travels. Adolescents don't give each other cancer or heart disease because they believe they are in love. But HIV is different.

And we have helped it along. We have killed each other—with our ignorance, our prejudice, and our silence. We may take refuge in our stereotypes, but we cannot hide there long. Because HIV asks only one thing of those it attacks: Are you human? And this is the right question: Are you human?

Because people with HIV have not entered some alien state of being. They are human. They have not earned cruelty and they do not deserve meanness. They don't benefit from being isolated or treated as outcasts. Each of them is exactly what God made: a person. Not evil, deserving of our judgment; not victims, longing for our pity. People. Ready for support and worthy of compassion.

My call to you, my Party, is to take a public stand no less compassionate than that of the President and Mrs. Bush. They have embraced me and my family in memorable ways. In the place of judgment, they have shown affection. In difficult moments, they have raised our spirits. In the darkest hours, I have seen them reaching not only to me, but also to my parents, armed with that stunning grief and special grace that comes only to parents who have themselves leaned too long over the bedside of a dying child.

With the President's leadership, much good has been done. Much of the good has gone unheralded. As the President has insisted, "Much remains to be done." But we do the President's cause no good if we praise the American family but ignore a virus that destroys it. We must be consistent if we are to be believed. We cannot love justice and ignore prejudice, love our children and fear to teach them. Whatever our role, as parent or policy maker, we must act as eloquently as we speak, else we have no integrity.

My call to the nation is a plea for awareness. If you believe you are safe, you are in danger. Because I was not hemophiliac, I was not at risk. Because I was not gay, I was not at risk. Because I did not inject drugs, I was not at risk. My father has devoted much of his lifetime to guarding against another holocaust. He is part of the generation who heard Pastor Niemoeller come out of the Nazi death camps to say, "They came after the Jews and I was not a Jew, so I did not protest.

They came after the Trade Unionists, and I was not a Trade Unionist, so I did not protest. Then they came after the Roman Catholics, and I was not a Roman Catholic, so I did not protest. Then they came after me, and there was no one left to protest."

The lesson history teaches is this: If you believe you are safe, you are at risk. If you do not see this killer stalking your children, look again. There is no family or community, no race or religion, no place left in America that is safe. Until we genuinely embrace this message, we are a nation at risk.

Tonight, HIV marches resolutely toward AIDS in more than a million

American homes, littering its pathway with the bodies of the young. Young men. Young women. Young parents. And young children. One of the families is mine. If it is true that HIV inevitably turns to AIDS, then my children will inevitably turn to orphans.

My family has been a rock of support. My 84-year-old father, who has pursued the healing of the nations, will not accept the premise that he cannot heal his daughter. My mother refuses to be broken. She still calls at midnight to tell wonderful jokes that make me laugh. Sisters and friends, and my brother Phillip (whose birthday is today), all have helped carry me over the hardest places. I am blessed, richly and deeply blessed, to have such a family.

But not all of you have been so blessed. You are HIV-positive but dare not say it. You have lost loved ones, but you dared not whisper the word AIDS. You weep silently. You grieve alone.

I have a message for you. It is not you who should feel shame, it is we. We who tolerate ignorance and practice prejudice, we who have taught you to fear. We must lift our shroud of silence, making it safe for you to reach out for compassion. It is our task to seek safety for our children, not in quiet denial but in effective action. Some day our children will be grown. My son Max, now four, will take the measure of his mother. My son Zachary, now two, will sort through his memories. I may not be here to hear their judgments, but I know already what I hope they are.

I want my children to know that their mother was not a victim. She was a messenger. I do not want them to think, as I once did, that courage is the absence of fear. I want them to know that courage is the strength to act wisely when most we are afraid. I want them to have the courage to step forward when called by their nation, or their Party, and give leadership, no matter what the personal cost. I ask no more of you than I ask of myself, or of my children.

To the millions of you who are grieving, who are frightened, who have suffered the ravages of AIDS firsthand: have courage and you will find support. To the millions who are strong, I issue the plea: Set aside prejudice and politics to make room for compassion and sound policy.

To my children, I make this pledge: I will not give in, Zachary, because I draw my courage from you. Your silly giggle gives me hope. Your gentle prayers give me strength. And you, my child, give me the reason to say to America, "You are at risk." And I will not rest, Max, until I have done all I can do to make your world safe. I will seek a place where intimacy is not the prelude to suffering.

I will not hurry to leave you, my children. But when I go, I pray that you will not suffer shame on my account. To all within the sound of my voice, I appeal: Learn with me the lessons of history and grace, so my children will not be afraid to say the word AIDS when I am gone. Then their children, and yours may not need to whisper it at all.

God bless the children, God bless us all. Good night.

(applause)

715

PEROT STATEMENTS ON ENDING AND REVIVING HIS CAMPAIGN
July 16 and October 1, 1992

After reaching heights no other independent candidate had ever attained, Dallas billionaire Ross Perot announced July 16 that he was dropping his undeclared bid for the presidency. Just as unexpectedly, on October 1, he returned to the race and went on to win 19 percent of the vote on November 3.

Before he dropped out temporarily, Perot actually led the two major candidates, President George Bush and Democratic challenger Bill Clinton, in nationwide polls throughout much of the late spring. His off-again, on-again candidacy sharply altered the nature of the 1992 election, leaving the experts to ponder whether he took more votes from Bush or the ultimate winner, Clinton. (Postelection Statements by Perot, Bush, and Clinton, p. 1019)

Although he won no states and therefore gained no electoral votes, Perot chalked up the most popular votes ever for an independent. It was also the highest percentage for a third-party candidate since 1912 when former president Theodore Roosevelt ran on his Progressive (Bull Moose) ticket and took 27.4 percent of the vote. Another former president, Millard Fillmore, ran as a Whig-American in 1856 and received 21.5 percent.

In the weeks before his July 16 announcement, Perot had been under intense media scrutiny, much of it unflattering, and he had slumped to third place in the polls. On July 15 his campaign co-manager, Edward J. Rollins, quit after disagreements with Perot on how to run the campaign.

When he came back in October, Perot said his departure had been a mistake. "I thought that both political parties would address the prob-

lems that face the nation," he said. "We gave them a chance. They didn't do it." Later, at a campaign stop in Pittsburgh, he said that he quit because he was told the Republicans planned to smear his daughter Carolyn just before her wedding and ruin the "happiest day of her life."

Began with a Call-in Show

The Perot candidacy, undeclared at first, was unconventional from the outset. It began February 20 with an appearance on CNN's "Larry King Live" show when Perot expressed a willingness to run for president. Under prodding, he said that if the people "register me in fifty states," he would personally finance a "world-class campaign."

Henry Ross Perot, a Naval Academy graduate who founded his own computer company after leaving IBM, had been in the public eye for years, financing expeditions to help find American prisoners in Vietnam and rescue his employees in Iran, reforming the Texas school system, trying to shake up the General Motors management, and more recently appearing on radio and TV talk shows to warn about the consequences of the mounting federal deficit.

By the time Perot (who by then had dropped his first initial) decided not to run, tens of thousands of volunteers were on their way to keeping their part of the bargain. According to the publication Ballot Access News, *Perot already had qualified for the ballot in twenty-four states—including California, Florida, New Jersey, and Texas—and had turned in signatures in eight other states.*

"He's let people down. He's betrayed them," said Matthew L. Lifflander, head of Perot's New York petition drive. "He's forced the alienated to be more alienated."

Perot, who had said he would spend upward of $100 million to launch his once-prospective presidential bid, shut down his operation after having spent, by his own estimation, roughly $10 million.

Rise and Fall

Perot scored as a political force in early June, when he signed Democrat Hamilton Jordan and Republican Rollins as strategists for his burgeoning campaign. It was a bipartisan coup. Jordan had managed Jimmy Carter's presidential runs in 1976 and 1980; Rollins directed Ronald Reagan's 1984 reelection campaign.

But the Perot campaign was unable to meld grass-roots amateurism with high-powered professionalism at a time when Perot's personal image was being battered by a spate of negative publicity, ranging from questions about his conduct as a young Navy officer to his lucrative business interests. To his critics in the media and the leadership of the two major parties, Perot was portrayed not as a savior of the political system but as a thin-skinned autocrat who could not be counted on to operate within it.

On several occasions Perot blamed Republican dirty tricks for his rising negatives. But some of the wounds were self-inflicted. He showed insensitivity to racial issues in an appearance before the annual convention of the NAACP on July 11 by referring to the audience as "you people" and "your people."

By the time Rollins quit the campaign, Perot was already thinking about it himself. ". . . I don't have any drive to be president of the United States," he said in bowing out. "I'm trying to do the right thing. It's that simple." He said he was also concerned that no candidate would get a majority in a three-way race, requiring the House of Representatives to decide the election, because the Democratic party had revitalized itself enough to split the traditional vote for Republican presidential candidates.

Star Debater

As a declared candidate Perot was accepted in the fall's three presidential debates, where he proved to be a formidable opponent. His folksy style and catch phrases ("it's just that simple" and "watch your wallet," among others) endeared him to viewers. Polls showed him winning the first debate and running a close second to Clinton in the third.

Perot's running mate, retired admiral James B. Stockdale, fared less well in the single vice presidential debate. Stockdale, a respected leader of American prisoners of war in Vietnam, was no oratorical match for Vice President Dan Quayle or his Democratic challenger, Senator Al Gore of Tennessee. (Presidential and Vice Presidential Debates, p. 907)

To get on the ballot in some states Perot had to have a running mate even before he became a declared candidate. He chose Stockdale to fill that role and then introduced him October 1 as his full-fledged vice presidential candidate.

> *Following are excerpts from the Reuter transcripts of statements given by independent presidential candidate Ross Perot on July 16, 1992, when he announced he would not declare his candidacy, and on October 1 when he did become a declared candidate:*

JULY 16 STATEMENT

Several million volunteers in all 50 states have done a brilliant job in reestablishing a government that comes from the people. Both political parties are now squarely focused on the issues that concern the American people. Being associated with the volunteers across this country in the last few months has been one of the great experiences of my life.

Their love of their country and their idealism just is apparent as you visit with them. And throughout this effort we have said repeatedly that our objective is to improve our country, not disrupt the political process.

We have said among ourselves, and publicly, that we must win in November. We must win a majority of electoral votes. As you know, if we cannot win in November the election will be decided in the House of Representatives, and since the House of Representatives is made up primarily of Democrats and Republicans, our chances of wining would be pretty slim.

Now that the Democratic Party has revitalized itself, I have concluded that we cannot win in November and that the election will be decided in the House of Representatives. Since the House of Representatives does not pick the president until January, the new president will be unable to use the months of November and December to assemble the new government.

I believe it would be disruptive for us to continue our program since this program would obviously put it in the House of Representatives and be disruptive to the country, in the states, so therefore I will not become a candidate.

And the states' petitions have not yet been turned in. I urge the volunteers to turn them in so that both parties can know exactly who the people are who are so concerned about their country's future.

If the petitions are turned in, both parties will continue to give a great deal of attention to the concerns of these fine people, and this is good for the people, for the parties to be very close to what the people want.

New York state is scheduled to start its petition signing today. I urge the volunteers in New York state to complete the process and turn in their petitions so that everybody running for president will know the names and addresses of all the people who are not happy with the way things are today.

I'd like to thank the members of the press who have been assigned to this effort. And again, I would like to thank the volunteers—the dedicated teams across the country—who have worked so valiantly to get this done. Nothing like this has ever occurred before in American politics.

I compliment you on your patriotism, your idealism, your creativity and your ingenuity. There is no question that you have changed politics in this country, and it is a change for the better. And all you have to do is listen to what both of the party candidates are saying now. They are basically focused totally on the things that so concerned you.

So, to all the volunteers, I'll always look back on this with the fondest of memories, and my memories will be focused on you and your greatness, because you are America. And I am certain that the Founding Fathers would be very proud of you. . . .

OCTOBER 1 STATEMENT

Good afternoon. The volunteers in all 50 states have asked me to run as a candidate for president of the United States. Jim Stockdale, our vice presidential candidate and I are honored to accept their request. . . .

I know I hurt many of the volunteers who worked so hard through the spring and summer when I stepped aside in July. I thought it was the right thing to do. I thought that both political parties would address the problems that face the nation. We gave them a chance. They didn't do it. But the volunteers on their own forged ahead and put me on the ballot in the final 26 states after July 16th.

The day we were on the ballot in all 50 states the volunteers requested that I come back in because the political parties had not responded to their concerns.

My decision in July hurt you. I apologize. I thought I was doing the right thing. I made a mistake. I take full responsibility for it.

There's only one issue now, starting today, and that is what's good for our country.

Looking back won't solve any of our problems. Looking forward, working together, we can fix anything. The American people are concerned about a government in gridlock. Our people are good. The American people are good. But they have a government that is a mess.

The American people are concerned about this government they pay for that doesn't produce results. Everybody in Washington makes excuses. Nobody takes responsibility, even when they have direct responsibility.

The American people have figured that out. They want that changed.

The American people are really concerned about a government where people go to Washington to cash in and not to serve. They want the government changed so that people go as servants of the people back home, and do not use government service as a stepping stone to financial success.

The people know that it is wrong to spend our children's money. Nothing could be more wrong. We know that we cannot constantly pass on a $4 trillion debt to our children. The people want this problem squarely dealt with. They want our financial house put back in order. . . .

And now to the American people, I don't belong to anybody but you. You the people own me. If you elect me I go as your servant. I will work night and day to see that the priorities that you have established are accomplished.

To the many young people—and it's a disproportionate number of very young people who have called me, written me, and some have even driven across country to Dallas to visit with me at their own expense, expressing concern about what kind of country they will live in as adults, wondering whether or not they will even have a job when they get out of school.

Now this is unthinkable, that you'd have a college degree and not be able to get a job in America.

When I think of all the sacrifices my parents and all the generations who came before them made in the earlier times for us so that we could live the American dream, certainly we all dedicate ourselves to seeing that you, the young people in our country, will have the American dream passed on to you. . . .

To the retired people who made it through the Depression, fought and won World War II—now how's that for a double hit? Grow up in the Depression and then as a bonus get to fight and win World War II. Worked and sacrificed most of their lives. I know you share my commitment to make sure that we pass the American dream on to our children and grandchildren. . . .

I look forward to squarely presenting these issues day after day to the American people. I would like to thank the American people. By choosing me as your candidate, you have given me the highest honor I could ever receive.

In closing, let me say this. I love this country. I love the American people. I love the principles on which this country was founded and I don't like to see those principles violated, and there are millions of folks out there just like me that are sick and tired of it.

I am totally committed to serving you, God bless you all, thank you for this honor, and now I would like to introduce Jim Stockdale, our vice presidential candidate, and his wife, Sibyl. Jim Stockdale is a hero's hero. He's a recipient of the medal of honor. In addition to that he is a scholar. He is a retired admiral. He suffered as a prisoner of war during Vietnam as few people have.

He provided leadership that caused our government to award him the medal of honor. . . .

CATHOLIC STATEMENTS ON HOMOSEXUAL RIGHTS LAWS

July 22 and 23, 1992

Saying that homosexuality is not a right, the Vatican counseled American Catholic bishops to oppose legislative proposals that might promote public acceptance of homosexual conduct. "There are areas in which it is not unjust discrimination to take sexual orientation into account," said an unsigned document the bishops received in June from the Congregation for the Doctrine of the Faith (CDF), the Vatican office for enforcement of Church doctrine. Those areas, "for example," included "the consignment of children to adoption or foster care, in employment of teachers or coaches, and in military recruitment."

The document was leaked to the press in mid-July by New Ways Ministry, a Catholic gay-rights group with headquarters in Mount Rainier, Maryland. A spokesman for the organization accused the Vatican of "playing to everyone's fears" and placing itself at odds with the views of most American Catholics. New Ways cited a Gallup poll in May indicating that 78 percent of the Catholics favored equal job opportunities for homosexuals.

Archbishop Daniel E. Pilarczyk of Cincinnati, president of the National Conference on Catholic Bishops, issued a statement in Washington on July 22 saying that the document was basically a restatement of previous positions taken by the church regarding homosexuality. It was the Vatican agency's concern that proposals to safeguard the legitimate rights of homosexuals not have the effect of creating a new class of legally protected behavior, the archbishop said. American bishops would continue to evaluate local legislation with those "considerations" clearly in mind, he added.

*However, Archbishop Rembert G. Weakland of Milwaukee observed
that although "previous documents have brought up the question of
legislation ... this is the first time I have seen anything so detailed."
Weakland had often been identified as a leader among a group of liberal-
minded bishops who worked to reconcile the church's disapproval of
homosexuality with compassion for individual homosexuals.*

Divisions Among Bishops

*On legislative matters affecting homosexuals, the bishops have not
spoken with a single mind. In 1991 Catholic bishops in Connecticut
dropped their opposition to a homosexual-rights bill after it was rewrit-
ten to apply only to employment, housing, and public accommodations.
Their shift was attacked by some conservative Catholics. Cardinal James A.
Hickey, archbishop of Washington, sought to overturn an ordinance
passed in 1992 by the District of Columbia City Council to let city
employees obtain health insurance for their "domestic partners"—
regardless of whether the partners were of the same or opposite sex.
Hickey's office praised the Vatican document.*

*On July 23 the Vatican released a revised text of the document—titled
"Observations Regarding Legislative Proposals Concerned with Discrimination Toward Homosexual Persons." The release was accompanied by a
statement by Vatican spokesman Joaquin Navarro-Valls, who said that
since the original text had been leaked to the news media, "for the sake of
an accurate report on the matter, the revised text ... is made public
today." The Catholic News Service quoted an unidentified Vatican
official as saying that the original text was issued for the bishops only,
and the second for a wider readership.*

Debate Beyond the Church

*The Catholic Church's concern with homosexual rights marked one
sphere of a debate being carried on nationally. Other churches also
struggled with the question—none too successfully. In June the government's General Accounting Office reported that the ban on homosexuals
in the armed forces was costly to maintain and "appears to be based on
the same type of prejudicial suppositions [formerly] used to discriminate
against women." Bill Clinton, the Democratic nominee for president, said
that if elected he would abolish the ban by executive order. President
George Bush favored the ban.*

*In the scientific community a century-old debate about the cause of
homosexuality was stirred anew by recent studies suggesting a biological
cause. To establish that homosexuality was genetic rather than an
acquired trait would presumably further the cause of homosexual
rights—because homosexuals "can't help it." The American Catholic
bishops suggested as much in a pastoral letter to their parishioners in
1991. They said that while homosexual activity was wrong, "such an
orientation in itself, because not freely chosen, is not sinful."*

Following are the statement by Archbishop Daniel E. Pilarczyk, issued July 22 in Washington, on the Vatican's document on homosexual rights, and a revised version of that document, titled "Observations Regarding Legislative Proposals Concerned with Discrimination Toward Homosexual Persons," preceded by a statement by Vatican spokesman Joaquin Navarro-Valls, both issued July 23 in Rome:

STATEMENT BY ARCHBISHOP DANIEL E. PILARCZYK

Attention has been drawn in recent days to a document from the Congregation of the Doctrine of the Faith entitled "Some Considerations Concerning the Catholic Response to Legislative Proposals on the Non-Discrimination of Homosexual Persons".

From time to time, various Roman Congregations communicate with individual bishops and individual bishops' conferences throughout the world on a variety of matters regarding Church teaching and discipline. Most often, these communications are elaborations of positions previously articulated by these same Congregations.

Several weeks ago, the Congregation for the Doctrine of the Faith sent some "considerations" to the bishops of this country for their reflection when dealing with legislative proposals concerning the rights of homosexual persons.

The Congregation's concern is that proposals to safeguard the legitimate rights of homosexual persons not have the effect of creating a new class of legally protected *behavior*, that is, homosexual behavior, which, in time, could occupy the same position as non-discrimination against *people* because of their race, religion, gender, or ethnic background. The document rightly warns against legislation designed more to legitimate homosexual behavior than to secure basic civil rights and against proposals which tend to promote an equivalence between legal marriage and homosexual lifestyles.

Bishops will continue to evaluate local legislation with these "considerations" clearly in mind. However, as the "considerations" note, "it would be impossible to foresee and respond to every eventuality in respect to legislative proposals in this area. . ."

I believe that the bishops of the various local Churches in the United States will continue to look for ways in which those people who have a homosexual orientation will not suffer unjust discrimination in law or reality because of their orientation. In our teaching, pastoral care, and public advocacy, bishops will, of course, continue to strive to be faithful to Church teaching on homosexuality, to uphold the values of marriage and family life, to defend the basic human dignity and human rights of all and to condemn violence, hatred and bigotry directed against any person.

NAVARRO-VALLS STATEMENT

For some time, the Congregation for the Doctrine of the Faith has been concerned with the question of legislative proposals advanced in various parts of the world to deal with the issue of the non-discrimination of homosexual persons. A study of this question culminated in the preparation of a set of observations which could be of assistance to those concerned with formulating the Catholic response to such legislative proposals. These observations offered considerations based upon relevant passages of the congregation's "Letter to the Bishops of the Catholic Church on the Pastoral Care of Homosexual Persons," which was published in the fall of 1986 and indicated certain applications which may be derived from them.

In view of the fact that this question is a particularly pressing one in certain parts of the United States, these considerations were made available to the bishops of that country through the good offices of the pronuncio for whatever help they might provide them. It should be noted that the observations were not intended to pass judgment on any response which may have been given already by local bishops or state conferences to such legislative proposals. The observations, then, were not intended to be an official and public instruction on the matter from the congregation but a background resource offering discreet assistance to those who may be confronted with the task of evaluating draft legislation regarding non-discrimination on the basis of sexual orientation.

With the idea that the publication of the observations would be something beneficial, a slight revision of the text was undertaken and a second version prepared. In the meantime, various references to and citations from the considerations have appeared in the media. For the sake of an accurate report on the matter, the revised text of "Some Considerations Concerning the Response to Legislative Proposals on the Non-Discrimination of Homosexual Persons" is made public today.

REVISED TEXT

Foreword

Recently, legislation has been proposed in various places which would make discrimination on the basis of sexual orientation illegal. In some cities, municipal authorities have made public housing, otherwise reserved for families, available to homosexual (and unmarried heterosexual) couples. Such initiatives, even where they seem more directed toward support of basic civil rights than condonement of homosexual activity or a homosexual lifestyle, may in fact have a negative impact on the family and society. Such things as the adoption of children, the employment of teachers, the housing needs of genuine families, landlords' legitimate concerns in screening potential tenants, for example, are often implicated.

While it would be impossible to anticipate every eventuality in respect to legislative proposals in this area, these observations will try to identify some principles and distinctions of a general nature which should be taken into consideration by the conscientious legislator, voter or church authority who is confronted with such issues.

The first section will recall relevant passages from the Congregation for the Doctrine of the Faith's "Letter to the Bishops of the Catholic Church on the Pastoral Care of Homosexual Persons" of 1986. The second section will deal with their application.

I. Relevant Passages from the CDF's "Letter"

1. The letter recalls that the CDF's "Declaration on Certain Questions Concerning Sexual Ethics" of 1975 "took note of the distinction commonly drawn between the homosexual condition or tendency and individual homosexual actions"; the latter are "intrinsically disordered" and "in no case to be approved of" (No. 3).

2. Since "[i]n the discussion which followed the publication of the (aforementioned) declaration . . ., an overly benign interpretation was given to the homosexual condition itself, some going so far as to call it neutral or even good," the letter goes on to clarify:

    "Although the particular inclination of the homosexual person is not a sin, it is a more or less strong tendency ordered toward an intrinsic moral evil; and thus the inclination itself must be seen as an objective disorder. Therefore special concern and pastoral attention should be directed toward those who have this condition, lest they be led to believe that the living out of this orientation in homosexual activity is a morally acceptable option. It is not" (No. 3).

3. "As in every moral disorder, homosexual activity prevents one's own fulfillment and happiness by acting contrary to the creative wisdom of God. The church, in rejecting erroneous opinions regarding homosexuality, does not limit but rather defends personal freedom and dignity realistically and authentically understood" (No. 7).

4. In reference to the homosexual movement, the letter states: "One tactic used is to protest that any and all criticism of or reservations about homosexual people, their activity and lifestyle are simply diverse forms of unjust discrimination" (No. 9).

5. "There is an effort in some countries to manipulate the church by gaining the often well-intentioned support of her pastors with a view to changing civil statutes and laws. This is done in order to conform to these pressure groups' concept that homosexuality is at least a completely harmless, if not an entirely good, thing. Even when the practice of homosexuality may seriously threaten the lives and well-being of a large number of people, its advocates remain undeterred and refuse to consider the magnitude of the risks involved" (No. 9).

6. "She (the church) is also aware that the view that homosexual activity is equivalent to or as acceptable as the sexual expression of conjugal love has a direct impact on society's understanding of the nature and rights of the family and puts them in jeopardy" (No. 9).

7. "It is deplorable that homosexual persons have been and are the object of violent malice in speech or in action. Such treatment deserves condemnation from the church's pastors wherever it occurs. It reveals a kind of disregard for others which endangers the most fundamental principles of a healthy society. The intrinsic dignity of each person must always be respected in word, in action and in law.

   "But the proper reaction to crimes committed against homosexual persons should not be to claim that the homosexual condition is not disordered. When such a claim is made and when homosexual activity is consequently condoned, or when civil legislation is introduced to protect behavior to which no one has any conceivable right, neither the church nor society at large should be surprised when other distorted notions and practices gain ground, and irrational and violent reactions increase" (No. 10).

8. "What is at all costs to be avoided is the unfounded and demeaning assumption that the sexual behavior of homosexual persons is always and totally compulsive and therefore inculpable. What is essential is that the fundamental liberty which characterizes the human person and gives him his dignity be recognized as belonging to the homosexual person as well" (No. 11).

9. "In assessing proposed legislation, the bishops should keep as their uppermost concern the responsibility to defend and promote family life" (No. 17).

II. Applications

10. "Sexual orientation" does not constitute a quality comparable to race, ethnic background, etc., in respect to non-discrimination. Unlike these, homosexual orientation is an objective disorder (cf. "Letter," No. 3) and evokes moral concern.

11. There are areas in which it is not unjust discrimination to take sexual orientation into account, for example, in the placement of children for adoption or foster care, in employment of teachers or athletic coaches, and in military recruitment.

12. Homosexual persons, as human persons, have the same rights as all persons, including the right of not being treated in a manner which offends their personal dignity (cf. No. 10). Among other rights, all persons have the right to work, to housing, etc. Nevertheless, these rights are not absolute. They can be legitimately limited for objectively disordered external conduct. This is sometimes not only licit but obligatory. This would obtain moreover not only in the case of culpable behavior but even in the case of actions of the physically or

mentally ill. Thus it is accepted that the state may restrict the exercise of rights, for example, in the case of contagious or mentally ill persons, in order to protect the common good.

13. Including "homosexual orientation" among the considerations on the basis of which it is illegal to discriminate can easily lead to regarding homosexuality as a positive source of human rights, for example, in respect to so-called affirmative action or preferential treatment in hiring practices. This is all the more deleterious since there is no right to homosexuality (cf. No. 10), which therefore should not form the basis for judicial claims. The passage from the recognition of homosexuality as a factor on which basis it is illegal to discriminate can easily lead, if not automatically, to the legislative protection and promotion of homosexuality. A person's homosexuality would be invoked in opposition to alleged discrimination, and thus the exercise of rights would be defended precisely via the affirmation of the homosexual condition instead of in terms of a violation of basic human rights.

14. The "sexual orientation" of a person is not comparable to race, sex, age, etc. also for another reason than that given above which warrants attention. An individual's sexual orientation is generally not known to others unless he publicly identifies himself as having this orientation or unless some overt behavior manifests it. As a rule, the majority of homosexually oriented persons who seek to lead chaste lives do not publicize their sexual orientation. Hence the problem of discrimination in terms of employment, housing, etc., does not usually arise.

Homosexual persons who assert their homosexuality tend to be precisely those who judge homosexual behavior or lifestyle to be "either completely harmless, if not an entirely good thing" (cf. No. 3), and hence worthy of public approval. It is from this quarter that one is more likely to find those who seek to "manipulate the church by gaining the often well-intentioned support of her pastors with a view to changing civil statutes and laws" (cf. No. 5), those who use the tactic of protesting that "any and all criticism of or reservations about homosexual people ... are simply diverse forms of unjust discrimination" (cf. No. 9).

In addition, there is a danger that legislation which would make homosexuality a basis for entitlements could actually encourage a person with a homosexual orientation to declare his homosexuality or even to seek a partner in order to exploit the provisions of the law.

15. Since in the assessment of proposed legislation uppermost concern should be given to the responsibility to defend and promote family life (cf. No. 17), strict attention should be paid to the single provisions of proposed measures. How would they affect adoption or foster care? Would they protect homosexual acts, public or private? Do they confer equivalent family status on homosexual unions, for

example, in respect to public housing or by entitling the homosexual partner to the privileges of employment, which could include such things as "family" participation in the health benefits given to employees (cf. No. 9)?

16. Finally, where a matter of the common good is concerned, it is inappropriate for church authorities to endorse or remain neutral toward adverse legislation even if it grants exceptions to church organizations and institutions. The church has the responsibility to promote family life and the public morality of the entire civil society on the basis of fundamental moral values, not simply to protect herself from the application of harmful laws (cf. No. 17).

QUESTION OF VALUE OF
A COLLEGE DEGREE
July 30, 1992

Stories of college graduates who ended up driving taxis or waiting tables have been a staple of conversation since the 1970s. Government studies indicate that as many as one-fifth of the graduate job seekers do not find work or take work below their abilities. And yet, other equally valid statistics have shown that overall those who went to college for four years earn much more than those who did not. In the 1980s the earnings gap actually widened. Average earnings of full-time workers with college educations stood at $42,524, some 60 percent above the pay of workers who finished only high school. Ten years earlier, the difference was but 33 percent.

How can it be that the pay bonus for holding a college degree had increased at a time when many degree-holders had to take jobs beneath their skill levels? Daniel E. Hecker, an economist, looked at that question and concluded that the college graduate appeared to fare so well only because the high school graduate—and especially the male high school graduate—had fared very badly in the 1980s. Adjusted for inflation, the college graduate's earnings rose about 4 percent during the decade, while the wages of the high school graduate fell by 14 percent.

Writing in the July 1992 edition of the Labor Department publication Monthly Labor Review, *Hecker drew on reams of statistics to rebut an argument advanced by some educators that the expansion of the wage gap during the past decade meant that college graduates were in short supply in the work force. They reasoned that employers were bidding up salaries because they could not hire enough young men and women fresh out of college.*

Oversupply of Grads in Work Force

Instead, Hecker found an oversupply. From 1969 to 1990, the proportion of college graduates in the labor market nearly doubled to 23 percent. The share of high school graduates in the work force barely inched upward to 39 percent. Job losses in manufacturing and mining, traditional outlets for young blue-collar males, forced many of them into lower-paying service jobs. They were more likely to flip hamburgers than to work on an assembly line.

Similarly, many college graduates entered lower-level jobs than they might have expected in other times. Hecker cited college graduate surveys conducted by the National Center for Educational Statistics that indicated almost 40 percent of the persons who were awarded bachelor's degrees in 1984 and 1986 reported that they thought a degree was not needed to obtain the job they held a year after graduation. "It is unlikely that this portion of graduates would be in jobs that did not require a degree if employers were having trouble filling college-level jobs," Hecker commented.

Question of Hiring Standards

With college graduates taking many jobs traditionally held by non-graduates, Hecker asked rhetorically whether employers had raised their hiring standards. A more likely case, he suggested, was that employers had determined that many of the current graduates were not well prepared for the job market despite their academic credentials.

In advancing this argument, the economist referred to "grade inflation" in both secondary and higher education. He cited instances of high grades being awarded to far more members of high school and college classes than in years past. Even though a college education does not necessarily open the door to a well-paying job, Hecker acknowledged that during the 1980s, "a college degree did pay off for the great majority of workers." But he noted that a study by Kristina Shelley, a colleague in the Bureau of Labor Statistics, concluded that through the year 2005 there would be more graduates entering the labor force than there would be jobs requiring a college degree.

Following are excerpts from Daniel E. Hecker's article, "Reconciling Conflicting Data on Jobs for College Graduates," in the July 1992 Monthly Labor Review, *published by the Bureau of Labor Statistics:*

Since the early 1970's, the data suggest a growing proportion of college graduates are in jobs that usually do not require at least a bachelor's degree. Bureau of Labor Statistics analysis of data related to the employment of college graduates indicates that there are more jobseekers with college degrees than there are openings in jobs requiring a degree. News reports and surveys by government agencies and private organizations on the employment patterns of recent college graduates support this conclusion. [The Bureau of Labor Statistics] projects that this divergence will continue through 2005.

In contrast to this apparent mismatch of jobs and jobseekers, articles in research and popular journals in recent years have pointed out that since 1979, earnings of college graduates have increased sharply relative to earnings of high school graduates. Some analysts have interpreted this to mean that employers were forced to bid up the wages of college graduates in order to fill vacant jobs—an action likely to occur only when there is a shortage of graduates.

Analysis of earnings data by educational level clearly confirm a sharp rise in earnings for college graduates relative to those of high school graduates during the 1980's. However, this article concludes that the relative earnings increase for college graduates was the result of a worsening job market for male high school graduates, not because of a shortage of workers with college degrees.

Identifying "College-Level" Jobs

It is not possible to precisely identify and measure the number of jobs that *require* a college degree. Standards of which jobs require a degree differ among employers, and ideas of what constitutes a "college-level" job also differ among employers, employees, and others. More important, occupational classification systems do not neatly distinguish between jobs that require a college degree and other jobs. However, surveys that asked workers what level of education they needed to qualify for their current jobs indicate that most jobs in retail sales; administrative support, including clerical; service; farm; precision production, craft, and repair; and operator, fabricator, and laborer occupational groups do not require a degree for entry, nor do they offer jobs duties attractive to most graduates. In contrast, the surveys show that most jobs in managerial, professional specialty, sales representative, and many technician occupations require a degree. These jobs involve specific skills (for example, the skills necessary to perform engineering and accounting tasks) or, at least, general analytic and communications skills typically learned in college. More important, employers generally recruit ... graduates for these occupations. ...

What the Data Show

The 1960's. During the 1960's, employers heavily recruited college graduates. Few graduates, regardless of their field of study, had difficulty finding college-level managerial, professional specialty, technical, and sales representative jobs. According to analyst Richard Freeman [in *The Overeducated American, 1976*], "jobs sought graduates." ...

The 1970's. The flow of graduates into jobs that do not traditionally require a degree largely resulted from a doubling in the number of college graduates in the labor force, coupled with slower employment growth during the 1970's than during the 1960's for school teachers—the largest occupation for college graduates—and in research and development, a very large employer of science and engineering graduates.

The poor job market for college graduates in the 1970's was reflected in their earnings. CPS data show that earnings increased slower for both males and females with 4 or more years of college than for males and females with 4 years of high school. The latter group is the largest educational group in the labor force, representing about 40 percent of all workers. During the 1969-80 period, earnings for high school graduates increased 119 percent for females and 114 percent for males. For college graduates, earnings increased 106 percent for females and 94 percent for males. Consequently, earnings premiums paid to female and male college graduates declined relative to the earnings of female and male high school graduates. . . .

Because college graduates were relatively less expensive to hire, employers might be expected to hire more of them. In fact, employers hired nearly all graduates who sought jobs, but many more than in the past were hired for retail sales, administrative support, and similar jobs that paid lower wages than the traditional college-level occupations.

The 1980's. From 1980 to 1990, the proportion of college graduates in the labor force who were either educationally underutilized or unemployed remained at about one-fifth of all graduates in the labor force, although their numbers rose from 3.6 million to 5.8 million. This implies that, as in the 1970's, the number of graduates in the labor force continued to exceed the number of college-level job openings.

Other data sources also suggest that there were more college graduates than there were openings in college-level jobs during the 1980's. The Recent College Graduates Surveys conducted by the National Center for Education Statistics indicate that almost 40 percent of the graduates awarded bachelor's degrees in 1984 and 1986 reported *that they thought* a degree was not needed to obtain the job they held a year after graduation. It is unlikely that this proportion of graduates would be in jobs that did not require a degree if employers were having difficulty finding graduates to fill college-level jobs. Surveys of graduates in 1977, 1980, 1984, and 1986 also reported occupational outcomes similar to those concluded from the CPS data—more than a quarter of graduates with bachelor's degrees were in retail sales, administrative support, service, and blue-collar jobs or were unemployed the year after graduation. Data on on-campus recruiting provide further evidence that a significant portion of new college graduates entered jobs that did not require a college degree.

However, during this period, the earnings of college graduates rose sharply relative to earnings of high school graduates, with greater increases for college men than for college women. By 1988, male college graduates had recovered the earnings premium they had held in 1967 relative to male high school graduates. As noted earlier, some analysts interpreted the sharp relative rise in earnings for college graduates to mean that employers competed for an insufficient number of college graduates. However, a review of the occupational employment patterns of college graduates leads to the opposite conclusion that an oversupply of college graduates existed because of the rising numbers of educationally underutilized and unemployed graduates.

Reconciling Contradictory Data

...Can this seemingly contradictory evidence—the increase of college graduates in jobs that do not require a college degree, and higher relative wages for college graduates—be reconciled? First, it is important to know whether demand for workers with 4 or more years of college really grew faster than supply, because this is a widely used definition of a shortage.... A review of employment data indicates that demand did not grow faster than supply over the 1979-90 period. In fact, during that period, supply, as measured by the number of college graduates in the labor force, grew from 17.9 million to 29 million, or 62 percent. At the same time, demand, as measured by employment of college graduates in managerial, professional specialty, technical, sales representative, and certain senior administrative support, police, blue-collar worker supervisor, and farm manager jobs that generally require a degree, increased 57 percent, or about as much as the supply of graduates. The number of college graduates who were in jobs that did not require a degree or who were unemployed increased more rapidly—81 percent. These data indicate that employers satisfied their demand for college graduates. If they did not, why did they not hire more unemployed or underemployed graduates to fill jobs requiring a degree? Is it possible that employers raised their hiring standards, and these graduates did not meet those standards?

Possible explanations. Poor educational preparation of college graduates for the work force could mean that many graduates did not qualify for available college-level jobs. And it is possible that many high school graduates were not educationally prepared for work, forcing employers to hire college graduates to fill jobs formerly filled by high school graduates.

However, available data do not support assertions that educational preparation has declined. In fact, data from the National Assessment of Educational Progress show modest increases in the reading and mathematics proficiency of 17-year-olds since the early 1970's. Data on SAT scores of high school graduates who plan to attend college showed modest decreases during the 1970's, and some recovery during the 1980's. The Graduate Record Examination, taken by bachelor's degree graduates planning to apply to graduate school, is the best broad-based measure of graduates' general learned abilities, but may not be applicable to those not planning graduate study. For this exam, scores dropped during the 1965-79 period, but by 1989, had regained their 1969 level. Now, of course, employers' educational needs may be rising, so that, relatively, scores are falling. Even so, it is not clear why employers would place so many of these admittedly less-qualified college graduates in jobs that do not require college-level skills if they had vacant college-level jobs. A logical explanation could be that the abilities of these graduates fell so far short of employers' needs that it was not reasonable to hire and train these workers, even at wages well below those paid to other graduates. However, we do not have evidence to this effect. . . .

A mismatch of skills, that is, too few graduates in some fields of training and too many in others could have caused the observed increase in wages. However, the number of college graduates in non-college-level occupations is so large, it is unlikely that this mismatch factor alone could be the sole reason. As indicated above, the number of college graduates employed in jobs that do not require a degree or who were unemployed increased from 3.2 million in 1979 to 5.8 million in 1990.

Occupational classification problems could have contributed to an incorrect picture of the employment patterns of college graduates through the 1980's. Researchers in the past have noted problems in the CPS, but there are reasons to doubt that data problems are a factor. First, the *proportion* of graduates in occupational groups that do not generally require a degree has grown steadily each year. These year-to-year changes seem a more reasonable conclusion from the CPS data than do year-to-year increases in misclassifications of respondents. . . .

Earnings Divergence

. . . An examination of actual earnings growth from 1979 to 1990 by educational attainment and gender show that earnings of female college graduates increased the fastest, followed by male college graduates, then female high school graduates. Earnings of male high school graduates increased much more slowly over the period. The premium for male college graduates over male high school graduates increased significantly over the 1979-90 period. . . .

In 1979, male high school graduates earned 22 percent more than female college graduates; by 1990, they earned 13 percent less. In 1979, the premium for male high school graduates over female high school graduates was 72 percent; by 1990, it had fallen to 45 percent. In other words, wages of female high school graduates rose sharply compared with those of male high school graduates, just, as noted above, did the wages increase for male college graduates. If rising wages for male college graduates relative to male high school graduates are simply interpreted as evidence of a shortage of male college graduates, why are rising wages of female high school graduates relative to male high school graduates not viewed as evidence of a shortage of female high school graduates? From 1979 to 1990, earnings increased slower for men with fewer than 4 years of high school than for any other demographic group. . . .

Research by a number of analysts conclude that a radical restructuring of the U.S. economy occurred during the 1980's. Many high-wage jobs which required a high school diploma or less education disappeared, or were taken by those with more education. Employment peaked in manufacturing in 1979 and in mining in 1981. The number of production-worker jobs in mining and manufacturing—industries which traditionally have provided high-earning jobs for those without a college education (particularly men)—declined by 2.3 million between 1979 and 1990. This represented a decline from 17.6 percent to 12.3 percent of all jobs in nonfarm establishments. Because a large proportion of these jobs had been held by men, their earnings growth slowed much more than that for women over the period.

Over the 1979-90 period, employment growth was above average in retail trade; finance, insurance, and real estate; and in business, professional, and health services. These industries provide many jobs for workers who are high school graduates, but most often the pay is less than that offered for jobs in manufacturing and mining occupations. Because female high school graduates were much more likely than male high school graduates to be employed in one of these industries than in a high-wage manufacturing or mining job, their earnings growth held up better than that of the males.

In addition, workers with at least some college education apparently took a growing proportion of the better paying jobs. College graduates and those with 1 to 3 years of college had higher increases in earnings in every occupational group and in almost every individual occupation than did high school graduates. . . . In 1979, 32 percent of all high-paid workers (those in the top one-fifth of all earners) were high school graduates. By 1990, only 21 percent were in the top one-fifth. High school graduates as a percent of employment declined by less than 1 percentage point over the period. . . .

Conclusions and Implications

The foregoing discussion indicates that during the 1980's, the earnings of college graduates increased relative to those with less education; an increasing number of college graduates were employed in jobs that did not usually require a degree; and employers had little difficulty hiring a sufficient number of college graduates to fill jobs that required a college degree. Analysts can reasonably conclude from the data presented in this article that rising relative wages of college graduates were not the result of a general shortage of college graduates, but rather a result of a restructuring of the economy. This restructuring affected particularly the earnings of high school graduates who in the past often found work in higher paying manufacturing and mining occupations.

Despite the large number of workers with 4 years of college education who were employed in jobs that did not require a degree, the data clearly show that college graduates were paid a premium for their skills and abilities, regardless of the occupation in which they are employed. Thus, on average, one can conclude that during the 1980's, a college degree did pay off for the great majority of workers. Some college graduates, however, earned substantially less than the average....

Kristina Shelley [a Bureau of Labor Statistics economist writing in the July 1992 *Monthly Labor Review*] projects that there will continue to be more graduates entering the labor force through 2005 than there will be openings for jobs that require a college degree, even under very optimistic assumptions about employment growth and upgraded job requirements....

August

August

OREGON HEALTH PLAN
August 3, 1992

An innovative Oregon plan that would have rationed health care to the poor while expanding Medicare coverage to include 120,000 more people was rejected August 3 by Secretary of Health and Human Services Louis Sullivan.

Oregon officials said the plan represented a trade-off that would help control medical costs while giving more people access to medical services. Under the proposal, Oregon would provide health care to every poor person in the state. That would add 120,000 people to the state's Medicaid rolls. The trade-off was that some medical services would not be covered. A panel ranked 709 medical services based on their costs and benefits. It then decided that the state's Medicare program would pay for the first 587 services but not the last 122. Treatment for bursitis and the common cold were some of the services eliminated under the plan. However, the congressional Office of Technology Assessment said the plan also failed to treat "a substantial number of medical conditions that in the absence of treatment have serious clinical consequences."

Backers of the plan included the state legislature, Oregon's two senators and five representatives, the Oregon Medical Association, some Oregon groups representing the disabled, and Democratic presidential candidate Bill Clinton. They contended that states had to set priorities for health-care spending because there was not enough money to provide all possible medical services to all people who needed them. They also said that health-care rationing already existed in many unofficial forms, particularly for the 120,000 state residents with no health insurance and no Medicaid benefits.

However, the plan drew widespread opposition from some advocates for the disabled, anti-abortion groups, the Roman Catholic Church, the Children's Defense Fund, and Senator Al Gore, Clinton's running mate on the Democratic ticket. Some opponents said the plan would force poor women and children to bear the brunt of containing health-care costs. Others contended that medical decisions about who to treat would be based on the patient's quality of life. Still others opposed the plan because it still paid for abortions.

Oregon needed federal approval for the proposal because it deviated from the federal Medicaid law, which provided medical care to poor people. But Sullivan refused to grant approval, contending that the plan violated the Americans with Disabilities Act of 1990 because it discriminated against the disabled. Sullivan cited two examples of alleged discrimination. He said an alcoholic suffering from cirrhosis of the liver would not be eligible for a kidney transplant, while a nonalcoholic would. He also said that a premature baby that weighed less than about eighteen ounces at birth would not receive the extensive life support that a larger premature baby would.

Oregon officials said the two examples showed sound medical reasoning, not discrimination. They said an alcoholic would still be eligible for a kidney transplant if he had stopped drinking. And they said that a baby weighing less than eighteen ounces at birth would still receive basic life support. However, it would not receive more expensive help that had little chance of prolonging the baby's life.

Some Oregon officials and health-care experts said the Bush administration's discrimination claim was simply a smokescreen. The real reason the administration rejected the plan, they said, was that it did not want to tackle such a touchy political issue so close to the presidential election. As evidence, they said that the administration had not raised the issue of the Disabilities Act until only days before Sullivan's decision was released.

Oregon Senate President John Kitzhaber, an emergency room physician who wrote the plan, denounced Sullivan's decision. He said the decision "constitutes a de facto endorsement of the current flawed and failing health care system—a system which excludes millions of Americans, many of whom suffer and die needlessly for want of basic care. While refusing to assume any accountability for the victims of today's silent rationing, the administration has delayed one state's effort to expand access."

Federal rejection also left in limbo a provision in the plan that would require all Oregon employers to offer basic health care benefits to their workers. With Clinton's win in the presidential election on November 3, however, Oregon officials were poised to resubmit the plan once Clinton took office in January 1993. Clinton said during the campaign that he would approve the proposal.

Following is the text of a letter that Dr. Louis Sullivan, secretary of Health and Human Services, sent to Oregon Governor Barbara Roberts August 3, 1992, and excerpts from the accompanying "Analysis Under the Americans With Disabilities Act (ADA) of the Oregon Reform Demonstration":

SULLIVAN LETTER TO GOVERNOR ROBERTS

Dear Governor Roberts:

Thank you for submitting your application entitled "Oregon Reform Demonstration" for review by the Department of Health and Human Services under section 1115 of the Social Security Act.

The Administration is firmly committed to encouraging innovation in state health care programs, and generally favors using states as "laboratories of democracy." With this application, Oregon has attempted to fashion a wide-ranging reform of its Medicaid program, many features of which have my strong support.

I regret, however, that I am unable to give your application final approval until a number of legal issues, which relate primarily to the Americans with Disabilities Act, are resolved. Particularly given the real possibility that Oregon's general approach will serve as a model for other states, it is critically important that it go forward only with strict adherence to the legal protections that President Bush has worked so hard to enact.

We have tried to provide as much guidance as possible for the future in the enclosed analysis. I urge Oregon to submit a revised application which addresses these concerns and I look forward to approving such a demonstration.

Sincerely,

Louis W. Sullivan, M.D.

ANALYSIS UNDER THE AMERICANS WITH DISABILITIES ACT ("ADA") OF THE OREGON REFORM DEMONSTRATION

The record regarding the manner in which the list of condition/treatment pairs was compiled contains considerable evidence that it was based in substantial part on the premise that the value of the life of a person with a disability is less than the value of the life of a person without a disability. This is a premise which is inconsistent with the ADA. Accordingly, the requested waiver cannot be approved until Oregon provides evidence that allows us to conclude that the program has been revised so that factors impermissible under the ADA had no effect on the list, thus bringing the program into conformity with the ADA. To assist Oregon in this undertaking, the following observations and suggestions are provided.

There are substantial indications in the material Oregon has provided that the quality of life data derived from the Oregon telephone survey quantifies stereotypic assumptions about persons with disabilities. Scholars who have examined quality of life surveys have concluded that as compared to persons who have the disabilities in question, persons without disabilities systematically undervalue the quality of life of those with disabilities. The Congressional Office of Technology Assessment found this bias against persons with disabilities in the Oregon survey results. The Commission itself stated that "those who had experienced the problem [impaired health state] did not feel it was as severe as those who had not experienced the problem." Commission Report at C-11. The Commission acknowledged that "[t]his response has been replicated in a number of studies." *Id.*

Oregon's counsel's submissions regarding the status of the program under the ADA do not dispute that the telephone survey allowed bias against persons with disabilities to be taken into account and that the telephone survey affected the final ranking of health services. In effect, Oregon argues that the biased telephone survey's impact on the ranking of health services was real but limited. However, Oregon's own statistical analysis—which itself may incorporate distinctions based on disabilities and may thus present independent questions under the ADA—shows that the survey had an appreciable impact on the final rankings, because more than 120 services would move at least 30 places on the prioritized list and more than 50 services would move at least 50 places on the list if constant values of 0.5 were substituted for values generated by the survey. One service would move 161 places. Unless Oregon funds all of the health services on its prioritized list every year, it is unlikely on the record Oregon submitted that the Commission could demonstrate that the telephone survey data will have no effect on which medical conditions are treated.

Accordingly, the rankings of condition/treatment pairs should be redone without using rankings derived from the telephone survey as a starting point.

Other aspects of the ranking process also reflect discrimination on the basis of disability. According to the Commission Report, the Commissioners ranked all categories and made hand adjustments to the list on the basis of certain community values, including "quality of life" and "ability to function." These two values place importance on "restored" health and functional "independence" and thus expressly value a person without a disability more highly than a person with a disability in the allocation of medical treatment. As the Commission itself notes, the adjustments also moved treatments for "severe or exacerbated conditions"—almost the very definition of a disability—to "relatively unfavorable positions." Commission Report at 28. The rankings should be redone without taking such factors into account. In addition, any methodology that would intentionally ration health care resources by associating quality of life considerations with disabilities does not comport with the mandate of the ADA.

Of course, there is a wide range of factors that Oregon may consider in allocating medical resources consistent with the ADA. These factors include, but are not limited to, the cost of medical procedures, the length of hospital stays, prevention of death, and prevention of contagious diseases. In general, Oregon may consider, consistent with the ADA, any content neutral factor that does not take disability into account or that does not have a particular exclusionary effect on persons with disabilities. . . .

GLASS CEILING REPORT
Aug. 11, 1992

While women and minorities were slowly moving into executive suites, a "glass ceiling" still prevented many from reaching their full potential in the business world.

That was the conclusion of "Pipelines of Progress: A Status Report on the Glass Ceiling," released August 11 by the U.S. Department of Labor. "Progress in the advancement of qualified minorities and women into mid and senior level management positions has taken place," the report said. "The success stories remain, however, the exception rather than the rule."

Women and minorities made up more than 50 percent of the nation's work force, according to the Labor Department. In the next decade, 80 percent of new entrants into the work force would be women, minorities, and immigrants. Yet many companies still made little or no effort to recruit, retain, and promote qualified women and minorities.

"Women and members of minority groups often find that working hard, sacrificing, paying their dues, will only take them so far," Secretary of Labor Lynn Martin said in a speech June 20 at Northwestern University. "They can see that next rung on the corporate ladder, but a glass ceiling keeps them from reaching it. That real, yet invisible, barrier keeps them from realizing their goal, from turning their dream into reality."

A 1992 Business Week *survey of 400 female managers found that 70 percent believed the male-dominated corporate culture was an obstacle to their success. That was up from 60 percent in a similar survey two years earlier. In addition, while nearly half said that large companies had done "somewhat better" in hiring and promoting female executives over the previous five years, more than half said the rate of progress had slowed down.*

In August 1991 the Labor Department kicked off a "Glass Ceiling Initiative" with an initial report that examined the status of women and minorities in corporations. The study found that corporations had erected barriers that blocked career advancement by minorities and women, the glass ceiling existed at a far lower management level than originally thought, and minorities plateaued at lower management levels than women.

"The glass ceiling, where it exists, hinders not only individuals but society as a whole," Martin said in releasing the 1991 report. "It effectively cuts our pool of potential corporate leaders by eliminating over one-half of our population. It deprives our economy of new leaders, new sources of creativity—the 'would be' pioneers of the business world. If our end game is to compete successfully in today's global market, then we have to unleash the full potential of the American work force."

After releasing the 1991 report, the Labor Department started conducting "glass ceiling compliance reviews" of federal contractors to ensure they were complying with laws barring discrimination in the workplace. The department also started a review of its own practices in hiring and promoting women and minorities.

In conjunction with release of the 1992 report, Martin signed an agreement with Small Business Administrator Patricia Saiki in which the two agencies pledged to work together to help small and medium-sized businesses eliminate barriers to diversity. The agreement's goal was to develop model programs that small and mid-sized firms could use to tackle their own glass ceilings. "I am convinced that small business owners are leading the way in adopting policies that are inclusive," Saiki said in signing the agreement, ". . . and that these small companies will continue to open paths of upward mobility for everyone."

In September 1992 Martin sent letters to twenty college presidents and twenty-six heads of leading media companies urging them to work with her to remove employment barriers. She asked them to meet with her to discuss how they could improve their own institutions and to make public commitments to remove glass ceiling barriers.

In October 1992 Martin chaired the first meeting of the congressionally mandated Glass Ceiling Commission. The twenty-one-member panel was charged with identifying obstacles that prevented qualified women and minorities from reaching executive suites. It planned to conduct hearings around the country and then prepare a report for Congress recommending ways to tear down the glass ceiling. The Glass Ceiling Commission was created as part of the Civil Rights Act of 1991, which President Bush signed into law in August 1991.

Also in October, a study by the U.S. Merit Systems Protection Board found that the same glass ceiling that blocked women in business also existed in the federal government. The report, titled "A Question of

Equity: Women and the Glass Ceiling in the Federal Government," found that women held nearly half the white-collar jobs in the federal government. However, only 25 percent of federal supervisors were women, and about 10 percent of senior federal executives were female. The report, like the study conducted by the Labor Department, found that advancement by women was blocked at a far lower level than previously believed.

Following is the executive summary of "Pipelines of Progress: A Status Report on the Glass Ceiling," released August 11, 1992, by the U.S. Department of Labor:

This report is largely focused on the steps companies can take and have taken to remove glass ceiling barriers. The companies discussed are those which have been subject to the Department's glass ceiling reviews as either part of the pilot reviews of last year, or as part of the ongoing reviews the Department now conducts. We believe this discussion should assist the entire corporate community, as individual companies identify their own glass ceiling barriers and implement strategies to remove them.

This report is also a good news, bad news document. The good news is that the participation rates of minorities and women in corporate management has improved. The bad news is that surveys in the corporate world do not point to an optimistic future unless commitments to positive change are sustained and enhanced. This report abounds with anecdotal evidence showing that glass ceiling barriers can be removed. It also demonstrates that the Department's enforcement effort must continue to be a critical component of the strategy to remove such barriers. But the report also underscores the fact that the challenge to shatter the glass ceiling takes far more time and effort than even the strongest of commitments can produce in one year.

I. Workforce Trends

Research data on workplace advancement has yielded mixed results. It is encouraging to note that there is an increased awareness of the issue of diversity in corporate America. They key to real progress in attaining this goal, however, still remains at the pipeline levels of advancement, well below senior level management.

A *Business Week* survey released this year of 400 female managers found that almost half of the respondents believed that large companies have done "somewhat better" over the last five years in terms of hiring and promoting women executives. More than half of these same respondents also believed that the rate of progress has slowed down. Seventy percent of those female managers polled believed that the male-dominated corporate culture was an obstacle to their success (up from 60 percent two years ago).

A recent study of career progressions of over 1000 male and female managers in 20 Fortune 500 companies by researchers at Loyola University of Chicago and the Kellogg Graduate School of Management found that while these two groups were alike in almost every way, the "women with equal or better educations earn less on average than men and there are proportionately fewer women in top management positions."

The Department's own analysis of data filed by those companies holding Federal contracts does show, however, that minorities and women have made progress over the past 10 years. The proportion of corporate officials and managers who are minorities and women significantly increased during this time period.

II. Corporate Management Reviews

During the past year, the Department has been monitoring the progress of the companies reviewed in the first round of pilot reviews through progress reports and follow-up visits.

The first round of reviews found that many of the Federal contractors believed they were in compliance, but when reviewed were found not to be. As a corrective measure, not only did the Department require progress reports, but it also conducted follow-up visits to substantiate the progress.

Some specific examples of the positive effects from the reviews and follow-up include:

- **Commitment Continues at the Top—Despite a Change in Leadership.** During our follow-up visit to this company, the new Chief Executive Officer (CEO) expressed concern that his corporation was still not where he wanted it to be with regard to diversity, but that they were actively attempting to monitor internal systems to ensure that qualified minorities and women could have access to the top based on merit. The company has made equal employment opportunity a performance appraisal standard for senior management and has experienced good results in expecting managers to make good faith efforts to include qualified women and minorities for promotional considerations.

- **Reaffirmation and Commitment to Inclusivity and Diversity.** Actions include a new performance appraisal system which contains a specific component appraising performance in the area of equal opportunity and making this an integrated management concern, not just a human resource function; corporate-wide diversity training to increase management understanding of the importance of nondiscrimination and good faith efforts in hiring, promotional and management development opportunities; and implementation of an employee opinion survey to provide confidential feedback.

- **One Company's Pipelines Yield Success.** A reorganization at this large Fortune 500 company resulted in the placement of all of the corporation's equal employment responsibility under a centralized management structure, and the establishment of critical measures to achieving workforce diversity. Since January 1, 1992, a number of women have been appointed to senior management positions, two of whom are members of a minority group. A minority male was also appointed to a group manager position.

III. Beyond the Pilot Reviews

Compliance reviews have continued in a measured, precise fashion. Results indicate that many of the companies audited since last year have changed their culture to one which values diversity. We continue to find that if the CEO is committed to ensuring diversity, it can happen. Such commitment notwithstanding, progress varies. Examples include:

- **A non-traditional industry for women,** a utility company in which the workforce had been primarily male for the past 100 years, is taking large strides to develop a diverse workforce through the new CEO's requirement of good faith efforts and accountability at each level of management. Actions include an executive recruitment effort which led to the hiring of women and minorities in high level positions; and the development of systems of mentoring, networking and identification of minorities and women with potential and providing them with information on career paths.
- **A company without a formal system for development** and few women and minorities in the pipelines for advancement, agreed to work to enhance the skills of all its employees, and appointed a top management team to monitor results of diversity efforts. Additionally, this employer is taking pro-active steps to recruit minorities and women through scholarships, outreach efforts, and greater visibility in the employment community.
- **A corporation with little emphasis on diversity** is changing the corporate culture to one that values diversity. A reorganization and the arrival of a new CEO from outside the corporation, have formed the groundwork for a corporate-wide commitment to developing a diverse workforce. The company agreed to many positive steps which include improving the workforce participation of minorities and women, monitoring for nondiscrimination, and ensuring that equal employment becomes an integrated business function of the corporation.

IV. Areas Warranting Greater Attention

Several of the barriers for women and minorities cited in the initial glass ceiling report continue to exist in companies reviewed this year.

- **A lack of consistent recruitment practices to attract a diverse pool of talent.** While entry level corporate hiring is generally well-documented, systems of recruitment and tracking generally did not exist above a certain level.
- **A lack of opportunity to contribute and participate in corporate development experiences.** Another *Business Week* survey, October 1991, further found that, "In regular B-school programs—

usually paid for by the participants, not an employer—there are plenty of women and minorities.... Yet in the prestigious programs paid for by corporations that round out a manager's credentials at a key career point, usually at age 40 or 45, companies are making only a token investment in developing female and minority executives. Only about 3 percent of the 180 executives in Stanford's recent advanced-management program were women."

• **A general lack of corporate ownership in affirming that the practice of equal employment opportunity is an organizational responsibility, not one persons's.**

Beyond those barriers, other issues have surfaced which appear to hinder the hiring and advancement of minorities and women. Some women expressed concern that they were not held to the same performance measures as men, and believed they had to work twice as hard. Mid level female managers in one company recently audited almost uniformly mentioned that the company was "not willing to take risks on women." These women felt they had to work twice as hard to prove they were as committed as men in the workforce, and had to stay in grade longer before promotion.

In many companies, the ability to relocate continues to be a requirement to career progression and advancement to the executive suite. The Department consistently states that if mobility is a requirement for career advancement, then management must also offer mobility opportunities to qualified minorities and women, ought to explain to them the benefits of acceptance, and must not make career assumptions for members of these groups.

V. What Works

There are a number of creative and effective approaches which employers are adopting in an effort to provide access into middle and upper management positions for qualified minorities and women. Indeed, the Department has recognized with annual awards several companies which have developed and implemented such approaches.

Some of these approaches include:

• Tracking Women and Minorities with Advancement Potential
• Ensuring Access and Visibility
• Ensuring a Bias-Free Workplace
• Entering the Pipeline (Corporate Attention Toward)

Conclusion

We are more convinced than ever that this decade must be the decade of dialogue between employers, employees, the Federal Government and the private sector. Employers have a responsibility to ensure that there are no artificial barriers to advancement of qualified minorities and women in their workplace. The Department of Labor not only has the legal responsibility to ensure no such barriers exist, but must also provide assistance to aid in compliance. And, of course, employees must take personal responsibility for their own careers—weighing personal and professional trade-offs.

It is only through greater understanding and heightened awareness to issues that true and lasting progress will occur. The Department of Labor continues to assist employers in identifying and eliminating barriers.

ETHICS COMMITTEE RESOLUTION REBUKING SENATOR HATFIELD
August 12, 1992

The Senate Ethics Committee formally rebuked Mark O. Hatfield, R-Ore., on August 12 for accepting and failing to report gifts worth nearly $43,000 between 1983 and 1988. Acting for the full Senate, the committee found that Hatfield had violated the 1978 Ethics in Government Act and Senate rules. It deemed his actions "improper conduct reflecting upon the Senate."

Most of the gifts cited by the committee were from Dr. James B. Holderman, former president of the University of South Carolina. While Hatfield chaired the Appropriations Committee in 1986, Congress approved a $16.3 million grant to the school.

In the course of its fifteen-month investigation, the ethics panel did not find evidence of criminal violations or willful wrongdoing by Hatfield, and it found no connection between his official actions and acceptance of the gifts. His shortcomings were instead attributed to "negligence" and "inattention."

Seemingly as a warning to others, the committee pointedly noted that even if the gifts were not linked to Hatfield's official actions, they were "inappropriate and cannot be condoned." Chairman Terry Sanford, D-N.C., and Vice Chairman Warren B. Rudman, R-N.H., said that the committee's action was a significant discipline.

Hatfield had served in the Senate since 1967 and before that had been governor of Oregon for eight years.

At an Oregon news conference hours after the Ethics Committee released its decision, Hatfield said, "I accept and agree with the committee's judgment.... My mistakes were many and my omissions serious."

Third Investigation

Hatfield's finances were similarly investigated in 1977 and 1984, but no improper conduct was found in the earlier cases. He had been reelected to a fifth Senate term in 1990, several months before newspapers in South Carolina and Oregon began reporting on the free-spending ways Holderman used to promote his school.

Hatfield filed amended financial disclosure reports, changed his office's procedures for filling out financial disclosure forms, and said that he would no longer accept gifts from anyone except family members and close friends having no stake in his official duties.

In addition to the gifts enumerated in the resolution, the committee reviewed the propriety of Hatfield's acceptance of low- and no-interest loans. His son's acceptance of a scholarship to the University of South Carolina was estimated to be worth at least $15,000. "We looked at everything," said Rudman.

The panel found no impropriety in the scholarship for Hatfield's son. Rudman and Sanford noted that Hatfield had been informed of the scholarship after it was awarded. Rudman also said that Hatfield's son was an "emancipated person"—over eighteen and financially independent—when he received the funds.

Unusual Dissenting Vote

The committee, divided equally between Democrats and Republicans, voted 5-1 to rebuke Hatfield. Democratic Senator Richard H. Bryan of Nevada said that while he agreed with the outcome, he wanted stronger language in the resolution. While Bryan refused to elaborate on his objections, his dissenting vote was highly unusual, a first according to Bryan. Typically the panel does not go public until its findings are unanimous.

Even in the 1990-1991 "Keating Five" investigation, Jesse Helms, R-N.C., who had scathingly denounced the committee's inclinations in the months leading up to its decision, chose to abstain rather than vote against the panel's recommendation.

The committee rebuke of Hatfield was a stronger action than that taken against four of the five senators involved with savings and loan magnate Charles H. Keating, Jr. The committee found them guilty of poor judgment and issued letters to that effect. The committee subsequently reprimanded one of the Keating Five senators, Alan Cranston, D-Calif., on November 19, 1991. It said his relationship with Keating showed "an impermissible pattern of conduct." Cranston did not seek reelection in 1992. (Senate Ethics Committee on "Keating Five," Historic Documents of 1991, p. 107)

In both the Cranston and Hatfield cases, the Ethics Committee said that it was acting "on behalf of and in the name of the United States Senate." There was no Senate floor vote in either case, but both rebukes were on a par with previous punishments that fell short of expulsion. Disciplinary precedents are somewhat vague because, over the years, the Senate has chosen different words—censure, reprimand, denounce, condemn—to describe similar actions.

Hatfield thus became only the thirteenth senator in history to be formally chastised, either by the Senate itself or by the Ethics Committee acting for the Senate.

> *Following is the resolution adopted by the Senate Select Committee on Ethics on August 12, 1992, rebuking Senator Mark O. Hatfield, R-Ore.:*

WHEREAS, the Senate Select Committee on Ethics has conducted a Preliminary Inquiry into allegations of misconduct by Senator Mark O. Hatfield, and has provided to Senator Hatfield all the rights provided under Senate Resolution 338 (88th Congress second session, as amended) and the Committee's procedural rules; and

WHEREAS, from 1983 through 1988 Senator Hatfield failed to disclose on his public financial disclosure reports the following:

1. a Boehm Carolina wren (value $725) from the University of South Carolina/Dr. James B. Holderman, former president of the University, in 1983;
2. a Steuben glass eagle (value $535) from the University of South Carolina/Dr. Holderman, in 1983;
3. a compact disc player (value $400) from Dr. Holderman in 1985;
4. a Steuben glass cross (value $3,875) from the University of South Carolina/Dr. Holderman in 1985;
5. a framed Audubon wild turkey print (value $3,336) from the University of South Carolina/Dr. Holderman in 1985;
6. $17,000 in home improvements for remodeling and expanding a bedroom from Mrs. Dorothy Cook in 1985;
7. the forgiveness of $4,415 interest due on loans from Mr. John Dellenback in 1987;
8. two signet rings (total value $5,500) from Mr. and Mrs. Herb Shapiro and Mr. Larry Packouz in 1987;
9. the forgiveness of $5,005 interest due on loans from Mr. Dellenback in 1988;
10. a bronze beaver sculpture (value $2,100) from Mr. Sang Hahn in 1988;
11. the reimbursement of travel expenses by the University of South Carolina in connection with an appearance at a park clean-up in Columbia, South Carolina, on or about March 1-3, 1985;
12. the reimbursement of travel expenses by the University of South Carolina in connection with University events honoring Sir Oliver

Wright on or about November 14-16, 1986;

13. the reimbursement of travel expenses by the University of South Carolina for delivering the commencement address at the university on or about December 18, 1987; and

WHEREAS, Senator Hatfield has acknowledged fault in connection with his failures to disclose; and

WHEREAS, the committee has found no credible evidence that Senator Hatfield's failures to disclose were intentional in nature; and

WHEREAS, Senator Hatfield has amended his annual financial disclosure reports to disclose each of the above enumerated items (with the exception of his calendar year 1983 report which is no longer of public record, having been destroyed by the Senate Office of Public Records as required by law);

It is therefore, RESOLVED, that:

Senator Hatfield's failure to disclose the above enumerated items violated the Ethics in Government Act of 1978 (Senate Rule 34), and his pattern of conduct in accepting and consistently failing to disclose the above enumerated items demonstrated a serious lack of concern for, and negligence in connection with, his legal obligation to disclose such gifts, violated established norms of behavior in the Senate, and was improper conduct reflecting upon the Senate as contemplated by Section 2(a) (1) of Senate Resolution 338, 88th Congress.

THEREFORE, the Senate Select Committee on Ethics, on behalf of and in the name of the United States Senate, does hereby rebuke Senator Mark O. Hatfield.

Additionally, the committee notes that Senator Hatfield accepted and failed to disclose gifts from the University of South Carolina/Dr. Holderman over a period of years when he was being asked to take routine official actions which affected the University of South Carolina/Dr. Holderman.

Although the Committee does not find any linkage between the gifts and these routine actions, including those with respect to appropriations affecting the University of South Carolina, the Committee concludes that Senator Hatfield's repeated acceptance of and failure to disclose gifts from the University of South Carolina/Dr. Holderman over a period of years when he was being asked to take routine official actions which affected the University of South Carolina/Dr. Holderman were inappropriate and cannot be condoned.

NORTH AMERICAN FREE TRADE AGREEMENT
August 12, 1992

The United States, Canada, and Mexico on August 12, 1992, agreed to a free-trade accord designed to erase, over a period of fifteen years, tariffs and other barriers to the movement of goods, services, and money among the three countries. The accord, the North American Free Trade Agreement (NAFTA), faced formidable hurdles—especially in legislatures in Canada and the United States—before it could be adopted. If adopted, the accord would take effect January 1, 1994.

The broad purpose of the agreement was to make the entire North American region better able to compete with its trading rivals in Asia and Europe. But many observers believed the accord's chief benefit to the United States would be to promote economic growth in Mexico, thus reducing the pressure of Mexican emigration to the north.

NAFTA would govern the sale and purchase of products and services throughout North America, stipulating the dates for the elimination of barriers to their free exchange among the three nations. Furthermore, it would open new markets in Mexico for American banks, insurance companies, and securities firms. In a provision of great interest to American and Canadian investors, the agreement would bar expropriation that was not compensated and would ensure that profits could be transferred out of Mexico without restrictions.

Announcing the agreement only hours after negotiations were concluded, President George Bush hailed the accord as "the beginning of a new era" for economic cooperation in North America that would "create jobs and generate growth in all three countries."

*Democratic Governor Bill Clinton of Arkansas, who was elected presi-
dent in November, said during the campaign that he supported NAFTA
if it provided "adequate protection for workers, farmers, and the environment on both sides of the border."*

*President Carlos Salinas de Gortari of Mexico had initiated the
negotiations that led to the agreement. Addressing his nation August 13,
1992, Salinas enthusiastically said the pact represented "one more step, I
repeat one more step, which will make it possible for us to create more
benefits for our children and our children's children."*

Support for the Agreement

*Many American labor leaders and some Democratic members of Con-
gress feared that, with liberalization of trade, American businesses would
move to Mexico to exploit low wages in that country. But Michael J.
Boskin, chairman of Bush's Council of Economic Advisers, and many other
analysts contended that the relatively low productivity of Mexican workers
made such a result unlikely. Boskin said that a "U.S. company that
moves to Mexico would have to hire more workers to achieve its desired
output...."*

*Carla Hills, the U.S. trade representative who led American negoti-
ators, said, "Mexico is our fastest growing export opportunity ... and this
agreement not only locks in the economic reforms and export opportunities that we have secured to date, but builds upon them and creates a real
job machine at our back door."*

*American manufacturers of automobiles, telecommunications equip-
ment, and computers believed that liberalized trade would vastly increase their sales in Mexico. For example, Robert C. Stempel, chairman
of General Motors Corp., said the agreement had the potential to create
jobs in the United States and to increase trade by all three countries.*

*NAFTA was attacked by some environmental groups especially worried
about pollution in the U.S.-Mexico border area. But William K. Reilly,
administrator of the Environmental Protection Agency, called the agreement the most environmentally sensitive trade agreement ever negotiated anywhere.*

An editorial in the Washington Post *Aug. 5, 1992, cited research by the
Institute of International Economics, which showed that NAFTA would
"probably create about 325,000 new jobs" in the United States during its
first five years. Yet the editorial also said the same research predicted
that NAFTA would cost 150,000 present jobs, for a net gain of 175,000
jobs. The editorial concluded that free trade was good for people with
advanced skills and bad for people without them.*

*A strongly supportive editorial in the same newspaper Sept. 8, 1992,
predicted that NAFTA would have the same effect on Mexico, encouraging democracy and productivity, that membership in the European
Community was having for Spain and Portugal. The editorial went on to
call NAFTA one of the best things that President Bush had done.*

Opposition Fears

Led by unions, opposition to NAFTA increased after the conclusion of negotiations. For example, Thomas Donahue, AFL-CIO secretary-treasurer, called NAFTA a bad deal for American workers, consumers, and the long-term health of the American economy. Most of all, the unions were fearful of runaway plants, that is, the loss of manufacturing plants to Mexico to take advantage of Mexican wages, estimated to be only one-seventh the wages in the United States.

Democratic Senator Donald W. Riegle Jr., who represented Michigan, where automobile plants were already being shut down, called NAFTA a "real danger to Michigan and the entire American economy ... because we will have plants closing all across America and moving to Mexico. . . ."

An influential Democratic leader in the U.S. House, Majority Leader Richard A. Gephardt, told reporters that NAFTA did not provide for adequate protection for workers, farmers, and the environment on both sides of the border. Gephardt called for renegotiation of NAFTA to correct what he perceived as its faults.

President Bush signed NAFTA on Dec. 17, 1992. He thus left to his successor, President Bill Clinton, the challenge of shepherding NAFTA through Congress, which had to enact implementing legislation before the agreement could take effect. President Salinas of Mexico and Prime Minister Brian Mulroney of Canada signed the agreement the same day in their countries.

> *Following are President Bush's remarks announcing the completion of negotiations on the North American Free Trade Agreement on August 12, 1992:*

Today marks the beginning of a new era on our continent, on the North American Continent. This morning the United States, Mexico, and Canada are announcing the completion of negotiations for a North American free trade agreement, NAFTA.

First, I want to express my deep appreciation to Ambassador Carla Hills, our United States Trade Representative, to Secretary Serra of Mexico, and to Minister Wilson of Canada for this outstanding achievement. Also standing next to me is Carla Hills' Deputy, my able friend Jules Katz, who had a very instrumental role in all these negotiations.

This historic trade agreement will further open markets in Mexico, Canada, and the United States. It will create jobs and generate economic growth in all three countries. Increased trade with North America will help our Nation prepare for the challenges and opportunities of the next century.

The cold war is over. The principal challenge now facing the United States is to compete in a rapidly changing, expanding global marketplace.

This agreement will level the North American playing field, allowing American companies to increase sales from Alaska to the Yucatan. By sweeping aside barriers, NAFTA will make our companies more competitive everywhere in the world. We've seen this happen with the U.S.-Canada Free Trade Agreement, and we'll see it even more with the NAFTA.

Open markets in Mexico and Canada mean more American jobs. Our Nation is the world's leading exporter, well ahead of Japan and Germany. Today over 7 million Americans are hard at work making products that will be sold around the world. Export-related jobs pay 17 percent more than the average U.S. wage. These jobs are the kind that our Nation needs to grow and prosper, the kind that showcase American talent and technology.

More than 600,000 Americans are now employed making products and selling them to Mexico, our fastest growing export market. We sold over $33 billion worth of goods to Mexico last year and are projected to sell $44 billion this year. In the last 5 years, as President Salinas has dismantled many longstanding Mexican trade and investment restrictions, our exports to Mexico have nearly tripled. In the last 5 years, let me repeat that, our exports to Mexico have nearly tripled. That's one-quarter of a million new American jobs. This agreement helps us lock in these gains and build on them.

Last year the Congress endorsed moving forward with NAFTA by extending the Fast Track procedures for congressional consideration and implementation of trade agreements. The rapid completion of the NAFTA talks shows how much can be accomplished when the executive branch and the Congress work together to do what is best for our Nation. And I'll work closely with the Congress for rapid implementation.

At the time Fast Track was extended, I outlined steps that we would take to address environmental and labor concerns. We've taken every promised step, and we are meeting or beating every commitment that I outlined. This is the first time a trade agreement has included stringent provisions to benefit the environment. The NAFTA maintains this Nation's high environmental, health, and safety standards. In fact, it goes even further and encourages all three countries to seek the highest possible standards.

The Environmental Protection Agency and its Mexican counterpart have already developed a comprehensive integrated border plan to clean up air, water, and hazardous wastes along the Rio Grande. These problems are serious, but they will be solved by environmental cooperation, increased trade, and higher levels of economic growth, not protectionism. Unfortunately, Congress has reduced the funding for our border plan in the appropriations process. I ask the Congress to fully fund these important environmental initiatives.

With NAFTA we're moving forward with our trade strategy. Trade is part of my long-term economic growth plan to create more opportunities for all Americans. In a changing world, we must give our workers the education and skills they need to compete and assistance and training to find good jobs. I've said many times: Level the playing field and the American worker can outthink, outproduce, and outwork anyone, anytime.

Today's historic agreement links our future with our past. Five centuries ago this very month, a man of courage and vision set sail from the Old World in search of new trade routes and opportunities. Christopher Columbus was an entrepreneur, and the journey he started 500 years ago continues to pay off abundantly today. By moving forward with the NAFTA, with the North American free trade agreement, we will replenish that investment, opening up new horizons of opportunity and enterprise in the New World.

So this is a good day for America, a good day for North America. Once again, I want to express my appreciation to Ambassador Hills and her extraordinarily able team, who have worked literally day and night for months to complete this negotiation phase of the agreement. It's good news, and as I understand it, the Ambassador will be having a briefing on the details of it in a few minutes from now.

Thank you all very much.

UN RESOLUTION ON
BOSNIAN RELIEF
August 13, 1992

Bowing to worldwide concern, the United Nations Security Council voted August 13 to "take all measures necessary" to deliver food and medicine to suffering civilians in Bosnia and Hercegovina, a war-ravaged former Yugoslav republic. The phrase was understood to mean the use of military force, if necessary, although the council resolution did not specifically call for the creation of a UN-led relief expedition. Instead it authorized member nations to undertake joint action to see that the relief aid was delivered.

The deliberately vague language of the resolution—Resolution 770— was similar to the phrasing of the United Nations resolution in November 1990 under which the United States led multinational forces against Iraq. (Deadline Pressure on Saddam Hussein, Historic Documents of 1990, p. 767) Resolution 770 made clear, however, that any force so raised "in coordination with the United Nations" would apply itself only to the delivery of goods and not to direct intervention in the Yugoslav civil war. And unlike in 1990, no countries promptly came forward to organize a military mission.

In fact, the reaction of UN Secretary General Boutros Boutros-Ghali to the resolution was negative. He warned that a UN-sanctioned use of military force could threaten an existing UN peacekeeping force of nearly 15,000 members in next-door Croatia, the scene of bitter fighting in 1991. Croatia and its neighbor Slovenia—two of the six Yugoslav republics— broke away from the Yugoslav state that June and separately declared their independence. The two republics were protesting a resurgent Serbian nationalism that was seeking to dominate the old federation. (Indepen-

dence of Yugoslav Republics, Historic Documents of 1991, p. 367)

Slobodan Milosevic, president of Serbia, espoused a strong brand of Serbian nationalism. The president of Croatia, Franjo Tudjman, pushed Croatian nationalism with equal fervor. Immediately after independence, fighting broke out in Croatia between Croats and Serbs, who formed a 700,000-member minority in that republic of 4.5 million people. Serbian rebels, backed by the Serbian-led Yugoslav army, gained control of several cities and about one-third of the territory. The campaign bogged down by the year's end and both sides acceded to the establishment of a UN peacekeeping force along cease-fire lines.

Bosnia-Hercegovina, an ethnically diverse republic with a large Moslem population, voted for independence in February 1992, but the referendum was boycotted by its Serbian residents, who quickly declared a Serbian state within Bosnia-Hercegovina. Serbian militias were armed, equipped, and often manned by Yugoslav army troops who had merely switched uniforms. They formed a fighting force superior to what either the Croats or Moslems could muster. Croats and Moslems, though supposedly allies in a common struggle against the Serbs, were sometimes fighting each other. According to reports, Serbia and Croatia had previously agreed to divide the conquered territory between themselves.

Sarajevo Under Seige

The Serbian militias soon laid siege to Sarajevo, the capital of Bosnia-Hercegovina, a city of nearly 400,000 people, and for months subjected it to bombardment. Cease-fire agreements were repeatedly invoked and violated. On May 30 the Security Council voted to impose economic sanctions against Serbia and Montenegro, all that remained of the former Yugoslav federation. Macedonia had meanwhile broken away. The council also voted to establish a "security zone" around the Sarajevo airport to enable relief supplies to be flown into the city. The previous November the European Community, followed by the United States, had similarly applied economic sanctions. News reports from Belgrade, capital of the Yugoslav federation and of Serbia, indicated that while sanctions had damaged the economy they had not cut off foreign supplies of oil or other critical war materiel for the Serbs.

By the time the Security Council acted on Resolution 770, reports of atrocities were multiplying in Bosnia-Hercegovina and public reaction in the West was putting pressure on European capitals and Washington to "do something." Mummahed Sacirbey, the republic's ambassador to the United Nations decried the Security Council action as a mere "attempt to appease public opinion." As he had before, Sacirbey pleaded for the Security Council to lift a ban on the export of weapons to the warring republics. He contended that the ban deprived Bosnia-Hercegovina of weapons to defend itself without hurting Serbia's ability to wage war. Most of Yugoslavia's arms industries were located in Serbia, the largest and, with 10 million people, the most populous of the Yugoslav republics.

Companion War Crimes Resolution

The Security Council on August 13 also passed another resolution, that one warning that persons who committed war crimes in the Yugoslav civil war would be held responsible for their deeds. The council returned to this subject again on October 6, going a step further by voting unanimously to set up a war crimes commission to collect evidence of atrocities.

The commission, first proposed by the Bush administration, was to be modeled on the Allied War Crimes Commission, which conducted the Nuremberg trials of Nazi leaders after World War II. However, the resolution made no provision for a tribunal at which accused persons would be tried. Similarly, onOctober 9 the Security Council —at American urging—banned all military combat flights over Bosnia-Hercegovina but provided for no enforcement mechanism. Serbian officials later said they would observe the "no-fly zone" and permit UN observers to verify that Serbian warplanes were grounded. Twelve of the fifteen Security Council members voted for Resolution 770. China, India, and Zimbabwe abstained, as they had on several other resolutions calling for UN action on Yugoslavia. Russia, with historic ties to Serbia, voted with the majority but reportedly insisted that the resolution make no references to Serbian aggression.

Following is Resolution 770, approved by the United Nations Security Council 12-0 (with 3 abstentions), August 13, 1992, authorizing member states to take "all measures necessary" to assure the delivery of humanitarian aid to Sarajevo and "wherever needed" to other parts of war-torn Bosnia-Hercegovina:

The Security Council,

Reaffirming its resolutions 713 (1991) of 25 September 1991, 721 (1991) of 27 November 1991, 724 (1991) of 15 December 1991, 727 (1992) of 8 January 1992, 740 (1992) of 7 February 1992, 743 (1992) of 21 February 1992, 749 (1992) of 7 April 1992, 752 (1992) of 15 May 1992, 757 (1992) of 30 May 1992, 758 (1992) of 8 June 1992, 760 (1992) of 18 June 1992, 761 (1992) of 29 June 1992, 762 (1992) of 30 June 1992, 764 (1992) of 13 July 1992 and 769 (1992) of 7 August 1992,

Noting the letter dated 10 August 1992 from the Permanent Representative of the Republic of Bosnia and Herzegovina to the United Nations (S/24401),

Underlining once again the imperative need for an urgent negotiated political solution to the situation in the Republic of Bosnia and Herzegovina to enable that country to live in peace and security within its borders,

Reaffirming the need to respect the sovereignty, territorial integrity and political independence of the Republic of Bosnia and Herzegovina,

Recognizing that the situation in Bosnia and Herzegovina constitutes a threat to international peace and security and that the provision of humanitarian assistance in Bosnia and Herzegovina is an important element in the Council's effort to restore international peace and security in the area,

Commending the United Nations Protection Force (UNPROFOR) for its continuing action in support of the relief operation in Sarajevo and other parts of Bosnia and Herzegovina,

Deeply disturbed by the situation that now prevails in Sarajevo, which has severely complicated UNPROFOR's efforts to fulfil its mandate to ensure the security and functioning of Sarajevo airport and the delivery of humanitarian assistance in Sarajevo and other parts of Bosnia and Herzegovina pursuant to resolutions 743 (1992), 749 (1992), 761 (1992) and 764 (1992) and the reports of the Secretary-General cited therein,

Dismayed by the continuation of conditions that impede the delivery of humanitarian supplies to destinations within Bosnia and Herzegovina and the consequent suffering of the people of that country.

Deeply concerned by reports of abuses against civilians imprisoned in camps, prisons and detention centres,

Determined to establish as soon as possible the necessary conditions for the delivery of humanitarian assistance wherever needed in Bosnia and Herzegovina, in conformity with resolution 764 (1992),
Acting under Chapter VII of the Charter of the United Nations,

1. *Reaffirms* its demand that all parties and others concerned in Bosnia and Herzegovina stop the fighting immediately;
2. *Calls upon* States to take nationally or through regional agencies or arrangements all measures necessary to facilitate in coordination with the United Nations the delivery by relevant United Nations humanitarian organizations and others of humanitarian assistance to Sarajevo and wherever needed in other parts of Bosnia and Herzegovina;
3. *Demands* that unimpeded and continuous access to all camps, prisons and detention centres be granted immediately to the International Committee of the Red Cross and other relevant humanitarian orga-

nizations and that all detainees therein receive humane treatment, including adequate food, shelter and medical care;

4. *Calls upon* States to report to the Secretary-General on measures they are taking in coordination with the United Nations to carry out this resolution, and *invites* the Secretary-General to keep under continuous review any further measures that may be necessary to ensure unimpeded delivery of humanitarian supplies;

5. *Requests* all States to provide appropriate support for the actions undertaken in pursuance of this resolution;

6. *Demands* that all parties and others concerned take the necessary measures to ensure the safety of United Nations and other personnel engaged in the delivery of humanitarian assistance;

7. *Requests* the Secretary-General to report to the Council on a periodic basis on the implementation of this resolution;

8. *Decides* to remain actively seized of the matter.

SENATE STAFF REPORT ON YUGOSLAV 'ETHNIC CLEANSING'

August 18, 1992

The Senate Foreign Relations Committee publicly released a staff report August 18 giving an account of wholesale murder and brutality in Bosnia-Hercegovina where Serb militias were engaged in "ethnically cleansing" that Balkan land of its Croat and Moslem inhabitants—slaughtering or driving them from their homeland. "Ethnic cleansing has been carried out with widespread atrocities" and "some organized massacres," especially among the Moslem population, the report said. It added: "We believe that the death toll associated with forcible removal [of Moslems] exceeds the death tolls from the bombardments of cities or from killings in prison camps" since the Yugoslav civil war erupted in 1991.

The report, based on the findings of two committee staff members who interviewed victims of the fighting and representatives of United Nations, Red Cross, and other international relief organizations, was one of the first detailed reports by the U.S. government on warring conditions in Bosnia-Hercegovina that lately had drawn world attention. It created pressure on the American and European governments, and on the United Nations, to do something to stop the bloodshed and suffering. The Bush administration, like governments in Europe, was reluctant to commit military forces to the Balkans and hesitant in a presidential election year to engage fully in a public debate on the question.

This hesitancy resulted in contradictory statements from State Department officials early in August as to whether the department had creditable information about torture and killings in Serb-run detention camps. Stories of such atrocities had appeared in several foreign and domestic new reports. In response to such stories, the Senate Committee *sent staff members Peter W. Galbraith and Michelle Maynard to assess human rights violations arising from the Serbian campaign.*

Background of the Struggle

The revival of Serbian nationalism followed the death in 1980 of Josip Broz Tito, who established a Communist regime in Yugoslavia after World War II. In recognition of the country's sharp ethnic divisions, the Communists adopted a federal system with six republics: Serbia, Croatia, Slovenia, Bosnia-Hercegovina, Macedonia, and Montenegro, plus the autonomous provinces of Kosovo and Vojvodina within the Serbian Republic. Although the boundaries were drawn mainly along ethnic lines, most republics had significant ethnic minorities. In Bosnia-Hercegovina, ethnic mixing among Serbs, Croats, and Slavic Moslems—descendants of converts to Islam during the Turkish Ottoman Empire's five-century occupation of that region made ethnically distinct boundaries impossible.

Tito's death removed the linchpin that held postwar Yugoslavia together. The disintegration was hastened by economic problems and the collapse of the Soviet Union. Serbia, the biggest republic, sought to reassert its former dominance. It harkened to the call of Slobodan Milosevic, who became Serbian Communist party chief in 1986 and asserted a strident brand of nationalism that survived the party's demise. The revival of Serbian nationalism led to a counterreaction among other Yugoslav peoples, especially the Croats, the second-largest ethnic group and bitter rivals of the Serbs.

In 1990 Croatia and its allied republic of Slovenia held free elections— the first in postwar Yugoslavia—and undertook fruitless negotiations with the Serbian-controlled federal government to reform the country into a confederation, giving each republic much more self-rule. Both republics on June 25, 1991, declared themselves independent states. (Independence of Yugoslav Republics, Historic Documents of 1991, p. 367) *Fighting immediately broke out in Croatia between Serbian guerrillas and Croatian forces and continued sporadically for months. Croatia lost about one-third of its territory and in January agreed to the deployment of a UN peacekeeping force in the areas of conflict.*

Shift of Fighting to Bosnia-Hercegovina

The next Yugoslav republic to be engulfed in fighting was Bosnia-Hercegovina. Elections there in late 1990 had led to a coalition government composed of Serbs, Croats, and Moslems. The government did not take sides in the fighting in Croatia but was unable to keep the Serbian-directed Yugoslav national army from using its territory to attack targets in Croatia. In December 1991 Bosnia-Hercegovina applied to the European Community (EC) for recognition as an independent state—something its Serbian population strongly opposed. Following EC recommendations, it held a referendum on the question. Independence was overwhelmingly approved, but Serb voters boycotted the election. The government at-

tempted to organize the newly independent republic into ethnically separate cantons—but lacking Serb cooperation was doomed to fail.

Ethnic Serbs launched attacks throughout the republic on April 4, and soon proclaimed their own Serbian Republic of Bosnia and Hercegovina. The federal army withdrew but left behind all Bosnian-born soldiers of Serb descent—about 80 percent of the total—and their equipment, including artillery. The Croat and Moslem defenders were no match for this well-armed force.

It laid seige to Sarajevo, the republic's capital, placing nearly 400,000 civilians under daily bombardments. The UN received permission to send in a peacekeeping unit to secure the Sarajevo airport on June 29 to permit flights of humanitarian aid to reach the city.

After that the focus of attention soon expanded beyond the city as a result of accumulating reports from Bosnia-Hercegovina of terrorized refugees, summary executions, gang rapes of female prisoners, beatings, torture, and starvation of prisoners.

Following are excerpts from "The Ethnic Cleansing of Bosnia-Hercegovina," a staff report to the Senate Foreign Relations Committee, released publicly August 18, 1992.

... Ethnic cleansing is the term the Serbs applied to a process of population transfers aimed at removing the non-Serbian population from large areas of Bosnia-Hercegovina. Ethnic cleansing has three main elements. First, there is the deliberate use of artillery and snipers against the civilian populations of the main cities including Sarajevo, Mostar, Bihac, Tuzla, and Gorazde. This is the most covered aspect of the policy but, numerically, the least deadly. Second, there is the forced movement of civilian populations. These have entailed the systematic destruction of homes, the looting of personal property, beatings, selective and random killings, and massacres. Third, there is mistreatment of prisoners and detainees, including beatings and executions.

All parties to the conflict have committed abuses against other ethnic groups. However, only the Serbian side has systematically targeted civilian populations.

Bosnian Serb leader Radovan Karadzic is the architect of the ethnic cleansing policy, although he now prefers the term ethnic shifting. Bosnian Serb and Serb military units, with varying degrees of organization and command, are actually implementing the ethnic cleansing policy. Some are local men who have picked up a gun to settle scores with neighbors. Others are police and paramilitary groups associated with the Bosnian Serb political leadership. Most importantly, the Bosnian Serbs are making use of Yugoslav People's Army units that remained in Bosnia-Hercegovina after the army officially pulled out on May 19.

The Bosnian Serbs have been joined by paramilitary groups from Serbia proper. These include groups headed by: (1) Mirko Jovic, leader of the Serbian National Renewal and whose paramilitary forces style themselves as the "white wolves"; (2) Vojislav Seselj, a member of the Serbian and Federal Parliaments and a former political prisoner often assisted by the United States, whose followers style themselves as "Chetniks"; and (3) Zeljko Raznjatovic, a former bank robber with the nom de guerre of "Arkan" and best known for his brutality and larceny in the Croatian War. The Serbian leader Slobodan Milosovic [sic] [president of Yugoslavia] has been a proponent of ethnic cleansing but now, with sanctions and the threatened use of military force, would like to disassociate himself from the consequences. . . .

Much information, including critical corroborating material, comes from U.S. Embassy sources in Belgrade and Zagreb, from the United Nations High Commission for Refugees, from the International Committee of the Red Cross, from human rights activists, and from conversations with Western journalists traveling throughout the region.

While we believe the main patterns of Bosnian Serb and Serbian behavior are clear, many additional interviews will be required to establish the veracity of specific stories cited. Some information, such as that on massacres and prison camp executions will require forensic excavations of mass graves as well as interviews.

Presenting a comprehensive picture of ethnic cleansing is a mammoth undertaking. Refugee witnesses are quickly being dispersed to the countries of Western Europe. We fear some witnesses may be killed and that other evidence is being manipulated or will remain inaccessible. Such comprehensive documentation can only be done if governments are prepared to commit resources to the necessary investigative work. Ideally, the United Nations Human Rights Commission should organize language proficient human rights investigative teams. However, because time is of the essence and mobilizing U.N. resources can be a lengthy process, an alternative approach is for the United States, in conjunction with the European states, to undertake immediately this work.

The Terror Begins

From February 29 through March 1, the Muslim and Croatian people of Bosnia-Hercegovina voted overwhelmingly for independence in free elections. The Serbs, one third of the population, opposed independence and boycotted the referendum. The stage was thus set for a confrontation that would be extremely bloody, if the previous 9 months in a disintegrating Yugoslavia was any guide.

On April 6, the European Community recognized the new nation of Bosnia-Hercegovina, on the grounds that it met the criteria for recognition that the European Community had set out the previous December. The next day, the United States followed suit. By the middle of April, Bosnian Serb forces, along with elements of the Yugoslav People's Army (JNA), began the shelling of Sarajevo. Television pictures of artillery attacks and sniper kills transfixed the world community on a city most recently in the spotlight as the agreeable host of the 1984 Winter Olympic Games.

Outside Sarajevo and mostly out of sight of the world press, something far more sinister and far more deadly had begun.

Bosnia-Hercegovina was at the beginning of April 1992, an ethnic melange of Serbs, Muslims, Croatians, and Yugoslavs, with a smattering of many smaller groups. Drawing boundaries for ethnically based cantons—one model proposed for a Bosnian state—would have been difficult. To break up the new nation with coherent international boundaries would have been impossible. The Croatian majority areas of Bosnia-Hercegovina are the Western Hercegovina districts adjacent to Croatia, which ironically, makes it possible to attach geographically Bosnia's 17 percent Croatian minority to Croatia. The Serbs, however, predominated in north and west Bosnia, geographically separated from Serbia by Muslim majority districts in northeast Bosnia and in the southern part of the new country.

If the Bosnian Serbs wanted to remain geographically tied to Serbia, they had to move to the Muslim majority districts and to remove the Muslims from those districts. This is what they set out to do.

On April 1, a bomb was thrown in a cafe in the Muslim majority town of Bijeljina a few kilometers from Serbia. Arkan, the former bank robber and now Serbian nationalist militant, entered the town with his paramilitaries. There were some killings and Muslims started to flee. Later in April, in nearby Zvornik, according to a U.S. Embassy source, an undetermined number of men were taken to the stadium and killed. . . .

Also in late April, Serbian forces entered the Bratunac area on the Drina River that forms the border with Serbia. There, we heard, tanks drove into Muslim villages, destroyed houses, and then Serb forces trapped and killed Muslim civilians.

On May 6-7, without much opposition, Serb forces took the large town of Brcko in Northeast Bosnia. According to our sources, the Muslim men were then herded to the center of town and given 2 to 3 minute summary trials. The trials were generally followed by executions. The number killed there over 2 days is indeterminate, but some sources say it may be as high as 500.

It is likely other massacres took place in April and May. Documentation will require systematic interviewing as well as access to sites where there may be mass graves. There is no sign that the killers gave much thought to hiding their crimes so locating physical evidence of killings may not be too hard if access can be arranged.

On May 19, the JNA announced its withdrawal from Bosnia-Hercegovina. Left behind were 85 percent of the officers and men, ostensibly because they were Bosnian-born Serbs, and all the army's equipment. After this date, the ethnic cleansing—that is the evacuation of Muslim villages—accelerated as did the killings.

After the JNA withdrawal, ethnic cleansing began in earnest in the northwest of Bosnia. The Serb plan was to connect the Krajina regions of Croatia and Bosnia to Serbia through an ethnically Serb corridor. Refugee interviews permit us to reconstruct what happened in one town in this corridor.

Kozarac and surrounding villages were a predominantly Muslim area of 25,000. Today the town is empty and most houses in ruins. H. H. (see interview No. 15) in Kozarac provides one account of what happened there: On May 24, Serb forces attacked with mortar and artillery, in an assault lasting all night. The people fled into the woods and to the river, where they eventually decided to surrender. The first attackers were primarily interested in collecting weapons and rather quickly released the captives. The next day, however, another paramilitary group showed up and again shelled the now defenseless villagers and townspeople. Men, women, and children were rounded up. Some of the men were severely beaten, and eventually separated from the women and taken to the Omarska prison camp. After some weeks detention and mistreatment, the women and children were released and fled to Croatia. Most of the men have not been accounted for.

A. H. (see interview No. 11), a 29-year-old mother from near Prijedor, describes another part of the same operation. After hiding in the forest, she and other villagers surrendered on the open road. The men were separated from the women and children. The women and children were force marched to buses. On the way she could see local policemen being pulled off the road. Later she heard screams and saw the flashing of knives but was ordered not to look. The women and children spent a harsh 2 weeks under detention and then went to Croatia. The men were taken to Omarska and Prijedor, and not seen again.

For H. O. (see interview No. 12), a 44-year-old mother also from Kozarac, the encounter with the ethnic cleansers came in the form of a Serbian neighbor. On or about May 18, she climbed a hill to bring food to her elderly parents in the nearby village of Barakovac. When she got to her parents house, she saw her neighbor, Nikola Przar, the 21-year-old son of a local Serb militant. The camouflage-clad young man summoned H. O.'s parents out of their house. Hand-in-hand, they came out. The father protested: "Please don't; we are not guilty. How can you do this to us?" The mother said nothing. Przar cut the couple's throats but for some reason let H. O. go. She had to leave her parents unburied and never learned the fate of her brother and son, both of whom lived with the elderly couple.

The true horror of ethnic cleansing is the sum of individual experiences like those of A. O., A. H., and H. H. There is every reason to believe these individual accounts are part of a story repeated throughout Muslim Bosnia-Hercegovina in April, May, and June.

... The Muslim Charity, Merhamet, has from its Zagreb bureau, video-taped more than 1,000 eyewitness accounts to atrocities committed in the course of village evacuations and in the various camps. Many survivors are unwilling to allow their names to be used out of fear for the safety of relatives left behind. That Merhamet should have so many accounts speaks volumes to the scale of the atrocities.

Neither Merhamet, nor any of the independent observers (United Nations, U.S. Embassy, journalists) believe the Serbian's campaign is aimed at the physical extermination of the Muslim and Croatian Bosnians. No one doubts, however, that murder and terror are tools in a campaign to grab territory and to remove non-Serbs from this territory.

The Camps

Muslims and Croatians driven from their homes often ended up in camps. Basically there are two kinds of camps: detention centers and prison camps.

Women and children typically ended up at the detention camps. These are in school buildings, gymnasiums, and other places that can accommodate large numbers of people. Sanitary conditions were appalling. If toilets were present, they were inadequate in number. According to many accounts, detainees had no toilets and, in some areas, defecated and urinated in the same room as they slept.

Food was always inadequate in these detention centers and medical care non-existent. In some centers, the women were free to go to adjacent towns to beg for food while in others, no one was permitted to leave the building.

We heard of very few accounts in which women and children were beaten. Some witnesses told us of instances in which women were shot in the camps, which seemed to be cases of sport killing (usually alcohol induced) or random shooting.

Merhamet, the Bosnian government, human rights groups, and some of our interviewees described the rape of girls and young women. Typically, armed Serbs would enter a detention center, select some girls, and rape them. In some cases the rapists killed their victims. In Islamic societies a raped woman often becomes an outcast and this may compound the shame rape victims typically feel. For this reason, it may be difficult to document the extent of rape in detention camps. Given the general lack of discipline of camp guards, there is every reason to suspect the practice was extensive.

The detention centers were usually a way station for women, children, and old men before going on to find refuge outside of the cleansed region. Generally, the stays in the detention centers were not long, in the range of one to two weeks.

Men, by contrast, are seen by the Serbs as potential fighters for the Muslim and Croatian cause. They were kept not in detention centers but in tightly guarded prison camps in secure places. Such places include an iron mine at Omarska, an army barracks at Prijedor, and a warehouse at Luka.

The treatment of male prisoners was generally very brutal. Almost all male prisoners were beaten, according to refugee accounts. In at least some of the prison camps, prisoners were provided little or no food. H. H., who spent one week in Omarska says that only 6 liters of water and one loaf of bread were provided daily for all of the 900 men in the Omarska barracks. The loaf was thrown in the air by the guards and only a lucky few got crumbs. Of course, the television images of emaciated men at Omarska and other camps would serve to confirm the accounts of no rations.

Killings occurred regularly in the prison camps. In many cases, the killings were recreational. R. B. (see interview No. 1), a 38-year-old mother spent 8 days at the Luka Camp at Brcko, not far from the Serbian border. According to her testimony, paramilitary groups from Serbia would enter the camp at night and make the men sing Chetnik songs. Those judged insufficiently enthusiastic would be pulled outside and made to fight in what was effectively a human cockfight. Two men would take turns slapping each other. The man judged the weaker slapper would be killed. One time, the Serbian paramilitaries cut off the loser's ears and nose before slitting his throat.

R. B. estimated that, during the 8 days she was at Luka, the Serb paramilitaries killed between seven and ten prisoners a day. The U.S. Embassy cites as credible an account that Luka prisoners were killed in groups of 50 and buried at a mass grave near Brejevo Polje. An investigator, with precise knowledge of the site has not been permitted to go there.

R. B.'s story supports accounts given to *Newsday* and the Senate Armed Services Committee by Alija Lujinovic, another Luka survivor. It is entirely possible that almost all of Luka's 1,000 prisoners perished in May and June.. . . .

Inspections of the Prison Camps

The stories and pictures out of Omarska, Luka and Prijedor outraged the world and intensified the debate over military intervention in Bosnia-Hercegovina. As the threat of a military response grew, the Bosnian Serb leadership promised to open all camps to international inspection. In addition to the ICRC, Western politicians and journalists visited the camps.

The Bosnian Serbs have done what they can to manipulate the visits. When a British politician visited the Prijedor Manjaca camp, he found the conditions poor but not those of a death camp. However, the politician did not see a number of buildings in the camp and spent just one half hour there. A journalist covering the visit told us that the prisoners looked remarkably fattened up since an earlier visit a week before. Assessments based on brief visits should be viewed with great skepticism.

In another case, the Kerateem camp was abruptly closed prior to international inspection and the prisoners taken east in a sealed cattle car. Firefights have been staged to keep journalists from visiting certain camps or suspected camp sites, and in Zvornik, a journalist trying to investigate a mass grave was briefly detained.

We believe the Bosnian Serbs are covering up the evidence of what went on in the camps. The international community should be cautious about absolving the Bosnian Serbs of the charge of running death camps.

Eyewitness accounts do provide compelling evidence that some camps, notably Luka and Omarska, were death camps. . . .

The Slow International Response

. . . The slow response to developing atrocities reflects, in our view, more than bureaucratic inattention. Rather, it is indicative of a systemic deficiency in both the United Nations and United States human rights machinery. Neither is geared to respond to developing large scale human rights crises such as those that overtook the Kurds in the late 1980's or are now occurring in Bosnia-Hercegovina.

The United Nations and its specialized agencies are hamstrung by the limitations of their mandates. . . .

The Human Rights Bureau of the U.S. State Department relies on embassies for reporting on human rights problems. Embassies, however, do not have the resources to undertake the kind of investigations required to assess large scale atrocity reports. . . .

Assuming a U.N. human rights investigative unit has the political independence to travel and to report to governments as it sees fit, this would be the preferable way to set up an early alert human rights monitoring system. However, if the U.N. route is not feasible, then the United States should consider establishing a small team within the State Department Human Rights Bureau that can investigate early on impending disasters.

Legal Consequences

Ethnic cleansing is itself illegal under international law. Protocol I to the 1949 Geneva Conventions prohibits the transfer of civilian populations except for their own security or military necessity. The Bosnian Serb policy of moving populations so as to make a territory ethnically pure falls far outside these exceptions.

The ways in which the Bosnian Serbs are carrying out ethnic cleansing violate many other provisions of Protocol I. The shelling of cities for the purpose of terrorizing the population and without any legitimate military target is a prohibited act under the Protocol. Also prohibited is the killing of prisoners, the use of torture, and deliberate starvation, all acts committed by the Bosnian Serb authorities.

Article 6 of the Charter of the Nuremberg Tribunal defines crimes against humanity as: "murder, extermination, enslavement, deportation, and other inhumane acts committed against any civilian population, before or during the war; or persecutions on political, racial or religious grounds in execution of or in connection with any crime * * * whether or not in violation of the domestic law of the country where perpetrated."

We believe there is a prima facie case that the Bosnian Serb authorities have committed crimes against humanity as well as war crimes. . . .

REPUBLICAN NATIONAL CONVENTION

August 17-20, 1992

Showing unshaken confidence in the strategy that had won five of the past six presidential elections, the Republican party renominated President George Bush at a 1992 convention dominated by conservative voices, notably on issues such as abortion, homosexuality, immigration, and school prayer.

Despite its surface optimism, the convention held in Houston's Astrodome August 17-20 was not the smooth gala Bush might once have hoped for. His position in preconvention polls had fueled a sense of desperation among some delegates and brought scrutiny to every aspect of his campaign and administration. Many senators made plans to be elsewhere, and relatively few House members chose to be delegates.

Preconvention polls had shown Bush's approval ratings hovering below those for Arkansas governor Bill Clinton, nominated by the Democrats a month earlier. But by week's end Bush campaign leaders felt that the convention had helped their cause. "We've got unity, we've got momentum. I think it's coming together just as we wanted," said campaign manager Fred Malek. (Democratic National Convention, p. 667)

Few could doubt that Bush had built up his standing by luring back disaffected conservatives from inside and outside his own party. And it was clear that "defining the differences" with Clinton, albeit on GOP terms, was having an impact. Speaker after speaker strafed Clinton and Tennessee Senator Al Gore, his running mate, as well as Hillary Clinton, the nominee's wife. As the week wore on, opprobrium also was heaped on the news media (teenagers marched through the news media working space chanting "No more lies" and "Tell the truth") and on selected other targets, including trial lawyers and the American Bar Association.

Maryland GOP chairman Joyce Terhes said Bush's acceptance speech was excellent because the president had been "hard-hitting on the attack, and that will be the difference in November."

Conservative Tilt

Conservatives' suspicions of Bush and his supporters were not easily assuaged. The main focus was the platform, written the week of August 10 and adopted August 17 without a floor debate.

A loosely organized group of abortion rights delegates and non-delegates tried to get six state delegations to support a floor debate on abortion. But after losing by lopsided margins in the platform process, the effort fizzled. That did not quiet dissent over the increasingly moral tone of the platform, however. "Most of America is not in the camp that supports an accelerating socialism of morality," said Rep. Jim Leach of Iowa. (Republican Party Platform, p. 799)

But the Bush-Quayle campaign did not cross swords with the religious right. The symbols of that movement—Phyllis Schlafly, Pat Robertson, and Jerry Falwell—were highly visible throughout convention week. "The Christian right is a very important part of the Republican coalition," said campaign chairman Robert Teeter. "They organize their own groups, speak and represent themselves as strong supporters of the president."

Still the Winning Formula?

But whether it was a smart move or a blunder to make the religious right so predominant at the convention remained an open question. "Normally, you would think they would be aiming for the broader voting public at this point," said Keith Hamm, a professor of political science at Houston's Rice University and a scholar of party history. Hamm attributed the party's continued fixation on its base to the scare it had received earlier in the year from Dallas billionaire Ross Perot. Perot, who folded his independent candidacy before the GOP convention but revived it afterward, had strong appeal among Republican voters. (Perot Statements on Ending and Reviving His Campaign, p. 717)

Bush's uncertain appeal—both to the party's base and across to other voters—called into question his reliance on the old formula. Analyst Kevin Phillips saw a "political vacuum" in the party that had prompted a week of "political archaeology"—highlighted by the nostalgic and triumphant appearance of former president Ronald Reagan on the convention's first night. The opening night lineup also included columnist Patrick J. Buchanan, Bush's former rival for the nomination.

The phrase "family values" was heard often during the week. Wednesday was devoted to a celebration of the family, with Bush appearing unannounced on stage to be surrounded by grandchildren. The party seemed to be almost physically wrestling back the icons of family and tradition the Democrats embraced at their convention. In so doing, the

GOP rebuked the Democrats for putting up a false front. "And they call me an actor," Reagan had said, his eyes wide with wonder.

Another speaker who held the delegates' attention was Mary Fisher, a woman afflicted by the virus that causes AIDS. Democrats heard a similar speech from Elizabeth Glaser, also HIV-infected. (Convention Speeches by Women Infected with HIV, p. 709)

Apology for Tax Compromise

On the final night Bush delivered a message rooted in Reagan's less-is-more philosophy of government, insisting that he would have carried Reagan's principles further into practice had it not been for "the roadblock at the other end of Pennsylvania Avenue." In his hour-long speech, Bush took credit for communism's collapse and other momentous world events, laying the nation's various domestic ills and economic doldrums at the Democrats' doorstep.

Recalling the mauling he had taken at the Democrats' convention in July, Bush laid into the Clinton-Gore ticket with a lash. Comparing his reaction to the 1990-91 Persian Gulf crisis with Bill Clinton's position, Bush said: "I bit the bullet, and he bit his nails." He said Clinton's decision making was "slippery when wet" and that a Clinton administration would amount to "a rubber-check Congress and a rubber-stamp president."

But the moment that proved just how determined Bush was to shore up the right, and the moment hundreds of delegates had come wanting to see, was the one in which he did what presidents almost never do. He apologized for a major policy decision—to sign a tax bill after pledging in 1988, "Read my lips. No new taxes." (Republican National Convention, Historic Documents of 1988, p. 589)

"I made a bad call," he said. "It was a mistake to go along with the Democratic tax increase" in the 1990 budget deal. Lowell B. Lynch, a Tennessee delegate for Buchanan, said Bush's admission of error was "unpleasant but necessary." It restored Bush's credibility among conservatives and "will let us go to work for him without apologies."

Vice President Dan Quayle gave a rousing twenty-minute acceptance speech showcasing the more polished, forceful persona he gained from four years in office. He also completed a weeklong embrace of the party's religious wing and its social issue agenda. He proclaimed himself "unbowed, unbroken, and ready to keep fighting for our beliefs." Quayle mentioned family ten times and values eight times.

Following are the renomination acceptance speeches delivered August 20, 1992, by President George Bush and Vice President Dan Quayle at the Republican National Convention in Houston. (The bracketed headings have been added by Congressional Quarterly to highlight the organization of the texts.):

BUSH ACCEPTANCE SPEECH

Thank you very, very much. Thank you, so much. Thank you all very, very much. Let's go to work. Thank you. Thank you so much. Thank you all very much. Thank you. Thank you very much.

And I am proud to receive, and I am honored to accept your nomination for president of the United States.

May I thank my dear friend and our great leader [Senate Minority Leader] Bob Dole for that wonderful introduction. Let me say this: This nomination is not for me alone. It is for the ideas, principles and values that we stand for.

And my job—my job has been made easier by a leader who has taken a lot of unfair criticism, with grace and humor—Vice President Dan Quayle.

I want to talk tonight about the sharp choice that I intend to offer Americans this fall, a choice between different agendas, different directions and, yes, a choice about the character of the man you want to lead this nation.

I know that Americans have many questions—about our economy, about our country's future, even questions about me. And I'll answer them tonight.

And first, I feel great.

And I am heartened by the polls, the ones that say I look better in my jogging shorts than the governor of Arkansas.

Four years ago—four years ago, I spoke about missions—for my life and for our country. I spoke of one urgent mission—defending our security and promoting the American ideal abroad.

Just pause for a moment to reflect on what we've done.

Germany has united, and a slab of the Berlin Wall sits right outside this Astrodome.

Arabs and Israelis now sit face to face and talk peace.

And every hostage held in Lebanon is free.

The conflict—the conflict in El Salvador is over, and free elections brought democracy to Nicaragua.

Black and white South Africans cheered each other at the Olympics. The Soviet Union can only be found in history books. The captive nations of Eastern Europe and the Baltics are captive no more. And today on—today, on the rural streets of Poland, merchants sell cans of air labeled "the last breath of communism."

["You Must Have Inhaled"]

If I had stood before you four years ago and described this as the world we would help to build, you would have said, George Bush, you must have been smoking something, and you must have inhaled.

This convention is the first at which an American president can say: The Cold War is over, and freedom finished first.

Now, some—some—we have a lot to be proud of. A lot. Some want to rewrite history, want to skip over the struggle, claim the outcome was inevitable. And while the U.S. postwar strategy was largely bipartisan, the fact remains that the liberal, McGovern wing of the other party—including my opponent—consistently made the wrong choices.

In the '70s, they wanted a hollow Army; we wanted a strong fighting force.

In the '80s—and you remember this one—in the '80s, they wanted a nuclear freeze; we insisted on peace through strength.

And from—from Angola—from Angola to Central America, they said, let's negotiate, deliberate, procrastinate. And we said, just stand up for freedom.

And now—now the Cold War is over and they claim, hey, we were with you all the way.

No. Their—their behavior—really, their behavior reminds me of the old con man's advice to the new kid. He said, "Son, if you're being run out of town, just get out in front and make it look like a parade."

Make no mistake—make no mistake—the demise of communism wasn't a sure thing. It took the strong leadership of presidents from both parties, including Republicans like Richard [M.] Nixon, Gerald [R.] Ford and Ronald Reagan.

And—and without their vision and the support of the American people, the Soviet Union would be a strong superpower today, and we'd be facing a nuclear threat tonight.

My opponents say I spend too much time on foreign policy. As if it didn't matter that schoolchildren once hid under their desks in drills to prepare for nuclear war. I saw the chance to rid our children's dreams of the nuclear nightmare, and I did.

Over the past four years, more people have breathed the fresh air of freedom than in all of human history. I saw a chance to help, and I did. And these—these were the two defining opportunities—not of a year, not of a decade, but of an entire span of human history.

I seized those opportunities for our kids and our grandkids, and I make no apologies for that.

Now—now—now, the Soviet bear may be gone, but there are still wolves in the woods.

We saw that when [Iraqi leader] Saddam Hussein invaded Kuwait. The Mideast might have become a nuclear powder keg—our energy supplies held hostage. So we did what was right, and what was necessary. We destroyed a threat, freed a people and locked a tyrant in the prison of his own country.

["I Bit the Bullet, and He Bit His Nails"]

Well, well, what about the leader of the Arkansas National Guard—the man who hopes to be commander in chief? Well, while I bit the bullet, and he bit his nails, and two days—two days—two days—listen to this, now, two days after Congress voted to follow my lead, my opponent said this, and I quote directly: "I guess I would have voted with the majority if it was a close vote. But I agree with the arguments the minority made."

Now, that sounds to me like his policy can be summed up by a road sign he's probably seen on his bus tour: slippery when wet.

Look—look, this is serious business. Think about the impact of our foreign policy failures the last time the Democrats controlled both ends of Pennsylvania Avenue. Gas lines. Grain embargoes. American hostages blindfolded.

There will be more foreign policy challenges like Kuwait in the next four years. Terrorists and aggressors to stand up to; dangerous weapons to be controlled and destroyed. And freedom's fight is not finished. And I look forward to being the first president to visit a free, democratic Cuba.

Who will lead the world—who will lead the world in the face of these challenges? Not my opponent. In his acceptance speech he devoted just 65 seconds to telling us about the world.

And then he said that America was, and I quote again—I want to be fair and factual—I quote, being "ridiculed" everywhere. Well, tell that to the people around the world, for whom America is still a dream. Tell that to leaders around the world, from whom America commands respect.

Ridiculed? Ridiculed? Tell that to the men and women of Desert Storm.

Let me make—let me just make an aside comment here because of what you've been reading in the paper. This is a political year, but there's a lot of danger in the world, and you can be sure I will never let politics interfere with a foreign policy decision. Forget the election—I will do what is right for the national security of the United States of America. And that is a pledge from my heart.

Fifty years ago—50 years ago this summer, I was 18 years of age—I see some young people in the audience tonight, and I remember how I felt in those days.

I believed deeply in this country, and we were faced with a world war. And so I made a decision to go off and fight a battle much different from political battles.

And I was scared, but I was willing. I was young, but I was ready. I had barely lived when I began to watch men die. I began to see the special place of America in the world, and I began to see, even then, that the world would become a much smaller place, and faraway places could become more and more like America.

And 50 years later, after change of almost biblical proportions, we know that when freedom grows, America grows. And just as a strong America means a safer world, we have learned that a safer world means a stronger America.

["Change Is Accelerating"]

This election is about change. But that's not unusual, because the American revolution is never-ending. Today, the pace of change is accelerating. We face new opportunities and new challenges. And the question is, who do you trust to make change work for you?

My opponent—my opponent—

My opponent says America is a nation in decline. Of our economy, he says, we are somewhere on the list beneath Germany, heading south toward Sri Lanka.

Well, don't let anyone tell you that America is second-rate, especially somebody running for president.

Maybe he hasn't heard—maybe he hasn't heard that we are still the world's largest economy. No other nation sells more outside its borders. The Germans, the British, the Japanese can't touch the productivity of you—the American worker and the American farmer.

My opponent—my opponent won't mention that. He won't remind you that interest rates are the lowest they've been in 20 years, and millions of Americans have refinanced their homes.

And you just won't hear that inflation—the thief of the middle class—has been locked in a maximum-security prison.

And you don't hear much about this good news, because the media also tends to focus only on the bad. And when the Berlin Wall fell, I half expected to see a headline: "Wall Falls, Three Border Guards Lose Jobs."

And underneath it probably says: "Clinton Blames Bush."

You don't—you don't hear a lot about progress in America. So let me tell you about some good things we've done together.

Just two weeks ago, all three nations of North America agreed to trade freely from Manitoba to Mexico. And this will bring good jobs to Main Street U.S.A.

We passed the Americans with Disabilities Act—bringing 43 million people into the economic mainstream. And I must say, it is about time. Our children will breathe easier because of our new Clean Air Act. We are rebuilding our roads, providing jobs for more than half a million Americans.

And we passed a child-care law, and we took a stand for family values by saying that when it comes to raising children, government doesn't know best, parents know best.

I have—I have fought against prejudice and anti-Semitism all my life. And I am proud that we strengthened our civil rights laws—and we did it without resorting to quotas.

And one more thing of vital importance to all. Today, cocaine use has fallen by 60 percent among young people. To the teenagers, the parents and the volunteers who are helping us battle the scourge of drugs in America, we say thank you, thank you from the bottom of our hearts.

Do I want to do more? You bet. Nothing hurts me more than to meet with soldiers home from the Persian Gulf who can't find a job. Or workers who have a job but worry that the next day will bring a pink slip. And what about parents who scrape and struggle to send their kids to college, only to find them back living at home, because they can't get work?

The world is in transition, and we are feeling that transition in our homes. The defining challenge of the '90s is to win the economic competition—to win the peace. We must be a military superpower, an economic superpower and an export superpower.

In this election—in this election, you'll hear two visions of how to do this. Theirs is to look inward, and protect what we already have. Ours is to look forward—to open new markets, prepare our people to compete, to restore our social fabric, to save and invest—so we can win.

We believe—we believe that now that the world looks more like America, it is time for America to look more like herself.

["Puts Faith in the Individual"]

And so we offer a philosophy that puts faith in the individual, not the bureaucracy. A philosophy that empowers people to do their best so America can be at its best. In a world that is safer and freer, this is how we will build an America that is stronger, safer and more secure.

We start with a simple fact: Government is too big and spends too much.

And I've asked Congress to put a lid on mandatory spending except Social Security. And I've proposed doing away with over 200 programs and 4,000 wasteful projects and to freeze all other spending.

The gridlock Democrat Congress said: "No."

So, beginning tonight, so beginning tonight, I will enforce the spending freeze on my own. And if Congress sends me a bill spending more than I asked for in my budget—I will veto it fast.

Veto it fast—faster than copies of Millie's book sold.

Congress won't cut spending but refuses to give the president the power to eliminate pork barrel projects that waste your money. Forty-three governors have that power. So I ask you, the American people: Give me a Congress that will give me the line-item veto.

Let me tell you about a recent battle I fought with Congress, in which I was aided by [House Minority Leader] Bob Michel and his troops and Bob Dole and his troops. This spring, I worked day and night to get two-thirds of its members to approve a balanced-budget amendment to the Constitution.

We almost had it, but we lost by just nine votes. Now, listen how. Just before the vote, the liberal leaders of Congress convinced 12 members who cosponsored the bill to switch sides and vote no. Keep in mind, they voted against a bill they had already put their names on.

Something fishy is going on. And look at my opponent on this issue. Look at my opponent, who says he's for balanced budgets. But he came out against the amendment. He's like that on a lot of issues, first one side, then the other. He's been spotted in more places than Elvis Presley.

After all these years—after all these years, Congress has become pretty creative at finding ways to waste your money. So we need to be just as creative at finding ways to stop them. And I have a brand new idea.

Taxpayers should be given the right to check a box on their tax returns so that up to 10 percent of their payments can go for one purpose alone: to reduce the national debt.

But we also—but we also need to make sure—we need to make sure that Congress doesn't just turn around and borrow more money to spend more money. And so I will require that, for every tax dollar set aside to cut the debt, the ceilings on spending will be cut by an equal amount.

And that way—that way, we will cut both debt and spending, and take a whack out of the budget deficit.

My feelings about big government come from my experience; I spent half my adult life in the private sector. My opponent has a different experience—he's been in government nearly all his life. His passion to expand government knows no bounds.

And he's already proposed—and listen to this carefully—he has already proposed $220 billion in new spending, along with the biggest tax increase in history—$150 billion—and that's just to start.

He says he wants to tax the rich, but folks, he defines rich as anyone who has a job.

You've heard of the separation of powers. Well, my opponent practices a different theory: the power of separations. Government has the power to separate you from your wallet.

["I Made a Bad Call" on Taxes]

Now, let me say this. When it comes to taxes, I've learned the hard way. There's an old saying. Good judgment comes from experience, and experience comes from bad judgment. Two years ago, I made a bad call on the Democrats' tax increase. I underestimated Congress' addiction to taxes, and with my back against the wall, I agreed to a hard bargain: one tax increase one time in return for the toughest spending limits ever.

Well, it was a mistake to go along with the Democratic tax increase.

And I admit it. But here's the question for the American people. Who do you trust in this election—the candidate who has raised taxes one time and regrets it, or the other candidate, who raised taxes and fees 128 times and enjoyed it every time?

Thank you very much.

When the new—OK. When the new Congress convenes—when the new Congress convenes next January, I will propose to further reduce taxes across the board—provided we pay for these cuts with specific spending reductions that I consider appropriate, so that we do not increase the deficit.

I will also continue to fight to increase the personal exemption and to create jobs by winning a cut in capital gains taxes.

That—that will especially help small businesses. You know, they create—small businesses, they create two-thirds of the new jobs in America. But my opponent's plan for small business is clear, present and dangerous. Besides new income taxes, his plan will lead to a new payroll tax to pay for a government takeover of health care, and another new tax—and another new tax to pay for training. And that is just the beginning.

And if he gets his way, hardware stores all across America will have a new sign up: "Closed for despair." And I guess you'd say his plan really is "Elvis Economics": America will be checking into the "Heartbreak Hotel."

I believe—I believe that small business needs relief—from taxation, regulation and litigation.

And thus, I will extend for one year the freeze on paperwork and unnecessary federal regulation that I imposed last winter. There is no reason—there is no reason that federal regulations should live longer than my friend George Burns. And I—I will issue an order to get rid of any rule whose time has come—and gone.

And I see something happening in our towns and neighborhoods. Sharp lawyers are running wild. Doctors are afraid to practice medicine. And some moms and pops won't even coach Little League anymore. We must sue each other less—and care for each other more.

I am fighting to reform our legal system, to put an end to crazy lawsuits. And if that means climbing into the ring with the trial lawyers, well, let me just say, Round 1 starts tonight.

After all—after all, my opponent's campaign is being backed by practically every trial lawyer who ever wore a tasseled loafer. He's not in the ring with them, he's in the tank.

There are other things we need to do to get our economy up to speed, and prepare our kids for the next century.

We must have new incentives for research and new training for workers. Small businesses need capital and credit, and defense workers need new jobs.

And I have a plan to provide affordable health care for every American, controlling costs by cutting paperwork and lawsuits, and expanding coverage to the poorest of the poor.

We do not need my opponent's plan for a massive government takeover of health care, which would ration care and deny you the right to choose a doctor.

Who wants health care—who wants a health-care system with the efficiency of the House Post Office and the compassion of the KGB?

What about our schools? What about our schools? My opponent and I both want to change the way our kids learn. He wants to change our schools a little bit—I want to change them a lot.

Take the issue of whether parents should be able to choose the best school for their kids. My opponent says that's OK—as long as the school is run by government. And I say every parent and child should have a real choice of schools—public, private or religious.

So—so we have a clear choice to fix our problems. Do we turn to the tattered blanket of bureaucracy that other nations are tossing away? Or do we give our people the freedom and incentives to build security for themselves?

Here's what I'm fighting for:

- Open markets for American products.
- Lower government spending.
- Tax relief.
- Opportunities for small business.
- Legal and health reform.
- Job training.
- And new schools built on competition, ready for the 21st century.

Now, OK, why are these proposals not in effect today? Only one reason—the gridlock Democratic Congress.

[Reacting to chants of "clean the House"] That's a very good idea. A very good idea.

Now, I know Americans are tired of the blame game, tired of people in Washington acting like they are candidates for the next episode of "American Gladiators."

I don't like it either. Neither should you. But the truth is the truth. Our policies haven't failed; they haven't been tried.

Americans want jobs. And on Jan. 28, I put before Congress a plan to create jobs. And if it had been passed back then, 500,000 more Americans would be at work right now. But in a nation that demands action, Congress has become the master of inaction.

And it wasn't always this way. I heard President Ford tonight. I served in Congress 22 years ago. Back then, we cooperated, we didn't get personal, we put the people above everything else. Heck, we didn't even have blow-dryers in those days.

At my first inauguration, I said that people didn't send us to bicker. I extended my hand—and I think the American people know this—I extended my hand to the congressional leaders, the Democratic leaders, and they bit it.

And the House leadership—the House leadership has not changed in 38 years. It is a body caught in a hopelessly tangled web of PACs, perks, privileges, partnership and paralysis.

Every day—every day, Congress puts politics ahead of principle and above progress.

Now, let me give you just one example. Feb. 20, 1991. It was at the height of the gulf war. On that very same day, I asked American pilots to risk their lives to fly missions over Baghdad. And I also wanted to strengthen our economic security for the future.

So that very same day, I introduced a new domestic energy strategy which would cut our dependence on foreign oil by 7 million barrels a day.

And how many days did it take to win the gulf war? Forty-three. And how many did it take Congress to pass a national energy strategy? Five hundred and thirty-two, and still counting.

I have ridden stationary bikes that can move faster than the United States House of Representatives and the United States Senate, controlled by the Democrat leadership.

[Reacting to chants of "hit 'em harder"] OK. All right. You wait. I'm fixing to.

Where—where does my opponent stand with Congress?

Well, up in New York at their convention, they kept the congressional leaders away from the podium—hid them away.

They didn't want America to hear from the people who really make the decisions.

And they hid them for a very good reason—because the American people would recognize a dangerous combination: a rubber-check Congress and a rubber-stamp president.

Gov. Clinton—Gov. Clinton and Congress know that you've caught on to their lingo.

They know when they say "spending," you say, "uh-oh."

So now they have a new word, "investment." They want to invest $220 billion more of your money, but I want you to keep it.

Gov. Clinton—Gov. Clinton and Congress want to put through the largest tax increase in history, but I will not let that happen.

Gov. Clinton and Congress don't want kids to have the option of praying in school, but I do.

Clinton and Congress don't want to close legal loopholes and keep criminals behind bars, but I will.

Clinton and Congress will stack the judiciary with liberal judges who write laws they can't get approved by the voters.

Gov. Clinton—Gov. Clinton even says that [New York Gov.] Mario Cuomo belongs on the Supreme Court.

Wait a minute. Maybe not a bad idea. If you believe in judicial restraint, you probably ought to be happy.

After all, the good governor of New York can't make up his mind between chocolate and vanilla at Baskin-Robbins. We won't have another court decision for 35 years. And maybe that's all right, too.

[Term Limits for Congress]

Are my opponent and Congress really in cahoots? Look at one important question: Should we limit the terms of Congress?

Gov. Clinton says no. Congress says no. I say yes.

We tried this—look, we tried this once before, combining the Democratic governor of a small Southern state with a very liberal vice president and a Democratic Congress. America does not need Carter II.

We do not want to take America back to those days of malaise. But Americans want to know, where's proof that we will have better days in Washington?

I'll give you 150 reasons. And that's how many members of Congress are expected to leave Washington this year. Some are tainted by scandal—the voters have bounced them the way they bounced their own checks. But others are good members. Republican and Democrat. And they agree with me. The place just doesn't work anymore.

One hundred-fifty new members—from both parties—will be coming to Washington this fall.

And every one will have a fresh view of America's future.

And I pledge today to the American people, immediately after this election, I will meet with every one of these new members, before they get attacked by the PACs, overwhelmed by their staffs and cornered by some camera crew.

And I—and I will lay out my case for change. Change that matters, real change that makes a difference. Change that is right for America.

You see, there is a yearning in America, a feeling that maybe it's time to get back to our roots.

Sure, we must change, but some values are timeless.

I believe in families that stick together, fathers who stick around.

And I happen to believe very deeply in the worth of each individual human being, born or unborn.

And I believe—

And I believe—and I believe—I believe in teaching our kids the difference between what's wrong and what's right, teaching them respect for hard work and to love their neighbors.

And I believe that America will always have a special place in God's heart, as long as he has a special place in ours. And maybe—

And maybe that's why I've always believed that patriotism is not just another point of view.

There are times in every young person's life, when God introduces you to yourself. And I remember such a time.

It was back many years ago, when I stood watch at 4 a.m. up on the bridge of the USS *Finback*.

I would stand there and look out on the blackness of the sky, broken only by the sparkling stars above. And I would think about friends I lost, a country I loved and about a girl named Barbara.

And I remember those nights as clearly as any in my life.

You know, you can see things from up there that other people don't see. You can see storm clouds rise and then disappear. The first hint of the sun over the horizon, and the first outline of the shore far away.

And now, I know Americans are uneasy today, there is anxious talk around our kitchen tables. But from where I stand, I see not America's sunset, but a sunrise.

And the world changes for which we've sacrificed for a generation have finally come to pass, and with them a rare and unprecedented opportunity to pass the sweet cup of prosperity around our American table.

Are we up to it? I know we are. As I travel our land, I meet veterans who once worked the turrets of a tank and can now master the keyboards of high-tech economy.

I see teachers, blessed with the incredible American capacity for innovation, who are teaching our children a new way to learn, for a new century.

And I meet parents, some working two jobs with hectic schedules, who—who still find new ways to teach old values to steady their kids in a turbulent world.

And I take heart from what is happening in America, not from those who profess a new passion for government but from those with an old and enduring faith in the human potential.

Those who understand that the genius of America is our capacity for rebirth and renewal. America is the land where the sun is always peeking over the horizon.

And tonight I appeal to that unyielding, undying, undeniable American spirit. I ask you to consider, now that the entire world is moving our way, why would we want to go back their way?

I ask not just for your support for my agenda but for your commitment to renew and rebuild our nation—by shaking up one institution that has withstood change for over four decades.

Join me in rolling away the roadblock—

Join me in rolling away the roadblock at the other end of Pennsylvania Avenue, so that in the next four years, we will match our accomplishments outside, by building a stronger, safer, more secure America inside.

Forty-four—forty-four years ago, in another age of uncertainty, a different president embarked on a similar mission. His name was Harry S Truman.

And as he stood before his party to accept their nomination, Harry Truman knew the freedom I know this evening, the freedom to talk about what's right for America, and let the chips fall where they may.

Harry Truman said this: This is more than a political call to arms. Give me your help, not to win votes alone but to win this new crusade and keep America safe and secure for its own people.

Well, tonight I say to you, join me in our new crusade to reap the rewards of our global victory—to win the peace—so that we may make America safer and stronger for all our people.

May God bless you, and may God bless the United States of America. Thank you very much.

QUAYLE ACCEPTANCE SPEECH

Mr. Chairman, delegates to this convention and friends around America.

With gratitude and a sense of mission, once again I accept your nomination as vice president of the United States.

Tonight—tonight I am stronger, more confident and more determined than ever to re-elect our great president, George Bush.

I know my critics wish I were not standing here tonight. They don't like our values. They look down on our beliefs. They're afraid of our ideas. And they know the American people stand on our side. And that's—that's why, when someone confronts them and challenges them, they will stop at nothing to destroy him. And I say to them, I say: You have failed.

I stand—I stand before you, and before the American people—unbowed, unbroken and ready to keep fighting for our beliefs.

I come from Huntington, a small farming community in Indiana. I had an upbringing like many in my generation—a life built around family, public school, Little League, basketball and church on Sunday. My brother and I shared a room in our two-bedroom house. We walked to school together. This was life in small-town America. Our people were strong, and we believed in the traditional values of middle America.

Marilyn and I have tried to teach our children these values, like faith in God, love of family and appreciation of freedom.

We have also taught them about family issues like adoption. My parents adopted twins when I was 10 years old. We have taught our children to respect single parents and their challenges—challenges that faced my grandmother many years ago and my own sister today.

And we have taught our children about the tragedy of diseases like breast cancer, which took the life of Marilyn's mother. Marilyn and I have hosted an annual event called the Race for the Cure of Breast Cancer. Two months ago, 20,000 runners, men and women, young and old, joined in our nation's capital to race for the cure. By leading the battle against breast cancer, in memory of her mother, Marilyn has taken a family tragedy and turned it into hope for others.

["Family Comes First"]

Like so many Americans, for me, family comes first. When family values are undermined, our country suffers. All too often parents struggle to instill character in their sons and daughters, only to see their values belittled and their beliefs mocked by those who look down on America. Americans try to raise their children to understand right and wrong, only to be told that every so-called "lifestyle alternative" is morally equivalent. That is wrong.

The gap—the gap between us and our opponents is a cultural divide. It is not just a difference between conservative and liberal; it is a difference between fighting for what's right and refusing to see what's wrong.

Families can also be strengthened by empowering our people—with low taxes, home ownership, parental choice in education, job training, safe streets, a clean environment and affordable health care. In all of these areas, we have a reform agenda, and it is time for Congress to get out of the way and pass the president's plan.

Speaking of reform: Our legal system — speaking of reform, our legal system is spinning out of control. The explosion of frivolous lawsuits burdens our economy and weakens our system of justice. America has 5 percent of the world's population and 70 percent of the world's lawyers.

I have nothing against lawyers—at least most of them. I'm a lawyer; I'm married to a lawyer. When we worked our way through night law school, Marilyn and I looked forward with pride to becoming part of the finest legal system in the world.

But today our country has a problem: Our legal system is costing consumers $300 billion a year. The litigation explosion has damaged our competitiveness; it has wiped out jobs; it has forced doctors to quit practicing in places where they are needed most. Every American knows this legal system is broken, and now is the time to fix it.

The President's Council on Competitiveness, which I chair, will continue to lead the charge against unnecessary federal regulation. We've worked to save jobs and to save lives. We've reformed the drug-approval process to speed up the availability of new medicines for people with life-threatening diseases like cystic fibrosis, cancer and AIDS.

And what is the response of the Democrats in Congress? They have tried to kill the Council on Competitiveness, which stands up for the American people and against the bureaucrats and the special interests. They think the Competitiveness Council should go. They don't get it. It is time for them to go.

You know, if the Democrats in Congress can't run their own restaurant, can't run their own post office and can't run their own bank, they sure can't be trusted to run our country.

I hope everybody who watched the Democratic Convention noticed how they hid their congressional leaders. You couldn't find them anywhere. Maybe it was a slick idea to keep those Democratic congressmen and senators under wraps. But on Election Day, but on Election Day, they're going to learn a hard lesson: You can run from a TV camera; you can even run from your own delegates; but you can't hide from the voters of America.

So again—so again, there is only one thing to say about the spend-everything, block-everything, know-nothing Democratic Congress: It is time for them to go.

And it's—and it's time—and it's time to change Congress for good. Almost 16 years ago, in my first speech as a member of the House of Representatives, I proposed limiting the terms of Congress. The Democratic Congress—the Democratic Congress tells us that it is good for the country to limit Ronald Reagan and George Bush to two terms as president. I say to them, if it is good for the country to limit Ronald Reagan and George Bush to two terms, then it would be great for the country to limit the terms of senators like [Majority Leader] George [J.] Mitchell and Ted [Edward M.] Kennedy, and the rest of that liberal Democratic Congress down there in Washington.

[Clinton and the Special Interests]

None of the reforms—none of the reforms I've just mentioned has any support from Bill Clinton. Bill Clinton talks about change, but he can't really change America because the special interests won't let him. He can't say a word—not one single word—about legal reform because the trial lawyers won't let him. He can't support—he can't support—he can't support school choice for parents because the education lobby in Washington won't let him. He will not join the majority of Americans in supporting term limits because the Democratic Congress won't let him. And he can't fight for the traditional family because his supporters in Hollywood and the media elite won't let him.

My friends: Bill Clinton and the special interests will never run America because we won't let them.

For more—speaking of the media, for more than a month, the media have been telling us that Bill Clinton and Al Gore are "moderates."

If they're moderates, I'm a world champion speller.

We are the true voice for change, and we do not take our marching orders from the special interests. On behalf of legal reform and education reform, we've taken on the strongest forces of the status quo, and we will not back down. On behalf of deregulation and term limits, we've taken on the Democratic Congress, and we will not back down. And on behalf of family values, we've taken on Hollywood and the media elite, and we will not back down.

It's been said—it's been said, and it is true, that a leader gives his people character. And once again, America is going to choose a leader who had judgment, experience and moral strength. Four years ago, none of us knew that the Berlin Wall would fall, the Iron Curtain would be lifted, the Baltic nations would be free, communism would be dead and buried, the Soviet Union would cease to exist and the threatening SS-18 ballistic missiles would be history. Nor did we know that we would be called upon to confront the aggression of a Middle East tyrant.

But four years ago we did know this: Whatever lay ahead, there was a clear choice to lead us. There was one man we could trust to guide our journey to a new century. And because we elected George Bush as our president, America is stronger, and the world is safer.

My friends—now, listen, listen, listen to this, listen to this, in an attempt, in an attempt to establish credibility in foreign policy, Gov. Clinton recently compared himself to former [Calif.] Gov. Ronald Reagan.

I know Ronald Reagan. Ronald Reagan is a friend of mine. And, Bill Clinton, you're no Ronald Reagan.

The Democratic—the Democratic—the Democratic nominee calls America "the mockery of the world," but he and his running mate are the only ones who believe that. To Gov. Clinton, I say this: America is the greatest nation in the world, and that's one thing you're not going to change.

These last four years, I have worked with a man who represents so much of what is good in our country, a man whose public and personal life are the embodiment of character. Every day in that Oval Office, I see the dedication of a husband, father and grandfather; the self-reliance of an entrepreneur; the courage of a Navy pilot; the dependability of a loyal friend; the compassion of a man of faith; and the wisdom of the man who married Barbara Bush.

George Bush has given us great victories abroad and performed great deeds at home. But, as Theodore Roosevelt said, the greatest victories are yet to be won, and the greatest deeds are yet to be done.

We will go on fighting for the values, the hopes and the dreams of our people. We will take this campaign to every American and to every state. We will win because of our principles; we will win because of our beliefs; and we will build an America more secure in the values of faith, family and freedom.

In these difficult times, America needs the very best: the best in character, the best in leadership and the best in judgment. And the very best is our nominee, our president, George Bush. Thank you very much. God bless you, and God bless America.

REPUBLICAN PARTY PLATFORM
August 17, 1992

Moving sharply to the right in keeping with the philosophy heard throughout the week, the Republican national convention on August 17 approved a tough, conservative platform that infuriated party moderates—especially on the issue of abortion. There were loud cries of "no" but no public debate as the delegates adopted the platform by voice vote at Houston's Astrodome.

If President George Bush found it difficult to run on the platform with its hard-line, no-exceptions abortion plank, he was not letting on. Within hours after the vote, Bush told NBC News: "Never mind. I'll be compatible with the platform in other ways." But he brushed off specifics, saying, "Well, I'll have to wait and read the platform, which I must confess I've not done."

Bush's seemingly offhand comments actually looked as carefully crafted and deliberately timed as those of his wife the week before. On August 13, the same day that platform writers finished drafting the document, Barbara Bush told reporters that she thought abortion had no place in it. Coming after four days in which antiabortion delegates hammered abortion rights supporters' every attempt to soften or delete the abortion plank, the statements by the president and first lady struck some as a deliberate attempt to placate the losers.

But abortion rights foes, noting Bush's record of vetoing abortion-related legislation, said Bush's actions spoke louder than off-the-cuff remarks. "I think the last thing George Bush wants to project is vacillation," said Rep. Henry J. Hyde, R-Ill., a leading antiabortion voice in Congress. "I think his convictions that at least he has acted on that have been very strong. The pro-life movement could not ask for more from any president."

Later in the week the convention nominated Bush and Vice President Dan Quayle to run for second terms against the Democratic ticket of Bill Clinton and Al Gore. (Democratic National Convention, p. 667; Republican National Convention, p. 781)

The GOP platform was four times longer than the Democrats' 1992 platform, which contained an abortion plank affirming "the right of every woman to choose, consistent with Roe v. Wade, *regardless of ability to pay."* (Democratic Party Platform, p. 685)

An Early Defeat

Abortion rights activists on the Republican platform committee were badly beaten the week of August 10 when they tried to rewrite the plank. Although similar language had been used in the 1984 and 1988 platforms, the group felt that times and conditions favored a more moderate stance in 1992. Pro-choice delegates hoped they might somehow attract enough delegate support to stage at least a brief floor debate during the convention's opening session August 17.

But there was not much chance activists would get their debate, let alone change the platform. Party operatives were so confident there would be no changes that they printed up an expensive-looking, bound version of the document that was ready for delegates and the media well before activists were scheduled to mount any floor challenge.

In the end, abortion rights supporters could not get the six delegations needed to support a floor motion. They rounded up only four: Maine, Massachusetts, New Mexico, and the Virgin Islands. "Many people said, 'I am pro-choice, but I didn't want to embarrass the president,' " said Maria M. Hustace, a delegate and 1988 U.S. Senate candidate from Hawaii.

Mary Dent Crisp, chair of the National Republican Coalition for Choice and a former national cochair of the GOP, said her antiabortion opponents had been working the grass roots for the better part of two decades. Her group had begun fighting back only when the Supreme Court's Webster *decision in 1989 scared abortion rights supporters by signaling that the Court might eventually strike down the constitutional protection for abortion. "The acceptance of this platform by the Republican national convention has provided a flash point for pro-choice Republicans on every level," Crisp said.*

Phyllis Schlafly, president of the Republican National Coalition for Life, said the plank would help Bush's campaign because "the American people will respect someone who stands up for a principle." Schlafly was widely credited with having helped to protect the antiabortion plank against any changes.

Other Major Planks

Consistent with the theme of the convention, the platform emphasized "family values" and sought to depict the Democrats' beliefs and programs as having contributed to breakdowns in traditional family unity and rising problems with AIDS, homelessness, teen pregnancies, and many other ills of modern society.

Among the major planks were:

- *Opposition to classifying homosexuals as a protected minority under civil rights statutes.*
- *Opposition to gun control.*
- *Support for Bush administration economic policies and rebuttal of Democratic assertions that economic conditions were poor.*
- *Support for the Bush administration's record in foreign affairs.*
- *Opposition to greater investment in public works as a "Democratic scam to raise taxes."*
- *Opposition to government control of health care.*
- *Support for greater reliance on the individual and private enterprise, and less on government.*

Following is an excerpted text of the Republican party platform adopted in Houston August 17, 1992:

Preamble

Abraham Lincoln, our first Republican president, expressed the philosophy that inspires Republicans to this day: "The legitimate object of government is to do for a community of people whatever they need to have done, but cannot do at all, or cannot so well do, for themselves in their separate and individual capacities. But in all that people can individually do as well for themselves, government ought not to interfere."

We believe that most problems of human making are within the capacity of human ingenuity to solve.

For good reason, millions of new Americans have flocked to our shores: America has always been an opportunity society. Republicans have always believed that economic prosperity comes from individual enterprise, not government programs. We have defended our core principles for 138 years. But never has this country, and the world, been so receptive to our message.

The fall of the Berlin Wall symbolizes an epochal change in the way people live. More important, it liberates the way people think. We see with new clarity that centralized government bureaucracies created in this century are not the wave of the future. Never again will people trust planners and paper shufflers more than they trust themselves. We all watched as the statue of Soviet hangman Feliks Dzherzhinsky was toppled in front of Moscow's KGB headquarters by the very people his evil empire sought to enslave. Its sightless eyes symbolized the moral blindness of totalitarians around the world. They could never see the indomitable spirit of people determined to be free from government control—free to build a better future with their own heads, hands and hearts.

We Republicans saw clearly the dangers of collectivism: not only the military threat but the deeper threat to the souls of people bound in dependence. Here at home, we warned against "big government," because we knew concentrated decision-making, no matter how well-intentioned, was a danger to liberty and prosperity. Republicans stood at the rampart of freedom, defending the individual against the domineering state. While we did not always prevail, we always stood our ground, faithful to our principles and confident of history's ultimate verdict.

Our opponents declared that the dogmas of the left were the final and victorious faith. From kremlins and ivory towers, their planners proclaimed the bureaucratic millennium. But in a tragic century of illusion, Five-Year Plans and Great Leaps Forward failed to summon a Brave New World. One hundred and fifty years of slogans and manifestos came crashing down in an ironic cascade of unintended consequences. All that is left are the ruins of a failed scoundrel ideology.

As May Day lapses back into just another spring festival, the Fourth of July emerges as the common holiday of free men and women. Yet, in 1992, when the self-governing individual has overcome the paternalistic state, liberals here at home simply do not get it. Indeed, their party seeks to turn the clock back. But their ideas are old and tired. Like planets still orbiting a dying star, the believers in state power turn their faces to a distant and diminishing light.

The Democrats would revise history to rationalize a return to bigger government, higher taxes and moral relativism. The Democratic Party has forgotten its origins as a party of work, thrift and self-reliance. But they have not forgotten their art for dissembling and distortion. The Democrats are trapped in their compact with the ideology of trickle-down government, but they are clever enough to know that the voters would shun them if their true markings were revealed.

America had its rendezvous with destiny in 1980. Faced with crisis at home and abroad, Americans turned to Republican leadership in the White House. Presidents Reagan and Bush turned our nation away from the path of overtaxation, hyper-regulation and megagovernment. Instead, we moved in a new direction. We cut taxes, reduced red tape, put people above bureaucracy. And so we vanquished the idea of the almighty state as the supervisor of our daily lives. In choosing hope over fear, Americans raised a beacon, reminding the world that we are a shining city on a hill, the last best hope for man on earth.

Contrary to statist Democrat propaganda, the American people know that the 1980s were a rising tide, a magnificent decade for freedom and entrepreneurial creativity. We are confident that, knowing this, they will never consciously retreat to the bad old days of tax and spend. Our platform will clarify the choice before our fellow citizens.

We have learned that ideas do indeed have consequences. Thus, our words are important not for their prose but for what they reveal about the thinking of our president and our party.

Two years ago, President Bush described the key elements of what he called "our new paradigm," a fresh approach that aims to put new ideas to work in the service of enduring principles—principles we upheld throughout the long twilight struggle, principles George Bush has acted decisively to advance. Thus we honor the Founders and their vision.

Unlike our opponents, we are inspired by a commitment to profound change. Our mission combines timeless beliefs with a positive vision of a vigorous America: prosperous and tolerant, just and compassionate. We believe that individual freedom, hard work and personal responsibility—basic to free society—are also basic to effective government. We believe in the fundamental goodness of the American people. We believe in traditional family values and in the Judeo-Christian heritage that informs our culture. We believe in the Constitution and its guarantee of color-blind equal opportunity. We believe in free markets. We believe in constructive change, in both true conservatism and true reform. We believe government has a legitimate role to play in our national life, but government must never dominate that life.

While our goals are constant, we are willing to innovate, experiment and learn. We have learned that bigger is not better, that quantity and quality are different things, that more money does not guarantee better outcomes.

We have learned the importance of individual choice—in education, health care, child care—and that bureaucracy is the enemy of initiative and self-reliance. We believe in empowerment, including home ownership for as many as possible. We believe in decentralized authority, and a bottom-line, principled commitment to what works for people.

We believe in the American people: free men and women with faith in God, working for themselves and their families, believing in the value of every human being from the very young to the very old.

We believe the Founders intended Congress to be responsive, flexible and foresighted. After decades of Democrat misrule, the Congress is none of these things. Dominated by reactionaries, obsessed with the failed policies and structures of the past, the Democrat majority displays a "do-nothing" doggedness: They intend to learn nothing and forget nothing. Seeking to build a better America, we seek to elect a better Congress.

Finally, we believe in a president who represents the national interest, not just the aggregation of well-connected special interests—a president who brings unity to the American purpose.

America faces many challenges. Republicans, under the strong leadership of President Bush, are responding with this bold platform of new ideas that infuses our commitment to individual freedom and market forces with an equal commitment to a decent, just way of life for every American.

With a firm faith that the American people will always choose hope over fear, we Republicans dedicate ourselves to this forward-looking agenda for America in the 1990s, transcending old, static ideas with a shared vision of hope, optimism and opportunity.

Uniting Our Family

As the family goes, so goes the nation. Strong families and strong communities make a strong America. An old adage says, "America is great because she is good; if America ceases to be good, she will cease to be great."

Our greatness starts at home—literally. So Republicans believe government should strengthen families, not replace them. Today, more than ever, the traditional family is under assault. We believe our laws should reflect what makes our nation prosperous and wholesome: faith in God, hard work, service to others and limited government.

Parents bring reality to these principles when they pass them on to their children. As the book of Proverbs proclaims, "Train up a child in the way he should go: and when he is old, he will not depart from it."

Imagine the America we could create if all parents taught their children the importance of honesty, work, responsibility and respect for others. We would have less violence in our homes and streets; less illegal drug use; fewer teen pregnancies forcing girls and boys to be adults before they have graduated from high school. Instead, we would have an America of families, friends and communities that care about one another.

That kind of future is not a matter of chance; it is a question of personal responsibility. Barbara Bush captured the importance of that stewardship when she said, "At the end of your life you will never regret not having passed one more test, not winning one more verdict, or not closing one more deal. You will regret time not spent with a husband, a child, a friend or a parent."

The Republican Party has espoused these principles since its founding. Families built on solid, spiritual foundations are central to our party's inspiration. At this time of great national and global transition, we renew our commitment to these fundamental principles, which will guide our family, our country, our world into the next century.

Family: The Home of Freedom

The Rights of the Family

Our national renewal starts with the family. It is where each new generation gains its moral anchor. It is the school of citizenship, the engine of economic progress, a permanent haven when everything is changing.

Change can be good, when it liberates the energy and commitment of family members to build better futures. We welcome change that corrects the mistakes of the past, particularly those at war against the family. For more than three decades, the liberal philosophy has assaulted the family on every side.

Today, its more vocal advocates believe children should be able to sue their parents over decisions about schooling, cosmetic surgery, employment and other family matters. They deny parental authority and responsibility, fracturing the family into isolated individuals, each of them dependent upon—and helpless before—government. This is the ultimate agenda of contemporary socialism under all its masks: to liberate youth from traditional family values by replacing family functions with bureaucratic social services. That is why today's liberal Democrats are hostile toward any institution government cannot control, like private child care or religious schools.

The Republican Party responds, as it has since 1980, with an unabashed commitment to the family's economic liberty and moral rights. Republicans trust parents and believe they, not courts and lawyers, know what is best for their children. That is why we will work to ensure that the Congress and the states shall enact no law abridging the rights of the family formed by blood, marriage, adoption or legal custody—rights that are anterior and superior to those of government. Republicans oppose and resist the efforts of the Democratic Party to redefine the traditional American family.

The Right to a Family

Every child deserves a family in a home filled with love and free from abuse. Today, many children do not enjoy that right. We are determined to change that. While government cannot legislate love and compassion, we can provide the leadership to encourage the development of healthy, nurturing families. We applaud the fine example of family values and family virtue as lived by the president and the first lady.

We will promote whole, caring families by eliminating biases that have crept into our legal and tax codes. We will advance adoption through significant tax credits, insurance reforms and legal reforms. We encourage adoption for those unprepared or unwilling to bear the emotional, financial or physical demands of raising a child, and will work to revive maternity homes to ensure care for both mothers and babies.

We applaud the commitment of foster-care parents who provide family environments for foster-care children. We abhor the disgraceful bureaucratic mismanagement of foster care. Big-city mayors have spent billions on social service bureaucrats who have lost track of many children. Many have no health records, no real residence, not even the simplest personal possessions. Shuttled from house to house, they lack discipline and identity, and are ripe for lives of crime. We are determined to reform this system to help these children.

Broken homes can have a devastating emotional and economic impact upon children and are the breeding ground for gang members. We urge state legislatures to explore ways to promote marital stability. Because the intergenerational family is a vital element of social cohesion, we urge greater respect for the rights and roles of grandparents.

Republicans recognize the importance of having fathers and mothers in the home. The two-parent family still provides the best environment of stability, discipline, responsibility and character. Documentation shows that where the father has deserted his family, children are more likely to commit a crime, to drop out of school, to become violent, to become teen parents, to take illegal drugs, to become mired in poverty, or to have emotional or behavioral problems. We support the courageous efforts of single-parent families to have a stable home.

Caring for Children

George Bush secured the American family's most important victory of the last four years: his child-care bill. He won landmark legislation—a voucher system for low-income households, allowing parents to choose what's best for their children, including care given by neighbors or churches. The Democratic Party opposed that legislation and instead sought government control of child care and fewer choices for parents.

The president also advanced equity for families that forgo a second income to care for their children at home through his Young Child Tax Credit. Congressional Democrats are already trying to repeal it.

The demands of employment and commuting often make it hard for parents to spend time with their children. Republicans advocate maximum flexibility in working and child-care arrangements so that families can make the most of their schedules. We support pro-family policies: job-sharing, telecommuting, compressed workweeks, parental leave negotiated between employer and employees, and flextime. We reject the Democrats' one-size-fits-all approach that puts mandates on employers and takes choices away from employees.

Most parents prefer in-home care of their children but often encounter government obstacles. Republicans will promote in-home care by allowing payment annually, instead of quarterly, of income taxes by employees and withholding taxes by employers. Our proposals for tort reform, now blocked by the Democrat Congress, will prevent excessive litigation that hampers the growth of child-care opportunities. By taking care of our children, we are taking care of our future.

Family Security

Over the last several decades, liberal Democrats have increasingly shifted economic burdens onto the American family. Indeed, the liberal Democrat tax-and-spend policies have forced millions of women into the workplace just to make ends meet. Because of their policies in Congress, fathers and mothers have a tougher time bringing home what they work so hard for.

Between 1948 and 1990, under the Democrat-controlled Congress for most of those years, federal taxes on the average family of four rose from 2 percent to 24 percent of income. When state and local levies are included, the tax burden exceeds one-third of family income. The increase in the effective federal tax rate since 1950 has now swallowed up an ever-increasing share of a family's earnings. Instead of working to improve their family's standard of living, they must work to feed government's gluttonous appetite.

This is a scandal. In the 1980s, two Republican presidents kept Democrats from making matters worse. Presidents Reagan and Bush led the way to increase the personal exemption for dependents. We pledge to go farther to restore the value, as a percentage of average household income, it had 50 years ago. The value of the dependent deduction has eroded to a fraction of its original worth to families. Republicans call for a complete restoration, in real dollars, to its original value. Rather than fatten government bureaucracies with new programs to "help" families, we want to expand the Young Child Tax Credit to $500 per child and make it available to all families with children under the age of 10.

When the Democrats establish tax policy that makes marriage more expensive than living together, they discourage traditional commitment and stable home life. We will remove the marriage penalty in the tax code, so a married couple will receive as large a standard deduction as their unmarried counterparts. Together, these changes will empower parents to care for their families in a way public services never can.

Achieving Educational Excellence

In the earliest American communities, pioneers would establish a church, then a school. Parents wanted their children to have the best possible education, to learn what they needed to know to make a better life. Virtually every newly arrived immigrant family thought of education as the American way from the back to the front of the line. Americans have come to believe that only a country that successfully educates its sons and daughters can count on a strong, competitive economy, a vibrant culture and a solid civic life. . . .

Recognizing what every parent knows, that our current educational system is not educating our children, President Bush is leading an educational revolution. We applaud the president's bold vision to change radically our education system. Our parents want it, our communities want it, our states want it, and our children want it—but the Democrat leadership in the House and Senate continue to thwart the will of the American people for radical change in the way we educate our children.

The Republican strategy is based on sound principle. Parents have the right to choose the best school for their children. Schools should teach right from wrong. Schools should reinforce parental authority, not replace it. We should increase flexibility from federal regulation. We should explore a new generation of break-the-mold New American Schools. Standards and assessments should be raised, not reduced to a lowest common denominator. Communities should be empowered to find what works. The pursuit of excellence in education is a fundamental goal. Good teachers should be rewarded for teaching well. Alternative certification can bring desperately needed new people into the teaching profession. America needs public, private and parochial schools.

Education is a joint responsibility of the individual, the family and the community. Parents are the first and most important teachers of their children. They should have the right not only to participate in their child's education but to choose for their children among the broadest array of educational choices, without regard to their income. We also support the right of parents to provide quality education through home-based schools.

The Bush administration has sent to Congress several legislative proposals embodying these principles. The proposals, in spite of the fact that 1,500 communities across the nation have developed local committees to support them through the America 2000 strategy, languish in the Democrat Congress. And they are opposed by special-interest unions that have a power grip on the failed policies of the past. . . .

The president has shown unprecedented leadership for the most important education goal of all: helping middle- and low-income families enjoy the same choice of schools—public, private or religious—that families with more resources already have. The president's proposed "GI Bill for Children" will provide $1,000 scholarships to middle- and low-income families, enabling their children to attend the school of their choice. This innovative plan will not only drive schools to excel as they compete, but will also give every parent consumer power to obtain an excellent education for his or her child.

Republican leadership has nearly doubled funds for Head Start, making it possible, for the first time, for all eligible 4-year-olds to participate, should their parents choose to enroll them. The Bush administration has put a college education within reach of millions more students, young and old. The president has proposed allowing families to deduct the interest they pay on student loans, and penalty-free withdrawal of IRA [individual retirement account] funds for educational expenses. . . .

Our Educational Beliefs

We are confident that the United States can, by the end of this decade, reach the six national education goals that President Bush and the nation's governors have established: that all children should arrive at school ready to learn; that high school graduation rates should be at least 90 percent; that all children learn challenging subject matter and become responsible citizens; that American children should be first in the world in math and science; that there must be a literate and skilled work force; and that schools must be disciplined and free of drugs and violence.

We have an uncompromising commitment to improve public education—which means assuring that our schools produce well-educated, responsible citizens—not the maintenance of a government monopoly over the means of educating. American families must be given choice in education. We value the important role played by our private, independent and parochial schools, colleges and universities. We believe that their quality is best encouraged by minimizing government regulation. . . .

Schools should be—as they have been traditionally—academic institutions. Families and communities err when by neglect or design they transfer to the school responsibilities that belong in the home and in the community. Schools were created to help and strengthen families, not to undermine or substitute for them.

Accordingly, we oppose programs in public schools that provide birth control or abortion services or referrals. Instead, we encourage abstinence education programs with proven track records in protecting youth from disease, pregnancy and drug use.

The critical public mission in education is to set tough, clear standards of achievement and ensure that those who educate our children are accountable for meeting them. This is not just a matter of plans or dollars. Competency testing and merit pay for teachers are essential elements of such accountability. . . .

Just as spiritual principles—our moral compass—help guide public policy, learning must have a moral basis. America must remain neutral toward particular religions, but we must not remain neutral toward religion itself or the values religion supports. Mindful of our country's Judeo-Christian heritage and rich religious pluralism, we support the right of students to engage in voluntary prayer in schools and the right of the community to do so at commencements or other occasions. We will strongly enforce the law guaranteeing equal access to school facilities. We also advocate recitation of the Pledge of Allegiance in schools as a reminder of the principles that sustain us as one nation under God. . . .

For Healthier Families: Promote Health, Prevent Disease, Reform Health Care

Americans receive the finest medical care in the world. We have the best health-care providers, the best hospitals and the best medical technology. People come here from Canada, from Europe, from every part of the globe, to seek procedures and treatments that are either unavailable or strictly rationed in their home countries.

But we must do better. Costs are soaring. Many Americans, responsible for children and aging parents, worry about the quality and price of care. The 1992 election presents all of us with a clear choice.

Democrats want a costly, coercive system, imported from abroad, with a budget set by Congress and policies set by bureaucrats. That is a prescription for misery. It would imperil jobs, require billions in new taxes, lower the quality of health care overall, drive health-care providers out of the profession, and result in rationing. . . .

Republicans believe government control of health care is irresponsible and ineffective. We believe health-care choices should remain in the hands of the people, not government bureaucrats. This issue truly represents a fundamental difference between the two parties.

We endorse President Bush's comprehensive health-care plan, which solves the two major problems of the current system — access and affordability—while preserving the high-quality care Americans now enjoy. The president's plan will make health care *more affordable* through tax credits and deductions that will offset insurance costs for 95 million Americans; and make health care *more accessible,* especially for small businesses, by reducing insurance costs and eliminating workers' worries of losing insurance if they change jobs. This plan will expand access to health care by:

- Creating new tax credits and deductions to help low- and middle-income Americans. These tax credits would be available in the form of vouchers for low-income people who work.
- Providing insurance security for working Americans by requiring insurers to cover pre-existing conditions.
- Making health insurance premiums fully deductible for the self-employed.
- Making it easier for small firms to purchase coverage for their employees. The proposal would allow small businesses to form health insurance purchasing pools that would make insurance more affordable. It also would guarantee the availability and renewability of insurance for small firms, set premium standards, pre-empt state mandated-benefit laws, establish minimum coverage plans, and require states to establish risk pools to spread risks broadly across health insurers.
- Addressing the medical malpractice problem by a cap on non-economic damage recoveries in malpractice claims and an alternative dispute resolution before going to court.

In short, the president aims to make coverage available to all, guaranteed, renewable, with no preconditions. Under his plan, no one will have to go broke to get well.

The Democrats' plan stands in stark philosophical contrast. Instead of preserving individual options, it would rely on government bureaucrats. Instead of preserving quality care, it would lead to rationing and waiting lines. And instead of enhancing the health-care security of American workers, it would require a massive increase in payroll taxes that would destroy hundreds of thousands of jobs.

The Democrats' so-called play-or-pay proposal would require employers either to provide health insurance for their workers or pay a new tax that would fund in part a new government-run health program. According to a study prepared by the Urban Institute, this mandate would require new federal taxes—or new federal borrowing—of $36 billion in the first year alone. Nearly 52 million Americans who now have private health insurance would be dumped by their employers onto the government-run plan. Additional costs to employers—particularly small employers—would total an estimated $30 billion in the first year. The Republican staff of Congress'

Joint Economic Committee estimates that 712,000 people would lose their jobs because of the play-or-pay mandate.

Republicans are also determined to resolve the crisis in medical liability, allowing physicians and certified midwives to deliver babies and practice in underserved areas. Meaningful medical tort reform would assure that doctors would not have to practice medicine under a cloud of potential litigation. We will reduce administrative expenses and paperwork by adopting a uniform claim and data system. We pledge our support for rehabilitation and long-term care coverage. We will curb costs through better prenatal and other preventive care. We encourage the application of the Good Samaritan law to protect health-care providers who wish to volunteer their time to provide patient care to the community. We encourage coordinated care in public programs and private insurance. We further support regulatory reforms to speed the development of new drugs and medical technology.

The health-care safety net must be secure for those who need preventive, acute and long-term care. Special consideration should be given to abolishing or reforming programs which prohibit or discourage individuals from seeking to work their way out of poverty and dependency. We will reduce paperwork burdens and redirect those resources to actual services. We will enhance access to medical care through community health centers, which provide primary care in medically underserved areas. We will modify outdated antitrust rules that prohibit hospitals from merging their resources to provide improved, cost-effective health care.

We encourage the use of telecommunications technology to link hospitals in larger communities with heath-care facilities in smaller communities. Advanced communications networks will facilitate the sharing of resources, will improve access to affordable health care through the transmission of medical imaging and diagnostics and will ensure that Americans living in rural areas have the same access to doctors and the latest medical procedures as Americans living in urban areas.

Republicans focus on health, not just health care. We want not only to treat disease and disability but to reduce and prevent them. Through funding for NIH [the National Institutes of Health], we invest in research to cure a range of diseases, from cancer to heart disease, from multiple sclerosis to lupus. We support efforts which foster early cancer detection. Even more important, we rely on individuals to lower the incidence of preventable illness and injury. A large part of our health-care costs, public and private, is caused by behavior. Good judgment can save billions of dollars—and perhaps millions of lives.

AIDS

The HIV/AIDS epidemic has exploded over the past decade into a crisis of tragic proportions. In our country, AIDS already has claimed more than 150,000 lives, and as many as 1 million more Americans may have been infected with the virus.

Epidemics have, throughout history, challenged governments, which have too often been powerless to combat them. Science—and human wisdom—have advanced, however, and we have met this crisis not only with a massive commitment of resources but also with a personal determination on the part of the president. That commitment and leadership will continue.

AIDS should be treated like any other communicable or sexually transmitted disease, while at the same time preserving patient confidentiality. We are committed to ensure that our nation's response to AIDS is shaped by compassion, not fear or ignorance and will oppose, as a matter of decency and honor, any discrimination against Americans who are its victims.

We encourage state legislatures to enact legislation which makes it a criminal act for anyone knowingly to transmit the AIDS virus.

We will seek to ensure that medical personnel, and the people who trust in their care, will be protected against infection.

This disease also challenges America scientifically. We must succeed in slowing the epidemic's spread. The administration has thus placed great emphasis on a variety of prevention efforts to do so. We must recognize, also, that prevention is linked ultimately to personal responsibility and moral behavior. We reject the notion that the distribution of clean needles and condoms are the solution to stopping the spread of AIDS. Education designed to curb the spread of this disease should stress marital fidelity, abstinence and a drug-free lifestyle. There must be a means for successfully treating the virus, and this has led to a threefold increase in research and steps to speed the approval process for new drugs that could make a crucial difference to those infected.

Above all, a cure must be found. We have committed enormous resources—$4.2 billion over the past four years for research alone, more than for any disease except cancer. In keeping with the American spirit, our fellow citizens with HIV/AIDS deserve our compassion and our care, and they deserve our united commitment to a cure. . . .

The Homeless

The Bush administration has worked vigorously to address this tragedy, believing that involuntary homelessness in America is unacceptable. Accordingly, the administration has proposed $4 billion in homeless assistance, an amount cut back by the Democrat-controlled Congress. We have also implemented a Shelter Plus Care program designed to assist homeless persons who are mentally ill, chemically dependent or stricken with AIDS. Republicans remain determined to help the homeless as a matter of ethical commitment as well as sound public policy. . . .

Promoting Cultural Values

The culture of our nation has traditionally supported those pillars on which civilized society is built: personal responsibility, morality and the family. Today, however, these pillars are under assault. Elements within the media, the entertainment industry, academia and the Democratic Party are waging a guerrilla war against American values. They deny personal responsibility, disparage traditional morality, denigrate religion and promote hostility toward the family's way of life. Children, the members of our society most vulnerable to cultural influences, are barraged with violence and promiscuity, encouraging reckless and irresponsible behavior. This undermines the authority of parents, the ones most responsible for passing on to their offspring a sense of right and wrong. The lesson our party draws is important—that all of us, individuals and corporations alike, have a responsibility to reflect the values we expect our fellow citizens to exhibit. And if children grow to adulthood reflecting not the values of their parents but the amorality with which they are bombarded, those who send such messages cannot duck culpability.

One example is the advocacy of violence against law enforcement officers, promoted by a corporation more interested in profits than the possible consequences of such a message. We believe, in the spirit of Theodore Roosevelt, that corporations—like individuals—have responsibilities to society, and that conscience alone should prevent such outrages.

We also stand united with those private organizations, such as the Boy Scouts of America, who are defending decency in fulfillment of their own moral responsibilities. We reject the irresponsible position of those corporations that have cut off contributions to such organizations because of their courageous stand for family values. Moreover, we oppose efforts by the Democratic Party to include sexual preference as a protected minority receiving preferential status under civil rights statutes at the federal, state and local level.

We oppose any legislation or law that legally recognizes same-sex marriages and allows such couples to adopt children or provide foster care.

We must recognize that the time has come for a national crusade against pornography. Some would have us believe that obscenity and pornography have no social impact. But if hard-core pornography does not cheapen the human spirit, then neither does Shakespeare elevate it. We call on federal agencies to halt the sale, under government auspices, of pornographic materials. We endorse Republican legislation, the Pornography Victims Compensation Act, allowing victims of pornography to seek damages from those who make or sell it, especially since the Commission on Pornography, in 1986, found a direct link between pornography and violent crimes committed against women and children. We also believe that the various state legislatures should create a civil cause of action against makers and distributors of pornography when their material incites a violent crime.

Government has a responsibility, as well, to ensure that it promotes the common moral values that bind us together as a nation. We therefore condemn the use of public funds to subsidize obscenity and blasphemy masquerading as art. The fine arts, including those with public support, can certainly enrich our society. However, no artist has an inherent right to claim taxpayer support for his or her private vision of art if that vision mocks the moral and spiritual basis on which our society is founded. We believe a free market in art—with neither suppression nor favoritism by government—is the best way to foster the cultural revival our country needs.

Individual Rights, Good Homes and Safe Streets

At a time when the rest of the world has rejected socialism, there are communities here at home where free markets have not been permitted to flourish. Decades of liberalism have left us with two economies. The pro-growth economy rewards effort, promotes thrift and supports strong families. The other economy stifles initiative and is anti-work and anti-family. In one economy, people are free to be owners and entrepreneurs. In the other economy, people are at the mercy of government. We are determined to elevate the poor into the pro-growth economy.

Republicans will lead a new national consensus around economic opportunity, greater access to property, home ownership and housing, jobs and entrepreneurship. We must bring the great promise of America to every city, every small town, and to all our people.

Our agenda for equality of opportunity runs throughout this platform and applies to all Americans. There is no such thing as segregated success. We reject the Democrats' politics of division, envy and conflict. They believe that America is split into classes and can be healed only through the redistribution of wealth. We believe in the economics of multiplication: free markets expand opportunity and wealth for all.

That is true liberation. It frees poor people not only from want but also from government control. That is why liberal Democrats have fought us every step of the way, refusing congressional action on enterprise zones until Los Angeles burned—and then mocking the expectations of the poor by gutting that critical proposal. They can kill bills, but they cannot kill hope. We are determined to pass that legislation for the sake of all who are awaiting their chance for the American Dream.

We will eliminate laws that keep Americans out of jobs, like the outdated ban on home work. The antiquated Davis-Bacon Act inflates taxpayer costs and keeps willing workers from getting jobs in federally assisted projects. It must go. Unlike the Democrats, we believe the private sector, not the federal government, should set prevailing wage rates....

In the tradition of Lincoln, President Bush has replicated the American dream of home ownership. For first-time home buyers, he has proposed a $5,000 tax credit. For lower-income families, he has worked to restore opportunity through HOPE, his initiative to help tenants now dependent on federal aid to buy their own homes; Mortgage Revenue Bonds, to assist more than 1.9 million families to buy a first home; Low-Income Housing Tax Credits, already producing more than 420,000 decent apartments at affordable prices; and HOME, a partnership among all levels of government to help low-income families secure better housing.

For everyone, but especially for the poor, the best housing policy is non-inflationary economic growth and low interest rates, the heart of our opportunity agenda....

We believe fathers and mothers must be held responsible for their children. We support stronger enforcement of child support laws. We call for strong enforcement and tough penalties against welfare fraud and insist that work must be a mandatory part of public assistance for all who are able to work. Because divorce, desertion and illegitimacy account for almost all the increase in child poverty over the last 20 years, we put the highest priority upon enforcement of family rights and responsibilities.

Among these responsibilities is the obligation to get an education—a key to avoiding dependency. Families on welfare with school-age children must be required to send them to school or provide adequate home education in keeping with various state laws in order to continue receiving public assistance. Young adult heads of welfare households should be required to complete appropriate education or training programs.

Safe Homes and Streets

One of the first duties of government is to protect the public security—to maintain law and order so that citizens are free to pursue the fruits of life and liberty. The Democrats have forsaken this solemn pledge. Instead of protecting society from hardened criminals, they blame society and refuse to hold accountable for their actions individuals who have chosen to engage in violent and criminal conduct. This has led to the state of affairs in which we find ourselves today.

Violent crime is the gravest domestic threat to our way of life. It has turned our communities into battlegrounds, playgrounds into graveyards. It threatens everyone, but especially the very young, the elderly, the weak. It destroys business and suffocates economic opportunity in struggling communities. It is a travesty that some American children have to sleep in bathtubs for protection from stray bullets. The poverty of values that justifies drive-by shootings and random violence holds us hostage and insecure, even in our own homes. We must work to develop community-help projects designed to instill a sense of responsibility and pride....

For too long our criminal justice system has carefully protected the rights of criminals and neglected the suffering of the innocent victims of crime and their families. We support the rights of crime victims to be present, heard and informed throughout the criminal justice process, and to be provided with restitution and services to aid their recovery.

We believe in giving police the resources to do their job. Law enforcement must remain primarily a state and local responsibility. With 95 percent of all violent crimes within the jurisdiction of the states, we have led efforts to increase the number of police protecting our citizens. We also support incentives to encourage personnel leaving the armed forces to continue to defend their country—against the enemy within—by entering the law enforcement profession.

Narcotics traffic drives street crime. President Bush has, for the first time, used the resources of our armed forces against the international drug trade. By our insistence, multilateral control of precursor chemicals and money laundering is now an international priority. We decry efforts by congressional Democrats to slash international anti-narcotics funding and inhibit the most vital control efforts in Peru. We support efforts to work with South and Central American leaders to eradicate crops used to produce illegal narcotics. . . .

We oppose legalizing or decriminalizing drugs. That is a morally abhorrent idea, the last vestige of an ill-conceived philosophy that counseled the legitimacy of permissiveness. Today, a similarly dysfunctional morality explains away drug dealing as an escape, and drive-by shootings as an act of political violence. There is no excuse for the wanton destruction of human life. We therefore support the stiffest penalties, including the death penalty, for major drug traffickers.

Drug users must face punishment, including fines and imprisonment, for contributing to the demand that makes the drug trade profitable. Among possible sanctions should be the loss of government assistance and suspension of drivers' licenses. Residents of public housing should be able to protect their families against drugs by screening out abusers and dealers. We support grass-roots action to drive dealers and crack houses out of operation.

Safe streets also mean highways that are free of drunken drivers and drivers under the influence of illegal drugs. Republicans support the toughest possible state laws to deal with drunken drivers and users of illegal drugs, who deserve no sympathy from our courts or state legislatures. We also oppose the illicit abuse of legal drugs.

White-collar crime threatens homes and families in a different way. It steals secretly, forcing up prices, rigging contracts, swindling consumers and harming the overwhelming majority of business people who play fair and obey the law. We support imprisonment for those who steal from the American people. We pledge an all-out fight against it, especially within the political machines that control many of our major cities. We will continue to bring to justice corrupt politicians and those who collude with them to plunder savings and loans.

New Members of the American Family

Our nation of immigrants continues to welcome those seeking a better life. This reflects our past, when some newcomers fled intolerance; some sought prosperity; some came as slaves. All suffered and sacrificed but hoped their children would have a better life. All searched for a shared vision—and found one in America. Today we are stronger for our diversity.

Illegal entry into the United States, on the other hand, threatens the social compact on which immigration is based. That is, the nation accepts immigrants and is enriched by their determination and values. Illegal immigration, on the other hand, undermines the integrity of border communities and already crowded urban neighborhoods. We will build on the already announced strengthening of the Border Patrol to better coordinate interdiction of illegal entrants through greater cross-border cooperation. Specifically, we will increase the size of the Border Patrol in order to meet the increasing need to stop illegal immigration and we will equip the Border Patrol with the tools, technologies and structures necessary to secure the border.

We will seek stiff penalties for those who smuggle illegal aliens into the country, and for those who produce or sell fraudulent documents. We also will reduce incentives to enter the United States by promoting initiatives such as the North American Free Trade Agreement. In creating new economic opportunity in Mexico, a NAFTA removes the incentive to cross the border illegally in search of work.

Individual Rights

The protection of individual rights is the foundation for opportunity and security.

The Republican Party is unique in this regard. Since its inception, it has respected every person, even when that proposition was not universally popular. Today, as in the day of Lincoln, we insist that no American's rights are negotiable.

That is why we declare that bigotry and prejudice have no place in American life. We denounce all who practice or promote racism, anti-Semitism or religious intolerance. We believe churches and religious schools should not be taxed; we defend the right of religious leaders to speak out on public issues; and we condemn the cowardly desecration of places of worship that has shocked our country in recent years.

Asserting equal rights for all, we support the Bush administration's vigorous enforcement of statutes to prevent illegal discrimination on account of sex, race, creed or national origin. Promoting opportunity, we reject efforts to replace equal rights with quotas or other preferential treatment. That is why President Bush fought so long against the Democrat Congress to win a civil rights bill worthy of that name.

We renew the historic Republican commitment to the rights of women, from the early days of the suffragist movement to the present. Because legal rights mean little without opportunity, we assert economic growth as the key to the continued progress of women in all fields of American life.

We believe the unborn child has a fundamental individual right to life that cannot be infringed. We therefore reaffirm our support for a human life amendment to the Constitution, and we endorse legislation to make clear that the 14th Amendment's protections apply to unborn children. We oppose using public revenues for abortion and will not fund organizations that advocate it. We commend those who provide alternatives to abortion by meeting the needs of mothers and offering adoption services. We reaffirm our support for appointment of judges who respect traditional family values and the sanctity of innocent human life.

President Bush signed into law the greatest advance ever for disabled persons: The Americans with Disabilities Act, a milestone in removing barriers to full participation in our country's life. We will fully implement it with sensitivity to the needs of small businesses, just as we have earlier legal protections for the disabled in federal programs. We oppose the non-consensual withholding of health care or treatment from any person because of handicap, age or infirmity, just as we oppose euthanasia and assisted suicide.

We support full access to the polls, and the entire political process, by disabled voters. We will ensure that students with disabilities benefit from America 2000's new emphasis on testing for excellence and accountability for results.

Promoting the rights of the disabled requires, before all else, an expanding economy, both to advance assistive technology and to create opportunities for personal advancement. That is another reason why Republicans are committed to growth.

We reaffirm our commitment to the Fifth Amendment to the Constitution: "No person shall be ... deprived of life, liberty, or property, without due process of law; nor shall private property be taken for public use, without just compensation." We support strong enforcement of this Takings Clause to keep citizens secure in the use and development of their property. We also seek to reduce the amount of land owned or controlled by the government, especially in the Western states. We insist upon prompt payment for private lands certified as critical for preserving essential parks and preserves.

Republicans defend the constitutional right to keep and bear arms. We call for stiff mandatory sentences for those who use firearms in a crime. We note that those who seek to disarm citizens in their homes are the same liberals who tried to disarm our nation during the Cold War and are today seeking to cut our national defense below safe levels. We applaud congressional Republicans for overturning the District of Columbia's law blaming firearm manufacturers for street crime.

We affirm the right of individuals to form, join or assist labor organizations to bargain collectively, consistent with state laws. We support the right of states to enact right-to-work laws.

A Republican Congress will amend the Hobbs Act, so that union officials will not be exempt from the law's prohibition against extortion and violence. We call for greater legal protection from violence for workers who stay on the job during strikes.

We support self-determination for Indian tribes in managing their own affairs and resources. Recognizing the government-to-government trust responsibility, we aim to end dependency fostered by federal controls. Reservations and tribal lands held in trust should be free to become enterprise zones so their people can fully share in the nation's prosperity. We will work with tribal governments to improve education, health, economic opportunity and environmental conditions. We endorse efforts to preserve the culture and languages of Native Americans and Hawaiians and to ensure their equitable participation in federal programs. . . .

Security and Opportunity in a Changing Economy

Our economy is people, not statistics. The American people, not government, rescued the United States from an economic collapse triggered by Democrats in the 1970s. Crippled by taxes, robbed by inflation, threatened by controls, stunned by interest rates, the people ended America's decline and restored hope across our country and around our world.

We launched an era of growth and prosperity such as the world had never seen: 20 million new jobs in the longest peacetime economic expansion in the history of the Republic. We curbed the size and power of the federal establishment. We lowered tax rates. We restored a sound dollar. We unleashed the might of free people to produce, compete and triumph in free markets. We gave them the tools; they completed the job.

During the 1980s and into the present decade, the U.S. economy once again became the engine of global growth. Inflation has fallen to its lowest level in 30 years. Interest rates dropped 15 percentage points. Productivity has sharply risen. Exports are booming. Despite a global downturn in late 1990, real economic growth resumed last year and has continued for five consecutive quarters. With low interest rates and low inflation, the American economy is poised for stronger growth through the rest of the 1990s. Keeping inflation and interest rates low and stable through a sound monetary policy is essential for economic growth. . . .

Keeping What You Earn

The test of economic policy is whether it promotes economic growth and expands job opportunities. Lower taxes and an expanding economy depend on long-term, consistent restraint in the growth of federal spending.

In 1990, as the deficit was threatening to balloon and further harm the economy, the president pushed for cuts in government spending overall and for caps on mandatory spending. The Democrat Congress insisted, however, on a tax hike as their price for controlling spending. In short, the Democrats held the U.S. economy—and U.S. jobs—hostage in order to raise taxes, much as they had done to President Reagan.

Just as they did with President Reagan, the Democrat-controlled Congress promised President Bush they would abide by binding controls on federal spending; and just as with President Reagan, they broke their word. Republicans will not again agree to such a program.

This year, to create jobs and promote growth, President Bush submitted a program of tax cuts and incentives designed to get the economy moving again—a program very similar to one he had sent to Congress in early 1990.

The Democrats' response was predictable—instead of cutting taxes, they passed a $100 billion tax increase that would have smothered growth and jobs. The president, true to our Republican philosophy, vetoed this tax hike, and sustained his veto with the support of Republicans in Congress.

Now a new Democrat nominee comes forward with his plan for the economy. With a clean piece of paper, and every opportunity to end his party's romance with taxes, he has instead proposed the largest tax increase in American history. His tax increases, his proposed mandated benefits on small firms, and his further reductions in defense would cost the jobs of 2.6 million Americans. With his present spending increases, his plan would greatly increase the federal budget and the deficit.

The simple truth for the American people is this: The only safeguard between themselves and Democrat tax increases is the use of the veto by George Bush and enough Republican votes in Congress to sustain it.

The truth is that the Democrat philosophy of bigger government and rigorous redistribution of income requires them to push for ever increasing spending and ever higher taxes.

The choice is clear—between George Bush, who vetoes tax increases, and his opponent, who proposes a $150 billion tax increase.

Our Republican position is equally clear: We will oppose any attempt to increase taxes. Furthermore, Republicans believe that the taxes insisted on by the Democrats in the 1990 budget agreement were recessionary. The Democrat Congress held President Bush and indeed all Americans hostage, refusing to take even modest steps to control spending, unless taxes were increased. The American economy suffered as a result. We believe the tax increases of 1990 should ultimately be repealed.

Just as history shows that tax increases destroy jobs and economic growth, it also shows that the proper path to create jobs and growth is tax rate reduction.

We commend those congressional and senatorial candidates who pledge to oppose tax rate increases.

As the deficit comes under control, we aspire to further tax rate cuts, strengthening incentives to work, save, invest and innovate. We also support President Bush's efforts to reduce federal spending and to cap the growth of non-Social Security entitlements.

Republicans want individuals and families to control their own economic destiny. Only long-term expansion of our economy and jobs can make the American dream a reality for generations to come. That is why we demand that the Congress do what President Bush called for last January: open a new era of growth and opportunity by enacting his comprehensive plan for economic recovery, including a reduction in the capital gains tax; an investment tax allowance; a $5,000 tax credit for first-time home buyers; a needed modification of the "passive loss rule"; a $500 increase in the personal income tax exemption; making permanent the research and development tax credit; and the passage of federal enterprise zone legislation.

We support restoring the deductibility of IRAs for all Americans, including full-time homemakers, and encourage savings for education and home ownership through Family Savings Accounts. The president's Family Savings Accounts will be an impetus to the economy. Let families use their IRAs for first-time home purchases, for college education and for medical emergencies.

We will cut the capital gains tax rate to 15 percent—zero in enterprise zones—and index it so government cannot profit from inflation by taxing phantom capital gains, literally stealing from savings and pensions.

We reject the notion advanced by Democrats that this enhances the wealthy. To the contrary, it would encourage investment, create new jobs, make capital available for business expansion and contribute to economic expansion.

Reducing the tax on investment will be the biggest possible boost for the new technologies, businesses and jobs we need for the next century. If government taxes capital gains at such a high rate that there is no incentive to take risks, to build businesses, to invest, to create jobs or to better oneself, then jobs and small businesses vanish, and everyone's opportunities are diminished.

Cutting the rate, on the other hand, will help supply seed capital where it is needed most—in our poorest communities. Refusing to cut it will handcuff America in international competition and will shackle aspiring entrepreneurs in inner cities and poor rural areas. To encourage investment in new technologies, we will make permanent the research and development tax credit. For the same reason, we want to expand deductibility for investments in new plant and equipment. . . .

Liberation through Deregulation

Government regulation is a hidden tax on American families, costing each household more than $5,000 every year. It stifles job creation and hobbles our national competitiveness. The "iron triangle" of special interests, federal bureaucrats and Democrat congressional staff is robbing consumers and producers alike.

We support President Bush's freeze on new regulations. We applaud his Competitiveness Council, under Vice President Quayle, for fighting the regulatory mania, saving the public $20 billion with its initial 90-day moratorium on new regulations and billions more under the current 120-day freeze. We call for a permanent moratorium until our regulatory reforms are fully in place. They include market-based regulation, cost-benefit analysis of all new rule-making, and a regulatory budget that will make Congress admit—and correct—the harm it does by legislation that destroys jobs and competitiveness. . . .

Homeownership

The best housing policy is a non-inflationary, growing economy that has produced low mortgage rates and has made housing more affordable.

We demand Congress enact President's Bush's housing program introduced as part of his pro-growth package in January.

Provide a $5,000 tax credit for first-time home buyers and allow them penalty-free IRA withdrawals.

Set a modified "passive loss rule" for active real estate investors.

Extend tax preferences for mortgage revenue bonds and low-income housing.

And allow deductions for losses on personal residences.

The average American's home is his or her primary asset. That asset should be completely shielded from federal taxation, allowing the homeowner to maintain it or access it as he or she sees fit. We call for the complete elimination of the capital gains tax on the sale of a principal residence.

Owning a home is not just an investment. It is a commitment to the community, a guard against crime, a statement about family life. It is a crucial component of upward mobility. To advance these goals, Republicans are determined to preserve deductibility of mortgage interest. . . .

For low-income families, the Republican Party stands for a revolution in housing by converting public housing into homes owned by low-income Americans. President Bush is eager to work closely with the states to fight and win a new conservative war on poverty. The truest measure of our success will not be how many families we add to housing assistance rolls but, rather, how many families move into the ranks of homeownership. . . .

Job Creation and Small-Business Opportunities

The engines of growth in a free economy are small businesses and jobs. Almost 99 percent of all businesses in America are considered small. Small business is the backbone of the American economy. For the past 12 years it has led the way in economic growth.

Small business generates 67 percent of all new jobs. Employment in industries dominated by small business increased more than twice as fast as in industries dominated by large businesses. Small business plays a critical role in America's economic health. What happens on Main Street drives what happens on Wall Street. . . .

To create jobs and keep small business growing, the Republican Party supports increased access to capital for business expansion, exporting, long-term investment, opportunity capital for the disadvantaged, and capital to bring new products and new technology to the market.

The Republican Party enthusiastically encourages the passage of federal enterprise zones. Enterprise zones have been effective programs for promoting growth in urban and rural America. Republicans believe that the concept of enterprise zones is based on unyielding faith in the entrepreneurial spirit of all Americans. Enterprise zones foster individual initiative and government deregulation. The states have come a long way in developing successful enterprise zone programs. State programs could only benefit from federal efforts. Congress should follow the lead of President Bush and HUD Secretary Jack Kemp in passing the federal enterprise zone program that will empower communities by reducing government regulation and taxation. . . .

Trade: A New World of Growth

Four years ago, the American people faced an historic decision: Compete or retreat. They chose, with President Bush, to compete in the international arena. Rather than retreat with the Democrats to the limits of yesteryear, they decided to attack the international marketplace with characteristic American vigor. Just as George Bush is a proven world leader on the military front, equally he is an economic world leader.

The results are spectacular. We have cut the trade deficit in half in just four years. The United States is again the world's top exporter. Exports drive our economy. Every $1 billion in exports creates 20,000 new jobs for Americans. Exports have created nearly 2 million new jobs at home since 1988.

We are tough free traders, battling to sweep away barriers to our exports. We are waging the Uruguay Round of the General Agreement on Tariffs and Trade (GATT) negotiations to win worldwide reductions in tariffs, elimination of subsidies and protection of American intellectual property rights. We are fighting to reduce farm subsidies in the European Community and to break up their government-industry collusion in production of civil aircraft. We firmly endorse President Bush's policy to support the Republic of China on Taiwan in international trade and her accession to GATT. Major market access gains have been made with Japan, with American manufacturing exports tripling since 1985. Throughout the world, we enforced greater compliance with U.S. trade rights. And we are making every effort to bring home a Uruguay Round agreement that is not only good for America, but great for tomorrow's entrepreneurs everywhere.

The free-trade agenda for the next four years starts with the signing of a North American Free Trade Agreement (NAFTA) with Mexico, completing the establishment of a free-trade area which already includes Canada. NAFTA will create the largest market in the world, greater than the European Community, with 360 million consumers and a total output of six trillion dollars. It means a net gain of hundreds of thousands of American jobs.

We acknowledge the possible effects on regional markets, specifically agriculture. We encourage our negotiators to be sensitive to those market concerns.

We will continue to fill the Pacific Rim with American exports, negotiating trade agreements with other Asian economies, and will complete our efforts—such as the Structural Impediments Initiative with Japan—to reduce barriers to American goods and services. And we will continue to negotiate the Enterprise for the Americas Initiative with Latin America as a first step in creating a hemispheric free-trade zone.

Congress should report to the American people the cost to workers, consumers and businesses of every Democrat trade restriction, trade tax or trade quota bill it considers. We will not tolerate their obstructing the greatest expansion of international trade in history. Republicans welcome this opportunity; for we know America's workers, thinkers and builders will make the most of it. . . .

Reforming Government and the Legal System

Two centuries ago, the American people created a miracle—a system of government, founded on limited authority and the rule of law, a system that made government the servant of the people. Today it is in shambles. Citizens feel overwhelmed by vast bureaucracies. Congress insulates incumbents from public judgment. Huge problems get worse while committee chairmen play partisan games. The current legal system tends to breed delay, cost, confusion and jargon—everything but justice. Many of our once-great cities are controlled by one-party machines that promote and encourage corruption and incompetence.

The Republic has not failed; the Democratic Party bosses failed the Republic.

The Republican Party, now as at its founding, challenges a debased status quo. In Congress, the states, our cities, our courtrooms, we fight for the basics of self-government.

We rely on what works, judging programs by how well they do instead of how much they spend. The Democrats believe in more government. Republicans believe in leaner, more effective government.

We decentralize authority, returning decisions to states, localities and private institutions. The Democrat bosses want to concentrate power on Capitol Hill. Republicans place it in town halls and the American home. . . .

Cleaning up the Imperial Congress

The Democrats have controlled the House of Representatives for 38 years—five years longer than Castro has held Cuba. They have held the Senate for 32 of those 38. Their entrenched power has produced a Congress arrogant, out of touch, hopelessly entangled in a web of PACs, perks, privileges, partisanship, paralysis and pork. No wonder they hid their congressional leaders during the Democrat convention of 1992. They didn't want Americans to remember who has been running the Congress.

The Democrats have transformed what the framers of the Constitution intended as the people's House into a pathological institution. They have grossly increased their staffing, their payrolls, their allied bureaucracies in little-known congressional agencies. Congress has ballooned to 284 congressional committees and subcommittees, almost 40,000 legislative branch employees and staff, and $2.5 billion in taxpayer financing, amounting to approximately $5 million per lawmaker per year. Incumbents have abused free mailing privileges for personal political gain. Twenty-two Democrats, with a total of 585 years in power, rule over a committee system that blocks every attempt at reform.

The Democrats have trampled the traditions of the House, rigging rules, forbidding votes on crucial amendments, denying fair apportionment of committee seats and resources. They have stacked campaign laws to benefit themselves. The Democrat leadership of the House has been tainted with scandal and has resisted efforts to investigate scandals once disclosed. Some in their leadership have resigned in well-earned disgrace.

The Democrat leadership of the Congress has turned the healthy competition of constitutional separation of powers into mean-spirited politics of innuendo and inquisition. Committee hearings are no longer for fact-finding; they are political sideshows. "Advise and consent" has been replaced by "slash and burn."

Republicans want to change all that. We reaffirm our support for a constitutional amendment to limit the number of terms House members and senators may serve. We want a citizens' Congress, free of bloated pensions and perpetual perks.

Congress must stop exempting itself from laws such as the minimum wage and the civil rights statutes, as well as laws that apply to the executive branch. The Independent Counsel Act is a case in point. It has permitted rogue prosecutors to spend tremendous amounts to hound some of the nation's finest public servants. If that act is reauthorized, it must be extended to Congress as well. Safety and health regulations, civil rights and minimum wage laws are further examples of areas where Congress has set itself apart from the people. This practice must end.

Congress must slash its own bureaucracy. Its employees operate in a maze of overlapping jurisdictions. A Republican Congress will cut expenses by 25 percent, reduce the number of committees and subcommittees, and assign staff in accurate proportion to party strength.

We will restore integrity to the House of Representatives, reforming its rules, allowing open debate and amendment. The committee system, both in Congress and in Democrat-controlled state legislatures, has been abused by chairpersons who have arbitrarily killed legislation that would have passed. Committees are a place for open and free discussion, not a closet for Democrats to stash Republican legislation. Democracy itself is endangered by these abuses, and Republicans condemn those practices. Both houses of Congress must guarantee protection to whistleblowers to encourage employees to report illegality, corruption, sexual harassment and discrimination.

The Democrat rulers of Congress have blocked or stalled presidential initiatives in many areas, including education, housing, crime control, economic recovery, job creation and budget reform. They care more about scoring petty partisan points for themselves and their party than about achieving real progress for the nation. To accomplish change, we need a change in Congress.

Reforming the Congressional Budget Process

At the heart of the Democrats' corruption of Congress is a fraudulent budget process. They do not want the public to understand how they spend the public's money. At a time when the nation's future depends on reduction of deficits, the lords of the Capitol still play the old shell game.

Republicans vigorously support a balanced budget, a balanced-budget constitutional amendment and a line-item veto for the president.

Republicans believe this balancing of the budget should be achieved, not by increasing taxes to match spending, but by cutting spending to current levels of revenue. We prefer a balanced-budget amendment that contains a supermajority requirement to raise taxes....

Cleaning Up Politics: Campaign Reform

We crusade for clean elections. We support state efforts to increase voter participation but condemn Democrat attempts to perpetrate vote fraud through schemes that override the state's safeguards of orderly voter registration. And it is critical that the states retain the authority to tailor voter registration procedures to unique local circumstances.

Most of all, we condemn the Democrats' shameless plots to make taxpayers foot the bills for their campaigns. Their campaign finance bill would have given $1 billion, over six years, in subsidies to candidates. President Bush vetoed that bill. Campaign financing does need reform. It does not need a hand in the public's pocketbook.

We will require congressional candidates to raise most of their funds from individuals within their home constituencies. This will limit outside special-interest money and result in less expensive campaigns, with less padding for incumbents. To the same end, we will strengthen the role of political parties to remove pressure on candidates to spend so much time soliciting funds. We will eliminate political action committees supported by corporations, unions or trade associations, and restrict the practice of bundling.

To restore competition in elections by attacking the unfair advantages of incumbency, we will stop incumbents from warding off challengers merely by amassing huge war chests. Congressional candidates will be forbidden from carrying campaign funds from one election to the next. We will oppose arbitrary spending limits—cynical devices which hobble challengers to keep politicians in office.

We will fully implement the Supreme Court's decision in the *Beck* case, ensuring that workers have the right to stop the use of their union dues for political or other non-collective bargaining purposes.

Managing Government in the Public Interest

The focus of government must shift from quantity to quality, from spending to service. Americans should expect measurable, published standards for services provided by government at all levels. Performance standards and rules, commonplace in the private sector, must be applied to government activities as well. Because federal government employees should not be a privileged caste, we will remove the bar to garnishing their wages to ensure payment of their debts....

Always trusting the initiative of the American people over the ways of government, we will not initiate production of goods or delivery of services by the federal government if they can be procured from the private sector.

We Will not Initiate Any Federal Activity That Can Be Conducted Better on the State or Local Level

In doing so, we reassert the crucial importance of the 10th Amendment. We oppose costly federal mandates that stifle innovation and force tax hikes upon states and localities. We require that Congress calculate the cost of mandated initiatives upon communities affected and provide adequate financial support for mandates invoked. We will continue the process of returning power to local voters by replacing federal programs with block grants.

Reforming the Legal System

The United States, with 5 percent of the world's population, has two-thirds of the world's lawyers. Litigation has become an industry, an end in itself. The number of civil cases in federal district courts has more than tripled in the past 30 years. It now takes more than a year to resolve the average lawsuit. Delays of three to five years are commonplace.

The current legal system forces consumers to pay higher prices for everything from basic goods to medical treatment. Direct litigation and inflated insurance premiums sock American consumers for an estimated $80 billion a year. All told, our legal system costs, directly and indirectly, $300 billion a year. What it costs us in the world marketplace, by hindering our competitiveness, is beyond calculation.

We therefore endorse the president's proposals for legal reform as developed by Vice President Quayle, and we salute his principled challenge to the American Bar Association to clean up its own house. We support the Fairness Rule, to allow the winning party to a lawsuit to recover the costs of litigation from the losing party. This will discourage needless suits, freeing legal resources for people with genuine cases. . . .

The Nation's Capital

We call for closer and responsible congressional scrutiny of the city, federal oversight of its law enforcement and courts, and tighter fiscal restraints over its expenditures. We oppose statehood as inconsistent with the original intent of the framers of the Constitution and with the need for a federal city belonging to all the people as our nation's capital. . . .

Our Land, Food, and Resources

We hold the resources of our country in stewardship. Our heritage from the past must be our legacy to generations to come. Our people have always known that, as they cherished their land and turned earth and rock into food, fiber and power. In the process, they built the world's most formidable economy, sustained by its raw materials, driven by its energy resources. They brought comfort to the home, transformed the nation and fed the world.

Agriculture and energy remain building blocks of modern life. Their vitality is crucial to the nation's growth. Indeed, to its survival. While supporting conservation, we reject the notion that there are limits to growth.

Human ingenuity is the ultimate resource, and it knows no limits. The true measure of America's economic success is not whether austerity can be shared by many, but whether prosperity can be achieved for all.

We advocate privatizing those government agencies and assets that would be more productive and better maintained in private ownership. We support efforts to decentralize government monopolies that poorly serve the public and waste taxpayers' dollars.

Agriculture

The Republican Party is the home of the farmer, rancher and forester. We have long championed their right to pursue growth, efficiency and competitiveness through market incentives, diversification and personal ingenuity. And for good reason. Their industry provides consumers with the highest-quality food and fiber for the smallest percentage of disposable income of any nation in the history of the world.

They have been pioneer environmentalists. They have turned over to their children and grandchildren land that has been nurtured to expand its productivity while conserving this vital resource. Even more important, they have cultivated in their homes strong family life and moral virtues. . . .

We pledge to fight unfair competition and to bring down the walls of protectionism around the world that unfairly inhibit competitiveness of U.S. farm exports. We pledge continued pressure to open world markets through the Uruguay Round, the North American Free Trade Agreement and bilateral negotiations.

We affirm that there will be no GATT agreement unless it improves opportunities for U.S. farmers to compete in world markets. We repeat our demands for cutbacks in export subsidies by the European Community and elsewhere, and we will fight the use of arbitrary health and sanitation standards to sabotage U.S. exports.

New markets for agricultural products will also be created as producers translate technological breakthroughs into new uses, such as soy oil diesel and biodegradable plastics. We support the widest possible use of ethanol in the U.S. motor fuel market, including in oxygenated fuels programs and as ethanol blends in reformulated gasolines. . . .

We value our nation's real wetlands habitat and the diversity of our native animal and plant life. We oppose, however, bureaucratic harassment of farm, ranch and timber families under statutes regarding endangered species and wetlands. When actions are required to protect an endangered species, we recognize that jobs can be lost, communities displaced and economic progress for all denied. Accordingly, prior to the implementation of a recovery plan for a species declared to be endangered, we will require the Congress to affirm the priority of the species on the endangered list and the specific measures to be taken in any recovery plan. These acts should not rest with the rubber stamp of a bureaucrat.

With regard to wetlands, following our principle that environmental protection be reasonable, land that is not truly wet would not be classified as a wetland. Protection of environmentally sensitive wetlands must not come at the price of disparaging landowners' property rights. Thus, we endorse, as President Bush has done, legislation to discourage government activities that ignore property rights. We also find intolerable the use of taxpayer funds, through the Legal Services Corporation, to attack the agricultural community.

Power for Progress

Energy sustains life as we know it: our standard of living, the prospect for economic growth, the way our children will live in the century ahead. Republican energy policy, now as in the past, reflects the common-sense aspirations of the American people.

Our goals address our fundamental needs: an energy supply, available to all, that remains reasonably priced, secure and clean, produced by strong energy industries on which the country can rely, operating in an environmentally responsible manner and producing from domestically available energy resources to the maximum extent practicable....

We broke the shackles of bureaucratic regulation by ending petroleum price and allocation controls, deregulating natural gas wellhead prices, and repealing restrictions on the use of clean-burning natural gas by industry and utilities. We repealed the windfall profit tax on crude oil that penalized investment in domestic oil production. We promoted free competition in an open marketplace and ended the public subsidy to the synthetic fuels program. And we broke the back of OPEC, the international energy cartel....

The domestic oil and gas industry saves us from total dependence on unreliable foreign imports. But over the past decade, it has lost more than 300,000 jobs. Drilling rigs are still. Crippled by environmental rules and taxes, independent producers have been devastated and major companies are moving operations overseas. We will reverse that situation by allowing access, under environmental safeguards, to the coastal plain of the Arctic National Wildlife Refuge, possibly one of the largest petroleum reserves in our country, and to selected areas of the outer continental shelf (OCS). We support incentives to encourage domestic investment for onshore and OCS oil and gas exploration and development, including relief from the alternative minimum tax, credits for enhanced oil recovery and geological exploration under known geological oil fields and producing geological structures, and modified percentage depletion rules to benefit marginal production. We will ensure that royalty payments on federal lands remain consistent with changing economic conditions.

Most important, unlike Democrat no-growth fanatics, we know what is most at stake in the energy debate: the family's standard of living, including job opportunities, household income and the environment in which we live.

That is why we have been supporting complete decontrol of wellhead prices for clean natural gas, which have already declined 10 percent in the last four years while consumption increased by the same amount. We support replacing government controls with the power of the market to determine transactions between buyers and sellers of natural gas. We encourage the use of natural gas for both vehicles and electricity generation, and the expansion of research, development and demonstration for end-use natural gas technologies. We will foster more public-private partnerships to advance use of natural gas. . . .

Public Lands

The millions of acres that constitute this nation's public lands must continue to provide for a number of uses. We are committed to the multiple use of our public lands. We believe that recreation, forestry, ranching, mining, oil and gas exploration, and production on our public lands can be conducted in a way compatible with their conservation. The United States has some of the richest mineral resources in the world. Our public lands should not be arbitrarily locked up and put off limits to responsible uses.

Approximately 50 percent of the lands in the West are owned by the federal government. These lands are a deeply intermingled patchwork built of public and private ownership. In order to provide an economic base for the people of the West, a public-private cooperative partnership on these lands for multiple use in an environmentally sound manner is imperative. . . .

Environment

Cleaning up America is a labor of love for family, neighborhood and the nation. In the Republican tradition of conserving the past to enrich the future, we have made the United States the world's leader in environmental progress.

We spend more than any other country on environmental protection. Over the last 20 years, our country has spent $1 trillion to clean its air, water and land. We increased GNP by 70 percent while cutting lead in the air by 97 percent. Our rivers run cleaner than ever in memory. We've preserved parks, wilderness and wildlife. The price of progress is now about $115 billion a year, almost 2 percent of GNP; and that will grow to 3 percent by 2000.

Clearly we have led the world in investment in environmental protection. We have taught the world three vital lessons. First, environmental progress is integrally related to economic advancement. Second, economic growth generates the capital to pay for environmental gains. Third, private ownership and economic freedom are the best security against environmental degradation. The ghastly truth about state socialism is now exposed in what used to be the Soviet Union: dead rivers and seas, poisoned land, dying people.

Liberal Democrats think people are the problem. We know people are the solution. Respecting the people's rights and views, we applied market-based solutions to environmental problems. President Bush's landmark Clean Air Act amendments of 1990, the toughest environmental law ever enacted, uses an innovative system of emission credits to achieve its dramatic reductions. This will save $1 billion over the Democrats' command-and-control approach. Other provisions of that law will cut acid rain emissions in half, reduce toxic pollutants by 90 percent, reduce smog and speed the use of cleaner fuels.

The president's leadership has doubled spending for real wetlands and targeted 1 million acres for a wetlands reserve through his farm bill of 1990. We have collected more civil penalties from polluters in two years than in the previous 20, begun the phaseout of substances that harm the ozone layer and launched a long-term campaign to expand and improve national parks, forests and recreation areas, adding 1.5 million acres. President Bush has dramatically increased spending for cleaning up past environmental damage caused by federal facilities.

Our reforestation drive will plant 1 billion trees a year across America. Our moratorium on offshore drilling in sensitive offshore areas has bought time for technology to master environmental challenges. Our farm policies have begun a new era in sound agricultural environmentalism.

Because the environment knows no boundaries, President Bush has accelerated U.S. research on global climate change, spending $2.7 billion in the last three years and requesting $1.4 billion for 1993, more than the rest of the world put together. Under his leadership, we have assisted nations from the Third World to Eastern Europe in correcting the environmental damage inflicted by socialism. We proposed a worldwide forestry convention and gave almost half a billion dollars to forest conservation. We won debt-for-nature swaps and environmental trust funds in Latin America and the Caribbean. We secured prohibitions against unilateral export or dumping of hazardous waste. We led the international ban on trade in ivory, persuaded Japan to end drift net fishing, streamlined response to oil spills and increased environmental protection for Antarctica.

Adverse changes in climate must be the common concern of mankind. At the same time, we applaud our president for personally confronting the international bureaucrats at the Rio Conference. He refused to accept their anti-American demands for income redistribution and won instead a global climate treaty that relies on real action plans rather than arbitrary targets hostile to U.S. growth and workers.

Following his example, a Republican Senate will not ratify any treaty that moves environmental decisions beyond our democratic process or transfers beyond our shores authority over U.S. property. The Democrats' national candidates, on the other hand, insist the United States must do what our foreign competitors refuse to do: abolish 300,000 to 1,000,000 jobs to get a modest reduction in "greenhouse gases.". . .

The Triumph of Freedom

No other president in the long history of our country has achieved so many of the enduring objectives of American foreign policy in so short a time as has George Bush. He made it look easy, even destined. It was neither.

Building on the legacy of Ronald Reagan, George Bush saw the chance to sweep away decadent communism. He was the first Western leader to declare his determination to fashion "a Europe whole and free." He took the free world beyond containment, led the way in aiding democracy in Eastern Europe and punched holes through the rusting Iron Curtain. We all remember the joy we felt when we saw the people of Berlin dancing on top of the crumbling wall that had symbolized four decades of communist oppression.

He championed Germany's right to become again one nation and orchestrated the diplomacy to make it happen, on Western terms, in one astounding year. Foreseeing revolutionary change in the Soviet Union itself, he carefully pushed its rules to open the way to the democratic future. When crisis came, in August 1991, George Bush, in the words of Boris Yeltsin, "was the first to understand the true meaning of the victory of the Russian people" and gave his decisive backing to the cause of democracy.

The world had never before faced the disintegration of a nuclear superpower. Today, thanks in large part to President Bush's initiatives, nuclear weapons are found in only four countries of the former Soviet Union—not 14. Because of his efforts, all but Russia are giving up any claim to these weapons, and Russia has agreed to destroy the most dangerous missiles ever built. The balance of terror is fading away. The ideals of liberty, both political and economic, are the dominant moral and intellectual force around the globe.

George Bush made it happen.

Yet now that we have won the Cold War, we must also win the peace. We must not repeat the mistake of the past by throwing away victory through complacency. A new world beckons, unlike any we have ever known, filled with uncertainties. Old passions have re-emerged. New democracies struggle to decide their destiny. Nations are torn asunder. Migrants and refugees strain the social fabric of continents. Tyrants work to build nuclear, chemical and even biological weapons to threaten us and our neighbors. Drug trafficking and terrorism, often linked, menace Americans at home and abroad.

Great transitions in world affairs are rarely tidy. They challenge statesmanship, require steadiness and wisdom. History teaches that when the United States shrinks from the world, we hasten the emergence of new dangers. Republicans remember the lesson taught by our Founders: that eternal vigilance is the price of liberty.

Meeting the Challenge

The gulf war showed the world how much is at stake when voters choose their president. George Bush had known war firsthand. So he tried the way of peace—months of negotiations and economic sanctions—then did what a president must do. He led from powerful convictions based on American values. The United States, in a pre-eminent position of world leadership, forged a new strategy of collective engagement which invigorated the United Nations.

This was not the same United States held hostage in 1980, when the Democrats controlled both the White House and the Congress. No helpless giant here. The president charted a path that wrecked Saddam Hussein's dreams of conquest and nuclear aggression while keeping America from the quagmire of indefinite military occupation of Iraq.

President Bush, trusting the military commanders he had chosen, was commander-in-chief of one of the finest achievements in the distinguished history of our armed forces. Americans will never forget that, of the 323 congressional Democrats, only 96 voted to support Operation Desert Storm and 227 voted to oppose it. If the Democrats had prevailed, Saddam Hussein would still be in Kuwait, armed with nuclear weapons. Everyone discovered what difference a vote for president can make.

Leadership through Partnership

A new era demands a new agenda. Our post-Cold War strategy both reflects our country's ideals and guards its interests.

Building a commonwealth of freedom differs greatly from the old concept of containment. It rests on a stable balance of power but goes beyond it to emphasize, above all, the supremacy of an idea: a common conception of how to make freedom work for all the nations moving with us into a radically changing future.

Republicans understand that objective cannot be pursued by the United States alone. We therefore have harnessed the free world's strength to American leadership. But such a strategy requires a president whose lead others will trust and follow. By forging consensus whenever possible, we multiply the impact of our nation's power and principles. But if necessary we will act alone to protect American interests. Consistent with our policy and traditions, we oppose any actions that would undermine America's sovereignty, either in political or economic terms. Leadership through partnership allows us to project American ideals and project American interests abroad, at less cost to our taxpayers.

That is how we will secure the victory of democracy as the best guarantee of a world without war. It is how we will open the world for American business to ensure prosperity in an open international economy.

And it is how we will banish the nuclear nightmare, limit the danger from weapons of mass destruction and safely manage a critical transition in our nation's defenses. . . .

In Western Europe, we reaffirm the NATO alliance. While we reduce our troop commitments on the continent—a thousand soldiers are coming home every week — we must keep a powerful force deployed there. The United States must remain a European power in the broadest sense, able to influence the policies and events that affect the livelihood and security of future generations of Americans.

The violence in what used to be Yugoslavia is an affront to humanity. We condemn those responsible for the carnage there and call for an immediate international investigation of atrocities. We support the United Nations peacekeeping effort and urge an immediate cease-fire by all parties. The United States should continue to demand respect for international law and fundamental human rights in this agonizing conflict. . . .

In the Middle East, prospects for peace have been transformed by the determined statesmanship of George Bush. Without the leadership of President Bush, Iraq would today threaten world peace, the peace and security of the Middle East, and the very survival of Israel with a huge conventional army and nuclear weapons. Direct peace talks, on terms Israel rightly had sought for more than four decades, would not be a reality. Soviet Jewish emigration likely would have been interrupted. The rescue of Ethiopian Jewry might not have happened. And the equation of Zionism to racism still would be a grotesque stain on the United Nations.

Although much has changed for the better, the Middle East remains an area of high tensions—many unrelated to the Arab-Israeli conflict— where regional conflicts can escalate to threaten the vital interests of the United States. As Saddam Hussein's aggression against Kuwait demonstrated, heavily armed radical regimes are capable of independent aggressive action. In this environment, Israel's demonstrated strategic importance to the United States, as our most reliable and capable ally in this part of the world, is more important than ever. This strategic relationship, with its unique moral dimension, explains the understandable support Israel receives from millions of Americans who participate in our political process. The strong ties between the United States and Israel were demonstrated during the gulf war when Israel chose not to retaliate against repeated missile attacks, even though they caused severe damage and loss of life. We will continue to broaden and deepen the strategic relationship with our ally Israel—the only true democracy in the Middle East—by taking additional concrete steps to further institutionalize the partnership. This will include maintaining adequate levels of security and economic assistance; continuing our meetings on military, political and economic cooperation and coordination; pre-positioning military equipment; developing joint contingency plans; and increasing joint naval and air exercises.

Consistent with our strategic relationship, the United States should continue to provide large-scale security assistance to Israel, maintaining Israel's qualitative military advantage over any adversary or coalition of adversaries. We also will continue to negotiate with the major arms supplying nations to reach an agreement on limiting arms sales to the Middle East and preventing the proliferation of non-conventional weapons.

We applaud the president's leadership in fostering unprecedented direct talks between Israel and its Arab neighbors. The United States is prepared to use its good offices to mediate disputes at their request. We do not believe the United States should attempt to impose a solution on the parties.

The basis for negotiations must be U.N. Security Council Resolutions 242 and 338. Peace must come from direct negotiations. It will be up to the negotiators to determine exactly what is required to satisfy these resolutions, but we firmly believe Israel has a right to exist in secure and recognized borders.

As President Bush stated in Madrid, our objective is not simply to end the state of war; rather, it is to establish real peace, one with treaties, security, diplomatic relations, trade, investment, cultural exchange, even tourism. We want the Middle East to become a place where people lead normal lives.

A meaningful peace must assure Israel's security while recognizing the legitimate rights of the Palestinian people. We oppose the creation of an independent Palestinian state. Nor will we support the creation of any political entity that would jeopardize Israel's security.

As Israelis and Palestinians negotiate interim self-government, no party will be required to commit itself to any specific final outcome of direct negotiations. Israel should not be forced to negotiate with any party. In this regard, the United States will have no dialogue with the PLO until it satisfies in full the conditions laid out by President Bush in 1990.

We believe Jerusalem should remain an undivided city, with free and unimpeded access to all holy places by people of all faiths. No genuine peace would deny Jews the right to live anywhere in the special city of Jerusalem.

Peace in the Middle East entails cooperation among all the parties in the region. To this end, we have worked to bring all of the states of the area together with Israel to hold multilateral negotiations on issues of common concern such as regional development, water, refugees, arms control and the environment. We support these forums as a means of encouraging Arab acceptance of Israel and solving common regional problems.

We continue to back legislation mandating that if the United Nations and its agencies were to deny Israel's right to participate, the United States would withhold financial support and withdraw from those bodies until their action was rectified.

Republicans believe freedom of emigration is a fundamental human right and that Jews from any nation should be free to travel to Israel.

Republicans are proud that we have maintained our historic and moral commitment to the resettlement in Israel of persecuted Jews. We congratulate President Bush and Secretary [of State James A.] Baker [III] on the agreement with Israel for a generous package of loan guarantees that will provide new immigrants with needed humanitarian assistance.

We also should maintain our close ties with and generous aid for Egypt, which properly reaps the benefits of its courageous peace with Israel. We continue to support Egypt and other pro-Western states in the region against subversion and aggression and call for an end to the Arab boycott of Israel. We also support establishment of a strong central government in Lebanon, democratically elected and representative of its citizens.

We salute all the countries in the Middle East who contributed to the success of Desert Storm and share our goal of stability in the region.

With them, we hope to build upon that triumph a new future for the Middle East, founded on mutual respect and a common longing for peace. To promote this goal, we should settle for nothing less than full, unconditional, immediate and verified Iraqi compliance with all aspects of the cease-fire laid out in U.N. resolutions.

In the Western Hemisphere, as elsewhere, we must promote democratic values. We will continue to seek cooperation in the common battle against the drug lords. We will also lower barriers to trade and investment, knowing that our exports to Latin America are helping to lead our economic recovery at home.

The president's Enterprise for the Americas initiative and the North American Free Trade Agreement mean, for the United States, billions of dollars in new trade, hundreds of thousands of new jobs, and a long-term solution to the economic pressures behind illegal immigration.

We welcome positive changes, economic and political, in Mexico and salute the people of Panama on their recovery of free institutions after Operation Just Cause. We commend President Bush for the decisive military action that led to the end of the corrupt [Manuel Antonio] Noriega regime and freedom for democratically minded Panamanians.

We will uphold free and unencumbered U.S. access to the canal. We hail the patriots of El Salvador and Nicaragua, whose bravery and blood thwarted communism and Castro despite the inconstancy of congressional Democrats. Together with other members of the Organization of American States, we will work to restore democracy to Haiti. . . .

Banishing the Nuclear Nightmare

The world has moved from the brink of disaster to the threshold of historic opportunity. For almost half a century, we lived under the shadow of nuclear destruction. Today, that specter is fading. We will not stop here. We will banish the threat of nuclear annihilation from the face of the earth—not by savaging our military, as some Democrats might insist but by building on the historic diplomatic achievements of Presidents Bush and Reagan.

This means ensuring stable command and control of the former Soviet arsenal, complete acceptance and verified implementation of all treaty obligations by the successor states to the Soviet Union, and achieving the additional 50 percent reduction in strategic forces now agreed upon. We must assist in dismantling weapons, transforming the massive Soviet war machine into an engine of peace and civilian revival. We will cooperate with our former adversaries both to curtail proliferation and to move beyond the ABM Treaty toward effective ballistic missile defenses.

We will not permit the Soviet nuclear nightmare to be replaced by another one. Outlaw nations—North Korea, Iran, Iraq, Libya and others—lust for weapons of mass destruction. This is the nightmare of proliferation: nuclear, chemical and biological weapons that, together with ballistic missiles, can deliver death across whole continents, including our own.

We will renew and strengthen the Nuclear Nonproliferation Treaty. We will design security policies to counter proliferation dangers. We will reinforce multilateral accords like the Missile Technology Control Regime. And most important, we will develop and deploy global defenses against ballistic missiles. Despite the opposition of the Democratic Party and congressional Democrats, we will deploy an effective strategic defense system for the American people.

America's Security

Because America won the Cold War, our homes and neighborhoods are more secure then they have been for half a century. Our children are safer. The greatest peace dividend is peace itself. For it, we thank God.

Victory was never inevitable. It was won in blood and treasure, over five decades, by the American people—from the military on the front lines to the taxpayers sustaining the forces of freedom. It was also secured, and the course of mankind profoundly changed for the better, because two successive Republican presidents, Ronald Reagan and George Bush, were dedicated to peace through strength.

"Peace through strength" was more than a slogan. It was the calculated Republican plan for, first, the survival, and then the triumph, of America. But freedom did not come cheaply, and the new world we celebrate today required great sacrifice.

In 1981 we inherited from Jimmy Carter and anti-defense Democrats a crippled military: demoralized, underfunded, ill-equipped. Republicans told the truth to the American people; they heeded our call to arms.

We restored our armed forces to their proper place in both the budget and the pride of the nation. Our men and women in uniform today are the equals of the finest soldiers, sailors and airmen who ever wore the uniform of our country.

Like earlier generations in 1918 and 1945, they won a great victory. Now, as in the aftermath of those earlier conflicts, comes the difficult task of reducing both the size and cost of defense without letting down America's guard. In the past, terrible mistakes were made, and we paid dearly for them when war came to Korea. We will not allow that to happen again.

America Challenged

The greatest danger to America's security is here at home, among those who would leave the nation unprepared for the new realities of the post-Cold War world. The ruthless demagogues in rogue regimes are real and so are the nuclear, chemical and biological weapons they seek. The danger of nuclear proliferation is real, especially with the dispersal of nuclear know-how after the collapse of the Soviet Union. That is why the Republican Party, whose leaders, such as Dan Quayle, insisted upon fielding a new Patriot missile in the 1980s, now calls for a new generation of defense against the Scuds of tomorrow.

Rather than admit their mistakes of the past, the same liberal Democrats who sought to disarm America against the Soviet threat now compound their errors with a new campaign—half audacity, half mendacity—to leave the nation unprotected in a still dangerous world.

Republicans call for a controlled defense drawdown, not a free fall. That is why President Bush proposes to carefully reduce defense spending over the next four years by an additional $34 billion, including $18 billion in outlays, with a 25 percent reduction in personnel. He has already eliminated over 100 weapon systems. Around the world, American forces are coming home from the frontiers of the Cold War. More than 550 overseas bases are being closed or realigned. Yet U.S. forces retain the ability to meet the challenge of another Desert Storm with equal success.

U.S. defense spending already has been reduced significantly. Five years ago, it was more than a quarter of the federal budget. By 1997 it will be less than a sixth. Spending on defense and intelligence, as a proportion of gross domestic product, will be the lowest it has been since before World War II.

Yet any defense budget, however lean, is still too much for the Democrats. They want to start by cutting defense outlays over the next four years by nearly $60 billion beyond the president's cuts, throwing as many as 1 million additional Americans out of work.

And this may be just the beginning, as the Democrats use the defense budget as a bottomless piggy bank to try to beat swords into pork barrels. This is folly. It would take us back to the hollow military of the Carter era. Once American defenses are allowed to decay, they cannot be rebuilt overnight. Effective arsenals, like effective leaders, require years of patient development. And our greatest asset of all, the people on whom our security depends, deserve a constant long-term investment in their quality, morale and safety. Republicans pledge to provide it.

America Secure

Because the United States will rely on a smaller force of offensive nuclear weapons to deter aggression in the post-Cold War era, we will maintain the triad of land, sea, and air-based strategic forces. We will continue to test the safety, reliability and effectiveness of our nuclear weapons.

With a smaller military, modernization of conventional forces is more important than ever. Desert Storm showed the importance of "force multipliers" like smart munitions, stealth technology and night-fighting capabilities.

We will upgrade existing weapons and selectively procure those that hold the promise of dramatic forward leaps in capability. Under no circumstances will we yield our technological superiority.

We must remain ready to defend American citizens and interests wherever they may be threatened. Essential to that readiness is maintenance of a strong global navy and modernization of vital airlift and sealift capacity. We remain committed to combating terrorism in all its forms wherever it threatens U.S. citizens or interests.

Republicans will preserve the nation's access to space for defense, as well as for other purposes, and ensure that space technology does not fall into dangerous hands.

Transformed by the collapse of communism, our Strategic Defense Initiative [SDI] is now designed to provide the United States and our allies with global defenses against limited ballistic missile attacks.

SDI is the greatest investment in peace we could ever make. This system will be our shield against technoterrorism. Russia has agreed to be our partner in it, sharing early warning information and jointly moving forward to stop those who would rain death upon the innocent.

We will use missile defenses to assure threatened nations that they do not need to acquire ballistic missiles of their own. We will move beyond the ABM Treaty to deploy effective defenses with the goal of someday eliminating, not merely reducing, the threat of nuclear holocaust.

We support efforts to reduce armaments, both conventional and otherwise, but the most effective arms control of all over the long run is democracy. Free nations do not attack one another. That is why the promotion of democracy on every continent is an essential part of the Republican defense agenda.

Managing the Peace

A new era in defense requires new approaches to management, to get more out of every dollar in a shrinking budget.

That calls for dramatically different ways of doing business. For example, President Bush's reforms in defense management and acquisition already mean massive savings—$70 billion through 1997—without sacrificing combat capability.

Our armed forces will still depend on our superb industrial base for everything from belt buckles to submarines. We cannot lose that engineering and manufacturing capability.

This is especially true of the high technology, demonstrated in Desert Storm, that made our enemies realize they had been left behind in the race for the future. We therefore pledge to maintain America's technological lead, preserve its defense industrial base, and maintain robust levels of investment in research and development.

We will attack the problem of waste in the military, especially at its root in the pork barrel politics of Capitol Hill. A Republican Congress will end the costly micromanagement of defense programs and reduce the number and scope of oversight committees.

We will urge the Department of Defense to encourage a broader constituency for saving and to continue genuine procurement reforms based on performance rather than unreasonable regulations imposed by the Democrat Congress. We will continue the successful effort to eliminate redundancy and streamline all facets of defense management.

We applaud the president's efforts to assist all individuals and communities adversely affected by the ongoing defense build-down, with more than 30 defense adjustment programs already in place and more than $7 billion committed to the effort in just the next two years.

The Men and Women of Defense

Republicans created the all-volunteer Army, and we hail its success. We pledge to keep faith with the men and women volunteers and with their families, for they are the backbone of the nation's defense. We oppose Democrat efforts to bring back the draft, whether directly or through the subterfuge of compulsory domestic service.

The armed forces are a colorblind meritocracy, a model for the rest of our society. Its enlistees should receive preference in federal education and retraining programs. We applaud the advancement of women in the military and single out for special recognition the outstanding contribution of women in Operations Desert Shield/Desert Storm.

However, we oppose liberal Democrat attempts to place women in combat positions just to make an ideological point. Unlike the Democratic Party and its candidate, we support the continued exclusion of homosexuals from the military as a matter of good order and discipline.

The Department of Defense will not be an exception to our assertion of family values. Republicans will not tolerate sexual harassment or misconduct toward any individual in the ranks. We demand both its prevention and its punishment.

To drive home that point, we urge a halt to the sale, in military facilities, of sexually explicit materials. We call for greater consideration of the needs of families when parents are called to duty.

We must ensure that all of the various benefits, including medical, that were promised to the men and women who chose to make the military and the defense of their nation a career are fulfilled even upon retirement.

In the Republican tradition of support for America's veterans, we proposed and created a Department of Veterans Affairs so their concerns would be represented at the Cabinet table. We affirm our support for veterans preference in federal employment and for sufficient funding to maintain the integrity of the veterans hospital and medical-care system. We strongly endorse programs to meet the needs of unemployed veterans. . . .

Proven Leadership

George Bush has been the most important architect of Western aspirations and designs for the challenging world we are now entering. His record is clear. President Bush has shown he understands how to lead in this new era, where the pre-eminent position of the United States offers new opportunities to build an international consensus on key issues. President Bush, with experienced Republican leadership, has proved he knows how to place our nation at the center of effective coalitions where our power is multiplied.

The test of international leadership is on the field, not in a playbook. The Oval Office is no place for on-the-job training—not in carrying out the presidential duty to protect and defend our nation, not in managing the arsenal of the supreme nuclear power.

There are those who talk and those who perform. George Bush has clearly performed for America, making the right calls in a series of tough decisions that helped transform the world.

Now that we have won the Cold War, we must secure the peace that follows. History has shown that the years following conflict are often critical—where the choices made can either lay the foundation for lasting peace or sow the seeds of the future war. In this period of high hopes and great challenges ahead, the nation needs the tested and experienced leadership of President Bush and the Republican Party.

HURRICANES ANDREW AND INIKI
August 24-25, September 1, 1992

Generating tornadoes at its edges and a politial storm in its wake, Hurricane Andrew smashed into the U.S. mainland August 24-25, devastating much of southern Florida and coastal Louisiana. Authorities classed Andrew as the country's worst natural disaster in terms of property damage, although adequate warning kept its death toll surprisingly low. Some thirty people were killed.

Less than three weeks later, Iniki, one of the most powerful hurricanes in Hawaiian history, battered the island of Kauai. On September 11 the hurricane's sustained winds of 130 miles an hour raked the island's eastern coast, where most of the resorts and development are concentrated.

Andrew, whose winds raged at up to 160 miles an hour, ranked in the next-to-highest class of severity, category 4. It virtually destroyed the community of Homestead, south of Miami, leaving a quarter of a million people without homes, jobs, food, or electricity.

Slow Federal Response Criticized

When emergency aid was slow in coming, the victims turned their wrath on the federal government, particularly the Federal Emergency Management Agency (FEMA), a unit already under fire as a political dumping ground for the Bush administration. (Report on the Federal Emergency Management Agency, p. 533)

President George Bush, trailing Democratic challenger Bill Clinton in the polls, visited the disaster area twice in the week following the storm in an effort to repair the political damage. The second time, on Septem-

843

ber 1, he dispensed good news, including pledges to rebuild Homestead Air Force Base and to have the federal government pick up the entire tab for eligible relief assistance, waiving the states' usual 25 percent share. That night he went on television and asked the nation to send help to the victims.

Earlier, Bush had finessed the FEMA controversy by placing Transportation Secretary Andrew H. Card, Jr., in charge of aid coordination, bypassing FEMA director Wallace E. Stickney.

Apparent tension between the Bush administration and Florida Governor Lawton Chiles added to local officials' frustration with the pace of disaster relief. Federal troops did not begin to arrive with emergency shelter and kitchens until four days after the hurricane struck, prompting Kate Hale, director of Dade County (Miami) emergency operations, to ask, "Where the hell is the cavalry on this one?"

Although disaster relief workers disputed administration claims that it sent help as soon as Chiles requested it, the governor later admitted he had delayed asking Washington for regular troops, believing the state's national guard would be adequate. But the guard was needed just to cope with widespread looting. Belatedly, both the governor and the White House recognized that the extent of the disaster necessitated a full- scale federal intervention.

The bitter criticism began to fade with the arrival of the first contingent of some 7,000 federal troops. And the president said August 28 that he was "not going to participate in the blame game, nor is Governor Chiles. What we're trying to do is help people, and it doesn't do any good to get into 'who shot John'."

Even before damage assessments in Louisiana were known, the Insurance Information Institute estimated the insurance industry would pay out $7.3 billion for insured losses in Florida, making Andrew the most costly hurricane in U.S. history. Hurricane Hugo, previously the most destructive hurricane, had cost the industry $4.2 billion.

Subsequent calculations by the institute, a nonprofit group supported by the property casualty industry, raised insurance costs in Florida from Andrew to $10.2 billion. With Louisiana's storm damage at $500 million, the total cost of the hurricane to the insurance industry was expected to be $10.7 billion. Officials estimated that the full monetary cost of Hurricane Andrew, including uninsured private property losses and damage to public and military facilities, would exceed $20 billion. (Hurricane Hugo, Historic Documents of 1989, p. 667)

Quick Response in Hawaii

In Hawaii the wind and torrential rains of Hurricane Iniki and the accompanying twenty-foot surf inflicted serious structural damage on an estimated 10,000 homes and virtually all seventy of Kauai's hotels. About 8,000 of the island's permanent population of 52,000 were made homeless. Damage was estimated at $1 billion or more. Oahu, the state's most *populated island, was spared the full force of the storm, but the famous Waikiki Beach was forced to close down. Governor John Waihee III called Iniki "probably the worst disaster we've ever had," although only three deaths were attributed to the hurricane.*

In contrast to Andrew, FEMA dispatched disaster teams to Hawaii even before Iniki struck Kauai and notified the U.S. Pacific military command to assist with emergency relief. Governor Waihee noted that his state probably was "the beneficiary" of the flap over FEMA's performance in Florida. President Bush declared the state a disaster area September 12 and, as with Andrew, waived the state matching requirement for federal assistance.

Hurricanes Andrew and Iniki were only two of a series of extraordinary natural and manmade disasters during the year. Scores of states suffered damage, some on two or more occasions, from intense wind and hail storms, tornadoes, and flooding. In April office buildings in downtown Chicago suffered $300 million in water damage from a leak in underground canals carrying water from the Chicago River. In May riots in Los Angeles caused $775 million worth of insured losses.

According to the Insurance Information Institute, the total cost of claims from these and other natural and manmade disasters through October was $16 billion, making 1992 the costliest year ever. The institute's figure excluded damage from Hurricane Iniki and a wave of tornadoes that cut a destructive path through twelve states from Texas to the Carolinas in mid-November, killing at least twenty-five people. The U.S. territory of Guam also suffered significant damage in 1992, when it was barraged by three separate typhoons. The worst was Typhoon Omar, which carried winds of 150 miles an hour.

> *Following is the text of President George Bush's address to the nation September 1, 1992, on disaster relief for Florida and Louisiana in the aftermath of Hurricane Andrew and also the text of the Insurance Information Institute's press release of September 1, 1992, giving a preliminary estimate of $7.3 billion for insured losses in Florida:*

ADDRESS TO THE NATION ON HURRICANE ANDREW DISASTER RELIEF

Eight days ago the people of south Florida and Louisiana were confronted by perhaps the most destructive natural disaster in our history. Tonight I want to report to the Nation on the aftermath of Hurricane Andrew and the effort required to help Andrew's survivors back on their feet.

In the past week I've twice visited Louisiana and Florida. And in Florida, where the storm was strongest, up to a quarter million people have lost their homes, many huddled beneath the busted timbers of what was once a living room or a kitchen. There's no running water, no electricity. Little children are left without even a toy to play with.

In the aftermath of Hurricane Andrew, a relief effort has risen, unprecedented in size and impact. And tonight as we speak, almost 20,000 troops are on the ground assisting in everything from providing meals to erecting tent cities. Basic human needs, food, water, shelter, and medical assistance, are being provided.

In Florida, a curfew is in place, and the National Guard and local police patrol the streets. It's a tribute to these officers and to the people of this region that looting has been kept to a minimum. Social Security checks are being delivered on time. Financial help is being made available to families who have lost their homes and their jobs.

This relief effort has generated incredible cooperation. My thanks go to so many people who slept so little the past 8 days, to State and local government officials, Federal Agencies, private charities, and the heroic men and women of the United States military. Most especially, my appreciation goes out to the volunteers. When we arrived in Florida, some of the first people we met were from South Carolina, victims of Hurricane Hugo who had spent the night driving so they could help others through their ordeal. We met doctors and firefighters spending sleepless vacations lending a helping hand. Through the eloquence of their action, I've been reminded that America will always be a Nation of neighbors.

Although the relief effort is well underway, urgent needs still exist. And so tonight I make a special appeal to the generous spirit of the American people. People in Florida and Louisiana want to stay in their homes. They're in desperate need of rolls of plastic to cover open roofs, lumber to board up walls, and cots to sleep on. They also need diapers, baby formula, and other infant supplies. And fresh volunteers are needed to staff medical facilities or help with the cleanup.

Right now, America's churches and charities are mobilizing to meet these needs. And I encourage all Americans to pitch in, in any way you can. If you don't know where to turn and you want to help right now, please call the American Red Cross at 1-800-842-2200.

Once our relief effort is complete, we will accelerate the process of recovery. Already today we announced plans to rebuild Homestead Air Force Base, the linchpin of the economy in devastated areas. And a distinguished Florida business leader, Alvah Chapman, has agreed to head a national private sector effort to help rebuild south Florida. It's called "We Will Rebuild." This effort has my strong support and the support of Florida Governor Chiles. All of us are in this for the long haul. If you want to be part of this effort, please write We Will Rebuild. And the address is Post Office Box 010790, Miami, Florida, and the ZIP Code is 33131.

In the past 8 days we've seen on our TV screens real tears, real sorrow, real hurt. Livelihoods have been destroyed. Lives, even young lives, have been tragically lost. But already in Florida and Louisiana, we're talking not just of relief but of recovery. This is a tribute to what is inside us. And yes, Andrew blew a whirlwind of devastation. But he could never extinguish the American spirit, a spirit of compassion and sacrifice and endurance. We have seen that spirit in action the past 8 days. And with this spirit and your enduring commitment, our neighbors in south Florida and Louisiana will recover.

Thank you for your generosity. And our prayers are with all who stood in Andrew's path. Good night.

INSURANCE INFORMATION INSTITUTE
PRESS RELEASE

MIAMI, Sept. 1—The property/casualty insurance industry will pay an estimated $7.3 billion in claims to victims of Hurricane Andrew in Florida, making the storm the costliest disaster in U.S. insurance history.

This preliminary estimate does not include insured losses from Hurricane Andrew in Louisiana or other areas affected by the storm.

Gary R. Kerney, director-catastrophe services, Property Claim Services (PCS) division of the American Insurance Services Group, Inc., provided the estimate at a news briefing at the Sheraton River House Hotel in Miami.

PCS also said that reports from the federal government's National Flood Insurance Program are that flood losses in Florida covered by NFIP are estimated at an additional $50 million.

Prior to Andrew, Hurricane Hugo, Sept. 17-22, 1989, had been the costliest hurricane, with insured losses estimated at $4.2 billion.

Hurricane Andrew, accompanied by high winds, flooding and tornadoes, struck the Bahamas and Florida on August 23-24, then moved across the open waters of the Gulf of Mexico and affected portions of Louisiana and other southeastern states on August 25-26.

The insured loss estimate for Florida does not include uninsured damage to government and military facilities or public property, including roads and bridges; utility equipment, such as power lines; the cost of emergency services; and economic losses, such as crop damage and lost taxes.

Kerney reported that more than 1,500 additional insurance company claims adjusters from across the country and specially trained catastrophe teams arrived in the storm-affected areas of Florida as quickly as possible to respond immediately in handling the huge number of claims arising from Andrew.

He estimated that approximately 685,000 claims will be reported in Florida alone as a result of the hurricane.

"The insurance industry began to settle claims immediately, making advance payments and providing assistance to storm victims in the recovery process," Kerney said.

"We believe the industry has an adequate number of adjusters on hand to cope with the situation as it now stands," he said. "Additional experienced adjusters will be brought into the area if needed."

Kerney said that PCS is working with the Federal Emergency Management Agency, the state insurance department, the governor's office, insurance industry associations and agents' groups, as well as other organizations to coordinate insurance company activities with the general recovery effort.

Heaviest insured damage occurred in counties on Florida's east coast. In Dade County alone, insured damage was estimated at more than $6 billion. The total estimated insured loss also includes damage that occurred in Broward, Palm Beach, Collier and Monroe Counties.

Insured loss estimates for Louisiana are expected to be available later in the week.

As a result of Hurricane Andrew's destruction in Florida, estimated insured catastrophe losses to date in 1992 total $11.2 billion. That already makes 1992 the worst year on record for catastrophe losses, topping the old record of $7.6 billion set in 1989—the year of Hurricane Hugo and the Loma Prieta earthquake in California.

The insurance industry designates an event a catastrophe when the insured loss is expected to exceed $5 million.

Hurricane Andrew was assigned Catastrophe Serial Number 27 by Property Claim Services.

NEW ALCOHOLISM DEFINITION
August 26, 1992

A new, more detailed definition of alcoholism appeared in the August 26 issue of the Journal of the American Medical Association (JAMA). *A twenty-three-member panel convened by the National Council on Alcoholism and Drug Dependence and the American Society of Addiction Medicine had actually approved the definition in April 1990, but it had received little attention until its publication in JAMA.*

The new definition emphasized that biological, psychological, social, and environmental factors played roles in the disease. It also noted that genetics made many drinkers vulnerable to alcoholism and listed some of the behaviors, especially denial, frequently engaged in by alcoholics.

The new emphasis on behavior was designed to help both doctors and the public recognize alcoholism earlier, Daniel Flavin, chief of the alcoholism and addictions outpatient program at St. Vincent's Hospital in New York and staff director for the committee, told the Washington Post. *"We're saying to a doctor or the guy in the street, 'Look, you can see behavior. You can recognize behavior. If you read this and it rings true in some way, get professional help,'" Flavin said.*

The committee included scientists, physicians, and lay experts. It defined alcoholism as "a primary, chronic disease with genetic, psychosocial, and environmental factors influencing its development and manifestations. The disease is often progressive and fatal. It is characterized by impaired control over drinking, preoccupation with the drug alcohol, use of alcohol despite adverse consequences, and distortions in thinking, most notably denial. Each of these symptoms may be continuous or periodic."

The previous definition, developed in 1976 by the National Council on Alcoholism and the American Medical Society on Alcoholism, emphasized biological factors in the disease. It said alcoholism was "a chronic, progressive, and potentially fatal disease. It is characterized by tolerance and physical dependency or pathologic organ changes, or both—all the direct or indirect consequences of the alcohol ingested."

The National Institute on Alcohol Abuse and Alcoholism estimated in 1990 that 17.7 million Americans had alcohol problems. That included 10.5 million who showed signs of alcoholism or alcohol dependence and 7.2 million who persistently drank so heavily that alcohol impaired their health or social functioning. Problem drinking was increasing, according to the institute. It estimated that by 1995 11.2 million Americans would be dependent on alcohol. In 1989 approximately 1.2 million people were enrolled in alcohol treatment programs.

Robert Morse, director of addictive disorders services at the Mayo Clinic and chairman of the panel that developed the new definition, said research on the causes and treatment of alcoholism was ongoing. This isn't the ultimate [definition]," Morse told the Post. *"If the field continues to evolve as it has, ten or twenty years from now we may have to put together another panel."*

Some members of Morse's committee reportedly wanted to go further and define specific criteria for a clinical diagnosis of alcoholism. The World Health Organization and the American Psychiatric Association had developed such diagnostic guides, although both groups were then revising their criteria. Ultimately, the panel decided not to develop a third set of competing standards. Instead, it chose to try to influence the work of the other two groups.

Less than two months after the definition was published, a study estimated that 50 to 60 percent of a woman's tendency toward alcoholism was genetic. The study examined 2,060 identical and fraternal twins. Among identical twins, the study found, a woman whose twin was an alcoholic was five times more likely than normal to be an alcoholic herself. Among fraternal twins, a woman whose twin was an alcoholic was 1.6 times more likely to be an alcoholic herself. The study was conducted by researchers at the Medical College of Virginia-Virginia Commonwealth University in Richmond. It appeared in the October 14 issue of the Journal of the American Medical Association.

Following is the text of an article, "The Definition of Alcoholism," prepared by a panel appointed by the National Council on Alcoholism and Drug Dependence and the American Society of Addiction Medicine that was published August 26, 1992, in the Journal of the American Medical Association:

Alcoholism is a primary, chronic disease with genetic, psychosocial, and environmental factors influencing its development and manifestations. The disease is often progressive and fatal. It is characterized by impaired control over drinking, preoccupation with the drug alcohol, use of alcohol despite adverse consequences, and distortions in thinking, most notably denial. Each of these symptoms may be continuous or periodic.

"Primary" refers to the nature of alcoholism as a disease entity in addition to and separate from other pathophysiologic states that may be associated with it. It suggests that as an addiction, alcoholism is not a symptom of an underlying disease state.

"Disease" means an involuntary disability. Use of the term *involuntary* in defining disease is descriptive of this state as a discrete entity that is not deliberately pursued. It does not suggest passivity in the recovery process. Similarly, use of this term does not imply the abrogation of responsibility in the legal sense. Disease represents the sum of the abnormal phenomena displayed by the group of individuals. These phenomena are associated with a specified common set of characteristics by which certain individuals differ from the norm and which places them at a disadvantage.

"Often progressive and fatal" means that the disease persists over time and that physical, emotional, and social changes are often cumulative and may progress as drinking continues. Alcoholism causes premature death through overdose; through organic complications involving the brain, liver, heart, and other organs; and by contributing to suicide, homicide, motor vehicle accidents, and other traumatic events.

"Impaired control" means the inability to consistently limit on drinking occasions the duration of the drinking episode, the quantity of alcohol consumed, and/or the behavioral consequences.

"Preoccupation" used in association with "alcohol use" indicates excessive, focused attention given to the drug alcohol and to its effects or its use (or both). The relative value the person assigns to alcohol often leads to energy being diverted from important life concerns.

"Adverse consequences" are alcohol-related problems, "disabilities," or impairments in such areas as physical health (e.g., alcohol withdrawal syndromes, liver disease, gastritis, anemia, and neurologic disorders), psychologic functioning (e.g., cognition and changes in mood and behavior), interpersonal functioning (e.g., marital problems, child abuse, and troubled social relationships), occupational functioning (e.g., scholastic or job problems), and legal, financial, or spiritual problems. Although the alcohol dependence syndrome may theoretically occur in the absence of adverse consequences, we believe that the latter are evident in virtually all clinical cases.

"Denial" is used in the definition not only in the psychoanalytic sense of a single psychologic defense mechanism disavowing the significance of events but more broadly to include a range of psychologic maneuvers that decrease awareness of the fact that alcohol use is the cause of a person's problems rather than a solution to those problems. Denial becomes an integral part of the disease and is nearly always a major obstacle to recovery. Denial in alcoholism is a complex phenomenon determined by multiple psychologic and physiologic mechanisms. These include the pharmacologic effects of alcohol on memory, the influence of euphoric recall on perception and insight, the role of suppression and repression as psychologic defense mechanisms, and the impact of social and cultural enabling behavior.

Our proposed definition should not be interpreted as a new set of criteria for making the diagnosis of alcoholism, even though certain criteria are implied in its terminology.

September

VINCENT'S RESIGNATION
AS BASEBALL COMMISSIONER
September 7, 1992

Yielding to the demands of a majority of Major League Baseball owners, Francis T. "Fay" Vincent, Jr., resigned September 7, 1992, as baseball commissioner. His decision came four days after an extraordinary vote of no confidence in him by club owners.

Elected unanimously September 13, 1989, to succeed the late A. Bartlett Giamatti, Vincent's term was to have run until April 1, 1994. Vincent was only the eighth commissioner in the history of baseball, but the third since October 1984. He was the third to be asked or forced to give up the post. The office of commissioner had been created in 1920 to run the Major Leagues in the aftermath of the 1919 Chicago White Sox gambling scandal.

Vincent's three-year tenure was stormy almost from the start. Just over a month after he became commissioner, an earthquake in San Francisco interrupted the 1989 World Series, being played at the city's Candlestick Park. He was widely praised for continuing the Series to completion after a reasonable delay. However, the turbulence created by his subsequent decisions directly affecting many influential baseball owners ultimately led to the September 3 vote calling for his resignation. Eighteen of the twenty-eight baseball owners voted, in effect, to fire him. While maintaining that the Major League Agreement barred the owners from firing him, Vincent September 7 said in a letter of resignation that it was in the best interests of baseball that he step down rather than wage a protracted court battle with the owners. He could not govern as commissioner, he said, "without the consent of owners to be governed." Earlier in the summer he had vowed never to resign.

Most baseball observers felt that with Vincent's forced dismissal the office of commissioner would never be the same. Club owners were expected to transform the office into something resembling a corporate chief executive officer who would report to the owners and would be answerable only to them. Owners also were likely to revamp the separate offices of president of the American and National leagues.

Long-running Conflicts

Vincent's conflicts with baseball management began in March 1990 when he helped arrange a new collective bargaining agreement with the Baseball Players Association, ending a thirty-two-day lockout of spring training. Many owners felt Vincent had been too accommodating to the union. Then in July that year he forced George M. Steinbrenner III to relinquish his position as managing partner of the New York Yankees. Steinbrenner had been implicated in dealings with Howard Spira, a known gambler, affecting his own ball club. (Rose's Sentencing and Steinbrenner's Removal, Historic Documents of 1990, p. 483)

In 1991 Vincent helped arrange a new four-year contract with the Major League Umpires Association. His actions later that year involving expansion of the National League angered some owners in both leagues, who charged that their share of the expansion fees was too small.

Another irritation was his refusal in June 1992 to relinquish his authority in labor relations. That request had been made by the Chicago White Sox and the Milwaukee Brewers and by the owners' chief labor executive. (Those two clubs, along with the Tribune Company that owned the Chicago Cubs, later initiated the campaign to remove Vincent.) That same month the owners, with Vincent's encouragement, arranged the controversial sale of the Seattle Mariners to Japanese interests. In June Vincent also permanently banned from baseball a New York Yankee pitcher for repeated drug abuse.

Vincent's disputes with the owners came to a head in July after he ordered the realignment of the National League to better reflect the actual geographical location of some teams. He put the Chicago Cubs and St. Louis Cardinals in the West division and the Cincinnati Reds and Atlanta Braves in the East division. The Cubs then sued the commissioner, and a judge temporarily blocked Vincent's order. It was the realignment brouhaha that sparked the move to seek the commissioner's removal.

Acting in "Best Interests of Baseball"

It was clear from his resignation letter that Vincent took literally the wording in the Major League Agreement giving the commissioner responsibility to act "in the best interests of Baseball," whether or not particular decisions adversely affected some or even all the owners. The office had been established to maintain the integrity of baseball, he stressed (the first commissioner, the strong-willed Judge Kenesaw Moun-

tain Landis, had set the tone), and thus it should remain independent of the owners. But some of them expected the commissioner to do their bidding on every issue, he said more in sorrow than in anger, a role which he could not accept. While it was obvious that some ball clubs wanted a figurehead as commissioner, he urged owners to retain a strong, hands-on commissioner—one who would act in the interests of the fans, players, and umpires as well as the owners.

Following is the text of Major League Baseball Commissioner Fay Vincent's September 7, 1992, letter to club owners announcing his resignation:

To: American and National League Owners

As requested in the owners' resolution of September 3, 1992, and in accordance with its terms, I tender my resignation as Commissioner of Baseball, effective immediately.

On August 20, I wrote each of the owners I would not resign the Office of the Commissioner of Baseball. I stated that, in my judgment, to do so would do a great disservice to the Office of the Commissioner and to Baseball itself. I strongly believe a Baseball Commissioner should serve a full term as contemplated by the Major League Agreement. Only then can difficult decisions be made impartially and without fear of political repercussions. Unfortunately, some want the Commissioner to put aside the responsibility to act in the "best interests of Baseball"; some want the Commissioner to represent only owners, and to do their bidding in all matters. I haven't done that, and I could not do so, because I accepted the position believing the Commissioner has a higher duty and that sometimes decisions have to be made that are not in the interest of some owners.

Unique power was granted to the Commissioner of Baseball for sound reasons—to maintain the integrity of the game and to temper owner decisions predicated solely on self-interest. The Office should be maintained as a strong institution. My views on this have not changed. What has changed, however, is my opinion that it would be an even greater disservice to Baseball if I were to precipitate a protracted fight over the Office of Commissioner. After the vote at the meeting last week, I can no longer justify imposing on Baseball, nor should Baseball be required to endure, a bitter legal battle—even though I am confident that in the end I would win and thereby establish a judicial precedent that the term and powers of the Commissioner cannot be diminished during the remaining 18 months of my term. But what would that really accomplish? What will the fight have been worth if, 14 months from now, prior to electing a new Commissioner, the owners change the Major League Agreement to create a "figurehead" Commissioner? This is certainly the goal of some. And while it is bad for Baseball, I cannot prevent that change.

A fight based solely on principle does not justify the disruption when there is not greater support among ownership for my views. While I would receive personal gratification by demonstrating that the legal position set out in my August 20 letter is correct, litigation does nothing to address the serious problems of Baseball. I cannot govern as Commissioner without the consent of owners to be governed. I do not believe that consent is now available to me. Simply put, I've concluded that resignation—not litigation—should be my final act as Commissioner "in the best interests" of Baseball.

I can only hope owners will realize that a strong Commissioner, a person of experience and stature in the community, is integral to Baseball. I hope they learn this lesson before too much damage is done to the game, to the players, umpires and others who work in the game, and most importantly, to the fans.

I am grateful to my friends, among the owners and around the country, for their warm and zealous support. I am especially grateful for all the messages of support from those in the game who care about me and who believe in what I have tried to accomplish. That support has meant a great deal to me—more than I can express. The game of Baseball can, and will, survive far more difficult times than these.

I bear no personal ill will toward any of the owners and I wish them well. At the same time I remind all that ownership of a Baseball team is more than ownership of an ordinary business. Owners have a duty to take into consideration that they own a part of America's national pastime—in trust. This trust sometimes requires putting self-interest second.

Sincerely
Francis T. Vincent, Jr.

FUJIMORI ON CAPTURE OF PERUVIAN SHINING PATH LEADER
September 13, 1992

A twelve-year manhunt for Peru's most wanted terrorist leader ended September with the capture of Abimael Guzman Reynoso. Guzman, the founder of the Shining Path insurrection, was arrested in a suburb of Lima, the nation's capital, along with several other rebel leaders. In a televised address to the nation September 13, President Alberto Fujimori praised the work of his intelligence and antiterrorist services and reiterated an earlier pledge to eliminate all terrorist groups in Peru by June 1995—the end of his presidential term. He was elected president in 1990.

Guzman's apprehension bolstered Fujimori's beleaguered regime. With the backing of the armed forces, Fujimori had suspended the Constitution and disbanded Peru's legislature and judiciary on April 5, 1992, on the ground that corrupt politicians and a weak-kneed judiciary were hindering his efforts to suppress the rebels. The United States supported Fujimori in his campaign against terrorism but insisted he restore a legitimate government.

While the arrest was seen as a significant personal victory for Fujimori, Peruvian observers said Guzman's capture would not end the Shining Path attacks. The rebels remained entrenched in much of the country. Allowed to talk to reporters following his incarceration, Guzman September 24 ordered his followers to continue their guerrilla tactics. Indeed, terrorist violence in Lima and in the countryside continued unabated in October and November 1992.

Demonstrating that it still was a major threat, the Shining Path set off several bombs throughout the capital November 22 as Peruvians went to

the polls for the first time since Fujimori suspended democratic govern-
ment. The election gave Fujimori and his allies a clear majority in the
new eighty-seat legislature. However, the two largest opposition parties
boycotted the election, saying it would only legitimize Fujimori's rule by
decree. And one in five voters turned in blank ballots. The new congress
was an interim body, convened to write a new constitution.

On October 7, 1992, after a ten-day trial that was closed to the public as
a security precaution, a newly created military court convicted Guzman
of treason. He was given the maximum sentence of life imprisonment
without parole. A 1979 law, and international treaties to which Peru was
a party, forbade the death penalty except in wartime. In related trials,
eleven other Shining Path leaders were sentenced to life imprisonment.
Guzman and two others also were fined $25 billion.

Once Guzman had exhausted all avenues for appealing his sentence, he
was expected to spend the rest of his life in a special jail cell at an island
naval base off the coast. Peruvian jails were notoriously lax and corrupt,
however, and authorities were apprehensive about the adequacy of
security measures for Guzman.

Reign of Terror

Considered the largest and most violent guerrilla insurgency in Latin
America, Shining Path, a Maoist splinter group of Peru's Communist
party, was responsible for the death of some 25,000 people since 1980, the
year Guzman's movement went underground. The country's economy was
virtually paralyzed. Property damage resulting from twelve years of
terrorism was estimated at more than $20 billion. By 1992 rebels were
believed to control an area containing about one-fifth of Peru's 22 million
people.

The Shining Path movement originated in the Upper Huallaga Valley
of central Peru, where it appealed to the indigenous Indian population.
It was closer to a cult than a political movement. Along with terrorism, it
gained control by exploiting racial divisions, and increasing social and
economic inequalities. It also took advantage of widespread corruption
and a weak central government. The government had clear evidence by
the mid-1980s of a link between the rebels and Peruvian coca growers and
international drug dealers. When Guzman was captured, officials esti-
mated Shining Path had about 5,000 active guerrillas and perhaps
another 25,000 persons actively cooperating with the rebels.

A Diabolical Genius

In this broadcast to the nation, Fujimori called Guzman a diabolical
and wicked genius, "a perpetrator of genocide" who had subverted a part
of Peru's population and fooled numerous foreign governments. Video
footage showing Guzman in captivity was also aired. Fujimori went to
great lengths to destroy Guzman's mystique and the aura of invincibility
that surrounded his life and actions. He portrayed Guzman as morally

weak, a drunkard, and womanizer living in luxury, rather than the idealistic revolutionary. Fujimori recited examples of Guzman's ruthless murders and tortures and his record as "the foremost hired assassin of drug trafficking in Peru." At the same time, he tried to reverse the prevalent feeling in the country that the government was powerless against the rebels, claiming that his regime had replaced years of distrust and hostility with genuine trust and collaboration between the government and the population.

Following are excerpts of President Alberto Fujimori's September 13, 1992, televised address to the nation on the capture of Shining Path leader Abimael Guzman Reynoso:

Good evening, my fellow citizens:

We Peruvians are all deeply aware of the significance of the apprehension of Abimael Guzman, alias "Comrade Gonzalo", because we know what his terrorist group, the Shining Path, stands for—destruction, death, drug trafficking.

This sinister character is the true embodiment of the means and ends used by his bloodthirsty organization. He has an extraordinarily complex and contradictory mind. A little more than a year ago, the people of Peru were able to meet Abimael Guzman through a video, and instead of the mythical revolutionary leader they expected, they saw a drunken individual, dancing clumsily, surrounded by a group of young women, also inebriated, against the backdrop of portraits of the founders of communism.

Since then, the intelligence services and Dincote (the elite anti-terrorist corps of the National Police) have tracked Guzman and the members of his entourage. Once again, his weaknesses did him in, and made this new and important success possible. It is interesting, how even the most cunning of criminals are taken by surprise in this manner and the leader of the Shining Path was no exception.

The National Police fell upon one of his hideouts when some of the top leaders of the Shining Path were engaging in pleasure-seeking activities which the members of an organization of this sort would have found to be inconceivable. It is indeed difficult to relate the marches of the militant members of the Shining Path, with their Maoist rituals, observed in the past in the jails and part of their export propaganda, with the debauchery of their top leaders, the parties where Greek music and Scandinavian vodka flowed in the midst of other luxuries and sophistication.

That is the moral fiber of this man, the same man who recruited young boys and young men by force to transport bombs and take part in suicide operations. That is Abimael, the exterminator, but it is also Abimael, the debauchee. In sum, a monster. We are before a monster. This is also the man who, with inhuman cold-heartedness, ordered the crime against Mrs.

Moyano, the killing at Tarata Street and as well as numerous genocidal raids against young people and peasant populations, where men and women were beheaded and mutilated.

This is the man who forsaking the principles enshrined in his revolutionary creed became the foremost hired assassin of drug trafficking in Peru.

The proceeds from drug-related activities, in addition to financing his personal luxuries and eccentricities and those of the closest members of his entourage, also financed narcoterrorist diplomacy in Europe.

Because part of the immense contribution from the drug cartels financed Shining Path ambassadors abroad, such as Adolfo Olaechea in Great Britain, Alberto Ruiz Eldredge, Jr. in France, Luis Arce in Belgium, Javier Mujica Contreras in Spain, Carlos La Torre Cordova in Sweden and many others throughout different European nations.

However, Guzman has led his youngest followers, those who truly bear the brunt of their struggle, to believe that his ties with drug trafficking are lies concocted by the Fujimori administration. And those young men, who are cannon fodder, have never seen or even dreamed of the luxuries of their leaders, and still believe that there is no connection between their movement and drug trafficking.

But we must acknowledge that Abimael Guzman is a diabolical genius. For 12 years he has been able to fool not only a sector of Peru's youth but also democratic governments and even international organizations which lent him their support in a number of ways, including the granting of asylum for his assassins.

It has taken the international community twelve years to realize that it was before a war criminal, a perpetrator of genocide, one who is on a par with the fascist war criminals of the Second World War.

During those 12 years, this wicked genius, "Comrade Gonzalo", planted the seeds of death and destruction under the protective mantle of silence of human rights organizations while Peru counted its dead, buried its dead, and remained impotent. The human rights of this terrorist and genocidal gang were more important than those of 22 million Peruvians.

Let the world know that that has been the cost we Peruvians have had to pay. Let the world hear and express its solidarity towards a people yearning for the advent of peace. Let the civilized governments of the world close their doors to those who have not only violated but desecrated human rights, these genocidal terrorists who under the guise of a Peruvian revolutionary movement have joined forces with the drug cartels and exterminated any who opposed them. This is the man, who with this shameful background, claimed to be the architect of a new democracy.

Fellow citizens:

I have pledged to defeat all terrorist groups by 1995. This should not be interpreted as "triumphalism". We must not be "triumphalist" for even a second or let down our guard against these fanatic criminals. We must at all times be realistic, but we must be convinced that with this new strategy and our firm resolve to come out victorious we will defeat an enemy which is becoming increasingly visible.

In spite of what some may say on television, presumably moved by their political interests, I know that you are aware of the fact that there is a new strategy and that it is bearing fruit. As long as you believe this we will continue implementing this strategy. I cannot provide you with any details, but you already know that this strategy rests on winning over the support of the population for its government, for its armed forces. Because if the population and the authorities are on a different course we will be incapable of defeating terrorism. . . .

The distrust and even rejection of the forces of law and order which existed in the past years are giving way to genuine trust and collaboration. In each of those places, places never visited by a president, there is no longer a fear of terrorists.

I am not saying that the people support me, this is not propaganda, I am simply stating that the people no longer feel that their government has forsaken them.

When we aired the now famous video of the Guzman hideout some time ago, I made an appeal to the population indicating that the people of Peru, numbering some 22 million, are dealing with a small group of fanatics. Today we Peruvians know that it is impossible for a small and drug-crazed sect to defeat a country.

Naturally, changes in an important set of conditions were necessary in order for the citizens to start believing in themselves. We must not ignore the fact that one of those apprehended with Guzman was Meche Zambrano, famous for having been set free prior to the fifth of April by the judiciary and the pseudo-democratic system prevailing at that time.

Since April the fifth, with our new antiterrorist legislation, these criminals no longer enjoy sham trials where they can threaten, as they in fact did, the authorities, but rather are judged by military tribunals, so that they can be speedily sentenced and if found guilty, jailed. . . .

All of these actions have been complemented by a new anti-terrorist legislation which, for the first time, prevents the fruit of police and law enforcement efforts from going up in smoke. The previous legislation, with its loopholes and contradictions, its ambiguities and evident obsolescence, served the Shining Path's interests. In this connection, we must not forget the number of terrorist criminals absolved in the most absurd of ways by the judicial branch. . . .

Fear has long been left behind. It has been replaced by indignation. I know that there is a victim of the Shining Path in every one of you. Not only because your loved ones may have fallen prey to those criminals, but also because you have also lost much or part of the fruit of your hard work. Twelve years of frenzied and savage destruction, and losses amounting to more than 20 billion dollars have taken a toll on this impoverished country, making it even poorer. To that we add the loss of 25 thousand lives.

I believe I can sense what fate the population wishes for this criminal, who has done such harm to Peru. You will not be disappointed. Have no doubt that he will have received the maximum sanction possible.

Fellow citizens:

We witness the birth of a new country, a country which believes in itself. We Peruvians are ready to put an end to this terror. Since the fifth of April the population stands united. Large majorities have rejected the vice and flaws of a false democracy and now embrace a genuine democracy to put an end to the greatest scourge in our republic's history once and for all.

On behalf of the nation of Peru, I extend my congratulations to Dincote, agency of the national police for its efficient and committed efforts.

And I again pay tribute to all the victims of the terrorist madness. My promise to the relatives left behind, orphan children, widowed mothers, is that their crimes will not go unpunished.

I thank you very much.

GAO REPORT ON PATRIOT MISSILE PERFORMANCE

September 22, 1992

It was impossible to determine how many Patriot missiles succeeded in shooting down Iraqi Scud ballistic missiles during the 1991 Persian Gulf War, the U.S. General Accounting Office (GAO) said in a report dated September 22. The GAO, the investigative arm of Congress, said strong evidence indicated that 9 percent of Patriot engagements during Operation Desert Storm resulted in Scud "kills." In April the U.S. Army had claimed there was strong evidence that Patriots had destroyed Scuds in a quarter of all engagements.

Because the Patriots were fired in a war zone, not on a test range, the GAO said, the Army could not collect accurate performance data for the missiles. As a result, there was "no way to conclusively determine how many targets the Patriot killed or failed to kill," the report said. Rep. John Conyers, chairman of the House Government Operations Committee and a critic of the Patriot, had requested the GAO report.

During the Persian Gulf War, the Patriot—a surface-to-air guided missile—was at least as important psychologically as it was militarily. Americans lined up before their television sets to watch breathtaking pictures of Patriots zooming into the sky to attack incoming Scuds. The Patriot quickly became a symbol of the United States' high-tech military power. On dozens of occasions, Defense Secretary Dick Cheney said the Patriot proved that "a decade of gloom-and-doom reporting" about problems with military technology was wrong.

Two weeks after the war started, General H. Norman Schwarzkopf, commander in chief of the allied forces, claimed the Patriots shot down every Scud they faced. An early Army report claimed that Patriots destroyed 96 percent of the Scuds the Iraqis fired at Saudi Arabia and Israel. Additional research, particularly by scientists at the Massachusetts Institute of Technology, forced the Army to shift its estimates downward twice. The Army eventually contended that Patriots were 70 percent successful in Saudi Arabia and 40 percent successful in Israel.

Part of the problem in assessing the Patriots' performance occurred because the missile did not actually have to hit a Scud to destroy it. The Patriots contained fuses that ignited when they sensed a Scud within a few yards.

The Army recorded a "probable kill" if the Patriot traveled to a point that computers said was close enough to kill the Scud and if after reaching that point the Patriot stopped communicating with the ground computer. Assessing kills was also difficult because some Scud missiles broke up as they re-entered the atmosphere. Especially when Iraq fired two or more Scuds at once, it was hard to determine whether Patriots hit Scuds or just debris.

The Patriot was first developed in the mid-1960s as an anti-aircraft weapon. Over the years developers modified it to defend against cruise missiles and short-range ballistic missiles as well. As Army officials repeatedly noted, though, the Patriot was not designed to defend large areas against the type of missiles that Iraq fired at Israel and Saudi Arabia.

The Pentagon did not specifically dispute the GAO findings. However, Pentagon spokesman Pete Williams said the report's "nitpicking and handwringing" would be "a little more on target if in fact the Patriot was designed originally as an anti-missile defense. It wasn't."

In a letter to the Washington Post, *the chief of public affairs for the Secretary of the Army strongly suggested that the Army's analysis was better than the GAO's. "The GAO report is the opinion of one auditor, supervised by three others in Atlanta and Washington," wrote Charles W. McClain, Jr. "The Army's assessment is based on a jury of nine officials, averaging almost 20 years of air defense experience, supported by a team of 27 technical experts in software, radar, computer, missile intelligence and weapons research."*

Whatever the Patriot's true success rate in the Persian Gulf, Pentagon officials clearly planned to retain it as a major component of the nation's defense arsenal. They said that lessons learned in the gulf would help them increase the missile's effectiveness.

> *Following is the text of a report entitled "Data Does Not Exist to Conclusively Say How Well Patriot Performed," dated September 22, 1992, and released September 29, 1992, by the General Accounting Office:*

The Honorable John Conyers, Jr.
Chairman
The Honorable Frank Horton
Ranking Minority Member
Legislation and National Security Subcommittee
Committee on Government Operations
House of Representatives

. . . As you requested, we reviewed the available information on the engagements that the Army is highly confident resulted in the destruction or disabling of Scud warheads. Our objective was to determine whether the Army's revised assessment of the Patriot's performance in these engagements is supported by the data.

Background

The Patriot is a surface-to-air guided missile system designed to protect U.S. forces from air strikes. Since the mid-1960s, it has evolved to defend against aircraft, cruise missiles, and, more recently, short-range ballistic missiles. The Patriot system consists of a ground radar, an engagement control station, an antenna, an electric power plant, and typically eight launchers. Each launcher contains four missiles in their individual storage-transportation launch containers.

When Iraq invaded Kuwait in August 1990, the Army deployed the Patriot to Southwest Asia to defend against the Iraqi-modified Scud missile—referred to as the Al-Hussein. The extended range of the Al-Hussein enabled it to travel faster than the Soviet missiles against which the Patriot had been designed to defend. The Al-Hussein travels at speeds of 2,000 to 2,200 meters per second, compared with 1,600 to 1,800 meters per second for the Soviet missile.

Although the Patriot was not originally designed to engage this extended range, high-speed ballistic missile, the Army quickly incorporated changes to provide the Patriot with this capability. In less than 1 week, the Army and the prime contractor, working closely with the intelligence community, identified, assessed, and incorporated software modifications to provide the Patriot the capability to engage the faster missiles. As a result of emergency production orders, the Army was able to supply the improved missiles to all units by the time of the first Scud engagement in January 1991. After the Patriot began to engage Scud missiles, the Army made two additional software modifications. These modifications were intended to (1) increase the altitude at which the Patriot intercepted the Scud and (2) reduce the number of false targets detected by Patriot fire units.

At the time of the Iraqi invasion, there were only three of the more capable Patriot missiles with this antitactical missile capability (PAC-2) in the Army's inventory. By the end of that month, about 600 improved Patriot missiles were in Southwest Asia. This number was substantially more than what was initially planned.

The Patriot missile does not have to hit the enemy warhead in order to destroy it. Each Patriot missile contains a fuze, which senses the presence of a target, and a warhead with (1) metal fragments to destroy or disable the target and (2) an explosive to propel the fragments to the target. When the Patriot missile flies close enough to the target to cause the Patriot's fuze to issue a detonation order, the fragments are propelled at high velocity toward the target. If they impact the target's warhead region at sufficient angle and velocity, the target's warhead will detonate. The Patriot fragments that do not cause the target's warhead to explode can damage the warhead to the extent that it will either not explode or will not explode with full force when it hits the ground or will go off course.

The Army has issued various reports that quantify the Patriot's performance during Operation Desert Storm. According to an early report, the Patriot destroyed about 96 percent of the Scuds engaged in Saudi Arabia and Israel. As more information became known, the Army reduced its assessment to 80 percent successful in Saudi Arabia and 50 percent successful in Israel. Now, as a result of the April 1992 revised assessment, the Army believes the Patriot was 70 percent successful in Saudi Arabia and 40 percent successful in Israel.

The Army used an improved methodology in its revised assessment of the Patriot's performance during Operation Desert Storm. The new methodology allowed the Army to (1) rank the available data according to the assessor's confidence in the data's accuracy; (2) use the ranked data to decide whether a Patriot engagement most likely resulted in a warhead kill, a mission kill, or a miss; and (3) assign a high, medium, or low confidence level to the assessed outcome. The Army assessed, with either low, medium, or high confidence, 52 percent of the Patriot's engagements as warhead kills.

The Army is highly confident that about 25 percent of the Patriot's Operation Desert Storm engagements resulted in warhead kills. According to the Deputy Project Manager, the assignment of a high confidence level to an engagement's outcome did not mean the Army was absolutely confident that the assessed outcome was correct. Rather, given the limited data available for assessment purposes, the Army scorers had higher confidence in the assessed outcome of these engagements than in others.

Results in Brief

The Army did not collect performance data during Operation Desert Storm that would permit an absolute determination of how many of its targets the Patriot killed or failed to kill because it was operating in a war zone rather than on a test range. As a result, the data that would be needed to conclusively demonstrate how well the Patriot performed during Operation Desert Storm does not exist and there is no way to conclusively determine how many targets the Patriot killed or failed to kill.

About 9 percent of the Patriot's Operation Desert Storm engagements are supported by the strongest evidence that an engagement resulted in a warhead kill—engagements during which observable evidence indicates a Scud was destroyed or disabled after a Patriot detonated close to the Scud. For example, the strongest evidence that a warhead kill occurred would be provided by (1) a disabled Scud with Patriot fragments or fragment holes in its guidance and fuzing section or (2) radar data showing evidence of Scud debris in the air following a Patriot detonation. The other 16 percent of the engagements the Army is highly confident resulted in warhead kills are not supported by such evidence. In these cases, however, radar tracking data collected proves that in some cases the Patriots came close to the Scuds, but it does not prove or disprove whether the Patriots came close enough to have a high probability of destroying, disabling, or diverting them.

Assessment Had Data Limitations

According to the Patriot Project Office Chief Engineer, the same types of equipment that are used on the test range would have been required to accurately assess the Patriot's performance during Operation Desert Storm. This equipment would have included high-speed photographic equipment, portable data recorders, and telemetry equipment. Except for data recorders that captured a few engagements in Israel, the Army did not collect such information. . . .

The Army obtained some data that proved helpful in assessing the Patriot's performance. The information collected by the Army included data generated by the Patriot's computers, operator reports, photographs, debris recovery, eyewitness accounts, media coverage, and various ground damage reports. Army scoring officials relied primarily upon computer-generated data and ground damage reports to support a high level of confidence that engagements had resulted in warhead kills. However, the computer data does not prove that the Patriot destroyed Scud warheads, and the ground damage searches were not sufficiently comprehensive to indicate how many warheads the Patriot killed.

Computer Data Could Not Prove
Patriots Destroyed Scud Warheads

During Operation Desert Storm, the Patriot computers generated target information that was sometimes preserved on tape or in hard copy. Although this information is useful in providing information about the target and, to some extent, the Patriot interceptor, it cannot irrefutably prove that the Patriot destroyed or failed to destroy the Scud warhead.

The Army sometimes, but not always, obtained computer-generated data to show the following:

- when the Patriot system detected a target;
- whether the target detected by the system met the speed criteria of the modified Scud, 2,000 to 2,200 meters per second;
- whether the Patriot system, or the system's operator, had determined

that the target would impact an asset being protected by the Patriot
and launched Patriot missiles toward the target (that is "engaged the
target"); and

- whether the Patriot system reported that it had probably killed or
failed to engage the target's warhead.

The Patriot system recorded a probable kill or an engagement failure at
the conclusion of each engagement. It reported a probable kill of its target
if the Patriot missiles traveled to a point in space that the system
computed to be the point of closest approach to the target (the intercept
point) and ceased to communicate with the ground system.

The system reported an engagement failure if the Patriot missile flew to
the intercept point and continued to communicate with the ground system.
When an engagement failed, the Patriot system, after a pre-set time delay,
caused its missile to self-destruct.

Computer-generated data may prove that the Patriot missile came close
to a Scud, but it cannot prove—even if the system reported a probable
kill—that the Scud warhead was destroyed. To have a high probability of
destroying a Scud warhead, the Patriot missile must detonate when it is
within a few meters of the Scud. However, only portable data recorders
provide a rough estimate of the distance between the Patriot and the Scud
(the "miss distance") at the time of the Patriot's detonation and this
information was available for only a few engagements in Israel.

Measuring miss distance is particularly important in determining
whether the Patriot destroyed a Scud warhead. The Chief Engineer said
that Patriot's fuze can sense its target and detonate at up to six times the
required miss distance, resulting in an extremely low or no probability of
kill. However, the system would still record a kill.

Also, a Missile and Space Intelligence Center engineer told us that the
Scud missile exhibited some unusual reentry anomalies that, according to
a Project Office system engineer, could have affected the Patriot's ability
to guide to its target. The Project Office engineer said that when the
anomalies were severe, the Patriot might not have been able to get within
the few meters where it had a high probability of destroying the Scud. Yet,
if the Patriot missile's fuze detected the Scud within the recognizable
distance, it could have detonated, and the system would have recorded a
probable kill.

Computer-generated data also does not provide information on whether
the Patriot's fuze reacted quickly enough to destroy the Scud. A Project
Office engineer told us the closing velocity, or the speed at which the
Patriot and Scud approach one another, helps determine whether the
Patriot's fuze had time to arm and detonate before the Scud passed the
intercept point. He said this information could be determined from
recorded data. However, the project officials did not develop the information because they did not believe it would benefit the assessment process.
The additional data would not have shown that the Patriot detonated

sufficiently close to the Scud to have a high probability of killing it.

In response to this data limitation, the engineer said that extensive computer simulation research was used to define the air and land area that the Patriot could be expected to successfully defend. He said studies showed that the Patriots intercepting Scuds within this zone should have a high probability of fuzing at the appropriate time. However, none of the available data proves or disproves this claim.

Searches for Ground Damage Were Not Comprehensive

The Army relied heavily upon ground damage assessments in determining the high confidence warhead kills. For example, if no ground damage was found after a Scud attack and other evidence indicated that the Patriot had intercepted the Scud, the scorers assumed the Patriot had destroyed the Scud in the air. If a Scud was found with Patriot fragments or fragment holes in its guidance and fuzing section, scorers assumed the Patriot had disabled the Scud. The scorers assumed the Patriot had missed the Scud if there was evidence of a warhead explosion on the ground. However, since all ground damage assessments were not equally comprehensive, the absence of identified ground damage could be a misleading indicator of a warhead kill.

A number of sources reported ground damage during Operation Desert Storm. The Army used the following reports in its revised assessment process to help determine whether the Patriot had destroyed or damaged a Scud warhead: a compendium of ground damage included in messages obtained by the Missile Space and Intelligence Center; investigative teams' reports; a Ballistic Research Laboratory ground damage assessment; and an Israeli Air Force ground damage assessment.

However, according to the Assistant Deputy Project Office Manager, while the Israelis conducted a coordinated, comprehensive ground search effort, the U.S. government did not make any single group responsible for ground damage searches in Saudi Arabia. Therefore, the extent and reliability of ground search efforts in Saudi Arabia—and consequently its reports—were seriously limited.

Message Traffic

Intelligence Center officials informed us that they had little confidence that the reports they had collected contained descriptions of all ground damage that had occurred or that all damage had been accurately portrayed. They said that many of the reports had been based on interviews with Saudi citizens—rather than with trained experts—who had observed or had been present during attacks but had not observed ground damage.

Intelligence Center officials said that the reports were not meant to provide performance data and do not provide conclusive proof that Scud or Patriot damage did or did not occur. They added that one of the agencies that generated ground damage reports from interviews recommended caution in using these messages, stating that they provided preliminary, often unverified, and sometimes contradictory information. The agency also said some messages included what are now known to be erroneous or misleading statements.

Investigative Team Reports

During Operation Desert Storm various individuals had attempted to locate impact points of Scuds or Scud debris. These individuals, whom the Army termed "investigative teams," viewed debris and craters. They tried to determine whether the debris was a part of a Patriot or a Scud and analyzed the size of the craters to determine whether they most likely resulted from a Scud warhead or some other Scud component, such as a fuel tank. However, these individuals did not investigate all engagements, and they did not prepare written reports at the time of the events. Rather, they prepared their reports from memory at the request of the Patriot Project Office months after the actual events occurred.

Ballistic Research Laboratory's Analysis

Our review of the Ballistic Research Laboratory's ground damage assessment revealed serious limitations in the Laboratory's analysis. For example, the assessment contained data on only about one-third of the Saudi engagements, and the data was collected by one engineer days or weeks after the Scud impacts occurred. The assessment also relied heavily upon photographs and interviews with military personnel assigned to the Patriot units. This methodology was necessary because by the time of the engineer's visit to the damage sites, the craters had often been filled and missile debris removed.

Strongest Evidence Exists for Relatively Few Engagements

While the assessment data collected by the Army cannot provide absolute proof that the Patriots killed Scuds, post-intercept observable data provides the strongest evidence that a warhead kill has occurred. For example, strong evidence that a Patriot has destroyed or disabled a Scud would include (1) a ground damage report that a Scud had been recovered with Patriot fragments or fragment holes in its guidance and fuzing section or (2) radar tracking evidence that the Scud has experienced a dramatic slowdown and that debris was present after a Patriot intercept.

Based on our analysis, this type of evidence of a warhead kill exists for about 9 percent of the engagements that the Army believes resulted in warhead kills. For one such engagement, data generated by the Patriot system computer and a unit report provide proof that the Patriot system detected, engaged, and intercepted a Scud, and ground damage reports showed no damage was reported that could be linked to the engagement. However, in this case, the Patriot's computers also provided information about the events that had occurred after intercept. Data shows that after the Patriot detonated, the system no longer saw a target of ballistic missile speed, but rather many small targets moving at much slower speeds. These are the characteristics of debris and stronger evidence for the contention that the Patriot did destroy the Scud.

In another engagement, an operator reported that the Patriot had intercepted and probably killed an incoming Scud. This report alone would be weak evidence of a kill. However, an Army warrant officer actually viewed the Scud on the ground and saw the Patriot's fragment holes in the warhead skin. His statement provides a high level of confidence that the Patriot disabled the Scud.

According to a Project Officer engineer, if the Patriot missile was highly accurate, evidence of the Patriot's success would probably not be preserved. For example, if a Scud was blown into very small pieces, the Patriot system would probably not be able to track the resulting debris, and radar tracking evidence of the Patriot's success would not be recorded. However, since extensive ground searches that would have ensured finding the debris were not conducted for most of the engagements, conclusive evidence is not available to prove or disprove this theory.

Engagements Supported by Lesser Evidence

Lesser evidence exists for the other 16 percent of the engagements that the Army classified as high confidence of a warhead kill. For several of the Army's high confidence warhead kills, for example, the Army used (1) computer-generated data to support its determination that a Scud had been detected, engaged, and intercepted and (2) ground damage reports that showed no ground damage relating to these engagements.

The computer data proves that the Patriot missiles came close to the Scuds, but it does not prove or disprove whether the Patriots came within the few meters necessary to have a high probability of killing the Scuds. Neither does the Army know whether the Patriots' fuzes armed and detonated before the targets passed the intercept points.

In addition, no evidence exists to clarify what happened to the Scuds after the intercept occurred. Radar tracking data does not indicate debris in the air, and since the ground damage reports for these events did not result from a systematic search for ground damage, they do not provide a high level of confidence that all ground damage was reported or that reported damage was accurate.

Scope and Methodology

We discussed the Army's methodology for the revised assessment with Army officials to determine how the Army assigned a high, medium, or low confidence level to the Patriot's Operation Desert Storm engagements that the Army believes resulted in warhead kills. For the Patriot engagements that the Army was highly confident had resulted in warhead kills, we examined documents—such as recorded Patriot computer data and ground damage reports—that the Army had used to make this judgment.

We obtained clarifying information through discussions with officials from the Patriot Project Office, the U.S. Army Missile Command's Research and Development Engineering Center, and the Missile Space and Intelligence Center, all located at Redstone Arsenal, Alabama. We also discussed ground damage information with individuals at the Ballistic Research Laboratory, Aberdeen, Maryland; the Training and Doctrine Command's Patriot System Manager's office, Fort Bliss, Texas; and the Eleventh Brigade, Riyadh, Saudi Arabia.

We conducted our review from April to July 1992 in accordance with generally accepted government auditing standards.

As requested, we did not obtain fully coordinated Department of Defense comments on this report. However, we discussed our findings with the Patriot Project Manager and other officials at the Patriot Project Office. They generally agreed with our findings.

Henry L. Hinton, Jr.
Director, Army Issues

UNITED NATIONS ON YUGOSLAVIA'S MEMBERSHIP

September 22, 1992

The United Nations General Assembly voted September 22 to vacate the seat held by Yugoslavia's truncated successor state. By an overwhelming vote of 127-6 the new Serb-controlled government in Belgrade was punished for fostering Serbian aggression among its neighbors, which too had been part of Yugoslavia before its breakup. Between June 1991 and the following April, four of the former republics in the Yugoslav federation declared their independence, leaving only Serbia and Montenegro to form a new Federal Republic of Yugoslavia, embracing about half the people and two-fifths of the 99,000 square miles of the former nation, the Socialist Federal Republic of Yugoslavia.

The Belgrade government, under both its old name and new, had been the object of a dozen or more UN resolutions decrying the ethnically inspired civil warfare that raged last year in Croatia between Croats and Serbs, and this year in Bosnia-Hercegovina among Serbs, Croats, and Moslems. In May the UN Security Council imposed economic sanctions on Belgrade and in August authorized the use of "all measures necessary" to deliver humanitarian aid to Sarajevo, the capital of Bosnia-Hercegovina under Serbian siege and bombardment. (UN Resolution on Bosnian Relief, p. 765, Senate Staff Report on Yugoslav 'Ethnic Cleansing,' p. 771)

Only once before in forty-seven years of United Nations operations had the General Assembly in effect expelled a member nation. The previous expulsion was in 1974 when South Africa's membership was suspended because of its separatist racial policies. The resolution ousting Yugoslavia did not use the word "expel," in deference to Russia, a historic ally of

Serbia. However, Russia voted with eleven other countries in the Security Council to approve the expulsion resolution and place it before the General Assembly. The Security Council vote drew no negative votes, but China, India, and Zimbabwe abstained from voting. The six votes against the resolution in the General Assembly were cast by Yugoslavia, Tanzania, Zambia, Zimbabwe, Swaziland, and Kenya.

The resolution declared that the new government in Belgrade could not "continue automatically" to hold the old Yugoslav federation's membership in the General Assembly but had to apply anew. There appeared little chance that such an application would be accepted as long as Slobodan Milosevic, president of Serbia, remained the dominant figure in the Serbia-Montenegro union. He had been accused by the United States and other Western governments of being the chief aggressor in the Yugoslav civil war.

Despite opposition from abroad—or possibly because of it—Milosevic retained and even strengthened his political power at home. He and his ultra-nationalist backers triumphed in presidential and parliamentary elections held by the new country December 20. Milosevic was re-elected president of Serbia over Milan Panic, the national prime minister who campaigned as a peace candidate and strongly denounced Milosevic as an instigator of war and economic ruin in Yugoslavia.

Panic, sixty-seven, who emigrated to America in 1956 and made a fortune in pharmaceuticals, returned to his native Serbia in July vowing to seek an end to the fighting. He was offered—and accepted—the prime ministership in what was regarded as an attempt by Milosevic to soften international opposition. When this did not happen, Panic became expendable. The national parliament removed him from office December 29 on a no-confidence vote.

Milosevic and the nation he led had been treated as international pariahs since its formal founding on April 27. American and European Community diplomats—except for a representative from Greece—boycotted the ceremony. China was the only major country to recognize the new government. In contrast, Western governments established diplomatic ties with the breakaway republics of Croatia, Slovenia, and Bosnia-Hercegovina—but not Macedonia. Greece contended that for historic reasons it had the sole right to the name, which is borne by a district in Greece. The Greek objection appeared to reflect a fear of conflicting claims likely to arise over the new state of Macedonia. It is made up mostly of Slavs and Albanians, people who are ethically akin to the natives of Serbia, Bulgaria, and Albania. By the end of 1992 it was frequently asserted that Macedonia was destined to become the next Balkan battleground. Others also predicted trouble in Kosovo, formerly an autonomous province in the Serbian republic. Serbs retained political control of Kosovo though constituting less than 10 percent of its 2 million people, who are mostly Albanian Moslems. The seventh-century Kingdom of Serbia was born in Kosovo, and Serbs still regard it as the cradle of their nation. Milosevic is believed to consider it a sacred duty to rid Kosovo of its Moslems.

Milosevic has repeatedly proclaimed a duty to protect Serbs not only in Serbia but in adjoining territories. He justified Serbia's invasion of Croatia in 1991 and its military involvement in Bosnia-Hercegovina in 1992 on that basis. Some 600,000 Serbs lived in Croatia and about 1.7 million in Bosnia-Hercegovina, forming the biggest collection of Serbs outside of Serbia. Milosevic speaks of a "Greater Serbia" that embraces all Balkan Serbs and conjures up images of Serbia's former glory. It was an independent state from 1830 until 1918, consisting of present-day Serbia and a portion of Bosnia-Hercegovina. The rest of Bosnia and Hercegovina, then separate provinces, were part of the Austro-Hungarian empire, as were Croatia and Slovenia. When that empire was broken up at the end of World War I, the territory that later became Yugoslavia was consolidated as the Kingdom of Serbs, Croats, and Slovenes—with Serbia the strongest partner. Yugoslavia emerged from World War II under Communist control; until his death in 1980, Marshal Tito ruled the country with an iron hand and tried to erase ethnic divisions. But within a decade of his passing the divisions resurfaced with pent-up fury and threatened to spread to other parts of the Balkans.

> *Following is the resolution approved September 22, 1992, by the United Nations General Assembly revoking the membership of the newly founded Federal Republic of Yugoslavia:*

The General Assembly,

Having received the recommendation of the Security Council of 19 September 1992 that the Federal Republic of Yugoslavia (Serbia and Montenegro) should apply for membership in the United Nations and that it shall not participate in the work of the General Assembly,

1. *Considers* that the Federal Republic of Yugoslavia (Serbia and Montenegro) cannot continue automatically the membership of the former Socialist Federal Republic of Yugoslavia in the United Nations; and therefore *decides* that the Federal Republic of Yugoslavia (Serbia and Montenegro) should apply for membership in the United Nations and that it shall not participate in the work of the General Assembly;
2. *Takes note* of the intention of the Security Council to consider the matter again before the end of the main part of the forty-seventh session of the General Assembly.

Recorded Vote on Resolution 47/1:

In favour: Afghanistan, Albania, Algeria, Antigua and Barbuda, Armenia, Argentina, Australia, Austria, Azerbaijan, Bahrain, Bangladesh, Barbados, Belarus, Belgium, Belize, Benin, Bhutan, Bolivia, Bosnia and Herzegovina, Brunei Darussalam, Bulgaria, Burkina Faso, Canada, Cape Verde, Chile, Colombia, Comoros, Congo, Costa Rica, Croatia, Cyprus, Czechoslovakia, Denmark, Djibouti, Ecuador, Egypt, El Salvador, Estonia, Federated States of Micronesia, Fiji, Finland, France, Gabon, Gambia, Germany, Greece, Grenada, Guatemala, Guinea, Guinea-Bissau, Haiti, Honduras, Hungary, Iceland, Indonesia, Iran, Ireland, Israel, Italy, Japan, Jordan, Kazakhstan, Kuwait, Kyrgyzstan, Lao People's Democratic Republic, Latvia, Liberia, Libya, Liechtenstein, Lithuania, Luxembourg, Madagascar, Malawi, Malaysia, Maldives, Mali, Malta, Marshall Islands, Mauritania, Mauritius, Mongolia, Morocco, Nepal, Netherlands, New Zealand, Nicaragua, Niger, Nigeria, Norway, Oman, Pakistan, Panama, Paraguay, Peru, Philippines, Poland, Portugal, Qatar, Republic of Korea, Republic of Moldova, Romania, Russian Federation, Rwanda, Saint Kitts and Nevis, Saint Vincent and the Grenadines, Samoa, San Marino, Saudi Arabia, Senegal, Singapore, Slovenia, Spain, Sudan, Suriname, Sweden, Thailand, Trinidad and Tobago, Tunisia, Turkey, Turkmenistan, Ukraine, United Arab Emirates, United Kingdom, United States, Uruguay, Vanuatu, Yemen.

Against: Kenya, Swaziland, United Republic of Tanzania, Yugoslavia, Zambia, Zimbabwe.

Abstaining: Angola, Bahamas, Botswana, Brazil, Burundi, Cameroon, China, Cote d'Ivoire, Cuba, Ghana, Guyana, India, Iraq, Jamaica, Lebanon, Lesotho, Mexico, Mozambique, Myanmar, Namibia, Papua New Guinea, Sri Lanka, Togo, Uganda, Viet Nam, Zaire.

Absent: Cambodia, Central African Republic, Chad, Democratic People's Republic of Korea, Dominica, Dominican Republic, Ethiopia, Equatorial Guinea, Georgia, Saint Lucia, Sao Tome and Principe, Seychelles, Sierra Leone, Solomon Islands, Somalia, Syria, Tajikistan, Uzbekistan, Venezuela.

PENTAGON REPORT ON TAILHOOK CONVENTION

September 24, 1992

Charges of sexual harassment by drunken aviators at the 1991 Tailhook convention led to the resignations of several senior Navy officials in 1992 and to a series of recommendations to reduce sexual abuse in the military.

The Tailhook Association's annual convention was a boisterous party in Las Vegas for present and past Navy and Marine Corps fliers. Although the association was a private group, it had close ties with the Navy. The Navy spent thousands of dollars flying aviators to the party, and senior Navy officials attended. The relationship continued despite the Navy's knowledge for years that the convention resulted in unruly and illegal behavior. Some Navy squadrons showed pornographic movies or provided prostitutes in their hotel suites. Heavy drinking, mauling of women, and extensive damage to the hotel were common.

At the 1991 convention, a large group of drunken junior officers formed a "gantlet" in a third-floor hotel hallway and sexually assaulted women who tried to pass through. The aviators grabbed the breasts and buttocks of the women, and in some cases tried to rip off their clothes. Half of the twenty-six women assaulted were Navy officers.

After the scandal became public in the fall of 1991, the Navy broke off its official relationship with the Tailhook Association. The Naval Investigative Service and the Navy's inspector general started separate investigations. The agencies refused to cooperate with each other, however; one victim complained that an investigator repeatedly pressured her for a date, and charges soon began to circulate that investigators were trying to protect senior officials from embarrassment. At the request of Navy

Secretary H. Lawrence Garrett III, the Pentagon's inspector general opened his own probe of the two investigations and of what happened at Tailhook.

Garrett was the first senior Navy official forced to resign because of the scandal. In his letter of resignation dated June 26, Garrett said he accepted responsibility "for the leadership failure which allowed the egregious conduct at Tailhook to occur...."

On July 2 J. Daniel Howard, under secretary of the Navy who was then serving as acting secretary, said Tailhook resulted from "a decaying culture" and the "toleration of stone-age attitudes about warriors returning from the sea." He also ordered a day-long "stand-down" so that everyone in the Navy and Marine Corps could receive training about the Navy's sexual harassment rules. The day before Howard made his comments, two senior officers were relieved of command over a party at the Miramar Naval Air Station near San Diego. The party featured a skit about Rep. Patricia Schroeder, D-Colo., and oral sex. Schroeder, a senior member of the House Armed Services Committee, was pushing the Navy to fully investigate Tailhook. The next month, a third officer lost his command over the skit.

On September 24 the Pentagon's inspector general sharply criticized the Navy's Tailhook investigations. The report said that "deficiencies in the investigations" occurred because of "an attempt to limit the exposure of the Navy and senior Navy officials to criticism regarding Tailhook 91." As a result of the report, the Navy forced two admirals who supervised the Tailhook investigations to retire and reassigned a third admiral. Howard, a civilian, was criticized for failing to "ensure that the Navy conducted a comprehensive investigation," but he remained in his job as under secretary. Acting Navy Secretary Sean O'Keefe, who replaced Howard as acting secretary on July 7, also ordered a restructuring of the Navy's investigative agencies and placed the Naval Investigative Service under civilian leadership.

Also in September, the House Armed Services Committee claimed that because the military had tolerated sexual harassment for so long, it could take five years to create an environment in which women did not feel threatened. On the same day the committee issued its report, the Department of Veterans Affairs announced that it would begin offering group therapy to female veterans who were victims of sexual harassment. And in October, the Navy announced creation of a hotline to provide information to victims of sexual harassment (Navy on Prevention of Sexual Harassment, p. 1003).

The Tailhook scandal added to the lengthy and growing debate over the role of women in the military. In 1987 a Pentagon report found widespread discrimination against women in the armed forces (Historic Documents of 1987, p. 671). *On June 2, 1992, the General Accounting Office [GAO] reported that sexual harassment was widespread at the U.S. service academies.* (GAO on Student Treatment at Military Academies,

p. 481) *The next month the* Army Times, *an independent newspaper, reported that at least twenty-four women serving with the U.S. Army were raped or sexually assaulted during Operations Desert Shield and Desert Storm.*

Despite the discrimination and assaults, women continued to press for the right to serve with military combat units. Admiral Frank B. Kelso II, the chief of naval operations, bolstered their case when he admitted that excluding women from combat may have contributed to the Tailhook incident. Nonetheless, most senior military officials remained strongly opposed to allowing women in combat. (Report on Women in Combat, p. 1029)

Following is an excerpt from "Tailhook 91—Part 1, Review of the Navy Investigations," prepared by the inspector general of the Department of Defense and released September 24, 1992:

Tailhook 91
Part I—Review of the Navy Investigations

Background

To provide the context in which the Navy investigations were conducted, the following is a brief discussion of the history of the Tailhook annual conventions and a cursory description of Tailhook 91. Much of this information was contained in media accounts of Tailhook 91 which appeared throughout the fall of 1991 and spring of 1992.

The Tailhook Association is a private organization composed of active duty, Reserve and retired Navy and Marine Corps aviators, Defense contractors, and others. The annual Tailhook Symposium began as a reunion of naval aviators in Tijuana, Mexico, in 1956. It was moved to San Diego in 1958 and then to Las Vegas, Nevada, in 1963 where it was expanded to include a number of professional development activities, such as the Flag Panel at which junior officers are given an opportunity to have a candid exchange of questions and answers with flag officers. Official Navy support for the Tailhook Association, especially for the annual convention, also grew. The majority of the planning for the convention's official functions was generally conducted by the office of the Assistant Chief of Naval Operations (Air Warfare). In addition, the Navy provided free office space for the Tailhook Association at Naval Air Station, Miramar, California, and used the Navy's extensive fleet of passenger aircraft to transport attendees to Las Vegas. In 1974, Senator William Proxmire presented his "Golden Fleece Award" to the Navy for using its aircraft to transport attendees to the Tailhook convention in Las Vegas. In 1991, the

Navy used some 27 C-9 flights to transport approximately 1,600 people to the convention.

It was also well known throughout the naval aviation community that the annual Tailhook convention was the scene of much drinking, general rowdiness and wild parties. The 1985 convention caused Vice Admiral Edward H. Martin, then Deputy Chief of Naval Operations (Air Warfare), to write to the Commander, Naval Air Force, Pacific Fleet, asking that he alert his subordinates to a number of concerns:

> The general decorum and conduct last year was far less than that expected of mature naval officers. Certain observers even described some of the activity in the hotel halls and suites as grossly appalling, "a rambunctious drunken melee." There was virtually no responsibility displayed by anyone in an attempt to restrain those who were getting out of hand. Heavy drinking and other excesses were not only condoned, they were encouraged by some organizations. We can ill afford this type of behavior and indeed must not tolerate it. The Navy, not the individual, his organization or the Tailhook Association, is charged with the events and certainly will be cast in disreputable light. Let's get the word out that each individual will be held accountable for his or her actions and also is responsible to exercise common sense and leadership to ensure that his squadron mates and associates conduct themselves in accordance with norms expected of naval officers. We will not condone institutionalized indiscretions.

In addition, a squadron commander then serving on the Tailhook Board of Directors brought his concerns over Tailhook 85 to the other Directors. In part, he wrote:

> 3 . . . I viewed with disdain the conduct or better put the misconduct of several officers and a lack of command attention which resulted in damage and imprudent action.

> A. The encouragement of drinking contests, the concept of having to drink 15 drinks to win a headband and other related activities produced walking zombies that were viewed by the general public and detracted from the Association/USN integrity.

* * *

> C. Dancing girls performing lurid sexual acts on naval aviators in public would make prime conversation for the media.

Despite the import of Admiral Martin's and the Board member's observations regarding the events at Tailhook 85, the activities that were of concern six years earlier continued to occur. After 1985, it became routine practice for the President of the Tailhook Association to write to squadron commanders prior to each convention exhorting them to ensure that conduct in the hospitality suites comported with standards of decency. Captain (CAPT) Frederic G. Ludwig, Jr., President of the Tailhook Association at the time of Tailhook 91, sent such a letter on August 15, 1991 (Enclosure 2). Especially significant is the paragraph warning against "late night gang mentality."

Estimates of total attendance at the 1991 convention range around 5,000 although official registration was approximately 2,000. The large difference in those numbers results from the fact that a substantial portion of the military personnel in attendance, plus civilians, came for the parties alone and did not register for the official functions that were part of the convention.

The parties centered around 26 hospitality suites on the third floor of the hotel. The suites were sponsored by individual Navy and Marine Corps aviation squadrons, combinations of squadrons and other Navy and Marine Corps organizations.

It is difficult to describe the atmosphere in and around the third floor hospitality suites without a full and complete description of the activities that took place there, which will be provided in our second report. However, investigative activity to date has confirmed more than isolated instances of men exposing themselves, women baring their breasts, shaving of women's legs and pubic areas, and women drinking from dildos that dispensed alcoholic beverages.

In addition, the Navy investigations confirmed the existence of a "gauntlet." The gauntlet was a loosely formed group of men who lined the corridor outside the hospitality suites, generally in the later hours of each of the three nights of the convention, and "touched" women who passed down the corridor. The "touching" ranged from consensual pats on the breasts and buttocks to violent grabbing, groping and other clearly assaultive behavior.

During the gauntlet on Saturday night, September 7, 1991, at approximately 11:30 p.m., a Navy helicopter pilot, Lieutenant (LT) Paula Coughlin, was assaulted. Then assigned as aide to Rear Admiral (RADM) John Snyder, the Commander, Naval Air Test Center (who had been president of the Tailhook Association from 1985 to 1987), she first complained to him of the assault during a telephone conversation on the following Sunday morning.

Some weeks later, dismayed by RADM Snyder's lack of action, LT Coughlin wrote to Vice Admiral Richard M. Dunleavy, the Assistant Chief of Naval Operations (Air Warfare), and reported the matter to him. Admiral Dunleavy immediately notified his superior, Admiral (ADM) Jerome Johnson, the Vice Chief of Naval Operations (VCNO). On reading LT Coughlin's letter, ADM Johnson recognized that the reported assault required immediate investigation. Accordingly, he summoned the Commander, Naval Investigative Service, and instructed him to open an investigation.

A final predicate to the discussion of the Navy investigations into Tailhook is an understanding that the senior officials who managed the investigations were well aware that the Secretary of the Navy, the Chief of Naval Operations, plus a large number of active duty and Reserve flag officers were in attendance at Tailhook 91 and that many of those individuals had attended previous Tailhook conventions.

The Commander of the NIS and the Naval IG Initiate
Investigations

The NIS opened a criminal investigation at the direction of the VCNO on October 11, 1991. On the same date, CAPT Ludwig wrote a letter (Enclosure 3) to the members of the Tailhook Association, commenting on the 1991 convention. In part, CAPT. Ludwig chastised the members:

> Let me relate just a few specifics to show how far across the line of responsible behavior we went.
>
> This year our total damage bill was to the tune of $23,000 ... We narrowly avoided a disaster when a "pressed ham" pushed out an eighth floor window ... Finally, and definitely the most serious, was "the Gauntlet" on the third floor. I have five separate reports of young ladies, several of whom had nothing to do with Tailhook, who were verbally abused, had drinks thrown on them, were physically abused and were sexually molested. Most distressing was the fact an underage young lady was severely intoxicated and had her clothing removed by members of the Gauntlet.

On seeing a copy of the letter, the Secretary of the Navy wrote to CAPT Ludwig on October 29, 1991, stating that he viewed Tailhook 91 as "a gross example of exactly what cannot be permitted by the civilian or uniformed leadership in the Navy, at any level." Accordingly, he notified CAPT Ludwig that he was immediately terminating all Navy support to the Association (Enclosure 4).

At the same time, by memorandum dated October 29, 1991 (Enclosure 5), the Secretary instructed his immediate subordinate, the Under Secretary of the Navy, Mr. Dan Howard, to direct that the Naval IG, Rear Admiral George W. Davis, VI, initiate an inquiry into any noncriminal abuses or violations of law or regulation associated with the Tailhook Association, or Tailhook 91. The Under Secretary, in turn, issued a memorandum to the Naval IG directing him to inquire into the organization and support of the Tailhook Association as well as the conduct of Tailhook 91, specifically, the use of naval resources; the nature, extent and propriety of the relationship between the Tailhook Association and the Navy; the professional climate of the symposium, including adherence to policies concerning alcohol consumption and sexual abuse; and other administrative or regulatory abuses or violations (Enclosure 6).

The Under Secretary modified his written tasking with oral direction to the IG to limit his inquiry to the details of the Navy "business relationship" with the Tailhook Association. Based on that direction, the Naval IG focused his initial efforts on determining the nature and extent of the Navy use of military aircraft to fly its personnel to Las Vegas, identifying the facts and circumstances surrounding the Association's occupancy of a building on the Miramar Naval Air Station in California, and obtaining information regarding prior Tailhook conventions.

The Naval IG told us that, about three weeks after that discussion with the Under Secretary, he recognized the Navy needed to do an "all-up investigation" of the Tailhook matter. He stated that he recommended to the Under Secretary that he (the Naval IG) form a large team to examine comprehensively three areas of concern to him: first, whether the Navy had a cultural problem that contributed to the assaults at Tailhook; second, whether the chain of command took appropriate action when notified of assaults by Navy victims; and third, whether there were noncriminal violations arising from Tailhook 91 that should be referred to the chain of command.

The Naval IG told us that in response to his recommendation for a comprehensive investigation, the Under Secretary told him that the Naval IG did not have the resources to conduct an investigation of that nature. The Under Secretary advised the Naval IG to let the NIS take the lead and conduct all interviews, which the Naval IG could then review, performing whatever follow-up was necessary. According to the Naval IG, he told the Under Secretary that if that was to be the procedure, the Under Secretary should task the NIS specifically with investigating the misconduct issues, because that was not an area NIS normally investigated. The tasking was never given. The Under Secretary told us he does not remember such a conversation with the Naval IG.

The Secretary of the Navy delegated to the Under Secretary the responsibility to oversee the conduct of the investigations. The Secretary of the Navy was briefed on the investigations' status in December 1991 but took no active role in the investigations until April 28, 1992.

At the outset of the investigations, the Under Secretary received separate briefings on the progress of the investigations from the Commander, NIS, and the Naval IG during the routine weekly meetings he held with each of them. However, within a few weeks the Under Secretary elected to combine the separate NIS and Naval IG briefings into a single weekly meeting to discuss the progress of the investigations.

In addition to the Under Secretary, the Naval IG, and the Commander, NIS, the weekly meeting was generally attended by the Judge Advocate General, Rear Admiral John E. Gordon, and the Assistant Secretary of the Navy (Manpower and Reserve Affairs), Ms. Barbara S. Pope.

Members of those senior officials' staffs also attended the weekly meetings from time to time as did Commander (CDR) Peter Fagan, Special Assistant to the Secretary of the Navy for Legal and Legislative Affairs. The significance of CDR Fagan's attendance will be discussed later in the report. The meetings continued more or less weekly from November 1991 until the reports were released at the end of April 1992.

The NIS Investigation

The NIS investigation was assigned to the Assistant Special Agent in Charge of the NIS Office at LT Coughlin's duty station, Patuxent River, Maryland. As the number of identified victims increased, a second agent was assigned to the case and the two agents relocated their activities to the NIS Regional Office in Arlington, Virginia.

The NIS interviewed some 2,100 witnesses during its investigation. The vast majority of the witnesses were interviewed by NIS agents worldwide responding to lead sheets the case agents had sent to their offices. The lead sheets provided a summary of the investigation and identified specific topics to be explored.

Despite the fact that the lead sheets were written to elicit only assault-related information, some NIS agents reported unsolicited information regarding other improprieties and possible crimes at Tailhook 91. The NIS managers failed to respond to that information, including indications of other violations of the Uniform Code of Military Justice such as Indecent Exposure (Article 134) and Conduct Unbecoming an Officer (Article 133). The managers neither expanded their investigation to encompass those reports nor did they ensure that the NIS forwarded the information to the Naval IG in a timely manner.

We found that with respect to the allegations of criminal assault, the NIS investigation was generally satisfactory. However, given the significance of the investigation and its potential impact on the Navy, the Commander, NIS, should have designated a larger full-time team of agents to the case to ensure that all aspects of Tailhook 91 were thoroughly and aggressively pursued.

With respect to reports that some officers refused to be interviewed or to have their photographs taken, we found that those instances were remedied fairly early. With respect to the "conspiracy of silence" engaged in by some of the officers NIS interviewed, we note that that problem is difficult to remedy without violating the prohibition against unlawful command influence. One effective remedy that the Commander, NIS, failed to consider in even a single instance is the grant of immunity in exchange for full and truthful testimony.

From the outset, the Tailhook investigation commanded the personal attention and involvement of the Commander, NIS, and his senior staff. The Commander's personal involvement in the matter included participation in basic investigative decisions such as the selection of photographs to be used for identification purposes. In addition, he closely monitored the progress of the case, going so far as to telephone the case agent several times while she was interviewing LT Coughlin and to have the agents bring the report to him on a Friday night so that he could read it immediately. Subordinate NIS managers were also unusually involved in the investigation and two members of the NIS headquarters staff were assigned to monitor the case agent's work.

We found two weaknesses in the investigation. First, as in the Naval IG investigation discussed later, senior officers who were present at Tailhook 91 were not interviewed. From an investigative standpoint, we believe that those officers should have been interviewed to determine what criminal activity or misconduct, if any, they witnessed or engaged in during Tailhook 91, or learned about subsequent to Tailhook 91. The NIS began its investigation with the group of people reportedly closest to the scene of the assault, i.e., the junior officers. Although NIS agents did not develop any leads suggesting that senior officers were involved in or had knowledge of the assaults, it does not appear from the interview sheets that that was information they were attempting to develop and, thus, the absence of such information is rather predictable. We believe thoroughness demanded the senior officers present be interviewed.

The other weakness is that, as evidence of nonassaultive criminal activity (such as indecent exposure or conduct unbecoming an officer) developed, the NIS investigative scope was not expanded to encompass it. The failure to expand the scope of the investigation or to ensure that the information was quickly passed to others (such as the Naval IG) meant that important information was not pursued.

The investigative findings were presented in the established NIS reporting format. That format provided for the use of "interim reports" that were composed of brief summary information accompanied by Investigative Actions (IA). The IAs covered completed investigative leads to include such things as witness interviews and record reviews. In addition to the interim reports, the case agents composed Prosecutive Summaries that outlined evidence in support of charges recommended against individual suspects. In this case, prosecutive recommendations were made with respect to four individuals. Information that was not contained in the Prosecutive Summaries or was received after its issuance was collected and eventually issued in a Supplemental Report.

Our review determined that, although NIS followed its standard format, the sheer volume of documents generated in this investigation—well over 2,000 pages—did not lend itself to that format. The format does not provide the reader with a comprehensive summary or a method of reviewing the data in a reasonable fashion. It is virtually impossible to determine whether specific interview information is contained in the report without a detailed and time-consuming review. Those deficiencies contributed to the omission from the NIS report of a critical report of interview involving the presence of the Secretary of the Navy in one of the suites. The omission is discussed later in this report.

The Naval IG Investigation

The Naval IG established a team of six staff members to conduct his investigation of Tailhook 91. The Naval IG viewed the Tailhook investigation as a collateral duty for the team members. For example, two team members were diverted to four routine inspections, each consuming about two weeks to conduct and report. Other team members similarly were sidetracked to other tasks during the Tailhook inquiry. We believe the Naval IG team was inadequately staffed to conduct an investigation of the magnitude required by the scope of events at Tailhook 91.

The Naval IG team produced two reports, one dealing with the Navy relationship with the Tailhook Association, the other dealing with the personal conduct that occurred at Tailhook 91.

In his report on the Navy relationship with the Tailhook Association, the Naval IG provided summary information on the history of the relationship, the recurring misuse of Navy aircraft to transport attendees to Las Vegas for convention activities, and the atmosphere in the hospitality suites. The Naval IG made several sound observations. In particular, we believe the Naval IG was correct in stating:

> A common thread running through the overwhelming majority of [NIS] interviews concerning Tailhook 91, was—"what's the big deal?"
> Those interviewed [by the NIS] had no understanding that the activities in the suites fostered an atmosphere of sexual harassment, and that actions which occurred in the corridor constituted at minimum sexual assault and in many cases criminal sexual assault. That atmosphere condoned, if not encouraged, the gang mentality which eventually led to the sexual assaults.

Similarly, we believe the Naval IG report regarding personal conduct at Tailhook 91 contains a good description of the general activities that occurred there and the environment in which they took place. Again, we found that the Naval IG identified a major problem when he stated:

> The activities which took place in the corridor and the suites, if not tacitly approved, were allowed to continue by the leadership of the aviation community and the Tailhook Association. Further, the conduct in the corridor was merely reflective of the atmosphere that was created by the activities in a number of the suites.

The major flaw in the Naval IG investigation is that, with very few exceptions, he failed to interview senior officials who attended Tailhook 91 and failed to assign any individual responsibility for the misconduct that occurred there. The Naval IG told us that he believed to do so would be perceived as a "witch hunt" that would detract from fixing the cultural problem identified in the reports. He stated he believed that would hurt the Navy rather than help it.

In a very telling comment, the Naval IG told us:

> ... once we determined we had a cultural problem, then it was our contention in that group around the table, the Under and all these people, that the corporate "we" had allowed this to take place. And to interview squadron [commanding officers], to ask them why they allowed that to happen didn't make any difference because the whole system allowed it to happen. And frankly, I think a Navy captain who had seen that over four or five years, had seen the Rhino room with a dildo hanging on the wall, is not going to walk in there in 1991 and change anything.

While it is easy to be sympathetic to the attitude—that the Navy had allowed that kind of activity to go on for so many years the attendees had become enculturated to it, could not be expected to change it, and therefore should not be held responsible for it—it must ultimately be rejected. For what the Naval IG failed to understand is that the time for attributing misconduct of that nature to a "cultural problem" had long since passed. At least a year prior to Tailhook 91, the Navy established a "zero tolerance" policy with respect to sexual harassment and sexual misconduct. For a cogent explanation of why it was critical to consider the responsibility of senior leaders for the misconduct that occurred at Tailhook 91, one need only read the memorandum written by the Secretary of the Navy to the CNO and the Commandant of the Marine Corps on June 2, 1992 (Enclosure 7). Unfortunately, the Secretary's initiative to consider personal accountability came too late and should have been addressed by the management team at the outset of the Navy investigations.

Conclusions

1. Although the Navy investigations into Tailhook 91 were generally satisfactory regarding the criminal assaults, the scope of the investigations was not broadened to encompass other violations of the law and regulation as they became apparent. Further, the investigations did not pursue issues of individual accountability for the leadership failure that created an atmosphere in which the assaults and other misconduct took place. The inadequacies in the investigations were due to the collective management failures and personal failures on the part of the Under Secretary, the Naval IG, the Navy JAG and the Commander of the NIS.

2. Because the Secretary of the Navy, the CNO, and more than 30 active duty flag officers were present at Tailhook 91, those managing the Navy investigations believed that the Navy as an institution could be vulnerable to considerable criticism. The principals in the Navy investigations erred when they allowed their concern for the Navy as an institution to obscure the need to determine accountability for the misconduct and the failure of leadership that had occurred. In our view, the deficiencies in the investigations were the result of an attempt to limit the exposure of the Navy and senior Navy officials to criticism regarding Tailhook 91.

3. It is inherently difficult for any organization to investigate allegations against the senior leaders of that organization. To address this difficulty, an existing Department of Defense directive requires that Military Departments and other Defense components notify the Inspector General, Department of Defense, on receipt of allegations against senior officials. In this case, the Naval Inspector General did not notify this office that senior Navy officials were involved or implicated in Tailhook 91.

4. The release of the Navy reports, contrary to the Secretary's instruction, set off a chain of events that made it impossible for the Navy to correct the weaknesses in their reports in terms of identifying individuals who may have engaged in misconduct or failed to provide appropriate leadership. Those shortcomings were recognized by the Secretary of the Navy and the ASN (M&RA) at the briefing on April 28, 1992.

5. The omission from the "final" NIS report of a report of interview stating that the Secretary of the Navy came by the Rhino suite

resulted from a decision by a NIS agent that the report of interview was irrelevant or redundant with respect to its prosecutive value relating to the assaults. Senior NIS officials showed poor judgment, if not professional incompetence, in viewing the witness statement as relevant only to the criminal case.

6. We considered whether organizational problems affected the Navy's handling of the Tailhook investigations. We considered a number of unique aspects of the Navy investigative structures, as well as whether the Navy's performance in the matter might be symptomatic of dysfunctional arrangements in other elements of the Department of Defense. We concluded that no particular organizational changes would have prevented the outcome in this instance or would preclude similar results in the future. Nevertheless, certain aspects of the Navy's investigative process—such as the lack of cooperation between the NIS and the Naval IG—could benefit from organizational changes or procedural modifications.

Recommendations

1. Consider whether the Under Secretary, the Judge Advocate General, the Naval Inspector General, and the Commander of the Naval Investigative Service should continue in their current leadership roles within the Department of the Navy.

2. Consider appropriate disciplinary action with respect to the Judge Advocate General and the Commander of the Naval Investigative Service for their failure to fulfill their professional responsibilities in the Navy's Tailhook investigation.

3. Consider whether any organizational changes or procedural modifications would improve the investigative process within the Department of the Navy and coordinate any changes with the Office of Inspector General, Department of Defense.

MAGIC JOHNSON'S RESIGNATION FROM AIDS COMMISSION

September 24, 1992

Only ten months after President George Bush appointed him to the National Commission on AIDS, basketball superstar Earvin "Magic" Johnson on September 24 charged that Bush had "dropped the ball" in battling the disease and resigned from the commission.

Johnson's frustration with what he perceived to be the administration's inattention to AIDS (acquired immune deficiency syndrome) had been growing for months. Two months before he resigned, Johnson told CNN he "probably" would quit soon because "every time we ask for meaningful funding or adequate funding we get shot down by the president."

Bush appointed Johnson to the fifteen-member, bipartisan commission in November 1991, only days after Johnson's stunning announcement that he had tested positive for the human immunodeficiency virus (HIV) that causes AIDS (Magic Johnson on His Retirement from Basketball, Historic Documents of 1991, p. 747). *The appointment of Johnson, one of the most admired sports stars in the world, greatly increased the commission's profile. However, Johnson and other commission members charged that the Bush administration ignored the panel's recommendations for fighting the disease. "AIDS is a crisis of monumental proportions," Johnson wrote to Bush, "and it cannot be fought with lip service and photo opportunities."*

White House spokeswoman Judy Smith said that the administration had made "a substantial investment" in fighting AIDS. She said proposed federal spending on AIDS in 1993 totaled nearly $5 billion, a 170 percent increase over funding in 1988.

Other commission members disputed the $5 billion figure. David E.

Rogers, who was appointed by Bush and served as vice chairman of the panel, called the figure "campaign rhetoric." Much of the money, he said, actually went toward Medicaid and other entitlements to help "sick, penniless people" with AIDS.

Rogers told the Washington Post *that the commission had been "categorically" disappointed with Bush's response to the disease. He said the administration deserved a grade of "B" for its efforts to expand research funding and a "D" for prevention and education programs. The commission, whose members were appointed by the president and Congress, had urged Bush to create a Cabinet-level agency on AIDS, provide additional help to people sick and dying from AIDS, and stop blocking people with HIV from traveling or immigrating to the United States.*

Bush responded to Johnson's resignation by criticizing him for allegedly attending only one meeting of the commission. The charge gained prominence when Bush repeated it during one of the fall presidential debates. However, the charge turned out to be untrue, and it was subsequently learned that Johnson had attended more commission meetings than some high-ranking members of the Bush administration who served on the panel.

Johnson was the only member of the commission who was infected with the HIV virus. To replace him, Bush appointed Mary D. Fisher, a 44-year-old Florida artist and mother of two who contracted the HIV virus from her former husband. Fisher gave an impassioned speech about AIDS at the Republican National Convention in August 1992 (Convention Speeches by Women Infected with HIV, p. 709).

On September 30, less than a week after resigning from the commission, Johnson announced that he would resume playing professional basketball with the Los Angeles Lakers. In November 1991, when Johnson announced he was HIV-positive, he immediately retired on his doctors' advice. They had feared that the strenuous nature of professional basketball could weaken Johnson and speed his death from AIDS. Johnson just could not stay away from the game, though. "Everybody knows that that [basketball] court is where I belong, no matter what happens," Johnson said at a press conference. During his retirement, he scored a spectacular twenty-five points in the NBA All-Star Game, and also played with the USA's "Dream Team" that won the gold medal at the summer Olympics.

AIDS activists, basketball officials, and doctors praised Johnson's decision to resume playing. Dr. Alfred Saah, an epidemiologist at the Johns Hopkins University School of Public Health, told the Washington Post *that large-scale medical studies had not yet found any factors such as physical activity that either accelerated or retarded the onset of AIDS. Saah said there was little risk to other players even if Johnson was cut during a game and bled on them. "No risk is zero in life," he said, "but there's a much greater risk of being struck and killed by lightning than of contracting AIDS at a sporting event."*

Johnson stunned the basketball world once again November 2, when he suddenly retired from the Lakers for a second time after playing in five preseason games. Johnson said he decided to retire for good because some of his peers were concerned about playing with him. "It has become obvious that the various controversies surrounding my return are taking away from both basketball as a sport and the larger issue of living with HIV for me and the many people affected," he said in a statement.

Following is the text of a letter that Earvin "Magic" Johnson sent to President George Bush September 24, 1992, resigning from the National Commission on AIDS:

Dear Mr. President:

I am writing to advise you of the decision which I have made regarding serving on the National Commission on AIDS.

I am grateful to have had the opportunity to serve on the commission because it has given me the chance to learn so much about AIDS and what must be done to fight it. My fellow commissioners are a wonderful group of caring and dedicated people who have worked hard and effectively to develop a bipartisan consensus and plan of action this country should follow in the fight against AIDS.

As I think you know, along with all of my fellow commission members I have been increasingly frustrated by the lack of support, and even the opposition, of your Administration to our recommendations—recommendations which have an urgent priority and for which there is a broad consensus in the medical and AIDS communities.

Your kind words to me aside, your Administration has not done what it could and should to address a situation which, day by day, poses an increasing danger to the well being of millions of Americans, and which threatens to cast an even wider pall across our nation. AIDS is a crisis of monumental proportions, and it cannot be fought with lip service and photo opportunities.

I cannot in good conscience continue to serve on a commission whose important work is so utterly ignored by your Administration.

Mr. President, when we met in January I gave you a letter in which I expressed my hope that you would become more actively involved in the fight against AIDS. No matter how good the team may be, I said, it won't win the championship without the owner fully in the game. I am disappointed that you have dropped the ball, and that your Administration is not doing everything that it must to fight this disease.

I am sorry to have to write this letter, but I am afraid that there is little that will be accomplished in the next four months. Accordingly, I have regretfully decided to resign your appointment to the National Commission on AIDS.

Sincerely,
Earvin Johnson, Jr.

October

REPORT ON ABUSES OF INDIGENOUS PEOPLE IN THE AMERICAS

October 6, 1992

Six days before the holiday marking the 500th anniversary of Christopher Columbus's voyage to the New World, Amnesty International October 6 released a report accusing governments in the Americas of flagrant human rights violations against indigenous people. In its 112-page report, the international human rights group said it "considers that 1992, the 500th anniversary of the arrival of Europeans in the Americas, is an appropriate time to focus special attention on human rights issues affecting indigenous peoples.... [I]t has therefore initiated a special program of activities ... to highlight the human rights violations—including extrajudicial executions, 'disappearances,' arbitrary arrests, torture and ill-treatment, unfair trials of political prisoners and the judicial death penalty—suffered by indigenous peoples in the Americas."

Legacy of Columbus Reassessed

Amnesty International's report reflected a widespread reassessment about the explorer and the impact of bringing European civilization to the New World. According to many observers, the legend of Columbus had been weakened by skepticism, multiculturalism, and environmentalism. Beginning in the 1970s, what really happened in 1492 has been the subject of an emotional debate among racial and ethnic groups, scholars, religious organizations, politicians, and environmentalists. Was Columbus the Great Discoverer, as schoolchildren had been taught for decades? Or was he a product of fifteenth century European greed and arrogance? "With Columbus, revisionism has carried the day," said Gilbert Sewall, director of the American Textbook Council, a New York organization that reviewed educational curricula. "Columbus has undergone what is perhaps the most dramatic reworking of any major historical figure in memory."

Skeptics of the "Columbus myth" contended that the Genoese did not so much "discover" the Americas as invade them. Moreover, he was only one in a series of many foreigners to do so. Various historians argue that not only did Columbus not discover a "new" world, but that he might well have been preceded by the Vikings, Africans, Irish, English, Welsh, and Chinese. Historians and others noted that by Columbus's own accounts, native Americans welcomed the Spaniards and openly shared the crops, gold, and other riches of the land with them. In return, however, Columbus is said to have enslaved them, killed those who resisted, and shipped many back to Spain.

In a book entitled Conquest of Paradise: Christopher Columbus and the Columbia Legacy, *author Kirkpatrick Sales contended that Columbus's voyage "may fairly be called the most important journey in the history of the human species: The journey that began the long process by which a single culture came to dominate as never before all the other cultures in the world. . . ." In an interview with the* Washington Post, *Sales said he viewed Columbus as a man of "rootlessness and melancholia . . . on a desperate search for salvation, with a lust for treasure . . . [and] a habit of violence," who viewed nature as a "place for exploitation for the enrichment of humans." "There's a sense of wanting to reclaim historicity. That yearning is occurring particularly by forgotten people . . . like Native Americans, like Hispanics" said Raul Yzaguirre, a Mexican American who was chairman of the National Hispanic Quincentennial Commission. Yzaguirre noted that a culture and governments were present in the Americas long before Columbus arrived. Others, however, observed that many native cultures also engaged in brutal activities, such as cannibalism and human sacrifice.*

The skeptical views about Columbus and his accomplishments were not totally pervasive, however. Shortly before the October 12 holiday, an Associated Press poll found that 64 percent of those surveyed said they viewed Columbus as a hero, compared with 15 percent who saw him as a villain. Nine percent felt he was both.

A number of Italian Americans took issue with those who characterized Columbus in negative terms. "Yes, he was involved in the enslaving of the native population and certain brutal acts," said Philip R. Piccigallo, executive director of the Order Sons of Italy in America. "But that was the norm, not the anomaly, of the 15th century world."

In a Columbus Day proclamation issued early in October, President Bush said Columbus was "one man who dared to defy the pessimists and naysayers of his day." The voyage "provides us the timeless lessons about faith and courage . . . and about the rewards of cultural and commercial exchange among nations."

Another defender of Columbus, former Treasury Secretary William E. Simon, said in a Columbus Day speech, that "the arrival of this glorious anniversary in the greatest democracy in the history of the world finds Columbus under siege and America divided." Countering revisionists who viewed Columbus as "a kind of seagoing Genghis Khan," Simon said, "Columbus was above all a man of deep faith. . . . He changed the fate of the whole world forever. And he changed it for the better."

William McNeill, a historian, questioned the influence of the explorer on the United States. "It is rather strange that the figure of Columbus should be so important to us. He . . . never actually set eyes on any part of the continental United States," McNeill said.

Changing Nature of Columbus Day

Originally expected to involve festivities throughout the hemisphere, the quincentennial of Columbus's landing was beset with problems. If they were held at all, celebrations and parades throughout the United States were generally low-key.

The national celebration planned by the Quincentenary Jubilee Commission was discredited when its chairman resigned in the face of charges that he received kickbacks from awarding contracts to his friends. Congressional investigations also brought to light disputes over licensing rights; as a result, a number of companies that had paid for licenses to produce souvenirs never manufactured them.

Plans for a Bob Hope Columbus Day television special were abandoned. The Spanish government cut short a scheduled tour of U.S. ports by replicas of the original Nina, Pinta, and Santa Maria because the venture lacked sponsors. An extravagant movie—"Christopher Columbus: The Discoverer"—released during the summer of 1992, was panned by numerous film critics and was a box office disaster. Even the lavish exhibit, "Circa 1492," at the National Gallery of Art in Washington, D.C., hardly mentioned Columbus and left town nine months before the anniversary.

Organizers of a Columbus Day Parade in Denver, scheduled to take place October 10, canceled the event after American Indians and their supporters warned they would disrupt the festivity. "We cannot countenance a parade dedicated to a despot, a man who didn't know where he was going, didn't know where he was when he got there, and didn't know where he had been when he got back to Spain," said Russell Means, executive director of the American Indian Movement of Colorado.

Alternatives to traditional Columbus Day events were planned in New York, Chicago, and other cities. In Columbus, Ohio—the largest city in the world named after the explorer—American Indians planned a memorial service in downtown Bicentennial Park. One of the biggest Columbus Day fiascos occurred in the Dominican Republic, the country many considered to be Columbus's first landing place in the "new world." Construction of a massive ten-story lighthouse by President Joaquin Balaguer as a memorial to the explorer sparked intense criticism over its cost—estimated at $70 million—borne by a nation whose annual per *capita income was $700. Thousands of Dominicans were evicted to make way for the memorial, which was the target of numerous large demonstrations by those who felt it was an insult to the memory of the Indian and black populations. The Balaguer government had counted on the celebration as a source of tourism revenue. However, the king and queen of Spain and all except one Latin American head of state declined to attend the ceremonies. The day before the celebration, Balaguer's sister and confidante died of a heart attack just after visiting the lighthouse. As a result, the president canceled his own appearance, and only a few hundred spectators—instead of the expected thousands—showed up at the dedication of the monument. The laser and fireworks shows planned to culminate the event also were canceled.*

Even Pope John Paul II, who was visiting the Dominican Republic, declined to celebrate Columbus Day mass at the controversial lighthouse. Although praising the evangelization of the Americas that resulted from Columbus's voyages, the pope acknowledged that abuses had occurred during the conquest. The Vatican also announced that the pontiff would meet October 13 with a delegation of Indians and blacks from around Latin America.

> *Following are excerpts from the report,* The Americas: Human Rights Violations Against Indigenous Peoples, *released October 6, 1992, by Amnesty International:*

Throughout history groups have dominated and colonized others, often at great cost to the subjugated culture. The region now called the Americas has been no exception. Before the arrival of Europeans, vast areas of the Americas were ruled by Indian empires, such as the Aztecas and the Toltecs, whose subjects risked enslavement and execution. Since colonization, indigenous peoples in the Americas have suffered gross and widespread human rights violations, including extrajudicial executions. Combined with the ravages of disease and starvation, these abuses have decimated and, in some cases, eliminated indigenous populations in the Americas. There is no longer an indigenous community on Hispaniola, the island where Columbus landed during his first visit to the "New World" and where many of the official ceremonies will be held in October 1992 to mark the quincentenary of his arrival in the Americas.

Mass killings of indigenous peoples may have reduced in scale over the past 500 years, but they have never stopped. Scholars agree that Indians were a particular target when the army broke the peasant revolt in El Salvador in 1932. Some 30,000 people are believed to have been killed, many of them indigenous. The great majority of the Indians who survived abandoned their communities and traditional dress to avoid summary execution, and from then on no longer spoke indigenous languages in public. The counter-insurgency tactics the Guatemalan army pursued to crush the armed opposition in the late 1970s and early 1980s claimed tens of thousands of non-combatant Indian peasants among its victims. Many of those who fled sought anonymity in the cities, abandoning the traditional clothing that would have identified them not only as indigenous, but also as natives of areas considered "subversive" by the authorities.

Throughout the Americas members of national security forces, either in uniform or in the guise of "death squads," and their civilian auxiliaries continue to be responsible for gross and widespread human rights violations against indigenous peoples. They are not the sole perpetrators. In several countries in the region private agents—hired gunmen, civilian vigilantes, armed groups of settlers, drug traffickers—are responsible for persistent abuses such as the abduction and murder of Indians. These otherwise common crimes become human rights violations when they are committed with official collusion or acquiescence, for example, when the state consistently fails to investigate them or to bring those responsible to justice. In countries racked by civil conflict members of armed opposition groups have also attacked indigenous people, often when they refused to take sides in the armed conflict between opposition groups and the government. Some of the most vulnerable indigenous groups are also the most isolated.

The circumstances in which indigenous peoples fall victim to human rights violations vary widely across the Americas. In Mexico and Ecuador, Indians involved in bitter struggles for land have been routinely arrested and tortured, and some have been extrajudicially executed. Native Americans in the USA await judicial execution in the horror of death row. In some countries Indians are living in a state of siege. The indigenous communities of Peru, caught in a decade of conflict between government forces and armed opposition groups, have suffered abduction, torture and killing on a mass scale.

Activists for indigenous rights throughout the Americas have paid for their commitment with their lives and liberty. Indigenous peoples have been victimized because they spoke out against the abuses suffered by their communities, or because they were active in groups protesting against those abuses. Others have been singled out because of their involvement in trade union or political organizations.

Sometimes abuses result from government actions directed at people of particular ethnic origin. In parts of the Americas, discrimination has forced indigenous peoples to the margins of society. In many contexts envangelization or assimilation has weakened their cultural identity. Indigenous peoples are often economically disadvantaged and marginalized from the societies in which they live by geographical, cultural and linguistic factors. Discrimination often renders them more vulnerable to abuse than other sectors of society. They may be more likely to be prosecuted or convicted for certain offenses than people from other racial groups and may have limited or no access to adequate legal representation. In some countries, they are apparently also more likely to suffer harsher penalties than non-indigenous people convicted of similar crimes. In a number of countries, indigenous prisoners allege that they are more likely to be ill-treated while in custody.

In theory, indigenous peoples in the Americas are protected against human rights violations by provisions in both national and international law. However, the degree to which protective legislation is enforced falls short of its potential. This is illustrated in country after country, in cases which range from direct involvement by state agents in human rights violations through to a general failure to protect indigenous peoples against abuses. Only rarely are the perpetrators brought to justice.

Amnesty International's primary emphasis is on governments because of their special responsibility under international law to respect human rights. However, the organization also unequivocally opposes and condemns deliberate and arbitrary killings, torture and hostage-taking by armed opposition groups. Deliberate and arbitrary killings include international killings of civilians, prisoners and others taking no part in hostilities. In Peru, for example, where indigenous people have repeatedly been victimized by both sides to the civil conflict, Amnesty International calls on both the government and the armed opposition to respect fundamental humanitarian standards.

Despite a 500-year legacy of abuse, throughout the centuries indigenous peoples in the Americas have struggled to preserve their cultures, their identities, and often their lives. Currently, there is a resurgence of indigenous organization, and groups throughout the region are working at community, national, regional and international level to ensure the protection of their civil, political, economic, social and cultural rights, and to bring their demands to public attention. As a result, some governments in the Americas, as well as intergovernmental bodies, are devoting increased attention to indigenous questions. Concern for indigenous affairs in the Americas has spread beyond the region. The United Nations (UN) Sub-Commission's Working Group on Indigenous Populations has met annually since 1982 to review developments which affect the rights of indigenous peoples and to develop standards concerning indigenous rights. The European Parliament, noting "reports from Amnesty International and Survival International of human rights violations against indigenous peoples," has instructed its human rights unit to appoint a rapporteur to "analyze the human, territorial and cultural rights of the indigenous peoples of the Americas."

Meanwhile, a growing international awareness of environmental and ecological issues coincides in some cases with indigenous peoples' traditional beliefs and practices concerning the protection of the environment, and has gained some indigenous organizations new allies on the national and international level. This has helped focus attention on the abuses which indigenous peoples suffer and the efforts they are making to protect their lives, their cultures, and their lands and resources.

Amnesty International and Indigenous Rights

Amnesty International has campaigned against the human rights violations suffered by indigenous people all over the world. The organization has, for example, repeatedly called for inquiries into killings of tribal people in the Chittagong Hill Tracts of Bangladesh by members of the security forces, including the Village Defence Party, a civilian defense force with official status. Amnesty International has repeatedly called for action against human rights violations inflicted on non-combatant indigenous people in Myanmar by government forces on counter-insurgency duty. In February 1992 the organization launched a campaign against political killings in the Philippines, where several members of tribal communities in the Cordillera region were killed in circumstances strongly suggesting official involvement. They were apparently singled out because of their work for tribal peoples' rights. In March 1992 Amnesty International launched a worldwide campaign against torture, rape, and death in custody in India, where many of the victims were tribal people. In Australia, where there is a high incidence of Aboriginal deaths in custody. Amnesty International has called on the government to fully investigate these deaths and to bring to justice any officials implicated in abuses.

For many years, Amnesty International has campaigned against the abuses suffered by indigenous peoples in the Americas. However, the organization considers that 1992, the 500th anniversary of the arrival of Europeans in the Americas, is an appropriate time to focus special attention on human rights issues affecting indigenous peoples, and those working with them, in that region. It has therefore initiated a special program of activities, "500 years on," to highlight the human rights violations—including extrajudicial executions, "disappearances," arbitrary arrests, torture and ill-treatment, unfair trials of political prisoners and the judicial death penalty—suffered by indigenous peoples in the Americas.

In the context of this program of activities and in line with its normal policy of responding to specific reports of human rights violations, Amnesty International has produced a series of special actions on abuses perpetrated against specific groups, such as the Mapuche of Chile, the Ticuna, Atikum and Truka of Brazil, and the Mixe, Zapotec, Ch'ol and Tzeltal of Mexico. In the first five months of 1992 the organization initiated 14 Urgent Action appeals on behalf of 78 indigenous people in the Americas whom it considered in imminent danger of suffering abuses such as torture, "disappearance" or extrajudicial execution.

In preparation for its "500 years on" campaign, Amnesty International has recently visited Brazil, Mexico, the USA and Canada, to research human rights violations against indigenous peoples. Other visits, to Panama, Bolivia and Argentina, for example, have included contacts with indigenous organizations among their objectives. Amnesty International also followed the deliberations of the UN Working Group on Indigenous

Populations with special interests at both its 1991 and 1992 sessions in Geneva in order to develop closer contacts with indigenous organizations. The organization also sent a delegation to the meeting held in Guatemala in October 1991 when indigenous organizations from throughout the Americas met to plan activities in 1992 to call attention to the plight of indigenous peoples in the region. In March 1992 Amnesty International representatives attended a conference in Caracas, Venezuela, which focused on women in the context of the 500th anniversary. . . .

Conclusions

Indigenous peoples in the Americas continue to be deprived of internationally recognized human rights: civil and political rights as well as economic, social and cultural rights. Deprivation and discrimination in areas such as health care, education, housing and land have been documented by others. In Amnesty International's area of expertise it has documented in this report and elsewhere gross and persistent human rights violations against indigenous peoples of the Americas including extrajudicial execution and the judicial death penalty, "disappearance," torture and ill-treatment (including rape and sexual abuse), unfair trial, and imprisonment as prisoners of conscience. The discrimination and economic deprivation which indigenous peoples suffer can render them particularly vulnerable to the human rights abuses Amnesty International works against; some sectors, such as refugees, displaced people and isolated groups, can be more vulnerable still.

No one is safe: the victims have included indigenous political, religious, and community leaders, women, children and old people. Those who work with indigenous peoples or support their cause, relatives of indigenous activists and those who have witnessed abuses have also become the victims of human rights violations.

Indigenous peoples suffer these violations for a variety of reasons. They may be singled out because of their ethnic or national origins or because they are outspoken activists on behalf of indigenous rights. In situations of internal conflict, indigenous people resident in contested areas may be subjected to abuses by both sides.

In other contexts, simply to be resident in areas where official security agents are engaged in anti-drugs operations, or where governments favor non-indigenous settlement in order to secure frontiers for reasons of "national security" may render indigenous people vulnerable to abuses.

Many violations directed against indigenous peoples stem from the struggle for land and resources: often their lands and resources; or lands and resources they claim, may be wanted by the state or commercial interests for economic exploitation. In such contexts, indigenous peoples may become vulnerable to abuses by state agents, or may find that the state does not investigate or prosecute effectively abuses carried out by non-state agents.

The discrimination and social and economic deprivation which many indigenous peoples suffer means they often have limited or no access to adequate legal representation, and makes it more difficult for them to seek redress when their rights are violated.

Members of the security forces have been named as responsible for human rights violations against indigenous peoples throughout the Americas. These violations have occurred in countries which have legal systems formally protective of the human rights of indigenous peoples. In some contexts, police officers and members of the armed forces have carried out abuses against indigenous peoples in the guise of so-called "death squads." Civil defense squads, formed at military behest and acting under military orders, have also been responsible for human rights violations against indigenous peoples. In some countries, the authorities have colluded or acquiesced in abuses carried out against indigenous peoples by private individuals, including hired gunmen.

In many countries of the Americas, those responsible for abuses, whether state or private agents, appear to benefit from virtual impunity for their deeds.

Throughout the Americas, there has been a resurgence of indigenous organization: groups have been formed at community, national, regional and international level to protect their rights and to bring their demands to public attention. A growing international awareness of environmental and ecological issues coincides in some cases with indigenous peoples' traditional beliefs and practices concerning protection of the environment and has gained indigenous organizations new allies at the international level. Some governments and intergovernmental bodies are in turn devoting increased attention to the demands and needs of indigenous peoples.

Although much has been accomplished, principally by indigenous peoples themselves, the human rights of indigenous peoples in the Americas continue to be massively abused, and much remains to be done at national and international level to redress the situation. . . .

PRESIDENTIAL AND VICE PRESIDENTIAL DEBATES

October 11, 13, 15, and 19

The three presidential and one vice presidential debates telecast live in October were a smash at the box office but seemed to reinforce, rather than revise, prevailing impressions of the candidates.

After presidential debates October 11, 15, and 19, Arkansas Governor Bill Clinton, the Democratic standard-bearer, retained his front-runner status. Although his appearance in the third debate was deemed his best, Republican President George Bush was unable to score the breakthrough that he needed to give him momentum going into the final two weeks of the campaign. Even before the debates began, political commentators were virtually unanimous in their agreement that Bush could no longer reverse his fortunes without a major news development or a Clinton misstep.

Independent candidate Ross Perot might have been helped the most by the debates, particularly the first and the third where his ability to toss off pointed one-liners came to the fore. By the end of the debates, Perot's standing in most public opinion polls had gone from single digits to the high teens. The vice presidential debate, held October 13, was marked by bickering between the two major party candidates, Democratic Senator Al Gore of Tennessee and Vice President Dan Quayle.

An estimated 81 million viewers saw the first presidential debate; more than 90 million watched the second; and an estimated 99 million saw the third. The numbers included those watching ABC, CBS, NBC, CNN, PBS, and the Fox Network. In contrast, the first presidential debate of the 1988 fall campaign drew an audience of 74 million. An audience of 76 million tuned in the October 13 vice presidential debate, an improvement of 8 million over 1988.

907

The debates almost did not occur. The bipartisan Commission on Presidential Debates, which had sponsored the debates in previous years, proposed a change in the format, from one in which a panel of reporters asked the candidates questions to one in which a single moderator posed the questions. The Clinton campaign accepted the proposed change, but the Bush camp objected. The commission canceled two scheduled debates, on September 22 and 29, because of the impasse. On September 29 the Bush campaign offered a new proposal, and after several days of negotiating between the two campaigns, a debate schedule was announced October 3. Each of the three presidential debates would be conducted under different formats.

Round One: Traditional Debate

On October 11, the three presidential candidates stood behind lecterns at Washington University in St. Louis and fielded questions from a panel of three journalists. Stiff and slightly hoarse, Clinton nonetheless was able to showcase his policy expertise and emphasize the need for change. Bush presented the less partisan side of his political persona. Although he criticized Clinton for participating in antiwar protests as a student in England, Bush did not press the attack. (Clinton Letter on Draft, p. 155)

The debate format, which limited responses to one or two minutes, seemed to best serve Perot, who used his well-practiced one-liners and homilies to great advantage. On the subject of experience, for example, he said, "Well, they've got a point. I don't have experience running up a $4 trillion debt." "Talk is cheap; words are plentiful, deeds are precious. Let's get on with it," he said at another point.

Round Two: The Town Hall Format

On October 15, the presidential candidates appeared on stage at the University of Richmond sitting on stools rather than standing behind lecterns. A single moderator, Carole Simpson of ABC News, directed the debate but let the audience of 209 voters ask most of the questions. This setting—suggestive of an afternoon TV talk show—put Clinton at ease. The Democrat ambled to the edge of the stage to address nearby members of the audience directly. He almost seemed to be having fun, in stark contrast to his cautious demeanor of the first debate.

Clinton also gained an advantage by letting Bush and Perot speak ahead of him on nine of the audience's thirteen questions. By speaking last, he was able to respond both to the question and the other answers. "Clinton was absolutely brilliant," said Doug Bailey, a Republican consultant and publisher of a news service. "He never was thrown off stride."

Neither Bush nor Perot showed the same mastery of the dynamics. The president had some difficulty connecting with the questioners and seemed unaware that the national TV audience could see him glancing repeatedly at his watch. Perot pursued much the same style he had used in the first debate, but the freer format seemed to take some of the snap out of his snippets. "I've never seen anyone who got so old in two nights," said Bob Beckel, a Democratic consultant who managed Walter F. Mondale's presidential campaign in 1984.

Round Three: A Mixed Format

The debate October 19, in East Lansing, Michigan, combined formats. A single moderator, Jim Lehrer of PBS, posed questions for the first half and then turned the debate over to a panel of three reporters.

Bush was widely acknowledged to have had the best ninety minutes of his campaign to date. He struck repeatedly at Clinton, labeling him untrustworthy and pronouncing his governorship a failure. Bush said that voters could not trust Clinton to limit tax increases to the wealthy— "watch your wallet," he warned—and suggested that a Democratic White House and Congress would bring back the days of 21 percent interest rates from the 1970s.

But the president showed defensiveness under attack. Perot ripped the president for supporting Saddam Hussein before Iraq invaded Kuwait in 1990. Perot also upbraided Bush about one-time support for former Panamanian strongman Manuel Noriega, for the collapse of the savings and loan industry, and for the weakened competitive position of U.S. airlines and banks.

The praises for Bush's performance in the final debate did not translate into new support in the national opinion polls. Some three-way national surveys even began to show the president slipping below 30 percent for the first time in the campaign.

Running Mates Joust

The debate between the three presidential contenders might more accurately have been called a fracas. Held October 13 in Atlanta, Georgia, the debate was conducted by a single moderator, Hal Bruno of ABC News, and the candidates were allowed to interact with each other directly. That led to squabbling between Gore and Quayle. For example, when Quayle attempted to cite proposals from Gore's book, Earth in the Balance, *Gore denied the accuracy of the citations. Quayle said Gore was "pulling a Clinton"—which he defined as refusing to stand by earlier statements.*

Quayle also focused closely on Clinton's integrity, suggesting repeatedly that the Arkansan could not be trusted. "The three words he fears most [are] 'tell the truth.' " Quayle said.

Throughout the debate Perot's running mate, retired Adm. James Stockdale, seemed detached. "Who am I? Why am I here?" Stockdale asked in jest as the debate began. At one point, watching an exchange between Gore and Quayle, Stockdale said he felt like "an observer at a pingpong game." But he did little to change his spectator status, demurring at one point by saying he was "out of ammunition."

*Following are excerpts from the transcripts of the presiden-
tial debates, held October 11, 15, and 19, and the vice
presidential debate, held October 13. (The bracketed headings have been added by Congressional Quarterly to highlight
the organization of the text.):*

OCTOBER 11 PRESIDENTIAL DEBATE

JIM LEHRER: Good evening, and welcome to the first of three
debates among the major candidates for president of the United States,
sponsored by the Commission on Presidential Debates.... I am Jim
Lehrer of the MacNeil-Lehrer Newshour on PBS, and I will be the
moderator for this 90-minute event.... Three journalists will be asking
questions tonight. They are John Mashek of The Boston Globe, Ann
Compton of ABC News, and Sander Vanocur, a freelance journalist....

The first topic tonight is what separates each of you from the other. Mr.
Perot, what do you believe tonight is the single most important separating
issue of this campaign?

PEROT: I think the principal that separates me is that five and a half
million people came together on their own and put me on the ballot. I was
not put on the ballot by either of the two parties; I was not put on the
ballot by any PAC money, by any foreign lobbyist money, by any special
interest money. This is a movement that came from the people. This is the
way the framers of the Constitution intended our government to be, a
government that comes from the people.

Over time we have developed a government that comes at the people,
that comes from the top down, where the people are more or less treated as
objects to be programmed during the campaign with commercials and
media events and fear messages and personal attacks and things of that
nature.

The thing that separates my candidacy and makes it unique is that this
came from millions of people in 50 states all over this country who wanted
a candidate that worked and belonged to nobody but them. I go into this
race as their servant, and I belong to them. So this comes from the
people....

GOVERNOR CLINTON: The most important distinction in this
campaign is that I represent real hope for change, a departure from trickle-
down economics, a departure from tax-and-spend economics to invest and
grow. But before I can do that, I must challenge the American people to
change and they must decide.

Tonight I say to the president, Mr. Bush, for 12 years you've had it your
way. You've had your chance and it didn't work. It's time to change. I want
to bring that change to the American people, but we must all decide first
we have the courage to change for hope and a better tomorrow.

PRESIDENT BUSH: Well, I think one thing that distinguishes is experience. I think we've dramatically changed the world. I'll talk about that a little bit later, but the changes are mind-boggling for world peace. Kids go to bed at night without the same fear of nuclear war.

And change for change sake isn't enough. We saw that message in the late '70s. We heard a lot about change. And what happened? The misery index went right through the roof.

But my economic program I think is the kind of change we want. And the way we're going to get it done is we're going to have a brand-new Congress. A lot of them are thrown out because of all the scandals. I'll sit down with them—Democrats and Republicans alike—and work for my agenda for American renewal which represents real change.

But I'd say if you had to separate out, I think it's experience at this level.

LEHRER: Governor Clinton, how do you respond to the president— you have two minutes—on the question of experience? He says that is what distinguishes him from the other two of you.

GOVERNOR CLINTON: I believe experience counts, but it's not everything. Values, judgment and the record that I have amassed in my state also should count for something. I've worked hard to create good jobs and to educate people. My state now ranks first in the country in job growth this year, fourth in income growth, fourth in the reduction of poverty, third in overall economic performance, according to a major news magazine. That's because we believe in investing in education and in jobs.

We have to change in this country. You know, my wife Hillary gave me a book about a year ago in which the author defined "insanity" as just as doing the same old thing over and over again and expecting a different result. We have got to have the courage to change.

Experience is important, yes. I've gotten a lot of experience in dealing with ordinary people over the last year, month. I've touched more people's lives and seen more heartbreak and hope, more pain and promise than anybody else who's run for president this year.

I think the American people deserve better than they're getting. We have gone from first to thirteenth in the world in wages in the last 12 years since Mr. Bush and Mr. Reagan has been in. Personal income has dropped while people have worked harder. In the last four years, there have been twice as many bankruptcies as new jobs created. We need a new approach.

The same old experience is not relevant. We're living in a new world after the Cold War and what works in this new world is not trickle down, not government for the benefit of the privileged few, not tax and spend, but a commitment to invest in American jobs and American education, controlling American health care costs and bringing the American people together. That is what works.

And you can have the right kind of experience and the wrong kind of experience. Mine is rooted in the real lives of real people and it will bring real results, if we have the courage to change.

PRESIDENT BUSH: I just thought of another big difference here between me—I don't believe Mr. Perot feels this way, but I know Governor

Clinton did, because I want to accurately quote him. He thinks—I think he said that the country is coming apart at the seams.

Now, I know that the only way he can win is to make everybody believe the economy is worse than it is, but this country's not coming apart at the seams, for heaven's sakes. We're the United States of America. In spite of the economic problems, we're the most respected economy around the world. Many would trade for it.

We've been caught up in a global slowdown. We can do much, much better, but we ought not to try to convince the American people that America is a country is coming apart at the seams.

I would hate to be running for president and think that the only way I could win would be to convince everybody how horrible things are. Yes, there are big problems, and yes, people are hurting, but I believe that this agenda for American renewal I have is the answer to do it. And I believe we can get it done now, whereas we didn't in the past, because you're going to have a whole brand new bunch of people in the Congress that are going to have to listen to the same American people I'm listening to.

LEHRER: Mr. Perot, a minute response, sir.

PEROT: Well, they've got a point. I don't have any experience in running up a $4 trillion debt.

I don't have any experience in gridlock government, where nobody takes responsibility for anything and everybody blames everybody else. I don't have any experience in creating the worst public school system in the industrialized world, the most violent, crime-ridden society in the industrialized world.

But I do have a lot of experience in getting things done.

So if we're at a point in history where we want to stop talking about it and do it, I've got a lot of experience in figuring out how to solve problems, making the solutions work and then moving on to the next one. I've got a lot of experience in not taking 10 years to solve a 10-minute problem.

So if it's time for action, I think I have experience that counts. If there's more time for gridlock and talk and finger-pointing, I'm the wrong man.

[The Character Issue]

LEHRER: President Bush, the question goes to you. You have two minutes. And the question is this: Are there important issues of character separating you from these other two men?

PRESIDENT BUSH: I think the American people should be the judge of that. I think character is a very important question. I said something the other day where I was accused of being like Joe McCarthy because I questioned—I put it this way. I think it's wrong to demonstrate against your own country or organize demonstrations against your own country in foreign soil. I just think it's wrong.

Maybe, they say, well, it was youthful indiscretion. I was 19 or 20 flying off an aircraft carrier, and that shaped me to be commander-in-chief of the armed forces. And I'm sorry, but demonstrating—it's not a question of patriotism. It's a question of character and judgment.

They get on me—Bill's gotten on me about "read my lips," and when I make a mistake, I'll admit it. But he has made—not admitted a mistake. And I just find it impossible to understand how an American can demonstrate against his own country in a foreign land, organizing demonstrations against it, when young men are held prisoner in Hanoi or kids out of the ghetto were drafted.

Some say, well, you're old-fashioned. Maybe I am, but I just don't think that's right. Now, whether it's character or judgment, whatever it is, I have a big difference here on this issue. And so we'll just have to see how it plays out, but I—I couldn't do that, and I don't think most Americans could do that.

And they all say, well, it was a long time ago. Well, admit it then. Say, I made a terrible mistake. How could you be commander-in-chief of the armed forces and have some kid say, when you have to make a tough decision, as I did in Panama or in Kuwait and then have some kid jump up and say, well, I'm not going to go, the commander-in-chief was organizing demonstrations halfway around the world during another era. . . .

PEROT: I think the American people make their own decisions on character, and at a time when we have work to do and we need action I think they need to clearly understand the backgrounds of each person. I think the press can play a huge role in making sure that the backgrounds are clearly presented in an objective way. Then make a decision.

Certainly, anyone in the White House should have the character to be there.

But I think it's very important to measure when and where things occurred. Did they occur when you are a young person in your formative years, or did they occur while you were a senior official in the federal government?

When you're a senior official in the federal government spending billions of dollars of taxpayers' money and you're a mature individual and you make a mistake, then that was on our ticket. If you make it as a young man, time passes.

So I would say just, you know, look at all three of us, decide who you think will do the job, pick that person in November, because, believe me, as I've said before, the party's over and it's time for the clean-up crew. . . .

GOVERNOR CLINTON: Ross gave a good answer, but I've got to respond directly to Mr. Bush. You have questioned my patriotism; you even brought some rightwing congressmen into the White House to plot how to attack me for going to Russia in 1969 and 1970 when over 50,000 other Americans did.

Now, I honor your service in World War II, I honor Mr. Perot's service in uniform, and the service of every man and woman who ever served, including Admiral Crowe who was your chairman of the Joint Chiefs and who's supporting me.

But when Joe McCarthy went around this country attacking people's patriotism, he was wrong—he was wrong. And a senator from Connecticut stood up to him named Prescott Bush. Your father was right to stand up to Joe McCarthy; you were wrong to attack my patriotism. I was opposed to the war, but I love my country.

And we need a president who will bring this country together not divide it. We've had enough division. I want to lead a unified country. . . .

[Taxes and the Deficit]

COMPTON: Governor Clinton, can you lock in a level here tonight on where middle-income families can be guaranteed a tax cut or, at the very least, at what income level they can be guaranteed no tax increase?

GOVERNOR CLINTON: The tax increase I have proposed triggers in at family incomes of $200,000 and above. Those are the people who in the 1980s had their incomes go up while their taxes went down.

Middle-class people, defined as people with incomes of $52,000 and down, had their incomes go down while their taxes went up in the Reagan-Bush years because of six increases in the payroll taxes. So that is where my income limit would trigger.

COMPTON: There will be no tax increases—

GOVERNOR CLINTON: Right. My plan—

COMPTON: —below 200,000—

GOVERNOR CLINTON: —notwithstanding my opponent's ad, my plan triggers in at gross incomes, family incomes of $200,000 and above. Then we want to give modest middle-class tax relief to restore some fairness, especially to middle-class people with families with incomes of under $60,000.

In addition to that, the money that I raise from upper-income people and from asking foreign corporations just to pay the same income on their income earned in America that American corporations do will be used to give incentives back to upper-income people. I want to give people permanent incentives on investment tax credit, like President Kennedy and the Congress inaugurated in the early '60s to get industry moving again; a research and development tax credit; a low-income housing tax credit; a long-term capital gains proposal for new business and business expansions.

We've got to have no more trickle down. We don't need across-the-board tax cuts for the wealthy for nothing. We need to say here's your tax incentive: if you create American jobs, the old-fashioned way. I'd like to create more millionaires than were created under Mr. Bush and Mr. Reagan, but I don't want to have four years where we have no growth in the private sector, and that's what's happened in the last four years. We're down 35,000 jobs in the private sector. We need to invest and grow, and that's what I want to do. . . .

PRESIDENT BUSH: Well, let me—I have to correct one thing. I didn't question the man's patriotism. I questioned his judgment and his character. What he did in Moscow, that's fine. Let him explain it. He did. I accept that. What I don't accept is demonstrating and organizing demonstrations in a foreign country when your country's at war. I'm sorry. I cannot accept it.

In terms of this one on taxes spells out the biggest difference between us. I do not believe we need to go back to the Mondale proposals or the Dukakis proposals of tax and spend. Governor Clinton says $200,000 but he also says he wants to raise $150 billion. Taxing people over $200,000 will not get you $150 billion. And then when you add in his other spending proposals, regrettably you end up socking it to the working man.

That old adage they use—we're going to soak the rich—we're going to soak the rich—it always ends up being the poor cab driver or the working man that ends up paying the bill. And so I just have a different approach. I believe the way to get the deficit down is to control the growth of mandatory spending programs, and not raise taxes on the American people. We've got a big difference there....

PEROT: We've got to have a growing, expanding job base to give us a growing, expanding tax base. Right now we have a flat to deteriorating job base and where it appears to be growing, it's minimum-wage jobs. So we've got to really rebuild our job base. That's going to take money for infrastructure and investment to do that. Our foreign competitors are doing it; we're not.

We cannot pay off the $4 trillion debt, balance the budget and have the industries of the future and the high-paying jobs in this country without having the revenue. We're going to go through a period of shared sacrifice. There's one challenge. It's got to be fair.

We've created a mess, don't have much to show for it and we have got to fix it. And that's about all I can say in a minute....

[Gasoline Tax]

MASHEK: Mr. Perot, you talked about fairness just a minute ago and sharing the pain. As part of your plan to reduce the ballooning federal deficit, you've suggested that we raise gasoline taxes 50 cents a gallon over five years. Why punish the middle class consumer to such a degree?

PEROT: It's 10 cents a year cumulative. It finally gets to 50 cents at the end of the fifth year. I think "punish" is the wrong word. Again, see, I didn't create this problem. We're trying to solve it.

Now, if you study our international competitors, some of our international competitors collect up to $3.50 a gallon in taxes, and they use that money to build infrastructure and to create jobs. We collect 35 cents, and we don't have it to spend.

I know it's not popular, and I understand the nature of your question. But the people who will be helped the most by it are the working people who will get the jobs created because of this tax.

Why do we have to do it? Because we have so mismanaged our country over the years, and it is now time to pay the fiddler. And if we don't, we will be spending our children's money. We have spent $4 trillion worth. An incredible number of young people are active in supporting my effort because they are deeply concerned that we have taken the American dream from them. I think it's fitting that we're on the campus of a university tonight. These young people, when they get out of this wonderful university, will have difficulty finding a job.

We've got to clean this mess up, leave this country in good shape, and pass on the American dream to them. We've got to collect the taxes to do it. If there's a fair way, I'm all ears—aah.

But—but—see, let me make it very clear. If people don't have the stomach to fix these problems, I think it's a good time to face it, November. If they do, then they will have heard the harsh reality of what we have to do. I'm not playing Lawrence Welk music tonight....

GOVERNOR CLINTON: I think Mr. Perot has confronted this deficit issue, but I think it's important to point out that we really have two deficits in America, not one. We have a budget deficit in the federal government, but we also have an investment, a jobs, an income deficit. People are working harder for less money than they were making 10 years ago, two-thirds of our people—a $1,600 drop in average income in just the last two years.

The problem I have with the Perot prescription is that almost all economists who've looked at it say that if you cut the deficit this much this quick it will increase unemployment, it will slow down the economy. That's why I think we shouldn't do it that quickly. We have a disciplined reduction in the deficit of 50 percent over the next four years, but first get incentives to invest in this economy, put the American people back to work. We've got to invest and grow.

Nine Nobel Prize-winning economists and 500 others, including numerous Republican and Democratic business executives, have endorsed this approach because it offers the best hope to put America back to work and get our incomes rising instead of falling....

PRESIDENT BUSH: Your question was on fairness. I just disagree with Mr. Perot. I don't believe it is fair to slap a 50-cent-a-gallon tax over whatever many years on the people that have to drive for a living, people that go long distances. I don't think we need to do it.

You see, I have a fundamental difference. I agree with what he's talking about in trying to get this spending down and the discipline, although I think we ought to totally exempt Social Security. But he's talking tough medicine, and I think that's good.

I disagree with the tax-and-spend philosophy. You see, I don't think we need to tax more and spend more, and then say that's going to make the problem better. And I'm afraid that's what I think I'm hearing from Governor Clinton.

I believe what you need to do is some of what Ross is talking about: control the growth of mandatory spending and get taxes down. He's mentioned some ways to do it—and I agree with those. I've been talking about getting a capital gains cut forever, and his friends in Congress have been telling me that's a tax break for the rich. It would stimulate investment. I'm for an investment tax allowance; I'm for a tax break for first-time homebuyers. And with this new Congress coming in, gridlock will be gone, and I'll sit down with them and say let's get this done.

But I do not want to go the tax-and-spend route. . . .

[Creating Jobs]

COMPTON: Mr. Perot, you talked a minute ago about rebuilding the job base. But is it true what Governor Clinton just said, that that means that unemployment will increase, that it will slow the economy? And how would you specifically use the powers of the presidency to get more people back into good jobs immediately?

PEROT: Step one, the American people send me up there, the day after election, I'll get with congressional—we won't even wait till inauguration, and I'll ask the president to help and I'll ask his staff to help me. And we will start putting together teams to put together—to take all the plans that exist and do something with them.

Please understand. There are great plans lying all over Washington nobody ever executes. It's like having a blueprint for a house you never built. You don't have anywhere to sleep.

Now our challenge is to take these things, do something with them. Step one, we want to put America back to work, clean up the small business problem, have one task force at work on that. The second, you've got your big companies that are in trouble, including the defense industries—have another one on that. Have a third task force on new industries of the future to make sure we nail those for our country and they don't wind up in Europe and Asia. Convert from 19th to 21st century capitalism.

See, we have an adversarial relationship between government and business. Our international competitors that are cleaning our plate have an intelligent relationship between government and business, and a supportive relationship.

Then have another task force on crime because, next to jobs, our people are concerned about their safety. Health care, schools—one on the debt and deficit. And finally in that 90-day period before the inauguration, put together the framework for the town hall and give the American people a Christmas present. Show them by Christmas the first cut at these plans. By the time Congress comes into session to go to work, have those plans ready to go in front of Congress. Then get off to a flying start in '93 to execute these plans.

Now, there are people in this room and people on this stage who've been in meetings when I would sit there and say, "Is this the one we're going to talk about or do something about?" Well, obviously, my orientation is let's go do it. Now, put together your plans by Christmas, be ready to go when Congress goes, nail these things. Small business—you've got to have capital, you've got to credit, and many of them need mentors or coaches.

And we can create more jobs there in a hurry than any other place.

GOVERNOR CLINTON: This country desperately needs a jobs program, and my first priority would be to pass a jobs program, to introduce it on the first day I was inaugurated. I would meet with the leaders of the Congress, with all the newly elected members of the Congress and as many others with whom I could meet between the time of the election and the inauguration, and we would present a jobs program.

Then we would present a plan to control health care costs and phase in health care coverage for all Americans. Until we control health care costs, we're not going to control the deficit. It is the number one culprit. But first we must have an aggressive jobs program.

I live in a state where manufacturing job growth has far outpaced the nation in the last few years, where we have created more private sector jobs since Mr. Bush has been president than have been created in the entire rest of the country, where Mr. Bush's labor secretary the job growth has been enormous.

We've done it in Arkansas. Give me a chance to create these kind of jobs in America. We can do it. I know we can. . . .

PRESIDENT BUSH: We've got the plan announced for what we can do for small business. I've already put forward things that'll get this country working fast, some of which have been echoed here tonight— investment tax allowance, capital gains reduction, more on research and development, tax credit for first-time home buyers.

What I'm going to do is say to Jim Baker when this campaign is over, all right, let's sit down now, you do in domestic affairs what you've done in foreign affairs, be kind of the economic coordinator of all the domestic side of the House, and that includes all the economic side, all the training side, and bring this program together.

We're going to have a new Congress, and we're going to say to them, you've listened to the voters the way we have. Nobody wants gridlock anymore, and so let's get the program through.

And I believe it'll work because, as Ross said, we got the plans. The plans are all over Washington. And I've put ours together in something called the agenda for American renewal, and it makes sense, it's sensible, it creates jobs, it gets to the base of the kind of jobs we need. And so I'll just be asking for support to get that put into effect. . . .

[Foreign Affairs]

LEHRER: All right. We're going to move—

We're going to move to foreign affairs. The first question goes to Mr. Perot for a two-minute answer, and Sandy will ask it.

VANOCUR: Mr. Perot, in the post-Cold War environment, what should be the overriding U.S. national interest, and what can the United States do, and what can it afford to do to defend that national interest?

PEROT: Well, again, if you're not rich, you're not a superpower. So we have two that I'd put as number one. I have 1 and 1(a). One is we've got to have the money to be able to pay for defense. And we've got to manufacture here. Believe it or not, folks, you can't ship it all overseas; you've got to make it here. And you can't convert from potato chips to airplanes in an emergency. See, Willow Run could be converted from cars to airplanes in World War II because it was here. We've got to make things here. You just can't ship them overseas anymore. I hope we talk more about that.

The second thing on priorities, we've got to help Russia succeed in its revolution, and all of its republics. When we think of Russia, remember we're thinking of many countries now. We've got to help them. That's pennies on the dollar compared to renewing the Cold War.

Third, we've got all kinds of agreements on paper and some that are being executed on getting rid of nuclear warheads. Russia and its republics are out of control or, at best, in weak control right now. It's a very unstable situation. You've got every rich Middle Eastern country over there trying to buy nuclear weapons, as you well know. And that will lead to another five-star migraine headache down the road.

We really need to nail down the intercontinental ballistic missiles, the ones that can hit us from Russia. We're focused on the tactical. We've made real progress there. We've got some agreements on the nuclear. But we don't have those things put away yet. The sooner the better.

So, in terms of priorities, we've got to be financially strong. Number two, we've got to take care of this missile situation and try to get the nuclear war behind us and give that a very high priority. And number three, we need to help and support Russia and the republics in every possible way to become democratic, capitalistic societies, and not just sit back and let those countries continue in turmoil because they could go back worse than things used to be—and, believe me, there are a lot of old boys in the KGB and the military that liked it better the way it used to be....

GOVERNOR CLINTON: In order to keep America the strongest nation in the world, we need some continuity and some change. There are three fundamental challenges. First of all, the world is still a dangerous and uncertain place. We need a new military and a new national security policy equal to the challenges of the post-Cold War era, a smaller permanent military force, but one that is more mobile, well-trained with high-technology equipment.

We need to continue the negotiations to reduce the nuclear arsenals in the Soviet Union, the former Soviet Union, and the United States. We need to stop this proliferation of weapons of mass destruction.

Second, we have to face that in this arm, economic security is a whole lot of national security. Our dollar is at a low-time low against some foreign currencies; we're weak in the world. We must rebuild America's strength at home.

And, finally, we ought to be promoting the democratic impulses around the world. Democracies are our partners, they don't go to war with each other, they're reliable friends in the future.

National security, economic strength, democracy. . . .

PRESIDENT BUSH: We still are the envy of the world in terms of our military, there's no question about that. We're the envy of the world in terms of our economy, in spite of the difficulties we're having. There's no question about that. Our exports are dramatically up. I might say to Mr. Perot, I can understand why you might have missed it because there's so much fascination by trivia, but I worked out a deal with Boris Yeltsin to eliminate, get rid of entirely, the most destabilizing weapons of all, the SS-18, the big intercontinental ballistic missile; I mean, that's been done. And thank God it has, because the parents of these young people around here go to bed at night without the same fear of nuclear war.

We made dramatic progress. And so we've got a good military. The question that says get a new military, get the best in the world—we got it. And they're keeping the peace, and they're respected around the world. And we are more respected, because of the way we have conducted ourselves. We didn't listen to the nuclear freeze crowd. We said peace through strength, and it worked, and the Cold War is over. And America understands that.

But we're turned so inward, we don't understand the global picture. And we are helping democracy, Ross. The Freedom Support Act is something that I got through the Congress, and it's a very good thing, because it does exactly what you say—and I think you agree with that—to help Russian democracy. And we're going to keep on doing that. . . .

[Use of Military Forces]

COMPTON: Mr. President, how can you watch the killing in Bosnia and the ethnic cleansing, or the starvation and anarchy in Somalia, and not want to use America's might, if not America's military, to try to end that kind of suffering?

PRESIDENT BUSH: Ann, both of them are very complicated situations. And I vowed something because I learned something from Vietnam. I am not going to commit U.S. forces until I know what the mission is, till the military tell me that it can be completed, and till I know how they can come out.

We are helping. American airplanes are helping today on humanitarian relief for Sarajevo. It is America that's in the lead in helping with humanitarian relief for Somalia.

But when you go to put somebody else's son or daughter into war, I think you got to be a little bit careful and you have to be sure that there's a military plan that can do this. You have ancient ethnic rivalries that have cropped up as Yugoslavia's dissolved or getting dissolved, and it isn't going to be solved by sending in the 82nd Airborne, and I'm not going to do that as commander-in-chief.

I am going to stand by and use the moral persuasion of the United States to get satisfaction in terms of prison camps, and we're making some progress there, and in terms of getting humanitarian relief in there. And right now, as you know, the United States took the lead in a no-fly operation up there in—no-fly order up in the United Nations. We're working through the international organizations.

That's one thing I learned by forging that tremendous and greatly—highly successful coalition against Saddam Hussein, the dictator. Use—work internationally to do it.

I am very concerned about it. I am concerned about ethnic cleansing. I am concerned about a tax on Muslims, for example, over there. But I must stop short of using American force until I know how those young men and women are going to get out of there as well as get in, know what the mission is, and define it. And I think I'm on the right track. . . .

PEROT: I think if we learned anything in Vietnam is you first commit this nation before you commit the troops to the battlefield. We cannot send our people all over the world to solve every problem that comes up.

This is basically a problem that is a primary concern to the European Community. Certainly we care about the people, we care about the children, we care about the tragedy. But it is inappropriate for us, just because there's a problem somewhere around the world, to take the sons and daughters of working people—and make no mistake about it, our all-volunteer armed force is not made up of the sons and daughters of the beautiful people; it's the working folks who send their sons and daughters to war, with a few exceptions. It's very unlike World War II, when FDR's sons flew missions. Everybody went. It's a different world now.

It's very important that we not just, without thinking it through, just rush to every problem in the world and have our people torn to pieces. . . .

GOVERNOR CLINTON: I agree that we cannot commit ground forces to become involved in the quagmire of Bosnia or in the tribal wars of Somalia. But I think that it's important to recognize that there are things that can be done short of that, and that we do have interests there. There are, after all, two million refugees now because of the problems in what was Yugoslavia, the largest number since World War II, and there may be hundreds of thousands of people who will starve or freeze to death in this winter. The United States should try to work with its allies and stop it. I urged the president to support this air cover, and he did—and I applaud that. I applaud the no-fly zone, and I know that he's going back to the United Nations to try to get authority to enforce it. I think we should stiffen the embargo on the Belgrade government, and I think we have to consider whether or not we should lift the arms embargo now on the Bosnians, since they are in no way in a fair fight with a heavily armed opponent bent on "ethnic cleansing."

We can't involved in the quagmire, but we must do what we can.

[Family Values]

COMPTON: Governor Clinton, can you tell us what your definition of the word "family" is?

GOVERNOR CLINTON: A family involves at least one parent, whether natural or adoptive or foster, and children. A good family is a place where love and discipline and good values are transmuted from the elders to the children, a place where people turn for refuge, and where they know they're the most important people in the world. America has a lot of families that are in trouble today. There's been a lot of talk about family values in this campaign. I know a lot about that. I was born to a widowed mother who gave me family values, and grandparents. I've seen the family values of my people in Arkansas. I've seen the family values of all these people in America who are out there killing themselves working harder for less in a country that's had the worst economic years in 50 years and the first decline in industrial production ever.

I think the president owes it to family values to show that he values America's families, whether they're people on welfare you're trying to move from welfare to work, the working poor whom I think deserve a tax break to lift them above poverty if they've got a child in the house and working 40 hours a week, working families who deserve a fair tax system and the opportunity for constant retraining; they deserve a strong economy. And I think they deserve a family and medical leave act. Seventy-two other nations have been able to do it. Mr. Bush vetoed it twice because he says we can't do something 72 other countries do, even though there was a small business exemption.

So with all the talk about family values, I know about family values—I wouldn't be here without them. The best expression of my family values is that tonight's my 17th wedding anniversary, and I'd like to close my question by just wishing my wife a happy anniversary, and thank you, my daughter, for being there. . . .

PRESIDENT BUSH: Well, I would say that one meeting that made a profound impression on me was when the mayors of the big cities, including the mayor of Los Angeles, a Democrat, came to see me, and they unanimously said the decline in urban America stems from the decline in the American family. So I do think we need to strengthen family. When Barbara holds an AIDS baby, she's showing a certain compassion for family; when she reads to children, the same thing.

I believe that discipline and respect for the law—all of these things should be taught to children, not in our schools, but families have to do that. I'm appalled at the highest outrageous numbers of divorces—it happens in families, it's happened in ours. But it's gotten too much. And I just think that we ought to do everything we can to respect the American family. It can be a single-parent family. Those mothers need help. And one way to do it is to get these deadbeat fathers to pay their obligations to these mothers—that will help strengthen the American family. And there's a whole bunch of other things that I can't click off in this short period of time. . . .

PEROT: If I had to solve all the problems that face this country and I could be granted one wish as we started down the trail to rebuild the job base, the schools and so on and so forth, I would say a strong family unit in every home, where every child is loved, nurtured, and encouraged. A little child before they're 18 months learns to think well of himself or herself or poorly. They develop a positive or negative self-image. At a very early age they learn how to learn. If we have children who are not surrounded with love and affection—you see, I look at my grandchildren and wonder if they'll ever learn to walk because they're always in someone's arms. And I think, my gosh, wouldn't it be wonderful if every child had that love and support. But they don't.

We will not be a great country unless we have a strong family unit in every home. And I think you can use the White House as a bully pulpit to stress the importance of these little children, particularly in their young and formative years, to mold these little precious pieces of clay so that they, too, can live rich full lives when they're grown....

[Racial Division]

MASHEK: Mr. Perot, racial division continues to tear apart our great cities, the last episode being this spring in Los Angeles. Why is this still happening in America, and what would you do to end it?

PEROT: This is a relevant question here tonight. The first thing I'd do is, during political campaigns, I would urge everybody to stop trying to split this country into fragments and appeal to the differences between us and then wonder why the melting pot is all broken to pieces after November the 3rd.

We are all in this together. We ought to love one another because united teams win and divided teams lose. And if we can't love one another, we ought to get along with one another. And if you can't get there, just recognize we're all stuck with one another because nobody's going anywhere, right?

Now, that ought to get everybody back up to let's get along together and make it work. Our diversity is a strength. We've turned it into a weakness.

Now again, the White House is a bully pulpit. I think whoever is in the White House should just make it absolutely unconscionable and inexcusable, and if anybody's in the middle of a speech at, you know, one of these conventions, I would expect the candidate to go out and lift him off the stage if he starts preaching hate—because we don't have time for it.

See, our differences are our strengths. We have got to pull together. In athletics, we know it. See, divided teams lose; united teams win.

We have got to unite and pull together, and there's nothing we can't do. But if we sit around blowing all this energy out the window on racial strife and hatred, we are stuck with a sure loser because we have been a melting pot. We're becoming more and more of a melting pot. Let's make it a strength, not a weakness....

GOVERNOR CLINTON: I grew up in the segregated South, thankfully raised by a grandfather with almost no formal education but with a heart of gold who taught me early that all people were equal in the eyes of God.

I saw the winds of hatred divide people and keep the people of my state poorer than they would have been, spiritually and economically. And I've done everything I could in my public life to overcome racial divisions.

We don't have a person to waste in this country. We are being murdered economically because we have too many drop-outs, we have too many low birthweight babies, we have too many drug addicts as kids, we have too much violence, we are too divided by race, by income, by region. And I have devoted a major portion of this campaign to going across this country and looking for opportunities to go to white groups and African American groups and Latino groups and Asian American groups and say the same thing.

If the American people cannot be brought together, we can't turn this country around. If we can come together, nothing can stop us....

PRESIDENT BUSH: Well, I think Governor Clinton is committed. I do think it's fair to note—he can rebut it—but Arkansas is one of the few states that doesn't have any civil rights legislation.

I've tried to use the White House as a bully pulpit, speaking out against discrimination. We passed two very forward-looking civil rights bills. It's not going to be all done by legislation. But I do think that you need to make an appeal every time you can to eliminate racial divisions and discrimination, and I'll keep on doing that and pointing to some legislative accomplishment to back it up.

I have to take ten seconds here at the end—the red light isn't on yet—to say to Ross Perot, please don't say to the DEA agents on the street that we don't have the will to fight drugs. Please. I have watched these people—the same for our local law enforcement people. We're backing up at every way we possibly can. But maybe you meant that some in the country don't have the will to fight it, but those that are out there on the front line, as you know—you've been a strong backer of law enforcement—really—I just want to clear that up—have the will to fight it, and, frankly, some of them are giving their lives....

[Fight Against AIDS]

MASHEK: Mr. President, yesterday tens of thousands of people paraded past the White House to demonstrate their concern about the disease AIDS. A celebrated member of your commission, Magic Johnson, quit saying that there was too much inaction.

Where is this widespread feeling coming from that your administration is not doing enough about AIDS?

PRESIDENT BUSH: Coming from the political process. We have increased funding for AIDS. We've doubled it on research and on every other aspect of it. My request for this year was $4.9 billion for AIDS—ten times as much per AIDS victim as per cancer victim.

I think that we're showing the proper compassion and concern. So I can't tell you where it's coming from, but I am very much concerned about AIDS and I believe that we've got the best researchers in the world out there at

NIH [National Institutes of Health] working the problem. We're funding them—I wish there was more money—but we're funding them far more than any time in the past, and we're going to keep on doing that.

I don't know. I was a little disappointed in Magic because he came to me and I said, "Now if you see something we're not doing, get ahold of me. Call me, let me know." He went to one meeting, and then we heard that he was stepping down. So he's replaced by Mary Fisher who electrified the Republican Convention by talking about the compassion and the concern that we feel. It was a beautiful moment and I think she'll do a first-class job on that commission.

So I think the appeal is yes, we care. And the other thing is part of AIDS—it's one of the few diseases where behavior matters. And I once called on somebody, "Well, change your behavior. Is the behavior you're using prone to cause AIDS? Change the behavior." Next thing I know, one of these ACT UP groups is out saying, "Bush ought to change his behavior."

You can't talk about it rationally. The extremes are hurting the AIDS cause. To go into a Catholic mass in a beautiful cathedral in New York under the cause of helping in AIDS and start throwing condoms around in the mass, I'm sorry, I think it sets back the cause.

We cannot move to the extreme. We've got to care. We've got to continue everything we can at the federal and the local level. Barbara I think is doing a superb job in destroying the myth about AIDS. And all of us are in this fight together, all of us care. Do not go to the extreme. . . .

PEROT: First, I think Mary Fisher was a great choice. We're lucky to have her heading the commission. Secondly, I think one thing that if I were sent to do the job, I would sit down with FDA, look at exactly where we are. Then I would really focus on let's get these things out. If you're going to die, you don't have to go through this ten-year cycle that FDA goes through on new drugs.

Believe me, people with AIDS are more than willing to take that risk. And we could be moving out to the human population a whole lot faster than we are on some of these new drugs. So I would think we can expedite the problem there.

Let me go back a minute to racial divisiveness. The all-time low in our country was the Judge Thomas-Anita Hill hearings, and those senators ought to be hanging their heads in shame for what they did there. . . .

Second thing, there are not many times in your life when you get to talk to a whole country. But let me just say to all of America: if you hate people, I don't want your vote. That's how strongly I feel about it. . . .

GOVERNOR CLINTON: Over 150,000 Americans have died of AIDS. Well over a million and a quarter Americans are HIV-positive. We need to put one person in charge of the battle against AIDS to cut across all the agencies that deal with it. We need to accelerate the drug approval process. We need to fully fund the act named for that wonderful boy Ryan White to make sure we're doing everything we can on research and treatment.

And the president should lead a national effort to change behavior, to keep our children alive in the schools, responsible behavior to keep people alive. This is a matter of life and death. I have worked in my state to reduce teen pregnancy and illness among children. I know it's tough.

The reason Magic Johnson resigned from the AIDS Commission is because the statement you heard tonight from Mr. Bush is the longest and best statement he's made about it in public.

I am proud of what we did at the Democratic Convention, putting two HIV-positive people on the platform, and I am proud of the leadership that I'm going to bring to this country in dealing with the AIDS crisis. . . .

[Governing]

COMPTON: Mr. Perot, even if you've got what people say are the guts to take on changes in the most popular, the most sacred of the entitlements, Medicare, people say you haven't a prayer of actually getting anything passed in Washington.

Since a president isn't a lone ranger, how in the world can you make some of those unpopular changes?

PEROT: Two ways. Number one, if I get there, it will be a very unusual and historical event—because the people, not the special interests, put me there. I will have a unique mandate. I have said again and again, and this really upsets the establishment in Washington, that we're going to inform the people in detail on the issues through an electronic town hall so that they really know what's going on.

They will want to do what's good for our country.

Now, all these fellows with thousand-dollar suits and alligator shoes running up and down the halls of Congress that make policy now—the lobbyists, the PAC guys, the foreign lobbyists, and what-have-you, they'll be over there in the Smithsonian, you know—because we're going to get rid of them, and the Congress will be listening to the people. And the American people are willing to have fair, shared sacrifice. They're not as stupid as Washington thinks they are. The American people are bright, intelligent, caring, loving people who want a great country for their children and grandchildren. And they will make those sacrifices.

So I welcome that challenge, and just watch—

—because if the American people send me there, we'll get it done.

Now, everybody will faint in Washington. They've never seen anything happen in that town.

This is a town where the White House says, Congress did it; Congress says, the White House did it. And I'm sitting there and saying, well, who else could be around, you know? Then when they get off by themselves, they say nobody did it.

And yet the cash register's empty and it used to have our money, the taxpayers' money, in it, and we didn't get the results.

No, we'll get it done. . . .

GOVERNOR CLINTON: Ross, that's a great speech, but it's not quite that simple.

I mean, look at the facts. Both parties in Washington, the president and the Congress, have cut Medicare. The average senior citizen is spending a higher percentage of income on health care today than they were in 1965, before Medicare came in.

The president's got another proposal to require them to pay $400 a year more for the next five years.

But if you don't have the guts to control costs by changing the insurance system and taking on the bureaucracies and the regulation of health care in the private and public sector, you can't fix this problem. Costs will continue to spiral.

And just remember this, folks. A lot of folks on Medicare are out there every day making the choice between food and medicine; not poor enough for Medicare—Medicaid, not wealthy enough to buy their medicine. I've met them, people like Mary Annie and Edward Davis in Nashua, New Hampshire. All over this country, they cannot even buy medicine.

So let's be careful. When we talk about cutting health care costs, let's start with the insurance companies and the people that are making a killing instead of making our people healthy. . . .

PRESIDENT BUSH: Well, first place, I'd like to clear up something because every four years, the Democrats go around and say, Republicans are going to cut Social Security and Medicare. They started it again.

I'm the president that stood up and said, don't mess with Social Security, and I'm not going to and we haven't and we are not going to go after the Social Security recipient.

I have one difference with Mr. Perot on that because I don't think we need to touch Social Security.

What we do need to do, though, is control the growth of these mandatory programs. And Ross properly says, okay, there's some pain in that. But Governor Clinton refuses to touch that, simply refuses. So what we've got to do is control it, let it grow for inflation, let it grow for the amount of new people added, population, and then hold the line.

And I believe that is the way you get the deficit down, not by the tax-and-spend program that we hear every four years, whether it's Mondale, Dukakis, whoever else it is. I just don't believe we ought to do that. So hold the line on Social Security and put a cap on the growth of the mandatory program. . . .

[Rationing Health Care]

VANOCUR: Governor Clinton, Ann Compton has brought up Medicare. I remember in 1965, when Wilbur Mills of Arkansas, the chairman of Ways and Means, was pushing it through the Congress. The charge against it was it's socialized medicine.

GOVERNOR CLINTON: Mr. Bush made that charge.

VANOCUR: Well, he served with him two years later, in 1967, where I first met him. The second point, though, is that it is now skyrocketing out of control. People want it. We say it's going bonkers.

Is not the Oregon plan applied to Medicaid rationing the proper way to go even though the federal government last August ruled that it violated the Americans with Disabilities Act of 1990?

GOVERNOR CLINTON: I thought the Oregon plan should at least have been allowed to be tried because at least the people in Oregon were trying to do something. Let me go back to the main point, Sandy.

Mr. Bush is trying to run against Lyndon Johnson and Jimmy Carter and everybody in the world but me in this race. I have proposed a managed competition plan for health care. I will say again: you cannot control health care costs simply by cutting Medicare. Look what's happened. The federal government has cut Medicare and Medicaid in the last few years, states have cut Medicaid—we've done it in Arkansas under budget pressures. But what happens? More and more people get on the rolls as poverty increases. If you don't control the health care costs of the entire system, you cannot get control of it.

Look at our program. We set up a national ceiling on health care costs tied to inflation and population growth set by health care providers, not by the government. We provide for managed competition, not government models, in every states. And we control private and public health care costs.

Now, just a few days ago a bipartisan commission of Republicans and Democrats—more Republicans than Democrats—said my plan will save the average family $1,200 a year more than the Bush plan will by the year 2000, $2.2 trillion in the next 12 years, $400 billion a year by the end of this decade. I've got a plan to control health care costs. But you can't just do it by cutting Medicare; you have to take on the insurance companies, the bureaucracies. And you have to have cost controls, yes.

But keep in mind we are spending 30 percent more on health care than any country in the world, any country, and yet we have 35 million people uninsured, we have no preventing and primary care. The Oregon plan is a good start if the federal government is going to continue to abandon its responsibilities. I say if Germany can cover everybody and keep costs under inflation, if Hawaii can cover 98 percent of their people at lower health care costs than the rest of us, if Rochester, New York, can do it with two-thirds of the cost of the rest of it, America can do it, too. I'm tired of being told we can't. I say we can. We can do better, and we must.

PRESIDENT BUSH: Well, I don't have time in 30 seconds, or whatever—a minute—to talk about our health care reform plan. The Oregon plan made some good sense, but it's easy to dismiss the concerns of the disabled. As president I have to be sure that those waivers, which we're approving all over the place, are covered under the law. Maybe we can work it out. But the Americans with Disabilities Act, speaking about sound and sensible civil rights legislation, was the most foremost piece of legislation passed in modern times, and so we do have something more than a technical problem.

Governor Clinton clicked off the things—he's going to take on insurance companies and bureaucracies. He failed to take on somebody else—the malpractice suit people, those that bring these lawsuits against—these frivolous trial lawyers' lawsuits that are running the costs of medical care up 25 to 50 billion. And he refuses to put anything, controls, on these crazy lawsuits.

If you want to help somebody, don't run the costs up by making doctors have to have five or six tests where one would do for fear of being sued, or have somebody along the highway not stop to pick up a guy and help him because he's afraid a trial lawyer will come along and sue him. We're suing each other too much and caring for each other too little.

PEROT: We got the most expensive health care system in the world; it ranks behind 15 other nations when we come to life expectancy, and 22 other nations when we come to infant mortality. So we don't have the best.

Pretty simple, folks—if you're paying more and you don't have the best, if all else fails go copy the people who have the best who spend less, right?

Well, we can do better than that. Again, we've got plans lying all over the place in Washington. Nobody ever implements them. Now I'm back to square one. If you want to stop talking about it and do it, then I'll be glad to go up there and we'll get it done. But if you just want to keep the music going, just stay traditional this next time around, and four years from now you'll have everybody blaming everybody else for a bad health care system.

Talk is cheap; words are plentiful, deeds are precious. Let's get on with it.

LEHRER: And that's exactly what we're going to do. That was, in fact, the final question and answer. We're now going to move to closing statements. Each candidate will have up to two minutes. The order, remember, was determined by drawing, and Mr. Perot, you are first.

PEROT: Well, it's been a privilege to be able to talk to the American people tonight. I make no bones about it. I love this country. I love the principle it's founded on. I love the people here. I don't like to see the country's principles violated. I don't like to see the people in a deteriorating economy in a deteriorating country because our government has lost touch with the people.

The people in Washington are good people. We just have a bad system. We've got to change the system. It's time to do it because we have run up so much debt that time is no longer our friend. We've got to put our house in order.

When you go to bed tonight, look at your children. Think of their dreams. Think of your dreams as a child and ask yourself, isn't it time to stop talking about it? Isn't it time to stop creating images? Isn't it time to do it? Aren't you sick of being treated like an unprogrammed robot? Every four years, they send you all kinds of messages to tell you how to vote and then go back to business as usual.

They told you at the tax and budget summit that if you agreed to a tax increase, we could balance the budget. They didn't tell you that that same year they increased spending $1.83 for every dollar we increased taxes. That's Washington in a nutshell right there.

In the final analysis, I'm doing this for your children when you look at them tonight.

There's another group that I feel very close to, and these at the men and women who fought on the battlefield, the children—the families—of the ones who died and the people who left parts of their bodies over there. I'd never ask you to do anything for me, but I owe you this, and I'm doing it for you. And I can't tell you what it means to me at these rallies when I see you and you come up and the look in your eyes—and I know how you feel and you know how I feel. And then I think of the older people who are retired. They grew up in the Depression. They fought and won World War II. We owe you a debt we can never repay you. And the greatest repayment I can ever give is to recreate the American dream for your children and grandchildren. I'll give you everything I have, if you want me to do it.

GOVERNOR CLINTON: I'd like to thank the people of St. Louis and Washington University, the Presidential Debate Commission and all those who made this night possible. And I'd like to thank those of you who are watching.

Most of all, I'd like to thank all of you who have touched me in some way over this last year, all the thousands of you whom I've seen. I'd like to thank the computer executives and the electronics executives in Silicon Valley, two-thirds of whom are Republicans who said they wanted to sign on to a change in America. I'd like to thank the hundreds of executives who came to Chicago, a third of them Republicans, who said they wanted to change. I'd like to thank the people who've started with Mr. Perot who've come on to help our campaign.

I'd like to thank all the folks around America that no one ever knows about—the woman that was holding the AIDS baby she adopted in Cedar Rapids, Iowa who asked me to do something more for adoption; the woman who stopped along the road in Wisconsin and wept because her husband had lost his job after 27 years; all the people who are having a tough time and the people who are winning but who know how desperately we need to change.

This debate tonight has made crystal clear a challenge that is old as America—the choice between hope and fear, change or more of the same, the courage to move into a new tomorrow or to listen to the crowd who says things could be worse.

Mr. Bush has said some very compelling things tonight that don't quite square with the record. He was president for three years before he proposed a health care plan that still hasn't been sent to Congress in total; three years before an economic plan, and he still didn't say tonight that that tax bill he vetoed raised taxes only on the rich and gave the rest of you a break—but he vetoed it anyway.

I offer a new direction. Invest in American jobs, American education, control health care costs, bring this country together again. I want the future of this country to be as bright and brilliant as its past, and it can be if we have the courage to change. . . .

PRESIDENT BUSH: Let me tell you a little what it's like to be president. In the Oval Office, you can't predict what kind of crisis is going to come up. You have to make tough calls. You can't be on one hand this way and one hand another. You can't take different positions on these difficult issues. And then you need a philosophical—I'd call it a philosophical underpinning. Mine for foreign affairs is democracy and freedom, and look at the dramatic changes around the world. The Cold War is over. The Soviet Union is no more and we're working with a democratic country. Poland, Hungary, Czechoslovakia, the Baltics are free.

Take a look at the Middle East. We had to stand up against a tyrant. The United States came together as we haven't in many, many years. And we kicked this man out of Kuwait. And in the process, as a result of that will and that decision and that toughness, we now have ancient enemies talking peace in the Middle East. Nobody would have dreamed it possible.

And I think the biggest dividend of making these tough calls is the fact that we are less afraid of nuclear war. Every parent out there has much less worry that their kids are going to be faced with nuclear holocaust. All this is good.

On the domestic side, what we must do is have change that empowers people—not change for the sake of change, tax and spend. We don't need to do that any more. What we need to do is empower people. We need to invest and save. We need to do better in education. We need to do better in job retraining. We need to expand our exports, and they're going very, very well, indeed. And we need to strengthen the American family.

I hope as president that I've earned your trust. I've admitted it when I make a mistake, but then I go on and help, try to solve the problems. I hope I've earned your trust because a lot of being president is about trust and character. And I ask for your support for four more years to finish this job.

Thank you very, very much. . . .

OCTOBER 15 PRESIDENTIAL DEBATE

CAROLE SIMPSON: Good evening and welcome to this second of three presidential debates between the major candidates for president of the United States. The candidates are the Republican nominee, President George Bush, the independent Ross Perot and Governor Bill Clinton, the Democratic nominee.

My name is Carole Simpson, and I will be the moderator for tonight's 90-minute debate, which is coming to you from the campus of the University of Richmond in Richmond, Virginia.

Now, tonight's program is unlike any other presidential debate in history. We're making history now and it's pretty exciting. An independent polling firm has selected an audience of 209 uncommitted voters from this area. The candidates will be asked questions by these voters on a topic of their choosing—anything they want to ask about. My job as moderator is to, you know, take care of the questioning, ask questions myself if I think there needs to be continuity and balance, and sometimes I might ask the candidates to respond to what another candidate may have said.

Now, the format has been agreed to by representatives of both the Republican and Democratic campaigns, and there is no subject matter that is restricted. Anything goes. We can ask anything.

After the debate, the candidates will have an opportunity to make a closing statement.

So, President Bush, I think you said it earlier—let's get it on.

PRESIDENT GEORGE BUSH: Let's go.

SIMPSON: And I think the first question is over here.

AUDIENCE PARTICIPANT: Yes. I'd like to direct my question to Mr. Perot. What will you do as president to open foreign markets to fair competition from American business and to stop unfair competition here at home from foreign countries so that we can bring jobs back to the United States?

ROSS PEROT: That's right at the top of my agenda. We've shipped millions of jobs overseas and we have a strange situation because we have a process in Washington where after you've served for a while you cash in, become a foreign lobbyist, make $30,000 a month, then take a leave, work on presidential campaigns, make sure you've got good contacts and then go back out.

Now, if you just want to get down to brass tacks, first thing you ought to do is get all these folks who've got these one-way trade agreements that we've negotiated over the years and say fellas, we'll take the same deal we gave you. And they'll gridlock right at that point because for example, we've got international competitors who simply could not unload their cars off the ships if they had to comply—you see, if it was a two-way street, just couldn't do it. We have got to stop sending jobs overseas.

To those of you in the audience who are business people: pretty simple. If you're paying $12, $13, $14 an hour for a factory worker, and you can move your factory south of the border, pay $1 an hour for labor, hire a young—let's assume you've been in business for a long time. You've got a mature workforce. Pay $1 an hour for your labor, have no health care—that's the most expensive single element in making the car. Have no environmental controls, no pollution controls and no retirement. And you don't care about anything but making money. There will be a job-sucking sound going south. If the people send me to Washington the first thing I'll do is study that 2,000-page agreement and make sure it's a two-way street.

One last point here. I decided I was dumb and didn't understand it so I called a "Who's Who" of the folks that have been around it, and I said why won't everybody go south; they said it will be disruptive; I said for how long. I finally got 'em for 12 to 15 years. And I said, well, how does it stop being disruptive? And that is when their jobs come up from a dollar an hour to six dollars an hour, and ours go down to six dollars an hour; then it's levelled again, but in the meantime you've wrecked the country with these kind of deals. We got to cut it out.

SIMPSON: Thank you, Mr. Perot. I see that the president has stood up, so he must have something to say about this.

PRESIDENT BUSH: Carole, the thing that saved us in this global economic slowdown has been our exports, and what I'm trying to do is increase our exports. And if indeed all the jobs were going to move south because there are lower wages, there are lower wages now and they haven't done that. And so I have just negotiated with the president of Mexico the North American Free Trade Agreement—and the prime minister of Canada, I might add—and I want to have more of these free trade agreements, because export jobs are increasing far faster than any jobs that may have moved overseas. That's a scare tactic, because it's not that many. But any one that's here, we want to have more jobs here. And the way to do that is to increase our exports.

Some believe in protection. I don't; I believe in free and fair trade, and that's the thing that saved us. So I will keep on as president trying to get a successful conclusion to the GATT Round, the big Uruguay Round of trade which will really open up markets for our agriculture particularly. I want to continue to work after we get this NAFTA agreement ratified this coming year. I want to get one with Eastern Europe; I want to get one with Chile. And free and fair trade is the answer, not protection.

And, as I say, we've had tough economic times, and it's exports that have saved us, exports that have built.

SIMPSON: Governor Clinton.

GOVERNOR BILL CLINTON: I'd like to answer the question, because I've actually been a governor for 12 years, so I've known a lot of people who have lost their jobs because of jobs moving overseas, and I know a lot of people whose plants have been strengthened by increasing exports.

The trick is to expand our export base and to expand trade on terms that are fair to us. It is true that our exports to Mexico, for example, have gone up and our trade deficit has gone down; it's also true that just today a record high trade deficit was announced with Japan.

So what is the answer? Let me just mention three things very quickly. Number one, make sure that other countries are as open to our markets as our markets are to them, and, if they're not, have measures on the books that don't take forever and a day to implement.

Number two, change the tax code. There are more deductions in the tax code for shutting plants down and moving overseas than there are for modernizing plant and equipment here. Our competitors don't do that. Emphasize and subsidize modernizing plant and equipment here, not moving plants overseas.

Number three, stop the federal government's program that now gives low-interest loans and job training funds to companies that will actually shut down and move to other countries, but we won't do the same thing for plants that stay here.

So more trade but on fair terms—and favor investment in America. . . .

[Deficit Reduction]

AUDIENCE PARTICIPANT: This is for Governor Clinton. In the real world, that is, outside of Washington, D.C., compensation and achievement are based on goals defined and achieved. My question is about the deficit. Would you define in specific dollar goals how much you would reduce the deficit in each of the four years of a Clinton administration and then enter into a legally binding contract with the American people, that if you did not achieve those goals that you would not seek a second term? Answer yes or no and then comment on your answer, please.

GOVERNOR CLINTON: No, and here's why. And I'll tell you exactly why. Because the deficit now has been building up for 12 years. I'll tell you exactly what I think can be done. I think we can bring it down by 50 percent in four years and grow the economy. Now, I could get rid of it in four years in theory on the books now, but to do it you'd have to raise taxes too much and cut benefits too much to people who need them and it would even make the economy worse.

Mr. Perot will tell you, for example, that the expert he hired to analyze his plan says that it will bring the deficit down in five years but it will make unemployment bad for four more years. So my view is, sir, you have to increase investment, grow the economy and reduce the deficit by controlling health care costs, prudent reductions in defense, cuts in domestic programs and asking the wealthiest Americans and foreign corporations to pay their fair share of taxes and investing and growing this economy.

I ask everybody to look at my economic ideas and nine Nobel prize winners and over 500 economists and hundreds of business people, including a lot of Republicans said, this is the way you've got to go. If you don't grow the economy you can't get it done. But I can't foresee all the things that will happen, and I don't think a president should be judged solely on the deficit.

Let me also say, we're having an election today. You'll have a shot at me in four years and you can vote me right out if you think I've done a lousy job and I would welcome you to do that.

PRESIDENT BUSH: Well, I'm a little confused here, because I don't see how you can grow the deficit down by raising people's taxes. You see, I don't think the American people are taxed too little. I think they're taxed too much. I went for one tax increase and when I make a mistake I admit it. I said that wasn't the right thing to do.

Governor Clinton's program wants to tax more and spend more—$150 billion in new taxes, spend another $220. I don't believe that's the way to do it.

Here's some thing that'll help. Give us a balanced budget amendment.

He always talks about Arkansas having a balanced budget and they do, but he has a balanced budget amendment. Have to do it. I've like the government to have that. And I think it would discipline not only the Congress, which needs it, but also the executive branch.

I'd like to have what 43 governors have—the line item veto, so if the Congress can't cut, and we've got a reckless spending Congress, let the president have a shot at it by wiping out things that are pork barrel or something of that nature.

I've proposed another one. Some sophisticates think it may be a little gimmicky. I think it's good. It's a check-off. It says to you as a taxpayer— say you're going to pay a tax of 1,000 bucks or something. You can check 10 percent of that if you want to, in the one box, and that 10 percent, $100, or if you're paying $10,000, whatever it is, $1,000, check it off and make the government, make it lower the deficit by that amount.

And if the Congress won't do it, if they can't get together and negotiate how to do that, then you'd have a sequester across the board. You'd exempt Social Security—I don't want to tax or touch Social Security. I'm the president that said hey, don't mess with Social Security, and we haven't.

So I believe that we need to control the growth of mandatory spending, back to this gentleman's question. That's the main growing thing in the budget. The program that the president—two-thirds of the budget, I as president never get to look at, never get to touch. We've got to control that growth to inflation and population increase, but not raise taxes on the American people now. I just don't believe that would stimulate any kind of growth at all.

PEROT: Well, we're $4 trillion in debt. We're going into debt an additional $1 billion, little more than $1 billion every working day of the year.

Now, the thing I love about it—I'm just a businessman. I was down in Texas taking care of business, tending to my family. This situation got so bad that I decided I'd better get into it. The American people asked me to get into it. But I just find it fascinating that while we sit here tonight we will go into debt an additional $50 million in an hour and a half.

Now, it's not the Republicans' fault, of course, and it's not the Democrats' fault. And what I'm looking for is who did it? Now, they're the two folks involved so maybe if you put them together, they did it.

Now, the facts are we have to fix it. I'm here tonight for these young people up here in the balcony from this college. When I was a young man, when I got out of the Navy I had multiple job offers. Young people with high grades can't get a job. People—the 18- to 24-year-old high school graduates ten years ago were making more than they are now. In other words, we were down to 18 percent of them were making—18- to 24-year-olds were making less than $12,000. Now that's up to 40 percent. And what's happened in the meantime? The dollar's gone through the floor.

Now, whose fault is that? Not the Democrats. Not the Republicans.

Somewhere out there there's an extraterrestrial that's doing this to us, I guess. And everybody says they take responsibility. Somebody somewhere has to take responsibility for this.

Put it to you bluntly, American people. If you want me to be your president, we're going to face our problems. We'll deal with the problems. We'll solve our problems. We'll pay down our debt. We'll pass on the American dream to our children, and I will not leave our children a situation that they have today. . . .

[The Character Issue]

AUDIENCE PARTICIPANT: Yes, I'd like to address all the candidates with this question. The amount of time the candidates have spent in this campaign trashing their opponents' character and their programs is depressingly large. Why can't your discussions and proposals reflect the genuine complexity and the difficulty of the issues. . . .

PEROT: I couldn't agree with you more, couldn't agree with you more. And I have said again and again and again let's get off mud wrestling, let's get off personalities and let's talk about jobs, health care, crime, the things that concern the American people. I'm spending my money—not PAC money, not foreign money, my money—to take this message to the people.

SIMPSON: Thank you, Mr. Perot. . . .

PRESIDENT BUSH: Well, in the first place, I believe that character is a part of being president. I think you have to look at it. I think that has to be a part of a candidate for president or being president. In terms of programs, I've submitted, what, four different budgets to the United States Congress in great detail. It's so heavy they'd give you a broken back. And everything in there says what I am for.

Now I've come out with a new agenda for America's renewal, a plan that I believe really will help stimulate the growth of this economy. My record on world affairs is pretty well known because I've been president for four years, so I feel I've been talking issues.

You know, nobody likes who shot John, but I think the first negative campaign run in this election was by Governor Clinton, and I'm not going to sit there and be a punching bag; I'm going to stand up and say, hey, listen, here's my side of it.

But character is an important part of the equation. The other night Governor Clinton raised my—I don't know if you saw the debate the other night. You did—suffered through that? Well, he raised the question of my father—it was a good line, well rehearsed and well delivered. But he raised the question of my father and said, well, your father, Prescott Bush, was against McCarthy, you should be ashamed of yourself, McCarthyism. I remember something my dad told me—I was 18 years old going to Penn Station to go on into the Navy, and he said write your mother—which I faithfully did; he said serve your country—my father was an honor, duty and country man; and he said tell the truth. And I've tried to do that in public life, all through it. That says something about character.

My argument with Governor Clinton—you can call it mud wrestling, but I think it's fair to put in focus is—I am deeply troubled by someone who demonstrates and organizes demonstration in a foreign land when his country's at war. Probably a lot of kids here disagree with me. But that's what I feel. That's what I feel passionately about. I'm thinking of Ross Perot's running mate sitting in the jail. How would he feel about it? But maybe that's generational. I don't know.

But the big argument I have with the governor on this is this taking different positions on different issues—trying to be one thing to one person here that's opposing the NAFTA agreement and then for it—what we call waffling. And I do think that you can't turn the White House into the Waffle House. You've got to say what you're for and you've got to—

SIMPSON: . . . I'm getting time cues and with all due respect—

PRESIDENT BUSH: Excuse me. I don't want to—

SIMPSON: I'm sorry.

PRESIDENT BUSH: I don't want to—

SIMPSON: Governor Clinton.

PRESIDENT BUSH: I get wound up because I feel strongly—

SIMPSON: Yes, you do. (Laughter)

GOVERNOR CLINTON: Let me say first of all to you that I believe so strongly in the question you asked that I suggested this format tonight. I started doing these formats a year ago in New Hampshire and I found that we had huge crowds because all I did was let people ask questions and I tried to give very specific answers. I also had a program starting last year. I've been disturbed by the tone and the tenor of this campaign. Thank goodness the networks have a fact check so I don't have to just go blue in the face anymore. Mr. Bush said once again I was going to have $150 billion tax increase. When Mr. Quayle said that all the networks said, that's not true. He's got over $100 billion of tax cuts and incentives.

So I'm not going to take up your time tonight, but let me just say this. We'll have a debate in four days and we can talk about this character thing again. But the Washington Post ran a long editorial today saying they couldn't believe Mr. Bush was making character an issue and they said he was the greatest quote "political chameleon" for changing has positions of all times. Now, I don't want to get into that—

PRESIDENT BUSH: Please don't get into the Washington Post.

GOVERNOR CLINTON: Wait a minute. Let's don't—you don't have to believe it. Here's my point. I'm not interested in his character. I want to change the character of the presidency. And I'm interested in what we can trust him to do and what you can trust me to do and what you can trust Mr. Perot to do for the next four years. So I think you're right and I hope the rest of the night belongs to you. . . .

[Gun Control]

AUDIENCE PARTICIPANT: My question was originally for Governor Clinton, but I think I would welcome a response from all three candidates. As you are aware, crime is rampant in our cities. And in the Richmond area—and I'm sure it's happened elsewhere—12-year-olds are carrying guns to school. And I'm sure when our Founding Fathers wrote the Constitution they did not mean for the right to bear arms to apply to 12-year-olds. So I'm asking: Where do you stand on gun control, and what do you plan to do about it?

SIMPSON: Governor Clinton?

GOVERNOR CLINTON: I support the right to keep and bear arms. I live in a state where over half the adults have hunting or fishing licenses, or both. But I believe we have to have some way of checking hand guns before they're sold, to check the criminal history, the mental health history, and the age of people who are buying them. Therefore I support the Brady bill which would impose a national waiting period unless and until a state did what only Virginia has done now, which is to automate its records. Once you automate your records, then you don't have to have a waiting period, but at least you can check.

I also think we should have frankly restrictions on assault weapons whose only purpose is to kill. We need to give the police a fighting chance in our urban areas where the gangs are building up.

The third thing I would say—it doesn't bear directly on gun control, but it's very important—we need more police on the street. There is a crime bill which would put more police on the street, which was killed for this session by a filibuster in the Senate, mostly be Republican senators, and I think it's a shame it didn't pass, I think it should be made the law—but it had the Brady bill in it, the waiting period.

I also believe that we should offer college scholarships to people who will agree to work them off as police officers, and I think, as we reduce our military forces, we should let people earn military retirement by coming out and working as police officers. Thirty years ago there were three police officers on the street for every crime; today there are three crimes for every police officer.

In the communities which have had real success putting police officers near schools where kids carry weapons, to get the weapons out of the schools, are on the same blocks, you've seen crime go down. In Houston there's been a 15-percent drop in the crime rate in the last year because of the work the mayor did there in increasing the police force. So I know it can work; I've seen it happen....

PRESIDENT BUSH: I think you put your finger on a major problem. I talk about strengthening the American family and it's very hard to strengthen the family if people are scared to walk down to the corner store and, you know, send their kid down to get a loaf of bread. It's very hard.

I have been fighting for very strong anti-crime legislation—habeas corpus reform, so you don't have these endless appeals, so when somebody gets sentenced, hey, this is for real. I've been fighting for changes in the exclusionary rule so if an honest cop stops somebody and makes a technical mistake, the criminal doesn't go away.

I'll probably get into a fight in this room with some but I happen to think that we need stronger death penalties for those that kill police officers.

Virginia's in the lead in this, as Governor Clinton properly said, on this identification system for firearms. I am not for national registration of firearms. Some of the states that have the toughest anti-gun laws have the highest levels of crime. I am for the right, as the governor says—I'm a sportsman and I don't think you ought to eliminate all kinds of weapons. But I was not for the bill that he was talking about because it was not tough enough on the criminal.

I'm very pleased that the Fraternal Order of Police in Little Rock, Arkansas endorsed me because I think they see I'm trying to strengthen the anti-crime legislation. We've got more money going out for local police than any previous administration.

So we've got to get it under control and there's one last point I'd make. Drugs. We have got to win our national strategy against drugs, the fight against drugs. And we're making some progress, doing a little better on interdiction. We're not doing as well amongst the people that get to be habitual drug-users.

The good news is, and I think it's true in Richmond, teenage use is down of cocaine, substantially, 60 percent in the last couple of years. So we're making progress but until we get that one done, we're not going to solve the neighborhood crime problem.

SIMPSON: Mr. Perot. . . . What are you going to do to get the guns off the street?

PEROT: On any program, and this includes crime, you'll find we have all kinds of great plans lying around that never get enacted into law and implemented. I don't care what it is—competitiveness, health care, crime, you name it. Brady Bill, I agree that it's a timid step in the right direction but it won't fix it. So why pass a law that won't fix it?

Now, what it really boils down to is can you live—we become so preoccupied with the rights of the criminal that we've forgotten the rights of the innocent. And in our country we have evolved to a point where we've put millions of innocent people in jail because you go to the poor neighborhoods and they've put bars on their windows and bars on their doors and put themselves in jail to protect the things that they acquired legitimately. That's where we are.

We have got to become more concerned about people who play by the rules and get the balance we require. This is going to take first, building a consensus at grassroots America. Right from the bottom up, the American people have got to say they want it. And at that point, we can pick from a variety of plans and develop new plans. And the way you get things done is bury yourselves in the room with one another, put together the best program, take it to the American people, use the electronic town hall, the kind of thing you're doing here tonight, build a consensus and then do it and then go on to the next one. But don't just sit here slow dancing for four years doing nothing. . . .

[Term Limits]

AUDIENCE PARTICIPANT: Please state your position on term limits, and, if you are in favor of them, how will you get them enacted?

PRESIDENT BUSH: Any order? I'll be glad to respond.

SIMPSON: Thank you.

PRESIDENT BUSH: I strongly support term limits for members of the United States Congress. I believe it would return the government closer to the people, the way that Ross Perot is talking about. The president's terms are limited to two, a total of eight years. What's wrong with limiting the terms of members of Congress to 12? Congress has gotten kind of institutionalized. For 38 years one party has controlled the House of Representatives, and the result, a sorry little post office that can't do anything right and a bank that has more overdrafts than all the Chase Bank and Citibank put together. We've got to do something about it.

And I think you get a certain arrogance, bureaucratic arrogance, if people stay there too long. And so I favor, strongly favor, term limits.

And how to get them passed? Send us some people that will pass the idea. And I think you will. I think the American people want it now. Every place I go I talk about it, and I think they want it done. Actually, you'd have to have some amendments to the Constitution because of the way the Constitution reads. . . .

GOVERNOR CLINTON: I know they're popular, but I'm against them. I'll tell you why. I believe, number one, it would pose a real problem for a lot of smaller states in the Congress who have enough trouble now making sure their interests are heard. Number two, I think it would increase the influence of unelected staff members in the Congress who have too much influence already. I want to cut the size of the congressional staffs, but I think you're going to have too much influence there with people who were never elected, who have lots of expertise.

Number three, if the people really have a mind to change, they can. You're going to have 120 to 150 new members of Congress.

Now, let me tell you what I favor instead. I favor strict controls on how much you can spend running for Congress, strict limits on political action committees, requirements that people running for Congress appear in open public debates like we're doing now. If you did that you could take away the incumbents' advantage because challengers like me would have a chance to run against incumbents like him for House races and Senate races, and then the voters could make up their own mind without being subject to an unfair fight.

So that's how I feel about it, and I think if we had the right kind of campaign reform, we'd get the changes you want.

SIMPSON: Mr. Perot, would you like to address term limitations?

PEROT: Yes. Let me do first on a personal level. If the American people send me up to do this job, I intend to be there one term. I do not intend to spend one minute of one day thinking about re-election. And as a matter of principle—and my situation is unique, and I understand it—I would take absolutely no compensation; I go as their servant.

Now, I have set as strong an example as I can, then at that point when we sit down over at Capitol Hill—tomorrow night I'm going to be talking about government reform—it's a long subject, you wouldn't let me finish tonight. If you want to hear it, you get it tomorrow night—you'll hear it tomorrow night.

But we have got to reform government. If you put term limits in and don't reform government, you won't get the benefits you thought. It takes both. So we need to do the reforms and the term limits. And after we reform it, it won't be a lifetime career opportunity; good people will go serve and then go back to their homes and not become foreign lobbyists and cash in at 30,000 bucks a month and then take time off to run some president's campaign.

They're all nice people, they're just in a bad system. I don't think there are any villains, but, boy, is the system rotten.

[Costs of Health Care]

AUDIENCE PARTICIPANT: I'd like to ask Governor Clinton, do you attribute the rising costs of health care to the medical profession itself, or do you think the problem lies elsewhere? And what specific proposals do you have to tackle this problem?

GOVERNOR CLINTON: I've had more people talk to me about their health care problems I guess than anything else, all across America—you know, people who've lost their jobs, lost their businesses, had to give up their jobs because of sick children. So let me try to answer you in this way. Let's start with a premise. We spend 30 percent more of our income than any nation on earth on health care, and yet we insure fewer people. We have 35 million people without any insurance at all—and I see them all the time. A hundred thousand Americans a month have lost their health insurance just in the last four years.

So if you analyze where we're out of line with other countries, you come up with the following conclusions. Number one, we spend at least $60 billion a year on insurance, administrative cost, bureaucracy, and government regulation that wouldn't be spent in any other nation. So we have to have, in my judgment, a drastic simplification of the basic health insurance policies of this country, be very comprehensive for everybody.

Employers would cover their employees, government would cover the unemployed.

Number two, I think you have to take on specifically the insurance companies and require them to make some significant change in the way they rate people in the big community pools. I think you have to tell the pharmaceutical companies they can't keep raising drug prices at three times the rate of inflation. I think you have to take on medical fraud. I think you have to help doctors stop practicing defensive medicine. I've recommended that our doctors be given a set of national practice guidelines and that if they follow those guidelines that raises the presumption that they didn't do anything wrong.

I think you have to have a system of primary and preventive clinics in our inner cities and our rural areas so people can have access to health care.

The key is to control the cost and maintain the quality. To do that you need a system of managed competition where all of us are covered in big groups and we can choose our doctors and our hospitals, a wide range, but there is an incentive to control costs. And I think there has to be—I think Mr. Perot and I agree on this, there has to be a national commission of health care providers and health care consumers that set ceilings to keep health costs in line with inflation, plus population growth.

Now, let me say, some people say we can't do this but Hawaii does it. They cover 98 percent of their people and their insurance premiums are much cheaper than the rest of America, and so does Rochester, New York. They now have a plan to cover everybody and their premiums are two-thirds of the rest of the country.

This is very important. It's a big human problem and a devastating economic problem for America, and I'm going to send a plan to do this within the first 100 days of my presidency. It's terribly important. . . .

PRESIDENT BUSH: I just have to say something. I don't want to stampede. Ross was very articulate across the country. I don't want anybody to stampede to cut the president's salary off altogether. Barbara's sitting over here and I—but what I have proposed, 10 percent cut, downsize the government, and we can get that done.

She asked a question, I think, is whether the health care profession was to blame. No. One thing to blame is these malpractice lawsuits. They're breaking the system. It costs $20-25 billion a year, and I want to see those outrageous claims capped. Doctors don't dare to deliver babies sometimes because they're afraid that somebody's going to sue them. People don't dare—medical practitioners, to help somebody along the highway that are hurt because they're afraid that some lawyer's going to come along and get a big lawsuit. So you can't blame the practitioners for the health problem.

And my program is this. Keep the government as far out of it as possible, make insurance available to the poorest of the poor, through vouchers, next range in the income bracket, through tax credits, and get on about the business of pooling insurance. A great big company can buy—Ross has got a good-sized company, been very successful. He can buy insurance cheaper than Mom and Pop's store on the corner. But if those Mom and Pop stores all get together and pool, they too can bring the cost of insurance down.

So I want to keep the quality of health care. That means keep government out of it. I want to do—I don't like this idea of these boards. It all sounds to me like you're going to have some government setting price. I want competition and I want to pool the insurance and take care of it that way and have—oh, here's the other point.

I think medical care should go with the person. If you leave a business, I think your insurance should go with you to some other business. You shouldn't be worrying if you get a new job as to whether that's gonna—and part of our plan is to make it what they call portable—big word, but that means if you're working for the Jones Company and you go to the Smith Company, your insurance goes with you. I think it's a good program. I'm really excited about getting it done, too. . . .

PEROT: We have the most expensive health care system in the world. Twelve percent of our gross national product goes to health care. Our industrial competitors, who are beating us in competition, spend less and have better health care. Japan spends a little over 6 percent of its gross national product. Germany spends 8 percent.

It's fascinating. You've bought a front row box seat and you're not happy with your health care and you're saying tonight we've got bad health care but very expensive health care. Folks, here's why. Go home and look in the mirror.

You own this country but you have no voice in it the way it's organized now, and if you want to have a high risk experience, comparable to bungee jumping, go into Congress some time when they're working on this kind of legislation, when the lobbyists are running up and down the halls. Wear your safety toe shoes when you go. And as a private citizen, believe me, you are looked on as a major nuisance.

The facts are you now have a government that comes at you. You're supposed to have a government that comes from you.

Now, there are all kinds of good ideas, brilliant ideas, terrific ideas on health care. None of them ever get implemented because—let me give you an example. A senator runs every six years. He's got to raise 20,000 bucks a week to have enough money to run. Who's he gonna listen to—us or the folks running up and down the aisles with money, the lobbyists, the PAC money? He listens to them. Who do they represent? Health care industry. Not us.

Now, you've got to have a government that comes from you again. You've got to reassert your ownership in this country and you've got to completely reform our government. And at that point they'll just be like apples falling out of a tree. The programs will be good because the elected officials will be listening to—I said the other night I was all ears and I would listen to any good idea. I think we ought to do plastic surgery on a lot of these guys so that they're all ears, too, and listen to you. Then you get what you want, and shouldn't you? You paid for it. Why shouldn't you get what you want, as opposed to what some lobbyist cuts a deal, writes a little piece in the law and he goes through. That's the way the game's played now. Till you change it you're gonna be unhappy.

SIMPSON: You wanted one brief point in there.

GOVERNOR CLINTON: One brief point. We have elections so people can make decisions about this. The point I want to make to you is, a bipartisan commission reviewed my plan and the Bush plan and there were as many Republicans as Democratic health care experts on it. They concluded that my plan would cover everybody and his would leave 27 million behind by the year 2000 and that my plan in the next 12 years would save $2.2 trillion in public and private money to reinvest in this economy and the average family would save $1,200 a year under the plan that I offered without any erosion in the quality of health care.

So I ask you to look at that. And you have to vote for somebody with a plan. That's what you have elections for. If people would say, well, he got elected to do this and then the Congress says, okay, I'm going to do it. That's what the election was about. . . .

[Personal Effects of Recession]

AUDIENCE PARTICIPANT: Yes. How has the national debt personally affected each of your lives? And if it hasn't, how can you honestly find a cure for the economic problems of the common people if you have no experience in what's ailing them?

PEROT: May I answer that?

SIMPSON: Well, Mr. Perot—yes, of course.

PEROT: Who do you want to start with?

AUDIENCE PARTICIPANT: My question is for each of you, so—

PEROT: It caused me to disrupt my private life and my business to get involved in this activity. That's how much I care about it. And believe me, if you knew my family and if you knew the private life I have, you would agree in a minute that that's a whole lot more fun than getting involved in politics.

But I have lived the American dream. I came from very modest background. Nobody's been luckier than I've been, all the way across the spectrum, and the greatest riches of all are my wife and children. That's true of any family.

But I want all the children—I want these young people up here to be able to start with nothing but an idea like I did and build a business. But they've got to have a strong basic economy and if you're in debt, it's like having a ball and chain around you.

I just figure, as lucky as I've been, I owe it to them and I owe it to the future generations and on a very personal basis, I owe it to my children and grandchildren.

SIMPSON: Thank you, Mr. Perot. Mr. President.

PRESIDENT BUSH: Well, I think the national debt affects everybody.

AUDIENCE PARTICIPANT: You personally.

PRESIDENT BUSH: Obviously it has a lot to do with interest rates—

SIMPSON: She's saying, "you personally"

AUDIENCE PARTICIPANT: You, on a personal basis—how has it affected you?

SIMPSON: Has it affected you personally?

PRESIDENT BUSH: I'm sure it has. I love my grandchildren—

AUDIENCE PARTICIPANT: How?

PRESIDENT BUSH: I want to think that they're going to be able to afford an education. I think that that's an important part of being a parent. If the question—maybe I—get it wrong. Are you suggesting that if somebody has means that the national debt doesn't affect them?

AUDIENCE PARTICIPANT: What I'm saying is—

PRESIDENT BUSH: I'm not sure I get—help me with the question and I'll try to answer it.

AUDIENCE PARTICIPANT: Well, I've had friends that have been laid off from jobs.

PRESIDENT BUSH: Yeah.

AUDIENCE PARTICIPANT: I know people who cannot afford to pay the mortgage on their homes, their car payment. I have personal problems with the national debt. But how has it affected you and if you have no experience in it, how can you help us, if you don't know what we're feeling?

SIMPSON: I think she means more the recession—the economic problems today the country faces rather than the deficit.

PRESIDENT BUSH: Well, listen, you ought to be in the White House for a day and hear what I hear and see what I see and read the mail I read and touch the people that I touch from time to time. I was in the Lomax AME Church. It's a black church just outside of Washington, D.C. And I read in the bulletin about teenage pregnancies, about the difficulties that families are having to make ends meet. I talk to parents. I mean, you've got to care. Everybody cares if people aren't doing well.

But I don't think it's fair to say, you haven't had cancer. Therefore, you don't know what's it like. I don't think it's fair to say, you know, whatever it is, that if you haven't been hit by it personally. But everybody's affected by the debt because of the tremendous interest that goes into paying on that debt everything's more expensive. Everything comes out of your pocket and my pocket. So it's that.

But I think in terms of the recession, of course you feel it when you're president of the United States. And that's why I'm trying to do something about it by stimulating the export, vesting more, better education systems.

Thank you. I'm glad you clarified it.

SIMPSON: Governor Clinton.

GOVERNOR CLINTON: Tell me how it's affected you again.

AUDIENCE PARTICIPANT: Um—

GOVERNOR CLINTON: You know people who've lost their jobs and lost their homes?

AUDIENCE PARTICIPANT: Well, yeah, uh-huh.

GOVERNOR CLINTON: Well, I've been governor of a small state for 12 years. I'll tell you how it's affected me. Every year Congress and the president sign laws that make us do more things and gives us less money to do it with. I see people in my state, middle class people—their taxes have gone up in Washington and their services have gone down while the wealthy have gotten tax cuts.

I have seen what's happened in this last four years when—in my state, when people lose their jobs there's a good chance I'll know them by their names. When a factory closes, I know the people who ran it. When the businesses go bankrupt, I know them.

And I've been out here for 13 months meeting in meetings just like this ever since October, with people like you all over America, people that have lost their jobs, lost their livelihood, lost their health insurance.

What I want you to understand is the national debt is not the only cause of that. It is because America has not invested in its people. It is because we have not grown. It is because we've had 12 years of trickle down economics. We've gone from first to twelfth in the world in wages. We've had four years where we've produced no private sector jobs. Most people are working harder for less money than they were making ten years ago.

It is because we are in the grip of a failed economic theory. And this decision you're about to make better be about what kind of economic theory you want, not just people saying I'm going to go fix it but what are we going to do?

I think we have to do is invest in American jobs, American education, control American health care costs and bring the American people together again. . . .

[New World Order]

AUDIENCE PARTICIPANT: We've come to a position where we're in the new world order, and I'd like to know what the candidates feel our position is in this new world order, and what our responsibilities are as a superpower?

SIMPSON: Mr. President.

PRESIDENT BUSH: Well, we have come to that position. Since I became president, 43, 44 countries have gone democratic, no longer totalitarian, no longer living under dictatorship or communist rule. This is exciting. New world order to me means freedom and democracy. I think we will have a continuing responsibility, as the only remaining superpower, to stay involved. If we pull back in some isolation and say we don't have to do our share, or more than our share, anymore, I believe you are going to just ask for conflagration that we'll get involved in in the future.

NATO, for example, has kept the peace for many, many years, and I want to see us keep fully staffed in NATO so we'll continue to guarantee the peace in Europe.

But the exciting thing is, the fear of nuclear war is down. And you hear all the bad stuff that's happened on my watch; I hope people will recognize that this is something pretty good for mankind. I hope they'll think it's good that democracy and freedom is on the move. And we're going to stay engaged, as long as I'm president, working to improve things.

You know, it's so easy now to say, hey, cut out foreign aid, we got a problem at home. I think the United States has to still have the Statue of Liberty as a symbol, caring for others. Right this very minute we're sending supplies in to help these little starving kids in Somalia. It's the United States that's taken the lead in humanitarian aid into Bosnia. We're doing this all around the world.

Yes, we got problems at home. And I think I got a good plan to help fix those problems at home. But because of our leadership, because we didn't listen to the freeze—the nuclear-freeze group, do you remember—freeze it, back in the late seventies—freeze, don't touch it; we're going to lock it in now or else we'll have war. President Reagan said no, peace through strength. It worked. The Soviet Union is no more, and now we're working to help them become totally democratic through the Freedom Support Act that I led on, a great Democratic ambassador, Bob Strauss, over there, Jim Baker, all of us got this thing passed—through cooperation, Ross—it worked with cooperation, and you're for that, I'm sure, helping Russia become democratic.

So the new world order to me means freedom and democracy, keep engaged, do not pull back into isolation. And we are the United States, and we have a responsibility to lead and to guarantee the security.

If it hadn't been for us, Saddam Hussein would be sitting on top of three-fifths of the oil supply of the world and he'd have nuclear weapons. And only the United States could do this. . . .

PEROT: Well, it's cost-effective to help Russia succeed in its revolution; it's pennies on the dollar compared to going back to the Cold War. Russia is still very unstable; they could go back to square one, and worse. All the nuclear weapons are not dismantled. I am particularly concerned about the intercontinental weapons, the ones that can hit us. We've got agreements, but they are still there.

With all this instability and breaking into republics, and all the Middle Eastern countries going over there and shopping for weapons, we've got our work cut out for us. So we need to stay right on top of that and constructively help them move toward democracy and capitalism.

We have to have money to do that. We have to have our people at work. See, for 45 years we were preoccupied with the Red Army. I suggest now that our number one preoccupation is red ink and our country and we've got to put our people back to work so that we can afford to do these things we want to do in Russia. We cannot be the policeman for the world any longer. We spent $300 billion a year defending the world. Germany and Japan spend around $30 billion a piece. If I can get you to defend me and I can spend all my money building industry that's a home run for me.

Coming out of World War II it made sense. Now, the other superpowers need to do their part. I'll close on this point. You can't be a superpower unless you're an economic superpower. If we're not an economic superpower, we're a used to be and we will no longer be a force for good throughout the world. And if nothing else gets you excited about rebuilding our industrial base maybe that will because job one is to put our people back to work.

SIMPSON: Governor Clinton, the president mentioned Saddam Hussein. Your vice president and you have had some words about the president and Saddam Hussein. Would you care to comment?

GOVERNOR CLINTON: I'd rather answer her question first and then I'll be glad to. Because the question you ask is important. The end of the Cold War brings an incredible opportunity for change. Winds of freedom blowing around the world, Russia demilitarizing. And it also requires us to maintain some continuity—some bipartisan American commitment to certain principles. And I would just say there are three things that I would like to say—number one—we do have to maintain the world's strongest defense. We may differ about what the elements of that are.

I think that defense needs to be—with fewer people in permanent armed services but with greater mobility on the land, in the air and on the sea, with a real dedication to continuing development of high technology weaponry and well trained people. I think we're going to have to work to stop the proliferation of weapons of mass destruction. Got to keep going until all those nuclear weapons in Russia are gone and the other republics. Number two, if you don't rebuild the economic strength of this country at home, we won't be a superpower. We can't have any more instances like what happened when Mr. Bush went to Japan and the Japanese prime minister said he felt sympathy for our country. We have to be the strongest economic power in the world. That's what got me into this race, so we could rebuild the American economy.

And number three, we need to be a force for freedom and democracy and we need to use our unique position to support freedom, whether it's in Haiti or in China or in any other place, wherever the seeds of freedom are sprouting. We can't impose it, but we need to nourish it and that's the kind of thing that I would do as president—follow those three commitments into the future. . . .

AUDIENCE PARTICIPANT: Yes. We've talked a lot tonight about creating jobs. But we have an awful lot of high school graduates who don't know how to read a ruler, who cannot fill out an application for a job.

How can we create high paying jobs with the education system we have and what would you do to change it?

SIMPSON: Who would like to begin—the education president?

PRESIDENT BUSH: I'd be delighted to, because you can't do it the old way. You can't do it with the school bureaucracy controlling everything and that's why we have a new program that I hope people have heard about. It's being worked now in 1,700 communities—bypassed Congress on this one, Ross—1,700 communities across the country. It's called America 2000. And it literally says to the communities, re-invent the schools, not just the bricks and mortar but the curriculum and everything else. Think anew. We have a concept called the New American School Corporation where we're doing exactly that.

And so I believe that we've got to get the power in the hands of the teachers, not the teachers' union. . . .

And so our America 2000 program also says this. It says let's give parents the choice of a public, private or public school—public, private or religious school. And it works—it works in Milwaukee. Democratic woman up there—taking the lead in this. The mayor up there, on the program. And the schools that are not chosen are improved—competition does that.

So we've got to innovate through school choice. We've got to innovate through this America 2000 program. But she is absolutely right. The programs that we've been trying where you control everything and mandate it from Washington don't work. The governors—and I believe Governor Clinton was in on this—but maybe—I don't want to invoke him here. But they come to me and they say, please get the Congress to stop passing so many mandates telling us how to control things. We know better how to do it in California or Texas or wherever it is.

So this is what our program is all about. And I believe you're right on to something, that if we don't change the education we're not going to be able to compete. Federal funding for education is up substantially—Pell grants are up. But it isn't going to get the job done if we don't change K through 12. . . .

GOVERNOR CLINTON: First of all, let me say that I've spent more of my time and life on this in the last 12 years than any other issue. Seventy percent of my state's money goes to the public schools, and I was really honored when Time magazine said that our schools have shown more improvement than any other state in the country except one other—they named two states showing real strides forward in the eighties. So I care a lot about this, and I've spent countless hours in schools.

But let me start with what you said. I agree with some of what Mr. Bush said, but it's nowhere near enough. We live in a world depends on what you can learn, where the average 18-year-old will change jobs eight times in a lifetime and where none of us can promise any of you that what you now do for a living is absolutely safe from now on. Nobody running can promise that, there's too much change in the world.

So what should we do? Let me reel some things off real quick, because you said you wanted specifics. Number one, under my program we would provide matching funds to states to teach everybody with a job to read in the next five years and give everybody with a job the chance to get a high school diploma, in big places on the job.

Number two, we would provide two-year apprenticeship programs to high school graduates who don't go to college. And community colleges are on the job.

Number three, we'd open the doors to college education to high school graduates without regard to income. They could borrow the money and pay it back as a percentage of their income or with a couple of years of service to our nation here at home.

Number four, we would fully fund the Head Start program to get little kids off to a good start.

And, five, I would have an aggressive program of school reform, more choices—I favor public schools or these new charter schools—we can talk about that if you want. I don't think we should spend tax money on private schools. But I favor public school choice, and I favor radical decentralization in giving more power to better-trained principals and teachers with parent councils to control their schools.

Those things would revolutionize American education and take us to the top economically. . . .

AUDIENCE PARTICIPANT: What are they going to cost?

SIMPSON: The question is, what is it going to cost?

GOVERNOR CLINTON: In six years—I budget all this in my budget, and in six years the college program would cost eight billion dollars over and above what—the present student loan program costs four; you pay three billion dollars for busted loans, because we don't have an automatic recovery system, and a billion dollars in bank fees. So the net cost would be eight billion six years from now in a trillion-plus budget—not very much.

The other stuff—all the other stuff I mentioned—costs much less than that. The Head Start program full funding would cost about five billion more. And it's all covered in my budget from—the plans that I've laid out—from raising taxes on families with incomes above $200,000 and asking foreign corporations to pay the same tax that American corporations do on the same income, from $140 billion in budget cuts, including what I think are very prudent cuts in the defense budget. It's all covered in the plan.

SIMPSON: Thank you. Mr. Perot, you on education, please.

PEROT: Yes, I've got scars to show for being around education reform. And the first word you need to say in every city and state, and just draw a line in the sand, is public schools exist for the benefit of the children. You're going to see a lot of people fall over it, because any time you're spending $199 billion dollars a year, somebody's getting it. And the children get lost in the process. So that's step one.

Keep in mind in 1960, when our schools were the envy of the world, we were spending $16 billion on them; now we spend more than any other nation in the world—199 billion a year—and rank at the bottom of the industrialized world in terms of education achievement. One more time you've bought a front-row box seat and got a third-rate performance. This is a government that is not serving you.

By and large it should be local—the more local, the better. Interesting phenomenon: small towns have good schools, big cities have terrible schools. The best people in a small town will serve on the school board; you get into big cities, it's political patronage, stepping stones—you get the job, give your relatives a janitor's job at $57,000 a year, more than the teachers make, and with luck they clean the cafeteria once a week. Now, you're paying for that. Those schools belong to you. And we put up with that.

Now, as long as we put up with that, that's what you're going to get. And these folks are just dividing up 199 billion bucks and the children get lost. If I could wish for one thing for great public schools, it would be a strong family unit in every home—nothing will ever replace that. You say, well, gee, what are you going to do about that? Well, the White House is a bully pulpit, and I think we ought to be pounding on the table every day. There's nothing—the most efficient unit of government the world will ever know is a strong loving family unit.

Next thing. You need small schools, not big schools. In a little school everybody is somebody; individualism is very important. These big factories? Everybody told me they were cost-effective. I did a study on it; they're cost-ineffective. Five thousand students—why is a high school that big? One reason. Sooner or later you get 11 more boys that can run like the devil that weigh 250 pounds and they might win district. Now, that has nothing to do with learning.

Secondly, across Texas, typically half of the school day was non-academic pursuits—in one place it was 35 percent. In Texas you could have unlimited absences to go to livestock shows. Found a boy—excuse me, but this gives the flavor—a boy in Houston kept a chicken in the bathtub in downtown Houston and missed 65 days going to livestock shows. Finally had to come back to school, the chicken lost its feathers. That's the only way we got him back.

Now, that's your tax money being wasted.

Now, neighborhood schools. It is terrible to bus tiny little children across town. And it is particularly terrible to take poor tiny little children and wait until the first grade and bus them across town to Mars, where the children know their numbers, know their letters, have had every advantage. At the end of the first day, that little child wants out.

I'll close on this. You've got to have world class teachers, world class books. If you ever got close to how textbooks were selected, you wouldn't want to go back the second day. I don't have time to tell you the stories.

SIMPSON: No, you don't.

PEROT: Finally, if we don't fix this, you're right. We can't have the industries of tomorrow unless we have the best educated workforce. And here you've got, for the disadvantaged children, you've got to have early childhood development. Cheapest money you'll ever spend. First contact should be with the money when she's pregnant. That little child needs to be loved and hugged and nurtured and made to feel special, like your children were. They learn to think well or poorly of themselves in the first 18 months.

SIMPSON: Thank you.

AUDIENCE PARTICIPANT: Thank you, Mr. Perot.

PEROT: And in the first few years they either learn how to learn or don't learn how to learn. And if they don't, they wind up in prison.

SIMPSON: Thank you, Mr. Perot.

PEROT: And it costs more to keep them in prison than it does to send them to Harvard. I rest my case.

SIMPSON: Thank you. President Bush, you wanted to answer.

PRESIDENT BUSH: I just had a word of clarification because of something Governor Clinton said.

My school choice program, GI Bill for Kids, does not take public money and give it to private schools. It does what the GI Bill itself did when I came out of World War II. It takes public money and gives it to families or individuals to choose the school they want. And where it's been done, those schools, like in Rochester, those schools that weren't chosen find that they then compete and do better.

So I think it's worth a shot. We've got a pilot program. It ought to be tried. School choice—public, private or religious. Not to the schools but to—you know, 46 percent of the teachers in Chicago, public school teachers, send their kids to private school.

Now, I think we ought to try to help families and see if it will do what I think—make all schools better.

GOVERNOR CLINTON: I just want to mention if I could—

SIMPSON: Very briefly.

GOVERNOR CLINTON: Very briefly. Involving the parents in the preschool education of their kids, even if they're poor and uneducated, can make a huge difference. We have a big program in my state that teaches mothers or fathers to teach their kids to get ready for school. It's the most successful thing we've ever done.

Just a fact clarification real quickly. We do not spend a higher percentage of our income on public education than every other country. There are nine countries that spend more than we do on public education. We spend more on education 'cause we spend so much more on colleges.

But if you look at public education alone and you take into account the fact that we have more racial diversity and more poverty, it makes a big difference. There are great public schools where there's public school choice, accountability and brilliant principals. I'll just mention one—the Beasley Academic Center in Chicago. I commend it to anybody. It's as good as any private school in the country.

SIMPSON: Thank you.... It is time now for the two minute closing statements and by prior agreement President Bush will go first.

PRESIDENT BUSH: May I ask for an exception because I think we owe Carole Simpson—anybody who can stand in between these three characters here and get the job done—we owe her a round of applause.

But don't take it out of my time!...

PRESIDENT BUSH: I feel strongly about it because I don't want it to come out of my time.

SIMPSON: Give this man more time.

PRESIDENT BUSH: No, but let me just say to the American people in two and a half weeks we're going to choose who should sit in this Oval Office, who to lead the economic recovery, who to be the leader of the free world, who to get the deficit down. Three ways to do that. One is to raise taxes. One is to reduce spending—controlling that mandatory spending.

Another one is to invest and save and to stimulate growth. I do not want to raise taxes. I differ with the two here on that. I'm just not going to do that. I do believe that we need to control mandatory spending. I think we need to invest and save more. I believe that we need to educate better and retrain better. I believe that we need to export more so I'll keep working for export agreements where we can sell more abroad and I believe that we must strengthen the family. We've got to strengthen the family.

Now, let me pose this question to America. If in the next five minutes a television announcer came on and said, there is a major international crisis—there is a major threat to the world or in this country a major threat—my question is, who, if you were appointed to name one of the three of us, who would you choose? Who has the perseverance, the character, the integrity, the maturity, to get the job done?

I hope I'm that person. Thank you very, very much.

SIMPSON: Thank you, Mr. President. And now a closing statement from Mr. Perot.

PEROT: If the American people want to do it and not talk about it, then they ought to—you know, I'm one person they ought to consider. If they just want to keep slow dancing and talk about it and not do it, I'm not your name. I am results oriented. I am action oriented. I've dealt my businesses. Getting things done in three months that my competitors took 18 months to do.

Everybody says you can't do that with Congress. Sure, you can do that with Congress. Congress—they're all good people. They're all patriots but you've got to link arms and work with them. Sure, you'll have arguments. Sure, you'll have fights. We have them all day every day. But we get the job done.

Now, I have to come back in my close to one thing because I am passionate about education. I was talking about early childhood education for disadvantaged little children. And let me tell you one specific pilot program where children who don't have a chance go to this program when they're three. Now we're going back to when the mother's pregnant and they'll start right after they're born.

Starting when they're three and going to this school until they're nine and then going into the public school in the fourth grade. Ninety percent are on the honor role. Now that will change America. Those children will all go to college. They will live the American dream. And I beg the American people, any time they think about reforming education to take this piece of society that doesn't have a chance and take these little pieces of clay that can be shaped and molded and give them the same love and nurture and affection and support you give your children and teach them that they're unique and that they're precious and that there's only one person in the world like them and you will see this nation bloom. And we will have so many people who are qualified for the top job that it will be terrific.

Now, finally, if you can't pay the bills you're dead in the water. And we have got to put our nation back to work. Now, if you don't want to really do that I'm not your man. I'd go crazy sitting up there slow dancing that one. In other words, unless we're going to do it, then pick somebody who likes to talk about it.

Now, just remember when you think about me—I didn't create this mess. I've been paying taxes just like you and Lord knows, I've paid my share—over a billion in taxes. And for a guy that started out with everything he owned in the trunk of his car—

SIMPSON: Mr. Perot, I'm sorry—

PEROT: —that ain't bad.

SIMPSON: —once again.

PEROT: But it's in your hands. I wish you well. I'll see you tomorrow night—

SIMPSON: And finally, last but not least—Governor Clinton.

GOVERNOR CLINTON: Thank you, Carole, and thank you, ladies and gentlemen.

Since I suggested this format I hope it's been good for all of you. I really tried to be faithful to your request that we answer the questions specifically and pointedly. I thought I owed that to you and I respect you for being here and for the impact you've had on making this a more positive experience.

These problems are not easy. They're not going to be solved overnight. But I want you to think about just two or three things. First of all, the people of my state have let me be their governor for 12 years because I made commitments to two things—more jobs and better schools.

Our schools are now better. Our children get off to a better start from pre-school programs and smaller classes in the early grades, and we have one of the most aggressive adult education programs in the country. We talked about that. This year my state ranks first in the country in job growth, fourth in manufacturing in job growth, fourth in income growth, fourth in the decline of poverty.

I'm proud of that. It happened because I could work with people— Republicans and Democrats. That's why we've had 24 retired generals and admirals, hundreds of business people, many of them Republican, support this campaign.

You have to decide whether you want to change or not. We do not need four more years of an economic theory that doesn't work. We've had 12 years of trickle down economics. It's time to put the American people first, to invest and grow this economy. I'm the only person here who's ever balanced a government budget and I've presented 12 of them and cut spending repeatedly. But you cannot just get there by balancing the budget. We've got to grow the economy by putting people first—real people like you.

I got into this race because I did not want my child to grow up to be part of the first generation of Americans to do worse than her parents. We're better than that. We can do better than that. I want to make America as great as it can be and I ask for your help in doing it. Thank you. . . .

OCTOBER 19 PRESIDENTIAL DEBATE

JIM LEHRER: Good evening. Welcome to this third and final debate among the three major candidates for president of the United States. Governor Bill Clinton, the Democratic nominee, President George Bush, the Republican nominee, and independent candidate Ross Perot.

I am Jim Lehrer of the MacNeil-Lehrer Newshour on PBS. I will be the moderator for this debate, which is being sponsored by the Commission on Presidential Debates. It will be 90 minutes long. It is happening before an audience on the campus of Michigan State University in East Lansing.

The format was conceived by and agreed to by representatives of the Bush and Clinton campaigns, and it is somewhat different than those used in the earlier debates. I will ask questions for the first half under rules that permit follow-ups. A panelist of three other journalists will ask questions in the second half under rules that do not.

As always, each candidate will have two minutes, up to two minutes, to make a closing statement. The order of those, as well as that for the formal questioning, were all determined by a drawing.

Gentlemen, again welcome and again good evening.

It seems, from what some of those voters said at your Richmond debate, and from polling and other data, that each of you, fairly or not, faces serious voter concerns about the underlying credibility and believability of what each of you says you would do as president in the next four years.

Governor Clinton, in accordance with the draw, those concerns about you are first: you are promising to create jobs, reduce the deficit, reform the health care system, rebuild the infrastructure, guarantee college education for everyone who is qualified, among many other things, all with financial pain only for the very rich. Some people are having trouble apparently believing that is possible. Should they have that concern?

GOVERNOR CLINTON: No. There are many people who believe that the only way we can get this country turned around is to tax the middle class more and punish them more, but the truth is that middle-class Americans are basically the only group of Americans who've been taxed more in the 1980s and during the last 12 years, even though their incomes have gone down. The wealthiest Americans have been taxed much less, even though their incomes have gone up.

Middle-class people will have their fair share of changing to do, and many challenges to face, including the challenge of becoming constantly re-educated.

But my plan is a departure from trickle-down economics, just cutting taxes on the wealthiest Americans and getting out of the way. It's also a departure from tax-and-spend economics, because you can't tax and divide an economy that isn't growing.

955

I propose an American version of what works in other countries—I think we can do it better: invest and grow.

I believe we can increase investment and reduce the deficit at the same time, if we not only ask the wealthiest Americans and foreign corporations to pay their share; we also provide over $100 billion in tax relief, in terms of incentives for new plants, new small businesses, new technologies, new housing, and for middle class families; and we have $140 billion of spending cuts. Invest and grow.

Raise some more money, spend the money on tax incentives to have growth in the private sector, take the money from the defense cuts and reinvest it in new transportation and communications and environmental clean-up systems. This will work.

On this, as on so many other issues, I have a fundamental difference from the present administration. I don't believe trickle down economics will work. Unemployment is up. Most people are working harder for less money than they were making ten years ago. I think we can do better if we have the courage to change.

LEHRER: Mr. President, a response....

PRESIDENT BUSH: Well, he doesn't like trickle down government but I think he's talking about the Reagan-Bush years where we created 15 million jobs. The rich are paying a bigger percent of the total tax burden. And what I don't like is trickle down government. And therein, I think Governor Clinton keeps talking about trickle down, trickle down, and he's still talking about spending more and taxing more.

Government—he says invest government, grow government. Government doesn't create jobs. If they do, they're make-work jobs. It's the private sector that creates jobs. And yes, we've got too many taxes on the American people and we're spending too much.

And that's why I want to get the deficit down by controlling the growth of mandatory spending. It won't be painless. I think Mr. Perot put his finger on something there. It won't be painless but we've got to get the job done. But not by raising taxes.

Mr. and Mrs. America, when you hear him say we're going to tax only the rich, watch your wallet because his figures don't add up and he's going to sock it right to the middle class taxpayer and lower, if he's going to pay for all the spending programs he proposes.

So we have a big difference on this trickle down theory. I do not want any more trickle down government. It's gotten too big. I want to do something about that.

LEHRER: Mr. Perot, what do you think of the governor's approach, what he just laid out?

PEROT: The basic problem with it, it doesn't balance the budget. If you forecast it out, we still have a significant deficit under each of their plans, as I understand them.

Our challenge is to stop the financial bleeding. If you take a patient into the hospital that's bleeding arterially, step one is to stop the bleeding. And we are bleeding arterially.

There's only one way out of this, and that is to stop the deterioration of our job base, to have a growing, expanding job base, to give us the tax base—see, balancing the budget is not nearly as difficult as paying off the $4 trillion debt and leaving our children the American dream intact.

We have spent their money. We've got to pay it back. This is going to take fair, shared sacrifice. My plan balances the budget within six years. We didn't do it faster than that because we didn't want to disrupt the economy. We gave it off to a slow start and a fast finish to give the economy time to recover. But we faced it and we did it, and we believe it's fair, shared sacrifice.

The one thing I have done is lay it squarely on the table in front of the American people. You've had a number of occasions to see in detail what the plan is, and at least you'll understand it. I think that's fundamental in our country, that you know what you're getting into.

LEHRER: Governor, the word "pain"—one of the other leadership things that's put on you is that you don't speak of pain, that you speak of all things—nobody's going to really have to suffer under your plan. You've heard what Mr. Perot has said. He's said it's got—to do the things that you want to do, you can't do it by just taking the money from the rich. That's what the president says as well.

How do you respond to that? They said the numbers don't add up.

GOVERNOR CLINTON: I disagree with both of them. For one thing, let me just follow up here. I disagree with Mr. Perot that the answer is to raise—put a 50-cent gas tax on the middle class and raise more taxes on the middle class and the working poor than on the wealthy.

His own analysis says that unemployment will be slightly higher in 1995 under his plan than it is today.

And as far as what Mr. Bush says, he is the person who raised taxes on the middle class after saying he wouldn't. And just this year, Mr. Bush vetoed a tax increase on the wealthy that gave middle class tax relief. He vetoed middle class tax relief this year.

And furthermore, under this administration, spending has increased more than it has in the last 20 years and he asked Congress to spend more money than it actually spent. Now, it's hard to out-spend Congress but he tried to for the last three years.

So my view is the middle class is the—they've been suffering, Jim. Now, should people pay more for Medicare if they can? Yes. Should they pay more for Social Security if they get more out of it than they paid in, they're upper income people? Yes. But look what's happened to the middle class. Middle class Americans are working harder for less money than they were making ten years ago and they're paying higher taxes. The tax burden on them has not gone down. It has gone up. I don't think the answer is to slow the economy down more, drive unemployment up more and undermine the health of the private sector. The answer is to invest and grow this economy. That's what works in other countries and that's what'll work here.

LEHRER: As a practical matter, Mr. President, do you agree with the governor when he says that the middle class, the taxes on the middle class—do your numbers agree that the taxes on the middle class have gone up during the last—

PRESIDENT BUSH: I think everybody's paying too much taxes. He refers to one tax increase. Let me remind you it was a Democratic tax increase, and I didn't want to do it and I went along with it. And I said I make a mistake. If I make a mistake, I admit it. That's quite different than some. But I think that's the American way.

I think everyone's paying too much, but I think this idea that you can go out and—then he hits me for vetoing a tax bill. Yes, I did. And the American taxpayer ought to be glad they have a president to stand up to a spending Congress. We remember what it was like when we had a spending president and a spending Congress, and interest rates—who remembers that? They were at 21.5 percent under Jimmy Carter, and inflation was 15. We don't want to go back to that.

And so yes, everybody's taxed too much and I want to get the taxes down, but not by signing a tax bill that's gonna raise taxes on people.

LEHRER: Mr. President, when you said just then that you admit your mistakes and you looked at Governor Clinton and said—what mistake is it that you want him to admit to?

PRESIDENT BUSH: Well, the record in Arkansas. I mean, look at it, and that's what we're asking America to have? Now look, he says Arkansas's a poor state. They are. But in almost every category they're lagging. I'll give you an example. He talks about all the jobs he's created in one or two years. Over the last ten years since he's been governor, they're 30 percent behind, 30 percent—they're 30 percent of the national average. On pay for teachers, on all these categories, Arkansas is right near the very bottom.

You haven't heard me mention this before, but we're getting close now and I think it's about time I start putting things in perspective. And I'm going to do that. It's not dirty campaigning because he's been talking about my record for a half a year here, 11 months here. So we've got to do that. I gotta get it in perspective.

What's his mistake? Admit it, that Arkansas is doing very, very badly against any standard—environment, support for police officers, whatever it is.

LEHRER: Governor, is that true?

GOVERNOR CLINTON: Mr. Bush's Bureau of Labor Statistics says that Arkansas ranks first in the country in the growth of new jobs this year, first.

PRESIDENT BUSH: This year.

GOVERNOR CLINTON: Fourth in manufacturing jobs, fourth in the reduction of poverty, fourth in income increase. Over the last ten years we've created manufacturing jobs much more rapidly than the national average. Over the last five years our income has grown more rapidly than the national average. We are second in tax burden, the second lowest tax burden in the country.

We have the lowest per capita state and local spending in the country. We're low spending, low tax burden. We dramatically increased investment and our jobs are growing. I wish America had that kind of record and I think most people looking at us tonight would like it if we had more jobs and a lower spending burden on the government.

LEHRER: Mr. Perot, if you were sitting at home now and just heard this exchange about Arkansas, who would you believe?

PEROT: I grew up five blocks from Arkansas. Let's put it in perspective. It's a beautiful state. It's a fairly rural state. It has a population less than Chicago or Los Angeles, about the size of Dallas and Forth Worth combined.

So I think probably we're making a mistake night after night after night to cast the nation's future on a unit that small.

LEHRER: Why is that a mistake?

PEROT: It's irrelevant.

LEHRER: What he did as governor of Arkansas is irrelevant?

PEROT: No, no, no, but I could say, you know, that I ran a small grocery store on the corner, therefore I extrapolate that into the fact that I can run Wal-Mart. That's not true.

I can't protect an Arkansas company, you notice there, Governor.

LEHRER: Governor?

GOVERNOR CLINTON: Mr. Perot, with all respect, I think it is highly relevant, and I think that a four-billion budget of state and federal funds is not all that small, and I think the fact that I took a state that was one of the poorest states in the country and had been for 153 years and tried my best to modernize its economy and to make the kind of changes that have generated support from people like the presidents of Apple Computer and Hewlett-Packard and some of the biggest companies in this country, 24 retired generals and admirals and hundreds of business executives, are highly relevant. And, you know, I'm frankly amazed that since you grew up five blocks from there you would think that what goes on in that state is irrelevant. I think it's been pretty impressive.

PEROT: It's not—

GOVERNOR CLINTON: And the people who have jobs—

The people who have jobs and educations and opportunities that didn't have them 10 years ago don't think it's irrelevant at all; they think it's highly relevant and they wish the rest of the country had them.

PRESIDENT BUSH: I don't have a dog in this fight, but I'd like to get in on this.

GOVERNOR CLINTON: Well, you think it's relevant.

PRESIDENT BUSH: Governor Clinton has to operate under a balanced budget amendment—he has to do it, that is the law. I'd like to see a balanced budget amendment for America, to protect the American taxpayers, and then that would discipline not only the executive branch but the spending Congress, the Congress that's been in control of one party, his party, for 38 years. And we almost had it done.

And that institution, the House of Representatives—everyone is yelling "Clean House!" One of the reasons is we almost had it done, and the speaker—a very, able, decent fellow, I might add—but he twisted the arms of some of the sponsors of that legislation and had them change their vote. What's relevant here is that tool, that discipline, that he has to live by in Arkansas, and I'd like it for the American people. I want the line-item veto. I want a check-off, so if the Congress can't do it, let people check off their income tax, 10 percent of it, to compel the government to cut spending. And if they can't do it, if the Congress can't do it, let them then have to do it across the board. That's what we call a sequester. That's the discipline we need, and I'm working for that—to protect the American taxpayer against the big spenders.

LEHRER: Mr. President, let's move to some of the leadership concerns that have been voiced about you. And they relate to something you said in your closing statement in Richmond the other night about the president being the manager of crises. And that relates to an earlier criticism, that you began to focus on the economy, on health care, on racial divisions in this country, only after they became crises.

Is that a fair criticism?

PRESIDENT BUSH: Jim, I don't think that's a fair shot. I hear it—I hear it echoed by political opponents. But I don't think it's fair. I think we've been fighting from day one to do something about the inner cities. I'm for enterprise zones. I have had it in every single proposal I've sent to the Congress. And now we hear a lot of talk, oh, well, we all want enterprise zones, and yet the House and the Senate can't send it down without loading it up with a lot of, you know, these Christmas tree ornaments they put on the legislation.

I don't think in racial harmony that I'm a laggard on that. I've been speaking out since day one. We've gotten the Americans for Disabilities Act, which I think is one of the foremost pieces of civil rights legislation. And yes, it took me to veto two civil rights quota bills because I don't believe in quotas, and I don't think the American people believe in quotas. And I beat back the Congress on that, and then we passed a decent civil rights bill that offers guarantees against discrimination in employment.

And that is good.

I've spoken out over and over again against antisemitism and racism, and I think my record as a member of Congress speaks for itself on that.

What was the other part of it?

LEHRER: Well, it's just that—you've spoken to it. I mean, but the idea, not so much in specifics, but that it has to be a crisis before it gets your attention.

PRESIDENT BUSH: I don't think that's true at all. I don't think that's true, but you know, let others fire away on it.

LEHRER: Do you think that's true, Mr. Perot?

PEROT: I'd like to just talk about issues, and so— ... I would rather not critique the two candidates.

LEHRER: All right. Governor, what do you think?

GOVERNOR CLINTON: The only thing I would say about that is, I think that on the economy, Mr. Bush said for a long time there was no recession, and then said it would be better to do nothing than to have a compromise effort with the Congress.

He really didn't have a new economic program until over 1300 days into his presidency, and not all of his health care initiative has been presented to the Congress even now.

I think it's important to elect a president who is committed to getting this economy going again, and who realizes we have to abandon trickle-down economics and put the American people first again, and who will send programs to the Congress in the first hundred days to deal with the critical issues that America is crying out for leadership on—jobs, incomes, the health care crisis, the need to control the economy. Those things deserve to be dealt with from day one. I will deal with them from day one. They will be my first priority, not my election year concern.

LEHRER: Mr. President?

PRESIDENT BUSH: Well, I think you're overlooking that we have had major accomplishments in the first term. But if you're talking about protecting the taxpayer against his friends in the United States Congress, go back to what it was like when you had a Democratic president and a Democratic Congress. You don't have to go back to Herbert Hoover. Go back to Jimmy Carter, and interest rates were 21 percent, inflation was 15 percent. The misery index—unemployment and inflation added together—it was invented by the Democrats—went right through the roof. We've cut it in half.

And all you hear about is how bad things are. You know, remember the question, are you better off? Well, is a homebuyer better off he can refinance the home, because interest rates are down? Is the senior citizen better off because inflation is not wiping out their family's savings? I think they are. Is the guy out of work better off? Of course he's not, but he's not gonna be better off if we grow the government, if we invest, as Governor Clinton says, invest in more government.

You've got to free up the private sector. You've got to let small businesses have more incentives. For three months—three quarters I've been fighting, three quarters been fighting to get the Congress to pass some incentives for small business. Capital gains, investment tax allowance, credit for first-time homebuyers. And it's blocked by the Congress. And then if a little of it comes my way, they load it up with Christmas trees and tax increases, and I have to stand up and favor the taxpayer.

LEHRER: I have to—we have to talk about Ross Perot now or he'll get me, I'm sure. Mr. Perot, on this issue that I have raised at the very beginning and we've been talking about, which is leadership, as president of the United States, it concerns—my reading of it, at least, my concerns about you, as expressed by folks in the polls and other places, it goes like this.

You had a problem with General Motors. You took your $750 million and you left. You had a problem in the spring and summer about some personal hits that you took as a potential candidate for president of the United States and you walked out.

Does that say anything relevant to how you would function as president of the United States?

PEROT: I think the General Motors thing is very relevant. I did everything I could to get General Motors to face its problems in the mid-'80s while it was still financially strong. They just wouldn't do it, and everybody now knows the terrible price they're paying by waiting until it's obvious to the brain-dead that they have problems.

Now, hundreds, thousands of good, decent people, whole cities up here in this state are adversely impacted because they would not move in a timely way. Our government is that point now. The thing that I am in this race for is to tap the American people on the shoulder and to say to every single one of you, fix it while we're still relatively strong. If you have a heart problem, you don't wait till a heart attack to address it.

So the General Motors experience is relevant. At the point when I could not get them to address those problems, I had created so much stress in the board, who wanted to just keep the Lawrence Welk music going, that they asked to buy my remaining shares. I sold them my remaining shares. They went their way. I went my way because it was obvious we had a complete disagreement about what should be done with the company.

But let's take my life in perspective. Again and again, on complex, difficult tasks, I have stayed the course. When I was asked by our government to do the POW project, within a year the Vietnamese had sent people into Canada to make arrangements to have me and my family killed. And I had five small children, and my family and I decided we would stay the course, and we lived with that problem for three years.

Then I got into the Texas War on Drugs program and the big-time drug dealers got all upset. Then when I had two people imprisoned in Iran, I could have left them there. I could have rationalized it. We went over, we got them out, we brought them back home. And since then, for years, I have lived with the burden of the Middle East, where it's eye for an eye and tooth for a tooth country, in terms of their unhappiness with the fact that I was successful in that effort.

Again and again and again, in the middle of the night, at 2 or 3 o'clock in the morning, my government has called me to take extraordinary steps for Americans in distress, and again and again and again I have responded. And I didn't wilt and I didn't quit.

Now, what happened in July we've covered again and again and again. But I think in terms of the American people's concern about my commitment, I'm here tonight, folks; I never quit supporting you as you put me on the ballot in the other 26 states; and when you asked me to come back in, I came back in. And talk about not quitting, I'm spending my money on this campaign; the two parties are spending your money, taxpayer money. I put my wallet on the table for you and your children. Over $60 million at least will go into this campaign to lead the American dream to you and your children, to get this country straightened out, because if anybody owes it to you, I do. I've lived the American dream; I'd like for your children to be able to live it, too. . . .

LEHRER: All right. Now we're going to bring in three other journalists to ask questions. They are Susan Rook of CNN, Gene Gibbons of Reuters and Helen Thomas of United Press International. . . .

[Clinton on the Draft]

HELEN THOMAS (UPI): Governor Clinton, your credibility has come into question because of your different responses on the Vietnam draft. If you had it to do over again, would you put on the nation's uniform, and if elected, could you in good conscience send someone to war?

GOVERNOR CLINTON: If I had it to do over again I might answer the questions a little better. You know, I'd been in public life a long time and no one had ever questioned my role and so I was asked a lot of questions about things that happened a long time ago and I don't think I answered them as well as I could have.

Going back 23 years, I don't know, Helen. I was opposed to the war. I couldn't help that. I felt very strongly about it, and I didn't want to go at the time. It's easy to say in retrospect I would have done something differently.

President Lincoln opposed the war and there were people who said maybe he shouldn't be president, but I think he made us a pretty good president in wartime. We've had a lot of other presidents who didn't wear their country's uniform who had to order our young soldiers into battle, including President Wilson and President Roosevelt.

So the answer is I could do that. I wouldn't relish doing it but I wouldn't shrink from it. I think that the president has to be prepared to use the power of the nation when our vital interests are threatened, when our treaty commitments are at stake, when we know that something has to be done that is in the national interest, and that is a part of being president.

Could I do it? Yes, I could.

LEHRER: A reminder now. We're back on the St. Louis rules, which means that the governor had his answer and then each of you will have one minute to respond. Mr. President.

PRESIDENT BUSH: Well, I've expressed my heartfelt difference with Governor Clinton on organizing demonstrations while in a foreign land against your country, when young ghetto kids have been drafted and are dying.

My argument with him on—the question was about the draft—is that there's this same pattern. In New Hampshire Senator Kerrey said you ought to level, you ought to tell the truth about it. On April 17 he said he'd bring out all the records on the draft. They have not been forthcoming. He got a deferment or he didn't. He got a notice or he didn't. And I think it's this pattern that troubles me, more than the draft. A lot of decent, honorable people felt as he did on the draft. But it's this pattern.

And again, you might be able to make amendments all the time, Governor, but you've got to, as president, you can't be on all these different sides, and you can't have this pattern of saying well, I did this or I didn't, then the facts come out and you change it.

That's my big difference with him on the draft. It wasn't failing to serve.

PEROT: I've spent my whole adult life very close to the military. I feel very strongly about the people who go into battle for our country. I appreciate their idealism, their sacrifices. Appreciate the sacrifices their families make. That's been displayed again and again in a very tangible way.

I look on this as history. I don't look on it personally as relevant, and I consider it really a waste of time tonight, when you consider the issues that face our country right now.

GENE GIBBONS (Reuters): Mr. President, you keep saying that you made a mistake in agreeing to a tax increase to get the 1990 budget deal with Congress. But if you hadn't gotten that deal, you would have either had to get repeal of the Gramm-Rudman Deficit Control Act or cut defense spending drastically at a time when the country was building up for the gulf war, and decimate domestic discretionary spending, including such things as air traffic control.

If you had it to do all over again, sir, which of those alternatives would you choose?

PRESIDENT BUSH: I wouldn't have taken any of the alternatives. I believe that—I believe I made a mistake. I did it for the very reasons you say. There was one good thing that came out of that budget agreement, and that is we put a cap on discretionary spending. One-third of the president's budget is at the president's discretion, or really the Congress, since they appropriate every time and tell a president how to spend every dime. We've put a cap on the growth of all that spending, and that's good and that's helped.

But I was wrong because I thought the tax compromise, going along with one Democratic tax increase, would help the economy. I see no evidence that it has done it.

So what would I have done? What should I have done? I should have held out for a better deal that would have protected the taxpayer and not ended up doing what we had to do, or what I thought at the time would help.

So I made a mistake, and I—you know, the difference, I think, is that I knew at the time I was going to take a lot of political flak. I knew we'd have somebody out there yelling "read my lips", and I did it because I thought it was right. And I made a mistake. That's quite different than taking a position where you know it's best for you. That wasn't best for me and I knew it in the very beginning. I thought it would be better for the country than it was. So there we are.

PEROT: 101 in leadership is be accountable for what you do. Let's go back to the tax and budget summit briefly. Nobody ever told the American people that we increased spending $1.83 for every dollar of taxes raised. That's absolutely unconscionable. Both parties carry a huge blame for that on their shoulders.

This was not a way to pay down the deficit. This was a trick on the American people. That's not leadership.

Let's go back in terms of accepting responsibility for your actions. If you create Saddam Hussein, over a ten-year period, using billions of dollars of U.S. taxpayer money, step up to the plate and say it was a mistake. If you create Noriega, using taxpayer money, step up to the plate and say it was a mistake. If you can't get your act together to pick him up one day when a Panamanian major has kidnapped him and a special forces team is 400 yards away and it's a stroll across the park to get him, and if you can't get your act together, at least pick up the Panamanian major, who they then killed, step up to the plate and admit it was a mistake. That's leadership, folks.

Now, leaders will always make mistakes. We've created, and I'm not aiming at any one person here, I'm aiming at our government—nobody takes responsibility for anything. We've gotta change that. . . .

GOVERNOR CLINTON: The mistake that was made was making the "read my lips" promise in the first place just to get elected, knowing what the size of the deficit was.

Knowing what the size of the deficit was, knowing there was no plan to control health care costs and knowing that we did not have a strategy to get real economic growth back into this economy. The choices were not good then. I think at the time, the mistake that was made was signing off on the deal late on Saturday night in the middle of the night. That's just what the president did when he vetoed the Family Leave Act.

I think what he should have done is gone before the American people on the front end and said listen, I made a commitment and it was wrong. I made a mistake because I couldn't have foreseen these circumstances and this is the best deal we can work out at the time. He said it was in the public interest at the time and most everybody who was involved in it, I guess, thought it was. The real mistake was the "read my lips" promise in the first place. You just can't promise something like that just to get elected if you know there's a good chance that circumstances may overtake you.

[Women in the Inner Circle]

LEHRER: All right, we're going to go on to another subject now, and the subject is priorities. The first question goes to you, President Bush, and Susan will ask it.

SUSAN ROOK: President Bush, gentlemen, I acknowledge that all of you have women and ethnic minorities working for you and working with you. But when we look at the circle of the key people closest to you, your inner circle of advisers, we see white men only. Why? And when will that change?

PRESIDENT BUSH: You don't see Margaret Tutwiler sitting in there with me today.

ROOK: The key people, President Bush.

PRESIDENT BUSH: Huh?

ROOK: The key people, the people beyond the glass ceiling.

PRESIDENT BUSH: I happen to think she's a key person. I think our Cabinet members are key people. I think the woman that works with me, Rose Zamaria, is about as tough as a boot out there and makes some discipline and protects the taxpayer.

Look at our Cabinet. You talk about somebody strong. Look at Carla Hills. Look at Lynn Martin, who's fighting against this glass ceiling and doing a first-class job on it. Look at our surgeon general, Dr. Novello. You can look all around and you'll see first-class strong women.

Jim Baker's a man. Yeah, I plead guilty to that.

But look who's around with him there. I mean, this is a little defensive on your part, Susan, to be honest with you. We've got a very good record appointing women to high positions and positions of trust, and I'm not defensive at all about it. What we got to do is keep working, as the Labor Department is doing a first-class job on, to break down discrimination, to break down the glass ceiling.

And I am not apologetic at all about our record with women. We've got, I think—you know, you think about women in government, I think about women in business. Why not try to help them with my small business program to build some incentives into the system? I think we're making progress here.

You got a lot of women running for office. As I said the other night, I hope a lot of them lose because they're liberal Democrats—and we don't need more of them in the Senate or more of them in the House. But nevertheless, they're out there. And we got some very good Republican women running. So we're making dramatic progress.

LEHRER: Mr. Perot, one minute.

PEROT: Well, I come from the computer business, and everybody knows the women are more talented than the men. So we have a long history of having a lot of talented women. One of our first officers was a woman, the chief financial officer. She was a director. And it was so far back, it was considered so odd, and even though we were a tiny, little company at the time, it made all the national magazines.

But in terms of being influenced by women and being a minority, there they are right out there, my wife and my four beautiful daughters, and I just have one son, so he and I are surrounded by women, giving—telling us what to do all the time.

And the rest of my minute, I want to make a very brief comment here in terms of Saddam Hussein. We told him that we wouldn't get involved with his border dispute, and we've never revealed those papers that were given to Ambassador Glaspie on July the 25th. I suggest, in the sense of taking responsibility for your actions, we lay those papers on the table. They're not the secrets to the nuclear bomb.

Secondly, we got upset when he took the whole thing, but to the ordinary American out there who doesn't know where the oil fields are in Kuwait, they're near the border. We told him he could take the northern part of Kuwait, and when he took the whole thing, we went nuts. And if we didn't tell him that, why won't we even let the Senate Foreign Relations Committee and the Senate Intelligence Committee see the written instructions for Ambassador Glaspie?

PRESIDENT BUSH: I've got reply on that. That gets to the national honor. We did not say to Saddam Hussein, Ross, you can take the northern part of Kuwait.

PEROT: Well, where are the papers?

PRESIDENT BUSH: That is absolutely absurd.

PEROT: Where are the papers?

PRESIDENT BUSH: Glaspie has testified—and Glaspie's papers have been presented to the United States Senate. Please, let's be factual.

PEROT: If you have time, go through Nexis and Lexis, pull all the old news articles, look at what Ambassador Glaspie said all through the fall and what-have-you, and then look at what she and Kelly and all the others in State said at the end when they were trying to clean it up. And talk to any head of any of those key committees in the Senate. They will not let them see the written instructions given to Ambassador Glaspie. And I suggest that in a free society owned by the people, the American people ought to know what we told Ambassador Glaspie to tell Saddam Hussein, because we spent a lot of money and risked lives and lost lives in that effort, and did not accomplish most of our objectives.

We got Kuwait back to the emir but he's still not his nuclear, his chemical, his bacteriological and he's still over there, right? I'd like to see those written instructions.

LEHRER: Mr. President, just to make sure that everybody knows what's going on here, when you responded directly to Mr. Perot, you violated the rule, your rules. Now—

PRESIDENT BUSH: For which I apologize. When I make a mistake I say I'm sorry.

LEHRER: I just want to make sure everybody understands. If you all want to change the rules, we can do it.

PRESIDENT BUSH: No, I don't. I apologize for it but that one got right to the national honor and I'm sorry. I just couldn't let it stand.

LEHRER: Governor Clinton, you have a minute.

GOVERNOR CLINTON: Susan, I don't agree that there are no women and minorities in important positions in my campaign. There are many. But I think even more relevant is my record at home. For most of my time as governor a woman was my chief of staff. An African American was my chief cabinet officer. An African American was my chief economic development officer.

It was interesting today. There was a story today or yesterday in the Washington Post about my economic programs and my chief budget officer and my chief economic officer were both African Americans, even though the Post didn't mention that, which I think is a sign of progress.

The National Women's Political Caucus gave me an award, one of their Good Guy Awards, for my involvement of women in high levels of government, and I've appointed more minorities to positions of high level in government than all the governors in the history of my state combined, before me.

So that's what I'll do as president. I don't think we've got a person to waste and I think I owe the American people a White House staff, a Cabinet and appointments that look like America but that meet high standards of excellence, and that's what I'll do.

[U.S. Relations with Iraq]

LEHRER: All right. Next question goes to you, Mr. Perot. It's a two-minute question and Helen will ask it. Helen?

THOMAS: Mr. Perot, what proof do you have that Saddam Hussein was told that he could have the—do you have any actual proof or are you asking for the papers? And also, I really came in with another question. What is this penchant you have to investigate everyone? Are those accusations correct—investigating your staff, investigating the leaders of the grassroots movement, investigating associates of your family?

PEROT: No. They're not correct and if you look at my life, until I got involved in this effort, I was one person. And then after the Republican dirty tricks group got through with me I'm another person, which I consider an absolutely sick operation. And all of you in the press know exactly what I'm talking about.

They investigated every single one of my children. They investigated my wife. They interviewed all of my children's friends from childhood on. They went to extraordinary sick lengths, and I just found it amusing that they would take two or three cases where I was involved in lawsuits and would engage an investigator—the lawyers would engage an investigator, which is common. And the only difference between me and any other businessman that has the range of businesses that I have is I haven't had that many lawsuits.

So that's just another one of those little fruit-loopy things they make up to try to, instead of facing issues, to try to redefine a person that's running against them. This goes on night and day. I will do everything I can, if I get up there, to make dirty tricks a thing of the past. One of the two groups has raised it to an art form. It's a sick art form.

Now, let's go back to Saddam Hussein. We gave Ambassador Glaspie written instructions. That's a fact. We've never let the Congress and the Foreign Relations, Senate Intelligence Committees see them. That's a fact. Ambassador Glaspie did a lot of talking right after July 25 and that's a fact and it's in all the newspapers. And you pull all of it at once and read it and I did, and it's pretty clear what she and Kelly and the other key guys around that thing thought they were doing.

Then at the end of the war, when they had to go testify about it, their stories are a total disconnect from what they said in August, September and October.

So I say this is very simple. Saddam Hussein released a tape, as you know, claiming it was a transcript of their meeting, where she said we will not become involved in your border dispute and, in effect, you can take the northern part of the country. We later said no, that's not true. I said well, this is simple. What were her written instructions? We guard those like the secrets of the atomic bomb, literally.

Now, I say whose country is this? This is ours. Who will get hurt if we lay those papers on the table? The worst thing is, again, it's a mistake. Nobody did any of this with evil intent. I just object to the fact that we cover up and hide things. Whether it's Iran-contra, Iraq-gate or you name it, it's a steady stream.

LEHRER: Governor Clinton, you have one minute.

GOVERNOR CLINTON: Let's take Mr. Bush for the moment at his word—he's right, we don't have any evidence at least that our government did tell Saddam Hussein he could have that part of Kuwait. And let's give him the credit he deserves for organizing Operation Desert Storm and Desert Shield. It was a remarkable event.

But let's look at where I think the real mistake was made. In 1988 when the war between Iraq and Iran ended, we knew Saddam Hussein was a tyrant, we had dealt with him because he was against Iran—the enemy of my enemy maybe is my friend.

All right, the war's over; we know he's dropping mustard gas on his own people, we know he's threatened to incinerate half of Israel. Several government departments—several—had information that he was converting our aid to military purposes and trying to develop weapons of mass destruction. But in late '89 the president signed a secret policy saying we were going to continue to try to improve relations with him, and we sent him some sort of communication on the eve of his invasion of Kuwait that we still wanted better relations.

So I think what was wrong—I give credit where credit is due—but the responsibility was in coddling Saddam Hussein when there was no reason to do it and when people at high levels in our government knew he was trying to do things that were outrageous....

PRESIDENT BUSH: Well, it's awful easy when you're dealing with 90-90 hindsight. We did try to bring Saddam Hussein into the family of nations; he did have the fourth largest army. All our Arab allies out there thought we ought to do just exactly that. And when he crossed the line, I stood up and looked into the camera and I said: This aggression will not stand. And we formed a historic coalition, and we brought him down, and we destroyed the fourth largest army. And the battlefield was searched, and there wasn't one single iota of evidence that any U.S. weapons were on that battlefield. And the nuclear capability has been searched by the United Nations, and there hasn't been one single scintilla of evidence that there's any U.S. technology involved in it.

And what you're seeing on all this Iraqgate is a bunch of people who were wrong on the war trying to cover their necks and try to do a little revisionism. And I cannot let that stand, because it isn't true.

Yes, we had grain credits for Iraq, and there isn't any evidence that those grain credits were diverted into weaponry—none, none whatsoever.

And so I just have to say, it's fine. You can't stand there, Governor Clinton, and say, well, I think I'd have been—I have supported the minority, let sanctions work or wish it would go away—but I would have voted with the majority. Come on, that's not leadership. . . .

[Government Reform]

LEHRER: All right, Mr. Perot, the next question—we're going into a new round here on a category just called differences, and the question goes to you, Mr. Perot, and Gene will ask it. Gene?

GIBBONS: Mr. Perot, aside from the deficit, what government policy or policies do you really want to do something about? What really sticks in your craw about conditions in this country—beside the deficit—that you would want to fix as president?

PEROT: The debt and the deficit. Well, if you watched my television show the other night, you saw it. And if you watch it Thursday, Friday, Saturday this week, you'll get more. A shameless plug there, Mr. President.

But in a nutshell we've got to reform our government or we won't get anything done. We have a government that doesn't work. All these specific examples I'm giving tonight—if you had a business like that, they'd be leading you away and boarding up the doors. We have a government that doesn't work. It's supposed to come from the people, it comes at the people. The people need to take their government back. You've got to reform Congress, they've got to be servants of the people again; you've got to reform the White House. We've got to turn this thing around. And it's a long list of specific items.

And I've covered it again and again in print and on television. But very specifically the key thing is to turn the government back to the people and take it away from the special interests and have people go to Washington to serve. Who can give themselves a 23-percent pay raise anywhere in the world except Congress? Who would have 1,200 airplanes worth two billions a year just to fly around in? I don't have a free reserved parking place at National Airport, why should my servants? I don't have an indoor gymnasium and an indoor tennis and an indoor every other thing they can think of; I don't have a place where I can go make free TV to send to my constituents to try to brainwash them to elect me the next time.

And I'm paying for all that for those guys. I'm going to be running an ad pretty soon that shows they promised us they were going to hold the line on spending at the tax and budget summit, and I'm going to show how much they've increased this little stuff they do for themselves. And it is silly putty, folks, and the American people have had enough of it.

Step one, if I get up there, we're going to clean that up. You say, how can I get Congress to do that? I'll have millions of people at my shoulder, shoulder to shoulder with me, and we will see it done work speed—because it's wrong. We've turned the country upside down.

LEHRER: Governor Clinton, you have one minute. Governor?

GOVERNOR CLINTON: I would just point out, on the point Mr. Perot made, I agree that we need to cut spending in Congress. I've called for a 25 percent reduction in congressional staffs and expenditures. But the White House staff increased its expenditures by considerably more than Congress has in the last four years under the Bush administration, and Congress has actually spent a billion dollars less than President Bush asked them to spend. Now, when you out-spend Congress you're really swinging.

That, however, is not my only passion. The real problem in this country is that most people are working hard and falling farther behind. My passion is to pass a jobs program and get incomes up with an investment incentive program to grow jobs in the private sector, to waste less public money and invest more, to control health care costs and provide for affordable health care for all Americans and to make sure we've got the best trained workforce in the world. That is my passion.

We've gotta get this country growing again and this economy strong again or we can't bring down the deficit. Economic growth is the key to the future of this country.

LEHRER: President Bush, one minute.

PRESIDENT BUSH: On government reform?

LEHRER: Sir?

PRESIDENT BUSH: Government reform?

LEHRER: Yes, exactly. Well, to respond to the subject that Mr. Perot mentioned.

PRESIDENT BUSH: Well, how about this for a government reform policy? Reduce the White House staff by a third after or at the same time the Congress does the same thing for their staff. Term limits for members of the United States Congress. Give the government back to the people. Let's do it that way. The president has term limits. Let's limit some of these guys sitting out there tonight.

Term limits. And then how about a balanced budget amendment to the Constitution? Forty-three—more than that—states have it, I believe. Let's try that. And you want to do something about all this extra spending that concerns Mr. Perot and me? Okay. How about a line item veto? Forty-three governors have that. And give it to the president, and if the Congress isn't big enough to do it, let the president have a shot at this excess spending. A line item veto. That means you can take a line and cut out some of the pork out of a meaningful bill.

Governor Clinton keeps hitting me on vetoing legislation. Well, that's the only protection the taxpayer has against some of these reckless pork programs up there, and I'd rather be able to just line it right out of there and get on about passing some good stuff but leave out the garbage. Line item veto—there's a good reform program for you.

LEHRER: All right.

Next question goes to Governor Clinton. You have two minutes, Governor, and Susan will ask it.

ROOK: Governor Clinton, you said that you will raise taxes on the rich, people with incomes of $200,000 a year or higher. A lot of people are saying that you will have to go lower than that, much lower. Will you make a pledge tonight below which, an income level that you will not go below? I'm looking for numbers, sir, not just a concept.

GOVERNOR CLINTON: My plan—you can read my plan. My plan says that we want to raise marginal incomes on family incomes above $200,000 from 31 to 36 percent, that we want to ask foreign corporations simply to pay the same percentage of taxes on their income that American corporations play (sic) in America, that we want to use that money to provide over $100 billion in tax cuts for investment in new plant and equipment, for small business, for new technologies, and for middle class tax relief.

Now, I'll tell ya this. I will not raise taxes on the middle class to pay for these programs. If the money does not come in there to pay for these programs, we will cut other government spending or we will slow down the phase-in of the programs. I am not gonna raise taxes on the middle class to pay for these programs.

Now furthermore, I am not gonna tell you "read my lips" on anything because I cannot foresee what emergencies might develop in this country. And the president said never, never, never would he raise taxes in New Jersey, and within a day Marlin Fitzwater, his spokesman, said now, that's not a promise.

So I think even he has learned that you can't say "read my lips" because you can't know what emergencies might come up. But I can tell you this. I'm not gonna raise taxes on middle class Americans to pay for the programs I've recommended. Read my plan.

And you know how you can trust me about that? Because you know, in the first debate, Mr. Bush made some news. He'd just said Jim Baker was going to be secretary of state and in the first debate he said no, now he's gonna be responsible for domestic economic policy.

Well, I'll tell ya. I'll make some news in the third debate. The person responsible for domestic economic policy in my administration will be Bill Clinton. I'm gonna make those decisions, and I won't raise taxes on the middle class to pay for my programs.

LEHRER: President Bush, you have one minute.

PRESIDENT BUSH: That's what worries me—that he's going to be responsible. He's going to do—and he would do for the United States what he's done to Arkansas. He would do for the United States what he's done to Arkansas. We do not want to be the lowest of the low. We are not a nation in decline.

We are a rising nation.

Now, my problem is—I heard what he said. He said I want to take it from the rich, raise $150 billion from the rich. To get it, to get $150 billion in new taxes, you got to go down to the guy that's making $36,600. And if you want to pay for the rest of his plan, all the other spending programs, you're going to sock it to the working man.

So when you hear "tax the rich," Mr. and Mrs. America, watch your wallet. Lock your wallet because he's coming right after you just like Jimmy Carter did and just like you're going to get—you're going to end up with interest rates at 21 percent, and you're going to have inflation going through the roof.

Yes, we're having tough times, but we do not need to go back to the failed policies of the past, when you had a Democratic president and a spendthrift Democratic Congress.

LEHRER: Mr. Perot.

GOVERNOR CLINTON: Jim, you permitted Mr. Bush to break the rules, he said, to defend the honor of the country. What about the honor of my state? We rank first in the country in job growth, we got the lowest spending, state and local, in the country, and the second lowest tax burden. And the difference between Arkansas and the United States is that we're going in the right direction and this country's going in the wrong direction. And I have to defend the honor of my state.

LEHRER: We've got a wash, according to my calculation. We have a wash. And we go to Mr. Perot for one minute. In other words, it's a violation of the rule, that's what I meant, Mr. Perot.

PEROT: So I'm the only one that's untarnished at this point?

LEHRER: That's right. You're clear.

PEROT: I'm sure I'll do it before it's over.

Key thing here, see, we all come up with images. Images don't fix anything. I think—you know, I'm starting to understand it. You stay around this long enough, you think about—if you talk about it in Washington, you think you did it. If you've been on television about it, you think you did it.

What we need is people to stop talking and start doing.

Now, our real problem here is they both have plans that will not work. The Wall Street Journal said your numbers don't add up. And you can take it out on charts, you look at all the studies the different groups have done, you go out four, five, six years, we're still drifting along with a huge deficit.

So let's come back to harsh reality, and what I—you know, everybody says, gee, Perot, you're tough. I'm saying, well, this is not as tough as World War II and it's not as tough as the revolution. And it's fair, shared sacrifice to do the right thing for our country and for our children. And it will be fun if we all work together to do it.

[Winning the Election]

THOMAS: Mr. President, why have you dropped so dramatically in the leadership polls, from the high 80s to the 40s? And you have said that you will do anything you have to do to get reelected. What can you do in two weeks to win reelection?

PRESIDENT BUSH: Well, I think the answer to why the drop, I think, has been the economy in the doldrums. Why I'll win is I think I have the best plan of the three of us up here to do something about it. Mine does not grow the government, it does not invest, have government invest.

It says we need to do better in terms of stimulating private business. We got a big philosophical difference here tonight between one who thinks the government can do all these things through tax and spend, and one who thinks it ought to go the other way.

And so I believe the answer is, I'm going to win it because I'm getting into focus my agenda for America's renewal, and also I think that Governor Clinton's had pretty much of a free ride. On looking specifically at the Arkansas record—he keeps criticizing us, criticizing me, I'm the incumbent, fine. But he's an incumbent, and we've got to look at all the facts. They're almost at the bottom on every single category. We can't do that to the American people.

And then, Helen, I really believe where people are going to ask this question about trust, because I do think there's a pattern by Governor Clinton of saying one thing to please one group, and then trying to please another group. And I think that pattern is a dangerous thing to suggest would work for the Oval Office. It doesn't work that way when you're president.

Truman is right. The buck stops there. And you have to make decisions even when it's against your own interest. And I've done that. It's against my political interest to say go ahead and go along with the tax increase, but I did what I thought was right at the time. So I think people are going to be looking for trust and experience.

And then, I mentioned it the other night, I think if there's a crisis, people are going to say, well, George Bush has taken us through some tough crises, and we trust him to do that.

And so I'll make the appeal on a wide array of issues. Also I got a philosophical difference. I got to watch the clock here. I don't think we're a declining nation. The whole world has had economic problems. We're doing better than a lot of the countries in the world. And we're going to lead the way out of this economic recession across this world and economic slowdown here at home.

PEROT: I'm totally focussed on the fact that we may have bank failures and nobody answered it. I'm totally focussed on the fact that we are still evading the issue of the Glaspie papers. I'm totally focussed on the fact that we still could have enterprise zones, according to both parties, but we don't. So I am still focussed on gridlock, I guess.

And I am also focussed on the fact that isn't it a paradox that we have the highest productivity in our workforce in the industrialized world and at the same time have the largest trade deficit, and at the same time rank behind nine other nations in what we pay our most productive people in the world, and we're losing whole industries overseas.

Now, can't somebody agree with me that the government is breaking business's legs with these trade agreements? They're breaking business's legs in a number of different ways. We have an adversarial relationship that's destroying jobs and sending them overseas while we have the finest workers in the world.

Keep in mind a factory worker has nothing to do with anything except putting it together on the factory floor. It's our obligation to make sure that we give him the finest products in the world to put together and we don't break his legs in the process.

GOVERNOR CLINTON: I really can't believe Mr. Bush is still trying to make trust an issue after "read my lips" and 15 million new jobs and embracing what he called voodoo economics and embracing an export enhancement program for farmers he threatened to veto and going all around the country giving out money in programs that he once opposed.

But the main thing is he still didn't get it, from what he said the other night to that fine woman on our program, the 209 people in Richmond. They don't want us talking about each other. They want us to talk about the problems of this country.

I don't think he'll be reelected because trickle down economics is a failure and he's offering more of it, and what he's saying about my program is just not true. Look at the Republicans that have endorsed me. High tech executives in Northern California. Look at the 24 generals and admirals, retired, that have endorsed me, including the deputy commander of Desert Storm. Look at Sarah Brady, Jim Brady's wife, President Reagan's press secretary, who endorsed me because he knuckled under to the NRA and wouldn't fight for the Brady Bill.

We've got a broad-based coalition that goes beyond party because I am going to change this country and make it better, with the help of the American people.

LEHRER: All right. Now, that was the final question and answer and we now go to the closing statements. Each candidate will have up to two minutes. The order was determined by a drawing. Governor Clinton, you're first. Governor.

GOVERNOR CLINTON: First, I'd like to thank the commission and my opponents for participating in these debates and making them possible. I think the real winners of the debates were the American people.

I was especially moved in Richmond a few days ago when 209 of our fellow citizens got to ask us questions. They went a long way toward reclaiming this election for the American people and taking their country back.

I want to say, since this is the last time I'll be on a platform with my opponents, that even though I disagree with Mr. Perot on how fast we can reduce the deficit and how much we can increase taxes on the middle class, I really respect what he's done in this campaign to bring the issue of deficit reduction to our attention.

I'd like to say to Mr. Bush, even though I've got profound differences with him, I do honor his service to our country. I appreciate his efforts and I wish him well. I just believe it's time to change.

I offer a new approach. It's not trickle down economics. It's been tried for 12 years and it's failed. More people are working harder for less, 100,000 people a month losing their health insurance, unemployment going up, our economy slowing down. We can do better.

And it's not tax and spend economics. It's invest and grow, put our people first, control health care costs and provide basic health care to all Americans, have an education system second to none and revitalize the private economy.

That is my commitment to you. It is the kind of change that can open up a whole new world of opportunities to America as we enter the last decade of this century and move towards the 21st century. I want a country where people who work hard and play by the rules are rewarded, not punished. I want a country where people are coming together across the lines of race and region and income. I know we can do better.

It won't take miracles and it won't happen overnight, but we can do much, much better if we have the courage to change. Thank you very much.

LEHRER: President Bush, your closing statement, sir.

PRESIDENT BUSH: Three weeks from now—two weeks from tomorrow, America goes to the polls and you're going to have to decide who you want to lead this country to economic recovery. On jobs—that's the number one priority, and I believe my program for stimulating investment, encouraging small business, brand-new approach to education, strengthening the American family, and, yes, creating more exports is the way to go. I don't believe in trickle-down government, I don't believe in larger taxes and larger government spending.

On foreign affairs, some think it's irrelevant. I believe it's not. We're living in an interconnected world. The whole world is having economic difficulties. The U.S. is doing better than a lot. But we've got to do even better. And if a crisis comes up, I ask who has the judgment and the experience and, yes, the character to make the right decision?

And, lastly, the other night on character Governor Clinton said it's not the character of the president but the character of the presidency. I couldn't disagree more. Horace Greeley said the only thing that endures is character. And I think it was Justice Black who talked about great nations, like great men, must keep their word.

And so the question is, who will safeguard this nation, who will safeguard our people and our children? I need your support, I ask for your support. And may God bless the United States of America.

LEHRER: Mr. Perot, your closing statement, sir.

PEROT: To the millions of fine decent people who did the unthinkable and took their country back in their own hands and put me on the ballot, let me pledge to you that tonight is just the beginning. These next two weeks we will be going full steam ahead to make sure that you get a voice and that you get your country back.

This Thursday night on ABC from 8:30 to 9, Friday night on NBC from 8 to 8:30, and Saturday night on CBS from 8 to 8:30, we'll be down in the trenches under the hood working on fixin' the old car to get it back on the road.

Now, the question is, can we win? Absolutely we can win, because it's your country. Question really is who do you want in the White House. It's that simple.

Now, you got to stop letting these people tell you who to vote for, you got to stop letting these folks in the press tell you you're throwing your vote away—you got to start using your own head.

Then the question is, can we govern? I love that one. The "we" is you and me. You bet your hat we can govern because we will be in there together and we will figure out what to do, and you won't tolerate gridlock, you won't tolerate endless meandering and wandering around, and you won't tolerate non-performance. And, believe me, anybody that knows me understands I have a very low tolerance for non-performance also. Together we can get anything done.

The president mentioned that you need the right person in a crisis. Well, folks, we got one, and that one is a financial crisis. Pretty simply, who's the best-qualified person up here on the stage to create jobs? Make your decision and vote on November the 3rd. I suggest you might consider somebody who's created jobs. Who's the best person to manage money? I suggest you pick a person who's successfully managed money. Who's the best person to get results and not talk? Look at the record and make your decision.

And, finally, who would you give your pension fund and your savings account to to manage? And, last one, who would you ask to be the trustee of your estate and take care of your children if something happened to you?

Finally, to you students up there—God bless you, I'm doing this for you: I want you to have the American dream.

To the American people, I'm doing this because I love you. That's it. Thank you very much.

LEHRER: All right, thank you, Mr. Perot; thank you, Mr. President; thank you, Governor Clinton—for being with us tonight and in the previous debates. Thank you to the panel.

VICE PRESIDENTIAL DEBATE

HAL BRUNO: Good evening from Atlanta and welcome to the vice presidential debate sponsored by the nonpartisan Commission on Presidential Debates. It's being held here in the Theater for the Arts on the campus of Georgia Tech. I'm Hal Bruno from ABC News and I'm going to be moderating tonight's debate. The participants are Republican Vice President Dan Quayle, Democratic Senator Al Gore, and Vice Admiral James Stockdale, who is the vice presidential nominee for independent candidate Ross Perot.

Now, the ground rules for tonight's debate. Each candidate will have two minutes for an opening statement. I will then present the issues to be discussed. For each topic, the candidates will have a minute and 15 seconds to respond. Then this will be followed by a five minute discussion period in which they can ask questions of each other if they so choose.

Now, the order of response has been determined by a drawing and we'll rotate with each topic. At the end of the debate, each candidate will have two minutes for a closing statement.

Our radio and TV audience should know that the candidates are given an equal allocation of auditorium seats for their supporters. So I'd like to ask the audience here in the theater to please refrain from applause or any partisan demonstration once the debate is under way because it takes time away from the candidates.

So with that plea from your moderator let's get started.

And we'll turn first to Senator Gore for his opening statement.

SENATOR GORE: Good evening. It's great to be here in Atlanta for this debate where America will be showcases to the world when the 1996 Olympics are put on right here. It's appropriate because in a real sense, our discussion this evening will be about what kind of nation we want to be four years from now. It's also a pleasure to be with my two opponents this evening. Admiral Stockdale, may I say it's a special honor to share this stage with you. Those of us who served in Vietnam looked at you as a national hero even before you were awarded the Congressional Medal of Honor.

And Mr. Vice President—Dan, if I may—it was 16 years ago that you and I went to the Congress on the very first day together. I'll make you a deal this evening. If you don't try to compare George Bush to Harry Truman, I won't compare you to Jack Kennedy.

Harry Truman—

VICE PRESIDENT QUAYLE: Do you remember the last time someone compared themselves to Jack Kennedy? Do you remember what they said?

SENATOR GORE: Harry Truman, it's worth remembering, assumed the presidency when Franklin Roosevelt died here in Georgia—only one of many occasions when fate thrust a vice president into the Oval Office in a time of crisis. It's something to think about during the debate this evening. But our real discussion is going to be about change. Bill Clinton and I stand for change because we don't believe our nation can stand four more years of what we've had under George Bush and Dan Quayle.

When the recession came they were like a deer caught in the head-lights—paralyzed into inaction, blinded to the suffering and pain of bankruptcies and people who were unemployed. We have an environmental crisis, a health insurance crisis, substandard education. It is time for a change.

Bill Clinton and I want to get our country moving forward again, put our people back to work, and create a bright future for the United States of America.

BRUNO: Okay, the next statement will be from Vice President Quayle.

VICE PRESIDENT QUAYLE: Well, thank you, Senator Gore, for reminding me about my performance in the 1988 vice presidential debate. This is 1992, Bill Clinton is running against President George Bush. There are two things that I'm going to stress during this debate: one, Bill Clinton's economic plan and his agenda will make matters much, much worse—he will raise your taxes, he will increase spending, he will make government bigger, jobs will be lost; second, Bill Clinton does not have the strength nor the character to be president of the United States.

Let us look at the agendas. President Bush wants to hold the line on taxes, Bill Clinton wants to raise taxes. President Bush is for a balanced budget amendment, Bill Clinton is opposed to it. We want to reform the legal system because it's too costly, Bill Clinton wants the status quo. We want to reform the health care system, Bill Clinton wants to ration health care. Bill Clinton wants to empower government, we want to empower people.

In St. Louis, Missouri, in June of this year, Bill Clinton said this: "America is the mockery of the world." He is wrong.

At some time during these next four years there is going to be a crisis—there will be an international crisis. I can't tell you where it's going to be, I can't even tell you the circumstances—but it will happen. We need a president who has the experience, who has been tested, who has the integrity and qualifications to handle the crisis. The president has been tested, the president has the integrity and the character. The choice is yours.

You need to have a president you can trust. Can you really trust Bill Clinton?

BRUNO: Admiral Stockdale, your opening statement, please, sir?

VICE ADMIRAL STOCKDALE: Who am I? Why am I here?

I'm not a politician—everybody knows that. So don't expect me to use the language of the Washington insider. Thirty-seven years in the Navy, and only one of them up there in Washington. And now I'm an academic.

The centerpiece of my life was the Vietnam War. I was there the day it started. I led the first bombing raid against North Vietnam. I was there the day it ended, and I was there for everything in between. Ten years in Vietnam, aerial combat, and torture. I know things about the Vietnam War better than anybody in the world. I know some things about the Vietnam War better than anybody in the world.

And I know how governments, how American governments can be—can be courageous, and how they can be callow. And that's important. That's one thing I'm an insider on.

I was the leader of the underground of the American pilots who were shot down in prison in North Vietnam. You should know that the American character displayed in those dungeons by those fine men was a thing of beauty.

I look back on those years as the beginning of wisdom, learning everything a man can learn about the vulnerabilities and the strengths that are ours as Americans.

Why am I here tonight? I am here because I have in my brain and in my heart what it takes to lead America through tough times.

BRUNO: Thank you, Admiral. I thought since you're running for vice president, that we ought to start off by talking about the vice presidency itself. The vice president presides over the Senate, he casts a deciding vote in case of a tie, but his role really depends on the assignments that are given to him by the president. However, if a president should die in office, or is unable to serve for any other reason, the vice president automatically becomes president, and that has happened five times in this century.

So the proposition I put on the table for you to discuss is this.

What role would each of you like to play as vice president, what areas interest you, and what are your qualifications to serve as president, if necessary?

In the case of Vice President Quayle, who we're starting with, I suppose you'd tell us the role that you did play in the first term and which you'd like to do in the second term. Go ahead, sir.

VICE PRESIDENT QUAYLE: Well, then I won't give you that answer.

Qualifications. I've been there, Hal. I've done the job. I've been tested. I've been vice president for four years. Senator Gore referred to us being elected to the Congress together in 1976. I've done the job. I've done many things for the president.

But even as vice president you never know exactly what your role is going to be from time to time, and let me just give you an example of where I was tested under fire and in a crisis.

President Bush was flying to Malta in 1989 to meet with President Gorbachev. It was the first meeting between President Bush and President Gorbachev. They had known each other before.

A coup broke out in the Philippines. I had to go to the situation room. I had to assemble the president's advisers. I talked to President Aquino. I made the recommendation to the president. The president made the decision, the coup was suppressed, democracy continued in the Philippines, the situation was ended.

I've been there. And I'll tell you one other thing that qualifies you for being president—and it's this, Hal—you've got to stand up for what you believe in. And nobody has ever criticized me for not having strong beliefs.

BRUNO: Admiral Stockdale.

STOCKDALE: My association with Mr. Perot is a very personal one and as I have stood in and finally taken his running mate position, he has granted me total autonomy. I don't take advantage of it, but I am sure that he would make me a partner in decision, in making decisions about he way to handle health care, the way to get this economy back on its feet again, in every way.

I have not had the experience of these gentlemen, but—to be any more specific—but I know I have his trust, and I intend to act in a way to keep that situation alive. Thank you.

BRUNO: Senator Gore.

SENATOR GORE: Bill Clinton understands the meaning of the words "teamwork" and "partnership." If we're successful in our efforts to gain your trust and lead this nation, we will work together to put our country back on the right track again. The experience that George Bush and Dan Quayle have been talking about includes the worst economic performance since the Great Depression. Unemployment is up, personal income is down, bankruptcies are up, housing starts are down. How long can we continue with trickle-down economics when the record of failure is so abundantly clear?

Discussions of the vice presidency tend sometimes to focus on the crisis during which a vice president is thrust into the Oval Office, and indeed, one-third of the vice presidents who have served have been moved into the White House.

But the teamwork and partnership beforehand—and hopefully that situation never happens—how you work together is critically important. The way we work together in this campaign is one sample.

Now I'd like to say in response to Vice President Quayle—he talked about Malta and the Philippines. George Bush has concentrated on every other country in the world. When are you guys going to start worrying about our people here in the United States of America and get our country moving again?

BRUNO: Again, I will ask the audience: please do not applaud, it takes time for the candidates. All right, now we have five minutes for discussion. Go ahead, Vice President Quayle.

VICE PRESIDENT QUAYLE: The answer to that is very simple: we are not going to raise taxes to create new jobs, we have a plan to create new jobs. But that wasn't the question. The question dealt with qualifications. Teamwork and partnership may be fine in the Congress, Senator Gore—that's what Congress is all about, compromise, teamwork, working things out. But when you're president of the United States or when you're vice president and you have to fill in like I did the night of the crisis in the Philippines, you've got to make a decision, you've got to make up your mind. Bill Clinton, running for president of the United States, said this about the Persian Gulf war. He said: "Had I been in the Senate, I would have voted with the majority, if it was a close vote. But I agreed with the arguments of the minority."

You can't have it both ways, you have to make a decision. You cannot sit there in an international crisis and sit there and say, well, on the one hand, this is okay, and, on the other hand, this is okay. You've got to make the decision. President Bush has made the decisions; he's been tested, he's got the experience, he's got the qualification, he's got the integrity to be our president for the next four years.

BRUNO: Thank you, Mr. Vice President. Admiral Stockdale, it's your turn to respond next, and then Senator Gore will have his chance to respond.

STOCKDALE: Okay. I thought this was just an open session, this five-minute thing, and I didn't have anything to add to this. But I will—

SENATOR GORE: Well, I'll jump in if you don't want—

VICE PRESIDENT QUAYLE: I thought anyone could jump in whenever they wanted to.

BRUNO: Okay, whatever pleases you gentlemen is fine with me. You're the candidates.

VICE PRESIDENT QUAYLE: But I want Admiral Stockdale's time.

BRUNO: This is not the Senate, where you can trade off time. Go ahead, Senator Gore.

SENATOR GORE: I'll let you all figure out the rules, I've got some points that I want to make here, and I still haven't gotten an answer to my question on when you guys are going to start worrying about this country, but I want to elaborate on it before—

VICE PRESIDENT QUAYLE: Why doesn't the Democratic Congress—why don't the Democratic Congress—

BRUNO: Mr. Vice President, let him say his thoughts, and then you can come in.

SENATOR GORE: I was very patient in letting you get off that string of attacks. We've been listening to—

VICE PRESIDENT QUAYLE: Good points.

SENATOR GORE: —trickle-down economics for 12 years now, and you all still support trickle-down to the very last drop. And, you know, talking about this point of concentrating on every other country in the world as opposed to the people of our country right here at home, when George Bush took former Secretary of State Baker out of the State Department and put him in charge of the campaign and made him chief of staff in the White House, Mr. Baker, who's quite a capable man, said that for these last four years George Bush was working on the problems of the rest of the world and in the next four years he would target America.

Well, I want you to know we really appreciate that. But Bill Clinton and I will target America from day one. We won't wait four years before we concentrate on the problems in this country.

He went on to say that it's really amazing what George Bush can do when he concentrates. Well, it's time that we had a president like Bill Clinton who can concentrate and will concentrate and work on the problems of real people in this country. You know, our country is in trouble. We simply cannot continue with this philosophy of giving huge tax cuts to the very wealthy, raising taxes on middle income families the way Bush and Quayle have done and then waiting for it to work. How much longer will it take, Dan, for trickle-down economics to work, in your theory?

VICE PRESIDENT QUAYLE: Well, we're going to have plenty of time to talk about trickle-down government, which you're for. But the question—

SENATOR GORE: Well, I'd like to hear the answer.

VICE PRESIDENT QUAYLE: But the question is—the question is—and which you have failed to address, and that is, why is Bill Clinton qualified to be president of the United States. You've talked about—

SENATOR GORE: Oh, I'll be happy to answer that question—

VICE PRESIDENT QUAYLE: You've talked about Jim Baker. You've talked about trickle-down economics. You've talked about the worst economy.

BRUNO: Now, wait a minute. The question was about—

VICE PRESIDENT QUAYLE: —in 50 years.

SENATOR GORE: I'll be happy to answer those. May I answer—

VICE PRESIDENT QUAYLE: Why is he qualified to be president of the United States?

SENATOR GORE: I'll be happy to—

VICE PRESIDENT QUAYLE: I want to go back and make a point—

SENATOR GORE: Well, you've asked me the question. If you won't answer my question I will answer yours.

VICE PRESIDENT QUAYLE: I have not asked you a question. I've made a statement, that you have not told us why Bill Clinton is qualified to be president of the United States. I point out what he said about the Persian Gulf War. But let me repeat it for you. Here's what he said, Senator. You know full well what he said.

SENATOR GORE: You want me to answer your question?

VICE PRESIDENT QUAYLE: I'm making a statement. Then you can answer it.

BRUNO: Can we give Admiral Stockdale a chance to come in, please...

VICE PRESIDENT QUAYLE: (Inaudible) here's what he said. I mean, this is the Persian Gulf War—the most important event in his political lifetime and here's what Bill Clinton says. If it's a close vote, I'd vote with the majority.

BRUNO: Let's give Admiral Stockdale a chance to come in.

VICE PRESIDENT QUAYLE: But he was the minority. That qualifies you for being president of the United States. I hope America is listening very closely to this debate tonight.

STOCKDALE: And I think America is seeing right now the reason this nation is in gridlock.

The trickle downs and the tax and spends, or whatever you want to call them are at swords points. We can't get this economy going. Over here we've got Dan whose president is going to take eight years to balance the budget and on my left, the senator, whose boss is going to get it half way balanced in four years. Ross Perot has got a plan to balance the budget five years in length from start to finish. And we're—people of the non-professional category who are just sick of this terrible thing that's happened to the country. And we've got a man who knows how to fix it, and I'm working for him.

[Economic Growth]

BRUNO: I was a little bit worried that there might not be a free flowing discussion tonight.

Let's move on to the economy. Specifically the economy was talked about at great length the other night in the presidential debate. Let's talk about a very particular aspect of the economy and that is, getting people back to work. For the average person, the great fear is losing his or her job and many Americans have lost jobs in this recession, which also means the loss of benefits, the loss of a home, the destruction of a family's security. Specifically, how would your administration go about getting people back to work and how long is it going to take? And we start with Admiral Stockdale.

STOCKDALE: The lifeblood of our economy is investment. And right now when we pay $350—we borrow $350 billion a year it saps the money markets and the private investors are not getting their share. What we do is work on that budget by an aggressive program, not a painful program, so that we can start borrowing less money and getting more investment money on the street through entrepreneurs who can build factories, who will hire people, and maybe we'll start manufacturing goods here in this country again. That's—that's my answer.

BRUNO: Okay. Senator Gore.

SENATOR GORE: Bill Clinton's top priority is putting America back to work. Bill Clinton and I will create good, high-wage jobs for our people, the same way he has done in his state. Bill Clinton has created high-wage manufacturing jobs at ten times the national average and in fact according to the statistics coming from the Bush-Quayle Labor Department, for the last two years in a role Bill Clinton's state has been number one among all fifty in the creation of jobs in the private sector.

By contrast, in the nation as a whole, during the last four years, it is the first time since the presidency of Herbert Hoover, that we have gone for a four-year period with fewer jobs at the end of that four-year period than we had at the beginning.

And look at manufacturing. We have lost 1.4 million jobs in manufacturing under George Bush and Dan Quayle. They have even—we learned two weeks ago—taken our tax dollars and subsidized the moving of U.S. factories to foreign countries. Now don't deny it because "Sixty Minutes" and "Nightline" and the nation's newspapers have investigated this very carefully.

When are you going to stop using our tax dollars to shut down American factories and move 'em to foreign countries and throw Americans out of work?

BRUNO: Vice President Quayle.

VICE PRESIDENT QUAYLE: Senator, don't always believe what you see on television.

Let me tell you: the media have been wrong before. We have never subsidized any country—or any company to move from the United States to Latin America. You know full well the Caribbean Basin Initiative, you've supported that.

SENATOR GORE: No.

VICE PRESIDENT QUAYLE: That is a program there—

SENATOR GORE: I voted against it.

VICE PRESIDENT QUAYLE: You voted for it and your record—

SENATOR GORE: No.

VICE PRESIDENT QUAYLE: Okay, Well, we'll—we'll have a lot of interesting debate after this debate. Our people will be glad to furnish the press, if they're interested, in Senator Gore's voting record on the Caribbean Basin Initiative. But let's talk—you know, you keep talking about trickle-down economics and all this stuff, about the worst economy since Hoover. It is a bad economy. It's a tough economy. The question isn't—it's not who you're going to blame; what are you going to do about it? Your proposal is to raise $150 billion in taxes. To raise $220 billion in new spending.

SENATOR GORE: No.

VICE PRESIDENT QUAYLE: How is raising taxes going to help small business? How is raising taxes going to help the farmer? How is raising taxes going to help the consumer in America? I submit to you that raising taxes will make matters much, much worse.

BRUNO: Admiral. We now throw it open for discussion. Admiral Stockdale, it's your turn to start the discussion.

STOCKDALE: Well, we've got to re—we've got to clean out the barn, if I may quote my boss, and start getting this investment money on the street so we can get, and encourage entrepreneurs to build factories. We—the program is out there. It's a put-together thing that requires some sacrifice, but not excessive, and we are willing to move forward in—on a five-year clip to put us back where we can start over and get—get this nation straightened out.

BRUNO: Senator Gore, getting people back to work.

SENATOR GORE: Well, the difference between the Perot-Stockdale plan and the Clinton-Gore plan is that Ross Perot's plan concentrates almost exclusively on balancing the budget and reducing the budget deficit, and the danger is that if that is the only goal it could throw our nation back into an even worse recession.

Bill Clinton and I have a detailed five-year budget plan to create good jobs, cut the budget deficit in half, and eliminate the investment deficit in order to get our economy moving forward again. We have a $20-billion infrastructure fund to create a nationwide network of high-speed rail, for example, and what are called information superhighways to open up a whole universe of knowledge for our young people and to help our universities and companies that rely on new advances in the information revolution. We also have tax incentives for investment in job-creating activities, not the kind of encouragement for short-term rip-offs like the proposal that we have had from George Bush.

But I want to return and say one more time: you have used our tax dollars to subsidize the recruitment of U.S. companies to move overseas and throw Americans out of work. In Decaturville, Tennessee, not very far from my home, a factory was shut down right there when they were solicited by officials paid with U.S. taxpayers' money, and then the replacement workers in a foreign country were strained with our tax dollars and then their imports were subsidized coming back into the United States.

When are you going to stop that program?

VICE PRESIDENT QUAYLE: We do not have any program that encourages companies to close down here and to go and invest on foreign soil. That is absolutely outrageous. Of course American businesses do have business abroad; we've got global competition. We want businesses to expand. Do you realize this, Senator, that every job that's overseas there's three jobs back here to support that.

But never have we ever, nor would we, support the idea of someone closing down a factory here and moving overseas. That's just totally ridiculous.

SENATOR GORE: It's going on right now; it happened in Tennessee, in Decaturville, Tennessee. When George Bush went to Nashville, the employees who lost their jobs asked to meet with—

VICE PRESIDENT QUAYLE: I want to get back—

SENATOR GORE: I talked with them. Let me tell you what they're feeling. Some of them are in their fifties and sixties. They want to know where they're going to get new jobs when their jobs have been destroyed. And there are 1.4 million manufacturing jobs that have been lost because of the policies of you and George Bush. Do you seriously believe that we ought to continue the same policies that have created the worst economy since the Great Depression?

VICE PRESIDENT QUAYLE: I hope that when you talked to those people you said: and the first thing that Bill Clinton and I are going to do is to raise $150 billion in new taxes.

SENATOR GORE: You got that wrong, too.

VICE PRESIDENT QUAYLE: And the first—that is part of your plan.

SENATOR GORE: No, it's not.

VICE PRESIDENT QUAYLE: A hundred and fifty billion dollars in new taxes. Well, you're going to disavow your plan.

SENATOR GORE: Listen, what we're proposing—

VICE PRESIDENT QUAYLE: You know what you're doing, you know what you're doing? You're pulling a Clinton.

And you know what a Clinton is? And you know what Clinton is? A Clinton is, is what he says—he says one thing one day and another thing the next day—you try to have both sides of the issues. The fact of the matter is that you are proposing $150 billion in new taxes.

SENATOR GORE: No.

VICE PRESIDENT QUAYLE: And I hope that you talk to the people in Tennessee—

SENATOR GORE: No, we're not.

VICE PRESIDENT QUAYLE: —and told them that—

SENATOR GORE: You can say it all you want but it doesn't make it true.

VICE PRESIDENT QUAYLE: —going to have new taxes. I hope you talked to them about the fact that you were going to increase spending to $220 billion. I'm sure what you didn't talk to them about was about how we're going to reform the health care system, like the president wants to do. He wants to go out and to reform the health care system so that every American will have available to them affordable health insurance.

I'm sure one other thing that you didn't talk to them about, Senator, and that is legal reform, because your position on legal reform is the status quo. And yet you talk about foreign competition. Why should an American company have to spend 15 to 20 times on product liability and insurance costs compared to a company in Japan or a company in Germany or somewhere else? That's not right. We have product liability reform legislation on Capitol Hill. It will create jobs. And a Democratic Congress won't pass it. . . .

[Environment and Jobs]

BRUNO: Let's talk about the environment—we'll get away from controversy. Everyone wants a safe and clean environment, but there's an ongoing conflict between environmental protection and the need for economic growth and jobs. So the point I throw out on the table is, how do you resolve this conflict between protection of the environment and growth in jobs, and why has it taken so long to deal with basic problems, such as toxic waste dumps, clean air and clean water?

And, Vice President Quayle, it's your turn to start first.

VICE PRESIDENT QUAYLE: Hal, that's a false choice. You don't have to have a choice between the environment and jobs—you can have both. Look at the president's record: clean air legislation passed the Democratic Congress because of the leadership of George Bush. It is the most comprehensive clean air act in our history. We are firmly behind preserving our environment, and we have a good record with which to stand. The question comes about: What is going to be their position when it comes to the environment? I say it's a false choice. You ought to ask somebody in Michigan, a UAW worker in Michigan, if they think increasing the CAFE standards, the fuel economy standards, to 45 miles a gallon is a good idea—300,000 people out of work. You ought to talk to the timber people in the Northwest where they say that, well we can only save the owl, forget about jobs.

You ought to talk to the timber people in the northwest, where they say that—well, we can only save the owl. Forget about jobs. You ought to talk to the coal miners. They're talking about putting a coal tax on. They're talking about a tax on utilities, a tax on gasoline and home heating oil—all sorts of taxes.

No, Hal, the choice isn't the environment and jobs. With the right policies—prudent policies—we can have both.

BRUNO: Admiral Stockdale.

STOCKDALE: I read Senator Gore's book about the environment and I don't see how he could possibility pay for his proposals in today's economic climate.

You know, the Marshall Plan of the environment, and so forth.

And also, I'm told by some experts that the things that he fears most might not be all that dangerous, according to some scientists. You know, you can overdo, I'm told, environmental cleaning up. If you purify the pond, the water lilies die. You know, I love this planet and I want it to stay here, but I don't like to have it the private property of fanatics that want to overdo this thing.

BRUNO: Senator Gore.

SENATOR GORE: Bill Clinton and I believe we can create millions of new jobs by leading the environmental revolution instead of dragging our feet and bringing up the rear.

You know, Japan and Germany are both opening proclaiming to the world now that the biggest new market in the history of world business is the market for the new products and technologies that foster economic progress without environmental destruction.

Why is the Japanese business organization—the largest one they have, ... arguing for tougher environmental standards than those embodied in U.S. law? Why is MITI—their trade organization—calling on all Japanese corporations everywhere in the world to exceed by as much as possible the environmental standards of every country in which they're operating?

Well, maybe they're just dumb about business competition. But maybe they know something that George Bush and Dan Quayle don't know—that the future will call for greater efficiency and greater environmental efficiency.

This is an issue that touches my basic values. I'm taught in my religious tradition that we are given dominion over the Earth, but we're required to be good stewards of the Earth, and that man ought to take care of it. We're not doing that now under the Bush-Quayle policies. They have gutted the Clean Air Act. They have broken his pledge to be the environmental president. Bill Clinton and I will change that.

BRUNO: Okay. Discussion period now. Again, leave time for each other, please. Vice President Quayle, go ahead.

VICE PRESIDENT QUAYLE: Well, I'm tempted to yield to Admiral Stockdale on this. But I—you know, that fact of the matter is that one of the proposals that Senator Gore has suggested is to have the taxpayers of America spend $100 billion a year on environmental projects in foreign countries—

SENATOR GORE: That's not true—

VICE PRESIDENT QUAYLE: Foreign aid—well, Senator, it's in your book. On page 30—

SENATOR GORE: No, it's not.

VICE PRESIDENT QUAYLE: It is there.

It is in your book. You know, Hal, I wanted to bring the Gore book tonight, because I figured he was going to pull a Bill Clinton on me and he has. Because he's going to disavow what's in his book. It's in your book—

SENATOR GORE: No.

VICE PRESIDENT QUAYLE: It comes out to $100 billion of foreign aid for environmental projects.

BRUNO: All right. Let's give him a chance to answer.

VICE PRESIDENT QUAYLE: Now, how are we going to pay for it? How are we going to pay for an extra $100 billion of the taxpayers' money for this?

SENATOR GORE: Dan, I appreciate you reading my book very much, but you've got it wrong.

VICE PRESIDENT QUAYLE: No, I've got it right.

SENATOR GORE: There's no such proposal.

VICE PRESIDENT QUAYLE: Okay, well, we'll find—

BRUNO: Let him talk, Mr. Vice President. Let the senator talk. Go ahead.

SENATOR GORE: There is no such proposal. What I have called upon is a cooperative effort by the United States and Europe and Asia to work together in opening up new markets throughout the world for the new technologies that are necessary in order to reconcile the imperatives of economic progress with the imperatives of environmental protection. Take Mexico City for an example. They are shutting down factories right now, not because of their economy, but because they're choking together on the air pollution. They're banning automobiles some days of the week.

Now what they want is not new laser-guided missile systems. What they want are new engines and new factories and new products that don't pollute the air and the water, but nevertheless allow them to have a decent standard of living for their people. Last year 35 percent of our exports went to developing countries, countries where the population is expanding worldwide by as much as one billion people every ten years.

We cannot stick our heads in the sand and pretend that we don't face a global environmental crisis, nor should we assume that it's going to cost jobs. Quite the contrary. We are going to be able to create jobs as Japan and Germany are planning to do right now, if we have the guts to leave.

Now earlier we hear about the auto industry and the timber industry. There have been 250,000 jobs lost in the automobile industry during the Reagan-Bush-Quayle years. There have been tens of thousands of jobs lost in the timber industry. What they like to do is point the finger of blame with one hand and hand out pink slips with the other hand. They've done a poor job both with the economy and the environment.

It's time for a change.

BRUNO: Admiral Stockdale, you had something you wanted to say here?

STOCKDALE: I know that—I read where Senator Gore's mentor had disagreed with some of the scientific data that is in his book. How do you respond to those criticisms of that sort? Do you—

VICE PRESIDENT QUAYLE: Deny it.

SENATOR GORE: Well—

STOCKDALE: Do you take this into account?

SENATOR GORE: No, I—let me respond. Thank you, Admiral, for saying that. You're talking about Roger Revelle. His family wrote a lengthy letter saying how terribly he had been misquoted and had his remarks taken completely out of context just before he died ... and just before he died, he co-authored an article which was—had statements taken completely out of context. In fact the vast majority of the world's scientists— and they have worked on this extensively—believe that we must have an effort to face up to the problems we face with the environment. And if we just stick our heads in the sand and pretend that it's not real, we're not doing ourselves a favor. Even worse than that, we're telling our children and all future generations that we weren't willing to face up to this obligation.

VICE PRESIDENT QUAYLE: Hal, can I—

SENATOR GORE: I believe that we have a mandate—

STOCKDALE: Sure. We've still got time.

SENATOR GORE: —to try to solve this problem, particularly when we can do it while we create jobs in the process.

BRUNO: Go ahead, Mr. Vice President, there's still time. Not much, though.

VICE PRESIDENT QUAYLE: I know it. We've got to have a little equal time here now, Hal. In the book you also suggest taxes on, gasoline taxes on utilities, taxes on carbon, taxes on timber. There's a whole host of taxes. And I don't just—I don't believe raising taxes is the way to solve our environmental problems.

And you talk about the bad situation in the auto industry. You seem to say that the answer is, well, I'll just make it that much worse by increasing the CAFE standards. Yes, the auto industry is hurting, it's been hurting for a long time, and increasing the CAFE standards to 45 miles per gallon, like you and Bill Clinton are suggesting, will put, as I said, 300,000 people out of work. . . .

[The Abortion Issue]

BRUNO: Abortion rights has been a bitter controversy in this country for almost 20 years. It's been heightened by the recent Supreme Court decisions. So I'll make it very simple in this question: Where do each of you stand on the issue? What actions will your president's administration take on the abortion question? Will it be a factor in the appointment of federal judges, especially to the Supreme Court? And I believe that Senator Gore goes first.

SENATOR GORE: Bill and I support the right of a woman to choose.

That doesn't mean we're pro-abortion; in fact, we believe there are way too many abortions in this country. And the way to reduce them is by reducing the number of unwanted pregnancies, not vetoing family planning legislation the way George Bush has consistently done.

The reason we are pro-choice and in favor of a woman's right to privacy is because we believe that during the early stages of pregnancy the government has no business coming in and ordering a woman to do what the government thinks is best. What Dan Quayle and George Bush and Jerry Falwell and Pat Robertson think is the right decision in a given set of circumstances is their privilege—but don't have the government order a woman to do what they think is the right thing to do.

We ought to be able to build more common ground among those who describe themselves as pro-choice and pro-life in efforts to reduce the number of unwanted pregnancies.

But, Dan, you can clear this up very simply by repeating after me: I support the right of a woman to choose. Can you say that?

BRUNO: Vice President Quayle, your turn.

VICE PRESIDENT QUAYLE: This issue is an issue that divides Americans deeply. I happen to be pro-life. I have been pro-life for my 16 years in public life. My objective and the president's objective is to try to reduce abortions in this country. We have 1.6 million abortions. We have more abortions in Washington, D.C., than we do live births. Why shouldn't we have more reflection upon the issue before abor—the decision of abortion is made. I would hope that we would agree upon that. I would hope that we would agree upon that. Something like a 24-hour waiting period, parental notification.

I was in Los Angeles recently and I talked to a woman who told me that she had an abortion when she was 17 years of age. And looking back on that she said it was a mistake. She said—she said I wished at that time, that I was going through this difficult time, that I had counseling to talk about the post-abortion trauma, and talk about adoption rather than abortion. Because if I had had that discussion, I would have had the child. Let's not forget that every abortion stops a beating heart. I think we have far too many abortions in this country, in this country of ours.

BRUNO: Admiral Stockdale.

STOCKDALE: I believe that a woman owns her body and what she does with it is her own business, period. Period.

BRUNO: That's it?

STOCKDALE: I don't—I, too, abhor abortions, but I don't think they should be made illegal, and I don't—and I don't think it's a political issue. I think it's a privacy issue.

BRUNO: You caught me by surprise. Let's go ahead with the discussion of this issue. Senator Gore.

SENATOR GORE: Well, you notice in his response, that Dan did not say I support the right of a woman to choose. That is because he and George Bush have turned over their party to Pat Buchanan and Phyllis Schlafly, who have ordered them to endorse a platform which makes all abortions illegal under any circumstances, regardless of what has led to that decision by a woman.

Even in cases of rape and incest, their platform requires that a woman be penalized, that she not be allowed to make a choice, if she believes, in consultation with her family, her doctor, and others, whoever she chooses, that she wants to have an abortion after rape, or incest. They make it completely—

VICE PRESIDENT QUAYLE: Senator, do you support a 24-hour waiting period?

SENATOR GORE: —illegal under any of those circumstances. Now they want to waffle around—

VICE PRESIDENT QUAYLE: Do you support a 24-hour waiting period?

SENATOR GORE: Let me finish this, briefly. Now—now you want to waffle around on it and give the impression that maybe you don't really mean what you say. But again, you can clear it up by simply repeating I support the right of a woman to choose. Say it.

BRUNO: Let him say it himself. Let him say his own words. Go ahead, Mr. Vice President.

VICE PRESIDENT QUAYLE: Thank you. Talk about waffling around. This issue is a very important issue. It has been debated throughout your public life and throughout my public life, and one thing that I don't think that it is wise to do, and that is to change your position.

At one time, and most of the time in the House of Representatives, you had a pro-life position.

SENATOR GORE: That's simply not true.

VICE PRESIDENT QUAYLE: In 1987, you wrote a letter, and we'll pass this out to the media—

SENATOR GORE: That is simply not true.

VICE PRESIDENT QUAYLE: You wrote a letter saying that you oppose taxpayer funding of abortion. Bill Clinton has the same type of a record.

SENATOR GORE: In some circumstances.

VICE PRESIDENT QUAYLE: You're going to qualify it now.

SENATOR GORE: And I still do.

VICE PRESIDENT QUAYLE: And Bill Clinton, when he was governor of Arkansas, also worked with the Right to Life people and supported Right to Life positions and now he has changed. Talk about waffling around. This is the typical type of Clinton response. Even on the issue like abortion. He's on both sides of the issue.

Take the NAFTA agreement—

SENATOR GORE: Well, wait—

BRUNO: Let's stick with the question, Mr. Vice President.

VICE PRESIDENT QUAYLE: How long did he have—

SENATOR GORE: I know you want to change the subject, Dan, but let's stay on this one for a while.

VICE PRESIDENT QUAYLE: How long did he have to wait—or how quickly did he change his position on education? He changes his position all the time.

SENATOR GORE: Let's stay with this issue for a while.

VICE PRESIDENT QUAYLE: Bill Clinton—Bill Clinton has trouble telling the truth. Three words he fears most in the English language.

BRUNO: Does anybody have any view about the appointment of judges on this?

VICE PRESIDENT QUAYLE: Tell the truth.

SENATOR GORE: Yea, I want to talk about this, because the question was not about free trade or education. The question—

VICE PRESIDENT QUAYLE: Talk about waffling. You're the one who brought up the—

SENATOR GORE: Now, I let you talk.

VICE PRESIDENT QUAYLE: —issue of waffling. He's waffled on the abortion issue.

SENATOR GORE: I let you talk. Let me talk now. It's going to be a long evening if you're like this, now.

VICE PRESIDENT QUAYLE: Oh, no it's not—

SENATOR GORE: Don't change the subject—

BRUNO: Let's get on with it. Gentlemen, let's get on with it.

SENATOR GORE: Don't change the subject—

VICE PRESIDENT QUAYLE: Well, answer my questions, then.

SENATOR GORE: What you have done—

VICE PRESIDENT QUAYLE: Answer my questions. On the 24 our waiting period—do you support that?

SENATOR GORE: I have had the same position—

VICE PRESIDENT QUAYLE: Do you support that?

SENATOR GORE: I have had the same position on abortion in favor of a woman's right to choose. Do you support a woman's right to choose—

VICE PRESIDENT QUAYLE: Do you support a 24 hour waiting period to have—

SENATOR GORE: You're still avoiding—

VICE PRESIDENT QUAYLE: How about avoiding the question?

SENATOR GORE: —the question. Now, wait a minute. Let me tell you why this is so important. There are millions of women in this country who passionately believe in the right of a woman to privacy. And they want to stack the Supreme Court with justices who will take away the right to privacy. Make no mistake about it. That is their agenda—

And if you support them, don't be surprised if that is exactly what they want to do and that is why Dan Quayle refuses to say this evening that he supports the right of a woman to choose.

I agree with Admiral Stockdale and the vast majority of Democrats and Republicans in this country. You know, one of the reasons so many Republicans are supporting the Clinton-Gore ticket is because they've turned over the party to this right wing extremist group which takes positions on issues like abortion that don't even allow exceptions for rape and incest.

BRUNO: Senator—

SENATOR GORE: Again, can't you just say you support the right of a woman to choose?

BRUNO: Could we give Admiral Stockdale a chance to jump in here if he wants to, if he dares to.

STOCKDALE: I would like to get in—I feel like I'm an observer at a pingpong game, where they're talking about well, you know, they're expert professional politicians that massage these intricate plots and know every nuance to 'em. And meantime, we're facing a desperate situation in our economy. I've seen the cost of living double in my lifetime. A new granddaughter was born in my family—my granddaughter—three weeks ago. And according to the statistics that we have—that is, the Perot group—the chances of her seeing a doubling of the standard of living are nil. In fact, her children will be dead before another—this standard of living is doubled. So what the heck! Let's get on with talking about something substantive.

BRUNO: All right. Mr. Vice President, you'll have a chance to— You'll have a chance in the closing statements.

VICE PRESIDENT QUAYLE: We need to get on—

BRUNO: No, let's move on to another topic.

VICE PRESIDENT QUAYLE: Just 15 second to respond.

SENATOR GORE: Well, can I have 15 seconds also?

BRUNO: No, let's move on, gentlemen.

VICE PRESIDENT QUAYLE: I'll tell you what. If—

BRUNO: Let's not—we're not horse trading. We're having a debate. Let's go on. Let's talk about the cities. Because that's where a majority of Americans live, in urban areas, and they're facing a financial and social crisis. They've lost sources of tax revenue. The aid that once came from the federal and state governments has been drastically cut. There's an epidemic of drugs, crime and violence. Their streets, the schools are like war zones. It's becoming increasingly difficult to pay for public education, for transportation, for police and fire protection, the basic services that local government must provide.

Now, everybody says, talks about enterprise zones, that may be part of the solution, but what else are your administrations really going to be willing to do to help the cities?

Vice President Quayle, it's your turn to go first.

[The American Family]

VICE PRESIDENT QUAYLE: Well, Hal, enterprise zones are important and it's an idea that the president has been pushing, and there's been very strong reluctance on, with the Democratic Congress. We'll continue to push it.

We also want, Hal to have home ownership. I was at a housing sub—a housing project in San Francisco several months ago and met with people that were trying to reclaim their neighborhood.

They wanted home ownership. They didn't want handouts. And I was with the Democrat mayor of San Franciso who was there supporting our idea. But when you look at the cities and you see the problems that we have with crime, drugs, lack of jobs, I also want to point out one of the fundamental problems that we have in American cities and throughout America today, and that is the breakdown of the American family.

I know some people laugh about it when I talk about the breakdown of the family, but it's true. Sixty percent of the kids that are born in our major cities today are born out of wedlock. We have too many divorces. We have too many fathers that aren't assuming their responsibility. The breakdown of the family is a contributing factor to the problems that we have in urban America.

BRUNO: Admiral Stockdale.

STOCKDALE: I think enterprise zones are good, but I think the problem is deeper than that. I think we are—you know, when I was—I ran a civilization for several years, a civilization of three to four hundred wonderful men. We had our own laws. We had our own, practically our own constitution. And I put up—I was the—I was the sovereign for a good bit of that. And I tried to analyze human predicaments in that microcosm of life in the—in the world. And I found out that when I really got down to putting out do's and don'ts, and lots of these included take torture for this and that, and this and that, and never take any amnesty, for reasons they all understood and went along with. But one of the—we had an acronym, BACKUS, and each one of those B-a-c-k was something for which you—you had to make them hurt you before you did it. Bowing in public, making, making—getting on the raid and so forth. But at the end it was US, BACKUS. You got the double meaning there.

But the US could be called the United States, but it was Unity Over Self, Loners Make Out. Somehow we're going to have to get some love in this country between races, and between rich and poor. You have got to have leaders—and they're out there—who can do this with their bare hands, with—working with, with people on the scene.

BRUNO: Senator Gore, please.

SENATOR GORE: George Bush's urban policy has been a tale of two cities: the best of times for the very wealthy; the worst of times for everyone else. We have seen a decline in urban America under the Bush-Quayle administration. Bill Clinton and I want to change that, by creating good jobs, investing in infrastructure, new programs in job training and apprenticeship, welfare reform—to say to a mother with young children that if she gets a good job, her children are not going to lose their Medicaid benefits; incentives for investment in the inner city area, and, yes, enterprise zones. Vice President Quayle said they're important, but George Bush eliminated them from his urban plan, and then—

VICE PRESIDENT QUAYLE: Well, that's not true.

SENATOR GORE: And then, when they were included in a plan that the Congress passed,—

VICE PRESIDENT QUAYLE: We have been for enterprise zones—

SENATOR GORE: —George Bush vetoed the enterprise zone law, the law that included them, for one reason: because that same bill raised taxes on those making more than $200,000 a year.

Let's face up to it, Dan: your top priority really, isn't it, to make sure that the very wealthy don't have to pay any more taxes. We want to cut taxes on middle-income families and raise them on those making more than $200,000 a year.

VICE PRESIDENT QUAYLE: What plan is that?

SENATOR GORE: And if we can take our approach, the cities will be much better off.

BRUNO: Let's start the discussion period right here. Go ahead.

VICE PRESIDENT QUAYLE: What plan is that that's just going to raise taxes on those making over $200,000 a year? You may call that your plan, but everyone knows that you simply can't get $150 billion in new taxes by raising the marginal tax rate to a top rate of 36 percent and only tax those making $200,000 a year. It's absolutely ridiculous. The top two percent which you refer to, that gets you down to $64,000; then you have about a $40-billion shortfall—that gets you down to $36,000 a year. Everybody making more than $36,000 a year will have their taxes increased if Bill Clinton is president of the United States.

And I don't know how you're going to go to urban America and say that raising taxes is good for you. I don't know how you're going to go to urban America and say, well, the best thing that we can offer is simply to raise taxes again. This is nothing more than a tax-and-spend platform. We've seen it before. It doesn't work.

Let me tell you about a story.

SENATOR GORE: Can I respond to some of that?

VICE PRESIDENT QUAYLE: I've got a very good example—

SENATOR GORE: Can I respond to some of that?

VICE PRESIDENT QUAYLE: —When we talk about families here, because I was meeting with some former gang members in Phoenix and Los Angeles and Albuquerque, New Mexico. And when I talked to those former gang members, here's what they told why they joined the gang. They said, well, joining a gang is like joining a family. I said, joining a family? Yet, because the gang offered support, it offered leadership, it offered comfort, it was a way to get ahead.

Where have we come if joining a gang is like being a member of the family?

BRUNO: Senator Gore, you wanted to respond?

VICE PRESIDENT QUAYLE: And that's why I think that families have to be strengthened, and you don't strengthen the American family by raising taxes.

SENATOR GORE: I do want to respond to that.

BRUNO: Go ahead, Senator, Admiral.

SENATOR GORE: George Bush and Dan Quayle want to protect the very wealthy. That is the group that has gotten all of the tax cuts under the Bush-Quayle administration. Nobody here who is middle income has gotten a tax cut because middle-income families have had tax increases under Bush and Quayle in order to finance the cuts for the very wealthy. That's what trickle-down economics is all about. And they want to continue it.

We're proposing to also require foreign corporations to pay the same taxes that American corporations do when they do business here in the United States of America. George Bush has not been willing to enforce the laws and collect those taxes. We want to close that loophole and raise more money in that way.

BRUNO: Senator, can we stick to the cities, sir?

SENATOR GORE: Excuse me?

BRUNO: Stick to the cities.

SENATOR GORE: All right. Well, he, he talked about ways to raise money to help the cities. What we're proposing is to invest in the infrastructure in cities and have targeted tax incentives for investment right in inner city areas. The enterprise zones represent a part of our proposal also, and strengthening the family through welfare reform. And you know the Bush administration has cut out—has vetoed family leave, they have cut childhood immunization and college aid.

If you don't support parents and you don't support children, how—how can you say you support families?

VICE PRESIDENT QUAYLE: How about supporting parents and the right to choose where their kids go to school, Al?

Do you support that

SENATOR GORE: We—

VICE PRESIDENT QUAYLE: Let the parents—let the parents—

SENATOR GORE: Do you want me to answer?

VICE PRESIDENT QUAYLE: —public or private schools?

SENATOR GORE: Want me to answer?

BRUNO: Go ahead.

SENATOR GORE: We support the public school choice to go to any public school of your choice. What we don't support—and listen to what they're proposing—to take U.S. taxpayer dollars and subsidize private schools. Now I'm all for private schools, but to use taxpayer dollars, when the people who get these little vouchers often won't be able to afford the private school anyway, and the private school is not—

VICE PRESIDENT QUAYLE: Al, I think, I think it's important—

SENATOR GORE: —under any obligation to admit them, that is a ripoff of the U.S. taxpayer.

VICE PRESIDENT QUAYLE: That's important. This is a very—this is a very important issue. Choice in education is a very important issue.

BRUNO: Let him respond.

VICE PRESIDENT QUAYLE: And he said that he was not for choosing—giving the parents the right to choose to send their children to public schools. But it's okay for the wealthy to choose to send the kids to private schools, but it's not okay for the middle class and the working poor to choose where they want to send their kids to school

I think that it's time that all parents in America have a right to choose where they send their kids to school to get an education.

BRUNO: Admiral Stockdale, would you like to have the last word in this period?

STOCKDALE: I—I come down on the side of freedom of school choice. The—and there's a lot of misunderstandings that I've heard here tonight, that I may have the answer to. The—starting at, you know, for the last, almost a decade, we've worried about our schools officially through Washington, and the president had a meeting of all the governors, and then they tried the conventional fixes for schools, that is, to increase the certification of—requirements for the teachers, to lengthen the school day, to lengthen the school year and nothing—this is a very brief overview of the thing—but nothing happened. And it's time to change the school's structure. In schools, bureaucracy is bad and autonomy is good. The only good schools—we have are those run by talented principals and devoted teachers, and they're running their own show. How many times have I thrived? You know, the best thing I had when I ran that civilization, it succeeded, and it's a landmark. The best think I had going for me was I had no contact with Washington for all those years.

SENATOR GORE: Could I respond?

BRUNO: We have to go on. What I'm about to say doesn't apply to the debate tonight; it applies to the campaign that's been going on outside this auditorium. With three weeks to go, this campaign has at times been very ugly, with the tone being set by personal negative attacks.

As candidates, how does it look from your viewpoint? And are these tactics really necessary? Admiral Stockdale—it's your turn to go first.

STOCKDALE: You know, I didn't have my hearing aid turned on. Tell me again.

BRUNO: I'm sorry, sir. I was saying that at times this campaign has been very ugly with personal negative attacks. As a candidate, how does it look from where you are and are these tactics really necessary?

STOCKDALE: Nasty attacks—well, I think there is a case to be made for putting emphasis on character over these issues that we've been batting back and forth and have a life of their own. Sure, you have to know where you're going with your government, but character is the big variable in the success. Character of the leads is the big variable in the success—long term success—of an administration.

I went to a friend of mine in New York some years ago and he was a president of a major TV network and he said, you know, I think we have messed up this whole—this election process—it was an election year—by stressing that—putting out the dogma that issues are the thing to talk about, not character.

He said, I felt so strongly about this, I went back and read the Lincoln-Douglas debates. Read those debates. How do they come down? Douglas is all character. He knows all of the little stinky numbers these guys do. Abraham Lincoln had character. Thank God we got the right president in the Civil War.

But that is a question that is a valid one, and you know, I would like to brag about the character of my boss.

BRUNO: Okay, Senator Gore.

SENATOR GORE: This election is about the future of our country, not about personal attacks against one candidate or another. Our nation is in trouble and it is appalling to me that with 10 million Americans out of work, with the rest working harder for less money than they did four years ago, with the loss of 1.4 million manufacturing jobs in our nation, with the health care crisis, a crisis of crime and drugs and AIDS, substandard education, that George Bush would constantly try to level personal attacks at his opponent.

Now, this, of course, just reached a new low last week when he resorted to a classic McCarthyite technique of trying to smear Bill Clinton over a trip that he took as a student along with lots of other Rhodes Scholars who were invited to go to Russia. It's a classic McCarthyite smear technique. I think the president of the United States ought to apologize. I think that he insulted the intelligence of the American people and I'm awful proud that the American people rejected that tactic so overwhelmingly that he decided he had made a mistake. Do you think it was a mistake, too, Dan?

BRUNO: Okay, Vice President Quayle.

VICE PRESIDENT QUAYLE: Let me answer the question.

BRUNO: Go ahead.

VICE PRESIDENT QUAYLE: Hal, you said—and I wrote it down here—"personal negative attacks." Has anyone been reading my press clippings for the last four years?

But I happen to—I agree with one thing on—with Senator Gore, and that is that we ought to look to the future, and the future is, who's going to be the next president of the United States. And is it a negative attack and a personal attack to point out that Bill Clinton has trouble telling the truth? He said that he didn't even demonstrate—he told the people in Arkansas in 1978. Then we find out he organized demonstrations. You know, I don't care whether he demonstrated or didn't demonstrate. The fact—the question is, tell the truth. Just tell us the truth. Today, Bill Clinton—excuse me—yesterday in Philadelphia on a radio show, must yesterday on a radio show, he attacked—Admiral, he attacks Ross Perot saying the media is giving Ross Perot a free ride. The press asked him when the klieg lights are on, said what do you mean by Ross Perot getting a free ride? He says I didn't say that at all.

I mean, you can't have it both ways. No, I don't think that is a personal attack. What I find troubling with Bill Clinton is he can't tell the truth. You cannot lead this great country of ours by misleading the people.

[Closing Statements]

BRUNO: All right, gentlemen, the control room advises me that in order to have time for your closing statements, which we certainly want, there simply is not going to be time for a discussion period on this particular topic.

So let's go to the closing statements. You have two minutes each. And we'll start with Admiral Stockdale.

STOCKDALE: I think the best justification for getting Ross Perot in the race again to say is that we're seeing this kind of chit-chat back and forth about issues that don't concentrate on where our grandchildren—the living standards of our children and grandchildren. He is, as I have read in more than one article, a revolutionary; he's got plans out there that are going to double the speed at which this budget problem is being cared for. It was asked how, if we would squeeze down so fast that we would strangle the economy in the process. That is an art, to follow all those variables and know when to let up and to nurse this economy back together with pulls and pushes.

And there's no better man in the world to do that then that old artist, Ross Perot. And so I think that my closing statement is that I think I'm in a room with people that aren't the life of reality. The United States is in deep trouble. We've got to have somebody that can get up there and bring out the firehouses and get it stopped, and that's what we're about in the Perot campaign.

BRUNO: Thank you.

Senator Gore, your closing statement, sir.

SENATOR GORE: Three weeks from today, our nation will make a fateful decision. We can continue traveling the road we have been on, which has led to higher unemployment and worse economic times, or we can reach out for change. If we choose change, it will require us to reach down inside ourselves to find the courage to take a new direction.

Sometimes it seems deceptively easy to continue with old habits even when they're no longer good for us. Trickle-down economics simply does not work. We have had an increase in all of the things that should be decreasing. Everything that should have been increasing has been going down. We have got to change direction.

Bill Clinton offers a new approach. He has been named by the other 49 governors, Republicans and Democrats alike, as the best and most effective governor in the entire United States of America.

He's moved 17,000 people off the welfare rolls and on to payrolls. He has introduced innovations in health care and education, and again, he has led the nation for the last two years in a row in the creation of jobs in the private sector.

Isn't it time for a new approach, a new generation of ideas and leadership, to put our nation's people first and to get our economy moving again?

We simply cannot stand to continue with this failed approach that is no good for us. Ultimately, it is a choice between hope and fear, a choice between the future and the past. It is time to reach out for a better nation. We are bigger than George Bush has told us we are, as a nation, and we have a much brighter future.

Give us a chance. With your help, we'll change this country and we can't wait to get started.

BRUNO: Vice President Quayle.

VICE PRESIDENT QUAYLE: Thank you, Hal. I'd like to use this closing statement to talk to you about a few people that I have met in these last four years. I think of a woman in Chicago when I was talking to parents about education where she stood up and said I'm sick and tired of these schools in this city being nothing but a factory for failure. And that's why we support choice in education.

I was in Beaumont, Texas, and met with small business people, and they wanted to reform the civil justice system because they think our legal system costs too much and there's too much of a delay in getting an answer.

I was in Middletown, Ohio, talking to a welfare women, where she said I want to go back to work and I had a job offered to me but I'm not going to take it because I have two children at home and the job that is offered to me doesn't have health insurance. Under President Bush's health care reform package that woman won't have to make a choice about going back to work or health care for her children, because she'll have both.

I was in Vilnius, Lithuania, Independence Square, speaking to 10,000 people in the middle of winter. Hundred of people came up to me and said: God bless America.

NAVY ON PREVENTION
OF SEXUAL HARASSMENT
October 13, 1992

The Navy announced October 13 that it was creating a toll-free hotline to provide information and advice to victims of sexual harassment. The hotline also offered information to alleged harassers and to co-workers of victims or harassers.

Creating the hotline was one of eighty recommendations made by the Standing Committee on Military and Civilian Women in the Department of the Navy. The committee was formed in July 1992 to provide advice to the navy secretary on ways to integrate women into the service.

The Navy created the hotline less than one month after the Pentagon's inspector general released a report blasting the Navy's investigation of the Tailhook scandal. (Pentagon Report on Tailhook Convention, p. 879) *At the 1991 Tailhook Association convention, drunken Navy and Marine Corps officers sexually assaulted at least twenty-six women as they passed through a "gantlet" in a hotel hallway.*

Tailhook was only the latest incident of sexual harassment or assault to plague the Navy in recent years. In earlier incidents male midshipmen at the United States Naval Academy chained a female classmate to a urinal; five naval fliers were accused of raping a woman at a bachelor party in Virginia; female students at a training center in Orlando, Florida, alleged that they had been harassed and raped; and Navy clubs in the Philippines allegedly welcomed prostitutes.

In July 1992 a Navy investigation found widespread discrimination against female sailors who worked on combat support ships in Hawaii. The captain of a salvage ship was relieved of his command because of "allegations of fraternization and sexual harassment" aboard his ship, according to a Navy statement.

Critics of the Navy said Tailhook and the other incidents were only symptoms of deep-set negative attitudes toward women. Acting Navy Secretary Sean C. O'Keefe agreed with this view at a September 24 press conference about Tailhook. "We know that the larger issue is a cultural problem which has allowed demeaning behavior and attitudes towards women in uniform to exist in the Navy," he said. Not everyone in the military agreed with O'Keefe, however. Defense Secretary Richard B. Cheney said it "would be a mistake" to look at Tailhook "as somehow indicating there's some kind of fundamental problem with the United States Navy."

In 1989 the Navy adopted a policy of "zero tolerance" toward sexual harassment, but because the penalties were light, the policy had little effect. In March 1992 the Navy toughened the penalties to make it possible to dismiss violators from the service.

Creating the hotline was only one action the Navy took in October to carry out the standing committee's recommendations. The Navy also established a "tiger team" to develop a department-wide system for tracking sexual harassment complaints. Some Navy commands previously tracked such complaints themselves, but there had not been a department-wide system. The purpose of the tracking system was to "provide a comprehensive, accurate yardstick to gauge the effectiveness of the Department's program to eliminate sexual harassment," according to the Navy.

The Navy established a second tiger team to develop a description of sexual harassment that everyone in the Navy and Marine Corps could understand. This second team was also charged with developing additional Navy policies on sexual harassment.

Other major actions by the Navy included:

- *Reevaluating career options available to women and determining if additional roles or assignments were possible.*
- *Acting to prevent service cutbacks from disproportionately affecting women.*
- *Creating a "User Skills" handbook to help personnel resolve sexual harassment problems themselves.*
- *Developing gender-neutral standards for nontraditional Navy jobs.*
- *Reviewing the sale of sexually explicit magazines at Navy exchanges.*
- *Reviewing policies about pregnancy and single-parent families.*

The Standing Committee sidestepped one of the biggest issues: whether women should serve in combat units. It said only that the Navy's policy on assigning women should be reviewed after the release of a report by the presidential Commission on the Assignment of Women in the Armed Forces. The commission was scheduled to complete its report in mid-November (Report on Women in Combat, p. 1029).

Following is the text of a press release titled "Navy Releases Information on Recommendations of the Standing Committee on Military and Civilian Women in the Department of the Navy," issued October 13, 1992, by the Department of Defense Public Affairs office:

Acting Secretary of the Navy Sean O'Keefe has announced several steps being taken by the Naval service to enhance professional opportunities for women and to eradicate sexual harassment. These steps are the result of recommendations developed by the Standing Committee on Military and Civilian Women in the Department of the Navy presented on September 30.

The Navy Department has established a "tiger team" to implement a department-wide reporting system to track formal sexual harassment complaints [and] incidents of sexual assault and rape. This tracking system will provide a comprehensive, accurate yardstick to gauge the effectiveness of the Department's program to eliminate sexual harassment.

A second tiger team has been established to translate the Department's definition of sexual harassment to terms more easily understood by personnel at all levels of the Navy and Marine Corps. This team is also responsible for developing additional Department of the Navy policy on preventing sexual harassment.

The Secretary has also directed the establishment of a toll-free advice and counseling line to provide information and advice to any member who might be involved in an incident of sexual harassment regarding their rights, and responsibilities, and options to resolve the situation.

Secretary O'Keefe has asked the Chief of Naval Operations and Commandant of the Marine Corps to develop plans to implement a number of other recommendations proposed by the Standing Committee. These plans will address actions necessary to implement roughly 80 recommendations made by the Committee. These include:

- Reevaluating, based on current law, the career options available to women to expand roles and assignments.
- Developing a "User Skills" handbook to provide individuals with information and techniques to empower them to resolve sexual harassment complaints informally, if appropriate.
- Providing service members and civilian employees with information about how alcohol can be a contributing factor in promoting inappropriate behavior, and reinforcing the choices of abstention and moderate, responsible use of alcohol.
- Evaluating the impact of current screening procedures for assigning women into non-traditional positions and developing appropriate gender-neutral job standards.

RESURGENCE OF TUBERCULOSIS
October 16, 1992

Tuberculosis, a scourge most Americans thought was a relic of the past, returned with a vengeance to the United States in the late 1980s and early 1990s. Most alarmingly, strains of tuberculosis developed that were resistant to most of the arsenal of drugs used to combat it. Science *magazine said the resurgence of the disease was "like the sequel to an almost forgotten horror movie."*

Tuberculosis was just one of a number of infectious diseases currently making a comeback. But it had the potential of being the deadliest. TB and other diseases once again posing severe public health threats, including Lyme disease and streptococcal bacteria, were discussed in a report released October 16, 1992, by the Institute of Medicine of the National Academy of Sciences. The 294-page report was called Emerging Infections: Microbial Threats to Health in the United States.

"We declared victory too soon," said Dr. Robert E. Shope of the reemergent diseases. Shope was a professor of epidemiology at Yale University School of Medicine and co-chair of the panel that prepared the report.

Nature of Tuberculosis

A disease that has afflicted mankind since ancient times, tuberculosis destroys lung tissue. Tuberculosis is usually caused by repeated exposure to tubercle bacilli, which are expelled into the air when a person with active pulmonary tuberculosis coughs, sneezes, talks, or laughs.

Most people who become infected do not develop the disease. The tubercle bacilli can lie dormant in the cells lining the lungs' air sacs, where the body may wall them up. Thus, a lifelong balance may be maintained. But if the body's resistance is lowered, the balance may be upset, and bacteria can enter the bloodstream, causing active tuberculosis.

The disease usually responds to proper medical care and drug treatment. But the number of patients with strands that resist treatment with the usual drugs has doubled since the early 1980s. Resistance to drug therapy develops when patients do not complete the full course of prescribed medication, thus allowing the most resilient strains of the bacteria to thrive.

Tuberculosis caused more deaths in the United States in the nineteenth century than any other disease. The number of Americans contracting tuberculosis declined after 1900. Still, 5 million tuberculosis deaths were recorded in this country during the first half of the twentieth century. Even in 1954, more than 110,000 hospital beds were available to tuberculosis patients. And in that year there were 84,300 cases. For those who could afford them, huge tuberculosis sanitariums, such as those in Saranac Lake, New York, provided rest, fresh air, and nutritious meals.

Better understanding of the disease and improved hygiene did much to cut the disease in the early twentieth century. The discovery of the antibiotic streptomycin in 1944 and the drug isoniazid in 1951 improved the likelihood that those with TB would be cured and thus reduced the incidence of the contagious disease even further. But the current resurgence of the disease has seen the number of cases grow from 22,201 cases in 1985 to 26,283 cases in 1991 (10.4 cases for every 100,000 people). What has become known as multidrug-resistant tuberculosis (MDRTB) is difficult to treat, requiring costly procedures and long hospitalization.

Inner City Problem

The Institute of Medicine report cited as factors contributing to the rise in cases: poverty, growing numbers of homeless individuals and families, substance abuse, the HIV-AIDS epidemic, and deterioration of the health care infrastructure for treating chronic infectious diseases. Writing in the October 11, 1992, New York Times, *Michael Specter said tuberculosis was occurring far more often in the country's largest cities than in the suburbs or in rural areas and fourteen times more frequently among blacks than among whites. Specter said the reported-case rates in central Harlem, in New York City, were 220 per 100,000 residents, thirty-five times the figure for residents of New York's affluent Upper East Side, not so many city blocks away. Specter added that as many as 40 percent of AIDS victims in New York City had active tuberculosis; their ravaged immune systems leave them far more likely to become infected, and they get sicker much more quickly. Among the homeless in the cities, public health officials said, 7 percent suffered from active tuberculosis and 50 percent had latent tuberculosis infection.*

Public Health Failure

Resurgence of the disease caught doctors and researchers off guard. "Everybody said the battle was won, so nobody really looked for a better cure for tuberculosis," Michael Iseman, chief of mycobacteriology disease at the National Jewish Hospital in Denver, told Science *magazine. "Pharmaceutical firms didn't follow up after the first good drugs were marketed. Academic scientists largely bailed out because it wasn't a good avenue for them to launch their careers. It just wasn't a disease with sex appeal, and now we're in a catch-up game."*

Barry Bloom, an investigator at the Albert Einstein College of Medicine, told the magazine that he viewed "this epidemic as a major indictment of the country's health care infrastructure. Why is it that the United States deals with health problems only when there is a crisis?"

Diminished funding at all levels of government played a crucial role. In the 1980s, the federal government replaced targeted tuberculosis grants with block grants to be used at local discretion. As a consequence, successful treatment programs were dismantled. Tuberculosis was not a priority under either the Reagan or Bush administrations. Although the federal Centers for Disease Control in 1989 proposed a tuberculosis "elimination plan" that would have cost $30-$34 million a year, the Department of Health and Human Services never asked for the money. In two subsequent budgets, the department sought a total of only $19 million. For fiscal 1993, the Bush administration requested $66 million, but public health experts were calling for $90-$125 million annually.

Following are excerpts from the report "Emerging Infections, Microbial Threats to Health in the United States," published by the Institute of Medicine on October 16, 1992:

Tuberculosis

Tuberculosis (TB) was the leading cause of death from infectious disease in the United States and Western Europe until the first decade of this century, and it remained the second leading cause from that time until the advent of antimicrobial drugs in the 1950s. At present, TB kills more people worldwide than any other infectious disease. Each year, according to the WHO [World Health Organization], 8 million new cases of clinical TB are diagnosed, and 2.9 million people die of the disease. In the United States, until 1985, TB incidence had been in decline for more than three decades. Between 1986 and 1991, however, 28,000 more cases were reported than were predicted to occur based on past experience.

TB is a bacterial disease whose principal manifestation is destruction of lung tissue; it is spread primarily though the respiratory route by patients with active pulmonary disease. One out of every 10 to 12 healthy individuals infected with the tubercle bacillus develops clinical disease.

The case fatality rate of untreated TB in people with clinical disease is 50 percent, and their average life span is six months to two years.

Multiple factors are contributing to the rise in cases of TB. Of major importance are increased poverty and a growing number of homeless individuals and families, substance abuse, a deteriorating health care infrastructure for treating chronic infectious diseases, and the HIV disease pandemic (perhaps the most significant factor at present). Complacency within the medical community and among the public at large and shortages of the drugs used to treat TB are additional factors in the increase.

TB is difficult to treat. Multidrug therapy is invariably necessary, with the drugs administered over at least six months to effect a clinical cure and prevent the emergence of drug-resistant organisms. Where health care infrastructure is adequate and compliance with treatment is maintained, cure rates should exceed 90 percent, even in HIV-infected individuals who have TB, providing resistant organisms are not present. When treatment is either inappropriate or inadequate, resistance to one or more of the treatment drugs often develops. The increased finding of resistant organisms reflects a major breakdown in the social and health care infrastructures.

When multidrug-resistant TB is present, case fatality rates can exceed 80 percent in immunocompromised individuals. The presence of multidrug-resistant organisms puts not only TB-infected individuals but also health care workers, social workers, corrections officials, families, and contacts at risk of contracting a disease that is difficult or essentially impossible to treat. Multidrug-resistant TB now represents a major threat to health in the United States.

In the 1950s, with the advent of antituberculosis drugs, TB became one of several newly treatable infectious diseases. The common assumption regarding such diseases has been that drugs that have been effective in treating them will continue to be so. Current experience with TB is causing many to question that assumption. Other organisms that have developed resistance to frontline drugs (probably for some of the same reasons) are also signaling the possibility of trouble ahead. Penicillin-resistant streptococcal Group A and Group C infections and penicillin-resistant pneumococcal infections have been documented, as have vancomycin-resistant staphylococcal and enterococcal infections. Without more careful prescription of antimicrobials by physicians and more consistent compliance with treatment regimens by patients, pathogenic bacteria are likely to undergo mutations that will enable them to resist available antibiotic therapy....

Tuberculosis (TB) is another example of an infection that can be reactivated during immunosuppression. The causative agent of TB, *Mycobacterium tuberculosis,* usually persists in the body long after primary infection. Although infection with this bacterium in a previously unexposed person is usually self-limiting, reactivated TB, which can occur years later, can cause life-threatening lung disease. In recent years, TB has stricken HIV-infected individuals with alarming severity, causing a rapidly disseminated disease involving organs throughout the body.

After declining steadily since the 1950s, the incidence of TB in the United States has recently begun to climb. Since 1986, reported cases have increased 16 percent. This trend is largely attributable to cases of TB among those infected with HIV. TB is also occurring with greater frequency among immigrants and refugees, substance abusers, the homeless, the medically underserved, and the elderly. The majority of the increase has been among racial and ethnic minorities (especially blacks and Hispanics), children and young adults, and immigrants and refugees.

The TB incidence rate among people infected with HIV is nearly 500 times the rate for the general population. In contrast to some fungal and other bacterial infections that occur only in the late stages of HIV disease, TB is a sentinel disease for HIV infection and tends to occur prior to other opportunistic infections, often before individuals realize they are HIV seropositive. In healthy individuals, pulmonary tuberculosis can be diagnosed and treated with relative ease (the cure rate is approximately 95 percent). In immunocompromised persons, however, the disease is often disseminated throughout the body, making it much more difficult to diagnose and treat.

Because of its persistence in the body, the tubercle bacillus is a notoriously difficult pathogen to control. Although bacille Calmette-Guerin (BCG) vaccine protects against severe tuberculous meningitis and disseminated TB in children, its efficacy against pulmonary TB in adults has varied widely in different parts of the world. Treatment of conventional TB is effective, but expensive, requiring daily treatment with multiple drugs for a minimum of six months. There is a universal tendency among TB patients to stop taking their drugs when the drugs begin to have their beneficial effect or to take the medications only intermittently. When this happens, relapses are frequent and very often are caused by drug-resistant tubercle bacilli that have survived the initial course of treatment. The emergence of drug-resistant *M. tuberculosis* is in many ways an index of individual compliance with antituberculosis chemotherapy and of the inability of the health care infrastructure to ensure adequate treatment. Many public health agencies that once could play key roles in this process have had their budgets cut drastically in recent years and hence are unable to perform this crucial service.

MDRTB is extraordinarily difficult to treat, and a majority of patients do not respond to therapy. Total treatment costs for an individual with MDRTB can be as much as $150,000, ten times the cost of traditional treatment; the cost of the treatment drugs alone can be as much as 21 times as great. In an outbreak of MDRTB in 1990 in Forth Worth, Texas, the cost of treating 10 patients was $950,433. The budget available that year to the Fort Worth/Tarrant County, Texas, Tuberculosis Control Program was less than one-fifth that amount.

The preferred treatment for classical TB consists of isoniazid, rifampin, and pyrazinamide. For patients whose tubercle bacilli are thought to be resistant to isoniazid, a fourth drug, ethambutol, should be added to the regimen until drug susceptibility results are know. Isolates of tubercle bacilli resistant to both isoniazid and rifampin, now representing about 20 percent in some cities, require specialized treatment with additional medications, which may include streptomycin and ciprofloxacin for almost two years. . . .

REPORT ON STUDENT DRUG USE

October 19, 1992

Despite the Bush administration's declaration of a "war on drugs," a study concluded that tobacco, alcohol, and other drug use among junior high and high school students was on the rise after a three-year decline. The report, prepared by the National Parents' Resource Institute for Drug Education (PRIDE), was based on a survey of 212,802 students in 1,588 schools in thirty-four states. Founded in 1977 as a nonprofit organization to provide drug prevention programs in schools, communities, and workplaces, PRIDE began its annual surveys in 1982.

The timing of the report's release—October 19, just two weeks before the presidential election in which George Bush lost his reelection bid to Democratic challenger Bill Clinton—generated some political flurry. PRIDE's president and cofounder, Thomas Gleaton, told a Washington Post *reporter that Terence J. Pell, chief of staff of the White House Office of National Drug Control Policy, had telephoned him to express concern that "the Clinton campaign has asked you for your data." After Gleaton responded that his organization was "considering" releasing the report, Pell said, "You know if you do that, it's going to hurt us." Gleaton said that, although Pell did not elaborate, it was "obvious" that the remark referred to Bush's reelection chances. He said he assured Pell that release of the report was "not something against the president."*

Report Findings: Rise in LSD Use

The 1992 study revealed that the use of drugs among students in junior high school (grades 6-8) rose in all ten categories surveyed: cigarettes, beer, wine coolers, liquor, marijuana, cocaine, "uppers," "downers," hallucinogens (principally LSD), and inhalants. LSD use among junior high students increased by 20 percent between 1990-91 and 1991-92, cocaine by 15 percent, and marijuana by 7 percent. In high school (grades 9-12), usage rose in seven of the ten categories, while it fell in three (wine coolers, marijuana, and cocaine).

Confirming widespread reports of rising student use of hallucinogens, the PRIDE survey found that far more high school students were using LSD and other hallucinogens than cocaine and crack. The survey found that 5.3 percent of all high school students reported using LSD, up from 4.9 percent the previous year. Fears that the drug of the psychedelic 1960s was making a comeback had previously prompted the Drug Enforcement Administration and other federal agencies to hold a summit on LSD in San Francisco in December 1991. Since then, increased LSD use by students had been corroborated by a number of reports throughout the nation, including widely publicized incidents involving suburban school students in California, Georgia, and Virginia. In addition, the PRIDE survey found that use of amphetamines ("uppers"), also popular in the 1960s, was on the increase.

The PRIDE survey also revealed an alarming increase in drug use by black students for all drug categories and all grade levels. Cocaine and marijuana use was up among black high school students, although the use of both drugs was down slightly among all students. However, previous studies by PRIDE and other researchers found that black students were less likely to use tobacco, alcohol, and other drugs than were their white counterparts.

More than one-third of all high school students (37.7 percent) said they had smoked cigarettes at least once in the past year, compared to 23.1 percent in the previous year. Liquor use also rose, to 50 percent from 48.7 percent among high school students and to 21.4 percent from 19.7 percent for junior high school students.

Despite the administration's emphasis on restricting the supply of drugs, more high school students told PRIDE that drugs in eight of the ten categories were "fairly easy" or "very easy" to obtain in 1991-92 than in the previous school year. Respondents said that cocaine and marijuana were more difficult to find. (President Bush had focused much of the administration's antidrug campaign on curtailing drug trafficking, meeting with leaders from six Latin American nations during February in an effort to forge greater cooperation in the effort to halt drug smuggling. (U.S.-Latin American Drug Summit at San Antonio, p. 201)

Controversy over Extent of Drug Use

"The 1991-92 data indicate a failure to adequately address the issue of drug use in America," commented Gleaton on the report's release. "As we focus on other issues like the economy and politics, shifting our focus from the drug epidemic, we should expect an increase in the use of alcohol and drugs by our youth." Despite the apparent rise in student

drug use, a report in the August 17, 1992, U.S. News & World Report found that only 2 percent of Americans in 1992 called drugs the nation's most important problem, compared with 64 percent in 1989.

Pell criticized the PRIDE survey as not being a "nationally representative" study. "The totality of all the surveys shows drug use among high school students going down dramatically," he said. Gleaton took issue with Pell's observation. "We at PRIDE are confident that these data reflect a conservative estimate of alcohol and drug use across the United States," he said.

Following are excerpts from a survey conducted by the National Parents' Resource Institute for Drug Education (PRIDE), released October 19, 1992, indicating that drug use was rising among junior high and high school students:

Summary of Findings

(1990-91 vs. 1991-92 Comparison Annual Reported Use)

High School Students (Grades 9-12)

1. An increase was noted in the following drug categories:

   - Cigarettes, up 7%
   - Beer, up 1%
   - Liquor, up 3%
   - Uppers, up 9%
   - Downers, up 7%
   - Inhalants, up 10%
   - Hallucinogens, up 8%

2. A decrease was noted in the following drug categories:

   - Wine coolers, down 3%
   - Marijuana, down 3%
   - Cocaine, down 3%

Junior High School Students (Grades 6-8)

   - Cigarettes, up 12%
   - Beer, up 3%
   - Wine coolers, up 2%
   - Liquor, up 9%
   - Marijuana, up 7%
   - Cocaine, up 15%
   - Uppers, up 15%
   - Downers, up 16%
   - Inhalants, up 20%
   - Hallucinogens, up 20%

Cigarette Use

a) 25.2 percent of 1991-92 NATIONAL SUMMARY students at the junior high level (6-8th) said they smoked cigarettes within the past year ('90 PRIDE Natl. Avg. 6-8th = 22.6%).

b) 37.7 percent of the 1991-92 NATIONAL SUMMARY students at the senior high level (9-12th) said they smoked cigarettes within the past year ('90 PRIDE Natl. Avg. 9-12th = 35.2).

Note: Senior high students (grades 9-12) who smoke cigarettes are eight times more likely to smoke marijuana than non-smoking senior high students (PRIDE 1990-91 National Summary).

Alcohol Use

a) Of the 31.6 percent of junior high students who drank beer within the past year ('90 Natl. Avg. 6-8th = 30.6%), 11.1 percent said they most often became "very high" or "bombed" when they drank.

b) Of the 56.4 percent of senior high students who drank beer within the past year ('90 Natl. Avg. 9-12th = 56.2), 23.9 percent said they most often became "very high" or "bombed."

Note: Beer and wine coolers are the favorite intoxicants of American students (PRIDE 1990-91 National Summary).

Marijuana Use

a) 16.4 percent of senior high students used marijuana within the past year ('90 Natl. Avg. 9-12th = 16.9%). Of those who used, 66.2 percent said they most often got "very high" or "bombed" when they used.

b) 12.6 percent of senior high students used marijuana on weekends and 2.3 percent used marijuana during school.

Note: The high school student who uses marijuana is about 100 times more likely to use cocaine than the non-marijuana user (grades 9-12). Marijuana is the most widely used illicit drug among American teenagers (PRIDE 1990-91 National Summary).

Cocaine Use

3.3 percent of senior high students reported using cocaine within the past year ('90 Nat. Avg. 9-12th = 3.4%). Of those who used, 74.0 percent said they most often got "very high" or "bombed" when they used.

November

POSTELECTION STATEMENTS
OF PEROT, BUSH, AND CLINTON
November 3 and 4, 1992

Savoring the excitement but mindful of the nation's grave problems, President-elect Bill Clinton hailed his victory November 3 as "a clarion call for the country to face the challenges of the end of the Cold War and beginning of the next century." Speaking in Little Rock shortly after midnight November 4, the Democratic Arkansas governor paid tribute to the Republican president he unseated, George Bush.

In Houston Bush conceded defeat after calling Clinton to congratulate him. He said that "the people have spoken, and we respect the majesty of the democratic system."

The third major candidate in the race, Texas billionaire Ross Perot, was the first to concede, at 10:30 p.m. in Dallas. Perot also congratulated Clinton, but he told cheering supporters to "forget the election, it's behind us. The hard work is ahead of us...."

During the campaign Clinton had portrayed himself as a different kind of Democrat, and the election produced a different kind of result. Clinton shredded the Republican-oriented electoral map that had been in place for most of the past quarter-century.

Clinton carried thirty-two states plus the District of Columbia, won 370 of the 538 electoral votes, and outscored President Bush by 5.6 percentage points in the popular vote (43.0 percent to 37.4 percent). It was the most sweeping triumph for any Democrat since President Lyndon B. Johnson in 1964 and the best showing for any Democratic challenger since Franklin D. Roosevelt ousted Republican Herbert Hoover from the White House in 1932.

Clinton benefited from a favorable backdrop, with voter attention

1019

focused on the struggling economy and the widespread perception that Bush was doing little about it.

The tide of discontent also lifted Perot, another apostle of change, who achieved the largest vote total (19,741,048) for an independent in presidential election history and the biggest vote share (18.9 percent) since 1912. A few weeks after the election Perot announced that he was keeping his grass-roots organization alive under the name United We Stand.

Feelings of economic anxiety helped Clinton to nail down the biggest electoral prize of all, California, where the economy was at a half-century low and where the Bush forces conceded early. California, with fifty-four electoral votes, led a list of nine states voting Democratic for president for the first time since 1964.

For the Record

The ticket of Clinton and Sen. Al Gore of Tennessee was the first successful all-southern slate since 1828 (Andrew Jackson and John C. Calhoun). Clinton also scored several other "firsts." He was the first:

- *Democrat to be elected president without carrying Texas since Texas joined the Union.*
- *candidate of either party since 1952 to be elected without having won the New Hampshire primary.*
- *president-elect from the baby boom generation born after World War II.*
- *president-elect since Franklin D. Roosevelt who had not served in military uniform.*

The election also set new benchmarks in Congress, with the addition of record numbers of women, blacks, and Hispanics. Democrats retained control of the House and Senate, but with a difference. The most obvious change was in the Senate—the most diverse in history. Carol Moseley-Braun of Illinois became the first black woman senator and for the first time both senators of a state were women, Democrats Barbara Boxer and Dianne Feinstein of California. A part American Indian, Ben Nighthorse Campbell, became Colorado's new junior senator.

Democrats increased their governorships to thirty, a net gain of two.

The Transition

In the weeks after the election, Clinton announced most of his cabinet choices and moved to cement a partnership with Congress in enacting the program he had sketched during the campaign. Foremost among the problems at hand was the $4 trillion national debt and the prospective $330 billion deficit for fiscal 1993. Clinton's campaign promise to halve the deficit in four years conflicted with his plans to cut taxes on the middle class and stimulate the economy with increased spending for highway and mass transit projects.

To head his economic team, Clinton chose Senate Finance Committee Chairman Lloyd Bentsen, D-Texas, as secretary of the Treasury. Another member of Congress, House Budget Committee Chairman Leon E. Panetta, D-Calif., was named director of the Office of Management and Budget.

The president-elect made clear that his wife, Hillary Rodham Clinton, would be a close adviser in his administration. Hillary Clinton, a lawyer, had been a Republican target during the campaign for her views on children's rights and her decision to campaign with her husband instead of staying at home to "bake cookies."

For White House chief of staff Clinton chose another member of his inner circle, Thomas F. McLarty III, a Little Rock gas company executive and Clinton friend since childhood.

Following, in chronological order, are the Reuter/News Transcripts Inc. texts (audience reactions omitted) of the concession statements given by independent candidate Ross Perot in Dallas and President George Bush in Houston on November 3, 1992, and the victory statement of President-elect Bill Clinton in Arkansas on November 4:

PEROT CONCESSION STATEMENT

I want to thank all of you who are here tonight and all the people who have come together across the nation. Starting last February, you did something that everybody said couldn't be done. Millions of you came together to take your country back. You gave Washington a laser-like message to listen to the people.

You have done an incredible job of getting this country turned back around to the type country our founders established, a country that came from the people. And you have changed this country through your massive efforts. And I compliment you for it, and it was brilliant the way you did it.

As I've said on a number of occasions, my role in life is that of the grain of sand to the oyster. It irritates the oyster, and out comes a pearl. I have been your grain of sand that you chose. It has been an honor to be your grain of sand in this process. And we will continue to work together to make pearls as necessary in the future. Fair enough?

The American people have spoken. They have chosen Governor Clinton. Congratulations.

Wait a minute. Oh, no, no. Wait a minute. Wait a minute. The only way we're going to make it work is if all team up together. So let's give Governor Clinton a big round of applause. He's won.

Now, let's forget the election. Forget the election, it's behind us. The hard work is in front of us, and we must all work together to rebuild our great country.

Thank you.

You the American people are the greatest people on the face of the earth, and if we will just put our differences aside and team up together, we can rebuild our job base, we can eliminate the deficit, we can eliminate the debt, and most importantly, we can pass on the American dream to our children, right?

And on the way, we can reform our government and get rid of some of these problems that are so damaging to all of us.

Now, to the millions of volunteers who asked me to serve as your candidate, as long as I live, one of the happiest memories of my life will be the memory of working with you. That memory will never dim. It's the nicest honor I ever received in my life. Thank you very much.

There are people here tonight and there are people across the country who literally gave it everything they had seven days a week since last February to take this country back and give it to the people, to pay its debts, to pass the American dream on to our children. And I want you to know how proud I am of you and how much all of us owe you for the tremendous effort you made.

So God bless you and thank you very much!

Now this is just the beginning, but the next step is we need to take all of our energy and harness it and try—see, time is not our friend. Time is our enemy. These problems our country faces need to be solved immediately. We need to all work together, and work with the new administration, and give it a world-class best effort to get these problems solved now because if we do, you benefit, the country benefits, your children benefit, and everybody wins. We've got to do it.

Spend about 10 minutes getting over being frustrated that your candidate didn't win, then take all of this enormous creativity and talent that you have displayed, and let's make our country work at the national state, county, city, the local, and neighborhood level, and at every single school across the country, right?

Absolutely.

Forty percent of the vote has been counted so far—and that is, is it good for our country, right? Is it good for the country? If it gets through that filter, then we'll back it hard and we'll use all of the enormous ability that you have to get things done for the benefit of our people and our country.

Now, the main thing—the main thing—is don't lose your enthusiasm, don't lose your idealism, don't lose your great love for this country, and please don't feel, gee, I'm powerless again. As long as we're together nationwide, you have enormous voice in this country.

So we will stay together and you will be a force for good for our country and our children.

Now, you remember—well, like the little children that are here tonight, the college students that have been at all the rallies all across the country—when you look at them, you're looking at tomorrow. And we must give them a brighter tomorrow than any other generation has ever had in our country. And if we keep it that simple and that pure and that clean, then we can make an enormous contribution, and that's what we must do.

We have our organization established, we have a nationwide network, a state-by-state network, a community-by-community network, and we will keep it in intact to be a force for constructive good throughout our country.

The best is in front of us, believe me!

This is no time to get discouraged, this is no time to throw in the towel, this is the time to redouble our efforts and work with the new administration to make sure that our country is a beacon to the rest of the world, to make sure that our cities are alabaster cities that gleam undimmed by human tears, and to make sure that every little child across America is only limited by his or her dreams and their willingness to pay the price and make the effort to make those dreams come true.

That's what America is all about.

And that's what you're all about. And God bless you. We love you. And I want you to know that our love for you and my love for you is permanent. And I will carry the memory of these past few months with me for the rest of my life. And I am available to you anytime, anyplace, anywhere, as long as I am around. God bless you, and thank you very much.

BUSH CONCESSION STATEMENT

Thank you. Thank you very, very much. Hey, listen, we've got to get going. Thank you. Thank you very much. Hey, listen, you guys. . . .

Hey, thank you very much. Look, thank you so much. Well, here's the way I see it. Here's the way we see it and the country should see it, that the people have spoken. And we respect the majesty of the democratic system.

I just called Governor Clinton over in Little Rock and offered my congratulations. He did run a strong campaign. I wish him well in the White House. And I want the country to know that our entire administration will work closely with his team to ensure the smooth transition of power. There is important work to be done, and America must always come first. So we will get behind this new President and wish him well.

To all who voted for us, voted for me here, especially here, but all across the country, thank you for your support. We have fought the good fight, and we've kept the faith. And I believe I have upheld the honor of the Presidency of the United States. Now I ask that we stand behind our new President. Regardless of our differences, all Americans share the same purpose: to make this, the world's greatest nation, more safe and more secure and to guarantee every American a shot at the American dream.

I would like to thank so many of you who have worked beside me to improve America and to literally change the world. Let me thank our great

Vice President, Dan Quayle. You know, in the face of a tremendous pounding, he stood for what he believes in. He will always have my profound gratitude and certainly my respect.

I would like to salute so many that did special work: Rich Bond up at the RNC; Bob Teeter, who ran the campaign; Bob Mosbacher; our entire campaign team. They've run a valiant effort in a very, very difficult year. I also want to salute the members of the Cabinet, all of whom who have served this Nation with honor, with integrity, and with great distinction. And I would like to single out two leaders who represent the ideal in public service. Together they've helped lead the world through a period of unprecedented transition. I'm talking, of course, about my National Security Adviser, Brent Scowcroft, and my good friend and fellow Texan, our Secretary of State, Jim Baker.

Finally, of course, I want to thank my entire family, with a special emphasis on a woman named Barbara. She's inspired this entire Nation, and I think the country will always be grateful.

But tonight is really not a night for speeches. But I want to share a special message with the young people of America. You see, I remain absolutely convinced that we are a rising nation. We have been in an extraordinarily difficult period. But do not be deterred, kept away from public service by the smoke and fire of a campaign year or the ugliness of politics. As for me, I'm going to serve and try to find ways to help people. But I plan to get very active in the grandchild business and in finding ways to help others. But I urge you, the young people of this country, to participate in the political process. It needs your idealism. It needs your drive. It needs your conviction.

And again, my thanks, my congratulations to Governor Clinton; to his running mate, Senator Gore. And a special thanks to each and every one of you, many of you who have been at my side in every single political battle.

May God bless the United States of America. Thank you very, very much. Thank you so much. Thank you.

CLINTON VICTORY STATEMENT

My fellow Americans on this day, with high hopes and brave hearts and massive numbers, the American people have voted to make a new beginning.

This election is a clarion call for our country to face the challenges of the end of the Cold War and beginning of the next century, to restore growth to our country and opportunity to our people, to empower our own people so that they can take more responsibility for their own lives, to face problems too long ignored, from AIDS to the environment to the conversion of our economy from a defense to a domestic economic giant.

And perhaps most important of all, to bring our people together as never before so that our diversity can be a source of strength in a world that is ever smaller, where everyone counts and everyone is a part of America's family.

I want to begin this night by thanking my family: my wife, without whom I would not be here tonight and who I believe will be one of the greatest first ladies in the history of this republic.

And I also want to say a special word of thanks to our daughter for putting up with our absence, for supporting our effort, for being brave in the face of adversity, and for reminding us every day about what this election is really all about.

I want to thank my mother, my brother, my stepfather, my mother-in-law and father-in-law, my brothers-in-law, and my sister-in-law, who carried this campaign across this country and stuck up for me when others were trying to put it down. I love them and I thank them.

I want to thank the people of this wonderful small state.

Time after time, when this campaign was about to be counted out, the Arkansas travelers exploded out of this state around the country to tell people the truth about what we had done here together, how we had pulled together, what we believed in and what we could do as a nation.

I have the best staff and cabinet you can imagine, and they kept this state together. And even when we weren't here, we continued to lead the country in job growth, in keeping taxes and spending down, and in pulling the people of Arkansas together to show what we could do if the nation pulled together and moved forward, too.

I want to thank the people who were in that infamous group, the FOBs, the Friends of Bill and the Friends of Hillary. No person who ever sought this office was more aided by the friends of a lifetime, and I will never forget you.

I want to thank the people in the New Democratic Party, headed by our chairman Ron Brown, the new members of Congress, the new blood, the new direction that we are giving.

And finally I want to thank the members of my brilliant, aggressive, unconventional but always winning campaign staff. They were unbelievable. And they have earned this.

I want to say, if I might, a special word of thanks to two people who lost their lives in the course of this campaign without whom we might not be here tonight, our friends Paul Telley and Vic Razor, our prayers are with them. They're looking down on us tonight and they're awful happy.

Not very long ago I received a telephone call from President Bush. It was a generous and forthcoming telephone call, of real congratulations and an offer to work with me in keeping our democracy running in an effective and important transition. I want all of you to join with me tonight in expressing our gratitude to President Bush for his lifetime of public service, for the effort he made from the time he was a young soldier in World War II, to helping to bring about an end to the Cold War, to our victory in the gulf war, to the grace with which he conceded the results of this election tonight in the finest American tradition. Let's give Mr. Bush and his family a hand.

I heard tonight Mr. Perot's remarks, and his offer to work with us. I say to you, of all the things that he said, I think perhaps the most important that we understand here in the heartland of Arkansas is the need to reform the political system, to reduce the influence of special interests and give more influence back to the kind of people that are in this crowd tonight by the tens of thousands. And I will work with him to do that.

And, finally, let me say how profoundly indebted I am tonight—beyond the folks at home, beyond the wonderful people that worked in this administration, the lieutenant governor and others, to keep our government going, beyond all the others I have to say a special word of thanks to my magnificent running mate, Senator Al Gore and his family.

I want to tell you that Al and Tipper, Hillary and I, have become friends. I admire them for what they stand for; they're enjoyable to be with, they believe in our country. Al Gore is a man of almost unparalleled combination of intelligence, commitment, compassion and concern to the people of this country, to our obligations to preserve our environment, to our duty to promote freedom and peace in the world. And together we're going to do our best to give you a new partnership for a new America.

I want to thank Al's children, his brother-in-law, and his wonderful parents. They made about as many votes in some states as we did. I think we carried every state that Senator and Mrs. Gore campaigned in. Their percentage was the best of all.

I want to say that we have established a partnership in this campaign that we will continue into this new administration.

For if we have learned anything in the world today, it is that we can accomplish more by teamwork, by working together, by bringing out the best in all the people that we seek—and we will seek the best and most able and most committed people throughout this country to be a part of our team.

We will ask the Democrats who believe in our cause to come forward, but we will look, too, among the ranks of independents and Republicans who are willing to roll up their sleeves, be a part of a new partnership, and get on with the business of dealing with this nation's problems.

I remind you again tonight, my fellow Americans, that this victory was more than a victory of party, it was a victory for the people who work hard and play by the rules, a victory for the people who feel left out and left behind and want to do better, a victory for the people who are ready to compete and win in the global economy but who need a government that offers a hand not a hand-out.

That is what we offer, and that is what tomorrow we will begin to work to provide to all of you.

Today, the steelworker and the stenographer, the teacher and the nurse, had as much power in the mystery of our democracy as the president, the billionaire, and the governor. You all spoke with equal voices for change. And tomorrow we will try to give you that.

You can trust us to wake up every day remembering the people we saw in the bus trips, the people we saw in the town meetings, the people we touched at the rallies, the people who had never voted before, the people who hadn't voted in 20 years, the people who'd never voted for a Democrat, the people who had given up hope, all of them together saying we want our future back. And I intend to help give it to you.

I say to all of those who voted for us, this was a remarkable coalition for change. Many of you had to put aside this or that personal ambition to be a part of a broad, deep commitment to change this country. I ask you to keep that commitment as we move from election to governing. We need more than ever for those of you who said let's put the public interest over personal interest to keep it right there for four years so we can turn this country around.

I say to all those who voted for Mr. Bush or Mr. Perot, those who voted for the president, those who voted for Ross Perot, I know you love your country, too. I ask you to listen to the voice of your leaders; I ask you to join with us in creating a re-United States, a united country, with a new sense of patriotism to face the challenges of this new time. We need your help, too, and we will do our best to deserve it.

When we seek to offer young people the opportunity to borrow the money they need to go to college and the challenge to pay it back through national service, when we challenge the insurance companies, the drug companies, the providers and the consumers, the government to give us a new health care system, when we offer those on welfare new opportunity in the challenge to move to work, when we ask companies to take the incentives we offer to put American people to work and export American products not American jobs—all of this is a part of a new patriotism to lift our people up and enable all of us to live up to the fullest of our potential.

I accept tonight the responsibility that you have given me to be the leader of this, the greatest country in human history.

I accept it with a full heart and a joyous spirit, but I ask you to be Americans again, too, to be interested not just in getting but in giving, not just in placing blame but now in assuming responsibility, not just in looking out for yourselves but in looking out for others, too. In this very place, one year and one month ago today, I said we need more than new laws, new promises or new programs. We need a new spirit of community, a sense that we're all in this together.

If we have no sense of community, the American dream will continue to wither. Our destiny is bound up with the destiny of every American. We're all in this together, and we will rise or fall together. That has been my message to the American people for the past thirteen months and it will be my message for the next four years.

Together we can do it. Together we can make the country that we love everything it was meant to be. I still believe in a place called Hope.

God bless America. Thank you all.

REPORT ON WOMEN IN COMBAT
November 15, 1992

A sharply divided Presidential Commission on the Assignment of Women in the Armed Forces said women should continue to be barred from nearly all combat roles. In a report issued November 15, the panel said the only combat role appropriate for women is service on Navy ships—except submarines and amphibious assault vessels. Even then, the panel recommended that women not be allowed to fly Navy combat aircraft.

The panel's recommendations, delivered to President George Bush two months before he left office, were not binding on Congress or the military. They were, however, a setback to supporters of an expanded role for women in the armed forces. Supporters contended that the strong performance of 40,000 female soldiers in the Persian Gulf War showed they could do the same jobs as men.

In May 1991 Congress voted to allow women to fly planes in combat, but Pentagon policies continued to keep women out of the cockpit during combat. Six other nations—Belgium, Canada, the Netherlands, Norway, Spain, and Great Britain—allowed women to fly planes in combat. By a vote of 8-7, the presidential commission said Congress should reverse its vote and go along with the Pentagon policy. By a 10-0 vote, the commission also urged Congress to pass a law barring women from ground combat assignments. In addition, the panel said the military should fire single parents with children under school age and bar spouses of military parents from joining the service.

Composition of Commission Criticized

Critics said the panel's conclusions were preordained when Bush selected its fifteen members. The Washington Post *reported that Defense Secretary Dick Cheney had developed a list of panelists that included both supporters and opponents of women in combat. Bush dropped the supporters, over Cheney's objections, and added Kate Walsh O'Beirne of the Heritage Foundation and Elaine Donnelly of Phyllis Schlafly's Eagle Forum, according to the newspaper.*

One of the two active-duty officers on the panel, Marine Brig. Gen. Thomas V. Draude, particularly criticized Donnelly. He told the Post *that she "uses facts the way a drunk uses a lamppost, not for illumination but for support." The other active-duty officer, Army Capt. Mary Finch, agreed. "If I was president, I would look at the makeup of the commission and throw a lot of the recommendations out," she said.*

Overall, the panel's debate frequently appeared to center more on questions of social policy than military preparedness. Conservative members, for example, contended that it was wrong to let women perform jobs that might involve killing. They also said women lacked the physical strength for combat, would face special hardships if they became prisoners of war, and would undermine the cohesiveness of male-dominated combat units.

The panel initially voted to recommend that women be barred from serving in any combat units at all. However, retired Air Force Gen. Robert T. Herres, the panel's chairman, argued that such a complete endorsement of current policy would harm the group's credibility. "A great number of people will not believe we credibly considered these issues," he said. The panel then voted to let women serve on all Navy combat ships except submarines and amphibious vessels.

An Issue for the Clinton Administration

In an editorial, the Post *called the report "a partisan mess." It said the incoming administration of President-elect Bill Clinton, which would have to address the issue of women in combat, "would do best to ignore most of the report and start again."*

The report added to the growing debate over women's role in and treatment by the military. Earlier in the year, the Navy's Tailhook sex-assault scandal cost two admirals their jobs and forced Navy Secretary H. Lawrence Garrett III to resign. Also in 1992, the Navy created a hotline to provide advice to both victims and perpetrators of sexual harassment (Pentagon Report on Tailhook Convention, p. 879; Navy on Prevention of Sexual Harassment, p. 1003).

Following are excerpts from the report by the Presidential Commission on the Assignment of Women in the Armed Forces, which was released November 15, 1992:

A: Quotas and Goals

Should a DoD [Department of Defense]-wide policy be established regarding the use of quotas or goals to influence gender-related personnel policies, e.g., recruitment, promotion, retention and assignment? If so, what should that policy be?

Recommendation: DoD should establish a policy to ensure that no person who is best qualified is denied access on the basis of gender to an assignment that is open to both men and women. As far as it is compatible with the above policy, the Secretary of Defense should retain discretion to set goals that encourage the recruitment and optimize the utilization of women in the Services, allowing for the requirements of each Service....

B: Voluntary v. Involuntary Duty

Should special conditions and different standards apply to service-women than apply to servicemen performing similar roles in the Armed Forces in the area of voluntary (women) versus involuntary (men) assignment policies?

Recommendation: The Services should adopt gender-neutral assignment policies, providing the possibility of involuntary assignment of any qualified personnel to any position open to them....

C: Fitness/Wellness Standards

Should special conditions and different standards apply to service-women than apply to servicemen performing similar roles in the Armed Forces in the area of general physical fitness requirements for purposes of wellness?

Recommendation: The Services should retain gender-specific physical fitness tests and standards to promote the highest level of general fitness and wellness in the Armed Forces of the United States, provided they do not compromise training or qualification programs for physically demanding combat or combat support MOSs [military occupational specialties]. ...

D: Occupational Physical Requirements

Should the Services establish and implement specific occupational, muscular strength/endurance, and cardiovascular capacity requirements where they are relevant to the duties of each specialty?

Recommendation: The Services should adopt specific requirements for those specialties for which muscular strength/ endurance and cardiovascular capacity are relevant....

E: Basic Training Standards

Should special conditions and different standards apply to service-

women than apply to servicemen performing similar roles in the Armed
Forces in the area of basic training?

**Recommendation: Entry level training may be gender-specific
as necessary. Each advanced training program should be classified according to the military specialties to which it is principally
dedicated, or to which it supplies personnel. Training programs
which are dedicated to combat specialties shall be governed by
policies which are consistent with laws and policies regarding the
use of women in combat....**

F: Pre-Commissioning Standards

Should special conditions and different standards apply to servicewomen than apply to servicemen performing similar roles in the Armed
Forces in the area of pre-commissioning training?

**Recommendation: Military pre-commissioning training may be
gender-normed in as much as post-commissioning training is
designed specifically for individual specialties, combat, combat
support and combat service support....**

G: Gender-Related Occupational Standards

Should special conditions and different standards apply to servicewomen than apply to servicemen performing similar occupational roles in
the Armed Forces in the area of muscular strength/endurance and cardiovascular capacity?

**Recommendation: The Services should adopt gender-neutral
muscular strength/endurance and cardiovascular capacity requirements for those specialties for which they are relevant....**

H: Parental and Family Policies

Should DoD policies, e.g., recruitment, retention, child care, and deployment policies, regarding single and dual-service parents be revised? What
effect do policies on the assignment of servicewomen have upon military
families, children, and the larger American society?

**Recommendation: During and after U.S. involvement in the Gulf
War, the American public and military community expressed
extreme disapproval of the deployment of single mothers/fathers
due to the possible effect on the children left behind. The Commission recommends that DoD review its policies and either adopt
new policies or better implement current policies to reflect concerns of the public and military communities. Specifically, the
Commission recommends that DoD consider the following
alternatives:**

- DoD should adopt a waivable policy that single parents with custodial
  care of children up to two years of age must accept assignment to a non-
  deployable position, if available, or be discharged from the Service with

the opportunity to re-enter the Service without loss of rank or position.
- For those single parents who have children older than two years and those parents who have been out for two years, they must have an approved and reliable child care package to re-enter the Service.
- In dual-service families, only one parent should be allowed to serve in a deployable position.
- Single parents with custody of children under school age should not be allowed to deploy.
- Single parents should not be permitted to join the Armed Forces (current situation).
- Spouses of military parents should not be allowed to enter the Service.
- One parent in a dual-service couple should be forced to separate from the Service.
- In order to reduce the number of children subjected to prolonged separation or the risk of becoming orphans during deployment, long-term DoD policies regarding the recruitment, deployment and retention of single and dual-service parents should be revised on a phased-in basis. Such policies should allow for voluntary or involuntary discharges at the discretion of local commanders, or reasonable incentives for separation. They may also include waivers by local commanders in certain circumstances.

In order to avoid severe separation, child care and deployability problems at at a time of mobilization, all family care plans must be regularly reviewed and evaluated by local commanding officers, with consideration given to the relationship of the potential caregiver to the child(ren) of deployable parents. Failure to ensure full compliance with family care requirements may constitute grounds for administrative or disciplinary action. . . .

I: Pregnancy and Deployability Policies

Should DoD rules regarding pregnancy, excluding deployability of servicewomen, be retained, modified or rescinded?

Should special conditions and different standards apply to service-women than apply to servicemen performing similar roles in the Armed Forces regarding deployability?

Should servicewomen who become pregnant continue to serve in deployable positions?

Should comparable restrictions on deployability be applied to servicemen?

Recommendation: The Commission reviewed the rules regarding pregnancy and found no specific areas of concern other than the problems associated with deployability and lost time; these problems are addressed in a separate issue. However, DoD should review rules regarding pregnancy to ensure consistency and force readiness.

Comparable deployability standards for each Service should be adopted by DoD and should be applied on a gender-neutral basis with exceptions for pregnancy.

A pregnant servicewoman should not be assigned to or remain in a position with a high probability of deployment. The Commission suggests that deployability for purposes of implementing such a policy be defined in terms of probabilities; a deployment-probability-designation coding system could be established to determine which positions have the higher probabilities of deployment and thus would be subject to restrictions under the recommended policy. Comparable restrictions should be applied to other servicemembers based on projected amount of time an individual will be unable to fulfill normal duties of his/her position because of injury, etc....

J: Combat Roles for Women

In view of American military history, experience of war, and religious and cultural values, should the U.S. under any circumstances assign any servicewomen to any combat position, on land, at sea, or in the air?

Recommendation: Yes. Military readiness should be the driving concern regarding assignment policies; there are circumstances under which women might be assigned to combat positions.

The American experience—military, religious, and cultural—and how that relates to the role of women in direct combat was of great interest to the Commission. American history is replete with examples of women defending the nation with courage and dedication, and as the Persian Gulf War experience indicated, there are women who, today, serve in combatant positions. Testimony from sociologists, ethicists, moralists, theologians, and clergy indicated that the U.S. is a country with a diverse set of beliefs and varied heritages. After eight months of consideration, the Commission decided that the "American experience" does not preclude assigning capable women to direct combat positions for which they are qualified.

It was noted by the Commission in examining the assignment of women to combat positions that women, although precluded from combat assignments by law and policy, are currently serving in combat positions in Air Force missile silos, in Army air defense units, and in other combat service support roles where they are exposed to enemy fire. To assess attitudes regarding women's roles in the military, the Commission conducted an extensive poll of public and military attitudes. The public survey revealed that the views of Americans on women in combat are as diverse as their backgrounds. The Commission's public poll on women in the military revealed that while the public is almost evenly split on the concept of women in direct combat generally; when asked about specific assignments such as combatant vessels and aircraft, they support the assignment of women to some combat roles.

One of the strongest sociological arguments in favor of women in combat focused on selecting the best qualified person for a position, regardless of gender. A number of witnesses, Members of Congress and senior military women advanced the belief that women should not be barred from any position in the military unless there is convincing evidence that they cannot meet the occupational demands. Testimony revealed maintained that the burden should be on those who would continue gender-based classifications. Other witnesses stated that placing the best qualified person in a specialty requires servicemembers should be judged as individuals—not as white or black, not as Italian or Greek or Jewish and not as men or women—they should be treated as individuals, and not members of groups.

Many other witnesses testified that the demand for full integration of women in the Armed Forces is about the advancement of a particular vision of culture and society that advocates gender-neutrality. A number of people testified that no human society has ever intentionally used female soldiers in extended combat except in cases of national survival. They viewed that placing women in combat arms as a reckless act when there are sufficient numbers of qualified men available to serve in those positions.

Theological testimony was received from representatives of a wide range of different religions and denominations. Among the major religious establishments in the U.S., none has adopted a position regarding women being assigned to combat positions on the basis of theology. The Commission concludes that although the U.S. has an undeniably strong religious heritage, it is not one that speaks clearly on the issue of women in combat.

There was general agreement among theologians, Catholic, Lutheran, Baptist, Jewish and Episcopalian that the military's policies should not unduly infringe upon the rights of the family. Similarly, there was a strong concern that in an effort to defend the country, the nation's internal values not be diminished. The conclusions varied as some stated that women should not be assigned to these positions under any circumstances, while others distinguished assignment between air, sea and land combat. Still others believed that, as long as American women must accept broad societal responsibilities, they have the right to be represented in all aspects of the military, including ground combat.

A great effort was made by the Commission to determine the attitudes of the public toward women in direct combat and the effect of such assignment on the public. Its review of the diverse testimony reveals no thread from which a definitive position can be drawn that would preclude roles for women in combat. As evident by the Commission's recommendations on air, sea and land direct combat positions, a majority of Commissioners believe that under some circumstances, American society not only allows, but actually encourages and approves the further integration of women into combat roles. . . .

K: Ground Combat

Should the existing service policies restricting the assignment of service-women with respect to ground combat MOS/specialties be retained, modified, rescinded, or codified?

Recommendation: The sense of the Commission is that women should be excluded from direct land combat units and positions. Further, the Commission recommends that the existing service policies concerning direct land combat exclusions be codified. Service Secretaries shall recommend to the Congress which units and positions should fall under the land combat exclusion.

The issue of whether to retain, modify, rescind, or codify the policies restricting the assignment of women in ground combat specialties was statutorily required to be considered by the Commission. In addressing the issue, the Commission found the effectiveness of ground units to be the most significant criterion.

American military women are prohibited by Service policies that preclude them from serving in direct ground combat positions. Current policy excluding women from ground combat is based, in part, on Congressional intent to preclude women from serving in combat aircraft or on combatant ships. The specialties that fall under the exclusion may be grouped into four major areas: infantry, armor, artillery, and combat engineers, all of which require a soldier to be prepared to fight in direct, close-quarters combat.

Through testimony and trips, the Commission heard and observed that the daily life of the ground soldier in combat circumstances is one of constant physical exertion, often in extreme climatic conditions with the barest of amenities and the inherent risks of injury, capture and death. The Commission learned that despite technological advances, ground combat has not become less hazardous and physically demanding.

The evidence before the Commission clearly shows distinct physiological differences between men and women. Most women are shorter in stature, have less muscle mass and weigh less than men. These physiological differences place women at a distinct disadvantage when performing tasks requiring a high level of muscular strength and aerobic capacity, such as hand-to-hand fighting, digging, carrying heavy loads, lifting and other tasks central to ground combat.

The Commission also heard from women of tremendous physical ability who expressed a desire to serve in the ground combat arms. There is little doubt that some women could meet the physical standards for ground combat, but the evidence shows that few women possess the necessary physical qualifications. Further, a 1992 survey of 900 Army servicewomen showed that only 12 percent of enlisted women and ten percent of the female noncommissioned officers surveyed said they would consider serving in the combat arms.

The Commission considered the effects that women could have on the cohesion of group combat units. Cohesion is defined as the relationship that develops in a unit or group where: (1) members share common values and experiences; (2) individuals in the group conform to group norms and behavior in order to ensure group survival and goals; (3) members lose their personal identity in favor of a group identity; (4) members focus on group activities and goals; (5) members become totally dependent on each other for the completion of their mission or survival; and (6) members must meet all standards of performance and behavior in order not to threaten group survival. The evidence clearly shows that unit cohesion can be negatively affected by the introduction of any element that detracts from the need for such key ingredients as mutual confidence, commonality of experience, and equitable treatment. There are no authoritative military studies of mixed-gender ground combat cohesion, since available cohesion research has been conducted among male-only ground combat units.

One research study reviewed by the Commission indicates that the following are areas where cohesion problems might develop:

1. Ability of women to carry the physical burdens required of each combat unit member. This entails an ability to meet physical standards of endurance and stamina.
2. Forced intimacy and lack of privacy on the battlefield (e.g. washing, bathing, using latrine facilities, etc.).
3. Traditional Western values where men feel a responsibility to protect women.
4. Dysfunctional relationships (e.g. sexual misconduct).
5. Pregnancy.

Of these, the prospect of sexual relationships in land units in direct combat with the enemy was considered to be dysfunctional and would encumber small unit ground combat leaders, noncommissioned officers, lieutenants and captains, in carrying out their military missions.

Ground combat incurs a high risk of capture by the enemy. The Commission's review of our nation's recent wars with respect to POWs suggests that potential enemies may not accord respect for the Geneva Convention and customary rules related to protection of prisoners. During our nation's major wars in this century, except Vietnam, the number of POWs has been greatest from the ground forces, the next largest number from downed aircraft and the least number from Navy ships. The Commission heard testimony from DoD representatives and POWs who indicated that the mistreatment of women taken as POWs could have a negative impact on male captives.

The Commission's enabling statute required examination of public attitudes toward the assignment of women in the military. Several surveys were conducted to determine what the American public and military attitudes were toward women in ground combat. The results of these surveys indicate that members of the military are strongly against women serving in all branches of ground combat, while the public has mixed views on service in different ground combat specialties. The Roper survey of the

American public showed that 57 percent of the American public polled said that women should not be assigned to the infantry, and 52 percent were against women in Marine infantry. However, 58 percent of the public surveyed were in favor of assigning women to both artillery and armor positions.

The Roper military poll reported that 74 percent of the military members surveyed did not think women should serve in the infantry, 72 percent rejected the idea of women in Marine infantry, 59 percent opposed women in tank crews, and 54 percent did not want women to serve in the artillery. When the same question was asked of military personnel who had actually served in the ground combat arms, the numbers increased to 83 percent against women in the infantry, 83 percent against women serving in Marine infantry, 71 percent against women in armor, and 64 percent against women in artillery.

Several countries have placed women in ground combat units with little success. Historically, those nations that have permitted women in close combat situations (the Soviet Union, Germany and Israel) have done so only because of grave threats to their national survival. After the crisis passed, each nation adopted policies which excluded the employment of women in combat. In more current times, the Commission learned that countries that have tested integrating women in ground combat units have found those tests unsuccessful.

The Commission also considered the effect on registration and conscription if women were allowed in ground combat units. In 1981, the Supreme Court upheld the male-only registration provision of the Military Selective Service Act, 50 U.S.C. App. 453, against a due process equal protection challenge from men who claimed that it was discriminatory because it required men, but not women, to register for the draft. The Court's opinion rested on the following argument: the purpose behind the registration requirement is to create a pool of individuals to be called up in the event of a draft; a draft is used to obtain combat troops; women are prevented, through law and policy, from serving in combat positions in any of the four Services; therefore, men and women are dissimilarly situated in regard to the registration requirement and it is permissible to treat them differently.

The Commission reviewed the assignment of draftees in our most recent conflicts, and according to statistics provided by DoD, 98 percent of draftees went to the Army during Vietnam, 95 percent during Korea and 83 percent during World War II. Because a draft is used to obtain combat troops and historically most draftees go into the Army, it can be deduced that the draft is used primarily to obtain a pool of ground combat troops. The Commission considered the possibility that lifting the ground combat exclusion pertaining to women may undermine the justification used by the Supreme Court to uphold the constitutionality of the all-male draft, because women would be eligible to serve in the positions which are filled through conscription.

The case against women in ground combat is compelling and conclusive. The physiological differences between men and women are most stark when compared to ground combat tasks. This is underscored by the evidence that there are few women, especially enlisted women, interested in serving in ground combat specialties. The overriding importance of small unit cohesion to ground military success, and the unknown but probably negative effect that the presence of women would have in those units were of critical concern to most Commissioners. Several polls revealed in most convincing terms that the public and military, especially the military people most familiar with its rigors, were fundamentally opposed to women in ground combat. The weight of international experience with women in ground combat units provides no conclusive evidence supporting the assignment of women in ground combat units. Finally, the legal implications of lifting the ground combat exclusion policy for the possible registration and conscription of women for ground combat were considered. The current ground combat exclusion policies, which are derived from Congressional intent to restrict the assignment of women in other Services, would be vulnerable if the remaining statute was repealed. The Commission therefore recommends that the ground exclusion policies be enacted into law for consistency and as sound public policy. . . .

L: Combat Aircraft

Should the existing service policies restricting the assignment of servicewomen with respect to aircraft be retained, modified, rescinded, or codified?

Recommendation: In view of the evidence gathered by this Commission with regard to the potential consequences of assigning women to combat positions, current DoD and Service policies with regard to Army, Air Force and Navy aircraft on combat missions should be retained and codified by means of the reenactment of Sec. 8549 of Title 10, U.S. Code which was repealed by Public Law 102-190, Sec. 531 for the Air Force, and reenactment of the provisions of 10 U.S.C. sec. 6015 prohibiting women from assignment to duty on aircraft engaged in combat missions, which was repealed by Public Law 102-190 for the Navy, and codification of Army policy.

Congress repealed 10 U.S.C. 8549 and amended provisions of 10 U.S.C. 6015 removing statutory restrictions of women aviators to fly combat aircraft. These actions and the strong performance of U.S. servicewomen in the Persian Gulf War warranted the Commission to develop a recommendation on the integration of women into combat aircraft.

During the discussion of the assignment of women to combat aircraft, this issue more than any other raised the question of "can versus should?" Although the evidence presented indicates that women are capable of flying and competing with men in combat aviation assignments, the Commission finds that concerns over cohesion and women as prisoners of war (POWs) were more persuasive and voted to recommend detention and codification of the Services' policies prohibiting the assignment of women to combat aircraft.

The Commission heard testimony from former POWs of the Vietnam War and one of the female POWs of the Persian Gulf War. The record of brutal treatment of POWs at the hands of the Vietnamese is incontrovertible. Iraq mistreated male POWs and indecently assaulted one U.S. woman POW.

Many experts and former POWs testified that the presence of women might cause additional morale problems for male prisoners. In Survival, Evasion, Resistance, and Escape (SERE) training, evidence indicates that men will try to protect women, to the detriment of the unit. The experience of foreign countries with women as POWs (the Soviet Union and Germany during WWII) also suggests that it would be detrimental to the military and the society. Some military experts and historians told the Commission that one of the major reasons for the exclusion of women from combat in Israel was the fear that female POWs would dishearten the Israeli people in wartime. The majority of Commissioners believe that the assignment of women to combat aircrews would inevitably require women aviators to conduct routine combat missions penetrating hostile air space over enemy territory, with the inherent risks of shoot-down, escape, evasion and capture.

A majority of Commissioners also believe that the introduction of women into air combat squadrons would disrupt the cohesion of their units, resulting in a lower quality force. Commissioners' views on the subject are contentious, as evidenced by the extremely close vote in favor of retaining and codifying the Services' existing prohibition against assigning women to fly combat aircraft. For several years, the U.S. military has had mixed gender aircraft squadrons, yet many men who have positive feelings about working with women in a noncombat unit, still believe women should not be integrated into air combat units. Across all Services, men in air combat units were against women entering those units. According to the Commission's worldwide survey of the U.S. military, 69 percent of all pilots (Air Force, Navy and Marines) believed that women should not be assigned to combat aircraft.

The Commission finds that there is no evidence in its review of scientific literature that defines a physiological basis to categorically restrict women from selection opportunity for combat aviation. In a number of informal studies measuring the capability of men and women aviators to withstand the rigors of flight, no information was found suggesting that women were at any kind of disadvantage vis-a-vis men. However, there are also concerns among several Commissioners that the effects of repetitive high G-stresses on aviators, both male and female, have not been adequately investigated under all relevant conditions.

The potential for pregnancy among female aviators was considered. The Commission found that there are suitable provisions by each of the

Services to restrict pregnant pilots from flying. The Commission also found that active duty female pilots have negligible pregnancy rates and thus the Commission discerned that pregnancy is not a major problem with regard to the pilotage issue.

The one vote margin by which this issue was resolved illustrates the deeply divided views that exist on the assignment of women to combat aircraft. Uncertainties about the ramifications of physiologically-driven performance differences, unit cohesion effects and the proportionately high probability of exposure to POW status were the major factors driving the exclusion recommendation. . . .

M: Combatant Vessels

Should the combatant vessel exclusions (law and policy) be retained, modified, or rescinded/repealed? Should the current policy be modified to conform with existing law?

Recommendation: Repeal existing laws and modify Service policies for servicewomen to serve on combatant vessels except submarines and amphibious vessels.

The Commission concludes that the current Navy law governing assignment of servicewomen is inconsistent because it allows women to serve as aviation officers aboard Navy ships, but prohibits their assignment to combatant ships in any other capacity. The law, 10 U.S.C. 6015, currently reads:

> The Secretary of the Navy may prescribe the kind of military duty to which such women members may be assigned and the military authority which they may exercise. However, women may not be assigned to duty on vessels engaged in combat missions (other than as aviation officers as part of an air wing or other air element assigned to such a vessel) nor may they be assigned to other than temporary duty on vessels of the Navy except hospital ships, transports, and vessels of a similar classification not expected to be assigned combat missions.

Since the late 1970s, women have served aboard tenders and service craft. In 1987, they began service in Combat Logistic Force (CLF) ships, which supply the combatant vessels, and in 1991, they began service aboard training frigates, all with no apparent changes in readiness or effectiveness. During that time, the Navy has accrued over 14 years of data regarding women's performance in the seagoing operational environment. The experiences of over 40,000 women, both officers and enlisted, serving in traditional and non-traditional billets and ratings on 66 ships, were a valuable resource for the Commission.

There are few differences between combatant and non-combatant ships in relation to physical strength tasks, with the possible exception of the flight decks of aircraft carriers. Many of the duties women perform on CLF and training ships are the same as those on a combatant ship. In general, men as a group perform better than women on military tasks requiring heavy lifting, carrying, pushing and pulling efforts. While there is a significant overlap in task performance between the sexes, debate over the importance of physical strength on ships continues to be an issue. The Commission generally believes that it is very important that women be integrated in accordance with the Commission's recommendations on Issues D and G, which emphasize the significance of meeting strength, endurance and cardiovascular requirements.

The Commission is well aware of the realities and dangers of serving at sea. Navy ships generally deploy for months at a time, are crowded and have few amenities. Space is at a premium aboard all Navy ships, especially in living facilities. Most ships have dozens of people berthing in one small compartment. Most ships require berthing modifications to accommodate the assignment of women, the cost of which varies greatly depending on the ship class. The Commission found that the costs can range from $66,000 to $4 million per ship. . . . Some argue that these costs waste dollars in a time of shrinking defense budgets.

Submarines are the most confined and crowded and would be the most difficult ships to modify. Modifying an SSN-688 attack or SSBN ballistic missile submarine to accommodate enlisted females could cost as much as $1 million per submarine depending on the number and mix of women assigned. Certain amphibious ships present serious habitability difficulties due to lack of complete privacy given that berthing areas of the embarked Marines are necessarily collocated with public passageways.

Opponents of assigning women to combatant vessels argue that women are incapable of excelling at physically demanding shipboard tasks. Research corroborates that many women have problems performing some of the training tasks related to the physically demanding shipboard tasks of damage control, like fire fighting, flood limitation, and emergency evacuation of wounded. However, 200 women performed well in an actual firefighting emergency aboard a Navy ship in 1988.

The Navy has no specific studies on mixed-gender crew cohesion. The Commission notes that there has been no comparative study showing that gender integration makes Navy ships equally or more efficient than all-male crews. Ship performance in the Navy is regularly rated on the basis of readiness criteria by inspection teams external to the command, and gender-integrated ships perform as well as those with only men.

Commissioners also are concerned with readiness problems that might occur because of pregnancy. While pregnancy is discussed in full in Issue I, the Navy's annualized pregnancy rate among enlisted members is 13.4 percent. The current Navy rule, which precludes pregnant women from deploying, has been a successful policy on the ships to which women are presently assigned.

The statute creating the Commission required examination of public attitudes toward the assignment of women in the military. Two surveys were conducted to determine what American public and military attitudes were toward women serving aboard combatant ships. When asked in the national public survey whether women should be assigned to combat ships,

83 percent of the public surveyed said that women should be assigned. Among those who had prior military experience, 72 percent said that women should be assigned to combatant ships. The results of the military poll showed that in today's Navy, 73 percent of those surveyed felt that women should be allowed to serve on combatant ships. In fact, one-half of Navy respondents felt that women should be required to serve on combatant ships.

The experience of gender integration in foreign navies was also studied by the Commission during its trips to Canada and Europe. Several European countries are at different stages of integrating women into surface combatant ships, and all countries visited reported they are continuing to integrate women in their respective navies.

The Commission notes that the U.S. Coast Guard has successfully integrated all ship classes and places no restrictions upon women regarding their number or the occupational specialties in which they serve.

The Commission recommends that the combatant vessel exclusion law (10 U.S.C. 6015) be repealed, with the exception of submarines and amphibious vessels. The contributions that women sailors have made on Navy support ships over the past 14 years were a major factor in the Commission's recommendation supporting opening combatant ships to women. Women's outstanding performances have resulted in a more capable force, and, during the process, changed traditional attitudes within the Navy. The Commission believes that women are well qualified for sea service. Their presence, it was successfully argued, will increase the military effectiveness of the Navy's surface warships. . . .

N: Special Operations

Should existing policies restricting the assignment of servicewomen with respect to Special Operations Forces be retained, modified, rescinded or codified?

Recommendation: Retain the existing policies. . . .

O: Risk Rule

Should the DoD "Risk Rule," which reduces servicewomen's risk of injury, death or capture be retained, modified, rescinded, or codified?

Recommendation: Retain the DoD Risk Rule as currently implemented. Navy policies which implement the Risk Rule should be modified to reflect the changes made in Issue M. . . .

P: Transition Process

What transition process is appropriate if servicewomen are to be given the opportunity to be assigned to combat positions in the Armed Forces?

Recommendation: The integration process should be accomplished in an orderly fashion and without undue haste. Any necessary modifications to vessels, equipment, and facilities should be done during the normal course of maintenance in a

fashion that minimizes cost. Additionally, the integration process should be consistent with the Commission's recommendations on Issues D and G....

Q: Conscription

Should women be required to register for and be subject to conscription under the Military Selective Service Act: (a) on the same basis as men, if women are provided the same opportunity as men for assignment to any position in the Armed Forces; (b) on the same basis as men, if women in the Armed Forces are assigned to combat positions only as volunteers; or (c) on a different basis than men if women in the Armed Forces are not assigned to combat positions on the same basis as men?

Recommendation: Women should not be required to register for or be subject to conscription.

STATE DEPARTMENT REPORT ON CLINTON'S PASSPORT SEARCH

November 18, 1992

An internal investigation conducted by the State Department determined that during the autumn presidential election campaign, some of its officials searched Bill Clinton's passport and counsular files for evidence that he once wanted to renounce his citizenship. Such files are subject to privacy laws and normally treated as confidential. Had such a letter from the Democratic nominee been found and disclosed, it might have sabotaged his election.

Sherman M. Funk, the department's inspector general, released an internal investigative report November 18 saying the manner of the search had brought "shame" to the department. But he insisted that his investigation had found no evidence that the search was "orchestrated" by the Republican-controlled White House "or any other external source." The report suggested the possibility of White House involvement, however.

Funk said the "genesis of the search" may have been "ordinary" requests from news organizations, filed under the Freedom of Information Act, seeking information about Clinton from government records. But "the manner in which it was carried out was anything but ordinary," he added. His report—formally titled "Special Inquiry Into the Search and Retrieval of William Clinton's Passport Files"—said the requests did not warrant the expedited and intense treatment they received. Never before, he said, had such a search been conducted "with such urgency, scope, thoroughness and grade-level of participants."

The search requests were made as rumors circulated in Washington that when Clinton was a Rhodes Scholar in England during the Vietnam

War he wrote the State Department renouncing his citizenship or, according to other variations, asking how to do so or saying he intended to renounce it. By some accounts, he planned to live in Norway, presumably to avoid military duty during the war. Because Clinton did not go into military service, his wartime draft status became a campaign issue—as did a trip he made to Moscow during his student days at Oxford University. The search for clues to such a letter extended to the passport files of Clinton's mother, Virginia Kelley. Her files likewise yielded nothing.

The day Funk released his report, Acting Secretary of State Lawrence S. Eagleburger said the department's handling of the search had "tarnished" its reputation. Consequently, Eagleburger revealed, he "personally" offered President George Bush his resignation before the November 3 election. Bush refused to accept it, Eagleburger added.

Firing of Key Search Officials

Eagleburger announced he was removing Steven K. Berry from his post as acting assistant secretary of state for legislative affairs, but not from the department. Eight days earlier at Bush's direction, Eagleburger dismissed Elizabeth M. Tamposi as assistant secretary of state for consular affairs and removed her from the department. Funk put the blame mainly on Berry and Tamposi, both political appointees. Consular Affairs, Tamposi's bureau, was responsible for passports. Eagleburger said disciplinary action would likely be taken against other employees, but he did not recommend that the criminal charges be filed against anyone.

Berry, a former Republican staff director of the House intelligence and foreign relations committees, moved to the State Department and worked two years as chief deputy to Janet Mullins, succeeding her in August when she was transferred to the White House as a political assistant to the president. Newsweek *magazine, in its November 23 issue, quoted Tamposi as saying that Berry told her that Mullins had requested the search of Clinton's files.*

Tamposi was also quoted as saying Margaret Tutwiler, a former State Department official who had been moved to the White House, also had advance knowledge about the search. Berry, Mullins, and Tutwiler all denied the allegations. Berry contended that he had asked for the search after repeated inquiries from right-wing Republicans in Congress.

FBI Inquiry into Phone Taps

The report noted that the State Department's Operations Center had monitored telephone calls between Tamposi and Berry without their knowledge. The departmental investigators became concerned that the wiretaps might be illegal and decided that the contents of the telephone conversations must be excluded from the report.

The Washington Post *reported on November 13 that the Tamposi-Berry phone conversations included "political discussions." The calls routed through the department's communications center had been routinely monitored without the caller's permission. That day the department acknowledged that the Federal Bureau of Investigation was investigating whether federal wiretap laws had been violated.*

Report Triggers New Investigations

The State Department's internal report, rather than closing the passport-search inquiry, appeared only to be the starting point for further investigations. "Many issues remain to be addressed," said Rep. Howard L. Berman, D-Calif., who with Sen. John Kerry, D-Mass., ordered a General Accounting Office review of the inquiry. Berman said the GAO, an investigative arm of Congress, would be asked to address unanswered questions raised by the report. The Washington Post *reported December 1 that the State Department subsequently found several "potentially criminal matters" arising from the investigation and asked the Justice Department to review them. A few days earlier it was disclosed that Justice was studying whether privacy laws had been violated in the passport search.*

In mid-December, about a month before leaving office and only a few days before the expiration of a law authorizing the appointment of special prosecutors, Attorney General William P. Barr arranged for the appointment of an independent prosecutor to conduct an independent investigation of the passport affair. Barr's decision reportedly shocked some politically conservative allies because he had often criticized that law. A three-judge panel promptly appointed Joseph E. di Genova the special prosecutor.

Following are excerpts from a "Special Inquiry Into the Search and Retrieval of William Clinton's Passport Files," issued November 18, 1992, by the State Department's Office of Inspector General to Acting Secretary of State Lawrence S. Eagleburger and released publicly:

INQUIRY INTO THE SEARCH AND RETRIEVAL OF WILLIAM CLINTON'S PASSPORT FILES

... In a very narrow sense, this special inquiry can be viewed as "much ado about very little." We spent considerable effort and resources examining in great detail a series of bureaucratic fumbles executed, in large part, by conscientious career public servants. We found no major fraud, no massive corruption, no rogue operations subverting American foreign policy.

In a broader sense, however, what we did find was more disturbing than any of these. What we found was an attempt to use the records and employees of a government agency, the U.S. Department of State, to influence the outcome of a presidential election.

As background: Early this fall, rumors began circulating widely on Capitol Hill, in the press and elsewhere, about a purported letter to the State Department from Bill Clinton, allegedly written while he was a Rhodes Scholar at Oxford. The letter, again purportedly, indicated that Clinton intended to renounce his U.S. citizenship, or requested information on how to renounce his citizenship, or flatly renounced his citizenship. All of these variations apparently included his plans to take up residence in Norway.

These were heady rumors in an election campaign at a time when the polls were running strongly in Clinton's favor. If such a letter existed in the files of the State Department and could be released, or even if its existence could be confirmed without its release, it might well have a profound, perhaps decisive, impact upon the election. If the fact of the letter could be authenticated, the only action seemingly required was to challenge Governor Clinton to authorize its release. A "yes or no" answer from Clinton at that point would be equally disastrous.

This, then, was the scenario motivating the intense interest on both sides in the Clinton letter. Did these rumors reflect a witting dirty trick? Or did they simply represent the dark side of human behavior, which seems to emerge as rumors in every election campaign? We don't know and will not seek an answer to such a boundless question.

What we do know is that these rumors began to gel in the media in the middle of September, prompting three Freedom of Information Act (FOIA) requests to the Department, the last of which, from the Associated Press, specifically asked for a supposed letter from Clinton stating his intention to renounce his U.S. citizenship. Because of botched work by the FOIA office, all three requests were bundled together and marked "expedite," although they clearly did not meet the Department criteria for such handling. Even though the FOIA office managers recognized that this marking was wrong, no attempt was made to correct it. In the upshot, the error made no difference. We were unable to find anyone participating in the subsequent searches who attributed the urgency of their efforts to the "expedite" marking—which, in itself of course, is a meaningful commentary on how the Department responds to such priorities.

The Office of Inspector General has determined that the search of Governor Clinton's passport files in response to FOIA requests was authorized in accordance with normal FOIA procedures. To respond to such requests, the Department has the authority, and indeed the obligation, to search appropriate files to determine if they contain anything that does not violate an individual's right to privacy and that may be released.

Because of their common focus on passport files, the actions taken in the FOIA office culminated in the bureau responsible for passports, Consular Affairs (CA). That bureau, spurred by the FOIA requests, by congressional correspondence and, at least in some part, by partisan hopes to derail the Clinton campaign, promoted a search for documents in Clinton's files of unprecedented scope, urgency, thoroughness, and seniority of participants.

The genesis of the search may have been ordinary FOIA requests; the manner in which it was carried out was anything but ordinary. Although aspects of the search made headlines for a month and a half, the entire search lasted but two days.

The Search: Day One

During the evening of September 30th, three senior employees from CA, Carmen DiPlacido, Richard McClevey, and Steven Moheban (the latter a Schedule C employee), acting under the direct authority of Elizabeth Tamposi, Assistant Secretary for Consular Affairs, and assisted by Washington National Records Center (WNRC) personnel, searched Governor Clinton's files. Tamposi had sought and received assurances from FOIA and passport experts in CA that a file search was required and appropriate.

The CA team retrieved Governor Clinton's original passport application files from WNRC late that evening. At Tamposi's instruction, Steven Moheban brought the file to Tamposi's home later that same night. Several of the team were concerned that something had been torn from a 1976 passport application, and Tamposi wanted to examine it personally. While Tamposi had the file that night, she called several people including the consular affairs officer in London and called Michael Brennan, the CA public affairs officer (also a Schedule C employee), whom she asked to come into work the following day even though he had just returned from Seattle, Washington, and was not scheduled to come in.

She also called Steven Berry, Acting Assistant Secretary for Legislative Affairs. Tamposi had been working with Berry to reply to an inquiry from Congressman Gerald Solomon regarding dual citizenship, and she suspected, based on an earlier telephone conversation with him, that Berry might be working on behalf of the White House to get into Clinton's records. Tamposi maintains that she told Berry she had Clinton's file, but that she did not reveal its contents. She said she only called Berry to discuss generalities about how to respond to Solomon's request. Berry, however, said that Tamposi told him about details of the search, said that something had been torn from a passport application, and asked him if he wanted to see it, something Berry claimed he refused to do. Berry further said that he and Tamposi had a political discussion that, if something were found concerning the Governor, it would certainly "get out." According to Berry, if something were found, both he and Tamposi wanted to see if the Congress would then clamor for Clinton to release his file to the public. Tamposi said no one else was in her home or had access to the file until she brought it into the office the next day.

Earlier, while her team was at the WNRC, Tamposi called the White House and tried to speak to Margaret Tutwiler about how to handle the press, should this search become public. Tamposi also wanted to know if Tutwiler was aware that Steven Berry was representing himself as acting on behalf of the White House in this matter. However, Tamposi did not reach Tutwiler, nor did the latter return her call.

At approximately 6:30 p.m., Tamposi told John F. W. Rogers, Under Secretary for Management, about the search. Rogers maintained he was concerned that anything Tamposi did could be misinterpreted in the charged political atmosphere prior to the presidential election. He said he cautioned Tamposi not to involve political appointees in the search and to ensure that everything she did was "by the book." However, by the time Tamposi called Rogers she had already dispatched a Schedule C employee to participate in the search. Later that evening she would call another Schedule C employee, Michael Brennan, and ask him to cancel his schedule leave for the following day; he was later assigned to assist in the October 1, 1992, search. Tamposi insisted that Rogers never instructed her not to involve political appointees; if he had, she claims she would not have done so.

The Search: Day Two

On the morning of October 1, DiPlacido told Tamposi that he and others should return to the WNRC to search classified files, which might contain information relating to Clinton's purported renunciation of citizenship. Tamposi concurred with this. DiPlacido, McClevey, Moheban, and Brennan spent the day searching classified and other records for any information on Governor Clinton, but found nothing. At approximately 5:00 p.m., Tamposi showed Clinton's file to John Rogers. Rogers maintained that he saw nothing unusual about its condition. Rogers said he again urged Tamposi to be cautious and not to involve political appointees. Rogers also saw Tamposi and others that evening to caution them again.

On October 1, shortly after 6:00 p.m., Tamposi, DiPlacido and Moheban showed Inspector General Sherman Funk Clinton's passport file and expressed their concern that something might have been removed from it. Funk agreed that the matter might be serious and urged them to secure the file. Instead, DiPlacido took the Clinton file to his home that night. DiPlacido maintained that only his wife and young daughter were at home and that the file was protected.

On October 2, Tamposi telephoned the Consular Officer in Oslo and told him to search for any records on Clinton.

Congressional/White House Involvement

Although the examination of Clinton's files was officially launched because of the FOIA requests, congressional interest accelerated the urgency and intensity of the search. According to Steven Berry, rumors were rampant among Republicans and Democrats that something potentially damaging to Clinton's presidential aspirations, such as a letter on dual citizenship or renouncing his American citizenship, was somewhere in some Federal agency. According to Tamposi, Berry called her on September 28 and discussed White House interest in a letter of renunciation of citizenship that Clinton may have written. Tamposi said Berry represented himself as working on behalf of Janet Mullins, Assistant to the President for Political Affairs. Tamposi said that Berry wanted to know if Tamposi could look through consular files on her own for the letter. Tamposi said she adamantly refused to do this and became frightened about its impropriety and the potential that the White House might be involved. Berry then asked what kinds of citizenship records and dual citizenship matters the Department had handled in the past, and Tamposi told him about several key cases, including one on President Panic of the former Republic of Yugoslavia. Berry asked Tamposi if she would respond to a congressional letter on dual citizenship and Tamposi agreed to consider it if one came. Berry said he would see that such a letter was delivered.

Berry told the Inspector General that members of the "congressional leadership on both sides of the aisle" were intensely interested in what might be in the Department's files concerning Governor Clinton. Congressman Solomon, in particular, wanted to know and had been working with Berry to determine how best to obtain access to Clinton's passport records. Berry freely admitted that he assisted Solomon in this regard and contacted Tamposi as the person who would be best able to respond. Berry claims that Congress was putting considerable pressure on the White House to access the files. Although Berry admits he may have told Tamposi about White House interest, and thereby given a misleading impression that he was working on behalf of the White House, he maintained that no one in the White House asked him to try to get Clinton's files.

Berry's friendship with Janet Mullins, a former colleague as well as supervisor, was well known, and he frequently talked with her about Clinton FOIA requests and other matters in the course of his official duties. Mullins' only advice to Berry was "not to get sucked into Clinton's trip to Moscow," a reference to the Governor's visit to Moscow when he was a student. Berry maintains that neither Mullins nor anyone else at the White House was orchestrating such an inquiry, although Berry freely admitted that the White House was trying to meet with Members of Congress about Clinton's Moscow visit. Berry said that the White House also would have been extremely pleased if information detrimental to Clinton had been discovered prior to the election.

During the course of our inquiry, we received many exhortations about direct White House or congressional involvement in the search of Clinton's files, but found few actual leads. We pursued all of these. Nobody, at any time, in or outside the State Department, declined to talk with us. We interviewed one Congressman and eight persons in the White House, three of them very senior. (In total, we conducted 107 interviews.) Other than the allegation from Tamposi about Berry's reference in their September 28th telephone conversation, for which Berry provided a reasonable explanation, and a continuing dialogue between Mullins and Berry which per se cannot be taken as conspiratorial, we found no evidence that the

White House—or any other external source—orchestrated an "attack" on the Clinton files.

Passport Files of Virginia Dell Blythe/Clinton

During the WNRC search in the evening of September 30, Governor Clinton's mother's passport file was briefly cross-checked on the off chance it might contain her son's alleged letter renouncing his citizenship or material relating to foreign travel. Nothing was found, and the file was returned to its place. Tamposi did not order Mrs. Clinton's files to be searched, nor, to the best of our knowledge, was she aware of the search until she read of it in the press.

H. Ross Perot's File

Because of her concern about possible tampering with Governor Clinton's file, Tamposi wanted to ensure that all other presidential candidates' files were adequately protected. Consequently, on October 1, she called her searchers at the WNRC and instructed them to obtain Perot's file and secure it. (President Bush's file had already been removed from the WNRC to secure storage in the K Street passport office shortly after his election in 1988.) Contrary to reports in the press, our inquiry uncovered no evidence which would suggest that Ross Perot's passport files were searched by Tamposi's aides with the hope of finding anything of political use.

However, Tamposi's aides were unable to obtain Perot's files on October 1st because they did not have accession numbers. Because of the press of other business, they did not return until October 13 to collect it and bring it to K Street. As of this date, Clinton's passport files are still with the Federal Bureau of Investigation.

* * *

There is always, in an event such as the search for Clinton's passport files—which attracted such extraordinarily intense media and congressional attention—a tendency to believe that there must be a correspondingly big and/or sinister cause. We did not find this here.

What we did find was bad enough: not a carefully thought-out conspiratorial plan but, rather, a general inability of the system in the State Department, of the people and procedures that make up some of the daily operations of the Department, to resist a kind of ad hoc attempt to politicize a process. This is dangerous at any time. During a presidential election campaign, in a matter relating directly to one of the candidates, it could have boiled over.

We found it encouraging, during our inquiry, to encounter so many Department employees, Civil Service and Foreign Service, who were outraged by what they had read about the search of the passport files. We were saddened, during our inquiry, to realize how easily the Department had begun to slide down a slippery slope.

WITHDRAWAL OF U.S. TROOPS FROM PHILIPPINES

November 24, 1992

In ceremonies laden with emotion, the American flag was lowered and the last of the few remaining U.S. troops sailed out of Subic Bay Naval Station on November 24, closing a major chapter in the ninety-four-year history of U.S.-Philippine relations. The departure occurred fourteen months after the Philippine Senate voted to reject renewing the lease on the largest U.S. overseas military base. In a speech delivered after a huge Philippine flag was unfurled, President Fidel V. Ramos called for "a new framework" to stimulate increased U.S.-Philippine economic cooperation, emphasizing that his country had "a continuing community of strategic and economic interests with the United States."

A History of Close Relations

The U.S. relationship with the Philippines began in 1898, when the United States defeated the Spanish to possess the Philippines—a Southeast Asian archipelago of 7,100 islands slightly larger than Nevada, with a population of 66 million. During World War II the Japanese occupied the islands; on July 4, 1946, the United States relinquished its only colony in accordance with an act passed by Congress in 1934, and an independent republic was established.

The United States continued to maintain military facilities on the Philippines, however. Located forty-two miles north of Manila at the port city of Olongapo, the Subic Bay facility and nearby Clark Air Force Base had provided major repair and supply depots for U.S. military operations in Vietnam and the Persian Gulf. Moreover, many of the 300,000 residents of the city had depended on the base for their livelihood, providing experienced labor at wages significantly below those paid to employees at U.S. bases in Hawaii and California; thousands of other Filipinos made a living working in bars, restaurants, and souvenir shops frequented by U.S. troops. With the end of the Cold War era and the break-up of the Soviet Union, however, U.S. security considerations in Southeast Asia had been transformed, more attention was being focused on economic issues, and increasing nationalism on the part of many Filipinos led them to view the base as a distasteful holdover from colonial times.

Most of the base had already been turned over to the Philippines in October 1992; during the year about 30,000 Filipino base workers had lost their jobs. Thousands of local residents turned out to bid farewell to the U.S. Navy in the formal closing ceremony, as Mayor Richard Gordon and Adm. Thomas Mercer, the base commander, led Navy officers and city officials on a half-mile parade from city hall to the base gates, passing en route cheering, saluting, and applauding spectators, waving Philippine and American flags. Some residents hung red, white, and blue buntings from windows, while loudspeakers broadcasted a rendition of "God Bless the U.S.A."

"In a real and profound sense, Subic Naval Base was a beacon to the parts of the globe which had not been illumined by the beneficent light of freedom," said President Ramos. "It also stood as a monument to the comradeship in arms of a developing nation, the Philippines, and a superpower, the United States of America, born out of a common commitment to democracy and freedom, nurtured by mutual respect and regard and sustained by shared experience and similar vision."

Prospects for New Relations Clouded

"We hope that there would be opportunities in the future for us to continue to cooperate, for us to continue to come here for aircraft landing, passing through, and ship visits," said Adm. Mercer. "We look ahead to an era where economic relations and new forms of military cooperation—cooperation without the bases— characterize United States-Philippine relations," said U.S. Ambassador Richard H. Solomon.

Mayor Gordon, chairman of the agency in charge of converting the base into an industrial zone and improving port facilities, called on public support for guarding the ecology of the 10,000-acre Subic forest, among the last remaining virgin stands in the country, which had been carefully protected by the United States. The mayor was also among the leading proponents of converting the $8-billion military complex into a free-trade zone to attract foreign investment. "Subic Bay is now open for business for the whole world," he declared.

"The Subic of tomorrow shall be the best manifestation of our primary focus on the economic concerns of the nation . . . a showcase of economic growth activities, from industries turning out quality products for export to resorts offering tourists nature's bounty and our renowned hospitality," said President Ramos.

Reflecting widespread concern over social problems that had been caused by the presence of U.S. troops, the president noted, "foremost among these is the welfare of what the people of Olongapo call 'the throw-away children' or the Amerasians in our midst. The Philippine government will do everything that it can [to help these offspring of American soldiers and Filipino women]. . . . In the final analysis, however," he added, "the welfare of these young Filipino-Americans remains the joint responsibility of both countries which does not terminate with the withdrawal of U.S. forces. . . ." An estimated 50,000 Filipinos of part-American parentage—among them Mayor Gordon—provided vivid testimony to the legacy of the U.S. military presence. Unlike Amerasian children in Vietnam, Cambodia, Thailand, and South Korea, Filipino children of U.S. servicemen were not eligible for U.S. citizenship or allowed to move to the United States unless the father legally acknowledged paternity.

Following are excerpts from the speech delivered by Philippine President Fidel V. Ramos on November 24, 1992, during ceremonies turning over the U.S. Naval Station at Subic Bay to the Philippines:

. . . In the long history of our people, it will be remembered that since Miguel Lopez de Legazpi took possession of the Philippine Archipelago in the name of the Spanish crown in 1571, there has been no day that foreign troops were not based on our soil. And so after 421 uninterrupted years, that epoch is about to be transformed. We can be sure that this day will forever be engraved in our memories.

Today's simple but moving ceremonies bring down the curtain on that long and storied era in Philippine history marked by the presence of American troops in our territory. They also open up new prospects in Philippine-American relations, which bear the creative innovation and constructive change.

For close to a century, American military facilities and forces in Subic Naval Base helped preserve the balance of power in this highly strategic area of the world. And up to the Persian Gulf War, Subic Naval Base served as a pivotal unit in the scheme of free world defense in the Asia and Pacific region.

In a real and profound sense, Subic Naval Base was a beacon to the parts of the globe which had not been illumined by the beneficient light of freedom. It also stood as a monument to the comradeship in arms of a developing nation, the Philippines, and a superpower, the United States of America born out of a common commitment to democracy and freedom, nurtured by mutual respect and regard, and sustained by shared experience and a similar vision.

From the welter of varied views on the future of U.S. involvement in regional affairs, our region of Asia and the Pacific, one portentous reality emerges, and that is, that the member nations of Asian uniformly hold the view that American power and influence continue to be essential to the preservation of peace and stability in the Asia and Pacific region.

The Future of RP-US Relations

Turning to Philippine-American relations, let me say in plain, unmistakable terms that we have a continuing community of strategic and economic interests with the United States. This central fact of life transcends fluctuations in the political and psychological climate of Philippine-American relations. It denotes invariable constants in bilateral affairs, which neither country can ill afford to subordinate to transient considerations and ephemeral exigencies.

Many of our eminent leaders have urged that the United States and the Philippines fashion a new framework for Philippine-American relations away, and I quote: "From the stultifying atmosphere of the bases issue." I fully and categorically subscribe to that view.

History has a way of validating ideas. We all can see how the result of the recent American presidential elections lends validity and urgency to the proposition that our two countries must now fashion a new framework for their relationship in keeping with the geopolitical realities prevailing in their common areas of concern and interest.

As one contemplates the picture of Philippine-American affairs, two massive and compelling facts instantly obtrude in one's mind: First, the United States market remains our biggest and most profitable. And second, the United States remains the undisputed leader of the free world.

At a time when the Philippines' export trade has continuously been in the doldrums, we have uninterruptedly enjoyed a whopping trade surplus with the United States, which was registered at $1.2 billion last year.

On the other hand, it should be pointed out that the mutual defense treaty, which lies at the core of the security arrangements between the Philippines and the United States, cries for a new, bracing breath of life. Framed and adopted at the height of the cold war, when American and free world strategy was based on the idea of surrounding the Soviet empire with bases of military and economic strength, the Mutual Defense Treaty has now to be reexamined in the context of the post-cold war era. Its concept, its thrust, and its scope have to be attuned to the realities of a world tormented by new conflicts and rivalries and faced with new trials and challenges.

Two matters, in particular, have to be clarified: When and where an attack on one party is to be regarded as an attack on the other party as well, and the precise point at which retaliation to attack is to be waged. It is well to bear in mind that these two matters have tended to be irritants in the relationship over the years between the Philippines and the United States.

The scope and the composition of bilateral trade and economic cooperation have to be reviewed and updated. The mechanism of bilateral economic affairs has to be re-engineered with a view to the progressive realization of expanding mutual progress.

At this moment in time, the Philippines and the United States are called upon to improve the structure of their historical and traditional relationship. They must reinforce its foundation, buttress its ramparts and shore up its weak spots.

And so as an earnest of their common desire to serve the ends of mutual defense, the Philippine and the U.S. Government through the RP-US mutual defense board have agreed to review so that it can be revitalized, the Philippine-American Mutual Defense Treaty under the auspices of which various programs and projects would be undertaken encompassing customary ship visits, joint military exercises, and similar cooperative arrangements. It should be stressed that these activities are to be undertaken within the accords of the Mutual Defense Treaty and do not entail the necessity of concluding any new and separate agreement.

Our Plans for Subic

What is reverted to the Filipino people today is certainly more than just a piece of real estate. It is a part of the nation's patrimony which we hope to consecrate to peaceful use and for the benefit of the Filipino people. The blueprint for transforming this military complex envisions, I must stress, both preservation and development. To be precise, we aim to maintain and secure its natural attributes—the pristine beauty of its forest cover and the clear deep waters of the bay.

This complex shall become the centerpiece of a conversion program that encompasses all the facilities and base lands relinquished by the United States. While its historical significance to our two countries will be deeply etched in the touchstone of our long-standing friendship, the Subic of tomorrow will acquire a universal identity as a major gateway for the world to our shores.

The Subic of tomorrow shall be the best manifestation of our primary focus on the economic concerns of the nation. Subic shall be a showcase of economic growth activities, from industries turning out quality products for export to resorts offering tourists nature's bounty and our renowned hospitality.

I confirm what Mayor Dick Gordon who is also the chairman of the SBMA has said here today that your president shall be your one-man oversight committee over the cabinet, over the SBMA council, and over the local government executives, as well as your one-man public relation's man towards our own people and our foreign friends so that indeed the promise of Subic and our vision for it will be fulfilled not too long from now.

Attention to Social Concerns

But while our plans are prioritized for the economic potential of this reverted territory, we shall not neglect the social concerns that have arisen from Subic's existence as a military base.

Foremost among these is the welfare of what the people of Olongapo call "The Throw-Away Children" or the Amerasians in our midst. The Philippine government will do everything that it can, not only to ensure them with enough opportunities to become educated, productive and useful citizens. And I will not allow them to end up in poverty, much less in street gangs. As Subic develops economically, hopefully we can provide these young children the means for gainful employment.

In the final analysis, however, the welfare of these young Filipino-Americans remains the joint responsibility of both countries which does not terminate with the withdrawal of U.S. forces from the Philippines.

This and other social concerns must be discussed in future talks on Philippine-U.S. relations. We will rely on the Americans' sense of civil responsibility so that the social effects of their stay are addressed to the mutual satisfaction of both parties.

As friends and allies, the Philippines and the United States stand on a promontory from which they have a commanding view of the past, the present, and the future. Behind them lie a long mountain range of shared experience in mankind's unending quest to expand freedom and progress. And ahead with them lies an entrancing vista of new promise, new frontiers, new horizons, and new opportunities.

I, for one, have high hopes that the leaders, the statesmen, the diplomats, the defense managers and the economic strategists of the Philippines and the United States, fired with a common inspiration and vision, will seize the opportunity before them to reinforce the bonds of friendship and mutual cooperation that unite them, to contribute to the enrichment of man's heritage of democracy and freedom, and to build a fortress of human liberty and well-being in this corner of the globe.

In sum, we bid "bon voyage" to the American servicemen represented here by their highest commanders and their ambassador. As we do this we ask the U.S. Government and the American people for the strengthening of our partnership on the basis of economic cooperation, social concern, mutual support and democratic commitment.

Let us not simply glory in history. Let us move on and make history! Thank you very much. . . .

QUEEN, PRIME MINISTER ON ROYAL FAMILY PROBLEMS

November 24, December 9, 1992

Members of the British royal family would clearly like to forget 1992. Queen Elizabeth II summed up the year at a November 24 luncheon celebrating the fortieth anniversary of her accession. "1992 is not a year I shall look back on with undiluted pleasure," she said. "In the words of one of my more sympathetic correspondents, it has turned out to be an 'annus horribilis,' "—Latin for a "horrible year."

Scandals and other troubles dogged the royal family all year. The event with the greatest consequences for Great Britain was the formal separation of Charles, heir to the throne, and Diana, the Prince and Princess of Wales. The two married in July 1981 in what was called "the wedding of the century," a ceremony of pomp broadcast to hundreds of millions around the world. In recent years, though, British tabloids and some books had reported the couple suffered in a loveless marriage and that Diana had repeatedly tried to commit suicide.

Buckingham Palace and Prime Minister John Major took pains to say the split would not affect Charles's and Diana's abilities to become king and queen. However, with many observers expecting that Charles and Diana would eventually divorce, it was unclear what would happen to the chain of succession. Some speculated that if Charles divorced, he would renounce the throne in favor of his oldest son, William. Even if he and Diana remained married, there were many questions about how a king and queen who lived separately could effectively serve the nation.

The announcement December 9 that Charles and Diana were separating was only the latest blow to the royal family. In the summer Princess Anne, the Queen's only daughter, divorced her husband, Mark Phillips.

Princess Anne remarried in December. The queen's second son, Andrew, the Prince of York, separated from Sarah Ferguson, the Duchess of York, better known as "Fergie." Their separation occurred as British and American tabloids printed pictures of Fergie cavorting topless on the Riviera with a man identified as her "financial adviser."

On November 20 a major fire struck Windsor Castle, which the queen used mainly as a weekend home. The castle had served as a home for British royalty for more than eight centuries. The fire gutted a large section of the structure and also damaged or destroyed parts of the queen's priceless art collection. Government officials announced that repairs would cost $90 million and that taxpayers would foot the bill. That drew howls of outrage from citizens. Many contended that the monarchy already cost too much and did little more than serve as a major embarrassment to the nation.

In response to growing public unhappiness, the queen in late November announced she would pay income taxes and more of the royal family's expenses. British law exempted the queen from paying taxes. The gestures by the queen, a multibillionaire who was thought to be the world's richest woman, were seen as an effort to improve the royal family's image amid Britain's longest recession since the 1930s. Yet many Britons were not appeased. A British polling firm found that only one in three believed the nation would be worse off without the monarchy. A similar survey conducted in 1984 found that three out of four thought abolishing the monarchy would hurt Britain. Despite the public discontent, however, there appeared little chance that Parliament would make any moves against the queen and her difficult family.

> *Following are the texts of a speech made by Queen Elizabeth II on November 24, 1992, at a lunch celebrating the fortieth anniversary of her accession to the throne and of an announcement on the separation of Charles and Diana, as delivered by Prime Minister John Major to the House of Commons on December 9:*

QUEEN ELIZABETH ON HER ANNIVERSARY

This great hall has provided me with some of the most memorable events of my life. The hospitality of the City of London is famous around the world, but nowhere is it more appreciated than among the members of my family.

I am deeply grateful that you, my Lord Mayor, and the corporation, have seen fit to mark the fortieth anniversary of my accession with this splendid lunch, and by giving me a picture which I will greatly cherish.

Thank you also for inviting representatives of so many organisations with which I and my family have special connections, in some cases stretching back over several generations. To use an expression more common north of the border, this is a real "gathering of the clans."

1992 is not a year I shall look back on with undiluted pleasure. In the words of one of my more sympathetic correspondents, it has turned out to be an "annus horribilis." I suspect that I am not alone in thinking it so. Indeed, I suspect that there are very few people or institutions unaffected by these last months of worldwide turmoil and uncertainty. This generosity and whole-hearted kindness of the corporation of the City to Prince Philip and me would be welcome at any time but, at this particular moment, in the aftermath of Friday's tragic fire at Windsor, it is especially so.

And, after this last weekend, we appreciate all the more what has been set before us today. Years of experience, however, have made us a bit more canny than the lady—less well-versed than us in the splendours of City hospitality—who, when she was offered a balloon glass for her brandy, asked for "only half a glass, please".

It is possible to have too much of a good thing. A well-meaning bishop was obviously doing his best when he told Queen Victoria: "Ma'am, we cannot pray too often, nor too fervently, for the royal family." The queen's reply was: "Too fervently, no; too often, yes." I, like Queen Victoria, have always been a believer in that old maxim "moderation in all things".

I sometimes wonder how future generations will judge the events of this tumultuous year. I dare say that history will take a slightly more moderate view than that of some contemporary commentators. Distance is well known to lend enchantment, even to the less attractive views.

After all, it has the inestimable advantage of hindsight. But it can also lend an extra dimension to judgment, giving it a leavening of moderation and compassion—even of wisdom—that is sometimes lacking in the reactions of those whose task it is in life to offer instant opinions on all things great and small. No section of the community has all the virtues, neither does any have all the vices. I am quite sure that most people try to do their jobs as best they can, even if the result is not always entirely successful. He who has never failed to reach perfection has a right to be the harshest critic.

There can be no doubt, of course, that criticism is good for people and institutions that are part of public life. No institution—City, monarchy, whatever—should expect to be free from the scrutiny of those who give it their loyalty and support, not to mention those who don't.

But we are all part of the same fabric of our national society and that scrutiny, by one part of another, can be just as effective if it is made with a touch of gentleness, good humour and understanding.

This sort of questioning can also act, and it should do so, as an effective engine for change. The City is a good example of the way the process of change can be incorporated into the stability and continuity of a great institution.

I particularly admire, my Lord Mayor, the way in which the City has adapted so nimbly to what the prayer book calls "the changes and chances of this mortal life". You have set an example of how it is possible to remain effective and dynamic without losing those indefinable qualities, style and character. We only have to look around this great hall to see the truth of that.

Forty years is quite a long time. I am glad to have had the chance to witness, and to take part in, many dramatic changes in life in this country. But I am glad to say that the magnificent standard of hospitality given on so many occasions to the sovereign by the Lord Mayor of London has not changed at all. It is an outward symbol of one other unchanging factor which I value above all: the loyalty given to me and my family by so many people in this country, and the Commonwealth, throughout my reign.

You, my Lord Mayor, and all those whose prayers—fervent, I hope, but not too frequent—have sustained me through all these years, are friends indeed. Prince Philip and I give you all, wherever you may be, our most humble thanks.

PRIME MINISTER MAJOR ON ROYAL FAMILY

With permission, Madam Speaker, I wish to inform the House that Buckingham Palace is at this moment issuing the following statement. It reads as follows:

"It is announced from Buckingham Palace that, with regret, the Prince and Princess of Wales have decided to separate. Their Royal Highnesses have no plans to divorce and their constitutional positions are unaffected. This decision has been reached amicably, and they will both continue to participate fully in the upbringing of their children.

Their Royal Highnesses will continue to carry out full and separate programmes of public engagements, and will from time to time attend family occasions and national events together.

The Queen and the Duke of Edinburgh, though saddened, understand and sympathise with the difficulties that have led to this decision. Her Majesty and His Royal Highness particularly hope that the intrusions into the privacy of the Prince and Princess may now cease. They believe that a degree of privacy and understanding is essential if Their Royal Highnesses are to provide a happy and secure upbringing for their children, while continuing to give a whole-hearted commitment to their public duties."

That is the text of the announcement.

I am sure that I speak for the whole House—and millions beyond it—in offering our support to both the Prince and Princess of Wales. I am also sure that the House will sympathise with the wish that they should both be afforded a degree of privacy.

The House will wish to know that the decision to separate has no constitutional implications. The succession to the throne is unaffected by it; the children of the Prince and Princess retain their position in the line of succession; and there is no reason why the Princess of Wales should not be crowned Queen in due course. The Prince of Wales's succession as head of the Church of England is also unaffected. Neither the Prince nor the Princess is supported by the civil list, and this position will remain unchanged.

I know that there will be great sadness at this news. But I know also that, as they continue with their royal duties and with bringing up their children, the Prince and Princess will have the full support, understanding and affection of the House and of the country.

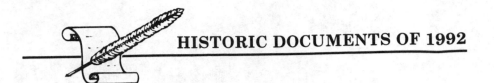

December

December

PRESIDENT'S ADDRESS
ON AID TO SOMALIA
December 4, 1992

Responding to a humanitarian crisis of immense proportions, President Bush December 4 went on national television and radio to announce that he was dispatching a "substantial number" of U.S. troops to the war-ravaged African nation of Somalia to assist United Nations forces in distributing food to the famine-stricken region. At least 300,000 Somalis had already died, and 2 million more were estimated to be at risk of dying.

The president's address outlining the U.S. action, called Operation Restore Hope, came after the UN Security Council voted unanimously on the night of December 3 to accept the U.S. offer, made November 25, to send troops; the council agreed to put U.S. military commanders in charge of the multinational effort. Adopting a resolution that "strongly condemns all violations of international humanitarian law occurring in Somalia, including in particular the deliberate impeding of the delivery of food and medical supplies essential for the survival of the civilian population," the council said it welcomed the U.S. offer "concerning the establishment of an operation to create . . . a secure environment" for the delivery of relief supplies.

The troop deployment took place only six weeks before the end of Bush's presidency. In seeking to justify—and circumscribe—the effort, Bush said, "I understand the United States alone cannot right the world's wrongs, but we also know that some crises in the world cannot be resolved without American involvement." The president added that U.S. forces "will not stay one day longer than is absolutely necessary" to ensure delivery of food and relief supplies.

President-elect Bill Clinton issued a statement from Little Rock, Arkansas, commending Bush for his "leadership on this important humanitarian effort." Clinton and his aides made clear that Bush, as president, was still the spokesman for and author of U.S. foreign policy, although they emphasized that the administration had kept them informed of events. According to House Speaker Thomas S. Foley, D-Wash., the consensus of congressional leaders who had been briefed on the decision was that "the president has acted wisely, and in circumstances where he had very little choice without grave humanitarian consequences resulting." Gen. Colin L. Powell, chairman of the Joint Chiefs of Staff, and Defense Secretary Dick Cheney had strongly supported the president's decision.

Background: End of Dictatorship Leads to Turmoil

Bordered by Ethiopia, Kenya, and the Indian Ocean, the Texas-sized nation of Somalia had been in turmoil since the January 1991 overthrow of Siad Barre, dictator for twenty-two years. Warfare among competing clans, particularly between rival leaders of the Hiwiye clan, for the right to run the country intensified the effects of a draught and led to widespread famine among the nation's 8 million people, most of whom belonged to the Hamitic ethnic group and were Sunni Muslims. With a per capita annual income estimated at $170, Somali was one of the poorest countries in the world even before the civil war and famine destroyed the the country's economic, political, and social fabric.

"Since Somalia began its descent into anarchy . . . ," reporter Keith Richburg wrote in the November 27 Washington Post, "it has been a place with no borders, no real armies, no particular meaning behind the chaos and—as yet—no hope. The stench of death hangs heavy in the air. Skeletal figures move along roadsides. Hollow-eyed children pick in the dirt. . . ."

The UN sent observers and relief ships to the area early in 1992, but efforts to arrange a cease-fire broke down, and, time and again throughout the year, ships attempting to deliver tons of food and medical supplies either were shelled and had to turn back or were thoroughly looted. In July the Security Council approved an emergency airlift to provide food for the estimated 30 percent of the population believed to be starving to death. But when the first four relief planes, provided by the United States, landed in the Somali capital of Mogadishu in August, gunmen killed three guards and wounded two UN military observers. The situation worsened as looters continued to confiscate food from warehouses and marauding freelance gunmen and "protectors"—described by many as "teen-age thugs"—of the feuding warlords roamed streets and roads in jeeps outfitted with AK-47 rifles and other weapons (many of which, ironically, had been provided by the cold war superpowers), firing at will on civilians and UN relief convoys.

As a result, the UN delayed its attempts to supply food while working to obtain a cease-fire agreement from the warlords. When that effort failed, the Security Council approved a marked change in policy and agreed to use offensive force if necessary to protect relief convoys. This change of policy represented the first time that the UN had agreed to use offensive force to help settle the internal affairs of a member country.

In a November 24 letter to members of the Security Council, UN Secretary General Boutros Boutros-Ghali acknowledged that it was impossible to negotiate because there were no "authorities" in the chaotic region "capable of maintaining law and order." Noting the widespread looting and the nonexistent economy, the secretary general said that the situation "is not improving" and that it had become "exceedingly difficult" for the UN to accomplish its mission. That set the stage for acceptance of the U.S. offer.

Scope of U.S. Mission

Speaking to reporters after the December 3 Security Council vote, White House spokesman Marlin Fitzwater said the administration hoped that the U.S. troops could be withdrawn by the time of president-elect Clinton's inauguration January 20, 1993. "We want to make it clear that this UN force would be designed to get humanitarian supplies in, not to establish a new government or resolve the decades-long conflict there or to set up a protectorate or anything like that," he said.

The mission of the American and other forces was to be limited to guarding ports, roads, and distribution points for relief supplies. (Other nations pledging support included Belgium, Canada, Egypt, France, Italy, Morocco, and Pakistan.) After accomplishing that task, the forces were to be withdrawn, leaving a much smaller UN contingent of about 5,000 to monitor the continuing flow of supplies.

The initial wave of U.S. troops—three teams of Navy Seals—waded ashore in camouflage make-up at Mogadishu on the night of December 9 under a full moon and the glare of scores of U.S. news photographers. They were followed by Marines, who were assigned to secure the port and airport so that supplies could be brought in, to accommodate both the troops and the relief delivery operation. Teams of American combat engineers, transportation crews, water purification experts, and other support troops were among the 28,000 American troops eventually involved in the operation.

At first, it was difficult to predict how much armed resistance the U.S.-led multinational forces would encounter. Apparently daunted by the display of force, gunmen and snipers sharply reduced their attacks in the first weeks of operation as the multinational troops moved quickly to secure essential areas. But sniper fire escalated as the year came to a close, and two U.S. soldiers and one civilian were killed.

Although Bush had stressed that the U.S. role had a limited objective—"to open the supply routes, to get the food moving, and to prepare *the way for a UN peacekeeping force to keep it moving"—the goal of removing U.S. forces from Somalia had not been met by the target date of January 20. Moreover, the multinational troops found that they had to act in a "protector" role that was more encompassing than originally envisaged. Although a substantial number of American forces were leaving, Defense and State Department officials predicted that others would remain until mid-1993. After that, the future of Somalia—a "nation" without a central governing authority and economy—was highly uncertain. Time and again, the principal warlords agreed to a cease-fire, only for one side or another to break it.*

Following is the text of President Bush's December 4, 1992, address on U.S. military efforts to assist UN forces in distributing food to alleviate the famine in Somalia:

I want to talk to you today about the tragedy in Somalia and about a mission that can ease suffering and save lives. Every American has seen the shocking images from Somalia. The scope of suffering there is hard to imagine. Already, over a quarter-million people, as many people as live in Buffalo, New York, have died in the Somali famine. In the months ahead 5 times that number, 1½ million people, could starve to death.

For many months now, the United States has been actively engaged in the massive international relief effort to ease Somalia's suffering. All told, America has sent Somalia 200,000 tons of food, more than half the world total. This summer, the distribution system broke down. Truck convoys from Somalia's ports were blocked. Sufficient food failed to reach the starving in the interior of Somalia.

So in August, we took additional action. In concert with the United Nations, we sent in the U.S. Air Force to help fly food to the towns. To date, American pilots have flown over 1,400 flights, delivering over 17,000 tons of food aid. And when the U.N. authorized 3,500 U.N. guards to protect the relief operation, we flew in the first of them, 500 soldiers from Pakistan.

But in the months since then, the security situation has grown worse. The U.N. has been prevented from deploying its initial commitment of troops. In many cases, food from relief flights is being looted upon landing; food convoys have been hijacked; aid workers assaulted; ships with food have been subject to artillery attacks that prevented them from docking. There is no government in Somalia. Law and order have broken down. Anarchy prevails.

One image tells the story. Imagine 7,000 tons of food aid literally bursting out of a warehouse on a dock in Mogadishu, while Somalis starve less than a kilometer away because relief workers cannot run the gauntlet of armed gangs roving the city. Confronted with these conditions, relief groups called for outside troops to provide security so they could feed people. It's now clear that military support is necessary to ensure the safe delivery of the food Somalis need to survive.

It was this situation which led us to tell the United Nations that the United States would be willing to provide more help to enable relief to be delivered. Last night the United Nations Security Council, by unanimous vote and after the tireless efforts of Secretary-General Boutros-Ghali, welcomed the United States offer to lead a coalition to get the food through.

After consulting with my advisers, with world leaders, and the congressional leadership, I have today told Secretary-General Boutros-Ghali that America will answer the call. I have given the order to Secretary Cheney to move a substantial American force into Somalia. As I speak, a Marine amphibious ready group, which we maintain at sea, is offshore Mogadishu. These troops will be joined by elements of the 1st Marine Expeditionary Force, based out of Camp Pendleton, California, and by the Army's 10th Mountain Division out of Fort Drum, New York. These and other American forces will assist in Operation Restore Hope. They are America's finest. They will perform this mission with courage and compassion, and they will succeed.

The people of Somalia, especially the children of Somalia, need our help. We're able to ease their suffering. We must help them live. We must give them hope. America must act.

In taking this action I want to emphasize that I understand the United States alone cannot right the world's wrongs. But we also know that some crises in the world cannot be resolved without American involvement, that American action is often necessary as a catalyst for broader involvement of the community of nations. Only the United States has the global reach to place a large security force on the ground in such a distant place quickly and efficiently and thus save thousands of innocents from death.

We will not, however, be acting alone. I expect forces from about a dozen countries to join us in this mission. When we see Somalia's children starving, all of America hurts. We've tried to help in many ways. And make no mistake about it, now we and our allies will ensure that aid gets through. Here is what we and our coalition partners will do:

First, we will create a secure environment in the hardest hit parts of Somalia, so that food can move from ships over land to the people in the countryside now devastated by starvation.

Second, once we have created that secure environment, we will withdraw our troops, handing the security mission back to a regular U.N. peacekeeping force. Our mission has a limited objective: To open the supply routes, to get the food moving, and to prepare the way for a U.N. peacekeeping force to keep it moving. This operation is not open-ended. We will not stay one day longer than is absolutely necessary.

Let me be very clear: Our mission is humanitarian, but we will not tolerate armed gangs ripping off their own people, condemning them to death by starvation. General Hoar and his troops have the authority to take whatever military action is necessary to safeguard the lives of our troops and the lives of Somalia's people. The outlaw elements in Somalia must understand this is serious business. We will accomplish our mission. We have no intent to remain in Somalia with fighting forces, but we are determined to do it right, to secure an environment that will allow food to get to the starving people of Somalia.

To the people of Somalia I promise this: We do not plan to dictate political outcomes. We respect your sovereignty and independence. Based on my conversations with other coalition leaders, I can state with confidence: We come to your country for one reason only, to enable the starving to be fed.

Let me say to the men and women of our Armed Forces, we are asking you to do a difficult and dangerous job. As Commander in Chief I assure you, you will have our full support to get the job done, and we will bring you home as soon as possible.

Finally, let me close with a message to the families of the men and women who take part in this mission: I understand it is difficult to see your loved ones go, to send them off knowing they will not be home for the holidays, but the humanitarian mission they undertake is in the finest traditions of service. So, to every sailor, soldier, airman, and marine who is involved in this mission, let me say, you're doing God's work. We will not fail.

Thank you, and may God bless the United States of America.

BUSH PARDON OF WEINBERGER, OTHERS IN IRAN-CONTRA CASE

December 24, 1992

One month after leaving office, President George Bush pardoned former defense secretary Caspar W. Weinberger and five other officials of the Reagan administration facing trial or sentencing for their involvement in the Iran-contra scandal. It was disclosed late in 1986 that U.S. arms had been secretly sold to Iran and some of the proceeds illegally diverted to rebels ("contras") attempting to overthrow the government in Nicaragua. In a Christmas Eve proclamation issued by the White House, Bush said he granted the pardons out of compassion for all six, especially Weinberger— "a true American patriot" who was seventy-five and ailing. But the president emphasized that his chief aim was to put "behind us" bitter passions aroused by the Iran-contra affair and its continuing investigation. It was time for the nation to "move on" to other matters, he said.

The full pardons prevented Weinberger from going on trial January 5 on charges of lying to Congress about his knowledge of the arms sales. Duane R. Clarridge, a former senior official in the Central Intelligence Agency (CIA), also pardoned, was similarly scheduled to be tried March 15 in federal district court in Washington, D.C. Clair E. George, former CIA deputy director, convicted of perjury, was due to be sentenced February 18. Other pardons set aside sentences imposed on Elliott Abrams, a former assistant secretary of state, Robert C. McFarlane, former national security adviser, and Alan D. Fiers, Jr., former CIA chief of a task force dealing with the contras. After pleading guilty to misdemeanor charges of withholding information from Congress, all three were placed on probation and assigned to community service work. McFarlane was also fined $20,000.

Walsh Denounces the Pardons

Lawrence E. Walsh, the special Iran-contra prosecutor whose inquiry began in 1986, angrily denounced the pardons. "The Iran-contra coverup, which has continued for six years, is now complete," he said. Weinberger's trial was expected to focus on his private notes that indicated both he and Bush—then Ronald Reagan's vice president—were aware of the arms sales. Bush had repeatedly said he was "out of the loop"—not privy to the Iran-contra dealings. Weinberger had similarly denied explicit knowledge of the unfolding events. In his pardon announcement, Bush said that "no impartial person has seriously suggested that my role in this matter was legally questionable."

Nevertheless, in a statement following the pardon announcement, Walsh hinted that Bush's role could be related to Weinberger's pardon. Walsh contended that Weinberger's notes included "evidence of a conspiracy among the highest ranking Reagan administration officials to lie to Congress and the American public." The prosecutor said that Weinberger's initial concealment of his notes—they later turned up in official files after he left office—may have "forestalled impeachment proceedings against President Reagan."

Walsh further said he had discovered "misconduct" by President Bush. The prosecutor disclosed that only on December 11 did he learn that Bush had kept "highly relevant contemporaneous notes, despite repeated requests for such documents." The notes were in the form of a campaign diary that Bush, as vice president, compiled after congressional elections in November 1986—losses in which some Republican losses were attributed to the Iran-contra scandal. C. Boyden Gray, the White House counsel, said Bush had voluntarily given his notes to Walsh and that they offered no new information about the matter. The White House promised that the material would later be made public.

According to press reports, former aides to Reagan had intensively lobbied for Weinberger's pardon. Many Republicans who had been angered by the Walsh prosecution were incensed when the prosecutor filed a new indictment four days before the November 4 election in which Bush was defeated by Democrat Bill Clinton. The indictment said Weinberger's notes contradicted Bush's denials of knowledge about the arms sales. Ironically, they indicated that Weinberger opposed sending arms to Iran.

The secret sales, intended to win the release of American hostages in Lebanon, were not illegal but ran counter to Reagan's proclaimed policy of refusing to negotiate for the hostages' release. The diversion of profits from the sales were used to help finance a covert weapons supply network for the contras after Congress barred direct military to them.

Other Iran-contra Convictions

Besides those pardoned by Bush, Walsh's staff had obtained seven other convictions or guilty pleas. But two of the most prominent convic-

tions—of Oliver L. North and John M. Poindexter—were later overturned because they had testified before Congress under grant of limited
immunity. North was a Marine Corps lieutenant colonel and National
Security Council staff member and Poindexter was a Navy rear admiral
who was Reagan's national security adviser. An eighth case, against
Joseph F. Fernandez, a former CIA station chief in Costa Rica, was
dropped when the government refused the defense's request for classified
documents. (Dismissal of Iran-Contra Charges Against Oliver North,
Historic Documents of 1991, p. 617)

Relevance of Former Pardons

Presidential pardons are permitted by Article II, Section 2, of the
Constitution, except to block impeachment proceedings or or to remove a
conviction of a state crime. In his pardon proclamation, President Bush
said he acted in the "healing tradition" of pardons issued by previous
presidents, including Andrew Johnson's pardon of former Confederate
soldiers, and Harry S. Truman and Jimmy Carter's pardons of men who
violated the draft laws in World War II and Vietnam. But the New York
Times noted "not since President Gerald R. Ford granted clemency for
former Richard M. Nixon for his possible crimes in Watergate has a
presidential pardon raised the issue of whether the president was trying
to shield government officials from the criminal justice system for
political purposes."

Reaction to Bush's pardons tended to follow partisan lines. George
Mitchell of Maine, the Senate Democratic leader, called the pardons a
mistake. "If members of the executive branch lie to Congress, obstruct
justice and otherwise break the law, how can policy differences be fairly
and legally resolved in a democracy?" In Little Rock, Arkansas, President-elect Clinton agreed: "I am concerned by any action which sends a
signal that if you work for the government you are above the law, or that
not telling the truth to Congress, under oath, is less serious than not
telling the truth to some other body, under oath." Clinton said he would
withhold further comment until he knew "all the details of the pardons."

In contrast, Reagan said he was pleased because the men who were
pardoned "have served their country for many years with honor and
distinction." Bob Dole, the Senate Republican leader, called the pardons
an "act of courage and compassion."

Weinberger called a news conference to express his gratitude to Bush
for granting the pardon, which his attorneys had formally requested in a
letter to the president. The former defense secretary considered the
pardon a confirmation of his innocence. He denounced Walsh as "lawless
and vindictive."

Following are President George Bush's proclamation pardoning six former government officials involved in the Iran-
contra scandal, issued December 24, 1992, by the White

House, and a statement issued later the same day by special
prosecutor Lawrence E. Walsh denouncing the pardons:

PROCLAMATION 6518—
GRANT OF EXECUTIVE CLEMENCY

Today I am exercising my power under the Constitution to pardon former Secretary of Defense Caspar Weinberger and others for their conduct related to the Iran-Contra affair.

For more than 6 years now, the American people have invested enormous resources into what has become the most thoroughly investigated matter of its kind in our history. During that time, the last American hostage has come home to freedom, worldwide terrorism has declined, the people of Nicaragua have elected a democratic government, and the Cold War has ended in victory for the American people and the cause of freedom we championed.

In the mid 1980's, however, the outcome of these struggles was far from clear. Some of the best and most dedicated of our countrymen were called upon to step forward. Secretary Weinberger was among the foremost.

Caspar Weinberger is a true American patriot. He has rendered long and extraordinary service to our country. He served for 4 years in the Army during World War II where his bravery earned him a Bronze Star. He gave up a lucrative career in private life to accept a series of public positions in the late 1960's and 1970's, including Chairman of the Federal Trade Commission, Director of the Office of Management and Budget, and Secretary of Health, Education, and Welfare. Caspar Weinberger served in all these positions with distinction and was admired as a public servant above reproach.

He saved his best for last. As Secretary of Defense throughout most of the Reagan Presidency, Caspar Weinberger was one of the principal architects of the downfall of the Berlin Wall and the Soviet Union. He directed the military renaissance in this country that led to the breakup of the communist bloc and a new birth of freedom and democracy. Upon his resignation in 1987, Caspar Weinberger was awarded the highest civilian medal our Nation can bestow on one of its citizens, the Presidential Medal of Freedom.

Secretary Weinberger's legacy will endure beyond the ending of the Cold War. The military readiness of this Nation that he in large measure created could not have been better displayed than it was 2 years ago in the Persian Gulf and today in Somalia.

As Secretary Weinberger's pardon request noted, it is a bitter irony that on the day the first charges against Secretary Weinberger were filed, Russian President Boris Yeltsin arrived in the United States to celebrate the end of the Cold War. I am pardoning him not just out of compassion or to spare a 75-year-old patriot the torment of lengthy and costly legal proceedings, but to make it possible for him to receive the honor he deserves for his extraordinary service to our country.

Moreover, on a somewhat more personal note, I cannot ignore the debilitating illnesses faced by Caspar Weinberger and his wife. When he resigned as Secretary of Defense, it was because of his wife's cancer. In the years since he left public service, her condition has not improved. In addition, since that time, he also has become ill. Nevertheless, Caspar Weinberger has been a pillar of strength for his wife; this pardon will enable him to be by her side undistracted by the ordeal of a costly and arduous trial.

I have also decided to pardon five other individuals for their conduct related to the Iran-Contra affair: Elliott Abrams, Duanne Clarridge, Alan Fiers, Clair George, and Robert McFarlane. First, the common denominator of their motivation—whether their actions were right or wrong—was patriotism. Second, they did not profit or seek to profit from their conduct. Third, each has a record of long and distinguished service to this country. And finally, all five have already paid a price—in depleted savings, lost careers, anguished families—grossly disproportionate to any misdeeds or errors of judgment they may have committed.

The prosecutions of the individuals I am pardoning represent what I believe is a profoundly troubling development in the political and legal climate of our country: the criminalization of policy differences. These differences should be addressed in the political arena, without the Damocles sword of criminality hanging over the heads of some of the combatants. The proper target is the President, not his subordinates; the proper forum is the voting booth, not the courtroom.

In recent years, the use of criminal processes in policy disputes has become all too common. It is my hope that the action I am taking today will begin to restore these disputes to the battleground where they properly belong.

In addition, the actions of the men I am pardoning took place within the larger Cold War struggle. At home, we had a long, sometimes heated debate about how that struggle should be waged. Now the Cold War is over. When earlier wars have ended, Presidents have historically used their power to pardon to put bitterness behind us and look to the future. This healing tradition reaches at least from James Madison's pardon of Lafitte's pirates after the War of 1812, to Andrew Johnson's pardon of soldiers who had fought for the Confederacy, to Harry Truman's and Jimmy Carter's pardons of those who violated the Selective Service laws in World War II and Vietnam.

In many cases, the offenses pardoned by these Presidents were at least as serious as those I am pardoning today. The actions of those pardoned and the decisions to pardon them raised important issues of conscience, the rule of law, and the relationship under our Constitution between the government and the governed. Notwithstanding the seriousness of these issues and the passions they aroused, my predecessors acted because it was time for the country to move on. Today I do the same.

Some may argue that this decision will prevent full disclosure of some new key fact to the American people. That is not true. This matter has been investigated exhaustively. The Tower Board, the Joint Congressional Committee charged with investigating the Iran-Contra affair, and the Independent Counsel have looked into every aspect of this matter. The Tower Board interviewed more than 80 people and reviewed thousands of documents. The Joint Congressional Committee interviewed more than 500 people and reviewed more than 300,000 pages of material. Lengthy committee hearings were held and broadcast on national television to millions of Americans. And as I have noted, the Independent Counsel investigation has gone on for more than 6 years, and it has cost more than $31 million.

Moreover, the Independent Counsel stated last September that he had completed the active phase of his investigation. He will have the opportunity to place his full assessment of the facts in the public record when he submits his final report. While no impartial person has seriously suggested that my own role in this matter is legally questionable, I have further requested that the Independent Counsel provide me with a copy of my sworn testimony to his office, which I am prepared to release immediately. And I understand Secretary Weinberger has requested the release of all of his notes pertaining to the Iran-Contra matter.

For more than 30 years in public service, I have tried to follow three precepts: honor, decency, and fairness. I know, from all those years of service, that the American people believe in fairness and fair play. In granting these pardons today, I am doing what I believe honor, decency, and fairness require.

Now, Therefore, I, George Bush, President of the United States of America, pursuant to my powers under Article II, Section 2, of the Constitution, do hereby grant a full, complete, and unconditional pardon to Elliott Abrams, Duane R. Clarridge, Alan Fiers, Clair George, Robert C. McFarlane, and Caspar W. Weinberger for all offenses charged or prosecuted by Independent Counsel Lawrence E. Walsh or other members of his office, or committed by these individuals and within the jurisdiction of that office.

In Witness Whereof, I have hereunto set my hand this twenty-fourth day of December, in the year of our Lord nineteen hundred and ninety-two, and of the Independence of the United States of America the two hundred and seventeenth.

George Bush

LAWRENCE WALSH'S STATEMENT

President Bush's pardon of Caspar Weinberger and other Iran-contra defendants undermines the principle that no man is above the law. It demonstrates that powerful people with powerful allies can commit serious crimes in high office—deliberately abusing the public trust—without consequence. Weinberger, who faced four felony charges, deserved to be tried by a jury of citizens. Although it is the president's prerogative to grand pardons, it is every American's right that the criminal justice system be administered fairly, regardless of a person's rank and connections.

The Iran-contra coverup, which has continued for more than six years, has now been completed with the pardon of Caspar Weinberger. We will make a full report on our findings to Congress and the public describing the details and extent of this coverup.

Weinberger's early and deliberate decision to conceal and withhold extensive contemporaneous notes of the Iran-contra matter radically altered the official investigations and possibly forestalled timely impeachment proceedings against President Reagan and other officials. Weinberger's notes contain evidence of a conspiracy among the highest-ranking Reagan administration officials to lie to Congress and the American public. Because the notes were withheld from investigators for years, many of the leads were impossible to follow, key witnesses had purportedly forgotten what was said and done, and statutes of imitation had expired.

Weinberger's concealment of notes is part of a disturbing pattern of deception and obstruction that permeated the highest levels of the Reagan and Bush administrations. This office was informed only within the past two weeks, on December 11, 1992, that President Bush had failed to product to investigators his own highly relevant contemporaneous notes, despite repeated requests for such documents. The production of these notes is still ongoing and will lead to appropriate action. In light of President Bush's own misconduct, we are gravely concerned about his decision to pardon others who lied to Congress and obstructed official investigations.

CUMULATIVE INDEX, 1988-1992

N